*Oracle Press*™

Oracle SOA Suite 12c
Handbook

About the Author

Lucas Jellema is an Oracle technology expert with wide and deep experience. He applies, extends, and shares his knowledge in his day job as solution architecture consultant and CTO at AMIS—an Oracle, Java, and SOA boutique technology consulting company and Oracle Platinum Partner from the Netherlands. Lucas is an almost compulsive enthusiast who will find opportunities to share his findings and excitement with his peers—through brainstorms and discussions, presentations and demonstrations, blog posts, web articles, and the book you are holding right now. Nominated Oracle ACE Director in 2006, Lucas has presented dozens of times at conferences such as Oracle OpenWorld, JavaOne, and Oracle user group meetings around the world. He contributed over 1,100 articles to the popular AMIS Technology Blog (http://technology.amis.nl). His Twitter handle is @lucasjellema.

About the Technical Editors

Guido Schmutz works for Trivadis, an Oracle Platinum Partner. He has more than 25 years of technology experience, including mainframes, integration, and SOA technologies in financial services, government, and logistics environments. At Trivadis, he is responsible for innovation in the areas of BigData & FastData and leads the Trivadis Architecture Board. He has longtime experience as a developer, coach, trainer, and architect in the areas of building complex Java EE and SOA-based solutions. Guido is an Oracle ACE Director for Fusion Middleware, SOA, and a regular speaker at international conferences, such as Oracle Open World, ODTUG, SOA & Cloud Symposium, UKOUG conference, and DOAG. He is also a coauthor of the books Oracle Service Bus 11g Development Cookbook; Do More with SOA Integration: Best of Packt, and Service-Oriented Architecture: An Integration Blueprint.

Ronald van Luttikhuizen Ronald van Luttikhuizen is one of the Managing Partners at eProseed Netherlands. eProseed is an Oracle Platinum Partner with in-depth expertise in Oracle Database, Oracle Fusion Middleware (FMW), and Oracle Hardware including Oracle Engineered Systems. Ronald has an MSc in computer science from Utrecht University. He has more than 15 years of experience in ICT in various roles such as coach, (lead) architect, (lead) developer, teacher, and team lead. Ronald focuses on architecture and security in BPM and SOA environments. He has in-depth knowledge of Oracle Fusion Middleware. Ronald is a speaker at (international) conferences such as Oracle OpenWorld and regularly publishes articles on Oracle Technology Network (OTN), Java Magazine, Optimize, and more. In 2008, Ronald was named Oracle ACE for SOA and Middleware, and in 2010 he became an Oracle ACE Director in that area. Ronald is co-author of SOA Made Simple, and was one of the technical reviewers for the Oracle SOA Suite 11g Handbook.

Oracle SOA Suite 12c Handbook

Lucas Jellema

New York   Chicago   San Francisco
Lisbon   London   Madrid   Mexico City   Milan
New Delhi   San Juan   Seoul   Singapore   Sydney   Toronto

Cataloging-in-Publication Data is on file with the Library of Congress

McGraw-Hill Education books are available at special quantity discounts to use as premiums and sales promotions, or for use in corporate training programs. To contact a representative, please visit the Contact Us pages at www.mhprofessional.com.

Oracle SOA Suite 12c Handbook

1 2 3 4 5 6 7 8 9 0   DOC DOC   1 0 9 8 7 6 5

ISBN 978-0-07-182455-2
MHID   0-07-182455-3

Sponsoring Editor
   Wendy Rinaldi

Editorial Supervisor
   Donna Martone

Project Manager
   Tanya Punj,
   Cenveo® Publisher Services

Acquisitions Coordinator
   Amanda Russell

Technical Editors
   Guido Schmutz
   Ronald van Luttikhuizen

Copy Editor
   Cenveo Publisher Services

Proofreader
   Cenveo Publisher Services

Indexer
   Jack Lewis

Production Supervisor
   Pamela Pelton

Composition
   Cenveo Publisher Services

Illustration
   Cenveo Publisher Services

Art Director, Cover
   Jeff Weeks

Contents at a Glance

v

PART V

Process Orchestration

Contents

PART I
Introducing Saibot Airport, SOA, and the Oracle SOA Suite

PART II
Elementary Services

PART IV
Asynchronous Services and Events

PART V
Process Orchestration

Foreword

Integration is the key driver for getting true return of IT investment in Enterprises. The advents of cloud-based applications, the proliferation of mobile devices, and the explosion of the API ecosystem are powering a new generation of integration requirements to solve the ever-increasing entropy and complexity in Enterprises today. The proliferation of cloud applications has reduced the time to market for Enteprises; however, it has clearly increased the entropy of applications. The proliferation of mobile devices has resulted in the need for consumers and employees to demand clean and relevant information to be pushed to their devices in real time. The advent of modern API-based development has clearly quickened time to market for app development, but increased the need for application integration and the simple and easy management of the integration infrastructure as well.

It is in this context that the 12*c* release of Oracle SOA Suite was born. This is a major milestone in the evolution of one of the cornerstone products in Oracle Fusion Middleware. Oracle SOA Suite helps organizations speed up time to integration, improve developer productivity, and lower TCO. With SOA Suite 12*c*, developers will be more productive and administrators will find even more capability to run highly available and scalable integrations for 24/7 support of the enterprise. Oracle Middleware continues to be the foundation for all of Oracle Applications and now is the foundation for Oracle Platform-As-A-Service in the cloud as well.

Upgrading to SOA Suite 12*c* is easier than ever before. Customers on the current patch releases and meeting other criteria can complete an in-place upgrade that allows their SOA composites to proceed right where they left off. Oracle SOA Suite 12*c* is truly the Service Integration Platform to power your Enterprise Applications, Internet of Things, Mobile, and Cloud.

The author of the book you are holding—Oracle ACE Director Lucas Jellema—has been publishing on Oracle SOA products for more than a decade. From blog posts on the initial BPEL Process Manager as early as 2004 and his widely used Oracle SOA Suite 11*g* Handbook in 2010, he now delivers the tome you are holding today. Maybe even more important: he brings a decade of practical experience to the table of utilizing Oracle Fusion Middleware in various challenging business environments. This experience shines through in the many examples and useful guidelines that Lucas provides in this book.

This book covers most areas of Oracle SOA Suite 12*c*. It starts from simple synchronous services and straightforward integration patterns and then gradually works its way through asynchronous interactions, event-driven exchanges to the implementation of complex business processes and human tasks. It discusses the technology adapters that provide essential integration with databases, queues, and other technology components. Run-time administration, DevOps, and Security are some areas touched upon as well.

The case of the airport that Lucas uses as the backdrop for the examples in this book is a fine example of an organization that has clear business objectives and an enterprise architecture to help realize those objectives. Lucas makes it quite clear how many pivotal aspects of the IT architecture of this airport can be implemented using the Oracle SOA Suite. The airport is imaginary—but the same applies to many organizations around the world, probably including yours.

I know that your organization can take important steps and make significant progress toward your main business objectives by applying service-oriented principles using Oracle SOA Suite 12*c*. I am convinced that this book, the many examples and practical tips provided by the author, will help you get started and become proficient with Oracle SOA Suite 12*c*.

I wish you the best as you embark on your journey to add value to your business. I know that Oracle SOA Suite 12*c* will power your innovation and that this book will provide you with expert guidance to make your project a success. We look forward to hearing from you as you use our products and services and are grateful that you chose Oracle to be your partner!

Inderjeet Singh
Executive Vice President,
Oracle Fusion Middleware Development

Acknowledgments

S uccess has many *fathers*, failure is an orphan. Many people contributed to this book and therefore its imminent success—including several who did so unconsciously and perhaps very indirectly. For example, during the OTN Yathra Tour of India in 2013, I met with two Oracle DBAs in Bangalore. They related to me how, by using my Oracle SOA Suite 11*g* Handbook, they had been introduced to Middleware in general and Oracle SOA Suite in particular. They thanked me for the book because of how it had propelled them in their career. They also could not stress enough how they would appreciate a successor describing the 12*c* release of SOA Suite. Although at the time I had no intention of committing to another book, this unexpected and heartwarming, if not outright flattering, conversation did much to convince me to get started on the book you have now in your hands.

Essential for the production of the book obviously has been the collaboration with the staff at Oracle Press/McGraw-Hill: Paul Carlstroem, Amanda Russell, and Brandi Shailer. The copy editing process was managed by Tanya Punj at Cenveo Publisher Services.

The support from within various teams at Oracle has been tremendous—through beta programs and early previews, frank discussions, and friendly banter, I have been given insights that helped me write the book and provide many details and clarification. Simone Geib has been my primary point of contact for SOA Suite. Vikas Anand, Robert Wunderlich, Ram Menon, Jay Kasi, Dave Berry, Ralf Müller, Lloyd Williams, Robin Smith, and Edwin Biemond are some of my other friends at Oracle who supported my efforts. Jürgen Kress is the tireless sponsor of AMIS and peer companies in his capacity as EMEA Oracle Fusion Middleware partner enabler. His energy, initiatives, and sometimes bold moves have frequently been motivating and helpful.

The Oracle ACE program is another constant source of inspiration. Discussions with my fellow ACEs and ACE Directors are invariably valuable and stimulating. I am grateful to the program's management: Victoria (Vikki) Lira, Lillian Buziak, and Jennifer Nicholson and the facilities they provide to us. I hope this book is up to the extremely high-quality expectations of the Oracle ACE(D)s.

I was fortunate to have two esteemed members of the Oracle ACE community as technical reviewers for this book. Ronald van Luttikhuizen and Guido Schmutz possess a great combination of technical expertise, patience, and willingness to share insights and to offer constructive feedback. Both of them are accomplished authors and helped me not just with the technical content but also with many other aspects of the book. Any mistakes, of course, are my own—and many things that are good about the book are so because of Guido and Ronald. Thanks so much for working on this together!

The trust from my colleagues at AMIS, the support from the entire company, and the many encouragements, contributions, and constructive criticisms have been wonderful. Thanks for 13 great years (so far) and your help in my endeavors. A special word of thanks to Chiel Ham, who tried out most of the samples introduced in the book and provided me with many corrections along the way.

Madelon has been crucial for the realization of this book. She came up with the airport case—mainly to shut me up so she could go to sleep, but still. More importantly, she is there for me. Our two sons—Lex and Tobias—are another wonderful constant in my life. Their curiosity into the book project provided a persistent drive and challenge.

Introduction

Service-Oriented Architecture is one of the major trends of our time in enterprise and IT architecture. The promise that SOA presents to business of business agility, lower costs, and improved quality of operations, based on concepts such as loose coupling, reuse, encapsulation, and interoperability, attracts many organizations. Complemented with Business Process Management (BPM) and Event-Driven Architecture (EDA), SOA can add real and sustained business value to enterprises.

Adopting SOA in an organization is a serious challenge that will require major efforts at various levels, from business to IT infrastructure. Crucial to the success of SOA adoption are sometimes intangible elements, including mindset, collaboration across departments and lines of business, communication, process orientation, and business analysis—in terms of interfaces and contracts, with focus on reuse and loose coupling and the implementation of proper governance.

When it comes to the actual implementation of the services and components that have been analyzed and designed, there is a need for an SOA platform—a run-time infrastructure that executes the applications and processes, handles service calls, and provides facilities around security, exception handling, and management. Enter Oracle SOA Suite 12*c*.

SOA Suite 12*c* is one of the key components in Oracle Fusion Middleware, a prominent platform to create and run agile and intelligent business applications and to maximize IT efficiency by exploiting modern hardware and software architectures—both on premises and in the cloud.

This book explains what SOA Suite 12*c* is and how its many features and components can be used to develop, deploy, and manage service-oriented artifacts.

About This Book

The book is primarily targeted at software developers and to some extent administrators and application or solution architects. Ideally, the reader has some knowledge of XML, SQL,

Java, and perhaps PL/SQL, but these are not required to benefit from most of the book's content. Readers with administrative responsibilities will find a lot of material supporting them in these tasks. Testers and (technical) architects will also learn a lot from large sections in this book. IT management staff and business analysts will mainly benefit from Part I; if they have a technical background, then others parts will prove worthwhile as well.

The book is organized into the following six parts.

Part I, "Setting the Stage," introduces the case of Saibot Airport and the business and IT challenges it faces. The path the airport has laid down for itself in order to create its future and the IT architecture and technology it has selected are discussed along with the core concepts that make up Service-Oriented Architecture. The history of Oracle Fusion Middleware is described as well as its current status. The focus then moves to a detailed overview of SOA Suite 12c, its main constituents, and closely associated products such as Managed File Transfer, API Catalog, API Manager, B2B, and Healthcare. This part concludes with a very quick start-up instruction which includes the installation of SOA Suite 12c development environment, ready for the creation and deployment of the HelloWorld equivalent in SOA applications.

Part II, "Elementary Services," provides the first iteration through Service Bus and SOA Composite applications using the Mediator component. This part discusses design and implementation of fairly simple services that are synchronous, single purpose, and short running, both with SOAP/XML and with REST/JSON style interfaces. The part introduces a number of outbound adapters: File, Database, UMS (for interaction with humans using email and chat), JMS, AQ, and EJB. The same services are implemented using both Service Bus and SOA Composites—to highlight the similarities and differences between the two approaches in SOA Suite 12c for service development.

In Part III, "Composite Services," more complex services are discussed that leverage more advanced facilities in the SOA Suite. The business process execution language BPEL is introduced as well as the Business Rule component. Complex message validation, making service call-outs for validation and enrichment, performing value lookups, and performing bulk operations in parallel are some mechanisms discussed in this part. Templates are introduced, providing reuse at various levels. Integration of custom Java in both Service Bus (Java Call Outs) and SOA Composites (Spring Java component) is demonstrated—demonstrated using interactions from SOA Suite with the Twitter and DropBox APIs. This part also discusses the use of the Coherence Adapter to improve response times and scalability and reduce load on backend systems.

Up to this point, all activities in SOA Suite were started and completed from a synchronous call on a single thread. In Part IV, "Asynchronous Services and Events," we discuss the asynchronous side of things. Asynchronous service interfaces that return a response through a callback at a later point in time are both consumed and published using both Service Bus and SOA Composite. Subsequently, the use of inbound technology adapters is discussed. These adapters cause services to be executed as a result of events detected in external components, such as database tables or advanced queues, JMS destinations, an email folder, or a file system directory. A time event can be another trigger to execute a service—as the chapter on the Enterprise Scheduling Service (ESS) explains. The ultimate decoupling mechanism in SOA Suite is the Event Delivery Network (EDN) that is introduced next. With EDN, we can implement the extreme decoupling concepts of Event-Driven Architecture for business events that are published and consumed from and by Mediator and BPEL inside the SOA Suite, and Java and PL/SQL components outside of it. How Service Bus can be made to interact with EDN is explained as well.

The last chapter in this part discusses Oracle Event Processor (OEP), a component that is included in the SOA Suite license, integrated with the Event Delivery Network, and implemented outside of the SOA Suite runtime, in its own container. With OEP, lightweight applications can be created that monitor and analyze signals across many run-time processes in real time. Using OEP, we can automate much of the human responsibility for observation, interpretation, and reaction.

In Part V, "Processes," we introduce the human actor into the mix. Recognizing that not all activities can be executed by automated service components, the SOA Suite is capable of engaging people. Through the Human Workflow Service, the SOA Suite can have tasks assigned, whose result—produced by the human actor(s)—is fed back into the automated process. An end-to-end business process—either true STP (straight through processing) or involving human activities—is implemented in SOA Suite using the BPEL component. As part of the process that gets implemented, interaction with a user directory is achieved using the LDAP adapter. User accounts are searched and new accounts get created.

A common consideration for organizations with a strong emphasis on automated business process execution is to acquire the Oracle BPM Suite on top of the SOA Suite and use Business Process Management and Adaptive Case Management (defined through BPMN and CMMN). This Part V makes a little excursion from its main scope—Oracle SOA Suite 12c—to discuss the BPM Suite and demonstrate how it facilitates the implementation of complex business processes as well as the notion of unstructured, content, and expert-driven processes through case management. Insight into the execution of business processes is usually highly desirable—for operational resource management and problem detection and intervention as well as for longer term process analysis and optimization. This chapter discusses how process analytics can be produced from both BPEL and BPMN processes and how these analytics are reported in Enterprise Manager Fusion Middleware Control and in Business Activity Monitoring (BAM). BAM is a standalone product that is included in the SOA Suite 12c license. It can be used to report on the analytics produced from SOA Suite and BPM Suite as well as on other data sources, as is demonstrated in this part.

In the final part, Part VI, "DevOps & Run-Time Administration," we switch gear a little. In parts II through V, we have primarily discussed the design and development of custom software to be deployed on the SOA Suite. In this part, we focus on the supporting software engineering processes that help govern and facilitate the creation of the custom software components as well as their delivery from development through test to production. This part discusses reuse of artifacts through MDS (the Meta Data Services), the mechanisms available for versioning, and some suggested practices for governance. Subsequently, the facilities are discussed for automated building, testing, and deploying of SOA Suite artifacts—for example, using Maven. Administrative responsibilities are an important topics in this chapter. The Enterprise Manager Fusion Middleware Control and its features to support run-time operations are introduced—for example, monitoring of SLAs, workload and performance, exception handling, metadata purging, and the extensive logging infrastructure in SOA Suite and WebLogic. The final subject in this part—and indeed the book—is security. The security of the SOA Suite run-time infrastructure and protection of its metadata is one aspect that is discussed. The protection of services from unauthorized access and the confidentiality and integrity of the messages that are exchanged is another one, both for the services exposed from the SOA Suite and for those invoked from it. The interaction with OPSS (Oracle Platform Security Services) and the OWSM (Oracle Web Services Manager) features prominently in this discussion.

Saibot Airport

Implementing SOA is meaningless without a tangible business context. Services address business requirements, as do composite applications and business processes. To illustrate SOA and Oracle SOA Suite, this book uses the case of a made-up airport, called Saibot Airport and located in the great city of Lexville. The exact location of the airport remains uncertain—hovering between the Netherlands and the USA, I would surmise.

The airport and its challenges, both at a business level and in terms of technology, provide the backdrop throughout the book against which SOA Suite features are discussed, examples are designed, and the implementation is done. This airport represents a series of business challenges that are found in organizations across industries and countries. It has interactions with external parties (including customers and business partners), strives to create more efficient business processes across departments that combine automated actions and manual tasks, needs to implement security, continually faces changing requirements with ever shorter times-to-market, and hopes to gain more real-time insight into the current state of affairs.

Many of the solutions discussed in this book for Saibot Airport set useful examples for similar requirements in other organizations. And at the very least, the airport provides a context that most readers from many different countries will be able to relate to.

How to Use the Book

This book is not intended as a reference manual that is used to look up specific details on an operation or feature in the SOA Suite, even though I suppose it could be used for that too.

This book is primarily a guide that invites you to come along and explore the SOA Suite. It introduces concepts and real-life requirements, using the imaginary Saibot Airport as the concrete example. It describes the functionality and features in particular components in the SOA Suite and applies them to actual business challenges. Through step-by-step cases that go beyond the archetypical Hello World and introductory order-processing examples, it demonstrates the application of product features, provides hints and tips for using them, and suggests best practices.

Even though you can read and practice individual chapters (in random order), be aware that they will often refer to decisions made in earlier chapters or features discussed in a previous stage. The chapters and topics are logically ordered in the sequence that feels most natural to me—adding scope and complexity as we work our way from simple synchronous interactions to asynchronous services and long-running business processes.

Most is gained from this book by not only browsing and reading it but also getting your feet wet by following along with the hands-on instructions in the book and the online resources. By having your hands do what your eyes are reading and your brain is processing, you will have a multichannel learning experience that delivers the most thorough and lasting results.

The Saibot Airport case provides the main storyline throughout the book. However, the examples discussed in each chapter stand on their own. You do not have to work your way through all chapters in order to implement the examples for a specific chapter. The environment in which the sources for any chapter run contains just whatever is discussed in that chapter without complex setup or dependencies on stuff from previous chapters.

Supporting Online Resources

Even though this is a sizable book, it does not contain all the SOA Suite 12c wisdom in the world. In fact, it does not even contain all information that is associated with the book itself. To allow the full breadth of the SOA Suite's functionality to be discussed in the book, some of the instructions in the book itself have been provided in summarized form or with a reduced number of illustrations. More detailed step-by-step instructions and full-color, higher-resolution screenshots, additional clarifications and links to videos, the official Oracle documentation, and alternative internet resources are provided on the book's website at www.soasuitehandbook.org.

Oracle SOA Suite Handbook Blog

resources complementing the Oracle SOA Suite Handbook

 Zoeken

| Home | Part 1 – Setting the Stage | Part 2 – Elementary Services | Part 3 – Composite Services |

| Part 4 – Asynchronous Services and Events | Part 5 – Processes | Part 6 – DevOps & Run Time Administration | Appendices |

Chapter 21 – Reuse, MDS, Versioning, Governance

Chapter 22 – Building and Deploying

Chapter 23 – SOA Suite run time operations

Chapter 24 – Security

Human Access to Run Time SOA Suite Tooling

Authentication and Authorization of Services

Confidentiality and Integrity of Message Content

Invoke Protected Services from SOA Suite

Auditing

Overview

The Oracle SOA Suite 12c Handbook serves as both an introduction and a reference to the SOA Suite 12c. The book is primarily targeted at software developers and to some extent administrators and application or solution architects.

The book is organized into the following six parts.

- Part 1 – Setting the Stage
- Part 2 – Elementary Services
- Part 3 – Composite Services
- Part 4 – Asynchronous Services and Events
- Part 5 – Processes
- Part 6 – DevOps & Run Time Administration

The menu structure on the blog section is organized according to the parts and chapters in the book. Each chapter has a dedicated page with relevant resources that support the content in the book. At specific points in the chapters, you will find references to the online resources on the book's website. These references apply to chapter-specific pages on this website.

The source codes for the examples in the book—the Saibot Airport case—are published from Github at the following URL: https://github.com/lucasjellema/soasuitehandbook.

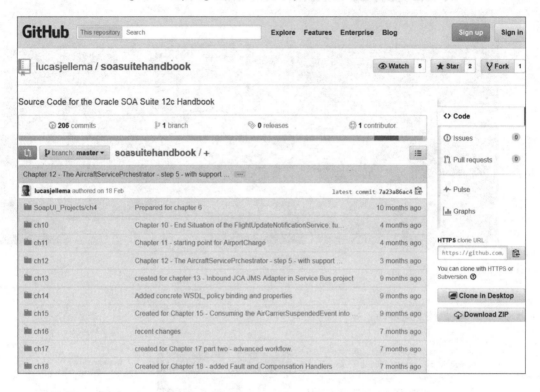

You can use the regular Git tooling to get hold of these sources in your local development environment. You can also make use of the Git support in JDeveloper to fetch the sources, use the option *Clone in Desktop* or simply download all sources in a single zip file.

If you want to provide any feedback on the book or ask questions related to the book's contents, you can post a comment on the blog or send a direct Twitter message to @lucasjellema.

PART
I

Introducing Saibot Airport, SOA, and the Oracle SOA Suite

CHAPTER
1

Saibot Airport Reaching for the Future

This book introduces you to Oracle SOA Suite 12c. It will show in great detail how the many features and functions of this rich set of products can be used and tied together. The book also tells the story of Saibot Airport—an ambitious international airport with a clear business vision about where it is going and a great need for IT solutions to enable these ambitions. Saibot Airport and its requirements constitute the case that provides the backdrop against which the SOA Suite is used. Various aspects of running and evolving the airport are used to illustrate the usage of the functionality offered by the SOA Suite.

This chapter introduces Saibot Airport as an organization with a vision and a business strategy, and one that depends heavily on IT to fulfill the strategy. The IT department itself is confronted by changing industry trends, changing regulations, new technology, and an evolution in the way it organizes its processes. From all of these, architecture consequences are derived. And finally, technology products have to be selected to start the realization of the information and application architecture designed to enable the IT and business objectives. Given the title of this book, it will come as no surprise that this made up Saibot Airport selects many components from the Oracle Fusion Middleware stack including the SOA Suite. The next chapter introduces this stack, the SOA Suite, and the role the SOA Suite plays.

Saibot Airport

Saibot Airport used to be just another mid-size airport near the great city of Lexville. It has been only a domestic hub for a long time, but for the last decade, its role in the region has become more prominent. It is very much the desire of the management team at the airport to continue and extend this trend and turn Saibot Airport into a major international hub, not dissimilar to what Dubai International Airport has achieved. The board of directors and the shareholders enthusiastically support this idea.

Like any airport, Saibot Airport offers facilities that enable airlines to provide services to passengers and logistics companies. The infrastructure includes terminal buildings, runways, parking space for planes, fuel depots, safety equipment, check-in desks and kiosks, various types of vehicles for transport inside the terminal as well as on the platform, luggage processing equipment, bird scaring machinery, and different types of flight information systems.

The airport primarily acts as a broker in services—bringing together parties offering services and parties looking for providers of such services. Examples of such services are cleaning, repairing, fueling and deicing the airplanes, handling luggage, providing security, catering, and safety. In the wake of the core activities at the airport, focused on flying, there is a wide range of other commercial activities. Saibot Airport has shops, restaurants, hotels, car rental companies, car parks, meeting rooms, office space, and entertainment areas—that are used to provide services to passengers and other visitors. Some of these services are offered by subsidiaries of Saibot Airport itself—but the vast majority are delivered by concession holders: companies that have paid for the (sometimes exclusive) right to provide certain services at the airport and rent facilities to do so. As a result, out of the many thousands of people working at the airport, only a minority is employed by Saibot Airport Corporation itself. Most are staff working at one of the hundreds of business partners active on the airport.

The airport may not do any flying itself and only execute a small portion of the activities, it does have a number of important and overarching responsibilities. These include overall safety and cleanliness of all facilities, for example, security on the ground, the technical condition of buildings and equipment, and up-to-date and accurate information with regard to flights and many other aspects of the operations on the airport.

Saibot Airport has interactions with many parties, both local and much further afield. These include the business partners active on the airport, travelers and their friends and relatives. Many interactions take place with local authorities and central government agencies, regarding topics such as environment, taxes, security, and safety.

Business Vision and Strategy

As mentioned before, Saibot Airport wants to expand and become a more important player at the *national* and *international* level. The associated increase in the number of flights to and from the airport and the number of passengers visiting the airport will drive up revenue and profit.

The potential for the growth is there, as extensive research has shown. In order to tap into that potential, the airport has to become more attractive for commercial airlines to use Saibot Airport as their hub. This is to be achieved in several ways, including offering attractive rates for using the airport facilities, ensuring a wide range of high-quality services, enabling airlines to operate very smoothly on the airport and making the airport especially appealing to travelers.

Attractive rates and smooth operations depend on a very efficient organization and implementations of processes and systems at the airport with a high rate of automation.

Getting very favorable traveler ratings is crucial. Traveler satisfaction depends on many qualities—and is not easy to obtain and retain. What matters most to passengers is a quick and painless check-in process and basic comfort in terminals. Other elements are airport accessibility, baggage claim, terminal facilities, security check, and food and retail services. Additionally, airport facilities have to be clean and good looking and within easy reach. Information plays a major role in the traveler's experience: info on how to get to the airport and how to find one's way around the airport, information on the flight and the check-in and boarding process, notifications on (changes in) the status of the flight and the ability to get quick and accurate responses to questions about airport facilities and flight details.

Any growth at Saibot Airport has to be coordinated with local and central government bodies. Safety, security, and logistics on and around the airport are to be orchestrated across the area. Especially, relevant for any growth scenario are environmental issues. Noise pollution, carbon dioxide emissions, energy consumption, and waste production are among the aspects that could constrain the growth in air traffic, unless handled carefully.

Business Objectives

To facilitate the longer term vision and goals, Saibot Airport has identified concrete business objectives it has to pursue. These are to be achieved or at least facilitated by the IT department

Modern interaction channels have to be introduced that allow 24/7 access that enable airlines to (re)schedule flights and to acquire services around these flights. Passengers and their relatives should have round-the-clock access to flight information as well as data on shops, restaurants, parking options, and travel times to and from the airport. Among these channels are to be a B2B service, a web portal, and a mobile application.

In 2018, Saibot Airport should be paperless. All information required, for example, for scheduling a slot, requesting a concession for a restaurant or renting a shop should be submitted in electronic format—both the forms and the supporting documents. Having all incoming information in digital format should reduce the workload on the inbound side of the airport's operation quite dramatically. The lead time from the moment the request is submitted to the moment a staff member can actually start working on it is should be shrunk to almost nothing thanks to the digitization. Furthermore, having multiple staff members work on the same request at the same time will finally be standard procedure—whereas today because of the single copy paper-based file this is only done in exceptional situations.

The learning curve for new staff should be much shorter than today. Saibot Airport's workforce is fairly flexible with a high turnover in several roles. A lot of money can be saved if new staff is productive in a much shorter period of time and will make fewer mistakes (currently caused by user interface unfriendliness). Management at the airport also requires more insight into the actual proceedings. It wants to be aware of delays in process execution, bottlenecks, and other process inefficiencies. Furthermore, it wants to be able to continuously improve business processes—without long lead times, massive development effort and high risks. They have heard the phrase "embrace change" at some agile seminar—and they like it. They desire the flexibility and short time to market promised by the agile evangelist.

Efficiency must be the name of the game. To be able to offer attractive rate to airlines and scale operations to the levels envisioned, the airport needs to make its operations more efficient. Marginal operational costs per flight must be reduced by at least 20 percent. Even though it is yet to be decided exactly where those costs are to be saved, it is obvious that downsizing the manual labor per transaction has to be a major part of the meeting the efficiency demands. By having business partners submitting all information in electronic format and by making all information about the progress of such requests available on line—a large part of the current workload will be taken away. Self-service through portals and mobile applications seems all about customer satisfaction—yet it can also work miracles in terms of cost savings on the part of the airport. Simpler applications with short learning curves and requiring less business understanding and process expertise should allow Saibot Airport to work with temporary workers—creating a flexible layer that can shrink and grow with the actual workload. This not only applies to the Saibot Airport organization itself but also to the many companies active on the airport. That in turn affects the airport—for example, through the frequent and usually urgent processing of security accreditation requests for new staff.

Smooth operations are crucial—from a cost perspective as well as the travelers' experience. Check-in, security, and boarding procedures are all too often hindered by inaccurate or incomplete information about the passengers or some flight details. This also applies to processing of luggage, informing all stakeholders of changes regarding the flight and coordination of catering, fueling, and cleaning the plane prior to departure. Ensuring the rapid electronic exchange of up-to-date and complete data regarding the flight schedule, the passengers and crew and the services to be provided to the air plane is crucial to be able to operate smoothly and efficient and to scale up these operations.

IT Objectives

The CIO—guided by his team of architects and with a clear link to the overall goals set by the board—has made sure that a number of specific IT objectives have been included in the program's design. She wants to ensure that the vital role IT plays for the operation of the airport is recognized and that a clear statement is laid down with regard to IT that serves as the starting point of the IT roadmap.

From the overhead objectives, it is already obvious that IT plays a large part in realizing the desired move toward the future. More specific statements in the program about IT are also included.

An enterprise architecture design has been created and serves as the foundation for all future projects. Modern IT architecture patterns will be adopted to translate the enterprise architecture into IT architecture and subsequently into designs of applications and infrastructure.

The architecture and the technology selected have to allow for flexibility: changing functionality should be possible in a simple, cheap, fast and risk free manner. Saibot Airport wants to go *agile*, both in business and in IT. Furthermore, the evolution of the systems, the transitions to new systems all have to take place while the shop stays open. The airport clearly cannot afford to close down, especially once 24/7 online channels (web, B2B, mobile) have been introduced.

Saibot Airport's IT should be based on current industry standards that are open and promote interaction and reuse. It should not be on the bleeding edge of technology and only use concepts and components that have been proven. At the same time Saibot Airport's IT has to be up to date in order to appeal to both staff and clients and allow the airport to find the right resources to help design, develop, and administrate the infrastructures and systems. There is neither special preference for nor aversion against open source software. However, Saibot Airport has found out the hard way that it should only use software that has a large community around it and one or more large commercial parties backing it.

It is the airport's intention to work with a small number of strategic vendors that have a broad product portfolio, a clear roadmap, ability and intention to keep evolving and a willingness to cooperate and ideally take responsibility for Saibot Airport's success with their products. Slideware won't do: the potential of the vendor's products has to be demonstrated through customer references. A technology (and vendor) selection has been made by the airport, which included consultation with industry analysts.

The airport is opening up to the outside world. In the past, many of its interactions beyond the perimeter of its physical site were on paper, through fax or telephone. Until not too long ago, its main online interaction comprised of email and a read-only website based on a database in the DMZ that was refreshed once a day from a file dump with real-time actual flight information. Now, however, real-time synchronous interactions with the enterprise systems will have to be supported, in the B2B exchange, for the mobile apps and for a much more interactive, real-time web application. Security has to be at the heart of these initiatives. It is imperative for certain information to be only made available to authorized parties—and hence it is crucial to identify any party dealing with the airport in a secure way.

The integrity of the data will also play an even more important role; automated processes do not have the same capacity as humans to cater for inconsistencies or simple typos in data. Furthermore, because the data from internal systems will be published directly to portal and B2B channels, without human checks and filters, the quality of the data has to improve beyond what it is today.

Part of the plans is reducing IT expenditure by consolidating onto a central infrastructure with a single source of truth for each data domain. This should also help with the quality of data—with far less data duplication and replication. This also should have the effect of lower hardware costs, lower software license expenses, and a downsized administration staff. In the initial stages of the program's execution, however, it is envisioned that IT spending will increase because of the many projects that will have to be carried out in order to meet the objectives. Saibot Airport is looking closely into the possibilities of making use of cloud service to achieve not only the consolidation but also the ability to achieve "web scale" IT operations that as a mid-size organization they would never be able to realize on their own. Leveraging cloud services would also allow the airport to graciously handle temporary increases in demand for IT infrastructure capacity without making structural investments.

The intended consolidation of all IT infrastructure and all data into a single instance means on the one hand a relief for the security officer as it means fewer sites, administrators, and environments to worry about. However, this consolidation means that availability, which in the 24/7 world of Saibot Airport is essential, becomes a much harder challenge. The consolidated systems, logically a single instance, are the critical factor in virtually all of the activities. It is a single point of failure—at least logically. Part of the IT roadmap is taking measures to safeguard the availability of all IT components—for example, through clustering and fail-over.

Architecture to Enable the Future

The architecture team at the airport leads the way in terms of technology evolution. This team has drawn up the high level IT architecture, selected and fine-tuned the architecture patterns that are to be applied and worked with developers to design the reference architecture. This reference architecture provides guidelines on how to make use of architectural patterns when designing system components and how to make use of the selected technology to implement these patterns. It also provides a common vocabulary with which to discuss implementations. A crucial architecture product is the roadmap that defines how Saibot Airport can go through the transition from the current to the to-be situation.

Partly based on these architecture designs, the strategic technology and vendor selection is made; it is after all imperative that the vendor and his product portfolio is capable of implementing the architecture as designed by the team.

The legacy at Saibot Airport involved a classic case of application *silos*: stand-alone units that consist of a database, business logic, and a user interface. Each application is implemented through its own silo—using distinct and sometimes very proprietary technologies and maintained by fairly inward facing, somewhat self-absorbed teams. Flexibly sharing resources between these teams is neither common nor easy. Technical integration between the silos for exchanging and ideally truly sharing data is hard to achieve too; frequently files are used to export and import data in an asynchronous batch process that may involve manual actions as well. Data replication is common as is the human task of typing to reenter data: even though data may already exist in one silo that does not mean it is accessible to another. Because data exchange is not readily available, manually keying in that same information is frequently the easy way out.

Breaking up the silos is an absolute requirement in the new architecture. Lasagna style is on the menu: a layered architecture with clear responsibilities assigned to each layer and well-defined interfaces describing the interactions between these layers. Figure 1-1 illustrates this transition.

No single team or application is owner of what essentially is and always should have been treated as enterprise data that can be used in many different processes. Teams and projects are not masters of their own destiny: decisions they make regarding technology, application layout, and implementation patterns are part of the enterprise landscape and have to fit in.
The layers identified in this architecture:

- User interface and programmatic interface layer—the interaction with the outside world through human-oriented as well as system-oriented interfaces
- Business layer—common interface to data and business logic reusable across user and programmatic interfaces
- Data layer—the persistency and integrity of all enterprise information assets including documents and other unstructured data

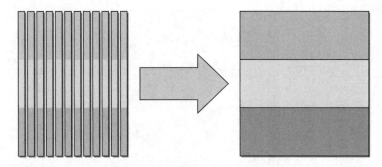

FIGURE 1-1.   *Transition from application silos to a layered architecture*

Identifying these layers will help to establish a clear *separation of concerns*. Each layer has its own role using its own design patterns and designated technology. The implementation of each layer is encapsulated to other layers. Layers can only invoke the next lower layer. Layers are unaware of any other layers except for the one directly underneath them. Communication is always started at the top, flowing downward.

Each layer should have clear interfaces defined that describe the interaction that it supports. Part of this interface description is the definition of the operations that can be invoked in the layer, the input they require and the output they return—including exceptions that can be thrown—as well as a description of side effects of the call, such as emails being sent, products being shipped, or data being persisted. Nonfunctional aspects of operations should also be described; these include availability (opening hours), costs, authorization and other security aspects, response time, and accepted volumes.

One of the key decisions made in the early stages of the architecture design was the adoption of many service-oriented architecture (SOA) principles. These principles include decoupling (well, loose coupling at the very least), abstraction and encapsulation, reusability, and location virtualization. Applying these principles will help to implement the layered architecture and will play a large part in the flexibility, short time to market, efficiency through reuse, and risk reduction that the business requires.

The Triangle

An increasingly important role in discussion about Saibot Airport's IT future was played by a very simple illustration. Basically nothing but a triangle, with its base at the top; see Figure 1-2.

This triangle visualizes the distinction between the layers in terms of their reuse potential and generic nature versus their multichannel support and level of customization.

The data layer is characterized by centralization and (logical) consolidation. Data assets have a single source of truth. This layer has a very high reuse potential and generic, enterprise-wide structure. As a core enterprise resource, requirements in quality, integrity, availability, and confidentiality are very high. The rate of change at this level is fairly low—at least at the meta-level. Data is not removed very frequently and the data structures evolve even slower. Note that big data and fast data are a special kind of data—raw data that serves very operational goals or undergoes substantial processing before ending up in this enterprise data layer.

The top layer that exposes interfaces to users and applications is quite different. It sports a large variety, catering to very specific channels, consumers, and user roles—allowing customization and

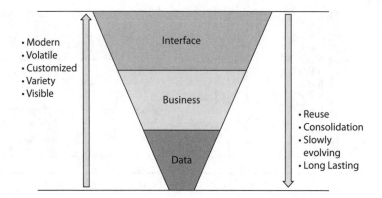

FIGURE 1-2. *The characteristics of the three main layers in the layered architecture*

personalization to meet special requirements. The average life time of components in this layer is fairly short, especially compared to the data layer, and the rate of change is much higher.

The business layer, the man in the middle, is also in the middle in terms of reusability and rate of change. It offers services that are aimed at reuse by various different interface components. This layer brings together various assets from the data layer, implements business logic, validates, processes and enriches data, and runs processes. The rate of change is higher than at the data layer as is the functional variety. Compared to the user and application interface layer, however, this layer evolves much slower, is much more focused at reuse and caters for far fewer specific, one-off needs.

Most business requirements are expected to find the majority of the required effort in the top layer, a sizable portion still in the middle layer and very little effort in the bottom layer. The triangle therefore also represents the work ratio in many development projects and therefore suggests a team composition.

The transition IT at Saibot Airport is undergoing is now characterized at a very abstract level by Figure 1-3.

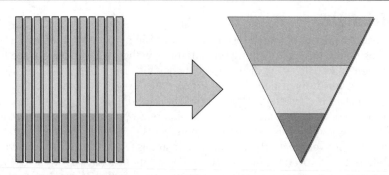

FIGURE 1-3. *From application silos to the layered architecture with varying degrees of consolidation and change*

Domains of Data

The enterprise architecture has identified domains within Saibot Airport—relatively independent areas. Data in each domain and services exposing that data are to be controlled by domain experts. There are no direct relationships between components in different domains. The thinking should be that at any time a domain could be reimplemented using a commercial off-the-shelf offering such as a SaaS CRM system or a third party expertise application.

Some of the domains identified by the architects are: common (reference data), relations, flight slots and schedules, security, concessions, documents, and finance.

Most interactions within and across domains will involve data. A common understanding of and language for interacting in terms of the data is essential. The architects have launched an initiative to create an Enterprise Data Model (EDM). This model describes all business objects that are meaningful to Saibot Airport's operations, including their properties and relationships. Common terminology as well as lists of reference values that are to be used to set the value of certain properties are defined in a standardized way and made available throughout the organization. Note: The model is defined at the business layer and it may not necessarily be fully aligned with the database structures and other technical assets inside each of the domains. The EDM is the common business language across all of Saibot Airport—stretching beyond IT. All interactions between the business layer and the data layer will be in terms of the EDM. Note that operations inside the data layer will probably use existing idiom and structures for quite some time to come—which is unavoidable and perfectly acceptable.

Service-Oriented Architecture

The decision to make service-oriented architecture the leading architecture principle has a number of consequences. Middleware is still fairly new at the airport. Teams used to be organized around applications—around the silos that were discussed earlier on. The business layer at the heart of the layered architecture will be the new focal point for all teams. This layer is made up of a number of different types of services. These services bring together all data from the data layer—structured and unstructured, across databases, document repositories, LDAP instances and mail servers—and expose access to the data in a standardized, unified way. Moreover, these services make business logic available to applications—both user interfaces and programmatic channels.

Part of the foundation of the business layer is the Enterprise Data Model (aka Canonical Data Model) and more specifically: an XML representation of that model, expressed in terms of a heavily annotated XSD (XML Schema Definition). All data structures handled by the services, both input and output, are defined in correspondence with business objects in this canonical XSD. The data domains are recognizable through the namespace structure used in these XSD definitions.

The architecture team came up with a service classification scheme that helps organize the services as well as the teams working on those services. Following this scheme, the business layer is subdivided in these types of services (as illustrated in Figure 1-4).

- Elementary services that provide atomic functionality within a domain; their reuse potential is high, their added value usually is low

- Composite services that combine two or more elementary services into business functions with higher added value; composite services come in two flavors:

  - Within a domain

  - Across domains—typically introducing the need for either global transactions or transaction compensation; even such cross-domain services should have a single owner—perhaps a designated domain

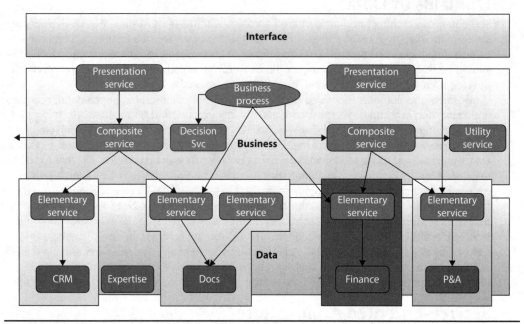

FIGURE 1-4. *Domains and service types at Saibot Airport*

- Process services that are often asynchronous and longer running (up to minutes, hours, or even days) and that will usually contain state while running

- Presentation services that are usually not meant for general reuse; instead they cater for specific needs of an application—either a user interface or a programmatic interface, speaking the language of that application as closely as possible

- Utility services—generic, domain independent, highly reusable services, frequently of an almost infrastructural nature; for example, logging, sending emails, value translation, and geocoding

Service design and implementation guidelines are created per service category. Governance, ownership, testing and many other aspects of the services also depend on the type of service. Saibot Airport ended up closely aligning its team structure with these categories of services—as we will see in a later section.

NOTE
Except for presentation services, the service interfaces are expressed in terms of the canonical data model. They are all recorded in a central service catalog where potential consumers will find information about the service including functionality, contract, nonfunctional aspects and status. At Saibot Airport, this service catalog started life as a simple Wiki that references the live WSDL (Web Service Definition Language) and XSD specifications of services.

Event-Driven Architecture

For the architecture layers it was stated that a layer cannot invoke a higher layer—or even be aware of it. The same applies to the service categories: a service is unaware—and therefore completely independent—of higher level services. It cannot directly initiate communications with higher level services. This means, for example, that an elementary service cannot invoke a composite service or process service; for all intents and purposes, it may not even know such higher level services exist.

This does not mean however that a lower level layer or service will never have something to tell that could be of interest to a higher level service. It means there has to be another way of communicating that information then telling it in a direct call. To address this challenge, the architects have adopted elements from Event-Driven Architecture (EDA). Events are used as the very decoupled vehicle to convey information without direct any dependencies between the source and the recipient(s) of the information.

In addition to defining the canonical data model and identifying the services, Saibot Airport's information analysts are working on discovering business events. A business event is a condition or situation that may come about somewhere in the airport's daily operations that is potentially of interest to other parties. Events of interest to a component within the Saibot Airport landscape can of course also take place in the outside world; these too classify as business event.

A business event is described by a name or type, a timestamp and a payload—data that clarifies what the event entails. Some examples of business events at the airport are: weather alert, (outbound) flight has been cancelled, airline has filed for bankruptcy, deadline has expired in some business process, business rule has been changed.

The reference architecture describes an event handling infrastructure—a generic facility that is available to all application components and services alike—as shown in Figure 1-5. Anyone can

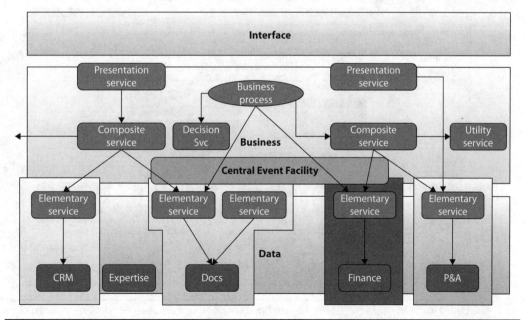

FIGURE 1-5. *The Central Event Facility handles events in an extremely decoupled approach*

publish a business event to this event handler—provided the event type is predefined and the payload has the predefined structure. After publishing the event, the publisher is not involved in any way with the delivery of the event and does not even know if the event is consumed by any party at all. Any component at any layer in the architecture can subscribe to selected types of business events. The event handler will push any published event to all subscribers to the type of this published event. Consumers of the event will receive the event with its payload and can do with it as they see fit. They are not aware of the component that published the event.

The perfect decoupling achieved through the events makes it extremely simple to add consumers of a particular type of event or to introduce new publishers of some event type. Removing subscribers to an event is another zero impact procedure, as is losing one or more publishers of events.

Through events, elementary services and even components in the data layer can tell their story that may be of great interest to composite or process services or even to user interface components—without ever knowing about them. The interaction can take place, but in an entirely decoupled fashion.

On Technology and Vendor Selection

The business objectives and the derived layered architecture as well as the more detailed architecture principles result in a clear image of the technology components required by Saibot Airport. Figure 1-6 shows the most important components that need to be implemented through technology products that will have to be selected and acquired from one or more vendors.

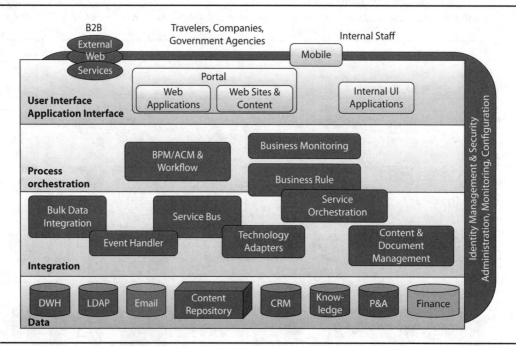

FIGURE 1-6. *An overview of the key technology components that Saibot Airport needs to select and acquire*

Saibot Airport has stated from the outset that it does not want to buy into a single integrated suite of products only because it is a single integrated suite. It wants the best of breed: the best product available in each category. It requires all products to be open, standards based and easily integratable.

A number of additional criteria were determined, based upon which products would be evaluated.

The airport does not have IT as its core activity. It wants to use proven and supported technology and products, backed by verifiable references. It needs a product to have a clear strategy as well as a strong community and an abundance of resources. The latter refers both to qualified IT professionals and to books, internet forums and blogs, training material, etc. The learning curve for a product should be clear and justifiable—judged against the existing workforce.

Any product should have strategic importance to its vendor. Besides, the vendor (or open source project) should be stable and future proof. Analyst reviews are retrieved and taken into consideration.

Saibot Airport does not want to have a large variety of technologies and platforms that require different skills. Even though it is a substantial organization, resources are limited. It wants to focus on a small number of major industry platforms—hardware, O/S, virtualization, database and middleware—as to prevent a nightmare for the administrators. All products selected should provide sufficient options for monitoring and configuration and they should allow for automated build and deployment.

Of course the cost of the software is an important part of the decision. Here, the selection process will look at a number of aspects. What is the license fee per pricing unit—user, CPU core—and what is the estimated number of pricing units. What is the yearly support fee and what are pricing elements play a role? What discounts can be negotiated? How long are the licenses valid for? What alternative constructions are available—such as a subscription fee? Furthermore, what assurances about the software behavior is the prepared to make? What SLAs will it enter? Is the vendor prepared to take some form of responsibility for the successful implementation of the software—possibly a no cure no pay construction or a fee that is partly based on the return on the investment. What are the options for using the software *from the cloud* to complement an on premises investment with a pay-per-use, scalable capacity?

Selection Approach

Saibot Airport had to make two selections that cannot be separated. It had to select one or more vendors and it needs to select the products that will implement the functions identified in the architecture.

It published a *Request for Information* in which it invited any vendor to answer questions for each of the components identified in the target architecture. This RFI focused on checklist on features, technical characteristics, implementation requirements, training, and order of magnitude pricing. Responses were received from vendors of niche products, specialists in very specific areas as well as reactions from vendors of suites of products that covered wide ranges of products. It also invited a number of parties to represent open source products.

In parallel with the RFI process, the airport gathered information from peer organizations—largely governmental—about product and vendor experiences. Saibot Airport also consulted market analysts—both online and in person.

The information received in this first round from the RFI and the parallel explorations was screened and evaluated, based on the criteria listed overhead. This resulted in a short list of both products and vendors. The vendors on this short list were invited for the next stage: *request for proposal*.

In this stage, vendors were asked to present a plan for how their product(s) could best be used by the airport—including the infrastructure topology, the licenses, the migration of systems and transition of processes and staff. The proposal needed to cover the overall price as well as any alternative compensation proposals such as deferred payment, result-based payment, subscription-based fee, and usage-based fee.

Each vendor had to present relevant customer reference cases that could be contacted and visited. It also had to lay down the product roadmap and longer term vision and strategy. Saibot Airport wanted to be convinced that the products presented were indeed future proof.

By this time, the airport had decided to take a slightly different approach. It defined several technology clusters that it wanted to select in somewhat separate stages. Roughly like this:

- Hardware—no immediate investment; virtualization using VM Ware was the short-term way forward; investigations are started into a multisite, disaster proof, very high availability data center setup.

- Database—consolidation on Oracle Database 12c—using the multitenancy option for consolidation (which means upgrading some databases and replacing some MySQL and SQL Server databases).

- Mobile—no strategic selection is made for now; given the volatility in the mobile market and the fact that mobile applications are on the very outside of the enterprise with little impact and a short lifespan, it was deemed unnecessary to make a strategic selection for mobile technology; being able to support mobile applications by exposing relevant (REST) services was deemed much more important.

- Internal user interface applications—for quite some time to come, some Oracle Forms applications will be used and maintained; one application has been migrated to (or rather rebuilt in) Oracle ADF 11g. The airport has evaluated its experiences with ADF and decided that for now it has no reason to select a different technology—only switch to the latest version of the framework (12c). It did of course verify the strategic importance of ADF for Oracle, the strength of the community, the roadmap and vision and the pricing, and found them satisfactory. The availability of external resources is somewhat worrying, although the realization that ADF is a Java EE framework that any Java Web Developer can quickly embrace by and large took care of that worry.

For the following clusters, a separate Request for Proposal is conducted:

- Service Oriented Middleware—Saibot Airport needs products to implement an enterprise service bus, service orchestration, Event-Driven Architecture, technology adapters; these products have to work together well and ideally use the same platform.

- Process and human workflow management—in this cluster, Saibot Airport identified the need for decision rules (aka business rules), business process orchestration, human tasks and workflow management, and business activity monitoring (BAM); these products have to be able to closely work together.

- Enterprise content management—one of the business objectives is the complete eradication of paper; working with digital documents is crucial for the organization. It requires products to store, search and publish, convert, tag and track, archive and protect digital documents in various formats. These products should of course fit in the service-oriented architecture that will be established.

■ Portals and external user interface applications—because of the decoupling achieved in the layered architecture and the use of services, the dependencies between portals and other external interfaces on the one hand and the products in the business layer on the other are minimal; that means that a decision on the products used for these portals can be made independently of the other product selections.

■ Identity and access management—Saibot Airport is opening up its enterprise applications to users outside the organization; this new situations calls for a new approach to management of identities, the implementation of authentication and the authorization based on the identity; the airport currently uses Active Directory for its internal staff and is not keen on abandoning that platform (as it is integrated into the overall office automation). It wants to introduce products that will handle identities and authorization for external users. It also requires products that handle encryption, digital signatures, and other security techniques that are to be applied to certain services.

Selections

Most of the products in the clusters *Service-Oriented Middleware* and *Process and Human Workflow Management* that made it onto the short list were based on the Java EE platform. Added to this, the fact that the technology for the internal applications was set as ADF 12*c*, another Java EE–based technology, and good old Oracle Forms—also running on the Java EE platform, Saibot Airport decided to choose Java EE as the platform for all its middleware. It also selected Oracle WebLogic 12*c* as the Java EE application server of choice. Only when a best of breed product would be selected with superior functionality that would be unable to run on WebLogic could another application server be considered. Note that the team at Saibot Airport very specifically kept open the possibility to support a different platform in the User and Application Interface layer. Some internal politics may have been part of that decision; there was some resistance against going Java all the way from some of the .Net-oriented teams.

The product selection for enterprise service bus and service orchestration (the latter quickly translated to BPEL) evaluated among other Microsoft BizTalk and various Tibco products as well as some open source offerings and then decided on Oracle SOA Suite including the Service Bus. This combination also brought in the required technology adapters and support for event handling—through the SOA Suite Event Delivery Network, as well as support for JMS and AQ (Advanced Queuing).

The support in SOA Suite for Decision (Business) Rules and Human Workflow as well as the strong integration with Oracle BPM Suite at both design time and run time weighed strongly in favor of the latter when the product selection was made for process orchestration and human workflow. The SOA Suite license includes most of the required functionality with rich (enough) functionality and a track record of many years. The BPM Suite adds support for true BPMN process modeling and execution and comes with a range of run time tools that help design, track and monitor, manage and collaborate on process instances. Saibot Airport ended up selecting BPM Suite because of its best of breed quality with the huge added bonus of perfect integration with SOA Suite.

NOTE
An on-site visit at St. Matthew's Hospital where SOA Suite 11g had been in use since early 2010 proved extremely helpful. The experiences at the hospital with almost all aspects of implementing the layered architecture using Oracle Fusion Middleware and in particular SOA Suite 11g were very valuable to the Saibot Airport staff. They were after all about to embark on a very similar journey that the hospital already had been on for the previous five years.

The product selection for content management did not go very smooth at all. This area is quite new at the airport and there is not a lot of grasp of the subject matter. An external consultant was hired—and quickly let go off again when he turned out to be quite biased (without making that clear up front). Then the definitions of what constitutes content—and what does not—in this selection process were contested. Some people had a vision of the static content of websites whereas others were thinking about all documents—or even all unstructured data—passing through the organization. Even the naming of the Oracle product—WebCenter Content—made some eyebrows go up; it sounded like that static website content thing that they had been able to get off the table after much debate. Only the reassurance that WebCenter Content was in fact the Universal Content Manager restored peace and quiet. In the end, it was decided to give WebCenter Content a go—not because it was such a clear winner but because of the integration in the Oracle Fusion Middleware Platform and the perceived lower risk and smaller effort resulting from that integration.

This next illustration, Figure 1-7, shows the products that were selected. The choice of the portal technology is yet to be made; for the time being, existing .Net and Sharepoint teams

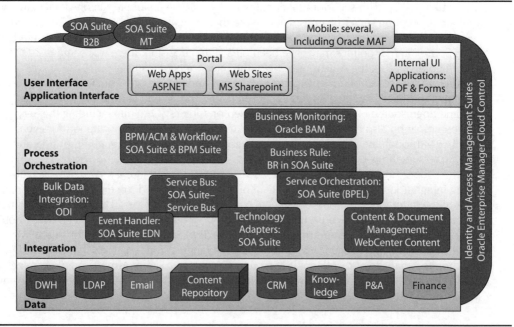

FIGURE 1-7. *Mapping the required components to actual products*

continue development work with their proven technology—connecting to the services offered from the business layer.

The decision on Identity Management and Security is proving difficult. Part of the complexity is the licensing conditions regarding all potential users of Saibot Airport's systems: anyone traveling through the airport is after all a potential user. The airport is negotiating with various vendors of IdM products on how to handle that particular situation in license terms. No final selection has been made. Fortunately, the Oracle Platform Security Services in the WebLogic Platform insulate applications running on the platform—such as ADF applications, SOA Suite Composite applications and Service Bus services—from the actual IdM technology. Any development work being done right now will not be impacted by a later decision on the specific products for identity management and authentication.

After the selections and the associated contracts have been approved by the board of directors, things moved forward and once the infrastructure was prepared, the software was actually installed and staff members educated. The business objectives that had lived on paper for several years now and the architecture design that decorated many a whiteboard were on the verge of getting real.

Processes and Organization

Saibot Airport has traveled part of the road mapped in their business plan. The first few of many projects for transitions of existing systems or the introduction of new business functionality through IT have been executed or are in progress. New technology has been introduced as well as a fundamentally changed way of approaching software development. While the road is bumpy, successes are far more abundant than failures. Reluctance was pretty widespread when the first steps with service orientation and layered architecture were taken and now the mood has changed. Many IT staff members are getting convinced of the approach in general and their ability to play a part in it. Enthusiasm is growing with self-confidence.

The way the airport is now perceived by its own staff, its many business partners, the travelers, liaisons in government bodies, etc. has improved substantially over the past few years. The modernization of applications appeals to all involved and an increase of the quality of service and information has been reported across the board. Shorter waiting times, fewer mistakes, and a better experience are among the results found in a recent survey. An internal evaluation under employees yielded similar outcomes with a higher satisfaction and a much higher score at the standard survey question "do you intend to work at Saibot Airport one year from now."

Among the very first steps in the program has been the consolidation of data into a single database and the centralization of all infrastructure in a single data center (which has two physical sites). All administration activities have been centralized as well. This has turned out to be much more efficient and also allows administrators to specialize. Instead of having to manage small pieces of everything—from network and storage all the way up to operating system and database—they now have responsibility for a much larger piece of one special area. External help is needed much less frequently because of this specialization. That in turn means costs are down and mean times to resolution are shorter.

The data consolidation is proceeding in several steps. First the data was stored in a single database—with the data still scattered across application schemas. Gradually, data becomes truly shared, reducing the duplication and resulting inconsistencies. This is not just a technical process—it also requires putting some pressure on the business representatives who are somewhat wary of sharing their data.

The transition from Oracle Classic [Forms, Data (CRUD-style) and Database oriented, SQL and PL/SQL, Discoverer, Designer] and waterfall approach to the new world of agile and service oriented along with Java and web user interfaces, Mobile, and BPM is scary and overwhelming. Guidance, reassurance, explanations, and almost spiritual support are absolutely necessary to motivate and enable staff in almost every role. For a long period, constant attention is required to engage people who are suspicious and frightened about what is happening. Communication is essential for the success of the kind of rapid evolution the airport is going through.

All roles, from business owner to administrator, need to be involved with the initial transition and with every new initiative involving software development. Support and involvement from C-level is crucial.

Embrace change is the adage of the agile approach to software development that Saibot Airport has adopted. That has been and still is a challenge for many of the parties involved. Even though it is acknowledged rationally that *change* is part of the game, changes in direction and planning are still frequently experienced as very disruptive. Involving the members of the Scrum-team early on whenever such changes occur is important in order to preserve their engagement and motivation.

The Scrum methodology has rapidly taken hold. The initial skepticism was quickly overcome for most and some of the early skeptics are now true Scrum believers—sometimes even bordering on the fanatical side. The commitment of team-members to the team and of the teams to the business objectives has increased dramatically. The constant focus on near rather than distant deadlines and rapid feedback from the business representative turns out to be very motivating for the teams and the quick feedback from the teams to the business also helps the business to adjust requirements. IT staff are usually pretty smart if somewhat overly focused people and their input is used to improve the plans and designs.

The responsibility the business needs to take on in order to gain agility and continuous delivery is substantial. In order for the Scrum approach to work well, the product owner needs to be available very frequently, needs to be thoroughly engaged and be able and authorized to make decisions on priorities and functional design choices. This role can make or break the software development endeavor.

The new way of working—both in terms of architecture and technology and also in terms of software development methodology and process—impacts all roles involved. Some roles, however, were far more changed in the transition. There is the role of the business owner—who has become far more actively involved throughout the project. Other roles undergoing substantial change are tester and administrator. Both are far earlier engaged in development initiatives and closer collaborating with or even embedded within the Scrum teams. New technologies and a broader scope of responsibilities make these roles more interesting as well as challenging.

One aspect of the Scrum way of working that Saibot Airport is still somewhat struggling with is the tension that frequently arises between the short-term focus of the sprints and the longer term architecture objectives. Technical debt is a term coined to describe the corners cut during sprints when functionality wins over coding standards and architectural guidelines. Technical debt should be settled before too long—and all parties agree on that principle—however, it proves a constant struggle to actually claim part of the team's capacity away from functional business value to longer term software quality and maintainability.

The database and SQL and PL/SQL continue to be incredibly important to the overall success of the application architecture. Performance, scalability, integrity can benefit from good or suffer from poor usage of the database capabilities.

It has proven extremely helpful to bring in real-world experience with as many aspects as possible of the transition and the target architecture and way of working; this helped prevent costly (and time-consuming) mistakes that would also cause frustration and undermine confidence in what is already a fragile environment. Experience helps to select and apply proven best practices. Experienced outsiders also allowed knowledge transfer in a hands-on situation—instead of just a classroom—and gives the trainer the opportunity to prove his salt.

Outsiders were brought in to initially show how things should be done, then later on to collaborate with the internal staff on equal footing and finally to act as part time coaches and quality assurers when the internal staff took over for real. The long-term objective is to build up the capabilities of the internal staff and in the short-term experiences outsiders can help boost productivity.

Service-Oriented Architecture

Even though the service orientation yields substantial returns in the long run—through reuse and agile development on top of existing services—there will be initial investments to put the architecture and the infrastructure in place. Some of the cost precedes the gain. Embracing the layered architecture and doing this SOA-thing has to be strategic decision and requires some steadfastness. Ideally of course, there is some low hanging fruit or an urgent business requirement that can lead to a first project that can be the carrier for the launch of the SOA implementation and have a quick and visible business value.

Encapsulation is a powerful notion. The implementation of a service is not relevant to its consumers. The contracts, both the functional interface and the nonfunctional usage aspects, are what consumers rely on. This means among other things that legacy applications can very well be embedded in the new architecture. As long as they can be wrapped inside standards-compliant interfaces that are mediated from to adapters on top of those legacy applications, they fit in quite well in the new world. Encapsulation makes it possible to then replace the legacy implementation of the service, along with its adapter, with a custom implementation using the technology of choice or perhaps with a COTS product.

The decoupled architecture approach also allows for specialized teams—working on isolated, clearly identified areas within the system landscape; that also means that not every developer needs to acquire skills for all tools and technologies involved (at once).

The layered architecture and the decoupled software design make it possible to outsource chunks of works to external partners. For example, once all service interfaces have been agreed upon, a nearby or even a far-away company can build a website or mobile application on top of these interfaces. Rapid development and flexible software engineering capacity—especially when a cloud-based development environment is used—are at the fingertips of the IT manager.

Governance is a critical element, especially in the mid to longer range. Governance is the approach for managing services and related assets (such as the canonical model) through their life cycle. It also includes identifying new services and changes to existing ones, cataloguing services in a way that makes them findable and ultimately reusable, and performing QA on design and implementation to ensure consistency and adherence to the standards specified as part of the governance initiative.

Tools

The short release cycles and frequent, near continuous, delivery can only be realized with automated build and deployment procedures that ideally include testing as well. These procedures for building and rolling out software deliverables should be coordinated and monitored.

Something similar applies to the environments in which the artifacts are deployed—the combination of platform and frameworks that make up the infrastructure in which the developed software runs. The environment consists both of standard software from third party vendors and the specific configuration this software as it applies to Saibot Airport. Controlling the creation, roll out of and updates to these environments is another process that requires automated execution and control in order to achieve an agile and managed delivery process.

The airport has selected a wide assortment of tools, most of them from open source projects, to aid with software engineering. Among these are tools that help with a variety of tasks, most in the area of DevOps. Bringing together the worlds of preparation (or development) and operations (aka ops) is tagged with the popular term DevOps. It is closely associated with an agile way of working that strives for quick time to market for updates in software, platform, and infrastructure. This can only be achieved by smooth communication, close collaboration, and a high degree of automation with regard to build, test, and deploy.

For orchestrating and monitoring the overall build process, Hudson was selected—and stuck to when the Jenkins fork occurred. The build actions themselves are largely done using Maven. In conjunction with Maven, the tool Artifactory is used as a repository for code artifacts. For controlled deployment, a tool called DeployIt has been acquired (this product is not open source). Rolling out environments has been tackled with Puppet.

For various types of testing activities, the following tools were selected:

- Web services: SoapUI (functional), JMeter, and LoadUI (load and stress)
- Java and ADF Business Components: jUnit (function and load)
- Web applications: JMeter (functional and primarily load); Selenium (functional); Oracle Application Testing Suite (under evaluation for both functional and load testing)

In addition, some of the built in testing features of the SOA Suite are used as well. Some attempts have been made to create unit tests for web components and composite services through the use of mock objects. EasyMock (for Java) and SoapUI with Jetty (for mock web services) were used for this.

Management of tickets—issues, requirements, enhancement requests—is done using Jira. This tool is also used for coordinating the Backlog (Product and Team Sprint) and the Scrum board.

Source code control is done using Subversion—although some investigation has been done into Git. No final decision has been made yet as to whether a migration to Git should be initiated.

With regard to the quality control of the code, a number of tools are applied—by and large only for Java code and not yet taking Service Bus, SOA Suite and BPM artifacts into account. Some of the frameworks used in this area are Sonar (for integrating the findings from various other QA tools), Checkstyle (for verifying adherence to coding conventions), PMD (spotting bad practices), and FindBugs (for finding potential bugs).

MediaWiki has been set up to allow teams and guilds (see below) to collaborate and share. The Wiki is used for checklists, how-to documents, configuration instructions, the catalog of services, records of design considerations, and motivated decisions. Also on the Wiki are architecture guidelines, coding conventions, descriptions of DTAP environments along with all URLs for the consoles and composers and associated tools for Service Bus, SOA Suite, WebCenter Content, and WebLogic Server.

Organization and Roles

The distinction between projects doing initial development and maintenance teams doing corrective and adaptive management is removed. With very short release cycles, the need for dedicated teams with special focus on maintenance working against a higher frequency release cycle than the projects teams largely disappeared. It seemed a waste to spread expertise in technology and application thin across development and maintenance. And it is considered a good idea that developers and teams take responsibility for evolving, which includes correcting, their own deliverables.

At the same time, the notion of project teams was dropped. Development teams would be created that focus on certain areas of functionality through development skills on a subset of all technology in use at the airport. These teams could be enlisted for user stories (features) defined by several business projects. They also were mandated to spend between 20 and 30 percent of their time on corrective and adaptive maintenance. Up to 10 percent of the time was free to use on "small effort, big gain" activities: business requests that are not really part of a formal user story or project back log but that can add substantial business value with very little risk and effort. Given the short release cycles, this flexibility easily provides happy faces among end users and developers.

The testers used to have their stage in the waterfall approach where—after plenty of preparations, based on detailed design documents—they would torture the software artifacts in order to verify its fitness. Testing was typically done in isolation—the only contact with the development team consisting of the issue tracking system. Testing focused almost exclusively on the user interface—by and large ignoring the internal components.

"Testing 2.0" in a Scrum way of working is very different. Testers are embedded in the Scrum teams. Testing is done as part of every sprint. Design documents are high level if at all available. Testing needs to be geared toward user expectations and interface designs. Testing involves a large chunk of nonuser interface services—such as web services and including database APIs. The use of tooling for automated (regression) testing is rapidly increasing. Communication and collaboration between testers and other team members such as analysts and developers grows from next to nothing to pretty intense. It is not uncommon for testers to engage in other activities in the early stages of a sprint—and for analysts and developers to pick up testing tasks near the end of a sprint. Feedback on software quality is much faster than in the old way of working. At the same time, testing may not be as rigorous as it used to be, although the gradual buildup of automatic test sets eventually brings testing to a fairly high level.

Similarly drastic are the changes for the administrators. For many years, administrators either did hardware and systems administration or database administration. By and large, activities were performed decoupled from development projects and only geared toward production systems. In a few years, a new world descended on the administrators. The introduction of virtualization made a huge difference to the administrators. New skills were required and new options became available, for quick deployment of new environments for example or easy rollback of an environment to a previous snapshot. Planning machines no longer meant the same thing as planning the hardware.

The next major wave of newness consisted of the introduction of middleware. The application server is the core element and then several engines run on the application server—each performing different functions that each required administrative effort in terms of installation, configuration, and monitoring. Expertise on WebLogic Server as well as administration for the Service Bus, the SOA Suite, WebCenter Content, and BPM Suite had to be built up.

Platform administration and infrastructure administration were identified as two individual and complementary disciplines and some steps are being taken to organize and offer the platform and infrastructure as private cloud services. Additionally, investigations have started into using external cloud facilities for testing purposes such as load and stress testing.

DevOps

Gradually the world at large as well as the parties involved at Saibot Airport realized that the gap between the project teams focusing on development and the administrators worried primarily about the running production systems was both artificial and unproductive. Upon closer inspection, it was realized that the stages visited for software development—design, build, test— also apply to platform development and infrastructure construction. For these two layers too, based on requirements, a design is created that is then implemented through installation and configuration and subsequently tested—as shown in Figure 1-8. Functional requirements are the main driver for the application development and nonfunctional requirements are the primary force in platform and infrastructure development. The three layers are closely related—and the way the work on them is performed and organized should reflect this close relation.

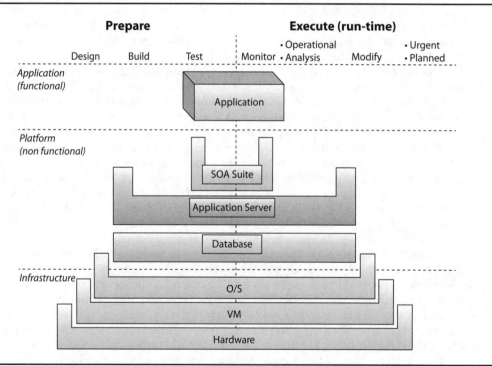

FIGURE 1-8. *The main stages in preparation and execution across the three main IT layers*

On the right side in Figure 1-8 is the run time phase—when custom software and COTS is deployed on the run time platform running on the production infrastructure. In this execution phase all preparations should come to fruition and actual value is delivered to the business. The entire stack is required to generate the business value—there can after all be no meaningful business value with any piece of the stack lacking or underperforming. Across the stack, the performance must be monitored to ensure the SLAs are met. Run time metrics are used for real time—and even predictive—assessment of the operations. These metrics are also analyzed for longer term trends.

Based on these operational findings as well as the longer term analysis and also fed by the ongoing activities in the preparation phase, modifications at various layers in the stack will be required. Some are urgent—instant responses to infrastructure or platform failures and urgent bug fixes in custom software—and some can be planned with more lead time.

As a result of the analysis overhead, some platform and infrastructure specialists were associated with and even embedded in software development teams and their activities were organized in a similar way. Other teams were set up to take on the right side of Figure 1-8—with members covering all layers of the stack. And both processes and tooling were instated to ensure easy communication and handovers between the worlds of preparation and execution. The agile approach with the frequent release of changes to applications, platform, and infrastructure made it imperative to close this traditional gap between the worlds of design time and run time and forced a much more integrated way of looking at the IT department at Saibot Airport.

Looking Forward

In the near future, Saibot Airport will continue executing the business program with the associated IT projects. A major new focus in addition to the introduction of SOA is going to be the introduction of BPM. Focus on business processes is strong—to ensure proper execution of procedures and provide management information about current affairs as well as the ability to optimize and partially automate the processes. It is hoped that new staff will require less training when they are guided to the processes. And some of the actions will be turned into self service activities to be executed by external parties.

Attracting new IT staff and building up internal expertise to reduce the dependency on external consultants is very important to Saibot Airport. It is actively approaching local specialist, trying to hire them away from their current employers. For its current staff, the airport is organizing development programs that will help them build up skills around the newly introduced technologies and methodologies. Staff can attend international conferences and workshops in order to meet with peers and learn the latest information. Renowned speakers are invited to conduct sessions at Saibot Airport itself—for internal staff as well as invitees that the airport hopes to hire. The opportunity to play a key role in this major technology evolution in combination with the facilities for personal development has already attracted a number of new Oracle Fusion Middleware specialists to the ranks of the airport's IT department.

In the slightly longer term, Saibot Airport hopes to do more with the data it is sitting on. It seems that this data may be interesting for external parties. And the airport also hopes to learn more itself about peak volumes and trends in order to streamline its processes and prepare its staff.

The development of mobile apps has only just started. Opening up multiple channels in earnest is among the near future plans. Saibot Airport expects to leverage the layered architecture and the reusable services to be able to quickly roll out new ways to interact.

Summary

The challenges for Saibot Airport are substantial—and very similar to those for many organizations around the world. The mission and business objectives may vary—the steps to go through in terms of IT close to identical across enterprises, industries, and countries. Agility and flexibility, digital, paperless interactions and processes, self-service, and 24/7 availability through multiple channels and near real-time operational insight are goals set by most organizations. At that broad level, the means to these ends are quite similar as well, in terms of IT architecture and the required technology components. Of course, many different vendors provide various products to address the challenges—and different combinations of these products could be used to do the job. Saibot Airport picked Oracle Fusion Middleware as its technology of choice—which makes it the perfect case study for this book. Starting in Chapter 3, we will see *how* the airport uses the Oracle SOA Suite in its quest for success. The next chapter first introduces the Oracle technology portfolio and zooms in on Fusion Middleware. Then it describes the SOA Suite in particular—as to set the scene for the remainder of the book.

CHAPTER
2

Overview of Oracle Fusion Middleware and SOA Suite 12c

Th
his book introduces you to the Oracle SOA Suite 12c product and how its many parts and features are used. This chapter provides a general introduction of SOA Suite 12c and its role within the Oracle Fusion Middleware stack, as well as the overall vision of Oracle regarding its portfolio and the part FMW plays in that vision. Saibot Airport is after all betting its future on FMW. This chapter will provide some insight as to why it is doing so.

Oracle Corporation clearly evolved from a one trick pony with its RDBMS product to what is arguably the vendor with the most extensive hardware and software portfolio in the world. Across all tiers—infrastructure, platform and (business) software—and across on premises and the cloud, Oracle has a large and growing presence—as depicted in Figure 2-1. And from a tentative player in the middleware arena at the start of the century, Oracle had grown into probably the most prominent player with magic quadrant listings in most middleware categories; with several of them categorized as "leading." SOA Suite is a pivotal element in Fusion Middleware, the foundation for many integration scenarios.

Oracle Technology Stack

Oracle offers software and hardware products to enterprises around the world that are complete, open, integrated and best in class.

Complete means that all capabilities in every enterprise IT area you can think of are provided by Oracle Corporation. And to put it even stronger, Oracle wants to make its offering a *best in class* offering. That means that even if an organization wants to pursue a best-of-breed strategy, it would have to select the Oracle product in every area because they are the best of breed in their own right. Oracle further strengthens the completeness claim with Fusion Applications running on its engineered systems as the living proof. Oracle has a unique ability—recognized by industry analysts—to maintain this completeness in the future, given its history, resources, dedication, and also its internal needs.

Open refers to the fact that components from the Oracle stack can be replaced by alternative products from other vendors. Oracle recognizes the fact that even though it claims to provide a complete, best-of-breed solution in every area, organizations may have current investments or

FIGURE 2-1. *The Oracle technology stack*

even deviating views as to which product is the best solution in a certain area. Another aspect of openness is the support for open standards. These make the products open in the sense that they can be interacted with in ways that are common across the industry.

Now let's consider *integrated*. Not only does Oracle offer virtually all enterprise IT capabilities (*complete*), it also has all these capabilities nicely integrated and working together. That may sound trivial—if a vendor offers a number of products, you would naturally expect them to work together. However, frequently that is not the case at all—and it wasn't necessarily the case for many of Oracle's products in the past. The slogan "Hardware and Software Engineered to Work Together" that is used to promote the engineered systems such as Exadata, Exalogic, and Exalytics is a good example of this high level of integration between Oracle products.

Cloud

Some pervasive trends in the IT industry have a clear effect on all players—vendors and their customers—and on Oracle as well. Big Data is one these trends—the drive to extract business value from the many (unstructured) data sources and streams that corporations have access to. Mobile is another trend that has a major impact on how business functionality is provided to actors: any place, any time and any device—with an effective, attractive, and consistent user experience.

The most fundamental change the industry at large and Oracle as a vendor is facing right now is adoption of *the (public) cloud*. Offering the capabilities of its products in the cloud way is a major change and a challenge for Oracle in terms of its technology and its business model. Delivering the capabilities from a centrally managed, multitenant environment with seamless scalability and round the clock, global availability would be quite an achievement. Turning the license based payment structure into a pay-per-use model is similarly tough.

Yet, the cloud *is* coming and Oracle will have to embrace it. Embrace in full, as expressed in its Cloud Mission (see Figure 2-2): *Bring Oracle's leading Infrastructure, Technology, Business Applications, and Information to customers and partners anywhere in the World through the Oracle Cloud.*

FIGURE 2-2. *Oracle mission in a single picture: bring all products to the cloud*

Oracle has declared its intention to offer services at all three generally recognized cloud levels: IaaS (*infrastructure* such as storage and compute), PaaS (*platform* such as database and middleware including the SOA Suite) and SaaS (*software* or business applications for example for marketing, sales, relationship management, human capital management).

Another important statement from Oracle regarding the cloud is that the same products are offered in the (public) cloud as are available on premises (private cloud). As a result—it will be very easy to lift and shift components back and forth between *on premises* and the cloud. Investments made in implementations on one end will be valid on the other. Mixing and mashing on premises instances with cloud environments will be a valid approach.

The availability of Oracle's PaaS services will have the potential of bringing the Oracle Platform within reach (again) of smaller and midsize organizations that currently cannot afford the on-prem licenses. Without substantial investment or long-term commitment, it should be possible for the Oracle platform to be flexibly entered, and left as well. This of course also applies to IaaS regarding to compute and storage infrastructure and SaaS for out of the box business functionality.

The fact that Oracle's SaaS products run on Oracle's PaaS services and are explicitly designed to be customized, extended and integrated with using these PaaS technologies creates a lot of opportunities for partners. For example, through the Oracle Cloud Marketplace, partners can offer reusable extensions and integrations that are deployed and run on the Oracle PaaS environment, integrating with the customer's SaaS instance.

Oracle Fusion Middleware

Middleware is crucial to the interaction between business applications and software components. It does not provide business value all by itself. Instead, Middleware is the infrastructure which facilitates creation of business applications, and provides core services like concurrency, caching, transactions, threading, and messaging. It also provides security and enables high availability functionality to the enterprise. Middleware, together with the RDBMS, forms the platform on top of which business applications are deployed.

History

Middleware at Oracle came first into existence as the new and middle tier in three tier (Java web) architectures: the tier that multiple web clients could connect to and interact with and that acted as the gateway to the underlying tier which usually consisted of primarily the database. Over time, this middle tier took on new responsibilities—for example, in the area of integration.

The application server was and is the foundation of middleware. Oracle has created one (Oracle Application Server or OAS), built one on top of external source code (iAS with OC4J at its core, on top of the Orion Application Server) and finally settled on WebLogic Server which it acquired as one of the key assets of BEA. Today, the term Cloud Application Foundation (CAF) is commonly used for WebLogic and some of its close associates.

The main purpose of middleware initially was to run web applications according to the Java EE standards (J2EE at that time). Application integration and messaging came a little bit later. An early (1999) initiative from Oracle was called InterConnect—an application integration platform that made a first stab at decoupled hub-and-spoke style integration. With the release of the BPEL Process Manager in 2004, based on the Collaxa acquisition, Oracle propelled itself to the forefront of standards-based middleware vendors.

Adding the homegrown ESB (Enterprise Service Bus) and Business Rule engine, Oracle released the SOA Suite 10*g* in 2006. The acquisition of BEA in 2008 yielded an enormous boost for the integration products (in addition to providing the WebLogic Server middleware foundation), as is visualized in Figure 2-3. BEA brought AquaLogic Service Bus to the party, as well as a BPM product (ALBPM, acquired through Fuego), a complex event processor (WebLogic Event Server), an enterprise repository (ALER, bought as Flashline), WebLogic Integration (WLINT) and several web portal products (acquired with Plumtree).

Meanwhile, other areas of middleware had been expanding as well. The availability of an application development framework for building Java web applications was crucial to Oracle—to empower its customers, obviously, and also to enable itself to develop the next generation of business applications. In 2004, the first incarnation of ADF (Application Development Framework) was released. Another product built from scratch at Oracle is WebCenter (2006). It leverages ADF to provide the foundation for creating enterprise portal, web-based mash ups of UI components—almost an ESB for UI services such as Portlets. In 2011, Oracle acquired FatWire to add web experience management to the WebCenter Suite as WebCenter Sites.

Since 2011, Oracle is actively pursuing development of mobile applications, first with ADF Mobile and later with the Mobile Application Framework (MAF).

Business Intelligence was transformed, driven by the acquisition of Siebel (2005) and its BI tools that resulted in OBI EE. The acquisition of Hyperion (2007) strengthened the BI offering, with the ESSBase OLAP Server. Enterprise content management (ECM) was added through the acquisition of Stellent (2006). Data discovery complemented the BI and Analytics portfolio when Endeca was acquired (2011).

Bulk data integration and ETL had been part at Oracle of the database division—through Warehouse Builder (OWB); with the acquisition of Sunopsis, this area was added to the middleware portfolio, through Oracle Data Integrator (ODI). Real-time data synchronization is contributed through GoldenGate (2009).

A series of smaller acquisitions helped build and strengthen some core capabilities in Fusion Middleware: management (MoniForce – 2007, AmberPoint – 2010, Nimbula – 2013) and security (Thor Technologies and Oblix – 2005, Bahrosa and Bridgestream – 2007, Vordel Gateway – 2011, Bitzer Mobile – 2014).

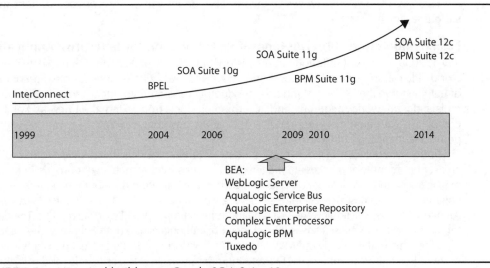

FIGURE 2-3.   *Historical build up to Oracle SOA Suite 12*c

Fusion

With the acquisition of PeopleSoft, Oracle announced its Fusion vision and roadmap. Later acquisitions had their impact, not so much on the vision itself but certainly on the roadmap and timelines. There has been a lot of confusion as to what Oracle's Project Fusion entailed. At the core, "Fusion" has these aspects:

- The integration of the acquired business entities into Oracle, reorganization as well as staff retention, especially among engineers.

- A newly developed next-generation application that is based on industry standards and the latest technology and that takes the best features, flows, and usability traits from the existing application products; this new product is known as *Fusion Applications*.

- Technology for making different products in the Oracle Applications portfolio— such as EBS, PeopleSoft, Siebel, Retek, and JD Edwards—work together, as well as the technology stack for the new Fusion Applications; this technology has been labeled *Fusion Middleware*.

No other software company has a track record comparable to Oracle's when it comes to acquiring companies and integrating both their staff and software products into its own organization and portfolio. From 2004 onwards, Oracle has made over one hundred acquisitions, across its stack. Many of these acquisitions concerned business applications and in recent years SaaS offerings. Another large portion of these acquisitions—most of them made before 2010— have been used to create what is Fusion Middleware today.

Oracle's ability to pick and choose and fuse together the best components from its own stack and each of its acquisitions as well as its capacity for integrating these bits and pieces really well, including the teams and staff responsible for these assets, is very impressive.

Figure 2-4 shows an overview of the most important and most recent acquisitions in the various layers in the stack.

Fusion Middleware 11g: The Innovative Foundation for Enterprise Applications

July 1, 2009, marked a milestone in the history of Oracle Corporation. On that day, the worldwide rollout of Oracle Fusion Middleware 11g was initiated, the culmination of many years of helping forge the industry standards, conducting research into interoperability, creating new tools and frameworks, acquiring and absorbing products from external parties, and architecting a complete stack of middleware products. The public unveiling of FMW 11g was one of the biggest product launches in Oracle's history.

Fusion Middleware 11g consisted of many different products that provide solutions in diverse areas, from identity and access management, business intelligence, event processing, content management and data integration to a data grid, web application development, enterprise portal and collaboration, business process management, governance, security, and, of course, Service-Oriented Architecture. Fusion Middleware 11g ran (and runs) on top of WebLogic Server 11g. The design time for most products in the stack was JDeveloper 11g, although some used Eclipse as their IDE.

Since this initial release of FMW 11g in 2009, Oracle published so called Patch Releases at more or less half-yearly intervals. Despite their name, these releases usually add not just fixes and small improvements but substantial new functionality as well.

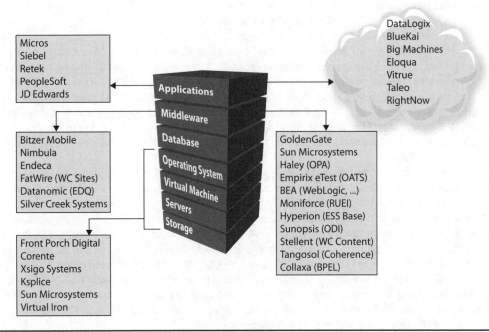

FIGURE 2-4.   *Most relevant or recent strategic acquisitions by Oracle Corporation in various layers in the stack*

Oracle Fusion Middleware: The Cloud Platform for Digital Business

The second generation of Fusion Middleware is labeled 12*c* – with a *c* for cloud. The motto for this release is *The Cloud Platform for Digital Business*. Cloud here refers to both private cloud (on premise) and public cloud.

For Fusion Middleware too, Oracle strives to be: Complete and integrated, best in class, open and standards based, available on premise and in the cloud. Additionally it states that Fusion Middleware provides the foundation for Oracle Fusion Applications and Oracle Cloud (SaaS and PaaS).

Fusion Middleware is not sold as single product with a simple price tag. Oracle understands that many organizations will, at least initially, only use specific components from the wide range of middleware products. Customers buy licenses for specific product suites, bundles of related products in specific areas of functionality. Among the FMW suites offered that are associated with SOA are the BPM Suite, EDA Suite, Identity Governance Suite, and, of course, SOA Suite. Note that these suites have a certain level of overlap. Also note that for most suites, several reduced-cost variations are offered that support usage of only specific products from the suite.

The biggest customer for Fusion Middleware is Oracle itself. The development of Fusion Applications and other products in the Oracle Applications portfolio is all done on top of the Fusion Middleware stack. Most organizations will have less stringent requirements for their development and integration efforts than the ones faced by Oracle's internal divisions. Because the exact same technology is available to external customers as is being used internally, Oracle is providing the proof in the FMW pudding by eating all of it itself.

An overview of Fusion Middleware is shown in Figure 2-5.

The foundation—or Cloud Application Foundation (CAF) as Oracle likes to call it—is provided by WebLogic Suite—the Java EE application server, along with Coherence, the enterprise data grid. Tuxedo is an application server for non-Java languages. It provides facilities—such as clustering, load balancing and transaction management—to build and deploy enterprise applications written in C, C++, COBOL, and with the SALT add-on applications written in Python and Ruby. Development for most components in Fusion Middleware is done in JDeveloper. A growing number of components support development also or sometimes even only through a browser interface.

User interfaces in FMW are typically developed using ADF—the Application Development Framework—from JDeveloper. This framework contains ADF Business Components for smooth interaction with the database and ADF Faces, with a rich Web 2.0 library of user-interface components based on the JavaServer Faces (JSF) industry standard. The rich web applications are agnostic when it comes to their data provider—the ADF Model abstracts the underlying business service—and work equally well with a persistence layer based on JPA and EJB as well as web services (SOAP and REST). ADF has facilities for very productive, declarative development with strong reuse mechanisms and support for advanced data visualization, active (event-driven, server-push) user interfaces, and "design time@run time" for application customization and personalization. Development of ADF applications is done with JDeveloper. The applications run on a Java EE application server, often WebLogic Server.

Note that user interfaces developed with non-Oracle Rich Web UI technologies such as HTML5, AngularJS or other frameworks can easily be used on top of FMW as well, adjacent to, integrated with or instead of ADF applications.

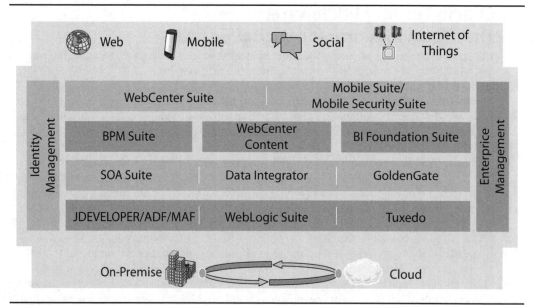

FIGURE 2-5. *Oracle Fusion Middleware—The Cloud Platform for Digital Business*

Mobile applications are developed in FMW using the Mobile Application Framework—also in JDeveloper—against RESTful services exposed from other FMW components—such as the SOA Suite—and using security services provided by the Mobile Security Suite.

GoldenGate is used for real-time fine-grained data synchronization. With low-impact, real-time change data capture, distribution, and delivery for transactional data across heterogeneous systems it helps to realize continuous availability, zero downtime migration, and integrated business intelligence. Data Integrator (ODI) is positioned for more batch-driven, high-volume integration and ETL use cases.

BPM Suite—discussed in this book in Chapter 19—orchestrates business processes and dynamic cases. WebCenter Content provides organizations with a unified repository to house unstructured content, and deliver it to business users in the proper format, and within context of familiar applications to fit the way they work. It supports end-to-end content lifecycle management from creation and capture to archiving. BI Foundation Suite is an integrated platform that provides comprehensive capabilities for business intelligence, including enterprise reporting, dashboards, ad hoc analysis, multidimensional OLAP, scorecards, and predictive analytics.

WebCenter Suite is a combination of WebCenter Portal and WebCenter Sites—both targeted at the integrated web experience of both internal staff as well as external parties such as customers, citizens, patients, and visitors.

Management of the FMW run time environment is done through Enterprise Manager. EM has many components that aid administrators in installing, configuring, and monitoring middleware components and the activities taking place through them.

Identity management enables organizations to effectively manage the end-to-end lifecycle of user identities across all enterprise resources, both within and beyond the firewall and into the cloud. The Oracle Identity Management platform delivers scalable solutions for identity governance, authentication, and access management (e.g., OAM and Entitlement Server) and directory services—Oracle Unified Directory (OUD) and Oracle Virtual Directory (OVD). The API Gateway as well as the Mobile Security Suite plays a role in protecting enterprise assets at the edge of and outside the enterprise perimeter.

Even though Figure 2-5 depicts various products as separate cells, mutually isolated, the fact is that in terms of functionality there is quite some overlap between many of the cells. Certain challenges can be met in several ways with different combinations of products. Additionally, there is a lot of integration between the products shown. They share a common infrastructure, participate in global transactions and end-to-end conversations and offer a very similar user experience. Based on open industry standards and architected in similar ways, the products in FMW easily exchange (meta-)data and interact in various ways.

Middleware from the Cloud

In addition to supporting various types of interactions with cloud based components, Oracle intends to make the functionality of Fusion Middleware available in the cloud. Instead of running FMW on premises—possibly as a private cloud service—it will be possible to run integration scenarios, business process, big data analysis, enterprise content management, rich web applications, and mobile enablement on the public cloud.

The objectives for the Oracle Cloud Services include:

- Broadest cloud offering covering SaaS, PaaS, and IaaS
- Built on industry standards—SQL, Java, HTML5, Web
- Transparently run (on premise developed components) in the cloud—zero application code changes

- Self-service control for users
- Complete data isolation and flexible upgrades
- Service-Oriented Architecture—on-premise integration
- Built-in business intelligence, social, and mobile

Oracle has launched or announced the following middleware PaaS service for its Public Cloud offering (also shown in Figure 2-6):

- Process Cloud Service (powered by BPM Suite)—to orchestrate business processes and workflows
- Integration Cloud Service (powered by SOA Suite)—to integrate SaaS applications to each other and to on premise applications
- Mobile Cloud Service—to define and expose mobile APIs to build mobile applications and rich client web applications against
- SOA Suite [as a Service | Cloud Service]—to run SOA Suite application in the Cloud
- Java Cloud Service (powered by WebLogic Server) and Node.js Cloud Service—to deploy Java EE and Node.js applications on
- Developer Cloud Service—a development platform that supports aspects of the complete development lifecycle such as issue management, source control, build management and continuous integration and deployment; it is integrated with, for example, the Java Cloud Service
- Document Cloud Service (powered by WebCenter Content)—to provide enterprise content management and collaboration
- Social Network—an enterprise equivalent to Facebook that is integrated into business applications as well as Process Cloud Service and Document Cloud Service
- Business Intelligence, Big Data, and Big Data Discovery (powered by BI Foundation Suite and Endeca)
- Messaging service—for asynchronous messaging, similar to JMS—over HTTP with push and pull support

| Process Management Services | Document Services | Social Services | Business Intelligence Services | Big Data Services |
| Database Services | Java Services | Developer Services | Mobile Services | Integration Services |

FIGURE 2-6. *Oracle Public Cloud PaaS offerings*

In addition to these middleware services, the Oracle Cloud includes the Database Cloud Service and underlying IaaS services: Compute Service and Storage Service.

As Oracle's SaaS offerings run on these same PaaS services, it is fairly straightforward to extend and integrate the SaaS products using the PaaS platform. Note that many of the SaaS products are already integrated with some of the PaaS services such as Document Cloud Service and Social network.

Overview of SOA Suite 12*c*

The SOA Suite 12*c* at its most fundamental is an orchestration and integration platform for receiving, processing and answering messages. These messages are frequently received over HTTP as web service requests in XML format—however, many other protocols and several other formats are supported as well. Processing these messages may involve call outs from the SOA Suite to back-end systems and other web services—using the same range of protocols and formats as available in the inbound direction. In addition to pure message processing, the SOA Suite contains facilities for orchestrating business processes and human tasks and workflows.

Figure 2-7 provides a schematic overview of the structure of the SOA Suite. Messages are sent from consumers or are pulled into the SOA Suite from external files or databases using inbound adapters. Services are responsible for dealing with these messages—typically applying validation and transformation on these messages before making call outs to gather the information or perform the actions required by the service based on the triggering message. More complex services may perform a series of orchestrated call outs to fulfill their responsibility. The distinction between complex services and business processes is not a very clear one with SOA Suite: as an asynchronous service takes longer to complete and involves more complexity, more call outs and perhaps some human interaction we will start calling it a business process. Business rules are used to make decisions on behalf of services and processes, following externalized algorithms defined and maintained by business representatives.

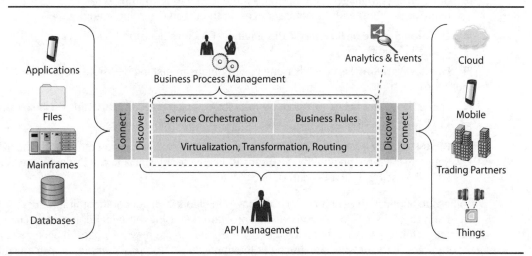

FIGURE 2-7.   *Overview of SOA Suite within Fusion Middleware 12c*

Through its support for (de facto) standards such as REST and WADL and the message format JSON in addition to SOAP and WSDL and XML, SOA Suite 12c can bridge the gap with mobile application infrastructures as well as cloud based systems such as SaaS products. SOA Suite integrated with Oracle B2B to interact with trading partners and industry hubs, using a wide variety of industry communication protocols and message formats. SOA Suite offers real time event processing; through this, live data can be processed and analyzed and turned into findings, recommendations and actions. This can be applied, for example, to the Fast Data produced by the IoT (Internet of Things) and also to monitor (across) business processes and service instances running in the SOA Suite itself. SOA Suite includes tools to also visualize process analytics and the analysis of events through live dashboards.

SCA Engine for Running SOA Composite Applications

One of the two core engines in SOA Suite 12c is the SCA container, a run-time engine that can execute composite service applications. Composite (service) applications are SCA-compliant applications that are assembled from various service components that are wired together internally based on WSDL contracts. Composite applications publish a service interface through which they can be invoked by external clients. This interface is frequently a (SOAP) web service interface, but other types of bindings are also possible, such as based on EJB/RMI and JMS. SOA Suite 12c can run multiple instances of every composite application in parallel. It can handle calls into applications, coordinate messages between components within an application, and facilitate calls from the application to external services.

A composite application can expose a web service binding at a specific URL to which an XML request message is sent. That message will be processed—possibly resulting in database manipulation, file creation, human task execution, email sending, and event publishing. At some point during the processing of the message, a response message may be sent out that can contain the results of whatever the application has been doing.

The composite applications running on the SOA Suite can make use of the following service languages and engines for executing its components:

- **BPEL Process Manager**   Orchestrates (potentially) long-running service composites with many interactions with external services, both outgoing and incoming.

- **Decision Service or Business Rules engine**   Executes decision logic that can be (re) defined at run time.

- **Human Workflow Service**   For engaging humans in making decisions or providing information.

- **Spring-based Java Beans**   Custom business logic implemented in Java acting on the messages.

- **Mediator**   For filtering, transforming, adapting, and routing messages.

- **BPMN**   Business process logic defined through BPMN can be executed inside the SOA Suite (by the same engine that also runs BPEL). Note: BPMN is not included in the SOA Suite license but instead is part of BPM Suite.

Composite applications (such as the one shown in Figure 2-8) accept incoming request messages and route them through components programmed using these technologies. Each component performs a service that may alter the message, create new messages, have external effects, or influence the onward processing in the application. Composite applications can call out to external web services—and receive asynchronous responses or other incoming messages

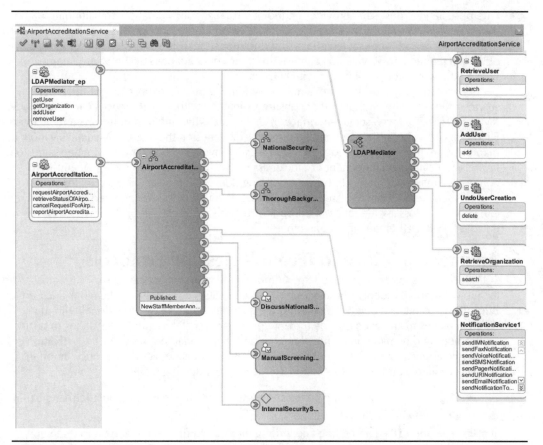

FIGURE 2-8. *Example of a fairly complex SOA composite application with BPEL, Business Rule, Human Task, and Mediator components; on the left the publicly exposed services and on the right the external references to an LDAP directory and the UMS messaging service , and in the middle the implementation using the various components.*

from these external services. Through technology adapters, composite applications cannot just invoke web services (and be invoked as a web service); other transport protocols are available as well, for example, JMS, EJB, File, JDBC (for database access) and AQ . Applications can also make use of the Event Delivery Network to publish business events as well as to consume such events.

Service Bus for Lean and Mean Message Processing

The second engine in SOA Suite for handling service calls is the Service Bus. This engine performs a similar task as the SCA container discussed in the previous section: it receives messages, processes them, performs relevant calls and (optionally) returns a response. There is overlap between the roles and functionality of the two engines: they can perform many of the same tasks.

Service Bus activities carry little overhead and it is considered the lean and mean machine (very good at doing almost nothing very fast). The Service Bus is typically used as the ESB or

Enterprise Service Bus—that provides endpoint virtualization, validation, transformation and routing as well as caching, monitoring, and SLA enforcement. Service Bus is a little awkward at dealing with asynchronous interactions and does not support long running processes or any form of human interaction. Service Bus can use the same set of adapters as the SCA container and—with a little work around—interact with EDN as well.

Service Bus projects (like the example shown in Figure 2-9) expose one or more proxy services; these are the endpoints that consumers interact with. Proxy services can expose a SOAP/XML or REST/JSON web service interface or one of the other inbound transports and adapters. Each proxy service calls a pipeline that performs activities on the message—such as validation, manipulation, transformation, logging—and usually invokes either another pipeline, a custom Java class, a split-join component or a business service for further processing. A split-join component makes it possible to have work being done on a message in parallel threads. A business service is a bridge to an external service. Through outbound adapters, a business service can connect across a wide range of transport protocols—from SOAP or REST web service to database, JMS, FTP, email, and many others.

Adapters to Bridge to Technologies and Protocols

SOA Suite 12c is integrated with a large number of adapters for accessing services across various technologies and protocols. These adapters allow the SOA composite applications and Service Bus projects to retrieve data from, forward messages to, and leverage functionality in many different places in and even outside the enterprise—from database and file systems to business applications and human communication channels. Some adapters allow for the activation of composite applications or Service Bus services from the outside world. The most important adapters available for use in SOA Suite 12c access the following targets:

- **Database** For accessing tables and views (query and data manipulation) and calling PL/SQL program units

- **File and FTP** For reading and writing files from a file system and an FTP server

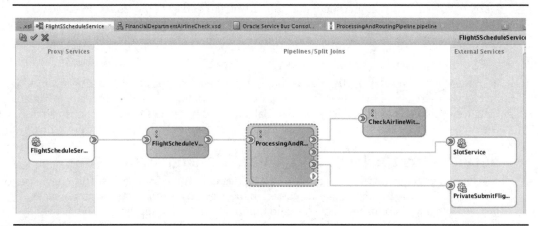

FIGURE 2-9. *An example of a Service Bus project; on the left the proxy service that exposes a public interface and on the right two business services that access back end services and systems; in between are pipeline to do the real work on the messages*

- **Queues**   For accessing queues through JMS, Oracle Advanced Queuing, and MQ Series (IBM) and MSMQ (Microsoft)

- **Enterprise Java Bean (EJB)**   To communicate with remote Enterprise JavaBeans

- **Sockets**   For reading and writing data over TCP/IP sockets

- **ADF-BC (Business Components)**   For interacting with an ADF BC–based Service Data Object service

- **LDAP** To read data from, maintain data in and be notified about changes in an LDAP directory

- **Coherence** To put data on, or read, query or remove data from a Coherence Data Cache

- **Oracle Applications (aka Oracle eBusiness Suite adapter)**   For retrieving data from and sending data to eBusiness Suite (11*i* and 12)

- **SAP R/3** For comprehensive, bidirectional, standards-based, real-time connectivity to SAP R/3 systems

- **JD Edwards World ERP System**

- **UMS** (User Messaging Services) For communication with human parties over email, SMS, VOIP and instant messaging (chat)

- **Cloud** Cloud adapters to communicate with SaaS applications such as SalesForce, Service Cloud (aka RightNow), Eloqua, Workday, and others. Note: Some of them require special licenses.

In addition to these adapters—that are all covered by the SOA Suite license—there are additional adapters that have to be licensed and installed separately. These include the adapters for Mainframe and TP-Monitoring as well as the Change Data Capture Adapters. The separate Oracle B2B Integration products provides adapters for electronic communication with e-commerce trading partners using industry standards such as RosettaNet, HL7, and various EDI protocols.

Also in addition we can use SOAP, REST, and EDN in services and references to integrate with SOAP web services, REST web services and events of the Event-Delivery Network.

Adapters will usually be called by the service components running in a composite application (outbound) or a business service in a Service Bus project. Note, however, that several adapters can also initiate a new instance of an application (inbound). The database adapter, for example, can "poll for changed records," and any new or changed record can start a new instance. Likewise, the file and FTP adapters can poll for new files to arrive on the file system or an FTP server, or for new lines in an existing file. This adapter, too, can instantiate a composite application instance when new data is read from a file that has changed. Other adapters that can act as "service clients" that create new instances of composite applications include the UMS adapter (upon the reception of an email or a chat message), the EJB adapter, the JMS adapter, the LDAP adapter, and the AQ adapter. Inbound adapters can also connect to (aka correlate with) running instances of composite applications.

TIP
Using the Enterprise Scheduling Service that is available in the run time infrastructure, almost any outbound retrieval action can be turned into an inbound polling activity that may lead to new instances. Thus, it would be easy to create inbound adapters that, for example, poll Twitter, Facebook, Dropbox, or the Oracle Community Forum on SOA Suite.

The Cloud Adapters SDK is made available to allow organizations to develop their own custom adapters for the SOA Suite. These custom adapters can integrate with SaaS products or on premise COTS or they can be created for repeatable interactions with 3rd party platform such as Microsoft Sharepoint or IBM's WebSphere or perhaps even Watson.

Event Delivery Network

Business events are situations of potential interest. Examples are the reception of an order, cancellation of a flight by the airline, the failure of a credit check, the crossing of a stock threshold (we are critically low on airplane fuel), and the acceptance of a job offer by a new member of staff. These events frequently occur in business processes when certain conditions are met or actions have been performed. Events can also come into existence during the execution of a service component. The business events may trigger the start of new composite application instances or could notify already running instances.

However, the burden of informing any potentially interested party of the event should not be on the service component that happens to encounter the situation. The producer of the event—the application or service component that causes or encounters the situation that is deemed to be of business interest—is not responsible for what happens with the published event, nor does or should it care. This keeps producers and consumers decoupled: Consumers can be added or removed without impact on the producers of events. Likewise, new producers can be introduced without any effect on the consumers. To make this happen, we need a "man in the middle" of sorts, a generic medium that deals with both consumers and producers.

A key part of SOA Suite 12*c* is the Event Delivery Network (EDN), an intermediary that takes on the responsibility of receiving events from producers and delivering them to interested parties. EDN is a generic business event handler built as an easy to use layer on top of JMS and AQ (Advanced Queuing).

Business events are defined across services and composite applications as an extension of the canonical data model. The definition of a business event comprises a name, possibly custom headers, and the definition of the payload. These definitions need to be registered with the EDN.

Service components—BPMN, Mediator, and BPEL—can publish events (occurrences of one of the predefined event types) to the Event Delivery Network. Events can also be published to the EDN from ADF applications, from the Oracle Event Processor and from any Java JMS Client. Using respectively the inbound JMS Transport and an outbound Java Callout, Service Bus services can both consume from EDN as well as publish to it.

Service components such as Mediator, BPMN, and BPEL register their interest in one or more of the centrally defined business events with the EDN. Such an interest can indicate all events of a specific type, but also can include more fine-grained selection rules that refer to the custom headers or payload to filter on specific occurrences of an event. When an event has been published, the Event Delivery Network will make sure that all interested parties will receive the event. Note that it is very well possible that an event is not delivered to any interested party at all. In that case, it simply disappears into the void.

Other Components in the Box

The SOA Suite 12*c* license covers a number of additional components that can be used in conjunction with the core engines for SOA composites (SCA) and Service Bus projects. Most notable are the Business Activity Monitor (BAM) and the Oracle Event Processor (OEP).

Business Activity Monitor (BAM)

Oracle BAM provides a framework for creating dashboards that display real-time data as it flows into the BAM server. This is typically data received from physical sensors (security gates, RFID scanners), trace details from computer applications (request logging in web applications, process progress signals from a BPM or workflow engine), or live data feeds with financial data, weather reports, or even sports statistics. Rules can be created in BAM to instruct the framework to highlight deviations and send alerts under specified conditions. BAM is primarily used to monitor aggregates against predefined thresholds for data recently received over relatively short periods (typically minutes to hours, rather than months to years). That, along with the built-in capability to trigger alerts and take actions, is the main distinction between BAM and traditional business intelligence, which tends to be more passive and more historically oriented. BAM tries to facilitate the operational control of business process execution.

Data used by BAM for the actual reports is managed in memory in an internal caching framework, based on Coherence. Data is loaded into this cache in real time via various channels, of which JMS is the most important one. Both BPEL and BPM processes can produce business metrics and process analytics that are directly recorded in BAM enabled database tables. BAM ships with out of the box dashboards to report on these process analytics.

Oracle Event Processor (OEP)

Oracle Event Processor is used to analyze messages in real time. Through filtering, aggregation, and pattern detection, OEP can quickly derive meaning from and suggest action based upon signals that range from measurements by physical sensors and social media updates to analytics produced by business processes or web site activity.

OEP is a light weight component with a fairly small footprint (one of the reasons it can be used in the embedded use case for example on a device the size of a Raspberry Pi). It holds relevant data in memory (or on a grid); most of the processing does not require I/O operations, allowing OEP to respond very fast. OEP can be integrated with SOA Suite through the EDN as well as JMS or HTTP.

Stream Explorer is a tool targeted at the Line of Business User (the nontechnical IT consumer). This tool provides a visual, declarative, browser-based wrapper around Oracle Event Processor and Oracle BAM. With Stream Explorer it is every easy to create explorations and dashboards on live (streams of) data—reporting in real time on patterns, correlations, aggregations, and deviations. The applications defined in StreamExplorer can be exported to JDeveloper for a developer to perform refinement of the underlying OEP sources.

Fusion Middleware infrastructure

SOA Suite 12*c* runs inside WebLogic Server 12*c*—the SCA and Service Bus engines live inside the Java EE container. The underlying run-time infrastructure of Fusion Middleware 12*c* the WebLogic Server platform, managed through its Administration Console. Several applications are installed into the WebLogic Server domain as part of SOA Suite 12c to support the FMW 12c run-time operations—as is visualized in Figure 2-10. The Oracle Enterprise Manager Fusion Middleware Control Console (from now on referred to as EM FWM Control) is the most important one of these—other examples are the SOA Composer, the BPM Worklist application for managing and performing human tasks, and the Service Bus Console. Other key components are the Enterprise Scheduling Service (ESS), the Web Services Manager (OWSM), Coherence, Platform Security Services (OPSS), and Meta Data Services (MDS).

Oracle Enterprise Manager Fusion Middleware Control Console (EM FWM Control)

The Oracle Enterprise Manager Fusion Middleware Control Console is the integrated console for virtually all run-time monitoring and administration of SOA composite applications and their instances. This console is an ADF 12c web application that runs on WebLogic and is accessed from a browser by the Fusion Middleware administrator and other actors to work on tasks in these main categories:

- **Configuring** Adjusting properties from SOA infrastructure and service engines down to components in composite applications.

- **Monitoring** Aggregating metrics, performance figures, and faults across applications, components, and service engines; reporting the current state of running instances; providing an audit trail per composite instance; drilling down to the steps through a component; and inspecting the log files.

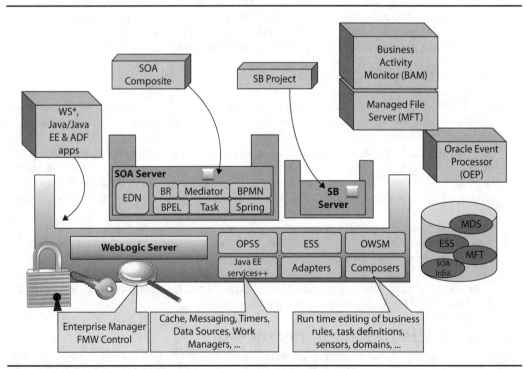

FIGURE 2-10. *An overview of the run time environment for SOA Suite 12c on top of WebLogic's Fusion Middleware infrastructure*

■ **Managing**   Deploying, stopping, and starting composite applications; recovering from faults; terminating application instances; unit testing of composite applications; and attachment of policies to SOA composite applications, service components, and binding components. The Oracle WSM Policy Manager is the integrated facility to attach policies regarding security, reliable messaging, addressing, and logging to web services and service composite applications.

The WebLogic Server Administration Console is used alongside the Enterprise Manager Fusion Middleware Control for normal and more infrastructural Java EE administrative tasks such as the configuration of data sources and JMS objects, administration of the security realm, and management of the technology adapters.

Platform Security Services (OPSS)

OPSS is the underlying security platform in WebLogic that provides security to Oracle Fusion Middleware including products like SOA Suite, WebCenter, and ADF. OPSS provides an abstraction layer in the form of standards-based application programming interfaces that insulate developers from security and identity management implementation details. With OPSS, developers don't need to know the details of cryptographic key management or interfaces with user repositories and other identity management infrastructures. Through OPSS, custom applications and Oracle FMW products benefit from the same, uniform security, identity management, and audit services across the enterprise.

Out of the box, OPSS is configured to use the embedded LDAP server in the WebLogic domain as its source for identities and role privileges. Other sources for user identities and role grants—such as LDAP directories or custom database schemas—can easily be configured.

Web Services Manager

Oracle Web Services Manager (OWSM) provides a policy framework to manage and secure web services consistently across your organization. It provides capabilities to build, enforce, run, and monitor web service policies, such as security, reliable messaging, MTOM, and addressing policies. OWSM can be used by both developers, at design time, and system administrators in production environments.

The policy framework is built using the WS-Policy standard. The OWSM Policy Enforcement Point (PEP) leverages Oracle Platform Security Service (OPSS) and the Oracle WebLogic Server authenticator for authentication and permission-based authorization. Custom policies can be implemented and enforced through OWSM to enforce constraints and provide pre- or postprocessing on inbound or outbound messages.

OWSM can be used to secure both SOA, Service Bus as Java Web Services.

Enterprise Scheduling Service (ESS)

The Enterprise Scheduling Service is an asynchronous, schedule based job orchestrator. Schedules can be complex calendar-based definitions about when an action should be triggered—ranging from simple instructions such as "every 5 minutes" or "at noon on the first day of each month" to far more complex statements. Job definitions can refer to web services to be invoked, PL/SQL packages to be called, operating system scripts to be executed and Java logic to be performed. Job definitions can take parameters. By combining schedules and job definitions, jobs can be scheduled to be run once or repeatedly. ESS is managed and monitored using a console that is integrated in the EM FWM Control.

ESS is integrated with SOA Suite in several ways. SOA composite applications and Service Bus services can be scheduled to be invoked and they can ESS themselves to schedule a job for execution. Inbound adapters can be activated and deactivated according to a schedule. The recovery of failed instances (of SOA composites) and the purging of data for historic instances can be scheduled through ESS.

Meta Data Services (MDS)

The Fusion Middleware run-time environment has at least one, and possibly multiple, metadata repositories that contain metadata for Oracle Fusion Middleware system components such as OWSM, ESS, and SOA Suite. A metadata repository contains metadata about the configuration of Oracle Fusion Middleware as well as metadata for different types of enterprise applications. Shared artifacts such as XSD documents describing the canonical data model, data value maps that describe mappings between business vocabularies in different domains, reusable transformations, human task definitions, security policies, business rule definitions, and business event definitions are deployed to and managed in metadata repositories. Artifacts in these metadata repositories can be used during development as well as at run time. Meta Data Services (MDS) provides a single interface across all repositories. MDS provides services to validate, version, tag and categorize, discover, and manage artifacts throughout their lifecycle.

A special facility in MDS is its support for customization. MDS can return specialized versions of artifacts that are created from a base version with context-sensitive deltas applied to it.

Close Associates

The following are products that are not enclosed in the SOA Suite license—yet that are very close to the product. They are almost always used in conjunction with the SOA Suite.

Oracle B2B Integration

Business-to-business (B2B) describes the electronic exchange of information between business partners. This can be orders and invoices exchanged between buyers and vendors. Or electronic tax forms submitted to the tax agency. Or details from a product catalog, requests for proposals or the proposals themselves, etcetera. In many industries, specific protocols and message formats have been developed and are used for B2B communication. Oracle B2B Integration builds on top of SOA Suite to support these industry specific protocols and it provides an architecture enabling a unified business process platform, end-to-end instance tracking, visibility, auditing, process intelligence, governance, and security.

Some of the supported message standards are EDIFACT, EANCOM, OAGIS, UB92, HL7, RosettaNet, and many more, besides custom documents. Besides this it also supports many interchange channel protocols like AS2, EBXML, Email, FTP, File, SMTP, in addition to (outbound) SOAP Web Service.

Healthcare Integration

Oracle SOA Suite for Healthcare Integration helps healthcare entities (both payers and providers) to securely exchange HL7 and HIPAA standard documents. It utilizes several features of SOA Suite to design, create and manage applications that process healthcare standard documents.

Managed File Transfer

Oracle Managed File Transfer (Oracle MFT) enables secure file exchange and management with internal departments and external partners. It protects against inadvertent access to unsecured files at every step in the end-to-end transfer of files. You can protect data in your DMZ by using the SSH/FTP reverse proxy. The built in reporting capabilities allow you to get quick status of a file transfer and resubmit it as required. MFT has an "Embedded" FTP(S)/SSH, FTP / FTP-SSL / SSH server to and from which files can be securely transferred.

It provides facilities for scheduling file transfer—both push and pull. Files can be pre- or postprocessed (e.g., encrypted and zipped or unzipped and decrypted). MFT integrates with (s) FTP, File, B2B, ODI, Healthcare and SOA Suite and plain web services. MFT runs as an application on its own WebLogic 12*c* managed server. For example, reception of a file can trigger activity for processing the file in SOA Suite. In the reverse direction, B2B and SOA Suite can also offer a file to MFT for onward handling. MFT helps process large files without clogging the SOA Suite infrastructure through unwieldy resource consumption.

Governance and API Management

Knowing that services exist, where and how they can be accessed and what exactly they can be used for is obviously crucial in establishing reuse of services in anything but the very smallest organizations. Managing the life cycle of services with a full grasp of the impact of the changes considered on consumers of these services is a vital activity. These are two aspects of what is called *governance*.

Oracle offers various products to support enterprise with establishing and executing governance. These integrate or at least collaborate with SOA Suite.

The flagship product is Oracle Enterprise Repository. OER is used as the single source of truth for information surrounding SOA assets and their dependencies. OER uses harvesting to acquire this information about relevant assets. Harvesting involves scanning and processing of source code and metadata documents.

TIP

At http://fusionappsoer.oracle.com you can see the Oracle Enterprise Repository in action with service-oriented architecture assets for Oracle Fusion Applications, such as service interfaces, business event definitions, business process models, table definitions and data diagrams.

The Oracle API Catalog is a browser-based wrapper around OER that hides much of its complexity to provide a user interface to easily collect and publish APIs from Oracle and non-Oracle environments to build up a catalog of APIs. Oracle API Catalog (OAC) streamlines processes and optimizes reuse to foster API adoption. OAC facilitates the discovery (through harvesting), understanding, and use of APIs. It provides the technical and nontechnical information needed to discover, understand, and use APIs.

NOTE

API (Application Programmatic Interface) is a well-known term that has recently taken on a new meaning in the worlds of SOA and SaaS. API refers to more or less the same thing we also call a service. APIs seem to be more used for public interfaces that enterprises expose to business partners and other external parties—and not so much to internal interfaces. APIs are more about the specific consumers that will use them, than services that are aimed at broad reuse. APIs can be created as consumer specific wrappers on top of these more generally reusable services.

Oracle API Manager is a brother in arms to OAC. It is an extension of the Service Bus component in SOA Suite 12*c*. In addition to supporting publication of APIs—based on selected Service Bus proxy services—and aiding the search for APIs, it is also used for collecting and analyzing metrics on the usage of the APIs and reporting these findings.

Unlike the previous three components, API Gateway is not oriented at design time at all. This product helps establish the enterprise gateway through which internal users and application assets are exposed to outside consumers—such as mobile applications or cloud-based applications. API Gateway helps secure these interactions, both in terms of access to APIs and of actual data exchanged. API Gateway monitors interactions and audits SLA agreements. A policy can be configured to send an alert when the conditions of the SLA are breached for quality of service monitoring. API Gateway can dynamically apply restrictions and throttling policies. API Gateway works with many different web service protocols (such as SOAP, MTOM, SwA, REST), message formats (XML, JSON) and transport protocols (TCP, HTTP 1.0 & 1.1, JMS, MQ, FTP, SFTP, SMTP, POP).

BPM Suite

Orchestration of business processes is the core objective of the BPM Suite. These processes can be highly structured, designed using the BPMN standard, or they can be much more dynamic, organized as adaptive cases, loosely following the CMMN approach. BPM Suite includes the SOA Suite. It adds the process orchestration capability that is integrated in SOA composite application and executed by the SCA run-time engine. BPM Suite also provides business architecture modeling capabilities, a framework for design of user interfaces to support human tasks and facilities to monitor, simulate and optimize business processes.

What Is New in SOA Suite 12*c*?

Many readers will probably have some familiarity with earlier versions of the SOA Suite. This book will cover release 12*c* on its own—not constantly comparing it to the previous release or discussing changes and differences with 11*g*. This section is the exception. It [briefly] outlines the most salient new features and changed functionality between 11*g* (up to Patch Set 7) and 12*c*.

- JDeveloper is now the single IDE used for not only SOA composite application but also Service Bus projects and OEP applications. The Integrated WebLogic Server in JDeveloper contains both SOA Suite run time engines for deploying and running SOA composites and Service Bus projects allowing for very quick development round trips.

- JDeveloper supports integrated debugging and a moderate degree of refactoring for both Service Bus and SOA composites.

- The design time, file-based MDS infrastructure can be used to transfer resources across applications.

- REST and JSON adapters support inbound and outbound interactions for both Service Bus and SOA composites; to expose REST interfaces, a REST-first as well as a generate REST-from-SOAP (and JSON from XML) approach can be adopted.

- The visual XSL Map editor has been enhanced, especially for large style sheets; it offers better support for using templates and for testing the map); XSL Maps are supported with Service Bus as well as with SOA composites.

- XQuery is available too in both Service Bus and SOA composites (BPEL and Mediator); the supported version of XQuery is still 1.0—however, valuable support for XQuery library modules has been added.

- Native Format Translation—available in Service Bus as well as BPEL and Mediator is functionality to convert from content in a native format such as JSON, CSV, any type XML, fixed positional and COBOL Copybook to regular, schema based XML that can be handled in the SOA Suite. The same conversion can be made from XML to these native formats. This format translation used to be available as part of the File Adapter for content read from or written to external files.

- Service Bus projects are visualized in JDeveloper using the Overview editor—similar to the composite editor for SOA composite applications. A new component in Service Bus project is the pipeline that contains a message flow with the activities acting on the message. Pipelines can be based on Pipeline Templates from which they inherit (part of their) definition. Multiple pipelines can be chained together. Pipeline can be reused: multiple proxy services and pipelines can invoke the same pipeline. All JCA Adapters are available in Service Bus, along with the original transports (largely for backward compatibility reasons). The *resequence* functionality already included in Mediator has been added to Service Bus as well, to ensure messages are processed in some specifically defined correct order.

- New in SOA composite applications is the use of Templates (at Project, Component, Custom BPEL Activity level). A new component is the BPEL Sub Process—that can be both inline and stand alone; this component helps break up complex BPEL process and allow for easy, local reusability. The new fault policy editor makes defining and binding fault policies much easier; fault policies can now also be associated with alerts to be sent to administration. The SOA Suite test framework for unit testing SOA composites has been improved, and now includes the ability to run tests within JDeveloper with detailed reports of every test run.

- Business Rule components cater for much easier testing of decision functions. Decision tables can be edited in Excel and reimported into JDeveloper. When using Business Rules in the context of BPM, more natural definitions of rules can be created in the form of verbal rules using business phrases. Business phrases provide the logic behind conditions that are used in the composition of the verbal rule.

- The Event Delivery Network has been made much more robust. It is now completely JMS, allows durable subscriptions (guaranteeing event delivery even in the temporary absence of a consumer) and supports event publication and consumption from outside the SOA Suite infrastructure using a JMS client—for example, Service Bus.

- Process analytics can be published through simple configuration of BPEL and BPM process definitions; the analytics are recorded in database tables that have been mapped to BAM Data Objects. Out of the box dashboards and reports leverage these data objects to provide insight in the execution metrics of business processes.

- The EM FMW Control console has been extended and improved in many ways. Operational details from Service Bus are exposed (such as Pipeline and SLA alerts and Message Reports). It presents a dashboard of relevant metrics, recent activities and instances waiting for recovery. It supports scheduled purge and fault recovery. Additionally, inbounds adapters can be scheduled for activation and deactivation.

- Through SOA Composer, composite sensor definition can be configured at run time; improvements were made to business rule and human task editing.

- Under the theme of industrialization, the resource footprint has been decreased or at least made smarter (through memory profiles and lazy loading) and workloads have been made more manageable using (per partition) work managers.

- Oracle SOA Suite 12*c* ships with a Maven plugin that allows development teams to use Maven to create, build, package and deploy SOA project: whenever an Application or Project is created, automatically the Maven pom.xml gets created.

- Oracle Event Processor application development is done in JDeveloper. Integration with the EDN has been provided. The browser tool StreamExplorer provides a user friendly UI for developing event processing applications.

- BAM has been redesigned—leveraging Coherence for data caching and the ADF Data Visualization components for presentation. BAM contains an embedded stripped down version of OEP that enables it to perform various types of aggregation and pattern detection. BAM is now supported on all major browsers and has a much revamped appearance.

- Several new JCA adapters have been added. On the technology side these are MSMQ, LDAP, Coherence and (substantial changes in) UMS. For Business Application and SaaS integration: SalesForce, RightNow, SAP R/3, JD EDwards with many more on the horizon: RightNow (aka Oracle Service Cloud), Oracle Sales Cloud, Eloqua (Oracle Marketing Cloud) and Big Machines (Oracle CPQ Cloud). The Cloud Adapters SDK is made available to allow organizations to develop their own custom adapters.

- Integration has been added with Enterprise Scheduling Services (ESS) and Managed File Transfer (MFT).

Bringing existing Service Bus projects or SOA composite applications from 11*g* to 12*c* does not mean a migration but merely a simple upgrade. Running instances can be upgraded while in flight.

Industry Standards for Middleware and Service-Oriented Architecture

To be *open* is one of the key characteristics for Oracle Fusion Middleware. This entails support for industry standards in order to allow integration with 3rd party products and easy application of skills and knowledge. FMW in general and SOA Suite 12*c* in particular support many standards—though in many cases not the most recent version of these standards. Table 2-1 provides an overview of some of the most relevant standards.

Standard	Year of Original Publication	Current Release and Year Published	Version Supported in SOA Suite 12*c* & FMW 12*c*	Standards Body	Purpose
XML	1998	1.1 (2nd edition), 2006	1.1	W3C	Flexible yet structured language for creating text documents
SOAP	1998	1.2, 2007	1.2 & 1.1	W3C	XML-based protocol specification for exchanging messages with web services
XPath	1999	3.0, 2014	2.0 & 1.1	W3C	Query language for retrieving information from XML documents
XSLT	1999	3.0, 2013 (working draft)	1.0	W3C	Style sheet language for describing transformations for XML documents
WSDL (Web Service Description Language)	2000	2.0, 2007	1.0	W3C	XML language for describing the web services interface
XSD	2001	1.1, 2012	1.1	W3C	Schema language for defining the valid structure and rules for XML elements (and successor to DTD)
Java Message Service (JMS)	2001	2.0, 2013	1.1	JCP	Java EE specification that describes a Java API for loosely coupled, asynchronous interactions through Message-Oriented Middleware
Java EE Connector Architecture (JCA)	2001	1.6, 2013	1.6	JCP	Java EE specification for creating adapters to connect Java with Enterprise Information Systems
Security Assertion Markup Language (SAML)	2002	2.0, 2005	1.0	OASIS	XML-based standard that describes how security-related information (identification, authorization) can be exchanged
WS-Reliable Messaging	2003	1.2, 2009	1.1	OASIS	A wire protocol used in SOAP messages to ensure reliable transport between sender and receiver
Business Process Execution Language (BPEL4WS/WS-BPEL)	2004	2.0, 2007	2.0	OASIS	Executable language for processes that interact with web services

TABLE 2-1. *Chronological Overview of Some IT Industry Standards and Specifications Relevant to Middleware and Service-Oriented Architecture (Continued)*

Standard	Year of Original Publication	Current Release and Year Published	Version Supported in SOA Suite 12c & FMW 12c	Standards Body	Purpose
Service Data Objects (SDO)	2004	2.0, 2005	2.0	OASIS	Data-programming architecture that facilitates working with structured data objects in Service-Oriented Architecture
Business Process Modeling Notation (BPMN)	2004	2.0, 2011	2.0	OMG	Standard for ways to graphically describe business processes—and as added bonus simulate or even execute those processes for real
WS-I Basic Profile	2004	2.0, 2010	1.1	WS-I (part of OASIS)	Specification on how to apply standards such as SOAP, WSDL, WS-Addressing and UDDI in order to achieve true interoperability across technology stacks
WS-Security [Policy]	2004	1.2, 2007	1.2	OASIS	Specification on how to apply security—for example, through SAML or Kerberos—to web services and SOAP messages
WS-Addressing	2006	1.0, 2006	1.0	W3C	Standard that provides transport-neutral mechanisms to address and identify web service endpoints and to secure end-to-end endpoint identification in messages
XQuery	2007	3.0, 2014	1.0	W3C	Programming language for querying collections of XML data (technically a subset of XPath)
Service Component Architecture (SCA)	2007	1.0, 2007	1.0	OSOA	Configuration language for describing composite applications based on service components
WS-Policy	2007	1.0-1.2, 2007	1.2	W3C	XML language for describing the policies—such as Security and Quality of Service—that apply to a web service
WS-I Basic Security Profile	2007	1.1, 2010	1.0	WS-I (part of OASIS)	Specification on how to apply security standards such as WS-Security in order to achieve true (security) interoperability across technology stacks
REST (Representational State Transfer)	2000	-	-	De facto	Provides an architecture for designing network applications. RESTful applications use HTTP requests to PUT data (create), POST data (update), GET data (e.g., make queries), and DELETE data. REST provides an alternative to using web services
JSON (JavaScript Object Notation)	2001	-	-	De facto (described by two competing standards, RFC 7159 and ECMA-404)	A human-readable text format to transmit data objects consisting of attribute–value pairs, arrays and nested objects. It is used primarily to transmit data between a server and web application, as an alternative to XML

TABLE 2-1.   *Chronological Overview of Some IT Industry Standards and Specifications Relevant to Middleware and Service-Oriented Architecture*

Standard	Year of Original Publication	Current Release and Year Published	Version Supported in SOA Suite 12*c* & FMW 12*c*	Standards Body	Purpose
CMMN (Case Management Modeling and Notation)	2014	1.0, 2014	-	OMG	A common meta-model and notation for modeling and graphically expressing a case, as well as an interchange format for exchanging case models among different tools
SAML (Security Assertion Markup Language)	2001	2.0, 2005	1.0	OASIS	An XML-based, open-standard data format for exchanging authentication and authorization data between parties, in particular, between an identity provider and a service provider
Web Application Description Language (WADL)	2009	-	-	De facto	Provides a readable XML description of HTTP-based web applications (typically REST web services). WADL simplifies the reuse of web services based on the existing HTTP architecture of the web. Can be seen as the RESTful counterpart to WSDL (for SOAP services)
Java SE&EE standards	1999	7,2013	6	JCP (Java Community Process)	
JAX-B	2003	2.2	2.2		
JAX-P	2000	1.3	1.3		
JAX-RS	2008	2.0	2.0		
Java API for WebSocket	2013	1.0	1.0		
JAX-WS	2006	2.2	2.2		
EJB	1997/1999	3.2	3.1		
Spring	2004	4.0, 2014	4.0, 3.1, 3.0	Pivotal/Spring Community	

TABLE 2-1. *Chronological Overview of Some IT Industry Standards and Specifications Relevant to Middleware and Service-Oriented Architecture (Continued)*

Getting Started with SOA Suite 12*c*

The quick start installation of JDeveloper 12*c* with the integrated WebLogic Server makes it very easy to make a flying start with your exploration of SOA Suite 12*c*. With a few simple steps, you are able get a development environment up and running with most of the SOA Suite 12*c* components at your disposal.

Creating a full blown SOA Suite 12*c* environment with all functionality enabled just like the production environment requires some additional steps—but is still not overly difficult.

Quick Starting the SOA Suite 12*c* Development Environment

The steps you have to go through in order to get your first HelloWorld SOA composite application running are simple, straightforward and take you less than 20 minutes—once the installation files are downloaded. The book's website contains a step by step instruction and a reference to the relevant documentation and software resources.

- Download the SOA Suite 12c installation file, a single zip file of some 3GB—either for the Windows 64 bit platform or for a generic JVM (on all other platforms). (http://www .oracle.com/technetwork/middleware/soasuite/downloads/index.html)

- Ensure that you have a supported JDK on the target machine (at least JDK 7.0 Update 55, but this may have changed for the specific release you will be installing).

- Run the installer from the command line; step through the installation wizard; there is just a single question of consequence: whether to install just SOA Suite or BPM Suite as well. After the installation is complete, close the installation wizard.

- Start JDeveloper. The design time for SOA Suite—as well as Java EE, ADF, and several other technologies—is available.

- To also create the *run time* for SOA Suite, you have to run the integrated WebLogic Server; this will first create the WebLogic domain and then extend that domain for SOA Suite (and BPM Suite if you selected that in the installation wizard). This process may take from 10 to 30 minutes or more, depending on the resources available on your machine. As the first step, you need to specify the credentials for the administrator and the hostname and port at which the server will listen (default are localhost and 7101).

- When the domain creation and extension is complete, the server is automatically started—ready to accept deployment of SOA Suite applications. The administration console is available at http://localhost:7101/console and the Enterprise Manager FMW Control can be accessed in a browser at http://localhost:7101/em. An application server connection for the integrated WebLogic Server is configured in JDeveloper—to be used for deployment of applications to the run time.

The run time environment you have thus created does not have support for Enterprise Scheduler, Managed File Transfer, B2B, or Healthcare, nor Business Activity Monitoring or OEP. It runs against an embedded JavaDB database rather than the Oracle RDBMS and as a result, a number of administration tasks are not available.

TIP
You can still configure JDBC data sources to reference other databases and in doing so enable the database adapter to be used from the local SOA Suite environment against these remote databases.

Creating the Full Blown SOA Suite 12c Run-Time Environment

Installing the standalone run time environment for SOA Suite 12c requires a little more effort than the use of the integrated WebLogic Server in JDeveloper. However, depending on your method, this extra effort can be very limited—and there are some rewards.

Using the integrated WebLogic Server as the SOA Suite run time environment makes installation very straightforward and it is a great way to get started very quickly. There are some disadvantages as well that after some time may make you prefer a standalone run environment instead. The integrated environment is not functionally complete. Additionally, it cannot run outside of JDeveloper and when JDeveloper is shutdown, it shuts down too. This tight relationship may get a little cumbersome.

The steps for the installation of the standalone run time environment entail preparation of an Oracle RDBMS (running the Repository Creation Utility to create some database schemas and a series of database objects), installation of WebLogic and SOA Suite software and the creation and configuration of the WebLogic domain. The book's website provides references to installation resources. It also has a reference to an instruction for using provisioning with Vagrant and Puppet to very rapidly implement a couple of VirtualBox VMs with the complete database and Fusion Middleware set up for SOA Suite along with BPM Suite, ESS, and BAM.

Summary

Oracle SOA Suite 12c is the long-awaited successor to the 11g release of 2009. It is the next step in a long evolution in the IT industry at large (and Oracle Corporation in particular).

This chapter gave you a glimpse of the rise of software for integration and later on middleware and the PaaS Cloud within Oracle. Standards were discussed as essential to the success of web services—the foundation for interoperability—and Service-Oriented Architecture. Oracle plays an important role in the specification process and the promotion of most industry standards.

Oracle itself is an interesting example of integration: The company has acquired and subsequently absorbed several dozens of other companies and their software offerings. Many important parts of today's software portfolio have roots in products from these "scalps." The most striking acquisitions in the area of middleware affecting the SOA Suite directly probably are Collaxa (2004), BEA (2008), and Sun Microsystems (2010). Oracle's success with the integration of these companies and their products is quite amazing.

A many-year process of innovation, integration, and interaction with customers, including the important internal Applications development teams, resulted in Fusion Middleware. On July 1, 2009, Fusion Middleware 11g was launched. Five years on, the 12c release brought the next generation of Fusion Middleware—a wide palette of middleware technology, ranging from business intelligence, web services, and content management, to enterprise collaboration, identity and access management, governance, event processing, and custom-developed user interfaces. SOA Suite 12c is an important element in the FMW 12c stack, with interactions with many of the other areas within FMW.

The SOA Suite has at its heart the SCA container that runs SOA composite applications and the Service Bus engine for execution of Service Bus projects. The SOA composite applications are built from components that run on specialized engines: BPEL, Mediator, BPMN, Business Rules, (Spring) Java, and Human Task. The components can interact with external web services and technology adapters to reach out to the database, file system, messaging infrastructures, and so on. The same applies to Service Bus projects.

The SOA Suite provides a framework for negotiating events between applications, offering a very decoupled way of making different applications interact. Other products in the SOA Suite are Business Activity Monitoring (BAM), and Oracle Event Processing (OEP).

Organizations that have adopted earlier generations of the SOA Suite only need to go through a very simple upgrade process when they want to adopt the 12c release.

This concludes Part I of the book. The next part introduces the components of the SOA Suite in detail and demonstrates how to create applications with them.

PART
II

Elementary Services

CHAPTER
3

Exposing
SOAP and REST Services
Using Service Bus

T he architecture team at Saibot Airport has decreed that all services are to be published through the Service Bus (SB). Any consumer of a service calls to a proxy endpoint exposed by the Service Bus and the bus routes that request to the actual service implementation The Service Bus is the common virtualization layer that hides the where, how, and even the if of services from consumers. The Service Bus virtualizes the real location of the service as well as its implementation. It makes all services available over standardized protocols and message formats. It also can hide the fact that a service is currently unavailable by rerouting the request to an alternative provider or producing a result from a cache. As part of the virtualization of services, the service does protocol mapping—for example, REST to SOAP or JMS to EJB—as well as message transformation.

The Service Bus as the common entry point provides a number of important run time facilities. All service access can be monitored, performance and SLA compliance can be tracked, authorization and security policies can be enforced and logging is done. The SB provides scalability through its stateless, easily clustered nature, which also prevents it becoming a single point of failure. The SB can do throttling on large volumes of service requests to prevent choking and general failure of the bus.

In this chapter, we meet the Service Bus. We will develop and deploy a number of simple services—some with SOAP/XML and one with a REST/JSON interface. JDeveloper and its Integrated WebLogic-with-SOA-Suite-Server will be our design time and run time environment.

Introducing Service Bus

The Service Bus component in the SOA Suite provides an enterprise service bus with all the common characteristics and patterns associated with an "Enterprise Service Bus." Simply put, the Service Bus in SOA Suite is a stateless, synchronous request/response engine that is a very fast, uniform intermediary between service consumers and heterogeneous services and backend systems, see Figure 3-1. The Service Bus implements the VETRO pattern. This acronym stands for Validate, Enrich, Transform, Route, and Operate. It has support for various other patterns, such as fan-in and fan-out, fire-and-forget, and so on.

Service consumers access an endpoint at the Service Bus using one of several supported transports and protocols. We will focus on HTTP as transport, SOAP and REST as protocols, and

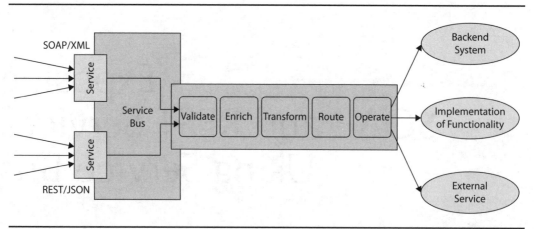

FIGURE 3-1. *Service Bus virtualizes access to services and implements the VETRO pattern*

XML and JSON as message formats. Note that the Service Bus can leverage the many JCA adapters available with Oracle SOA Suite for receiving inbound messages, as well as a number of the native transports inherited from previous incarnations of the product.

The endpoint is exposed by a Proxy, the inbound end of a service in the Service Bus, as shown in Figure 3-2. The Proxy receives the incoming request message and, regardless of transport, protocol, or format, will set up a message context that gives the impression that all messages are SOAP messages and all payloads are XML. This context consists of a number of variables—$header, $body, and $attachments. These wrapper variables contain the Simple Object Access Protocol (SOAP) header elements, body element, and Multipurpose Internet Mail Extensions (MIME) attachments, respectively. Another variable—$inbound—provides metadata about the incoming message, such as transport and security.

The message context is handed over by the Proxy to the Pipeline—the central message processing unit in the Service Bus providing routing and transformation capabilities. The pipeline can be seen as a simple function that is invoked with a message context—based on the initial request—and returns the modified message context—based on the response of the underlying service implementation and whatever processing takes place in the pipeline.

The pipeline is a special type of program, visually constructed using a number of built in operations, many of which operate on the predefined message context variables or on custom XML variables. Among these standard operations are common programming instructions such as assign (value to variable), replace (value in variable), if else, forEach, call out (to Java Class or external service), and publish (a log message or some alert or report).

The first half of a pipeline processes the request message received from the Proxy—available through the message context variables. It typically ends with a Routing action that invokes a *business service* (which is the local bridge in the Service Bus to external services) or another SB pipeline. The values of the $body, $header, and $attachments variables at the time of this routing action determine the contents of the request message sent in the invocation.

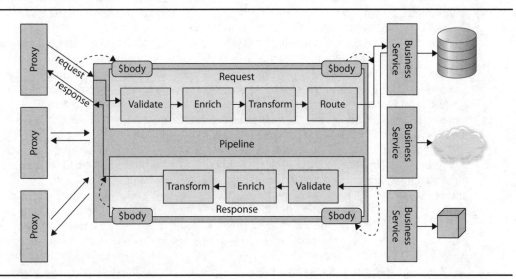

FIGURE 3-2. *Message processing from proxy through pipeline to business service and the four roles played by $body variable regarding the inbound and outbound payload from and to proxy and business service*

The response from the routing call to either the business service or the pipeline sets the values of the three message context variables for the second half of the pipeline: the response flow. After the possible manipulations of the variables, their values at the end of the pipeline are used to compose the response message returned from the proxy to the service consumer. Note that response processing takes place in a different (Java) thread than the request processing.

A business service in Service Bus terms is a reference to an enterprise resource that provides (part of) the implementation of the functionality exposed by the proxy. This resource is invoked by the pipeline through the local representation provided in the SB by the business service component. Part of the business service definition is the adapter or transport over which the underlying service can be invoked, the endpoint(s) and possible load balancing and failover strategy to be used when accessing the enterprise service and the security measures that may have to be used for making calls to the service.

Simple services can do without a call to a business service. For example, when the functionality a service offers can be implemented through a transformation of the request message, there is no need to route to an external service. Note that is largely a theoretical possibility that we will use for our very first implementation only and that is not commonly used in real life.

Note that the Proxy, the Pipeline, and the Business Service are stand-alone components that are developed independent from one another and that are only loosely coupled. Several proxies can be associated with the same pipeline. A pipeline can be used by various proxies as well as other pipelines and a business service can be invoked from multiple pipelines.

Airport Information Desk Is the Human Service Bus

The Service Bus plays a similar role toward service consumers in the Service-Oriented Architecture at Saibot Airport as the Airport Information Desk does with regard to people with enquiries. The Service Bus is the entry point for parties invoking services published by Saibot Airport. It will sometimes provide the implementation of the service itself and relay the request to back-end systems in the majority of cases.

The Information Desk is very alike. It is the first point of call for anyone with a question concerning the airport. Questions can be asked over different channels, what we would call transports for the Service Bus: in person at the desk itself, via telephone, or through chat. The Service Bus supports different formats and the desk will process questions in English, Spanish, and French. The Service Bus is stateless and does either one-way messages (without response) or synchronous request-reply. The Information Desk does not call back; one has to stay on the line or at the desk in order to get one's answer.

Staff at the Information Desk makes use of various enterprise resources to get questions answered. These include internal IT systems, phone calls to colleagues, email forwarding to other staff members or even external contacts, lookup in manuals, the use of dictionaries, and of course use of Google and other public websites. The Service Bus enlists the help of various types of business services to fulfill service requests. It is the responsibility of the bus—like the desk—to decide which resource to call and how to ask the question from that particular resource given the original request—transforming that request to the format and wording understood by that resource.

When the internal systems change—the people working at the desk will change the way in which they find the answers to the questions. However, when that happens, nothing changes for the customers of the desk. Similarly, when the implementation for a service changes, consumers of the public services exposed by the Service Bus will not be impacted. That is what we call encapsulation and separation between interface and implementation.

When the Information Desk starts to support a new channel (e.g., Twitter) or hires people who speak a new language (Dutch), nothing will change for the internal systems; all operations continue just like before, only the people at the desk have to adapt.

The Information Desk can easily scale up when demand increases: multiple people can man the desk and there are no special relationships between the clients and the staff. When someone at the desk gets sick, someone else will take over—or the remaining staff will have to work just a little bit harder. This of course is exactly parallel to the clustering capabilities of the Service Bus as well as its fail-over capacity.

In this comparison, the people at the desk are both the proxy and the pipeline; their avenues to answers to the questions asked can be regarded as the business services at their disposal. This includes the people they can call, computer applications they can check and manuals they can look into.

Developing the Temperature Conversion Service

The value of a service is the product of the functionality it provides—how much does it do—and its reuse potential—how frequently will it be invoked to make its contribution. Unfortunately, the two factors are almost inversely proportional. It is up to the service architect and designer to strike the optimal balance between coarse and fine grainedness and determine the functional scope of each service. Of course, you will end up having services with all levels of grain size in your environment.

NOTE
Flexibility in the implementation of services that allows easy change upon future requirements is also a large factor in determining its value—or rather its cost reduction potential. Sacrificing reuse for lower maintenance costs may well be justified.

At Saibot Airport, a number of fine grained functions with very high reuse potential have been identified. These functions are utility services that offer conversions between the various appearances of the many physical units that international airports have to deal with, such as speed, height, distance, weight, and temperature. Utility services such as these offer generic, often not business domain specific, functionality that can be reused throughout the enterprise and even beyond. The implementation is typically fairly straightforward and light weight.

We will start by creating a Service Bus pipeline that is exposed with a SOAP Web Service proxy to provide temperature conversions between Celsius and Fahrenheit. A simple transformation is all it takes to make the conversion. This means that the pipeline does not need to invoke any business services to produce its answer.

Starting a New Service Bus Project

Development of any SOA Suite 12c component is done through JDeveloper with the SOA Suite extension installed. The first step therefore is to start JDeveloper. Create a new application, for example, using the menu option File | New | Application… This will bring up the New Gallery.

From the Categories tree, click on General > Applications. Select *Service Bus Application with Service Bus Project* from the Items field.

The wizard for creating a Service Bus project appears. Enter the Application Name as ConversionServices. Enter a directory to create the application in. Click on the Next button. On the next page, enter the name of the Service Bus project: TemperatureConversionService. Accept the default directory. Verify that the Service Bus project feature is selected. Press Finish. JDeveloper will now create the folders you specified if they do not already exist. The .jws file that holds the application definition and the .jpr file that represents the project are created. The Service Bus editor—shown in Figure 3-3—opens for the TemperatureConversionService. The editor is driven by the file overview.xml that is created in the project directory.

Create Folders

In Service Bus applications, folders are used to organize artifacts within a project. These folders will not be automatically created in Service Bus. It is recommended though to use a standardized folder structure that is the same across all Service Bus projects as well as similar where relevant with the structure used for SCA Composite applications.

At this moment, create the following folders in the TemperatureConversionService project: *Schemas*, *WSDLs*, *Transformations*, and *Proxy*.

A folder is created through the New Gallery. Open the New Gallery from the context menu on the project node in the application navigator. Note that this context menu will contain the option Folder after the first time you have created one. In the Gallery, select Folder in the list of items shown when the General Category node is selected. Click on OK. Enter the name of the desired folder in the Create Folder dialog. Accept the default directory to create the folder in. Then press OK. The project should now look like Figure 3-4.

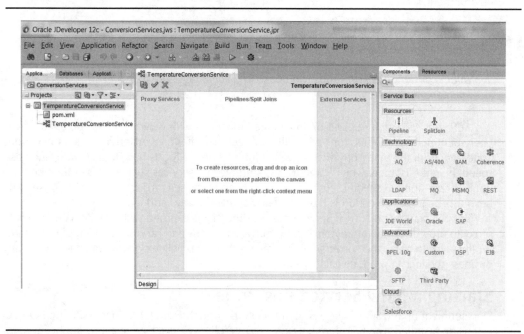

FIGURE 3-3. *JDeveloper showing the Service Bus project TemperatureConversionService*

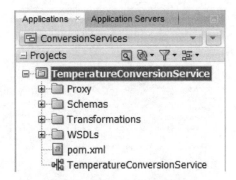

FIGURE 3-4. *Folder structure in TemperatureConversionService project*

NOTE
Folders Adapters *and* Business Service *will be added at a later stage.*

Importing the Design Resources

The designers at Saibot Airport have created not only the XSD documents representing the canonical data model, but also the specific service interface for the TemperatureConversionService. This contract consists of a WSDL document that defines the interface of the service and an associated XSD document with the definitions of the request and response messages prescribed for the operations in the service interface. This schema definition makes use of the file common.xsd that contains some basic canonical types used throughout Saibot's services landscape. In this chapter, we will take a somewhat naïve view in that both XSDs are located locally, in the same directory. In later chapters we will reference generic, reusable resources such as common.xsd from the MDS (Meta Data Services) repository.

Select the option Import on the context menu for the WSDLs folder node. From the Import dialog, choose *Service Bus Resources*. Click on OK. Select Configuration Jar on the first page of the wizard Import Service Bus Resources. Select the jar-file TemperatureConversionServiceResources.jar in the source directory for Chapter 3. Click on Next. The wizard will present an overview of what resources it will import into the project—see the left part of Figure 3-5. Accept all (three) resources and click on Finish.

When the import wizard is complete, the two XSD files and the WSDL file are imported into the project. The application navigator tree looks as is shown on the right in Figure 3-5.

Let's take a brief look at the TemperatureConversionService interface, starting with the WSDL for this service. The meat of the WSDL is found in the portType element. This service exposes a single operation, called *getTemperatureCelsiusToFahrenheit*, which is evidently offering to convert a temperature value in degrees Celsius into the Fahrenheit equivalent.

The input message to be passed into the operation is named *temperatureCelsiusToFahrenheitRequestMessage* and the result is returned in the form of a *temperatureCelsiusToFahrenheitResponseMessage*. These messages are defined in the messages element. The definitions of the both messages contain a single part, based on XSD elements in the imported XSD document TemperatureConversionService.xsd.

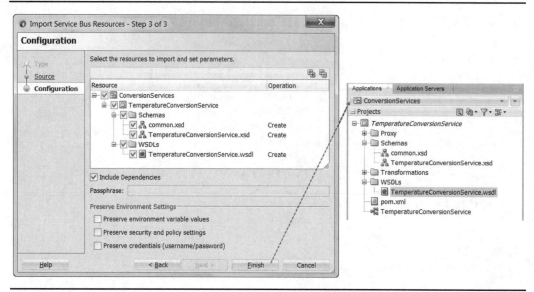

FIGURE 3-5. *The TemperatureConversionService project after importing the design resources*

Exploring dependencies from the context menu on the WSDL file quickly reveals the file level dependencies, as is shown in Figure 3-6.

Create the Proxy

What we are doing here is essentially contract-first development: based on the definition of the contract, that was created first, we are now ready to develop the service implementation. The Service Bus project will expose a proxy service as its entry point. This particular proxy will support an SOAP/XML over HTTP transport and protocol style.

A straightforward way to create the proxy for the TemperatureConversionService is using the option *Generate Proxy Service* on the context menu for the TemperatureConversionService.wsdl. When you activate that option, a wizard occurs—see Figure 3-7. On the first page, set the *Location* (where the proxy is to be generated) to the Proxy folder you have created earlier on in the project. Uncheck the check box *Generate Pipeline* that would instruct the wizard to automatically create a pipeline (with the same interface as the proxy) and link the proxy to the

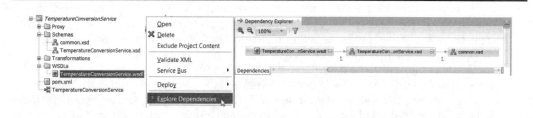

FIGURE 3-6. *The Dependency Explorer for TemperatureConversionService.wsdl*

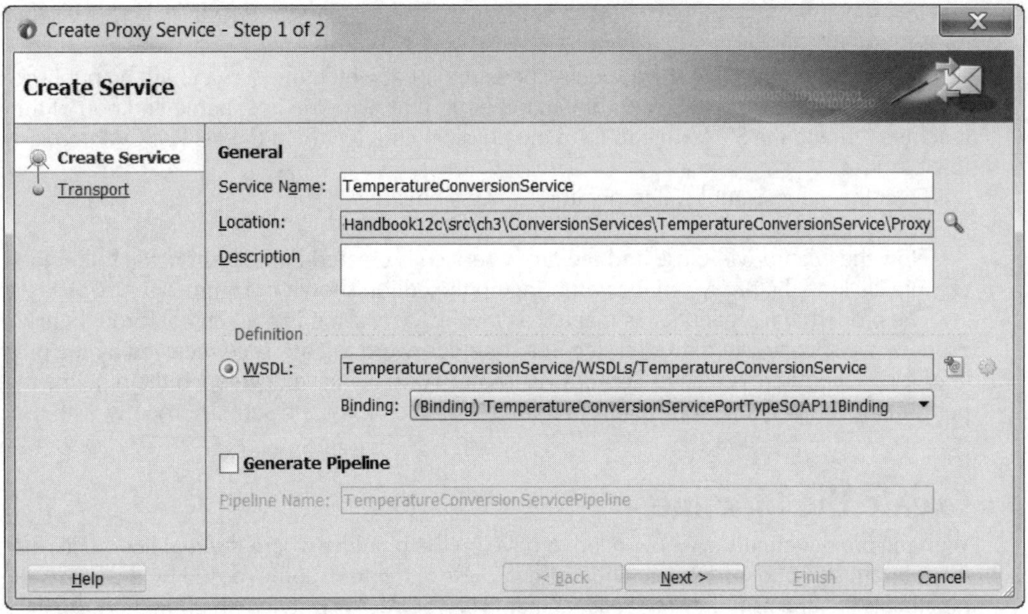

FIGURE 3-7. *The wizard for creating a Proxy Service*

pipeline. In later situations, we will use that option—as it is actually quite convenient. Right now, it is important to understand the various constituents of a Service Bus project.

Click on next.

In the second page of the Proxy Service wizard (Figure 3-8), we can specify the transport to be supported by this proxy service. Among the options are *jca*—for when we use the inbound mode of one of the technology adapters available with the SOA Suite, *local*—for proxies that are only

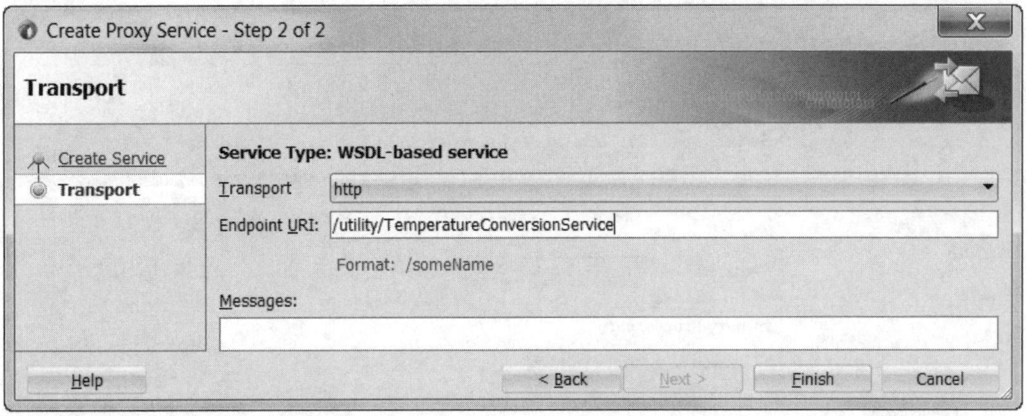

FIGURE 3-8. *Specifying the transport details for the new Proxy Service*

invoked by other proxies and pipelines-, *jms* and *ws*—for interactions according to the Web Services Reliable Messaging (WSRM) specification. For regular SOAP/XML style proxy services, we will use the default option of *http*.

In the Endpoint URI field we specify the endpoint at which this service will be published. The value we provide here will be combined at the run time with the host name and port of the actual machine running the SOA Suite to form the physical URL to which the HTTP/SOAP requests are to be sent.

Enter the value as /utility/TemperatureConversionService.

Then press Finish.

Now the wizard will close and the proxy service is created in the designated folder Proxy. Double clicking the proxy service will bring up the editor, shown in Figure 3-9.

The property Target Service is marked as invalid, because it is not yet set. Through this property we specify where the Service Bus should forward the message received by the proxy after it has been normalized to SOAP/XML format. After we have developed the pipeline that will perform the temperature conversion, we will revisit the proxy and set this property with a reference to the pipeline.

Create the Pipeline

With the proxy defined, we now need to develop the pipeline where the real action takes place—the relevant subset of VETRO activities. Regardless of the transport exposed by the proxy, the pipeline is created as if the service is regular HTTP/SOAP/XML-style (which in this case the proxy's transport happens to be too). A pipeline in general is created without any special consideration for the proxy service(s) and other pipelines that will invoke it.

Create the pipeline using the menu option Service Bus | Generate Pipeline on the context menu for the wsdl document.

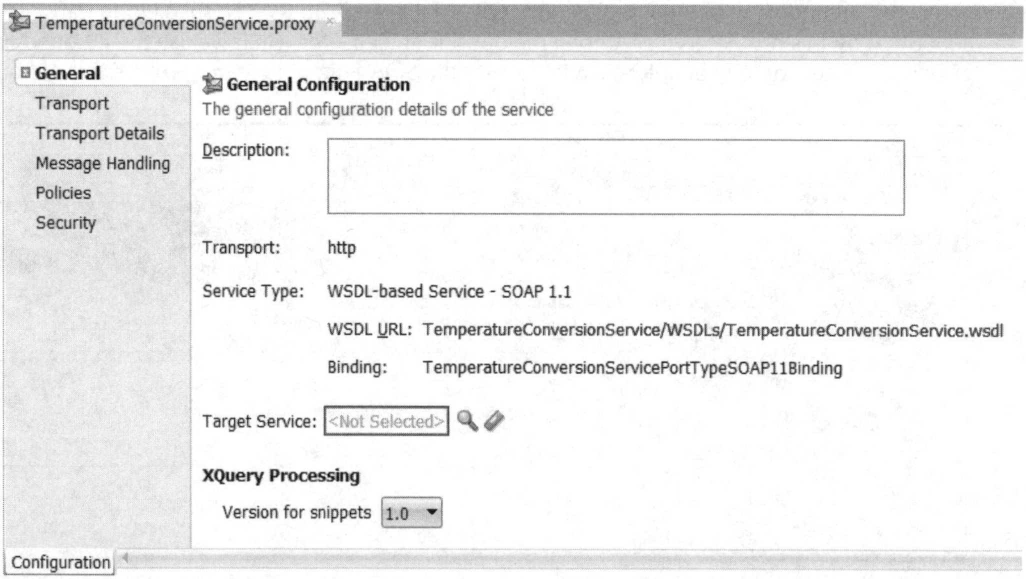

FIGURE 3-9. *The proxy editor for the TemperatureConversionService proxy*

The wizard for creating a service bus pipeline opens. On the first page, set the Name to *TemperatureConversionPipeline* and the Location to a new *Pipeline* folder that you create from the browse dialog. Click on the Next button. Accept the already selected Service Type settings, derived from the wsdl. Uncheck the check box *Expose as a Proxy Service*. In this case, the proxy already exists and is waiting to be connected to the pipeline. Press *Finish*. The wizard will now create the pipeline that supports the interface defined in the WSDL document TemperatureConversionService.wsdl.

The pipeline editor has two tabs, labeled *design* and *configuration* respectively. On the design tab, the message flow through the pipeline is visualized. The component palette exposes all the actions we can make use of when programming the pipeline. We can drag and drop these actions to the visual flow editor to add them to the pipeline. This is shown in Figure 3-10.

The configuration tab allows to set properties for various aspects of the pipeline's behavior. This includes settings for how to deal with large messages and attachments, the transactional behavior, the way the pipeline determines from a request message which operation in the service interface is invoked, as well as optionally the strategy to use for ensuring the sequence for processing messages. For the very simple TemperatureConversionService we will accept all default configuration settings.

On the design tab, add a Pipeline Pair to the message flow by dragging it from the component palette and dropping it below the *TemperatureConversionPipeline* icon. A pipeline pair is a container component used to organize part of the message flow through the pipeline—as illustrated in Figure 3-2. The word pair in the name refers to the fact that there is a matching couple of flows: one that describes the journey of the incoming request message on its way through the VET (Validate-Enrich-Transform) stages to possibly some routing to an onward destination, and a matching one for the response message received back from the next step in the pipeline and the validation, enrichment, and transformation it undergoes before being handed back as response to the next step up the call chain. Note that the earlier discussed variables $body, $header, and $attachments can be read and operated on in the activities in the pipeline.

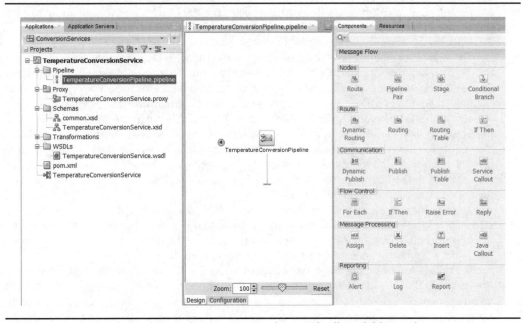

FIGURE 3-10. *Pipeline editor and Component Palette with all available pipeline activities*

Inside each of the two flows in the pipeline is currently a single stage included. A stage is the smallest activity container available in pipelines. In the pipeline editor, stages are used to optimally organize, present, and navigate the pipeline. A stage has a user defined name, it can contain one or more activities. It can have an error handler. Stages can be expanded or collapsed, moved around, copied and pasted, removed and recreated. Stages cannot be nested.

In the *TemperatureConversionPipeline* we will initially do just one thing with the request message: transform it into a response message with the properly converted temperature value. Before we can configure this transformation through the replace activity, we will first create the XSLT document that handles this particular transformation.

Create the Transformation

Manipulation of variables that hold XML data is very common in Service Bus pipelines. This XML content is frequently read from the body or headers of incoming messages or written to outgoing messages. Custom variables can also be defined in pipelines; these too hold XML content that is assigned and manipulated. Manipulation of variables is done using XQuery or XSLT. Both are equally well supported in the SOA Suite, in SCA composites as well as in Service Bus projects. XQuery is better suited for fine-grained manipulation of individual nodes in XML documents and XSLT is more appropriate for transformation of the entire documents. Deciding which of the two to use for wholesale transformation of the contents of a variable seems a matter of preference; both XQuery and XSLT do such transformations well and there is no inherent preference for either from the run time engine.

In the case of the *TemperatureConversionPipeline* we will develop an XSLT stylesheet that we will use to transform the contents of the $body variable. The value that is passed into the pipeline is based on the XSD element *temperatureCelsiusToFahrenheitRequestMessage*. The value that the $body variable should have at the end of the [response part of the] pipeline—the value that is returned as the response from the pipeline—has to be based on the element *temperatureCelsiusToFahrenheitResponseMessage*. The XSLT stylesheet we are about to create has to perform a transformation between these two elements.

Click on the node Transformations. Open the context menu and select New | XSL Map.

The wizard for creating an XSL Map File appears—Figure 3-11. It supports version 1.0 of XSLT. Set the File Name to temperatureCelsiusToFahrenheitRequestToResponse.xsl. First set the Primary Source, which in this case is also the only source used in the transformation. Press the Browse button in the Sources frames. Browse to the *temperatureCelsiusToFahrenheitRequestMessage* element in the TemperatureConversionService.xsd file, and select it as the source element. Using the Browse button in the Target frame, select the *temperatureCelsiusToFahrenheitResponseMessage* element as the target element. This instructs the tool that the map we are creating should produce an XML document with the structure of the target element—and that it may expect an XML input document of the source type. Note for future reference that an XSL Map can also use auxiliary XML sources and input parameters. Press OK.

The XSL Map editor opens for the newly created XSL document. On the left side, the map editor shows the source structure providing the input to the transformation. On the right side is the target structure that the transformation will produce. In the middle we will add the map itself—the XSLT instructions for constructing the target from the source.

For simple source element to target element mappings, the Design view of the mapping editor is well suited, as we will experience now: drag the temperature source element to the temperature target element. This does not do any value conversion, as it will perform a straight copy of the temperature value. Applying the actual conversion formula is easier in source mode. Switch the map editor to source mode and change the expression

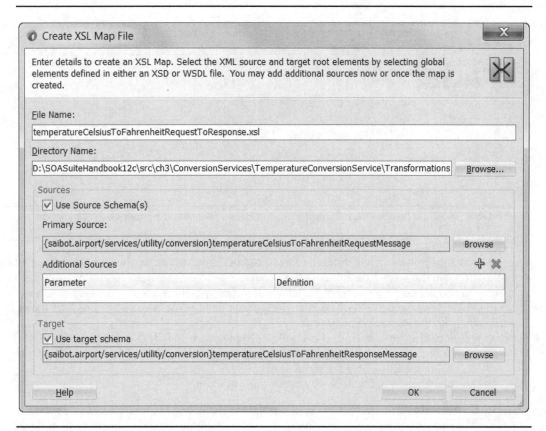

FIGURE 3-11. *The wizard for creating the XSL Map file (an annotated XSLT document)*

```
<xsl:value-of select="/ns0:temperatureCelsiusToFahrenheitRequestMessage/
ns0:temperature"/>
```
that was created when we dragged the temperature element to the following expression that actually performs the conversion:
```
<xsl:value-of select="(/ns0:temperatureCelsiusToFahrenheitRequestMessage/
ns0:temperature * (9 div 5) +32)"/>
```

Back in the Design mode, the editor looks as is shown in Figure 3-12. It is probably easy to understand why creating this particular conversion is easier in source mode than in design mode.

We can test this transformation. Click on the icon as is indicated in Figure 3-12. The XSL Map tester is opened. Select—or generate—a source XML file. Press OK to run the transformation on the source document. The transformation result is shown, with the Fahrenheit temperature value.

Add the Transformation to the Pipeline

Now that we have created the XSLT stylesheet that will do the required transformation of the contents of the $body variable, it is time to add a *Replace* activity to the pipeline that will use the stylesheet to manipulate the variables value.

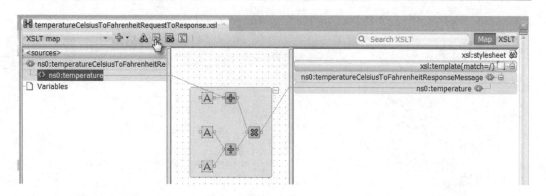

FIGURE 3-12. *The XSL Map editor for the Celsius to Fahrenheit temperature conversion*

Drag the Replace activity from the Message Processing section on the Components palette and drop it in the *stage 1* container in the Request Pipeline. Note: Because this pipeline does not route to another component, the Request and Response pipelines are directly sequential and we could have positioned the Replace in the Response pipeline just as easily. Figure 3-13 shows the pipeline with the Replace activity.

The Properties window is used to configure the Replace activity. Note: If the Properties window is not currently shown, it can be made to appear using the Window | Properties menu option or using the Ctrl + Shift + I shortcut key.

The configuration of the Replace activity consists of:

- *Location* (which variable is to be manipulated and what part of the variable's XML content)—in this case, as in most, that is the *body* variable; the specific part of the XML content of the variable that is to be replaced is indicated using an XPath expression that selects the XML node to be manipulated. Here, as is common, the XPath expression is left empty, indicating the entire contents of the variable.

- *Value* (what is the expression used to derive the value to be applied to the Location)—the combination of the source value retrieved from the $body variable using the XPath expression $body/con:temperatureCelsiusToFahrenheitRequestMessage and the XSLT stylesheet used for the transformation of that source value: temperatureCelsiusToFahrenheitRequestToResponse. xslt—as shown in Figure 3-14.

- *Replace Option* (either *Replace entire node*—to specify that the nodes selected by the XPath expression you defined are replaced along with all of its contents, or *Replace node contents*—to specify that the node is not replaced but only the contents are). In this case, only the node's contents are replaced. Note: Selecting *Replace node contents* and leaving the XPath field empty is more efficient than selecting *Replace entire node* and setting the XPath to `./*`, even though the two have the same effect.

The pipeline can be tested too, just like the XSL Map. The context menu on the pipeline node in the application navigator offers the item *Run*. Selecting this option will deploy the entire Service Bus project to the integrated WebLogic Server-with-Service-Bus-run-time, and it will open

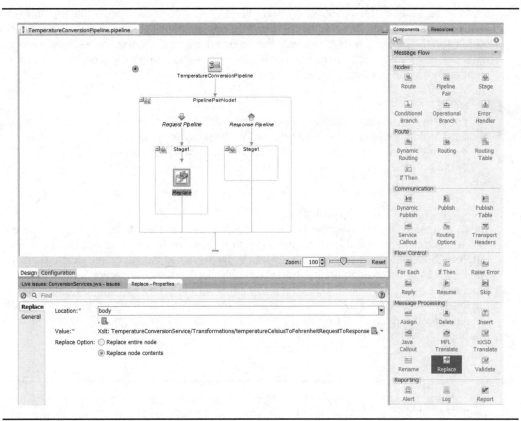

FIGURE 3-13. *The Replace activity that transforms the body variable's contents to the response format with Fahrenheit temperature value*

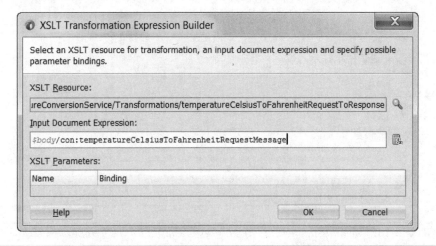

FIGURE 3-14. *Configure the XSLT Transformation to be performed by the Replace activity*

the Pipeline Tester in JDeveloper. This tester allows us to specify the input to the pipeline—an XML temperatureCelsiusToFahrenheitRequestMessage element. We can then press the Execute button and the pipeline will be invoked. The tester subsequently shows the response produced by the pipeline, as well as the invocation trace which is a step by step execution overview of what went on inside the pipeline. Figure 3-15 demonstrates this.

NOTE
The pipeline can only be tested when the project does not have any outstanding compilation errors. At this point, the proxy is still in error because it does not have its Target Service *set. See the next section to fix this.*

Link the Proxy to the Pipeline

When we created the proxy earlier on, we unchecked the checkbox to auto generate a pipeline into which the proxy would feed the messages it receives. To get a good understanding of the different constituents of a Service Bus project, we have created the proxy and pipeline separately. Now is the moment to establish the link between the TemperatureConversionService proxy and the pipeline we have just created. Open the proxy editor for this proxy and on the General tab open the Resource Chooser for the Target Service property. Select the *TemperatureConversionPipeline* as the target for this proxy, as shown in Figure 3-16. Note that the icon signaling an open issue now disappears from the proxy.

```
⚙ Invocation Trace

📧 ⊟ (receiving request)
    Initial Message Context
    ➕ ⊟ added $body
        <soap:Body xmlns:soap="http://www.w3.org/2003/05/soap-envelope">
            <con:temperatureCelsiusToFahrenheitRequestMessage xmlns:con="saibot.airport/services/utility/conversion">
                <con:temperature>-25</con:temperature>
            </con:temperatureCelsiusToFahrenheitRequestMessage>
        </soap:Body>
    ➕ ⊞ added $header
    ➕ ⊞ added $inbound
    ➕ ⊞ added $messageID
⇕ PipelinePairNode1
    ⬦ ⊞ stage1
📧 ⊞ (echoing request)
⇕ PipelinePairNode1
    ⬦ ⊟ stage1
        Message Context Changes
        △ ⊟ changed $body
            <soap:Body xmlns:soap="http://www.w3.org/2003/05/soap-envelope">
                <ns0:temperatureCelsiusToFahrenheitResponseMessage xmlns:common="saibot.airport/data/common" xmlns:
                    <ns0:temperature>-13</ns0:temperature>
                </ns0:temperatureCelsiusToFahrenheitResponseMessage>
            </soap:Body>
        △ ⊞ changed $inbound
```

FIGURE 3-15. *Demonstrating the Pipeline Tester output for the TemperatureConversionPipeline*

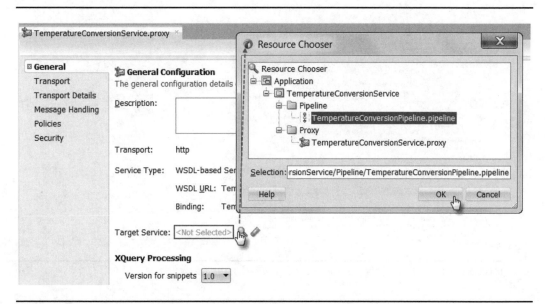

FIGURE 3-16. *Configuring the Pipeline as the Target Service for the Proxy*

This completes the implementation of the TemperatureConversionService. With a proxy linked to a pipeline that transforms from the input format—with a Celsius temperature—to the output format—with a Fahrenheit temperature—we have a completely functional service, shown in Figure 3-17. Or that is what we will try to establish in the next section.

Run the TemperatureConversionService

The TemperatureConversionService could be deployed to a stand-alone SOA Suite run time environment with Service Bus engine support. However, far easier would be to run the service on the integrated WebLogic Server in JDeveloper. Simply run the service from the context menu on the TemperatureConversionService proxy node. If the Integrated Server is running, the project will be deployed and a window will be displayed, ready for testing. If the Integrated Server is not running, then it will be started, the project will be deployed and a window labeled Proxy Service

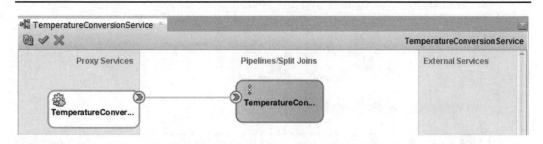

FIGURE 3-17. *The Service Bus project overview with the proxy service wired to the pipeline*

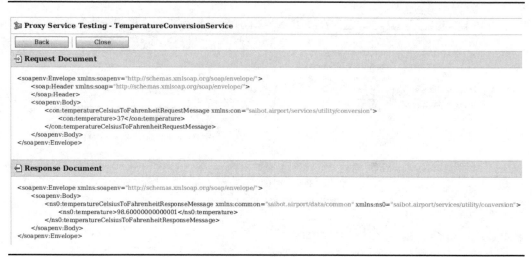

FIGURE 3-18. *Testing the TemperatureConversionService*

Testing will be displayed in JDeveloper, as shown in Figure 3-18. Complete the XML payload with a suitable value for the temperature and press Execute. The service is invoked and the Service Bus will produce the Fahrenheit temperature value.

Alternatively, we can invoke the service at its endpoint http://localhost:7101/utility/TemperatureConversionService, using tools such as the Http Analyzer in JDeveloper – as illustrated in Figure 3-19 - or the popular freeware test tool SoapUI that we will be using throughout this book.

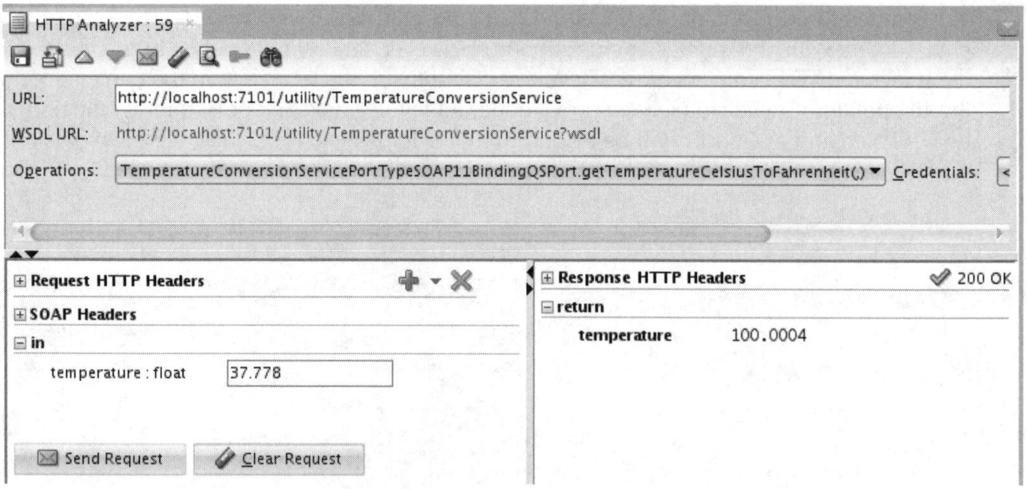

FIGURE 3-19. *Testing the TemperatureConversionService using the Http Analyzer tool in JDeveloper*

NOTE
The WSDL URL consists of the service endpoint with the string ?WSDL concatenated to it.

Extending the Temperature Conversion Service with Validation, Exception Handling and Reporting

The TemperatureConversionService is a real service, but it hardly scratches the surface in terms of the capabilities of the Service Bus it leverages. In this section, we will make use of some of those capabilities to enhance the service. First we will add validation to check if incoming request messages satisfy the interface. Then we will add exception handling to the pipeline in order to appropriately respond to such contract breach by the service consumer. Finally we take a brief look at how we can monitor the activity in the SB with regards to the TemperatureConversionService.

The V in VETRO—Adding Validation

The *temperatureCelsiusToFahrenheitRequestMessage* that is the input to the TemperatureConversionService's *getTemperatureCelsiusToFahrenheit* operation contains a temperature element that is defined in the common.xsd schema definition, shown in Figure 3-20.

This makes clear to any invoker of the operation that the value for the temperature element should be numerical—a float—and the value should not be lower than –273.15, the absolute minimum temperature on the Celsius scale.

However, the current implementation of the service does nothing to stop calls from coming in that contain quite invalid temperature values. You can easily verify this by making test calls with non-numerical values or values below the absolute minimum. Nonsensical Celsius temperature values are happily converted by the service into equally ridiculous Fahrenheit temperatures.

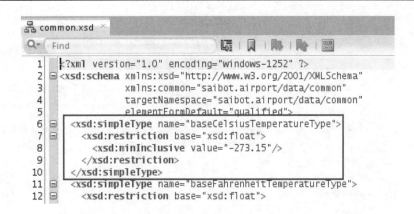

FIGURE 3-20. *The XML Schema Definition for the baseCelsiusTemperatureType*

When a non-numerical string value is used for temperature, the Service Bus built-in fault processing takes over to return a decent NaN (not a number) indication—that is basically the tip of the stack trace produced during the failed XSLT transformation.

Validation is required here, as in most cases, to prevent incorrect messages to even reach the hinterland and put an unnecessary load on pipeline activities and underlying business services. Additionally, explicit validation allows us to control what happens in case of incorrect request messages, rather than having to rely on whatever Service Bus mechanism kicks in.

Add a Validate Activity to the Pipeline

Open the pipeline editor. Drag the Validate activity from the component palette to *stage 1* and drop it above the Replace activity (after all it is VeTro and not TeVro). Configure the Validate activity in the property editor, as shown in Figure 3-21. It should verify if the contents of the

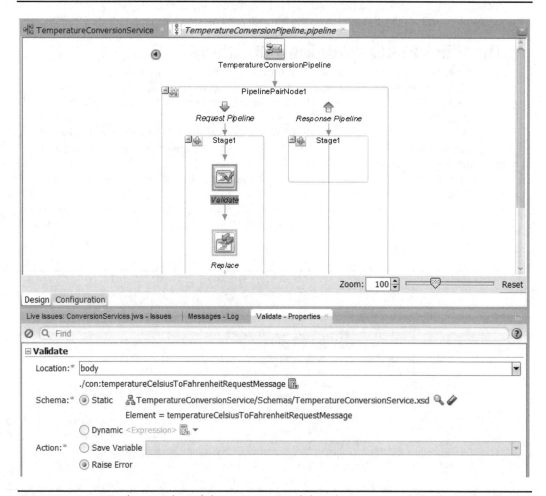

FIGURE 3-21. *Configuring the Validate activity to validate the contents of $body against the temperatureCelsiusToFahrenheitType in the TemperatureConversionService.xsd document*

$body variable—which at this point contains the incoming request message—is indeed correctly based on the *temperatureCelsiusToFahrenheitRequestMessage* XSD element.

Set the *Location* property to body—since the $body variable's contents is to be validated. The XPath expression is set to ./con:temperatureCelsiusToFahrenheitRequestMessage using the XPath expression editor. This indicates that the validation concerns the con:temperatureCelsiusToFahren heitRequestMessage child element in the contents of the variable.

Select the *Static* radio button for the *Schema* property, because this validation is always based on the same XSD element. With the *Dynamic* option we can configure how at run time the required XSD Element to validate against should be determined. Select the *temperatureCelsiusToFahrenheitRequestMessage* element in the TemperatureConversionService .xsd schema definition as the definition against which the Location—the *temperatureCelsiusToFahrenheitRequestMessage* child element in the $body variable— should be validated.

The *Action* property is used to specify what should happen in case of validation failure. The options are to save the result of the validation—a boolean result—in a custom variable or to raise an error in case of failed validation. Select the Raise Error radio button for the current pipeline.

Test the TemperatureConversionService with Validation

It is easy to see the effect of the validate activity. Just run the proxy again in order to redeploy the Service Bus project with the TemperatureConversionService. The service tester opens in JDeveloper. Now deliberately provide an incorrect value for the temperature element—for example, a numerical value smaller than –273.15 or a non-numerical value—and invoke the service. The response from the service this time will be a standard SOAP Fault message that the Service Bus produces in case of an unhandled exception. This fault message contains a child element called ValidationFailureDetail that indicates exactly what the validation failed on. In Figure 3-22, the temperature element's value –900 was found to be less than the minimum (–273.15) allowed for elements of type baseCelsiusTemperatureType.

The service interface does not include a fault message for the *getTemperatureCelsiusToFahrenheit* operation, so returning one may not be expected by the service consumer. We can resolve this inconsistency by either modifying the definition of the operation in the service interface or adding an exception handler to the pipeline and deal with the validation failure in some other way.

NOTE
A distinction can be made between functional faults and technical faults. Functional faults represent situations that have been identified in our functional analysis. These are cases where due to business circumstances or even illogical combinations of data in the request message an operation cannot perform its task as expected. Such faults are explicitly defined in the service interface as faults of an operation. Service consumers should implement logic to handle these faults.

Technical faults are caused by some form of (temporary) system failure. These indicate that "at the present time, the service cannot fulfill the request, but it is not caused by the consumer's request." Typically, the request can be retried after some time has passed. Technical faults are also thrown as SOAP faults, but they are not explicitly defined in the interface.

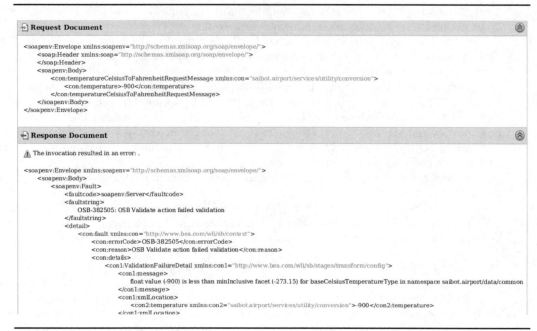

FIGURE 3-22. *Example of a validation failure reported by the service bus*

Exception Handling in the Pipeline

Almost all programming languages provide a mechanism for catching exceptions and handling them. This also applies to Service Bus projects. An error handler can be configured at each of the following levels: message flow (global), pipeline, route node, and stage. An error is handled at the lowest possible level. If an exception occurs or is explicitly raised in a stage, the error handler at the stage level is invoked for handling the error. If no stage-level error handler exists or it is not able to definitively handle a given type of error, the next level error handler—at the pipeline level—is invoked. If the pipeline-level error handler does not exist or also fails to handle the error, the service-level error handler is invoked. If the service-level error handler also fails, the error is handled by the system (the Service Bus run time framework). An error handler makes short work of an error if it ends with either a resume (continue as if nothing happened) or a reply activity (send a response and immediately end pipeline processing altogether).

A predefined context variable—called $fault—is populated with information about the error that triggered execution of the error handler. The XML structure of the content of this variable depends on the type of error that occurred. The fault variable is defined only in error handler pipelines. We can build business logic in the error handler based on the content of the fault variable.

An error handler is a pipeline and is therefore configured like any other pipeline. For example, you can use the Publish action to send error notifications to other services, use the Assign action to modify the context variables, Report on whatever is troubling the service, or perform other common pipeline actions.

Three commonly used error actions are *Raise Error*, *Reply*, and *Resume*. These actions should be the last one in an error handler. If an error handler does not contain a Reply, Resume or Raise

Error activity, it will be treated as if the error that triggered its execution is re-raised—which is implicitly equivalent to Raise Error.

Raise Error is used to throw a selected exception with a specified error code and description. This can be a form of preprocessing before a global error handler kicks in.

Reply is used to cease further processing and return the response. The response is composed using the contents of the $body, $header, and $attachments variables as they are at the time of executing the Reply action. This means, for example, that by replacing the contents of the body variable with a SOAP Fault element just prior to the Reply activity, we can ensure that a fault is returned by the pipeline with the exact structure and contents that we want it to have.

The Reply activity is configured with one of two options: Success or Failure. Depending on this setting, the result code in the transport header returned from the pipeline is set to 0 or 1, respectively. A proxy with an HTTP transport will derive the HTTP 200 or 500 response code from that value. Note that success or failure does not influence the contents of the returned message at all. Selecting the option *With Failure* for example does not make Reply return a SOAP Fault message. For that to happen, a SOAP message has to be assigned to $body before the reply. It is typically considered good practice to always use a reply with failure if the $body contains a Fault message. Otherwise it is not as clear for the consumer that a fault is returned by the service provider and it would depend on the client implementation if the occurrence of a Fault in the body triggers its fault handling. The interoperability standard for Web Services (WS-I) also states that a SOAP fault should be signaled by a HTTP status 500 response.

Resume is the third way to conclude an error handler—but only at the stage or pipeline level and not at service level. It instructs the Service Bus to continue processing the next container at the same level as the error handler's current container (stage or pipeline). After the Resume is performed, there are no lasting effects from the fact that an error has occurred. Note that activities that come after the failed activity in the same container—the one that was interrupted by the error—are not executed.

In the *TemperatureConversionPipeline* we will add an error handler to take care of any validation errors. We will take the somewhat unsophisticated tit-for-tat approach of returning a SOAP Fault that has not been announced in the service interface to inform the invoker that the request message did not comply with the service interface.

Drag the *Error Handler* from the component palette to the pipeline editor and drop it on *stage1* in the request pipeline. This will create the stage level error handler. Next, drag the *Raise Error* activity from the component palette and drop it inside the just created error handler for *stage1*. Specify the error code this activity should report, for example SAIBOT-001, and potentially a message as well. The pipeline should now look as is shown in Figure 3-23.

 NOTE
stage1 *contains both Validate and Replace activities, so errors from within Replace and the XSLT execution would also be handled by this error handler. In this example that might be okay, but in real life, validation should typically have its own stage so it can have a special error handler that only gets triggered in case of a Validation error.*

It is easy to see the effect of the error handler in action. Just run the Proxy Service to have the service with modified pipeline deployed and the tester opened. Invoke the service with a temperature value of less than −273.15. The result should be a SOAP Fault that contains the SAIBOT-001 code value—see Figure 3-24.

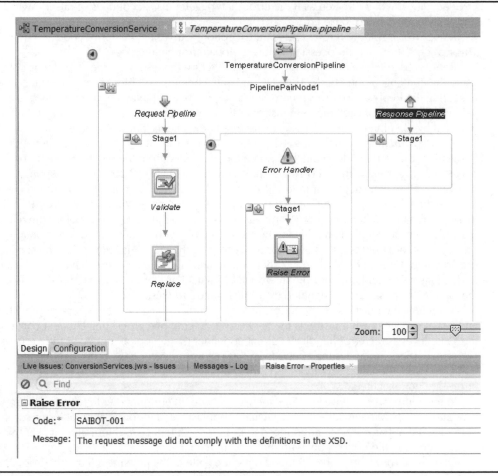

FIGURE 3-23. *The Error Handler at stage level will raise a generic error in case of an exception in the stage*

To get a better insight in what exactly happens inside the pipeline, you can also run the pipeline itself. This gives us not just the response with the SOAP Fault from the pipeline: It also produces the trace of the activity inside the pipeline, as shown in Figure 3-25.

The trace in this case is pretty simple, because it only consists of stage 1—where validation takes place—and its stage-level error handler where the validation exception is handled. For more complex pipelines, this execution trace is very valuable.

Monitoring Service Bus Activity

The Service Bus is not built for comfort but for speed. Fast, stateless processing of messages, taking those messages as quickly as possible from reception to outbound routing (if applicable) and back to response is what it does in a highly optimized fashion. All overhead has been stripped from that process, including all forms of default reporting on the message processing.

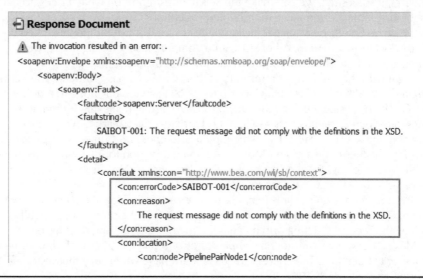

Response Document

⚠ The invocation resulted in an error: .

```
<soapenv:Envelope xmlns:soapenv="http://schemas.xmlsoap.org/soap/envelope/">
    <soapenv:Body>
        <soapenv:Fault>
            <faultcode>soapenv:Server</faultcode>
            <faultstring>
                SAIBOT-001: The request message did not comply with the definitions in the XSD.
            </faultstring>
            <detail>
                <con:fault xmlns:con="http://www.bea.com/wli/sb/context">
                    <con:errorCode>SAIBOT-001</con:errorCode>
                    <con:reason>
                        The request message did not comply with the definitions in the XSD.
                    </con:reason>
                    <con:location>
                        <con:node>PipelinePairNode1</con:node>
```

FIGURE 3-24.   *The response from the Raise Error activity in the Error Handler*

```
✉ ⊞ (receiving request)
⇵ PipelinePairNode1
   ⇄ ⊟ stage1
      Message Context Changes
         ⚠ ⊞ changed $body
         ⚠ ⊞ changed $inbound
      ⚠ ⊟ Stage Error Handler
         $fault:     <con:fault xmlns:con="http://www.bea.com/wli/sb/context">
                        <con:errorCode>OSB-382505</con:errorCode>
                        <con:reason>OSB Validate action failed validation</con:reason>
                        <con:details>
                            <con1:ValidationFailureDetail xmlns:con1="http://www.bea.com/wli/sb/stages/transform/config">
                                <con1:message>
                                    float value (-300) is less than minInclusive facet (-273.15) for baseCelsiusTemperatureType in namespace
                                    saibot.airport/data/common
                                </con1:message>
                                <con1:xmlLocation>
                                    <con2:temperature xmlns:con2="saibot.airport/services/utility/conversion">-300</con2:temperature>
                                </con1:xmlLocation>
                            </con1:ValidationFailureDetail>
                        </con:details>
                        <con:location>
                            <con:node>PipelinePairNode1</con:node>
                            <con:pipeline>
                                request-7894665277143958754--35381876.14315a23ed8.-7fc4
                            </con:pipeline>
                            <con:stage>stage1</con:stage>
                            <con:path>request-pipeline</con:path>
                        </con:location>
                    </con:fault>
```

FIGURE 3-25.   *The execution trace for the TemperatureConversionPipeline in case of a validation error*

However, if so desired, we can make the Service Bus report on what it does, to help us get more insight in volume, performance metrics, and exceptions.

Open the Enterprise Manager Fusion Middleware Control for the Integrated WebLogic Server at http://localhost:7101/em. All of SOA Suite components including the Service Bus can be managed by administrators from this single unified console.

Login with the *weblogic* administrator account and the password that was set when the Integrated WLS was first created. Click on the SOA | service-bus node in the Target Navigation tree. On the right side, click on the Operations tab. Press the Search button, to show a list of all operations—pipelines, business services, and proxies. The list contains the proxy *TemperatureConversionService* and the pipeline *TemperatureConversionPipeline*. Click the check box in the header of the column Monitoring, to enable monitoring for all (two) operations listed. Enable Msg Tracking, Pipeline Alerts, Logging, Reports, and Exe Tracing as well. Press Apply. Figure 3-26 shows what the page looks like.

If you now click on the link *TemperatureConversionService*, the dashboard with metrics for this proxy service is shown. Since no calls were made to the proxy since enabling all monitoring, tracing, and reporting settings, no meaningful metrics are presented at this point.

Make a number of calls to the *TemperatureConversionService*, including some with invalid values for temperature. Then refresh the dashboard page with proxy metrics to see some metrics reported—see Figure 3-27.

Through monitoring we can get an aggregate impression of the activity per service or pipeline in the Service Bus. However, we do not get to see information about individual service calls. There are several reporting activities—Alert, Log, Report—that we can make use of in the pipeline to produce some operational information from within.

The *Log* activity is used to write information to the log files produced by Service Bus through the Web Logic logging framework.

Report publishes information to the built in reporting framework. The information is tagged with one or more search keys that help filtering and searching specific messages. Service Bus has an internal report handler that stores messages in a database (asynchronously, as to not add overhead to the request processing) and exposes them through the EM FMW Control console. Custom report handlers can be plugged in as well.

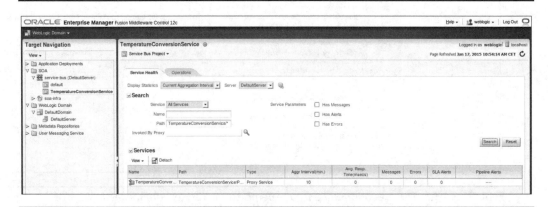

FIGURE 3-26. *The Service Bus Operations tab in the Enterprise Manager Fusion Middleware Control 12c console*

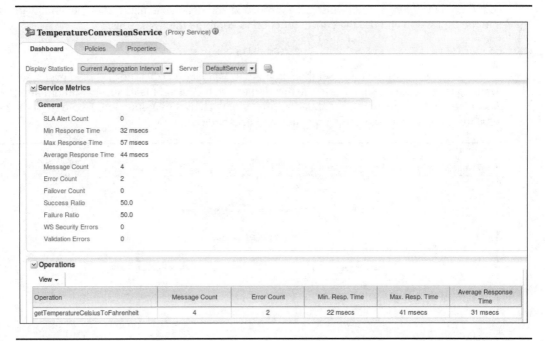

FIGURE 3-27. *The Dashboard for the Proxy Service TemperatureConversionService in EM FMW Control*

Alert is used to publish messages associated with a certain severity level—ranging from *information* to *fatal*—to an alert destination. An alert destination captures a list of recipients that can receive alert notifications from the Service Bus. An alert destination can include one or more of the following types of destinations: Alert Logging (meaning the EM FMW Control), Reporting, SNMP trap, one or more email addresses, one or more JMS queues or topics. If you specify Reporting, alerts are sent to the Service Bus Reporting module and can be captured using a custom Reporting Provider that can be developed using the Reporting APIs. Note that the alert destination can be configured independent of the alert activities used in pipelines, even at run time.

Using Alerts to Provide Details about Validation Errors

We will now make use of an alert to make more details available in the administration console about any errors handled by the error handler in the *TemperatureConversionPipeline*.

As a first step, create a new folder called *Alerts*. From the context menu on this folder, select the option New | Alert Destination. A window appears that has you enter the name of the new alert destination, for example *PipelineAlertDestination*. When you press Finish, the alert destination is created and the editor appears to allow further editing of the destination's properties. The default settings are fine, because Alert Logging is set. This means that we will be able to monitor the messages published to this destination in the EM FMW Control.

Return to the pipeline editor for the *TemperatureConversionPipeline*. Add an Alert activity from the component palette to the Error Handler, dropping it above the Raise Error activity. Configure the activity in the property editor to report some fault details. Open the expression editor for the *Content* property. Insert the errorCode and details elements from the $fault variable into the expression and use the concat function to combine them, like this:

```
concat($fault/ctx:errorCode, ' ', $fault/ctx:details)
```

Close the expression editor. Set the Summary to *Validation Error*. The Severity Level is set to Warning in this case, to slightly elevate the alert above the level of least severity (Information). Select the Alert Destination you created a short while ago as the Destination. Figure 3-28 shows what the pipeline with the configured alert activity should now look like.

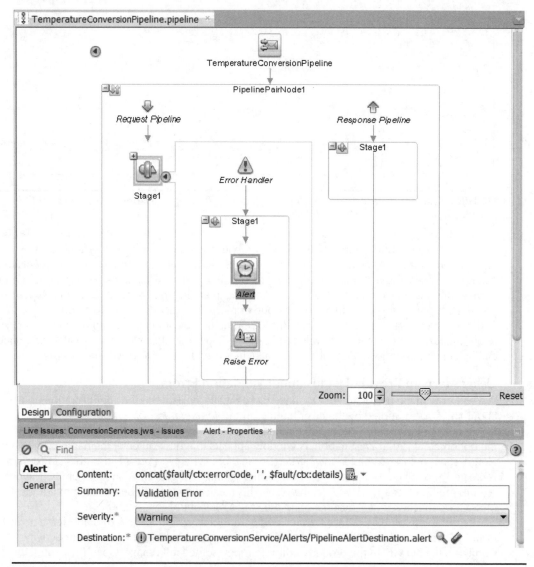

FIGURE 3-28. *The TemperatureConversionPipeline with the Alert activity and its properties*

Run the pipeline or the proxy. It will be redeployed, this time with the Alert activity that will report on validation errors. Make some service calls with incorrect temperature values. Then open the Alert History tab of the Service Bus dashboard in the EM FMW Control.

Set the Alert Type drop down to Pipeline Alerts. Then press the Search button. A list of recent pipeline alerts is shown, including instances resulting from the recently failed temperature conversion attempts. If you click on the link Validation Error in the Alert Summary column, a popup window appears with details for the pipeline alert, as is shown in Figure 3-29.

NOTE
The Service Bus is configured per individual pipeline to keep track of pipeline alerts [or not] and starting at what severity level. In the EM FMW Control console, select the node SOA | service-bus | TemperatureConversionService. Click on the Operations Tab. Click on Search. Then click on the link for the TemperatureConversionPipeline; this takes you to the dashboard for the pipeline. Finally, click on the Properties tab—as shown in Figure 3-30. Here are the pipeline level operational properties that govern things like monitoring [level], logging, and reporting for this pipeline. The Pipeline Alerting Enabled checkbox should be checked and the Pipeline Severity should not be higher than Warning.

Using Message Reporting

The Report action lets you extract information from each message handled by a pipeline and write it to the Service Bus Reporting Data Stream, from where they can be handled in various ways. In the Report action, key value pairs are used to define key identifiers and values that can be extracted from any message context variable or message payload. The keys provide a convenient way to find and identify messages.

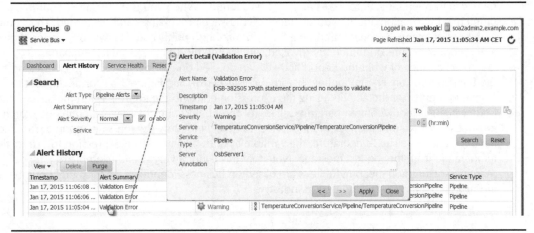

FIGURE 3-29. *Details for a Pipeline Alert published from the Error Handler in response to a validation error*

FIGURE 3-30. *Pipeline level properties for monitoring, reporting, logging and alerting*

Messages are published to a JMS Queue with little overhead to the reporting thread—the one processing the request. The default reporting provider consumes the messages from that queue and writes data to a database table. The messages stored in the database can be searched and reviewed through the Enterprise Manager FMW Control. When you use Message Reporting, a lot of internal information about (various stages of) message processing can be exposed. This comes at the cost of some overhead: preparing the information to publish adds some processing time and reporting actions on frequently invoked service will fill up the SOA INFRA database.

To get an idea of what the Report activity can do, add one for example to the Error Handler in the TemperatureConversionPipeline, before the Raise Error. See Figure 3-31 for details. Set the Content property for the activity using the expression editor to the entire request message in the body variable: $body/con:temperatureCelsiusToFahrenheitRequestMessage. Define one search key to use as a tag on instances of the service, to quickly identify the message report at runtime. Set the name to celsiusTemperature, the variable to body and the XPath expression to extract the temperature from the request message. Note that this is not a very useful example of a report search key. Common meaningful keys are based on business identifiers, such as flight number or airline code in the case of the airport industry.

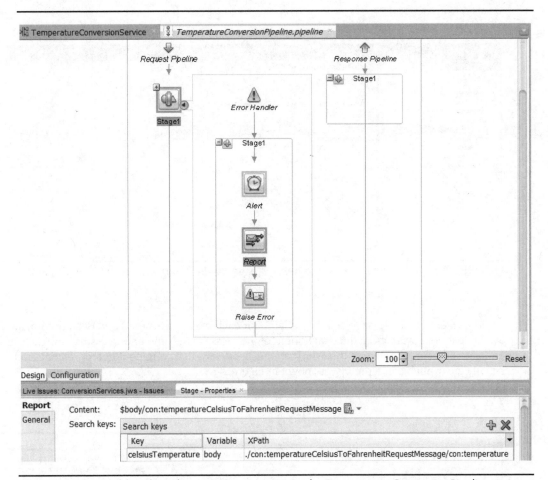

FIGURE 3-31. *Add and configure a Report action in the TemperatureConversionPipeline*

After adding the Report activity, run the *TemperatureConversionService*. Make some calls that include invalid temperature values, in order to trigger the error handler and thereby the Report activity. The Message Reports thus produced can be viewed in the EM FMW Control. Go to the console, select the node SOA | service-bus | TemperatureConversionService. From the drop-down menu labeled Service Bus Project (almost at the top of the right side of the page), select the option Message Reports (Figure 3-32).

Press the Search button on the page that appears next, to find all available message reports. An overview of the reports is presented. The search keys (aka report index) for each report are listed along with timestamp, origin of the report, and error code if applicable (Figure 3-33). By clicking on the Report Index link you can navigate to the page with message details.

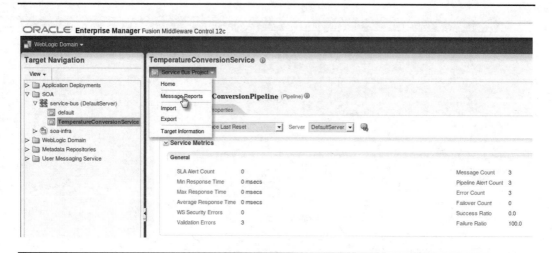

FIGURE 3-32. *Opening the Message Reports page for the TemperatureConversionService*

The extent of the message details available for each message is broad and deep. Information is available for example about the exact origin of the message, its time of processing, and the status and about the fault if one was thrown. The message details that were configured in the Report activity are available in a popup, as shown in Figure 3-34.

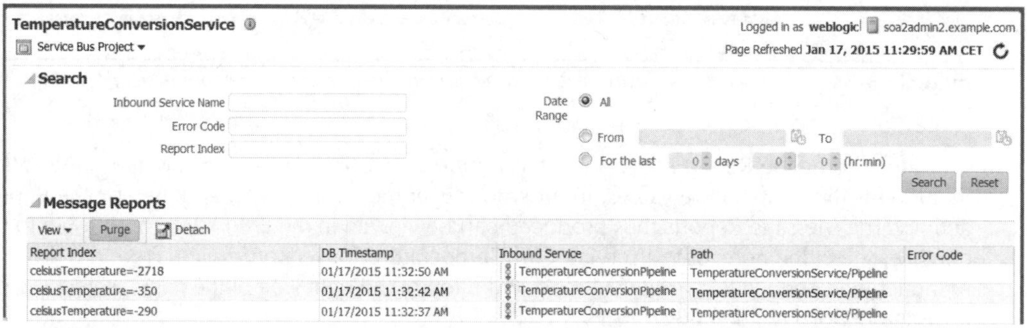

FIGURE 3-33. *Searching for Message Reports for the TemperatureConversionService*

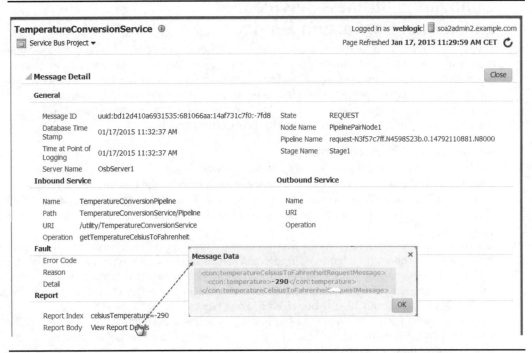

FIGURE 3-34. *Message details in the EM FMW Control as a result of a pipeline Report activity*

Speed and Distance Conversions through Routing to External Services

The temperature conversion service we have discussed so far is about the simplest service imaginable. This service hides the encapsulations of the implementation of the business logic, but instead of invoking that business logic in the form of a business service, the temperature conversion service also implements the logic itself. In this section, we will move beyond that very simple case. We will develop another conversion service on the Service Bus, this time one that calls upon external services to do distance, height, and speed conversions. The pipeline will now implement both halves—the one leading up to the routing action calling the business service as well as the second half that deals with the response from the business service.

Additionally, the service that is preferably called to do the conversion, may not always be available. The business service will be configured to automatically fail-over to a local conversion service whenever the number one choice is not available. Note: The assumption here would be that the local conversion is not as accurate or quick as the preferred service, otherwise of course we would not need the external service.

Configure a Business Service for an External Conversion Service

The website http://www.webservicex.net offers a number of public SOAP web services. Some of these will support the unit conversions we are looking for. Conversions of height and distance for example are provided by the Length/Distance Unit Converter. In order to leverage this web service in a Service Bus project, there has to be a Business Service configured as the local stub representing the external service. In a pipeline we can call out to or—more commonly—route (a message) to a business service and hence to the external service.

Import the Web Service Contract

The WSDL for the external service has to be locally available. Under formal governance we would probably make use of an UDDI style service directory or the Fusion Middleware MetaData Services (MDS), but for now we will keep things simple. From the context menu on the WSDLs folder select the option Import. In the popup window that appears select the option *Service Bus Resources*.

The Import wizard opens. On the first page, select the option Resources from URL and press Next. On the second page (Figure 3-35) select WSDL as the Resource Type. Paste the URL for the WSDL of the external convertor service: http://www.webservicex.net/length.asmx?WSDL into the Source URL property. Enter the name for the resource as LengthDistanceUnitConvertorService. The WSDLs folder should already be selected. Press Next.

The wizard presents an overview of its intentions on the third page: creating a new WSDL resource with the specified name based on the document found at the URL for the external service. Press Finish to mandate this action.

The WSDL document is created in the WSDLs folder.

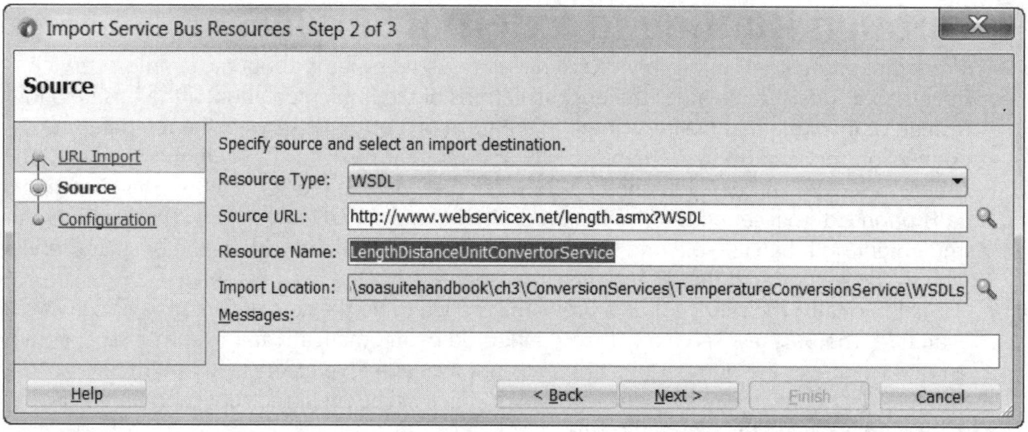

FIGURE 3-35. *Import an external WSDL (with associated resources such as imported XSD documents)*

Create Business Service

Create a new folder called Business Service. Next, right click on the newly created WSDL document LengthDistanceUnitConvertorService to open its context menu. From the menu select Service Bus | Generate Business Service.

Another wizard appears to assist you in the creation of the business service based on the WSDL. Ensure that the Location field specifies the Business Service folder (Figure 3-36). Because this document contains four different port definitions, we have to make explicit which of these the business service will represent. Make sure that you select the *lengthUnitSoap* port. Then press Next.

Accept the default transport type and endpoint url on the second page and press finish to create the Business Service.

We can now test the business service. The option Run on the context menu for the new business service LengthDistanceUnitConvertorService will redeploy the entire ConversionService project and open the business service tester in JDeveloper, from which you can test make test calls to the Business Service that in turn means making test calls to the external service.

Business Service Fail-Over

The business service can be seen as the local representative of the external service. It takes care of relaying requests to the remote end point. It can, however, be more than a simple messenger boy. For example, it can be configured with multiple endpoints for the external service and employ a load balancing algorithm for distributing the requests over these endpoints. Various other aspects of the communication with the external service can be configured on the business service as well, including transport specific properties, security details, and result cache options.

When the business service is invoked from a pipeline and the remote service is not available at the endpoint that is invoked, then depending on the retry settings the business service will

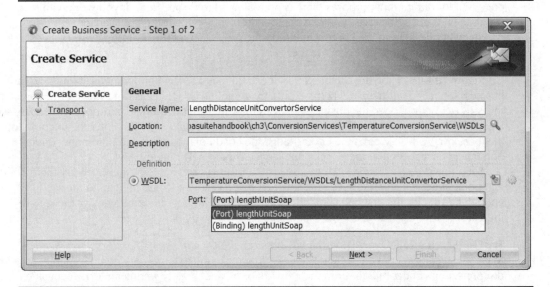

FIGURE 3-36. *Configuring the Business Service for the external SOAP Web Service*

attempt fail-over to other endpoints if these are configured—or it will retry the same endpoint again if no other endpoints are defined. Note that the alternative endpoints can refer to entirely different service instances on quite different locations, as long as they implement the same port or binding from the WSDL that the business service is referencing.

To see the fail-over in action, we will now create a local mock service that implements the same contract as the external *LengthDistanceUnitConvertorService*. We will then configure the business service to use the local service as a fail-over destination.

NOTE
We only do this to see the fail-over mechanism in action. In actual practice it would be silly to have an external service and then implement a local equivalent that we use as a fail-over destination only.

Generate and Deploy Local Mock Conversion Service   Open the context menu for the WSDL document LengthDistanceUnitConvertorService.wsdl. Select the item Create Web Service. This will start a wizard that will generate a Java (JAX-WS) Web Service based on the same contract as the remote service. In the wizard go to step 2—Target Project—and press on the button New Project. Set the name of the new project to LocalLengthDistanceUnitConvertorService and accept the default target directory. Accept all defaults in all subsequent steps of the wizard and press Finish to start generation of the Java Web Service. The new project is created, with annotated Java classes to implement and publish the web service.

You can now test the local web service by running the class LengthUnitSoapImpl. This will deploy the web (service) application. The service can now be tested at http://localhost:7101/ ConversionServices-LocalLengthDistanceUnitConvertorService-context-root/lengthUnitSoap, for example using the HTTP Analyzer. All conversions will currently return 0.0, as we have not yet implemented any logic in the Java class to do any real conversion. You could enhance the Java code, but for our current purposes there is no real need to do so. Note: If you work with a stand-alone WebLogic Server, you can deploy the Web Service using the WebServices deployment profile from the context menu on the project. The URL for testing will be the same, except for the hostname and port number.

Configure Fail-Over for the Business Service   There is a second endpoint available now for the business service to fail-over to when the primary, remote web service is not available. To configure this fail-over option, open the business service editor for *LengthDistanceUnitConvertorService* (see Figure 3-37). Click the green plus icon in the area labeled *Endpoint URIs* . Enter the endpoint of the local Java Web Service as the URI. Change the Load Balancing Algorithm to none: under normal circumstances, the local convertor service should never be invoked.

Set property *Retry Count* to 2—to instruct the business service to immediately try the second end point (the local mock service) after the first one has failed. When the call to the second endpoint also fails, the first one should be attempted again, but only after waiting for as long as is indicated in the *Retry Iteration Interval*.

Try Out Service Fail-Over   Run the business service *LengthDistanceUnitConvertorService*. Make a few calls to convert some distances. Now make the external service unavailable, either by disconnecting your computer from the network or by deliberately setting an incorrect value for the external service's endpoint—for example, in the run time Service Bus Console. Verify if your

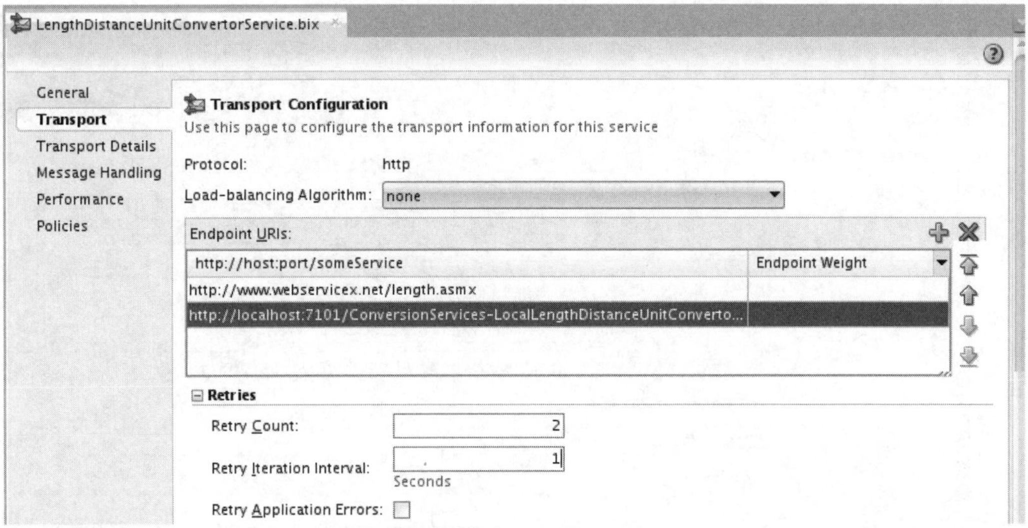

FIGURE 3-37. *Configuring the business service for fail-over to a local (mock) conversion service*

next service call returns successfully, even if with a value that is not to be trusted (0.0 if you have left the mock service above with the default implementation). If so, fail-over to the local service will have been performed upon the business service's connection problem to the primary, remote end point.

Create Proxy ConversionService

The *ConversionService* as specified by Saibot's designers in the WSDL document offers a range of specialized, frequently used conversion operations that will convert distance, height (just another form of distance), speed, weight, and temperature. The service will use a variety of local and external services for its implementation, but that of course is encapsulated—hidden from view for consumers of conversion functionality. A Service Bus Proxy Service is exposed for such consumers, based on the functional service interface and using a regular HTTP/SOAP transport.

Generate the Proxy Service using the menu item Service Bus | Generate Proxy Service on the context menu for the ConversionService.wsdl document.

The Create Proxy Service wizard opens—Figure 3-38. Set the Service Name to *ConversionServicePS*—following the standing naming convention of using the PS suffix for proxy services. Set the location to the Proxy folder. Ensure that this time the checkbox Generate Pipeline is checked. Set the name of the Pipeline to *ConversionPipeline*. Press Next.

On the second page of the wizard, change the endpoint to /utility/ConversionService. Press Finish to complete the wizard.

The proxy service and the pipeline are generated, both in the same folder Proxy, which for the pipeline is not the correct location. From the context menu on the *ConversionPipeline*, select the item Refactor | Move and relocate the pipeline to the Pipeline folder.

The default algorithm used by proxy services in the Service Bus to determine which of the operations defined in the service interface should be executed is by looking at the incoming

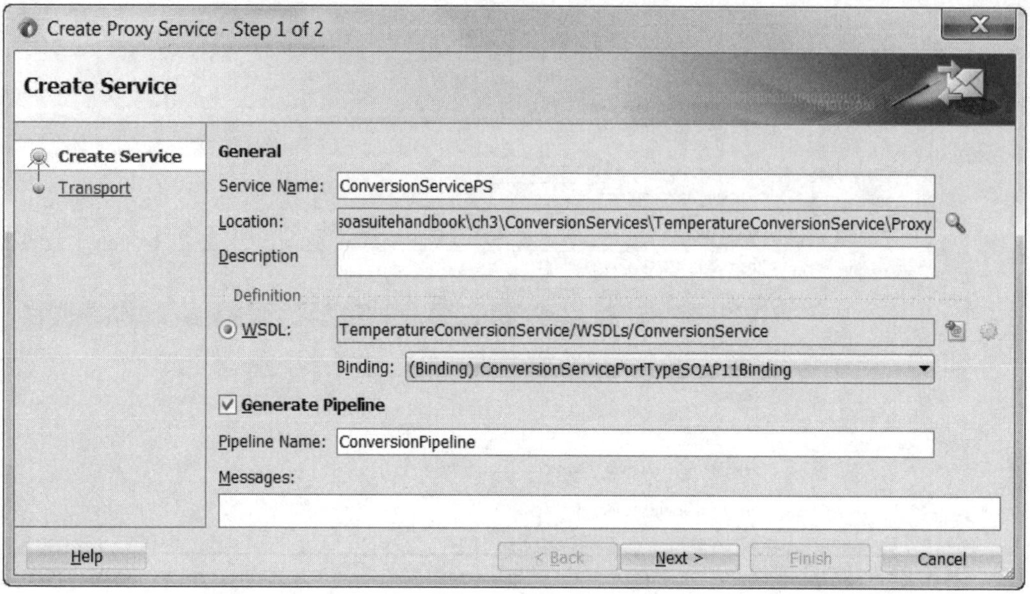

FIGURE 3-38. *Configure the Proxy Service for the Conversion Service*

message type. In this case, that approach will not do, because several operations expect the same message type. Therefore we have to open the Operation Selection tab in the proxy editor and set the Selection Algorithm to SOAP Action Header (see Figure 3-39). This means of course that service consumers will have to set that SOAP Action Header in their calls.

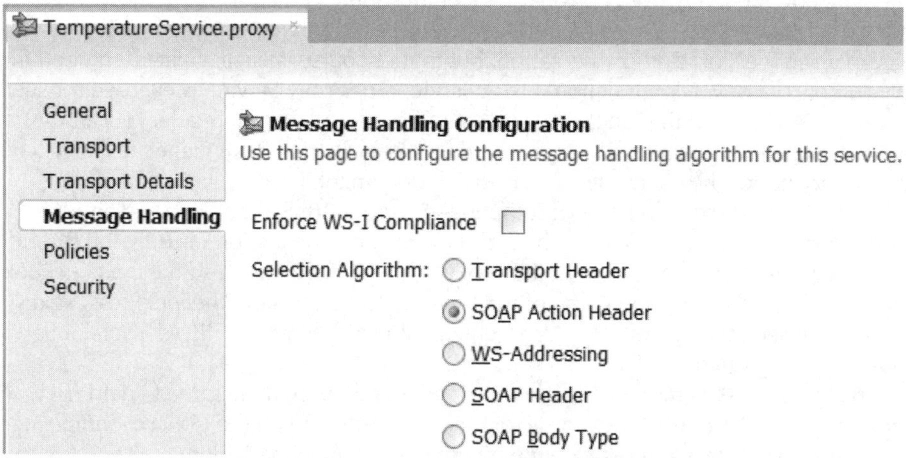

FIGURE 3-39. *Set the Operation Selection algorithm for the ConversionService proxy*

Implement the Generated ConversionPipeline

The *ConversionPipeline* is going to be a bit more interesting than the *TemperatureConversionPipeline*. Not only does the *ConversationPipeline* have to support multiple operations, it will also actually perform Routing to a business service and therefore have to cater for both the request and the response pipeline in the pipeline pair.

We will first focus on the operation *getDistanceFeetToMeter* that will be used to convert heights, typically expressed in either feet or meter. We need to be able to discern between different operations and implement activities to cater to each of them. Because the request message defined in the ConversionService's interface for the *getDistanceFeetToMeter* operation does not have the same XML structure as the message we need to send to the *LengthDistanceUnitConvertorService* business service, we have to implement a transformation in the request pipeline. Similarly, the response from that business service is not based on the same XSD definition as the response expected from the proxy service, and therefore another transformation is needed to produce the required structure for the response message.

Configuring the Operational Branch

Open the designer for the *ConversionPipeline*. Drag the Operational Branch activity to the pipeline. This node is a minimal configuration branching node that contains branches and associated logic for selected operations defined in the WSDL. The Service Bus determines from the operation indicated in the request message which of the flows in the Operational Branch to execute. There is a *default* flow that will be executed if for the indicated action there is no operation-specific flow.

After adding the Operational Branch to the pipeline, configure the first (non-default) flow for the *getDistanceFeetToMeter* operation by selecting that operation from the drop-down list in the property editor (as is shown in Figure 3-40).

Add a Pipeline Pair to the *getDistanceFeetToMeter* flow and set its name to *VET*. In this pair we will add the transformations of the request to, and response from, the business service.

Configure Routing to the Business Service

Add a Route node to the flow for operation *getDistanceFeetToMeter*; drop it after the VET activity. Set the name of the Route node to RO. This container node will implement the call to the business service. For now, these names signify how the VETRO pattern is implemented in the pipeline. In the future, we will use more functional names for these nodes.

Drag the Routing component from the palette and move it to the Route node. Select the new Routing activity, as shown in Figure 3-41. Click on the magnifying glass for the *Service* property in the property editor. Browse to the business service *LengthDistanceUnitConvertorService* and select it as the target for the Routing activity. The only operation supported by the business service is *ChangeLengthUnit*; therefore this operation is automatically selected to be invoked by the Routing.

End-to-End Test of the ConversionService

Add this point we can try out the end to end chain, from proxy service to the pipeline all the way to the business service, the external service and back again. This flow is visualized in the overview editor, see Figure 3-42. Note that the link between the proxy service and the pipeline was established when we had the proxy service wizard also generate the pipeline.

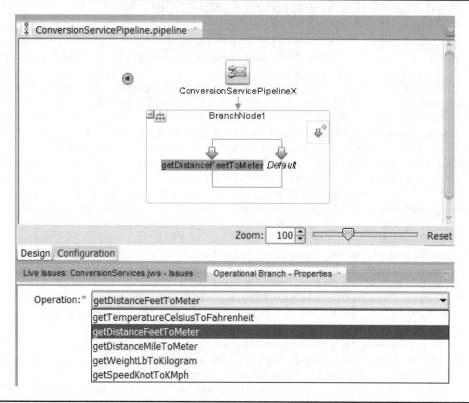

FIGURE 3-40. *Configuring the flow for operation getDistanceFeetToMeter in the operational branch*

This will not yet result in meaningful responses with accurate converted values, because we have not yet added the transformations. However, the flow for a request message with its action set to *getDistanceFeetToMeter* should already be functioning.

Run the *ConversionServicePS* proxy and invoke the operation *getDistanceFeetToMeter*.

The response, though meaningless, should contain an XML element called *ChangeLengthUnitResponse* in the namespace *http://www.webserviceX.NET/*. This is proof that the end-to-end call succeeded; this XML element is returned by the external service invoked by the business service.

Add Request and Response Transformations

In order to produce a meaningful response we need to add a little processing in both request and response pipeline. The request message that arrives at the pipeline, held in the $body variable, is not of the XML type expected by the business service. Therefore, the $body variable's contents should be replaced—using a transformation. Create a new XSL Map, called *distanceFeetToMeterRequestToChangeLengthUnit.xsl*. This map will transform from the source element *distanceFeetToMeterRequestMessage* to the *ChangeLengthUnit* element that is the root of the request message to be sent to the business service.

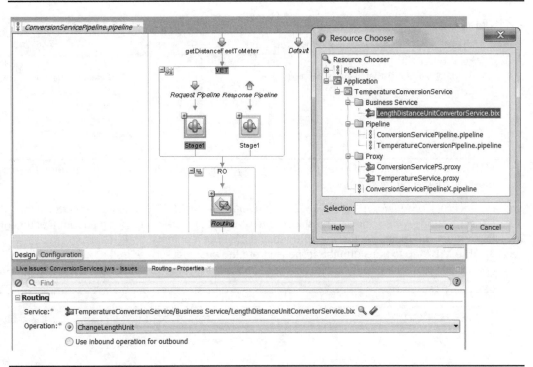

FIGURE 3-41.   *The pipeline editor with the Routing activity in the operational branch*

The mapping simply copies the value of the *distanceFeetToMeterRequestMessage* element to the *LengthValue* element in the target structure. It also has to set the *fromLengthUnit* and *toLengthUnit* in the target message with text values *Feet* and *Meters* respectively, as shown in Figure 3-43.

A Replace activity should be added to the Stage in the Request pipeline, as is shown in Figure 3-44. The Replace activity is configured with Body as the Location, the XSL Map file

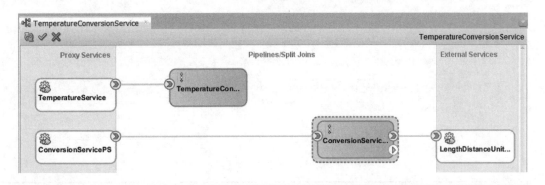

FIGURE 3-42.   *Service Bus overview editor with the wires between proxy, pipeline, and business service*

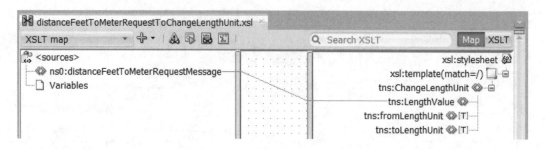

FIGURE 3-43. *The XSL Map for the transformation of the $body contents to produce the request message for the business service*

distanceFeetToMeterRequestToChangeLengthUnit.xsl as the XSLT Expression to perform the transformation—with $body/con:distanceFeetToMeterRequestMessage for the Input Document Expression. The replace activity should replace the node contents.

The XSL Map to transform the response from the business service in the body variable to the appropriate structure is called *changeLengthUnitResponseTodistanceFeetToMeterResponse.xsl*.

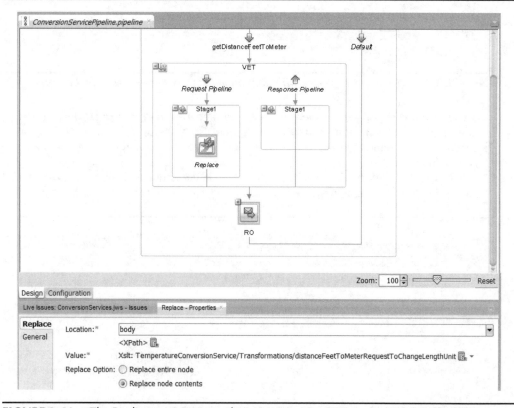

FIGURE 3-44. *The Replace activity turns the proxy service request message into the business service input*

It maps the value from the *ChangeLengthUnitResult* element in the *ChangeLengthUnitResponse* root to the *distanceFeetToMeterResponseMessage* element. A replace activity is added to the stage in the Response pipeline to apply this transformation to the contents of $body—that holds the response from the business service at that point.

Run/Test Service

The *ConversionService* is now completely implemented—at least for the operation *getDistanceFeetToMeter*. The proxy receives the request and hands it to the pipeline to have it first transformed and then routed to the business service. The business service delivers to it the external service. The response is delivered by the business service to the pipeline, that processes it in the response pipeline by transforming it into the desired XML structure, before conveying it to proxy service. The proxy service will finally send the response over the current transport method to the consumer.

Try out the *ConversionService*—either by running it from within JDeveloper or using the HttpAnalyzer tool or SoapUI. Request the conversion from feet to meter for various values.

Routing Messages to the TemperatureConversionPipeline

The *ConversionPipeline* supports the ConversionService's interface as defined in the WSDL document. The pipeline has an operational branch that determines from the operation indicated in the request message which of the branches in the pipeline to execute. At this point, the branch for the *getDistanceFeetToMeter* operation has been implemented. Calls to other operations are currently handled by the *default* branch—meaning that such calls would simply return the request message to the caller.

It should be simple to have the *ConversionPipeline* also provide support for the operation *getTemperatureCelsiusToFahrenheit*. After all, earlier in this chapter we developed the *TemperatureConversionService* that can be used as the implementation behind this operation.

To add a flow for this operation in the operational branch, click on the icon in the upper right hand corner. This will add a flow to the diagram. Ensure that the *Operation* property for this flow is set to *getTemperatureCelsiusToFahrenheit*. Add a Route component to the flow and drag a Routing activity inside this component.

Configure the Routing node to invoke the *TemperatureConversionPipeline*. Note: Pipelines can invoke other pipelines, just like they can route to business services. Pipelines are reusable building blocks that can not only serve multiple proxy services but other pipelines as well. In this case, we could also have wrapped the *TemperatureConversionService* in a business service that we can then invoke from the *ConversionPipeline*. However, it does not seem likely that we want to use any of the facilities business services provide in this current case—such as fail-over, result cache, security and transport settings—so the overhead is not justified.

Because the request and response messages exchanged with the *TemperatureConversionPipeline* are the same as those supported by operation *getTemperatureCelsiusToFahrenheit*, we do not have to perform transformative actions on the contents of the body variable, neither on the way to the *TemperatureConversionPipeline* nor on the way back.

The overview editor now visualizes the reference from the *ConversionPipeline* to the *TemperatureConversionPipeline*—as well as the external reference to the *LengthDistanceUnitConvertorService* business service (Figure 3-45). The project publishes two service endpoints—both based on SOAP—through two proxy services. Because the *ConversionService* also offers an operation to convert Celsius to Fahrenheit temperatures, we could consider removing the almost redundant *TemperatureConversionService* proxy altogether.

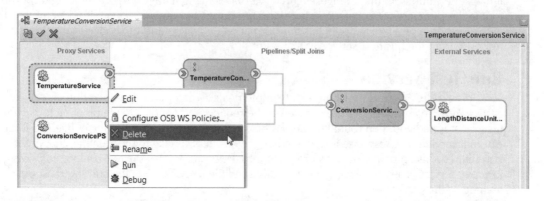

FIGURE 3-45. *Overview of the Service Bus project with the ConversionPipeline invoking the TemperatureConversionPipeline to provide the implementation of the getTemperatureCelsiusToFahrenheit operation*

That would be as easy as activating the menu option Delete on the context menu for the Proxy Service in the overview diagram.

Now try out the conversion of Celsius temperatures by invoking the *getTemperatureCelsiusToFahrenheit* operation in the *ConversionService* proxy, to find out that you experience no difference whatsoever from having temperatures converted through calls to the *TemperatureConversionService* proxy.

Exposing a REST/JSON Endpoint for the Temperature Conversion Service

An increasing number of service consumers—for example, applications running on mobile devices or HTML5 rich client/thin server web applications—have a desire to be able to consume services through a REST interface rather than the full blown SOAP protocol, frequently preferring JSON as the payload format over XML. SOA Suite provides native support to cater for these wishes: using the REST Adapter it is straightforward to provide REST/JSON endpoints in addition to or instead of SOAP/XML endpoints.

In this section, we will use this REST Adapter to expose the *ConversionService* as a REST-style service that accepts a simple HTTP GET request with a single URL parameter holding the Celsius temperature to convert and returns the calculated Fahrenheit temperature in a JSON message.

Creating a REST Conversion Service Interface with JSON Response

There are two approaches we can choose from:

■ Top-down, where we start by defining a Proxy Service with a REST interface with the exact JSON or XML message structures that we require (potentially based on a predefined WADL—the REST equivalent of the WSDL)

■ Bottom-up, where we have JDeveloper take an existing pipeline or business service and expose it as a REST service; we have control over the names of the resource and the service itself, and over the names of URL parameters but we cannot specify the exact structure of the response messages because these are automatically derived (XML or JSON) from the response messages defined in the interface we are exposing

In this section, we will go for the bottom-up approach. It offers less refined control—but it is a lot faster. We do not have to create the transformations between the request and response definitions specified for the REST service and the corresponding messages used in the pipeline.

Expose the ConversionPipeline as REST Service

Right click on the *ConversionPipeline* that is to be exposed in a RESTful manner. Select the menu option Expose As REST (shown in Figure 3-46).

The REST Binding Adapter wizard appears, see Figure 3-47. Set the name to *RestService*, set Resource Path to /Temperature, remove all operations except *getTemperatureCelsiusToFahrenheit* and click on the icon to edit this operation binding.

In the REST Operating Binding editors, elect GET as the HTTP Verb, accept the request settings, and on the Response tab select [only] the JSON Payload checkbox for the response, as shown in Figure 3-48.

Click on OK (twice) to complete the configuration of the RestService.

Test the REST Interface of the ConversionService

The implementation of the REST-style interface of the ConversionService is complete—with currently only support for the temperature conversion and with an auto-derived payload format. This interface can easily be tested from any browser: the request message is as simple as a URL with a single parameter that is sent as an HTTP GET request by the browser to the endpoint operated by the RestService proxy.

Open a browser and type in the address bar the following URL:

http://localhost:7101/TemperatureConversionService/RestService/Temperature?temperature=0

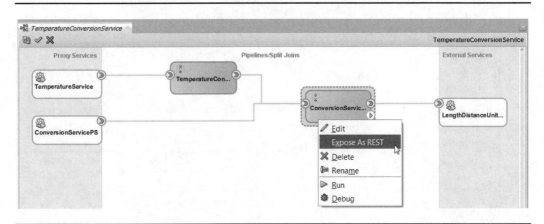

FIGURE 3-46. *Expose a Pipeline as a RESTful service—with limited control over the structure of the URL parameters and the JSON or XML response message*

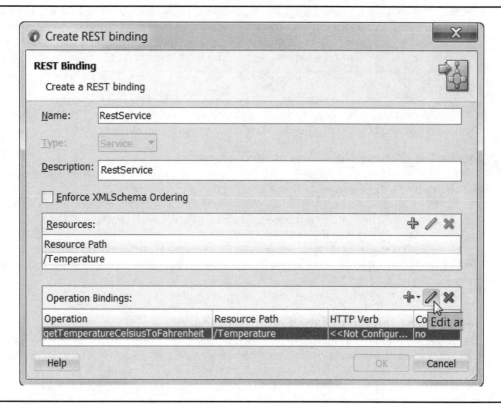

FIGURE 3-47. *Edit the REST binding—set Name and Resource [path], then edit one operation*

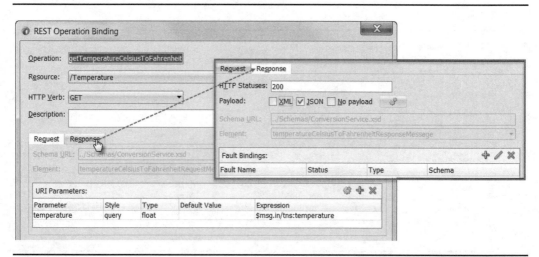

FIGURE 3-48. *Edit the getTemperatureCelsiusToFahrenheit operation binding—set HTTP Verb and configure Payload [type]*

```
{
    "temperature" : 32
}
```

FIGURE 3-49.   *Example of REST style call to the RestService to get the converted temperature value and the resulting JSON response*

then press enter to make the browser send this request. See Figure 3-49 for the result.

The Service Bus receives the request. It derives the resource from the request—resource—and knows how to process the HTTP GET call: an XML document is constructed from the URL parameter temperature and the *ConversionPipeline* is invoked with this XML document set up in the $body variable. The response from that pipeline is transformed internally into the JSON message that is handed to the *RestService* Proxy that will return it.

The endpoint for the *RestService* (Proxy Service) is set to /TemperatureConversionService/ RestService—a combination of the name of the current project and the name of the service. We are free to set a different value for this endpoint though, by editing the Endpoint URI on the Transport tab of the Proxy Service editor.

NOTE
You can also make test calls to REST services from the HTTP Analyzer in JDeveloper, SoapUI, and plugins for various browsers. The WADL address is: http://localhost:7101/sbresource?PROXY/ TemperatureConversionService/Proxy/RestService.

Summary

The Service Bus provides a platform for exposing all your services to (future) service consumers. It provides features such as protocol and data transformation, virtualization of the backend services and integration capabilities. To do this, the Service Bus is light-weight and capable of handling large volumes of service requests. The Service Bus is not meant as a platform to *implement* complex services, although for simple services you could use it.

More about the Service Bus

The Service Bus can obviously do much more than is discussed in this chapter. We have seen though what the core is of the Service Bus; receive requests over one of several transports like SOAP/XML or REST/JSON, perform selected aspects of VETRO on the request contents and after routing to the downstream component such as a pipeline or a business service do some VETRO on the response before return that response over the initial transport to the original caller. And do all of this really fast with very little overhead and even if we really want to, produce some operational data about what is going on.

In subsequent chapters, we will learn how the Service Bus will frequently be the front end of services whose implementations use various components, including Java classes, PL/SQL packages, 3rd party applications as well as SCA composite applications with BPEL and Business Rule components and Technology Adapters. We will see more in-depth information about additional functions and advanced facilities in the Service Bus for both developers and administrators.

CHAPTER

4

Accessing Database
and File System
through Outbound
Technology Adapters

Many services require interaction with enterprise resources such as databases, legacy applications, file systems, and FTP servers as part of their implementation. The SOA Suite is shipped with a wide range of adapters that help the integration from Service Bus projects (and the SOA composite applications we will first meet in Chapter 5) with these back-end systems. These adapters facilitate both inbound and outbound interactions. The former starts with an event in the enterprise resource that through the adapter triggers the service implementation. The latter is initiated in the Service Bus and goes out to the back-end system—to retrieve, publish, or push out data.

One of these adapters is the database adapter. This adapter allows integration from the Service Bus to relational databases to perform SQL queries, do data manipulation, and call stored procedures. We will do all of the above in this chapter with some of the Saibot Airport core databases.

The file adapter is used for outbound interactions such as to read files from and write them to the file system. These files can be in various formats such as delimited—like comma separated values (csv) -, fixed length, JSON, and XML. The files to be processed can contain multiple records, even of different types. In this chapter, we use the file adapter to create and update flight event log files and to expose the contents of an event log file in a service.

This chapter only demonstrates the outbound mode of the adapters. See Chapter 13 for examples of the inbound or polling mode of the technology adapters.

Note that the technology adapters are not only supported with Service Bus but also with SCA composite applications, as well as other Fusion Middleware components such as Oracle Data Integrator (ODI).

Introducing Technology Adapters

The Oracle Technology Adapters are stand-alone applications, deployed in the J2CA container of WebLogic as a type of application called Resource Application. The adapters implement the Java EE JCA 1.5 standard. This standard describes a number of aspects of connecting to enterprise systems, including connection and transaction management, security, and lifecycle management and handling of events and incoming messages from the enterprise system. Any application running on the WebLogic platform can engage these adapters for enterprise integration purposes. The SOA Suite is one such application. Note that the JCA adapters can also be deployed on the JBoss and WebSphere platforms.

The collection of technology adapters includes (see Figure 4-1) Database, Advanced Queuing (AQ), MQ Series, JMS (Java Messaging System), File and FTP (File Transfer Protocol), Sockets, Coherence, LDAP *(Lightweight Directory Access Protocol)*, and User Messaging Service (UMS) for email, VoIP, FAX, and text message. Custom JCA adapters can be used from the SOA Suite too. In addition to technology adapters, Oracle also offers Application Adapters (SAP, PeopleSoft, JD Edwards, Siebel, Oracle Applications for E-Business Suite), B2B Adapters (RosettaNet, EDI, Healthcare, and ebXML), Mainframe and TP-Monitor and Changed Data Capture Adapters. The technology adapters are included in the SOA Suite license; all other adapters are licensed separately.

Adapters provide the bridge to other technologies and communication protocols than those native to the SOA Suite. Note that other integrations—for example, to BAM, EJB, HTTP, and REST—are provided in the SOA Suite by special transports in the SOA Suite itself rather than through separate JCA adapters. These transports are listed in the component palette intermingled with the separately deployed adapters, which might be a little confusing.

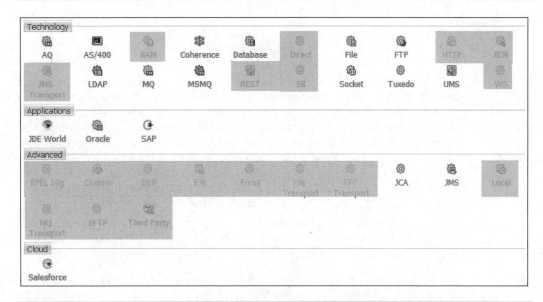

FIGURE 4-1. *Overview of Technology Adapters and other JCA adapters in SOA Suite 12c (grayed out are the Service Bus transports)*

The initiative for an interaction with an enterprise system can come from within the SOA Suite. The SOA Suite composite application invokes the adapter and has it contact the external resource to read or perhaps manipulate data. This is called the outbound mode of the adapter.

From the perspective of the SOA Suite, the inbound mode is the situation where the composite application is invoked by the JCA adapter, at which point a new instance of the service is created in the SOA Suite. The JCA adapter can be registered as a listener for events in enterprise systems or it can be configured to periodically poll an enterprise resource for specific changes. When the adapter receives an event or identifies a relevant change through polling, it calls the proxy service (Service Bus) or service binding (SCA) over the JCA transport and thus triggers a new instance.

Design Time

The SOA Suite design time in JDeveloper has extensive support for the technology adapters as well as the B2B and Applications Adapters. That means that the configuration of adapters is supported through developer friendly wizards and that integration of the adapter configuration as proxy service or business service (in Service Bus projects) or as service binding or reference binding (in SCA composites) is seamless. The operation performed by the technology adapter is exposed in terms of a regular service using a WSDL interface definition and an XSD to describe the data input and output. Using technology adapters requires a service developer to configure the design time settings of the adapter; when that has been done, there is no adapter specific knowledge required because the adapter looks like any other service in the composite. Note, however, that this adapter-derived service is only to be used as a private contract inside the service. Also note that some run-time configuration is necessary to make the adapter connection to the enterprise resource.

The adapter configuration wizard generates a number of files. These largely fall into three categories:

- Adapter metadata files that instruct the Resource Adapter application at run time on what exactly to do (which SQL to execute, which JMS Queue to publish to, which file to read)

- XSD that describes the XML data structure for the data that is passed into and/or is received from the adapter; a crucial aspect of the adapters is their ability to communicate in XML terms with the SOA Suite, regardless of the format used for interacting with enterprise systems. For many adapters, the configuration wizard will invoke the Native Format Builder. This wizard gathers some details from the developer on the native data format the adapter will have to deal with (e.g., in its dealings with the file system or the JMS queue or the User Messaging Service) and then creates the NXSD document that contains the mapping definition between the native data format (delimited text, fixed length text, JSON, XML, COBOL Copybook) and an XML representation thereof.

- WSDL that describes the operations performed by the adapter in web service terms that can easily be interpreted by the SOA Suite design time and run time; this definition references the relevant elements in the XSD documents.

The design time configurations of adapters contain a reference to the JNDI name of a Resource Adapter connection in the target deployment WebLogic platform—as shown in Figure 4-3. This connection describes exactly which physical endpoint the adapter will interact with—which database, JMS queue or Socket it connects to. The design time definition of the adapter does not contain such physical, environment specific run-time aspects. This makes it easier to promote applications using Resource Adapters through your development, test, and production environments.

Run Time

The run-time component of Oracle technology adapters is the J2CA 1.5 resource adapter for the specific type of back-end application. The technology adapters are deployed into the J2CA container of the Oracle WebLogic Server. Oracle Fusion Middleware integrates with these J2CA 1.5 adapters through the JCA Binding Component, which converts web service messages into J2CA interactions and back.

Each binding of an adapter to a Service Bus project or a SOA composite involves the configuration of a specific adapter action and the connection factory entry whose JNDI name is included in the configuration. These connections are managed through the WebLogic administration console. Note that these run-time adapter connections not only specify the connection details for an enterprise resource to interact with—for example, using a reference to a JDBC Data Source or a JMS Destination. They can also govern specific aspects of the behavior of the adapter. For example, high availability requirements on specific adapter operations can be configured on these connections, as well as thread management, transaction, and throttling details.

Saibot Airport and Its Data

Data is an important asset for any business in the 21st century. It is certainly an essential aspect in many applications running in the SOA Suite. Carefully structuring and organizing data is essential. This starts with the metadata: the description of the data itself in terms of structure and relations, integrity constraints, and interpretation. Next are designing the logical storage of the data along with ownership, information life cycle management and security.

Some data will live for a very short time—such as the temperature registration in a waiting area or the clicks by a visitor of the website—and other records may be retained for many years. These differences obviously impact the way such data is stored, processed, and managed.

Data used at Saibot Airport may not be owned or managed by the airport itself. Examples are the IATA registrations of airports, air carriers, air craft models, and individual air crafts. The list of countries and cities, nor the weather information (both local and worldwide) is owned by Saibot Airport. Yet the airport has a need for that data and it may or may not be feasible or practical to rely on real-time access of such data from their respective owners.

Data quality is an important challenge for the airport. For historical and sometimes still valid practical reasons, some data sets are replicated across the organization. This means there is a risk at data inconsistency through incomplete replication. The consequences range from mild embarrassment to substantial business costs and even safety threats.

As part of the enterprise architecture effort at Saibot Airport, a number of relatively independent business domains have been identified. Each domain covers clusters of business processes that provide an important function to the organization. Associated with each business domain is a data domain that contains the data processed, recorded, and managed by the functions in the domain. Ownership of each domain is clearly identified.

Within the data domain, the owner decides how to organize, store, manage, and enforce the integrity of the data. There is certainly no one to one mapping between logical domains and physical databases. While implementing services, we assume that every data domain is a stand-alone logical data store. Data from the domain is exposed through services that communicate in terms of the canonical Enterprise Data Model. These services cater for the required data aggregation and historical perspective. Services in other domains can only access data from a domain through these data services—never directly in the underlying data store. This decoupling means that integrity can be enforced anywhere from the data service level to the data store and that whenever the underlying implementation of (part of) a domain changes, there will be no impact on consumers outside the domain unless of course the change itself needs to be exposed.

Sometimes even though joins would be possible in a query that spans across tables that are in the same physical database but in different domains, we cannot use the table joins because we work from the assumption that these tables are actually in separate databases. And one day they may indeed be in different databases. Or one data domain may be implemented through a third party system or a remote web service. When that happens, the impact on Saibot's service architecture will be limited. Only the implementation of the elementary data services will have to change—from accessing one database to integrating with another or to invoking a third party API or remote service interface. Nothing changes for the consumers of these elementary services.

There is therefore a price to pay for the increased control over the data: Logical references from data records in one domain to entities in a different domain cannot be implemented at database level through meaningless, system-derived identifiers and foreign key constraints, as was customary in the past. Joins in SQL queries cannot be used either, to enrich data from one domain with information from another. Filtering records from a large database table based on attributes of related records in other domains is not possible. Composite services, first discussed in Chapter 7, will deal with such cross domain relations. In the long term, this will turn out to be a fairly small consequence considering the rewards.

NOTE
Several service design patterns have evolved that help further alleviate the burden. Examples are the use of business identifiers instead of the meaningless keys often used in relational databases, Domain Value Mapping and Cross Referencing (features in the SOA Suite, introduced in Chapter 5), service call outs to gather lookup details to use in the main routing call.

The data domains identified by the IT staff at Saibot Airport include equipment, property, concessions, finance, HR, flights, reference, see Figure 4-2. Many of these domains have been subdivided in more fine grained components. The domains or these more refined components also shine through in the XML namespaces used in the canonical data model XSD definitions and in the namespaces used for domain level services.

The Flights domain is one we will have many dealings with in this chapter and the remainder of the book. This domain contains information regarding the slots that have been registered for air carriers—the future flights. It also holds the flights that are scheduled for the next 24–48 hours—the present—and flights that took place in the recent past. The implementation of the data domains is done through various mechanisms for storing and processing data, including NoSQL storage and data grids, content management systems and relational databases. The Flights domain at Saibot uses among others three distinct relational databases for future (slots), present, and past. Over the course of the book, we will investigate if for the live data regarding the present it could be useful and attainable to use a Coherence data grid to increase performance and availability.

Retrieving Information from the Database

One important requirement in service implementations with regard to databases is the need to retrieve data from them. Services frequently expose search operations, making relevant data available in canonical data formats to various consumers. In order to actually deliver the goods, these services require database interaction, and a straightforward way of achieving that in the Oracle SOA Suite is through the use of the database adapter.

In this section, we will create the AirportService that exposes reference data regarding airports. All flights coming into Saibot Airport or leaving from it connect with a remote airport. There are many details about all these connecting airports that are relevant to invoking systems. The database in the Common data domain contains a table CMN_AIRPORTS with stores details about airports. The AirportService will expose the data from this table, as well as the

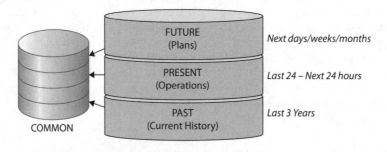

FIGURE 4-2. *Overview of Saibot's core data domains*

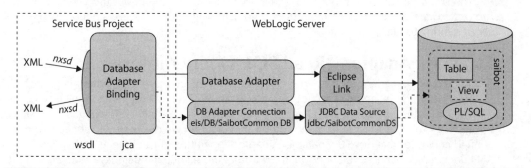

FIGURE 4-3. *The anatomy of an outbound Database Adapter binding—configured with JCA, WSDL, and XSD files referencing a runtime Database Adapter connection that uses a JDBC Data Source to connect to a database schema*

CMN_COUNTRIES table that provides lookup data about the host country of the airport. The database adapter will provide the translation from SOAP to JDBC, from WSDL to SQL, and from relational data to XML, as shown in Figure 4-3.

Get Going with Application and Service Bus Project

Create a new application in JDeveloper using the New Gallery (CTRL + N). Select Category General | Applications and then the item *Service Bus application with Service Bus project*.

Name the application *ReferenceDataServices*. Call the Service Bus project *AirportService*.

Create the familiar folder structure: schemas, business service, proxy, WSDLs, pipeline, transformations. Also add a folder Adapters. Import the resources AirportService.xsd, common.xsd, reference.xsd (into folder Schemas), and AirportService.wsdl (into folder WSDLs) from the jar file AirportServiceInitialResources.jar, to make it look like Figure 4-4.

FIGURE 4-4. *The AirportService project with the imported resources*

The WSDL document—supported by the XSD definitions—describes the interface of the *AirportService*. Take a moment to familiarize yourself with the *findAirports* operation that we are about to bring to life.

Database Adapter—Read SQL Query Airports

Open the overview editor for the *AirportService*. From the component palette, drag the Database [Adapter] from the Technology section and drop it in the External References lane, see Figure 4-5.

The editor for configuring the Database Adapter reference appears. It will gather details from us on what exactly is the nature of the database interaction we desire. It will generate the configuration files that drive the database adapter's operation at run time as well as WSDL and XSD documents that describe in normalized format the service the database adapter is to provide.

Set the name of the Database Adapter Reference to *QueryAirportsDB*. Press Next.

The Service Connection step in the configuration wizard (Figure 4-6) has a double purpose. It can be a little confusing to have both these purposes handled on the same page. The first one is to provide the database connection that is used at design time to gather metadata about the database and the objects we want to interact with. This database connection is used only by the wizard at design time. It is not relevant in any way to what will happen at run time. Select or create a database connection that connects to the database schema that holds the Saibot Common tables.

The second purpose is to provide the JNDI Name of the Database Adapter connection to be used at runtime, which we will configure in the target WebLogic platform—more details in the next section. It is common for this JNDI Name to start with eis/DB/ and to be followed by a descriptive name that indicates which logical database environment (database, schema, role) it is associated with. Note that this is *not* the JDBC Data Source name. Set the JNDI Name to eis/DB/SaibotCommonDB.

Press Next.

On the next page (Figure 4-7) we set the Operation Type. This is obviously quite important: do we want the adapter to operate in inbound (polling) mode or in outbound mode. And in outbound mode, do we want it to manipulate data, to invoke a stored procedure or to query data. And if—as in our case—we want to query data, what exact data retrieval method do we want to employ.

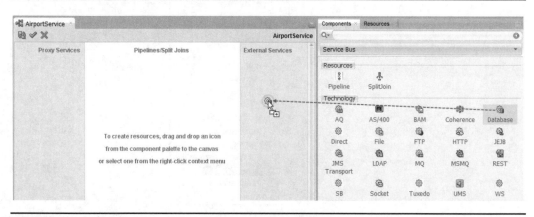

FIGURE 4-5. *Drag the Database Adapter to the External References lane*

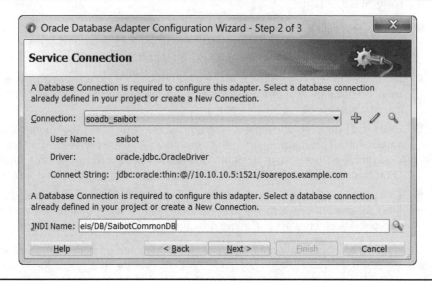

FIGURE 4-6. *Configure the design time database connection and the run-time JNDI Name of the DB Adapter connection*

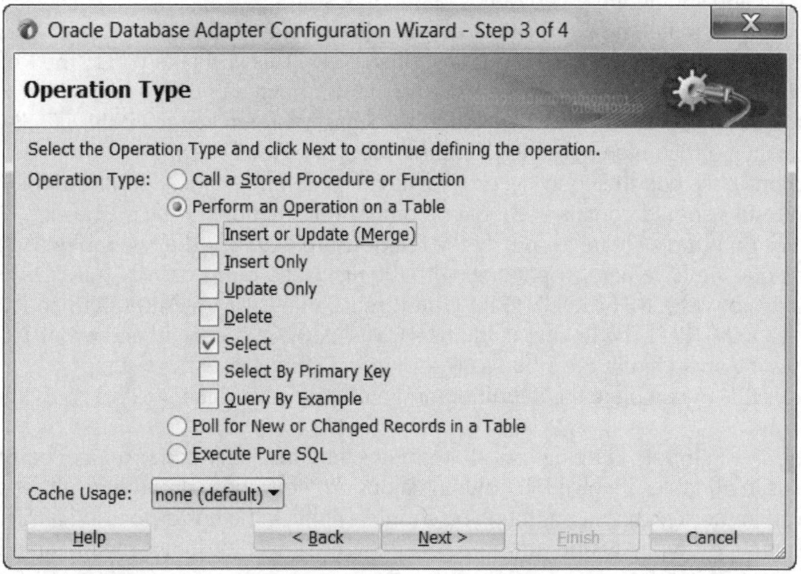

FIGURE 4-7. *Selecting the operation type for the Database Adapter Reference*

The retrieval options are:

- Select—we define a SQL query that typically contains one or more bind parameters; the input to the adapter at run time consists of the values for these parameters and based on these values, the query will return a specific result set.

- Select By Primary Key—similar to the previous option, except that only one parameter is used: the primary key; this operation benefits from use of the Coherence integration with the database adapter, available only on Exalogic systems.

- Query by Example—a sample XML record in the structure of the query results provides values that all produced query results should have in the corresponding columns; this operation provides a lot of flexibility, that comes at a performance cost, because a new SELECT statement must be prepared and hard parsed by the database for each execution.

- Execute Pure SQL—provide the exact SQL statement that should be executed, including bind parameters to use; this type is especially useful when dealing with arbitrarily complex statements, aggregate queries, and XMLType columns or other database types.

Additionally, and frequently quite valuable, a call to stored procedure or function can be used to retrieve a result set. This makes it possible to encapsulate the SQL inside the stored program. On an Oracle database, this also allows us to prepare arbitrarily complex, multilevel data structures—using objects and collections—that can be returned in a single round trip. We will see this mechanism in action later in this chapter.

In this case, pick operation type Select.

In step 4, import tables CMN_AIRPORTS and CMN_COUNTRIES. Click the button Import Tables, press query to bring up a list of all tables available in the database connection you defined earlier on and shuttle these two tables to the right side.

It will take a little time for the wizard to process all metadata associated with these tables. When you can again operate the buttons, press Next. This will take you to the Relationships page. This is where we have to specify how the two tables hang together.

The situation is that table CMN_AIRPORTS has a foreign key to CMN_COUNTRIES, based on column cty_id that references the id column in CMN_AIRPORTS. We want to be able to search for airports based on the country code—which is a column in the countries lookup table. And the search results should contain the lookup country information for each airport.

Click on button Create to specify the relationship between the two tables. A lookup relation like the one we have here is specified with the first radio button: CMN_AIRPORTS has a 1:1 Relationship with CMN_COUNTRIES. The Parent Table is CMN_AIRPORTS and the Child Table is CMN_COUNTRIES. The linking columns—CMN_AIRPORTS.cty_id and CMN_COUNTRIES. id—must be specified in the table, as is shown in Figure 4-8.

Press OK to complete the definition of the relationship. Then Next to go to the next step in the wizard.

The step Attribute Filtering lists all attributes that the query can produce, based on the columns in all tables involved. If column values are not required in the result set and are not involved in the search criteria, then you should uncheck the corresponding attributes for reasons of design time simplicity and run-time performance: fewer attributes means simpler transformations at design time and smaller data sets at run time.

Press Next when you have determined which attributes to include and exclude.

The next step is Define Selection Criteria (Figure 4-9), which really means composing the where clause for the SQL query. The wizard allows you to declaratively construct the selection criteria. However, you can also manually edit the SQL statement on this page.

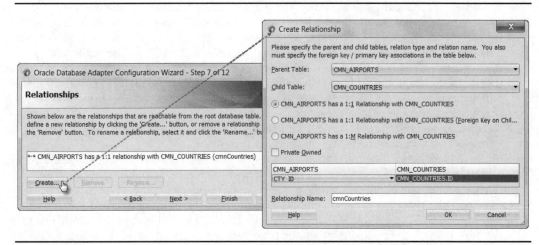

FIGURE 4-8. *Configuring the relationship between tables CMN_AIRPORTS and CMN_COUNTRIES*

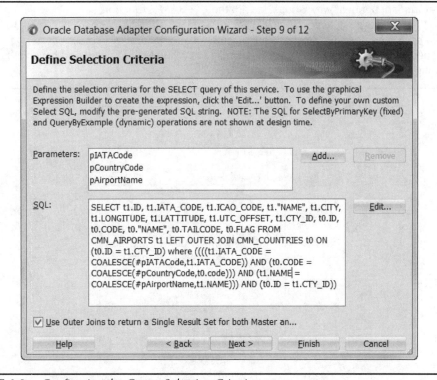

FIGURE 4-9. *Configuring the Query Selection Criteria*

When you manually edit the statement, then you are introducing hard-coded SQL that may result in maintenance overhead at a later stage and you may lose database platform independence by using vendor specific SQL. As long as you stay in declarative mode, the database adapter will translate the declarative search definition into platform specific SQL for the run-time target database, using relevant capabilities in TopLink. A preferred method of using advanced platform specific SQL capabilities without losing platform independence would be to encapsulate such SQL in database views that can be queried against by the database adapter using standard SQL, or use stored procedures to encapsulate the SQL.

Because Saibot Airport is hooked on Oracle Databases and is fictitious to boot, we will have no qualms in this book to edit SQL statements as we see fit.

First, press button Add thrice to create three parameters, called pIATACode, pCountryCode, and pAirportName. These parameters represent the run-time input to the database adapter reference. They can be used as bind parameters in the SQL query.

Check the checkbox to use outer joins to return a single result set. The effect of this setting is that TopLink will use a single SQL query to return results from both tables, instead of one query per table or even one query for the master table and one query on the lookup table for each master record.

When you press the Edit button you can declaratively compose the where condition, using the three parameters. The editor does not have built in facilities to deal with optional parameters not having a value. After using the declarative editor, you will have to manually refine the SQL condition to deal with that. The easiest way is using the Oracle specific NVL function; the platform independent way would be with the COALESCE function.

When the SQL statement is complete, press Next. The following two steps are for configuring advanced options (JDBC settings such as timeout and maximum number of rows) and JCA properties (retry strategy). Finally, press Finish to complete the wizard and have the adapter configuration files generated (see Figure 4-10).

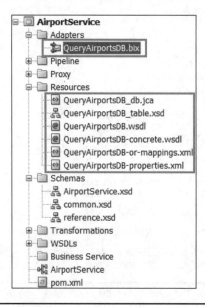

FIGURE 4-10. *The files generated by the Database Adapter configuration wizard*

The generated file QueryAirportsDB_db.jca is the root of the database adapter configuration for this service. It contains references to the other files that were generated as well as the core properties required at run time by the database adapter to do the job. Crucial among these is the location attribute (the JNDI name) in the connection-factory element that refers to the DB Adapter connection defined in the runtime WLS platform (see next section).

The generated QueryAirportsDB.wsdl file contains the normalized, web service representation of the functionality offered by this (database) adapter reference: it makes the database adapter reference look like an ordinary web service. The corresponding concrete WSDL adds a binding of type JCA transport and a port at the endpoint that was specified through the JNDI name entered in the wizard. The generated QueryAirportsDB_table.xsd is imported from the wsdl document. It contains the definition of the XML structure for the input—the parameters—and output—the query results—of the adapter operation. The files QueryAirportsDB-properties.xml and QueryAirportsDB-or-mappings.xml contain definitions used by TopLink, including the actual SQL query and details about the parameters and columns involved. Any advanced TopLink specific refinements that are not supported in the adapter configuration wizard can be made in these files. Note: re-running the wizard can overwrite such changes.

The wizard will also generate a Service Bus business service QueryAirportsDB, configured for this database adapter reference (using the JCA transport and referencing the QueryAirportsDB _db.jca file). See how these files hang together in the dependency overview in Figure 4-11.

NOTE
*A business service can also be generated from the context menu on
any JCA adapter configuration file, in this case by right clicking on
QueryAirportsDB_db.jca.*

Configuration of Run-Time Server

The WebLogic Server on which the Service Bus engine runs needs to be prepared for the use of the database adapter, or at least for using the adapter to access a new target database. Typically this will be a two-step process that requires us to configure a JDBC Data Source—that describes the connection to the database account—and a Database Adapter Connection that defines specific adapter behavior and references the JDBC Data Source. Both steps are done from the WebLogic Server Administration console. You access this console at http://localhost:7101/console for the Integrated WLS or from the context menu on the Integrated WebLogicServer connection in the Application Servers window in JDeveloper.

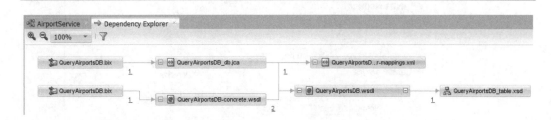

FIGURE 4-11.   *Explore dependencies for the JCA Adapter specific WSDL file
QueryAirportsDB.wsdl*

Configure JDBC Data Source

To configure the JDBC Data Source, click on Data Sources on the home page in the console. Click on the New button and select the option Generic Data Source, to create a new JDBC Data Source. See Figure 4-12.

Define the Name as SaibotCommonDS and the JNDI Name as jdbc/SaibotCommonDS. Press Next—assuming the Database Type is indeed Oracle.

Following up on that assumption, accept the default driver on the second page of this wizard. Click Next again. Provide the Database Name (the SID of the target database), the Host Name, and the Port. Then provide the name of the database account to which the Data Source should connect and the associated password (twice). Press Next. Press the button Test Configuration to verify if the connection was configured correctly. If not, return and correct the settings.

Otherwise, press Next again. We now need to associate the Data Source definition with the managed server(s) we want to deploy it to. For the Integrated WebLogic Server, check the box in front of DefaultServer. Then press Finish.

This will create the Data Source and deploy it to the DefaultServer, making it available for applications that want to use it.

Configure Database Adapter

The database adapter is deployed as an application to WebLogic where it runs independently from the SOA Suite. Any Java EE application running on the WebLogic Server can enlist the help of the database adapter or any other of the JCA adapters to integrate with enterprise resources.

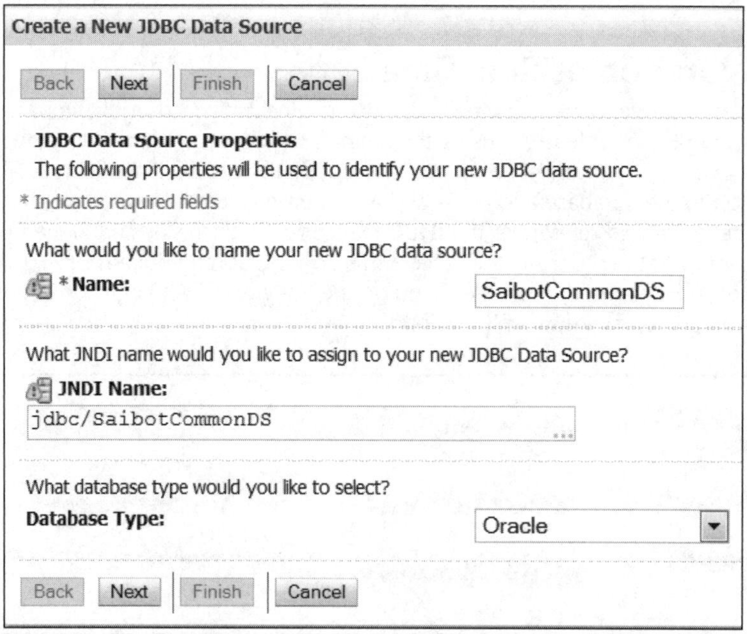

Create a New JDBC Data Source

| Back | Next | Finish | Cancel |

JDBC Data Source Properties
The following properties will be used to identify your new JDBC data source.

* Indicates required fields

What would you like to name your new JDBC data source?

* Name: SaibotCommonDS

What JNDI name would you like to assign to your new JDBC Data Source?

JNDI Name:
```
jdbc/SaibotCommonDS
```

What database type would you like to select?

Database Type: Oracle

| Back | Next | Finish | Cancel |

FIGURE 4-12. *Configure JDBC Data Source, name and JNDI name*

In order to invoke the adapter successfully, it requires a set of JCA properties that instructs the adapter on what action it should execute. Among the properties used by the database adapter is a reference to the JNDI name of a connection that should be used. This connection is configured for the database adapter through the WebLogic Administration Console. The configuration includes some settings regarding the use of database sequences for generating unique numbers and some other specific JDBC operations. The most important property is the reference to the JDBC Data Source that should be used by this DB Adapter connection to access the target database.

To configure the DB Adapter connection, go to the home page of the WLS console and list the deployments. Locate the DB Adapter deployment and click on it. Open the Configuration tab and then the sub-tab labeled Outbound Connection Pools. Click on the New button.

A wizard page appears on which you can specify the JNDI name for the new DB Adapter connection. This is the same name used in the JNDI name field in the Database Adapter configuration wizard in JDeveloper (that was saved in the location attribute of the connection-factory element in the .jca properties file). Set the JNDI Name to eis/DB/SaibotCommonDB and press Finish to create the new connection. When this is your first change to the database adapter deployment, WebLogic will prompt you to create a deployment plan file to save this and future configuration changes to. This file should be called Plan.xml and is commonly located in a directory called Middleware Home/SOA Suite home/soa/DBPlan, although you are free to choose any location on the server that runs the WebLogic platform.

The console will take you to a page that assures you that all changes have been activated and no restarts are necessary. Let's make a few refinements to the connection definition.

Return to the tab Configuration | Outbound Connection Pools and click on the connection eis/DB/SaibotCommonDB you have just added. Click on the property value for the property XADataSourceName. The field is editable now. Type the JNDI name of the JDBC Data Source that you created earlier on: jdbc/SaibotCommonDS. Then press enter to set the value. Then press the Save button. This completes the configuration of the Database Adapter connection configuration.

NOTE
In general, if a data source is used for nontransactional database access—read only—or will not be used for operations to participate in global transactions, it is best to configure it as "Non XA" (by selecting a database driver that does not do XA) to avoid the overhead associated with the XA transaction. In the Database Adapter configuration, you should then set the DataSourceName property instead of XADataSourceName. For the purpose of the Saibot Airport case in this book, working with an XADataSource at all times will be the simplest approach.

Test Business Service

When the Database Adapter binding is configured in JDeveloper and a Service Bus business service is created for it, we can test it without first having to create a pipeline and a proxy service. One provision is that the configuration of the Database Adapter connection has been completed, as described in the previous section.

To test the database interaction, select the option Run on the context menu for the QueryAirportsDB business service in the Service Bus overview.

The Service Bus project will be deployed to the Integrated WLS. The Business Service tester appears, which allows us to enter values for the search parameters used in the query against the Airports and Countries tables.

When you press Execute, the XML document is handed to the DB Adapter by the Service Bus along with the JCA properties that tell it which connection to use and thereby indirectly which JDBC Data Source to leverage. The Database Adapter uses TopLink to construct the SQL query that is executed over the JDBC connection against the Saibot Common database (schema) and to return the results in XML format as described by the XSD document QueryAirportsDB_table.xsd. This XML document is returned to the Business Service Tester in the Response, as is shown in Figure 4-13.

TIP
If instead you get a response message that contains a Missing Property Exception, the name used in the location property of the connection-factory element in the QueryAirportsDB_db.jca file may not exactly correspond to the JNDI name assigned to the DB Adapter connection in the WLS Console; alternatively you may have to restart the WebLogic Server after all.

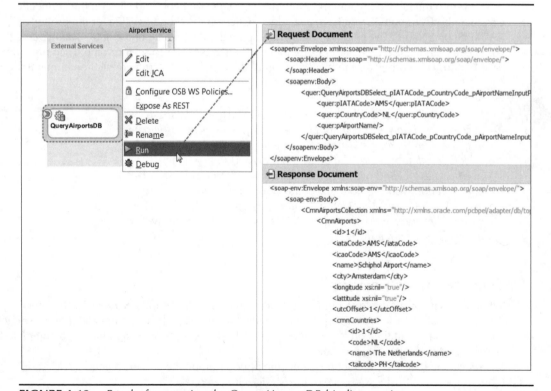

FIGURE 4-13. *Results from testing the QueryAirportsDB binding service*

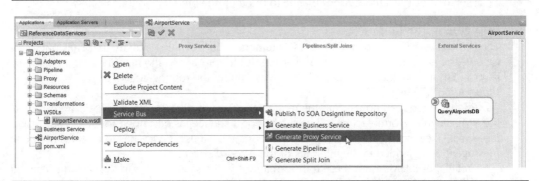

FIGURE 4-14.   *Generate the Proxy for the Airport Service based on the AirportService.wsdl document*

Implement Proxy Service and Pipeline

The next step on our way to the implementation of the *AirportService* is the implementation of the Proxy Service and Pipeline in the Service Bus project.

Generate Proxy Service

The *AirportService* that we are implementing here is described by the AirportService.wsdl document. Based on that document, we can let JDeveloper generate the proxy service as well as the pipeline. Bring up the context menu on the wsdl document and activate Service Bus | Generate Proxy Service, as shown in Figure 4-14.

In the Create Proxy Service editor, set the name to *AirportServicePS*, following the naming convention that Saibot have chosen for proxy services. Have the Pipeline generated as well by checking the relevant checkbox; call the Pipeline *AirportPipeline*.

Press Next. Set the Endpoint URI to /reference/AirportService.

Press Finish. The proxy service and the pipeline are generated, both in the WSDLs folder. Use the Refactor | Move option on the context menu for both definitions to relocate them to the appropriate folders.

The AirportService overview shows the new AirportServicePS wired to the equally new AirportPipeline. Create a wire from the AirportPipeline to the QueryAirportsDB business service, as shown in Figure 4-15.

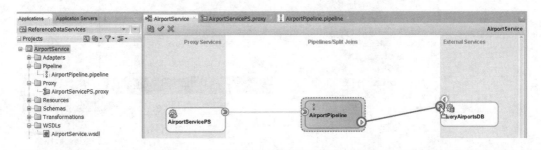

FIGURE 4-15.   *Wiring the AirportPipeline to the QueryAirportsDB business service in the AirportService project*

Then double click the *AirportPipeline* to bring up the pipeline editor.

Implement Pipeline

The *AirportPipeline* already contains a Route node with a Routing activity that calls out to the QueryAirportsDB business service. This is the result from wiring the pipeline to the business service. Ensure that the right operation is invoked from the routing activity: *QueryAirportDBSelect*.

All that is required now is that the request received from the proxy service is transformed to the XML technical format expected by the business service, as described in QueryAirportsDB_table.xsd. Likewise, the technical response from the business service has to be transformed to the message format defined in the interface of the *AirportService*.

Create the XSL Maps for these transformations in the same way as in the previous chapter.

In the mapping of the response from the Database Adapter to the response message format, you will have to deal with a repeating set of nodes using the XSLT for-each operator. Every node represents a result row of the select statement. When the XSL Map editor first opens: click on the tns:airport node in the target tree and from the context menu select Insert Parent | XSL | for-each (see Figure 4-16). This will add a for-each node to the tree.

Map the node ns0:CmnAirports to the xsl:for-each node. Subsequently, map all child nodes to their respective counterparts—optionally using the *auto map* feature that you can engage by dragging node ns0:CmnAirports to node tns:airport. Figure 4-17 shows part of the mapping result.

In the pipeline's Routing node, add Replace activities to both the Request and Response actions, using the two XSL Maps you have just created (as shown in Figure 4-18). Both replace the node contents of the body using an XSLT resource and feeding $body/*[1] as the input document expression into the transformation.

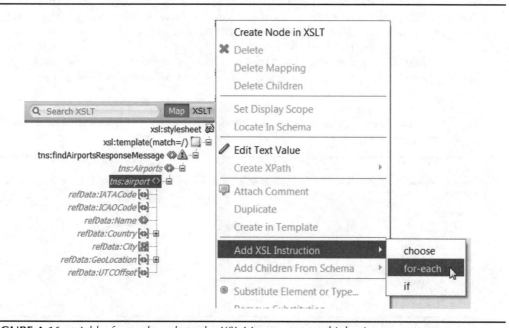

FIGURE 4-16.   *Add a for-each node to the XSL Map to map multiple airports*

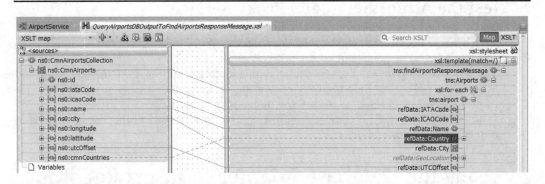

FIGURE 4-17.   *Mapping multiple airports queried from the database to the response message format*

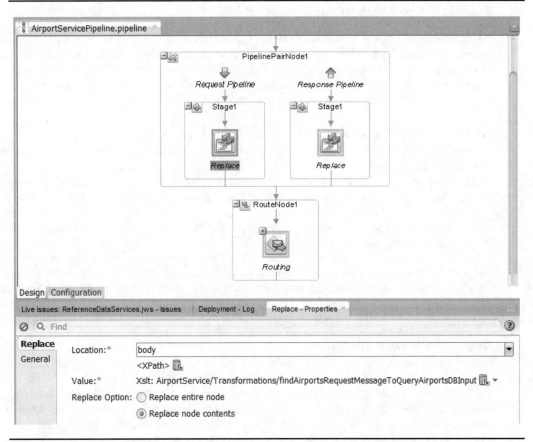

FIGURE 4-18.   *The AirportPipeline with the Routing Node and two Replace activities—on the way in and on the way out*

Test the AirportServicePS Proxy Service

The complete *AirportService* can now be tested by running the *AirportServicePS* proxy. The Service Bus project is deployed and the Proxy Service Tester is displayed. Provide input in the format prescribed by the interface of the *AirportService*.

Press Execute to invoke the service. Through a transformation of our request message followed by an SQL query against the Saibot Common database and finally a transformation of the query results to the required response format, the output will be produced.

The end-to-end chain is complete—allowing us to expose services that use a database for most of their implementation.

Using the Database Adapter to Insert Records

In addition to querying data, the database adapter is well suited to support data manipulation. It can do Insert, Update, Delete, and Merge operations—and it performs the manipulation(s) as part of the same transaction that was started for handling the service request by the Service Bus if we want it do (or alternatively create a dedicated transaction for the database operation).

More complex data manipulations—such as those involving multiple tables—can be implemented using stored procedures. Calls to stored procedures made by the database adapter are included in the global transaction too when an XA Data Source is used. Stored procedures should not perform Commit operations: any data manipulations they perform are committed or rolled back along with the (global or dedicated) transaction, orchestrated from the Service Bus.

In this section, we will look at both types of data manipulation with the database adapter: straightforward DML and calls to stored procedures that indirectly perform DML.

Simple Database Record Insert or Update

In the case of Saibot Airport, reference data is not only exposed through reference services, it is also managed through these services. For example, countries: the *CountryService* is used to search countries, retrieve country details as well as manage the data. Even though reference data for countries does not change a whole lot, still there are regular changes—34 new countries since 1990, such as the recent birth of South Sudan, the break-up of the Netherlands Antilles, the new flags of Paraguay and Malawi and several areas around the world where relevant changes may be the result of animosities.

The *CountryService* is defined through a WSDL document—CountryService.wsdl—with an associated XSD definition. The country data is held in table CMN_COUNTRIES in the Saibot Common domain. The table has columns for the country code, its name, the tail code assigned to aircrafts registered in the country and a BLOB column to hold a picture of the flag. We will now create the service to maintain country records, using the database adapter and the Service Bus.

Prepare the Service Bus Project

Back in the JDeveloper application *ReferenceDataServices*, create a new Service Bus project using the New Gallery—Category: General | Projects, Item: Service Bus Project.

Call the new project *CountryService*. Optionally, create folders WSDLs, Schemas, Proxy, Adapters, Pipeline, Transformations, and Business Service. Import the resources CountryService.wsdl and CountryService.xsd and also reference.xsd and common.xsd from the JAR file *CountryServiceInitialResources.jar*.

Create the Proxy Service and a Pipeline

From the context menu on the file CountryService.wsdl, generate a proxy service and associated pipeline.

The proxy service should be called *CountryServicePS* and the pipeline *CountryPipeline*. The location for the proxy service is the Proxy folder.

On the Transport page, set the Endpoint URI for the proxy service to /reference/CountryService.

Finish the wizard and have the proxy service and the pipeline generated in the project.

In the Service Bus overview editor, the result—an exposed proxy service wired to the CountryPipeline—is displayed. What we need next is the business service based on a Database Adapter reference, wired to the pipeline.

Configure a Database Adapter Reference for Inserting Country Records

In the Service Bus overview editor, drag the Database Adapter from the component palette to the External References lane, to bring up the wizard that will configure the outbound DB Adapter reference, and create the business service on top of it.

Set the name of the Database Adapter Reference to *CreateCountryDB*.

On page 2, use the IDE database connection to the Saibot Common database. The Database Adapter connection that we used for the AirportService can be used again, because the current DB Adapter reference will access the same target database in a similar fashion. Either type the JNDI name of that connection—eis/DB/SaibotCommonDB—or browse this connection using the JNDI Browser against the Integrated WLS, provided it is actually running (as shown in Figure 4-19).

Select Insert Only as the Operation Type in step 3.

Import table CMN_COUNTRIES in the next step. Press Next. There are no relationships to add, so press Next again. Accept all attributes based on table columns to be included in the insert operation, and press Next.

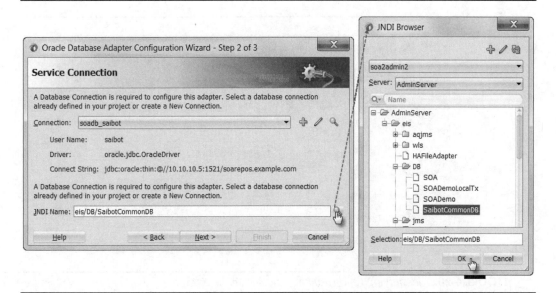

FIGURE 4-19.   *Browsing the JNDI name for the DB Adapter connection in the Integrated WLS*

In step 7, we specify how for each new COUNTRY record, the next value from a database sequence CMN_CTY_SEQ will be used to set the value of the ID column—which is the primary key. If this sequence does not yet exist, it will not be in the drop-down list in this page. In that case simply type the name of the sequence in the Sequence field—and it will be created by the wizard in the database schema linked to by the IDE Database Connection, see Figure 4-20.

Complete the wizard, accepting all default settings after this step.

The Database Adapter configuration files are generated, as is the *CreateCountryDB* business service that is based on the JCA transport defined by the adapter configuration.

NOTE
One of the properties of the Database Adapter connection defined in the WebLogic console is the SequencePreAllocationSize. It is necessary for this value to be equal to the increment by property of the database sequence. The default setting in the adapter connection is 50.

Test the Business Service

At this point, even though the pipeline is not implemented nor is it wired to the business service, we can already test the business service and thereby the configuration of the database adapter. Because the DB Adapter connection is already set up in the Integrated WebLogic Server (or the stand-alone managed server you are using) earlier in this chapter, we can now simply activate Run on the context menu for the business service in the Service Bus editor and have the Service Bus project deployed and the business service tester console launched.

The request document is of course not of the XML structure *createCountryRequestMessage* that we need for the proxy service, but of the technical structure generated by the Database Adapter configuration wizard, corresponding to the SQL operation insert into CMN_COUNTRIES. Provide details, for example for the UK (tail code is G) and execute the business service.

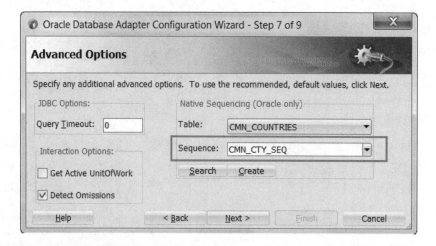

FIGURE 4-20.   *Identifying (and Creating) the sequence to derive the primary key values from for newly inserted records*

The Response document shows the country record as it was created, including the value derived from the sequence and assigned to the ID column.

You can verify in the database if the new Country record was indeed created. Later in this section we will use SoapUI to test the *CountryService* and also submit binary data for a picture of a flag that will be stored in the BLOB column in the CMN_COUNTRIES table.

Complete the Pipeline

In the Service Bus overview editor, wire the pipeline to the CreateCountryDB business service. This will add a Route node and Routing activity (linked to the business service) to the pipeline.

All we need to do now is to add transformations to the Routing activity, to transform the request message based on the XSD element *createCountryRequestMessage* to the input for the *CreateCountryDB* business service (== Database Adapter) and the response from the latter into the *createCountryResponseMessage* structure. Create the necessary XSL Maps and add Replace operations to the Routing node. You can test the proxy service as soon as the Replace for the request action is in place: the response will not have the correct XML structure, but the request does and the country should be added to the database table.

Note that the *CountryService* defines three operations in its interface specification. There is no distinction in the pipeline between these operations. That means that the pipeline will always do the same thing—invoke the *CreateCountryDB* business service—regardless of what operation was actually invoked. We need to add an operational branch node to add support for all three operations when we get round to completing the pipeline.

Test the Create Country Operation in the CountryService

When the pipeline is complete, with transformations in both request and response action, then run-the Proxy Service and create a request message, for example, to add France with tail code F. This time, we compose a *createCountryRequestMessage* XML element, according to the interface definition of the service.

After executing the service, the response message will be of the specified type— *createCountryResponseMessage*—containing a *resultCode* element with the assigned id value for the new country.

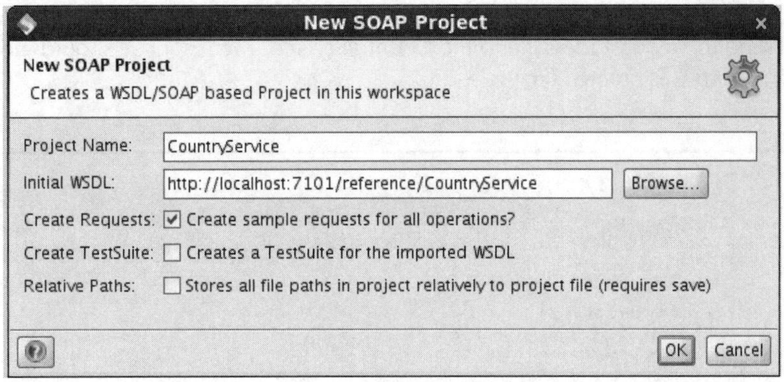

FIGURE 4-21. *Create new SOAP UI Test Project configured for the CountryService*

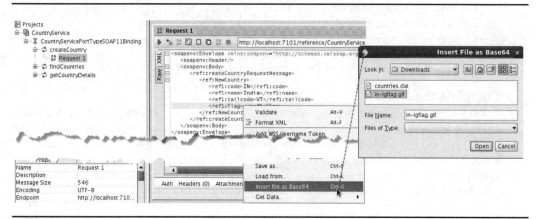

FIGURE 4-22. *Add the binary content from a file as Base64 encoded data to a request message*

Create a SoapUI Test Project for the CountryService

SoapUI (http://www.soapui.org/) is a valuable tool for testing services—so valuable it has become the de facto standard among developers. We can use SoapUI to see whether the CountryService handles images well. With SoapUI it is very easy to include, for example, the contents from image files as base64 encoded content in the XML request message.

Start SoapUI and create a new Soap project for the CountryService—its WSDL is exposed at http://localhost:7101/reference/CountryService?wsdl (see Figure 4-21).

Have sample requests created for all operations. Then open the test request for the createCountry operation. Enter the NewCountry record for India (IN, India, VT). Then remove the random data for the Flag element. Open the context menu for the Flag element and select the option Insert file as Base64 that allows us to add the contents from a binary file as base64 encoded content to the request message, as shown in Figure 4-22.

A file browser dialog window opens. Select an image file that holds the flag of India, such as in-lgflag.gif, downloaded from https://www.cia.gov/library/publications/the-world-factbook/docs/flagsoftheworld.html.

SoapUI adds the base64 equivalent of the binary file to the request message. Press the Run icon to send the request message to the CountryService. The response should indicate that a new Country record was created (Figure 4-23).

FIGURE 4-23. *Request to and Response from the CountryServie*

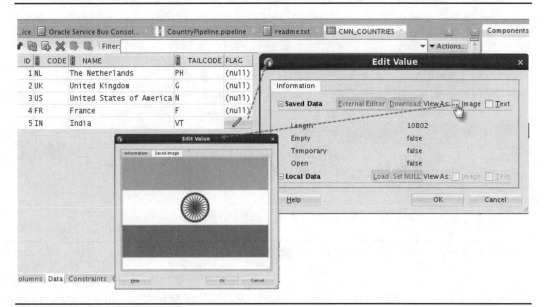

FIGURE 4-24.   *Inspecting the new Country record including the BLOB column with the flag contents*

In JDeveloper, in the Databases Window, when we open the connection to the Saibot Common database schema and list the tables, we can easily verify the data in the CMN_COUNTRIES table. This reveals that the test from SoapUI created the country record for India, including a value for the FLAG column of type BLOB (Figure 4-24). We can inspect the value of the BLOB column and display that value as an image, by checking the Image checkbox in the Edit Value window.

Invoke Stored Procedure

The simple SQL data manipulations and select operations can be quite powerful, but they are limited. Data manipulations access only a single table—unless that table actually is a multitable view with an instead of trigger to handle multitable manipulation from PL/SQL—and do not handle multiple records of different types. The select operation can return records multiple types—for example, nested master-detail structures, such as countries with all their airports. However, because we have to perform all data gathering in a single SQL statement, we still are somewhat limited in bringing in data from various tables.

One common way and even best practice to work around these limitations is through the use of stored procedures. The database adapter is equally good at invoking these database program units as it is as performing SQL. The DB Adapter also knows how to deal with stored functions or procedures that return a (ref) cursor; using a cursor is an elegant way of encapsulating the SQL required to gather data while still making the data available in an efficient manner. PL/SQL programs in an Oracle Database can use complex parameters, defined on top of Object and Collection definitions, that make it possible to transfer multilevel and heterogeneous record

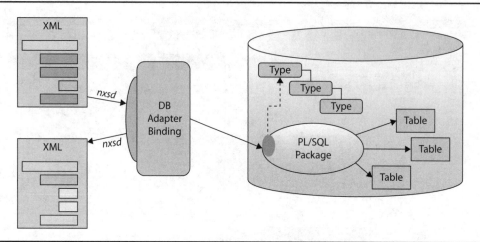

FIGURE 4-25. *The DB Adapter can easily expose complex PL/SQL program units and nested data structures*

structures—composed through simple or highly ingenious PL/SQL logic—in a single round trip, as Figure 4-25 visualizes.

The stored procedure can perform multiple queries and DML statements, against multiple tables, allowing for arbitrarily complex data manipulations. As a bonus, all database actions are encapsulated in the stored procedure; the only dependency between the database adapter and the Service Bus project using it on the one hand and the database on the other is the interface specification of the stored procedure.

In this section, we will use a PL/SQL package to take care of the database actions required for allocating one or more slots to an air carrier in the Saibot Future database with mid-term plans and forecasts. The *SlotService* is invoked to record and retrieve details about allocated slots as agreed in contracts between air carriers and Saibot Airport. This PL/SQL package provides the implementation for the *allocateSlots* operation in the *SlotService*. The response from that operation indicates for each slot if the registration of the allocation was successful.

Create Stored Procedure to Create Slot Allocations

The PL/SQL package FUT_FLIGHT_API contains procedure ALLOCATE_SLOTS. This procedure's interface has two parameters:

- Input: p_slots based on database type slot_tbl_t, defined as a table of slot_t
- Output: p_slot_allocations of type slot_allocation_tbl_t, a table of slot_allocation_t

These types are defined as objects—similar to XML elements or Java Classes—with DDL statements such as:

```
create or replace
type slot_t force
as object (
  aircarrier_code          varchar2(3)
, timeblock                timeunit_t
```

```
, arrival_or_departure      varchar2(1)
, aircraft_model_iata_code varchar2(3)
, aircraft_model_iaco_code varchar2(4)
)
```

where timeunit_t is a nested object type that itself references the collection type weekday_tbl_t (see Figure 4-26). Obviously, these types support the definition of complex, nested data structures. These types can be used as the data type for database columns, for column expressions in select statements and for PL/SQL variables. When used as the foundation for input and output parameter as is the case here, quite large and complex data packets can be transferred into and from PL/SQL procedures and functions. That fact, and the ability of the Database Adapter to work well with such parameters, make them very suitable for use in the interaction between the SOA Suite and the database.

The PL/SQL code in procedure ALLOCATE_SLOTS takes care of some simple validations, lookups and finally record creation in table FUT_SLOTS.

Prepare Application FlightFuture

Create a new JDeveloper application called *FlightFuture* of type Service Bus application with Service Bus project. Call the Service Bus project *SlotService*.

Create folders Adapter, Schemas, Transformations, and WSDLs in the *SlotService* project. Import the resources SlotService.wsdl, SlotService.xsd, common.xsd, and reference.xsd from the file SlotServiceInitialResources.jar.

Configure Database Adapter

Drag the Database Adapter to the lane with external reference. Configure a database adapter reference called *AllocateSlotsDB*, using the same IDE database connection as before, to the Saibot Common database, and using the same JNDI name eis/DB/SaibotCommonDB to use the same Database Adapter connection as before. Select Operation Type *Call a Stored Procedure or Function* in step 3 of the wizard.

Select procedure ALLOCATE_SLOTS in package FUT_SLOT_API in step 4 of the wizard, labeled Specify Stored Procedure (Figure 4-27).

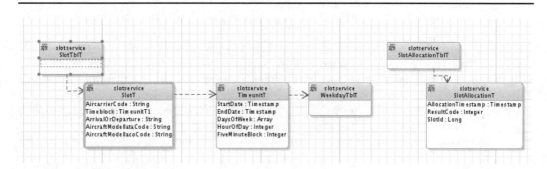

FIGURE 4-26. *Database types (Objects and Nested Table Collections) for Slot Allocation details*

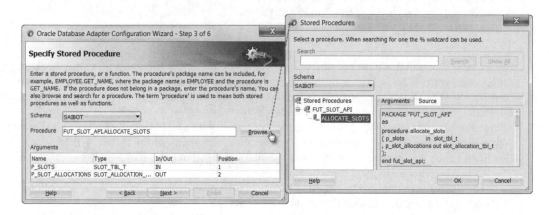

FIGURE 4-27. *Specify a stored procedure to have invoked by the DB Adapter*

The wizard inspects the signature of the procedure—deriving metadata about the parameters. Later on, it will generate an XSD document that represents the structure of the parameters. The ability to map these parameters defined in terms of database objects and collection to and from XML is an extremely powerful and frequently undervalued capability of the database adapter.

Accept all further defaults in the wizard and press Finish on the first opportunity. The adapter configuration files are generated, as is the business service *AllocateSlotsDB* that links to it.

If you feel like it, you can test the business service to verify if the configuration of the database adapter was successful; just right click on the business service in the overview editor and select the run option.

Implement Proxy and Pipeline

Generate the Proxy Service *SlotServicePS* from the context menu on the SlotService.wsdl document.

Also let the wizard generate the pipeline for this Proxy Service, called *SlotPipeline*. Set the Endpoint URI for the proxy service to /flight/SlotService.

In the overview editor for the *SlotService*, wire the pipeline to the business service *AllocateSlotsDB*.

Create the XSL Map transformation that maps from the *allocateSlotRequestMessage* to the *InputParameters* element generated for the database adapter binding (see Figure 4-28). Also create the mapping from the *OutputParameters* element defined in AllocateSlotDB_sp.xsd document to the *allocateSlotResponseMessage* to be returned by the Proxy Service.

Add Replace operations to the routing node in the *SlotPipeline* and have them operate on the $body on the way in and on the way out respectively (Figure 4-29 shows the latter).

This completes the implementation of pipeline *SlotPipeline*. Save all sources.

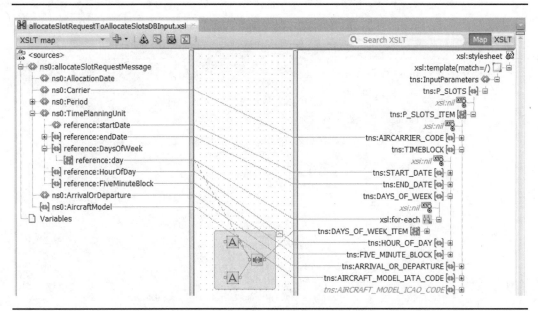

FIGURE 4-28. *Mapping the request message to the InputParameters element generated by the DB Adapter wizard based on the Objects and Nested Table definitions in the database*

Test the Allocation of Slots through the SlotService

The *SlotService* is now completely implemented and is ready for testing. Run the *SlotServicePS* proxy service. Provide the details for a slot allocation in the request message, including one or more weekdays and the IATA code for an air carrier (see Figure 4-30). Press Execute to invoke the *SlotService*.

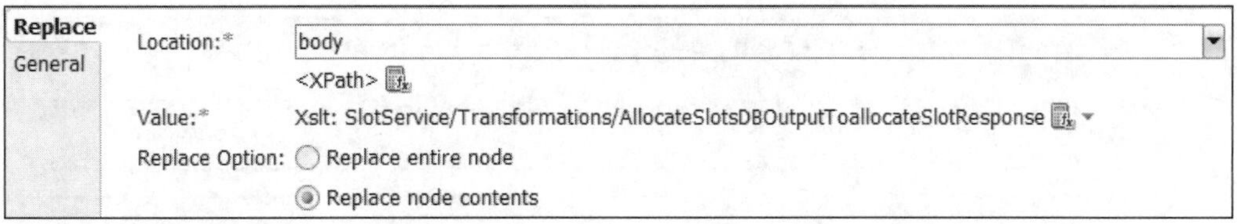

FIGURE 4-29. *Replace activity in the Response flow to transform the contents of $body based on the AllocateSlotsDBOutputToAllocationSlotResponse.xsl map*

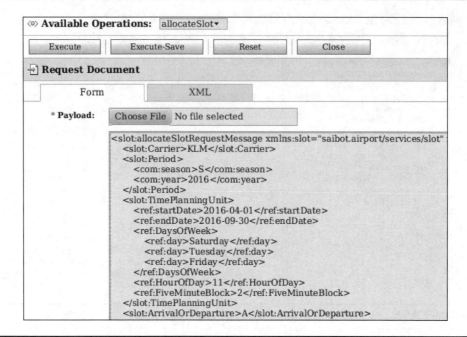

FIGURE 4-30. *Example of a Slot Allocation request message destined for the SlotService*

The response message will indicate if the registration of the slot allocation succeeded with a Result code (0 means success, > 0 indicates an error of some sort). In case of success, the identifier value for the registered slot is returned as well. Querying the FUT_SLOTS table will then produce the newly created SLOT record, as shown in Figure 4-31.

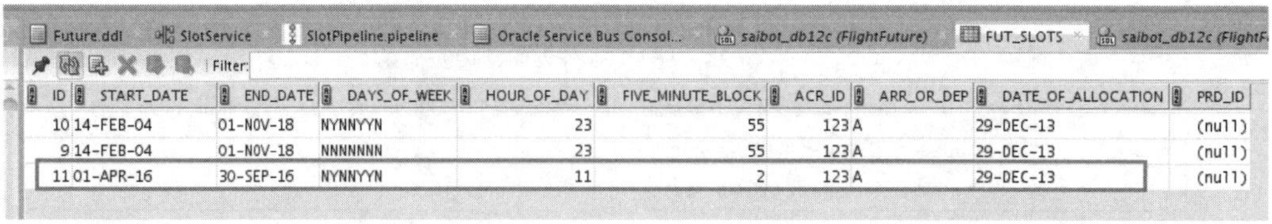

	ID	START_DATE	END_DATE	DAYS_OF_WEEK	HOUR_OF_DAY	FIVE_MINUTE_BLOCK	ACR_ID	ARR_OR_DEP	DATE_OF_ALLOCATION	PRD_ID
	10	14–FEB–04	01–NOV–18	NYNNYYN	23	55	123	A	29–DEC–13	(null)
	9	14–FEB–04	01–NOV–18	NNNNNNN	23	55	123	A	29–DEC–13	(null)
	11	01–APR–16	30–SEP–16	NYNNYYN	11	2	123	A	29–DEC–13	(null)

FIGURE 4-31. *New Slot record in FUT_SLOTS table, created by the SlotService through the PL/SQL Package*

Alternative Way: Invoking Database through REST

Database can be invoked in various ways from the SOA Suite, that not all involve the database adapter.

From the SOA Suite we can call out an intermediary component—such as an Enterprise Java Bean (EJB) or a JAX-WS or JAX-RS-based Java Web Service—that in turn interacts with databases. This database interaction could be implemented using JPA (e.g., with EclipseLink, TopLink, or Hibernate), Oracle ADF Business Components (ADF BC), or plain JDBC.

Another example is simple HTTP Requests from the SOA Suite directly to the HTTP port of an Oracle Database. Such calls are handled by stored PL/SQL units registered with the Embedded PL/SQL Gateway (the same mechanism that facilitates the Oracle APEX product). These calls cannot participate in a global transaction: they are a transaction of their own. This type of interaction does not require a Database Adapter connection or JDBC Data Source to be configured, or even the ability to establish a connection at all; the requests travel through firewalls and into clouds.

Using the dbms_epg package to create a Database Access Descriptor (DAD) and configuration of the path-alias and path-alias-procedure attributes for that DAD with a PL/SQL program unit that handles HTTP requests for specific URLs, we can construct a REST style service that can be invoked using typical REST URLs, such as http://DBhost:DB_HTTP_port/saibotapi/rest/flights/10-10-2016/flight/KL103/ to request the flight details for flight KL 103 on the 10th of October 2016.

We can implement a PL/SQL package that prepares flight information based on the parameters—date and flight number—passed through this type of URL, and returns that data constructed as a JSON message. A Service Bus business service can use the REST adapter to construct the URL to invoke this REST service and to retrieve the flight information from the database and convert from JSON to XML (or have the database return XML if that is more convenient).

Alternatively, we can use the ORDS (Oracle REST Data Services) product to expose REST services directly from the database.

File Adapter for Updating Files

One of the enterprise resources that can be integrated into the SOA Suite by a JCA Technology Adapter is the File System adapter. Through the File Adapter, Service Bus projects and SCA Composite applications can interact with a file system (that is accessible from the host of the SOA Suite run time) to read files and directories and write new or append to existing files. Additionally, the file adapter can be used in inbound or polling mode, where the adapter will trigger the execution of a service upon the detection of a new file. The File Adapter is also integrated with Oracle Data Integrator (ODI), where it is typically used to handle large batches.

The file contents handled by the file adapter can be both XML and non-XML data formats. When the file adapter is configured at design time, a mapping is created between the file format and a corresponding XML structure. This results in a Native XSD (NXSD) document that describes the XML structure to be used by the Service Bus (or SOA composite) for interacting with the file adapter. The NXSD document also provides instructions to the file adapter itself for converting the native file contents into XML and vice versa.

The FTP adapter has largely the same functionality as the file adapter, interacting with remote file systems through use of the File Transfer Protocol (FTP). For the transfer of large files to and from remote locations, the SOA Suite interacts with MFT (Managed File Transfer). MFT is a Fusion Middleware component to process (potentially very large) documents that can be passed to SOA, B2B, or Service Bus. It uses its own embedded FTP server to receive files onto before further processing and routing them. Its operations can be scheduled as batch jobs.

In this section, we will use the file adapter to write an event log file with all status changes and events with regard to the flights that are scheduled to arrive and depart from Saibot Airport. The file adapter is used in the implementation of the *FlightReportService* that exposes an operation for updating that flight event log with new flight information.

Initially, all flight events are written (or appended) to a single file. In a second iteration, the file adapter is instructed to write events to a flight specific file located in a date specific directory.

Prepare Service Bus Project for FlightReportService

Create a new JDeveloper application *FlightPresent* with a Service Bus project called *FlightReportService*. Create folders Schemas, WSDLs, and Transformations. Import the sources FlightReportService.wsdl, FlightReportService.xsd, and the canonical XSD documents common.xsd, reference.xsd, and flight.xsd from the file FlightReportServiceInitialResources.jar.

Create a new file—sampleFlightEventLog.txt—with some sample data in the intended format of the flight event log file that the file adapter is going to create. You can use any of a number of format styles, including COBOL Copybook, Binary, Fixed Position, JSON, XML, and delimited such as comma separated. For the flight event log file, we will use a CSV file format, with event entries composed like this:

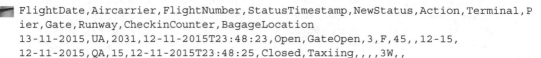

```
FlightDate,Aircarrier,FlightNumber,StatusTimestamp,NewStatus,Action,Terminal,P
ier,Gate,Runway,CheckinCounter,BagageLocation
13-11-2015,UA,2031,12-11-2015T23:48:23,Open,GateOpen,3,F,45,,12-15,
12-11-2015,QA,15,12-11-2015T23:48:25,Closed,Taxiing,,,,3W,,
```

Configure Outbound File Adapter

Open the editor for the FlightReportService project. Drag the File Adapter to the External References lane (see Figure 4-32).

The File Adapter configuration wizard opens. Set the name to *FlightEventLogFileWriter*. Press Next.

In step 2, choose Define [Interface] from operation and schema (specified later). In step 3 accept the default for the File Server JNDI Name (eis/FileAdapter).

In step 4, select the operation *Write File*. On this page (Figure 4-33) you see all other supported operations: Read File (polling, inbound), Synchronous Read File, List Files and Chunked Read (to process large files in chunks, only available from within a BPEL process). Set the operation name to *WriteFlightEventLogEntry*.

In step 5 (Figure 4-33), set the directory to be specified as a logical name. This means that the real [physical] directory name is not hard coded in the adapter configuration but instead will be provided via a property that is typically set at deployment time (as it depends on the target deployment environment which directory should be used).

Set the logical name to FLIGHT_EVENTLOG_DIRECTORY. Set the file name of the file to which the adapter will write messages to *flightEventLog.txt*. Check the check box *Append to File*.

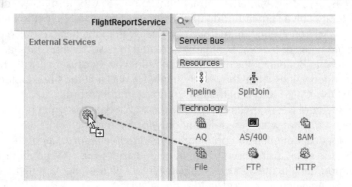

FIGURE 4-32. *Add outbound File Adapter to the FlightReportService Service Bus project*

This means that instead of creating a new file every time the adapter is executed, the file adapter will now add new messages to the end of the existing file. Only when the file adapter finds that the file specified does not yet exist, will it create the file.

The name of the file that is written to can be determined by dynamically using wild cards that either resolve to a unique sequential number (%SEQ%) or to a string based on the timestamp at the moment of writing (%yyyy% or %dd.mm.yyyy'T'HH:mm%). Examples of valid file names with wild cards are eventsFor%yyyy.mm.dd%.txt and uniqueLogFile%SEQ%.log). In this case, use the fixed file name flightEventLog.txt.

Press Next to go to the Messages definition page.

When you check the box "Native format translation is not required (Schema is Opaque)," the file adapter will not attempt to translate the contents read from or written to the file, from or to a native format. Instead, the contents are passed without interpretation as Base64 Encoded. This allows binary content such as image files or PDF documents to be read and written, without content parsing thereby increasing performance.

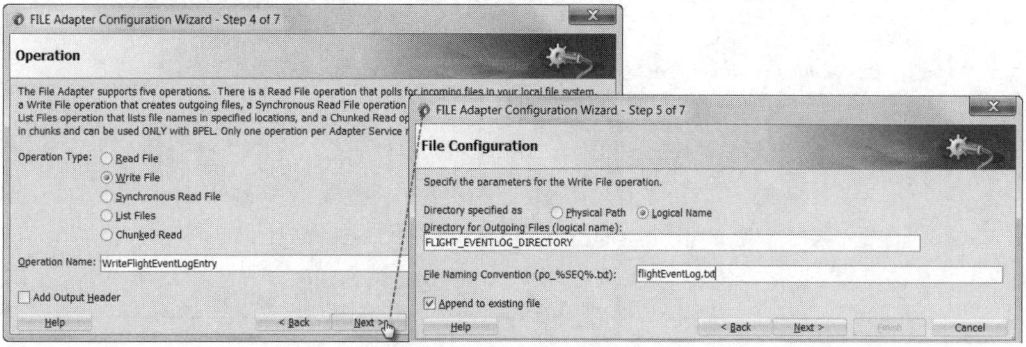

FIGURE 4-33. *Operations available with the File Adapter*

In this case, we do want native format translation—to CSV format—so click on the little gears icon to start the Native Format Builder that will help create an NXSD file that maps the native file format to an XML representation that we can deal with in the Service Bus pipeline.

Set the file name of the NXSD file to be created to nxsd_FlightEventLogFile.xsd in step one of the Native Format Builder. Select the Delimited file type, because we will create a file with comma delimited values. Note the variety in file formats that the file adapter can create for us, including JSON, XML, Fixed Length, and Complex (multi record).

In step 3 (Figure 4-34), specify the file with sample data that you created earlier. Accept all other settings—most of which are relevant only for file reading.

In step 4, accept the default configuration of *multiple records, all of the same type*. In step 5 you can provide some instructions for creating an easier-to-use XSD definition. Set the namespace to saibot.airport/data/flight/FlightEventLogFileWriter, the root element name to *FlightEventLog* and the record level element name to *FlightEventLogEntry*.

The delimiters to use to identify fields and records, and the rules for filtering records, are defined in step 6 (Figure 4-35). These rules can be quite complex when the native format is to be used for *reading* files (with not straightforward structures). In our case, we can accept all default settings that stipulate that fields are delimited by commas and that records are delimited by an EOL (end of line).

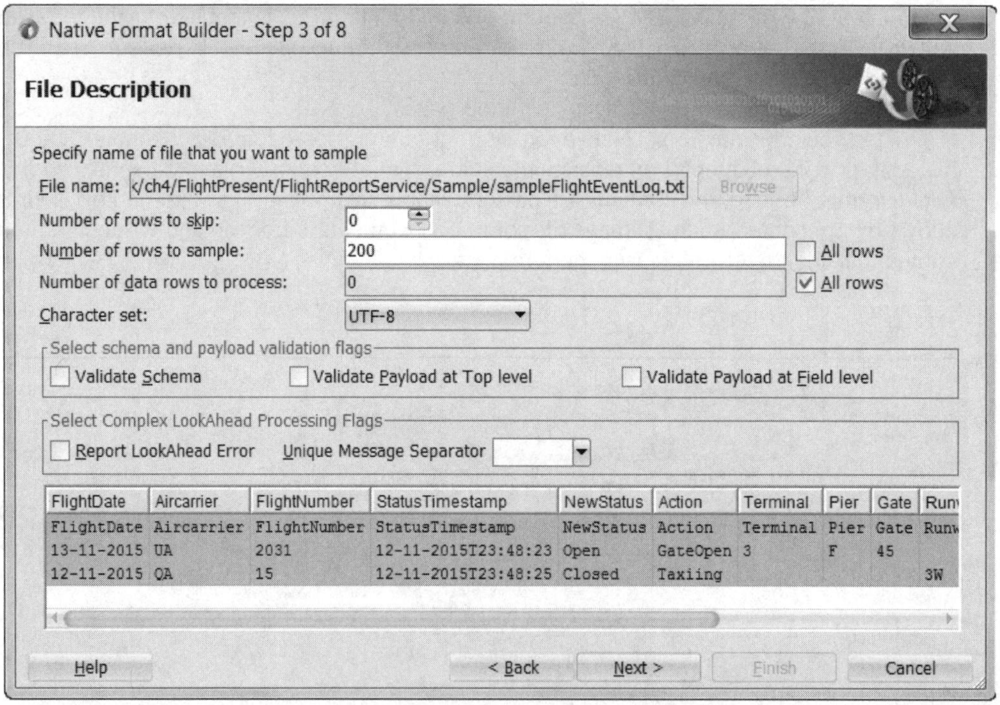

FIGURE 4-34. *Configuring the Native Format for the delimited file type*

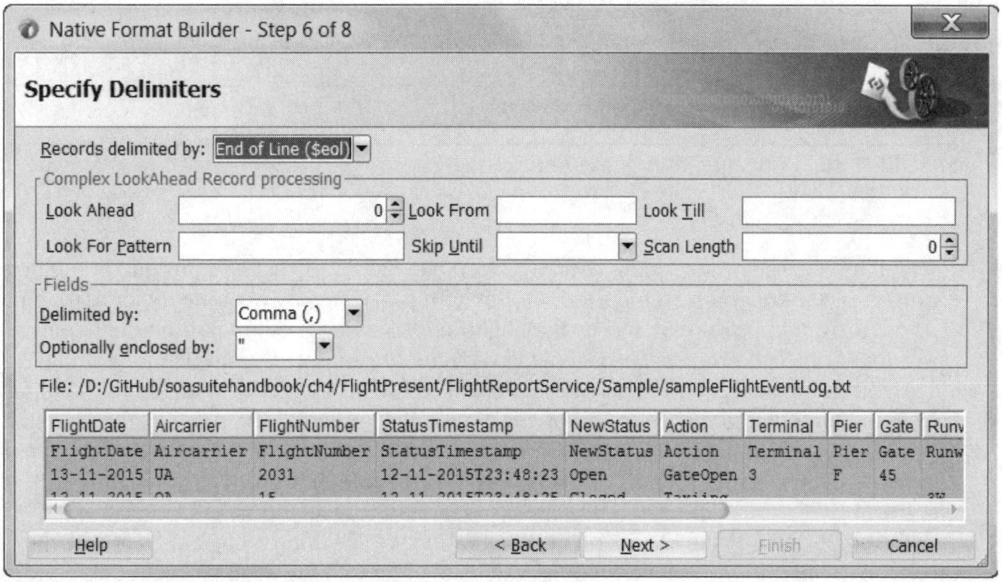

FIGURE 4-35. *Specify the delimiters to use to separate fields and records when writing the file*

In step 7, we can specify the names of the XML elements that the wizard will create in the NXSD file. In this case, we can derive the names from the field names in the first record (the header) in the sample data file.

In step 8, the wizard presents the NXSD source it is about to generate. You can inspect, modify, and accept or go back to previous wizard steps or cancel the wizard. Press Finish to complete the wizard and generate the NXSD file.

You are returned to step 6 of the File Adapter configuration wizard where the link is set to the *FlightEventLog* element in the generated NXSD document. Press Next. Then press Finish to complete the file adapter configuration and the associated business service.

Implement Proxy and Pipeline

Generate a proxy service *FlightReportServicePS* and associated pipeline *FlightReportPipeline* from the FlightReportService.wsdl document. Set the Endpoint URI for the proxy service to /flight/ FlightReportService. In the overview editor, wire the pipeline to the business service *FlightEventLogFileWriter*.

Create an XSL Map, for example, called reportFlightStatusUpdateRequestToNXSDFlightEventLog.xsl. In this map, transform from the *reportFlightStatusUpdateRequestMessage* to the *FlightEventLog* element that was generated in the NXSD definition.

Open the pipeline. Add a Replace activity to the request action in the routing activity. Configure the replace to transform the contents of the $body variable using the XSL Map to provide the NXSD formatted input for the request message sent to the business service and mapped onwards to a csv-style record entry in the log file.

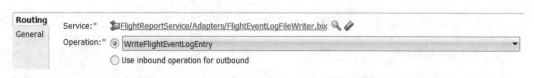

FIGURE 4-36. *Configuration of the Routing activity to the File Adapter Business Service*

Edit the Routing node: set the operation to *WriteFlightEventLogEntry* (instead of the default setting of *Use inbound operation for outbound*). This is necessary because the operation name *reportFlightStatusUpdate* exposed by the FlightReportService is different from the name of the operation *WriteFlightEventLogEntry* generated by the file adapter wizard (Figure 4-36).

At this point, the request message is received by the proxy service, handed to the pipeline and transformed into the format specified by the Native XSD schema. The pipeline routes to the business service that hands the XML document to the file adapter that converts it into the native comma separated values record. When it next tries to write the record to the flightEventLog.txt file, it will fail.

Remember how in the file adapter configuration we specified a Logical Name for the target directory, in order to prevent hard coded values to enter into the adapter configuration for settings that are environment specific. In Chapter 22, we will discuss environment specific deployment. For now, we will set the value for the FLIGHT_EVENTLOG_DIRECTORY property on the Transport Details tab of the business service editor for the *FlightEventLogFileWriter* (Figure 4-37). Set the property to a directory on the local file system of the runtime SOA Suite platform. Note: The directory—and its parents if necessary—will be created at run time by the file adapter, if it does not already exist. This requires that the operating system account, under which the SOA Suite runs, has the required privileges to do so.

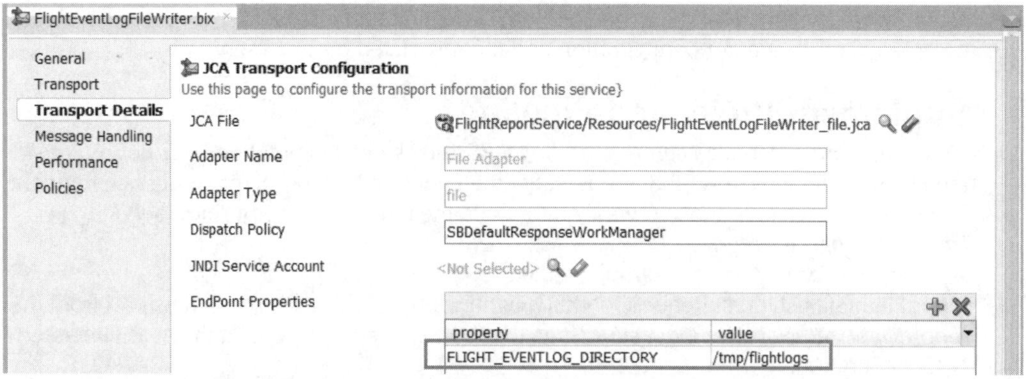

FIGURE 4-37. *Set the value for the logical directory property FLIGHT_EVENT_DIRECTORY on the Transport Details tab of the business service*

Test the FlightReportService

Run the *FlightReportServicePS* proxy. Select operation *reportFlightStatusUpdate* to invoke and provide some sensible data for the *reportFlightStatusUpdateRequestMessage*. Press the Execute button to invoke the service.

The response message is the raw output from the file adapter—because we did not yet implement any manipulation of the body variable in the response pipeline.

When you check the file system, you should find a file called flightEventLog.txt with the data from the *reportFlightStatusUpdateRequestMessage*. This file is located in the directory specified in the FLIGHT_EVENTLOG_DIRECTORY property; this directory is created by the file adapter if it did not already exist beforehand.

Enhance FlightReportService to Use Dynamic Directory and File Names

A single flight event log file soon will become unwieldy. It would be far more convenient to create separate log files per date and flight. We will change the configuration of the file adapter to achieve the following: flight event log files are created per flight per date. They are created in a directory that is dedicated to the date on which the flight was scheduled to take place, for example, 12-25 for Christmas Day. The log files will be called <Air Carrier><Flightnumber>FlightEventLog.txt.

Compose the Name for the Flight Event Log File

Add an Assign activity to the Request pipeline, before the Replace activity that manipulates the $body contents. Configure the activity to assign the name of the log file to write to. This name should be assigned to a local pipeline variable *flightEventLogFileName*. Use a concatenation of the month and day of the flight—with the XQuery functions fn:month-from-date and fn:day-from-date—followed by the / separator, followed by the air carrier code and the flight number, concluding with the string FlightEventLog.txt. Note that the first part of this value—anything leading up to the directory separator—determines the target directory within the directory specified using the FLIGHT_EVENTLOG_DIRECTORY property.

The complete XQuery expression is:

```
concat(fn:month-from-date($body/flig:reportFlightStatusUpdateRequestMess
age/flig:flightStatusEvent/flig:FlightDate),'-',fn:day-from-date($body/
flig:reportFlightStatusUpdateRequestMessage/flig:flightStatusEvent/
flig:FlightDate),'/',$body/flig:reportFlightStatusUpdateRequestMessage/
flig:flightStatusEvent/flig:Carrier,$body/flig:reportFlightStatusUpdateRequest
Message/flig:flightStatusEvent/flig:FlightNumber, 'FlightEventLog.txt')
```

Set Filename through Transport Header

Many JCA properties can be manipulated at run time. That means that within the pipeline, we can dynamically derive values that steer the behavior of the JCA adapter. One of these properties is jca.file.FileName that is interpreted by the File Adapter as the name of the file that should be processed.

JCA properties can be set in a Service Bus pipeline with the Transport Header activity. Add this activity to the request pipeline, under the Replace activity (Figure 4-38). Make sure that the Direction property on this activity is set to Outbound.

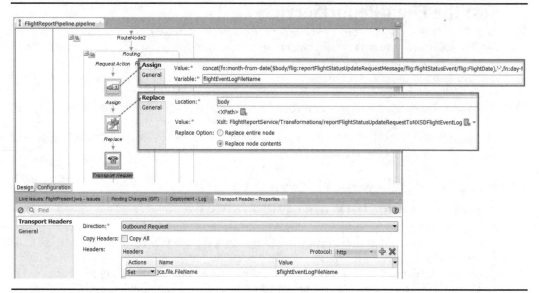

FIGURE 4-38. *Transport Header activity to set the name of the file to write to at run time*

Set the protocol dropdown in the Headers table to JCA. Click on the green plus icon to add a header. The action for this new entry should be Set. Click on the field in the Name column. A dropdown becomes available with a listing of all known outbound JCA properties. You can either select or simply type property name jca.file.FileName. The Value expression should be set to $flightEventLogFileName.

Run the Enhanced Service

With these changes, you can run and test the *FlightReportService*. However, with file names that are dynamically set, the file adapter does not create the target directories if they do not already exist. That means that you will have to create date specific directories inside the directory indicated by property FLIGHT_EVENTLOG_DIRECTORY for each day for which event log files will be generated.

TIP
The File Adapter may sometimes have to deal with files that require pre or post processing. For example, when files are compressed or encrypted or both, the mapping of native file content to an XML document can only be done when decompression and decryption have been performed after reading the file. Or in the outbound case the data mapped from XML to the native file format should be encrypted and/or compressed before the file can be written and perhaps a target directory has to be created. For such intermediate processing of file contents, the File Adapter has a feature called File Valves. With this feature, we can hook custom Java code into the processing pipeline of the File Adapter—to inspect and manipulate the data after having been read or just before being written.

Reading from the File System Using the File Adapter

The File Adapter can read files in two different modes. One is the inbound, polling mode where the adapter periodically inspects specific directories on the file system for new files and starts reading and processing them when they are found. The other is the synchronous read mode where the adapter is engaged to retrieve the contents from one or more files and deliver them to the invoker, which is typically a Service Bus business service or an SCA composite.

We will now use this second mode to read data from flight event log files created through the *FlightReportService* as discussed in the previous section. This file adapter configuration is integrated into the *FlightReportService* to provide all event information available on a certain flight to satisfy the need of the *getFlightReport* operation.

Configure File Adapter for Synchronous Read

The first step is the configuration of a second file adapter configuration in the *FlightReportService* project. Open the editor and drag the file adapter to the external references lane. In the file adapter configuration wizard, set the name to *FlightEventLogFileReader*. Accept the defaults in steps 2 and 3. In step 4, select operation type *Synchronous Read File*. This means that the file adapter will read the contents from an existing file, typically convert it to an XML representation and make it available to the invoker.

Set the operation name to *ReadFlightEventLogHistory*. Do not check the box to *read the file as an attachment*, because we want to use the file contents as the body of the response from the business service that wraps the file adapter configuration.

Specify the same logical directory name as previously mentioned in step 5, using the logical name FLIGHT_EVENTLOG_DIRECTORY. The logical name is exposed as a property on the business service's transport details tab. Ensure that the check box for deleting files after reading them is unchecked, as well as the option to archive the files. Both actions are primarily intended for use with the inbound polling mode of the file adapter. Note: If the checkbox is read only, you will have to set the corresponding property DeleteFile to false in the JCA file FlightEventLogFileReader_file.jca in the text editor in source mode.

Specify a random file name—for example, UNSPECIFIED—in step 6 of the wizard. We will dynamically determine the name of the file to read—because it depends on the flight for which the event history is requested.

The Native XSD nxsd_FlightEventLogFile.xsd that was created when we configured the file adapter to write the flight event log file can be reused in step 7. For reading the log file, the same mapping from comma separated values to XML can be reused. Select the *FlightEventLog* element in that XSD document, to instruct the file adapter on how to make the data from the log file available.

Note that in the NXSD definition, we can include special reading instructions for the file adapter to skip records from the source file or map records in different ways depending on conditions regarding the data in specific fields.

Complete the wizard.

Open the Transport Details tab for the business service *FlightEventLogFileReader* that has been created by the wizard. Set property FLIGHT_EVENTLOG_DIRECTORY to the appropriate value for your environment.

Implement Operational Branch for getFlightHistory

The interface of the *FlightReportService* defines a second operation, next to *reportFlightStatusUpdate*. The pipeline should therefore have an operational branch activity with branches for each of these operations. Open the *FlightReportPipeline* (Figure 4-39). Add the operational branch with branches for the operations *reportFlightStatusUpdate* and *getFlightReport*. Move the routing node previously implemented to implement the *reportFlightStatusUpdate*—to the appropriate branch. Add a new routing node to the branch for *getFlightReport*. Add a routing activity and configure it to invoke the *FlightEventLogFileReader* business service's *ReadFlightEventLogHistory* operation.

Add an assign activity in the request pipeline of the routing node. This derives the name of the file to read the requested flight event log entries from and assigns it to a new variable *flightEventLogFileName*. The file to read can be found in a flight date specific directory, named according to the <month number>-<day number> pattern. The request message sent to the getFlightReport operation contains a FlightDate element from which the directory name is derived. The filename itself is composed from the IATA code of the air carrier and the number of the flightboth elements in the request messagefollowed by the fixed string FlightEventLog.txt. The following XQuery expression is used in the assign activity to concatenate all pieces together:

```
concat(fn:month-from-date($body/flig:getFlightReportRequestMessage/
flig:FlightDate),'-',fn:day-from-date($body/flig:getFlightReportRequest
Message/flig:FlightDate),'/',$body/flig:getFlightReportRequestMessage/
flig:Carrier,$body/flig:getFlightReportRequestMessage/flig:FlightNumber,'Fligh
tEventLog.txt')
```

The name of the file to read, set by the assign activity in $flightEventLogFileName, should be passed to the file adapter as a transport header property. Add a transport header to the request pipeline, after the assign. With direction is Outbound Request, add a header for jca.file.FileName that takes its value from this variable, as shown in Figure 4-39.

To complete the pipeline, the response from the file adapter needs to be transformed into the proper format. To that end, create an XSL Map called nxsdFlightEventLogTogetFlightReportResponse.

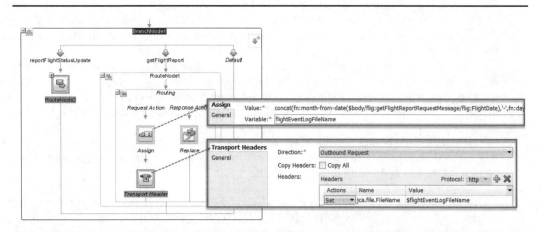

FIGURE 4-39. *Pipeline with Operational Branch and Routing activity for the getFlightReport operation*

xsl that maps from the *FlightEventLog* element in the Native XSD created for the file adapter to the *FlightReportResponseMessage* element in FlightService.xsd.

Add a replace activity to the response pipeline of the branch for *getFlightReport*. Have it replace the $body contents using the new XSL stylesheet acting on $body/*[1].

Run getFlightReport in FlightReportService

At this point we can run the FlightReportService and invoke the getFlightReport operation to retrieve all events regarding a specific flight.

If we provide a combination of flight date, air carrier code, and flight number for which earlier on flight events were reported, we will get an overview of such events in the response message. If no event log file exists for the flight indicated, the file adapter will not find the requested file and instead of a proper response message, the service will return a soap fault. We could add an error handler to the pipeline for that situation and if we were really developing the production systems for the good people of Saibot Airport in Lexville, then of course we would.

Remote File Adapter—Retrieving Data from Internet Resources

Data offered as internet resource in a structured XML or non-XML format (such as JSON, CSV, or fixed position)cannot be retrieved by the File Adapter, but it can be read by the Service Bus. Using a combination of an HTTP transport style Business Service, a Service Callout, and a Native XSD mapping, it turns out to be fairly easy to implement what is best described as a *remote file adapter*. This section describes the implementation of a *findCountries* operation that reads a comma separated values file with countries, accessed with a simple HTTP GET request to the website OurAirports.com.

The FTP adapter can be used to access remote files, if these are located on an FTP server. SOA Suite does not contain an out of the box WEBDAV adapter that could be used for a similar operation. One could be implemented as Custom JCA adapter.

Create Business Service to Retrieve File Contents

Open the *ReferenceDataServices* application and the *CountryService* project. Create a business service *OurAirportsCountriesBS*, with transport set to http.

On the second page of the wizard, pick the option Messaging with both Request and Response set to Text as the content type (Figure 4-40).

On the third page of the wizard, set the Endpoint URI for this business service to the URL at which the comma separated countries file can be accessed: http://www.ourairports.com/data/countries.csv.

Press Finish to close the wizard and complete the creation of the business service.

Create the Native XML Schema Definition

The SOA Suite has the capability to come up with an XML representation of data in all kinds for formats that are not XML. Native XML Schema Definitions—indicated with NXSD—are created that describe both the XML structure that best represents the native data format and provide mapping instructions on how to convert from the native format to that XML structure and vice

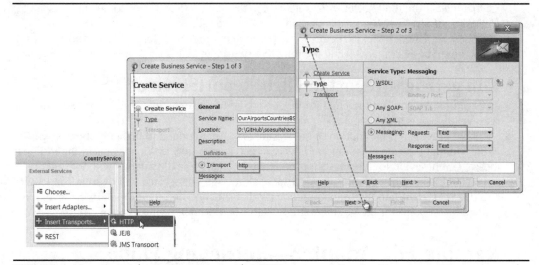

FIGURE 4-40. *Create business service with HTTP transport, Service Type set to Messaging and the content type as Text for request and response*

versa. This capability is used in various adapters, as we already have seen with the File Adapter and the REST Adapterand can be used in Service Pipelines as well.

In our current implementation, we need to convert the countries.csv file into an XML structure that we can filter for the countries that should be returned. To that end, first create a sample file of the data in the CSV file. You can do this by downloading the file to your local file system or creating a new file in the *CountryService* project, opening the countries.csv file and copying a few records to the new project file.

From the New Gallery, select General | XML | NXSD Schema. This will bring up the Native Format Builder Wizard that introspects a sample of the data in native format and with your guidance creates the native schema that represents it.

Create an NXSD schema for the sample file—in the same way as we created the NXSD schema for the sampleFlightEventLog.txt file.

Update Pipeline to Retrieve Remote Data into a Local XML Variable

Open the *CountryPipeline*. Add an operational branch to enable the pipeline to handle requests for different operations. Create a branch for operation *createCountry* and move the existing pipeline pair and route node to this branch. Add a branch in the operational branch for the *findCountries* operation. Add a pipeline pair to this new branch.

Add a service callout activity to the request pipeline (Figure 4-41). This type of activity is used in pipelines to help perform enrichment or validation prior to and after routing takes place. We use it here to take over from the routing node, to make the call that brings in the remote CVS document and loads it into a pipeline variable.

Configure the Service Callout to invoke the business service *OurAirportsCountriesBS*. Check the radio button marked *Configure Payload Document*. Set the *Body* field to body in the request

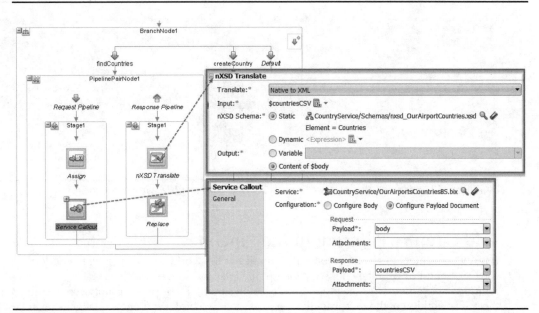

FIGURE 4-41. *Configuring the Service Call out to fetch the file returned from the remote website into the custom variable countriesCSV and the nXSD Translate to process the contents in $countriesCSV*

document indicating that the request should use the content of the $body variable as its payload (which is irrelevant since the callout does an HTTP GET request that carries no payload). Set the *Response Body* to *countriesCSV*. This means that the body from the response returned by this callout should be used to populate the custom pipeline variable *countriesCSV*. Subsequent activities in the pipeline can access the contents of this variable using the familiar $countriesCSV notation.

Add an NXSD Translation activity to the Response Pipeline. This activity is used in general to use a Native XSD to map data in native format into the corresponding XML representation, or vice versa. In this case, it maps the contents of the $countriesCSV variable as XML to the $body variable, using the Native XSD that was created earlier based on the sample countries file.

Configure the NXSD Translation as is shown in Figure 4-41: *Apply Translation* should be configured as *Native to XML*. The input is variable $countriesCSV, populated by the Service Callout. The NXSD Schema to use for this mapping is the *Countries* element in nxsd_OurAirportsCountries.xsd. The result of the translation should be set as the content of the $body variable.

The *CountryService* project is shown in Figure 4-42. The Service Callout has introduced a new wire from the pipeline to the business service *OurAirportsCountriesBS*.

At this point, you can test the CountryService's *findCountries* operation by running the *CountryService*. The search criteria you pass in the request message will be completely ignored and the response message will not be according to the service's interface definition, but you should get an XML representation of all countries provided by OurAirports.com.

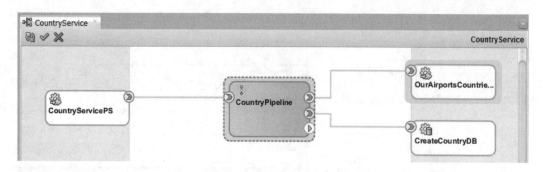

FIGURE 4-42. *Service Bus project CountryService with doubly wired pipeline*

Add Country Filtering to the Pipeline

It is not convenient to always receive *all* countries in the world when invoking the *findCountries* operation and it is definitely not what the service interface suggests with its *findCountriesRequestMessage* input. Besides, at this point the response is not even according to the XSD definition of the response message. Let's kill two birds with one stone by using an XSLT transformation to map the response into the right format and filter for only those countries that satisfy the search condition.

Create an XSL Map—nxsdOurAirportsCountriesTofindCountriesResponse.xsl—that maps from the Countries element in the Native XSD to the *findCountriesResponseMessage* in the CountryService.xsd. Define three parameters, simple without Schema reference, called *continent*, *countryName*, and *countryCode*, as shown in Figure 4-43.

Map the source to target as shown in Figure 4-44 using a for-each node as parent for the tns:Country element to which the *Country* element from the source is mapped. Map the code and name fields from the source to the their counterparts. Note the three source nodes available for mapping, created for the three input parameters. Then open the source mode tab to add the filter condition to the for-each node.

Add the following expression to the select attribute of the for-each node:

```
/ns0:Countries/ns0:Country[(($countryName='*') or starts-
with(ns0:name,$countryName)) and (($countryCode='*') or
starts-with(ns0:code,$countryCode)) and (($continent='*') or
(ns0:continent,$continent))]
```

This results in only countries whose name starts with the value passed in the $countryName parameter are returned, unless that parameter is set to the * wildcard. And only countries whose code starts with the value passed in the $countryCode parameter are returned, unless that parameter is set to the * wildcard. And finally, only those countries whose continent is set to the value in the $continent parameter are returned, unless that parameter is set to the * wildcard.

NOTE
When you have to resort to filter expressions like this, it may be a reason for considering the use of XQuery mapping, with its quite powerful FLOWR expressions.

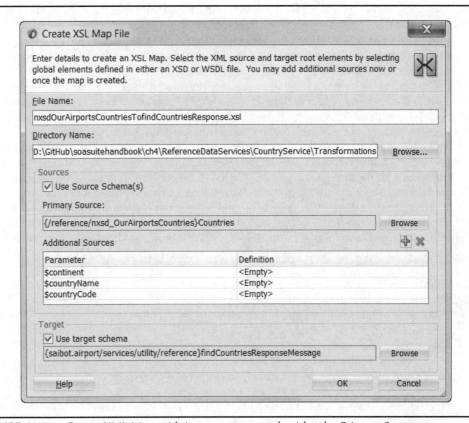

FIGURE 4-43. *Create XML Map with input parameters besides the Primary Source*

This mapping can be applied to the $countriesCSV variable—provided we have the values for the three parameters. These values are taken from the request message sent to the *findCountries* operation, so initially they can be found in the contents of the $body variable. We should save this initial message into a custom variable early on in the pipeline. If we do not, manipulation of

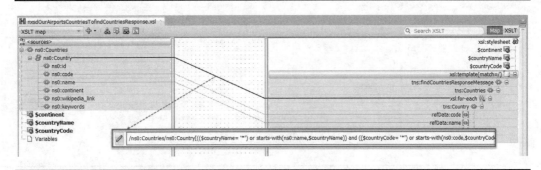

FIGURE 4-44. *Mapping the countries read from the remote countries file to the response format*

the $body variable—as is done by the NXSD Translation that writes its result to $body—would overwrite the data, before we get to the replace activity.

Add an Assign activity before the Service Callout. Configure the Assign action to use the *findCountriesRequestMessage* element in the $body variable to set the value of the custom variable *findCountriesRequest*.

At this point we have made all the necessary preparations and we can add the Replace activity in the response pipeline, right after the NXSD Translation. Configure the replace activity (Figure 4-45) with the location set to body, the XPath expression empty, and the replace option set to Replace node contents. Configure the Value using an XSLT Resource. Select the nxsdOurAirportsCountriesTofindCountriesResponse.xsl map we have just created as the resource to perform the transformation with. Set the Input Document Expression to $body/*[1]. Then also set the values for the three parameters, using XPath expressions to retrieve the relevant element value from the $findCountriesRequest variable: $findCountriesRequest/ref:continent/text(),$findCountriesRequest/ref:code/text() and $findCountriesRequest/ref:name/text().

This completes the *findCountries* branch in the *CountryPipeline*. You can now again test the *findCountries* operation in the *CountryService* and this time you should get a response in the proper XML format and containing only the countries you actually asked for.

NOTE
Retrieving the countries.csv file from the remote website can take fairly long. Additionally, the site may not always be available. And the data in the file is relatively stable. These are indications that we should consider the use of the Service Result cache for the OurAirportsCountriesBS business service. The result cache is a facility that keeps a local, in-memory (actually in Coherence grid) copy of the data returned by the business service. This copy can be used by the business services instead of the remote data, for as long as was specified as retention time. The Service Result Cache is discussed in more detail in Chapter 9.

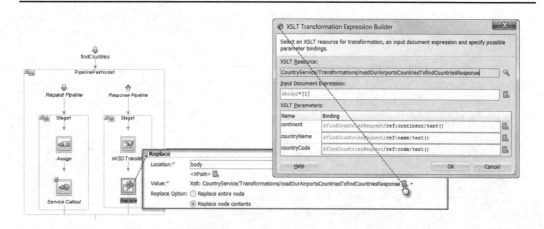

FIGURE 4-45. *Configure the Replace activity to transform and filter the country records*

Summary

It is quite common for services to rely on enterprise resources to provide (part of) their implementation. Such resources—like database, file system, queue, ERP system, SaaS application—are usually accessed in other ways and with other technologies than HTTP and SOAP or REST. Frequently they handle data in different formats than XML. The SOA Suite works with Technology Adapters to cross the gap between the world of the Service Bus (and SOA) composite and the enterprise resources. Through these adapters, service developers in SOA Suite can interact with these resources on familiar web service terms and have the adapter do the translation from these terms to whatever native format and protocol the resource uses.

In this chapter, we have seen how outbound interactions—initiated from within the Service Bus use the File Adapter and Database Adapter to access external files and interact with tables and stored procedures in a relational database. An important part of that interaction is the translation of messages from the native format utilized by the enterprise resource and XML used by the Service Bus. The Native Format Builder and the Native Transformations are important tools to work with native formats such as relational data, JSON, and CSV. The translation from and to native formats can be done as part of the adapter operation or as activity in a Service Bus pipeline.

Apart from the File Adapter and the Database Adapter, the SOA Suite also works with technology adapters for Advanced Queuing, MQ Series, JMS, FTP, Sockets, Coherence, LDAP, and User Messaging Service (UMS) for email, VoIP, fax, and text message. Additionally, Custom JCA adapters can be used from the SOA Suite. Most of these adapters will be discussed in later chapters.

Many adapters can be used in an inbound interaction. This means that an event outside the SOA Suite is detected by a technology adapter and results in a service initiation by the adapter, based on that event. Examples are the file polling mode in the File and FTP adapter, incoming messages on a queue received by the JMS and AQ adapter, incoming emails and chat messages intercepted by the UMS adapter and new or updated records detected by the polling Database adapter. Inbound actions are discussed in Chapter 13.

CHAPTER
5

Introducing SOA
Composite Applications

The Service Bus is typically used to virtualize service implementations: to expose an end point and perhaps a normalized interface for services that are implemented using a choice of technologies. The implementation of services can be realized outside the organization, inside the organization in legacy applications or platforms—exposed through technology adapters—or custom built using some programming language like Java (for example EJB or JAX-WS) or .NET technologies (e.g., Windows Communication Foundation or WCF and C#).

The SOA Suite offers another option for implementing services in the form of SOA composite applications, based on the SCA (Service Component Architecture) standard. These applications can leverage the service component engines in the SOA Suite—BPEL, Mediator, Business Rule, Human Task, Spring Java—to implement functionality, and they can easily integrate with external services and enterprise resources.

SOA composite applications expose a service interface. In many respects they are very similar to Service Bus composites. In this chapter, we will get started with these composite applications by implementing the ConversionService again. In Chapter 3, we did an implementation with the Service Bus, and this time we will use the SCA approach using the Mediator component to implement the same functionality. This should make it clear what the similarities are and where some differences lie between Service Bus projects and SOA composite applications.

We will add a composite sensor to achieve a little run-time monitoring support and we add validation and fault handling. The chapter concludes with the common pattern of publishing the SOA composite in the Service Bus, thereby virtualizing the service implementation.

Service Component Architecture

SCA is the industry standard Service Component Architecture for composing applications in a service oriented way. In SCA, all business resources—web services, Enterprise Information System (EIS) service assets, workflows, databases, and so on—are presented in a service-oriented way, with a service interface. SCA aims at separating business integration logic from implementation so that an integration developer can focus on assembling an integrated, composite application rather than on the implementation details. Specialists create the service components using, for example, BPEL, Java, or Business Rules or whichever component technology is best suited for the job. They then make these components available for wiring together and assembly into composite applications. These composites hide their implementation—they only expose their service interface and their dependencies. Deployment of the bundled composites is easier and more efficient than deployment of every individual component would be.

Even though SCA is an industry standard, it does not provide portability of composite applications between SCA containers. An SCA application that has been developed for the Oracle SOA Suite will not run on Apache Tuscany or IBM WebSphere. Applications running on those platforms will have a similar structure, using the same SCA artifacts, but leveraging platform-specific service engines and bindings. The portability of developers and administrators across different vendors' SCA containers is much enhanced, though, because of the common concepts.

Some Background on SCA

SCA is an industry standard that prescribes a structured approach for composing applications from service components. Service components are pieces of (potentially fairly coarse-grained) business logic that are used as building blocks when composite applications are assembled. The composite applications are the reusable functional units that provide meaningful business functionality, in the form of services.

The components, their assembly into composite applications, and their mutual dependencies and interaction within the composites are described in the SCA standard and defined by a series of XML files, created at design time and interpreted by the SCA container at run time. The core elements of an SCA composite are (also see Figure 5-1):

> Service—how the composite is exposed (interface, protocol binding)
>
> References—on what other services the composite depends
>
> Components—the internal components that provide the implementation of the service(s) (interface, binding and endpoint)
>
> Wires (how the service components hang together and how they relate to the externally service interfaces and service references

The composite.xml file is the file that describes the composite application as a whole—in terms of these elements. It is from this file that all other files are directly or indirectly referenced, and it is also this file that an SCA container—such as the SOA Suite—will interpret first at deployment time.

Service Components

Each service component is described in the composite.xml file. It has a name, an implementation— a combination of an implementation type that references a service component engine such as BPEL or mediator—and a reference to an implementation file or the program that should be executed by the engine. The component definition contains a componentType element that specifies the service(s) exposed by the component—through references to portTypes in WSDL documents or alternatively with references to Java interfaces.

However, a service component not only explains what it can do for the world; it also indicates what it needs the world to do in return. Every service component can specify one or more references. A reference is a dependency from within the component that needs to be satisfied. It is similar to the power plug that comes with electrical devices: the device promises to deliver a service, but only when you provide it with an electricity service. For Java developers, this mechanism of advertising a dependency and relying on it to be fulfilled in order to properly function is well known as "dependency injection," as performed by the Spring Bean Container or the JSF managed bean framework, for example.

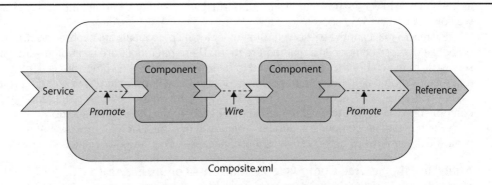

FIGURE 5-1.   *The core elements of an SCA composite application*

References are, like services, usually described in terms of a portType defined in WSDLs or a Java interface: The service component describes the interface it requires the injected service to implement in order to utilize it.

Additionally, a component can advertise the fact that it has properties that can be set by anyone who is including the component in a composite application or doing deployment, or even administering the composite at run time. A property has a name, type, and possibly a (default) value. Typically, the value of a property governs part of the behavior of the component.

Service Composites

Components cannot exist on their own—or at least not in the SCA run-time environment. They need to be part of a service composite (application) because that is the unit of deployment and invocation. Usually a composite will contain more than just a single component, but it does not have to.

Composites are described through the composite.xml file as per the SCA standard, which is rendered in JDeveloper in the visual composite editor. This composite.xml file includes entries for service components and the wires between these components.

A composite application usually exposes at least one service—a public interface for consumers of the composite. Note that a composite application could have as its only "interface" a component that consumes an event. In that case, there is no explicit public service interface that external consumers should invoke.

Multiple services containing multiple operations can be published by a single composite application. A public service exposed by a service composite application is a service published by one of the service components inside the composite that has been promoted to the composite level. Inbound adapter services are the special case in the SOA Suite—they provide entrance points into SOA composite applications, but frequently in a slightly indirect way that does not allow for direct invocation. Examples are the file system and database adapters that poll for new files or records and in response initiate a new composite instance with the new or modified data acting as the implicit request message. The JMS and AQ adapter do something similar with messages arriving on a topic or queue.

Components declare their dependencies through references. Some of these references are satisfied by other components within the composite. These references can therefore remain private, hidden from public view—an example of encapsulation. Compare this with a desktop computer that has a motherboard inside with a dependency on electricity—a fact that is not advertised externally because it can be satisfied internally with a wire (quite literally in this case) to the internal power adapter that itself is published as a reference through the power cord that we connect to the power socket.

References that cannot be resolved using other local components are exposed by the composite on behalf of those components that require them. These references are promoted—just like services—to the composite level and need to be satisfied when the composite is deployed. At that time, it should be indicated in the composite.xml how those references are to be resolved. Component-level references have to be wired to their provider—which is either another internal component or a composite-level reference that gets bound to an implementation.

Whether another component, another composite or some external provider fulfills the service is mostly determined by aspects such as reuse, encapsulation, and ownership.

Analyzing the Service Composite Definition—composite.xml

Next follows a simplified snippet from a composite.xml file that defines a service composite *ConversionService* that exposes a service called *ConversionService* that is exposed with a SOAP

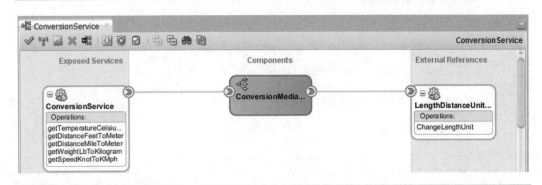

FIGURE 5-2. *The visualization of the ConversionService SCA composite*

Web Service binding according to the port and with the functional interface as specified in the associated WSDL and XSD documents.

The composite contains a single component, *ConversionMediator*, that implements the service interface we just discussed, described by the *ConversionServicePortType*. The component also exposes a reference—a need for some service injection—described by PortType *lengthUnitSoap*. From the implementation element, we derive that this component is to be executed by the mediator service component engine and that this engine should execute the *ConversionMediator* *.mplan* file.

The composite itself has a reference binding, which is component's reference promoted to the composite's level and satisfied with a binding (SOAP 1.1 Web Service) to the external *LengthDistanceUnitConvertorService*. This promotion is necessary in this case because there is no component available in the composite that can provide the service required by the *ConversionMediator*.

Figure 5-2 shows the visualization of this same service composite in the JDeveloper SOA composite editor.

```
<composite name="ConversionService" revision="1.0">

  <import namespace="saibot.airport/services/utility/conversion"
location="WSDLs/ConversionService.wsdl"
          importType="wsdl"/>
  <import namespace="http://www.webserviceX.NET/" location="WSDLs/length.asmx.
wsdl" importType="wsdl"/>
  <service name="ConversionService" >
    <interface.wsdl interface="saibot.airport/services/utility/
conversion#wsdl.interface(ConversionServicePortType)"/>
    <binding.ws port="saibot.airport/services/utility/conversion#wsdl.
endpoint(ConversionService/ConversionServicePort)">
    </binding.ws>
  </service>
  <property name="someRunTimeProperty" type="xs:string" many="false">some
value</property>

  <component name="ConversionMediator">
    <implementation.mediator src="Mediators/ConversionMediator.mplan"/>
```

```
      <componentType>
        <service name="ConversionMediator" >
          <interface.wsdl interface="saibot.airport/services/utility/
conversion#wsdl.interface(ConversionServicePortType)"/>
        </service>
        <reference name="LengthDistanceUnitConvertorService" >
          <interface.wsdl interface="http://www.webserviceX.NET/#wsdl.
interface(lengthUnitSoap)"/>
        </reference>
      </componentType>
  </component>
  <reference name="LengthDistanceUnitConvertorService" >
      <interface.wsdl interface="http://www.webserviceX.NET/#wsdl.interface(leng
thUnitSoap)"/>
      <binding.ws port="http://www.webserviceX.NET/#wsdl.endpoint(lengthUnit/
lengthUnitSoap)"
                    location=»WSDLs/length.asmx.wsdl» soapVersion=»1.1»>
</binding.ws>
  </reference>
  <wire>
      <source.uri>ConversionService</source.uri>
      <target.uri>ConversionMediator/ConversionMediator</target.uri>
  </wire>
  <wire>
      <source.uri>ConversionMediator/LengthDistanceUnitConvertorService</source.
uri>
      <target.uri>LengthDistanceUnitConvertorService</target.uri>
  </wire>
</composite>
```

The two wire elements at the end of this snippet describe the link between the service exposed by the composite and the service provided by the *ConversionMediator* on the one hand and the relation between the reference published by the mediator and the composite level reference. This instructs the SCA engine to channel message received at the *ConversionService* to the *ConversionMediator* and to send messages from the *ConversionMediator* to the reference configured to invoke the external *LengthDistanceUnitConvertorService*.

SCA Composites in Oracle SOA Suite

The SOA Suite contains two run-time service engines. One is the Service Bus engine that we first met in Chapter 3 and the other one is the SCA engine that processes SOA composite application definitions. SOA composite applications are developed in JDeveloper. They can make use of several SCA service component engines—BPEL, Mediator, Human Task, Business Rule, Spring Java—that the SCA run time knows how to invoke.

The actual work done in a composite application takes place in these engines, based on the respective component implementations created by, for example, BPEL, Business Rule, or Java developers. The published interfaces of both the services and references at composite as well as component level are defined in one or more WSDL files with associated XSD documents. These interfaces and contracts are typically created before the implementation for each component is created; this approach is sometimes referred to as "contract first" development. The interface or contract provides the context within which the developer will create the implementation.

SOA Suite developers are usually not very aware of the fact that they are working on SCA artifacts. Most of the SCA specific terminology and configuration files are hidden from view by visual editors in JDeveloper.

 NOTE
In the context of SOA Suite, it is common to use the term SOA composite [application] instead of SCA composite application—and we will use the former in the remainder of this book.

Compare SOA Composite with Service Bus Project

The core of the functionality offered by SOA composites is very close to what Service Bus provides. Both expose services, handle requests—frequently using call outs to other applications or third party services—and return responses. Some measure of XML validation and manipulation is involved and at run time some degree of fault handling and monitoring support is available. In fact, there are few things that Service Bus allows us to do that we cannot accomplish with an SOA composite (albeit not always in a very efficient or straightforward manner). Many of the things we can do in SOA composites can also be done with Service Bus, although there are areas that Service Bus does not touch; these include long running and stateful services (or processes). Asynchronous interactions can be dealt with to a certain extent by Service Bus, but not as smoothly as with the BPEL component in an SOA composite. The special engines for business rules and human interaction (per definition asynchronous and long running) available for SOA composites can also not be embedded in Service Bus composites, although the service they expose can be invoked from a Service Bus project.

Because any organization that has acquired the SOA Suite has full access to both SOA composites and Service Bus projects, they are at liberty to pick the best option for a challenge, based on the respective strengths of the two engines for that particular task.

Service Bus is typically positioned as the lean mean business machine: very good at doing very little, extremely fast, and scalable. It is best used for its core qualities:

- Receiving messages over a variety of transports as part of one way or synchronous two-way exchanges

- Performing validation, transformation, enrichment, and routing over multiple transports to external systems

- Processing responses through transformation, enrichment, and returning them to the calling party

The Service Bus is capable of thus processing high message volumes with short processing time per message. Additionally, the Service offers valuable run-time facilities for monitoring the message traffic and looming SLA violations, for applying security policies that govern access to services as well as message encryption/decryption, for dealing with peak volumes in message traffic, for load balancing outgoing requests and handling unavailability of external services and for transparently engaging a local cache for efficiently reproducing service responses without having to call the external system all the time.

The implementation of the functionality of a service, especially when it is getting more elaborate, is not ideally developed inside the Service Bus composite. It is preferable to create the implementation in a different component—which could be a SOA composite—and engage that component from the Service Bus. A best practice has arisen among SOA Suite developers to have only lean Service Bus projects that can benefit from the core strengths of the Service Bus for message processing and for run-time operations and have these composites route to the actual implementation of the service.

It is also common to expose all services through the Service Bus and not access service implementations directly—or at least not allow such direct interactions across domains. Under that guideline, all SOA composites would be registered on and exposed by the Service Bus and only ever accessed through the Service Bus. In that way, all run-time goodies in the Service Bus are applicable to requests to the SOA composite. Additionally, consumers are insulated from changes in the implementation, including one so dramatic as a migration from an SOA composite to a standard application to provide the service functionality, because the Service Bus can still offer the same contract but routes to a different implementation.

Your first composite application

In this section, we will create a SOA composite application. Such an application is created in a JDeveloper project. This project can be deployed to a SOA Suite run-time environment, either into the Integrated WebLogic Server or into a remote, stand-alone server. The service interfaces declared by the composite are exposed as service endpoints by the run time once the application has been deployed. In this case, the composite application will implement the temperature conversion in the *ConversionService*.

Prepare the JDeveloper Project

To get started, create a new JDeveloper application. Pick the application template *SOA Application*. Call the application *ConversionServices*. The application wizard will prompt you for the creation of an SOA Suite project. Call the project *ConversionService*. On the page *Configure SOA Settings* (see Figure 5-3), select the option *Composite with Mediator*. Press Finish to create the application, the project, and the mediator component.

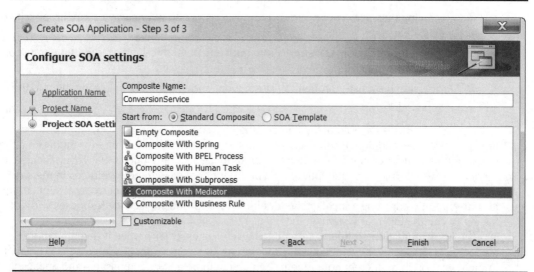

FIGURE 5-3. *Create SOA composite application with a Mediator component inside*

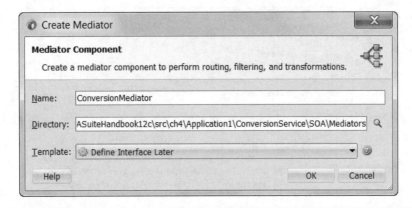

FIGURE 5-4. *Quick configuration of the ConversionMediator component*

A wizard opens (Figure 5-4) to have you configure the Mediator component that gets created. Set its name to *ConversionMediator* and accept the default template *Define Interface Later*.

Press OK to create the Mediator.

The composite editor opens for the *ConversionService* composite, as shown in Figure 5-5. It visualizes the current structure of the SCA composite, that is specified through the file composite.xml. Note: The application navigator lists this file as *ConversionService*. Also note that in the project some predefined folders have been created, such as WSDLs, Transformations, and Schemas.

From the *ConversionService* project from Chapter 3, copy the XSD files common.xsd and ConversionService.xsd to the Schemas directory, the XSL files to the Transformations directory and the ConversionService.wsdl file to the WSDLs directory. Figure 5-6 shows what the project contents should now be.

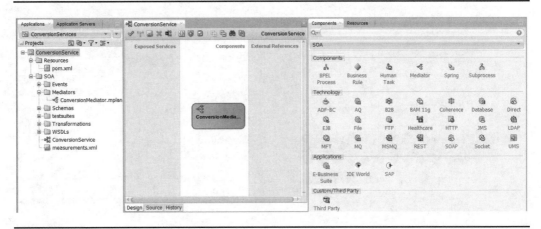

FIGURE 5-5. *Overview of the JDeveloper IDE after the initial configuration of the SOA composite application*

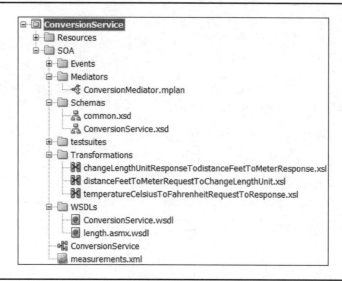

FIGURE 5-6. *Project navigator after copying the relevant files to the ConversionService project*

The project contains both the original service interface used for the Service Bus implementation, as well as the XSL Maps that were created for that implementation. We will be reusing these transformations in the SOA composite, from the Mediator component.

Configure the Service Binding

Right click in the Exposed Services lane. Select the option Insert | SOAP Service, to indicate that this composite should expose a SOAP web service. In the dialog that pops up (Figure 5-7), set the

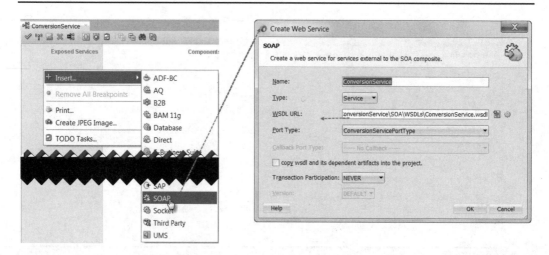

FIGURE 5-7. *Configure the ConversionService SOAP Web Service interface exposed by the SOA composite*

name of the service to expose to *ConversionService*. Select the ConversionService.wsdl file that was copied into the WSDLs directory from the Service Bus implementation for the WSDL URL field. The ConversionServicePortType will automatically be set. Press the OK button to create the service binding.

The composite overview will display the *ConversionService* SOAP binding that the composite now exposes to external consumers. However, the service binding is not yet wired to any service component to provide the implementation.

The *ConversionMediator* will have to be the component implementing this *ConversionService*. Wire the service binding to the Mediator to establish that fact, as shown in Figure 5-8.

Configure the ConversionMediator

At this point, the file composite.xml contains the wire definition that instructs the SOA Suite engine to pass any request messages received on the *ConversionService* SOAP binding to the *ConversionMediator*. At this moment, the Mediator has no clue as to what to do with such requests.

The mediator component is similar to the pipeline in Service Bus: it performs the core VETRO operations, typically routing transformed messages to the component delivering the actual functionality for a service operation. The mediator does not have the same rich support for error handling, message manipulation, use of variables, looping, and call out found in the pipeline. It is simple, straightforward and has some advanced features such as integration with Schematron for complex validation of messages, content based filtering, parallel routing, message resequencing, and hooks for Java Callouts to perform custom operations on messages before or after processing. The Mediator is configured with routing rules: instructions that specify for a specific service operation how an incoming message should be processed in terms of validation, transformation, and routing. The transformation can be implemented with both XSLT (XSL Map), XQuery of direct value assignments, and can leverage Domain Value Maps (DVM) and Cross References (XREFs) through advanced XPath functions.

Double click on the Mediator component. The editor opens and displays stubs for the creation of routing rules for each of the five operations specified in the ConversionService contract. Messages arriving at the SOAP endpoint for this SOA composite application are handed to this

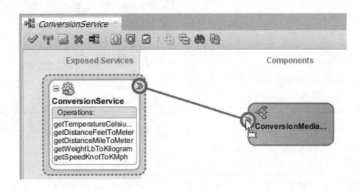

FIGURE 5-8.   *Wiring the ConversionMediator to the ConversionService—to specify that the former provides the implementation of the latter*

mediator. The mediator determines the required operation—from the SOAP action specified in the request message—and executes the routing rule(s) set up for that operation. For each routing rule, we can specify a boolean filter condition; only when the expression—that typically inspects the contents of the request message (content-based routing) —evaluates to true, is the routing rule executed. Note that multiple routing rules can be executed for an operation, resulting in the sequential or even parallel delivery of messages to multiple destinations.

Click on the green plus icon for the operation getTemperatureCelsiusToFahrenheit that we want to create routing rule for. This brings up a dialog—as shown in Figure 5-9—in which we can select the target type for the routing rule. The mediator can invoke an existing service or generate a new SCA reference to invoke, or it can publish an event to the Event Delivery Network when the rule is executed (see Chapter 15 for more on events) or it can simply Echo the request—after doing a transformation—back to the caller. In a Service Bus pipeline, when no Routing activity is executed, we also effectively do an echo of the request message—potentially after transformation.

Select the Echo Reply Target Type and click on OK.

The routing rule is created. No filter expression is required, nor do we need Schematron-based validation, transformation to native format or assignment of values to header variables. All we need is a simple transformation of the request message, using the XSL Map created in Chapter 3 for the *TemperatureConversionService*. Click on the icon behind the field labeled Transform Using. Select the temperatueCelsiusToFahrenheitRequestToResponse.xsl file in the Transformations folder, as shown in Figure 5-10.

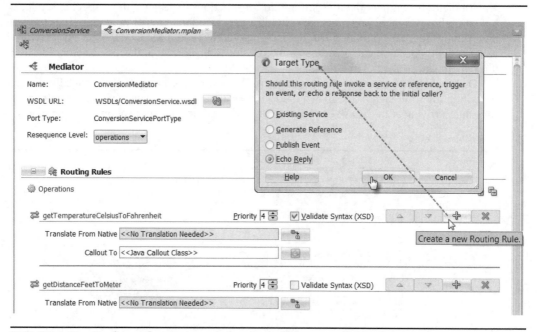

FIGURE 5-9. *Configure the routing rule for the getTemperaturCelsiusToFahrenheit operation to be of type Echo Reply*

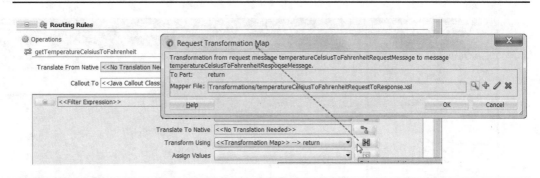

FIGURE 5-10.   *Configure the transformation for the routing rule, using an XSL Map*

This map performs the Celsius to Fahrenheit conversion and creates the required response message format.

The mediator has similar support for mapping to and from native data formats as has the Service Bus pipeline through the NXSD Translation activity. Some selected section of the content of the request message that contains data in some special format such as CSV or JSON can be mapped to XML using an NXSD map—as is specified in the Translate from (or to) Native field in the operation. This XML is then taken as the input for the transformation configured in the routing rule. Similarly, a routing rule can be configured to produce a native output format that is routed to a target service or echoed back to the invoker.

Save all changes and close the mediator editor.

Deploy the SOA Composite and Test the Temperature Conversion

Right click the *ConversionService* project node and select the option Deploy. This deploys the SOA composite *ConversionService* to the SOA domain on the Integrated WebLogic Server. Note that the logging for the SOA build action, shown in the console, rightly displays warning messages, indicating that the mediator does not contain routing rules for four of the five operations in the *ConversionService* interface. Ignore these warnings—we will simply not invoke those operations.

When the deployment is complete, login to the Enterprise Manager FMW Control as user *weblogic*. Open the node SOA | soa-infra | default to see the SOA Composites that have been deployed to the default partition on the integrated server's SOA domain. The *ConversionService* composite should be listed, as shown in Figure 5-11.

Click on the node for the *ConversionService*. Then click on the Test button that appears in the *ConversionService* detail page.

A simple web service testing page opens (see Figure 5-12), similar to the Proxy Service tester used for the Service Bus. Select the operation *getTemperatureCelsiusToFahrenheit*—the only one currently implemented by the mediator. Enter a value for the temperature in Celsius and press the button Test Web Service.

FIGURE 5-11. *Enterprise Manager Fusion Middleware Control with the freshly deployed ConversionService composite*

FIGURE 5-12. *Page in EM FMW Control to test the web service exposed by the SOA composite ConversionService*

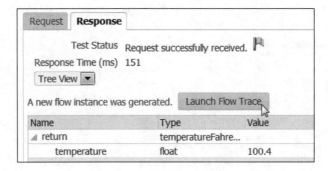

FIGURE 5-13. *The response to the test call to the web service*

After a short while, the response from the web service should be displayed, with the Fahrenheit equivalent of the Celsius temperature—as shown in Figure 5-13.

The first time you invoke the service, the response may take a little time because of various initializations going on. Perform the test again and you will probably experience a much faster reaction. You may also want to try out the other operations that are currently not yet implemented by a routing rule in the mediator, to see what will happen.

Detailed Execution Trace

The SOA Suite records and makes available quite a bit of detail about the execution of composite applications. This information can be very useful during development as well as for monitoring purposes in a production environment. Note that this information comes at the cost of performance overhead as well as potentially large storage requirements. The Audit Level settings govern how much trace details are recorded, and these should be set with some care in your production environment.

Click on the Launch Flow Trace button to get details about the internals of the execution that took place when the *ConversionService* SOA composite was invoked, as shown in Figure 5-14.

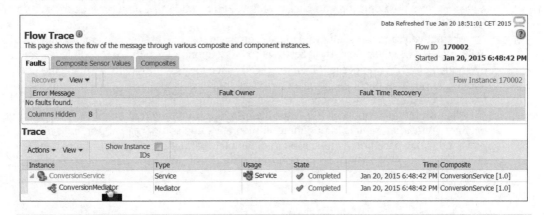

FIGURE 5-14. *The message flow trace through the SOA composite for the test call to the ConversionService*

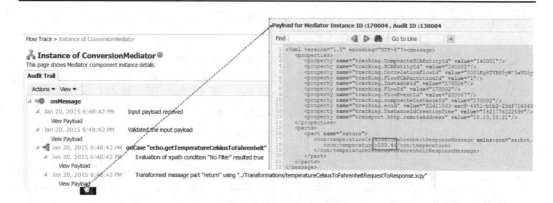

FIGURE 5-15. *Details on the ConversionMediator execution for the ConversionService composite*

Clicking on the *ConversionMediator* link will reveal additional details about the actions taken by the mediator in this particular instance or execution of the *ConversionService* composite, as shown in Figure 5-15.

We can even check the message payload at each step of the execution of the mediator—both before and after transformation for example.

Configuring the Audit Level

The level of detail of the trace information recorded and retained for instances of SOA composite applications is configurable at run time. Three Audit Levels are available: Development (full record of payload and instance trace), Production (complete instance trace but no payload details), and Off. To set the Audit Level globally, select the soa-infra node and from the context menu click on SOA Administration | Common Properties (see Figure 5-16).

Alternatively, and especially valuable to administrators of a production environment that will typically have the global Audit Level set to Production or even Off, the audit level can be overridden per SOA composite. Open the details page for a composite by selecting the node for the composite in the target navigation tree, as shown in Figure 5-17. Click on Settings. The first option in the drop-down menu allows setting the audit level for the composite.

All audit information for SOA composite instances is captured in the SOA Suite run-time database infrastructure. It is important to implement some sort of regular purging scheme to prevent this database from getting too large. Simple, manual purging of instances can be done through the EM FMW Control console. More details in Chapter 23.

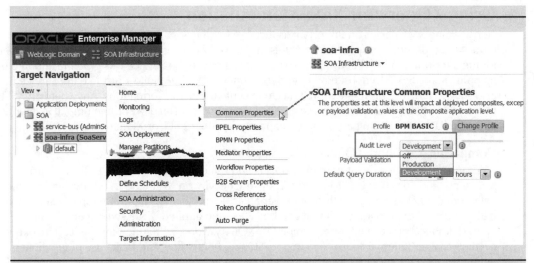

FIGURE 5-16. *Configuring the system wide auditing settings through the EM FMW Control*

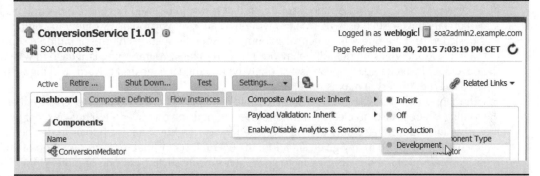

FIGURE 5-17. *Define the audit level setting for the ConversionService composite (overriding the system wide setting)*

Extending the Initial SOA Composite Application

We have seen a complete iteration for the *ConversionService* composite application—from development through deployment and runtime execution. In this section, this application is extended—as is our understanding of SOA composite application development. Until this point, we have only used XSLT for transformation of XML data. XQuery is introduced as an alternative. Validation of request messages in the Mediator comes up next, either using the XSD Schema Definition or using the more advanced Schematron definitions. Fault handling in SOA composites is introduced—to deal with validation errors. And finally, to aid our run-time understanding of the instances of the SOA composite application, Composite Sensors are used to add metadata to these instances.

Using XQuery for XML Manipulation

Transforming XML data is an important aspect of what the SOA Suite does when it handles requests and produces responses. Until this point, we have used XSL Mapping (XSLT stylesheets) for the transformation of the XML, in the replace actions in the Service Bus pipeline and in the mapping in the SOA Composite mediator component. The SOA Suite—just like the Service Bus—also supports the use of XQuery functions to execute these transformations. Anywhere an XSLT resource can be engaged, we can use an XQuery resource instead. At design time, JDeveloper offers similar visual tooling for creating mappings in either XSLT or XQuery.

Comparing XSLT and XQuery

XSLT and XQuery are similar in many respects and quite different in some. Both work from an XML input and construct an XML result. They rely heavily on XPath 2.0 to retrieve and manipulate data from the XML sources. Both support variables, looping and if-then-else logic. XSLT works with templates as a program unit that can be called and applied. XSLT stylesheets can import other stylesheets and use imported templates. XQuery works with functions that can invoke each other. An XQuery resource can import XQuery library files and make use of functions defined in such library modules. Recursion is supported in both XQuery and XSLT—and used frequently enough.

XSLT seems best suited for transforming a single source XML document in its entirety, the default approach of its built-in tree walking engine. XSLT is not a strongly typed language, because its origin lies in text processing. Based on the assumption that it would be used to generate documents in a markup language—such as XML, XSLT is written as an XML vocabulary. XQuery in contrast was designed to run a query in which you zoom into specific sections of one or multiple source documents. XQuery has no default behavior; it is more like a programming language in which the developer is in charge. XQuery is a strongly typed language, geared toward working with typed data. The XQuery syntax is not XML.

The support for XQuery and XSLT in SOA Suite is on par—there is no preference for either in the tooling. There is also no clear performance benefit of using one over the other—except when the streaming support in XQuery can be leveraged in Service Bus. So it is up to us to decide which of the two to use in any given situation. In general it seems that for transformation of entire messages, using XSLT is the easiest way to go. When specific sections of one or more XML sources are to be processed, inspected, or validated, XQuery probably offers more freedom to the developer to achieve the desired results. Additionally, XQuery expressions can readily be used in SOA Suite applications for simple evaluations or assignments.

Create the XQuery Transformation for the Celsius to Fahrenheit Conversion

We will now explore how a simple XQuery transformation can be created and integrated in the SOA composite application to do the temperature conversion. Open the context menu for the Transformations folder and click on New | XQuery File ver 1.0 to create a new XQuery. The dialog window shown in Figure 5-18 opens, in which we have to specify the details for the XQuery file.

Set the name to temperatureCelsiusToFahrenheitRequestToResponse.xqy. Check the box to generate a function. Specify the name of the function as *temperatureCelsiusToFahrenheitRequestToResponse*. Accept the defaults for namespace URI and prefix. An XQuery function can take from zero to many input parameters. Frequently it will have a single input parameter: the source document that is to be processed into some form of output.

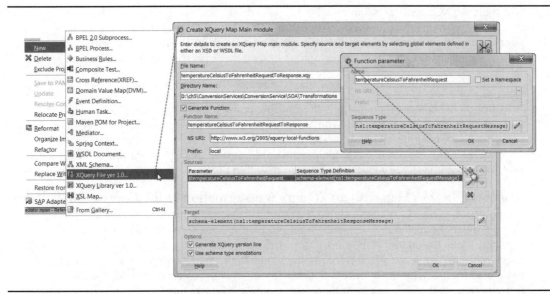

FIGURE 5-18. *Create the XQuery Map to transform from XSD type temperatureCelsiusToFahrenheitRequestMessage to temperatureCelsiusToFahrenheitResponseMessage*

Add an input parameter called *temperatureCelsiusToFahrenheitRequest*, based on the XSD type *temperatureCelsiusToFahrenheitRequestMessage*.

Set the type of the target—the outcome of the function—to the XSD type *temperatureCelsiusToFahrenheitResponseMessage*. Press OK to complete the setup of the XQuery Map Main module. JDeveloper will now create the xqy file and open the editor.

The mapping editor for XQuery is very similar to the mapper for XSLT, see Figure 5-19. The sources that were specified for the XQuery function are shown on the left. The target element's structure is presented on the right. Through simple drag (from source) and drop (on target), we can create a straightforward mapping of sources values into the target XML structure. Drag the source temperature element to the target element. Then, click on the created line. The properties editor

FIGURE 5-19. *Creating the XQuery mapping that converts the temperature*

will show the XQuery expression that the drag and drop operation produced— fn:data($temperat ureCelsiusToFahrenheitRequest/con:temperature). This expression will simply copy the temperature value from the source. That is not good enough, as we have to actually convert the temperature from the Celsius scale to Fahrenheit. Edit the expression in the property editor to:

```
fn:data($temperatureCelsiusToFahrenheitRequest/con:temperature) * (9 div 5) + 32
```

Click on the commit icon to apply this change to the XQuery source.

Note that you can go straight to the XQuery Source view to directly edit the source instead of using the visual mapping tool and property editor.

Save the XQuery source. Note: Unlike the XSLT Mapper, this editor unfortunately does not offer the option to test the XQuery function from within the IDE.

Replacing the XSL Map with an XQuery Transformation in the ConversionMediator

We now have two ways of transforming the request message for the temperature conversion. The routing rule in the mediator is currently set up to use the XSLT stylesheet for mapping the request message. Open the editor for the *ConversionMediator*. Click on the mapping icon for the routing rule for the *getTemperatureCelsiusToFahrenheit* operation. A dialog appears where the mapper file to be used for the Request Transformation can be set, as Figure 5-20 demonstrates. Click on the browse icon, set the File Type to XQuery Files (*.xqy) and select the temperatureCelsiusToFahrenheitRequestToResponse.xqy file that contains the XQuery function to perform the transformation.

Unlike an XSL map, that simply takes the entire request document as its input, we have to explicitly configure the values used for the input parameters of the XQuery function. Click on the row for *temperatureCelsiusToFahrenheitRequest* in the table with External Variables. Click on the edit icon. Derive the value for this parameter from an expression and set the expression to $in.in/ conversion:temperatureCelsiusToFahrenheitRequestMessage.

Click on OK to close the Request Transformation Map dialog. The routing rule has now been updated to engage the XQuery transformation to process the request message.

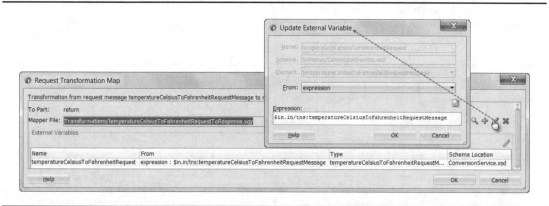

FIGURE 5-20. *Configure (how) to use the XQuery transformation for transforming the Celsius temperature request message*

Deploy and Test the ConversionService with XQuery Inside

Deploy the ConversionService project to the Integrated WLS. Then test the web service from the Enterprise Manager FWM Control, using the HTTP Analyzer in JDeveloper or with an external tool such as SoapUI.

Obviously, you will not notice any change in the way the service is invoked or in the response. Only when you check the detailed flow trace will you notice that the Mediator did not do the XSL transformation but an XQuery manipulation instead did the honors.

Validation of Request Messages

The mediator supports two types of message validation. One is the straightforward validation of incoming messages against the XSD—similar to what the Validate action in a Service Bus pipeline does. The second type of validation is support for Schematron. These two options are shown in Figure 5-21, in the Mediator editor. Schematron is a validation language in which rules are specified that the contents of an XML document should comply with. These rules are expressed in XPath expressions that are used to inspect the existence or absence, number of occurrences, and values of XML elements and attributes. Schematron goes beyond XSD validation because of its ability to apply rules conditionally or work with rules that refer to multiple elements.

When validation is enabled for a particular routing rule, every request message arriving at the mediator and processed by that rule is validated and a fault is produced if the message contents violates the validation through either or both the XSD definition or the Schematron rules.

NOTE
A service interface stipulates through an XSD definition what the structure should be of any message passed into it. However, the SOA Suite does not—for either Service Bus or for SOA composites—actually enforce that the request messages comply. This validation has to be performed explicitly.

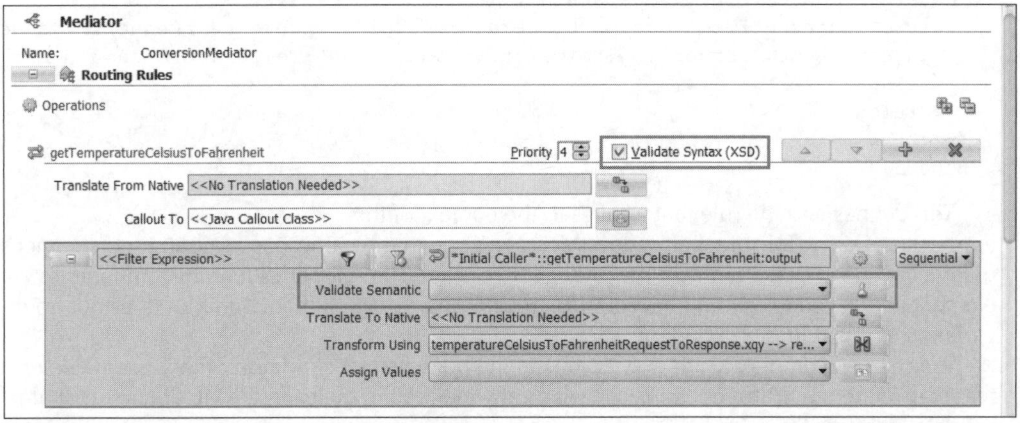

FIGURE 5-21.   *Validation can be done by the Mediator based on the XSD Schema or a Schematron rule library*

Even more advanced validation could be implemented using Java Callouts. We can specify a Java Class that will be invoked by the Mediator for a number of specific stages in the message processing—pre- and postvalidation, transformation, and routing of a message. In this class, we can implement validation logic through custom Java code that has full access to the message content. Note: Chapter 10 introduces the Spring component that will frequently the better option for message preprocessing in custom Java.

Enabling XSD Validation

To enable the validation of request messages against the XSD they are based on, all we need to do is check the checkbox *Validate Syntax (XSD)* at the operation level. This setting applies to all routing rules that may be created for the operation.

Schematron-Based Validation

Schematron validation rules are specified in an XML document created according to the 1.5 version of Schematron that uses the namespace http://xml.ascc.net/schematron/ (which also happens to be the URL at which more information can be found).

Schematron-based validations can introduce substantial performance overhead because of potentially complex, fine grained rule evaluations. They are typically used to inspect messages originating from systems and entities outside the trusted enterprise landscape—including third party COTS applications, and not so much for the internal interactions between services running on the SOA Suite.

Any XPath condition can be used to specify the test condition of a Schematron rule, that is, the boolean expression that should evaluate to true in order for the document to be considered valid with respect to that rule.

Create a new XML document in the Schemas folder. Call it ConversionServiceValidationRules .sch. The extension.sch is used to identify Schematron files.

Add the following content to ConversionServiceValidationRules.sch:

```
<?xml version="1.0" encoding="UTF-8" ?>
<schema xmlns="http://www.ascc.net/xml/schematron">
 <ns uri="saibot.airport/services/utility/conversion" prefix="conversion" />
 <pattern name="Celsius Temperature Values not under -100">
    <rule context="//conversion:temperatureCelsiusToFahrenheitRequestMessage">
     <assert test="conversion:temperature &gt; -100">Temperature should not be
below -100</assert>
    </rule>
 </pattern>
</schema>
```

This defines a single rule that applies to the context of the temperatureCelsiusToFahrenheitRequestMessage node in the namespace saibot.airport/services/ utility/conversion (specified with the prefix conversion). The rule states that the temperature element in this context should have a value greater than −100. If that condition does not hold, a violation of this rule is reported.

We can use complex XPath expressions in the boolean test condition of the assert element, that may reference XPath functions as well as any element in the source XML document that is validated through the rule.

The Schematron document may contain many rules that apply to various context element. If an XML document is validated using a Schematron document, only those rules applicable to the elements in the XML are processed and all other are ignored.

To configure the routing rule to perform validation using this Schematron document, bring up the mediator editor. Click on the stamp like icon behind the Validate Semantic field in the routing rule for the getTemperatureCelsiusToFahrenheit operation. Select the ConversionServiceValidationRules.sch as the Schematron file to use to validate the request message, as shown as in Figure 5-22. Each message part can be associated with a different Schematron document. Note that Schematron validation is configured per routing rule—not at the operation level like is the case for XSD validation.

Validation in Action

Both types of Validation have now been configured—against XSD and according to Schematron. Deploy the project. Send a test message with the temperature value set to –300, which is invalid according both the XSD schema and the Schematron rule.

The result is a SOAP fault with a message that reads: "oracle.tip.mediator.infra.exception .MediatorException: ORAMED-01303:[Payload default schema validation error]XSD schema validation fails with error "Invalid text '-300' in element: 'temperature'"." This clearly is the outcome of the XSD validation, which is apparently the first—and in this case only—validation to take place.

When you send a second test message with a temperature value of –150, the XSD validation is passed. Now the Schematron rule kicks in and the result is again a SOAP Fault, with a payload stating "oracle.tip.mediator.infra.exception.MediatorException: ORAMED-01301:[Payload custom validation]Schematron validation fails with error "Temperature should not be below -100"."

Clearly these are not the faults we would like to return to the consumer of our service—if for no other reason than that the SOAP Fault betrays far too many details about the implementation to consider the service anywhere near encapsulated.

In the Enterprise Manager FMW control, details on the faulted instance can be found in the instances tab for the *ConversionService* (see Figure 5-23) and the flow trace for the faulted instance. The column *recovery* lists the fault as nonrecoverable—obviously, because in this synchronous service the fault has already been returned to the caller.

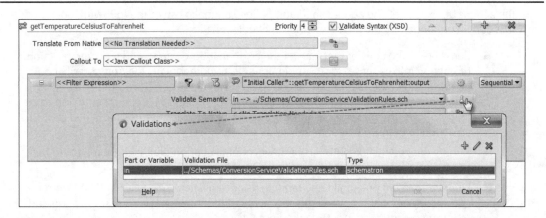

FIGURE 5-22.   *Configuring validation according to a Schematron constraint definition file*

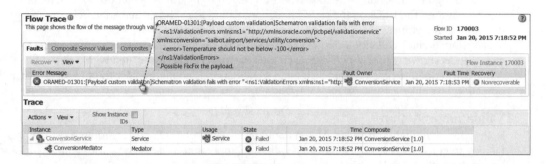

FIGURE 5-23. *Flow trace for a ConversionService instance that returned with a [Schematron validation] fault*

Fault Handling

Fault handling in SOA Composite applications is to some extent handled inside components—for example in BPEL and to a lesser degree in Mediator. SOA Suite has a generic framework for handling faults in SOA composite applications, using fault policies and bindings that are configured and executed outside the components. The bindings associate the fairly generic policies with specific composites and components. The policies specify what should be done under which conditions.

Fault Policies

Fault policies are defined in the file fault-policies.xml in the root directory of the SOA composite project—or in a file with a different name in a different location (typically MDS, see Chapter 21) that is specified through the oracle.composite.faultPolicyFile in the composite.xml file. This file contains one or more fault-policies, identified through a unique id. These policies are typically reusable across composites.

A fault policy contains actions—*what* should be done—and conditions—*when* should one of the actions be executed. The actions in a fault policy can make use of the following operations that can be performed by the SCA container to handle a fault:

- Retry—retry the activity that caused the error, in a new thread and a new transaction; this action makes sense, for example, for calls to components that temporarily could be unavailable; the retry action is configured with details on how often and with what delays a retry should be attempted. Additionally, we can specify another action in the fault policies file to execute when the maximum number of retries has failed as well as an action to perform when the retry was successful.

- Abort—the generic exception FabricInvocationException fault is thrown back to the caller, and the state of the composite instance is set to terminated.

- Human intervention—make the faulted instance available in the EM FWM Control console for manual recovery; this recovery could include payload manipulation and restarting the instance at a suitable moment.

- Custom Java Code—invoke a custom Java Class to execute custom logic to deal with the fault; for each possible return value from the class, we can configure a subsequent action in the fault policy file to be invoked. Additionally, we can associate a property set with an action entry of type custom Java to pass context settings to the Java code. This class should implement the Java interface IFaultRecoveryJavaClass.

- Rethrow—the final resort to simply rethrow the same SOAP fault that triggered the policy, when all else fails.

For synchronous interactions such as the one in the *ConversionService* composite, only Abort, Rethrow and Custom Java Code are appropriate operations to execute.

The conditions in the fault policy file identify an error or fault condition and then indicate the action to be taken when that particular condition occurs. The condition identifies a fault—either a predefined generic SOA Suite fault such as mediatorFault or remoteFault—or a specific custom fault. Note: Every Mediator fault is wrapped into the mediatorFault, which acts as a generic container for all the mediator faults. The condition can contain a test that inspects the fault details—for example, those inside mediatorFault—using a boolean XPath expression. When this expression evaluates to true, the condition applies and the action associated with the condition is executed.

Mediator Error Groups can be used in test conditions while defining the Fault Policy. There are six mediator error groups: TYPE_ALL, TYPE_DATA, TYPE_METADATA, TYPE_FATAL, TYPE_ TRANSIENT and TYPE_INTERNAL. Each of these groups contains several error codes, that each start with the name of the group. Examples of these error codes that can be tested for are TYPE_ DATA_FILTERING, TYPE_DATA_TRANSFORMATION and TYPE_FATAL_DB. An example of a test condition that would trigger for a validation violation is given next

```
contains($fault.mediatorErrorCode, "TYPE_DATA_VALIDATION")
```

Multiple conditions in a fault policy can evaluate to true for a fault occurrence. The first condition that applies is the one for which the action is executed. Other conditions are ignored. The order in which conditions are defined in the fault-policy is therefore meaningful.

Fault Bindings

Fault policies are defined in the file fault-bindings.xml in the root directory of the SOA composite project—or in a file with a different name in a different location that is specified through the oracle.composite.faultBindingFile in the composite.xml file.

The fault bindings file contains one or more entries that associate a fault policy with the entire composite, with a specific component or with a specific reference (to an adapter or other binding to an external service).

Such an association is very straightforward. To associate the entire SOA composite with a particular fault policy, the syntax is as follows

```
<composite faultPolicy="SaibotFaultPolicy"/>
```

To associate one or more components in the composite with a fault policy, the syntax is:

```
<component faultPolicy="SynchronousMediatorPolicy">
   <name>ConversionMediator</name>
   <name>SomeOtherComponent</name>
</component>
```

Specifying that a fault policy is associated with a reference is similarly straightforward:

```
<reference faultPolicy="UsuallyReliableExternalServicePolicy">
  <name>QueryAirportsDB</name>
  <name>AllocateSlotsDB</name>
</reference>
```

When a fault occurs at runtime, the fault bindings are checked to determine the fault policy for the current component. If none is specifically associated with the component, the policy at composite level is picked. If a fault policy is found, then the conditions are inspected to find the action to execute. If no fault policy binding is located, then no action is performed and the behavior is the same as if the fault policies did not exist.

If there is no fault policy defined the error is thrown back to the caller for synchronous interactions. For parallel routing rules in the Mediator and other one-way or asynchronous interactions, the default action of human intervention is performed. Note: When fault handling has been implemented inside the component and the fault does not get published outside of it, then the fault handling framework does not get triggered at all.

Fault Handling in the ConversionService

In the context of the *ConversionService* SOA composite, open the New Gallery. Create a new SOA Tier | Faults—Fault Policy Document. A file fault-policies.xml is created and the fault policy editor opens, see Figure 5-24.

Set the name of the (first) fault policy to *SynchronousMediatorPolicy*. Click on the Actions tab. Here are the predefined actions—default-termination, default-manual, default-retry, and

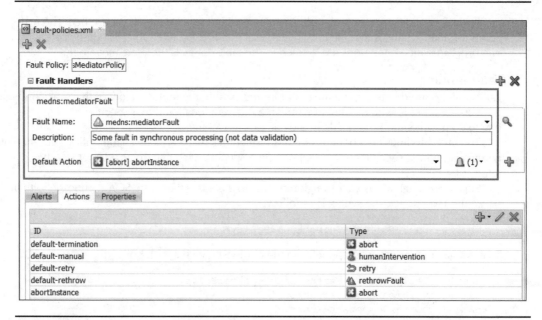

FIGURE 5-24. *Fault Policy editor showing a fault policy for the medns:mediatorFault*

default-rethrow. Each of these predefined actions is associated with one of the five action types available in fault policies. Add a new action with an ID of *abortInstance* and of type *abort*.

Add a fault condition by clicking the green plus icon. Select the medns:mediatorFault from the drop-down list. Provide a description that explains to the developers and administrators what this condition is for and then set the Default Action to *abortInstance*.

This fault policy now specifies that when the mediatorFault occurs, the abortInstance action should be executed. We have not yet specified to which composite or component this policy applies. That is what fault-bindings.xml file is for.

Open the composite overview for *ConversionService*. Click on the little icon for editing the composite fault policies. Figure 5-25 shows the popup that appears. Set the policy to *SynchronousMediatorPolicy* for the *ConversionMediator*. At this moment, binding the policy at composite level would have exactly the same effect.

Through these two editors, the fault-policies.xml and fault-bindings.xml files have been created. You may want to take a look at the source of these files, to get a good understanding of what was done behind the covers.

Deploy the composite. Test the temperature conversion operation in the service with a temperature value outside the valid range, which means under –100 degrees Celsius. The invocation will fail, like before. Only this time, the instance will abort because of the fault policy, as Figure 5-26 demonstrates. The SOAP Fault does not reveal detailed information. The end status of the *ConversionMediator* instance is now Terminated.

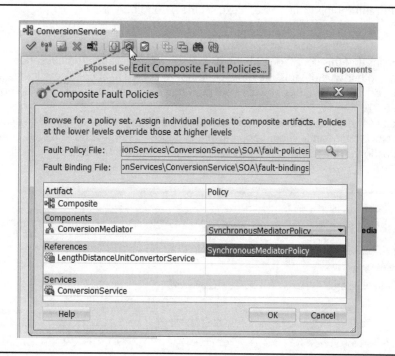

FIGURE 5-25. *Binding Fault Policy SynchronousMediatorPolicy to the ConversionMediator component*

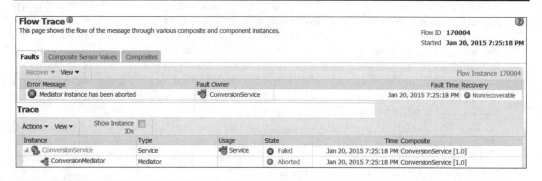

FIGURE 5-26. *Flow trace for an ConversionService instance that was aborted because of the fault policy binding*

Return to JDeveloper and change the action for the one condition in the fault policy to *default-rethrow*, the predefined action to rethrow the fault. Deploy the composite again and execute the same test with the invalid temperature value. This time, the response will be the same SOAP Fault we saw in the previous section. The fault policy kicked in—and this time the action was to rethrow.

Return to the fault policy editor in JDeveloper. Add a new condition. Choose again the mediatorFault for the Fault Name. Next, set the *If* condition to

```
contains($fault.mediatorErrorCode, "TYPE_DATA_VALIDATION")
```

This means that this condition only holds true in case of a validation exception from the Mediator. From any other type of fault, the other condition will kick in and execute the default-rethrow action. For validation faults however, set the *Then* action to *abortInstance*, as shown in Figure 5-27.

Deploy the composite once more and invoke the temperature conversion again with an invalid value. Now the instance should abort again, because the fault condition we just added—to abort for validation errors—trumps the generic one that is defined below it in the fault-policies.xml file.

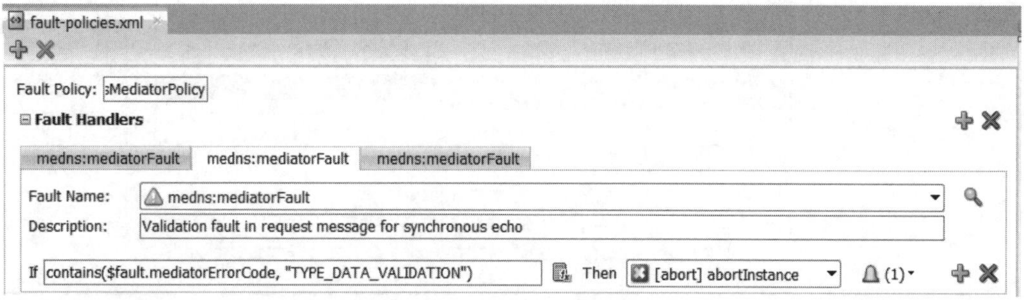

FIGURE 5-27. *Adding a conditional action for the mediatorFault*

More on Fault Handling

Compared with the error handling in a Service Pipeline, the Mediator lacks a number of important facilities. There is not the option to perform an alternative way of processing the faulted request and still return a valid response, nor can we change from the actual SOAP Fault to a fault of our own choosing. We cannot throw a business fault when neither the validation, the transformation, or the routing resulted in a technical exception or SOAP Fault, even if the contents of the request or response would suggest that we do so. Only by using Java callouts and/or a Custom Java Action to handle a fault do we get a little more grip. As we discuss later in this chapter, many organizations will decide to expose their SOA composites through the Service Bus—and not have any direct calls to the service exposed by the composite. The fault handling— including encapsulation and picking the appropriate fault—can then be done using the richer capabilities at that level, which is usually the preferred option over dabbling in custom Java Callouts.

TIP
The BPEL component that we also can use in SOA composites has much richer fault handling capabilities (see Chapter 8).

The fault-policies.xml file allows us to define fault alerts, configure them through a property set and associate these alerts with individual fault conditions. Alerts send notifications to a Logger, a JMS destination, or an email address. When an alert has been associated with a fault condition, whenever that condition is satisfied by a fault occurrence and it triggers an action, the alert is executed as well and a notification with fault details is sent to the alert destination.

Add Composite Sensors for Instance Identification

Instances of a SOA composite are identified through a rather meaningless technical numeric identifier, that is of little use when trying to find a particular instance. In SOA Suite, we have the option of associating other, more meaningful tags with instances of a composite through a feature called composite sensors. A sensor is defined at design time—or at run time—with a name, an XPath expression that derives the value for the sensor from the request message sent to the composite instance or the response returned from it and a filter that can be used to track the sensor value for selected instances only. In the Enterprise Manager FMW Control, composites instances display their sensor values and we can search for instances of SOA composites with specific values for the composite sensors. Additionally, the value of the sensor can be sent to a JMS destination, to allow external parties to keep track of specific activities. The composite sensor is quite similar to the message reports introduced for Service Bus pipelines in Chapter 3.

The ConversionService is not the most logical candidate to tag through a composite sensor, but in order to get a feel for the mechanism, we will apply one anyway.

Specifying a Composite Sensor for the ConversionService

A sensor is defined on a SOA composite through the dialog opened from the Composite Sensor icon above the SOA composite editor, as shown in Figure 5-28. Click on the icon. In the Composite Sensors window that appears, select the Service node ConversionService. Then click on the plus icon. The Create Composite Sensor window appears.

Set the name to celsiusTemperatureValue. Select the operation getTemperatureCelsiusToFahrenheit. Define an XPath expression using the expression builder. Have it return the temperature element

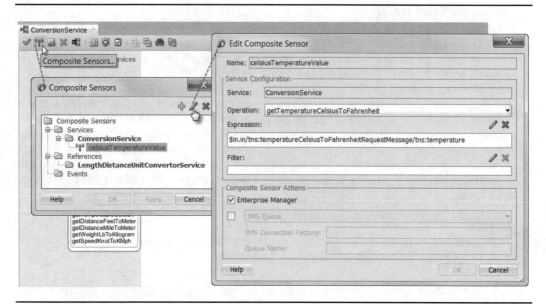

FIGURE 5-28. *Creating a Composite Sensor celsiusTemperaturValue for the ConversionService SOA composite*

in the request message. Ensure that the sensor action checkbox for Enterprise Manager is checked. Leave the checkbox for the JMS action unchecked. Press OK to complete the definition of the Composite Sensor. Then press OK to close the Composite Sensors window. You will notice that a small icon has been added to the ConversionService element in the Exposed Services swimlane, indicating the existence of at least one composite sensor.

Deploy the SOA composite to the Integrated WLS. Make one or more calls to convert a Celsius temperature. Then open the overview page for the *ConversionService* composite in the EM FMW Control. Click on the Flow Instances tab. Search for all recent instances. Click on the last instance. On the bottom part of the page, activate the Sensor Values tab. There you will find the value for the *celsiusTemperatureValue* sensor, as shown in Figure 5-29.

Instances can be filtered by the value of their sensors, both at the level of a single composite as well as at the level of the entire SOA Suite node.

On the search tab, by clicking the Add/Remove Filters link, a popup window is brought up. In this window, the checkbox labeled Flow Instances should be checked in order to be able to filter instances by composite sensor. With that checkbox checked, up to six composite sensors can be used to filter on.

Browse for, or type the name of the sensor. In the browse dialog, you can specify which operator should be used in conjunction with the values of this sensor: equality, like, less than (or equals) or greater than (or equals). In the search tab itself, the value is set with which the composite sensor values for all composite instances should be compared. Figure 5-29 shows a filter that searches for instances that have a composite sensor *celsiusTemperatureValue* with a value of exactly 67.

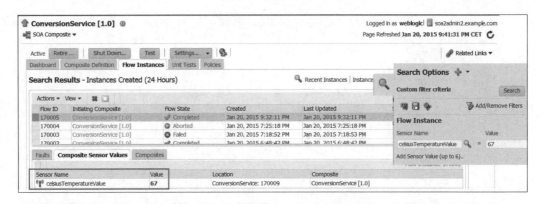

FIGURE 5-29. *Composite Sensor values providing additional context for instances of SOA composites—note how you can search for instances with a specific value for the composite sensor*

Add Height and Distance Conversion Support Using an External Service

The SOA composite *ConversionService* has only support for one of five operations in the service interface: the temperature conversion that is locally implemented using the Echo routing rule and a simple message transformation. Just like the Service Bus pipeline in chapter 3 that used an external service to implement the operation *getDistanceFeetToMeter*, we will now add support for that operation to the SOA composite. To that end, we will add a reference to the external service that does the actual distance conversion and define a new routing rule in the mediator that maps and routes messages received for operation *getDistanceFeetToMeter* to the reference. We will be able to reuse some of the artifacts we used with the Service Bus pipeline in Chapter 3.

Create a Reference for the External Conversion Service

Service Bus projects use a Business Service to locally represent an external service and configure details about how to access the service. In SCA, this is done using a Reference (binding). Such a reference is created in the composite editor by dragging the appropriate component from the component palette and dropping it in the External References swimlane. Create a reference binding in this way using the SOAP binding component, as is shown in Figure 5-30.

A dialog appears for configuring the Web Service binding (Figure 5-31). Set its name to *LengthDistanceUnitConvertorService*. Set the WSDL URL to http://www.webservicex.net/length .asmx?WSDL. Select Port Type *lengthUnitSoap* from the drop-down list that is populated from the WSDL document. Check the checkbox to copy the WSDL document and associated artifacts into the project. Press OK to complete the configuration.

The Reference binding *LengthDistanceUnitConvertorService* is now created in the External References swimlane. Connect the *ConversionMediator* to this reference. In the Choose Operations dialog, map the *getDistanceFeetToMeter* operation from the *ConversionService* interface to the *ChangeLengthUnit* operation in the reference binding, as shown in Figure 5-32.

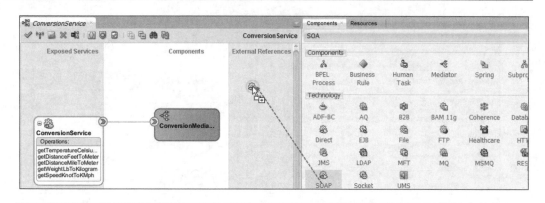

FIGURE 5-30. *Add a SOAP Web Service Reference Binding to the SOA composite*

Wiring the mediator to the reference has caused an update in the composite.xml file—you may want to take a look how this wire is configured. It has also resulted in a new routing rule in the mediator—one that routes request messages for the *getDistanceFeetToMeter* operation to the *ChangeLengthUnit* operation on the reference. We need to further configure this routing rule, to have it perform the necessary transformations of the request and response messages.

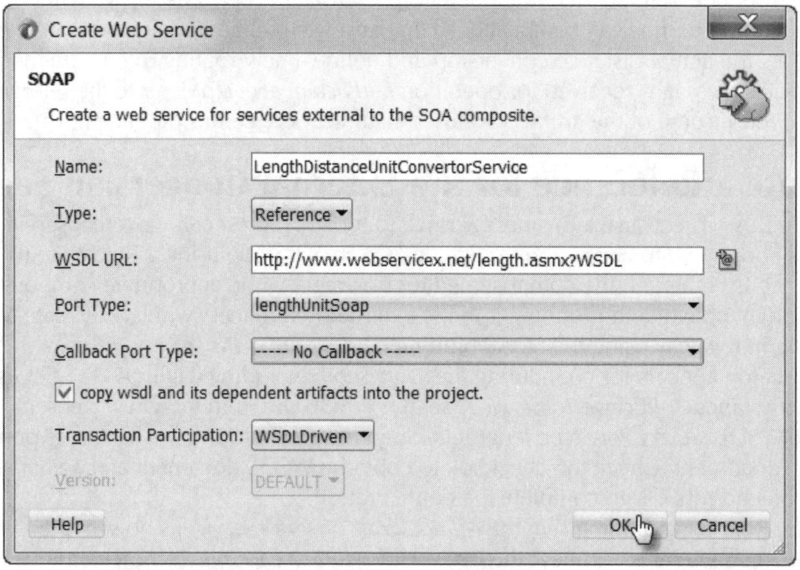

FIGURE 5-31. *Configuring the Web Service binding for the external service (dependency)*

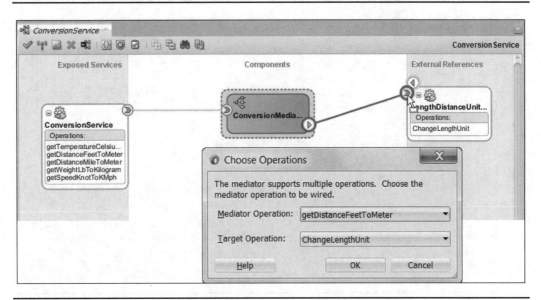

FIGURE 5-32.   *Wiring the ConversionMediator to the LengthDistanceUnitConvertorService reference and mapping the operations*

NOTE
Many organizations adopt as a best practice that all access to external services is routed through the Service Bus. For each external service invoked from the enterprise, a proxy service is published on the Service Bus. The proxy routes to a business service that is set up for the external service. The same practice is generally adopted for services in different domains inside the organization.

This proxy is the local endpoint for the external service that all consumers can make use of. It virtualizes the external service—its location, its availability and other aspects. If a new provider of the external service is engaged, this change will not impact internal consumers of that service, since their only dependency is on the proxy.

Using this practice, SOA composites would never directly reference external services such as the LengthDistanceUnitConvertorService. The limitations in the Reference binding compared with the Service Bus business service—such as runtime property adjustment, load balancing, fail over, result cache, service throttling, and SLA monitoring that are only available on the Service Bus—are then irrelevant because there still is a business service between the composite and the external service.

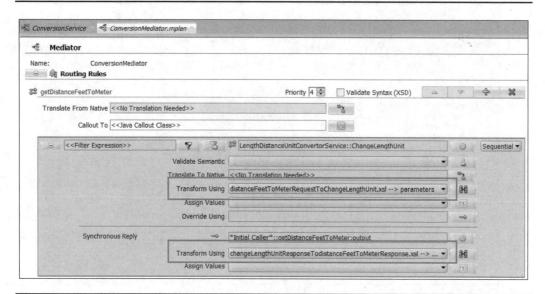

FIGURE 5-33. *The routing rule for the getDistanceFeetToMeter operation with the two transformations set up*

Configure Routing Rule in Mediator

Edit the *ConversionMediator*. You will find the new routing rule for the *getDistanceFeetToMeter* operation. Click on the transformation icon for the request message. Select the XSLT file distanceFeetToMeterRequestToChangeLengthUnit.xsl in the Transformations folder to perform the transformation of the request message. This is the same mapping that was used in Chapter 3 in a Replace activity in the Service Bus pipeline and which we have copied into the project earlier.

Next, set up the file changeLengthUnitResponseTodistanceFeetToMeterResponse.xsl to perform the mapping of the response message. The routing rule is shown in Figure 5-33.

Deploy and Test

Deploy the *ConversionService* composite to the Integrated WLS. Test the service—this time calling the *getDistanceFeetToMeter* operation to convert a 1000 feet into the meter equivalent. Once you have received the response, you can check the instance flow trace. See Figure 5-34.

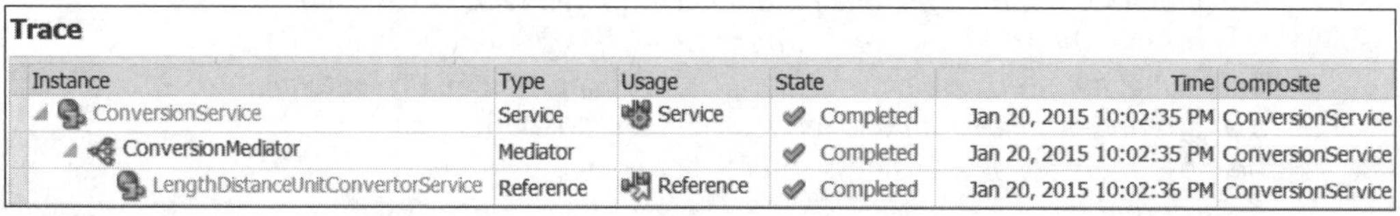

Trace

Instance	Type	Usage	State	Time	Composite
ConversionService	Service	Service	✔ Completed	Jan 20, 2015 10:02:35 PM	ConversionService
ConversionMediator	Mediator		✔ Completed	Jan 20, 2015 10:02:35 PM	ConversionService
LengthDistanceUnitConvertorService	Reference	Reference	✔ Completed	Jan 20, 2015 10:02:36 PM	ConversionService

FIGURE 5-34. *The flow trace for the ConversionService composite handling a call to the getDistanceFeetToMeter operation and engaging the external reference for the LengthDistanceUnitConvertorService*

Short-Cut to Run SOA Composite from JDeveloper

When you are doing development work on the SOA composite—for example, working on transformations or validations—it is helpful to frequently try out the intermediate results from your most recent changes. It would be very convenient to be able to quickly do deploy-and-run cycles from within JDeveloper. For Service Bus composites, the IDE provides the Run option on the context menu for proxy service, pipeline, and business services. Activating that option will deploy the composite and open the service tester, poised for the right service. This facility however is not available for SOA composites, but there turns out to be a pretty good alternative.

For SOA composites, the SOA Suite has a built in testing framework for conducting unit tests. A quick first introduction to this framework follows next—more details are in Chapter 22.

A SOA composite can have one or more associated test suites. A test suite contains one or more test cases. Each test case represents a call to one of the operations in a service exposed by the composite. Part of a test case are a request message, the expected response message and optionally the emulated replies from external references or components within the composite. Assertions can be added to test case to verify if the results conform to the expectations. A test suite is deployed along with the SOA composite and can be run from the Enterprise Manager FMW control. It can also be run directly from JDeveloper. When the latter is done, the SOA composite is redeployed if it has been changed since the last deployment, the test calls are made from JDeveloper to the freshly deployed composites and the results are shown in JDeveloper. A new instance of the SOA composite is created and can also be inspected in EM FMW control.

This means: by running the test from JDeveloper, we achieve the goal of build-deploy-run (and show results). Note that we do not necessarily want to test the outcomes of the service call in detail—we only use this as a short-cut to try out the current state of the composite.

The steps for the *ConversionService* are as follows:

Click on the icon to Create Composite Test—shown in Figure 5-35.

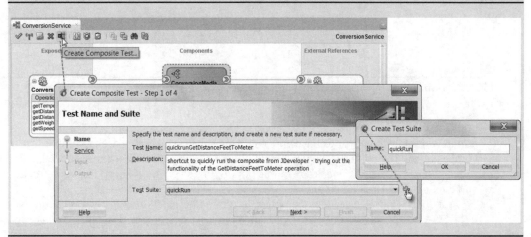

FIGURE 5-35. *Creating a Composite Test [Case] for the ConversionService composite*

A wizard for creating a Composite Test [Case] appears. Provide the name of the Test Case, for example, *quickrunGetDistanceFeetToMeter* for a test case we will use to try out the *getDistanceFeetToMeter* operation. Provide a description. This is the first test case in our composite, so click on the icon to create a Test Suite, as shown in Figure 5-35.

Set the name of the new Test Suite to quickRun; this will be a test suite with shortcuts for all operations in the composite.

In step 2 of the wizard, select the operation to call in this test. In step 3, provide the content for the request message to use in this test. In step 4, specify the expected response message (or accept the default if you do not actually need to test the results but merely want an easy way to fire off the operation). Press Finish to complete the wizard. The Test Suite is created as a new folder under the *testsuites* project folder.

The new test case is created as a file in the test suite folder. In its context menu, the option Run Test can be used to run the test. The file can also be opened through double click. In that case, the composite editor opens in a special mode (see Figure 5-36) that has an overlay with details of the test case. The test case can be further refined in this mode—emulations of response messages and assertions on intermediate results can be added to the wires.

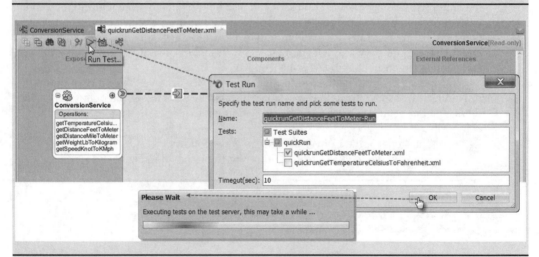

FIGURE 5-36. *Run the Test Suite from the SOA composite editor in Test Mode*

With the run icon in the top menu bar, the test case can be kicked off. The first time a popup window will appear to have you select the server on which to deploy the SOA composite and run the test. Usually this will be *localhost*—where the Integrated WLS is running. If you check the checkbox in this popup, this selection is saved in the preferences and the question is not asked again.

A second window gives you the option to refine the selection of test cases to run. Next, if the SOA composite has been changed since the last deployment, a window appears to have you confirm that redeployment should take place. Then, build and deploy steps are executed and the test(s) are run. A dialog appears to inform you that the tests are in progress. When running the tests is done, a tab opens in JDeveloper with the test results. You can inspect the response message produced by the composite instance.

You can also inspect the composite instance and its flow trace details in EM FMW control. Note that instances created by running test cases are marked with a yellow indicator in the instances overview, as shown in Figure 5-37.

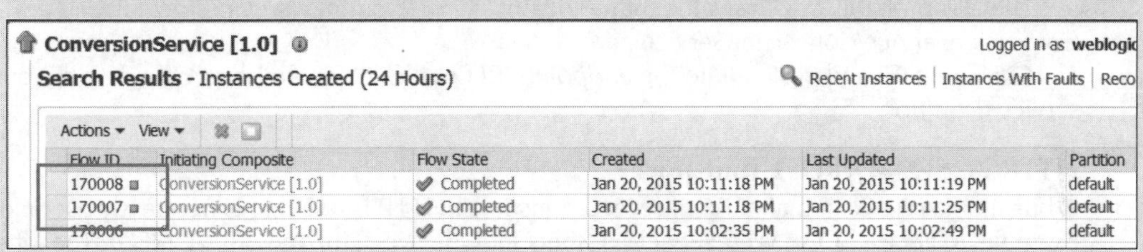

🏠 **ConversionService [1.0]** ⓘ					Logged in as **weblogic**
Search Results - Instances Created (24 Hours)				Recent Instances	Instances With Faults	Reco

Actions ▾   View ▾   ✖ ☐

Flow ID	Initiating Composite	Flow State	Created	Last Updated	Partition
170008 ■	ConversionService [1.0]	✔ Completed	Jan 20, 2015 10:11:18 PM	Jan 20, 2015 10:11:19 PM	default
170007 ■	ConversionService [1.0]	✔ Completed	Jan 20, 2015 10:11:18 PM	Jan 20, 2015 10:11:25 PM	default
170006	ConversionService [1.0]	✔ Completed	Jan 20, 2015 10:02:35 PM	Jan 20, 2015 10:02:49 PM	default

FIGURE 5-37.   *Test instances of the ConversionService, marked with the test indicator: a yellow square*

Exposing SOA Composites through the Service Bus

A SOA composite is one of several ways to create a service implementation. Others include JAX-WS, ADF BC, EJB, JAX-RS, and third party technologies. Services can be exposed through the Service Bus, that takes care of virtualization of the location and underlying implementation. Service Bus will also help scale the services to handle higher volume of requests, monitor their activity, and provide caching and fail over. It is a best practice to not have consumers directly access SOA composites. Instead, the SOA composite's service is registered on the Service Bus and thus exposed to consumers.

In this section, we will register the SOA composite ConversionService on the Service Bus and expose its interface through a proxy service. Consumers can then invoke ConversionService operations on that proxy and have the SOA composite take care of handling their request, without dealing with that composite directly.

Create Service Bus Project

In JDeveloper, create a new Service Bus Application with a new project, both called *ProxyConversionService*. Create the two folders WSDLs and Schemas. Copy files ConversionService.wsdl, ConversionService.xsd and common.xsd from the SOA composite to these two folders.

NOTE
In real life, we would use MDS (Meta Data Services) to hold and provide access to these artifacts, instead of copying and moving them around. We will discuss MDS in Chapter 21.

Register SOA Composite as Business Service

Drag the HTTP component from the palette to the external references swimlane and drop it. In the Create Business Service wizard that appears, set the name of the business service to *ConversionServiceBS*. Click Next. On the second page, select the WSDL as the service type. Browse for the file ConversionService.wsdl in the SOA composite project *ConversionService*. The correct port type is automatically selected. Click Next.

On the third page of the wizard, you have to provide the endpoint URI for the *ConversionService*. You can find the URI for the service exposed by the SOA composite *ConversionService* in the Enterprise Manager FMW Control. Select the *ConversionService* composite in the navigation tree. Then click on the icon to the right of the settings button, as shown in Figure 5-38.

The URI probably has this value: http://localhost:7101/soa-infra/services/default/ ConversionService/ConversionService.

Copy the URI and paste it into the *endpointURI* field. Click on Finish to complete the business service definition.

HTTP vs. SOA-DIRECT Transport

A business service can make use of several transports. HTTP is one that is frequently used, for example, to access SOAP Web Services. Others include JMS, EJB, and SOA-DIRECT. The latter is a transport that connects a Service Bus Business Service to a direct binding service exposed by a SOA composite. This transport exchanges messages over a remote method invocation (RMI), and is the recommended transport if you need transaction or security propagation. For interactions between Service Bus and SOA composites where transaction or security propagation are not relevant, HTTP is the preferred transport.

Expose Proxy Service

Right click on the ConversionService.wsdl and select the menu option Service Bus | Generate Proxy Service, to generate the Proxy Service and Pipeline for this WSDL.

The Create Proxy Service wizard appears. Set the name of the proxy service to *ProxyConversionServicePS* and the name for the pipeline to *ProxyConversionPipeline*. Change the endpoint for the proxy service to /utility/ConversionService, on the second page of the wizard. Press Finish to complete the creation of the proxy service and pipeline.

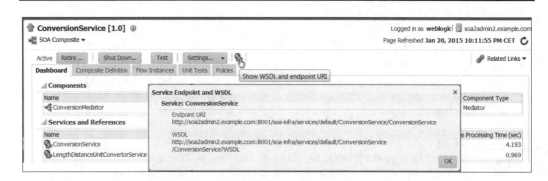

FIGURE 5-38. *Finding the endpoint of the SOA composite web service from the EM FMW Control*

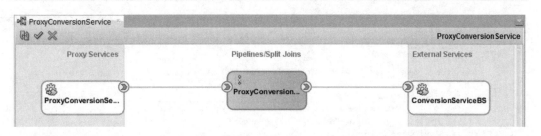

FIGURE 5-39. *Service Bus project to expose the ConversionService SOA composite*

JDeveloper will now inform you about the need to change the operation selection configuration, because two operations use the same request message and therefore the message type cannot be used as the basis for the operation selection. On the tab for Operation Selection Configuration in the proxy service editor, select SOAP Action Header as the algorithm for picking the operation to execute.

In the *ProxyConversionService* overview editor, wire the pipeline to the business service. The project now looks as shown in Figure 5-39.

This will create a route node with a routing activity in the pipeline that routes every request message through the business service, to the SOA composite. At this point, no validation, enrichment or transformation is required, just routing—as shown in Figure 5-40.

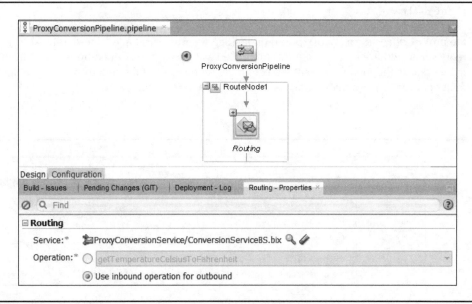

FIGURE 5-40. *The ProxyConversionPipeline only has to do routing to the business service for the SOA composite*

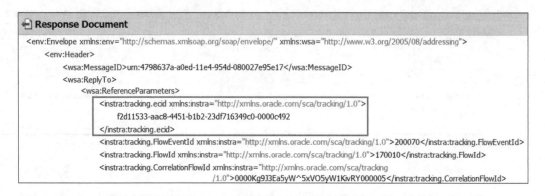

FIGURE 5-41. *Header details that betray the passage through the SOA composite*

Deploy and Invoke

Run the proxy service from within JDeveloper using the context menu. This will automatically trigger deployment of the Service Bus project to the Integrated WLS, and open the test dialog. Either invoke the operation to convert feet to meters or Celsius to Fahrenheit. You should receive a response message—that also contains information in the header about the trip the message took through the SCA container when processed by the SOA composite, such as the unique ECID or execution context identifier (a unique identifier assigned to a request by Fusion Middleware that can be used to track a request or transaction across tiers—more on ECID in Chapter 23) (see Figure 5-41).

This same ECID is used to compose the message flow trace that you can inspect for the call to the proxy *ConversionService* exposed on the Service Bus. This trace (Figure 5-42) shows how the request traveled from the Service Bus (indicated as OSB) to the SOA composite and from there to the Mediator and in the case of the feet to meter conversion if the request was for the feet to meter conversion also the invocation of the external reference.

Trace   Flow ID **170010**

Actions ▾   View ▾   Show Instance ☐   Started **Jan 20, 2015 10:42:44 PM**
                                IDs

Instance	Type	Usage	State
◢ 🗐 ServiceBus	ServiceBus		
◢ 🖲 ConversionService	Service	🖳 Service	✔ Completed
◢ 🖧 ConversionMediator	Mediator		✔ Completed
🖲 LengthDistanceUnitConvertorService	Reference	🖳 Reference	✔ Completed

FIGURE 5-42. *Flow trace of a message sent to the Service Bus proxy and routed to the SOA composite*

Failed Deployment Because of Conflicting Endpoint

The deployment might fail because the endpoint configured for the proxy service is the same one we used for the Service Bus project we developed in Chapter 3, and that may still be deployed to the Integrated WLS. The Service Bus cannot listen on one endpoint on behalf of two different services, so if that is the case, let's remove that Chapter 3 *ConversionService* project to make way for the current project.

In order to do so, open the Service Bus Console—at http://localhost:7101/servicebus. Select project *ConversionService* in the project browser. Click on the Create button to start an editing session. Click on the red cross-shaped delete icon. Confirm your decision. The click on Activate to apply these changes for real.

Suggested Guidelines

Most organizations define guidelines that describe how they make use of technology components. Common guidelines around the SOA Suite include:

Keep the Service Bus clean, mean, and lean—have the pipelines do their essential (VETRO) task and as little else as possible. The implementation of services is not what the Service Bus should be used for. This may go as far as ban all outbound adapters from the Service Bus—and only use them in SOA composites.

Consumers should only invoke services exposed on the Services Bus and never call implementations or external services directly. The Service Bus virtualizes all services, provides additional functionality—including monitoring, caching, fail over—and is the decoupling point that allows implementations to be modified or completely swapped in and out. This would mean that calls to SOA composites should only come through the Service Bus—and never directly. A slightly less strict guideline could make a distinction between different domains or functional areas and allow direct calls between SOA composites within a domain but not across.

Summary

This chapter introduced SOA composite applications. SOA composites are based on the SCA (Service Component Architecture) standard. SCA composites expose services, consume references and implement their logic using service components, such as the mediator. Other SCA service components in the SOA Suite are BPEL, Human Task, Business Rule, and Spring Java.

The SOA Suite contains two run-time engines that run services—one for SCA composites and one for Service Bus projects. Interactions between the two engines are easily implemented through simple service calls—that could propagate transaction and security context if required. A common approach is to implement all but the simplest services through SOA composites and virtualize access to all services through the Service Bus. Nearly all SOA composites are then registered on the Service Bus and exposed through a proxy.

Administration tasks for both engines and both types of applications are performed in the same console: Enterprise Manager Fusion Middleware Control. Development is done in JDeveloper for both types of applications.

The structure of a SOA composite with a mediator component is very similar to that of a Service Bus composite with a pipeline. The SOA composite exposes services—called proxy service in Service Bus terminology—and consumes external references—called business service in the context of Service Bus. A mediator looks a lot like a pipeline: it does validation, transformation, and routing. Compared to the pipeline, a mediator adds parallel routing rules and dynamic routing rules based on a Business Rule, content based filtering, asynchronous operations, and built-in Schematron validation as well as the SOA composite fault handling framework. In that same comparison, mediators have less capabilities to manipulate messages, handle faults locally, implement enrichment and use programming logic to tune the message flow.

This chapter introduced semantic message validation based on Schematron, that goes beyond what XSD can do. It also discussed the fault handling framework for SOA composites, using fault policies and fault bindings. The chapter describes how composite sensors can be used to add tags to instances of a SOA composite, that can be used to find and identify instances in the EM FMW control.

In subsequent chapters, we will discuss how SOA composites can use multiple interconnected service components to implement complex functionality, that for example allow long running, stateful processes and asynchronous interactions.

More on Mediator

This chapter scratched the surface with regard to the Mediator component. Its core features were shown. Many more interesting options and capabilities have not yet been discussed, including these:

- Native transformation—support for native, non-XML data such as JSON or CSV; mediators can take native input and map it to XML prior to the regular transformation and also produce native output from the outcome of the regular transformation and send it onward.

- Leverage Domain Value Maps and Cross References in transformations and value assignments

- One way and Asynchronous—handling requests for which no response is expected or for which the response is sent through an asynchronous callback.

- Response forwarding—forward the response from a target to another target (instead of sending a response to the invoker).

- Resequencing—rearrange incoming messages (per time interval) in the proper order according to custom logic.

- Parallel rules—execute multiple routing rules at the same time in parallel threads.

- Condition-based routing—executing routing rules according to conditions that inspect the headers or contents of messages using boolean XPath expressions.

- Assign values (headers)—manipulation of header properties, for example to dynamically influence JCA Adapter behavior.

- Callouts—hooks for adding message processing in custom Java classes at predefined moments in the Mediator processing lifecycle (before and after executing routing rules), for example, to add advanced validation, enrichment, and transformation as well as custom logging and tracking.

- Dynamic Routing Rules—using a business rule component to implement the routing logic external to the mediator using a decision table to determine the endpoint of the target service.

- Attachments—support for processing attachments to request and response messages.

CHAPTER
6

One-Way Services and
More Protocols

Alll services we have discussed in the previous chapters share at least one characteristic: they are all synchronous, two-way, request/reply services. This means that consumers of these services are blocked for the duration of the service execution, waiting for a response. There are many situations where a service does not need to return a response, or at least not synchronously. One-way (aka fire and forget) services have operations defined in their interface with an input but no output or fault. When invoked, the service returns an HTTP 200 acknowledgment (without payload) of the reception of the message, before it starts processing the request. It will not return a response message. That means the consumer is blocked for only a very short period of time. It also means that the connection between service and consumer is severed and no result can be returned (in a regular way). In Chapter 12, we will discuss two-way asynchronous services—that have the benefit of the nonblocking execution of the service in combination with the ability to return a response in the form of a call-back message. Various mechanisms are available to deliver deferred results to consumers, including events, correlation, and (temporary) storage such as data grid, queue, and database table.

The SOA Suite supports several outbound transports that are intrinsically one way: they hand over a message to an external resource without waiting for a response. The technology adapters for JMS, MQ, UMS (User Messaging Service), and AQ support this one-way, fire and forget message exchange pattern—illustrated in Figure 6-1. The adapter for JMS is introduced in this chapter, used in its outbound mode for sending messages to a JMS destination where it will be consumed by a financial application for collecting details to calculate landing fees for incoming aircrafts. To learn about the similarities between various outbound adapters, especially those for asynchronous actions, we will replace that JMS adapter with an AQ adapter as an alternative implementation.

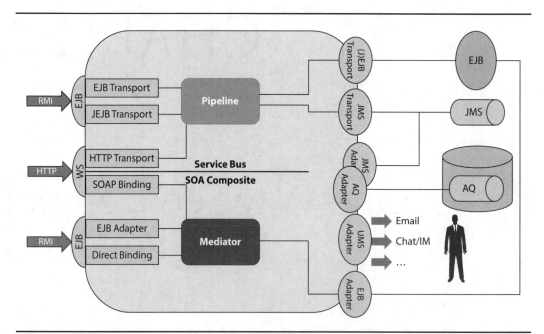

FIGURE 6-1. *Overview of the Outbound JCA Adapters and Service Bus Transports for EJB, JMS, AQ, and User Messaging*

The external resource targeted by the SOA Suite component can be a human. We people are extremely asynchronous in the eyes of automated systems: if we respond at all, we do so rather tardily. The SOA Suite caters for humans through the User Messaging Service (UMS) and the UMS adapter. Through UMS, we can have messages sent from composites through email, instant messaging (chat), and text message (SMS). In this chapter, we will see how flight updates—changed gate, adjusted ETA, new status—can be communicated by a service to an interested (human) party through either email or instant messaging.

The UMS Adapter also supports inbound interactions. This means that services can be triggered through the reception of an email or chat message. We will discuss this in Chapter 13.

An important type of communication in a Java EE environment is based on EJBs. Both Service Bus and SOA composites can invoke Enterprise Java Beans that run locally or remotely. Additionally, they can also both expose an inbound EJB service, allowing Java clients to consume the composite in a native way that can even propagate transaction scope and security context. All four EJB interactions—inbound and outbound and both Service Bus and SOA composite—are discussed.

Flight Updates through Email and Chat Using the UMS Adapter

One example of a one-way (or at least asynchronous) communication is from machine to human. It is not easy for an automated system to draw the attention of a human resource, let alone have that human respond to a request within typical time out periods. In this section, we will focus on the one-way interaction from the world of automated systems and human actors.

The mechanisms for this interaction include email, instant messaging (IM), SMS, and VoIP. Additionally, social media—Twitter, Facebook, and so on—expose APIs that could also be leveraged by SOA Suite components to inform their human partners of relevant developments and questions.

The SOA Suite ships with the UMS adapter, a JCA adapter that makes the User Message Service (UMS) functionality available from within Service Bus and SOA composites. Through UMS, messages can be sent over various channels, such as email, IM, SMS, and VoIP. The UMS adapter also supports an inbound mode. In this mode, incoming emails and chat messages can be forwarded to a running SOA composite instance or they can trigger execution of a service exposed by a Service Bus project or an SOA composite instance.

In this section, we will implement the *FlightUpdateNotificationService* through an SOA composite that uses an outbound UMS adapter binding to send emails and chat messages (IM). The composite exposes a service interface that expects a flight update message. The information about the changed flight status is transformed into a human readable format and then sent through the channel specified in the request message. The composite contains a mediator component that makes use of content-based routing to route the message to the UMS adapter binding for the selected channel.

Flight Updates Reported through Email Notifications

The first step en route to the composite that handles both *email* and *chat* communication is the implementation of the email channel. This requires the definition of the service, the implementation of the composite and the configuration of the email driver properties for the UMS adapter. In a few steps, we can start informing interested parties through email about the latest flight status.

Prepare SOA Composite Application and Project

Create a new SOA application called *FlightUpdateNotificationService* with an SOA composite project with that same name. Initially, the composite can be left empty. We will add a mediator component later on.

When the composite editor has opened, add a UMS adapter to the external services swim lane. The adapter configuration wizard opens to allow us to configure an outbound adapter binding that supports sending emails (to parties that are to be informed about a flight update).

Set the name to *EmailSender*. Press Next. Accept the default JNDI name for the UMS adapter connection to use in the run-time environment (eis/ums/UMSAdapterOutbound). Press Next. Accept the preselected Operation Type (*Outbound Send Notification*) and the default Operation Name *SendNotification*. Press Next.

The page *Outbound Notification Details* (Figure 6-2) contains many properties that are typically specified at run time. On this page, set the type of notification to email—that is the one thing that will not change. You could set the subject—to something like "Flight Update" — although in reality you may want to add the flight number to that subject at run time. The *From* and *Reply To* email address can perhaps be set, although these two can be set at run time as well. However, the wizard will not let you proceed unless you provide a value for the To email address. Use a dummy value, like dummy@design.time.

Press Next. Check the check box for *Message is String Type*. Press Next and press Finish. The outbound UMS adapter binding is created, poised for sending emails (to a dummy address).

Our next step will be to create a mediator that exposes the interface of the *FlightUpdateNotificationService*, routes to the UMS adapter with the proper destination email address set and performs the transformation from XML message with flight status update to a human readable message in between.

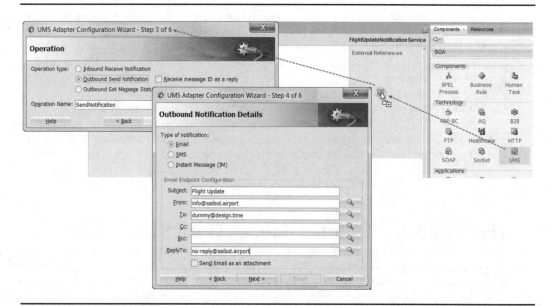

FIGURE 6-2. *Configuration of the outbound UMS adapter for sending email notifications*

Add the MachineToHumanMediator Component

Drag a mediator component to the SOA composite. Configure the mediator with its name set to *MachineToHumanMediator*. Set the template to *Interface Definition from WSDL* and select the FlightUpdateNotificationService.wsdl interface definition from the source folder for this chapter. Leave the checkbox *Expose as an SOAP service* checked; this will result in a service wired from the mediator to the exposed services swim lane and therefore the service published at the composite level. Press OK to create the mediator. Wire the mediator to the *EmailSender* reference, as shown in Figure 6-3. This will create the routing rule in the mediator.

Right click the exposed service and use the option Rename on the context menu, change the name of the service to *FlightUpdateNotificationService*.

Next, we need to create a way to transform the incoming request message into a proper email body. The easiest way is through an XSL Map that maps from the *sendFlightUpdateNotificationRequestMessage* to the message payload expected by the *EmailSender*—which could well be an XHTML snippet for a rich mail body. Compose the payload element with a suitable message, using at least the salutation element in the *communicationMetadata* section of the request message.

XQuery may be more suitable for composing the text of the email body, because of the relative ease with which we can extract data from the source and combine it with text and html elements. You are encouraged to give that a try.

Configure the routing rule in the mediator to make use of the appropriate transformation.

The destination email address also needs to be set. This is done through the Assign [Properties] dialog in the mediator editor. Click on the icon behind the Assign Values field. The editor shown in Figure 6-4 pops up. On the left side, select the ToAddress property in the CommunicationMetadata element in the request message. On the right side, locate and select the property jca.ums.to.

This will make the Mediator pass to the UMS adapter the email address to send the email to. You would typically also add a rule for the *jca.ums.subject* property in order to dynamically assign a value to the subject of the email.

The SOA composite is now complete. It can be deployed to the Integrated WLS. However, we will not yet be able to send any mails, because the email driver used by UMS for emails sent on behalf of SOA Suite has yet to be configured with the mail server details.

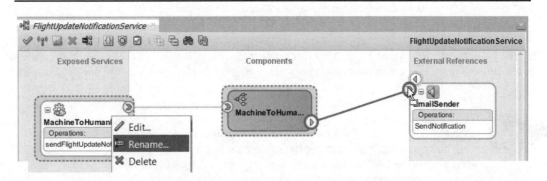

FIGURE 6-3.   *Wire the mediator to the outbound UMS adapter binding and rename the exposed service*

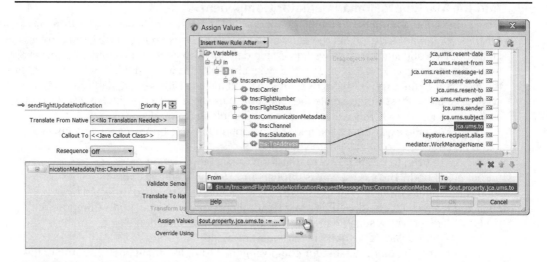

FIGURE 6-4. *Configuring the jca.ums.to property with the destination email address.*

Configure UMS Email Driver

Outbound emails are sent from a mail server—the SOA Suite does not act on its own. Therefore, at domain level, the UMS email driver has to be configured for both outbound (and inbound if so desired) interaction with the email server that handles the actual communication with the outside world. This configuration is done through the EM FMW Control. Instructions are provided on the book's website.

Before doing the upcoming configuration, you need to have the access details for a mail server—both host and port as well as a mail account from which the emails sent by the SOA Suite are going to originate.

NOTE
For inbound emails, you would have to configure the mail account in which the incoming messages are gathered. This is discussed in Chapter 13.

Apply all settings of the email driver properties. This will enable the SOA Suite to properly process outbound email interaction from UMS adapter bindings such as the one we are about to create.

TIP
In Chapter 17, Human Tasks are introduced. Communication about these tasks is typically done using the same User Messing Service leveraged by the UMS adapter. Mails sent to inform our users about tasks assigned to them, are sent through the mail server that is configured as per the online instruction.

FIGURE 6-5. *Email sent by the FlightUpdateNotificationService*

Test the Email Sending Capability of the FlightUpdateNotificationService
After deploying the *FlightUpdateNotificationService* composite and configuring the email driver, now is the time to try out how a flight status update is turned into a notification sent to the indicated email address.

Send a request message to the *FlightUpdateNotificationService*, see whether it processes successfully and then wait for an email to arrive, like the one shown in Figure 6-5.

Add Flight Updates through Instant Messaging
Not all interested parties prefer email as their (only) notification channel. Therefore, we will extend the *FlightUpdateNotificationService* with support for the IM channel that uses chat conversations to push messages. IM is also supported by the UMS adapter. That means that to support this channel, we can make use of a second outbound UMS adapter binding. The service interface of the SOA composite does not change. However, the mediator has to be extended to also cater for both the new channel as well as the message format expected by the new UMS adapter binding.

Configure the UMS Driver for Instant Messaging
In much the same way as we have configured the UMS driver for email, we also should configure the driver for instance messaging. To use the XMPP driver in UMS, you must have access to a Jabber/XMPP server and an XMPP account for the UMS XMPP driver instance with which to log in. All instant messages sent from any SOA composite in the SOA Suite are going to be sent from a single UMS driver configuration. We need to specify an XMPP server and port as well as the username and password on that server. Note: You may enter a complete Jabber ID if its domain name is different from the Jabber/XMPP server hostname (e.g., saibotInfoDesk or saibotInfoDesk@jabber.lexville). See the book's website for instructions on how to configure the UMS XMPP driver—including suggestions for how to create chat accounts on XMPP servers and which client tools to use.

Add an Outbound UMS Adapter Binding for Chat
Open the SOA composite editor. Drag the UMS adapter once more to the external references swim lane. Set the name to *ChatClient*. Press Next. Accept the default JNDI name. Press Next. Accept the defaults for Operation Type and Operation Name. Press Next. On the tab for Outbound Notification Details (Figure 6-6), set the Type of Notification to Instant Message (IM). Only one property can be set now: the To property that specifies the IM endpoint to which the message is to be sent. We will set this destination at run time. Therefore, it is best to provide a dummy value. Then press Next. Specify that the message is a string, press Next and press Finish.

Configure Content-Based Routing in the MachineToHumanMediator
Some of the request messages handled by the mediator will have to be routed to the new ChatClient, because they are destined for the *IM* channel. Therefore, wire the mediator to the ChatClient UMS adapter binding.

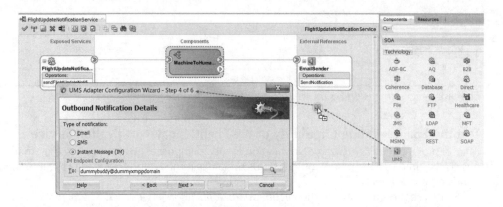

FIGURE 6-6. *Configuration of the outbound UMS adapter for instance messaging*

Open the mediator editor. There are now two routing rules that both process all messages and passes them to their respective UMS binding. That is not what we desire: all messages that have the *email* channel set in the request message should go to the *EmailSender*—but the routing rule for the *EmailSender* should not process messages with their channel set to *IM*. Likewise, the routing rule for the *ChatClient* should ignore the requests that contain Email as the channel. This conditional processing based on the content of the request messages is called *content-based routing*. In the mediator component, this is implemented using filter conditions that determine whether or not a message should be processed by a routing rule.

Click on the *filter* icon in the routing rule to the *EmailSender*. Set the filter expression to

```
$in.in/tns:sendFlightUpdateNotificationRequestMessage/
tns:CommunicationMetadata/tns:Channel='email'
```

Do the same thing for the routing rule for the ChatClient. Replace the string *email* with *IM* in this case (Figure 6-7).

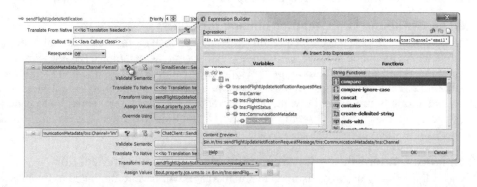

FIGURE 6-7. *Configuring the filter expression for content-based routing to the ChatClient*

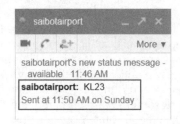

FIGURE 6-8. *Reception of the chat message from the FlightUpdateNotificationService*

The routing rule for the chat client has to be refined in two additional ways to have the required values set at run time:

■ The jca.ums.to property has to be assigned a value, based on the *ToAddress* element in the request message (just like we did for the email routing rule)

■ A transformation should be configured that turns the request message with the flight status into a proper chat message

Once these alterations have been applied, the SOA composite is ready for deployment.

Deploy and Test Flight Status Updates via the Chat Channel

Deploy the SOA composite. Subsequently, invoke the *FlightUpdateNotificationService* with a request message that specifies *IM* as the Channel. Verify that content-based routing did indeed kick in and routed the message to the *ChatClient* (and not to the *EmailSender*).

Also check if a chat message is indeed received at the destination address, containing the expected information about the flight status—similar to Figure 6-8.

Also invoke the *FlightUpdateNotificationService* with a request message that specifies *email* as the Channel. Verify that content-based routing did indeed kick in and route the message to the *EmailSender* this time and ignored the routing rule for the ChatClient. Check what happens if you set Channel to an unknown value, such as *bloemkool*.

Feeding the Financial Queue through JMS

Saibot Airport charges airlines for the use of the airport and its facilities. The fees charged are based on several factors, including date and time of day, weight of the aircraft—Maximum Take-off Mass of the aircraft (MTOM)—as well as its noisiness, number of passengers, origin or destination, and the airline involved. The financial department will process all reports of landings and take-offs and prepare invoices for the airlines accordingly. This department operates rather independently of other divisions at Saibot Airport, and at its own pace. For its technical implementation it has a backend system that will read accounts of aircraft movements from a JMS Queue. Since it involves a fire-and-forget process it won't return a response.

We will create a Service Bus project that puts the aircraft movements on the financial queue. A proxy service is exposed by this project that consumers can invoke to report landing and taking-off of aircrafts, with the required details. The composite will convey these messages in the appropriate text-based format to the JMS queue.

The Service Bus has two ways of interacting with JMS destinations. One is through the JMS transport and one uses the JCA adapter for JMS (that is also available for SOA composites). Both methods support outbound as well as inbound interactions. They also both implement request/response message exchange over JMS that allows them to do synch-to-asynch bridging and expose a synchronous interface on top of a JMS-based business service.

The functionality of these two options is similar but not entirely the same. The Oracle product team indicates that the JMS transport is the preferred option whenever its functionality suffices for the task at hand. That is the reason this option is part of the *Technology* category in the component palette, rather than the *Advanced* category. The underlying explanation lies in the history of the two major components in the SOA Suite (Service Bus and SCA engine) that were independently developed—Service Bus originated at BEA Systems—and have been converging ever since Oracle acquired BEA.

For educational purposes, we will use both approaches in the *AircraftMovementsService* Service Bus project—one with the JMS transport and one with the JCA adapter for JMS. Instead of a Service Bus project, we could use an SOA composite with a mediator component to provide the same functionality. Which implementation to choose is largely a matter of taste, as laid down in the guidelines an organization has adopted.

Introducing JMS

JMS (Java Message Service) is a Java EE standard (JSR-194) that describes an API for interacting with a messaging infrastructure. Many open source projects and commercial vendors offer messaging technologies—such as Apache ActiveMQ, SonicMQ, WebLogic JMS, WebSphere MQ (aka MQSeries) from IBM, Oracle AQ, or EMS from Tibco—that can be accessed via JMS, either directly or through adapters. Java EE Application Servers also contain messaging frameworks that publish a JMS API—including JBoss Messaging, Glassfish Sun Java System Message Queue, and Oracle Enterprise Messaging Services (based on WebLogic JMS or Advanced Queuing).

Messaging according to JMS comprises two main models:

- Publish a message to a *queue* and have it consumed by one and only consumer.
- Publish a message to a *topic* from where it can be consumed by potentially many consumers.

This fundamental model is embellished and refined in many ways, including topics that persist messages until all registered consumers have consumed it—even when they were unavailable at the time of publication, various retry patterns for delivering messages, high availability and performance features, transactional support, etc.

JMS and SOA Suite

The SOA Suite supports interactions from and to JMS destination in various ways, both in Service Bus projects and in SOA composites. For Service Bus we can use the special JMS transport to configure a business to send messages to JMS or a proxy service to receive inbound messages over JMS. Both Service Bus and SOA composites use the JCA adapter for JMS for both outbound and inbound interactions. Note that behind the scenes, the Service Bus and SOA Suite also use JMS on various levels and for multiple functions in their internal infrastructure. One example of this is the Event Delivery Network (EDN) that we will discuss in Chapter 15.

Setup the JMS Destination for AircraftMovement Reports in WebLogic

JMS destinations, queues and topics, are created at WebLogic level—for example, through the WLS Admin Console. These are not specific to SOA Suite but can be used by all components and applications running on WebLogic. For the next sections on creating SOA Suite projects that interact with JMS for publishing messages, it is assumed that you follow the detailed instructions that are published on line, resulting in a JMS queue with a JNDI name of jms/finance/AircraftMovementsQueue in the SOAJMSModule and a Connection Factory called jms/finance/FinanceConnectionFactory in that same JMS Module. Note: In real life you should be creating your own JMS Module instead of using the SOAJMSModule that SOA Suite uses itself; the online instructions describe this as well.

Implementation of the AircraftMovementService with the JMS Transport

The JMS queue that was set up in the previous section provides a buffer between the operational division of Saibot Airport and the financial department. Messages are put on the queue, entrusted to the platform infrastructure. The operations side of things can continue with their responsibilities and in due time and in their own way, the financial systems will take care of those messages. Decoupling in optima forma. Whenever systems inside an enterprise require interaction that can be asynchronous (either fire and forget or callback in your own time), this type of JMS based-communication is a good option, especially when the availability or processing speeds differ between the systems involved.

We will create a Service Bus project that implements the *AircraftMovementService*. This is a regular SOAP Web Service with a single one-way operation that is invoked with a SOAP/XML message that contains details about the landing or take-off of an aircraft. The Service Bus project ensures that this message ends up on the JMS queue.

Prepare the Application and Project

From the New gallery, create a new Service Bus application with a Service Bus project. Call both *AircraftMovementService*.

Import Service Bus Resources from the file aircraftMovementServiceStartpoint.jar. This will create the folders WSDLs and Schemas with the interface definition of the *AircraftMovementService*.

Create the Business Service with JMS Transport

The essential aspect of this project is the business service that uses the JMS transport to connect to the world of JMS. Open the overview editor for the *AircraftMovementService*.

Drag the JMS Transport component from Technology category on the component palette to the External References lane, as shown in Figure 6-9. When you drop it, the business service wizard appears. Set the name of the business service to *FinanceAircraftMovementsReporter*. The transport is already set to jms.

Click Next.

Set the Service Type to Messaging. For the Request, select Text as the Messaging type. Set it to None for the Response, as we are implementing a one-way service where we expect no response. In an asynchronous JMS request/response scenario setting the response is necessary, in order to define the JMS message being returned and correlated to the request message.

Press Next.

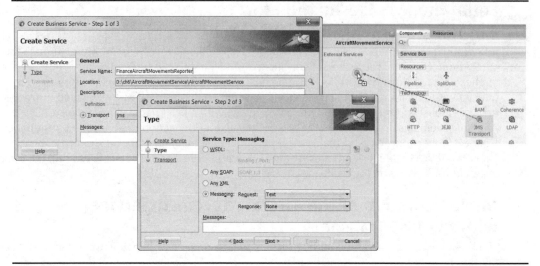

FIGURE 6-9.   *Drag the JMS Transport to the External References area in the Service Bus project*

The Endpoint URI for the JMS destination that this transport will interact with has to be set on the third page (Figure 6-10). The format of this URI is: jms://host:port/<JNDI name of Connection Factory>/<JNDI name of the destination queue>. Note that in the JNDI names, the slashes have to be replaced with periods. You have created this destination according to the online instructions. The Endpoint URI in this case should therefore probably be set to: jms://localhost:7101/jms .finance.FinanceConnectionFactory/jms.finance.AircraftMovementsQueue.

Press Finish.

The business service is created and added in the project overview.

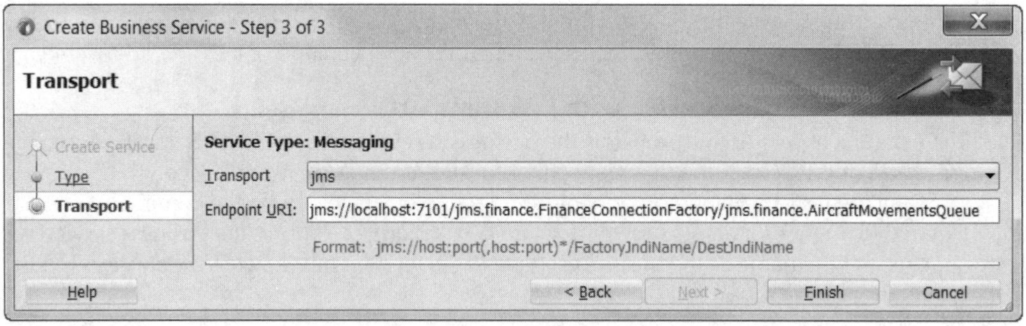

⚙ Create Business Service - Step 3 of 3	✕

Transport

Create Service	**Service Type: Messaging**
Type	Transport [jms ▼]
Transport	Endpoint URI: [jms://localhost:7101/jms.finance.FinanceConnectionFactory/jms.finance.AircraftMovementsQueue]
	Format: jms://host:port(,host:port)*/FactoryJndiName/DestJndiName

| Help | < Back | Next > | Finish | Cancel |

FIGURE 6-10.   *Set the JMS Endpoint URI for the outbound JMS transport*

Test the Business Service

Run the business service from its context menu. The Service Bus composite is deployed and the familiar test interface displays. You can enter the contents of the message to be published to the JMS destination. The message is of type text with no further constraints—so you type anything you like. Press Execute. There is no response message—obviously, because this is a one-way operation. There is, however, some response metadata and a response code with value 0 if the interaction was successful or a fault if it was not.

To find out if indeed the message was published to the *AircraftMovementsQueue*, we can do several things. We can run a Java Client to retrieve messages from the queue, we can use a convenient tool like QBrowser, Hermes, or JMSBrowser to inspect the contents of the queue or we can simply inspect the queue in the WebLogic Console.

Open the console. In the Domain Structure window, select Services | Messaging | JMS Modules. In the list of JMS Modules, click on *SOAJMSModule*. In the Summary of resources, locate queue jms/finance/AircraftMovementsQueue. Click on it. Then open the Monitoring tab. This tab presents an overview with all messages that are currently on the queue and have been published to the queue in the past. Whenever you re-execute the business service from the tester in JDeveloper and subsequently refresh this monitoring tab, the messages total listed should increase by one. You can also drill down and inspect the metadata of individual messages as well as their contents.

Proxy Service and Pipeline

Completing the Service Bus composite is pretty straightforward now, because it is not really different from creating a proxy service and pipeline for any other type of Business Service. The fact that this business service communicates to a JMS destination is not relevant to either pipeline or proxy service.

The WSDL document AircraftMovementService.wsdl was imported during the initial preparation of the project, along with the referenced XSD-documents, and are now in the appropriate folders (WSDLs and Schemas). Generate a proxy service *AircraftMovementServicePS* from the WSDL and an associated pipeline *AircraftMovementPipeline*. Set the Endpoint URI for the proxy service to /monitor/AircraftMovementService.

Wire the pipeline to the business service *FinanceAircraftMovementsReporter* (see Figure 6-11).

You can easily test the proxy service, by running it from the context menu. The composite is again redeployed and the service tester opens with a sample XML message. Because the contents of the request message will simply end up on the JMS queue, you can press execute to invoke the AircraftMovementService with the sample message.

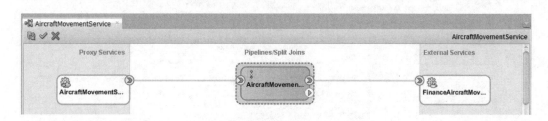

FIGURE 6-11.   *Wiring the AircraftMovementPipeline to the FinanceAircraftMovementReporter business service*

The meta response code should be 0—to indicate a successful transfer of the request message to the one-way service. Check the contents of the queue to verify whether the message was delivered; this can be done through the Admin Console for the Integrated WLS (http://localhost:7101/console) or through external tools such as QBrowser.

Alternative Implementation Using the JCA JMS Adapter

SOA Suite ships with a JCA adapter for JMS that can be used with both Service Bus and SOA composites. In Service Bus projects, the JMS transport is the preferred choice for JMS interaction, although the differences with using the JCA adapter are fairly small. When the requirement is to synchronously read (rather than poll) a message from a JMS queue, the outbound JCA adapter is the only option available.

The next sections describe how to use the JCA adapter for JMS with a Service Bus project—to perform the same operation that we previously used the JMS transport for.

To use the JCA JMS adapter, we have to configure the JMS adapter deployment in the WebLogic Server that also runs the SOA Suite. Subsequently, a JMS adapter binding is added to the Service Bus project. This binding is configured with the JMS destination it should target and the JMS adapter connection it should leverage.

Configure the JMS Adapter Connection

Just as with the Database Adapter and other JCA adapters, some generic, cross-service configuration of the adapter is done on the adapter deployment in the target WebLogic Server. A connection is created in that deployment—that forms the link between the usage of the JMS adapter in the service implementation and a specific JMS connection factory that is to be used by the JMS adapter.

In the WLS Admin console, show the list of deployments. Locate the JmsAdapter. Click on it. This brings up a pane titled *Settings for JmsAdapter*. Open the Configuration tab. Click on the New button to create a new outbound connection. This is a prescription for the JMS adapter to connect to a JMS Connection Factory from which it can gain access to Queues and Topics.

A two-step wizard starts for creating the connection. Accept the default (and only) option in the first step. Set the JNDI name to eis/Finance/Queue in the second step, as shown in Figure 6-12. Then press Finish.

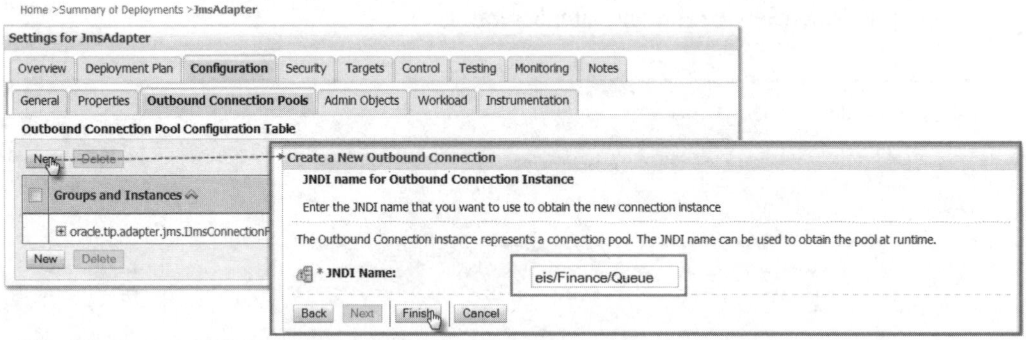

FIGURE 6-12. *Configure a new outbound connection for the JMS adapter*

The list of all connections appears. Click on the newly created connection eis/Finance/Queue to configure its reference to a JMS Connection Factory (Figure 6-13). A list with Outbound Connection Properties appears. Click on the property value for the *ConnectionFactoryLocation*. Enter the value jms/finance/FinanceConnectionFactory. Press enter to set the value. Then click on the Save button to commit it.

At this point, even though the changes have been activated, the JmsAdapter still needs to be redeployed in order for the changes to become effective.

Go to the Deployments summary, mark the checkbox for the JmsAdapter, and click on the Update button above the table. On the Update Application Assistant page, select "Redeploy this application using the following deployment files" and press Finish. After a few seconds, you will get a message that the selected deployment was updated. At this point, the new JMS Adapter connection can be used.

Configure the Outbound JMS Adapter Binding

Drag the JCA JMS adapter from the Advanced category to the External References lane. When you drop it, the adapter configuration wizard appears, to configure the JMS adapter binding. Detailed instructions in the online chapter complement.

On the first page, set the name of the Reference to *FinanceAircraftMovementsReporterJCA*. Set the Service Directory to the Adapters folder. Click Next.

Select the Oracle Enterprise Messaging Service JMS provider and specify the Oracle WebLogic JMS option on page two. Press Next.

On the third page, select the AppServer connection to the Integrated WLS. This connection is used to browse for the JMS adapter connection and the JMS queue. Press Next. Select *Import an existing WSDL* and select the AircraftMovementService.wsdl as the source.

On the Operation page, set the Operation Type to Produce Message. The name of the operation is derived from the WSDL and is set to *reportAircraftMovement*.

The next page of the wizard (Figure 6-14) is titled Produce Operation Parameters. Set the Destination Name to the JNDI name of the JMS queue the adapter binding should publish messages to: jms/finance/AircraftMovementsQueue. Accept the defaults for Message Body Type (JMS_PP_TEXT_TYPE) and Delivery Mode (Persistent). Set the TimeToLive to 15 seconds.

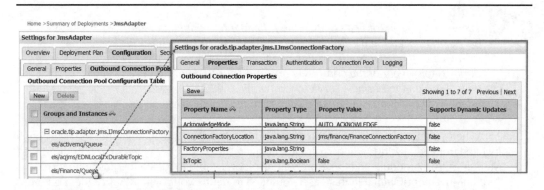

FIGURE 6-13. *JMS adapter connection properties—set the value for the ConnectionFactoryLocation property*

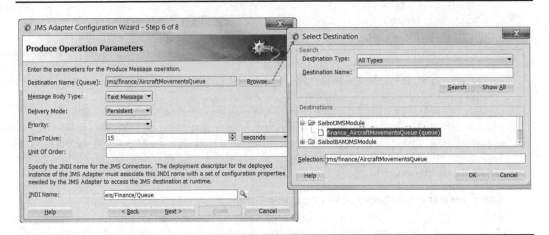

FIGURE 6-14. *Configure the outbound JMS adapter binding*

The JNDI Name [of the JMS adapter connection] should be set to eis/Finance/Queue—the name specified for the new connection that was configured for the JMS adapter.

Press Next. In the next page, if we have not yet defined the Adapter Interface, we can specify the format of the messages that the JMS adapter should pass onward to the JMS queue. Checking the checkbox *Native format translation is not required (Schema is Opaque)* is used when a base64 payload should be passed. Alternatively, we can specify a native XSD definition for whatever format the JMS message payload should have. In this case, the WSDL specifies the *reportAircraftMovementRequestMessage* and this page in the wizard is disabled.

Press Next, then press Finish to complete the configuration of the outbound JMS adapter binding.

JDeveloper will create a business service with JCA transport that references the JMS adapter binding configuration file FinanceAircraftMovementsReporterJCA.jca. You can test this business service—by activating the run option in the context menu on the business service in the Service Bus composite overview.

NOTE
There is no reason for first creating the JMS adapter connection and only then configuring the JMS adapter binding in the composite. The reference to the JNDI Name eis/Finance/Queue is only validated during deployment of the composite and used at run time. However, when you run the business service from within the IDE, the JMS adapter connection has to be in place in the target WebLogic Server.

When you use separate managed servers for Service Bus and SCA engine, the JMS adapter invoked from Service Bus will run on the managed server for OSB where it will not find the JMS Module SOAJMSModule and therefore will also not be able to locate the jms/finance/AircraftMovementsQueue. In this case, you need to define your own JMS Module, add the *AircraftMovementsQueue* to it and target this JMS Module to the managed server running Service Bus. Details are explained in the online instructions.

Redirect the Routing

The new business service for the JCA adapter is not yet used in the Service Bus composite. Open the pipeline editor and click on the routing activity (Figure 6-15). Browse for the *FinanceAircraftMovementsReporterJCA* business service as the new target for this activity. The reportAircraftMovement operation should be selected as the one to invoke.

Check the new wiring in the project overview (right side in Figure 6-15).

Run the Service

Run the proxy service, provide the details for an aircraft movement, and submit the request. No response is returned. In fact, you will not notice any difference in calling the proxy from when the JMS transport was used.

Verify the contents of the JMS queue to see whether a message was indeed published.

Comparing JMS Transport and JCA Adapter for JMS

The configuration details for the JMS transport is stored entirely in the business service. This means they are part of the service implementation and deployed along with it. With the JMS JCA adapter, similar settings are specified. Some of these are part of the JMS adapter binding—that is part of the implementation that gets deployed. Other properties are set on the connection that is configured on the JMS adapter (deployment) on the WebLogic server; these properties are set and managed outside of JDeveloper and the deployable unit. The connection can be reused across multiple JMS adapter bindings.

Alternative Implementation Using an SOA Composite

The JCA adapter for JMS is also available with SOA composites, but the JMS Transport is not. Creating an SOA composite that is functionally equivalent to the *AircraftMovementService* Service Bus project turns out very simple indeed, using the exact same JCA adapter configuration. The steps for this (details and step-by-step screenshots) are provided in the online chapter resources.

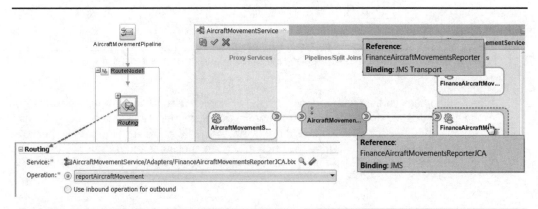

FIGURE 6-15. *Configure the routing node in the pipeline to route messages to the outbound JMS business service; The pipeline is wired now to the new business service (based on the JMS adapter); the original business service (based on the JMS Transport) is currently not used*

Asynchronous Processing or the Mini-Batch

Asynchronous processing of a request is a good way of decoupling (almost releasing) the consumer from the actual processing performed by a service. If the service is not going to respond—not with a result message nor with a fault—there is really not a good reason for a service to be implemented synchronously and have the consumer wait for the processing to complete. Instead, each service request will trigger a mini-batch to be started in the background. The work is ideally started pretty much instantaneously—in most cases, but on a separate thread—so as to not block the invoker.

However, one thing consumers should be able to rely on, is a promise that their message is not only received but is also securely stored and will be processed, if not immediately. The HTTP-200 acknowledgment only specifies reception by the Service Bus but does not give any guarantee about safe storage for subsequent processing.

In a common pattern for providing both asynchronous processing and a guarantee of safe storage (illustrated in Figure 6-16), the service that receives the request message will start a transaction, send the message to a JMS (or AQ) queue, complete the transaction and send a response message. In this way, the service interface is not one-way: it is synchronous. The work done synchronously is minimal: perhaps validation of the request message, then securing the message by enqueuing it on a queue and sending a response message (typically with a unique tracking number that identifies the conversation) that signifies: your message was received and understood; we are now committed to processing it, at some later point in time. If this asynchronous message processing will result in a message to be sent to the original service consumer, the tracking number is used to refer to the original conversation.

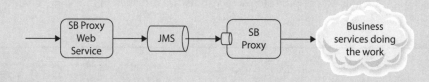

FIGURE 6-16. *Synchronous operation for reliable, asynchronous processing*

At the back end, an inbound JMS (or AQ) adapter is used to listen to new messages on the queue that require processing. An incoming message triggers a service—Service Bus or SOA composite—that does the actual processing. When that background processing fails there is no easy way of informing the original service consumer and it usually falls to the service provider to handle the problem.

Content-Based Routing in Service Bus Pipelines

Earlier in this chapter, we have seen how the Mediator component supports content-based routing—through filter expressions on routing rules that determine whether or not a routing is executed. In Service Bus pipelines too, we can implement conditional routing.

We have already seen operational branches that define a path based on the operation that was invoked on the pipeline's interface. A similar construct, called conditional branch, can be configured with multiple branches, one of which is executed according to an XPath expression. Whichever condition is satisfied first determines which branch is executed. If none of the branch conditions is satisfied, then the default branch is performed. Routing Table is a similar activity where multiple routing options are configured, one of which is executed depending on the evaluation of an XPath expression.

The *dynamic routing* activity is another mechanism with which a form of content-based routing can be realized. The business service or pipeline to route the message to is determined using an XQuery expression—one that could for example read a routing table from an XML file or Domain Value Map.

We will use content-based routing in the *AircraftMovementPipeline* to easily switch between the JMS Transport and JCA JMS adapter as business service to route the *AircraftMovementReport* messages to. Then we will add an Advanced Queue Adapter to the mix.

NOTE
This example of content-based routing is used for educational purposes. In real-life systems, it would make no sense at all to have this kind of conditional routing between three mechanisms that are basically the same. You would normally pick one and be done with it.

Switching between JMS Transport and JCA JMS Adapter Using Conditional Branching

A conditional branch is introduced into our pipeline to implement content-based routing. Depending on the value set in a pipeline variable $channel, the conditional branch will either execute the branch that routes to the JMS Transport (business service) or the JCA JMA Adapter (business service). First we add the variable and its assignment, next we use the variable in the conditional branch.

Add a pipeline pair called SetChannel as the first node in the pipeline. Add an Assign activity. Configure this activity to assign a value

```
<ChannelValue>JMSTransport</ChannelValue>
```

to variable *channel*, as shown in Figure 6-17. Alternatively, the values JMSJCA and AQ can be assigned to the ChannelValue element in this expression.

By setting the value of variable $channel, we want to govern the routing of the request through the pipeline. The pipeline activity we use to implement that behavior is called Conditional Branch.

Drag the Conditional Branch from the component palette and drop it in the pipeline, right after the pipeline pair *SetChannel*. Set the Expression field to channel (to indicate that this expression operates in the context of that variable). Set the expression itself to ./text()—or

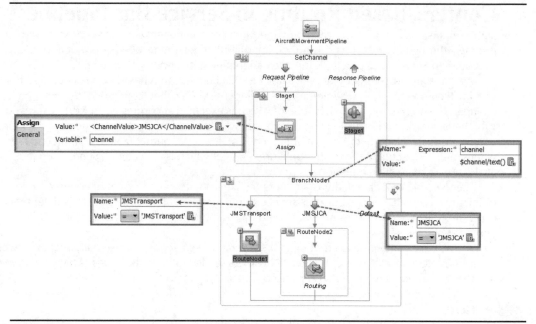

FIGURE 6-17. *Assign activity to set the $channel variable that governs the routing and configure a conditional branch with branches for various conditions based on $channel*

$channel/text(). This instructs the conditional branch to derive the text value in the root element of the $channel variable. This evaluates to one of the values JMSTransport, JMSJCA, or AQ. Note: Conditional branching is driven by an XPath expression (not XQuery).

Add branches inside this activity that are labeled JMSTransport and JMSJCA. Configure them to trigger on the values "JMSTransport" and "JMSJCA," respectively, by setting the operator to the equality operator and the XPath expression to the appropriate string value.

Add the Route node with Routing activity to the JMS JCA business service—including the Replace activity—to the JMSJCA branch, by simply dragging and dropping it. Add a route node with routing activity to the JMS Transport business service to the JMSTransport branch.

The Service Bus project overview will now display two wires from the pipeline to the business services.

You can test the implementation by running the pipeline and check in the trace whether the expected business service as engaged.

Conditional Pipelines

Instead of performing the necessary logic directly in the conditional branch—such as the transformation of the request message in the JMS JCA branch—we could instead create pipelines for each conditional branch and include the logic in the designated pipeline. The first pipeline would only hold the conditional branch and the logic for invoking the required pipeline, whereas the actual work for each condition is done in the condition-specific pipeline that ends with doing the routing to the associated business service. Note: The communication between local pipelines is very efficient; there is no noticeable difference in performance overhead between the single pipeline and this multi-pipeline approach.

The result of that approach is shown in Figure 6-18.

NOTE
Service Bus composites offer yet an alternative implementation of content-based routing, through the Dynamic Routing activity. A dynamic routing activity determines at run time which business service to route a message to. A target can be both a business service or a pipeline, as well as a split-join or a proxy service.

The dynamic routing activity is configured with an XQuery expression that has to produce the Business Service and Operation to invoke in the following format:

```
<ctx:route>
    <ctx:service>AircraftMovementService/Business Service/
FinanceAircraftMovementsReporter
    </ctx:service>
<ctx:operation>report</ctx:operation>
</ctx:route>
```

The service element contains the fully qualified name of the business service, in the format <project name>/<foldernames>/<name of business service [file without .bix extension]>.

Routing to a pipeline requires a similar XML snippet:

```
<ctx:route>
    <ctx:pipeline>Pipelines/AircraftMovementPipelineJMSTransport</ctx:pipeline>
</ctx:route>
```

With this dynamic routing to pipelines, instead of using a conditional branch we can use a dynamic routing action to determine which pipeline to invoke, assuming that for each condition we have a separate pipeline.

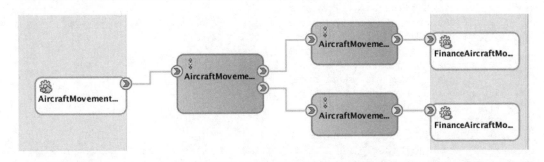

FIGURE 6-18. *First pipeline with the conditional branch, routing to condition specific pipelines to handle the work*

Using AQ instead of JMS

Advanced Queuing is the enterprise queuing mechanism in the Oracle Database. Its role and use cases are very similar to JMS—with one large difference: PL/SQL handlers can be associated directly with AQ queues, and not with middleware-based JMS destinations. If the messages queued are to be processed by stored procedures inside an Oracle Database, then publishing them to AQ could be preferred.

From the perspective of the SOA Suite, there is hardly any distinction between JMS and AQ as destinations. After setting up the AQ queue and backing table, we will configure the AQ adapter deployment on WebLogic—similar to how we did it for the Database Adapter and the JMS adapter. The outbound AQ adapter binding is configured in very much the same way as the JMS adapter binding was. We will modify the Service Bus composite created in the previous section by adding a new branch. Instead of JMS as destination, we will use AQ as the target for the *AircraftMovement* messages. And this requires very little work with very little impact.

> **NOTE**
> *JMS Queues in Web Logic can be backed by an Advanced Queue*
> *in the Oracle Database. Publishing messages to the JMS Queue then*
> *indirectly means publishing them to the underlying Advanced Queue.*
> *PL/SQL handlers could pick up messages from that queue as well.*

Configure Advanced Queue in Database

We assume a user SAIBOT_FINANCE has been set up in the database. As a DBA (e.g., as user SYS), grant the aq_administrator_role to user saibot_finance. Also execute this statement:

```
EXECUTE dbms_aqadm.grant_type_access('saibot_finance');
```

These next statements are to be executed by the user SAIBOT_FINANCE in order to create the type that defines the payload for messages on the queue, and also create the queue and the queue table and subsequently start the queue.

```
CREATE TYPE aircraft_movement_report_t AS OBJECT (
     message_id       NUMBER(15)
  ,  movement_timestamp    timestamp
  ,  flightnumber          number(3)
  ,  carrier_iata_code     varchar2(3)
  ,  airport_iata_code     varchar2(3)
  ,  arrival_or_departure varchar2(1)
  ,  aircraft_iata_equipment_code       varchar2(3)
  ,  number_of_passengers number(4,0)
);
BEGIN
    DBMS_AQADM.CREATE_QUEUE_TABLE (
        queue_table           => 'saibot_finance.aircraft_movements_qt'
      , queue_payload_type => 'saibot_finance.aircraft_movement_report_t'
    );
    DBMS_AQADM.CREATE_QUEUE (
        queue_name            => 'aircraft_movements_queue'
```

```
        , queue_table          => 'saibot_finance.aircraft_movements_qt'
        , queue_type           => DBMS_AQADM.NORMAL_QUEUE
        , max_retries          => 0
        , retry_delay          => 0
        , retention_time       => 1209600
        , dependency_tracking  => FALSE
        , comment              => 'Aircraft Movement Reports Queue'
        , auto_commit          => FALSE
    );
    DBMS_AQADM.START_QUEUE('aircraft_movements_queue');
END;
```

At this point the AQ queue *aircraft_movements_queue* has been created and started. It accepts messages with a payload of type *aircraft_movement_report_t*. The queue is backed by a queue table called *aircraft_movements_qt*.

Configure AQ Adapter Connection in WebLogic Server

First create a JDBC Data Source connecting to the database schema that either owns the queue or has at least a usage grant on the queue. Set the JNDI name for this Data Source to jdbc/SaibotFinanceDS.

Then find the AQ adapter deployment in the summary of deployments. Click on this deployment to go to the Settings. Open the Configuration tab and within that the Outbound Connections Pool. Click on the New button, to create a new connection.

Another two step wizard, in which you accept the default and only Outbound Connection Group on the first page and set the JNDI name for this new connection on the second page. This name will be referenced from the outbound Adapter binding in the service implementation. Set the name to eis/aq/SaibotFinance.

Press Finish to complete the creation of the connection. Next, return to the *Properties* tab for the connection. The DataSourceName or XADataSourceName (depending on how you created the data source—XADataSource if you accepted the default driver) property has to be set with the JNDI name of the data source: jdbc/SaibotFinanceDS.

Press enter and press the Save button. Now to ensure the new AQ adapter connection is available for use, update the AqAdapter deployment. See for more details and screenshots for all steps described here the online chapter complement.

Configure AQ Adapter Binding

The JCA AQ adapter too can be used in both Service Bus projects and SOA composite applications. We will add it to the *AircraftMovementService* project that contains the Service Bus artifacts. The configuration of the adapter binding is exactly the same in the context of an SOA composite.

Open the overview editor for the *AircraftMovementService*. Drag the AQ adapter to the External References lane and drop it (see Figure 6-19).

The AQ adapter configuration wizard appears. Set the name of the reference to *FinanceAircraftMovementReporterAQ*. Click Next.

Select or create a database connection to the SAIBOT_FINANCE database schema that contains the queue to publish to. Set the JNDI name [of the AQ adapter connection] to eis/aq/SaibotFinance. Click Next.

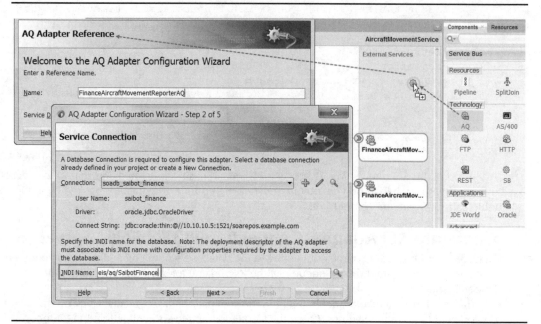

FIGURE 6-19. *Add the outbound AQ adapter to the Service Bus project AircraftMovementService*

Click Next again on the Adapter Interface page: we will define the interface from the operation and schema (specified later).

Set the Operation Type to *Enqueue*. Set the name of the operation to *Report*. Click Next.

Browse for the AIRCRAFT_MOVEMENTS_QUEUE in the SAIBOT_FINANCE database schema, as shown in Figure 6-20. Messages will be enqueued by the newly created AQ adapter binding to this queue.

Press Next.

Do not specify a correlation id, because the enqueue operation we configure for this adapter binding is not in response to previously dequeued message that it should be correlated with. Press Next.

The payload type for the queue is set in the database to AIRCRAFT_MOVEMENT_REPORT_T. The AQ adapter can either publish a message with a payload based on that entire object or one that contains but a single field in that object. In this case, select the *Whole Object* option. Press Next. And press Finish.

The AQ adapter binding is generated—both the JCA configuration and the business service that leverages it. The interface of the business service is described by the WSDL and XSD files that were generated by the AQ adapter wizard.

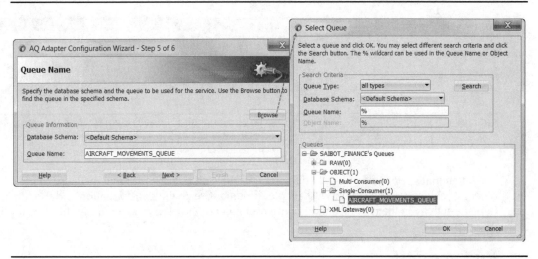

FIGURE 6-20. *Configuring the AIRCRAFT_MOVEMENTS_QUEUE to publish messages onto*

Add the AQ Path to the Conditional Branch in the AircraftMovementPipeline

Open the *AircraftMovementPipeline*. Add a new branch to the Conditional Branch node. Set the label of the new branch to AQ. Set the operator to "=" and the expression to "AQ," as visualized in Figure 6-21.

Add a Route node with a Routing activity inside. Configure the routing activity for the *FinanceAircraftMovementReporterAQ* business service because we want the pipeline to route messages to this business service for the AQ adapter and have it publish the reports on the Advanced Queue instead of the JMS Queue.

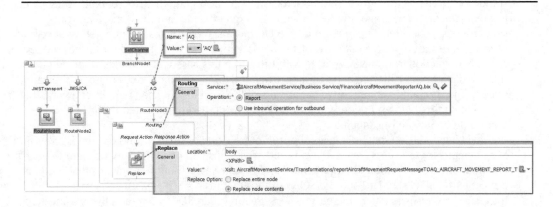

FIGURE 6-21. *Configuring the branch for the AQ channel*

FIGURE 6-22. *Verifying the contents of the AIRCRAFT_MOVEMENTS_QUEUE in the JDeveloper Database Navigator*

Additionally, we need a slightly different transformation of the message, because of the different schema required by the AQ adapter binding. Create the transformation and use it in a Replace activity in the request action of the routing node, to prepare the request message for the AQ adapter.

Run and Test

Change the assign activity in the SetChannel step—assign a value of AQ to the ChannelValue element in the $channel variable. This ensures that when we next deploy and run the service, our message is routed through the AQ branch of the conditional branch and hence to the AQ adapter binding.

Now run the pipeline or the service and send a message with an *AircraftMovementReport*.

At this point, there should be a new message on the AQ Queue in the Saibot Finance database. We can verify this in several ways, including the Database Navigator view in JDeveloper (as shown in Figure 6-22) and a simple SQL statement performed against the Saibot Finance database schema (select * from AIRCRAFT_MOVEMENTS_QT).

Invoking an Enterprise Java Bean (EJB)

In this section, we will assume that the financial department considers publishing an EJB as the interface to send reports of aircraft movements to—possibly because it allows them to perform some validations on the reports sent in before actually accepting them. Apparently they receive too many incorrect messages to their liking on the queue and want to do more upfront—synchronous—checking. The method on the EJB has a similar role as the queue has: accept an object that describes an aircraft movement, validate it, and pass it onward for further processing.

The interaction from the SOA Suite with the EJB in this case will be synchronous, because the finance department will raise an exception when the input to the EJB does not pass the validation checks. The *AircraftMovementService* that calls out to the EJB will itself remain one way. That means that in real life exception handling would have to be implemented in the SOA Suite composite or Service Bus pipeline.

Invoking an EJB—whether it is local or remote—is one of several ways for Service Bus and SOA composites to access external Java-based code. EJBs can be SDO (Service Data Objects) enabled, or can be defined through a (remote) Java interface. The former means that the EJBs adhere to the SDO standard and the SOA composite transfers SDO parameters to the EJB in order to operate on business data. One easy way of creating such SDO powered EJBs is using ADF Business Components.

NOTE
*Interaction through EJBs is much more tightly coupled of course
than JMS-based interaction, although the EJB to be invoked can be
designated asynchronous.*

Prepare the Financial Enterprise Java Bean to Invoke

To set the stage, we will first create a rather simple EJB that we deploy as a stand-alone Java EE
application. This EJB represents the service published by the financial department as an
experimental alternative to the decoupled communication based on JMS queues.

The steps are straightforward: create a new project, develop the interface to be published,
configure the EJB—such as its mapped name—and implement the EJB according to that interface.
Finally, deploy the application.

Implementing the Financial EJB

Create a new JDeveloper project of type EJB project under the *AircraftMovementService*
application. The name of the project is *FinanceAicraftMovementEJB*. The default package is
saibot.airport.finance.

Accept the defaults on the third page of the EJB project wizard, indicating that EJB 3.1 is the
release we are working with and annotations are the preferred way of configuring the EJBs.

Create a Java bean called *AircraftMovement*, with a toString() implementation, that
implements the Serializable interface.

```
public class AircraftMovement implements Serializable {
    @Override
    public String toString() {
        return "Aircraft Movement: at "+movementTimestamp+" for flight "+
carrierIataCode;
    }
    Date movementTimestamp    ;
    Integer flightnumber      ;
    String carrierIataCode  ;
    String airportIataCode ;
    String arrivalOrDeparture ;
    String aircraftIataEquipmentCode ;
    Integer numberOfPassengers ;
...
// accessor methods for these properties
}
```

Add fields and accessors for the bean properties.

Create a Java interface *FinanceAircraftMovementReporter* and add the @Remote annotation.
This will be the remote interface exposed by the EJB as stateless session bean.

```
package saibot.airport.finance;
import javax.ejb.Remote;
@Remote
public interface FinanceAircraftMovementReporter {
    public void reportAircraftMovement( AircraftMovement aircraftMovement);
}
```

Implement class FinanceAircraftMovementReporterBean that implements the
FinanceAircraftMovementReporter interface. Implement method reportAircraftMovement:
make it write some text to the output in order to show proof that the bean has been accessed:

```
package saibot.airport.finance;
import javax.annotation.Resource;
import javax.ejb.SessionContext;
import javax.ejb.Stateless;
@Stateless(name = "FinanceAircraftMovementReporterEJB", mappedName =
"FinanceAircraftMovementReporter")
public class FinanceAircraftMovementReporterBean implements
FinanceAircraftMovementReporter
  {
    @Resource
    SessionContext sessionContext;
    public FinanceAircraftMovementReporterBean() {
    }
    @Override
    public void reportAircraftMovement(AircraftMovement aircraftMovement) {
        System.out.println("AircraftMovement has been reported "+
aircraftMovement);
    }
}
```

Deploy and Test the EJB

Deploy the project, using the EJB deployment profile that was added when the project was first
created as an EJB project.

Generate a sample client using the option New Sample Java Client on the context menu for the
FinanceAircraftMovementReporterBean. A Java class is generated with the necessary statements to
lookup the EJB. Add some code to actually invoke the method *reportAircraftMovement* of the EJB,
for example:

```
    ...
        final Context context = getInitialContext();
            FinanceAircraftMovementReporter financeAircraftMovementReporter =
                (FinanceAircraftMovementReporter) context.lookup("FinanceAircra
ftMovementReporter#saibot.airport.finance.FinanceAircraftMovementReporter");
            AircraftMovement am = new AircraftMovement();
            am.setMovementTimestamp(new Date());
            am.setCarrierIataCode("KLM");
            financeAircraftMovementReporter.reportAircraftMovement(am);
    ...
```

Run the sample Java client just locally, in JDeveloper, and see if the expected line is written by the
EJB to the console, by inspecting the logging of the running Integrated WLS. Note: You may have
to add the library WebLogic 12.1 Remote Client to the project.

If a log entry was indeed written, the EJB is active at the mapped name used in the sample
client code.

Calling Out to EJBs from Service Bus Composites

Callouts from a Service Bus composite are typically handled through a business service. The business service can leverage an adapter or a transport (preferred). And for callouts to EJBs, we even have two transports at our disposal. One is the JEJB transport and the other is the EJB transport. Both interact over RMI in terms of (serialized) Java objects with the remote EJB.

The JEJB transport interacts internally in terms of Java objects. That means that a pipeline that calls a JEJB business service has to pass a Java POJO payload. This is useful when the proxy service exposed by the composite and wired to the pipeline is also based on the JEJB transport— the message is never turned to XML and can stay a Java object all the way. We will discuss the JEJB transport in a later section, when we talk about an inbound EJB interface for a Service Bus composite. For now, we will use a business service based on the EJB transport.

Business Service with EJB Transport

Drag the EJB transport to the outbound references swim lane and drop it. The configuration wizard appears. Set the name of the business service to *FinanceAircraftMovementsReporterEJBTransport*.

On page two of the wizard, specify the Endpoint URI for the Enterprise Java Bean that is to be invoked, as shown in Figure 6-23. This URI pattern in the case of a locally deployed EJB (local means that the EJB is running on the same WLS domain as the SOA Suite run time) follows a pattern of: ejb::jndi_name. For remote beans, this pattern is ejb:jndi_provider:jndi_name. We will discuss this in a later section.

For EJB 3.x beans on Oracle WebLogic Server, jndi_name takes the form of mappedName#BusinessInterface. Therefore, in this current case, the Endpoint URI should be set to the local format: ejb::FinanceAircraftMovementReporter#saibot.airport.finance .FinanceAircraftMovementReporter

Complete the wizard. Then double click the newly created business service and go to the Transport Details tab (Figure 6-24).

Select the checkbox for EJB 3.0. Click on the browse icon for the Client jar. Browse for the jar file AircraftMovementService_FinanceAircraftMovementEJB_ejb.jar that was generated in the deploy directory of FinanceAircraftMovementEJB project when that project was deployed. The Import Service Bus Resources wizard appears. Import this jar file into the Resource folder of the project.

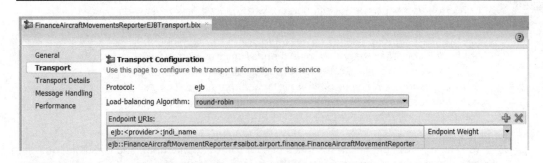

FIGURE 6-23. *Configuration of the outbound EJB transport to the FinanceAircraftMovementReporterBean*

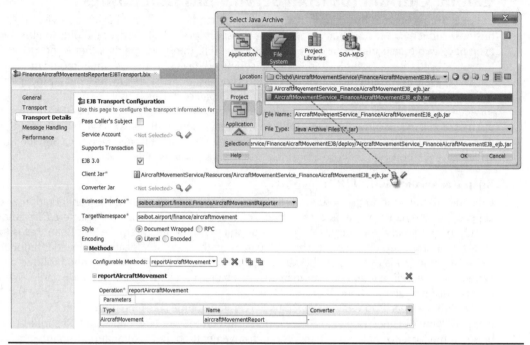

FIGURE 6-24. *Transport details for the EJB transport of the Business Service*

Set the Business Interface to the remote EJB interface saibot.airport.finance
.FinanceAircraftMovementReporter. Set the Target Namespace to saibot.airport/finance/
aircraftmovement.

The only available method is already selected. Change the parameter name to
aircraftMovementReport.

This completes the configuration of the transport.

NOTE
*Converter classes can be specified to convert the Java payloads when
the parameters exchanged with the EJB are too complex for the JAX-
RPC engine to automatically convert them, for example, when they
hold collections that are not strongly typed. The converter classes
are packaged in a single jar file. They must implement the com.bea
.wli.sb.transports.ejb.ITypeConverter interface that prescribes a single
static method called convert that accepts a single input parameter.
We do not need that in this case.*

You can now run the business service, feed it some sample input, and check the output in the
console window that indicates that the EJB was indeed invoked from the Service Bus composite.

Create the Routing to the EJB Business Service

In order to be able to map the request message that is sent into the *AircraftMovementService* to the XML message expected by the business service, we need to know the WSDL interface of the business service. JDeveloper can generate this WSDL for us. Right click on the business service node in the project browser and activate Service Bus | Generate WSDL (Figure 6-25).

Specify the location for the WSDL document—for example, the WSDLs folder. The WSDL gets generated and it contains the XSD definitions that we need for creating the XSL or XQuery transformation.

Create a pipeline *AircraftMovementPipelineEJBTransport*—based on the same *AircraftMovementService* interface used for all other pipelines. Add a route node with a routing activity inside this pipeline. Configure the latter to invoke the business service *FinanceAircraftMovementsReporterEJBTransport*.

Create an XSL Map to transform between the *reportAircraftMovementRequestType* and the {saibot.airport/finance}AircraftMovement. Add a Replace action in the request pipeline to transform the body contents to the XML format required by the business service's WSDL interface generated from the EJB interface using that XSL Map.

We now need to modify the dispatcher *AircraftMovementPipeline* in order to have it connect to the *AircraftMovementPipelineEJBTransport* pipeline. Change the assign activity inside this pipeline and have it set $channel/ChannelValue to EJB—to ensure that in our next test run, the conditional routing brings us to the EJB branch.

Add a branch to the conditional branch. Set its label to EJB and have its expression test for the value "EJB." Add a route node with a routing activity to the branch, the latter wired to the *AircraftMovementPipelineEJBTransport*. The Service Bus project overview at this stage is shown in Figure 6-26.

Test the AircraftMovementService with the EJB Callout

Run either the new EJB business service, the proxy service, or one of the pipelines *AircraftMovementPipelineEJBTransport* or *AircraftMovementPipeline*. Each of these actions will deploy the Service Bus composite and invoke the EJB. The effect in each case is the same: a message is written to the console.

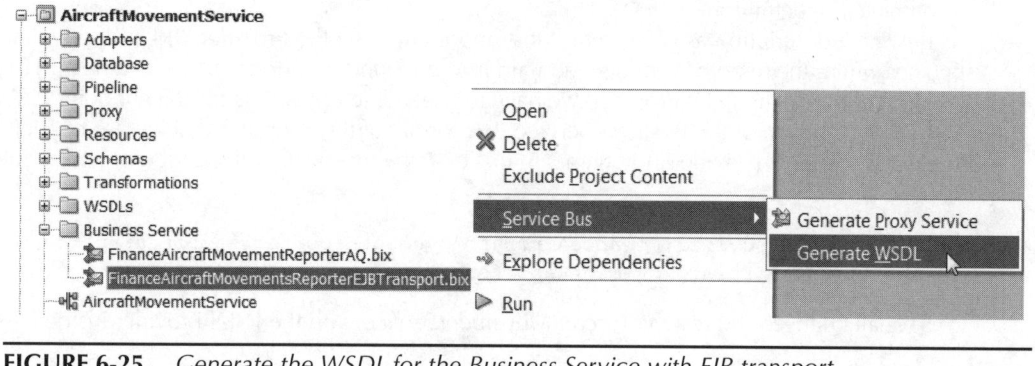

FIGURE 6-25. *Generate the WSDL for the Business Service with EJB transport*

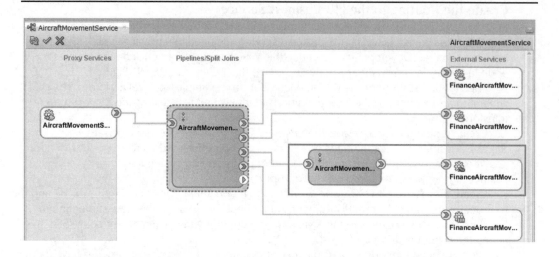

FIGURE 6-26. *Service Bus project with the dispatcher AircraftMovementPipeline and the channel specific pipelines*

Invoking a Remote EJB Using a JNDI Provider

If your EJB is remote—running on a different Java EE Server (than the local WLS that also runs the SOA Suite)—then you need to add a JNDI provider for your EJB. A JNDI Provider resource allows you to specify the communication protocols and security credentials used to retrieve EJB stubs bound in the JNDI tree of remote Oracle WebLogic Server domains or third party application server instances.

In our case, where the EJB is really local, we can still configure a JNDI Provider that references the local EJB container and pretend it is remote, just for educational purposes.

Right click on the Resources folder. Select the context menu option New | JNDI Provider. The JNDI Provider wizard appears. Set the name of the JNDIProvider to *FinanceJNDIProvider*. Click Finish. The JNDI Provider is created—without configuration details. The editor opens to allow you to complete the definition.

Provide a description as you see fit. Most importantly: set the Provider URL property that specifies where the remote WebLogic domain is to be found. In our case: t3://localhost:7101.

In order to use the JNDI Provider, we have to use a different setting for the endpoint URI in the Transport section of the Business Service. The format of the endpoint URI in case of a JNDI Provider is: ejb:jndi_provider:jndi_name. In this case that means that the endpoint URI should be changed to:

```
ejb:FinanceJNDIProvider:FinanceAircraftMovementReporter#saibot.airport.
finance.FinanceAircraftMovementReporter
```

Save all changes and test the *AircraftMovementService* with the JNDI Provider inside.

Calling Out to EJBs from SOA Composite Applications

SOA composites can call out to external services over an SOAP and REST binding—both over HTTP—as we have seen in the previous chapters. Using JCA adapters, they also can talk to file system, database, JMS destination, and email server. There is support too for EJB bindings that interact over RMI with local or remote Enterprise Java Beans.

The EJB binding reference in SOA composites is configured through the EJB Adapter wizard. The wizard asks for the JNDI lookup name for the EJB, the Java Remote EJB Interface, and whether the EJB Binding is WSDL (SDO) based or Java based. In case of an SDO style EJB the wizard requires the WSDL that describes the service provided by the EJB. The parameters sent into the EJB service and returned by it in that case are SDO types. That means that they are described in an XSD that follows the SDO specifications. As we have the parameter definitions generated for us, it is not too large a burden on the developer to work with these SDO enabled EJBs. However, it means that we have the EJB has to be implemented in the SDO way—which may not be possible or desired at all. Working with a Java (interface) based EJB Binding is usually the easier option.

Implement the Outbound EJB Interaction

Open project *AircraftMovementServiceSOAcomposite* and open the SOA composite editor. Drag the EJB Adapter from the Technology section of the component palette to the External References lane and drop it.

The EJB Adapter Configuration wizard appears, see Figure 6-27. Set the name of the adapter binding to *FinanceAircraftMovementReportEJB*.

Set the Type to *reference* (for outbound) and Version to EJB 3. The interface is Java. The JNDI name is the same as before with the EJB transport in the Service Bus composite: FinanceAircraftMovementRe porter#saibot.airport.finance.FinanceAircraftMovementReporter. Select the jar file that was deployed in the EJB project and that was previously imported into the Service Bus project. Again, JDeveloper prompts you to import the JAR file. Accept the offer to have the file copied to the SCA-INF/lib directory.

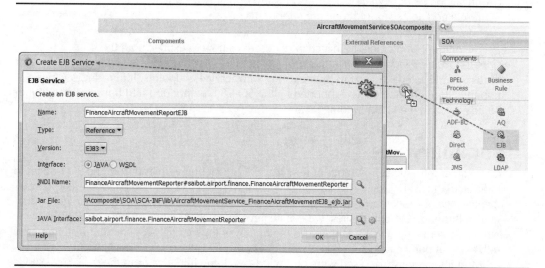

FIGURE 6-27. *Configuring the EJB Reference binding for the EJB FinanceAircraftMovementReporter*

Browse for the Java interface saibot.airport.finance.FinanceAircraftMovementReporter. Then press the OK button to have the EJB Adapter binding generated.

Next, create a wire from the mediator component to the new EJB Adapter binding.

At this point, we can choose: either the Mediator will have a single routing rule to the JMS adapter or the EJB binding, or it will have two routing rules that are both executed. In the latter case the aircraft movement is reported to both the JMS queue and the Financial EJB. Mediators can have multiple routing rules—as we have seen in the beginning of this chapter—and they can all be executed (in case of a one-way service interface).

Ensure that at least one routing rule in the mediator is set up to invoke the EJB binding. Then deploy the SOA composite and invoke its *AircraftMovementService*. Verify the message flow trace or the console window with the logging from the Integrated WLS to establish whether indeed the EJB has been invoked.

Expose Inbound EJB Interfaces

Services exposed from the SOA Suite—whether they are implemented through Service Bus or SOA composites—can be exposed in various ways. The most common is the web service binding or transport that supports SOAP/XML calls over HTTP. We have discussed support for RESTful services, also over HTTP. And now we will look at exposing the service as an EJB over RMI. Both Service Bus composites—using the JEJB transport and SOA composites, through the EJB adapter—can easily be exposed as EJBs. Consumers of these services interact with such EJBs like they do with regular EJBs—no specific SOA Suite aspects are involved. The onus of translating from the world of the Java interface and serialized Java objects to WSDL and XML is on the SOA Suite.

NOTE
With the ever increasing support for web service interaction in Java— through for example JAX-WS and JAX-RS—the relevance of direct EJB interaction is somewhat decreasing. EJBs are primarily used when transaction and security scope are important.

The online complement to this chapter describes how to expose both the *AircraftMovementService* Service Bus project and the *AircraftMovementServiceSOAComposite* through an EJB interface, next to their existing web service endpoints. It introduces various inbound EJB interaction styles supported by the SOA Suite: inbound JEBJ transport, the inbound EJB adapter, and the direct binding facility.

Summary

This chapter introduced a number of new ways of interacting with and from the SOA Suite. In addition to the HTTP-based REST and SOAP style web services we had encountered in previous chapters, we have seen how using special transports in Service Bus or with JCA adapters in both Service Bus and SOA composites, we can achieve interaction over JMS, AQ, and EJB/RMI with external systems. The UMS adapter adds the option of interacting over email or instant messaging with external human actors.

Most interactions discussed were outbound—with the initiative from the SOA Suite service. These services were all asynchronous and more than that: one way (only). A request message is delivered at the SOA Suite's endpoint to be handled after the HTTP handshake is completed and without the invoker waiting for the result. This message exchange pattern adds a level of decoupling that is frequently desirable to simplify in complex architectures. Of course, most of these adapters and transports can also be used for inbound interactions and for other message exchange patterns such as request/reply.

Additionally, this chapter demonstrated how we can publish services from the SOA Suite with an EJB interface over the RMI protocol—using the JEJB transport in Service Bus or the EJB adapter and the Direct Binding API with SOA composites.

A topic on top of all these protocol discussions is content-based routing or the ability to handle messages in a way that is dictated by their specific contents. The conditional branch in Service Bus proves an excellent way of routing messages based on conditions evaluated against the message contents. In SOA composites, the filter expressions on routing rules in the mediator do a very similar thing.

PART
III

Composite Services

CHAPTER
7

Composite Services
with Service Bus

C omposite services are a step beyond the elementary services that were discussed in the previous part. Composite services are services that combine two or more other services to create a service that provides more added value. Composite services invoke elementary services and other composite services, they may access multiple domains, coordinate a global transaction with multiple local transactions. An even simpler definition of composite service: do (substantially) more than straightforward request/reply VETRO. One reason for creating composite service is to prevent the same or very similar combinations of service orchestrations from being duplicated.

Note that the classification in elementary and composite is just one of many ways to classify services. It is a type of classification with which design and implementation guidelines can be associated. The SOA Suite itself does not employ the concept of elementary or composite at all.

In this chapter, we discuss the implementation of composite services with Service Bus. A number of facilities at our disposal for creating more advanced flow logic than we have seen in previous chapters is introduced. Conditional steps, iterations, message transformation, value translation, and callouts are important elements in a composite service. The ability to execute parts of the message processing in parallel—with the Split-Join components—is discussed as well.

With two major options—Service Bus and SOA Composite—at our disposal for implementing services we have to choose how and where to implement composite services. In Chapter 8, we will look at implementing composite services with SOA composites, using the BPEL component. This component has its strength in service orchestration—including asynchronous services—and long running operations. With Service Bus, we can create quite complex services with many actions performed, many callouts made, and a lot of data processing going on. These services however are synchronous or one way, stateless and not long running. They do not interact very easily with asynchronous business services. Deciding when to implement a composite service with Service Bus and when with an SOA composite is to some extent a matter of personal preference: often times they can both do the job perfectly well. In general, the more complex the processing, the more likely an SOA composite will be used.

This chapter looks at the submission of a flight schedule by an airline carrier. Earlier, in Chapter 4, we developed the *SlotService*. Through this service, a specific time slot is assigned to an airline for a departure or arrival. This assignment results in a placeholder in the airport's seasonal flight schedule, which actual scheduled flights can be linked to. The composite *FlightScheduleService* that is the subject of the current chapter takes a request for actually planning a flight. Such a planned flight has to be an implementation of a slot.

The implementation of the *FlightScheduleService* involves the use of multiple pipelines—that handle various stages of validation and enrichment. The set of Service Bus activities used includes validation, service callout and Java callout, error handling, for..each iteration, some complex XQuery processing, if..then..else logic, and the use of DVM (Domain Value Mapping). The Split-Join component is used to speed up the execution by making some of the processing execute in parallel.

Creating the Bare Bones FlightScheduleService

This section discusses the initial creation of the *FlightScheduleService*, making use of a Service Bus template created by some team at Saibot Airport—that provides some of the implementation basics. We will then add some activities to implement a number of validation steps.

In a planned flight, flight details that are not defined in a slot allocation are stated. These include the actual dates on which a flight takes place (within the perimeters set by the slot), the aircraft model used for the flight, the connecting airport, the assigned flight number, the (provisionally) assigned terminal, pier and potentially even gate and the connecting planned flight: most flights are either the prequel to a departing flight or the sequel to an arriving flight—unless the airplane is parked after or was parked before the flight.

Along with the scheduled flight, details about code sharing are provided: one scheduled flight is associated with the operating airline. Other airlines may cooperate the flight and each have their own flight numbers to identify the flight. These details have to be recorded—if for no other reason than to present the information on the flight information monitors in the airport buildings.

The *FlightScheduleService* has to validate the details that were provided, it will then have to enrich some of the information before it can finally invoke the business service that will actually assign the flight identification and record the flight.

Set Up the FlightScheduleService

Open application *FlightScheduleService*. This application has two predefined projects.

Create Local Proxy PrivateSubmitFlightSchedule

Open project *PrivateSubmitFlightSchedule*. This project contains a pipeline that implements a service interface that will be invoked by the publicly exposed *FlightScheduleService*. The pipeline currently contains a dummy implementation.

Right click the Pipeline and activate the run option in the context menu. This will deploy the project and open the tester. Invoke the service exposed by the pipeline. The input consists of details for a flight to be scheduled by Saibot Airport. The response contains the flight identifier assigned by Saibot along with the tentatively (and currently hard coded) allocated gate.

Eventually, this implementation could be extended with a database adapter to record the scheduled flight in the database. It will then invoke a database procedure to have the scheduled flight created as a record in table fut_planned_flights with possible details in detail table fut_code_shares; the service should return the identifier of the created flight and possibly the tentatively assigned gate details.

We will expose the pipeline as a locally available service—a proxy that can only be invoked by other Service Bus services running on the same server. This can be done in the Service Bus overview editor by dragging the input icon from the pipeline to the Proxy Services swim lane.

The Create Proxy Service dialog appears. On the first page, set the name of the proxy service to *PrivateSubmitFlightSchedulePS*. Accept all defaults regarding the service type and the WSDL interface on the second page. On the third page, set transport to *local*, in order to expose this pipeline as a proxy service with transport *local*. This effectively turns it into a private service—a container of reusable Service Bus logic that is only accessible to other Service Bus projects. Note that for the local transport, there is no Endpoint URI; calls to local proxy services are configured by fully qualified name—as we will see later on.

Press Finish to create the Proxy Service. The resulting Service Bus project overview is shown in Figure 7-1.

Run the proxy service *PrivateSubmitFlightSchedulePS*—to verify it is working and to make sure it is deployed on the Integrated WLS environment, ready to be invoked from other Service Bus projects.

FIGURE 7-1. *PrivateSubmitFlightSchedulePipeline exposed as [local] proxy service*

Outline of FlightScheduleService

Open the *FlightScheduleService* project in the *FlightScheduleService_***step0** application that forms the starting point for the development of this project. It contains various artifacts, such as WSDLs, Schema definitions and a proxy service *FlightScheduleService*, based on the FlightScheduleService.wsdl and the interface with a single operation: *submitFlightSchedule*. The proxy service is currently not wired and can therefore not be deployed nor invoked.

Create a pipeline, called *FlightScheduleValidationPipeline*, based on the same WSDL as the proxy service. Wire the proxy service to this new pipeline.

Create another pipeline based on the same WSDL document, this one called *ProcessingAndRoutingPipeline*.

Wire FlightScheduleValidationPipeline to *ProcessingAndRoutingPipeline*.

Open the *ProcessingAndRoutingPipeline*. Add a Route node to the pipeline. Drag a Routing activity inside the node. Configure the Routing activity to invoke the local proxy *PrivateSubmitFlightSchedule*, as shown in Figure 7-2.

The *PrivateSubmitFlightScheduleService* does not actually look at the request it receives—it just produces a hard-coded response. So whether we transform the request into the proper

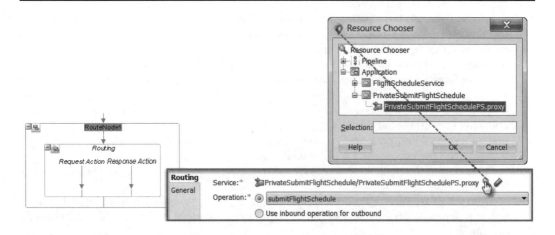

FIGURE 7-2. *Configuring the routing to the local (private) proxy service PrivateSubmitFlightSchedule*

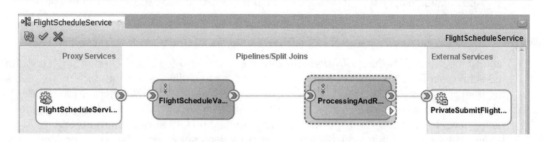

FIGURE 7-3. *The outline of the FlightScheduleService*

message format before sending it, will not make any difference. But of course the proper thing to do is add a *Replace* activity in the request action pipeline of the Routing activity to make sure $body contains the input message stipulated by the private service. Use the XSLT templates in the folder Transformations. Use hard coded values for now for the three input parameter for the submitScheduledFlightRequestToprivateSubmitScheduledFlightRequest.xsl template; the values required for these parameters will be gathered using callouts in the next sections.

The overview of the *FlightScheduleService* should now look like Figure 7-3. Note how the call to the local proxy service is visualized and remember that we did not create the business service as our local intermediate to that local proxy.

Run the *FlightScheduleService* proxy service and verify that a response message is returned that is prepared in the *PrivateSubmitFlightSchedule*. This proofs that the end-to-end chain is working—even though it does not do anything useful yet.

Implementing Validation

Processing a scheduled flight is not a trivial thing. First, the incoming message should be validated against the XSD Schema definition. Then a number of constraints that cannot be expressed in an XSD have to be checked. Subsequently, some of the values provided in the request message have to be verified against a list of allowable values. These values may also have to be converted to a different domain.

In order to provide our consumers with as complete a list of problems as possible with their request for a scheduled flight, we do not want to immediately abort processing in the validation pipeline upon the first issue we run into. Instead, we compile the results from each of the three steps into a list of processing results. If no issues were encountered, we can proceed to the next pipeline. If, however, one or more issues were found during XSD validation, constraint checking or domain value checking and mapping, we will not continue to the next stage but instead return a response that contains all the issues that were discovered.

In this section, we will implement the three validation stages as well as the mechanism for collecting all issues. The starting point is the *step1* application in the online sources.

Add XSD Validation

Open the *FlightScheduleValidationPipeline* editor. Add a pipeline pair—called Validations—and a stage in the request pipeline, called *SchemaValidation*.

Add a Validate activity to this stage. Configure this activity—as shown in Figure 7-4—to validate in Location *body* the expression

```
$body/flig:submitScheduledFlightRequestMessage
```

against the *submitScheduledFlightRequestMessage* in the XSD file FlightScheduleService.xsd in the Schemas folder. Note that in order to be able to successfully use a namespace prefix such as flig in expressions, such a prefix has to be explicitly defined. While in the Expression Builder, click on the tab which reads *Namespaces*. Click on the green plus icon, to add a user defined namespace. In the popup that appears, set Prefix to flig and URI to saibot.airport/services/flightschedule. Press OK to add this new namespace declaration. From this point on, the prefix flig: can be used in expressions anywhere in this stage.

Specify in the Validate activity that an error should be raised when validation errors are found.

Next, we add an error handler to the stage. We want to trap the validation error, save the validation results, and continue processing with the next stage in the pipeline.

Drag the error handler from the component palette to the *SchemaValidation* stage. Rename the stage in the error handler to *AddErrorToProcessingResults*. Add an Insert activity that will add the summary of validation errors to a variable. Configure this activity with this value:

```
<fse:ProcessingResult  xmlns:fse="saibot.airport/services/flightschedule">
    <fse:ResultCode>{$fault/ctx:errorCode}</fse:ResultCode>
    <fse:Description>{$fault/ctx:reason}</fse:Description>
    <fse:ContextTrace>{$fault}</fse:ContextTrace>
</fse:ProcessingResult>
```

to be inserted as [the] first child of the processingResults variable.

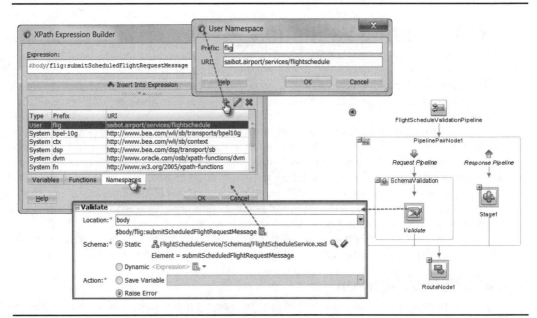

FIGURE 7-4. *Configuring the Validate activity to validate the submitScheduledFlightRequestMessage; a User [defined] Namespace with prefix flig is defined*

Add the Resume activity to the error handler, to ensure that once the validation fault details have been added to the *processingResults* variable, the next stage in this pipeline will be executed.

The error handler is shown in Figure 7-5.

The *processingResults* variable that is updated in the error handler has to be initialized first. We cannot insert a child into an uninitialized variable. Therefore, add a stage called *Initialization* to the request pipeline, before the *SchemaValidation* stage. Add an Assign activity to this stage. In this activity, assign the value of

```
<fse:ProcessingResults xmlns:fse="saibot.airport/services/flightschedule">
</fse:ProcessingResults>
```

to variable *processingResults*, thus initializing this variable.

Stop or Go

Before we add two more stages for additional validation activities, let's first add a stage that determines if the request is suitable to be routed to the next pipeline or whether validation errors have been found and therefore processing should cease and the validation outcome should be reported.

Add a stage called *ContinueOrReturn* as the last in the pipeline, just before the Route node.

Add an *If Then* activity to this stage. This activity does what you expect it to do: depending on the outcome of a Boolean condition, one of two branches is executed.

Configure the If condition with

```
fn:count($processingResults/*) gt 0
```

to determine whether or not any children have been added inside the variable *processingResults*.

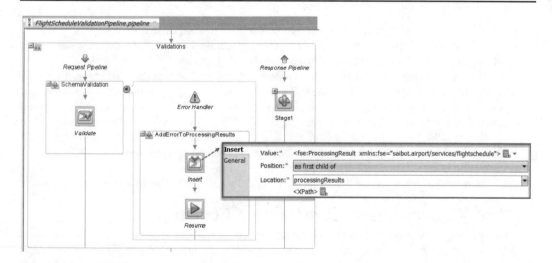

FIGURE 7-5.   *The error handler for the SchemaValidation stage, resuming processing after updating the processingResults variable*

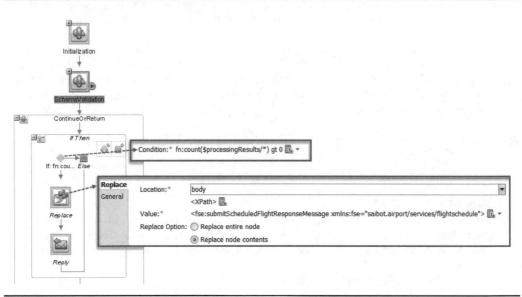

FIGURE 7-6. *The ContinueOrReturn stage that deals with processingResult if there are any*

Next, add a Replace activity to the *If*-branch. Configure this activity to replace the contents of the body variable with this expression:

```
<fse:submitScheduledFlightResponseMessage xmlns:fse="saibot.airport/services/
flightschedule">
 {$processingResults}
</fse:submitScheduledFlightResponseMessage>
```

This adds the value of variable *processingResults* to the response message.

Finally, add a Reply activity to the same *If*-branch, below the Replace step. Configure the activity to return with success. The stage is shown in Figure 7-6.

The logic we have now implemented ensures that when the Schema Validation finds errors, these errors are added to the $processingResults variable. When that happens, the if-then activity will trigger. The response is prepared in the $body variable—with the current contents from variable *processingResults*—and processing is halted with the sending of the response.

Run the Pipeline to try out this logic. The default message prepared in the tester contains some schema validation. Just press execute. Check the response message. Also verify the invocation trace, as shown in Figure 7-7.

Now we are ready to add two additional validation stages in this pipeline.

Add XQuery-Based Constraints Checking

Many of the constraints that apply to request messages cannot be expressed in XSD. This also holds true for the *submitScheduledFlightRequestMessage*. We require of this message for example that

■ The start date is prior or equal to the end date.

■ The start date is at least three days from today.

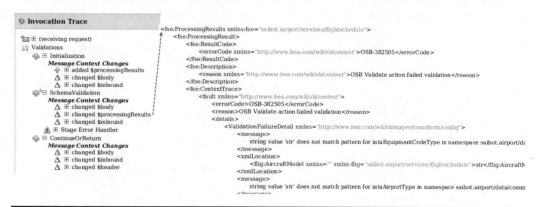

FIGURE 7-7.   *Invocation Trace for the FlightScheduleValidationPipeline—showing validation violation findings*

- The element FiveMinuteBlock is an integer times five.
- The element hour of the day is not empty.

These and similar constraints are not enforced by the Validate activity that we used in the previous section, because they cannot be specified in terms of the XSD definition.

The mediator component supports advanced validation using Schematron. In Service Bus, that option is not out of the box available to us. However, with XQuery we have a formidable tool at our disposal. We can create an XQuery function that inspects the XML contents of a variable and return a list of validation errors with zero, one or more errors. Using an Assign activity, we can invoke the XQuery function with the contents of the *submitScheduledFlightRequestMessage* and get a list of all (which could be none) validation errors.

Create a new XQuery file in a new folder called *Validations*. Call the XQuery file ValidateSubmitScheduledFlightRequest.xqy. Set the function name to *validateSubmitScheduledFlight*. Set a single source parameter, based on the *submitScheduledFlightRequest* element in FlightScheduleService.xsd. The target is based on Validation in Validation.xsd.

Add the following lines to the generated .xqy file:

```
xquery version "1.0" encoding "utf-8";

(:: OracleAnnotationVersion "1.0" ::)

declare namespace fse="saibot.airport/services/flightschedule";
(:: import schema at "../Schemas/FlightScheduleService.xsd" ::)
declare namespace ns1="saibot/validation";
(:: import schema at "../Schemas/Validation.xsd" ::)
declare namespace ref="saibot.airport/data/reference";
(:: import schema at "../Schemas/reference.xsd" ::)

declare variable $submitScheduledFlightRequest as element() (:: schema-element
(fse:submitScheduledFlightRequestMessage) ::) external;
```

```
declare function local:validateSubmitScheduledFlight($submitScheduledFlightReq
uest as element() (:: schema-element(fse:submitScheduledFlightRequestMessage)
::)) as element() (:: element(*, ns1:Validation) ::) {
    <ns1:Validation>
     <ns1:Payload>{$submitScheduledFlightRequest/.}</ns1:Payload>
     <ns1:ValidationErrorList>
       {
       (: Validations of required fields:)
       if (empty($submitScheduledFlightRequest/fse:TimePlanningUnit/
ref:HourOfDay/text())) then
       <ns1:ValidationError>
       <ns1:code>1</ns1:code>
       <ns1:message>Hour of Day is required</ns1:message>
       </ns1:ValidationError>
       else ''
       }
       </ns1:ValidationErrorList>
    </ns1:Validation>
};

local:validateSubmitScheduledFlight($submitScheduledFlightRequest)
```

At this point this XQuery function performs only a single validation: it checks if the Hour of the Day element does indeed contain a value. If it does not, a validation error is returned in the *ValidationErrorList* element. We will make the XQuery file a little bit more interesting a little later on.

First, add a stage to the pipeline called *CustomValidations*. In the stage, add an Assign activity. Configure the activity to invoke the ValidateSubmitScheduledFlightRequest.xqy document and pass $body/flig:submitScheduledFlightRequestMessage as the input parameter. Assign the outcome from that call to a new local variable called *validationResults*.

When the Assign activity is executed, the variable *validationResults* has been set with a *ValidationErrorList* element that may contain zero, one or more *ValidationError* elements. And for each of these elements, we want to add an entry to $processingResults.

Whenever we want to do something for each of the elements in a list, we can make use of the For Each activity. Add such an activity to the stage, dropping it below the Assign activity. Configure the activity according to Figure 7-8: the source of the For Each is the variable *validationResults*. The expression used to retrieve elements from this variable is: ./val:ValidationErrorList/val:ValidationError.

The *Value Variable*—that is the variable populated in each iteration with the current element from the list—is called *ValidationError*. The *Index Variable* and *Count Variable* are automatically set by the Service Bus engine. We do not make use of these values in this situation.

Add an Insert activity inside the For Each. This activity is configured to add as a *First Child of* variable *processingResults* this expression:

```
<fse:ProcessingResult  xmlns:fse="saibot.airport/services/flightschedule">
   <fse:ResultCode>{$ValidationError/val:code}</fse:ResultCode>
   <fse:Description>{$ValidationError/val:message}</fse:Description>
   <fse:ContextTrace>{$ValidationError}</fse:ContextTrace>
</fse:ProcessingResult>
```

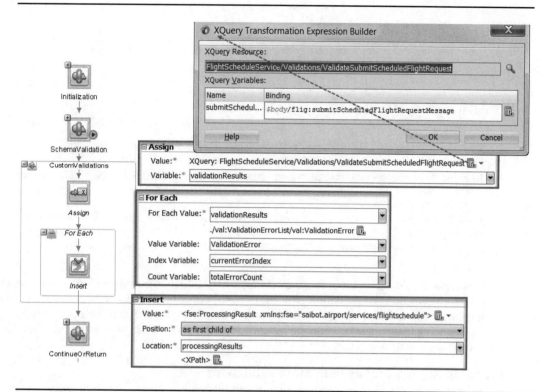

FIGURE 7-8.   *Configuring the For Each activity to look over each and every ValidationError*

This means a ProcessingResult element is created for every validation error and added to $processingResults.

The request side of the pipeline now looks as is shown in Figure 7-8. Now is a good time to run the pipeline—with a request message that does not contain a value for the Hour of Day element. Verify that meaningful information about the missing data is included in the response message.

Create a Local XQuery Function with Additional Validations

To bring more structure to XQuery files, we can make use of functions that contain reusable logic. These functions can be invoked from other functions—to contribute to the overall result.

Return to the XQuery file ValidateSubmitScheduledFlightRequest.xqy. Create a new function using this code:

```
declare function
local:validateSubmitScheduledFlightDateAndTimeConstraints($submitScheduledFlightRequest as
element() (:: schema-element(fse:submitScheduledFlightRequestMessage) ::)) as element()  (::
element(*, ns1:ValidationErrorList) ::) {
    (: Validations of date and time constraints for ScheduledFlight submission :)
    <ns1:ValidationErrorList>
    {
    if (true() and (  xs:date($submitScheduledFlightRequest/fse:TimePlanningUnit/
```

```
ref:startDate) lt (fn:current-date() - xs:dayTimeDuration('P3D')))) then
    <ns1:ValidationError>
    <ns1:code>21</ns1:code>
    <ns1:message>Start date should be more than three days from now</ns1:message>
    </ns1:ValidationError>
    else ''
    }
    </ns1:ValidationErrorList>
};
```

This function takes a *submitScheduledFlightRequestMessage* element and verifies if the startDate is at least 3 days from today. If it is not, a validation error is produced.

To enlist this function, add the following lines to function *validateSubmitScheduledFlight*:

```
    {for $validationError in
local:validateSubmitScheduledFlightDateAndTimeConstraints($submitScheduledFlightRequest)/
ns1:ValidationError
        return $validationError
    }
```

This code should come just before the closing </ns1:ValidationErrorList> element. The result from the local function is a validation error list that may contain *ValidationError* elements. Each of these elements should be added to the final result of function *validateSubmitScheduledFlight*.

After making these changes rerun the pipeline with a request message in which the start date is not at least three days into the future.

Create an XQuery Library with More Validations

Local functions in XQuery files can be reused locally. It helps to structure an otherwise unwieldy XQuery function—but it does not contribute to reuse. We can, however, also create a library module with XQuery functions that can be reused across XQuery files.

From the New Gallery, create an XQuery Library. Set the name to TimePlanningUnitValidations.xqy. Set the function name to *validateTimeplanningUnit*. Set the target namespace to *validateTimeplanningUnit*. The source parameter is called *timePlanningUnit*. The result is again of type *ValidationErrorList*.

Complement the generated source, to the following code:

```
xquery version "1.0" encoding "utf-8";

(:: OracleAnnotationVersion "1.0" ::)

module namespace ns3="airport.saibot/validations/dateAndTime";

declare namespace ref="saibot.airport/data/reference";
(:: import schema at "../Schemas/reference.xsd" ::)
declare namespace val="saibot/validation";
(:: import schema at "../Schemas/Validation.xsd" ::)

declare function ns3:validateTimeplanningUnit($timePlanningUnit as element() )
as element() (:: element(*, val:ValidationErrorList) ::) {
    (: Validations of date and time constraints :)
```

```
      <val:ValidationErrorList>
        {
        if (  (not(empty($timePlanningUnit/ref:endDate))) and
($timePlanningUnit/ref:endDate lt $timePlanningUnit/ref:startDate)  ) then
        <val:ValidationError>
        <val:code>11</val:code>
        <val:message>End date should be empty or equal to or later than start
date</val:message>
        </val:ValidationError>
        else ''
        }
        {
        if (  ( $timePlanningUnit/ref:FiveMinuteBlock mod 5 !=0  )) then
        <val:ValidationError>
        <val:code>15</val:code>
        <val:message>The five minute block should be an integer number times
5</val:message>
        </val:ValidationError>
        else ''
        }
      </val:ValidationErrorList>
};
```

This function performs two validations on a *TimePlanningUnit* element:

- If the end date value is set, is the date equal to or later than the start date
- Is the numerical value in the element *FiveMinuteBlock* an integer number times 5?

In order to make use of this function, we have to make two changes in the XQuery file ValidateSubmitScheduledFlightRequest.xqy.

1.   Add this line to import the library module:

```
import module namespace ns3='airport.saibot/validations/dateAndTime' at
"TimePlanningUnitValidations.xqy";
```

2.   Call the function in the library from function *validateSubmitScheduledFlight*:

```
        {
        for $validationError in ns3:validateTimeplanningUnit($submitSche
duledFlightRequest/fse:TimePlanningUnit)/ns1:ValidationError
          return $validationError
        }
```

After making these alterations and saving all files, please run the pipeline once more. Define an end date in the request message that is set before the start date and make sure to set the *FiveMinuteBlock* to 42. Check the contents of the response message and ensure that all validation errors are properly reported.

Airline Checks and Mapping with Domain Value Map

The airline for which the scheduled flight is requested, is specified through the *carrier* element. This element is defined in the XSD document as a string. It is not further restricted in the schema. However, the values recognized for airlines by the business service are only the two letter IATA airline designators. This means therefore that we have to check:

- If the length of the airline value > 3 or <2; if so, it is incorrect.
- If the length of the airline value == 3 then it is probably an ICAO code and it should be mapped to an IATA code.
- If the length is two, it is probably an IATA code; we should ensure it is a valid IATA code.

To implement this validation, we need a new stage, a little if-then-else logic and this thing called a DVM or Domain Value Map.

Prepare the Stage AirlineValueMap

Add a stage called *AirlineValueMap* to the pipeline, between the stages *CustomValidation* and *ContinueOrReturn*. Add an If..Then activity to the stage, with the condition set to

```
fn:string-length($body/flig:submitScheduledFlightRequestMessage/flig:Carrier) lt 2 or
fn:string-length($body/flig:submitScheduledFlightRequestMessage/flig:Carrier) gt 3
```

This condition traps values for the carrier element that are shorter than two or longer than three characters, neither of which is good.

Add a Raise Error activity to the Then branch, with the code set to FSE-10 and the message to "The carrier element has the wrong length—it can neither be a valid IATA code nor a correct ICAO code."

We do not want this stage to cause the pipeline to abort because of this error, so we have to add an error handler to the stage. Inside the error handler, just like in the error handler for stage *SchemaValidation*, add an insert activity to add an entry for the error to variable *processingResults* and a Resume activity to continue on with the next stage.

Add another If..Then activity to the Else branch. Set the condition for this activity to

```
fn:string-length($body/flig:submitScheduledFlightRequestMessage/flig:Carrier) = 3
```

When the value for the carrier element has three characters, we assume it is an ICAO code and we have to find the corresponding IATA designator. In the Then branch, we will use a domain value map to perform that feat.

Domain Value Map to Map ICAO Codes to IATA Designators

Mapping of values from one range of values (or domain) to another can be implemented in SOA Suite using a DVM or Domain Value Map. Such a DVM is an XML document that contains records for each point-to-point value mapping. A record contains one or more qualifiers used to identify the record (in the source domain) along with one or more values in the target domain. XPath functions are available that can be used in XPath and XQuery expressions and in both XQuery functions and XSL stylesheets to lookup an entry in a specific DVM and retrieve the associated mapped values. Domain Value Maps can be edited at run time using the out of the box SOA Composer console.

In the case at hand, we want to map from the three-character ICAO codes for airlines to the corresponding two-character IATA designators. If such a designator is not found, the request cannot be successfully processed because the carrier is unknown.

Create a new DVM called *ICAOToiataAirlineMapping* in the folder Validations. Specify three domains called ICAOAirlineCode, iataAirlineCode, and airline respectively. Create a few records, as shown in Figure 7-9. For example, mapping AFR to AF for Air France, AIC to AI for Air India Limited and DLH to LH for Lufthansa.

Add an Assign activity to the Then branch. Set the Value field to:

```
dvm:lookup('FlightScheduleService/Validations/
ICAOToiataAirlineMapping', 'ICAOAirlineCode', $body/flig:submitScheduledFl
ightRequestMessage/flig:Carrier, 'iataAirlineCode', 'XXX')
```

Set the Variable to *iataAirlineCode*. This activity will use the DVM that was just created and look in the *ICAOAirlineCode* qualifier column with the value in the *Carrier* element in the *submitScheduledFlightRequestMessage* to locate the appropriate airline record. When found, the value in the *iataAirlineCode* column will be returned. If the record is not found—which means that the value in the Carrier element is not a known ICAO code—the default value "XXX" is returned, which clearly indicates the failure of the lookup.

Add an If..Then activity below the Assign, as is indicated in Figure 7-10.

Set the condition to $iataAirlineCode= 'XXX'. This will determine if the value in the carrier element was not found as a valid ICAO code in the DVM. For that case, add a Raise Error activity (in the Then branch). Set an error code and a message indicating that the Carrier element does not contain a known ICAO code.

In the Else branch, add a Replace activity to enrich the request message with the retrieved IATA equivalent to the ICAO code in the Carrier element. Set the location to body and the expression to ./flig:submitScheduledFlightRequestMessage/flig:Carrier. The value should be $iataAirlineCode and only the node contents should be replaced.

This stage requires an error handler, to prevent the Raise Error activities from ruining our carefully constructed $processingResults. Add the error handler at stage level. Specify the same Insert activity as in the *SchemaValidation* stage, to insert a new *ProcessingResult* element based on the contents of $fault as the first child of variable *processingResults*. Also add a Resume activity, to continue pipeline processing with the next stage.

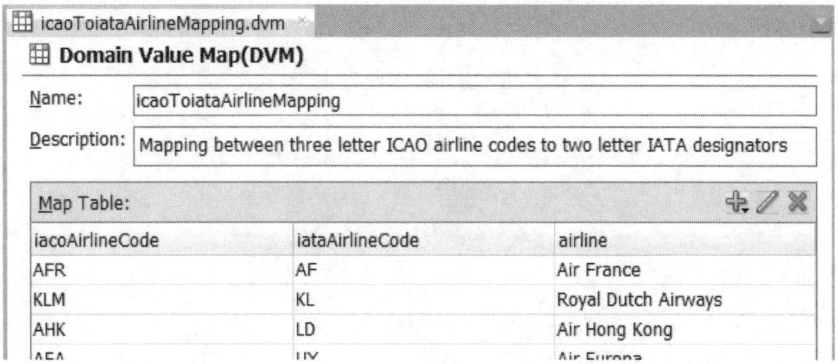

icaoToiataAirlineMapping.dvm		
Domain Value Map(DVM)		
Name: icaoToiataAirlineMapping		
Description: Mapping between three letter ICAO airline codes to two letter IATA designators		
Map Table:		
iacoAirlineCode	iataAirlineCode	airline
AFR	AF	Air France
KLM	KL	Royal Dutch Airways
AHK	LD	Air Hong Kong
AEA	UX	Air Europa

FIGURE 7-9.   *Domain Value Map between ICAO airline codes and IATA designators*

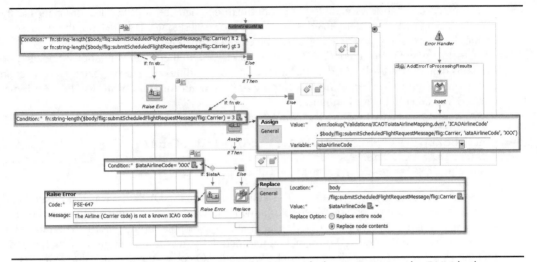

FIGURE 7-10. *The complete stage AirlineValueMap with the Assign using the DVM lookup*

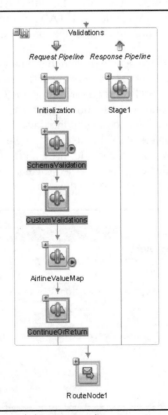

FIGURE 7-11. *The complete Validations Pipeline*

Now is a good time to run the pipeline (Figure 7-11) again. Provide a three letter (uppercase) value for the carrier element. If you use a value that occurs in the DVM, you should see the proper value of the corresponding IATA designator being assigned to the $iataAirlineCode variable. If your value is in fact a pretend ICAO code, this variable will have been assigned the value XXX and the error hander will have kicked in, once more.

Using Callouts for Validation and Enrichment

The second pipeline in the *FlightScheduleService*—the *ProcessingAndRoutingPipeline*—can rely on the data it receives being valid. Not just in terms of the XSD definition but also the custom validations on start date, end date, and 5-minute time block as well as the IATA designator for the air carrier. It is now up to this pipeline to perform several enrichment steps that are to precede the final routing to the *PrivateSubmitFlightSchedule* local proxy service.

■ The number of flights has to be established that are to take place in the requested flight schedule.

■ The identifier of the allocated slot with which the flight schedule is to be associated must be retrieved.

■ The Financial Department has to approve of the requested flight schedule—based on the credit status, solvency, and safety status of the airline.

Service Bus has the concept of Callouts to invoke services, from any stage, prior to or after executing the routing activity. Callouts can invoke Java Classes, Pipelines, Local Proxy Services, and Business Services.

In this section, we will look at three types of callouts:

■ Java Callout to a custom Java Class, to calculate the number of flights

■ Service Callout to a Business Service, to find the slot with which to associate the scheduled flight

■ Service Callout to a Pipeline, to check if the airline is not blacklisted with the finance department

Java Callout to Execute Content-Based Logic

A Java Callout activity can be used to invoke a static method in a custom Java Class. This class can be deployed as part of the Service Bus project or to the classpath of the run-time WLS. XPath expressions are used to determine the values passed to this method as input parameter. The value returned from the Java code can be assigned to a stage level variable.

The Java Class we will create takes the start date and the end date for the requested flight schedule and—taking the weekdays into account—calculates the actual number of flights this request represents. This number has to be passed to the local proxy that processes the request.

Prepare for the Java Class to Be Called Out To

The Java Class receives the *TimePlanningUnit* element from the request message and it does so in the form of an XmlObject, a class from the Apache XmlBeans library. To work with such an object we need to add a library to the project, just like we did in Chapter 6 for working with the JEJB transport. The JAR file that contains the required definitions for the XmlBeans library ships with

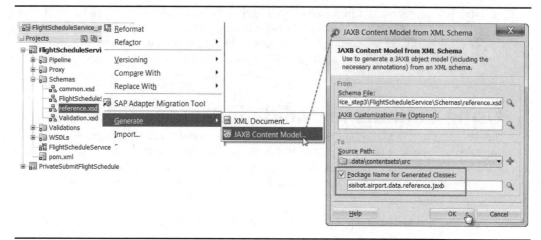

FIGURE 7-12. *Generating the JAXB Content Model for XSD document reference.xsd*

the SOA Suite. It can be found as com.bea.core.xml.xmlbeans_1.0.0.0_2-6-0.jar under MIDDLEWARE_HOME/Oracle_Home/oracle_common/modules. Add this JAR file to the *AircraftMovementService* project.

To conveniently work with the XML content in our Java code, we can leverage JAXB—the Java standard for binding XML to Java and vice versa. Right click on the reference.xsd document in the Schemas folder. Select the option Generate | JAXB Content Model. See Figure 7-12.

In the dialog that appears, set the Java package name for the generated classes to saibot .airport.data.reference.jaxb. Accept the other defaults and press OK to have the JAXB object model generated.

Verify that the classes were indeed generated for the elements in the reference.xsd document.

Finally, create a new deployment profile called *JavaCalloutJar* of Profile Type JAR file for the project *FlightScheduleService*.

Implement Class ScheduledFlightProcessor

Create a new Java Class called ScheduledFlightProcessor, using the following code:

```java
package saibot.airport.flightscheduleservice;

import java.io.ByteArrayInputStream;
import javax.xml.bind.JAXBContext;
import javax.xml.bind.JAXBElement;
import javax.xml.bind.JAXBException;
import javax.xml.bind.Unmarshaller;
import javax.xml.datatype.XMLGregorianCalendar;
import org.apache.xmlbeans.XmlObject;
import saibot.airport.data.reference.jaxb.TimePlanningUnitType;
public class ScheduledFlightProcessor {

    public static int calculateNumberOfFlights(XmlObject timePlanningUnit) {
        int numberOfFlights = 0;
```

```
        JAXBContext jc = null;
        try {
            jc = JAXBContext.newInstance(TimePlanningUnitType.class);
            Unmarshaller unmarshaller;
            String xml = timePlanningUnit.toString();
            // this string starts with <xml-fragment xmlns:ref="saibot.airport/
data/reference" xmlns:flig="saibot.airport/services/flightschedule">
            // the xml-fragment has to be replaced with ref:TimePlanningUnit
            xml = xml.replaceAll("xml-fragment", "ref:TimePlanningUnit");
            unmarshaller = jc.createUnmarshaller();
            byte[] bytes = xml.getBytes();
            ByteArrayInputStream bais = new ByteArrayInputStream(bytes);
            TimePlanningUnitType tpu = (TimePlanningUnitType) ((JAXBElement)
unmarshaller.unmarshal(bais)).getValue();
            XMLGregorianCalendar startDate = tpu.getStartDate();
            if (tpu.getEndDate() == null) {
                numberOfFlights = 1;
            } else {
                XMLGregorianCalendar endDate = tpu.getEndDate().getValue();
                if (endDate.equals(startDate)) {
                    numberOfFlights = 1;
                } else {
                    int diffInDays = (int)Math.ceil((endDate.
toGregorianCalendar().getTimeInMillis() - startDate.toGregorianCalendar().
getTimeInMillis())/(1000*60*60*24));
                    // determine number of days per week
                    int daysPerWeek = tpu.getDaysOfWeek().getDay().size();
                    numberOfFlights = (diffInDays* daysPerWeek/7);
                }
            }
        } catch (JAXBException e) {
            e.printStackTrace();
        }
        return numberOfFlights;
    }
}
```

The class contains a single static method *calculateNumberOfFlights* that accepts an XmlObject. This object is expected to contain a *TimePlanningUnit* element. Using that XML content, an instance of class *TimePlanningUnitType* is retrieved. From this object, we can easily get hold of start date, end date, and the list of weekdays included in the flight schedule. The total number of flights is calculated and returned as an int value.

At this point, deploy the JavaCalloutJar profile—to create jar file JavaCalloutJar.jar in the deploy folder of the project. This jar file is needed for the configuration of the Java Callout. The contents of the jar file will also be deployed along with the Service Bus project when that is deployed.

Configure the Java Callout

Open the *ProcessingAndRoutingPipeline*. Add a Pipeline Pair. Change the name of the auto-created stage to *DeriveNumberOfFlights*. Add a Java Callout activity to the stage, and configure it as shown in Figure 7-13.

Select the JavaCalloutJar.jar in the deploy folder of the project. Select the *calculateNumberOfFlights* method in the ScheduledFlightProcessor.

Set the XPath expression for the input parameter to:

```
$body/flig:submitScheduledFlightRequestMessage/flig:TimePlanningUnit
```

Make sure to add the user defined namespace "**saibot.airport/services/flightschedule**" and prefix: flig.

Set the name of the return variable to *numberOfFlights*. This means that the outcome of the Java Callout is stored in $numberOfFlights.

At this point, you can run the *ProcessingAndRoutingPipeline* and see the Java Callout in action. Depending on the start date, end date, and the week days, the value for *numberOfFlights* is calculated.

NOTE
Using a Java Callout is not the only way of executing custom logic implemented through Java in a Service Bus service. Creating a custom XPath function is another. Almost any static method can easily be registered as a function that can be used in XPath expressions in Service Bus. In the above example, we could easily have used such an XPath function in a simple Assign expression, rather than using a Java Callout. In fact, the logic currently implemented in the Java class could be handled using a very simple XQuery function without any custom Java code.

Many aspects of Service Bus projects can be inspected and edited at run time—including XQuery functions, XPath expressions and other elements that drive the behavior of services. This does not apply to Java code invoked in Java Callouts. That should be a consideration when deciding on using a Java Callout. Heavy use of such callouts is not considered a good practice.

Custom XPath functions are deployed in a JAR file on the WLS server and require a server restart in order to be available to Service Bus projects. As such, they are highly reusable and (almost) part of the run-time infrastructure of the Service Bus.

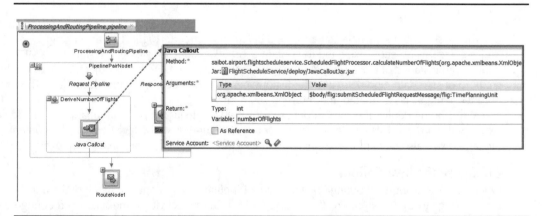

FIGURE 7-13. *Configuration of the Java Callout to the ScheduledFlightProcessor class*

Service Callout to a Business Service to Find the Allocated Slot

A Service Callout is an activity that invokes a service. Like a Java Callout, this activity can be used anywhere in a stage, both in the request pipeline or the response pipeline. Service Callouts are synchronous. That means that all other processing in the pipeline blocks until the callout has received its response. Service Callouts are used, for example, for validation and enrichment, logging, and auditing. A Service Callout can invoke a business service or local proxy service as well as a pipeline or split-join.

We will first look at a Service Callout to a business service to find the slot with which to associate the scheduled flight.

Create Business Service SlotService

The *SlotService* that was developed in Chapter 4 to record slot allocations in the database with future flights data, has been upgraded to also allow slot identifiers to be searched and retrieved. To that end, the interface of the *SlotService* has been extended with an operation *findSlot*. The *step3* source application contains a simple, almost mock implementation of the SlotService (that does not do any database interaction). Deploy and run the *SlotService* and invoke the *findSlot* operation to find out it has a mock-implementation that always returns the same slot identifier.

Open the overview editor for the *FlightScheduleService* project. Drag an HTTP technology component to the External Services swim lane. Call the business service *SlotService* and configure it to invoke the *SlotService*: select the WSDL for the *SlotService* from the Application Server and have it imported to the *FlightScheduleService* project along with the resources required because of dependencies or import the SlotService.wsdl file from the SlotService project. In that case, you have to configure the endpoint for the business service: http://host:port/flight/SlotService.

You can now run the newly added business service straight from the overview editor, to see if you can retrieve the slot identifier.

Add Service Callout to SlotService

Add a stage *RetrieveSlotIdentifier* directly under the stage *DeriveNumberOfFlights* that contains the Java Callout. Add a Service Callout activity to this stage.

Configure this activity to call out to the *findSlot* operation on the business service *SlotService*. Set the Configuration radio button to *Configure Body*. The body field under Request should be set to *findSlotRequestMsg* and the body under Response should be set to *findSlotResponseMsg*. These two settings indicate that new variables are created that hold the request message to be sent in the service callout, respectively, the response that will be received from the service callout.

Add an Assign activity in the Request Action of the Service Callout activity.

This should assign the value

```
<soapenv:Body xmlns:soapenv="http://schemas.xmlsoap.org/soap/envelope/"/>
```

to variable *findSlotRequestMsg*. Add a Replace activity underneath this Assign to update the contents of the variable with the request message to be sent to the *SlotService*.

The location for this Replace is variable *findSlotRequestMsg*. The Value is an XSLT Resource FlightScheduleService/Transformations/submitScheduledFlightRequestMessageTofindSlotRequestMessage .xsl to which $body/flig:submitScheduledFlightRequestMessage is fed as the Input Document Expression.

Then, add an Assign activity to the Response Action. This activity retrieves the slot identifier from the Service Callout response and exposes it in a new variable called *slotIdentifier*.

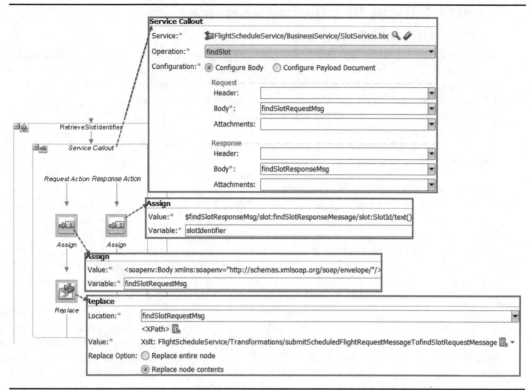

FIGURE 7-14. *Configuration of the Service Callout to the SlotService*

Use the following XPath expression to extract the slot identifier:

```
$findSlotResponseMsg/slot:findSlotResponseMessage/slot:SlotId/text()
```

Make sure to define in the expression editor a new user defined namespace. Its prefix should be *slot* and it is to be associated with namespace saibot.airport/services/slot.

At this point, the Service Callout is complete (Figure 7-14). It is visualized in the overview editor through a wire from the pipeline to the business service (Figure 7-15).

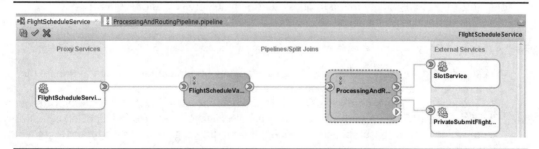

FIGURE 7-15. *Overview of Service Bus project with the wire to the SlotService based on the Service Callout*

You can run the *ProcessingAndRoutingPipeline* again to see in the trace how the slot identifier is retrieved through the Service Callout to the *SlotService*. A little later on we will use the $slotIdentifier variable to complement the message routed to the *PrivateSubmitFlightScheduleService*.

TIP

At pipeline level, we can define the so called Shared Variables. These variables can shared across multiple pipelines—provided each pipeline defines these shared variable with the same name and the same type (supported types are String, Boolean, or XML data type). Sharing of variables works even across local proxies and through Split-Join services. The latter means that when pipeline A invokes a Split-Join service that invokes pipeline B, there can be a variable shared between A and B. However, this shared variable cannot be accessed inside the Split-Join service itself.

Service Callout to a Pipeline within the Service Bus Project

A Service Callout can also be used inside a Service Bus project, to invoke a pipeline or Split-Join component. Pipelines are standalone, reusable containers of logic inside Service Bus projects. A pipeline implements its own interface, defines its own variables, and is well encapsulated. Pipelines cannot be reused outside the project—unless they are exposed through a proxy service. Pipelines are defined in their own file. That means that several developers can each work on a different pipeline in a Service Bus project at the same time. Having multiple developers work simultaneously within the same pipeline is usually not a very good idea: they would be working on the same file.

We will now create a new pipeline based on a template. The logic of that pipeline has been implemented in a different project, perhaps by a different team. The pipeline was then published as a template—a file with extension .ptx. This makes it reusable in other Service Bus projects where local pipelines can be created that inherit the contents of the template. At run time, the pipeline that is based on a template will be deployed with a reference to the template, that itself also has to be deployed in the run-time server. Any change to that template is immediately inherited by all pipelines based on that template.

In this case, the project *FinancialDepartmentPipelines* contains the pipeline template *FinancialDepartmentAirlineCheckPipeline*. You can open the pipeline template, inspect it, and edit it. Let's not make any changes right now.

Create Pipeline Based on a Template

Open the overview editor for the *FlightScheduleService*. In the center area, right mouse click and click on the option Insert | Pipeline in the context menu. Set the name of the new pipeline to *CheckAirlineWithFinancialDepartmentPipeline*. Check the checkbox *From Template*. Then select the *FinancialDepartmentAirlineCheckPipeline* template using the template browser (Figure 7-16), from either the local file system or the WebLogic domain.

On the second page of the Create Pipeline Service wizard, set the Service Type to WSDL and select the FinancialDepartmentAirlineCheck.wsdl file in the WSDLs folder in the *FinancialDepartmentPipelines* project. Click on Finish to generate the pipeline.

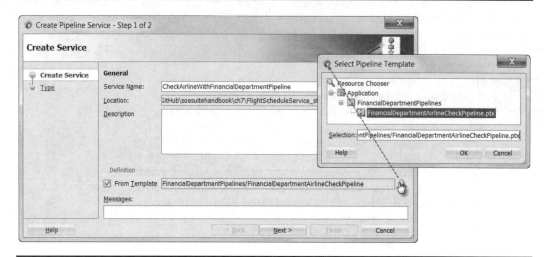

FIGURE 7-16. *Create a pipeline based on the FinancialDepartmentAirlineCheckPipeline template*

The overview editor displays the new, not yet connected pipeline. You can edit the pipeline, even though it is based on a template. When you open the editor, you will see the pipeline definition with a pipeline pair and two activities. It is inherited from the template. Because no placeholders were added in the template definition, you cannot actually add or remove any stages or activities to or from the pipeline. You can, however, change the properties of the activities that are in the pipeline.

You can run the pipeline. Regardless of the values in the request message, it will run for approximately three seconds and return the string value "OK" as well as a unique identifier that represents the financial department's approval stamp.

Create a Service Callout to the Pipeline

Open pipeline *ProcessingAndRoutingPipeline*. Add a stage *CheckAirlineWithFinancialDepartment* just above the RouteNode1. Add a Service Callout activity to this stage.

Configure the Service Callout activity to invoke the *CheckAirlineWithFinancialDepartmentPipeline*. Define variables *checkAirlineRequest* and *checkAirlineResponse* to be used for the callout request and response message respectively, as is shown in Figure 7-17.

Add an Assign activity in the Request Action of the Service Callout, and assign the following expression to the variable *checkAirlineRequest*:

```
<soapenv:Body xmlns:soapenv="http://schemas.xmlsoap.org/soap/envelope/">
<fin:checkAirlineRequestMessage xmlns:fin="saibot.airport/services/financial">
 <fin:Carrier>
    <ref:IATACode xmlns:ref="ref:saibot.airport/data/reference">{$body/flig:su
bmitScheduledFlightRequestMessage/flig:Carrier}</ref:IATACode>
 </fin:Carrier>
</fin:checkAirlineRequestMessage>
</soapenv:Body>
```

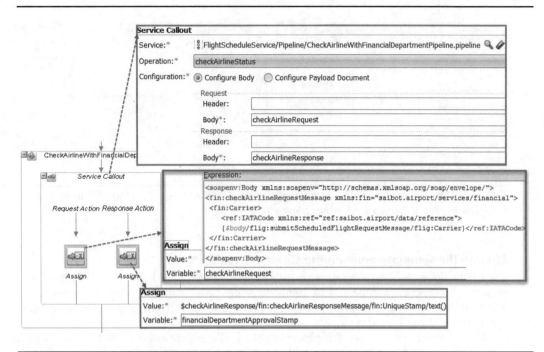

FIGURE 7-17. *Configure the Service Callout activity to invoke the CheckAirlineWithFinancialDepartmentPipeline*

Also add an Assign activity to the Response Action. This activity retrieves the financial approval stamp from the response message and stores it in the variable *financialDepartmentApprovalStamp*. Set the Value field to

```
$checkAirlineResponse/fin:checkAirlineResponseMessage/fin:UniqueStamp/text()
```

This XPath expression takes the value from the *UniqueStamp* element that will be set by the FinancialDepartment when they approve of the airline. Make sure that a user defined namespace is set up for namespace saibot.airport/services/financial with prefix fin.

The project as it currently stands is shown in Figure 7-18.

You can now run the *ProcessingAndRoutingPipeline* and from the flow trace see not only the number of flights calculated and the slot identifier retrieved but also the blessing from the financial department begotten and stored in $financialDepartmentApprovalStamp. The three parameters can now be used to provide the appropriate input to the XSL stylesheet that we use for the transformation of the message sent from the final Routing activity to the *PrivateSubmitFlightService*.

It does take an uncomfortable long time to arrive at the final result though. Apparently, some of the processings in either the *SlotService* or the financial department's pipeline—or both, as it turns out—is somewhat slow. We will address this slowness to some extent using parallelization through split-join a little bit later on.

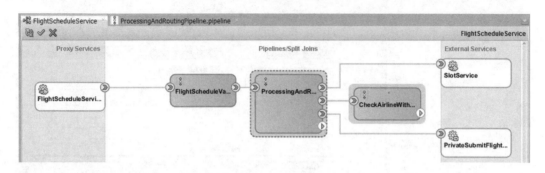

FIGURE 7-18. *Overview of the entire FlightScheduleService including the callout to the CheckAirlineWithFinancialDepartmentPipeline*

Update the Template and See the Change Trickle Down

The *CheckAirlineWithFinancialDepartmentPipeline* is created based on a Template. The link between this pipeline and the original template is retained—until such time as we sever it. This can be done as shown in Figure 7-19 by right clicking on the pipeline and choosing the option Service Bus | Break Template Link.

If we do not break the link, this pipeline and all other pipelines based on the same template, will inherit any change made to the template.

Open the template pipeline FinancialDepartmentAirlineCheckPipeline.ptx in project *FinancialDepartmentPipelines*. Drag an If..Then activity to the SetAirlineStatus stage in the response pipeline and drop it above the existing Assign activities. Set the condition to

```
$body/*[1]/*:Carrier/*:IATACode/text()='XX'
```

This tests for the condition that the IATACode is set to XX. Copy the first Assign activity and paste it in the Then branch. Modify it to make it apply the value "NOK" to the variable called *status*. Move the first two Assign activities—that assign values to $status and to $uniqueApprovalStamp— to the Else branch.

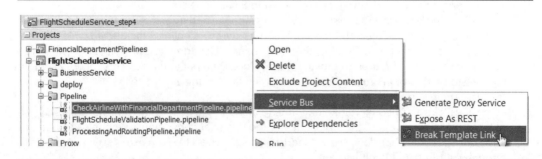

FIGURE 7-19. *Breaking the link between a pipeline and the template is was created from*

Copy the Assign activity and one of the Alert activities from the *Logging* stage to the error handler. Change the Alert activity's severity to Major. Also change the Summary.

Add a Report activity. Set the content to $fault. Define one search key called *messageKeyFaultReport*. Its value is taken from variable *messageKey* using the XPath expression . (a single period).

The last activity in the error handler should be a Raise Error activity. Have it set a generic error code and message. All activities in the stage *PipelineErrorHandler* should be locked: pipeline developers working on children of this template have no business making changes to these action.

Add a Logging Pipeline to the FlightScheduleService

Open the overview editor for the *FlightSchedulerService*. Drag the pipeline component from the palette to the central area. The Create Pipeline wizard appears. Set the Service Name to *LoggingPipeline*. Check the checkbox *From Template*. Then browse for the *LoggingPipelineTemplate* in the *CommonPipelines* project.

Click Next. The Service Type is WSDL. Browse for the FlightScheduleService.wsdl, because we want this pipeline to expose exactly the same interface as the Validation pipeline currently invoked by the proxy service. Uncheck the checkbox for exposing the new pipeline as a proxy service. Press Finish to have the pipeline created. It is added as a standalone pipeline component in the overview editor.

Double click the *LoggingPipeline* to open the editor. The gray background indicates that this is not a regular pipeline, but instead one derived from a template. When you click on any of the activities in the *Logging* stage or the *PipelineErrorHandler* stage, you will see the effect of earlier locking these actions during template development: the activities can be inspected but not edited.

To make the *LoggingPipeline* useful, a number of activities do have to be edited. First, configure the Routing activity to make it route to pipeline *FlightScheduleValidationPipeline*. In the overview editor, the wire has been added. Delete the wire from the proxy service to *FlightScheduleValidationPipeline*. Then create a wire from the proxy to the *LoggingPipeline*, as shown in Figure 7-22.

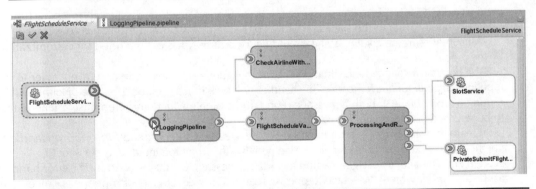

FIGURE 7-22. *Rewiring the proxy service to the LoggingPipeline that intercepts requests and routes them through*

The template is now changed—to return a value of NOK for airline XX. This change is immediately inherited by any pipeline based on the template. Run pipeline *CheckAirlineWithFinancialDepartmentPipeline* in the *FlightScheduleService*. Provide a value of XX for the carrier and see the value of NOK returned.

Add a Template-Based Logging Pipeline

In the previous section, we have seen a first example of a pipeline template. Such template is a predefined pipeline that new pipelines can be cloned or—better yet—inherited from. A template contains stages, activities, error handlers, variables, and other elements found in any regular pipeline. When a new pipeline is defined based on a pipeline template, the pipeline already includes all the stuff from the template. Some of these elements in the template can be locked: not to be changed in derived pipelines (unless the link is broken). Others can be open for editing. Template developers can predefine stages that are placeholders for template consumers to add elements to. Through these placeholders, the template designer guides the pipeline developer through a number of predefined and documented steps.

Pipeline templates are very useful for boosting productivity and stimulating the use of best practices for Service Bus service design. Templates can be used to capture and share design patterns. They can also be used to easily distribute reusable pieces of configurable logic.

In this section, we will first create a template for a logging pipeline. The template predefines a number of elements that perform logging in the way Saibot Airport considers desirable practice. By simply including a pipeline based on this template as the first step in each Service Bus project following the proxy service, developers ensure that they adhere to the logging guidelines. Some aspects of the logging pipeline have to be configured for the specific project—such as the logic to determine if the service request was processed successfully and the actual contents to include in log entries.

We will then use this pipeline template in the *FlightScheduleService* to quickly add logging functionality. As we have seen before: any change in the pipeline template, applied even after the template has been used to create new pipelines from, is inherited by each derived pipeline—as long as the link to the template has not been broken.

Create the Pipeline Template with Logging Capabilities

Open the project *CommonPipelines*. This project is the container for reusable pipelines. Right click on the project node. Click on New | Pipeline Template in the context menu (Figure 7-20).

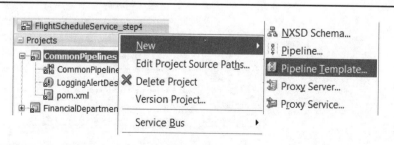

FIGURE 7-20. *Create a new Pipeline Template*

The Create Pipeline Template wizard appears. Enter *LoggingPipelineTemplate* as the name for the new template. Press Next. Select SOAP 1.1 as the Service Type. Press Finish to have the template generated.

The Pipeline Template editor opens. It is very similar to the normal pipeline editor—with some differences. The background, a grid, makes it obvious that the pipeline editor is in a special (template) mode. The component palette contains a special section, titled Template Placeholders.

These components—nodes, stages, actions, route, conditional, operational—are used to create a placeholder in the template where the actual pipeline instance derived from the template can have zero, one, or multiple elements included of the type indicated by the placeholder. The template developer will typically add documentation on the placeholder to explain what type of activity is expected at that point in the template.

Figure 7-21 shows the implementation we will subsequently add to the currently empty template.

Add a Route component with a Routing activity to the pipeline template. We expect pipelines based on this template to be injected in existing wires from Proxy Services to regular pipelines. Our pipeline template exposes the Any service type interface and should also contain the Routing action to connect to the first regular pipeline. Also add a Pipeline Pair above the Route node. This is where the real logging action will take place.

The routing action should not be locked of course: the pipelines based on the tem to be configurable for the specific routing that applies in the services where they are i

Change the name of the stage in the Request Pipeline to *Initialize and Retain*. Cha stage name in the Response Pipeline to *DefineStatusAndToBeLogged*. Add a second s Response Pipeline, called *Logging*.

Add an Assign activity to stage *Initialize and Retain*. Set the value to *fn:current-da* the variable to *startTime*. Add a second Assign activity that will retain the original req future use. The value should be *$body* and the variable is *originalBody*. Lock both act right clicking them and selecting Lock Action from the context menu. These activities be modified by the developers creating pipelines based on this template.

Add an Assign activity to stage *DefineStatusAndToBeLogged*. This activity sets value variable *status*. It is up to pipeline developers to override the configuration of this activit their own logic to derive the value of $status. Based on the value assigned to status—eit some other value—the Logging stage will produce logging at severity level normal (all is minor (something is not well). Add a second Assign activity in this stage. This one assign variable *toBeLogged*. Anything this variable contains is used in logging messages in the stage. The default value used for $toBeLogged is the expression $body/*[1]—or the cont response message. It is likely to be overwritten in concrete pipeline instances based on t

Add an Assign activity to stage *Logging*. It calculates the total processing time, usin

```
fn:current-dateTime()- xs:dateTime ($startTime)
```

and assigns the result to variable *totalProcessingTime*.

Then add an If..Then activity in stage *Logging*, below the Assign activity. Set the co

```
$status='OK'
```

Add an Alert activity to both the Then and the Else branch. Both can refer to the, *LoggingAlertDestination*, Alert Destination that is prepared in the project. Set the Alert to Normal in the Then branch and to Minor in the Else branch. Set appropriate Summ. Use the same Content for both Alert activities:

```
fn:concat('Start Processing: ',$startTime,' Total Processing Time ',
$totalProcessingTime  ,$toBeLogged)
```

Here we see the $startTime that was created in the request pipeline, the $totalProcessir was calculated earlier in the stage and $toBeLogged that was defined in the previous st

All activities in the *Logging* stage should be locked; they are not intended for custor by the pipeline developers.

We have now reached the situation shown in Figure 7-21. Next, add an error handl pipeline *LoggingPipelineTemplate*. This handler will kick in if a fault occurs. The pipelin report all fault details in both a message report and a pipeline alert and then raise a gen to be returned to the service invoker.

Create two stages in the error handler: *SetMessageKeyForReport* and *PipelineErrorH* The first one should contain a single Assign activity (that the pipeline developer should customize). The activity assigns a value to variable messageKey that is used by the error as the key under which a Message Report is created. Only developers of pipeline instan determine what a meaningful message key is for the current service. Use "yourKey" as t value to be overridden by the pipeline developer.

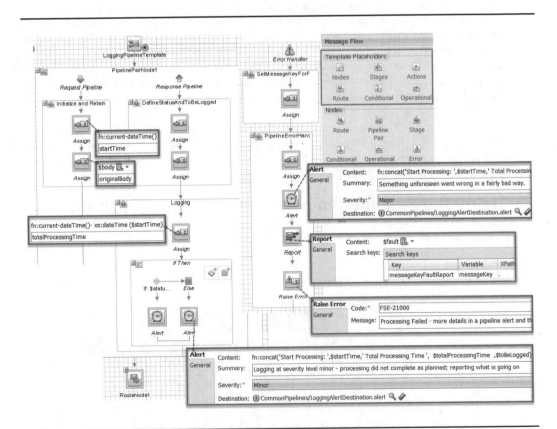

FIGURE 7-21.   *The request and response pipelines for the LoggingPipelineTemplate*

Return to the *LoggingPipeline* editor, where we have to configure a number of activities.

Click on the first Assign activity in stage *DefineStatusAndToBeLogged*. Set the Value—the expression used to derive the value of variable status—to the following XQuery expression:

```
let $errorCount := fn:count($body/flig:submitScheduledFlightResponseMessage/
flig:ProcessingResults/flig:ProcessingResult)
return if ($errorCount = 0)
        then 'OK'
        else 'NOK'
Define user namespace saibot.airport/services/flightschedule with prefix flig.
```

Next, edit the second Assign activity in the same stage, the one that assigns a value to variable *toBeLogged* that determines what will be visible in the pipeline alert. Use the following expression for the Value:

```
if ($status= 'OK')
then
fn:concat('Successful processing; assigned flight id: ', $body/flig:submitSche
duledFlightResponseMessage/flig:FlightSchedule/flig:FlightId)
else
$body/flig:submitScheduledFlightResponseMessage/flig:ProcessingResults
```

In case of a successful scheduled flight registration, only the identifier of that flight is reported. In case of unsuccessful processing, all process results are reported.

Test the FlightScheduleService with LoggingPipeline

With these simple configuration steps, the new *LoggingPipeline* is embedded in the *FlightScheduleService*. Any request the service handles is processed by the pipeline and will surface somehow in pipeline alerts and whatever channels the *LoggingPipelineTemplate* uses now or in the future.

Run the *FlightScheduleService* and submit a request message that you expect will be processed successfully. The only evidence from the *LoggingPipeline* will be visible in pipeline alerts. Note: If instead of running the proxy service you run the *LoggingPipeline*, you can check the flow trace for details on the actions by the *LoggingPipeline*. Run either the proxy service or the *LoggingPipeline* with a request message that will fail during validation.

Open the Enterprise Manager FMW Control. Click on the node SOA | service-bus in the Target Navigation frame. On the Dashboard, set the Alerts dropdown to Pipeline Alerts. The Alert History appears (Figure 7-23) and should contain two pipeline alerts for the last two requests. The last one (that failed) at level Minor and the one before that at severity Normal.

Click on the alerts to verify if the Description contains the information that was defined in the $toBeLogged variable.

Right click on the Service Bus drop-down link above the dashboard link. Select the option *Message Report* from the drop-down menu. On the overview page that appears, click on the Search button to retrieve all [recent] message reports. Note: If your request to the *FlightScheduleService* caused the *ProcessingAndRoutingPipeline* to abort, then the error handler in the *LoggingPipeline* will have kicked in and a Message Report is produced. In that case, the pipeline alert is created at severity Major. If the request did not make it passed the validation pipeline, then the alert is of severity level Minor and it did not trigger the error handler in the *LoggingPipeline*.

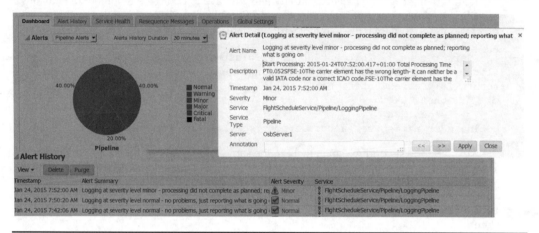

FIGURE 7-23. *Alert details produced from the inherited Logging Pipeline Template*

NOTE
At this point, we can make additional changes in the LoggingPipelineTemplate in project CommonPipelines and see how these changes would automatically appear in the FlightScheduleService. We can also create pipelines in other services based on the LoggingPipelineTemplate—to further demonstrate the reuse potential of pipeline templates.

Reaching Out from a Pipeline with Routing, Service Callout and Publish Activities

There are several activities that can be used to reach out from a pipeline to a business service, a local proxy service, a Split-Join component, or a pipeline. Service Bus developers can use routing, service callout and publish. Even though they essentially do the same thing, there are some distinctions you should be aware of.

Routing is used as the last node in a pipeline. It is the bridge between the request pipeline and the external component that continues processing the contents of $body and $header. The routing activity will receive the response and trigger the response pipeline. A pipeline can contain only a single routing activity. This activity is synchronous: Service Bus will wait for the Route call to finish before continuing to process.

The threading model of the Service Bus consists of different threads being used for the request and the response pipeline. Routing is done by a Transport Provider that may or may not use the request thread to wait for the provider's response. The latter case means that the transport is blocking and this applies to the EJB transport and the JCA Database Adapter.

The HTTP transport is nonblocking, which means that the request thread is released as soon as the transport provider has sent the request. The answer from the synchronous business service is handled by a newly allocated response thread.

A Service Callout can be used like Routing to callout to local proxy service, pipeline, business service, and split-join. A pipeline can contain multiple Service Callout activities, both in the request as well as in the response pipeline. Service callouts are synchronous. *The pipeline processor will block the thread until the response arrives asynchronously. The blocked thread then resumes execution of the pipeline. An important purpose of a Service Callout is to retrieve values for variables that can later be used in pipeline actions to perform business logic.* That means that while the Service Callout is being processed, nothing else can happen in the pipeline in terms of processing the current request.

The Publish activity is also used to invoke a local proxy service, pipeline, business service, and split-join. This activity can be used multiple times in a request and a response pipeline. Calls by Publish can be synchronous or asynchronous. Publish action is used for request-only scenarios where you don't expect a response back. The exact nature of the Publish action depends upon the target service you are invoking. For example, with the Quality of Service (QoS) defined as "best effort" (the default setting), Publish is a true fire and forget and the thread will not be blocked.

A Publish Table activity can be used when the service to invoke has to be selected at run time. Switch-style condition logic is used to determine at run time which of the predefined services are to be invoked. Additionally, Dynamic Publish activities are used to invoke a single service; at run time is determined through an XQuery expression which service that should be.

Parallel Processing Using Split-Join

A pipeline can contain many activities. Some of these are sequential by necessity, because one builds on the results of another. Activities have to wait on their predecessor in such cases. However, it is not uncommon to have activities that could be processed in parallel, because they do not depend on each other in any way. Especially when these activities interact with external services whose response time determines the duration of the activity—and no local resources are involved—we can speed up the overall processing by executing these unrelated activities simultaneously.

Service Bus provides the Split-Join component, which allows us to implement such parallelism. It comes in two flavors: static and dynamic. In the static case, each parallel thread performs its own task and the number of parallel activities is known beforehand. In the dynamic case, the same set of activities is performed on multiple elements that are identified in a for..each loop. The iterations of this loop can (to some degree) be executed in parallel.

In the next two sections, we will first use a static Split-Join service to do a reimplementation of the *RoutingAndProcessing* pipeline that leverages the fact that its three key stages are actually unrelated and are good candidates for parallel execution. The second section introduces the *MultipleFlightScheduleService* that is capable of handling multiple flight schedule requests in one go. This service will use a dynamic split-join to process these requests in parallel.

Implementing the Aggregator Pattern through a Static Split-Join

The aggregator design pattern describes how multiple *individual messages are collected and retained through individual service calls until all required information is available to process and ultimately publish a single message distilled from the individual messages.*

The implementation of this pattern—where we retrieve results in parallel from various back end systems and subsequently aggregate the results together—can be done easily in a Service Bus project using the Split-Join component. Figure 7-24 shows how we could leverage this pattern in the *ProcessingAndRoutingPipeline* for the three sequential actions slot retrieval, calculation of the number of flights, and the airline check.

In the overview editor for the *FlightScheduleService*, create a Split-Join component—either by dragging it from the component palette or from the context menu Insert | Split Join.

The Create Split-Join Service wizard appears. Set the name to *ParallelEnrichmentSplitJoin*. Click Next. Select the ParallelFlightEnrichmentService.wsdl in the WSDLs folder. Operation *enrichFlightSchedule* in binding execute_bind is selected. Uncheck the checkbox for exposing the split-join as a proxy service. Click Finish to create the Split-Join service.

Double click on the Split-Join component to start editing it. The editor is similar to the pipeline editor—but quite different as well. Split-join is a different beast—as the component

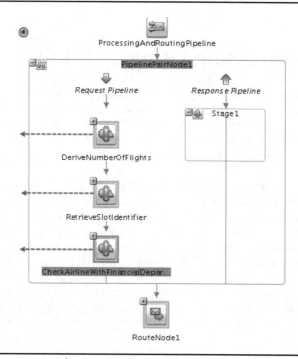

FIGURE 7-24. *Three sequential actions in the ProcessingAndRoutingPipeline that are candidate for parallel invocation*

palette should tell you; when you check the .flow source file, you will see that this component uses BPEL as its definition language.

We want to have several enrichment operations executed in parallel. Therefore, add a Parallel component from the component palette and drop it between Receive and Reply, as shown in Figure 7-25.

Set the names of the two predefined scopes in this parallel flow to the same names used for the stages in the *ProcessingAndRoutingPipeline*: *DeriveNumberOfFlights* and *RetrieveSlotIdentifier*. Add a third scope, called *CheckAirlineWithFinancialDepartment*.

Implementing the Three Parallel Scopes

Add a Java Callout assign operation to the scope *DeriveNumberOfFlights*. Configure the method in the same way as when we implemented the Java Callout in the *ProcessingAndRoutingPipeline* (see Figure 7-13): invoke method *calculateNumberOfFlights* in class *ScheduledFlightProcessor* available in Jar file JavaCalloutJar.jar. Set the value expression of the argument to $request.in/bind:TimePlanningUnit. This refers to the request message received by the Split-Join service. In a pipeline we would use $body instead of $request.in. For the Return value, click on the green plus icon and generate a new global variable *numberOfFlights* of type integer.

Next, drag the Invoke Service component to the scope *RetrieveSlotIdentifier*. Configure this action (as shown in Figure 7-14) to call the operation *findSlot* on the business service *SlotService*. For the request variable, create a local variable called *findSlotRequestMsg*. For the response variable, create a global variable *slotIdentifier*.

Add an assign action prior to the Invoke Service. Configure this action to assign the value

```
<soapenv:Body xmlns:soapenv="http://schemas.xmlsoap.org/soap/envelope/"/>
```

to $findSlotRequestMsg.in.

Add a replace action, following the assign. Have it operate on location *findSlotRequestMsg.in*, replacing only the node contents. Use the XSLT resource submitScheduledFlightRequestMessageTofindSlotRequestMessage.xsl in folder Transformations on $request.in.

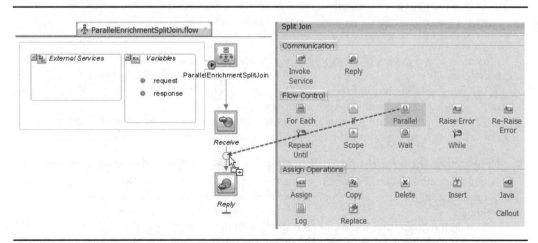

FIGURE 7-25.   *Initial implementation of the ParallelEnrichmentSplitJoin component*

Moving to the third scope: *CheckAirlineWithFinancialDepartment*. Add another Invoke
Service action and configure it as shown in Figure 7-17: Have it invoke the
FinancialDepartmentPipeline and specifically the *checkAirlineStatus* operation. Create a local
variable *checkAirlineRequest* for the Request variable and a global variable
checkAirlineFinanceResponse for the Response Variable.

Add an assign action to the scope preceding the service invocation. The Variable is set to
checkAirlineRequest.in. The expression used for setting the variable is:

```
<soapenv:Body
xmlns:soapenv="http://schemas.xmlsoap.org/soap/envelope/">
<fin:checkAirlineRequestMessage xmlns:fin="saibot.airport/services/financial">
  <fin:Carrier>
    <ref:IATACode xmlns:ref="ref:saibot.airport/data/reference">{$request.in/
bind:Carrier}</ref:IATACode>
  </fin:Carrier>
</fin:checkAirlineRequestMessage>
</soapenv:Body>
```

Here we include the *Carrier* element from the request message sent to the Split-Join service in
the request message for the *FinancialDepartmentPipeline*.

Complete the Split-Join Service

All three scopes are defined—in a way that is very similar to the sequential stages in the
ProcessingAndRoutingPipeline. The results from the scopes are stored in three global variables.
What is left for us to do is create an Assign action that constructs the response message—in global
variable $response, and not in $body as we are used to in pipelines. Add an Assign action,
outside the parallel container and above the Reply action. The expression

```
<flig:EnrichmentDetails xmlns:flig="saibot.airport/services/flightschedule">
  <flig:SlotId>{$slotIdentifier.return/ns1:SlotId/text()}</flig:SlotId>
  <flig:NumberOfFlights>{$numberOfFlights}</flig:NumberOfFlights>
  <flig:FinancialDepartmentApprovalStamp>
    {$checkAirlineFinanceResponse.out/ns3:UniqueStamp/text()}
  </flig:FinancialDepartmentApprovalStamp>
</flig:EnrichmentDetails>
```

is to be assigned to variable $response.out (the wrapping body and
enrichScheduleFlightResponseMessage element are added automatically). Here we construct the
SOAP Body with the required response message, injecting the three global variables that have
been assigned values by the three parallel scopes.

At this point, you can run the Split-Join service to see if it produces the desired result. Simply
right click, either in the project navigator, the Split-Join editor, or the overview editor.

Reorganize the ProcessingAndRoutingPipeline to Utilize the Split-Join Service

The real benefit from the *ParallelEnrichmentSplitJoin* will only emerge when we replace the
current logic in the *ProcessingAndRoutingPipeline* with a call to the Split-Join service. That is
easily done.

Open the *ProcessingAndRoutingPipeline* for editing. Add a new stage
InvokeParallelEnrichmentService as the first in the request pipeline. Add a Service Callout

activity to this stage. Configure it to invoke the *ParallelEnrichmentSplitJoin* service, specifically the operation *enrichFlightSchedule*, as shown in Figure 7-26.

Set the Configuration radio button to Configure Body. Define body variables *parallelEnrichmentRequest* and *parallelEnrichmentResponse* for the Request and Response, respectively.

Next, add an Assign activity to the request pipeline in the Service Callout. This assign has to copy $body to the variable *parallelEnrichmentRequest*.

Disable the three stages *DeriveNumberOfFlights*, *RetrieveSlotIdentifier*, and *CheckAirlineWithFinancialDepartment*.

TIP
Disabling and enabling stages or activities in a Service Bus pipeline can be done from the context menu on the relevant stage or activity in the pipeline editor. When disabled, a node is completely ignored by the run-time engine, as if the node does not exist at all.

Add a new Replace activity in the Request Action of the Routing activity and disable the current one (or update the current one with new settings). This [new or edited] Replace activity acts on Location body. It replaces the node contents, using an XSLT resource (submitScheduledFlightRequestToprivateSubmitScheduledFlightRequest.xsl). The three input parameters for this transformation—*numberOfFlights*, *financialDepartmentApprovalStamp,* and

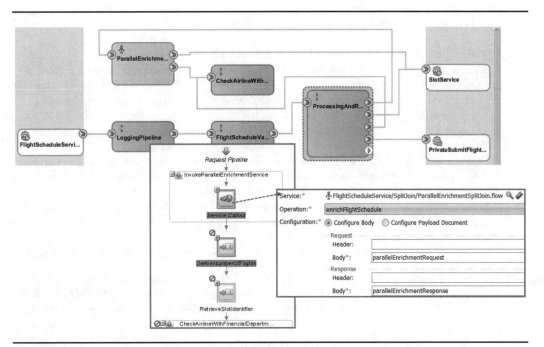

FIGURE 7-26. *Configuring the Service Callout to the Split-Join component*

slotIdentifier—are now to be configured using the following binding expressions, all based on the response from the Split-Join service:

```
$parallelEnrichmentResponse/*[1]/flig:NumberOfFlights/text()
$parallelEnrichmentResponse/*[1]/flig:FinancialDepartmentApprovalStamp/text()
$parallelEnrichmentResponse/*[1]/flig:SlotId/text()
```

At this point you can try out the newly configured *ProcessingAndRoutingPipeline* with the callout to the Split-Join service, either by running the pipeline directly or any of the pipelines that precedes it or even the proxy service. Check what has happened with the overall response time: has it gone down now that we do multiple things in parallel using the Split-Join service?

Dynamic Split-Join for Parallel Processing of Multiple Scheduled Flights

In the previous example, we used a Split-Join service to perform three distinct tasks in parallel. Another common situation is where a message contains a number of details that should each be processed in the same way. This could apply to order items in an order, line items in an invoice or passengers on a flight boarding plan. Split-join can also be used in these cases—where the same operation has to be performed on a number of elements. The number is unknown at design time. The processing of each item is unrelated to each other item—therefore the processing can be performed in parallel—provided enough threads are available.

This section, we will look at this dynamic application of split-join. We will implement a new service interface *MultiFlightScheduleService*. This service is the versatile cousin of the *FlightScheduleService* that can process multiple requested scheduled flights in a single service request. Each scheduled flight request can be processed independently of the others—and this could be done in parallel to speed up the overall process.

Create Split-Join and Expose a Proxy Service for It

Open the overview editor for the *FlightScheduleService*. Either using drag and drop from the component palette or using right mouse click and Insert | Split Join, add a Split-Join component. Set the name to *MultiFlightScheduleSplitJoin*. Press Next to advance to the second page.

Select MultiFlightScheduleService.wsdl in the WSDLs folder as the interface for this split-join. Select operation *submitMultiFlightSchedules*. Have the split-join exposed through a Proxy Service called *MultiFlightScheduleServicePS*, to be created in the *Proxy* folder.

Press Finish to have the split-join created. Double click the split-join to edit its definition.

A request and response variable have already been created and the request and reply steps are also already present. Create a new global variable *tempResponse* based on the *submitMultiScheduledFlightsResponseMessage* element in the FlightScheduleService.xsd file. We will collect all intermediate results—gathered during parallel processing of the flight schedule requests—into this variable.

Add an Assign operation below the Receive activity. Configure the assign to assign this value

```
<flig:submitMultiScheduledFlightsResponseMessage xmlns:flig="saibot.airport/
services/flightschedule"> <flig:SubmittedFlightScheduleResults></flig:Submitte
dFlightScheduleResults> </flig:submitMultiScheduledFlightsResponseMessage>
```

to variable *tempResponse*.

Add a For..Each action below the Assign. This action is where the parallel processing will take place. Set the Execution Mode of the For..Each to Parallel. Call the counter variable name *counter*. Set the Counter Start Value to *number(1)*. Set the Final Counter Value to

```
count($request.in/bind:SubmittedFlightSchedules/bind:SubmittedFlightSchedule)
```

Add an Assign, an Invoke Service and an Insert action inside the For..Each scope. The assign will set the request message to be used in the Invoke Service and the insert will take the response from the service invocation and add part of it to the *tempResponse* variable.

Configure the Invoke Service to call the *submitFlightSchedule* operation on the *FlightScheduleValidationPipeline*, as shown in Figure 7-27. Create and set local Request Variable *submitFlightScheduleReq* and Response Variable *submitFlightScheduleRes* for this action.

Next, configure the preceding assign activity to set variable *submitFlightScheduleReq* with the expression

```
$request.in/bind:SubmittedFlightSchedules/bind:SubmittedFlightSchedule[$counter]
```

This means that in each iteration, the next *SubmittedFlightSchedule* element from the request message received by the split-join is used for the subsequent service call to *FlightScheduleValidationPipeline*.

Configure the insert action with the value:

```
<bind:SubmittedFlightScheduleResult>
<bind:Carrier>{$submitFlightScheduleReq.in/bind:Carrier/text()}</bind:Carrier>
<bind:FlightNumber>{$submitFlightScheduleReq.in/bind:FlightNumber/text()}</
bind:FlightNumber>
<bind:SubmissionOutcome>
<bind:FlightSchedule> <bind:FlightId>{$submitFlightScheduleRes.out/
bind:FlightSchedule/bind:FlightId/text()}</bind:FlightId> <bind:SlotId>{$submi
tFlightScheduleRes.out/bind:FlightSchedule/bind:SlotId/text()}</bind:SlotId>
</bind:FlightSchedule>
{$submitFlightScheduleRes.out/bind:ProcessingResults} </
bind:SubmissionOutcome>
</bind:SubmittedFlightScheduleResult>
```

Set *as first child of* as the Position and the XPath expression *./*[1]* and variable *tempResponse* as the (target) location (see Figure 7-27).

This means that in each iteration, variable *tempResponse* is extended with an additional *SubmittedFlightScheduleResult* element.

Add a final assign activity after the For..Each and before the Reply. Assign the value $tempResponse to variable response.out to copy the final result to the response message returned from the Split-Join service.

Figure 7-28 shows the overview for the *FlightScheduleService* project, with the pipelines, the two Split-Join components, the two exposed proxy services, and the two business services—and all their interdependencies—including the logging pipeline that will be added in the next section. Each of these components can be run from within JDeveloper.

You can now run either the proxy service or the split-join itself. Feed a request message with two or more *SubmittedFlightSchedule* elements and see the response with entries for each of them. Try out a request message with a combination of correct *SubmittedFlightSchedule* elements

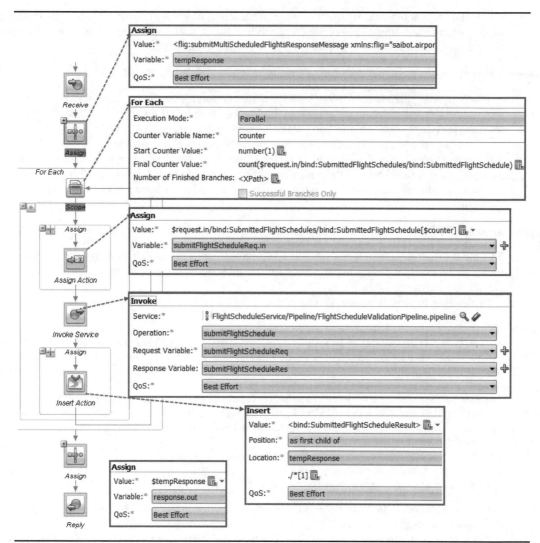

FIGURE 7-27. *The Split-join for parallel processing multiple flight schedules using a For..Each activity*

and elements that will fail validation. The response will contain a combination of *SubmissionOutcome* elements and *ProcessingResults* entries.

Note that the response time is not the sum of the processing time of each *SubmittedFlightSchedule*. Thanks to parallel processing, the total response time should be considerably lower than that—depending on the number of threads the Service Bus has at its disposal for doing the work in parallel.

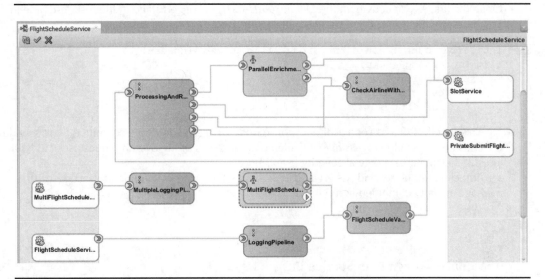

FIGURE 7-28. *Overview over the FlightScheduleService project*

NOTE
An alternative to the dynamic split-join in case of one-way processing: post each element on a queue and do the processing in a second Service Bus service that listens to that queue. This is a nice approach when the processing part is reusable (and can be exposed as a separate service). This decoupled approach will also help to throttle the number of threads used to process elements in parallel and it allows the Split-Join component to complete more rapidly.

Add Logging Pipeline

As a final step in this chapter, we will now reuse the logging pipeline template to also insert logging in the *MultipleFlightSchedule* service processing. Create a new pipeline in the *FlightScheduleService* project. Call the pipeline *MultipleLoggingPipeline* and associate it with the *LoggingPipelineTemplate* in project *CommonPipelines*. The pipeline should implement the same interface implemented by the *MultipleLoggingPipeline* and the *MultiFlightScheduleServicePS* proxy service, as defined in the MultiFlightScheduleService.wsdl.

Edit the new pipeline and configure the Routing activity to invoke the *MultiFlightScheduleSplitJoin*. Rewire the proxy service *MultiFlightScheduleServicePS* to this pipeline.

At this point, you can run the proxy service. The multiple flight schedule requests will be processed and some basic logging is performed, including a pipeline alert that tells you the time it took to process the request.

To tailor the output in the new logging pipeline, double click on the *MultipleLoggingPipeline*. Specify the expression that determines whether we should log at normal or minor severity level.

Open the first Assign activity in the *DefineStatusAndToBeLogged* stage in the response pipeline. Set the expression to

```
let $errorCount := fn:count($body//flig:ProcessingResults/
flig:ProcessingResult)
return if ($errorCount = 0)
        then 'OK'
        else 'NOK'
```

This specifies that as soon as the response from processing multiple submitted flight schedules contains even a single *ProcessingResult* element, the status of the overall request is set to NOK. As a result, logging takes place at severity level Minor.

You can edit the second Assign activity to define the value of variable $toBeLogged—the message actually contained in the Pipeline Alert.

Modular Design with Service Bus

Service Bus has several levels of granularity at which functionality can be encapsulated. The most fine-grained level is the stage, which is easily identifiable in the visual editor and can have its own variables and error handling. A stage is not invoked—it is executed when within the request or response pipeline its turn has arrived. Stages are not reusable.

The pipeline is the next level of encapsulation granularity. Pipelines can contain multiple stages, have their own variables that are global throughout the pipeline and can have their own error handling. When a pipeline is based on a template, it inherits the template's functionality. Shared variables can be shared across pipelines within the same project. Pipelines are reusable within the Service Bus project. Pipelines are invoked through the service interface they expose. That interface can be exposed as proxy service to external consumers as well. Note that Pipelines are very similar to Mediator or BPEL components in SOA composite applications.

Private proxy services that are invoked over the local transport offer the next level of encapsulation. These services are reusable across Service Bus projects within the same run-time environment. The local transport ensures efficient, low-overhead calls can be made to these services, that allow transaction and security context to be shared. Shared variables can be shared between pipelines in the calling project as well as the called, private service project.

Public proxy services are the highest, coarsest grained level of reusable functionality in the Service Bus. Any pipeline can invoke a public proxy service, either a local one or a remote one. In both cases, nothing is shared between the calling and the called service—no variables and no security or transaction context, unless the transport protocol used has explicit support for such propagation.

When designing services and their implementation, these levels of encapsulation should be considered. For example, from the perspective of reuse, testing, team development, deployment, debugging, and continuous delivery.

Summary

Service Bus is the lean and mean machine that is very good at processing messages quickly and efficiently, and without too much fuss. Earlier chapters demonstrated fairly simple Service Bus projects with minimal VETRO activity. This chapter makes clear that a Service Bus pipeline can do much more than just a little transformation. Implementing composite services is very well possible too. Callouts, error handling, if..then..else logic, for-loops and such make a pipeline into a little program that can perform quite complex tasks. Multiple pipelines can be linked together, to form a larger process constructed from fairly encapsulated reusable pieces.

Determining how to organize the logic in a Service Bus project and what granularity to use for stages, pipelines, and local proxies is both important and something of challenge. Deciding what to do in Service Bus projects and when to engage an SOA composite application is even more important. To keep the Service Bus lean and mean, we probably should refrain from implementing too much complexity and composition in Service Bus projects—even when that can be done.

Pipelines can be based on pipeline templates. These templates—as we have seen—provide inheritable chunks of logic that can be fine-tuned in each realization of a pipeline based on the template. The logging pipeline template that we discussed contains generic functionality—best practices as laid down by the Saibot Airport competence center on SOA Suite—that can easily be applied in pipelines across many Service Bus projects. These pipelines each customize and complement the contents from the template to the specific context in which they are used. When the pipeline template is modified and deployed, all derived instances will inherit these changes automatically without redeployment.

The Split-Join service can be used as another type of reusable component that can be called from either pipelines, proxy services, or other Split-Join services. The split-join is similar to a Pipeline. However, it uses a different syntax and set of activities (based on BPEL). Its main purpose in Service Bus is to provide of parallel processing capabilities that are used to speed up processing of messages.

The next chapter will demonstrate how composite services can also be implemented in SOA composites. We will see how the BPEL component is another great tool for implementing complex message processing, XML oriented logic, and service orchestration.

CHAPTER
8

Composite Services with SOA Composites Using the BPEL Component

The previous chapter demonstrated how composite services can be implemented through Service Bus projects, using Pipelines and Split-Join components. We welded several of these components together to realize the *FlightScheduleService*—using activities to validate messages, do parallel processing on parts of messages, and to call out to custom Java classes and local and remote web services.

The BPEL component that can be used in SOA composites is also very well and probably even better equipped for the implementation of such composite services. Orchestrating service calls, manipulating XML messages, performing flow logic with if-then-else and for-loops, handling exceptions as well as performing parallel processing are the sweet spot for this component. A BPEL component has many characteristics in common with Service Bus Pipelines and Split-Join components. In addition to orchestrating synchronous services, BPEL is also good at asynchronous interactions as well as longer running (stateful) conversations. These latter two subjects—that are both not the strong suit of Service Bus—are addressed in later chapters.

BPEL (Business Process Execution Language) is a standard, defined by OASIS, and supported by many IT vendors. BPEL is a language for creating a piece of service and process logic—logic that exposes a service interface and that typically orchestrates multiple service calls. At the same time, BPEL has many of the traits of general-purpose programming languages, as we will see in this chapter and the next.

A BPEL process can be fairly long-running, can contain state, and can receive incoming messages in addition to the original request that instantiated the process. In addition, BPEL can perform its orchestration as part of a single global (XA) transaction. This chapter introduces BPEL and the development of BPEL service components.

In this chapter, we will revisit the *FlightScheduleService* and the *MultiFlightScheduleService* that were introduced in Chapter 7. These services take a single one or multiple of these requests for actually planning a flight that is the implementation of a slot. We will implement them again, this time using a SOA composite application and the BPEL component, as well as many of the same artifacts used in the previous chapter, for example, for transformation and Domain Value Mapping.

The sources for this chapter provide several stages in the development of this service (from the starting point *step0* through *step7* with the final result). Each step is both the end result of the previous stage as well as the starting point for the next. This chapter covers a lot of ground. It does not provide screenshots or detailed explanations for every step along the way. You are encouraged to take a close look at the steps in the source code to get a good understanding of how the end result is arrived at.

Using BPEL to Create the Bare Bones FlightScheduleService

This section discusses the initial creation of the *FlightScheduleService*, using a BPEL component. At first it will be a hollow shell: the service interface is exposed and the barest of implementations is provided. Later on we will add more details to this implementation. Start this section from the *step0* sources.

Quick Introduction to BPEL

BPEL is a programming language for implementing process flows and composite (or orchestrated) services. The program created with BPEL is called a (BPEL) process. This term reflects the fact that BPEL was initially positioned to implement business processes. Over the years, business processes have predominantly become the domain of BPMN (and for Oracle of the BPM Suite)—see Chapter 19, with BPEL being used more in a similar way as Service Bus pipelines: service oriented programs that manipulate XML, invoke business services and perform logic around those. BPEL is therefore a fine candidate for implementing composite services. One major difference with Service Bus pipelines is BPEL's natural ability to interact with asynchronous services, as we will discuss in Chapter 12, and to capture state during longer running processes.

BPEL is a standard maintained by OASIS and supported by all major players in the IT industry, including Microsoft, Oracle, IBM, Software AG, Adobe, and SAP. A BPEL program—referred to as a *BPEL process definition*—can be run by a BPEL engine, just like a Java program can be run by a Java Virtual Machine and a PL/SQL program by the Oracle RDBMS. BPEL is one of the first-class citizens for component implementation included in the SCA standard, along with Java, Spring, PHP (SOAP) web services, and C++. Services implemented using BPEL can easily be configured in SCA components and linked with references provided by other SCA components.

A BPEL process is often published as a web service. It then has an associated WSDL document with XSD definitions and one or more operations on a *portType* that can be called through SOAP messages. Note that we will later discuss other ways to call and communicate with BPEL components.

A typical BPEL process contains the following items:

- Calls to services. A service in this sense can be a task performed by a human staff member, hiding behind the service interface of a workflow engine, or an automated Web Service, although for the BPEL process, the distinction is not important.

- Specific BPEL activities, including data manipulation (calculation and transformation of variables associated with the process) and flow logic, including decision point (if-then-else and switch/case, iteration, parallelism, wait).

- Event handlers and fault (or exception) handlers.

In SOA Suite 12c, BPEL components often work closely together with other service components in a composite application, such as Mediator, and Business Rule service components, to facilitate interaction with other services and provide complex, externalized decision logic. Human Task components are also frequently wired to BPEL processes for the manual handling of activities in potentially complex workflows. Another regular partner for BPEL components is the Notification Service for sending messages to human users via email, SMS, and instant messaging (internally connected to the User Messaging Service, or UMS).

Its a good fit with business processes notwithstanding, BPEL primarily provides a powerful way for implementing composite services that do not necessarily directly relate to an automated business process. Of course, services can be implemented using a variety of technologies. Especially when a service component has to invoke multiple services—either external to the composite application or provided by other service components inside the composite, and potentially asynchronous and long-running—BPEL is typically a good way to implement the component. This holds especially true when over the course of the component's lifetime some state is built up in variables and process flow logic is involved to loop or conditionally branch.

A BPEL component has the capability to receive additional messages, beyond the first invocation that initiated the component instance, and respond to them. This allows clients to interact with the process—for example, to check on its progress, provide additional information, or get a hold of intermediate results.

First Steps with the FlightScheduleService and with BPEL

Open project *FlightScheduleService* in application *FlightScheduleServiceSOA*. This is a SOA composite project. It currently exposes the *FlightScheduleService*—based on the same WSDL and XSDs we used in Chapter 7. This service is to be invoked with details about a flight schedule that is the implementation of an existing slot allocation. The scheduled flight should be registered, once it has been validated and enriched. Upon successful registration, the assigned Saibot Airport flight identifier is to be returned, along with a tentative gate assignment.

The initial implementation will simply accept the request message and return a hard-coded response. No validation, enrichment, or onwards processing is performed yet. It will be a first taste of BPEL.

Implement the Minimal FlightScheduleService

Open the composite editor for the *FlightScheduleService*. From the component palette, drag the BPEL component and drop it in the Components section, to add the component to the SOA composite.

The editor for creating a BPEL process appears, as shown in Figure 8-1. Call the BPEL component *FlightScheduleProcessor*. Set the namespace to saibot.airport/services/flightschedule/private/FlightScheduleProcessor. Select the Template *Base on a WSDL* and select the FlightScheduleService.wsdl in the WSDLs folder. Note that the Port Type is automatically set. Set the Service Name to *FlightScheduleProcessor* and uncheck the checkbox *Expose as a SOAP service*. Press OK to complete the creation of the BPEL component.

The BPEL component is added to the composite overview and to the underlying composite .xml file. Wire the exposed service to this new component. This means that when the composite is deployed and the *FlightScheduleService* is invoked, the request message is passed to the BPEL engine to process using the *FlightScheduleProcessor*. It is up to this BPEL component to perform

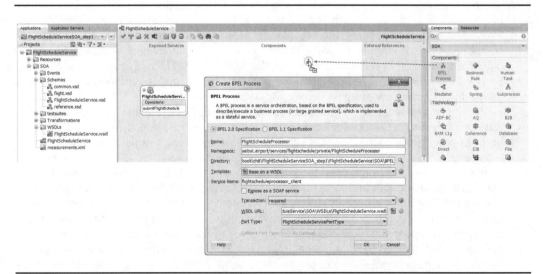

FIGURE 8-1. *Add a BPEL component to the FlightScheduleService SOA composite application to provide the implementation of the FlightScheduleService*

the required logic and come up with a meaningful response message that will travel from the BPEL engine over the SCA fabric to be returned to the service consumer.

Double click the BPEL component to bring up the editor. You will see something similar to Figure 8-2—and not all that different from the Service Bus Split-Join editor discussed in Chapter 7.

The BPEL process should be read from top to bottom. It contains a single, largely sequential flow that starts with the *receive* activity. This activity gets handed the incoming request message, initiates a new instance of the BPEL process, and assigns the request message to a global variable—default name is *inputVariable*. This variable was created automatically—based on the request message for operation *submitSchedule* as defined in the FlightScheduleService.wsdl document.

At this moment, the only other activity is a Reply activity. This activity takes the value from one of the variables in the BPEL process—by default called *outputVariable* and based on the response message defined in the FlightScheduleService.wsdl document—and returns it to the caller as the response message.

Note the component palette with activities that can be added to the BPEL process. Many are similar to the activities available in Service Bus pipelines, used for messaging validation and processing, for service callouts and for typical programming operations such as iterations, conditional logic, and exception handling.

All interactions between a BPEL process and the outside world—both incoming and outgoing—are regulated through Partner Links, such as the *FlightScheduleProcessor* partner link shown on the left in Figure 8-2.

NOTE
Interactions through the Event Delivery Network (see Chapter 15) are the exception to this statement: these do not take place through Partner Links.

Partner Links represent service interfaces that are either implemented by or accessed from the BPEL process. The definition of exactly which interface is associated with a Partner Link is defined

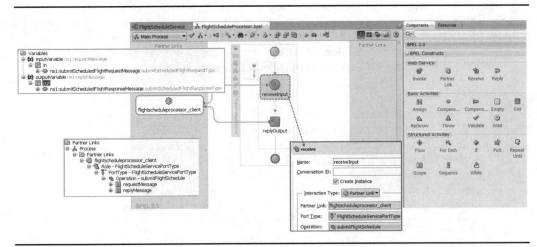

FIGURE 8-2.   *The default implementation of a BPEL process based on a synchronous service definition*

in a wrapper WSDL document. In this case that is FlightScheduleServiceWrapper.wsdl—generated by JDeveloper when the BPEL component was first created, based on the FlightScheduleService. wsdl and implementing the *FlightScheduleServicePortType*.

A *PartnerLinkType* specifies "role" elements. Each role element introduces a role that either the BPEL process or the external partner can assume in their mutual interaction: service consumer or service provider. That role is linked to a *portType* that the partner playing the role should implement. These roles associated with *portTypes* are a BPEL specific extension to vanilla WSDL documents.

If the BPEL process is asynchronous, the partner link type contains two role elements: The partner is initially the consumer of the service, sending a SOAP message to the BPEL process and subsequently the receiver of the response message sent to the callback interface. Asynchronous services are discussed in Chapter 12.

Both the Receive and the Reply activity are associated with the *submitFlightSchedule* operation on the *FlightScheduleProcessor* partner link.

Although you could already deploy the SOA composite and test the service, what is still lacking from the BPEL process is an activity that assigns a value to the *outputVariable*. At this moment, the response message would be empty.

Add an Assign Activity to Provide Content for the Response Message

In BPEL, the Assign activity is used to manipulate variables. Add an Assign activity from the component palette and insert it between the Receive and Reply activity. Set the name of the activity to *setHardcodedReply*. This name has no relevance for the BPEL engine—it is only used for human readability when working in the design time, or when looking at the audit trail at run time.

Double click on the Assign activity to bring up the editor. On the right-hand side, you will see the variables that can be manipulated in the current scope. On the left is a similar list that shows all available variables from which data can be used to help construct the data to be applied to the target. We can draw direct mappings from the left to the right, to have values copied over to the target variables.

Alternatively, we can assign static values or entire XML fragments and we can use expressions to produce the values of (elements of) target variables. These expressions can enlist advanced XPath functions that can do both XQuery- and XSLT-based transformations, deal with binary content or map from native formats to XML or vice versa. Assign rules can also remove elements from the target variable or rename or recast them (both local name and namespace). Check the documentation for some details on all the many intricacies of the Assign activity and the copy rules.

For now, set hard coded values for all elements in the *FlightSchedule* node in the *outputVariable*, by dragging literals to the relevant target elements.

TIP
BPEL differs from Service Bus pipeline in this area in several ways: in BPEL, variables have to be predefined before they can be used in an Assign activity. Additionally, the Assign activity in BPEL is used both for the initial assignment of a value to a variable as well as for manipulating and replacing the current value of a variable, unlike Service Bus that has separate activities for this—assign and replace respectively. In both cases, variables contain XML structures—although BPEL also supports simple types such as String and Integer.

Deploy and Test

Deploy the SOA composite *FlightScheduleService* to the Integrated WLS, in exactly the same way as first introduced in Chapter 5. A test call to the service exposed by this composite can be made from a tool like SoapUI, from the test tab in the EM FMW Control and from with JDeveloper, using the HTTP Analyzer. If you open the *Application Servers* window and expand the node for the IntegratedWebLogicServer all the way down to IntegratedWebLogicServer | SOA | DefaultServer | default | FlightScheduleService [1.0] | FlightScheduleService (ws), you can right click on this node and select *Test WebService* on the context menu. Figure 8-3 illustrates this.

NOTE
The [1.0] for the SOA composite application is an indication of the version of the composite. Multiple versions could be deployed at once, all of them running in parallel (also see Chapter 21). This is a distinction between Service Bus and SOA composites: the Service Bus does not have any concept of versioning at all.

The HTTP Analyzer will appear. This is a tool integrated in JDeveloper for making test calls to HTTP services, including SOAP and REST services. Since the HTTP Analyzer is invoked in the context of the *FlightScheduleService*, it opens with the correct WSDL and Service URL (endpoint) and presents a form where the values for the elements of the request message can be set, see Figure 8-4. The XML content can be directly edited on the tab labeled HTTP Content.

To see what happened during the execution of the service request in the composite instance, we can inspect the SOA composite flow trace and the detailed BPEL audit flow in the EM FMW Control. The latter allows us a step by step audit trail of exactly what went on in the BPEL process instance, see Figure 8-5.

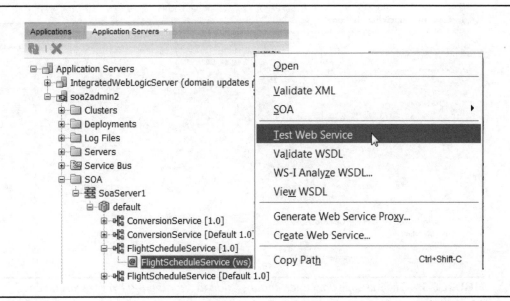

FIGURE 8-3. *Invoking a service exposed by a deployed SOA composite from within JDeveloper*

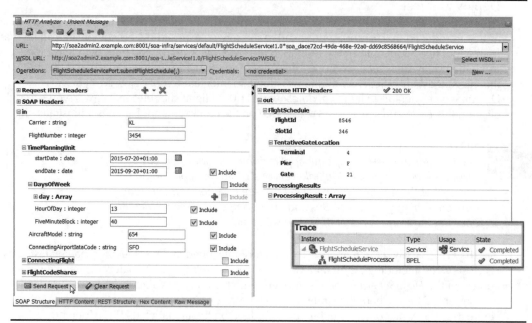

FIGURE 8-4. *Test call to the FlightScheduleService SOA composite's exposed service interface*

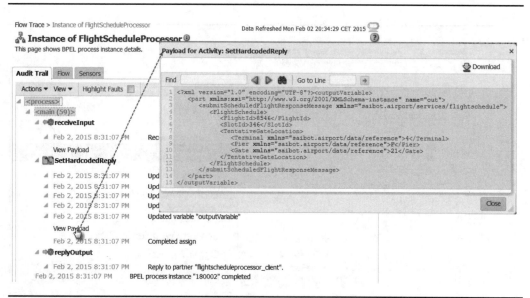

FIGURE 8-5. *The message flow trace and the audit trail for the BPEL process instance*

NOTE
We can also make use of debugging the SOA composite and the BPEL component to closely inspect exactly what goes on inside.
*   The Flow tab provides a graphical report on the BPEL process instance, illustrating in the same language as used in the BPEL design editor how a particular instance progressed.*

Implementing Validation on Requested Flight Schedules

Processing a scheduled flight is not a trivial thing. First, the incoming message should be validated against the XSD Schema definition. Then a number of constraints, that cannot be expressed in an XSD, have to be checked. Subsequently, some of the values provided in the request message have to be verified against a list of allowable values. These values may also have to be converted to a different domain. This was the situation in Chapter 7—where we dealt with the challenges in a Service Bus pipeline—and it is again the situation now as we will use a BPEL component to implement the desired logic.

In order to provide our consumers with as complete a list of problems as possible with their request for a scheduled flight, we do not want to immediately abort processing upon the first issue we run into. Instead, we compile the results from each of the three steps into a list of processing results. If no issues were encountered, we can proceed to the next phase of the BPEL process: enrichment. If, however, one or more issues were found during XSD validation, constraint checking, or domain value checking and mapping, we will not continue to this next stage but instead return a response that contains all the issues that were discovered.

In this section, we will implement the three validation stages as well as the mechanism for collecting all issues. Start this section from the *step1* sources.

Prepare the Multiphase BPEL Process Structure

A BPEL process contains activities. In the most basic case, these activities are organized in a single sequential flow. The BPEL language provides the Scope activity, an important element in structuring processes. A scope is a container that contains one or more activities. A scope can also define local variables—private to the scope—and define scope level fault handling and compensation logic (to deal with failed transactions) as well as scope level event handlers. Unlike a Sequence activity in BPEL, a Scope is more therefore than just a container or package of related activities.

Scopes are quite useful when developing large BPEL processes in a structured fashion. Scopes can be nested to any level. They allow clustering of related activities with meaningful labels, making the BPEL process diagram much easier to understand. You can open or collapse scopes in the visual BPEL editor, which allows you to focus on details where you need to and stick to a high-level overview where that is more appropriate. Scopes also help with a top-down design of the BPEL process.

We want to execute three types of validations, and each of these three may result in a fault. However, these faults should not cause the process instance to completely abort but instead have to lead to an update of a variable that contains processing results. This leads inevitably to a process design with a scope for each of these three validation steps. Additionally, it makes sense to make an explicit distinction between the validation phase of the process and the processing and routing phase. In Service Bus, we used separate pipelines for this high-level service implementation structure and used stages for the more fine-grained organization. In BPEL we have more options. Scopes, unlike Service Bus stages, can be nested—so we can use top level scopes for one level of organization and a deeper level for more fine grained structure. Additionally, we can use a subprocess—either inline or stand-alone—to be called from the main BPEL process, as a means of structuring the BPEL process.

For now, let's just work with scopes—top level and nested.

Open the BPEL editor and add two top level scopes, called *Validations* and *ProcessingAndRouting*. Open the *Validations* scope and add four nested scopes, called *SchemaValidation*, *CustomValidation*, *AirlineValueMap*, and *ContinueOrReturn*, respectively, as seen in Figure 8-6.

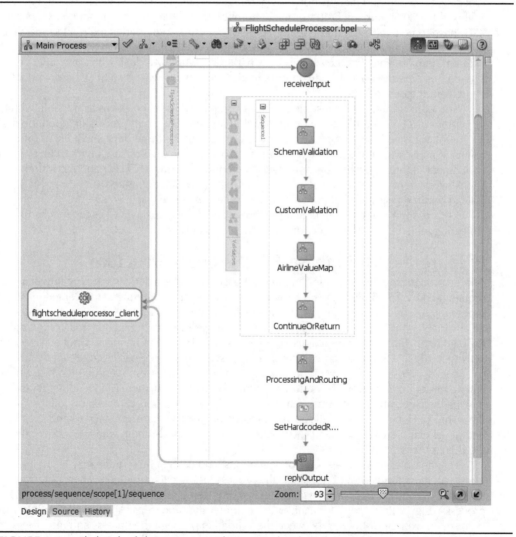

FIGURE 8-6. *FlightScheduleProcessor with two top level scopes and four nested scopes*

TIP
A scope must contain at least one activity in order to be valid. New scopes will therefore be marked with an alert icon as long as they do not have that first activity. To make a scope valid without having to implement its functionality, we can use the BPEL activity called Empty. This activity does what you would expect it to do: nothing. By giving this activity a logical name that describes what the eventual activity in that spot should do, it can be used to design the structure of the process early on. At a later stage, the real activities doing the actual work can replace these empty activities.

When the scopes are created, they will automatically contain a *sequence* activity. A sequence contains one or (usually) multiple BPEL activities that are executed sequentially. A sequence can be named and it can be expanded or collapsed in the visual editor, just like a scope. Unlike a scope, a sequence does not have its own variables or handlers—all it has are the sequentially executed activities. Sequences are frequently used for grouping activities inside containers, such as Scope and Flow, which can contain only a single [direct] child activity.

Add Schema Validation

Instructing the BPEL engine to perform validation of the contents of a variable against the underlying XSD schema is straightforward: there is an activity called Validation for precisely that purpose. Drag a Validation activity from the component palette to the *SchemaValidation* scope. Double click the activity. On the *General* tab, add variable *inputVariable* as the variable whose content should be validated against the XSD definition. This will make the BPEL engine perform the *Schema Validation*. When a violation is detected, the BPEL engine will throw a bpelx:invalidVariables run-time fault.

You can deploy the SOA composite and invoke the *FlightScheduleService* with a request message that contains a violation of the XSD, for example, by using a one-digit numerical value for the *AircraftModel* element. An HTTP 500 response will be the result, containing a SOAP Fault that reports on the validation error.

We do not want the process to abort, however. Therefore, we have to add fault handling to the *SchemaValidation* scope.

Fault Handling for Scope SchemaValidation

The main process activity, as well as every scope in a BPEL process, can have a *faultHandler* associated with it that contains one or more Catch activities that can each handle a specific type of fault (or all faults) when it occurs in the scope they are defined against—or in one of that scope's descendants or nested scopes. Each fault type in a BPEL process is identified through its fully qualified name. Catch activities specify the fault type they want to catch through that name. A Catch activity for a fault that has associated data can specify a *faultVariable* that will be initialized with the fault's data when the Catch is activated. We will use this for the *invalidVariables* fault that is thrown when a validation error occurs.

The variable used as the fault variable needs to have been defined earlier in the scope or on some higher level. It needs to be based on a message type—not a simple or complex XML element—in one of the WSDL documents associated with the application.

In addition to fault-specific Catch elements, we can add a catchAll—similar to "when others" in PL/SQL and "catch(Throwable exception)" in Java. When no fault-specific Catch is around to take care of the current fault, this all-purpose safety net steps in to handle it. We can find out the name of the fault that our catchAll is dealing with using the Oracle BPEL-specific XPath function bpelx:getFaultAsString(), which we can use, for example, to assign the name of the fault to a local variable.

Add Fault Handler to Scope SchemaValidation

Click on the Add Catch icon in the *SchemaValidation* scope's icon bar as shown in Figure 8-7. The Catch editor appears. Enter *handleValidationFault* as the documentation only name of this Catch. Select the predefined *invalidVariables* fault for the Fault Name. Type *validationFault* as the user defined name for the Fault Variable; that is the variable into which the BPEL engine will store the fault when it occurs. From that variable will we be able to read some details about the fault inside the Catch.

Click on OK to close the Catch editor. Next, create the variable called *validationFault* at scope level. This variable is of type Message Type. It is to be based on the message *RunTimeFault* in the RunTimeFault.wsdl document that is available in the type browser.

It is our objective to be able to return a response message that contains the processing results from this and other validation stages in the BPEL process. To that end, we have to create a global variable to which each validating scope can add its findings.

Create a global variable—at process level—called *processingResults*. This message should be based on type *processingResultsType* in FlightScheduleService.xsd. The scopes can insert *ProcessingResult* elements into this variable if they have found violations of some sort. Add an Assign activity – immediately after the receiveInput activity - to initialize the variable with a literal XML snippet. The value to assign to processingResults is

```
<processingResults xmlns:def="saibot.airport/services/flightschedule"
xmlns:xsi="http://www.w3.org/2001/XMLSchema-instance" xsi:type="def:processing
ResultsType"></processingResults>
```

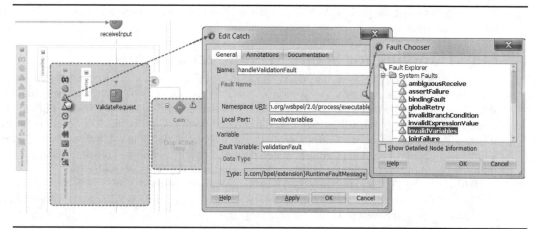

FIGURE 8-7. *Add Catch (fault handler) to scope SchemaValidation, handling fault invalidVariables*

Return to the Catch in scope *SchemaValidation*. Add an Assign activity. This activity has to create a *ProcessingResult* element inside the global variable *processingResults*.

First, drag the Literal icon to the *processingResults* variable. In the editor, specify the literal value as:

```
<fse:ProcessingResult xmlns:fse="saibot.airport/services/flightschedule">
    <fse:ResultCode>SBT-011</fse:ResultCode>
</fse:ProcessingResult>
```

Next, wire the *summary* element in the *validationFault* variable to the *Description* element under the *ProcessingResult* node. Right click on the copy rule that is created and check the option *insertMissingToElement*. This ensures that the *Description* element gets created in the target variable.

Finally, wire the *in* node under *inputVariable* to the *ContextTrace* element in the *processingResults* variable. Check option *insertMissingToElement* for this copy rule too.

The Assign activity should now look as is shown in Figure 8-8.

Close the editor.

You can now deploy the SOA composite and invoke the *FlightScheduleService*. The response message will not yet contain any indication of validation errors though. Only in the BPEL audit trace in the Enterprise Manager FMW Control will you be able to verify that the fault handler was triggered and variable *processingResults* was set. In the next section, we will ensure that the response message is set appropriately.

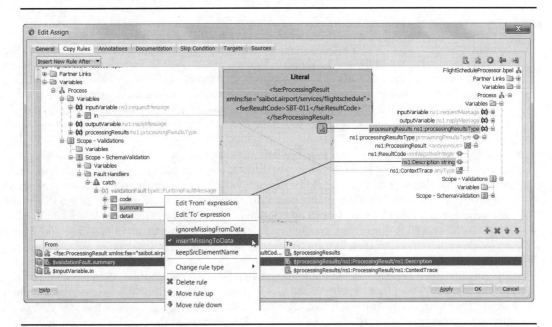

FIGURE 8-8. *Assign activity that populates variable processingResults based on the validation findings*

Return Processing Results upon Validation Failure or Continue

As the last step in the top level scope *Validations*, we will determine if all validations were passed successfully and we can therefore move on to the second top-level scope *ProcessingAndRouting*, or if one or more validation issues were encountered and the process should therefore terminate and return the processing results to the service consumer.

Implement Scope ContinueOrReturn

Open scope *ContinueOrReturn*. Add an If activity to the scope. We will configure this activity with a condition to check if variable *processingResults* contains any *ProcessingResult* entries. If it does, clearly one of the validating scopes has reported an issue and we cannot proceed with processing the flight schedule request.

Set the name of the If activity to *IfValidationErrors*. Set the condition to

```
count($processingResults/ns1:ProcessingResult) > 0
```

This condition will evaluate to true when at least one *ProcessingResult* has been added to global variable *processingResults*.

The process will enter the If branch if a validation error was reported. In that case, the outputVariable on which the response message is based should be updated, the response should be sent, and the process should be terminated.

Add an Assign activity to the If branch. Double click this activity to edit it. Set the name to UpdateOutputVariable.

Map a literal value to the out part in outputVariable. Set the literal value to

```
<fse:ProcessingResults xmlns:fse="saibot.airport/services/flightschedule"/>
```

The copy rule should be of type append, meaning that this literal should be appended to the contents of the out part of the *outputVariable*.

Add a second copy rule—also of type append—that maps the *ProcessingResult* element in variable *processingResults* to the *ProcessingResults* element in the *outputVariable*.

Add a reply activity to the If branch, right after the assign activity. Link this activity to the [FlightScheduleProcessor] partner link. Select the *outputVariable* as the one to provide the data for the response message.

This activity will send the response, but that does not prevent the BPEL process from continuing. If we would not forcibly interrupt the process, it would continue onwards and send another reply. That second reply would be the only one that consumers receive as it supersedes the first one. That is not what should happen. Add a Terminate activity underneath the Reply. This will ensure that the BPEL process stops and nothing is done after the reply has been sent.

The *else* branch is simple and straightforward: nothing has to happen in that case and we can move on to the second top level scope. However, the *else* branch must contain at least one activity, so add an Empty activity.

An alternative implementation could be: move all subsequent processing to the *else* branch. In that case, both the Empty activity in the *else* branch and the Terminate activity in the If branch would not be necessary. The result would be somewhat different: instances of the SOA composite that ran into validation errors would be marked as *aborted* when the Terminate executes or as *completed* in the alternative implementation.

The scope *ContinueOrReturn* should now look as in Figure 8-9.

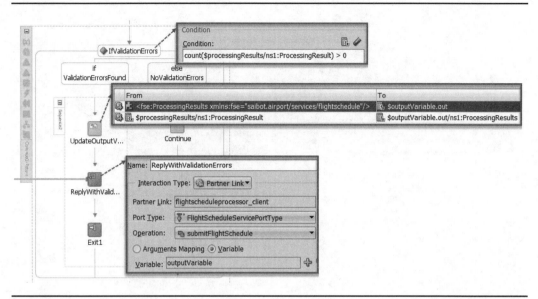

FIGURE 8-9. *The If activity that determines whether validation errors were reported and acts accordingly*

Test the FlightScheduleService with Validation and Premature Termination Inside
Deploy the *FlightScheduleService* composite. Then invoke the service from either the HTTP Analyzer, the EM FMW Control test page, or any other tool. Send a request message that does not satisfy the XSD definition.

This time this call should result in a response message that contains the *ProcessingResults* element with contents that explains what the problem was with the request message. The flow trace in the EM FMW Control as well as the BPEL audit trail (Figure 8-10) should make clear which path was taken. The SOA composite instance is listed in the console as *aborted* because of the terminate that ended the instance.

Implement Custom Validations Using XQuery
The BPEL process *FlightScheduleProcesor* now has a mechanism for performing validations in a scope, handling validation errors at that scope level, and adding them to the global *processingResults* variable. The *ContinueAndReturn* scope inspects that variable and determines whether to continue or to report back the processing results and subsequently abort the process instance.

We next will implement the *CustomValidation* scope, to do the more advanced validations of the request message and report any violations in the same way. We can make good use of the XQuery functions that we used in Chapter 7 in an Assign activity in the Service Bus pipeline. This time, we will create a BPEL Assign activity that sets the value of a local scope variable using the contents of the request message and these XQuery files. The outcome is used to update the global variable *processingResults* in case of errors.

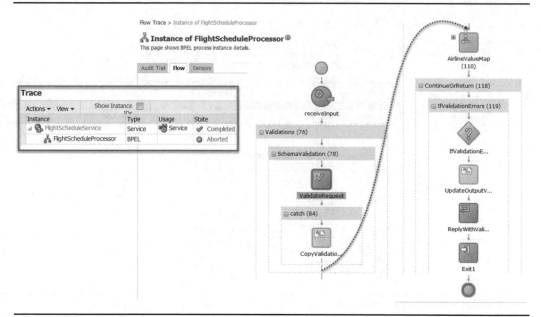

FIGURE 8-10. *The Audit Trail of a BPEL process instance that ran into Schema Validation issues—through Fault Handling at the SchemaValidation scope, through two more Validation scopes to the If-branch in the ContinueOrReturn scope, terminating the process instance*

Add Assign Activity to Perform Custom Validation Using XQuery Function

The XQuery documents ValidateSubmitScheduledFlightRequest.xqy and TimePlanningUnitValidations .xqy were introduced in Chapter 7. These files are in the Validations folder of the current *FlightScheduleService* project. They perform several custom validations on the requested flight schedule that go beyond the XSD validation. The XQuery-based validation is invoked with the submitScheduledFlightRequest and it produces a *Validation* element as defined in Validation.xsd. Check for more details in Chapter 7.

Create a scope level variable in scope *CustomValidation* that is called *validationResults*. The variable is based on the same Validation type that is returned by the XQuery function.

Next, add an Assign activity to scope *CustomValidation*. Call the activity *ValidateScheduledFlightWithXQuery*. Open the editor and drag an expression to variable *validationResults*. Set the expression to

```
ora:processXQuery10('../Validations/ValidateSubmitScheduledFlightRequest.xqy',
'submitScheduledFlightRequest',$inputVariable.in)
```

This expression stipulates that the main function in XQuery document ValidateSubmitScheduledFlightRequest.xqy is invoked and that the contents of part *in* for *inputVariable* is passed as the value for the input parameter *submitFlightScheduleRequest* of the XQuery function. The result from this call—an instance of Validation—is stored in variable *validationResults*.

This means that additional validation errors have to be reported in variable *processingResults* when after the Assign activity executes, variable *validationResults* contains one or more ValidationError elements.

TIP
In addition to using an Assign activity with the processXQuery function, we can also make use of the XQuery Transform activity which you will find in the component palette in the section Oracle Extensions | Transform, along with the activity XSLT Transform. When the number or complexity of the assign rules increases or the same set of assign rules is used multiple times, it may be interesting to resort to a transformation.

Add If Activity to Handle Any Validation Errors

Add an If activity labeled *IfCustomValidationError* with its condition set to

```
count($validationResults/ns3:ValidationErrorList/ns3:ValidationError) > 0
```

which is a test for the existence of any *ValidationError* elements.

Add an *Empty* activity to the *else* branch—since in that case (no *ValidationError* elements and therefore nothing to report) the process can simply proceed.

In the If branch, we have to loop over all *ValidationError* elements and add a *ProcessingResult* element for each one of them. BPEL provides us with three iterating activities—For Each, While, and Repeat Until. The first one will do nicely in our case, so add a For Each activity to the If branch. Double click the For Each to bring up the editor, as is shown in Figure 8-11. Set the name to *ProcessAllValidationErrors*. Set the Counter Name to *counter*. This is the local index variable that inside the For Each keeps the iteration count.

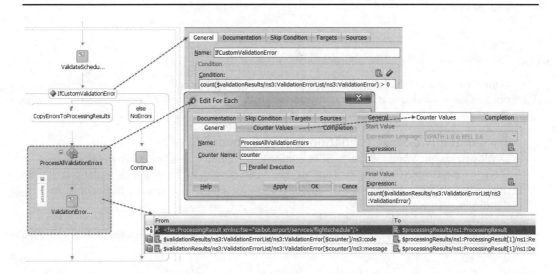

FIGURE 8-11.   *Configuration of the For Each activity*

Notice the check box labeled *Parallel Execution*. This little checkbox represents a serious piece of functionality, similar to what we saw in the dynamic split-join case of the previous chapter. When the activities performed in each iteration involve for example calls to external resources or other actions that make sense to carry out in parallel, this checkbox is how to unleash that power.

Now open the Counter Values tab. Because of the condition on the If activity, we know there is at least one *ValidationError*. That means we can configure our iteration to start at 1 and continue for as many times as there are *ValidationError* elements. In other words, set the Expression for *Start Value* to 1 and for *Final Value* to

```
count($validationResults/ns3:ValidationErrorList/ns3:ValidationError)
```

Finally, add an Assign activity to the scope inside the For Each activity. Create a first copy rule of type *InsertBefore*, mapping a literal value to $processingResults/ns1:ProcessingResult. The literal value creates a new *ProcessingResult* element as the first one under the root:

```
<fse:ProcessingResult  xmlns:fse="saibot.airport/services/flightschedule"/>
```

Next add rules to insert values for *ResultCode* and *Description* to this node. Both rules have their *insertMissingToData* option set. The first copy rule copies

```
$validationResults/ns3:ValidationErrorList/ns3:ValidationError[$counter]/
ns3:code
```

to

```
$processingResults/ns1:ProcessingResult[1]/ns1:ResultCode
```

And the second one in a similar vein

```
$validationResults/ns3:ValidationErrorList/ns3:ValidationError[$counter]/
ns3:message
```

to

```
$processingResults/ns1:ProcessingResult[1]/ns1:Description
```

Figure 8-11 shows what scope *CustomValidation* should look like, after adding the *Assign* that does XQuery validation, the *If* that checks for any validation errors and the *For Each* that adds a *ProcessingResult* for every validation error reported by the XQuery-based validation.

Try Out the Two-Stage Validation in FlightScheduleService

Deploy the *FlightScheduleService* SOA composite. Then invoke *submitSchedule* operation in the service, for example from the HTTP Analyzer. Make sure to include several violations of the rules—both in terms of XSD and additional rules—to see the effect of the two scopes each performing their own validation.

This could look like Figure 8-12.

Checking in the EM FMW Control's BPEL audit trail clearly visualizes the flow that was taken through the BPEL process instance.

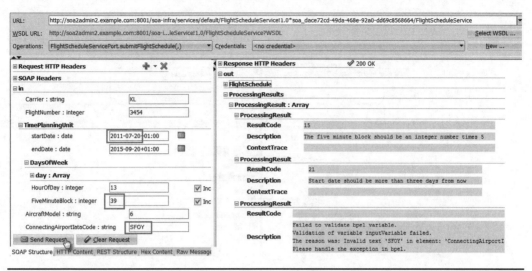

FIGURE 8-12. *Testing the FlightScheduleService with incorrect data produces the expected processing results*

Airline Checks and Mapping with Domain Value Map

The following will sound familiar from Chapter 7. The airline for which the scheduled flight is requested, is specified through the *carrier* element. This element is defined in the XSD document as a string. It is not further restricted in the schema. However, the values recognized for airlines by the business service are only the two letter IATA airline designators. This means therefore that we have to check:

■ If the length of the airline value > 3 or < 2; if so, it is incorrect.

■ If the length of the airline value == 3 then it is probably an ICAO code and it should be mapped to an IATA code.

■ If the length is two, it is probably an IATA code; we should ensure it is a valid IATA code.

To implement this validation, we need a new stage, a little if-then-else logic and this thing called a DVM or Domain Value Map. In Chapter 7, the DVM was first introduced and specifically the DVM to map from ICAO to IATA codes was introduced. This DVM will be reused in the BPEL process.

Map ICAO Code to IATA Code Using a Domain Value Map

Open scope *AirlineValueMap*. Create a scope level variable of type string called *iataCode*. This will be our target for the mapping of the ICAO airline code.

Add an If activity with a condition to check for an incorrect length of the incoming carrier element. In the *else* branch, add another If activity that checks if the length of the carrier element happens to be 3. In that case, it may well be an ICAO code and we will try to map the value to the corresponding IATA airline code. Add an Assign activity—called *MapAirlineCode*—to the If branch of this second If activity, as is shown in Figure 8-13.

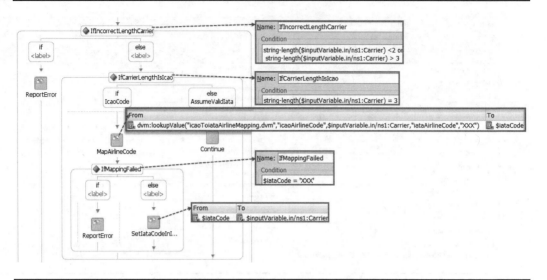

FIGURE 8-13. *Scope AirlineValueMap with If (incorrect length) and nested If (length equals three) activities*

Configure a single copy rule mapped to variable $iataCode that uses the following expression `dvm:lookupValue('icaoToiataAirlineMapping.dvm', 'icaoAirlineCode', $inputVariable.in/ns1:Carrier, 'iataAirlineCode', 'XXX')` This instructs the BPEL engine to read the DVM file, locate in domain *icaoAirlineCode* the value contained in the Carrier element in the request message and return the corresponding *iataAirlineCode*. When the value from the request message cannot be found in the DVM document, the value XXX is returned to indicate that apparently the input was not a valid *icaoAirlineCode*. Add an If activity after *MapAirlineCode* that tests for the string 'XXX' in variable $iataCode. In the if-branch, we face the situation that the three character carrier value could not be (domain value) mapped to a valid IATA code.

We now need to report a *ProcessingResult*—shown in Figure 8-13 through the *ReportError* activities—in case the carrier length was neither 2 nor 3 and in case the carrier element with length 3 could not be mapped to an IATA code. If the length was 2, we ideally should test for the existence of the value as a valid IATA code, but we will save that for another time.

Instead of adding assign activities in many different places in the BPEL process to update variable $processingResults and perhaps perform additional error reporting activities such as logging, we will introduce in the next section an inline subprocess to capture that logic in a reusable unit that can be called from different places in the BPEL process.

Reusable Logic through Inline Subprocess

An inline subprocess can best be thought of as a callable scope. It is a scope that is not part of the normal process flow, but rather a unit of encapsulated logic that can be called zero, one or multiple times from anywhere within the BPEL process—even recursively from within itself. It is in effect very similar to a private member function in a Java class or a procedure in the body of a PL/SQL package.

An inline subprocess can define arguments to be passed in. These can be passed by reference, which means the subprocess can alter their values as well. Additionally, the inline subprocess can access all global process variables. The inline subprocess is a scope which as such can define local variables and nested scopes, use partner links, and have event handlers etcetera.

An inline subprocess is created from a normal scope that is promoted using the context menu option *Convert to subprocess*. At that time, at the location in the BPEL process where the scope used to be, a call to the subprocess can be inserted. Later on, such calls can be added in other places as well. Of course the subprocess can be further refined after its initial creation.

TIP
In addition to the Inline Subprocess, the BPEL component also supports stand-alone Subprocesses. These are defined in a separate file (with extension .sbpel) and appear as components in their own right in the composite overview. They can be called from multiple other BPEL components (but only from BPEL components). They cannot access global elements of these calling BPEL processes, unlike the Inline Subprocess. However, for every other intent and purpose, they act as if merged into the calling process.

An important advantage of the stand-alone subprocess, apart from its ability to be reused across multiple BPEL process components, is the fact that because the subprocess has its own definition file, developers can work in parallel on subprocesses.

Start this section from the *step2* sources.

Create Inline Subprocess to Report a Validation Error

An inline subprocess can easily be created from a scope. Create a scope called *ReportError* in the If branch of the *IfIncorrectLengthCarrier* activity. Copy the Assign activity *CopyValidationFaultToProcessingResults* from the Fault handler on scope *SchemaValidation* to this new scope *ReportError*.

Select the scope and click on the icon *Convert to a Subprocess*—or select that option from the context menu, as shown in Figure 8-14.

The dialog box appears to create the Inline Subprocess. Provide a name—such as *ReportMessageToProcessingResults*—and a label and comment (for documentation purposes). Press OK to create the inline subprocess.

The scope *ReportError* has been replaced with a Call Activity that invokes the new subprocess. In order to inspect and further edit the subprocess, you have to select it from the drop-down list in the upper left-hand corner, as shown in Figure 8-15.

Click on the global scope for the subprocess. Next, click on the *variables* icon that displays as an x between parentheses: (x). Specify three variables for the subprocess—for message code, message summary and description, each of type string.

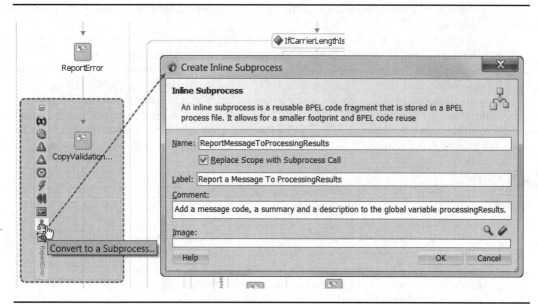

FIGURE 8-14. *Convert a Scope to an inline Subprocess and a call to the Subprocess*

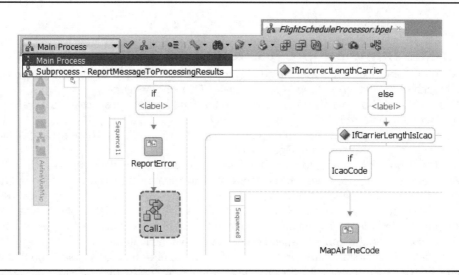

FIGURE 8-15. *Toggling the BPEL editor to one of the inline subprocesses*

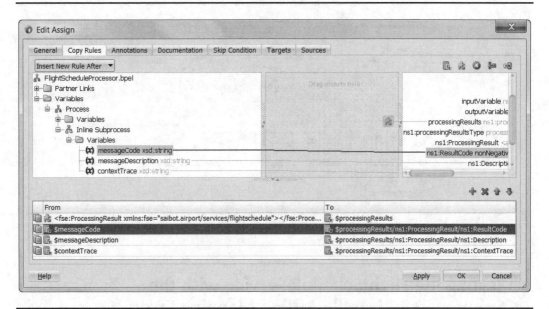

FIGURE 8-16. *Create the ProcessResult element using the values from the input variables to the subprocess*

Edit the Assign activity. Take the values from the three (input) variables of the subprocess to provide the values for the new *ProcessResult* element, as illustrated by Figure 8-16.

Set the flag *insertMissingToData* on each of the three copy rules, to have all elements in the nested XML structure specified in the target XPath expression constructed if they do not exist, instead of throwing a *selectionFailure* fault if the XPath expression does not return exactly one element. Note that the first copy rule should be of type insertBefore rule in order to prevent overwriting previous errors.

Call the Inline Subprocess from Scope AirlineValueMap

Return to the main process and to the call activity that replaced the scope. Edit the call activity. Specify the values for the three input variables, as "FSS-32," concat('Incorrect length for Airline Carrier: ', $inputVariable.in/ns1:Carrier) and string($inputVariable.in) respectively. See Figure 8-17 for an example. Copy these values by value—because it is not our intention to have the subprocess manipulate these values.

Next, copy the call activity and paste it in the *IfMappingFailed* branch of scope *AirlineVaueMap*, also shown in Figure 8-17. Here it will call the subprocess to report an incorrect length for the carrier element. Update the values passed to the subprocess accordingly.

You may also want to use the call activity in the fault handler in scope *SchemaValidation* and in the *For Each* activity *ProcessAllValidationErrors* in scope *CustomValidation*.

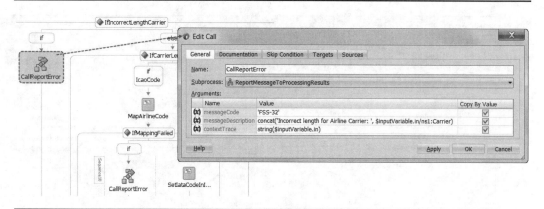

FIGURE 8-17. *Configuration of the Call activity that calls the inline subprocess*

Testing the FlightScheduleService with the Subprocess to Handle Airline Mapping Errors

Deploy the *FlightScheduleService* composite. Invoke the service with a perfectly valid flight schedule request message, with a three letter airline carrier that exists in the DVM. Note how the response does not mention any processing results. When you check the BPEL process audit trail or flow overview, you will find how the DVM produced the two letter IATA code for the carrier.

Now provide either a carrier value of less than two or more than three characters length or with a three character value that does not exist as a source value in the DVM. In the response you will find at least one *ProcessResult* this time. In the EM FMW Control console, you will see how the inline subprocess is invoked to write the processing result element, see Figure 8-18.

Common next steps are both the addition of new functionality to or the refinement of existing functionality in the subprocess as well as the creation of more calls to the subprocess in various spots in the main process.

Using Embedded Java for Validation and Enrichment

The second top level scope in the *FlightScheduleProcessor*—the *ProcessingAndRouting* scope—can rely on the data it receives as being valid. Not just in terms of the XSD definition but also the custom validations on start date, end date, and five minute time block as well as the IATA designator for the air carrier. It is now up to this scope to perform several enrichment steps that are to precede the final registration of the flight schedule:

- The number of flights has to be established that are to take place in the requested flight schedule.

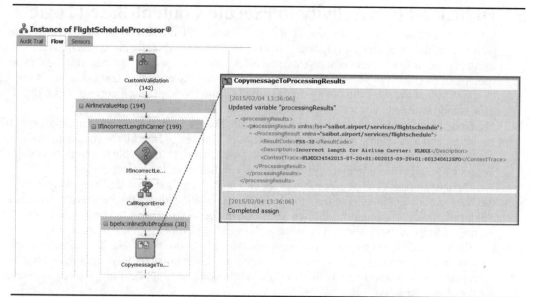

FIGURE 8-18. *The call to the inline subprocess is presented inline in the BPEL audit trail and flow overview*

- The identifier of the allocated slot with which the flight schedule is to be associated must be retrieved.
- The Financial Department has to approve of the requested flight schedule—based on the credit status, solvency, and safety status of the airline.

BPEL processes can perform various types of call outs. Through Partner Links, the process can invoke both other components within the SOA composite as well as adapter bindings and references to external services. Similar to Java Call Outs in Service Bus, BPEL process can also use the Embedded Java activity.

In this and the next two sections we will look at three types of interactions:

- Embedded Java activity calling to a custom Java class to calculate the number of flights.
- Partner Link that connects to a reference to an external service to find the slot with which to associate the scheduled flight.
- Partner Link that connects to another service component in the SOA composite to check if the airline is not blacklisted with the finance department.

Start this section from the *step3* sources. First add three nested scopes to scope *ProcessingAndRouting* for these three tasks: *DeriveNumberOfFlights*, *RetrieveSlotIdentifier,* and *CheckAirlineWithFinancialDepartment*. For now, these scopes are sequential. A little bit later on we will see how easy it is in a BPEL process to organize these scopes into parallel activities. Also add variables numberOfFlights (int) and slotIdentifier (string) to scope *ProcessingAndRouting*.

Embedded Java Activity to Execute Content-Based Logic

We can embed Java snippets in special activities inside BPEL process components—at a more granular, tighter integrated, less formal (no service interface), typically more specialized level than using partner links to other components or even external services. We do this with the Oracle-specific BPEL extension activity Exec. This activity contains a snippet of Java code that is executed by the JVM that executes the BPEL process—in the same JTA transaction context as the BPEL process and without any context switches.

Embedding Java like this is primarily useful for advanced validation and manipulation of BPEL variables, and for auditing and debugging purposes. One usage is to fill the metadata attributes in the instance table in the dehydration store with functional data to be able to correlate composite instance IDs with meaningful instance data. This can be handy for error recovery.

The Java snippet can use a number of special built-in methods that facilitate integration with the BPEL process instance. These methods, for example, allow direct read and write access to BPEL variables. Java exceptions thrown and not handled in the Embedded Java activity are converted to BPEL faults and can be dealt with in the BPEL process in the normal way.

The Embedded Java snippet can do JNDI lookup operations that make it possible to invoke EJBs from within the Exec activity. Note that although this is possible, it is certainly not the recommended way to interact with EJBs from within composite applications, except sometimes for the SOA Suite's own API.

It sounds too good to be true: the power of Java in the best-performing, transaction-preserving way. Wow! Well, although it seems pretty good, it is very tightly coupled. Before you get too excited about the ability to use Java inside BPEL, remember why we do not use Java for all the functionality of our composite applications. We strive for decoupled, reusable components that bring us business agility. Embedding small or even large chunks of Java code inside BPEL processes threatens this ambition: The code is not reusable at all, and it is difficult to develop, test, and subject to version control, as it is pretty much hidden inside the BPEL process. However, for relatively localized and fairly small operations, it can be quite powerful.

TIP

The SCA Spring component can be used to embed Java-based logic in an SOA composite application in a more explicit way that is to be preferred as it is more aligned with the SCA specification. More on this component is in Chapter 10.

In our current case, we want the embedded Java code to take the start date and the end date for the requested flight schedule and—taking the weekdays into account—calculate the actual number of flights this request represents and write that number to a BPEL process variable.

Create Java Code That Does the Job

Our first step will be to create a stand-alone Java application—well, Java class—that has the logic we need to embed later on. We have no easy way to test the Embedded Java—only by deploying the composite and testing it, can we test the Java logic in a very indirect way. It is a best practice to have as little Java code inside the Exec tag—only the direct interaction with the BPEL process and a call to a custom class that does the actual work. Note that this custom class has to be explicitly imported in the BPEL process. The same applies to other classes used in the Java code in the Exec activity.

Create Java class *FlightScheduleProcessor*—in package saibot.airport.flightscheduleservice—with a static public method *calculateNumberOfFlights,* as shown below. The method takes the string representation of a start date and end date as well as the *numberOfDaysPerWeek* on which flights will be executed and it returns the number of (days with) flights in that period.

```java
public class FlightScheduleProcessor {
  public static int calculateNumberOfFlights(String startDateString, String
endDateString, int numberOfDaysPerWeek) {
DateFormat formatter = new SimpleDateFormat("yyyy-MM-dd");
int numberOfFlights = 0;
if (endDateString == null||endDateString.length()==0) {
   numberOfFlights = 1;
} else {
   if (endDateString.equals(startDateString)) {
      numberOfFlights = 1;
   } else {
      try {
         Date startDate = formatter.parse(startDateString);
         Date endDate = formatter.parse(endDateString);
         long dayDiff = getDateDiff(startDate, endDate, TimeUnit.DAYS);
         numberOfFlights = (int)(dayDiff* numberOfDaysPerWeek/7);
      } catch (ParseException e) {
      }
   }
}
return numberOfFlights;
}

   public static long getDateDiff(Date date1, Date date2, TimeUnit timeUnit) {
long diffInMillies = date2.getTime() - date1.getTime();
return timeUnit.convert(diffInMillies,TimeUnit.MILLISECONDS);
   }
}
```

When you add a main method to this class or create a test class, you can test the *calculateNumberOfFlights* outside the context of the BPEL process or the SOA Suite. There is nothing yet in this class that indicates that soon it will be integrated into a BPEL component.

Embed the Java Logic in the BPEL Process

We have the Java code working on its own; we can now leverage it from an Exec activity in the BPEL process and integrate it with the BPEL variables in that process.

Open the BPEL process *FlightScheduleProcessor* and add two import elements as direct children of the process root element. These elements make the Java classes XMLElement and *FlightScheduleProcessor* available for use in embedded Java activities:

```xml
<import location="oracle.xml.parser.v2.XMLElement" importType="http://schemas.
oracle.com/bpel/extension/java"/>
<import location="saibot.airport.flightscheduleservice.
FlightScheduleProcessor" importType="http://schemas.oracle.com/bpel/extension/
java"/>
```

Add an Embedded Java activity to the BPEL process and set its name to *CalculateNumberOfFlights*. Next, set the Code Snippet of this activity to the following snippet:

```
XMLElement flightNumberElement = (XMLElement) getVariableData("inputVariab
le", "in", "/ns1:submitScheduledFlightRequestMessage/ns1:FlightNumber");
  String flightNumber = flightNumberElement.getTextContent();
  XMLElement startDate = (XMLElement) getVariableData("inputVariable",
"in", "/ns1:submitScheduledFlightRequestMessage/ns1:TimePlanningUnit/
ns2:startDate");
  XMLElement endDate = (XMLElement) getVariableData("inputVariable", "in", "/
ns1:submitScheduledFlightRequestMessage/ns1:TimePlanningUnit/ns2:endDate");
  XMLElement daysOfWeek = (XMLElement) getVariableData("inputVariable",
"in", "/ns1:submitScheduledFlightRequestMessage/ns1:TimePlanningUnit/
ns2:DaysOfWeek");
  int numberOfDaysPerWeek = daysOfWeek.getElementsByTagName("day").
getLength();
  int flightCount = FlightScheduleProcessor.calculateNumberOfFlights(startDa
te.getTextContent(), endDate.getTextContent(),numberOfDaysPerWeek);
  addAuditTrailEntry("Java Embedding - Calculated number of flights for
flightnumber "+ flightNumber +" as "+ flightCount);
  setVariableData("numberOfFlights", flightCount);
```

In the first line, the built-in method *getVariable* is used to retrieve a specific element from one of the variables in the BPEL process. More specifically: an XPath expression is used to access the *FlightNumber* element *in* for the *in* message part of the *inputVariable*. The result is an XMLElement—that is stored in a local Java variable defined in the snippet. The next line retrieves the actual value from that element.

The same *getVariableData* is used to retrieve the values for *startDate*, *endDate,* and *daysOfWeek*. The latter holds zero, one or more children and *numberOfDaysPerWeek* is set with that number of child elements.

Finally, the call is made to the public static method *calculateNumberOfFlights* on class *FlightScheduleProcessor*. Inside this class, as we have seen, the context of the BPEL process is no longer available.

Method *addAuditTrailEntry* is another built-in operation that can be used in embedded Java snippets, to add entries to the audit trail that can be inspected in the EM FMW Control (as well as through the APIs). Finally, through *setVariableData*, the actual number of flights is pushed back to the BPEL process context and set on scope variable *numberOfFlights*.

Run the Composite with Embedded Java Inside

With the code in place, we can deploy the composite application. The custom Java class is deployed along with the application, and any libraries you would add to the project would also have been deployed along with the composite.

Invoke the *FlightScheduleService*, perhaps with a little variation in the start date and end date values. You will not see an effect of the calculated number of flights in the response message. However, when you inspect the audit trail (Figure 8-19), there will be evidence of the Java activity and the additional audit trail entry.

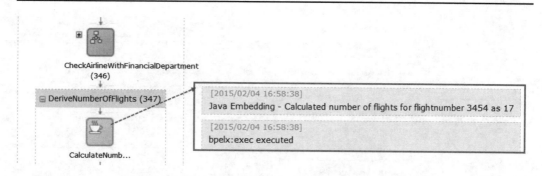

FIGURE 8-19. *Evidence in the flow trace of the execution of the Embedded Java activity*

TIP
BPEL processes can send signals out through so-called BPEL sensors. These signals inform the world of the progress in the process. Sensors can be targeted at a database table, a JMS queue or topic, BAM (Business Activity Monitoring) or a custom Java class. Note that such a custom Java class is called and notified; it cannot respond to the process and it cannot manipulate its data or impact its flow.
  Composite sensors by contrast—first introduced in Chapter 4— are defined at the composite level rather than the level of a BPEL component, and do not support custom Java actions.

External Callouts or Invoking Services from a BPEL Process

Calling out to web services or other components is the most natural thing for a BPEL process. The Invoke activity is used for making such calls. And just like the Receive and Reply are associated with a partner link, so is the Invoke. The partner link represents the service interface that the invoke calls out to—without bothering the invoke activity with details about transport or location.
  Start this section from the *step4* sources.

Invoke the SlotService from the BPEL Process

The *ProcessingAndRouting* scope contains the scope *RetrieveSlotIdentifier*. In this scope, we will add the invoke activity that will indirectly—through the partner link and the reference binding— interact with the same *SlotService* that the Service Bus pipeline in the previous chapter did a Service Callout to.

Create Reference for SlotService

Open the SOA composite overview editor. Right click in the External References zone and select Insert | SOAP or drag the SOAP component to this area, as shown in Figure 8-20. The *Create Web Service* editor appears. Enter the name—*SlotService*—and the WSDL URL (for the *SlotService* exposed on the Service Bus), presumably: http://localhost:7101/flight/SlotService?wsdl. After entering this value—or browsing for it using the icon—the wizard will auto-select the Port Type.

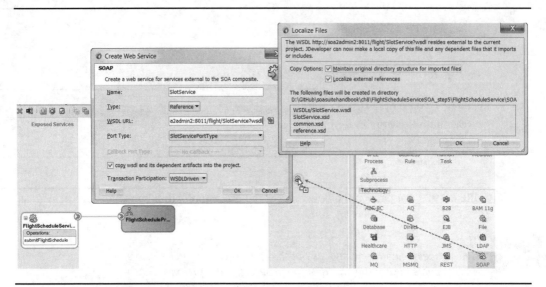

FIGURE 8-20.   *Add a reference binding for the external SlotService*

The little check box marked *copy wsdl and its dependent artifacts into the project* is actually quite important. It determines whether the project will have design time dependencies on the live service and its artifacts or will be stand alone. Both options have their merits: only being able to do development work on the composite when the *SlotService* is deployed and the server is up and running can be quite cumbersome. Then again, locally creating copies of all service artifacts—including some that are truly shared artifacts—and running the risk that these go out of synch with the real service definition is not attractive either. In a later chapter, we will discuss the MDS (Meta Data Services) that provides a solution to many of these challenges.

Let us for now check the checkbox and create a stand-alone reference to the *SlotService*. Press OK to create the reference binding.

The *SlotService* reference is added to the composite, in the External References swim lane. The SlotService.wsdl document is added to the WSDLs folder and it references SlotService.xsd that is created in the root of the project. Also created in the project root are common.xsd and reference .xsd—which are duplicates from files already available in the project. We need to reorganize things a little. Delete common.xsd and reference.xsd in the root folder. Move SlotService.xsd to a new folder called *LocalizedExternalResources*. Edit the import statements in SlotService.xsd to have them reference the common.xsd and reference.xsd files in the Schemas folder.

Finally, to prevent problems with multiple instances of the XSD documents at build time, you also need to edit the composite.xml file. Edit the *reference* element for the *SlotService*: remove the *location* attribute on the binding.ws element and add a property called endpointURI to reference to the endpoint for the *SlotService*:

```
<reference name="SlotService" ui:wsdlLocation="WSDLs/SlotService.wsdl">
...
    <property name="endpointURI" type="xs:string">http://localhost:7101/
flight/SlotService?wsdl</property>
  </binding.ws>
</reference>
```

Next, create a wire from the *FlightScheduleProcessor* BPEL component to the new SlotService reference. This will create a new partner link definition in a newly created file SlotServiceWrapper.wsdl, clearly associated with SlotService.wsdl. Note that this will make the partner link available inside the BPEL process, to for example connect *Invoke* activities to.

Add Invoke Activity in BPEL Process

Open the editor for BPEL component *FlightScheduleProcessor*. Open the scope *RetrieveSlotIdentifier* and add an Invoke activity. Wire this activity to the *SlotService* partner link, as demonstrated in Figure 8-20.

The invoke activity editor appears. Set the name of the activity to *InvokeSlotService*. Select operation *findSlot* on the *SlotServicePortType*. On the Input tab—where the variable or arguments mapping for the call out to the *SlotService* is configured—set the radio button to Input Variable and click on the green plus icon to have a new local variable created that will contain the data to pass to the *SlotService*. Accept the default name for this variable, as shown in Figure 8-21.

TIP
A local variable is defined at the scope level. It can only be accessed inside the scope. As soon as the scope is completed, the local variable is removed from memory. Local variables in BPEL are very similar to private variables in Java methods. It is good practice to define variables as local if they only are used within a certain scope.

Do the same thing on the Output tab: have a local variable created to hold the result returned from the *SlotService*. Click OK to complete the configuration of the invoke activity.

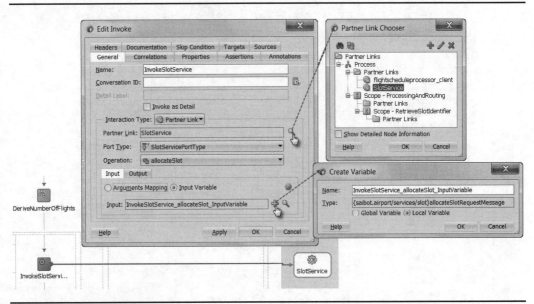

FIGURE 8-21. *Configure the invoke activity including new default local variables for the input to and output from the SlotService*

Next, add two assign activities to the current scope, one to go just prior to the invoke activity and one to immediately follow the invoke activity. This is a common pattern: these assign activities will copy from the process variables to the local input variable and from the local result variable to the process variables. You can use Sequence activities to group these together.

Configure the first assign activity to set the *Carrier, TimeplanningUnit,* and *AircraftModel* elements from the *inputVariable*—that holds the request message that was sent to the *FlightScheduleService*—to the variable created locally to provide the input to the *SlotService.*

Configure the second assign activity to copy the *SlotId* element returned from the *SlotService* and stored in the local output variable to the *slotIdentifier* variable.

With these steps, we have extended the *FlightScheduleProcessor* with the callout to the *SlotService*: first we created the reference binding at SOA composite level and wired the reference to the BPEL component (which created the partner link). Next, we created and configured the invoke activity, wired it to the partner link and configured assignments to and from the local variables.

Test FlightScheduleService with the Call to the SlotService Inside

It is easy to deploy and test the *FlightScheduleService* composite once more. The Flow will show (Figure 8-22) how this time, right after the embedded Java activity is executed, the invoke activity does its thing. The returned SlotId is 4592.

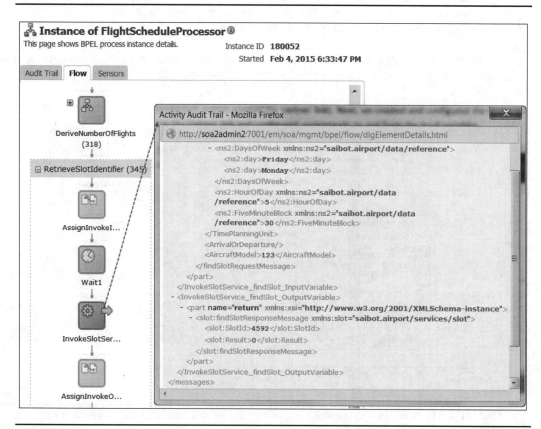

FIGURE 8-22. *BPEL process flow that visualizes the InvokeSlotService activity*

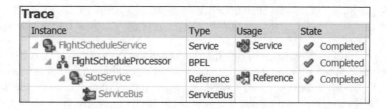

| Trace | | | |
Instance	Type	Usage	State
▲ 🔷 FlightScheduleService	Service	🔳 Service	✔ Completed
▲ 🔷 FlightScheduleProcessor	BPEL		✔ Completed
▲ 🔷 SlotService	Reference	🔳 Reference	✔ Completed
🔷 ServiceBus	ServiceBus		

FIGURE 8-23. *Message flow trace after calling the FlightSchedule service that invokes the SlotService*

All we can see from the flow is that the Invoke does something. From the BPEL process definition we know that the invoke calls a partner link that is based on and wired to the SlotService reference binding in the SOA composite. The SOA composite message flow trace in Figure 8-23 reveals that this reference resolves to a service exposed on the Service Bus. This trace does not reveal the name of the particular proxy service. Detail trace information about what goes on inside the Service Bus can for example be generated using pipeline alerts. This information is not available from this flow trace though.

Dependencies from BPEL Component

In this chapter, we create a BPEL component based directly on the external service interface *FlightScheduleService*—WSDL plus XSD—exposed by the SOA composite. It is certainly convenient—as we can simply wire the exposed service directly to the BPEL component. However, there is a drawback: the BPEL component has a direct dependency on the external WSDL and XSD as a result. The variables and activities in the BPEL components lean on the WSDL and XSD definitions. That means that when there is a change in the external service interface, this change may have a direct impact on BPEL process—and a much larger impact than *should* be the case. Often, BPEL components have a lot of activities that work on payloads (as defined in XSDs) so changes to XSDs can be disruptive to BPEL components.

The same is true in the other direction: we want to have the freedom to change the implementation of the BPEL process without having to worry about disrupting the external service interface. Additionally, it is convenient to have a separate BPEL component for each operation in the external service interface—which of course means that no single BPEL process implements the same WSDL as the SOA composite exposes.

To eliminate this direct dependency, we could determine to use a Mediator between the exposed service and the BPEL component, as is shown in Figure 8-24. The BPEL component would have its own WSDL and XSD that are of course very similar to interface definitions of the exposed service and of the Mediator. The transformation in the Mediator is therefore almost trivial (completely auto-mapped). Yet, when the external interface changes, there is no immediate impact on the BPEL component. Depending on the changes in the service definition, several strategies can be used to revise the SOA composite to provide the implementation. These may or may not include modifying the BPEL component. By decoupling we have ensured at least we have this choice.

Something similar can be said about the outgoing partner links of a BPEL component. These can be wired directly to the external references—such as the *SlotService*—and outbound adapter bindings of the SOA composite. That is easy enough. However, this too causes the BPEL component to be directly dependent on the WSDL and XSD of the external service or adapter binding. That means that even a small change in these definitions may break the BPEL component and have a far larger impact than should be the case.

The BPEL component can be insulated from such direct effects by using a Mediator component between the BPEL component and the outbound dependencies. The Mediator implements the internal interface that the BPEL component is designed for, using SOA composite specific definitions. The Mediator translates to and from whatever external service is enlisted to provide the implementation of the external need of the BPEL component. When we decide to use a different external provider, this does not affect the BPEL component, but only requires an update of the Mediator.

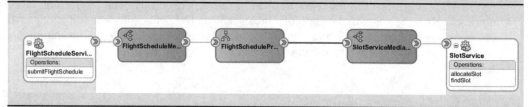

FIGURE 8-24. *The BPEL component decoupled from both the service interface and the external references*

FinancialDepartmentAirlineCheck from the BPEL Process

The *FlightScheduleServiceSOA_step5* application contains a second project, called *FinancialDepartmentProcesses*. This project contains a SOA composite and the single component in the composite application is a BPEL process called *FinancialDepartmentAirlineCheckProcess*. This component implements the service interface *FinancialDepartmentAirlineCheckService*, as specified in the WSDL document with that name. The interface has a single operation: *checkAirlineStatus*.

In this section, we are going to take this BPEL component and turn it into a Component Template that we publish to be reused across different projects. Note that unlike a Service Bus pipeline template, there is no lasting relationship between the template and components derived from the template. Using an SOA component template is more like a complex copy and paste operation than an inheritance definition.

Next, we will create a new BPEL component in the *FlightScheduleService* composite, based on this template. The new component is wired to the existing *FlightScheduleProcessor* component and invoked from the last remaining empty scope *CheckAirlineWithFinancialDepartment*. This in turn completes the *ProcessingAndRoutingScope*.

Start this section from the *step5* sources.

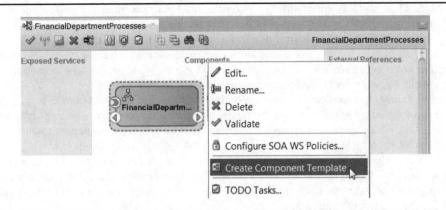

FIGURE 8-25.   *Starting to create a component template from a BPEL process component*

Turn BPEL Component into Component Template

Open composite overview editor for the *FinancialDepartmentProcesses* project. Right click the BPEL process component. From the context menu, select option *Create Component Template*, as shown in Figure 8-25.

The Create Component Template wizard appears, to collect your input about the template (Figure 8-26). You can specify the name, the description, and (optionally) the palette icon. This is

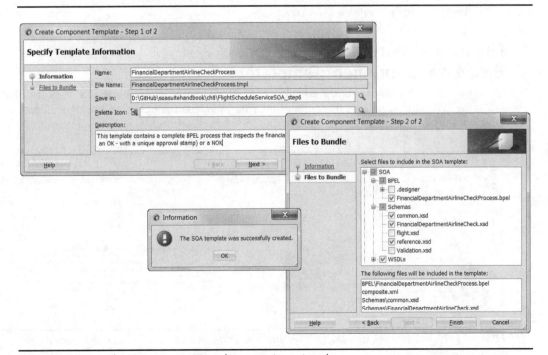

FIGURE 8-26.   *The Component Template creation wizard*

important because this information will be presented in the component palette and has to allow other developers to decide whether or not to reuse this template.

Press Next to go to the second step of the component template creation. In this step, the wizard lists all files in the project and allows you to decide which ones to include in the template. All files you select here will be bundled as part of the template and will be copied to an SOA composite target project when the template gets used in that project.

Press Finish to complete the creation of the template. The template bundle is now created and saved on your local file system (from which it can be uploaded to a central share or into Subversion, Git or some other source code management system). Templates can also be stored in MDS (see Chapter 21).

In JDeveloper, from the main menu Windows | Preferences, you can bring up the SOA | Templates preferences page. On this page, you can specify which locations can contain SOA templates—not just component templates but also SOA composite application templates and BPEL scope (activity) templates.

NOTE
Given the low reuse potential of this FinancialDepartmentAirlineCheckProcess, it is not a logical candidate at all to create a template of. Typically, templates will contain the outline of a process according to the development guidelines in an organization, with predefined scopes and embedded logging and fault handling. They will generally have to be completed with the specific functionality required of the component based on the template.

In this case, the template serves as a container for quickly injecting a number of artifacts into an SOA composite.

Create and Wire the BPEL Process Based on Component Template

Open the SOA composite overview editor for the FlightScheduleService. Open the SOA Templates tab in the Components palette. It should list the *FinancialDepartmentAirlineCheckProcess* template. Drag the template from palette and drop in the Components section, as shown in Figure 8-27.

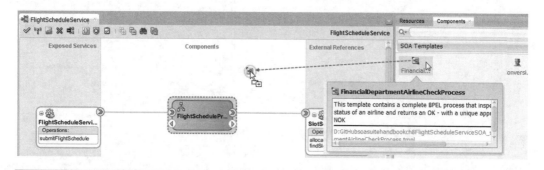

FIGURE 8-27. *Use SOA Component Template to add a predefined BPEL component to the FlightScheduleService*

Another editor manifests itself—one that helps you create an SOA component from a Component Template, see Figure 8-28. Set the name of main component (note that from one template, multiple components can be created) to *FinancialDepartmentAirlineCheckProcess*. Review the list of template entries: these are the artifacts that are about to be added to the project.

Click on Next to review the conflicts: artifacts in the template bundle that already exist in the target project. For each of the conflicts, we need to decide whether to retain or overwrite the current project artifact. In the current case, choose *skip* for each conflict—which means that in each case the existing resource is retained. Click on Finish to complete the creation of the component based on the template.

Create a wire between the *FlightScheduleProcessor* and the new BPEL component *FinancialDepartmentAirlineCheckProcess*.

Invoke the Financial Department Check of the Airline

Open the editor for the BPEL component *FlightScheduleProcessor*. Open the scope *CheckAirlineWithFinancialDepartment*. Remove the *Empty* activity from the scope and add an *Invoke* activity. Wire this activity to the new partner link for the *FinancialDepartmentAirlineCheckProcessor* component, as Figure 8-29 shows.

TIP
It may feel more natural to have the outgoing partner links displayed on the right side of the BPEL diagram. Using the option Display | Move To Opposite Swim Lane, you can manipulate the position where a partner link is shown.

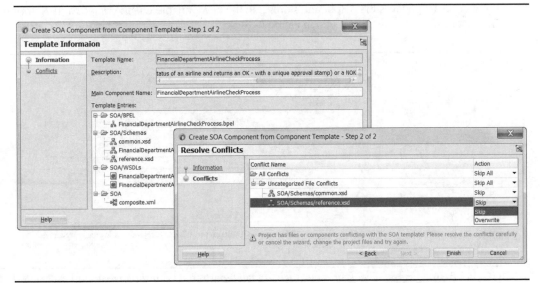

FIGURE 8-28.   *Creating an SOA Component by importing a Component Template*

FIGURE 8-29. *Wire invoke activity to partner link for the FinancialDepartmentAirlineCheckProcessor component*

Configure the invoke activity, including two local variables for the input and output to the second BPEL component.

Next, in scope *ProcessingAndRouting*, create a scope level variable called *checkAirlineFinanceResponse*, based on the *checkAirlineResponseType* in the FinancialDepartmentAirlineCheck.xsd schema definition.

Then, add assign activities to scope *CheckAirlineWithFinancialDepartment*, one before and one after the invoke activity. As before, the first assign has to set the input variable for the invoke activity. The second assign takes the output and stores it in the new variable *checkAirlineFinanceResponse*. The scope now looks as is displayed in Figure 8-30.

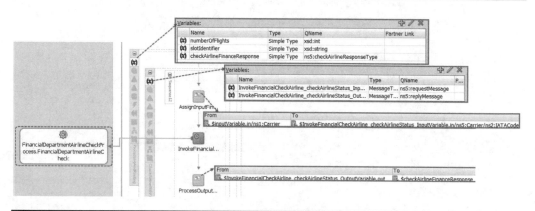

FIGURE 8-30. *Scope CheckAirlineWithFinancialDepartment with the invoke and associated assign activities*

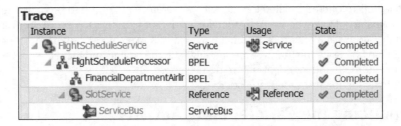

FIGURE 8-31. *Composite message flow through two BPEL process components and one reference binding*

Deploy and Test

Deploy the SOA composite and invoke the *FlightScheduleService* once more. Depending on the request message and specifically the carrier code, the airline check with the financial department returns either an OK or NOK status.

Note that the message flow trace for the entire composite visualizes the additional step that was introduced with the new BPEL component that performs the financial department's airline check, see Figure 8-31.

Reorganizing Scope ProcessingAndRouting with Parallel Activities

At this moment, scope *ProcessingAndRouting* has three sequential scopes. However, just as we concluded in the previous chapter leading to the decision to introduce a Split-Join component, these scopes could also be executed simultaneously. They do not depend on each other; results from one scope do not influence the other scopes. By configuring the scopes to be executed in parallel, we allow the BPEL engine to assign system resources in a more flexible an potentially efficient way. For example, in situations where one scope has to wait long for an asynchronous response, the engine can speed up the overall processing time by running a second scope while the first one is waiting.

The BPEL language comes equipped with the Flow activity. This activity contains one (not useful) or more parallel branches. One fact you have to aware of: one BPEL instance is executed by at most one thread. That means there is never real parallelism, even with this Flow activity: only when the first branch that was started is blocked (waiting for an asynchronous response or just waiting) can the thread be assigned to the second parallel branch. Branches cannot actually execute at the same time, but one branch's wait time can be used to allow another branch to run.

Ideally, each branch writes to a separate variable. When the Flow is complete, the contents from these variables-per-branch could be combined into a single global variable.

The property *nonBlockingInvoke* can be set on a partner link to specify that an invoke of that partner link should not be blocking. This property will cause a new thread to be created for each invocation of the partner link, which will then callback to the main thread once it has completed, resulting in true parallelism: the newly spawned thread is the one waiting for the synchronous response, not the main one that can continue to spawn additional thread to make invokes from. This does mean your process instance may consume many threads which reduces the scalability of the application.

Our current scopes do not make asynchronous calls or have other long-running activities. The semi-parallelism offered by the Flow-activity is therefore not going to be of any serious help in our current situation. However, we will still take a brief look at how to use the Flow activity. We may extend the scopes at a later moment in a way that will make them suitable for more serious parallel behavior. And by using the flow, we are sending both the engine and the fellow developers a message about the mutually independent nature of the scopes.

Start this section from the *step6* sources.

Introducing the Parallel Flow Activity to the ProcessingAndRouting Scope

Open scope *ProcessingAndRouting* in the *FlightScheduleProcessor*. Add a Flow activity to the scope. Initially it contains two parallel sequences. Add a third sequence. Drag each of the three scopes—*DeriveNumberOfFlights, RetrieveSlotIdentifier,* and *CheckAirlineWithFinancialDepartment*—to one of the parallel Flow sequences, see Figure 8-32.

TIP
It is very easy to restructure a BPEL process. Activities can easily be moved around from one scope to another and new activities can be added anywhere in the process.

There is no additional configuration required.

When you next deploy and run the *FlightScheduleService*, you will not notice any difference. The visual flow looks a little bit different from before. By adding Wait activities of, for example,

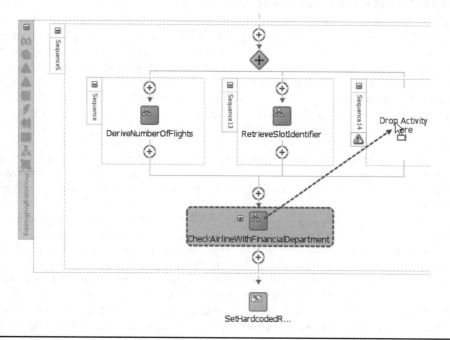

FIGURE 8-32. *Three parallel scopes within the Flow activity*

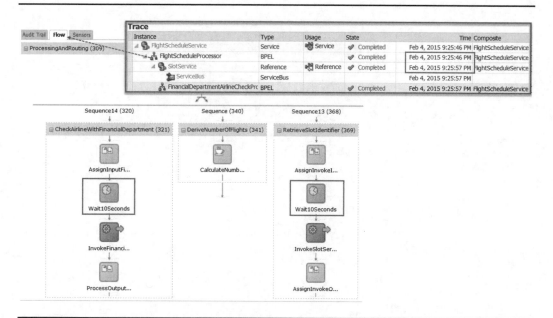

FIGURE 8-33. *BPEL Flow in the EM FMW Control—showing the parallel processing of a Flow activity with two 10-second-long Wait activities*

10s to each of these three scopes, we can see the effect of the parallel flow very clearly—as visualized in Figure 8-33. Instead of the overall processing taking longer than 20 seconds—which would have been the case when no parallel scope processing would take place at all, the response is received in about 11 seconds.

Summary

This chapter introduced the BPEL component in SOA composite applications. With BPEL, we have a language at our disposal that is very good at calling services—synchronous or asynchronously—and processing XML data. BPEL also provides many of the features expected from any programming language—including iterations, fault handling, conditional logic as well as parallel processing. Additional features we have encountered are the embedded Java activity, the callable inline subprocess, and the use of a component template to rapidly create a new BPEL component.

Creating a composite service that receives a request message and performs a number of actions before producing a response, potentially interacting with multiple local components or remote services, is quite straightforward with the BPEL component. Still to come in later chapters are asynchronous interactions, long-running BPEL process instances, event consumption, compensation, interaction with human actors, and correlation.

There are many similarities between BPEL processes and Service Bus pipelines. This chapter implemented the same *FlightScheduleService* with BPEL that we developed in Chapter 7 using Service Bus pipelines. When we start discussing how to implement true, long-running processes using BPEL, the difference between Service Bus and BPEL will become more apparent.

CHAPTER
9

Coherence Integration to Reduce Load and Speed Up Response

The service implementations we have seen until now have no memory: they are stateless. Once they are done, they are done. They don't store intermediate state in memory, in the database, or in any other medium other than for purposes of monitoring (e.g., by recording audit trails). Ask them a question and they will process the request and usually (except for one-way operations) prepare a response. And next time for the same request, they will go through exactly the same motions again. However, there are many situations where the same question is indeed asked from a service quite frequently, in fact, much more frequently than the response is likely to change.

A simple example would be the current dollar to euro conversion ratio (set once per day at Saibot Airport) or the weather forecast (set per hour) or the status of a flight. During the day, for each scheduled flight, the status may be asked for thousands of times. By the application that powers the web portal and from the application that runs all the information terminals and by the many hand held devices used by security staff, cleaning super visors, baggage handlers, and so on. For every request about the flight status, the service will still access the enterprise resources that hold the flight details, even though this puts a load on the back-end system, adds time to the request processing, and usually returns the same value as upon the previous round trip. The status of the flight does not change very often. However, the service is stateless and has no memory.

Enter Coherence. Coherence is part of the Fusion Middleware infrastructure. It provides an in-memory multinode grid that can be accessed through a Java API, RESTful APIs, and the JCA Coherence adapter. Additionally, Coherence is the foundation for the out-of-the-box Result Cache feature on Service Bus business services.

Coherence can be used as the (shared, cross cluster) memory for services. A service can easily store a result on the Coherence grid and reuse that result for more quickly handling a future request, provided the stored result is still deemed valid and fresh enough. Values that do not have to be recalculated or retrieved again from back-end systems can be made available much faster for service consumers and obviously reduce the load on the enterprise resources that would otherwise have had to cough them up.

This chapter shows how Coherence can be integrated into SOA composites through the Coherence adapter. Using the example of the flight status, it shows how a typical pattern emerges: put data in the cache when first queried and either expire the cache after a set time or refresh the cache when the value changes in the underlying system. With Service Bus, we will see that the first approach is available declaratively for any business service using Result Caching.

TIP
This chapter is fairly technical in nature. It does not introduce new functional behavior in the SOA Suite, but merely describes nonfunctional aspects. As such, you could easily skip the chapter for now and return to it later.

Introducing Cross Instance Shared Memory Using Coherence

As a first step, we will create a new SOA composite with a simple BPEL process that creates a single string response for a single string request. Producing the response takes 5 seconds—because of a Wait activity in the BPEL process. Into this SOA composite, we introduce two BPEL subprocesses that together with a Coherence cache act as the shared memory across instances of the composite. Using Coherence, the subprocesses are capable of recording a value associated with a certain key and retrieving a previously registered value.

This cache does not just exist across instances of the same SOA composite, it is also available across different SOA composites, across different applications—including Service Bus and custom Java applications—and across cluster nodes.

Create Slow SOA Composite

Create a new SOA Application with project, both called *QuickAndSlowHello*. Choose the Template Composite with BPEL Process. Set the name of the BPEL process to *QuickAndSlowProcess*. Select *Template Synchronous Service* and accept all defaults.

Add the following type definition in the XSD document QuickAndSlowProcess.xsd.

```
<complexType name="intermediateResultType">
  <sequence>
    <element name="result">
      <complexType>
        <sequence>
          <element name="ValueOne" type="string"/>
          <element name="ValueTwo" type="string"/>
        </sequence>
      </complexType>
    </element>
  </sequence>
</complexType>
```

We will use this definition to define the payload of the calculated result that is to be stored in and retrieved from the cache.

Open the BPEL editor for the *QuickAndSlowProcess*. Add a global variable called *intermediateResult*, based on the `intermediateResultType` that was just added to QuickAndSlowProcess.xsd.

Add a scope *ComputeValue* between the request and reply activities. Add an assign activity to this scope, in which the following XML literal is assigned to variable *intermediateResult*:

```
<intermediateResult xmlns=" http://xmlns.oracle.com/QuickAndSlowHello/
QuickAndSlowHello/QuickAndSlowProcess">
<result xmlns="http://xmlns.oracle.com/QuickAndSlowHello/QuickAndSlowHello/
QuickAndSlowProcess">
  <ValueOne>Bonjour</ValueOne>
  <ValueTwo>Goedendag</ValueTwo>
  </result>
</intermediateResult>
```

Also add a wait activity to the scope, configured to wait for 5 seconds. This activity represents the long time it may take to access back-end systems and process some result. In the next section, we will be able to retrieve the value from the cache instead of having to recreate it—thereby shaving off almost 5 seconds from the over-all processing time. Although in real life this nonsensical wait would of course never be introduced, it is an easy way to demonstrate the effect of introducing a Coherence cache.

Add a second Assign activity, below the scope. In this activity, set the result element in the payload message part of the *outputVariable*.

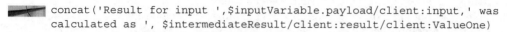

```
concat('Result for input ',$inputVariable.payload/client:input,' was
calculated as ', $intermediateResult/client:result/client:ValueOne)
```

Figure 9-1 shows the extremely simple BPEL process as it currently stands.

Deploy the SOA composite and make a test call from the HTTP Analyzer. After a considerable waiting time of at least 5 seconds, the response should become available.

If you execute the same request again—and again, and again—the response time will not vary substantially: it will be a little over 5 seconds for every call, because on each occasion, the intermediate result has to be recalculated—at a cost of a little more than 5 seconds.

Speed It Up with Cache Support

SOA composites as well as Service Bus applications can make use of Coherence as a caching infrastructure embedded in the SOA Suite. Using the Coherence Adapter, composites can easily interact with this infrastructure. The contents of the cache can be shared across all instances of all SOA composites and Service Bus projects, and across all cluster nodes.

Retrieve from Cache

Add the file Cache.xsd to the *Schemas* directory in the *QuickAndSlowHello* project. This schema defines types for key used for storing objects in the cache and for the cached object itself.

Open the SOA composite editor. Drag the Coherence Adapter from the component palette to the External References swimlane, as shown in Figure 9-2. The Coherence Adapter editor opens.

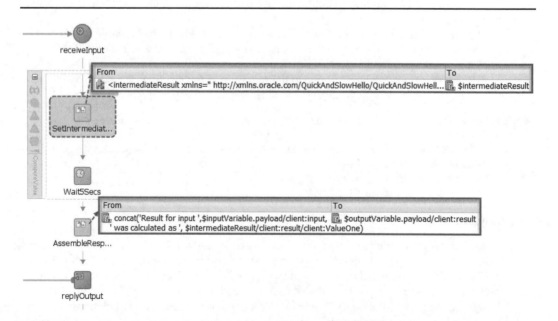

FIGURE 9-1. *The initial BPEL process that primarily waits for 5 seconds*

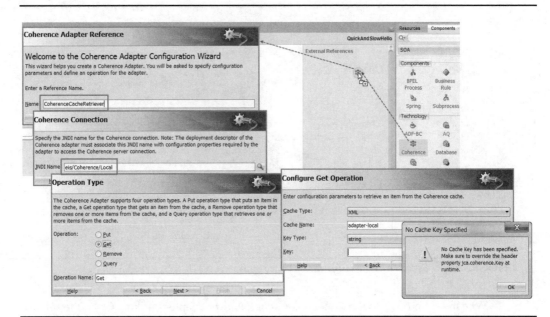

FIGURE 9-2. *Adding the Coherence Adapter binding to read from an external cache*

Set the name of the adapter binding to *CoherenceCacheRetriever*. Set or select the JNDI name of the Coherence connection to eis/Coherence/Local. This name corresponds with one of the connections configured in the Coherence Adapter deployment in the Integrated WebLogic Server. Select *Get* as the operation type and the operation name.

In step 4 of the wizard, set *Cache Type* to XML. Set the *Cache Name* to adapter-local. This cache is preconfigured—ready to use for straightforward situations where no special configuration is required. Set the Key Type to String and leave the Key field empty. Press Next. A popup appears with a message, instructing us on setting the value for the key at run time using the JCA header property jca.coherence.Key. Acknowledge the message and continue.

NOTE
Check in the WebLogic Admin Console whether the Coherence Adapter deployment is active. Initially its status can be New or Prepared. In those case, select the Coherence Adapter application deployment and click on the Deploy button.

In the next page of the wizard—*Specify Schema*—select element *CacheResult* from the Cache.xsd document as the schema element (for objects to retrieve from the cache). Click Next and click Finish. The Coherence Adapter reference is created.

In order to clearly separate the cache interaction from the logic of our main BPEL process and to also make that cache interaction reusable across processes, we create a BPEL subprocess, as visualized in Figure 9-3. Drag a BPEL subprocess component to the central area in the composite editor. Call the subprocess *CacheRetriever*. Set the namespace to saibot.airport/ services/generic/soacomposite. Click OK to have the subprocess created.

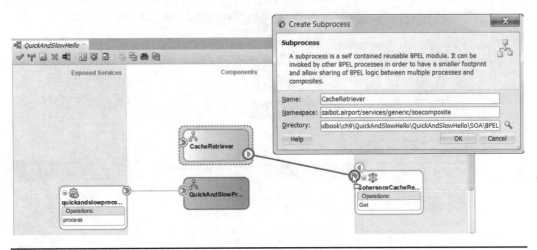

FIGURE 9-3. *Create a BPEL subprocess as a separate unit of (reusable) logic*

Wire the subprocess to the *CoherenceCacheRetriever* adapter binding. Open the subprocess by double clicking the icon.

Create global variables *key* and *cacheResult*, based on the *CacheTagType* and *CachedObjectType* types in the Cache.xsd document. The *key* variable will be the input to the subprocess and the *cachedResult* variable is used as the output.

Add a scope to the BPEL subprocess. Inside the scope, add an Invoke activity, linked to the Partner Link *CoherenceCacheRetriever*. In the Invoke activity editor, specify two local variable to be created for the input and the output. Note that we will not actually use the input variable—because the key value we need to pass to the partner link and indirectly the Coherence Adapter binding is passed using a header property.

Open the *Properties* tab in the Invoke editor. Click on the green plus icon to add a property to pass. Select property jca.coherence.Key from the drop-down list. Specify the following expression to derive the value for the Key property:

```
$key/ns2:tag
```

This means that the Coherence Adapter is asked to retrieve an object that was stored using a key with the string found in the tag element.

Click on OK to complete the definition of the invoke activity.

Under the Invoke, add an Assign activity to copy the output returned by the Coherence Adapter to global variable *cacheResult*. The subprocess now looks like Figure 9-4.

NOTE
A subprocess does not start with a Receive nor does it end with a Reply activity: the subprocess is more or less merged at runtime into the calling BPEL process.

Open the editor for *QuickAndSlowProcess*. Add a scope *ProduceResult*, directly under the Receive activity. Create a scope level variable called *cacheTag*, based on the *cacheTagType* in

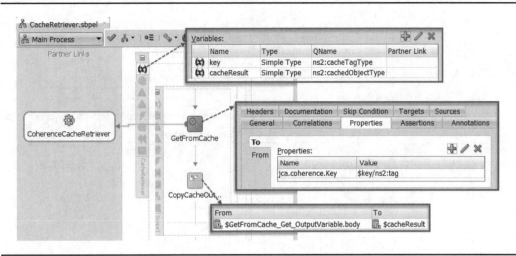

FIGURE 9-4. *Subprocess CacheRetriever that invoked the CoherenceCacheRetriever and copies the result to the result variable*

schema definition Cache.xsd. This variable will hold the key with which an object is retrieved from and if needs be stored into the cache.

Add an Assign activity to set the *cacheTag* variable, based on the input element in the request message. Also add a new scope *FetchFromCache* inside this scope. Later on, we will add a test on whether the result was found in the cache. If not, the result has to be calculated—and stored on the cache.

Open the scope *FetchFromCache*. Create a scope level variable called *localCacheResult* and base it on type *cachedObjectType* in Cache.xsd.

These steps are all visualized in Figure 9-5.

Add a call activity to invoke the subprocess *CacheRetriever*. Map the *key* argument of the subprocess to variable *cacheTag*. Map the *cacheResult* to variable *localCacheResult*, as shown in Figure 9-6. Because this argument represents the output from the subprocess and only input variables can be copied by value, you have to uncheck the checkbox for Copy by Value.

Add an Assign activity under the (call to the) subprocess. Map the payload element in the variable *localCacheResult* to variable *intermediateResult*. Set the type of the copy rule to append. Check the *ignoreMissingFrom* option on the copy rule.

The payload element is an XSD anyType: it can contain any valid XML fragment. In order to derive from this element the actual contents we know to find there, we have to refine the copy rule in the BPEL source editor. In this case, we want to copy the result element from the payload to the *intermediateResult* variable. Refine the *from* expression as shown in the next code snippet:

```
<assign name="CopyCacheOutcomeToIntermediateResult">
  <extensionAssignOperation>
    <bpelx:append ignoreMissingFromData="yes">
            <bpelx:from>$localCacheResult/ns1:payload/client:result</bpelx:from>
      <bpelx:to>$intermediateResult</bpelx:to>
    </bpelx:append>
  </extensionAssignOperation>
</assign>
```

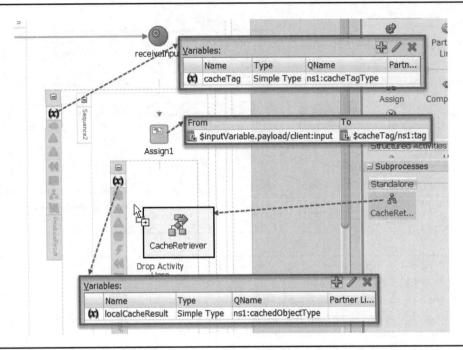

FIGURE 9-5. *Preparing the BPEL process for the call to the CacheRetriever subprocess*

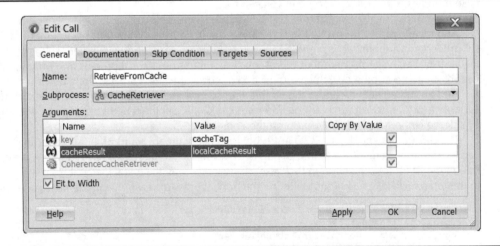

FIGURE 9-6. *Configuring the arguments for the call to the CacheRetriever subprocess*

Extend the Flow Logic

The SOA composite can be deployed and invoked at this point. It will perform just like before, because even though we attempt to retrieve the result from the cache, it is never actually put on the cache. All attempts to retrieve it are in vain, so we have not yet gained anything.

There are two approaches to a solution:

- A process outside the current composite takes care of computing results and storing them in the Coherence cache; the *QuickAndSlowHello* composite may be able to benefit from such values.

- The *QuickAndSlowProcess* will store itself any value it calculates on the Coherence cache, in order to *remember* it in any future instances (for the same input).

To benefit from the cache whenever a result is found on it and to implement the second option, we need to make a few extensions in the *QuickAndSlowProcess*.

Add an If activity under the *FetchFromCache* scope. Set the label of the activity to *IfDataInCache* and set the condition to

```
$intermediateResult/client:result
```

which is a test for the existence of the result element in variable *intermediateResult*.

If the data was found on the cache, it has been loaded into $intermediateResult and we do not need to do anything else in the If activity. Therefore, a simple Empty activity suffices in the If branch.

In the Else branch, the intermediate result has to be computed. Therefore, drag scope *ComputeResult* to the Else branch. Under that scope, add a new scope *PutValueInCache*. This scope will be implemented in the next section, to actually record any computed results. Figure 9-7 shows the salient sections of the *QuickAndSlowProcess*.

Write Computed Result to Cache

Configure a second Coherence Adapter binding in the SOA composite. This one is called *CoherenceCacheWriter*.

Use the same settings—except the operation type—as for the first Coherence Adapter: set the JNDI name of the Coherence connection to eis/Coherence/Local. Select Put as the operation type. In step 4 of the wizard, set *Cache Type* to XML. Set the *Cache Name* to adapter-local. Uncheck the checkbox for auto generating the key. Set the Key Type to String and leave the Key field empty. Accept the default for *time to live*. Press Next. Select element *CacheResult* from the Cache.xsd document as the schema element (for objects to put in the cache). Click Next and click Finish. The Coherence Adapter reference is created.

Drag a BPEL subprocess component to the central area in the composite editor. Call the subprocess *CacheWriter*. Set the namespace to saibot.airport/services/generic/soacomposite. Click OK to have the subprocess created. Wire the subprocess to the *CoherenceCacheWriter* adapter binding.

Open the subprocess by double clicking the icon.

Create global variables *key* and *cachePayload*, based on the CacheTagType and CachedObjectType types in the Cache.xsd document. Both variables provide input to the subprocess and there is no output.

Add a scope *PutOnCache* to the BPEL subprocess. Inside the scope, add an Invoke activity, linked to the Partner Link *CoherenceCacheWriter*. In the Invoke activity editor, specify two local variable to be created for the input and the output. Note that we will not actually use the output variable.

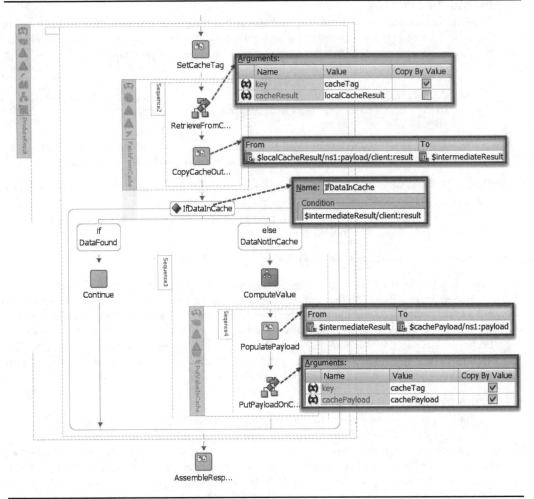

FIGURE 9-7. *The flow logic that attempts to find a result in the cache and that computes and stores the result if it was not yet found*

Open the Properties tab in the Invoke editor. Click on the green plus icon to add a property to pass. Select property jca.coherence.Key from the drop-down list. Specify the following expression to derive the value for the Key property:

```
$key/ns2:tag
```

This means that the Coherence Adapter is asked to store an object using a key with the string found in the tag element. Click on OK to complete the definition of the invoke activity.

Before the invoke, add an assign activity to copy the content of global variable *cachePayload* to the generated local input variable for the invoke to the Coherence Adapter. Figure 9-8 shows the complete subprocess.

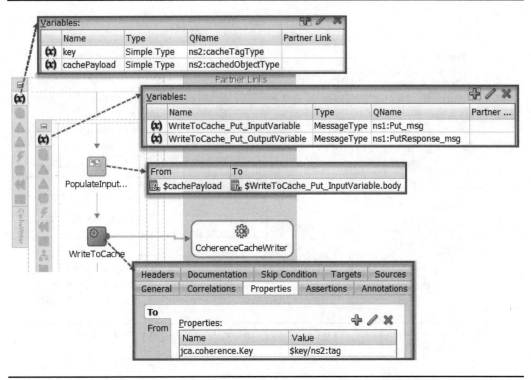

FIGURE 9-8. *Subprocess CacheWriter, to store payloads on the Coherence grid*

Return to the BPEL process editor for *QuickAndSlowProcess*. Open scope *PutValueInCache*. Create a scope level variable called *cachePayload*, based on type *cachedObjectType* (in Cache.xsd).

Add (a call to) the *CacheWriter* subprocess to the scope. Map the *key* argument of the subprocess to variable *cacheTag*. Map the *cachePayload* argument to the new local scope variable *cachePayload*.

Finally, almost done now, add an assign activity just before the call to the subprocess. In this activity, copy variable *intermediateResult* to the payload element in variable *cachePayload*. Check the option *insertMissingToData* on the copy rule.

This completes the BPEL process *QuickAndSlow*—now with full cache support. It also is final piece in the *QuickAndSlowHello* composite application. Time to deploy the entire composite, and invoke the service it exposes. The first call—for input string "Jean" —takes more than 5 seconds. Subsequent calls—for that same input—are just over 0.1 second (Figure 9-9). When the input is changed to "Luc," the service response takes again over 5 seconds to arrive and the second call for that same input takes again some 100 milliseconds. The impact of using cached results instead of recalculated results is clearly visible.

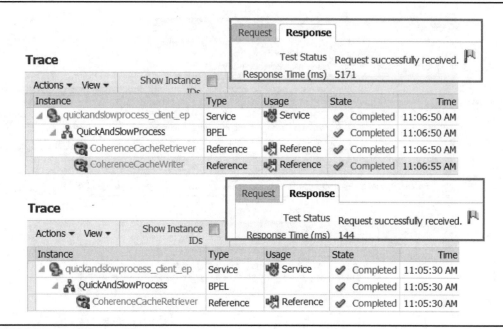

FIGURE 9-9. *What a difference caching can make (comparing first and sub sequent calls for a certain request message)*

Create Reusable Subprocesses for the Cache Support

The entire composite is shown in Figure 9-10. It consists of a specific part—the QuickAndSlowProcess—and a generic section: the two subprocesses with associated Coherence Adapter bindings.

These generic elements—for writing to the cache and retrieving values from it—can be turned into component templates that make them easily reusable in other SOA composites. That allows us, for example, to reuse them in the next section, when we will spice up the *FlightStatusService*.

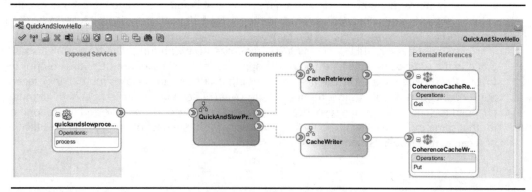

FIGURE 9-10. *The QuickAndSlowHello composite application*

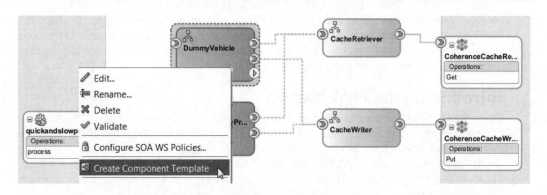

FIGURE 9-11. *Create a Component Template for the DummyVehicle BPEL process to actually create a template with the two subprocess components and their associated Coherence Adapter bindings*

However, JDeveloper does not allow us to create a Component Template for a BPEL subprocess. We can bring the subprocess components along in a template created for a different component though. So, as a workaround, add a BPEL component to the *QuickAndSlow* composite, for example, called *DummyVehicle*—not to be exposed as SOAP Web Service. Open the BPEL editor for *DummyVehicle*. Add calls to the two subprocess components—just through drag and drop, no further configuration is required. Close the BPEL editor.

Right click on the *DummyVehicle* component, as shown in Figure 9-11. From the context menu, select option Create Component Template.

The Create Component Template wizard appears. On the first page, provide the name—for example, *CoherenceCacheSupport*—and a description that lets potential users of the template know what exactly it provides. You may change the location where the template will be created, or accept the default. On the second page, an overview is given of all files that will be bundled with the template—including the two BPEL subprocess components, the Coherence Adapter configurations and the relevant XSD files. Accept this selection. The template is now created. You could remove the *DummyVehicle* again, as it no longer serves any purpose.

NOTE
You can review and manage the templates from the menu option
Tools | Preferences | SOA | Templates.

Add Some Coherence-Powered Memory to the FlightService

The *FlightService* provides the current status for any flight that is scheduled to arrive or depart in a 36-hour time range. It is a crucial service—providing up-to-date flight information to hundreds of systems and tens of thousands of consumers. It is this service that we want to make faster—and this service that we would like to query the enterprise database far less frequently.

Using the generic component templates that were created in the previous section, we should be able to substantially reduce the load on the enterprise resources by fetching the flight status from the cache most of times. Having achieved that first goal, we have to deal with a second challenge: how to ensure that the cache does not serve information that is no longer valid because it is out of synch with the updated back end.

Introducing the FlightService

Open the *FlightService* application and project from the FlightService_step0 folder. The implementation is simplified: instead of a call to a real back-end system, the core BPEL process in this composite calls a local BPEL component—*DetermineFlightStatusFromBackendSystems*—to get the status of a specific flight. This implementation—shown in Figure 9-12—will suffice to demonstrate the use of the cache on a business service—and has the benefit of being easy to deploy and try out.

After inspecting the composite, deploy it to the Integrated WLS. Invoke the *FlightService* using the HTTP Analyzer for various flights. Retrieving the status of each flight takes about the same time—just a little over 4 seconds.

Add Cache Support

Instead of having to contact the back-end systems—through the *DetermineFlightStatusFromBackendSystems* component—we want our core BPEL process to only contact the back-end systems if it does not know the status of a particular flight. And the status is considered known if it is available from the cache. Fetching the status from the cache is both much faster and far less of a burden on the back-end systems.

Our first step will be to extend the *FlightService* composite with two BPEL subprocesses, based on the component template created in the previous section. This will create the link with the Coherence cache. Next, we will somewhat reconfigure the *FlightStatusProcessor*, in very much the same way as we did with the *QuickAndSlowProcess* in the previous section, leveraging the two subprocesses for reading from and writing to the cache.

Add CacheReader and CacheWrite Subprocess from Templates

Drag the *CoherenceCacheSupport* component template from the component palette—panel SOA Templates—to the Components area in the composite editor, as shown in Figure 9-13.

The wizard for creating a component based on a component template appears. It lists all files it is about to merge into the *FlightService* project, together with potential conflicts. In this case,

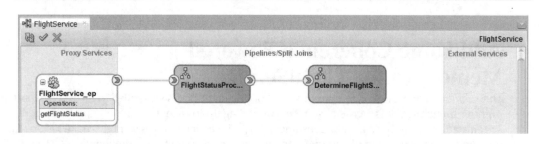

FIGURE 9-12. *The initial FlightService composite, without caching support*

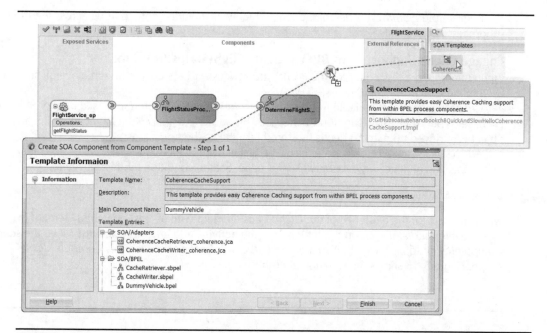

FIGURE 9-13. *Adding Component Template CoherenceCacheSupport to the SOA composite*

almost all files are new so there will be few conflicts. The exception is the composite.xml file that will be merged into the existing composite.xml.

Press Finish to have the BPEL subprocess components as well as the Coherence Adapter bindings added to the project. When components have been created for from the template, the composite looks as is shown in Figure 9-14.

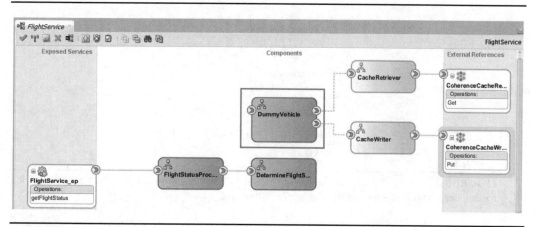

FIGURE 9-14. *FlightService composite with foundation for cache support created from component template*

Remove the *DummyVehicle* component, which was included only to bring across the BPEL subprocess components.

Engage Cache Support from BPEL Process FlightStatusProcessor

Open the BPEL process editor for the *FlightStatusProcessor*. Let's create the same overall structure used in the *QuickAndSlowProcess*.

Create a scope level variable in scope *ProduceResult* called *cacheTag*, based on the *cacheTagType* in schema definition Cache.xsd. This variable will hold the key with which an object is retrieved from and if needs be stored into the cache.

Add a scope called *FetchFromCache* as the first activity in the scope *ProduceResult*. Underneath that scope, add an If activity, labeled *IfDataInCache*. Set the condition for this activity to:

```
$intermediateResult/ns1:result/ns1:FlightStatus/*[1]
```

which is a test for the existence of the *FlightStatus* element with at least one child element in variable *intermediateResult*. In the If branch of the activity, add an Empty activity. Move the scope *ComputeResult* to Else branch. Add a scope *PutValueInCache* following this *ComputeResult* scope. Figure 9-15 shows the situation after these edits.

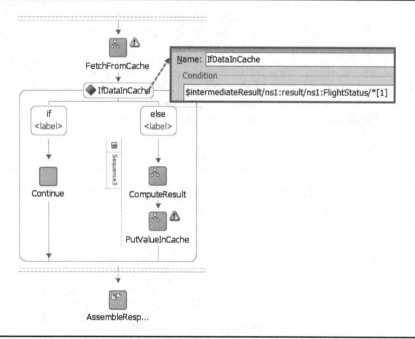

FIGURE 9-15. *The outline for the cache support: try to fetch from the cache and when not found, compute and save on the cache for future use*

Add an assign activity just prior to the *FetchFromCache* scope. Set the tag element in the *cacheTag* variable with a concatenation of the carrier, the flight number and the date:

```
concat($inputVariable.in/ns1:Carrier,':',$inputVariable.in/ns1:FlightNumber,':
',string($inputVariable.in/ns1:FlightDate))
```

Open the scope *FetchFromCache*. Create a scope level variable called *localCacheResult* which is based on type *cachedObjectType* in Cache.xsd.

Add (a call to) the subprocess *CacheRetriever*. Map the *key* argument of the subprocess to variable *cacheTag*. Map the *cacheResult* to variable *localCacheResult* and make sure to uncheck the checkbox for Copy by Value—because this is the output that should come back from the subprocess.

Add an assign activity after the *CacheRetriever* subprocess, to take the output in *localCacheResult* and copy it to variable *intermediateResult*. Map the payload element in the variable *localCacheResult* to the result element in variable *intermediateResult*. Check the *ignoreMissingFrom* option and the *insertMissingTo* option on the copy rule.

The payload element is an XSD anyType: it can contain any valid XML fragment. In order to retrieve from this element the actual contents we know to find there, we have to refine the copy rule in the BPEL source editor. Refine the *from* expression as shown in the next code snippet:

```
<assign name="CopyCacheOutcomeToIntermediateResult">
    <copy bpelx:insertMissingToData="yes" ignoreMissingFromData="yes">
        <from>$localCacheResult/ns5:payload/ns1:result</from>
        <to>$intermediateResult/ns1:result</to>
    </copy>
</assign>
```

These steps are visualized in Figure 9-16.

Open scope *PutValueInCache*. Create a scope level variable called *cachePayload*, based on type *cachedObjectType* (in Cache.xsd).

Add (a call to) the *CacheWriter* subprocess to the scope. Map the *key* argument of the subprocess to variable *cacheTag*. Map the *cachePayload* argument to the new local scope variable *cachePayload*.

Finally, almost done now, add an assign activity just before the call to the subprocess. In this activity, copy variable *intermediateResult* to the payload element in variable *cachePayload*, and copy the expression xp20:current-dateTime() to the *creationTimestamp* element in $cachePayload.

Try Out the Cache-Enabled FlightService

Deploy the *FlightService* composite, which now looks like Figure 9-17. It has cache support enabled. That means that the first call for a combination of carrier, flight number, and data will still take over 4 seconds, but every subsequent call for that same combination should return well within 1 second. The result in those cases does not have to be reconstructed from back-end systems but instead can be reproduced from the cache.

Calling the *FlightService* three times in a row for the same combination of carrier, flight number, and flight date will make the effect of the cache quite obvious: the first call takes over 4 seconds, the other two should take no more than a fraction of a second.

Another telltale sign of the effect of the cache can be seen from the element *creationTimestamp*: if a timestamp is returned that is distinctly in the past, the flight status was retrieved from the cache.

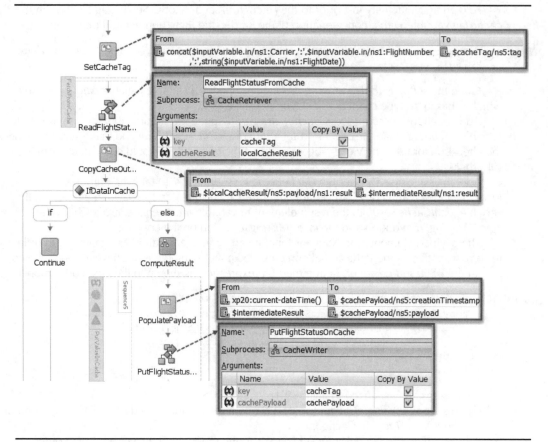

FIGURE 9-16. *The BPEL process FlightStatusProcess with caching support*

Add Refresh Cache Strategy

The flight status can efficiently be retrieved from the cache. That is good. What is less good is that as soon as that status is stored in the cache—it could become stale. Stale means that the situation in the cache deviates from the actual status in the back-end systems. Clearly, the flight service should not produce stale or incorrect data. Therefore, a mechanism is required that removes data for a flight from the cache that is known to be stale. The next time the status is requested for that flight, it will be retrieved from the back-end systems and stored anew in the cache.

NOTE
The mechanism introduced here for guarding the freshness of the cache could even take responsibility for calculating and caching the fresh value. For now we take a somewhat simpler approach of merely ensuring the cache will not produce stale values.

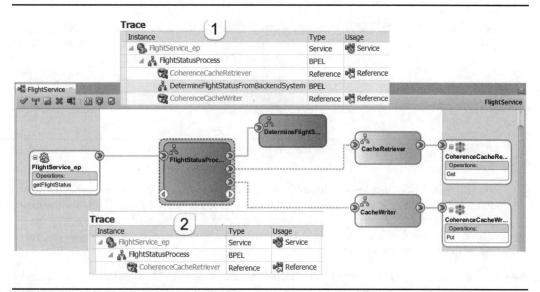

FIGURE 9-17. *FlightService composite with cache support based on subprocesses and Coherence Adapter bindings created from component template; trace 1 indicates a request that could not be serviced with a an existing cache value and trace 2 is for one that did leverage the cache*

In our current case, we will publish a service *FlightStatusCacheService* on the Service Bus that should be invoked whenever the status of a flight changes—much like the *FlightUpdateNotificationService* introduced in Chapter 6 is invoked when a flight status is updated. For now, we will not go into detail as to what agent will take responsibility for calling. Note that this same service could perhaps expose operations for preloading the cache at midnight with the flight status for all the flights of the coming day and for querying flights with specific characteristics.

Create FlightStatusCacheService to Reset the Cache

Open the Service Bus project *FlightStatusCacheService* in the *FlightStatusCacheService_step0 application*. It contains the WSDL for this service along with the associated Schema definitions.

Right click in the External Service lane. Select Insert Adapters | Coherence from the context menu. The Coherence Adapter configuration wizard appears. Call the adapter reference *RemoveFromCache*. Set the JNDI connection to eis/Coherence/Local. Select Operation Type *Remove*. Set the Cache Name to *Adapter-Local*. Type *dummy* into the Key field and leave the Filter field empty. We will use a JCA header property to specify the key of the object to be removed from the cache. Click Finish to complete the creation of the Adapter binding and the business service.

Next, right click the FlightStatusCacheService.wsdl file and select Service Bus | Generate Proxy Service from the context menu. Check the checkbox to also generate a pipeline. Set the name of the pipeline to *FlightStatusCachePipeline*. Set the endpoint URI to /flight/FlightStatusCacheService. Click Finish to create the proxy service and the pipeline. Then, wire the pipeline to the business service *RemoveFromCache*, as shown in Figure 9-18.

Open the pipeline. Modify the routing activity: configure it to invoke the *Remove* operation on the *RemoveFromCache* business service.

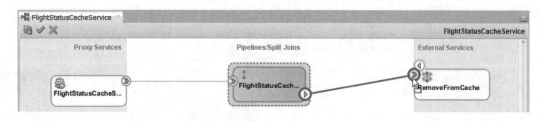

FIGURE 9-18. *Wire pipeline FlightStatusCachePipeline to the Coherence Cache business service*

Add a Transport Header activity to the Request Action section in the Routing activity. Add a Header for the jca protocol. Select or set the name to jca.coherence.Key. Then edit the expression to derive the value for the property. It should contain the equivalent of the concatenation of carrier, flight number, and flight date that we used in *FlightService* to put flight data on the cache and retrieve it from the cache:

```
fn:concat($body/flig:getFlightStatusRequestMessage/flig:Carrier,':',$body/flig
:getFlightStatusRequestMessage/flig:FlightNumber,':',$body/flig:getFlightStatu
sRequestMessage/flig:FlightDate)
```

TIP
SOA Suite allows the creation of custom XPath functions through the implementation and registration of a simple Java class. Whenever you find yourself reusing the same, complex XPath expression over and over again, you could consider creating such a reusable custom XPath function for it.

Figure 9-19 shows the pipeline and specifically the configuration of the Transport Header activity.

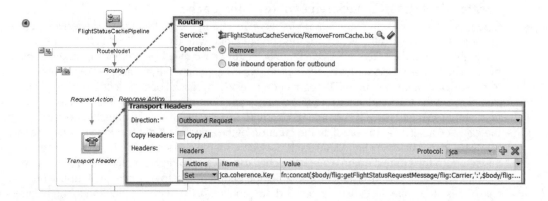

FIGURE 9-19. *Configuration of the FlightStatusCachePipeline—set the jca.coherence.Key transport header*

Deploy the FlightStatusCacheService.

TIP
The logic provided above in a Service Bus project could just as easily be implemented in an SOA composite application using a mediator and the same Coherence Adapter binding. The source code for this chapter has the FlightStatusCacheServiceAlternative *folder with this alternative implementation.*

Test the Forced Cache Refresh
What we want to verify is the following scenario:

- Invoke *FlightService* for a specific flight X—response takes more than 4 seconds and the cache is loaded.

- Invoke *FlightService* for the same flight X—response is received in less than half a second, as it is produced from the cache.

- Invoke *FlightService* for a specific flight Y—response takes more than 4 seconds because the status for this flight is not yet found in the cache; subsequently the cache is loaded with the status of flight Y.

- Invoke *FlightService* for the same flight X—response is still received in less than half a second.

- Invoke *FlightStatusCacheService* for flight X—there has been a status update for that flight and the information has to be removed from the cache.

- Invoke *FlightService* for flight X again—response takes more than 4 seconds because the status is retrieved afresh from the back-end systems because it was previously removed from the cache; the newly derived status is stored in the cache.

- Invoke *FlightService* for the same flight X—response is received in less than half a second, as it is produced from the cache.

- Invoke *FlightService* for the flight Y—response is received in less than half a second because earlier on the status for this flight was produced and stored in the cache. Note that the cache reset for Flight X did not affect the information for Flight Y.

Walk through these steps to verify whether the behavior you are experiencing is in accordance with your expectations.

Leverage Service Bus Result Cache
The Service Bus has a built in integration with Coherence that doesn't require the use of the JCA Coherence adapter. It is called Service Result Cache. Business services can be configured with the Service Result Cache, to cache the response from the business service for future use. The expiration time of the cached response is configured, as is the expression to derive the key under which the response is cached. All that is required to leverage this Service Result Cache is a little declarative configuration. Compared to the Coherence adapters we have seen in action earlier in this chapter, we lack the ability to explicitly reset the values in the Service Result Cache, for example when

some event tells us the cached data has grown stale. Simply put, Result Cache is easier to configure, but more limited in functionality than the explicit use of the Coherence Adapter.

We will see the Service Bus service result cache in action for a wrapper *FlightService* on the Service Bus that routes to the *FlightService* SOA composite. We will disable the cache support in the SOA composite, feel the effects and then switch on the service result cache to provide the cache fueled response acceleration again.

Expose FlightService on the Service Bus

Create a Service Bus application and project, both called *FlightServiceProxy*. Copy the folders WSDLs and Schemas from the *FlightService* SOA composite project to the *FlightServiceProxy* project.

In the project overview editor, right click on the External Services swim lane. Select Transports | HTTP from the context menu, to create a business service that invokes the *FlightService* exposed by the SOA composite. Set the name of the business service to *FlightServiceSOAcomposite*.

On the second page, set type to WSDL and browse for the WSDL for the SOA composite *FlightService*. Use the URL with port 7101 over HTTP, instead of the URL for 7102 over HTTPS. The wizard will propose to import a number of resources associated with the *FlightService*. Accept this proposal. Click on Next and click on Finish to create the business service. At this point, you can already test the business service by simply running it from the context menu.

Open the folder WSDLs and click on FlightService.wsdl to open the editor. Add a SOAP 1.1 binding to the WSDL, by clicking the green plus icon in the frame labeled bindings. This is necessary because the composite's WSDL is abstract and a Service Bus proxy service has to be associated with a binding element from the WSDL definition. Save the changes.

Right click on the FlightService.wsdl file and select Service Bus | Generate Proxy Service from the context menu. The wizard appears to help create a proxy service and a pipeline from the WSDL interface definition. Call the service *FlightServicePS*. Call the pipeline *FlightPipeline* and check the checkbox to generate a pipeline wired to the proxy service. Click on Next. Set the Endpoint URI to /flight/FlightService. Click Finish.

Wire the freshly created pipeline to the business service, see Figure 9-20. Because the interface definition is the same for the proxy service, the pipeline, and the business service, you do not have to make any additional changes. You can run each of these three to verify whether the reference to the SOA composite works as expected and benefits from the cache support in the composite. The latter should mean that if you make two calls to either the proxy service, the pipeline, or the business service, at least the second should complete in less than 0.5 second.

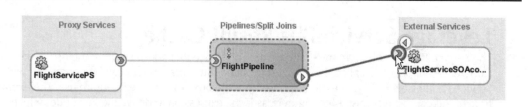

FIGURE 9-20. *The FlightServicePS proxy wraps the Flight Service SOA composite through a business service with Service Result Cache configured*

Disable Cache Support in FlightService SOA Composite

Open the *FlightService* SOA composite. Open the *FlightStatusProcess* BPEL component. Change the condition in the If activity to false().

This ensures that even when the requested flight status is retrieved from the cache, the BPEL process will still recompute the status. The cache support has effectively been disabled.

Deploy the composite and make a few test calls to the Service Bus proxy service *FlightService* to verify that each request now takes similarly long: more than 4 seconds.

Switch on Service Result Cache

Let's now configure the result cache on the business service for calling the SOA Composite *FlightService*. Open the editor for the business service and bring up the Performance tab, as shown in Figure 9-21.

Check the checkbox labeled *Enable Result Caching*, to indicate that responses from the underlying service—the SOA composite *FlightService*—can be reused for subsequent requests. Set Cache Token Expression to the following XQuery expression—that derives a key based on the same components we used before: carrier, flight number. and flight date:

```
fn:concat($body/flig:getFlightStatusRequestMessage/flig:Carrier,':',$body/flig
:getFlightStatusRequestMessage/flig:FlightNumber,':', $body/flig:getFlightStat
usRequestMessage/flig:FlightDate)
```

Set the *Expiration Time* to a duration of 30 seconds. That means that any cached results are good for reuse during 30 seconds. After that period, these values should not be reused again and should eventually be removed from the cache. Alternatively, the expiration time can be derived dynamically in an XQuery expression that can use elements in either the request or the response message. The setting Default refers to a value specified in the configuration file osb-coherence-config.xml for element expiry-delay; initially that value is set to 5 minutes.

By adding the cache-ttl metadata element to the request sent to the business service, we override the cache-ttl that was derived from the Expiration Time expression configured on the business service at design time:

```
<tran:cache-ttl xmlns:tran="http://www.bea.com/wli/sb/transports">PT5S</
tran:cache-ttl>
```

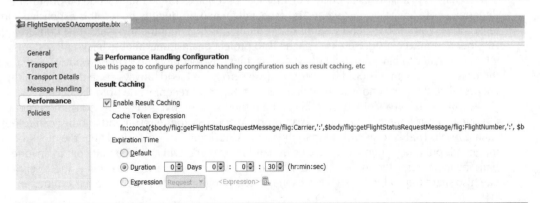

FIGURE 9-21. *Configuration of result caching for the business service*

When you invoke the business service, the response metadata that is shown in the Service Bus console contains header elements called cache-token and cache-originated. The former shows the cache token as derived from the expression specified for the result cache and the latter indicates whether the response could be retrieved from the cache or not.

Deploy the Service Bus project. Make a few calls to the Service Bus proxy service *FlightService* to verify that each first request for a specific flight (carrier, flight number, and flight date) still takes a little more than 4 seconds and that each subsequent request for a specific flight returns a response in less than 0.5 second. The latter is the effect of the result caching that has been enabled on the business service that wraps the SOA composite *FlightService*.

NOTE
The service result cache does not expose cache refresh operations. Only through the expiration expression defined for the cached value can we influence the caching behavior. There is no direct access path to reset entries in the service result cache. That may be a good reason to work with relatively short expiry times, depending of course on the expected rate of change.

Summary

Recalculating the same result over and over again is a waste of resources and causes the response time to be longer than is necessary and can cause overloads in (back-end) systems. Use of a cache, where previously produced values are stored for reuse is a common mechanism to lower the load on back-end systems and improve the performance of the system.

SOA Suite is shipped with Coherence—an in-memory, multinode data grid. This grid can be used as a cache to easily store and retrieve objects to and from. Values in the cache can have an associated expiry time, can be XML fragments or Plain Old Java Objects and are available across different instances of composites, across different composites, and Service Bus projects and across different nodes in a SOA Suite cluster. SOA composites and Service Bus project can use the Coherence Adapter to interact with the cache. Additionally, a business service in a Service Bus project can be configured with the Result Cache option. This is a simplified integration with Coherence through which caching can be enabled in a straightforward, easy, and declarative way, with somewhat limited capabilities regarding refresh strategies.

Caching is primarily useful when the number of requests for a certain value far outnumbers the number of changes to that value and especially when producing the result is expensive—in terms of load on the back-end systems or even in terms of actual money—and time consuming. Another reason to consider use of a cache is to protect against unavailable back-end systems when it is better to have a potentially stale but still fairly recent value than no value at all. If that is the case, the algorithm should be: retrieve always from back end, always store the value in the cache; when the back end is unavailable: retrieve the most recent value from the cache.

Anything put on a Coherence grid can be retrieved from that grid by any consumers, not just the one that put it there. One service can produce and record the result and another can retrieve such a result. That is somewhat akin to the Claim Check pattern—so called after the cloakroom that hands out a tag when a coat has been handed over and will produce that coat to anyone handing in the tag later on. So instead of handing a value from service to service, these services can also share that value through the cache, by exchanging the key to that cached value.

Note that when large documents or a large number of objects are put on the cache, this may result in quite substantial memory consumption. The Coherence cache used through the adapter or in conjunction with the business service result caching option can either be local on the same server as SOA Suite, which is the default, or it can be configured on remote clusters, possibly only used for caching.

CHAPTER
10

Embedding Custom Logic Using Java and Spring Component

The SOA Suite is a platform on which Service Bus projects and SOA composites can be deployed to run and process requests. This platform provides many out of the box components that are configured through declarative programs into processing XML, calling out to services, performing logic, and so on. Occasionally, these components and the declarative approach fall just short of what we need for a specific service implementation. In those cases, we can make use of custom Java components to complement the out of the box capabilities.

We have seen how we can call out to Enterprise JavaBeans and how both a Service Bus pipeline and a BPEL process can call out to a Java class. However, the transition from the service implementation to these Java contexts was not entirely smooth, and required us to jump through some hoops.

In this chapter, the Spring component is introduced. This is a first class citizen in the SCA fabric of SOA composites, along with BPEL, Mediator, Business Rules, and Human Task components that are discussed in subsequent chapters. This component allows custom Java classes and third party Java libraries to be easily integrated into SOA composite applications. We will discuss use of the Twitter4J library for interacting with Twitter as well as the Java SDK for Dropbox.

An important component in this chapter is the Mediator component. We will discuss how a mediator can forward a response it has received to another service component—instead of returning a response message. The mediator can make use of simple *assign values* steps to construct the routed message, instead of XSL, or XQuery-based transformations.

Simple intro—First Steps with the Spring Component

A service interface describes operations and for each operation the input and output parameters. A Java interface does the same thing for the Java methods it exposes. It is, therefore, fairly easy to convert a Java interface into a web service interface described by a WSDL document with XSD types.

SOA Suite works from this notion and allows us to create Java classes that implement one or more interfaces and have these classes expose the web service equivalent of the Java interface(s) they implement in a SOA composite application. To that end, Java classes need to be configured in a Spring context component, defined through an extended Spring framework bean definition file. Beans configured in this component can publish any Java interface they implement as an SCA service to be invoked by other components in the SOA composite.

The Spring framework has at its core an IoC or Inversion of Control container, that can construct beans that are instances of Java classes into which property values and dependencies can be injected. Multiple beans can be configured in a single Spring component—with some beans being injected into others, to satisfy the dependencies of these objects. When a bean has a dependency that cannot be satisfied by another bean in the Spring context, this dependency can be promoted and exposed as an SCA reference that other components in the composite can provide the implementation for.

This must all sound very abstract, to those who do not know the Spring framework, so let us start with a very simple example.

The Greeter Service Based on the Java Greeter Interface

Create a new SOA composite application, called *SpringGreeter*, initially empty. This composite will expose a *GreeterService*, based on a Java interface that is exposed by a bean in a Spring context component and implemented by a simple Java class. The service will take a string input and return it with a simple greeting—"Hello <name>"—added to it. In a second iteration, we will define a dependency in the class on a decorator. At first, this decorator will be provided by a local bean in the Spring context—based on a Java class that returns the all capitals version of the string with an exclamation mark added to it. Next, the dependency is promoted to a reference that a mediator component outside the Spring context is brought in for. Note: Create all classes and interfaces in a package called *springgreeter*.

Quick GreeterService Implementation

Create a Java interface called *Greeter*—in the same project as the SOA composite—with a single method that accepts a String and returns a String:

```
public interface Greeter {
    public String greet(String input);
}
```

Next, create a Java Class GreeterImpl that implements this interface:
```
public class GreeterImpl implements Greeter {
    @Override
    public String greet(String input) {
       return "Hello "+input;
    }
}
```

Make the project—which takes care of compiling these two Java artifacts.

Open the SOA composite editor. Drag a Spring context component from the component palette to the central area in the SOA composite. Create the Spring context component as *GreeterSpring*.

Double click the new component and configure the bean configuration file as follows:

```
<bean id="greeterBean" class="springgreeter.GreeterImpl" />
<sca:service name="Greeter" target="greeterBean" type="springgreeter.Greeter" />
```

This defines through the second line that the *GreeterSpring* component exposes a service called *Greeter*, based on the Java Interface *Greeter* and implemented by a Spring bean identified as *GreeterBean*. The first line tells the Spring container that this *GreeterBean* can be constructed using the *GreeterImpl* class.

When you save the file, you will notice that the Spring component exposes a service now, as shown in Figure 10-1. Drag this service to the External Services swim lane on the left-hand side, and drop it. JDeveloper will show a popup, indicating that it is about to generate a WSDL document describing the web service derived from the *Greeter* interface. Click OK.

This completes the composite. Deploy it and make a test call to the operation *greet*. In XML terms, you should see the results from your own Java code's operations.

Working with a Locally Satisfied Dependency

Create a second Java interface, called Decorator, with a single method *prettifyString*:

```
public interface Decorator {
    public String prettifyString(String input);
}
```

Open the GreeterImpl class and extend the implementation like this:

```
public class GreeterImpl implements Greeter {

    private Decorator decorator;

    public void setDecorator(Decorator decorator) {
        this.decorator = decorator;
    }

    @Override
    public String greet(String input) {
        return decorator.prettifyString("Hello "+input);
    }
}
```

The *GreeterImpl* class has a dependency now: before using the *GreeterBean,* someone should inject a Decorator into it. An obvious solution is the creation of a Java class that implements the Decorator interface on which a second Spring bean can be based that is injected:

```
public class RealDecorator implements Decorator {
    @Override
    public String prettifyString(String input) {
        return input.toUpperCase()+"!!";
    }
}
```

Change the contents of the *GreeterSpring* context definition like this:

```
<bean id="greeterBean" class="springgreeter.GreeterImpl" >
  <property name="decorator" ref="decoratorBean" />
</bean>
<bean id="decoratorBean" class="springgreeter.RealDecorator" />
```

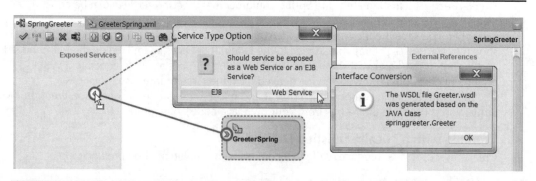

FIGURE 10-1.   *Promote the service exposed by the Spring Context to an external web service published by the SOA composite application*

Nothing changes in the sca:service element. The new dependency in the *GreeterBean* is resolved internally for now, between the Spring beans themselves.

Deploy the composite and make a test call. The effects from the injected Decorator are visible.

Satisfy a Bean Dependency with an SCA Component

The decorator that is now provided by another Spring bean, can also be provided by a mediator or BPEL component in the SOA composite, or even by an adapter or external reference at composite level. To bring this about, the dependency has to be promoted in the Spring context definition like this:

```
<bean id="greeterBean" class="springgreeter.GreeterImpl">
    <property name="decorator" ref="StringDecorator"/>
</bean>
<sca:reference name="StringDecorator" type="springgreeter.Decorator"/>
```

Here, the decorator property is no longer set using a local bean but instead it refers to the sca:reference element. When you save the changes and return to the SOA composite editor, you will see that the *GreeterSpring* component now exposes a reference.

In order to satisfy this dependency, create a new mediator component called *StringDecorator*. Indicate that the interface will be defined later.

Wire the reference from the *GreeterSpring* component to the new *StringDecorator* mediator, as is shown in Figure 10-2. JDeveloper generates the WSDL definition for the *Decorator* interface that this reference requires. This WSDL will automatically become the service interface for the mediator component.

All that is left to do, is provide the implementation of a routing rule in the Mediator. Open the editor for *StringDecorator*. Add a routing rule of type *echo*. Click on the Assign Values icon for this routing rule and have the output derived as the lowercase value from the input, as is shown in Figure 10-3.

We now have a an example of an SOA composite that exposes a web service implemented by a Spring bean that relies on an implementation of the *Decorator* interface that is provided by a

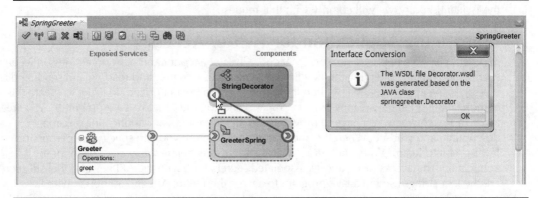

FIGURE 10-2.   *Mediator StringDecorator satisfies the dependency from the GreeterSpring component (and indirectly from the GreeterImpl Java class)*

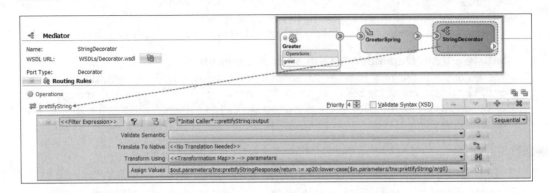

FIGURE 10-3. *Configure the Echo Routing Rule That Returns the Lower Case String*

mediator component. These are the essential ingredients of the integration of custom Java classes through the Spring component in SOA Suite.

Deploy the composite and make a test call. Verify that you see the effect of the *StringDecorator* (lower case output). Inspect the message flow trace for the test call in the Enterprise Manager FMW Control. You will see the Spring context invoked as well as the mediator component. There is no trace of individual Java classes inside the Spring component.

Add the Twitter Channel to the FlightNotificationService

In Chapter 6, we have created the *FlightNotificationService*. This service sends notifications of updates in the status of a flight to an indicated recipient over the specified channel. Currently, this service leverages the outbound UMS adapter to send notifications over channels Email and Chat (IM). The marketing department of Saibot Airport has expressed an interest in adding Twitter (direct messages) as a channel for sending such notifications. Using the Spring component and the Twitter4J library, we will comply with that request.

Prepare the Application for Twitter Access

In order to be able to programmatically access a Twitter account and perform actions on its behalf such as reading and querying the timeline, posting status updates, and reading and sending direct messages, the application that will do these things has to be authorized. In order to create this authorization, go to https://apps.twitter.com/ and click on the Create New App button. You are taken to a page where you have to provide some details about your application—name, description, and website. When the application is registered, you can specify the permission level—set it to Read, Write, and Direct Messages. Next, generate the access token for the application. The access token and its associated secret along with the API key and the API secret are the four strings used in a Java program to access the Twitter API and authorize with it.

TIP
The online resources for this chapter have step by step instructions and screenshots illustrating these actions. They also describe the certificate that has to be configured in the JVM Key Store to be able to access Twitter over a secure connection.

Download Twitter4J from http://twitter4j.org, for example, twitter4j-4.0.4.zip. Extract file twitter4j-core-4.0.4.jar (or whatever more recent version is available) from the zip file to the SOA/ SCA-INF/lib folder under the *FlightNotificationService* project. This JAR file contains the Java library that makes interaction with the Twitter API fairly easy.

Open the *FlightNotificationService* application and project. Open the project properties editor, from the context menu on the project node. Open the Libraries and Classpath tab. Click on Add JAR/Library. Browse for twitter4j-core-4.0.4.jar and add it to the project.

Create the Java Class to Send Twitter Direct Messages

Create Java Interface *TwitterMessageSender*:

```
package saibot.airport.services.spring;
public interface TwitterMessageSender {
    void sendDirectMessage(String message, String recipient);
}
```

Create a new Java Class, called *TwitterClient* that implements the interface, using this code:

```
package saibot.airport.services.spring;
public class TwitterClient implements TwitterMessageSender {
    private final String consumerKey = "ZdDrYourKey";
    private final String consumerSecret = "srkVo4oYourSecret";
    private final String accessToken = "12YourAccessToken";
    private final String accessTokenSecret = "yZYYourTokenSecret";

    private ILoggerBean logger;
    public void setLogger(ILoggerBean logger) {
        this.logger = logger;
    }
    private Twitter constructTwitterInstance() {
        ConfigurationBuilder cb = new ConfigurationBuilder();
        cb.setDebugEnabled(true)
          .setOAuthConsumerKey(consumerKey)
          .setOAuthConsumerSecret(consumerSecret)
          .setOAuthAccessToken(accessToken)
          .setOAuthAccessTokenSecret(accessTokenSecret);
        Twitter sender = new TwitterFactory(cb.build()).getInstance();
        return sender;
    }
    public void sendDirectMessage(String message, String recipient) {
        Twitter sender = constructTwitterInstance();
        try {
```

```
            DirectMessage directmessage = sender.sendDirectMessage(recipient,
message);
            if (logger!=null) {
                logger.log(Level.INFO, "Sent: " + directmessage.getText() + "
to @" + directmessage.getRecipientScreenName());
            }
        } catch (TwitterException e) {
            e.printStackTrace();
            if (logger!=null) {
                logger.log(Level.WARNING, "Failed to send Direct Twitter
Message to "+recipient,e);
            }


        }
    }
    public static void main(String[] args) throws TwitterException {
        SimpleDateFormat sdf = new SimpleDateFormat("hh:mm aa");
        new TwitterClient().sendDirectMessage("FLight - KL 423 - Status
Update at " + sdf.format(new Date()) + " - Boarding at Gate 45 ",
"yourTwitterAccount");
    }
}
```

Provide the values for the consumer API Key, the consumer API secret, AccessToken and AccessTokenSecret that you generated when registering the application with your Twitter account.

NOTE
The preferred way of providing these values would probably be to define them in a property file and from there have them injected as defined in the Spring configuration file into the twitterMessageMaster bean. That is a little more involved for the purpose of this chapter and would make it a little harder to test the Java Class—so we choose the plain, less elegant approach here.

Run the Java class to see whether a first direct message is sent to the recipient you specify (this could be your own Twitter account).

The *ILoggerBean* interface referred to in this code is an interface of a bean that is preregistered in the SOA Suite. That bean is our gateway to the logging infrastructure of the SOA Suite. It can be configured in Spring components in SOA composites to be injected into our beans, as we will see in a little while.

Configure the Spring Context Component

Open the SOA composite editor for the *FlightUpdateNotificationService*. Drag a Spring component to the central section and drop it, as is shown in Figure 10-4.

The Create Spring [Context Component] editor appears. Set the name of the component to *TwitterChannel* and create a new context. Press OK to have the context created.

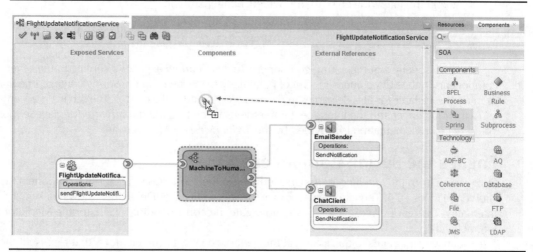

FIGURE 10-4. *Add Spring component to the composite application*

Double click on the new Spring component, to bring up the editor for the Spring context file. Under the comment line Spring bean definitions go here, add a bean definition, as follows:

```
<bean class="saibot.airport.services.spring.TwitterClient"
id="twitterMessageMaster" >
    <property name="logger" ref="loggerBean" />
</bean>
```

This defines a bean that will be identified with the string *twitterMessageMaster*. The bean is implemented by the *TwitterClient* class (which should have a no-argument constructor to be instantiated). The bean defines a property logger—and will have a *setLogger* method. Another bean identified by the string *loggerBean* will be injected into this *twitterMessageMaster* bean to provide the value for this property.

NOTE
The identifier loggerBean *is predefined in SOA Suite. It refers to the generic implementation of the* ILoggerBean *interface. The SOA Suite run time will recognize the identifier and will know what object to inject. Two additional preregistered beans are available:*

- *headerHelperBean*: For getting and setting header properties
- *instanceHelperBean*: For getting the following information: instance ID of the composite instance currently running, instance ID of the component instance currently running, composite distinguished name (DN) containing the name of the spring service component

Next, add the following entry to the TwitterChannel.xml file.

```
<sca:service name="TwitterMessenger" target="twitterMessageMaster"
type="saibot.airport.services.spring.TwitterMessageSender" />
```

Here we specify that the Spring component *TwitterChannel* exposes a service to the other components in the SOA composite. Out of potentially many beans in the Spring context, one makes its interface available for outside parties to create a wire to and make calls to. The service is advertised as *TwitterMessenger* and the interface it implements is the Java Interface *TwitterMessageSender*. The service implementation is provided by the *TwitterMessageMaster* bean.

Engage the Spring Component

Drag a wire from the *MachineToHuman* Mediator to the *TwitterChannel* Spring component, as is shown in Figure 10-5. The latter exposes exactly one service, so JDeveloper knows for which Java Interface—*TwitterMessageSender*—it should create the corresponding WSDL for the Mediator to interact with.

You may want to take a quick look at the generated WSDL. The elements that represent the arguments have fairly meaningless names such as arg0 and arg1.

Next, create an XSL Map to transform from the input to the Mediator—the *sendFlightUpdateNotificationRequestMessage*—to the *sendDirectMessage* element in the generated TwitterMessageSender.wsdl file, that represents the input to the *TwitterMessageMaster*. Map the *ToAddress* element to the recipient and use the carrier, flight number, and assorted other elements to construct a meaningful direct message about the current flight status. Make sure it stays within 140 characters, as Twitter restricts a message to this length.

Open the Mediator editor for the *MachineToHuman* component. A new routing rule was added when you created the wire from the Mediator to the Spring component. Set the filter condition on this routing rule to

```
$in.in/tns:sendFlightUpdateNotificationRequestMessage/
tns:CommunicationMetadata/tns:Channel='twitter'
```

to ensure that whenever the channel is specified as *twitter*, this routing rule is triggered. Set the Transformation to use the XSL Map that was just created. These settings are shown in Figure 10-6.

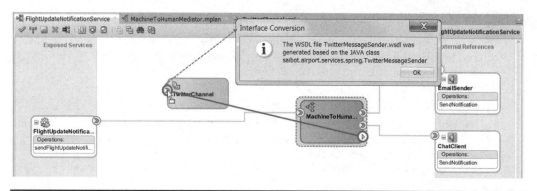

FIGURE 10-5. *Creating a wire from the Mediator to the Spring component causes a WSDL to be generated for the Java Interface exposed by the Spring component*

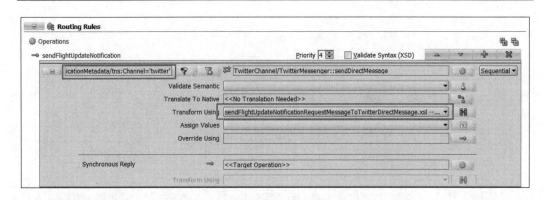

FIGURE 10-6.   *Configuring the routing rule that filters on the twitter channel*

This completes this next iteration for the composite application.

Try Out the Twitter Message Master

Deploy the SOA composite to the Integrated WLS. Make a few calls to the *FlightUpdateNotificationService* with the *channel* set to *twitter* and a *ToAddress* that specifies a valid Twitter account (yours or one of a friend or even @SaibotAirport).

The messages should be sent when the SOA composite instance executes, as shown in Figure 10-7.

NOTE
In this case, the custom Java code that is invoked could also have been implemented in an EJB or even a plain Java Servlet that is invoked through a Reference binding, or alternatively in a custom JCA Adapter or as a custom channel implementation in the UMS Adapter. All those solutions would have been more cumbersome in terms of implementation and deployment—but have advantages because of reuse potential. The largest benefit of using the Spring component in SOA composites compared to these alternatives is achieved when the Java code in the Spring beans makes use of services that are injected into the Spring component through references to other components, allowing the Java code to directly call out to BPEL components and JCA adapters. We will see this happening in the next section.

Logging Configuration and Monitoring
In the Java code for the *TwitterClient* we made use of the *loggerBean* to send logging details to. These details are fed into the logging infrastructure of the SOA Suite run time that is integrated with the WebLogic Server logging mechanism.

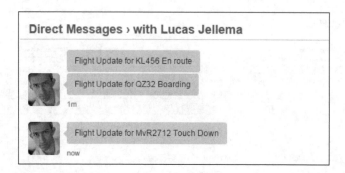

FIGURE 10-7. *Some direct messages sent from the SOA composite and received over Twitter*

To configure the logging level for the *LoggerBean*, open the Enterprise Manager FMW Control. Right click on the node SOA | soa-infra under Target Navigation and activate menu item Logs | Log Configuration, as shown in Figure 10-8.

The Log Configuration page that appears is used to configure the settings for logging by various components of the run time platform. Enter the term *LoggerBean* in the search field and press the search button. The search action should return the [oracle.integration.platform.blocks. java.beans.impl]LoggerBean class. For this class, you can specify the desired Logging Level— meaning the minimum level for which log messages will be written to the specified log handler. On the Log Files tab, the configuration of the log handlers can be changed as well as the mapping between loggers (classes that produce logging) and log handlers.

When this configuration has been applied and the composite is invoked once more to send a FlightStatus update in the form of a Twitter message, we can find the associated log entry in the log file (obviously) as well as through the console on the Log Messages page (Figure 10-9): right click on the node SOA | soa-infra under Target Navigation and activate menu item Logs | Log Messages.

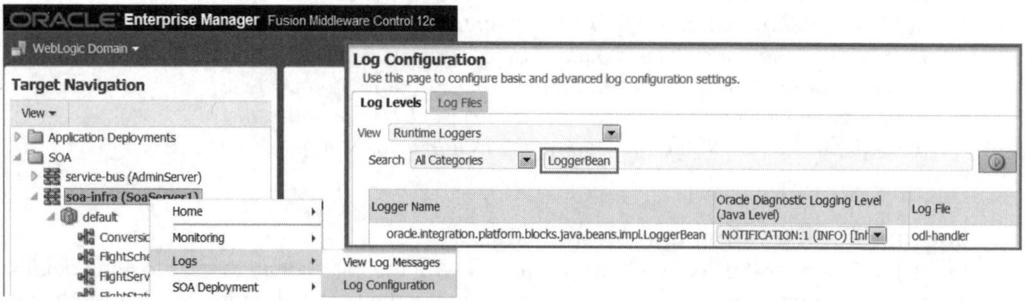

FIGURE 10-8. *Configure the log settings for the LoggerBean*

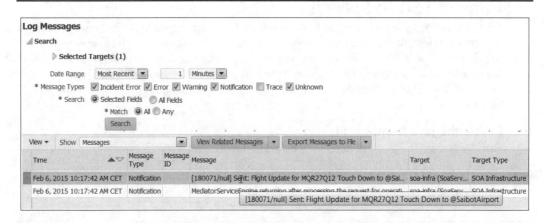

FIGURE 10-9. *Log Messages overview including the log entry through the LoggerBean from the TwitterClient class*

Create Spoken Flight Status Announcement and Put in Dropbox

In this section, we will wire together a number of Spring components and inject services into them. Together these components will implement the following functionality:

- Turn the FlightUpdateNotification message into the verbal text for an announcement.
- Turn the announcement into an MP3 stream using the *Google Text To Speech* API.
- Put the MP3 file for the announcement in the Airport's Public Dropbox folder (and return a direct link to it).

Using this combined functionality, we can extend the *FlightUpdateNotificationService* with a new channel that publishes a public tweet regarding the flight status change with a link to the audio file.

NOTE
This chapter only includes the salient code snippets because including the full classes would take up too much space. The online resources for this chapter have every line of code. The starting point for this section is the step1 application—the final result is step2.

TIP
An interesting extension would be to also include translation of the flight update announcement into different languages. Using the Google Translate service (paid for) or Microsoft's Bing Translator (free), it is fairly simple to include such functionality.

Convert Text to Speech

There are various ways to turn text to speech from Java. Open source projects such as MaryTTS support local installation of a text to speech convertor. Alternatively, on line services like NeoSpeech, iSpeech and Cereproc provide text to speech conversion through HTTP calls. That also applies to the Google TTS API, which we will use in this section. This API is free. It allows a maximum of 100 characters per call. It supports multiple languages, through a simple HTTP GET API.

Create the Java Components

First, let's create the Java interface for the Text to Speech converter:

```
public interface TextToSpeechConverter {

    public byte[] convertTextToSpeech(String text, String language);

    public String convertTextToSpeechAndHandle(String text, String language,
String title);
}
```

The second method is akin to an implementation of the claim check pattern: the text string passed in is turned to MP3 data. This data is then taken care of by the content handler that has been configured (see next); this content handler returns a string—the claim—that is a reference to the MP3 document. The content handler is defined through this Java Interface:

```
public interface ContentHandler {
    public String handleContent(byte[] content, String title);
```

The Java Class GoogleTextToSpeechConverter is created to implement the *TextToSpeechConverter*. It is based on a blog article by Jeff Chien (http://bit.ly/1sW95lv).

```
public class GoogleTextToSpeechConverter implements TextToSpeechConverter {

private ContentHandler contentHandler;

    public void setContentHandler(ContentHandler contentHandler) {
        this.contentHandler = contentHandler;
    }
    @Override
    public byte[] convertTextToSpeech(String text, String language) {
        try {
            return makeAudio(language, text.replaceAll(" ", "+"));
        } catch (IOException e) {
            e.printStackTrace();
        }
        return null;
    }

    private byte[] makeAudio(String language, String text) throws IOException
{
        byte[] mp3Buffer = null;
```

```java
    try {
        byte[] buffer = new byte[1 << 8];
        Path file = Paths.get(System.getProperty("user.home"), "temp.mp3");
        SeekableByteChannel sbc =null;
        sbc =


            Files.newByteChannel(file,
                                    EnumSet.of(StandardOpenOption.
CREATE,StandardOpenOption.TRUNCATE_EXISTING,
                                            StandardOpenOption.WRITE));
        InputStream in = null;
            URLConnection connection =
    new URL("http://www.translate.google.com/translate_tts?tl=" + language +
"&q=" + text).openConnection();
            //simulate a browser because Google doesn't let you get the mp3
without being able to identify it first
            connection.setRequestProperty("User-Agent",
                                        "Mozilla/4.0 (compatible;
MSIE 6.0; Windows NT 5.1; .NET CLR 1.0.3705; .NET CLR 1.1.4322; .NET CLR
1.2.30703)");
            connection.connect();
            in = connection.getInputStream();
            int count;
            ByteBuffer bb;
            while ((count = in.read(buffer)) != -1) {
                bb = ByteBuffer.wrap(buffer);
                sbc.write(bb);
                bb.clear();
            }
            in.close();
        in.close();
        SeekableByteChannel byteChannel = Files.newByteChannel(file);
        ByteBuffer bb = ByteBuffer.allocate((int) byteChannel.size());
        byteChannel.read(bb);
        mp3Buffer = bb.array();

    } catch (FileNotFoundException e) {
        e.printStackTrace();
    } catch (IOException e) {
        e.printStackTrace();
    }
    return mp3Buffer;
}


    @Override
    public String convertTextToSpeechAndHandle(String text, String language,
String title) {
        byte[] buffer =
            convertTextToSpeech(text, language);
        String result="NONE";
```

```
        if (contentHandler!=null) {
            result  = contentHandler.handleContent(buffer, title);
        }
        return result;
    }
}
```

This code is the simplified version of the code included in the online resources.

Configure the TextToSpeechConverter Spring Context Component

Create a new Spring content component in the SOA Composite, called *TextToSpeechConverter*.
Configure the following definition:

```
    <bean class="saibot.airport.services.spring.GoogleTextToSpeechConverter"
id="googleTextToSpeechConverterBean">
        <property name="contentHandler">
            <ref bean="ContentHandler"/>
        </property>
    </bean>
    <sca:service name="TextToSpeechConverter" target="googleTextToSpeechConver
terBean"
                 type="saibot.airport.services.spring.TextToSpeechConverter"/>
    <sca:reference name="ContentHandler" type="saibot.airport.services.spring.
ContentHandler"/>
```

This specification declares the *TextToSpeechConverter* component to expose one service—
TextToSpeechConverter—based on the Java Interface with that same name, provided by bean
GoogleTextToSpeechConverterBean implemented by the Class *GoogleTextToSpeechConverter*.
This class has a method *setContentHandler*. When the bean is instantiated, this property is set
using the reference injected by the SCA engine based on the reference *ContentHandler* exposed
by this Spring component. That means that in order to successfully use this Spring component, we
have to make sure to wire a component to the *ContentHandler* reference, a component that
implements the *ContentHandler* interface.

Publish File to Dropbox

Dropbox provides a cloud-based document service for storing and sharing documents. This
service can be accessed from various devices, using apps and agents and a browser interface.
Additionally, the Dropbox service can be accessed programmatically through a REST API and a
number of SDKs. One of these is a Java SDK. Using this SDK, accessing the Dropbox service for
operations such as upload and download file is very simple.

Getting Ready to Access Dropbox

Just as with Twitter, you need to register the application that will use the Dropbox API. Then each
user whose Dropbox account is to be accessed from that application will have to explicitly
authorize the application. The results from these steps are an application key and secret, and for
each user an access token. The steps are described here: https://www.dropbox.com/developers/
core/start/java.

Next, go to https://www.dropbox.com/developers/core/sdks/java to download the Java SDK for
Dropbox. Add the Dropbox-core-sdk-x.y.z.jar and the Jackson-core-x.y.z.jar to the SCA-INF/lib

folder of the project. Also add both jar files to the project in the Project Properties | Libraries and Classpath page.

To work around a class issue with HttpsURLConnection on WebLogic—note that this does not happen when you run the Dropbox client locally in JDeveloper—you have to make a configuration change in the setDomainEnv.sh or setDomainEnv.bat file in the $DOMAIN_HOME/ bin directory. Add the following system property to the JAVA_OPTIONS (to force WebLogic to use standard Sun's implementation of SSL):

```
JAVA_OPTIONS="${JAVA_OPTIONS} -DUseSunHttpHandler=true"
```

This property only takes effect after a restart of the server.

Creating the Dropbox Java Client

The Java Interface our Dropbox Java Client will implement is a simple one:

```java
public interface DropboxAdapter {

    /**
     * @param fileContents the bytes that for the contents of the file
     * @param fileName the name of the file that should be created on Dropbox
     * @param path the target folder on Dropbox into which the file should be
created (for example /Public)
     * @return the public, shareable URL where the file can be accessed on
Dropbox
     */
    public String writeFileToDropbox( byte[] fileContents, String fileName,
String path);
}
```

The Java class that will do the actual file uploading through the Dropbox Java SDK is implemented as follows:

```java
public class DropboxClient implements DropboxAdapter, ContentHandler {

    private final String accessToken = "YourToken";
    final String APP_KEY = "YourAppKey";
    final String APP_SECRET = "YourAppSecret";

private DbxRequestConfig config ;
    public DropboxClient() {

        DbxAppInfo appInfo = new DbxAppInfo(APP_KEY, APP_SECRET);
        config = new DbxRequestConfig(
            "SaibotAirport0", Locale.getDefault().toString());
    }

    @Override
    public String writeFileToDropbox(byte[] fileContents, String fileName,
String path)  {
        DbxClient client = new DbxClient(config, accessToken);
        String shareableURL="";
```

```
            ByteArrayInputStream contentStream = new ByteArrayInputStream(fileConte
nts);
        try {
            DbxEntry.File uploadedFile = client.uploadFile(path +"/"+fileName,
                DbxWriteMode.add(), fileContents.length, contentStream);
            shareableURL = client.createShareableUrl(uploadedFile.path);
            DbxUrlWithExpiration tempurl = client.createTemporaryDirectUrl(uplo
adedFile.path);
            shareableURL = tempurl.url;
        } catch (DbxException e) { //TODO: implement
        } catch (IOException e) { //TODO: implement
        } finally {
            try {
                contentStream.close();
            } catch (IOException e) { //TODO: implement
            }
        }
        return shareableURL;
    }


    @Override
    public String handleContent(byte[] content, String title) {
        String url = writeFileToDropbox(content, title, "/Public");
        return url;
    }
}
```

Note that this class not only implements the *DropboxAdapter* interface, but also the *ContentHandler* interface that was specified in the previous section and that will be used to have this class process the results from the *TextToSpeechConverter*.

Configure the Dropbox Adapter Spring Component

Create a new Spring Component, called *DropboxAdapter*. Configure the following specification:

```
<bean class="saibot.airport.services.spring.DropboxClient"
id="dropboxAdapterBean" >
</bean>
<sca:service name="DropboxAdapter" target="dropboxAdapterBean" type="saibot.
airport.services.spring.DropboxAdapter" />
```

The component exposes a single service, based on Java Interface *DropboxAdapter* and implemented through the *DropboxClient* Class that is used to define the *dropboxAdapterBean*. Components inside the SOA composite can be wired to this *DropboxAdapterService*. They can pass the contents of files to have them uploaded to a Dropbox folder in the preconfigured account. Before too long, we still create our first wire to this component.

Compose Flight Announcement

The composition of the actual announcement that should be voiced will take a place in a Java class that is embedded in a Spring component that will be invoked from the

MachineToHumanMediator. The class receives a *Flight* object with the details about the latest flight status (this is a Java Bean with a number of properties, included in the on line sources). It uses a helper class to convert a number of values—status, airline—to proper read-out-loud values. This helper class in turn has several dependencies that are satisfied in part by local beans and in part through external references. To the helper class, it makes no difference whether another Spring bean is the provider of a dependency or whether that is a Mediator component (or some other SCA component) wired to the external reference.

The Custom Java Classes for Composing the Flight Announcement

The external interface that is to be exposed for the Announcement Component is:

```java
public interface Announcer {

    public String composeFlightStatusAnnouncement( Flight flight);
}
```

The Java class that implements this interface is fairly simple. In part because it does not create very refined announcements and in part because it engages a helper class—*FlightDetailProvider*—to do some of the heavy lifting:

```java
public class FlightAnnouncementComposer implements Announcer {

    private FlightDetailProvider flightDetailProvider;

    public void setFlightDetailProvider(FlightDetailProvider
flightDetailProvider) {
        this.flightDetailProvider = flightDetailProvider;
    }

    @Override
    public String composeFlightStatusAnnouncement(Flight flight) {
        String airline = flightDetailProvider.getCarrierAnnouncementName(flig
ht.getCarrier());
        String action = flightDetailProvider.getActionAnnouncementTerm(flight.
getAction());
return "Announcement about flight "+flight.getCarrier()+"
"+getSeparateNumbers(flight.getFlightNumber())+" operated by "+airline+
" This flight is "+action;
    }

    private String getSeparateNumbers(String flightNumber) {
        String spelledOutFlightNumber ="";
        for (int i=0;i< flightNumber.length(); i++) {
            spelledOutFlightNumber = spelledOutFlightNumber+ flightNumber.
substring(i,i+1) + " " ;
        }
        return spelledOutFlightNumber;
    }
}
```

The FlightDetailProvider class is defined as follows:

```
public class FlightDetailProvider {
    private ValueMapper airlineMapper;
    private ValueMapper flightActionMapper;

    public void setAirlineMapper(ValueMapper airlineMapper) {
        this.airlineMapper = airlineMapper;
    }

    public void setFlightActionMapper(ValueMapper flightActionMapper) {
        this.flightActionMapper = flightActionMapper;
    }

    public String getCarrierAnnouncementName( String carrier) {
        return airlineMapper.mapValue("carrier", carrier);
    }
    public String getActionAnnouncementTerm( String action) {
        return flightActionMapper.mapValue("flightAction", action);
    }
}
```

The interface ValueMapper:

```
public interface ValueMapper {
    public String mapValue(String domain, String sourceValue);
}
```

And one implementation of the ValueMapper interface is the class:

```
public class FlightActionMapper implements ValueMapper {
    @Override
    public String mapValue(String domain, String sourceValue) {
        String mappedValue = "";
        switch (sourceValue) {
        case "FinalApproach":
            mappedValue = " almost at our airport. It is in its final approach
and ready for touch down shortly. ";
            break;
        case "GateOpen":
            mappedValue = " open for boarding at the gate. ";
            break;
        case "GateClosing":
            mappedValue = " currently closing its door. Final passengers have
to come to the gate immediately. ";
            break;
            ...
        case "AtGate":
            mappedValue = " safely arrived at the gate where off loading will
commence shortly. ";
            break;
        default:
            mappedValue = sourceValue;
```

```
        }
        return mappedValue;
    }
}
```

Spring Component FlightAnnouncementComposer

Create a new Spring component in the SOA composite, called *FlightAnnouncementComposer*. Configure the following beans, service and reference:

```
<bean class="saibot.airport.services.spring.FlightAnnouncementComposer" id="Fl
ightAnnouncementComposerBean">
    <property name="flightDetailProvider">
        <ref bean="FlightDetailProviderBean"/>
    </property>
</bean>
<bean class="saibot.airport.services.spring.FlightDetailProvider"
id="FlightDetailProviderBean">
    <property name="airlineMapper">
        <ref bean="CarrierMapper"/>
    </property>
    <property name="flightActionMapper">
        <ref bean="FlightActionMapperBean"/>
    </property>
</bean>
<bean class="saibot.airport.services.spring.FlightStatusMapper"
id="FlightStatusMapperBean"/>
<sca:service name="FlightAnnouncementComposer" target="FlightAnnouncementC
omposerBean"
            type="saibot.airport.services.spring.Announcer"/>
<sca:reference name="CarrierMapper" type="saibot.airport.services.spring.
ValueMapper"/>
```

The *FlightAnnouncementComposerBean* has a single property whose value is provided by the *FlightDetailProviderBean*. This bean has two properties or two dependencies. One is satisfied by local bean *FlightStatusMapperBean* and the other—*airlineMapper*—is promoted to the level of the sca:reference *CarrierMapper*. This means that the Spring component itself does not have the implementation of the *CarrierMapper* and it relies on the SCA engine to provide such an implementation through the reference. In the next section we will have a mediator wired to this reference, to provide the *CarrierMapper* functionality.

Create a CarrierMapper

The *CarrierMapper* performs a fairly simple task: based on the IATA carrier code, it provides the proper name for an airline to be used in the flight status announcements. That is a task for which the SOA Suite provides an easy solution: the Domain Value Map or DVM that we have encountered in earlier chapters. A DVM defines one or more domains. A domain consists in its simplest form of source values for which a translated or mapped value is provided.

Create a new Domain Value Map Airlines.dvm in the folder DVM. Configure the DVM to have columns *IATACode* and *FullName*. Provide some entries for airlines that you will use later on in your flight status updates. Note that through SOA Composer, the contents of DVMs can be edited at run time.

Create a new mediator called *CarrierMapper* and specify that the interface will be created later on. When this mediator is later on wired from the *CarrierMapper* reference in the *FlightAnnouncementComposer* component, it will get its interface defined. At that moment, a routing rule will be defined that is next configured to leverage the DVM.

Extend TwitterChannel to Publish Updates

The Java class *TwitterClient* has to be extended to also publish status updates, that is, tweet messages. And, in order to make this new functionality available to other components in the SOA composite, we have to extend an existing or define a new Java Interface that is specified in the Spring component's definition file.

We choose to create a new Java Interface:

```java
public interface TwitterStatusUpdater {
    void updateStatus(String message);
}
```

The class TwitterClient is modified to also implement this interface:

```java
public class TwitterClient implements TwitterMessageSender,
TwitterStatusUpdater {

    @Override
    public void updateStatus(String message) {
        Twitter sender = constructTwitterInstance();
        try {
            sender.updateStatus(message);
        } catch (TwitterException e) {
            e.printStackTrace();
            if (logger!=null) {
                logger.log(Level.WARNING, "Failed to update Twitter Status",e);
            }
        }
    }
}
```

Then the Spring component definition file TwitterChannel.xml is updated with this new definition:

```xml
 <sca:service name="Tweeter" target="twitterMessageMaster" type="saibot.
airport.services.spring.TwitterStatusUpdater" />
```

This defines the Spring component to publish a second service, described by the *TwitterStatusUpdater* interface and provided by the *twitterMessageMaster* bean (that is based on the *TwitterClient* class).

Wiring the Pieces Together

The composite application now looks as is shown in Figure 10-10. The new components *DropboxAdapter, TextToSpeechConverter,* and *FlightAnnouncementComposer* stand ready to be engaged. Notice how the latter two do not only expose services to be invoked but also references to be injected.

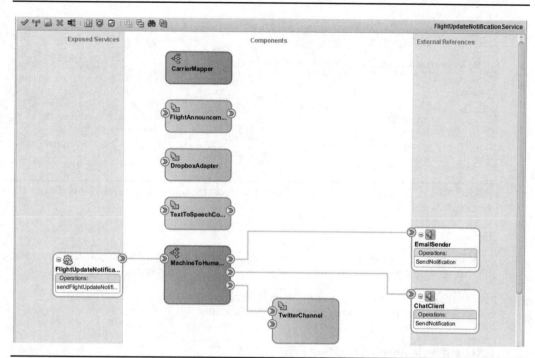

FIGURE 10-10.   *FlightUpdateNotificationService SOA composite prior to wiring the components together*

Create Wires to and from the FlightAnnouncementComposer

Wire *CarrierMapper* to *FlightAnnouncementComposer*, to fulfill the requirement from the latter to have a *ValueMapper* implementation that will take a string value (with in this case the IATA code for a carrier) and turn it into the name of the airline as it should be used in spoken announcements. When this wire is created, JDeveloper will generate the ValueMapper.wsdl file that describes in web services terminology what the Java Interface *ValueMapper* entails. The WSDL file contains the XSD definition of the input to and output from the *mapValue* method that *CarrierMapper* mediator is promising to implement.

Open the editor for mediator *CarrierMapper*. Add a routing rule of type *Echo Reply*. Click on the icon for Assign Values. Drag an expression to the mapValueResponse/return element in the output, as shown in Figure 10-11. Double click on the expression icon to bring up the editor. Set the expression to:

```
dvm:lookupValue('DVM/Airlines.dvm','IATACode', $in.parameters/tns:mapValue/
arg1,'FullName', $in.parameters/tns:mapValue/arg1)
```

Here we specify how the return value is derived using the Domain Value Map Airlines.dvm with the source value—the IATA code for an airline—and locating the corresponding FullName in the DVM. If the airline cannot be found in the DVM, we will stick to the input code as the next best thing for the return value.

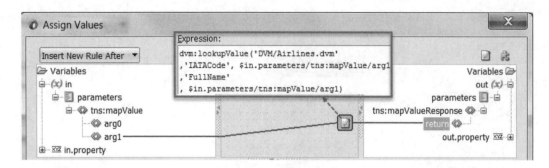

FIGURE 10-11. *Specify how the response from mediator CarrierMapper is derived from the input and the DVM*

Wire Spring component *FlightAnnouncementComposer* to mediator *MachineToHumanMediator*. This creates a new routing rule in the latter. Set the filter condition on this routing rule to

```
$in.in/tns:sendFlightUpdateNotificationRequestMessage/
tns:CommunicationMetadata/tns:Channel='audio'
```

TextToSpeechConverter

The *TextToSpeechConverter* exposes a reference that should implement the *ContentHandler* interface. The *contenthandler* that is injected will be invoked after the MP3 has been generated, to take good care of the audio stream. The handler will return a string that can be seen as a claim to the audio content that it has been stored somewhere. In our scenario, this will be a URL to the MP3 file as it has been uploaded to the Public folder in the *Saibot Airport Dropbox* account.

Instead of wiring the *DropboxAdapter* directly to the *TextToSpeechConverter*, we will use a mediator in between. One reason is that the interface exposed by the *DropboxAdapter* may well not be a precise match to the interface required by the reference on the *TextToSpeechConverter*. Another reason is that in a mediator we can add additional routing rules to also route the MP3 content to other handlers.

Create mediator *MP3Router* and indicate that the *Interface will be created later*. Create a wire from the reference on *TextToSpeechConverter* to this *MP3Router* component. At this point, the interface ContentHandler.wsdl will be generated. As far as the *TextToSpeechConverter* is concerned, its dependency has been satisfied now. The buck has passed to the *MP3Router*, to handle the audio content.

The *DropboxAdapter* is of course the component we have in mind to receive the MP3 data and store them in the Public folder. Wire the reference on the *MP3Router* to the service on the *DropboxAdapter*—as is shown in Figure 10-12. JDeveloper will generate the DropboxAdapter. wsdl document to describe what the *DropboxAdapter* has to offer.

We need to configure the routing rule in the *MP3Router* mediator to make the output from the *TextToSpeechConverter* fit the input of the *DropboxAdapter*. Open the mediator editor for *MP3Router*. Open the Assign Values dialog for the routing rule, see Figure 10-13. Wire the arg0 element in the input (as described by the ContentHandler interface) to the arg0 (file contents) element in the out

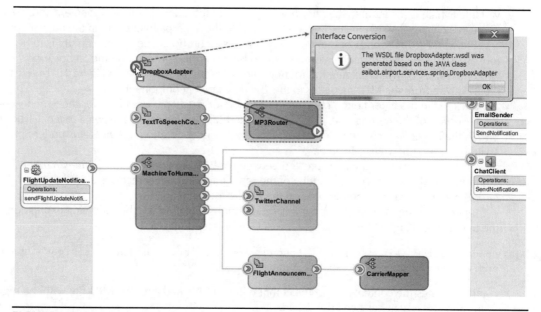

FIGURE 10-12.   *Creating the wire between MP3Router and DropboxAdapter*

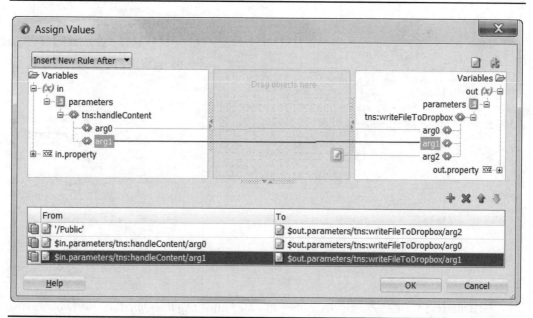

FIGURE 10-13.   *Setting the values to be passed to the Dropbox adapter*

variable (which is the input to the *DropboxAdapter*). Do the same for the arg1 element and the arg1 (filename) element. Assign the expression "/Public" to the arg2 (path) element in the out variable.

The *writeFileToDropbox* operation is a two way synchronous operation. Its reply is to be forwarded to the *TwitterChannel* component, to be turned into a Tweet on the *SaibotAirport* twitter stream. We will configure the routing rule accordingly, as shown in Figure 10-14. First, create a wire from the MP3 mediator to the *TwitterChannel* component.

Back in the mediator editor, click on the *Browse for Target Services* icon for the Synchronous Reply section of the routing rule. In the popup titled Target Type select *Existing Service*. Click on OK. In the Target Service browser that appears next, select operation *updateStatus* under Springs | TwitterChannel | Services | Tweeter.

When you click OK, a wire is created between the *MP3Router* and the *TwitterChannel* components. This visualizes the routing of the reply the *MP3Router* receives after the *DropboxAdapter* has put the MP3 file on the Public folder.

Open the Assign Values dialog for this synchronous reply. Assign the following expression to the updateStatus/arg0 child element in the out variable:

```
concat('Saibot Airport Flight Announcement was published at ',$in.parameters/
tns:writeFileToDropboxResponse/return)
```

This defines the contents of the Tweet that will be published after the MP3 file with the flight status announcement has been published.

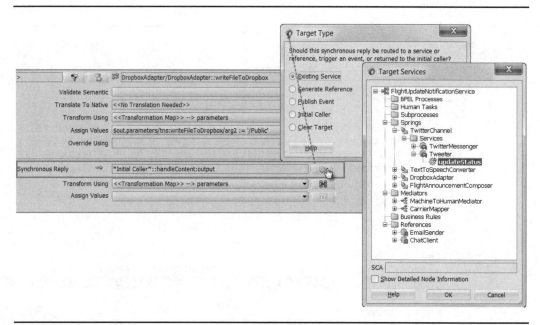

FIGURE 10-14. *Configuring the routing rule for forwarding the reply from the DropboxAdapter to the Tweeter component's updateStatus operation*

Route the Announcement to the TextSpeechConverter

We have strung together the *TextToSpeechConverter, MP3Router, DropboxAdapter,* and *TwitterChannel* components. However, this string does not yet have a happy beginning. For that to happen, we have to configure the routing rule for the *audio* channel in the *MachineToHumanMediator*. First, create a wire from the mediator to the *TextToSpeechConverter* component. Then open the editor for the mediator. Configure the target service for the synchronous reply on the "audio" routing rule to be the *TextToSpeechConverter*—the operation *convertTextToSpeechAndHandle* to be exact.

Use the Assign Values dialog to set the input values for the *TextToSpeechConverter*. The text element is to be derived from the `composeFlightStatusAnnouncementResponse/return` element returned from the *FlightAnnouncementComposer* component. Set the language and title to "en" and "FlightAnnouncement.mp3," respectively.

TIP
In the Assign Values dialog, we cannot use data from the original request message to set values in the message based on the forwarded reply. However, when we use a transformation, we can use the original request as a source next to the response message that is being forwarded. That would allow us, for example, to define a filename that contains the flight number of the flight that the announcement is about.

File Adapter to Locally Write the MP3 File

In addition to the MP3 file that is put on the Dropbox, it may be convenient to also create that MP3 file locally. Using the File Adapter, it is of course very straightforward to create such a local file.

Drag a File Adapter to the External Reference swim lane in the composite editor, as shown in Figure 10-15. Set the name to *MP3Writer*. Accept the default JNDI name. Select the *Write* operation. On the File Configuration page in the File Adapter wizard, select *Logical Name* for the Directory and set the logical name as MP3_ANNOUNCEMENTS_FOLDER. Set the File Naming convention to FlightAnnouncement.mp3—or any arbitrary value, because we will dynamically set the file name. Set the number of messages per file to 1.

On the Messages, check the checkbox for *Native format transformation is not required* (Schema is Opaque). The contents of the file is binary—and no attempt should be made by the File Adapter to transform that binary data in any way. Click Next and click Finish to complete the File Adapter configuration.

Next, create a wire from mediator *MP3Router* to this File Adapter. This adds a second routing rule to the mediator, to carry the MP3 data received from the *TextToSpeechConverter* to a second target. Open the mediator editor to configure the data mapping for this routing rule. Click on the Assign Values icon for the routing rule. Wire element handleContent/arg0 in the *in* variable to the *opaqueElement* in the out variable. Assign the value from element handleContent/arg1 to the header property $out.property.jca.file.FileName.

In the composite editor, [single] click on the MP3Writer (Figure 10-16). Ensure the properties palette is displayed. Open the tab Composite Properties. This tab presents the property MP3_ANNOUNCEMENTS_FOLDER—the logical name of the directory into which the file adapter should deposit the files it writes. Set an appropriate value for your local environment for this property. The value you define is saved in the composite.xml file.

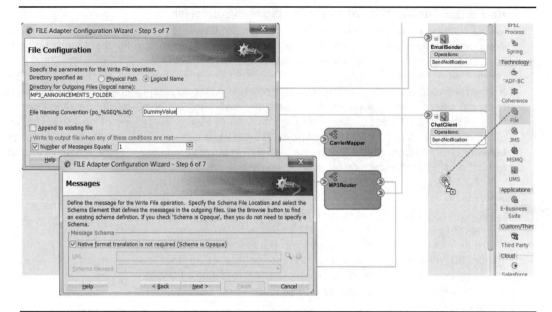

FIGURE 10-15. *Add an outbound File Adapter binding to write raw binary input to a file*

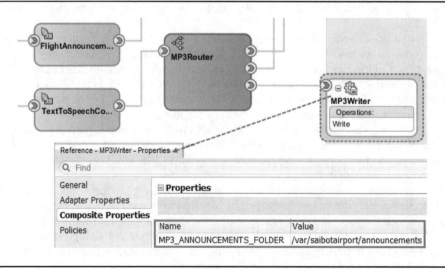

FIGURE 10-16. *Set a value for the property MP3_ANNOUNCEMENTS_FOLDER*

TIP
After deployment, the value of this and other properties can be modified in the Enterprise Manager FMW Control, on the Properties tab for the specific component under the FlightUpdateUpdateNotificationService composite—as discussed in detail in Chapter 23.

The Complete End-to-End Audio Channel

With the steps described in the previous sections, we now have an SOA composite that implements an audio channel to announce flight status updates in the form of audio that can be fed to the Airport's PA system. Figure 10-17 shows the composite and highlights the flow for the audio channel through the composite.

It starts with the routing rule for the *audio* channel in the *MachineToHumanMediator*. This rule routes the flight status message to the *FlightAnnouncementComposer* (1). This Spring component makes use of the *CarrierMapper* mediator with DVM inside to derive the full name of the airline (2). The announcement is passed back to the *MachineToHumanMediator* that forwards it to the *TextToSpeechConvertor* (3). This Spring component generates the MP3 file and passes it to the injected *MP3Router* component (4). This mediator calls the *DropboxAdapter* to create a file in the Public Dropbox folder and return the URL for that file (5). The *MP3Router* forwards this reply from the *DropboxAdapter* to the *TwitterChannel* component (6), to publish a Tweet on the SaibotAirport twitter stream.

The *MP3Router* also calls the file adapter *MP3Writer* (7) with the content received from the *TextToSpeechConverter*, to write the MP3 file on a local environment. By configuring the routing

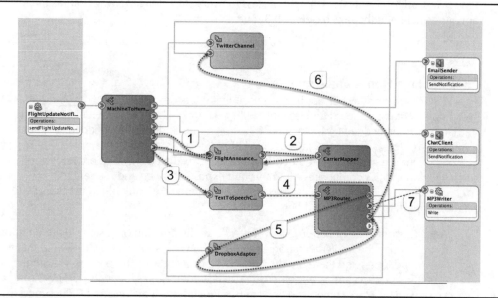

FIGURE 10-17. *The FlightUpdateNotificationService composite with the entire flow for the audio channel*

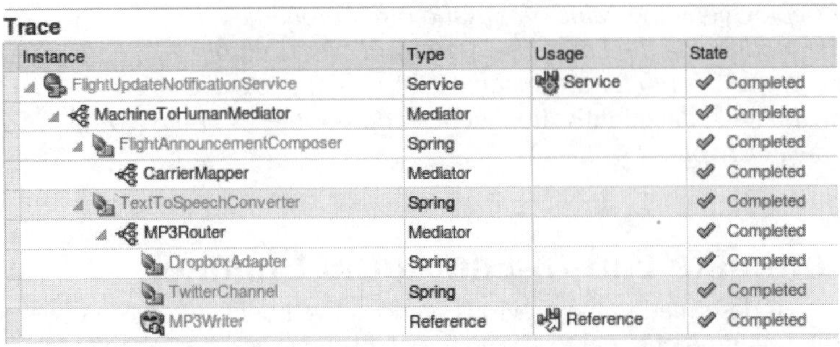

Trace

Instance	Type	Usage	State
▲ 🔷 FlightUpdateNotificationService	Service	🔹 Service	✓ Completed
▲ 🔶 MachineToHumanMediator	Mediator		✓ Completed
▲ 🔹 FlightAnnouncementComposer	Spring		✓ Completed
🔶 CarrierMapper	Mediator		✓ Completed
▲ 🔹 TextToSpeechConverter	Spring		✓ Completed
▲ 🔶 MP3Router	Mediator		✓ Completed
🔹 DropboxAdapter	Spring		✓ Completed
🔹 TwitterChannel	Spring		✓ Completed
🔷 MP3Writer	Reference	🔹 Reference	✓ Completed

FIGURE 10-18. *The message flow trace for the audio channel route through FlightUpdateNotificationService*

rule filters on the *MP3Router*, we can disable or enable one or both routes for the MP3 file, for example, to try to the generation of the MP3 files before publishing these files to the world.

Deploy the SOA composite. Invoke the service exposed by the composite with some made-up combination of flight data. The results of your call should be manifold:

- An MP3 file put on the Public folder in Dropbox
- A Tweet published with a URL referring to the file in the Dropbox
- A local MP3 file with the same contents as the one on the Dropbox

and of course an SOA composite instance with a full message flow trace to be inspected in the EM FWM Control (Figure 10-18), with access to every step along the way such as the text of the announcement and the raw, base64 MP3 data.

Other Java Hooks and Crannies

The SOA Suite is a Java EE application itself that offers developers many opportunities to complement the standard functionality with customized behavior implemented using Java. Call outs to embedded Java—in Service Bus pipelines and using Embedded Java activities in BPEL—as well as to external Java code—EJB, JMS—are but simple examples. The Spring component is a great way to embed Java in an encapsulated way that provides good integration in SOA composites, both through exposed service and references.

Several other options for Java based customizations are available in the SOA Suite. The most important ones are listed here:

- *Custom XPath function:* SOA Suite allows the creation of custom XPath functions through the implementation and registration of a simple Java Class. Such XPath functions—and therefore the underlying Java code—can be invoked from Service Bus projects and SOA composites, in XSL-Maps and XQuery transformations as well as in assignments in Service Bus Pipelines, Mediators, and BPEL processes.

- *Mediator Callout:* Associated with an Operation in a Mediator can be Java Callout class that has to implement the IJavaCallout interface or for convenience can extend from class AbstractJavaCalloutImpl. In the callout, the headers, payload and properties can be inspected, validated, and manipulated both before the routing takes place and after the response from the target service comes in.

- *File Adapter Valve:* A File Adapter binding—both inbound and outbound—can be configured with one or more Valves: custom Java classes that implement the interface Valve or StagedValve or—to make life easier—simply extend from AbstractValve. These classes perform pre-processing of the file content (on the inbound side) before it enters the file adapter proper or post processing (outbound) on the content that has left the file adapter before it is written to the file system. Valves can be used for file processing operations like decrypt/encrypt, decompress/compress and transformation.

- *Custom OWSM Policy* (attached at the very edge of service implementations): In Chapter 24, we will discuss security and the role of OWSM (Oracle Web Service Manager) policies in the protection of inbound or outbound services and references, for both Service Bus services and SOA composites. In addition to all out of the box policies, we can add custom policies and use custom Java Classes for the implementation of such policies. These policies live and execute on the very edge of the service—either before the service is even entered (inbound) or at the very last moment before the request message is sent to an external service (outbound). Policies can be used to inspect the contents of messages and also to manipulate the said contents. When all else fails, extreme pre- and post-processing of messages can therefore be implemented using custom policies.

- *Custom JCA Adapter:* The JCA adapter framework is a generic Java EE facility in WebLogic that Oracle itself has made use of to create and integrate the various JCA adapters we have met—JMS, UMS, Database, AQ, File, and FTP. We can also create our own JCA adapter—using custom Java classes and adhering to the rules of the JCA framework. For example, an outbound adapter that publishes files to Dropbox, as an alternative to the out of the box File and FTP adapters would be valid to create. Or an inbound adapter that polls a particular RSS feed or Twitter stream and triggers new composite instances when an entry is found that satisfies certain conditions.

Summary

The SOA Suite ships with a large collection of out of the box features and functions, catering for many situations, requirements, and interactions. However, there will still be the occasional challenge where the shipped components do not do the job at hand. For those situations, the SOA Suite offers developers many options to complement, customize, and extend the default platform through the use of custom Java logic. Embedded Java, Java Callouts, Custom Java based Security policies, Custom JCA Adapters, Custom XPath functions are some examples of such extension points.

The Spring component is another way of introducing custom Java classes into SOA composite application. Such Java classes can perform virtually any specific custom function imaginable, using third party libraries if needed, configured according to the Spring framework. Selected operations from the Spring content can be exposed as [SCA] services that can be invoked by other components in the composite application. Some dependencies can similarly be exposed as [SCA] references, which can be satisfied through wires to other components in the composite application. Through these references, it becomes easy to inject a mediator, BPEL component, or any JCA adapter into a custom Java class, where it will be accessed through a standard Java interface, in the same way as any other Spring bean. The Spring context component is capable of working with Groovy and AspectJ classes just as well as regular Spring beans.

Using custom Java classes should not be your first option. Using out of the box functionality is the preferred alternative—when available. Such functionality is better integrated, has been tested, probably performs better, and will be easier to upgrade. However, when the standard platform capabilities do not suffice, the use of the Spring context and the other Java extension options almost always ensure a way forward.

CHAPTER
11

Business Rules to Capture Business Logic to Automate Decisions

S OA composite applications contain various forms of logic. These have some overlap, but they also have their own specific actors, implementation technologies, and maintenance cycles. There is, of course, implementation logic written by programmers in programming languages such as BPEL, XPath and XSLT, Java, and even PL/SQL. There is also process logic, designed perhaps using the Business Process Analysis Suite, modeled in BPMN or BPEL by business analysts.

Another type of logic is business logic—describing and implementing derivations, validations, calculations, and other business rules. Frequently this last type of logic is described by the analysts—in free format text—and then implemented by developers as part of the programs they write. It is fairly common to find the implementation of business logic done in several places in the application using hard-coded values and references. The business logic cannot easily be told apart from the implementation logic of the computer program, cannot be modified without the help of the programmers, and cannot be deployed without redeploying the entire application. This is a problem since business logic—especially business rules tend to change in a faster pace than other logic.

This chapter introduces the Decision Service component in SOA Suite, also known as the Business Rule service component. We will use the name Business Rule from now on. This type of component implements business logic and exposes it as an SCA component that can easily be integrated into other components such as BPEL processes, Human Workflows, and Mediators. This business logic can also be invoked through a Java API. Implementing business logic in a central, encapsulated, reusable component makes it much easier to manage and maintain and actually reuse such logic.

Oracle Business Rules is very good at evaluating the business logic expressed in the special RL (Rule Language) language—with high performance and good scalability, especially compared to alternative implementations of the same logic in, for example, XPath. Business rules created within SOA composite applications usually work with the RL language, which allows definition of rules in a very declarative way that is even accessible to non-programming business analysts. The run-time infrastructure—through the SOA Composer tool—allows editing the business logic after the application has been deployed, contributing to business agility, because the frequency with which this type of logic changes is typically different from—and usually higher than—the frequency in which the other types of logic change. It is a huge boon to be able to modify business rules at run time without redeploying your process.

We will meet the Business Rule component in this chapter and see how business rules can be implemented and integrated in composite applications or exposed as elementary services. In part 5, when we discuss [business] processes, we will discuss the Business Rule component again—to encapsulate the decision logic required to steer the process flow.

Calculating the Airport Charge for a Flight—Round One

The calculation of the airport charge for a particular flight is not trivial. Various considerations play a part in the airport charge, including regulations, scarce resources, long-term strategy and short-term stimuli and of course the fierce competition in the airport market. The formulas for calculating the charge are fairly complex and are susceptible to frequent change and to business driven exceptions. The documents describing the calculation of the charge are frequently lengthy and contain many if/then clauses. The IT architects at Saibot Airport were quick to realize that a business rule is a good way of implementing the business logic that calculates the charge. The business rule encapsulates the derivation logic for the charge, makes it easy to reuse and gives the business easy access to the key parameters driving the calculation.

In its bare form, the airport charge is calculated based on the weight of the aircraft, using the following formula: if the weight is under 20,000 kg, then the charge is (currently) set at 94 euros. Else the charge is calculated as 4.70 euro per 1000 kg of weight. In two iterations we will later on introduce considerations around cargo versus passengers, noise category of the aircraft, time of the day and landing versus take off.

Prepare SOA Composite Application

Create a new SOA composite application with a SOA project called *AirportCharge*. Create it as initially empty. Add the file AirportChargeCalculation.xsd to the Schemas folder. Then drag a Business Rule component from the component palette to the composite editor. When you drop it, the dialog shown in Figure 11-1 appears. Set the name of the business rule component to *AirportChargeArbiter*. Set the package to saibot.airport.finance.airportcharge. Define an input parameter called *Flight*, based on the *FlightType* in the XSD file. Also define an output parameter called *AirportCharge* based on the *AirportChargeType* in said XSD file. Click OK to complete the creation of the business rule component and its associated rule dictionary.

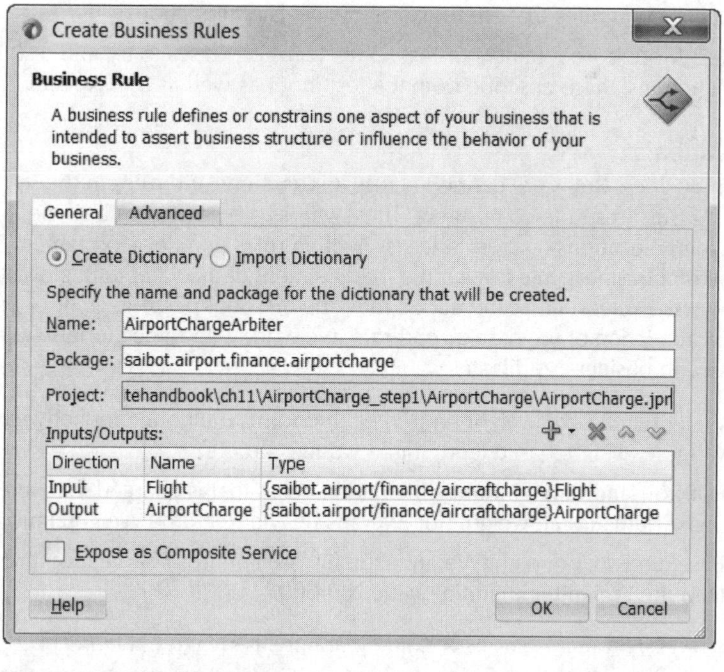

FIGURE 11-1.   *Initial creation of the AirportChargeArbiter business rule component*

Implement Business Rule

Double click on the business rule component in the SOA composite editor to start refining the details for this business rule dictionary, in order to provide the business logic behind this *AirportChargeArbiter* component.

The dictionary consists of a number of elements:

- Facts and their properties—the definitions of the business entities that are evaluated and manipulated by the rules; the input and output defined for the Business Rule component—based on XSD types—resulted in Fact definition. Additional Facts can be added—based on Java Classes, XSD Types, RL (Rule Language) definitions or ADF BC View Objects.

- Functions—encapsulated logic expressed in RL; a number of predefined functions are available by default

- Globals—constants with a name and a value; these globals can be referenced throughout rule definitions by their logical name that at run time is substituted with their value. Updating the business logic can be as simple as changing the value of a global

- Value Sets—named lists of allowable values that are associated with properties in facts; a value set association can be used for validation of input facts (at run time) and can be used at design time for quick rule editing and for conflict analysis on decision tables

- Decision Functions—special functions that define the external interface of the Business Rule dictionary in terms of rule sets, input and output facts and initializations

- Rules Sets with General (if/then) Rules and Decision Tables—the actual decision logic captured in rules that are triggered by Decision Functions

- Test Models—containers of Test Suites with Test Cases to try and test the logic in Decision Functions; these describe both the test input as well as the expected outcome

Define Globals

Globals in Business Rules are defined across all functions and rules in the dictionary created for a single [SCA] Business Rule component. These values are defined in a single location and can be reused in many locations—across rule sets, if-then rules and decision tables. The most common refinement of a business rule is a simple readjustment of the value of a global that is used as a parameter in the rule, such as the cut off rate, the discount percentage or upper limit.

In the calculation of the base airport rate, we work with three globals—that can easily be modified when business so dictates:

- WeightLimit—the weight limit in kg that forms the boundary between the flat fee and the variable, weight based feed; initial value is 20,000.

- PerThousandKilogramRate—the rate in euros that is charged for every 1000 kg MTOW (maximum aircraft weight) for aircrafts heavier than the WeightLimit; initial value is 4.70.

- BaseRateForUnderLimitWeight—the flat fee in euros charged for aircrafts with less weight than the WeightLimit; initial value is 94.00.

Define these *globals* in the Business Rule dictionary as shown in Figure 11-2.

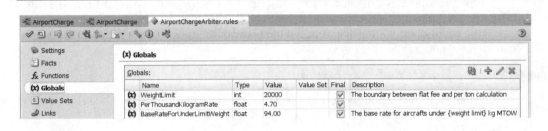

FIGURE 11-2.   *Defining global business parameters that are to be referenced in business rules*

Facts Generated from Schema

Click on the Facts tab. This tab contains all fact types that we can base variables on in the business rule dictionary. These fact types can be defined in four categories: based on XML Types, on Java Classes, on ADF BC ViewObjects and defined as native Business Rule Fact. When facts are used in the decision function that is exposed as web service, they should be XML facts. For internal functions, other fact types can be used as well.

When we initially created the business rule with input and output based on the elements in the schema definition AirportChargeCalculation.xsd, facts were immediately generated based on the underlying XSD types *AirportChargeType* and *FlightType*, as shown in Figure 11-3. You may change the name of the aliases for the facts and their properties—to bring them more in line with the business terminology that you want to use in the business rule definitions. However, if the XSD definition was created in business friendly terms there is little need for making changes here.

If you click on the edit icon, you can inspect and change the details for the fact types and their attributes.

IF/Then Rule Set to Calculate the Base Rate

We will work initially with two rule sets: one to calculate the base rate, based on the weight of the aircraft and the second to calculate the total charge. At this moment, the total charge is equal to the base rate. In the next section, we will make the calculation a little more realistic by introducing several surcharges.

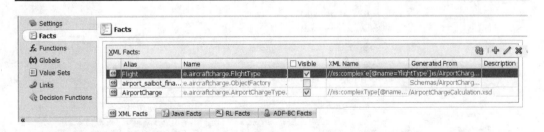

FIGURE 11-3.   *The XML facts generated from the XSD types on which the input and output are based*

Open the Rule Sets tab. Click on the initial rule set. Change its name to *CalculateBaseRate*. Click on the green plus sign under General Rules to add a simple If/Then rule, as shown in Figure 11-4.

The editor opens for the new rule. Set the name of the rule to *UnderWeightLimit*. Enter a *simple test* under IF. Set the test equal to:

```
Flight.aircraftMTOW < WeightLimit
```

using the code completion support to select the aircraftMTOW property on the Flight Fact as well as the global WeightLimit.

Set the THEN action to:

```
Assert new AirportCharge( baseRate: BaseRateForUnderLimitWeight,
totalCharge:0)
```

Click on the green plus icon to create a second IF/THEN rule. This second rule will trigger when the aircraft's MTOW is equal to or larger than the WeightLimit. When that happens, it will assert a new AirportCharge fact with the baseRate set to

```
PerThousandKilogramRate*Flight.aircraftMTOW/1000
```

Figure 11-5 shows these two rules.

Now create a second Rule Set called *CalculateTotalCharge*. Add a single IF/THEN rule.

This rule is triggered by the assertion of the new *AirportCharge* fact by one of the rules in the previous rule set.

Set the IF condition to

```
AirportCharge.totalCharge == 0
```

And the THEN action to

```
assign.AirportCharge.totalCharge = AirportCharge.baseRate
```

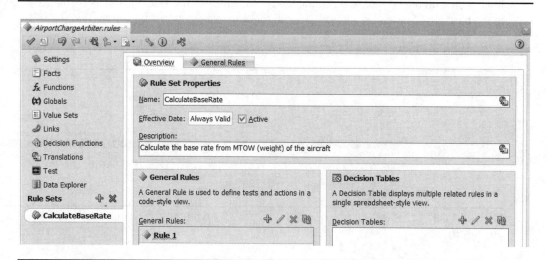

FIGURE 11-4. *Create rule set CalculateBaseRate with a first If/Then Rule*

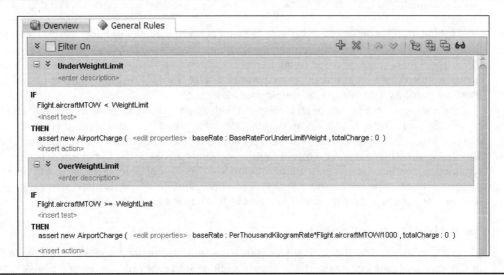

FIGURE 11-5. *The two IF/THEN rules in the CalculateBaseRate rule set*

These steps are shown in Figure 11-6.

This simple calculation will be replaced with a more complex one that involves surcharge percentages in a later section.

Edit the Generated Decision Function

Rule Sets cannot be invoked directly. We can create decision functions in the business rule dictionary that can trigger rule sets. In fact, when we first created the business rule component, a default decision function was generated, called DecisionService_1. Click on the tab labeled

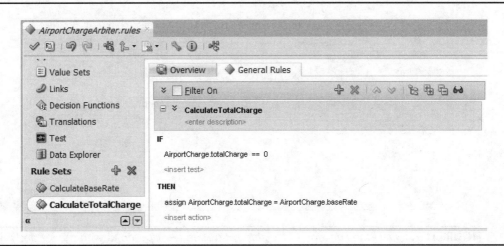

FIGURE 11-6. *The rule CalculateTotalCharge to calculate the final charge for an aircraft movement*

Decision Functions. Change the name of the generated function into *CalculateAirportCharge*, see Figure 11-7.

This function is configured to be exposed with a [web] service interface, as you can tell from the checked checkbox labeled Web Service. Through this interface, other components—Mediator, BPEL, and BPMN—can be wired to the Business Rule. It is recommended to not expose the Business Rule component directly as an external service from the SOA composite, but to always use a Mediator as wrapper around the Business Rule.

The decision function has been configured with an input parameter—called Flight and based on the Flight Fact Type. It also has an output parameter called after and based on the AirportCharge Fact Type. The tab *Rule Sets & Decision Functions* contains the collection of Rule Sets that is to be triggered when this decision function is invoked. The initial rule set—now renamed to CalculateBaseRate is listed. Add the Rule Set CalculateTotalCharge to the selected set on the right side. Now, when this function is invoked, after the Flight fact has been asserted, both Rule Sets are active to be triggered. Click on OK to close the Decision Function editor.

Test the Business Rule

It is pretty simple to take the decision function for a spin. Testing facilities are integrated in the design time environment for the business rule dictionary. We do not have to deploy the SOA composite before we can check out the implemented functionality.

On the Decision Functions tab, click on the decision function *CalculateAirportCharge*. Click on the Test icon, as shown in Figure 11-8. In the test editor pop up, click on the green plus icon to create a new test suite. Assign a probable name. Then click OK to return to the table with test suites. Select the new test suite and click on the edit icon.

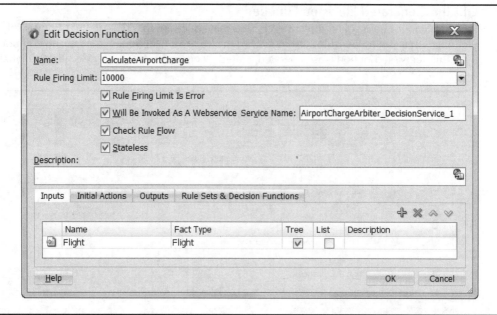

FIGURE 11-7. *Decision Function CalculateAirportCharge—exposed as web service and associated with two rule sets*

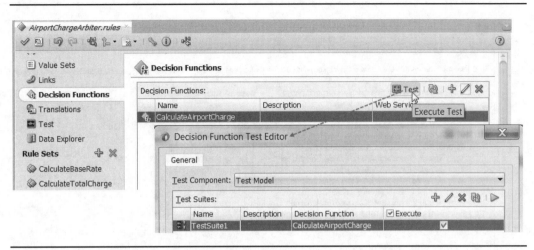

FIGURE 11-8. *Create a Test Suite for the CalculateAirportCharge rule set*

This brings up the Test Suite editor. Click on the green plus icon in the test case table to create a new test case. Indicate in the name of this test case that it handles about an under-the-weight-limit aircraft. Then edit the test case by setting values for both the input Flight fact—aircraftMTOW : 15000 and numberOfPassengers : 150—and the expected output AirportCharge fact—baseRate and totalCharge both equal to the global BaseRateForUnderLimitWeight, as shown in Figure 11-9.

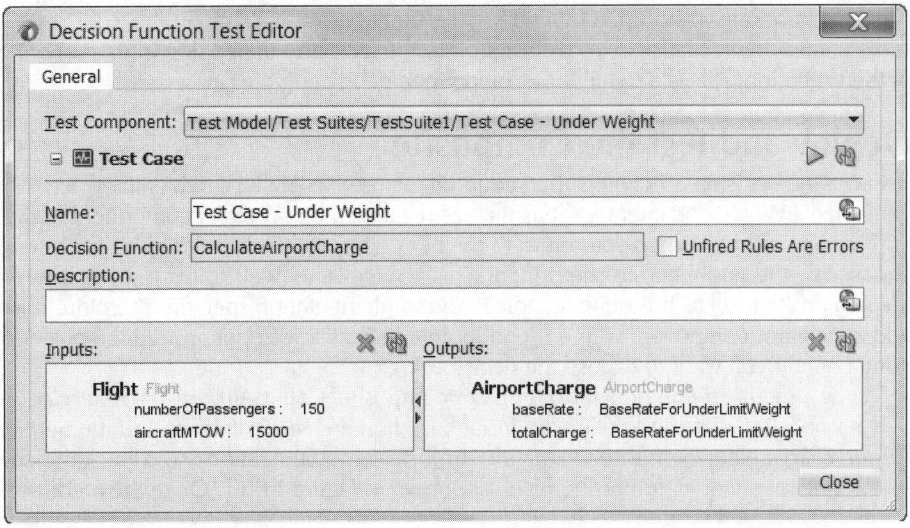

FIGURE 11-9. *Configuration of the Under Weight test case*

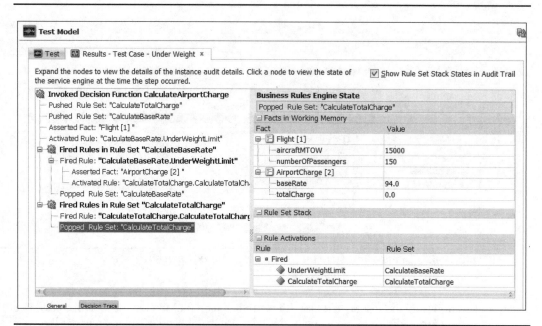

FIGURE 11-10. *Execution trace for the CalculeAirportCharge decision function*

Click on the green play icon to execute this test case. The result should be a passed test case, as well as an interesting trace of the execution of the test case, as shown in Figure 11-10. This overview makes it clear what exactly went on during the execution of the decision function. Note: It should be read inside-out, where first rule UnderWeightLimit in the rule set CalculateBaseRate was fired, followed by rule CalculateTotalCharge in the Rule Set with that same name. The trace also gives us insight into the facts and their value in memory at each stage of the execution. This is a tremendous help when debugging the rules.

Deploy and Test the Composite

Because the decision function is marked to be exposed as a web service, JDeveloper has generated a WSDL document for it as well as registered it as an SCA component in the component.xml file. When you return to the SOA composite editor, you will see a service exposed by the business rule component. This service is not well suited to be exposed directly at the composite level as it is quite technical and implementation specific. Therefore it is useful to add a mediator component with a friendlier interface as a wrapper around the business rule component if you want to expose the decision logic.

Drag a mediator component to the SOA composite. Call it *AirportChargeService*. Select the Synchronous Interface and define the input based on the *Flight* element and the output on the *AirportCharge* element in the schema file AirportChargeCalulcation.xsd. Check the checkbox to expose the mediator at composite level, as shown in Figure 11-11. Once the mediator is added to

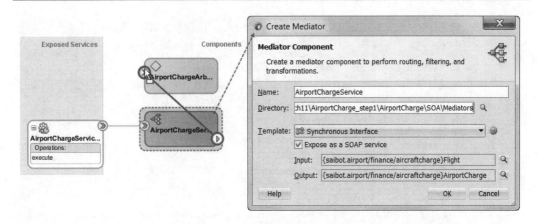

FIGURE 11-11.   *Edit the new mediator and wire it to the business rule AirportChargeArbiter*

the composite, wire it to the business rule component and connect it to the operation *callFunctionStateless*.

Double click the mediator to bring up the editor. Open the Assign Values dialog for the request step in the routing rule. Map the *Flight* element in the input to the corresponding *Flight* element in the *parameterList* element. Also configure Assign Values for the reply. Set the *AirportCharge* element in the output based on the corresponding element in the *resultList* element in the reply from operation *callFunctionStateless*.

Deploy the SOA composite to the Integrated WLS. When the deployment is complete, make a few test calls from for example the HttpAnalyzer or SoapUI. You can check the message flow trace and audit trail in the Enterprise Manager FMW Control; the output is similar to what the test case produced earlier in Figure 11-10.

Extend Business Rule with Cargo Consideration

Now suppose—as is the case for many airports around the world—that the airport charge is lower for cargo planes than for passenger flights. In that case our calculation of the base rate has to be adjusted. First of all, we introduce a new global that defines the number of passengers that is the maximum for a flight to be still considered a cargo flight. This number could be zero, but we could also allow a few passengers and still charge the flight as a cargo flight.

Define this new global of type int, called *MaxNumberOfPassengersOnCargoFlight*. Set the value to 5 for now.

Open the rule set *CalculateBaseRate*. Add a rule called *CargoCorrection* like this (and as shown in Figure 11-12):

```
IF Flight.numberOfPassengers <= MaxNumberOfPassengersOnCargoFlight
THEN modify AirportCharge ( baseRate: Airport.baseRate/2)
```

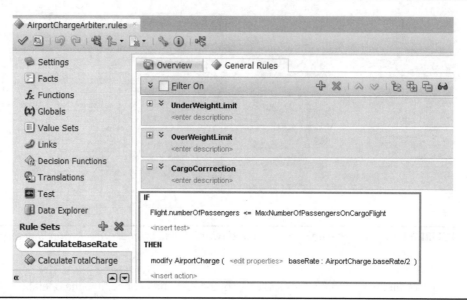

FIGURE 11-12. *Add the If/Then rule CargoCorrect*

Create a new test case in the test suite for the decision function *CalculateAirportCharge* for a flight with 5 or less passengers. Verify that the calculated charge is half of the value previously expected. Also check the trace to confirm that the new rule *CargoCorrection* is indeed executed.

You may want to deploy the composite and verify that the *AirportChargeService* now exhibits the modified behavior when it comes to cargo flights.

Use SOA Composer for Online Manipulation of Business Rule Parameters

The SOA Composer tool is a browser based tool that allows run-time access to a number of aspects of SOA composites, including Domain Value Maps, Composite Sensors, and Business Rules. On the Integrated WLS and running against JavaDB, the SOA Composer will only allow read only access to these definitions. On the full server install with the Oracle Database backed MDS, business rules and other definitions can be manipulated as well. That means that without having to open JDeveloper to change the business rule and deploy the modified composite, the business rule logic can be edited at run time. Changing global values, for example, is very simple to do. Rolling out new airport rates per 1000 kg MTOW, for example, is done in minutes, as is setting the new cut off weight or the flat fee for aircrafts below that cut off weight.

The URL for this tool on the Integrated WLS is http://localhost:7101/soa/composer.

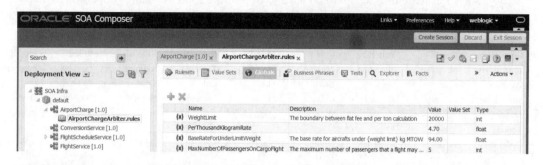

FIGURE 11-13. *Inspecting and possibly editing the values of globals or other aspects of business rule definitions through the SOA Composer*

When you open the SOA Composer on the full server installation, you can change, for example, the global *PerThousandKilogramRate* that is crucial in calculating the airport charge for heavy airplanes (see Figure 11-13). Open an edit session, change the global's value, commit the session and reinvoke the *AircraftChargeService* to see the effect of the changed value.

Introduction of the Decision Table

Business logic can be quite complex. Up until now in this chapter, we have seen fairly simple, straightforward IF/THEN rule sets with a limited number of variations. However, it is not hard to imagine more convoluted rules, for situations where multiple dimensions influence the outcome and several options may apply along each dimension. The decision table–style rule set in Oracle Business Rules helps to manage such situations.

Decision Table for the Daily Starbucks Decision-Making Process

Take, for example, the decision-making process the CEO of Saibot has to go through at the Starbucks counter. Several factors influence the process and help determine the outcome. In the morning, coffee is the obvious choice. Afternoons usually are for tea, and coffee again at night. However, in the winter she may opt for hot chocolate drinks in the afternoon and in the spring she typically picks soy milk in the evening. When she has plenty of time and is not stressed at all, she may take the largest drink on offer, except when it is raining. When she has very little time, she may take a cold drink—although never in the fall. And on and on and on.

We see at least four dimensions in the decision-making process—time of day, weather conditions, stress level, and season—and along each dimension, one of several cases may be true. This decision-making process can be turned into a long list of IF/THEN rules, with the likes of if season = "SUMMER" and stresslevel = "relaxed" and time_of_day = "MORNING" and weather="HOT" THEN assert new Order (drink: "grande latte").

Such a list would be a pain to create and even more so to maintain. A decision table does more or less the same, but is much easier to read and maintain. For this example, it works like this (with only a subset of the 3*3*2*4 = 72 columns):

Conditions	Rule R1	Rule R2	Rule R3	Rule R4	Rule R5	Rule R6	Rule R7	Rule R8
Time of day	Morning	Afternoon	Evening	Morning	Afternoon	Morning	Evening	Afternoon
Weather	Cold	Cold	Cold	Hot	Cold	Cold	Normal	Hot
Stress level	Relaxed	Relaxed	Relaxed	Harried	Harried	Harried	Harried	Relaxed
Season	Winter	Winter	Winter	Winter	Fall	Fall	Spring	Summer
Actions								
Order drink	Large cappuccino	Large hot chocolate	Double espresso	Small iced coffee	Small hot chocolate	Small black coffee	Small soy milk	Large hot tea (earl grey)
Order snack	Oatmeal cookie	Chocolate chip cookie	Bar of dark chocolate	—	—	Blueberry muffin	—	Biscuit

Every column can be read like a single IF/THEN rule. For example, the first column: if time of day="morning" and weather ="cold" and stress level = "relaxed" and season="winter" then assert new Order (drink: large cappuccino; snack: oatmeal cookie).

Every row contains a condition—all possible states that may apply to a certain property. A column (rule) is matched for the input record when each row in that column matches the data. Note that the input does not necessarily contain the exact values used in this matrix. In this coffee counter example, it might very well be that the input record contains the current date and time, a temperature, and an indication of Saibot Airport's CEO's stress level. The first three values do not directly match the options in the matrix. We need to convert time, date, and temperature to the terminology used in the decision table:

```
(10AM, 4th July, 86F, relaxed) => (morning, Summer, Hot, relaxed)
```

We make use of value sets for this, defined as part of the business rule dictionary. Every property is associated with a value set—a set of allowable values or allowable ranges. Well-known value sets include Boolean, Gender, and Color of Traffic Light. Instead of a single allowable value, each entry in a value set can be an allowable range. When the value for the property falls within the allowable range entry in the value set, the associated label or alias can be assigned. For example, the Season value set has four entries, each an allowable date range that will convert the date to the season. In a similar way, three time ranges in the Time of Day value set help choose between morning, afternoon, and evening.

Extended Airport Charge Calculation— Using a Decision Table

The calculation of the airport charge is not as simple as we discussed in the previous section. There is more at stake than just the weight and the type of flight. The formula also takes into account a surcharge for which the calculation depends on the noise category of the aircraft, the timeslot of the flight and whether the flight takes off or touches down. Simply put: for each combination of noise category, time slot and arrival or departure, a different surcharge percentage is determined. The total charge is calculated from the base rate corrected with this surcharge percentage.

Just as in the Starbucks example, various factors play a role in the derivation of the surcharge, each having a value in a specific category. We could either implement the derivation with a large number of IF/THEN rules or introduce a decision table to deal with this derivation. As discussed earlier, for a large number of variations, decision tables are generally the better choice.

Prepare Business Rule for the Decision Table

The factors that weigh in for the calculation of the surcharge have to be provided to the business through an extended version of the *Flight* fact. This fact as well as the web service interface exposed by the decision function is based on complex type *flightType* in the AirportChargeCalculation.xsd. We have to modify that type then refresh the fact and prepare the Value Sets.

Modify the XSD and Update the Facts Accordingly

Open this file and add these lines to the *flightType*:

```
<xsd:element name="SlotTime" nillable="false" type="xsd:time" minOccurs="1"
maxOccurs="1"/>
<xsd:element name="ArrivalOrDeparture" nillable="false" type="xsd:string"
minOccurs="1" maxOccurs="1"/>
<xsd:element name="AircraftNoiseCategory" nillable="false"
type="fac:noiseCategoryType" minOccurs="1" maxOccurs="1"/>
```

and this single line to the *airportChargeType*:

```
<xsd:element name="surchargePercentage" nillable="false" type="xsd:int"
minOccurs="1" maxOccurs="1"/>
```

Also add this simple type:

```
<xsd:simpleType name="noiseCategoryType">
  <xsd:restriction base="xsd:string">
  <xsd:enumeration value="MCC3"/>
  <xsd:enumeration value="A"/>
  <xsd:enumeration value="B"/>
  <xsd:enumeration value="C"/>
  </xsd:restriction>
 </xsd:simpleType>
```

Save these changes to the XSD document.

To synchronize the *Flight* and *AirportCharge* facts in the business rule with the updated definitions of the underlying XSD types, open the Facts tab in the business rule editor. In the upper right hand corner of the Fact table is a little icon. Click on it and pick the first option in the drop-down menu. This option says *Reload Facts based on Modified Schema* and that is what it will do: update the facts in accordance with the changes applied to complex types in the AirportChargeCalculation.xsd document.

When the reload action is complete, you can double click the *Flight* fact to check whether new properties have been added for the *slot time*, the *noise category* and the *arrival or departure* of the flight. The property *aircraftNoiseCategory* should be associated with a Value Set called *NoiseCategoryType*. This Value Set describes the allowable values for this property. It is derived from the simple type with enumeration in the XSD document.

Create Value Sets

A Value Set in the business rule dictionary describes a set of values or value ranges. Each value or value range in the set can be labeled with an alias that can be referred to in, for example, rule test expressions and actions and also in conditions in decision table. Value Sets can be associated with fact properties as well as with input and output parameters to [decision] functions and globals. The value set can be used to enforce that only allowable values are set in these variables.

We need Value Sets to define the possible values for each of the conditions defined in the rows of the decision table. In this case that means that for all of the following we need to define a value set that contains the possible values: noise category, slot time, and arrival/departure.

TIP

If a fact property can have values that are irrelevant for the business rules, these values can all be grouped under the value set entry called otherwise. *In decision table conditions, we can check for the* otherwise *value in fact properties—evaluating to true when the property does not have any of the explicitly defined values in the value set.*

Open the Value Sets tab. The value set for the noise category is already created. Open this value set. It contains five values—including one with alias "null." Change this alias to "Unknown" and click OK to save this change.

New Value Sets are needed for *Time of Day* (associated with *SlotTime*) and *Arrival Or Departure*. Figure 11-14 shown the definition of the latter. Click on the green plus icon and select Value Set from the drop-down list. Specify the name of the new Value Set as *ArrivalOrDeparture*. Click on the edit icon to bring up the Value Set editor. Define three values: "D" (with alias "Departure"), "A" (with alias "Arrival") and otherwise. Press OK to close the editor.

Click again on the green plus icon and this time select Range Value Set from the drop-down list. Specify the name of the new Value Set as *SlotTime*. Click on the edit icon to bring up the value set editor. Set the Data Type to *Time*. Add three Range Values, in addition to –Infinity, as shown in Figure 11-15. The End Points should be 05:30:00+00:00, 07:00:00+00:00, and

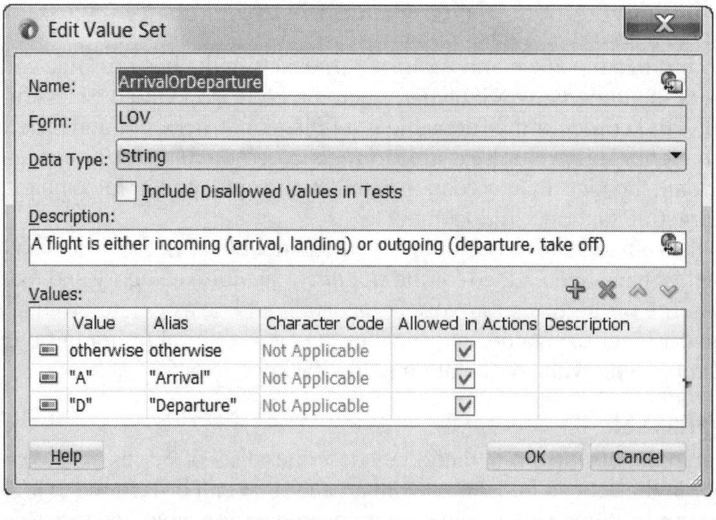

Edit Value Set

Name:	ArrivalOrDeparture
Form:	LOV
Data Type:	String

☐ Include Disallowed Values in Tests

Description:

A flight is either incoming (arrival, landing) or outgoing (departure, take off)

Values:

	Value	Alias	Character Code	Allowed in Actions	Description
	otherwise	otherwise	Not Applicable	☑	
	"A"	"Arrival"	Not Applicable	☑	
	"D"	"Departure"	Not Applicable	☑	

Help   OK   Cancel

FIGURE 11-14. *Editing the Value Set ArrivalOrDeparture*

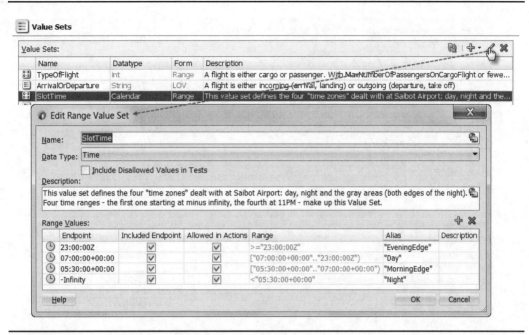

FIGURE 11-15.   *The definition of the SlotTime Range Value set*

23:00:00Z. The four aliases used for the Range Values should be Night, MorningEdge, Day, and EveningEdge.

Open the Fact editor for *Flight*—as shown in Figure 11-16. Associate properties *arrivalOrDeparture* and *slotTime* with the Value Sets *ArrivalOrDeparture* and *SlotTime,* respectively.

Update Rule CalculateTotalCharge

The calculation of the total charge in rule set *CalculateTotalCharge* has to be altered, to include the surcharge percentage that is to be established by the decision table. Open the rule set and change the implementation of the THEN action in the rule to:

```
Assign AirportCharge.totalCharge = AirportCharge.baseRate * (1 +
AirportCharge.surchargePercentage/100)
```

as shown in Figure 11-17.

Create the Decision Table for Deriving the Surcharge Factor

All the preparations have been made. The one thing lacking is the rule set with the decision table to determine the surcharge percentage in the *AirportCharge* fact.

Create Rule Set and Decision Table

Create a new rule set called *FlightSurchargeCalculation*. Add a decision table to the rule set, called *FlightSurchareDecisionTable*—as shown in Figure 11-18.

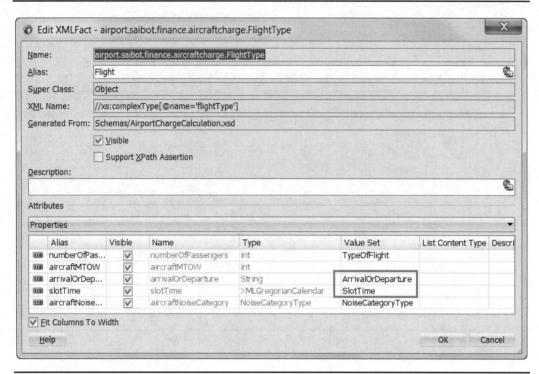

FIGURE 11-16. *Edit the Flight fact type—set the Value Set property for attributes ArrivalOrDeparture and SlotTime*

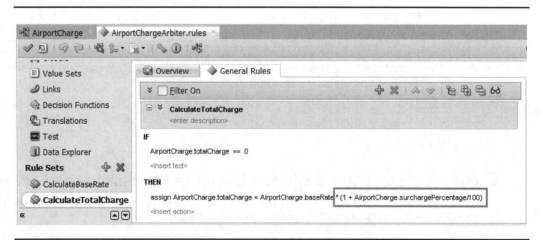

FIGURE 11-17. *Add the surchargePercentage to the calculation of the total charge*

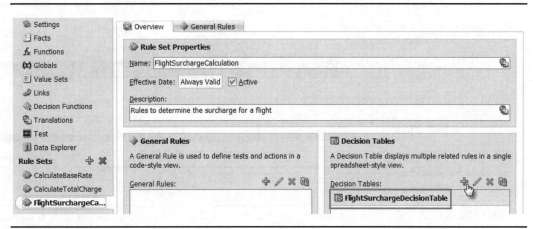

FIGURE 11-18. *New rule set FlightSurchargeCalculation with a DecisionTable called FlightSurchareDecisionTable*

The table has three areas: the conditions and the actions (rows) and the rules (columns). Optionally a fourth section can be shown, called *Conflict Resolution*. Conflicts can occur when business rules are incomplete or contain contradicting rules.

A condition is a value that is the result of an expression, usually based on one or more input values (or the current date or time), and associated with a Value Set. Conditions in our example are the flight properties *slotTime, aircraftNoiseCategory,* and *arrivalOrDeparture*. The decision table for establishing the surcharge percentage will have one condition for each of these three factors contributing to that percentage.

Click on the green plus icon to create a new condition C1. Define the condition as Flight. aircraftNoiseCategory.

A rule is defined through a column with in the cell values for each of the conditions—the rows that each represent a *Flight* property. When the values in the *Flight* fact match with all cells in a rule—and this should happen with any Fact for exactly one rule—then the actions in the bottom half of the decision table are activated within that rule column. When a rule has no value in a specific row (for a condition), it means the rule will match for every value the condition may have (in other words, the rule does not care about that particular condition).

Rule [column] R1 is already defined. Configure its cell for condition C1 to match on values MCC_3 and Unknown, as shown in Figure 11-19.

The action is usually defined using one or more parameters—whose values depend on the specific rule (or column) that matches the conditions. Our decision table for deriving the surcharge percentage for a flight has a generic action of type *modify* that assigns a value to the *surchargePercentage* property in the *AirportCharge* fact, as shown in Figure 11-20.

The actual value to be set is defined for each rule specifically, in the bottom section for that rule's column. Set this value to 60, because the surcharge on top of the base rate for aircrafts in the noisiest category MCC3 is set at 60 percent.

Add rules R2 through R4 that trigger on the other values A, B, and C for noise category. The associated surcharge percentage values are 40, 0 and −20. Figure 11-21 shows the current situation in the decision table.

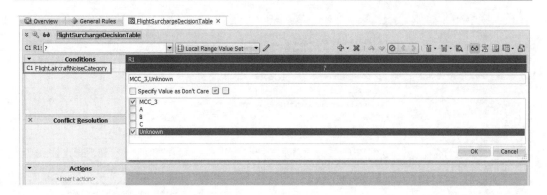

FIGURE 11-19. *Configuring the cell that defines when Rule R1 triggers for condition C1: for MCC_3 and Unknown noise category values*

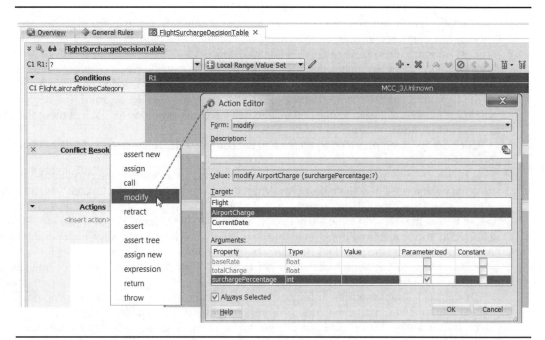

FIGURE 11-20. *Defining the generic action to set the surchargePercentage on the AirportCharge; note that the actual value is parameterized which means: set at each individual rule*

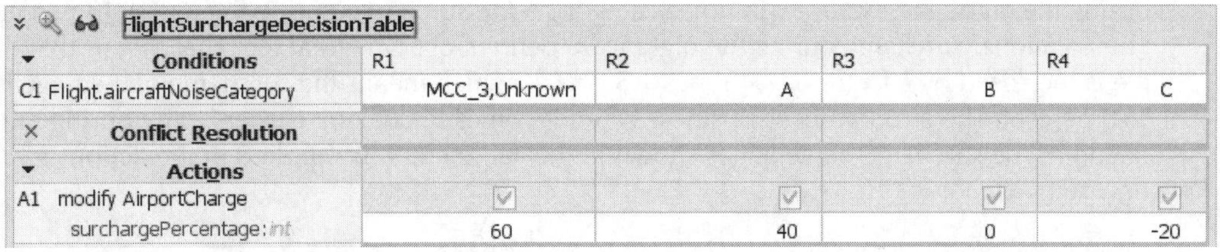

FlightSurchargeDecisionTable				
Conditions	R1	R2	R3	R4
C1 Flight.aircraftNoiseCategory	MCC_3,Unknown	A	B	C
× **Conflict Resolution**				
Actions				
A1 modify AirportCharge	☑	☑	☑	☑
surchargePercentage: *int*	60	40	0	-20

FIGURE 11-21. *Decision table with one condition and four rules triggering on the possible values and setting the surchargePercentage*

Click on the green plus icon and add a second condition: Flight.slotTime. This adds a row C2 in the decision table. Each rule column currently has a question mark for the cells in this row—because we have not yet specified on which value for the *slotTime* condition these columns should trigger. Change all question marks into the value "day."

A flight during the day does not get an extra surcharge. However, we do not currently cater for the other values the *slotTime* condition may have: Night, MorningEdge, and EveningEdge. Click on the *Gap Analysis* icon—as shown in Figure 11-22. This brings up a popup that indicates which rules are missing from the decision table (assuming a complete coverage is sought for all possible values for all conditions).

Check the boxes on top of each of the columns to have JDeveloper add the missing rules. Click on OK. This will create rules R5 through R8 for the four values of noise category combined with the set of all three slot time values.

Right click on cell C2-R5 (currently associated with all slot time values for the MCC_3 and unknown noise categories). Because the surcharge is not the same for all slot times, click on Split Selected Cell in the context menu. R5 will be split into three columns (R5, R6, and R7), one for each value in the Cell. The surcharge is the same for early morning and late evening. Therefore, select the cells for MorningEdge and EveningEdge and click on Merge Selected Cells in the context menu. Go through the same steps for the noise categories A, B, and C.

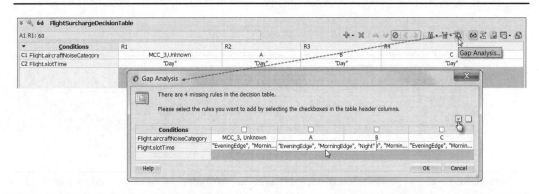

FIGURE 11-22. *Gap Analysis indicating the missing rulers for the other slotTime conditions (besides Day)*

The surcharged is elevated with an additional 20 percent during edge hours and 50 percent during the night. For example: in noise category A the surcharge during the day is 40 percent. The additional surcharge during the night is 50 percent over the total fee. That means that the fee is increased by a factor of 1.4 times 1.5 or 2.1, which means the surcharge percentage is 110 percent. The airport means business when it comes to coaxing carriers to fly during the daytime! The surcharge percentages shown in this table are to be applied in the actions for the new rules R5..R12:

MCC3		A		B		C	
Edge	Night	Edge	Night	Edge	Night	Edge	Night
92	140	68	110	20	50	−4	20

Configure the action column in rules R5-R12 to align with these percentages, as shown in Figure 11-23.

NOTE
In addition to splitting and merging the cells for condition C2, to achieve the situation in Figure 11-14, some rules were moved sideways (to bring all rules with the same noise category closer together) and some cells for condition C1 were merged.

We now introduce the final piece of business logic. For flights during the night or the edge periods, it depends whether the flight is arriving or departing. The surcharge percentage for flights arriving during the night is set at 25 percent. Night or edge time departures are considered bad form—much worse than arrivals during those hours.

This means we have to add a third condition to the decision table, based on the *Flight* fact property *arrivalOrDeparture*. Nothing changes for day time and night edge flights. That means that for all rule columns with the value day or edge (morning or evening) in their C2 cell, we can set the C3 cell to "I do not care." For all rule columns with the value *Night* in their C2 cell, we have to split their C3 cell—to create separate columns for arriving and departing flights. Subsequently, we have to lower the surcharge percentage in the arriving flight column, to the following values: MCC3: 100, A: 75, B: 25, C: 0. Figure 11-24 shows the final result for the FightSurchargeDecisionTable.

FlightSurchargeDecisionTable

	R1	R2	R3	R4	R5	R6	R7	R8	R9	R10	R11	R12
Conditions												
C1 Flight.aircraftNoiseCategory	MCC_3,Unknown			A			B			C		
C2 Flight.slotTime	"Night"	"MorningEdge"...	"Day"	"Night"	"MorningEdge"...	"Day"	"Night"	"MorningEdge"...	"Day"	"Night"	"MorningEc."	"Day"
Conflict Resolution												
Actions												
A1 modify AirportCharge	☑	☑	☑	☑	☑	☑	☑	☑	☑	☑	☑	☑
surchargePercentage:int	140	92	60	110	68	40	50	20	0	20	−4	−20

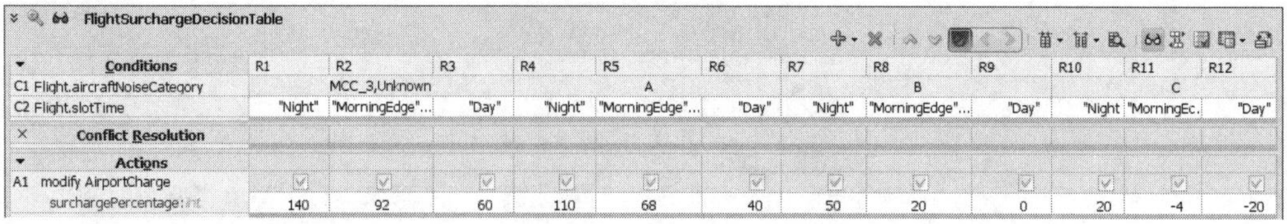

FIGURE 11-23. *Twelve rules covering all relevant combinations of noise category and slot time, with the applicable surcharges*

Conditions	R1	R2	R3	R4	R5	R6	R7	R8	R9	R10	R11	R12	R13	R14	R15	R16
C1 Flight.aircraftNoiseCategory	MCC_3,Unknown				A				B				C			
C2 Flight.slotTime	"Day"	"Morning...	"Night"		"Day"	"Morning...	"Night"		"Day"	"Morning...	"Night"		"Day"	"Morning...	"Night"	
C3 Flight.arrivalOrDeparture	-	-	"Arrival"	"Departure"	-	-	"Arrival"	"Departure"	-	-	"Arrival"	"Departure"	-	-	"Arrival"	"Departu...
✕ **Conflict Resolution**																
▾ **Actions**																
A1 modify AirportCharge	☑	☑	☑	☑	☑	☑	☑	☑	☑	☐	☐	☐	☑	☑	☑	☑
surchargePercentage:	60	92	100	140	40	68	75	110	0	20	25	50	-20	-4	0	20

FIGURE 11-24.   *Decision Table for the derivation of the flight surcharge percentage based on three factors*

Analyzing the Decision Table

Note that the order of the rules in the table is not important. The decision table editor will sometimes move the rule columns around, to combine cells where it can do so in order to present a more compact, easier-to-interpret picture. We can also do that manually using the move [column] left and right icons and the drop-down menus for merging and splitting cells, as we have been doing.

Compacting the table can reduce the number of rules we have created by eliminating the rules that are redundant while preserving the no gap, no conflict properties for the decision table. The split operations create additional rules, one for each of the values in the cell that is split. Splitting a cell that currently matches on [Arrival, Departure] produces two cells, and therefore columns, one for each of the two values. If a cell has the "do not care" value, splitting the cell produces a cell for every value in the value set. The merge operations do the opposite from what split does: They combine various condition values into a single cell.

The decision table editor in JDeveloper has several interesting features. One is the Gap Analysis. This helps us inspect the decision table we have composed to see whether we have forgotten rules, given the combinations of condition values that may occur. We have used the analysis when we added the second condition to the decision table. Note that we can decide to allow gaps, for example, when we know for sure that certain combinations of values from different value sets will never occur—such as MCC_3 aircrafts in the middle of the night—and therefore need not have rules to cater for them. If that situation should occur after all, no rules will match and no value is assigned as an outcome of the business rule.

Another valuable feature is conflict resolution. The decision table editor can find rules that may trigger for the same set of conditions—and that may try to assign different, conflicting result values. It may be intentional or by mistake. In the latter case, this check allows us to correct the oversight. When the rule conflict is intentional, we have to indicate how the conflict should be resolved. Various methods of conflict resolution are available to us, for each conflict detected by the tool. Through Override and OverriddenBy, we can indicate that one rule overrules the other one (the overridden rule is ignored altogether). With RunBefore and RunAfter, both rules may be activated—in the order specified—and both actions may be executed. Finally, using NoConflict we can instruct the business rule engine to ignore what it thinks is a conflict.

We could have a potential conflict in our decision table: say we want to implement a fallback option as a final resort that should trigger when no other rules have triggered. This fallback rule will assign the surcharge percentage value 200. The fallback rule accepts all values for all conditions—and therefore has a conflict with every other rule.

When we double-click the cell that shows the conflicts, the Conflict Resolution window pops up. We can select the resolution for every conflict for this rule. In this way, all other rules will override this fallback rule—when any other rule has fired, this rule is overridden, which means ignored. Only when no other rule was activated will this rule come in action to assign a 200 surcharge percentage.

Use Excel for Editing the Decision Table

The business rule editor in JDeveloper has a little Excel icon in its top bar. Through this icon, we get access to two options, for exporting decision tables to an Excel document and importing an [edited] Excel document with the updated definition of the decision table.

Through Excel it becomes much easier for business representatives and function analysts who are not JDeveloper users, to work on the business logic captured in the decision table. Especially for large tables with many factors and values per factor, the table can become quite big and unwieldy to work on in the business rule editor. Figure 11-25 shows the export dialog. Note that only decision tables are exported, not the regular IF/THEN rules.

The exported Excel document contains the definition of a special Excel plugin with its own ribbon (Figure 11-26). It also has instructions on how to edit the decision table and the value sets. The value set definitions are included and can be edited, as well as of course the decision table itself.

Add Decision Table to Decision Function

To ensure that the decision function leverages the decision table for calculating the surcharge, we have to explicitly add the *FlightSurchargeCalculation* rule set to the list of selected rule sets in the decision function, between the two other rule sets, as shown in Figure 11-27.

Update Test Suite

The existing test cases are no longer valid, because they have not been configured with appropriate values for the new fact properties in the Flight fact. To reinstate these test cases, we also have to provide values for the *SlotTime* property, which is of type *XMLGregorianCalendar*. To allow easy configuration of test values for *SlotTime* based on a simple time string, we will create a helper function *getTimeFromString*. Using the function, we can subsequently refine the test cases.

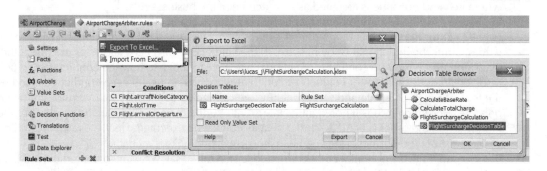

FIGURE 11-25. *Exporting a decision table to an Excel document for review and manipulation outside JDeveloper*

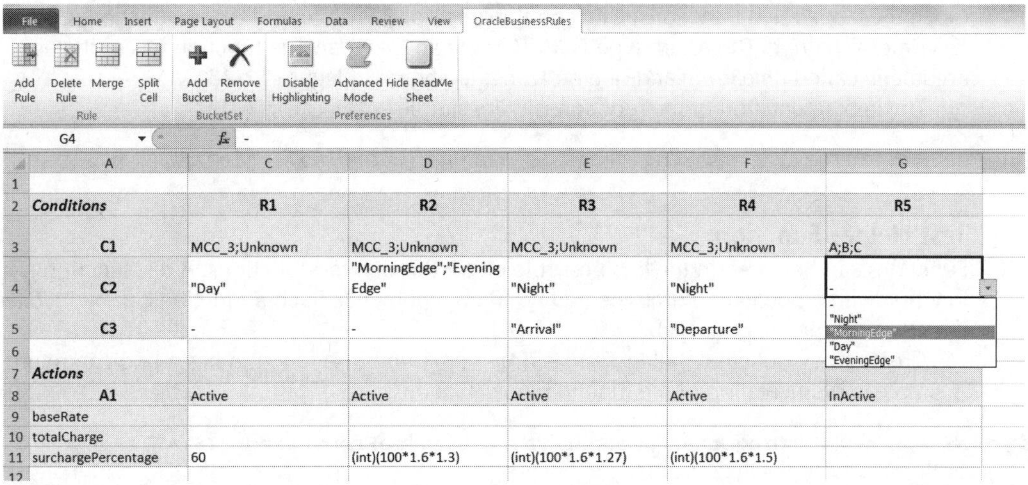

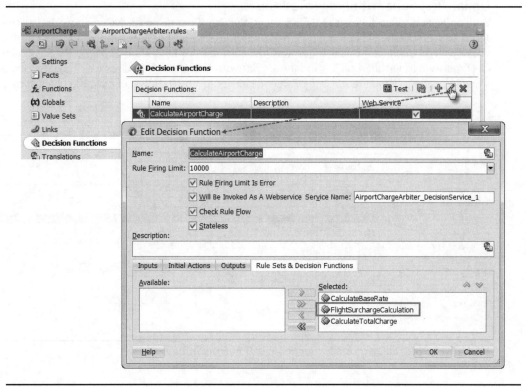

	A	C	D	E	F	G
1						
2	**Conditions**	R1	R2	R3	R4	R5
3	C1	MCC_3;Unknown	MCC_3;Unknown	MCC_3;Unknown	MCC_3;Unknown	A;B;C
4	C2	"Day"	"MorningEdge";"Evening Edge"	"Night"	"Night"	-
5	C3	-	-	"Arrival"	"Departure"	
6						
7	**Actions**					
8	A1	Active	Active	Active	Active	InActive
9	baseRate					
10	totalCharge					
11	surchargePercentage	60	(int)(100*1.6*1.3)	(int)(100*1.6*1.27)	(int)(100*1.6*1.5)	
12						

FIGURE 11-26. *Editing the decision table in Excel*

FIGURE 11-27. *Add rule set FlightSurchargeCalculation to decision function CalculateAirportCharge*

Create Helper Function to Produce XMLGregorianCalendar

Open the tab labeled Functions. Click on the green plus icon to add a new function. Call it *GetTimeFromString*. The return type is *XMLGregorianCalendar*. The function has a single argument, called *timeString* and of type *String,* as shown in Figure 11-28.

The implementation of the function is quite simple:

```
return XMLDate.fromstring("2015-12-31T"+ timeString + ":00Z" )
```

Test Helper Function

Functions can be tested in the business rule editor through test functions. A test function is any function with a boolean return type and no input arguments. Such a function can be invoked directly from the Functions tab.

Create a new function called *TestGetTimeFromString*. The function has a boolean return type. A simple implementation of the function looks like this:

```
assign new XMLGregorianCalendar var = GetTimeFromString("15:45")
call print (message: var)
return true
```

Figure 11-29 shows the test function and its output.

Update Test Suite with Proper Test Cases

With a function to produce an XMLGregorianCalendar at our disposal, we can now update the Test Cases. Before the Flight input only had properties for *numberOfPassengers* and *aircraftMTOW*. We now need to provide values for *arrivalOrDeparture* (A or D), the *slotTime*—using a call like GetTimeFromString("hh24:mi")—and the *aircraftNoiseCategory* (A, B, C, or MCC_3). The output has a new property as well: the *surchargePercentage*. Figure 11-30 shows an example of a test case.

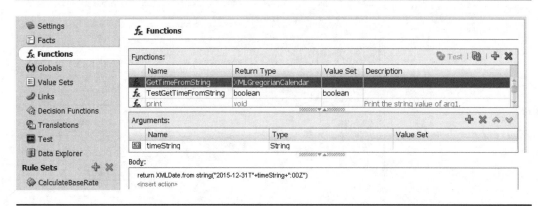

FIGURE 11-28. *Create custom function GetTimeFromString*

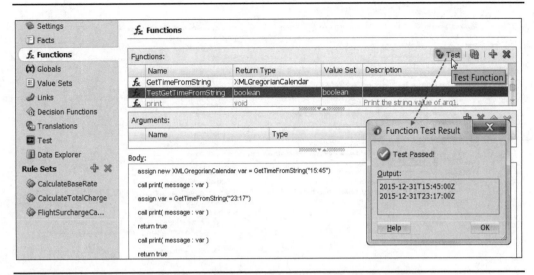

FIGURE 11-29. *Using a test function to try out function GetTimeFromString*

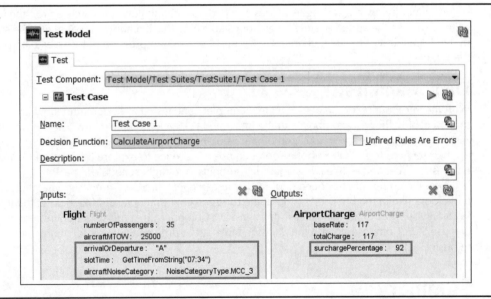

FIGURE 11-30. *Test case for decision function CalculateAirportCharge—with the three new properties to derive the surcharge percentage*

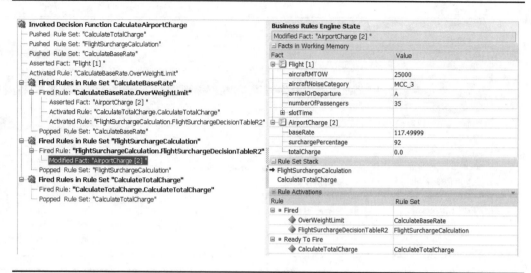

FIGURE 11-31. *Trace details for test case execution for decision function CalculateAirportCharge*

After modifying the existing test cases and perhaps adding new ones, we can run the test suite to witness the added business logic for establishing the surcharge and applying the surcharge in the calculation of the total charge. Figure 11-31 gives an impression of the trace details for the test case.

Deploy and Test

With the introduction of the decision table complete and tested at design time, now is a good time to deploy the SOA composite to the Integrated WLS and to make a few test calls to the *AirportChargeService* for various combinations of input parameters. Airlines considering signing up their services to slots at Saibot Airport can use this service to explore the costs of their various options and scenarios—tweaking slot times, aircrafts, and flight schedules.

After the composite has been deployed, you can check in SOA Composer what the decision table looks like in the browser on top of the run-time environment. And like before: the Integrated WLS only supports read only access through SOA Composer. In a full server environment, you can use SOA Composer to edit the decision table at run time and very rapidly implement changes in business policies.

Summary

Separation of concerns is a crucial element in the SOA Suite. Externalizing business logic out of technical implementations into metadata that can easily be changed and redeployed without changing the code leveraging that logic is a good way to help achieve that separation—especially given the different pace of change in the logic (fast) and the services using the logic (much slower).

The Business Rule component in SOA composite applications is the embodiment of that notion. This component can be used to take on the responsibility of performing potentially complex, reusable calculations, validating data, and making decisions given a certain input based on advanced business logic. A special aspect of Business Rules is their ability to be edited at run time. Through the SOA Composer, developers or business analysts can refine the definition of a business rule. Such modifications take immediate effect and do not require a redeployment of the application.

Business Rules can be leveraged from other components, such as Human Task, BPEL, and BPMN processes, as we will see in future chapters. They can play an important role in assigning tasks, dynamically determining where to route messages or deciding which paths to take in a business process. In adaptive case management, a business rule component is even at the heart of the case, acting as a *state engine* that drives the case from start to finish. Note that business rules can also be invoked from external applications as a web service and from Java applications through a Java-based API.

PART
IV

Asynchronous
Services and Events

CHAPTER
12

Asynchronous Services
with SOA Composites
and Service Bus

"Let me write down your number and get back to you" can be much more efficient than "please hold the line." The former is a typical example of asynchronous communication. This can be much more efficient than actually holding the line, which is the synchronous way of conversing. While holding the line, waiting for a response, you are blocked—unable to engage in useful activities.

In real life, when you tell something to a person, you don't mind waiting for answer (beyond some form of acknowledgement that your message was heard and understood) if and when:

- You asked a question that you want an answer to.
- You cannot meaningfully continue with your life until you receive the response.
- You do not have to wait too long (a little subjective).
- You will lose the opportunity to receive the answer at all if you do not wait for it.
- You can afford to wait (because of the time or cost of resources involved with waiting).

However, if these considerations do not apply, you want to continue with your life as soon as possible after saying your piece or asking your question.

In the world of services, very similar considerations apply. Replace "you" in these bullets with "the service consumer" and you have a checklist that will help you decide when interactions must be synchronous and when perhaps they could be handled asynchronously.

Synchronously waiting for a response that it is not absolutely required is not just a waste of time: it is also a waste of scarce system resources such as memory and primarily processing threads. Synchronous interactions also add to the fragility of a system. When instead of a long, complex, all-dependent chain we can work with multiple, smaller, simpler, decoupled chains that would be far preferable. So after having discussed synchronous interactions in most of the preceding chapters, we will focus in this chapter on how we can expose asynchronous interfaces from the SOA Suite. These interfaces will take a request, cease the communication, proceed with the execution of the request and provide a response in a callback. BPEL as we will see provides the easiest way to implement such operations, although using only Service Bus or Mediator we can achieve similar results.

Due to the fact that a BPEL process can be long running, we can speak of instances of a process and we can engage in communication with such an instance. This can be, for example, to learn something about the (status of the) instance, to feed additional information to the instance or to abort the instance. Ensuring that requests end up in the correct instance is one of our challenges—handled in BPEL through a mechanism called correlation.

As a practical show case we will look at the *AircraftServiceOrchestrator*—the intermediate between airlines and providers of fuel, cleaning, catering and repair services on Saibot Airport that helps parties negotiate agreeable terms for services to be rendered under specified conditions.

Exposing Asynchronous Services

The term asynchronous service is perhaps somewhat misleading. We use it to indicate a category of services that are associated with two interfaces. One is the interface implemented by the service itself with one or more one-way operations that only take an input. The other interface is the callback interface: the interface that the service expects when it calls back to deliver the response message. This interface has to be implemented by the party invoking the service. The address of the implementation has to be delivered along with request message—so the service knows where to call with the response. In human interactions, the callback interface is, for example, the telephone or fax machine and their wired or wireless connection.

Only if you have the ability to be called back in the manner described by the service provider, can you make a successful call to the asynchronous service and get the response you are looking for.

NOTE
A service operation may define an output (that is returned synchronously) and also specify a callback interface. The service operation can be implemented in such a way that it first returns a synchronous response and subsequently makes a call to the callback service and deliver an additional message. In this chapter, we will assume the asynchronous service operations will be one way and deliver a single, asynchronous response message to the callback service.

The implementation of an asynchronous web service requires some steps in addition to what a synchronous service implementation has to do. These steps concern the interpretation of the request headers to extract the address to send the response to as well as a message identifier used for identification of the conversation. Additionally, the service implementation will have to make a service call itself—to the address dynamically extracted.

This section discusses the implementation of the asynchronous service with Service Bus projects, Mediator, and first of all BPEL. We will also look at invoking asynchronous services from these three environments. Mediator and Service Bus can both expose an asynchronous interface on top of a synchronous and an asynchronous back end or business service. BPEL in addition can present a synchronous interface on top of an asynchronous back end.

The online resources for this chapter describe the implementation of an asynchronous web service using only Java and JAX-WS, as well as the invocation of an asynchronous web service from a Java SE program.

The service we will implement is an asynchronous form of hello world: *ThoughtfulGreeterService* (Figure 12-1).

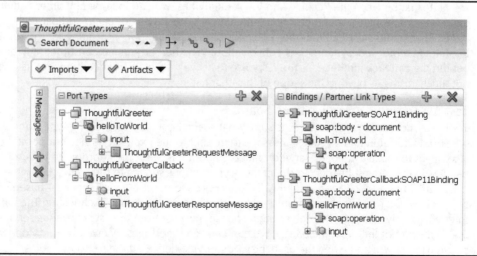

FIGURE 12-1. *The WSDL definition for the ThoughtfulGreeterService*

The service definition describes two interfaces: the primary one, implemented by the service itself and the callback one, implemented by the service consumers. The former interface has a single one way operation—*helloToWorld*—that takes a simple request message with a name element as key aspect. It does not return any output.

The callback interface also contains a single operation, this one called *helloFromWorld*. This operation is also one way: it takes as input the response message from the *ThoughtfulGreeterService* and does not return any output. This operation should only be invoked by implementations of the *ThoughtfulGreeterService*'s primary interface.

Implement the Asynchronous ThoughtfulGreeterService with a BPEL Component

The *ThoughtfulGreeterService* is just a *hello world* service that takes its time to respond. More precisely: it completes the synchronous interaction with the consumer accepting the request message, it composes the response messages through whatever processing it has to perform and then calls back to the address specified to hand over the response—which is sent as a request to the callback service. This could indeed take some time. However, it could also be near instantaneously. Asynchronous does not necessarily mean slow or delayed. It *does* mean decoupled: receiving the response takes place in a different interaction than the one in which the service was first invoked.

The steps for the BPEL implementation of this service are straightforward (see the result in Figure 12-2):

- Create a new SOA composite application—Empty Template.
- Add BPEL component, based on the ThoughtfulGreeterService.wsdl.
- Check the BPEL process created (Receive and Invoke rather than Reply).
- Choose roles to implement.
- Create SOAP Service Binding at the composite level, based on WSDL.
- Add Assign activity to set the output variable.

Note that between the Receive and Invoke activities, we can include any other activity—including synchronous or asynchronous service calls, iterations (for each) and parallel scopes (flow). There is no risk of a time out—because there is no component waiting for the result—at least not in a blocked, synchronous conversation. Whether the service consumer may be waiting behind the callback interface for the response to arrive—with a fixed deadline and its own time out mechanism—is beyond the scope of this chapter.

Test Asynchronous Service from SoapUI

Testing asynchronous web services is somewhat special compared to testing synchronous services because in addition to the request message to be sent to the exposed service endpoint, SoapUI also needs to make a callback service available and it has to set the appropriate WS-Addressing headers in the request headers to direct the asynchronous service to the callback service.

SoapUI has a Mock Service facility. This allows us to publish a web service—based on a port type in a WSDL document and published at a port and endpoint of our choosing. The callback interface is only one way: it receives the response message from the asynchronous service and that is the end of the story. In SoapUI, we can check all messages received by the Mock Service, so we will know if and when the asynchronous service delivered the response.

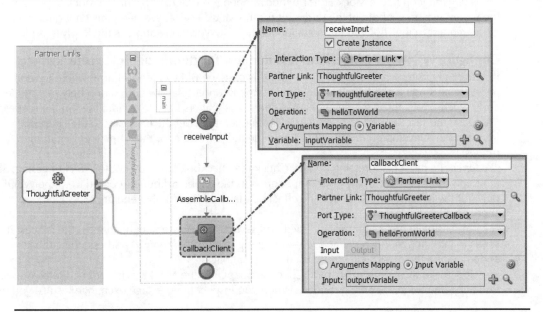

FIGURE 12-2.   *The BPEL process that implements an asynchronous interface (the final activity is an Invoke instead of a Reply—and it invokes a different portType on the ThoughtfulGreeter partnerLink)*

TIP
The online resource explains and shows in detail how to set up the test project with mock service for the ThoughtfulGreeterService.

Create a new SoapUI project—based on the WSDL document exposed by the deployed *ThoughtfulGreeter* service (at the address shown as WSDL URL in the EM FMW console after deployment of the SOA Composite, for example: `http://localhost:7101/soa-infra/services/default/AsynchronousSOAComposite/ThoughtfulGreeter_ep?WSDL`).

The project is created with test cases and requests for both bindings in the WSDL.

Next, we need a MockService in SoapUI—to implement the callback interface (PortType *ThoughtfulGreeterCallback*) for the *ThoughtfulGreeterService*. Right click on the project in SoapUI. Select New SOAP MockService from the context menu. Set the name of the MockService to *ThoughtfulGreeterCallbackService* and click on OK. Add a MockOperation from the context menu for the *helloFromWorld* operation.

Open the MockService Editor, from the context menu on the Mock ServiceOpen the options window for the Mock Service. Set the Path and Port for the Mock Service to appropriate values—such as */MockThoughfulGreeterCallback* and 8081.

Start the Mock Service. Note that we do not have to specify a response message for this mock service and operation. The operation is one way—only to be invoked in order for the asynchronous service to deliver its response.

Using the icon in the Mock Editor window, open the WSDL page for the Mock Service. It is the easiest way to get hold of the endpoint for the MockService. We need this endpoint, to pass it in the request to the ThoughtfulGreeterService.helloToWorld operation as the ReplyTo address.

Configure WS-Addressing in the Test Request for the ThoughfulGreeterService

In order to let the asynchronous service—in this case the BPEL engine—know where to send its response message and what messageId to include in order to allow correlation between request and asynchronous response, several WS-Addressing headers have to be included in the request.

Open the Test Request for the *helloToWorld* operation. Set the endpoint to the endpoint found in the JDeveloper console after deployment. Set a value for the name element in the request message.

Open the tab for Addressing details. Check the checkbox labeled Enable WS-Addressing. Set the ReplyTo property with the endpoint address in the clipboard buffer (copied from the WSDL page for the Mock Service). Check the checkbox labeled Randomly generate MessageId, as shown in Figure 12-3.

This basically means that SoapUI will add several WS-Addressing headers to the request it sends to the *ThoughtfulGreeterService*—including one for the *ReplyTo* address (the callback endpoint) and the message ID to be used in the callback.

Now make the call from SoapUI. Check in SoapUI in the MockService editor. Here you will find a log line for an incoming request. When you inspect the message exchange results, you will

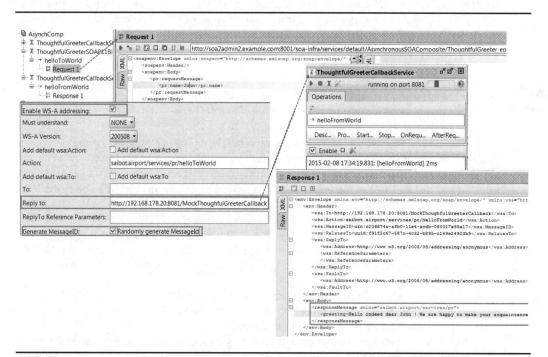

FIGURE 12-3. *Configure the SoapUI Test Request (with the WS-Addressing properties to guide the callback message) and the Mock Service receiving the asynchronous response from ThoughtfulGreeterService*

find the response message as well as the *RelatesTo* header property with the same message Id that was sent in the request message.

You can of course also check the flow trace and BPEL audit trail for the SOA composite instance that was created when the SoapUI test request was sent for the asynchronous service.

Note that in the implementation of the service in BPEL did we at no point have to deal with WS-Addressing headers or other low level details concerning the callback location or the correlation ID. The BPEL engine takes care of all that.

Implement Asynchronous Service with Mediator

A Mediator can also implement an asynchronous service. It does so not as elegantly as a BPEL component can. The developer has to read and set WS-Addressing settings from the request and to the message sent as response to the callback service. We will briefly discuss this approach.

Add a Mediator component to the SOA composite. Call it *ThoughtfulGreeterMediator*. Choose the *Interface Definition from WSDL* template, check the checkbox *Expose as a SOAP service* and select the ThoughtfulGreeter.wsdl document. Select the *ThoughtFulGreeter* interface as PortType and the *ThoughtfulGreeterCallback* as the Callback Port Type, as shown in Figure 12-4.

Also add a SOAP Reference Binding to the component, based on callback interface in the WSDL document. Note: The endpoint set for this binding at design time is irrelevant. At run time, the endpoint will be set based on the WS-Addressing ReplyTo header received from the service consumer to make the callback to deliver the asynchronous response.

Wire the Mediator to this SOAP binding, as is shown in Figure 12-5.

Open the Mediator editor. It shows a routing rule to a (dummy) SOAP Reference that implements the *ThoughtfulGreeterCallback* interface.

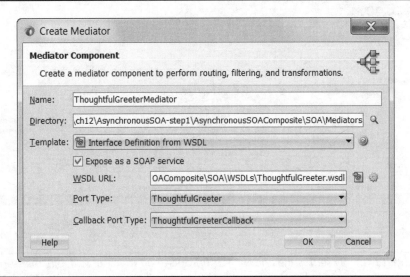

FIGURE 12-4.   *Configuration of Mediator with asynchronous interface*

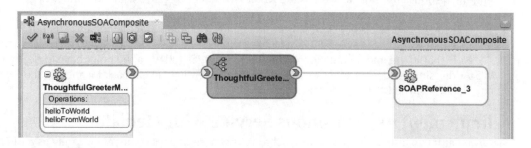

FIGURE 12-5. *ThoughtfulGreeterMediator exposing an asynchronous interface and using a SOAP Reference binding to perform the callback.*

Open the Assign Values dialog, see Figure 12-6. Set the *endpointURI* property (in the $out variable) with the value in the *replyToAddress* property in the $in variable (received as header in the request message). Map the *wsa.messageId* property in the $in variable to the *wsa.relatesTo* property in the $out variable. Also set an XPath expression to derive the value for the (greeting element in the) response message.

Deploy the SOA composite. Use the same SoapUI Test Request as before to test the service and verify that the Mediator sends a response message to the callback (mock) service.

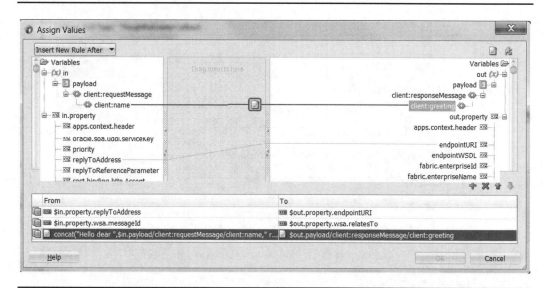

FIGURE 12-6. *By setting the endpointURI property on the $out variable, the response is guided to the correct callback service endpoint; the relatesTo property is set with the incoming messageId—to allow correlation by the consumer between the request and the asynchronous response to the callback service*

Expose Asynchronous Service Interface with Service Bus

The Service Bus implements an asynchronous interface in a similar way as the mediator does: after an initial one-way incoming conversation, the request is processed in a pipeline and the result of that processing—which may involve calls to one or more business services—is sent to a business service that represents the callback service. The headers in the request message contain the information required to instruct the business service on which endpoint to send the response to.

The steps for implementing the *ThoughtfulGreeterService* with Service Bus are fairly straightforward.

Create a new Service Bus project. Import the WSDL and XSD into the project. Create a proxy service based on the *ThoughtfulGreeter* port binding and a business service based on *ThoughtfulGreeterCallback*. Note that the endpoint address set for the business service is irrelevant—because as with the mediator, this endpoint will be set at run time from the ReplyTo header property received from the service consumer.

Create a pipeline, also based on *ThoughtfulGreeter*. Wire the proxy service to this pipeline and the pipeline to the business service, as shown in Figure 12-7.

The pipeline gathers the ReplyTo address and MessageId from the request headers, then processes the body to prepare the response and then uses a Publish operation to invoke the one-way callback interface, after manipulating the header with the appropriate values, as shown in Figure 12-8.

NOTE
This Publish action could instead of calling the outgoing business service also invoke a Service Bus proxy service, which uses its own pipeline to do processing on a decoupled, *separate thread. As long as the WS-Addressing properties are passed along, this pipeline could route to a business service that invokes the Callback interface.*

The first stage—GatherCallbackToandMessageId—contains Assign activities that assign values from the $header variable to local variables:

```
$header/wsa05:ReplyTo/wsa05:Address/.  =>  callbackToAddress
```

and

```
$header/wsa05:MessageID/. => MessageId
```

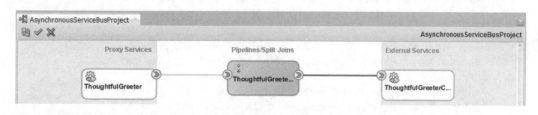

FIGURE 12-7.   *The ThoughtfulGreeter Service Bus project for asynchronous responses*

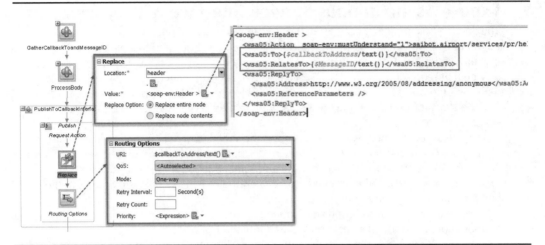

FIGURE 12-8. *Pipeline implementing the ThoughtfulGreeter functionality in three steps: retrieve WS-Addressing properties, prepare response and publish to the business service that does the callback*

Note that in a Service Bus pipeline we always have access to both the body and the header element from the request message, in the $body and $header variables respectively.

The response message is prepared in the second stage *ProcessBody* using a replace activity on the $body variable, replacing the node contents with a greeting message that contains the name from the request.

The third stage initiates the callback through the publish action to the business service. The publish action is configured to invoke the business service. It contains a replace activity to replace the entire node in the header variable using the gathered WS-Addressing information.

The Routing Options activity is where the endpoint address is set that the publish action uses to send its message to. The URI property is set based on the $callbackToAddress variable that we set earlier on based on the request header. Note that the endpoint address specified on the business service is completely ignored as it is overwritten by the value set in the Routing Options activity.

This completes the implementation Service Bus style of the *ThoughtfulGreeterService*. Run it from JDeveloper, then invoke it from SoapUI using the same test project as used for testing the SOA composite—only with the endpoint set for the service exposed on the Service Bus. The result should of course be exactly the same.

TIP
We tend to think of the ReplyTo address as the "return to sender" location—a location that should somehow be related to and located near by the component the asynchronous service. However, we could just as well consider it as the "forwarding address" —a service endpoint that can be completely unrelated to the location from which the service is invoked.

Additionally, it is of course custom to use the WS-Addressing header properties *RelatesTo* and *ReplyTo* to specify the message ID or correlation identifier and the endpoint to which the asynchronous response should be sent. And for the automatic handling of the asynchronous interactions in BPEL, this is required. However, you have seen how for the Mediator and Service Bus implementations, we have specified ourselves how to retrieve and assign these values. That means that we can read the forwarding address and the correlation identifier in other ways than from the WS-Addressing header properties, if we are so inclined.

Interacting with Asynchronous Interfaces

Exposing and implementing an asynchronous interface requires something extra compared to synchronous services. Invoking these interfaces and preparing for the callback response is even more of a challenge, as we will see next when we invoke an asynchronous operation from both a BPEL component as well as a Service Bus project.

Invoke an Asynchronous Service from a BPEL Component— Synchronous Interface on Top of Asynchronous Back End

BPEL is a language designed for web service orchestration. This includes an ability to handle interactions with asynchronous web services. The manipulation of the WS-Addressing headers as well as the correlation of the asynchronous [call back] response from the asynchronous service back to the invoking BPEL process instance is all handled by the BPEL engine. The developer simply deals with a partnerLink that is invoked as well as received from.

The asynchronous buck stops with the BPEL process: the BPEL process can expose a synchronous interface to its consumers, even when internally it engages in asynchronous interactions. Of course, when the asynchronous response takes a long time to arrive, then the synchronous conversation may time out.

We walk through a simple example of a BPEL process that exposes a synchronous variation of the *ThoughtfulGreeter*: it receives a request message with a name and returns a synchronous response with a greeting. This BPEL component invokes the asynchronous *ThoughtfulGreetingService*—either of the ones implemented earlier in this chapter using BPEL, Mediator and Service Bus, respectively.

The steps are again straightforward:

- Create a new SOA composite application *LessThoughtfulGreeterService*.

- Create or import the synchronous WSDL definition for the *LessThoughtfulGreeterService* (of course, even though this service is synchronous, it cannot really be considered less thoughtful because for the creation of the response it enlists the so called *ThoughtfulGreeterService*).

- Create a Web Service Reference Binding for the ThoughtfulGreeterService.

- Create a BPEL component called *LessThoughtfulGreeterProcess* based on the *LessThoughtfulGreeterService.wsdl* document; have this component exposed as a SOAP Web Service.

- Wire the BPEL component to the *ThoughtfulGreeterService* reference.

The composite now looks like Figure 12-9.

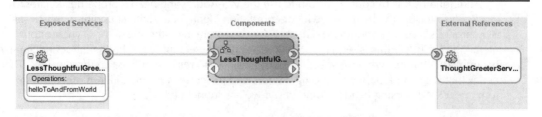

FIGURE 12-9. *The SOA composite that exposes a synchronous interface that is backed by an asynchronous back end—with the synchronous-asynchronous decoupling handled by the BPEL component*

Open the editor for the BPEL component. Add an *invoke* activity that calls the partner link for the *ThoughtfulGreeterService*. Configure the activity to call the *helloToWorld* operation on the *ThoughtfulGreeter* portType. Create an input variable for this call. Because this is a one-way operation, there is no output variable to be configured.

The BPEL component will subsequently have to wait for the asynchronous response to come in. To make this happen, we need to add a *receive* activity, just under the *invoke*, and also wire it to the *ThoughtfulGreeterService* partnerlink. However, this time the activity is configured for the *helloFromWorld* operation in the *ThoughtfulGreeterCallback* Port Type, as Figure 12-10 shows.

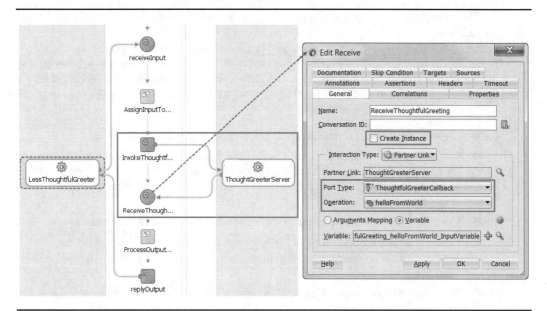

FIGURE 12-10. *Configuring the Receive activity that handles the reception of the asynchronous callback*

Make sure that the checkbox *Create Instance* is unchecked in the *receive* configuration: in this case we want to receive the message via the partner link in an existing instance and not create a new instance. Unchecking this checkbox means that the BPEL engine upon reception of the asynchronous callback message will attempt correlation with a running instance—based on the RelatesTo WS-Addressing header property.

NOTE
When the asynchronous service that gets invoked does not support use of the WS-Addressing Relates To property, we can manually define the correlation identifier in the callback message that should be used to associate that message with a running instance. This correlation mechanism is introduced in the next section.

Finally, add *assign* activities to prepare the input to the *ThoughtfulGreeterService* and to set the *outputVariable* based on the callback message that gets received. Figure 12-9 shows the complete BPEL process.

The SOA composite can now be deployed and its (synchronous) service interface tested. This will demonstrate how BPEL can easily adapt from an asynchronous conversation style to a synchronous one. It can also do the reverse: publish an asynchronous interface while itself interacting with synchronous services.

TIP
There is no reason why there cannot be other activities between the invoke and the receive activity. When the thread executing the BPEL process instance gets to the receive activity, the instance is dehydrated, or compressed and stored, and the thread released. When the callback message arrives, another thread is given the task of reviving the instance and executing the receive activity.

Invoking an Asynchronous Service in Service Bus

The previous section described how elegantly a BPEL component can interact with an asynchronous service. The heavy lifting is done by the engine and as a developer, there is hardly any difference between invoking a synchronous service or an asynchronous one.

Service Bus is stateless and does not have these same facilities for correlating incoming messages. When the callback message comes into to the Service Bus runtime, it is no different from any other (request) message. The callback message needs to be handled by a proxy service, just like any other message. Note that the asynchronous business service can be HTTP/SOAP, but also JMS, EJB, AQ among others.

Service Bus cannot invoke an asynchronous service in the implementation of a synchronous interface. There can be no link between the original synchronous request and the processing of the callback message from the asynchronous business service.

Calling an asynchronous service from Service Bus in the implementation of a one-way service is perfectly possible. The endpoint of the callback proxy service is passed in the ReplyTo header property. This proxy is invoked by the asynchronous service and may continue the next stage in the one-way service implementation.

If the Service Bus should virtualize an asynchronous back end—it can only do so with an asynchronous interface, as shown in Figure 12-11; unlike BPEL it cannot adapt from asynchronous to synchronous. At the end of the processing that starts at the proxy service that handles the callback message, we need to callout to the callback service endpoint stipulated by the external consumer that started the whole conversation. That in turn requires us to transfer the ReplyTo and MessageId properties received in the original call to the asynchronous business service and hope to receive them back in the callback message. Figure 12-12 shows the two-step dance we have to perform in Service Bus.

This means that in order for the Service Bus to completely virtualize the asynchronous business service, it is required that the original ReplyTo value—the address of the *ThoughtfulGreeterCallback* service in Figure 12-12—is somehow passed to the proxy service that is invoked by the business service with the callback message.

There seem to be two main ways to approach this challenge:

1. Have the asynchronous business service pass on the original ReplyTo value—for example, by including it in a (custom) header property that is passed unchanged or by concatenating this value to the message identifier.

2. Have the first proxy service save the ReplyTo address to a (cross cluster) cache— associated with the message identifier as key—and have the second (callback) proxy service retrieve this ReplyTo address from the cache, using the RelatesTo property in the callback message as the key value.

If you have control over the asynchronous service, then the first approach is the easiest. Simply agree on the header property that the invoker may pass in and the asynchronous business service

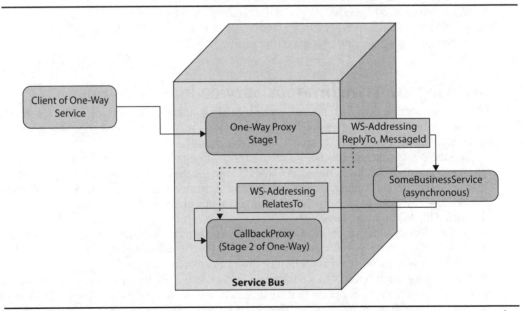

FIGURE 12-11. *Calling an asynchronous business service from a Service Bus project; passing the endpoint of the "next stage proxy service" as the callback service in the ReplyTo header property*

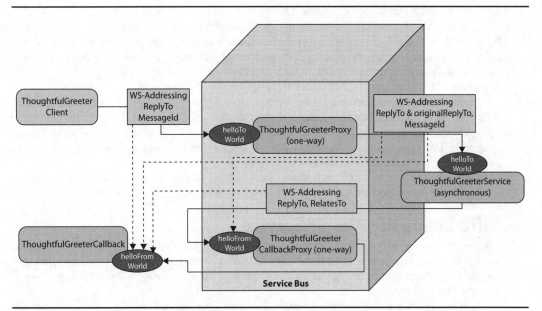

FIGURE 12-12.   *Virtualizing an asynchronous business service in Service Bus using two one way proxy services*

will pass through. If the asynchronous service to virtualize cannot be changed in this way, you can either manipulate the message identifier (if the business service sets the RelatesTo property based on the MessageId), or resort to the second approach.

The story for Mediator component is largely the same. This component too is stateless and does not have engine-level infrastructure to handle asynchronous callback correlation. The solution would be similar to what is described for the Service Bus.

Request Proposal for Airport Service

The COO of Saibot Airport is anxious that operations on the airport run smoothly. Not just when Saibot Airport itself is involved in interactions with airline carriers or other parties performing business activities on or around the airport, but also when various parties have direct interaction without involvement from Saibot. To increase the attractiveness of Saibot for passengers, business partners and especially airline carriers, it is deemed crucial to foster fast, efficient, flexible and consistent business operations.

One area where this desire to have business run smoothly is around aircraft services. Every plane requires a number of services after arrival and before departure. Examples of these are baggage handling, fueling, power and water supply, cleaning (inside and out), small repairs, and catering. Many airlines request these services and a substantial number of companies active on Saibot Airport offer (a subset of) these services.

Saibot has taken the lead in organizing automated, electronic exchange around these services, by specifying a web service interface that any company has to offer if they want to be eligible for performing aircraft services for the airline carriers. When the carriers have scheduled a flight for which they need help with catering or cleaning, they will send requests for proposal to the web services exposed by all companies that can supply aircraft facilities. The service specified by Saibot is an asynchronous service where a carrier can request a quote for some (combination of) services regarding a flight. After whatever internal processing the aircraft service providers have to go through in order to prepare their response to the RFP, the callback with the price quote is made to the airline carrier that initiated the RFP.

In this section we will briefly introduce the service interface that Saibot's IT staff has defined. Next, we will look at an implementation of the *AircraftService* using BPEL to make the asynchronous callback. We then create a second SOA composite to acts as the requestor of the proposals. This composite also contains a BPEL process—that invokes the *AircraftService* provider and waits for the asynchronous callback to arrive.

Finally, we extend this BPEL process to simultaneously call out to multiple *AircraftServiceProviders* and wait for their proposals in parallel.

Introducing the AircraftService

The *AircraftService* defines two portTypes—the "normal" one that is implemented by the aircraft service provider and the callback portType that will be invoked by that provider and that therefore has to be implemented by anyone who invokes the *AircraftService* and wants to receive the asynchronous response.

The *requestProposal* operation is invoked to request a proposal from a supplier of aircraft services. The request contains information about the services to be provided—fuel, cleaning, catering, baggage handling, etc. —for which flight—aircraft type, time slot, flight number, destination, number of passengers—and what the deadline is for the quote. The one-way *submitProposal* operation in the callback interface is invoked with a message that contains an indication from the supplier whether he is able to provide the requested services, what the price is for these services and until what time the offer is valid.

Implementing the Asynchronous AircraftService with BPEL

The starting point of this implementation of the *AircraftService* interface that the airport people came up with is obviously the WSDL with its associated XSD documents. Using these, we can create an SOA composite application that exposes a service based on that interface, implemented by a BPEL component that adheres to the same interface.

In just a few steps, we have the foundation of the composite application:

- Create a new SOA application in JDeveloper—called *AircraftServices*—with SOA composite called *AircraftServiceProvider*—based on the *Empty Template*.
- Add a BPEL component called *AircraftServiceRequestProcessor*; this component is based on the AircraftService.wsdl document. The BPEL component is exposed as a SOAP Service at the composite level

The SOA composite is shown in Figure 12-13. The BPEL component exposes the one-way interface and invokes the callback interface to deliver the proposal.

Open the BPEL editor for the *AircraftServiceRequestProcessor* component. The receive and asynchronous invoke (i.e., the callback) activities are already created and wired to the PartnerLink. All we need to add are an Assign activity—to provide some semi-meaningful content

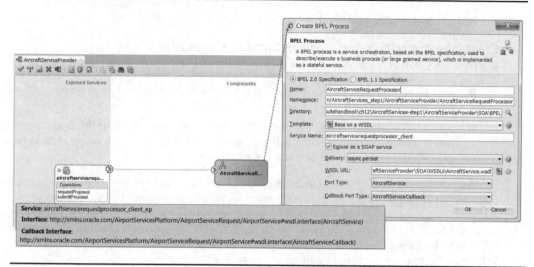

FIGURE 12-13. *A BPEL based implementation of the asynchronous AircraftService interface*

for the callback message and a Wait activity—to appear not too eager and to simulate real life at least to a little extent.

This is all that is required to implement the asynchronous interaction. Because the BPEL engine takes responsibility for the asynchronous details such as manipulating the WS-Addressing headers, the developer hardly even notices that the interaction is in fact asynchronous rather than straightforward synchronous request/reply.

You can deploy the composite and test it using EM FMW Control. There will not be a visible response, but by checking the flow trace you will be able to verify if the call back response took place. Using SoapUI with a mock service to implement the callback interface and providing the proper WS-Addressing header properties, we can find out if the callback message is correctly returned.

Implementing the AircraftServiceOrchestrator

An airline carrier—or a party that acts as a broker between carriers and service providers—has to implement an orchestrator: a mechanism to coordinate the search for a party to deliver the required aircraft services. This mechanism has to invoke the *AircraftService* exposed by as many applicable service providers as possible, handle the actual proposals they submit through their asynchronous callbacks, keep an eye on deadlines and collect the results and make or recommend a selection.

We have seen how BPEL is good at invoking asynchronous services and handling the callbacks that deliver the responses. Dealing with multiple parallel activities and maintain the state of the overall activity for some time is definitely something BPEL is well equipped for. Hence we will create an *AircraftServiceOrchestrator* composite to organize the RFP interactions for an airline carrier.

This composite exposes a web service with two operations—*arrangeAircraftService* and *cancelAircraftService*. The first one initiates and coordinates the proceedings to ask aircraft service suppliers for their proposals and collect their responses. The second is used to abort the proceedings and is discussed in a later section.

Create the AircraftServiceOrchestrator SOA Composite

The steps for creating this composite are very similar to those seen in the previous section:

■ Add an SOA project called *AircraftServiceOrchestrator* to the application AircraftServices; have the project be based on the *Empty Template*.

■ Add a BPEL component called *AircraftServiceNegotiationProcessor*; this component is based on the AircraftServiceNegotiation.wsdl document. The BPEL component is exposed as a SOAP Service at the composite level

We want the BPEL component to be able to call out to aircraft service suppliers who expose their implementation of the *AircraftService* that was implemented and deployed in the previous section. Obviously, in real life, there will be many implementations of this service, each with the same interface and their own endpoint. We will deal with that situation later on. For now, we will just create the interaction from the BPEL component with the one *AircraftService* instance we know of—the one we deployed in the previous section.

Drag the SOAP component from the palette to the references swim lane, to create a reference binding for the external *AircraftService*. Set the name of the reference to *AirportServiceProvider*. Select the AircraftService.wsdl document. Select the *AircraftService* and *AircraftServiceCallback*, respectively, for the Port Type and Callback Port Type properties. Press OK.

JDeveloper will show a warning about the abstract nature of the WSDL document: because it only describes the functional interface without providing a port with an actual endpoint where the service is available, we do not yet have enough information to successfully deploy and run our composite. However, to continue its implementation, there is no problem. Acknowledge the warning and continue.

Wire the BPEL process to the *AircraftServiceProvider* Reference Binding. The SOA composite is shown in Figure 12-14.

Implement the AircraftServiceNegotiationProcessor Component

The BPEL process accepts a request message—with a service request identifier and details about the required aircraft amenities—and replies immediately with a response that contains that same identifier and also the final time at which the process will summarize all proposals.

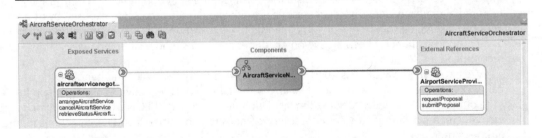

FIGURE 12-14. *The AircraftServiceOrchestrator that uses AircraftService Providers to collect proposals to deliver a type of aircraft service*

When this synchronous reply is returned to the invoker, the BPEL process will invoke one *AircraftServiceProvider*, passing the details from the aircraft service request as well as the RFP identifier and the deadline for responding. This call is one way; it initiates an asynchronous conversation that ends with the callback from the service provider. However, when the asynchronous response is not received before the deadline, then the process will cease waiting and complete immediately. At this point, we focus on the asynchronous interaction and the wait-until-deadline-or-callback and the BPEL process does not actually collect and further process the proposals.

Open the BPEL editor to implement the process as described above. The *receive* and *reply* activities are already created. Define two global variables—*RFPIdentification* of type xsd:string and *Deadline* of type xsd:dateTime. Add an Assign activity—called *SetGlobals*—following the Receive. Set these two variables to:

- RFPACS<ServiceRequestIdentifier><DDMMYY>
- 36 hours before the actual service delivery date—which would be done using the expression: xp20:add-dayTimeDuration-to-dateTime($inputVariable.part1/ ns3:ServiceDeliveryDate, '-P1DT12H'); for testing purposes you can also just set the current time plus 5 minutes

Next, add an Assign activity to set the *outputVariable* for the synchronous response. This variable contains the service request identifier and the deadline by which the proposals will be gathered. Finally, add a scope called *ExecuteRFP* underneath the Reply activity. This is where the actual collecting of proposals will be done. The BPEL process now looks as is shown in Figure 12-15.

Next, add an Invoke activity—wired to the one way interface of the *AircraftServiceProvider* partner link; have this activity use a local input variable. Also add a Receive activity for consuming the callback message from the *AircraftServiceProvider* partner link. This is where BPEL

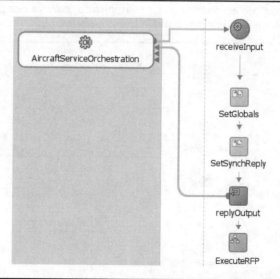

FIGURE 12-15.   *The synchronous first part of the AircraftServiceNegotiationProcessor*

really shines: receiving a callback message (i.e., an asynchronous response) is about as simple as receiving a synchronous reply. Create another local variable, to hold the callback response.

Add an Assign activity—called *SetInputForRFP*—prior to the Request. In this Assign step, make the necessary mappings between the *inputVariable* and the two globals (*RFPIdentifier* and *Deadline*) to the local input variable for the call to the *AircraftServiceProvider*.

The second part of the BPEL process is shown in Figure 12-16.

At this point, we can almost deploy and run the composite. In a later section we will add the "wait for deadline" functionality that is currently lacking. At that moment, we will add parallel call to a second *AircraftServiceProvider*.

Complete, Deploy and Run the AircraftServiceOrchestrator

The composite is not yet ready for deployment. Remember how the reference binding for the *AircraftServiceProvider* was based on the abstract WSDL that we selected from the file system. This WSDL did not provide a concrete port and endpoint which means our composite knows what the service looks like but does not know where to find it. Before we can successfully deploy, we have to specify the exact address of the service.

In later chapters, we will discuss the use of a configuration plan, to provide during deployment the environment specific endpoints for external services. For now, let's make simple modification to the composite.xml file.

First, open the WSDL document for the *AircraftService* composite that was deployed earlier in this chapter. You can do so from the EM FMW Control. Locate the Port element in the WSDL document. The combination of the *name* attributes of the Service and Port elements in the live WSDL document supplies the value for the wsdl.endpoint in the *port* attribute of the binding.ws element (Figure 12-17). The *location* attribute of the binding.ws element is set based on the *location* attribute in the soap:address element in the *port* element of the live WSDL and indicates the real endpoint address.

When the binding.ws element in the composite.xml file has been completed, we can deploy the composite to the SOA Suite run time. After the deployment, we can invoke the *arrangeAircraftService* operation to commence the proceedings for enlisting an aircraft service provider to help out with fuel, cleaning, catering, and baggage handling for a specific flight.

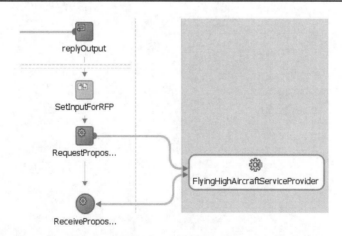

FIGURE 12-16.   *The asynchronous interaction with a single AircraftServiceProvider*

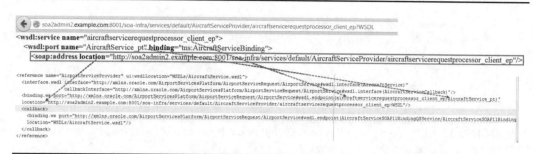

FIGURE 12-17. *Derive the concrete binding for the composite.xml reference definition from the live WSDL document for the AircraftServiceProvider*

The trace flow for a request to this operation could look like Figure 12-18.

Implementing the Asynchronous AircraftService with ServiceBus

A second implementation of the *AircraftService* can be created using Service Bus. Earlier in this chapter, we have seen how an asynchronous interface is implemented in Service Bus using a callout to a business service after setting the endpoint address based on the WS-Addressing header in the original request. The steps are as follows:

- Create a new application with a Service Bus project *AircraftServiceProvider*.
- Add the AircraftService.wsdl and the associated XSD document.
- Add bindings to the WSDL for both the port types.
- Create a Proxy Service *AircraftServicePS* for the one way port type and generate an associated pipeline; set the endpoint to */FlyingHighAircraftService/ AircraftServiceProvider*.

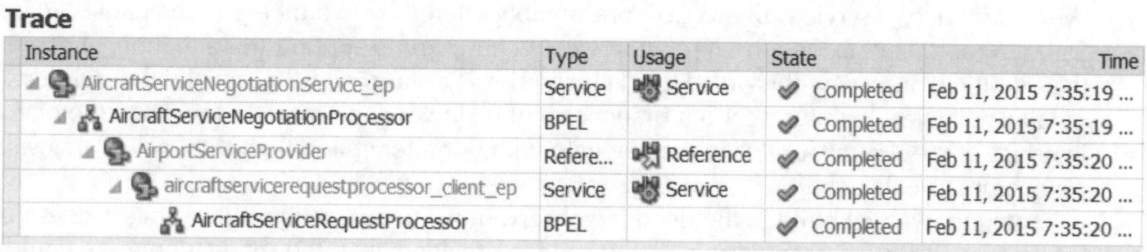

Trace

Instance	Type	Usage	State	Time
AircraftServiceNegotiationService_ep	Service	Service	Completed	Feb 11, 2015 7:35:19 …
AircraftServiceNegotiationProcessor	BPEL		Completed	Feb 11, 2015 7:35:19 …
AirportServiceProvider	Refere...	Reference	Completed	Feb 11, 2015 7:35:20 …
aircraftservicerequestprocessor_client_ep	Service	Service	Completed	Feb 11, 2015 7:35:20 …
AircraftServiceRequestProcessor	BPEL		Completed	Feb 11, 2015 7:35:20 …

FIGURE 12-18. *A call to operation arrangeAircraftService on the AircraftServiceOrchestration service triggered the AircraftNegotiationProcessor and its asynchronous interaction with the AircraftServiceProvider; the callback message from the AircraftServiceProvider is smoothly fed back into the right instance of the AircraftNegotiationProcessor by the BPEL run-time framework*

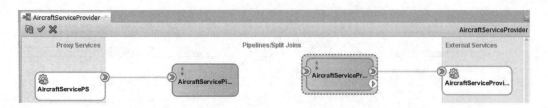

FIGURE 12-19. *The Service Bus project that implements the asynchronous AircraftService—with one way request and deferred callback*

■ Create a Business Service (*AircraftServiceProviderCallbackBS*) based on the callback port type. Also create a second pipeline (*AircraftServiceProviderCallbackPipeline*), based on the one way interface also implemented by the proxy service and the other pipeline. Add a *publish* activity in this second pipeline and have it publish to the business service and its *submitProposal* operation.

The Service Bus project is shown in Figure 12-19.

The first pipeline will publish its request to the second pipeline. Through this publish operation, the thread that is handling the reception of the incoming request is immediately released.

This second pipeline contains three stages—as is shown in Figure 12-20:

1. Gather WS-Addressing details in local variables.

2. Prepare the $body with the callback message.

3. Publish to the callback business service; however, before the call to the business service is actually made, we dynamically set the endpoint for this call to have it routed to the callback endpoint found in the WS-Addressing headers in the original request message instead of to the callback pipeline.

Details about the exact implementation can be found online.

We can test this asynchronous service using SoapUI, in the same way we have seen before.

Extend the AircraftServiceOrchestrator

We now have two services to invoke—presumably offered by two different companies active at Saibot Airport. Let's extend the *AircraftServiceOrchestrator* to support this situation. That means that our BPEL process will have a Flow activity. This is a standard BPEL activity that supports parallel activities. In this case, both branches in the Flow will perform an Invoke to the one way interface of the *AircraftService* to request help with our aircraft and then they will both await the asynchronous callback.

Later on, we will build in the deadline observation—to ensure the BPEL process does not wait longer for callback messages from aircraft service providers than the set deadline. We could even further extend this example to dynamically derive a list of services to invoke, instead of working with just these two hard coded ones.

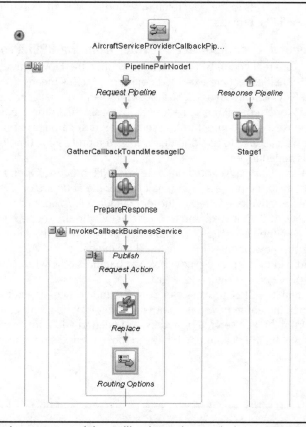

AircraftServiceProviderCallbackPip...

PipelinePairNode1

Request Pipeline   Response Pipeline

GatherCallbackToandMessageID   Stage1

PrepareResponse

InvokeCallbackBusinessService

Publish

Request Action

Replace

Routing Options

FIGURE 12-20. *Implementation of the Callback Pipeline with three stages: extract WS-Addressing headers, compose callback message and publish callback message to dynamically selected endpoint*

Integrate the Asynchronous Service Bus-Based AircraftService into the Composite

First, we have to determine the endpoint for the *AircraftServicePS* exposed from the Service Bus. Navigate to the Application Servers window and open the Service Bus node for the Integrated WebLogicServer. Under this node, expand the project folder for *AircraftServiceProvider*. Right click in the *AircraftServicePS* node and select Open from the context menu.

The WSDL document is retrieved from the run time and opened in JDeveloper. The location attribute in the address element in the port yields the endpoint. Add ?WSDL to this URL to get the WSDL location.

Open the SOA composite editor for the *AircraftServiceOrchestrator* composite. Add a SOAP Reference binding in the External References swim lane. Set the name to *FlyingHighAircraftServiceProvider*. Paste the endpoint determined in the previous step into the WSDL URL field. The Port Type is selected automatically. Press OK to create this Reference binding.

Wire the BPEL process to the new reference binding; it is after all our intention to invoke this reference from the BPEL process.

Invoke the Second AircraftService Provider from the BPEL Process

Parallel activities are realized in BPEL processes through the Flow activity. A Flow contains two or more Sequence activities that are executed concurrently. This means, for example, that in two branches in the Flow activity an asynchronous call to an external service can be made with both branches waiting for a reply at the same time. Obviously this is more efficient than having to wait for the first response to come in before the second request can be sent out. With a flow, the time it takes for the slowest service to respond determines the processing time of the overall flow, not the times of all calls added together.

Open the *AircraftServiceNegotiationProcessor* BPEL process. Open the scope *ExecuteRFP*. Add a Flow activity to the process, immediately after the *SetInputForRFP assign* activity. Drag the invoke and receive activities—wired to the *AircraftServiceProvider* partner link—to the first branch in the flow. Add an invoke and a receive activity to the second flow branch. Associate these activities with the *FlyingHighAircraftService* partner link. The same input variable can be used for calling this new partner link as is used for the call to the *AircraftServiceProvider* partner link. The second part of the process now has two parallel activity branches—one for each *AircraftService* provider, see Figure 12-21.

At this moment, the BPEL process can only continue processing activities that come after the *flow* activity when the entire flow has completed. That is, when both callback proposals have been received from the two service providers. We need to add a mechanism to monitor our deadline: when we hit the deadline, we have to move on and stop waiting for these callback messages to arrive.

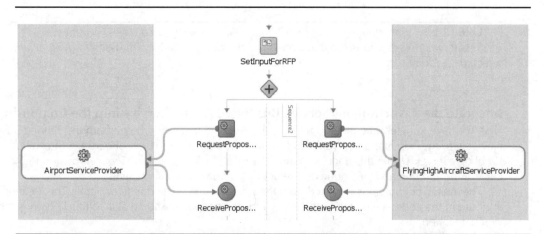

FIGURE 12-21. *Flow activity with parallel branches to do the asynchronous interaction with two different service providers simultaneously*

Introduce Some Asynchronous Interaction to the BPEL Process

A BPEL process can engage in various forms of asynchronous activity. We have seen how the process can wait for the callback message that is effectively the reply from an asynchronous partner [link]. Such a callback message is expected—even though we do not know when—and even if—it will arrive.

Another asynchronous activity we can introduce into the BPEL process is a background timer that runs for a certain period or until a certain deadline. When the timer fires, specified action is taken. The *AircraftServiceOrchestrator* will be made to wait no longer than until the deadline for deciding on a service provider arrives.

And in a similar way, we can have background message listeners that listen for request messages—not callback responses in reaction to previous service invocations from the BPEL process but unexpected new messages.

In this section, we will allow the airline carrier that initially called the *AircraftServiceOrchestrator* composite to invoke a cancel operation on the *AircraftServiceOrchestrator* service to stop the RFP proceedings. This should result in a similar message being sent to all aircraft service providers to inform them of the cancellation of the RFP. This last call, however, is outside the scope of this chapter.

Along similar lines we could have the carrier ask for the status of the proposal and even provide additional information such as an updated number of passengers or a changed slot time.

The ability to call a running instance of an SOA composite is quite special. It relies on a mechanism in BPEL called *correlation*. Through correlation, a request message can be associated with an existing BPEL process instance, rather than initiate a new one as normally would happen.

Add Deadline Monitor to AircraftServiceOrchestrator

A *scope* in BPEL is like an encapsulated unit that in addition to a set of activities can have its own local variables, fault handlers, compensation handlers as well as (asynchronous) event handlers. An event handler specifies an asynchronous agent that runs for as long as the scope is running and can do one of two things: wait for a specific moment in time and then act, or receive an incoming message of a specific type and act on it.

Select the *scope* in the *AircraftServiceOrchestrator* BPEL process that contains the flow with the two calls to AircraftServiceProviders. In the icon palette on the left side of the scope, click on alarm clock icon to add an OnAlarm event handler, as shown in Figure 12-22. JDeveloper adds the handler to the scope. Click on the OnAlarm activity to open its editor. Set the radio button to Until—to trigger the alarm at a specific moment—and specify $Deadline as the expression for the time at which the alarm should be triggered. Rename the scope in the event handler to *HandleDeadlineExpiry*. As a first and ultimately crude way of dealing with the deadline expiry, add an *exit* activity to this scope. Note that the OnAlarm handler is only ever activated when not all aircraft service providers send their proposal callback message before the deadline.

In order to see the OnAlarm in action, you want to change the deadline values and manipulation a little bit—or make the *AircraftServiceProvider* a bit slower.

After redeploying *AircraftServiceOrchestrator* composite, we can try out the added logic. Invoke the *arrangeAircraftService* operation with perhaps an early deadline. If the OnAlarm

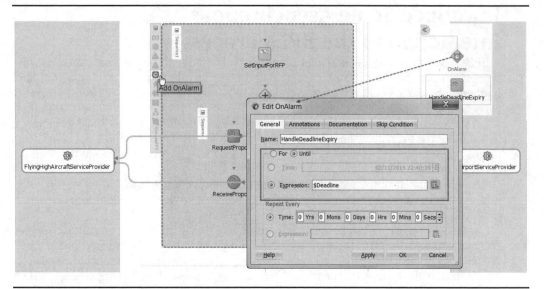

FIGURE 12-22. *Configuring an OnAlarm event handler for scope ExecuteRFP, to be triggered when the deadline is reached*

trigger fires, the flow trace and audit flow will indicate this. See Figure 12-23. Note: Since we did nothing to inform the *AircraftServiceProviders* about the deadline expiry, their process instances completed normally—even though their responses could not be handled by the negotiator because of the alarm that terminated normal processing.

Use Correlation to add a Cancel Operation to the AircraftServiceOrchestrator

BPEL has a unique capability among all the service engines and languages in the SOA Suite: a BPEL process can receive even after it has started running—and this goes beyond processing synchronous or even asynchronous responses to service invocations. Most computer programs are initiated by an original invocation and return a result once they are complete—they cannot easily or at all be accessed from the outside while they are running. A BPEL process can expose multiple operations—one of which will initiate the instance while others feed messages into a running instance.

We have already seen how BPEL processes can continue to run after they have returned a synchronous or asynchronous response message. To this special behavior we now add the capability of receiving subsequent messages—either by explicitly waiting for them to arrive or by handling them as unsolicited events. In both instances, the key ingredient to this functionality is a BPEL mechanism called correlation—the ability to match an incoming message with one of potentially many running instances.

Receiving messages into a running instance can be done using a Receive activity. Another method is through an onMessage event handler that we can attach to a scope in the BPEL process.

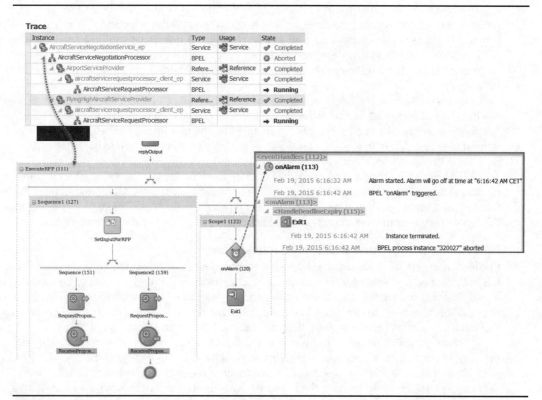

FIGURE 12-23. *Message Flow Trace and Audit Trail for AircraftServiceOrchestrator after asynchronous OnAlarm event handler has triggered—and has cut short the execution of the scope*

TIP

A third method for a running BPEL process instance to deal with incoming messages is inside the Pick activity. A BPEL Pick activity is included in a sequence like any other BPEL activity. It, too, deals with events: It instructs the BPEL engine to pause the BPEL process instance until one of potentially many events occurs. The events, as in the case of the event handlers, are either the elapsing of a certain time duration or the reception of a specific message. Unlike the event handlers that sit idle in the background for the entire lifespan of the scope, impacting the BPEL process only when the event they are listening for occurs, the Pick activity stalls the process—or at least the branch in which it lives, because there can be other branches in a common Flow parent—until one of the events for which it is configured takes place. No activity that follows the Pick activity is executed unless one of the Pick events occurs.

The cancellation can arrive at any time, from the moment the initial request for aircraft services was submitted until the time the RFP is complete and the selection of a service provider is made. It enters our SOA infrastructure as a web service request that should be fed into the BPEL process instance that was created and is still running for that particular aircraft. The BPEL process instance receives the request in the relevant event handler and should then complete the instance entirely.

The cancellation web service request needs to specify exactly which aircraft service request has to be cancelled—just like we would have to do when we cancel such an earlier request by telephone or email. The service request is identified by the identifier that was part of the initial request message. Alternatively, we could also determine an identifier inside the BPEL process and return it in the synchronous reply.

This identifier is used by the SOA Suite run time to associate the incoming cancellation request with the correct running SOA composite application instance. A precondition for this is that the used identifier should be unique across all process instances. The mechanism that makes this match between an inbound request and an existing instance is called correlation.

Correlation for the AircraftServiceOrchestrator

Correlation in general deals with the following scenario: A request message arrives at the SOA Suite. It is not intended to start a new composite application instance. Instead, it needs to be routed to an already running instance. It is up to the engine to find the correct instance to hand the message to. In this case, the request to cancel an RFP needs to be handed to the instance that was created for that particular aircraft service request. Refer to Figure 12-24 for an illustration of this.

Of course, the engine needs to be able to extract some sort of identifier from the request message to correlate that message with a running instance. In our example, the *AircraftServiceOrchestrator* was initially invoked with a message that contains a *ServiceRequestIdentifier* which for the purpose of this discussion we assume to unique across all calls to the *AircraftServiceOrchestrator*.

Any subsequent interactions regarding the service request should contain this identifier, and each running instance of the *AircraftServiceOrchestrator*, too, should be identifiable through that identifier. It is the linking pin to correlate new request messages with running instances.

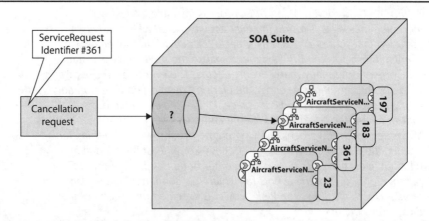

FIGURE 12-24. *Correlation between an incoming message and running composite application instances through a BPEL component*

Correlation of instances of composite applications is built on the correlation of BPEL process instances; a composite application without a BPEL service component does not support correlation. The message that needs to be correlated to a running composite application instance needs to be sent into the BPEL component—and therefore be sent to a service exposed by the application that is wired to the BPEL component.

In order to make the correlation mechanism work, we have to configure the BPEL process to recognize the *serviceRequestIdentifier* as that correlation key.

An instance of a BPEL process can be identified for correlation using a correlation set. Such a correlation set is a combination of one or more properties, in a way that is very much like a composite primary or unique key database constraint. Properties are defined at the process level, are of a certain type, and are mapped to values in the messages sent from or received by the process. A BPEL process can have multiple correlation sets—just like a database table can have multiple unique keys.

The *AircraftServiceNegotiationProcessor* has a single correlation set that consists of a single property. Let's call this set the *ServiceRequestIdentifierSet*. We can create a correlation set from the drop-down menu in the bar on top of the BPEL process editor, shown in Figure 12-25.Call the correlation set *ServiceRequestIdentifierSet*. Add a single property called *ServiceRequestIdentifier*, of type String.

Hereby we specify that instances of the *AircraftServiceNegotiationProcessor* BPEL process can be uniquely identified by correlation set *ServiceRequestIdentifierSet* using only the value of this property.

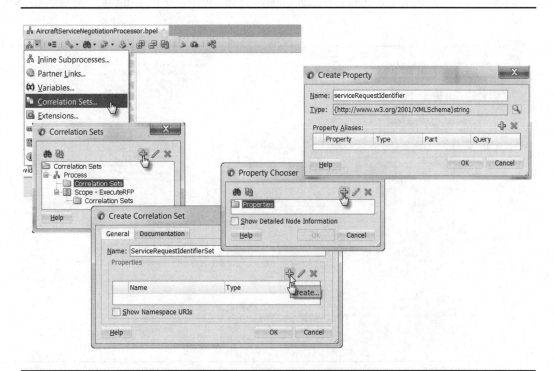

FIGURE 12-25. *Creating the correlation set ServiceRequestIdentifierSet and the ServiceRequestIdentifier property for the AircraftServiceNegotiationProcessor*

However, what is the value of that property? When and how is that determined? How does the property relate to the variables in the BPEL process or the messages sent to or from the process?

Correlation always takes place in the context of a message exchange. Either when the BPEL process is receiving a message (onMessage and Receive activities) or when it is sending a message (Invoke and + Reply) does correlation come into play. And only at such times does the engine need to establish the values of the properties in the correlation set that is attached to the message exchange.

The value of a property is associated with the content of the messages sent to or from the process at such exchange moments. For example, the *serviceRequestIdentifier* property gets its value from the outgoing *ArrrangeAicraftServiceResponseMessage* that is returned from the process in the first, synchronous Reply activity. When the cancellation message exchange takes place, the property will get its value from the incoming *CancelAircraftServiceRequestMessage*.

These associations between the property and a particular message exchange are specified using property alias definitions. A BPEL process can contain one or more property aliases that map a property to a specific message part—and to be precise, a specific XPath expression to extract a value from within that message part. This message part is used in the exchange through one of the partnerLinks in the process.

In the case of the *AircraftServiceNegotiationProcessor*, we will have two property aliases, because the *ServiceRequestIdentifier* is associated with two message exchanges (initial aircraft service request and cancellation). These property aliases can be created from the *edit* property window that can be opened using the edit property icon on the correlation set window. This is shown in Figure 12-26. In the Query field, we must specify the XPath expression to retrieve the

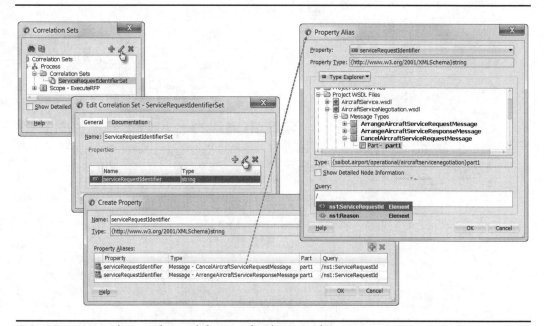

FIGURE 12-26. *The correlation definitions for the AircraftServiceNegotiationProcessor: the correlation set, the property, and the two property aliases*

value for the property. Hint: Pressing ctrl-spacebar brings up a list of available XML elements to add to the XPath expression.

The identity of the process instance (the values in the correlation set) is established only once—obviously, because that cannot change later on. Establishing the identity takes place through initialization of the correlation set and capturing the values of the properties in the set at that moment in time. In our case, this happens when the *ArrrangeAicraftServiceResponseMessage* is sent by the synchronous reply operation labeled *arrrangeAicraftService*. The value of the *ServiceRequestId* element in the *ArrrangeAicraftServiceResponseMessage* element in the response message is read and set as the value for the *ServiceRequestIdentifier*—a value that will never change for the instance of the BPEL process.

On each subsequent message exchange, the identification of the process instance, as determined in the correlation set, can be compared to the value as extracted from incoming messages. That allows the engine to link the incoming message to the instance with the same value for the correlation set.

The steps in the correlation processes are as follows:

1.   The synchronous Reply activity initiates the correlation set, and the value is extracted from the response message and used to set the instance identifier.

2.   The value for the *ServiceRequestIdentifierSet* correlation set is extracted from the incoming Cancellation Request message based on the property alias defined for that message and compared with the identifiers for all running instances to find the matching instance.

The final step in making correlation work like this is to configure the activities that send (Reply) and receive (onMessage handler) the messages that need to be correlated.

First of all, the Reply activity. This activity is special because it needs to instantiate the correlation set. Open the editor by double-clicking the Reply activity. Go to the Correlations tab. Click the green plus icon to add a correlation set that is associated with this message exchange. Select the *ServiceRequestIdentifierSet*. You need to set Initiate to *yes* to indicate that this Reply step is the moment when this correlation set is instantiated and the identifier for this process instance is set. Figure 12-27 illustrates these steps.

Through this definition, we have ensured that when this Reply activity is executed, an instance of this BPEL process is assigned an identity that can be used for correlation purposes.

As an aside, a BPEL process can have multiple identities through multiple correlation sets that have different properties and different values, and can be established at different points in time. The *AircraftServiceNegotiationProcessor*, for example, could have a second correlation set that also identifies the aircraft service request through a combination of the flightNumber and the date and time of the slot.

Correlation for the Aircraft Service Request Cancellations

We have laid the foundation for the capability to receive a cancellation request for an aircraft service request. We have configured a correlation set and ensured that the instance identity is determined when the synchronous reply takes place.

Next, we have to add an on [message] event handler to the scope *ExecuteRFP* to handle reception of an *CancelAircraftServiceRequestMessage* when the *cancelAircraftService* operation is called on the *AircraftServiceNegotiation* service. Then we need to configure this onMessage handler to support correlation for this message exchange. Double-click the on event icon to configure the message exchange it will implement. Figure 12-28 illustrates these steps.

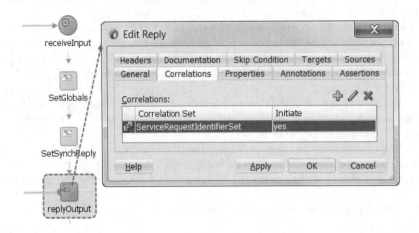

FIGURE 12-27. *Configuring the correlation set ServiceRequestIdentifierSet and its initiation for the Reply activity*

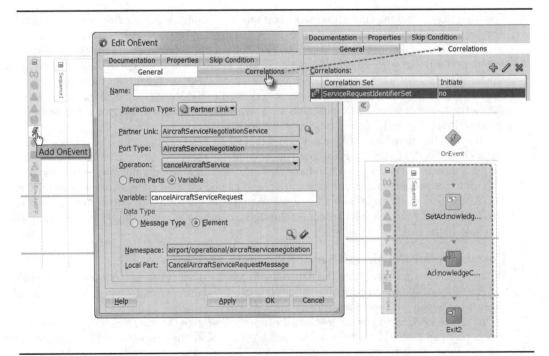

FIGURE 12-28. *Configuring the message exchange and correlation for the onMessage branch that will handle the cancellation requests*

The partner link involved in the on (message) event activity is the *AircraftServiceOrchestration*. The relevant operation in the port type associated with this partner link is the *cancelAircraft* operation. Specify the (input) variable as *cancelAircraftServiceRequest* based on the *CancelAircraftServiceRequest* element on which the request message is based.

Next, click the Correlations tab. The only correlation set that is involved with this on event activity is the *ServiceRequestIdentifierSet*. It should not be initiated, because that already happened through the outgoing message sent from the Reply activity; for cancellations, we will use the value assigned to the property in the correlation set at that time to correlate with the incoming cancellation message's property value.

To add some degree of decent cancellation handling, add a *reply* activity to the scope inside the onEvent handler. This activity provides the synchronous reply to the cancellation request; it is associated with the *AircraftServiceOrchestration* partner link. Have a local variable generated to hold the response and add an *assign* activity to set the value for this variable with some form of acknowledgement of the cancellation request. Then, as a very crude way that suffices for now, add an *exit* activity to terminate the instance of the *AircraftServiceNegotiationProcessor*.

Deploy the AircraftServiceOrchestrator composite. Invoke the service on its arrangeAircraftService operation. Then, shortly after that call, call the service again, this time on its cancelAircraftService operation, passing in the same value for ServiceRequestId as in the first call. This should result in an AircraftServiceOrchestration process instance being started and being interrupted and aborted by the cancellation request. Figure 12-29 shows the flow trace and the audit trail for this process instance. Note the second call to the AircraftServiceOrchestration_ep service binding; this one does not start a new instance of the composite but is correlated with and fed into the running instance, based on the ServiceRequestId.

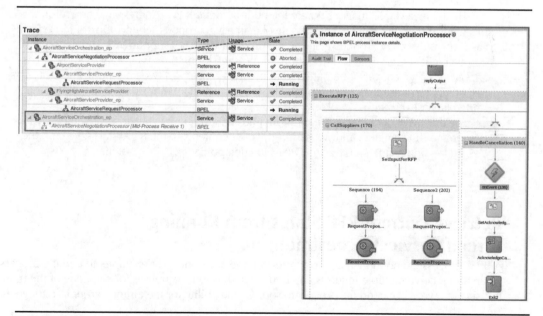

FIGURE 12-29. *Flow trace and BPEL audit trail for the AircraftServiceOrchestration composite instance that is cancelled through a correlated service call*

Correlation and Asynchronous Service Calls

Correlation is the primary mechanism used by the SOA Suite run time to match up incoming messages with existing instances of composite applications. Yet we did not discuss correlation when we introduced the implementation of our calls to asynchronous services, even though the response from an asynchronous service such as the *AircraftServiceProvider* is returned in the form of a service call to the *AircraftService* callback portType, handled through the partnerlink by the *AircraftServiceNegotiationProcessor*.

The reason for this is that the BPEL engine handles this automatically under the covers using the WS-Addressing standards. In other scenarios we have to implement/configure this ourselves because the components we interact with are not BPEL components. We do not need to make any changes to the BPEL process, the composite definition, or the WSDL file in order to leverage the WS-Addressing method for correlation between BPEL process instances and the asynchronous services they invoke. The BPEL engine run-time framework will add headers to the SOAP message that is sent when an asynchronous Web Service is invoked. These headers—based on the WS-Addressing specification—contain the endpoint location (reply-to address) that specifies the location at which a BPEL client is listening for a callback message and the Conversation ID, which is a unique identifier for the BPEL process instance that sent the request.

When the asynchronous service sends the response by invoking the callback service, it can use the information from the WS-Addressing headers to target the response at the right client. When the asynchronous service is itself a BPEL process, like one of our *AircraftService* providers, the headers are leveraged automatically by the BPEL engine, completely transparently to us as developers.

There are several situations where the built-in, default WS-Addressing correlation mechanism does not suffice when we invoke an asynchronous service. One of those is the case where the asynchronous web service provider does not support WS-Addressing and correlation is required to map the response message to the process instance. Another case is a more complex conversation pattern that involves more than two communication partners and a final response that is not returned by the partner that received the original call that started the conversation.

See the FMW documentation for more information about WS-Addressing, the way it is used in the BPEL engine, and ways to inspect the contents of the SOAP message (and the WS-Addressing headers) using an OWSM logging policy or TCP/IP Listener.

Retrieve Current RFP Status from Running AircraftServiceOrchestrator

A BPEL process cannot only receive a correlated message once, for example, to end the process, it can also receive multiple requests and return synchronous responses for each one of them. In this section, we will extend the process to support the ability for the airline carrier to retrieve the status of the RFP while the orchestrator is still doing the negotiations. We will make use of a BPEL Inline Subprocess that is invoked from each of the parallel branches in the flow to add the aircraft service proposal to a global collection of all proposals. Then we will add a second OnEvent handler to the *ExecuteRFP* scope that receives another correlated message—for the *retrieveStatus* operation that we will add to the portType in the WSDL.

Extend the Service Interface Definition

Open the AircraftServiceNegotiation.xsd document. It contains the proposalsListType that is used in the RetrieveStatusAircraftServiceNegotiationResponseMessage. The RetrieveStatusAircraftServiceNegotiationRequestMessage contains a ServiceRequestId element—that should be somewhat familiar by now.

Open the AircraftServiceNegotiation.wsdl document. Add two messages and also one operation in the portType:

```
    <wsdl:message name="RetrieveStatusAircraftServiceNegotiationRequestMessage">
        <wsdl:part name="part1"
element="acsn:RetrieveStatusAircraftServiceNegotiationRequestMessage"/>
    </wsdl:message>
    <wsdl:message name="RetrieveStatusAircraftServiceNegotiationResponseMessage">
        <wsdl:part name="part1"
element="acsn:RetrieveStatusAircraftServiceNegotiationResponseMessage"/>
    </wsdl:message>
        <wsdl:operation name="retrieveStatusAircraftServiceNegotiation">
            <wsdl:input
message="tns:RetrieveStatusAircraftServiceNegotiationRequestMessage"/>
            <wsdl:output
message="tns:RetrieveStatusAircraftServiceNegotiationResponseMessage"/>
        </wsdl:operation>
```

Extend the AircraftNegotiationProcessor Process

Open the BPEL editor for the *AircraftNegotiationProcessor*. Create a new variable, called *collectedProposals*, based on the proposalsListType in the XSD document. In this variable, we will collect all proposals received from our suppliers of aircraft services.

Add a Scope activity to one of the flow branches. In this scope, add an Assign activity. This activity has to append a proposal element to the *collectedProposals* variable. Right click the scope and select the option *Convert to Subprocess*.

Define two variables for the subprocess—as its input parameters; see Figure 12-30 for details. One is called *proposal*—based on SubmitProposalCallbackMessage that is received from the aircraft service providers—and the other is called *supplier* and is of type string.

Edit the Assign activity to copy all values from the proposal variable to the global *collectedProposals* variable, including the name of the supplier. Figure 12-31 shows this Assign activity.

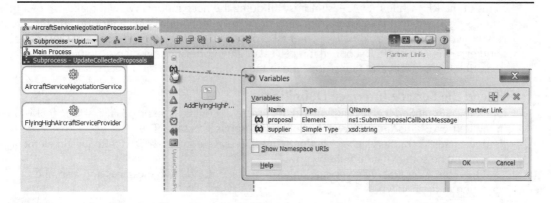

FIGURE 12-30. *Define the input parameters for the UpdateCollectedProposals sub process: the received proposal and the name of the supplier who made the proposal*

Add and edit calls to the subprocess from each flow branch. Map local variables to the input parameters to the subprocess, as shown in Figure 12-32.

Add a property alias for property *ServiceRequestIdentifier* to allow correlation of messages sent to the *getStatusRFP* operation. This time, the property is mapped to the *ServiceRequestId* element in the *RetrieveStatusAircraftServiceNegotiationRequestMessage*, as shown in Figure 12-33.

Add an OnEvent handler to scope *ExecuteRFP* for the *retrieveStatus* operation in the *AircraftServiceOrchestrator* service. Configure the correlation set to hook into this event handler, as shown in Figure 12-34.

Add a reply activity for the *retrieveStatus* operation with a generated local variable and add an assign activity to add the contents from the *collectedProposals* variable to this output variable.

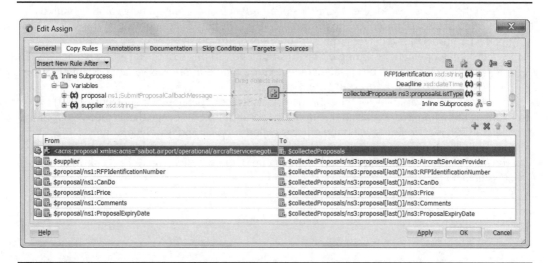

FIGURE 12-31. *The Assign activity that copies details about a supplier's proposal to the collectedProposals collection*

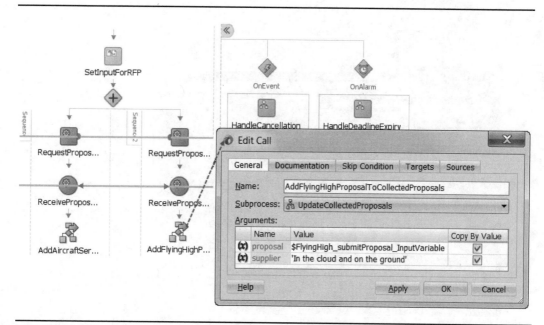

FIGURE 12-32. *Configuring the call to the BPEL inline Subprocess to add the received proposal to the collection of proposals*

TIP
To have a little more time to ask for the status of a running instance, you could add a wait *activity after the flow activity inside scope* ExecuteRFP *to force the instance to run a little longer.*

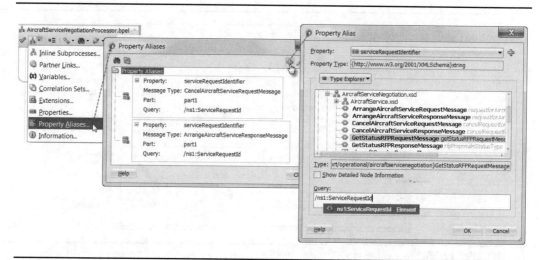

FIGURE 12-33. *Adding a property alias for the GetStatusRFPRequestMessage*

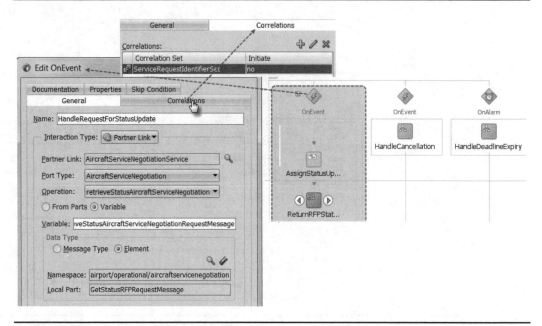

FIGURE 12-34. *Configure the OnEvent handler to handle the request message to the retrieveStatusAircraftServiceNegotiation operation with correlation enabled*

Deploy the composite. Invoke the *AircraftServiceOrchestrator* composite as before, calling the arrange operation. Now you can invoke the composite again, this time invoking the *retrieveStatus* operation and passing the same identifier as in the call to the arrange operation. The current status should be returned; its value depends of course on whether the aircraft service providers have already sent their proposal to the orchestrator. Figure 12-35 shows the

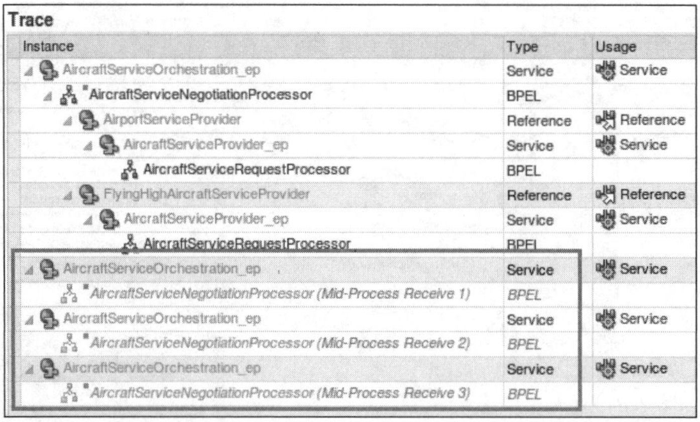

Trace		
Instance	Type	Usage
⊿ ◳ AircraftServiceOrchestration_ep	Service	Service
⊿ ⅄ *AircraftServiceNegotiationProcessor	BPEL	
⊿ ◳ AirportServiceProvider	Reference	Reference
⊿ ◳ AircraftServiceProvider_ep	Service	Service
⅄ AircraftServiceRequestProcessor	BPEL	
⊿ ◳ FlyingHighAircraftServiceProvider	Reference	Reference
⊿ ◳ AircraftServiceProvider_ep	Service	Service
⅄ AircraftServiceRequestProcessor	BPEL	
⊿ ◳ AircraftServiceOrchestration_ep	Service	Service
⅄ *AircraftServiceNegotiationProcessor (Mid-Process Receive 1)	BPEL	
⊿ ◳ AircraftServiceOrchestration_ep	Service	Service
⅄ *AircraftServiceNegotiationProcessor (Mid-Process Receive 2)	BPEL	
⊿ ◳ AircraftServiceOrchestration_ep	Service	Service
⅄ *AircraftServiceNegotiationProcessor (Mid-Process Receive 3)	BPEL	

FIGURE 12-35. *Message flow trace with three mid-process, asynchronous calls to the retrieve status operation*

message flow trace for the *AircraftServiceOrchestrator*; the three asynchronous, mid-process status retrieval calls are indicated.

Note that you can invoke the *retrieveStatus* operation multiple times. When you invoke the operation before the *arrange* operation is called—that initiates the composite—then the BPEL engine will remember the request and process it as soon as the *arrange* operation has been invoked to instantiate the BPEL process.

The BPEL audit trail for the interactions shown in Figure 12-35 are shown in Figure 12-36.

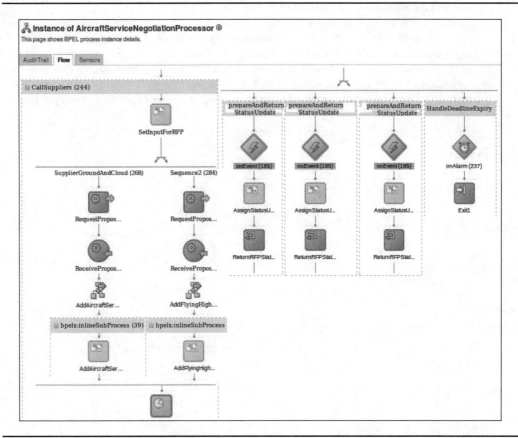

FIGURE 12-36.   *The BPEL flow trace for the AircraftServiceNegotiationProcessor with two asynchronous interactions with aircraft service providers and three correlated mid-process status retrieval requests*

Summary

Asynchronous interactions are important in the real world as well as in a service oriented architecture. Tying up resources in synchronous exchanges when the synchronicity is not required is a waste. SOA Suite provides good support for asynchronous message exchanges—both for accessing asynchronous service provides as well as for implementing asynchronous service interfaces.

While Mediator and Service Bus have some support for asynchronous interactions, it is a little lower level and requires manipulating WS-Addressing headers. BPEL is ideally equipped for asynchronous exchanges—both for implementing them as well as for initiating them. The BPEL engine handles all addressing and correlation details; as a result, the developer hardly even notices that an interface is asynchronous rather than synchronous.

In addition to an asynchronous "request followed by callback" pattern, we have in seen this chapter how BPEL can accept subsequent requests into an already running process instance through correlation. Such requests can be explicitly waited for in the main process 'thread' or they can arrive as asynchronous events in the process, handled by an event handler. Another type of asynchronous or background event handler is provided by the OnAlarm mechanism that can interrupt the main flow when a deadline has been reached or a certain period of time has passed.

CHAPTER
13

Inbound Adapters—
Polling Database,
Consuming JMS, and
Receiving Emails

S OA composites or Service Bus projects do not have to be triggered through a request message from an external consumer. The adapters we have discussed for outbound operations towards databases, file systems, JMS destinations, Advanced Queues, and people (UMS through email, SMS and chat) also operate in an inbound direction. In this direction, external events activate the adapter to trigger the proxy service or SOA composite. This includes events such as a new file appears, a database record is updated, a message is published on a JMS queue or topic or an email or chat message arrives.

This chapter demonstrates the use of these inbound adapter actions. These are quite valuable to have our SOA applications quickly respond to events in boundary systems—even though these are not explicitly published as business events. The inbound mode of the adapters mean we do not have to write all kinds of polling logic to keep track of what is going on in various channels and systems around us.

Specifically, this chapter discusses the inbound database adapter mode to spot new or changed database records, the JMS queue listener, and the inbound mode for the UMS adapter, which will monitor incoming emails and chat messages.

Database Polling for Staged Slot Requests

Data manipulation is ideally done through services only. However, the reality is that in many organizations there are existing applications that directly update database tables—without going the proper service route. It is very well possible that these direct inserts or updates of database records should trigger activity at service and process level—in the SOA Suite. These data manipulations may represent business events that our services need to respond to.

The database adapter was first introduced in Chapter 4. Then we used this adapter to reach out from the Service Bus project or the SOA composite to the database—to invoke PL/SQL stored programs or to query data from tables and views. This adapter also supports an inbound mode— where the initiative lies with the adapter instead of with the service. In this section we will use the inbound mode to inspect a table where an external Portal application and an internal application for Saibot's account managers can write slot requests—database records that represent a desire from an aircraft carrier to take possession of a certain slot.

In this section, we have to develop a SOA composite that will find these slot request records in the database table and process them—making a call to the *SlotService* for proper registration of the slot allocation in the Future data domain. This composite will poll the table with slot requests. For each record found, a new instance of the SOA composite will be initiated.

Prepare Environment

For the SOA composite we are about to develop to poll records from a database table, we need of course to first create that table. The table we will be checking for new records is called *PORTAL_SLOT_ALLOCATIONS*. It is created through the DDL scripts in the on line resources for Chapter 13. The table contains 10 columns that describe a slot allocation request for a particular air carrier.

Additionally, just like the outbound database adapter bindings we discussed in Chapter 5, the inbound adapter binding references (the JNDI name of) a connection specified in the database adapter deployment, that itself uses a JDBC Data Source that connects to the database schema that contains the table. The required configuration steps for the database adapter are described on line.

Create SOA Composite

Create a new SOA application *InboundProcessing* with an SOA composite project called *PortalSlotRequestProcessor*. Select the template *Composite with Mediator*. Set the name of the Mediator to *PortalSlotRequestMediator* and choose to define the interface later.

The inbound interface for this mediator will be defined by the inbound database adapter binding in a little while.

Configure Inbound Database Adapter

Drag the Database Adapter to the Services swimlane—because in this case the adapter binding will initiate the SOA composite instance and as such act as the service in the SCA meaning of that term. Set the name of the adapter binding to *PortalSlotRequestPoller*. Use the same Saibot database connection as in chapter 4 and set the JNDI Name to eis/DB/SaibotCommonDB—corresponding to the JNDI name of one of the connections defined for the Database Adapter deployment in the run time SOA Suite environment. In step 3 we have a novelty: select *Poll for New or Changed Records in a Table* as the operation type. This operation is only meaningful for inbound database adapter bindings.

On the next page, you have to indicate the table that should be polled: PORTAL_SLOT_ALLOCATIONS. Then, in step 8, you can specify the behavior for the Database Adapter after processing a record, see Figure 13-1. Depending on how the records to be processed are identified and which privileges the SOA composite application has on the source table, we can choose from a direct update of the database record that was processed (an update or even a delete) or we can indicate that the identifier for each record that has been processed showed be inserted in a different table (in the same or another database as the one being polled) or in a file (locally on the SOA Suite environment).

Whenever possible, it is common to use the logical delete option that will update a particular column for the records that have been processed.

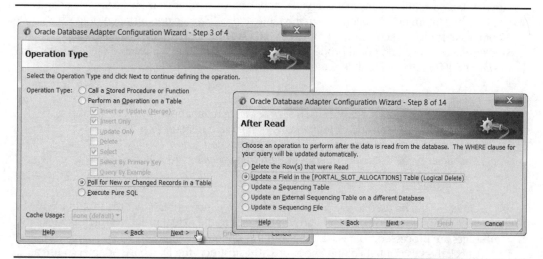

FIGURE 13-1.   *The inbound mode of the database adapter will poll for new or changed records*

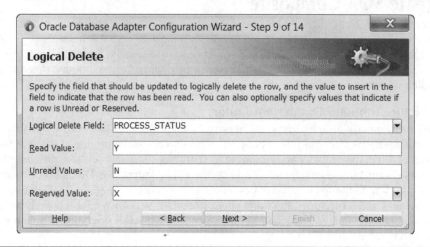

FIGURE 13-2. *Configure the details for the Logical Delete on processed database records*

If we pick the option to Logically Delete records after processing, we get to specify the details for this logical delete in step 9 (Figure 13-2). Select column PROCESS_STATUS as the column that will indicate the status of the record. The value Y will indicate the record has been read and processed. The value N for this column identifies records that have not yet been processed. The Reserved Value X is used to mark records that are currently being processed. Records will have this value only briefly.

The next step in the wizard is for the Polling Options (Figure 13-3). In this step we specify the polling frequency; every 20 seconds in this example will do. We set the number of database records that will be passed in a single SOA composite instantiation; we set this property to one, as will usually be the case. The number of database rows picked up in a single transaction is set to two in this case; this means that every 20 seconds, every instance of this database adapter will fetch a maximum of two records from the table and will create one instance of the SOA composite for each record. The number of workers—instances of the database adapter—is determined by two additional properties: *activationInstances* in a clustered environment and *NumberOfThreads* in a multithreaded single node set up.

TIP
If you want to implement your own logical delete mechanism, you can. In that case, select Delete the Row(s) that were Read in step 8 and after the wizard is completed, edit the generated ..-or-mappings .xml file and edit a <delete-query> section that specifies the SQL to execute for each record to be logically deleted.

Order by can be used to specify the sort order in which unread records should ideally be processed. However, no guarantees are available as to the actual order in which the resulting messages are processed, so it is best to avoid this option altogether.

Check the Distributed Polling check box. This instructs the Database Adapter to use a SELECT .. FOR UPDATE SKIP LOCKED syntax when fetching records from an Oracle database, a syntax that optimizes throughput and reduces negative impact from multiple workers.

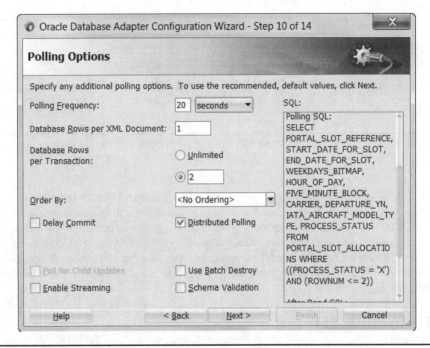

FIGURE 13-3. *Configure the polling options to indicate how often the table should be inspected and how many records should be processed per service instance and per transaction or polling event*

Check the documentation for the other, more advanced and/or exotic options. Press Next to go to step 10—Defined Selection Criteria. This step allows us to further refine the SQL statement that should be executed to fetch records to process. Accept the default statement and continue to press Next until the Finish button is enabled. Accept all intermediate defaults and press Finish to complete the configuration of this inbound database adapter binding.

Create Reference Binding for Slot Service

We want to invoke the *SlotService* that was created in Chapter 4 (and reused in Chapter 7) for each slot allocation request that the inbound database adapter will hand to the current SOA composite. Therefore, a Reference binding should be added to the composite for the *SlotService*.

Right click in the External References swimlane can select Insert | SOAP from the dropdown menu. Enter the URL for the *SlotService's* WSDL: http://localhost:7101/flight/SlotService?wsdl. Set the name of the reference to *SlotService*. Press OK. Allow the localization of all files. As a result, the WSDL document and associated resources are copied to the project.

Configure the Mediator

In this case, as so often, the mediator component is really the man in the middle. Wire the inbound database adapter binding to the mediator, as shown in Figure 13-4. Wire the mediator the *SlotService* reference binding.

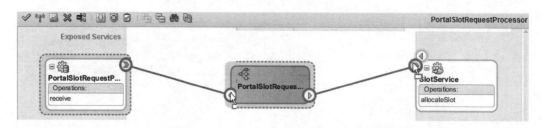

FIGURE 13-4. *The PortalSlotRequestProcessor composite with an inbound database adapter*

All we need to do now is map the XML message (structure) that the database adapter will feed into the SOA composite to the message structure expected by the *SlotService*. The former is described by the PortalSlotRequestPoller_table.xsd file that was generated by the Database Adapter wizard. Create a new XSL Map file inboundPortalSlotRequestToallocateSlotRequestMessage.xsl that maps between the *PortalSlotAllocationsCollection* and the *allocateSlotRequestMessage*.

Edit the Mediator: configure the routing rule to use this XSL Map for the transformation of the request message.

Deploy and Test

With the SOA composite application complete, we can deploy it. When done, there is not a service interface that we can invoke for this composite. Its entrance is through the inbound database adapter, which polls the database table.

After deployment, the polling of the database will immediately commence. After the polling interval passes, the *PORTAL_SLOT_ALLOCATIONS* table is inspected for any (new) records with status equal to N. For each record retrieved, a new instance of the SOA composite will be created that gets handed the XML representation of the database record as its request message, with a maximum of two instances per polling interval (in the case of a single adapter instance). The composite transforms the message and passes it on to the *SlotService* for proper processing. The outcome of entire transaction is that a new record is added to table *FUT_SLOTS*.

When we insert three or more records into table *PORTAL_SLOT_ALLOCATIONS* and wait for approximately 20 seconds—we can find the flow trace shown in Figure 13-5 in the EM FMW Control.

Additional unprocessed records will have to wait for the next polling interval to be also retrieved and handled.

Inbound Adapters and Exceptions

When processing of inbound messages fails, there is no explicit party to send an error message to. The inbound database adapter is only the man in the middle—picking up records from a table and handing them to the SOA composite. When exceptions occur in or beyond the SOA composite, the SOA composite instance fails. We have to set up fault policies or manual procedures to deal with those failed instances.

Additionally, the inbound adapter can be configured with a rejection handler to deal with rejected messages. A distinction is made between retryable errors—caused for example by

Trace

Instance	Type	Usage	State
PortalSlotRequestPoller : 10044	Service	Service	Completed
PortalSlotRequestMediator : 10045	Mediator		Completed
SlotService : 10046	Reference	Reference	Completed
ServiceBus : E10272	ServiceBus		
PortalSlotRequestPoller : 10047	Service	Service	Completed
PortalSlotRequestMediator : 10048	Mediator		Completed
SlotService : 10049	Reference	Reference	Completed
ServiceBus : E10279	ServiceBus		

FIGURE 13-5.   *A single polling action by the inbound database has fetched two database records and created an instance of the SOA composite for each of them; these instances invoked the SlotService (on the Service Bus) that used the outbound database adapter to created records in table FUT_SLOTS*

connection issues—and non-retryable faults, as a result for example of transformation errors or even unhandled business exceptions. A special category of rejection that can be handled is when the inbound adapter does not even get to the stage of handing a message to an SOA composite because of internal issues, for example with the transformation of the native data into the XML format configured with the adapter binding.

A database record that is fetched by the inbound adapter will be logically deleted (have its logical delete status set to *Read*) when the processing leads to a failed SOA composite instance. The recovery has to take place for the SOA composite; at that point, the database record is considered done.

Scaling Inbound Adapter Activity

An inbound database adapter could cause a large load to be put on the SOA Suite server: if, for example, an import operation or some batch creates or updates a large number of database records or the inbound database adapter becomes active after a long downtime, you might expect that a large number of SOA composite instances could be created almost instantaneously. Fortunately, there are tuning parameters available on the adapter binding definition:

- *activationInstances*—the number of concurrent instances of the DB Adapter that is created to process database records in a distributed cluster scenario. In a multithreaded single node scenario, configure *NumberOfThreads* instead.

- *MaxTransactionSize*—the maximum number of records an DB Adapter instance will process in a single transaction and therefore in a single polling interval.

- *PollingInterval*—the wait time between reads by an DB Adapter instance.

- *MaxRaiseSize*—the number of database records that is to be processed by a single SOA composite instance.

From these parameters, we can calculate the maximum load the SOA Suite engine can be put under as a result from the inbound DB Adapter binding:

The largest number of database records processed per second is calculated as MaxTransactionSize/PollingInterval * activationInstances. For example: with a MaxTransactionSize of 150, 6 activationInstances and a PollingInterval of 5 minutes, no more than 150/300 * 6 = 3 records can be processed per second (although we handle this in bursts per 5 minutes per instance).

We can compare this to the traffic we expect to see whether our set up will be able to cope in the long run. This does not tell us however how large the effort is to process a single database record so we do not know if in terms of throughput and resources we will actually get those three records processed per second.

To increase scalability and decrease mutual impact from concurrent instance of the DB Adapter, use the Distributed Polling strategy. On an Oracle Database this means that records are fetched using "SELECT FOR UPDATE SKIP LOCKED" which means that polled records are locked, locked records are ignored and no wait time is incurred because of existing locks. This is the by far most efficient way of reserving and fetching batches of records for a DB Adapter instance without any impact on other instances.

Just so you know: inbound adapters can be switched on and off through the embedded Enterprise Scheduler. This allows us for example to respect maintenance windows of external systems. Chapter 14 will provide more details on this.

Breaking up BPEL Processes Using Inbound Database Adapter

A BPEL process can be long running. This happens typically when the BPEL process will wait for external actions—either messages to arrive from external systems or actions performed by human agents. The BPEL infrastructure however is not ideally suited to very long running process instances. Some considerations include the size of the dehydration store, the deployment of new versions of the SOA composite and an upgrade of the SOA Suite run time environment. Instances that run for days or (much) longer are ideally avoided.

Sometimes the logic of the BPEL process dictates the long running nature. That is just the way the business functionality is defined. At various moments, spread over time, stages of the process have to be performed, each one triggered by a certain external event—which can be just the passing of time. And each stage needs access to at least some of the state of the process (instance).

If the stages in the BPEL process are activated by deadlines or by events other than correlated message exchanges, then it may be an option to create separate BPEL processes for each stage and have each of these stage-processes activated through in inbound database adapter that watches for deadlines and status changes. Each stage starts by retrieving the state information and concludes by recording the updated state information for the process instance.

Figure 13-6 visualizes this approach. The original BPEL process—indicated by the surrounding rounded rectangle—has been split into multiple stage-specific process definitions. Stage 0 initiates the process instances in the regular way, based on a SOAP request. When stage 0 is done, the BPEL component records the state that should carry over to the next stage, using a reusable BPEL subprocess. This subprocess uses a custom format (probably XML based) to record the relevant state in a custom table in a database schema.

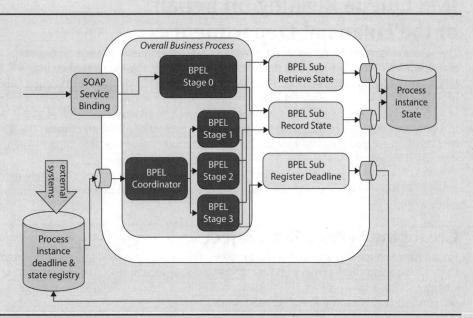

FIGURE 13-6. *Breaking up a long-running BPEL process into multiple stages—triggered by an inbound database adapter based on deadline or status changes*

The inbound database adapter monitors a table that holds records for process instances of this specific SOA composite. Each record represents a (running) process instance. The records can trigger the database adapter, either through a status or through a deadline. When a deadline is passed or the status is set to a specific value, the inbound database adapter triggers a new instance of the SOA composite and invokes the Coordinator BPEL process. The coordinator determines from the current process status read from the database which stage should be executed. It then invokes the BPEL process component for that stage—passing the instance identifier of the process.

The BPEL process for the selected state uses this instance identifier to retrieve the process state from the custom process state repository. When the state has been restored, the actions for this stage are executed by the BPEL process. When the stage is complete, the component will record the state the process instance has now reached. It may also write a deadline record or a new status value for the process instance. At that point, the composite instance is done processing. No running instance is left around at the level of the SOA Suite. Only in the custom table we may still have the potential for a next stage to be executed for the business process.

Each stage specific process instance will run for a short duration. The entire business process consists of all stages and may run for days, weeks or even months—without introducing all the drawbacks of such long running instances (but introducing a nonstandard process coordinator mechanism that will not produce an end to end message flow trace—because to the SOA Suite, each stage is a new conversation). Using composite sensors is at least a way to be able to quickly find all related SOA composite instances for a single business process instance. Note that this approach is similar to what we can do in the BPM Suite with BPMN processes and probably even more so with adaptive cases.

JMS Queue Reading on Behalf of the Financial Department

The *AircraftMovement* messages that were put on the JMS queue in Chapter 6 make a reappearance here when through the inbound mode of the JMS adapter, they trigger a Financial Department's Service Bus service. Note: We are using the JCA adapter for JMS in a Service Bus project, only to see how inbound adapters can be used as easily with Service Bus projects as with SOA composites—there is no special preference from the products themselves to use inbound JCA adapters with one or the other. The Service Bus project can instead of using the JCA adapter for JMS also leverage the JMS Transport in inbound mode—that is a little lighter weight than the JCA-based approach.

We will see how to the pipeline in the Service Bus project, it makes absolutely no difference whether its input originates with an inbound adapter or with a more common incoming SOAP request.

Create the Service Bus Project

Create new Service Bus application and project, both called *FinancialAircraftMovementProcessor*. Copy the Schemas folder from the *AircraftMovementService* project that you worked on in Chapter 6 to this new project. This folder contains the schema definition for the messages that the new project will consume from the JMS Queue.

Add the Inbound JMS Adapter Binding

Drag the JMS Adapter from the Advanced category in the Component palette to the Proxy Services swimlane.

The adapter configuration wizard appears. Set the name for the inbound service to *ConsumeAircraftMovementMessages*. In step 2, choose Oracle Enterprise Messaging Service and select Oracle WebLogic JMS as the implementation.

On the Adapter Interface step, accept the default of Define from operation and schema (specified later). Press Next. In the Operation page, select the *Consume Message* radio button. Set the operation name to *ConsumeAircraftMovementMessage* (this value is quite arbitrary). Click next to go to the Consume Operation Parameters page, shown in Figure 13-7.

Select the jms/finance/AircraftMovementsQueue as the [JMS] Destination Name. Despite the confusing name—Destination—we are configuring the JMS queue or topic here from which we want this adapter binding to consume messages. The message body type is *TextMessage*. We will not use a MessageSelector. The JNDI name for the JMS [Adapter] Connection is eis/Finance/ Queue (also see the next section). Click Next to proceed.

The last page of the wizard is for specifying the schema that describes the message that is consumed from the queue. Select the *reportAircraftMovementRequestMessage* element from the AircraftMovementService.xsd. Click Next and then Finish. The Proxy Service is now created as is the JCA file with the adapter configuration.

Right click in the central area of the Service Bus overview editor. Select Insert | Pipeline. Call the new pipeline *ProcessAircraftMovementPipeline*. Click next to go to the second page of the wizard, see Figure 13-8. Select the WSDL radio button. Click on the gears icon to generate the

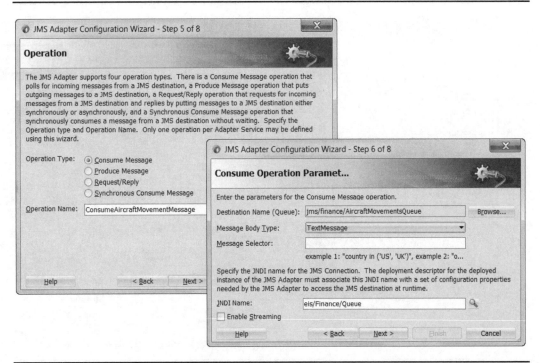

FIGURE 13-7. *The crucial steps in the inbound JMS adapter configuration wizard*

WSDL that this pipeline will expose. Accept all defaults—including the One Way Interface type. Specify a single input parameter, based on the same *reportAircraftMovementRequestMessage* from the AircraftMovementService.xsd that we used in the JMS adapter configuration.

Also expose the pipeline through a Proxy Service called *ProcessAircraftMovementPS*. Click Finish to create the pipeline.

Wire the proxy service *ConsumeAircraftMovementMessage*—created with the inbound JMS adapter—to this pipeline. This means there are now two channels to the pipeline: one through the one-way SOAP Web Service exposed through the *ProcessAircraftMovementPS* and the other from the JMS queue through the inbound adapter and the *ConsumeAircraftMovementMessage* proxy service, as shown in Figure 13-9.

Double click on the pipeline to open its editor. Create a really simple implementation right now, because all we want to show is how the inbound JMS adapter will allow the financial department at Saibot Airport to consume the aircraft movement message that were published by a service in an entirely different department.

Add a pipeline pair. Add a [Message] Report action to the request pipeline. Set the content to $body—so you will be able to see the entire message that is retrieved from the JMS Queue. Define a search key called *FlightnumberForAircraftMovement* and have it return the flight number from the body variable. Save your changes.

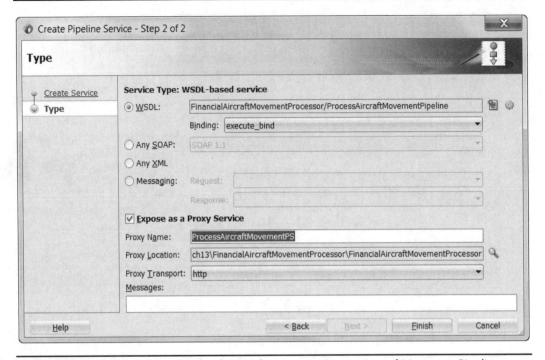

FIGURE 13-8. *The configuration for the Pipeline Service ProcessAircraftMovementPipeline*

Configure JMS Adapter

Before we can meaningfully deploy the Service Bus project, we have to prepare the JMS Adapter deployment.

In Chapter 6 we already configured the JMS Adapter on the WebLogic Server for the queue we are now discussing. A connection was added through the WebLogic Console to

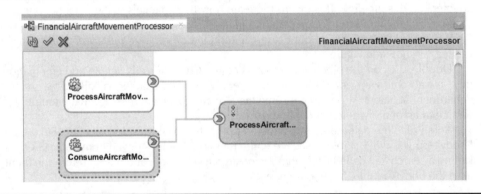

FIGURE 13-9. *Two channels into the pipeline, including one from the inbound JMS adapter*

the JMS Adapter's set of connections with the JNDI name of *eis/Finance/Queue*. This connection refers to the *FinanceConnectionFactory* that facilitates access to resources such as the *AircraftMovementsQueue* that we are now going to listen to with the inbound mode of the JMS Adapter. No more configuration is required if we simply reuse this connection.

Deploy and Test

You can test the pipeline directly—right click and press run—or indirectly through the *ProcessAircraftMovementPS* proxy service. The proxy service *ConsumeAircraftMovementMessage* based on the inbound JMS adapter cannot be directly tested. Instead, we have to deploy the Service Bus project—which will register the adapter binding as a subscriber on the *AircraftMovementsQueue*. When we next publish a message on that queue, this should activate the adapter binding and indirectly invoke the pipeline.

By invoking the *AircraftMovementService* that was developed in Chapter 6, we can have the message published on the JMS queue—provided that this service picks the correct path in the conditional branch. Alternatively, we can use a tool such as QBrowser, SoapUI (with HermesJMS) or the WebLogic admin console to publish a message on the *AircraftMovementsQueue*.

After you publish a message on the queue, check in the EM FMW Control whether the expected new Message Report is published with details from the message you put on the JMS Queue as proof that the inbound adapter did consume the message and activated the pipeline in the Service Bus project.

The Airport Information Desk—Receiving Emails

Questions regarding the flight status can be answered over instant messaging (chat) and email, as we have seen in Chapter 6. In this section, we will see how these questions can also be asked over human interaction channels, focusing on email.

The UMS adapter does not only have an outbound mode for initiating interactions with people. It also supports an inbound mode, where it polls email servers, XMPP servers and other messaging engines to allow incoming messages to trigger a new SOA composite instance or a call to the Service Bus. We will use this UMS adapter's inbound mode to monitor an Inbox for a mail account on a mail server. For each email received in this inbox, there will be an instance of the SOA composite.

Create the SaibotHelpdesk SOA Composite

Create a new SOA application called *SaibotHelpdesk*. Create a new project with the same title, using the empty template.

Drag the UMS adapter to the left hand services swimlane, to create an inbound adapter binding. The configuration wizard appears. Set the name to *HelpdeskEmailProcessor*. Accept the default inbound Connection JNDI Name (eis/ums/UMSAdapterInbound). In step 3, the operation type should be *Inbound Receive Notification*. Accept the default operation name *ReceiveNotification*.

Step 4 is for configuring the inbound operation details such as the polling settings, shown in Figure 13-10. Set 30 seconds as the polling interval—or any other value you think appropriate. Given the slow volume in our development environment, we should not need configure multiple threads to handle the incoming emails. Note: Instead of polling mode, we can also choose listener mode. That latter mode allows us to receive email messages in near real time, having the UMS Server perform dedicated work for this composite.

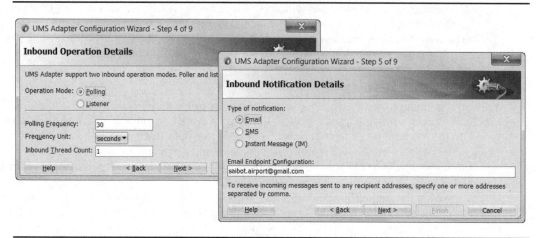

FIGURE 13-10. *Configuring the polling operation and the Email Endpoint aka the email account whose Inbox to poll*

In step 5, we specify the email account whose Inbox we want to listen in to. We can provide multiple accounts, in a comma separated list. Provide the email address in the Email Endpoint Configuration property—in Figure 13-10 set to saibot.airport@gmail.com. The email address(es) provided here have to be configured in the UMS Email Driver, as discussed in the next section.

Step 6 of the wizard is for configuring the message handling. The payload of the email can be passed into the composite application as a string or even a base64 binary object, or it can be natively transformed when the email contents is XML, JSON or some other structured format that can be converted into proper XML. Note that in addition to the email message contents, the SOA composite received a broad selection of JCA header properties that provide details from the subject, to and cc to messageID, reply to, language, encoding, and attachment indication. Mail attachments are also available in the SOA composite for further processing.

In this case, check the box Message is String Type.

In step 7, we can specify Message Filters. These are used to instruct the UMS adapter on which emails to actually process and create an instance of the SOA composite for, and which to ignore. Message filters can make use of white lists (specifically process mails from these senders), black lists (process all but emails from these senders) and text filtering on subject, content, sender, recipient, and reply to. Additionally, in step 8, we can even configure a callout to a custom Java class that performs our own specific inspection of the incoming message to determine whether or not to forward it to the SOA composite.

In this case, do not configure any filtering at all.

Press Next and the Finish, to complete the wizard and create the adapter binding.

Drag a Mediator component to the composite application. Call it *EmailMediator*. Wire the inbound adapter binding to the mediator.

Add a BPEL process component to the application, called *EmailProcessor*. Configure this component with a one way interface, accepting the default simple single string input.

Wire the *EmailMediator* to the *EmailProcessor*. The application will look now as shown in Figure 13-11.

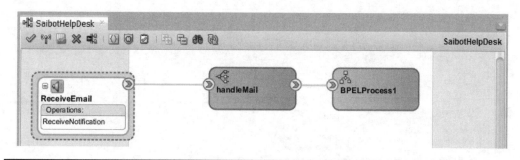

FIGURE 13-11. *SaibotHelpdesk composite with the Inbound UMS adapter to intercept incoming emails, handing them off to the Mediator for filtering, transformation and routing, and finally a BPEL process for processing*

Edit the routing rule in the EmailMediator: use the Assign Values option to pass the contents of the email to the BPEL process. This will allow us to see whether we are able to intercept incoming emails, have them trigger new SOA composite instances and passing on the email payload to a BPEL process for processing. A more meaningful usage of the email is discussed later on.

Configure Email Driver

In order to configure our SOA Suite run time environment for polling an Inbox for a certain email account on some email server, we have to configure the UMS Email Driver Properties on the managed server. Depending on the mail server that is being used, the IMAP or POP3 protocol are configured, to read messages received on the mail server. The host and port have to be configured as well as the users whose mail accounts are to be polled, the folder that should be polled and the password(s) for the accounts that should be polled.

The online resources describe the details for this configuration.

Deploy and Test

Deploy the SOA composite to the SOA Suite run time. As with the composite with the inbound database adapter, there is no direct way to test the composite. It does not have a service interface. It can only be activated through the inbound UMS adapter that is triggered through the reception of an email.

Send an email to the email address that is configured for inbound interactions. After a little while—depending on the polling time configured for the UMS inbound adapter binding—the email will be picked up and handed to a new instance of the SOA composite, as visualized in Figure 13-12.

The SOA composite we have created for processing incoming emails is quite simple—especially since we do not really do any message handling right now. But even so, it might come as a surprise how little effort is required to have the SOA Suite activated through an email. Note that for incoming chat messages we have to go through very similar steps.

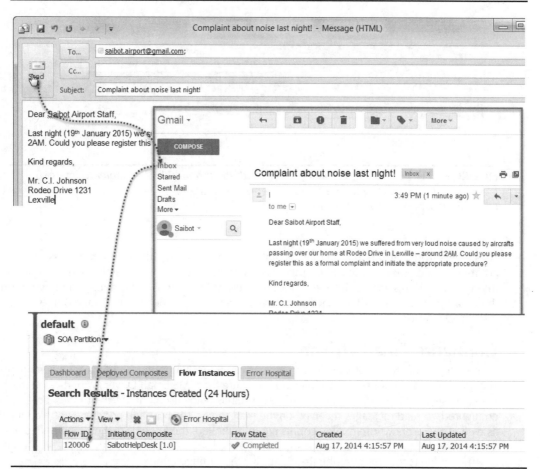

FIGURE 13-12. *Sending an email to saibot.airport@gmail.com triggers an instance of the SaibotHelpdesk composite through the inbound UMS adapter binding that picks up the email from the Inbox*

Miscellaneous Inbound Interactions

In addition to the inbound interactions through database adapter, JMS adapter, and UMS adapter (for emails), there are several other inbound actions. We will briefly look at some of these.

The AQ adapter is obviously very similar to the JMS adapter; it subscribes to an Advanced Queue in a database and triggers an SOA composite or Service Bus proxy service whenever a message is consumed from the queue. In this area, there are also the MS (Microsoft), MQ, and MQ Series adapters that have an inbound mode triggered by messages arriving on a queue.

The File and FTP adapters both support file polling. Whenever a new file arrives in a configured directory, it will be retrieved by the File Adapter—from the local [shared] file system— or the FTP Adapter—from a (potentially remote) FTP server – at the end of the polling interval.

The contents from the file are processed as specified, for example, using native format transformation or rather opaque for binary files. Additionally, we can configure File Valves, custom Java classes that perform preprocessing on the retrieved files.

TIP
We can instruct the File Adapter in inbound mode to only start polling once a "trigger file"—a dummy file with a predefined name—is found. In this way we can ensure that a file is only processed when it is complete.

In addition to the out-of-the-box JCA adapters, you can create your own Custom JCA adapters, to, for example, poll a DropBox folder, an RSS feed or any other resource whose changes you may want to trigger a Service Bus project or an SOA composite instance. A custom adapter leverages the JCA 1-way inbound interaction with activation mechanism for polling activities. The Custom Adapter wizard in JDeveloper can be used to configure the adapter binding for a custom inbound adapter.

Of course, any scheduled process that polls, gathers, aggregates and then triggers a service exposed by Service Bus or an SOA composite can perform an operation very similar to an inbound adapter. In the next chapter, we will look at the Enterprise Scheduling Service (ESS). We can use this service to schedule the execution of services implemented using Service Bus and SOA composites, the activation and deactivation of (inbound) adapters and the execution of external programs—that could perform a polling operation and based on the results, invoke a Service Bus or SOA composite service.

The Event Delivery Network (EDN) is the foundation of an important inbound mechanism for SOA composites. Events published to the EDN can be delivered to running instances or to newly created instances. The EDN provides a functional, more business oriented layer on top of the somewhat more technical JMS messaging infrastructure. We will discuss the EDN in Chapter 15.

Summary

Inbound adapters are used in cases where the initiative for action in the Service Bus or SOA composite does not lie with some external party who is interested in a response or feels an obligation to call a one way service. Instead, it is the adapter that is configured to periodically inspect external systems for relevant changes—such as new files, new emails or chat messages, changed or new database records, or message on a queue—and upon finding such changes to initiate an SOA composite instance or invoke a Service Bus proxy service. Inbound adapters can play an important role in the implementation of (asynchronous) Straight Through Processing (STP).

This chapter showed the configuration of various inbound adapter bindings. It became obvious that once the adapter has forwarded the payload it retrieved from the external system, the processing of that payload in a pipeline (in Service Bus) or a Mediator or BPEL process (in SOA composites) is no different from processing payload received in normal request messages that were actively sent by external partners.

The configuration of inbound adapters can require some considerable care. To ensure timely action, polling times should not be set to high values. The size of transactions—how large is the chunk processed in a single go—and the number of polling threads concurrently active are very important in tuning the workload and preventing an overload on the server.

CHAPTER
14

Using the Enterprise
Scheduler Service

The Fusion Middleware 12.1.3 platform contains the ESS or Enterprise Scheduler Service. This service can be used as an asynchronous, schedule-based job orchestrator. It can execute jobs that are Operating System actions, Java calls (local Java or EJB), PL/SQL calls, and web service calls (synchronous, asynchronous and one-way) including calls to SOA composite, Service Bus and ADF BC web services. Schedules used for planning the execution of a job can define a single, future point in time or may describe a periodically repeating pattern for the execution of the job. The finest granularity of schedules is at the level of minutes and hours. ESS is clearly not intended for very rapid polling or high frequency tasks.

ESS has the concept of Job Sets. A Job Set consists of multiple job step steps where a job set step can be a job or another job set. Execution of job set steps can be configured as sequential or as parallel. Using a serial job set Enterprise Scheduler supports conditional branching between steps based on the execution status of a previous step. Additionally, output from one job set step can be used as the input for the next step.

Jobs and schedules can be defined from client applications that access a Java API, through the Enterprise Manager FMW Control user interface for ESS and through a web service. This web service through which (predefined) jobs can be scheduled can be invoked from BPEL processes in SOA composites, using a special Schedule Job activity. Additionally, a Service Bus business service for invoking the ESS Web Service can be created and a Mediator or Spring component can make that call from an SOA composite.

The ESS is used in at least two more ways from SOA Suite 12c, besides invoking services from a scheduled job and being invoked from a service to schedule a job.

One is the bulk recovery of faulted instances. This can be planned using a schedule—to ensure that recovery is performed in the near future, on a convenient moment and spread out over time to prevent sudden a sudden peak load. Behind the covers, the Enterprise Scheduler Service is used to coordinate the execution of the recovery according to the schedule.

The second use case for ESS is the activation and deactivation of (inbound) adapters based on a schedule. Key reasons for scheduling the availability of adapters are the availability of back-end systems—why start processing messages on a queue at any moment when we know that the ERP system that needs to be invoked is down every night—and the load on the system—let's handle the low-priority inbound flow of documents at a time when the system is not swamped with a peak load of more important processes.

The ESS complements the database scheduler in the area of "middleware jobs." It collaborates with the database scheduler for the execution of PL/SQL jobs. Note that the scheduled purging of SOA composite instances is done directly through the database scheduler, without ESS involvement. The periodic clean-up of historical job data in contrast is handled by ESS itself.

Switch Off the Inbound Database Adapter for Processing Portal Slot Requests

The Enterprise Scheduler Service supports a number of administration activities around the SOA Suite. Although we will discuss administration in more detail in Part 6, we will look at one particular use case regarding environment management using the ESS.

In the previous chapter, we introduced the inbound database adapter. We have created the *PortalSlotRequestProcessor* SOA composite that uses a database poller looking for new records in table *PORTAL_SLOT_ALLOCATIONS*. The polling frequency was set to once every 20 seconds. And that goes on and on for as long as the SOA composite remains deployed and active.

Imagine the situation where every day during a certain period, there is a substantial load on the SOA Suite, and we would prefer to reduce the resource usage from noncrucial processes. Further suppose that the slot allocation requests arriving from the portal are considered not urgent, for example, because the business service level agreed with our account managers is that these requests have to be processed within 24 hours—rather than once every 20 seconds. We do not want to create a big batch, and whenever we can, we strive to implement straight through processing. But between 1 and 2 AM on every day, we would like to pause the inbound database adapter.

In this section, we will use the Enterprise Scheduler Service to achieve this. We will create the schedules that trigger at 1 AM every day, used for deactivating the adapter, and 2 AM, used for activating the adapter. In fact, in order to make testing more fun, we will use schedules that trigger at 10 past the hour and 30 past the hour. These schedules are then associated in the Enterprise Manager Fusion Middleware Control with the inbound database adapter binding *PortalSlotRequestPoller*.

Create Schedules

An ESS Schedule is used to describe either one or a series of moments in time. A schedule can be associated with one or many job definitions to come to describe when those jobs should be executed. A recurring schedule has a frequency that describes how the moments in time are distributed over time. A recurring schedule can have a start time and an end time to specify the period during which the recurrence should take place.

To create the schedules that will govern the inbound database adapter, open the EM FMW Control and select the node Scheduling Services | ESSAPP. From the drop-down list at the top of the page, select Job Requests | Define Schedules, as is shown in Figure 14-1.

Click on the icon to create a new schedule. Specify the name of the schedule as At10minPastTheHour. Set the display name to "10 minutes past each hour." The schedule has to be created in the package [/oracle/apps/ess/custom/]soa. This is a requirement for schedules used for adapter activation.

Select the frequency as Hourly/Minute, Every 1 Hour(s) 0 Minute(s) and the start date as any date not too far in the future (or even in the past) with a time set to 10 minutes past any hour. An example is shown in Figure 14-2.

Note that using the button Customize Times, we can have a long list of moments in time generated and subsequently manually modify them if we have a need for some exceptions to the pattern.

Click on OK to save this schedule.

Create a second schedule called *At30minPastTheHour*. The definition is very similar to the previous one, except for the start time that should 30 minutes past some hour. Click OK to save this schedule definition.

Note that more sophisticated recurrence schedules can be created through the Java API exposed by ESS as well as through the IDE support in JDeveloper. These options that allow specific week days or months to be included or excluded can currently not be set through the EM FMW Control.

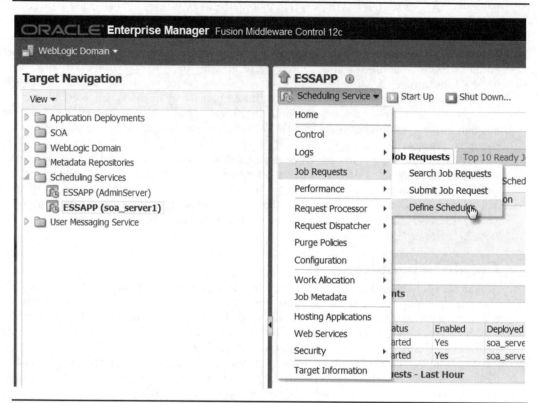

Figure 14-1. *Open the page to Define the ESS Schedules*

Apply Schedules for Activation and Deactivation of Inbound Database Adapter

Select node SOA | soa-infra | default | PortalSlotRequestProcessor—the composite we created in the previous chapter. Under Services and References, click on the *PortalSlotRequestPoller*, the inbound database adapter binding, as shown in Figure 14-3.

The *PortalSlotRequestProcessor* appears. Click on the icon for adapter schedules. In the Adapter Schedules popup that appears (Figure 14-4), we can select the schedule that is to be used for deactivating and for activating the adapter binding. Use the *At10minPastTheHour* schedule for deactivation and *At30minPastTheHour* for activation. Press Apply Schedules to confirm the new configuration.

From this moment on, the inbound database adapter binding that polls table *PORTAL_SLOT_ALLOCATIONS* is active only for 40 minutes during every hour, starting at 30 minutes past the hour.

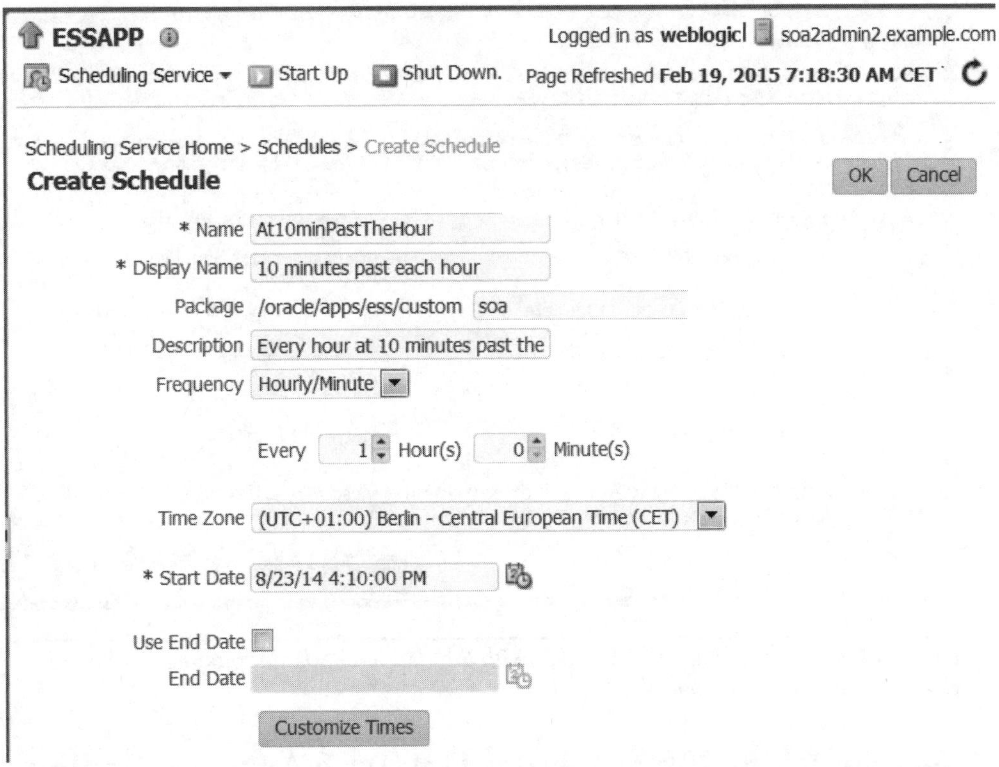

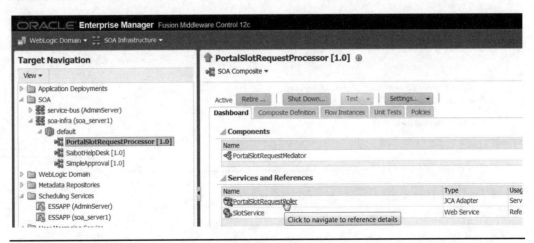

ESSAPP ⓘ

Logged in as **weblogicl** soa2admin2.example.com

Scheduling Service ▾   Start Up   Shut Down.   Page Refreshed **Feb 19, 2015 7:18:30 AM CET** ↻

Scheduling Service Home > Schedules > Create Schedule
Create Schedule

OK   Cancel

* Name	At10minPastTheHour
* Display Name	10 minutes past each hour
Package	/oracle/apps/ess/custom soa
Description	Every hour at 10 minutes past the
Frequency	Hourly/Minute ▾

Every   1 ▴▾ Hour(s)   0 ▴▾ Minute(s)

Time Zone   (UTC+01:00) Berlin - Central European Time (CET) ▾

* Start Date 8/23/14 4:10:00 PM

Use End Date ☐

End Date

Customize Times

Figure 14-2. *Configure the Schedule At10minPastTheHour*

Figure 14-3. *Drill down to the configuration of the inbound database adapter binding*

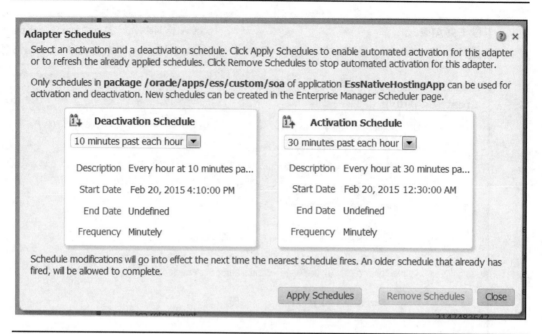

Figure 14-4. *Associating ESS Schedules with the database adapter binding to schedule deactivation and activation*

Test Switching Off and on of Database Adapter Binding

When the schedules for activation and deactivation have been applied, they are immediately in effect. You can test this in the Dashboard page for the inbound database adapter binding, as is shown in Figure 14-5.

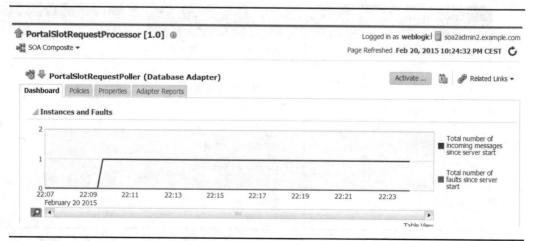

Figure 14-5. *Dashboard showing the status of the PortalSlotRequestPoller Database Adapter binding*

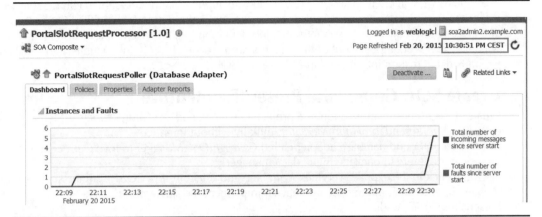

Figure 14-6. *At 30 minutes past the hour, the adapter binding is activated again and it processes four records—inserted at 22:11 and 22:12—in two polling cycles*

Here we see how a single record was processed by the adapter binding, insert at 10:09 PM. Four more records were inserted into table PORTAL_SLOT_ALLOCATIONS at 10:11 and 10:12. However, because the adapter binding is currently not active, so these records have not yet been processed.

At 30 minutes past the hour—10:30 in this case—the adapter becomes active again and starts processing the records it will then find in the table. Because the adapter was configured to pass just a single record to an SOA composite and not process more than two records in a single transaction, it will take two polling cycles to process the four records that were inserted between 10:10 and 10:30. Figure 14-6 illustrates this.

When you check in the ESS UI in EM FMW Control, you will find two new Job Definitions, generic Jobs for executing SOA Suite management tasks. In the Job Requests overview, instances of these jobs appear, every hour one of each. And the details of these job requests specify which adapter binding in which composite is the target of the SOA administrative action performed by the job.

You can submit requests for these Job Definitions yourself, providing different values for the application properties, to activate or deactivate selected inbound adapters.

Schedule Daily Flight Data Transfer

At Saibot, the Future database [schema] holds data about current and future slot allocations. From the data in this schema, Saibot derives every day the flights that are to take place in the next 24 hours. Details about these flights are loaded into the Present database [schema] that is the source for the flight information system presented to travelers in the terminals, on the website and in the mobile app. A third database [schema] used by Saibot is called Past. It holds data from flights and aircraft movement as they took place a week or more ago. Every day, data is moved from Present to Past—in order to keep Present, the live operational database—as lean as possible.

The two daily data movements described above are good candidates for scheduled orchestration by ESS. We will focus on the first one. A PL/SQL package is provided in the online sources that is called with a date parameter and will create the flight records in Present based on the slot allocation details in Future.

Initially, we will create a simple SOA composite application that uses the database adapter to call out to this package. Then we will create an ESS Job Definition for calling the SOA composite and create a job request that associates that job definition to a daily schedule. Subsequently, we will take the SOA composite out of the equation and create a PL/SQL Job Definition to carry out the daily data creation job directly from ESS to PL/SQL.

Create SOA Composite PresentFromFuture

Create SOA composite application and project called *PresentFromFuture*. Create a Mediator called *PreparePresentFromFutureMediator*, initially without interface.

Add an outbound database adapter called *CallFlightDataManager* to invoke procedure derive_present_from_future in package flight_data_manager.

Right click in the exposed services swim lane and select Insert | SOAP. Call the service *PreparePresentFromFutureService* and have it implement the single port type in PresentFromFuture.wsdl.

Wire the service to the Mediator and the Mediator to the outbound database adapter binding. Figure 14-7 shows the state of the composite.

Use the Assign Values settings in the Mediator to pass values from the request message to the database adapter binding and subsequently to the PL/SQL procedure.

Deploy the SOA composite. Make a test call and see if it completes successfully—and does in the database what you expect it to do. Note: We do not intend to make such direct calls in the future—that is what ESS will do for us.

Create and Schedule daily execution of PresentFromFuture with ESS

We will now create the Job Definition to invoke the *PresentFromFuture* composite and schedule it for execution once per day.

Create the Job Definition CreateCurrentFlightData

Open the EM FMW Control and go to the ESS page. From the drop-down menu, select Job Metadata | Job Definitions. Click on the create button.

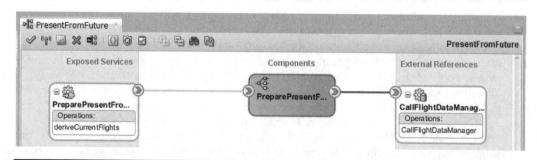

Figure 14-7. *SOA composite PresentFromFuture—a simple web service to PL/SQL package flow*

Edit the new job definition. Name is *CreateCurrentFlightData*, display name is "Derive current flights" and package is [oracle/apps/ess/custom/]saibot/flight. Job Type is *SynchWebserviceJobType*. Click on Select Web Service. A popup appears. Enter the URL for the WSDL for the service exposed by the *PresentFromFuture* composite. Set the Web Service Type to SOA. Press the Go button.

The WSDL is retrieved and processed. A list of (one) services is shown—click on *PreparePresentFromFutureService*. The drop-down element labeled *Port Type* is now populated. Select the *PreparePresentFromFutureService_pt* option. This will extend the dialog to include a drop-down list with operations. Select operation *deriveCurrentFlights*. A sample request message to this operation is shown. Set the value of the *PeriodDuration* element to ${ESS_REQ:NUMBER_OF_HOURS}. This is a placeholder that tells ESS to replace it with the actual value of the application property *NUMBER_OF_HOURS* set for the specific job request. See Figure 14-8 for the complete Job Definition.

Finally, add an Application Defined Property to the job definition. This property is called NUMBER_OF_HOURS and is of type Integer. The initial value is 24 and the property is not read only.

Create the Once per Day Schedule

Use Job Requests | Define Schedules in the drop-down menu on the Scheduling Service page in EM FMW Control. Click on the create icon. The page for creating a new schedule appears, see Figure 14-9. Set the name to OncePerDayAt1AM and the display name to something similar.

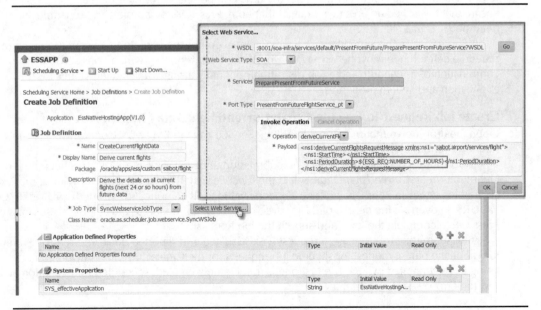

Figure 14-8. *Configure the Job Definition CreateCurrentFlightData that involves invoking a synchronous web service exposed by SOA composite PresentFromFuture*

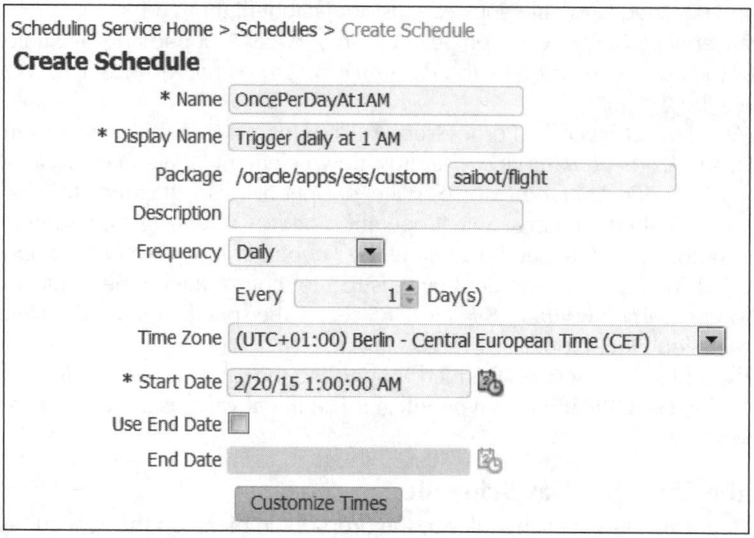

Scheduling Service Home > Schedules > Create Schedule
Create Schedule
```
              * Name   OncePerDayAt1AM
      * Display Name   Trigger daily at 1 AM
           Package   /oracle/apps/ess/custom  saibot/flight
        Description
         Frequency   Daily              ▼

                 Every              1 ▲▼ Day(s)

         Time Zone   (UTC+01:00) Berlin - Central European Time (CET)   ▼
      * Start Date   2/20/15 1:00:00 AM           📅
      Use End Date   ☐
          End Date                                📅
                       Customize Times
```

Figure 14-9.   *Configuring the OncePerDayAt1AM schedule*

Set package to [/oracle/apps/ess/custom/]saibot/flight. Set the frequency to daily and the start date to any date in the past or near future. Set the time component of the start date to 01:00:00 AM to ensure that this schedule fires every day at that time. Press OK to complete the schedule definition.

By just creating this schedule, we have not yet accomplished anything, except providing this schedule definition for anyone who wants to submit a job request—which consists of the combination of a schedule and a job definition optionally along with specific values for application and system properties.

Create Job Request to Execute CreateCurrentFlightData Once per Day
Open the drop-down menu on the Scheduling Service page in EM FMW Control. Click on Job Requests | Submit Job Request.

The form for creating the Job Request submission appears, see Figure 14-10. Select the Job Definition *CreateCurrentFlightData*. Select the *OncePerDayAt1AM* Schedule. Provide some submission notes and perhaps provide a special value for the application property NUMBER_OF_HOURS, to override the default of 24 for every execution of the job as a result of this submission. Press OK to complete the form and submit the Job Request.

After submitting this request, a request ID is assigned and reported back. The request with this id will be the parent request for specific job requests for the CreateCurrentFlightData job that are going to be generated by ESS. The first one is immediately created, scheduled for execution at 1 AM tomorrow, see Figure 14-11.

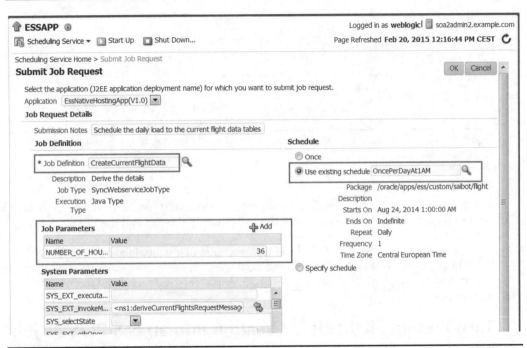

Figure 14-10. *Configuring the Job Request for CreateCurrentFlightData according to the OncePerDayAt1AM schedule*

Testing Our Job Request

In terms of testing, there is really not a lot we can do—except wait for the first 1 AM to arrive and see whether an instance of the *PresentFromFuture* SOA composite is created. Of course, we can speed up things a little, by tampering just a little with the schedule—for example, by changing the frequency from daily to hourly. Note that you have to reassign the (same but now modified) schedule to the job request in order for the change in frequency to have an

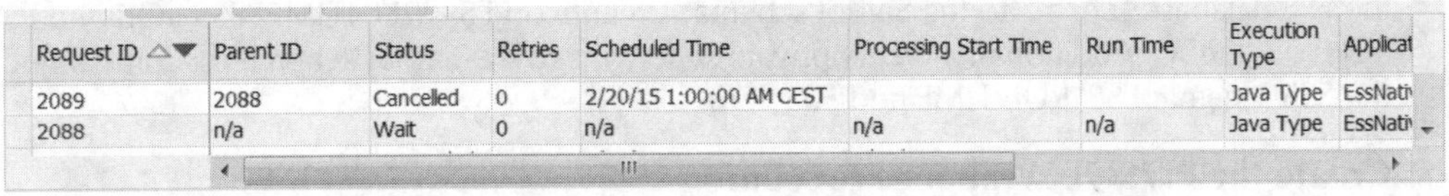

Request ID △▼	Parent ID	Status	Retries	Scheduled Time	Processing Start Time	Run Time	Execution Type	Applicat
2089	2088	Cancelled	0	2/20/15 1:00:00 AM CEST			Java Type	EssNati
2088	n/a	Wait	0	n/a	n/a	n/a	Java Type	EssNati

Figure 14-11. *The Job Requests records created by ESS as a result of submitting the Job Request*

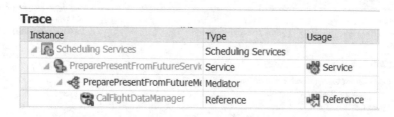

Figure 14-12. *Flow trace of the scheduled execution of the (call to the) SOA composite PresentFromFuture*

effect. Alternative, you can submit a single execution request for the Job Definition. That will not test the schedule, but it will ensure the execution of the job and therefore the SOA composite.

At the scheduled time, ESS will trigger the execution of the job, leading to an invocation of the SOA composite that will call the PL/SQL package to perform the data creation in the tables with current flight information, see Figure 14-12. And at the next scheduled moment, that will happen again.

Turn Present Flight Data Creation into an ESS PL/SQL Job

In the previous section, we have created an SOA composite to invoke a PL/SQL procedure to perform data creation. Subsequently, we have scheduled a call to the service exposed by the SOA composite. And sure enough, it all works smoothly enough. However, the value of having the SOA composite between the Enterprise Scheduler Service and the PL/SQL procedure is extremely small. It produces some additional logging, which is basically it. It could do enrichment, fault handling, and post processing, but these are currently not required. So we are putting load on the SOA Suite that is not valuable at all. Additionally, the work done in the PL/SQL package might take considerable time and could even lead to a transaction time out for the SOA composite.

In short, it might be a much better idea to simply schedule the current flight data creation as a PL/SQL Job Type without involving the SOA Suite at all. In a few simple steps, that is exactly what we will be doing in this section.

Prepare the Saibot Database Schema for ESS PL/SQL Jobs

In order to successfully create and execute the PL/SQL wrapper around the PL/SQL package flight_data_manager that ESS can invoke, we have to grant some privileges on database objects in the ESS database schema to the Saibot schema: Execute on ESS_RUNTIME, ESS_JOB and ESS_SCHJOB_PROC. Additionally, create private synonyms in the Saibot schema for some objects in the ESS schema: ESS_RUNTIME and ESS_JOB.

Create the PL/SQL Wrapper Procedure

A PL/SQL procedure that is to be invoked from ESS as a PL/SQL Job has to implement a specific signature: a single input variable of type varchar2 that provides the ESS request identifier. Input values can be read by the PL/SQL procedure from the ESS request context using that identifier, through package ess_runtime. That same package ess_runtime can be used to pass results from the PL/SQL procedure back to the ESS engine.

Note that the PL/SQL procedure handles its own transaction management—the ESS engine does not coordinate a transaction. The next code fragment is a stripped down version of the one you will find in the sources for this chapter: all exception handling that should part of it is taken out for readability purposes.

```
create or replace
procedure ess_job_derive_pres_from_fut
( request_handle in varchar2
) is
  l_number_of_hours    number(5,0);
  l_number_of_flights number(5,0);
  l_request_id         number := null;
begin
  l_request_id := ess_runtime.get_request_id(request_handle);
  l_number_of_hours := ess_runtime.get_reqprop_int(l_request_id, 'NUMBER_OF_
HOURS');
  flight_data_manager.derive_present_from_future
    ( p_start_time   => trunc(sysdate)
    , p_hours        => l_number_of_hours
    , p_number_of_flights => l_number_of_flights
    );
  -- Update an existing request property with a new value.
  ess_runtime.update_reqprop_int(l_request_id, 'NUMBER_OF_FLIGHTS_PROCESSED',
                                    l_number_of_flights);

  commit;
end ess_job_derive_pres_from_fut;
```

Create ESS Job Definition of PL/SQL Job Type

Open the EM FMW Control and go to the ESS page. From the drop-down menu, select Job Metadata | Job Definitions. Click on the create button.

Edit the new job definition, as is shown in Figure 14-13. The name is *CreateCurrentFlightDataPLSQL* and package is [oracle/apps/ess/custom/]saibot/flight. Choose your own display name and description. Set the Job Type to PlsqlJobType. Set the procedure name to saibot.ess_job_derive_pres_from_fut. Create to Application Defined Properties, called NUMBER_OF_HOURS and NUMBER_OF_FLIGHTS_PROCESSED. Both are not read only and both are of type Integer.

Press the OK button to create the Job Definition.

Schedule the PL/SQL Job for Daily Execution

The PL/SQL job that we have just created will take over from the SOA job *CreateCurrentFlightData* that we created earlier on and that we submitted a job request for. This job request can be withdrawn, using the Action | Cancel option on the request details page.

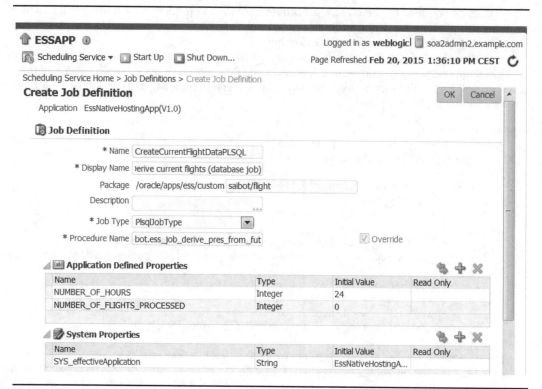

Figure 14-13. *Creating the CreateCurrentFlightDataPLSQL Job Definition of type PL/SQL Job Type to invoke PL/SQL wrapper procedure ess_job_derive_pres_from_fut*

Submit a new Job Request for the PL/SQL job *CreateCurrentFlightDataPLSQL* in the same way as before: Click on Job Requests | Submit Job Request in the drop-down menu. The form for creating the Job Request submission appears. Select the Job Definition *CreateCurrentFlightDataPLSQL*. Select the *OncePerDayAt1AM* Schedule. Provide some submission notes and perhaps provide a special value for the application property NUMBER_OF_ HOURS, to override the default of 24 for every execution of the job as a result of this submission. Press OK to complete the form and submit the Job Request, as shown in Figure 14-14.

Once again, we can do little to test, except wait for the schedule to trigger the first execution of the job. Alternatively, you can submit a second job request that executes only once—just to try out the job definition itself.

Once the job request has completed, the job request parameter NUMBER_OF_FLIGHTS_ PROCESSED will contain the number returned from the PL/SQL procedure and stored in the job request by the wrapper procedure. We will find no trace of the request and its execution in the SOA composite flow trace—because the SOA Suite is not involved. The ESS pages in EM FMW Control provide the details about each child Job Request spawned by the request we submitted in Figure 14-15.

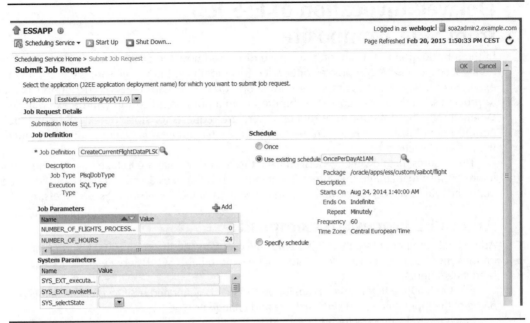

Figure 14-14. *Submitting a job request for job definition CreateCurrentFlightDataPLSQL*

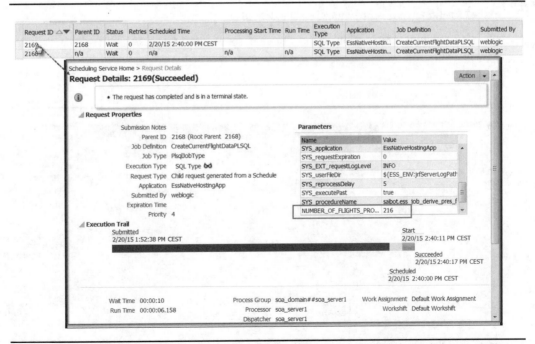

Figure 14-15. *Details on the request for PL/SQL Job Definition CreateCurrentFlightDataPLSQL*

Delayed Invocation of ESS Job from SOA Composite

In the introduction to this chapter, we have discussed how the ESS Scheduler Web Service can be invoked from SOA composites or Service Bus pipelines. In this section, we will see an example of this. The SOA composite *PortalSlotRequestProcessor* that we created in Chapter 13 to process slot allocation requests submitted from a portal application will be extended. When among the slot allocation requests there are requests for slots in next 48 hours, the composite will instruct ESS to run the *CreateCurrentFlightDataPLSQL* job that was defined in the previous section.

This ensures that new flights derived from these requests that are to take place in the very near future are also loaded into the current flight tables. This happens asynchronously, outside the SOA Suite and will have very little impact on the execution of the *PortalSlotRequestProcessor*.

Add BPEL Process to Composite

Add a BPEL component—called *IfDoRunPresFromFutJob*—to the composite. It should be based on the One Way BPEL Process template, not be exposed as a SOAP Service and it can use the predefined input.

Edit the XSD file IfDoRunPresFromFutJob.xsd that is generated by JDeveloper. Change the name of the input element to *slotStartDate* and change its type to *dateTime*.

Open the BPEL process for editing. Add an If activity with an expression that tests if the *slotStartDate* is within 48 hours from now.

```
$inputVariable.payload/client:slotStartDate <=  xp20:add-dayTimeDuration-to-
dateTime(xp20:current-dateTime(),'PT48H')
```

Add a *Schedule Job* activity to the *if* branch, see Figure 14-16. Drag an Empty activity to the *else* branch.

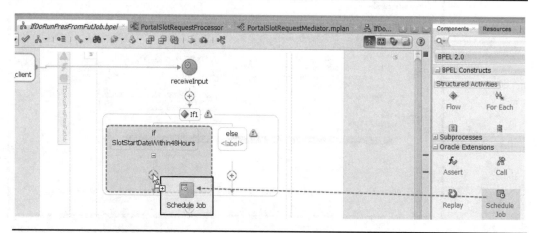

Figure 14-16. *Add a Schedule Job activity to the BPEL process*

The next step to take is editing the *Schedule Job* activity. Note that for doing so, there needs to be a special connection available in JDeveloper: an MDS Database connection that connects to the *essUserMetadata* partition in the MDS.

With that connection set up, double click the Schedule Job activity. Set the name of the activity as *ScheduleJobPresentFromFuture*. Select the job *CreateCurrentFlightDataPLSQL*; this will populate the Application field. Do not select a Schedule: this means that we want the ESS to execute this job immediately. See Figure 14-17 for the complete dialog. Click OK to complete the definition of the activity.

When you close the dialog, a warning appears about the fact that the WSDL for the ESS Service is an abstract one. Click Yes to acknowledge this message—we will fix this problem a little bit later on.

Forward Response from DB Adapter to BPEL Process

Return to the composite editor and double click on the Mediator. In the routing rule, click on the gears icon behind the field for Synchronous Reply, to set the destination to route a request to once the reply is received from the outbound database adapter. Select the (existing) service exposed by the BPEL process as this destination.

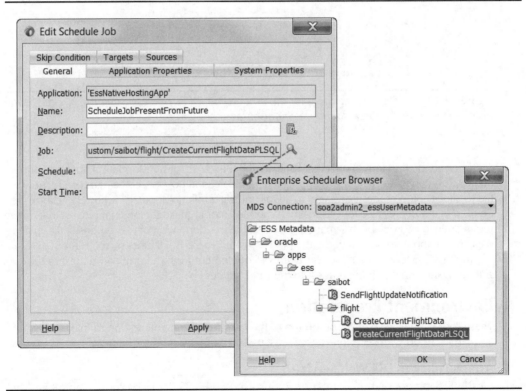

Figure 14-17.   *Editing the Schedule Job activity to have ESS immediately run the CreateCurrentFlightDataPLSQL job*

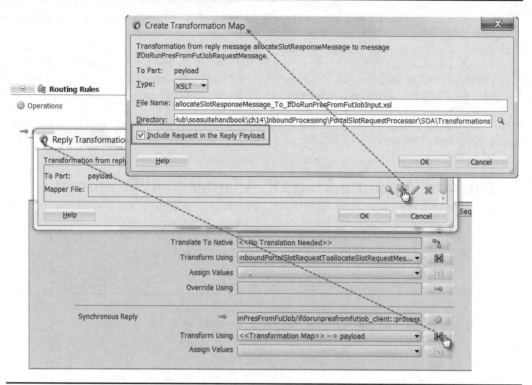

Figure 14-18. *Create the mapping for the input to the BPEL process using the original request from the inbound database adapter as input parameter*

Click on the transformation icon to specify the file to use for transformation. In the popup, click on the plus icon to create a new mapping file. In the second popup, set the name of the new mapper file to allocateSlotResponseMessage_To_IfDoRunPresFromFutJobInput.xsl. Check checkbox *Include Request in the Reply Payload*. This instructs the Mediator to make the original request that entered the routing rule to be available as a parameter when the transformation of the response takes place—so we can take input from the request and pass it onward to the BPEL process, see Figure 14-18.

In the XSL Mapper, map the *startDateForSlot* element from the original request to the *slotStartDate* element in the request to the BPEL process.

Environment Preparation

There some things we have to do on top of the functional implementation to make this all work. Some have to do with security—a topic discussed in more detail in Chapter 24.

Attach Policy to ESS Web Service

Jobs in ESS cannot be run as an anonymous user. So if ESS does not know who makes the request for scheduling a job, it will not perform the request. To ensure a user's identify is established when our BPEL process schedules a job, we have to attach a WSM security policy to the ESS Web Service and pass a WS Security Header with valid username and password in our request.

The steps are: in EM FMW Control, click on the node for the Scheduling Service | ESSAPP on the relevant managed server. From the drop-down menu on the right side of the page, selection option Web Services. You will be taken to the Web Service overview page. Click on the link for the *SchedulerServiceImplPort*. This brings you to another overview page for the *SchedulerServiceImplPort*. Open the tab labeled WSM Policies. Click on the icon labeled Attach/Detach. Now you find yourself on the page where policies can be attached to this Web Service (port binding). Find the security policy oracle/wss_username_token_service_policy in the list of available policies. Click on the Attach button to attach this policy to the ESS Web Service. Click on OK to confirm this new policy attachment.

At this point, the ESS Scheduler Service can only be invoked by parties that provide a valid username and password. As a result, the web service's operations are executed in the context of a real user—just like job-related operations performed through the EM FMW Control's UI for ESS are or actions from a client application through the Java API.

Set Concrete WSDL URL for ESS Web Service Binding

To resolve the warning about the abstract WSDL for the *EssService*, we need to get hold of the WSDL for the live ESS Web Service. On the page in the EM FMW Control where you just added the security policy, there is also a link to the WSDL document—it is called *SchedulerServiceImplPort*. Click on that link to review the WSDL document and more importantly, to get hold of its URL.

Return to the composite editor. Right click the *ESS Service* Reference Binding and select Edit from the menu. Set the WSDL URL in the field in the Update Reference dialog.

Attach Policy to ESS Reference Binding

Because the ESS Scheduler Web Service is protected by a WSM Security Policy, it requires callers to pass the appropriate WS Security Header. We can simply attach a WSM policy (of our own) to achieve that effect. We can even do so through EM FMW Control, in the run-time environment, rather than right here at design time. But this time we will go for the design time, developer route.

Right click the *EssService* reference binding. Select Configure SOA WS Policies | For Request from the menu. The dialog for configuring SOA WS Policies appears. Click on the plus icon for the Security category. From the list of security policies, select oracle/wss_username_token_client_policy. Then press OK. The policy is attached to the reference binding. Press OK again.

What we have configured at this point will cause the OWSM framework to intercept the call from our SOA composite to the *EssService* and inject WS Security policies into it. Or at least, that is what it would like to do. But the policy framework needs access to credentials to put in the WS Security header. The normal approach with this is for the policy framework to inspect the configured credential store for the username and password to use.

There is a short cut however, that we will use here. Instead of using a credential store, our security policy can also simply use a username and password that are configured as properties on the reference binding to which the policy is attached. Click on the reference binding once more. Locate the section Composite Properties | Binding Properties in the properties palette, as shown in Figure 14-19.

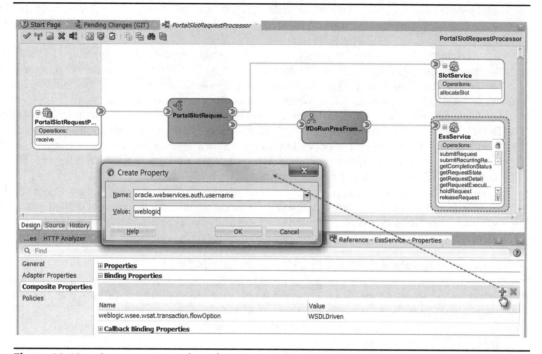

Figure 14-19. *Set property oracle.webservices.auth.username on the Reference Binding for the EssService*

Click on the green plus icon to add a new property. Its name is oracle.webservices.auth .username and the value is for example weblogic. Then add a second property, called oracle .webservices.auth.password and set its value. You will notice that these two properties are not displayed in the property palette. However annoying that is, it is not a problem: the properties are added to the composite.xml file all the same.

Deploy and Test

Deploy and make sure to override the existing PortalSlotRequestProcessor that was deployed in Chapter 13.

Next, insert a record into table PORTAL_SLOT_ALLOCATIONS and make sure that the START_DATE_FOR_SLOT column has a value within the next 48 hours—as that should trigger the BPEL process into scheduling a job. After committing the transaction and waiting some time for the inbound database adapter to do its polling (ensure that it is not currently deactivated!), you should find a new SOA composite instance with the flow trace similar to Figure 14-20.

When you check the Job Requests in the ESS management pages, you will see that a one off request for the *CreateCurrentFlightDataPLSQL* was created and has been executed. When you inspect the ESS request log for this request, you will find the SOA Flow Id for the SOA composite instance that triggered this job request—which sure enough corresponds with the instance of the *PortalSlotRequestProcessor* that was created by the inbound database adapter.

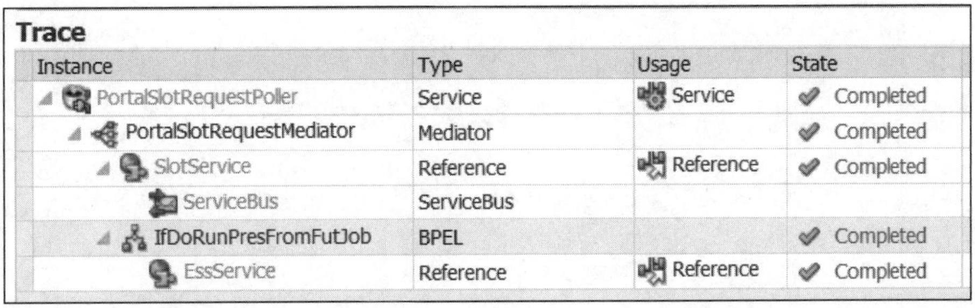

Trace			
Instance	Type	Usage	State
▲ 🔲 PortalSlotRequestPoller	Service	📇 Service	✔ Completed
▲ ◆ PortalSlotRequestMediator	Mediator		✔ Completed
▲ 🔲 SlotService	Reference	📇 Reference	✔ Completed
📨 ServiceBus	ServiceBus		
▲ 🔲 IfDoRunPresFromFutJob	BPEL		✔ Completed
🔲 EssService	Reference	📇 Reference	✔ Completed

Figure 14-20.   *The message flow trace resulting from the new Portal Slot Allocation request record that was processed by the inbound database adapter and resulted in a job request being submitted to ESS*

Summary

The Enterprise Scheduler Service provides a means to schedule the execution of SOA composites—as well as several other job types—according to a specific schedule. This opens up options for having work done in the background, periodically and at appropriate moments—such as the implementation of custom inbound adapters, to poll, for example, Dropbox, Twitter, or an RSS Feed.

A powerful option is the ability to associate inbound adapters with an ESS schedule for deactivation and activation. This means we can bring the adapter binding up and down in accordance with the availability of external systems and or the capacity of our own environment. Activating or deactivating an adapter binding can be done from the ESS console or from an SOA composite as well.

From within an SOA composite or a Service Bus pipeline, we can invoke the ESS Scheduler web service, to submit job requests. This means that our service implementations can easily request various types of postprocessing to be performed asynchronously, outside the (transaction) boundaries of the service execution—at a selected moment in time. We could for example schedule the Performance Review Process service to be invoked 30 days after the first working day of a new employee in the baggage handling department. And also run Operating System processes that an SOA composite does not directly have access to.

CHAPTER
15

The Event
Delivery Network

S OA is about decoupling and reuse, leading to business agility. In the previous chapters, we have seen many examples of decoupling, both within and between our SOA composite applications, as well as between these composites and external services and systems.

The use of XML and web service standards is good for decoupled interoperability across heterogeneous technology stacks—for example, file systems, databases, Java applications, packaged applications, and SOA Suite. The integration between service components based on the WSDL contracts and the SCA infrastructure allows us to use the best tool for the job—Business Rules for business logic, Mediator for routing and transformation, BPEL for stateful processes, and technology adapters to leverage functionality in other platforms.

The asynchronous capabilities that queues such JMS and AQ, as well as the events introduced in this chapter, provide us with also allow for temporal decoupling where consumer and provider can communicate without having to be available at the same time.

In terms of decoupling, we have at least one other challenge left: How do we make sure that services are called at the right time? Some services provide clear value to their invoker, such as the requests for the latest flight information. Such services will be called whenever their functionality is desired by an application. The application is functionally decoupled from the service—the canonical model and reusable web service contract as well as end point virtualization by the Service Bus take care of that. However, the application still needs to explicitly invoke the service, needs to know some endpoint location, and work according to the service contract.

The story is even more interesting for one-way services, which may need to perform some action when a flight is cancelled or no service provider bids on a contract offered by a certain air carrier. Who is responsible for calling these services? No one will call them to get something out of them—because they do not return a response. Other services and applications may possess the information that the one-way services need to get. But whose responsibility is it to get it to them? How should these information owners know which one-way services are interested in their data? And should the onus be on them to explicitly call these services? Surely we do not want to modify and redeploy applications whenever a new consumer of their information comes along—or an existing one loses interest. That would not be decoupling at all!

This chapter introduces the Event Delivery Network (EDN) in SOA Suite—a facility that provides advanced decoupling by mediating events between producers and consumers that are unaware of each other. Composite applications can subscribe to one or more of the centrally defined business event types and are notified by the EDN whenever an instance is published of one of those types. More specifically, both Mediator and BPEL components can produce and consume events. Events can also be correlated into running composite instances through BPEL components. The EDN can be listened to or published onto from local and remote Java clients as well as from Oracle Event Processor (see the next chapter) and BPM processes (see Chapter 19). Note: Service Bus does not natively interact with the EDN; however, the underlying implementation of EDN is JMS and of course Service Bus can interact with a JMS Topic.

Event-Driven Architecture for Super Decoupling

Event-Driven Architecture (with the obvious acronym of EDA) made a lot of heads turn. Seen as the successor to SOA by some and as a welcome complement to SOA by others, EDA is clearly on to something. Extremely Decoupled Architecture would be a perfect secondary meaning of the acronym—because extreme decoupling is one of the things that EDA adds to "traditional"

SOA. In the world of EDA, events are the messages, replacing direct service calls. Events are not targeted to a specific service provider. Events are published with some logical name on some central, generic infrastructure that the event producers use in a fire-and-forget mode. After publishing their event, these producers have no more responsibility for it. They have done their job by handing the event to the central event-coordinating facility and no longer have strings attached to the event. In fact, they may later on even consume their own event just like any other consumer—because their origin is unknown to event consumers. Events typically have a header and a payload. The header contains metadata such as the event type and a timestamp. The body or payload contains the details that describe the facts of the event instance that business logic in the consumer will process.

Anyone interested in occurrences of a specific type of event can subscribe to it, registering their interest in that event type with a central facility that coordinates events. This coordinating facility receives all events that get published, relieving the event publisher of the responsibility for the event. After receiving an event, it will traverse all subscriptions for the particular event type, taking into account any filters that may have been defined on such subscriptions to see whether the specific event occurrence should actually be forwarded to the subscription's consumer, and propagate the event to all qualifying consumers. The event coordinator may support mechanisms to retry delivery of an event upon initial failure or deferred delivery for currently unavailable consumers.

NOTE
None of the producers of events are aware of subscriptions for events.
They should continue to publish their events even if no subscriptions
exist at all. They should neither know nor care.

The terms SOA 2.0 and Event-Driven SOA have made some inroads into the SOA community. They both indicate a service-oriented architecture where event mechanisms are used to further decouple applications and services from each other. Instead of coupling applications and services that are sources of business events to the (often one-way) services that have a need for the information, events are used to convey the data through a generic facilitating medium: an event coordinator. In the SOA Suite, the role of event coordinator is implemented by the Event Delivery Network.

Introducing the Event Delivery Network

Oracle SOA Suite comes with the Event Delivery Network (EDN), an infrastructure that provides a declarative way of defining, publishing, and registering for consumption of business events. The EDN enables implementation of the EDA patterns in the SOA Suite.

The Event Delivery Network is a man-in-the-middle, a central coordinator that interacts with three types of entities: publishers of events, consumers of events, and the events themselves. The publishers—composite SOA applications or external parties such as Java applications or PL/SQL code running in the database—create an event and publish it by telling the man-in-the-middle about it.

However, before events can be published, their meta-definition needs to be in place, consisting of a (fully qualified) name and an XSD definition of their payload. The payload of an event is the data associated with it, provided by the publisher and available to the consumer. The meta-definitions of the business events are defined in EDL—the Event Definition Language. EDLs are deployed inside composites or stored in MDS. These event-definition files typically import one or more XSD documents that provide the element definitions on which the event payload is based.

EDL is just another XML language—based itself on an XSD (edl.xsd in the JAR file bpm-ide-common.jar) that is registered with JDeveloper. Note that there are no explicit references to EDL files, not from composite.xml or from any of the components' definitions files. All EDL files in a project help provide events that the components can subscribe to or publish, and all EDL files deployed to an SOA Suite instance are available to all composites in that SOA Suite. One EDL file can contain multiple definitions of event types.

The Event Delivery Network works across and beyond the SOA Suite, coordinating events from and to all composites running in the SCA container. The event definitions should therefore ideally be generic, based on canonical data model definitions.

Once event definitions have been registered with the EDN, subscriptions can be created on those events. SOA composite applications register their interest in events of a specific type with the EDN through Mediator or BPEL components that consume such events. BPMN components—which will be introduced in Chapter 19—can also subscribe to EDN events that are consumed as BPMN signal events. Many different composite applications can subscribe to the same event. Each of these applications will receive notification of the events from the Event Delivery Network.

Upon deployment of an application with event-consuming components, the subscriptions are automatically detected by the EDN and used to distribute the published instances of those events. These subscriptions are durable—they continue to exist when the composite is deactivated for some reason. Upon reactivation, the events published during the composite's downtime are delivered. Undeploy ends subscription of an SOA composite, as does Retire.

Publishers of events do not have to be registered beforehand; anyone can publish an event of a type that is defined through EDL. Events of a specific type can be published by many different publishers, both inside the SCA container and outside of it. Primary publishers of events to the Event Delivery Network are Mediator, BPMN, and BPEL service components as well as OEP applications and Java Clients. Additionally, ADF Business Components can be configured to publish events to the EDN when data manipulations on entity objects occur. The EM FMW Control has a facility for publishing events for test purposes—we will be using that feature later in this chapter.

The FlightStatusUpdate Event

One of the key business events at Saibot Airport is the *FlightStatusUpdate* event. Every time something happens around a flight, when it is within 20 minutes of landing, touches down or arrives at the gate, when the cleaning crew completes the job or the baggage hits the belt, an event is published. Many different parties at the airport make use of these events to coordinate their own activities. All companies, for example, who have a contract to provide some sort of aircraft service to a particular flight. And everyone involved in informing humans who have expressed an interest in the flight.

In this section, we will define the *FlightStatusUpdate* event in an EDL file, the definition format for EDN. We will then create a new SOA composite that registers on this event using a Mediator and that makes calls to the *FlightUpdateNotificationService* for every person and channel—email, Twitter, chat—for which an active interest in the flight is registered. We will first use the test facility in EM FMW Control to publish the event on the EDN and then we will look at publishing the event from a Service Bus service.

Define the Business Event FlightStatusUpdate

The *FlightStatusUpdate* event is defined in an EDL file—as an airport-wide event type with a canonical payload—not specific to any application or service and based on elements defined in the canonical data model. Note that the EDL file has to be created and deployed as part of an SOA composite application, even though it does not really belong to any one application— it is applicable throughout the SOA Suite container and is more or less "community property." In Chapter 21, we will see how MDS can be used to centrally store, share, and manage EDL definitions.

Create SOA Application *FlightStatusRelay* with an SOA composite project with that same name using the Empty Composite template.

Right click on the folder SOA | Events and select New | Event. Enter *FlightEvents* as name for the EDL file. Set the namespace to saibot.airport/events/flight. Click the green plus icon to add the first event definition. Select the element *FlightStatusUpdate* from the XSD FlightEvents.xsd, in the Type Chooser pop-up window. Enter *FlightStatusUpdateEvent* as the name for the event, as shown in Figure 15-1. Click OK to complete the event creation.

At this stage, the business event has been defined. There are no consumers yet, the run time EDN does not know of it and there is no one publishing the event.

Consume FlightStatusUpdate from EDN

In order to consume a specific event such as the *FlightStatusUpdateEvent* from the Event Delivery Network, an SOA composite needs to have a subscription for that event with EDN. A subscription can be created in two ways: through a Mediator or a BPEL component (or a BPMN component as we will see in Chapter 19). A Mediator routing rule can have an event as its source, rather than a request message passed in over a wire from a service binding or another SCA component. A BPEL component can have a Receive or (mid process) OnMessage activity listen to an event instead of a partner link.

Add a Mediator component called *FlightStatusUpdateEventHandler* to the application—without interface at this time. Right click on the created Mediator and select Add Subscribed Events. Click on the green plus icon in the dialog that appears and browse for the *FlightStatusUpdateEvent*, as

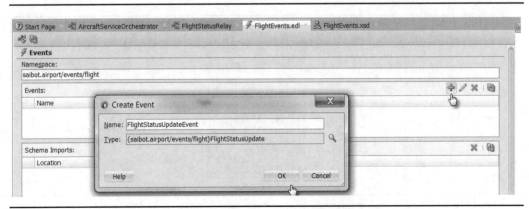

FIGURE 15-1. *Defining the FlightStatusUpdateEvent in the FlightEvents.edl file*

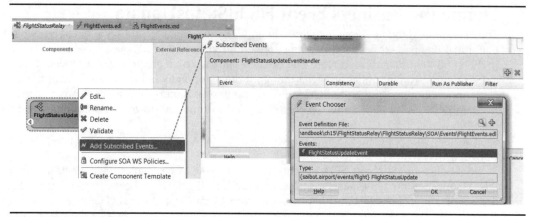

FIGURE 15-2. *Configuring the Mediator to consume the FlightStatusUpdate event*

shown in Figure 15-2. Then click OK and OK to confirm the Mediator's subscription on the event—with default settings for Consistency (one and only one), Durable (yes), Run as Publisher (yes), and Filter (none).

With this event subscription, a new instance of this *FlightStatusRelay* composite will be created whenever the *FlightStatusUpdateEvent* is published on the EDN. The payload of the event is transferred to this new instance and will be the input to the Mediator. At that point, there is no distinction in the subsequent processing of the event payload with a regular request message that arrives.

Because the default settings that we accepted configure the subscription as *Durable*—the events are guaranteed to be delivered to the composite. Even when it is temporarily off line, the events are stored and will be forwarded to the composite once it comes back on line. The other default setting we have accepted is to run the event processing in the security context of the publisher of the event.

Next, create a reference binding in the SOA composite for the *FlightUpdateNotificationService*, last seen in Chapter 10. Wire the Mediator to this reference, as shown in Figure 15-3. Next, open the Mediator for editing. Use the Assign Values dialog to copy

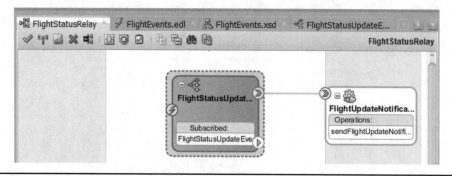

FIGURE 15-3. *The FlightStatusRelay composite that is initiated by the FlightStatusUpdateEvent and invokes the FlightUpdateNotificationService*

the *Carrier*, *FlightNumber* and *FlightStatus* from the event to the input for the
FlightUpdateNotificationService. Also define values for the communication meta data, especially
the *to* address and the *channel* (email, im, twitter).

Deploy the SOA composite. This will make the run time EDN environment aware of the
FlightStatusUpdateEvent and its one and only consumer at present. Time to let the events come in.

Publish Test Event from EM FMW Control

Open the EM FMW Control. Click on the node SOA | soa-infra. From the drop-down menu,
shown in Figure 15-4, select *Business Events*.

You will find a list of all know event definitions, containing a single event:
FlightStatusUpdateEvent. You can inspect the definition of the event and browse the subscriptions
for this event, as well as their status. In the EM FMW Control, you can view the service
components that have subscribed to business events. Service component subscriptions are created
in Oracle JDeveloper during design time and cannot be modified in Oracle Enterprise Manager
Fusion Middleware Control.

You can also publish the event, by clicking the Test button. You have to provide an XML
message that forms the payload of the event. In this case, that means an XML fragment based on
the *FlightStatusUpdate* element, see Figure 15-5.

Press Publish to transfer the event to the Event Delivery Network. A popup will appear that
informs you that the event was successfully published.

FIGURE 15-4.   *Open the Business Events console in EM FMW Control*

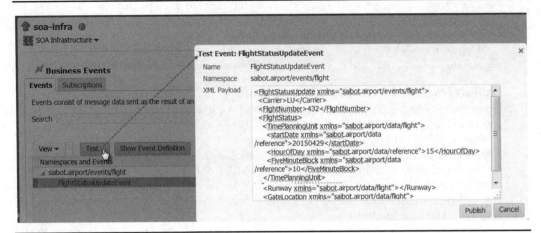

FIGURE 15-5. *Publish the FlightStatusUpdateEvent to EDN from EM FMW Control*

EDN absorbs the event, checks the subscribers and delivers the event to each of the subscribers. In this case, the *FlightStatusRelay* composite is instantiated because of its subscription and the event's payload is transferred to the *FlightStatusUpdateEventHandler* Mediator component, see Figure 15-6 for the message flow trace that started with the event.

Under the Covers: JMS

When you open the WLS Administration Console and you check the *EDNTopic* in the *SOAJMSModule*, you will find one durable subscriber in the Monitoring tab. This represents the event subscription in the Mediator component in the *FlightStatusRelay* composite.

Open the EM FMW Control and click on the node SOA | soa-infra. Navigate to the tab Deployed Composites. Click on the *FlightStatusRelay* composite. Then click on the button Shutdown, to temporarily deactivate the composite.

Publish the FlightStatusUpdateEvent again.

The subscription for the composite is still there. But the composite is not up and running. What happens now is that the event is held in the JMS Topic, until such time as the composite is ready to

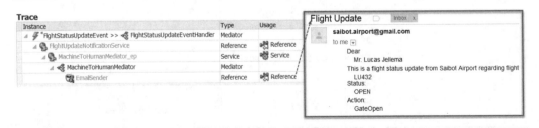

FIGURE 15-6. *The FlightStatusUpdateEvent triggered the FlightStatusRelay composite that invoked the FlightUpdateNotificationService that sent the email to the interested traveler*

consume again. In the WLS Admin Console, in the Monitoring tab for the *EDNTopic*, you will now find this message-in-transit when you click the button *Show Messages* for the durable subscription.

When you next start up again the composite, this message will disappear from the topic because it can be delivered to the composite. You will find a new composite instance, initiated right after the composite becomes active again.

Air Carrier Suspended Event

Due to international tensions and resulting sanctions as well as financial turmoil and escalating business disputes, there is a real possibility of air carriers being suspended. When that happens— a business event to that effect should be published.

In this section, a BPEL process will subscribe to this event. When the event is consumed, the BPEL process will retrieve all flight numbers of current flights by that air carrier and will publish their cancellation through the publication of instances of the *FlightStatusUpdateEvent*.

Subsequently, the *AircraftServiceOrchestrator* BPEL process that was introduced in Chapter 12, will be extended to also consume that event. When it does, it will immediately cease the RFP process it has started for the air carrier. The event is consumed through correlation into a running instance for the air carrier—it does not start a new instance.

Consume EDN Event into New BPEL Process

Find all open flights and publish the *FlightStatusUpdateEvent* for all now cancelled flights by the suspended carrier.

Preparation

First we define the SOA application, the project and the *AirCarrierSuspended* event definition. We also create a simple BPEL process that returns a (static, dummy) list of flights for a given carrier.

Create the SOA Application and Project   Create new SOA Application called *CarrierWatcher* with an SOA composite (project) called *CarrierWatcher*, based on the empty template. Copy the file CarrierWatcher.xsd to the Schemas folder.

Define the AirCarrierSuspendedEvent EDN Event   Right click Events folder. Select New | Event Definition from the context menu. Set the name [of the edl file] to *AircarrierEvents* and the namespace to saibot.airport/events/aircarrier.

Click green plus icon to create a new event. Define the event name as *AirCarrierSuspendedEvent*. Select element *carrierSuspension* from CarrierWatcher.xsd as the event payload.

Click OK and OK to complete the definition of the event and the .edl file.

Create BPEL Component to Gather All Current Flights   Create a synchronous BPEL process component called *CurrentFlightsRetriever* that is not exposed as a SOAP service. The input is based on the *CurrentFlightsRequest* element in CarrierWatcher.xsd and the output on *CurrentFlightsResponse* in that same file. This component accepts criteria for current flights—in this case only the air carrier— and returns a list of all current flights in a 48 hour time window.

In a real-world airport and a real end to end application, this component would call out to various business services that in turn query the *present* database where flight details are stored. However, in the scope of this chapter where we focus on events, we create a very simple dummy implementation that returns a few flights for the air carrier whose IATA code is passed in.

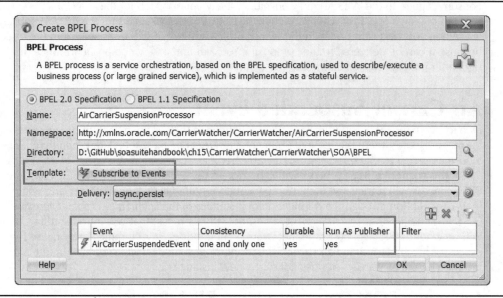

FIGURE 15-7. *Creating a BPEL process component that is initiated by the consumption of the AirCarrierSuspendedEvent from the Event Delivery Network*

Open the BPEL process. Add an Assign activity. Open the editor. Drag the icon for a literal [XML fragment] to the *outputVariable/payload* element. Use the contents from the CurrentFlights.xml document in the Samples directory to populate the fragment.

Create BPEL to Consume AirCarrierSuspendedEvent

Add a new BPEL component to the composite. Set the name to *AirCarrierSuspensionProcessor*. Select the Template *Subscribe to Events*. Click on the green plus icon to create an event subscription. Subscribe the BPEL component to the *AirCarrierSuspendedEvent*, as shown in Figure 15-7. Accept the default settings. Click OK to complete the creation of the BPEL component.

Wire the BPEL component to the *CurrentFlightsRetriever*. Next, open the component for editing. Add an Invoke activity to the *CurrentFlightsRetriever* component. Have the input and output variable generated. Add an Assign activity to map the air carrier code from the event that triggers the BPEL component to the input variable that flows to the *CurrentFlightsRetriever*.

Add a For-Each activity. Configure the activity to loop over all Flight elements in the *CurrentFlights* list returned from the invoke activity. Check—in an If activity—for each flight if its status is unequal to cancelled and closed—because those flights do not require further action. Add an Invoke activity to the If branch. Configure this activity to not invoke a partner link but instead to publish the *FlightStatusUpdateEvent*. Have the input variable created that is used to set the payload for the event. Add an Assign activity—just above the Invoke activity that publishes the event—to set the value of this input variable from the current flight element in the For Each loop. Figure 15-8 shows what the BPEL process should look like.

The entire composite looks as shown in Figure 15-9. There are no service or reference bindings. Instead: the input and output into and from this composite consists of the EDN events consumed and published by the first BPEL component.

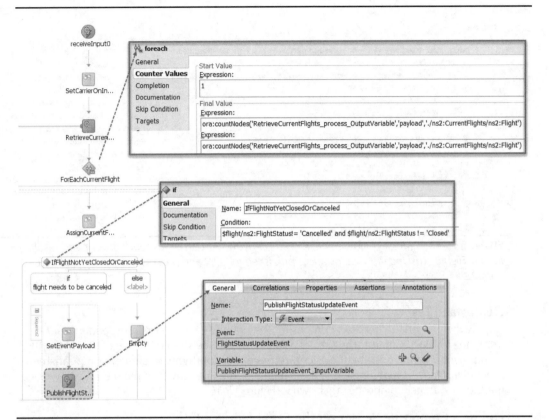

FIGURE 15-8. *The BPEL process that retrieves the current flights for the suspended carrier and published the FlightStatusUpdateEvent for each relevant flight*

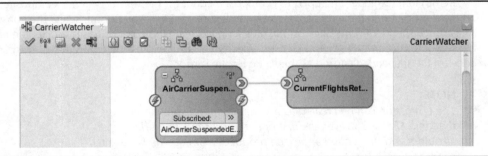

FIGURE 15-9. *The CarrierWatcher composite that subscribes to the AirCarrierSuspendedEvent and published the FlightStatusUpdateEvent for the air carrier's current flights*

Trace

Instance	Type	Composite
◢ ⚡ ＂AirCarrierSuspendedEvent >> ⚘ AirCarrierSuspensionProcessor >> ⚡ ＂FlightStatusUpdateEvent	BPEL	CarrierWatcher [1.0]
⚘ CurrentFlightsRetriever	BPEL	CarrierWatcher [1.0]
◢ ⚡ FlightStatusUpdateEvent >> ◀ FlightStatusUpdateEventHandler	Mediator	FlightStatusRelay [1.0]
◢ 🔋 FlightUpdateNotificationService	Reference	FlightStatusRelay [1.0]
◢ 🔋 MachineToHumanMediator_ep	Service	FlightUpdateNotificationService [1.0]
◢ ◀ MachineToHumanMediator	Mediator	FlightUpdateNotificationService [1.0]
📧 EmailSender	Reference	FlightUpdateNotificationService [1.0]
◢ ⚡ FlightStatusUpdateEvent >> ◀ FlightStatusUpdateEventHandler	Mediator	FlightStatusRelay [1.0]
◢ 🔋 FlightUpdateNotificationService	Reference	FlightStatusRelay [1.0]
◢ 🔋 MachineToHumanMediator_ep	Service	FlightUpdateNotificationService [1.0]
◢ ◀ MachineToHumanMediator	Mediator	FlightUpdateNotificationService [1.0]
📧 EmailSender	Reference	FlightUpdateNotificationService [1.0]
▷ ⚡ ＂FlightStatusUpdateEvent >> ◀ FlightStatusUpdateEventHandler	Mediator	FlightStatusRelay [1.0]
▷ ⚡ ＂FlightStatusUpdateEvent >> ◀ FlightStatusUpdateEventHandler	Mediator	FlightStatusRelay [1.0]

FIGURE 15-10. *Message flow trace, kicked off by the AirCarrierSuspendedEvent and resulting in four FlightStatusUpdateEvent instances published to EDN and processed by the FlightStatusRelay composite*

Deploy and Test
Deploy the *CarrierWatcher* SOA composite. Then publish an *AirCarrierSuspendedEvent* instance from the EM FMW Control. The *CarrierWatcher* composite should be triggered and the BPEL component should consume the event, retrieve a list of flights to cancel and publish the *FlightStatusUpdateEvent* for each of these flights. Verify this activity in the message flow trace for the *CarrierWatcher* composite, as shown in Figure 15-10.

Define a Composite Sensor on the Event Subscription
Composite sensors—first seen in Chapter 5—can be defined on service and reference bindings to publish relevant and typically identifying details on an instance of a SOA composite—much like message reports in Service Bus pipelines. Such sensors can also be defined on event subscriptions, to track (relevant information for) composite instances that have consumed an event.

Return to JDeveloper and open the composite editor for the *CarrierWatcher* composite. Click on the sensor icon in the icon bar, as shown in Figure 15-11. In the popup, select the consumed *AirCarrierSuspendedEvent*. Click on the plus icon to create the composite sensor. Set the name of the sensor to *AirCarrierSuspensionSensor*. Specify an XPath expression that retrieves the carrier code (of the suspended carrier) as the value for the sensor.

NOTE
The expression can be created as a Variable or an Expression using the same XPath. However, the first option results in a iataAirlineType as output and the second approach produces a String. The latter is far easier to search for.

Redeploy the composite. Publish another instance of the *AirCarrierSuspendedEvent*. Check whether an instance of the composite is created. Then find out if the composite sensor value is available in the EM FMW Control, as is shown in Figure 15-12.

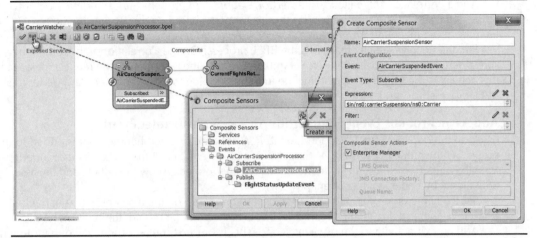

FIGURE 15-11. *Creating a composite sensor that exposes the carrier code on all instances of the CarrierWatcher composite triggered by the AirCarrierSuspendedEvent*

Consume into Running BPEL Process AircraftServiceNegotiationProcessor

The *AircraftServiceOrchestrator* composite engages one or usually more than one provider of aircraft services to solicit proposals for an airline carrier. The services that the composite invokes are asynchronous—a response can take several hours to multiple days to come in. The whole RFP can and should be terminated as soon as the air carrier that requested it has been suspended. That means that the BPEL component *AircraftServiceNegotiationProcessor* should consume the *AirCarrierSuspendedEvent* into a running instance for the suspended carrier (if there is one) and terminate that instance.

We have seen in the previous section how a BPEL process can be instantiated through the reception of an event. We will now go one step further and use an event instead of an mid process incoming request message, to correlate into the instance.

Define Correlation Set for BPEL Process

Open the AircraftServiceOrchestrator composite. Open BPEL component AircraftServiceNegotiationProcessor for editing.

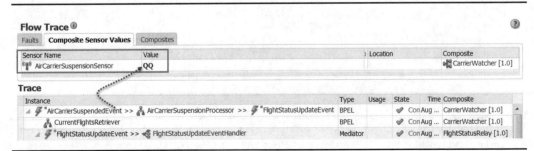

FIGURE 15-12. *The composite sensor value derived from the AirCarrierSuspendedEvent*

Add a correlation set, called *AirCarrierCorrelation*. Add property *AirCarrierIataCode* of type String to the set. Define a property alias for this property, based on the *RequestingCarrierIATACode* element in the incoming *ArrangeAircraftServiceRequestMessage*.

Edit the Receive activity that starts the BPEL process. On the Correlations tab, add the new *AirCarrierCorrelation* correlation set. Set initiate to true—the reception of the request message by this activity is the trigger for specifying the identifying value for the *AirCarrierIataCode* for this BPEL process.

Add Asynchronous Event Handler for AirCarrierSuspendedEvent

Click on the *onEvent* icon for scope *ExecuteRFP*. Edit the *onEvent* handler that is added to the scope. Set the name to *ConsumeAirCarrierSuspendedEvent*. Select the *AirCarrierSuspendedEvent* from the AircarriersEvents.edl file in the *CarrierWatcher* project. Allow the edl file and the associated XSD files to be copied to the current project.

Set the name of the variable to *carrierSuspension*, based on the element of that name in the CarrierWatcher.xsd document. Figure 15-13 shows the configuration of the *onEvent* handler.

Add an Exit activity to the *onEvent* scope. This is our first, rather crude way of handling the *AirCarrierSuspendedEvent*. Ideally of course we would inform all aircraft service providers that are participating in the RFP and whose asynchronous responses we are still awaiting. Those are refinements we ought to add in the real world. In this example, they do not add to our understanding of correlating EDN events into running BPEL process instances, so we ignore them.

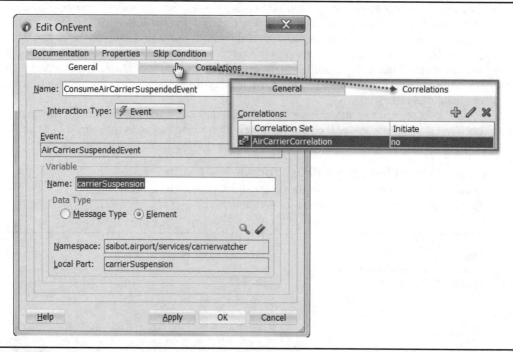

FIGURE 15-13. *Configuring the onEvent handler to consume the AirCarrierSuspendedEvent into an instance with the corresponding air carrier value for the correlation set AirCarrierCorrelation*

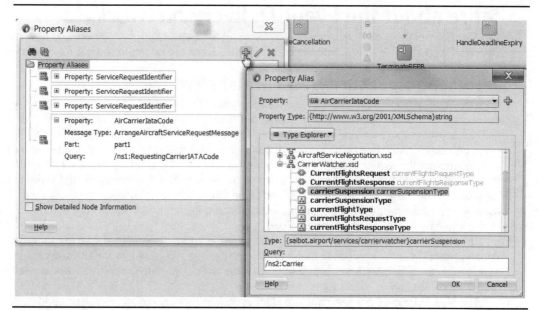

FIGURE 15-14.   *Adding a property alias for property AirCarrierIataCode based on the Carrier element in the payload of the AirCarrierSuspendedEvent*

Finally, add a property alias to the correlation set that maps the Carrier element in the payload of the *AirCarrierSuspendedEvent* to the property *AirCarrierIataCode*, as shown in Figure 15-14.

Deploy and Test

Deploy the SOA composite *AircraftServiceOrchestrator*. Invoke operation *arrangeAircraftService* with a value of XX for element *RequestingCarrierIATACode* in the request message.

When you inspect in the EM FMW Control, you will find a running *AircraftServiceOrchestrator* instance, initiated by your request.

Use the Business Events console in the EM FMW Control to publish an instance of the *AirCarrierSuspendedEvent*. Set the *Carrier* element in the payload for this event to XX. The running *AircraftServiceOrchestrator* instance should consume this event in the new *onEvent* handler that we have just added. This in turn should result in the immediate termination of the instance.

NOTE
Correlation in BPEL assumes uniqueness of the correlation set among all running instances. That means in this case that only one instance of the AircraftServiceOrchestrator can be running at any one time for a specific air carrier. In reality it will frequently occur that an event should be consumed into more than one running instance—and we need a somewhat more involved approach than this described above. The book's website contains a reference to an article introducing a way to "fan out EDN events" so as to have one event impact multiple instances.

More about the Event Delivery Network

This section contains a number of useful details about the Event Delivery Network and how it can be used. Of course, it is only a limited collection. Check out the on line resources for more details.

Transactions, Security, and Scalability

With the "Consistency" setting on an event subscription, do we indicate whether the delivery of the event is part of the transaction in response to the event (one and only one) or whether the delivery is in separate transaction (guaranteed). The former (and default) setting means that the event delivery is rolled back when errors occur in the consumer (and the event can be delivered again), whereas the latter causes the event to be lost for this subscription when the consuming transaction is rolled back. The third value—immediate—specifies that events are delivered to the subscriber in the same global transaction and same thread as the publisher, effectively (and usually very undesirably) coupling the publisher to the consumer. Stay away from that option, unless you have a very good reason for using it.

The setting "Run as publisher" is set to yes to have the consumer executed with the same security context (identity) as the composite that published the event. According to the documentation, alternatively an Enterprise Role can be set to execute the consuming composite with. However, the IDE does not appropriately support this.

The SOA Suite does not keep track of EDN events, in the form of an archive or audit trail or something along those lines. When an event is consumed by a composite, the composite flow trace will reflect the event occurrence. Events associated with durable subscriptions by currently unavailable consumers are retained at JMS level.

If your SOA composite application includes a business event subscription, and you deploy different revisions of the composite, all event subscriptions from all revisions of the composite are active and receive messages.

An Oracle WebLogic Server JMS topic (default) and an AQ JMS topic are automatically configured for EDN use after installation. The default JMS type can be switched from Oracle WebLogic Server JMS (default) to AQ JMS in Oracle Enterprise Manager Fusion Middleware Control. You can map business events to JMS topic destinations on the Business Events page in Oracle Enterprise Manager Fusion Middleware Control—to reduce the risk of bottlenecks when all events flow through a single JMS Topic.

TIP
A human task component—to be introduced in Chapter 17—can be configured to publish events to the Event Delivery Network for every task and workflow event. This includes task assigned, claimed, rejected, escalated, and completed.

NOTE
Events are not subject to authorization mechanisms: Any composite can register for any event type on the EDN and every instance of events is delivered to every consumer—when allowed by the optional filter expression on the subscription. No authorization can be specified or enforced.

Missing Event Detection

An event indicates that something happens—or so you would think. However, it is quite possible to have a meaningful event when something does not happen. When the expected does not occur, that can be quite an event indeed. If the sun or the tide forgot to rise, we would have major events indeed.

On a slightly smaller scale, we, too, have the situation where the fact that something we expected did not actually happen in itself is a meaningful event. The invoice was sent but the payment never materialized; the suitcase went into the baggage-handling system but never came out; the complaint was filed but a response was never sent. Such an event is often called a nonevent. The absence of an event is an event in its own right.

A common challenge in event processing is the detection of nonevents: events that should take place (before a certain moment in time) but do not happen. SOA Suite does not have support for this detection out of the box. We have to implement some logic to find the nonevents and turn them into real EDN business events. Here is one way of approaching this challenge.

When an aircraft touches down and starts taxiing towards the gate, an event is published to the Event Delivery Network (say, the *AircraftLandedEvent*) with the flight number as payload. A composite application is subscribed to this event and a new instance is initiated upon consumption. This composite contains a BPEL component that consumes event. It enters a Pick activity with two branches: One is a Wait activity that will wait for 30 minutes. The other branch is an *onMessage* that will wait for an *AircraftAtGateEvent*. The *onMessage* will correlate this latter event on the flight number.

When an aircraft arrives at the gate, this *AircraftAtGateEvent* should be published. When it is, the BPEL component will consume it, conclude the Pick activity, and terminate the instance altogether. However, if after 30 minutes this event is still not received, the wait branch of the Pick activity is activated and it will publish the "nonevent" *AircraftDidNotArriveAtGateEvent*. The BPEL component turns the absence of the business event—after the specified period—into another business event, which subsequently can be responded to by all consumers.

Event Exchange with EDN from Other Channels

Publishing and consuming EDN events can easily be done from a Mediator and a BPEL process. Oracle Event Processor has an adapter to interact with EDN, ADF Business Components can be configured to publish to EDN and anyone capable of communicating over JMS can interact with EDN. This makes it possible to, for example, publish events to EDN from Service Bus, despite the fact that Service Bus does not understand the EDL file nor has a native EDN integration.

In this section, we will first look at the interaction from a simple Java Client with the Event Delivery Network. Next, we will focus specifically on Service Bus as consumer and producer of events.

Publish FlightStatusUpdateEvent from Java Client to EDN

Java clients can make use of the EDN Java API that Oracle ships with the SOA Suite. By using this API, most details surrounding the communication and event definition are taken care of. Alternatively, we could communicate at plain JMS level—which leaves us with far more responsibility regarding EDN intricacies.

Create a Service Bus application called *EDNandAlternativeChannels*. Create a new Java project called *EDNJavaClient*. Add the following libraries and jar files to the project:

- Libraries: SOA Runtime, WebLogic 12.1 Remote-Client, JRF Runtime
- Jar-files: Tracking-core.jar and Jca-binding-api.jar (note: these jar files can be found in the directory FMW_HOME\Oracle_Home\soa\soa\modules\oracle.soa.adapter_11.1.1 and FMW_HOME\ Oracle_Home\soa\soa\modules\oracle.soa.fabric_11.1.1, respectively

Create a Java class called *FlightStatusUpdateEventPublisher*. Add the following code that will publish the *FlightStatusUpdateEvent* to the Event Delivery Network. Note the address and login details of the SOA Suite managed server that are provided; you need to adapt them for your environment. Note that the import statements have been left out for the sake of brevity. You will of course find the correct imports in the on line sources:

```java
package saibot.airport.events.client;
public class FlightStatusUpdateEventPublisher {
 public static void main(String[] args) {
  Properties props = new Properties();
  props.put(Context.PROVIDER_URL, "t3://soa2admin2:8001/soa-infra");
  props.put(Context.INITIAL_CONTEXT_FACTORY, "weblogic.jndi.
WLInitialContextFactory");
  props.put(Context.SECURITY_PRINCIPAL, "weblogic");
  props.put(Context.SECURITY_CREDENTIALS, "weblogic1");
  String FlightStatusUpdateEventBody =
  "<FlightStatusUpdate xmlns=\"saibot.airport/events/flight\">\n" + "
<Carrier>ZQ</Carrier>\n" +
  "  <FlightNumber>1134</FlightNumber>\n" + "  <FlightStatus>\n" +
  "    <Action xmlns=\"saibot.airport/data/flight\">GateOpen</Action>\n" +
  "  </FlightStatus>\n" + "</FlightStatusUpdate>";
  try {
   Element eventBody = XMLUtil.parseDocumentFromXMLString(FlightStatusUpdateEv
entBody.toString()).getDocumentElement();
   BusinessEventConnectionFactorySupport.setJndiProperties(props);
   EdnConnection ec = (EdnConnection) BusinessEventConnectionFactorySupport.
                      findRelevantBusinessEventConnectionFactory(true).
                      createBusinessEventConnection();
  String namespace = "saibot.airport/events/flight";
  String eventName = "FlightStatusUpdateEvent";
  BusinessEventBuilder builder = BusinessEventBuilder.newInstance();
  builder.setEventName(new QName(namespace, eventName));
  builder.setBody(eventBody);
  ec.publishEvent(builder.createEvent(), 4);
  ec.close();
  } catch (Exception e) {
            e.printStackTrace();
  }
 }
}
```

When you run this Java class, its main method is executed. It builds up an EdnConnection to the SOA Suite run time server—without having to know a lot about the configuration of EDN in terms of JMS Topics and connection factories. Through the EdnConnection, it is easy to publish an event. Setting the right namespace and event name are of course crucial to instruct EDN on the nature of the event.

Run the class and verify whether a new instance of SOA composite *FlightStatusRelay* is created.

Consume FlightStatusUpdateEvent from EDN to a Java Client

With the JDeveloper project that we created in the previous section to publish an EDN event, we are already well underway to also consume an event from EDN. We can fairly easily create an event subscription and register one of our own objects as a listener. We can specify the event type to listen for and also use an event filter. The EDN API takes care of creating the appropriate durable JMS Topic subscription and transferring the event to our listener. With the subscription, we can specify a time out that indicates if and for how long our code should block waiting for the event we subscribe to.

Create a Java Class *FlightStatusUpdateEventSubscriber*. The following code also establishes an EDN Connection. It then creates a subscription on the *FlightStatusUpdateEvent*—registering itself as listener. The Class implements the interface *BusinessEventHandler* that is defined in the EDN API. The method *onEvent* has to be implemented in the Class, to satisfy the interface. This method is called whenever the event is published on EDN.

```java
public class FlightStatusUpdateEventSubscriber implements BusinessEventHandler {
  public static void main(String[] args) {
    Properties props = new Properties();
    props.put(Context.PROVIDER_URL, "t3://soa2admin2:8001/soa-infra");
    props.put(Context.INITIAL_CONTEXT_FACTORY, "weblogic.jndi.
WLInitialContextFactory");
    props.put(Context.SECURITY_PRINCIPAL, "weblogic");
    props.put(Context.SECURITY_CREDENTIALS, "weblogic1");
    BusinessEventConnectionFactorySupport.setJndiProperties(props);
    EdnConnection ec = (EdnConnection) BusinessEventConnectionFactorySupport.
                        findRelevantBusinessEventConnectionFactory(true).
                        createBusinessEventConnection();
    String namespace = "saibot.airport/events/flight";
    String eventName = "FlightStatusUpdateEvent";
    ec.setEventHandler(new FlightStatusUpdateEventSubscriber());
    ec.setTimeout(12000);
    ec.subscribe(new QName(namespace, eventName),
"mySubscriptionForFlightStatusUpdateEvent");
  }

  public void onEvent(BusinessEvent be) throws FabricInvocationException {
    System.out.println("Hey, I received an event of type " + be.getEventName()+";
payload = " + be.getBodyAsText());
  }
}
```

Run this class. Now either publish the *FlightStatusUpdateEvent* from the EM FMW Control or using the Java class *FlightStatusUpdateEventPublisher* created in the previous section. Check if the *onEvent* method does indeed receive the event.

Interact with EDN from Service Bus

As was stated before, Service Bus does not have out of the box integration with the Event Delivery Network. Having said that, because EDN can be accessed through a Java API to publish events and uses JMS to deliver events, it turns out not incredibly difficult to interact with EDN from Service Bus. Using a Java Callout to a Java class very similar to the one created in the previous section, we can publish EDN events from a Service Bus Pipeline. Subsequently we will subscribe a Service Bus proxy service to a specific EDN event using an inbound JMS transport.

Use Java Callout to Publish to EDN

Create Java project *EDNServiceBusCalloutLibrary*. Add the same libraries and JAR-files as in the *EDNJavaClient* project. Also add the XML Beans jar-file we previously used to construct a Java Callout in Chapter 7 (com.bea.core.xml.xmlbeans_x.y-z.p.jar). Finally, create a new deployment profile for the project called *EDNServiceBusCalloutLibraryJAR* of Profile Type JAR file.

Create Java class *EDNEventPublisher* with static method *publishEDNEvent* that takes an *XmlObject* with the payload of the EDN event and strings for the namespace and [local] event name of the EDN event. (The final input parameter is the name of the root element—to work around the SB characteristic of using xml-fragment as root element.)

Implement this method much like the main method in Java class *FlightStatusUpdateEventPublisher* discussed before, only make the code generic: not tied to the *FlightStatusUpdateEvent*.

```
public static void publishEDNEvent(XmlObject eventPayload, String
ednEventNamespace, String ednEventName,
                                   String rootElementName) {
    String xml = eventPayload.toString().replaceAll("xml-fragment",
rootElementName);
    Properties props; // define properties as before
    try {
        Element eventBody = XMLUtil.parseDocumentFromXMLString(eventBodyXML.
toString()).getDocumentElement();
        BusinessEventConnectionFactorySupport.setJndiProperties(props);
        EdnConnection ec =
            (EdnConnection) BusinessEventConnectionFactorySupport.findRelevantBusi
nessEventConnectionFactory(true).createBusinessEventConnection();
        BusinessEventBuilder builder = BusinessEventBuilder.newInstance();
        builder.setEventName(new QName(ednEventNamespace, ednEventName));
        builder.setBody(eventBody);
        ec.publishEvent(builder.createEvent(), 4);
        ec.close();
    } catch (Exception e) {
        // implement exception handling ...
    }
}
```

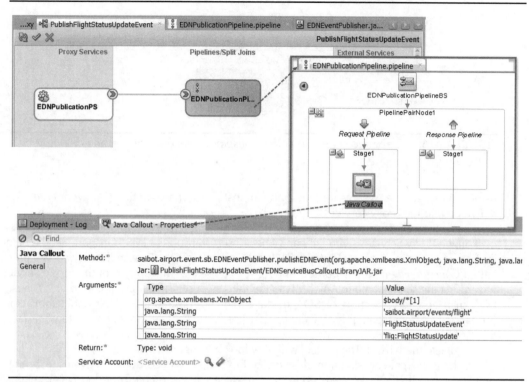

FIGURE 15-15. *Configuring the Service Bus project to publish events to EDN*

Deploy the project according to the *EDNServiceBusCalloutLibraryJAR* deployment profile, producing a JAR file.

Create a new Service Bus project called *PublishFlightStatusUpdateEvent*. Create a ProxyService *EDNPublicationPS* with service type Any XML. Generate a pipeline called *EDNPublicationPipeline* for this proxy service. Add a pipeline pair in the pipeline. Add a Java Callout in the request branch. Configure the callout to call method *publishEDNEvent* in *EDNEventPublisher* Class in JAR file EDNServiceBusCalloutLibraryJAR.jar. The first argument is set with the first element in the $body variable, the other three are set to saibot.airport/events/flight, FlightStatusUpdateEvent, and flig:FlightStatusUpdate, respectively, see Figure 15-15.

Run the Pipeline or the Proxy Service. Set the input to an XML document that is the payload for the *FlightStatusUpdateEvent*. The event should be published and, for example, consumed by a new instance of the *FlightStatusRelay* composite.

Consume EDN Events in Service Bus Using Inbound JMS Transport
Consuming EDN events can be done in Service Bus projects using a simple inbound JMS Transport. A Service Bus proxy service is subscribed as durable listener on the *EDNTopic* and

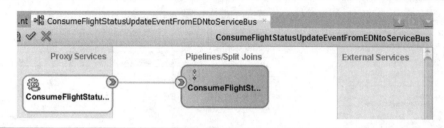

FIGURE 15-16. *The Service Bus project that consumes EDN events using an inbound JMS Transport*

using a message filter we ensure that (only) all instances of a specific EDN event type are delivered into the proxy service.

Create Service Bus project *ConsumeFlightStatusUpdateEventFromEDNtoServiceBus*. Right click in the Proxy Services swim lane and select Insert Transports | JMS Transport. Set the name of the proxy service to *ConsumeFlightStatusUpdateEventFromEDN*. Expose the service as a pipeline, called *ConsumeFlightStatusUpdateEventFromEDNPipeline*. In step two of the Proxy Service wizard, set the service type to Any XML. In the third step, set the Endpoint URI to jms://<host_of_SOA_managed_server>:<port_of_SOA_managed_server>/jms.fabric.xaEDNConnectionFactory/jms.fabric.EDNTopic (e.g., jms://localhost:7101/jms.fabric.xaEDNConnectionFactory/jms.fabric.EDNTopic).

Complete the wizard. The project will now look like Figure 15-16.

With the current configuration, this Service Bus project will consume all events that published on EDN, regardless of type. We need to set a message selector on the Transport Details page for the proxy service. We can find the required expression by inspecting the durable subscription for the Mediator *FlightStatusUpdateEventHandler* in the *FlightStatusRelay* composite:

```
(JMS_WL_DDForwarded IS NULL OR (NOT JMS_WL_DDForwarded)) AND EDN$namespace =
'saibot.airport/events/flight' AND EDN$localName = 'FlightStatusUpdateEvent'
```

Also set the Destination Type to Topic and check the box for Durable Subscription, as shown in Figure 15-17.

At this point, the event is consumed but nothing is done with it. In order to at least prove that EDN events of type *FlightStatusUpdateEvent* do indeed trigger the *ConsumeFlightStatusUpdateEventFromEDN* proxy service, we can add a Report activity in a Pipeline Pair in the *ConsumeFlightStatusUpdateEventFromEDNPipeline* that publishes a report with the entire event payload (which is loaded in the $body variable inside in the pipeline).

Deploy the project. Then publish the *FlightStatusUpdateEvent* using either the EM FMW Control or the Java Client or Service Bus project *PublishFlightStatusUpdateEvent* that were created in the previous sections.

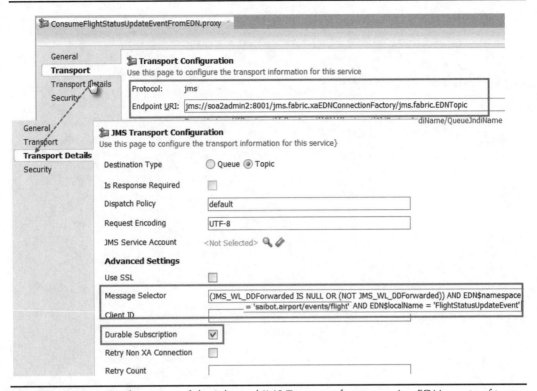

FIGURE 15-17.   *Configuration of the inbound JMS Transport for consuming EDN events of type FlightStatusUpdateEvent*

Summary

Events add an important element to a service-oriented environment: they provide a means of interacting in a truly decoupled way. Consumers and publishers do not know about each other—yet they are hugely important to one another. The Event Delivery Network enables the exchange of events, from SOA composites through Mediator and BPEL components as well as other parties, including Service Bus and remote Java clients. This chapter demonstrated some of the key aspects of using EDN for publishing and subscribing and consuming events.

However, this only scratches the surface. Using events as integral part of the SOA opens up a lot of questions, challenges, and opportunities that require careful investigation. Note that events and the EDN will make appearance in some upcoming chapters, including the next one—on continuous event processing—and Chapter 19 on BPM.

CHAPTER
16

Fast Data Processing with
Oracle Event Processor

U nderneath the tier of business events discussed in the previous chapter exists a world of fine-grained signals, measurements, and facts. This is the world of fast data where streams of time stamped data statements flow continuously through the IT systems. Live data is produced by the IoT (Internet of Things)—all kinds of connected sensors, cameras, wearables, and other devices, as well as by social media such as Twitter and Facebook, and by sensors on mobile apps, web applications, administrative software systems, and business process engines.

By processing these streams, we may be able to learn important business information. Aggregation, filtering, missing event detection, and pattern matching are some of the operations we can apply to promote findings from this avalanche of signals to the business level. Event processing typically produces business events that provide insight and trigger action. The interpretation of streams of data facts typically has to be done in (near) real-time, which adds to the challenge and necessitates the use of specialized technology.

A typical companion to event processing is business activity monitoring (BAM). Through BAM—both the act of monitoring and the product (to be discussed in Chapter 20), operational insight is provided through live dashboards and near real-time reports. It is common for results produced by event processing to be reported through a BAM dashboard.

The Oracle Event Processor (OEP) is a component integrated in SOA Suite that provides the capability to process fast data and produce business events from continuous streams of fine-grained data events. OEP can consume fast data from various channels—including JMS, EDN, HTTP/REST, RMI—and supports creation of custom adapters for collection fast data from, for example, Twitter, messaging systems such as Tibco Rendezvous, Sockets, APIs from financial data feeds, etc. Similar adapters are used to publish the outcomes produced by OEP. The integration between OEP and SOA composites and Service Bus hinges on JMS and EDN.

OEP is not only for processing huge volumes of events. It will also be the tool of choice for detection of predefined patterns that span cross process instances and service calls. OEP can be made to remember business events for quite some time and rapidly correlate additional (or missing) events to produce a relevant insight or alert.

Stream Explorer (SX) is a tool on top of OEP, targeted at the Line of Business User (the nontechnical IT consumer). This tool provides a visual, declarative, browser-based wrapper around Oracle Event Processor, and Oracle BAM. With Stream Explorer it is every easy to create explorations and dashboard on live (streams of) data—reporting in real time on patterns, correlations, aggregations, and deviations.

In this chapter, we will use OEP to process a simulated feed with car park events that report cars entering and leaving one of the car parks at Saibot Airport. These events are processed to produce messages on JMS whenever a car park is close to filling up. Using the event stream, OEP will detect towing candidates: cars that have been abandoned or that at least have stayed in the car park for longer than 48 hours. OEP will also produce *car stay* events—derived from the base *car entry* and *car leaving* events—that are then aggregated to produce *average car stay duration* reports.

Finally, OEP is used by the security department at Saibot Airport—to detect a string of suspicious credit card transactions in the airport's shopping area, following a specific pattern identified in earlier theft cases. Such findings are reported as business events on EDN to be taken care of by one or more SOA composite applications.

Sorting Out the Real-Time Data Avalanche

The term ongoing events can refer to many different things—from fairly high-level business events such as signing a long-term agreement with some vendor or the arrival of a large order from a wholesaler, to tiny crumbs of information such as the current temperature in a fridge, a click on a navigation link in the patient self-service web application, the heartbeat of some device, or the fact that some security badge was scanned to gain entry into a storage room. The higher-level events typically have a much lower frequency—counted in occurrences per hour or day—than the lowest-level data grains, arriving in up to thousands per second. The information contents of these two ends of the events spectrum tend to range from rich for the high-level, low-frequency events, to quite sparse for highly frequent packets.

An important aspect of the processing of these events is that much of it must be done in real time. Ongoing business leads to continuous streams of events that may require instantaneous actions. We cannot afford to just dump all the data into data warehouses that we will analyze later on, even though for some of the (derived) data that is, of course, exactly what we will do. The urgency of some of the reactions the events may prompt us to come up with is one reason. The sheer volume of the data is another: Thousands of low-level events occurring every second represent tons of data that a data warehouse cannot comfortably handle—and should not handle, as the vast majority of those events represent entirely useless information, especially when considered by themselves.

Therefore, we need a way to process the zillions of events that the business operation keeps on producing. A processor that turns these events into information—usually by producing a higher-level type of event that has some special business meaning, carries a larger information payload and is produced at much lower frequencies. This is illustrated in Figure 16-1. Typically the events produced by the processor are propagated in a more generic, canonical way, both in terms of protocol and channel as well as information structure.

After the first stage of event processing, downstream consumers absorb the higher-level events. These consumers can do several things, including sending out alerts or notifications, updating a real-time report or dashboard, taking actions such as invoking a web service or starting a human task, or loading data into a data warehouse. These downstream consumers can also further process the events—into even higher-level, more meaningful events. These events are then propagated through a next iteration of event processing.

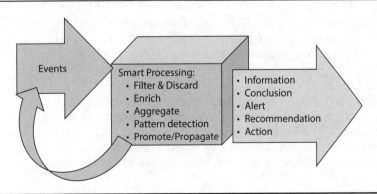

FIGURE 16-1. *Event processing—increasing information content and decreasing frequency*

Complex Event Processing

Finding the (missing) needles in the haystacks of large volumes of continuously arriving, largely individually meaningless events is the purpose of Complex Event Processing (CEP), also known as Intelligent Event Processing (IEP). CEP is a field that came to existence in the early 1990s, first in academic circles, such as Stanford University and the California Institute of Technology, and later in the IT industry. Many large vendors are active in this space (some after recent acquisitions), including SAP, Microsoft, Software AG, IBM, Tibco, JBoss, and EsperTech. These vendors offer various software products that provide "operational intelligence" through real-time computing that involves pattern matching with their respective intelligent or complex processors of event streams.

Event processors consume events from heterogeneous sources—such as JMS queues, JMX MBeans, incoming HTTP requests and WebSockets and native API calls, Message Driven Beans, data grids, Hadoop/NoSQL, and relational databases. The outcome of processing consists primarily of another, high-level generation of events that are sent through usually more homogenous channels in canonical data formats. Note that the event processors are decoupled from both the producers of the events they process and the consumers of the events they produce.

The processors perform the following operations on incoming events resulting in the events they publish:

- *Filter* Finding the needles in the haystack, those rare events that indicate exceptions.

- *Enrich* Adding context and thereby (business) meaning to events.

- *Aggregate* Counting events or determining a sum, an upper or lower limit, or an average over a metric that the events carry in their payload.

NOTE
An aggregate is frequently calculated over a window that consists of all events in the specific timeframe or a specified number of the latest events.

- *Pattern detection* Spotting a trend by comparing correlated events over a period of time, finding a special sequence of values or value changes that is known to herald a certain incident, and discovering the absence of an event that should have occurred are all examples of the detection of meaningful patterns among a string of correlated events.

- *Promote or propagate* The result of the preceding operations can be to propagate the event, either as is or in an enriched or promoted state, or to publish entirely new events that carry an aggregated value, some indicator, or an alert.

TO BE CLEAR
The word complex in Complex Event Processing does not refer to the events—they are usually extremely simple—but rather to the processing that takes place. Especially the detection of patterns can be very advanced, considering the complexity of the patterns and the addition of the challenges of continuously processing very large volumes of events in real time.

The Event Processing Language

Event processors need to be programmed. They are like query engines that need to query streams of events—not static sets of records, but incessantly changing collections of data granules. Event queries are not executed just once. They are instead attached to an event stream and continuously executed. Every new arriving event may cause the event query to produce a new result. Results are constantly being published in the form of events.

Over time, special languages have evolved for programming the event processors under the generic label of Event Processing Language (EPL). However, no single standard unified EPL has emerged in the industry. Several quite dissimilar EPLs are used for various CEP products. Some EPLs are derived from or inspired by Business Rule Languages. Other EPLs are inspired by, derived from, or even integrated with SQL. The widespread knowledge of SQL can be leveraged when programming event processing queries. It also turns out to be quite handy to be able to combine event streams and relational data sources in a single query (e.g., to join historical and reference data with the live event feed). This union of SQL and EPL, resulted in CQL, the Continuous Query Language, which has its roots at Stanford University. CQL is the core technology used in OEP applications for processing and producing events.

TIP
The Match_Recognize operator introduced in Oracle Database 12c to perform pattern matching on relational data sets also makes use of the CQL syntax to construct the pattern query.

CQL queries select from an event channel, often with some range or time window applied, using a where clause to filter on the events that are returned by the query. The select clause refers to event properties and uses functions and operators to derive results. Note that multiple channels and other data sources can be joined—yes: even outer joined—together in a single CQL query.

Here is a simple example of a CQL query that produces an output event whenever the number of input events in the *someEventStream* with a payload value larger than 15, changes, considering a time window that ranges over the last 5 seconds:

```
select count(payloadValue) as countEvents
from    someEventStream [range 5]
where   payloadValue > 15
```

The number of results produced by this query cannot be predicted: it depends on the frequency and irregularity with which events appear in the event stream. When, for example, exactly one event per second is published to the stream, the number of events in a 5-second window will not change and after the first 5 seconds of running the query, no additional events would be produced by the query.

Downstream Event Consumers

The Event Processor brings us only part of the path from data to insight and action. It only speaks in events on channels such as JMS—not directly with people or even web services—and it has no user interface of its own—except the browser-based Visualizer that is used as administration and monitoring console. The events published by OEP—no matter how advanced and enriched they may have become—need to be consumed and turned into something else: a report or dashboard, an alert or an action.

OEP applications typically publish their findings in the form of fairly generic messages on a JMS queue, messages to the EDN or HTTP channel, as data packets on a data grid or as record into a NoSQL database, or as requests to a web service interface or to some other standard facility. Many different products can therefore be used downstream of OEP to absorb the events and do something with them: load in a data warehouse, use to refresh a real-time dashboard, update a database record, notify a web service, send an email or text message, create a human task, or publish on a website or RSS feed. Note that it is not uncommon to have multiple chained OEP instances, each one processing a decreasing volume of higher business level events.

In this chapter, we will use the most common channels: JMS and the SOA Suite Event Delivery Network (EDN) for publishing the OEP outcomes.

Oracle Event Processor and SOA Suite

The Oracle Event Processor is part of the SOA Suite license. However, it is not part of the SOA Suite SCA container—it does not even run in the same WebLogic Server as the SOA Suite does. It runs on its own streamlined, lightweight server—which is POJO based, founded on Spring DM and an OSGi-based framework to manage services. This server comes with Jetty, an HTTP container for running servlets, and support for JMS and JDBC. It has caching and clustering facilities—possibly backed by an Oracle Coherence grid. OEP can handle thousands of concurrent queries and process hundreds of thousands of events per second. The average message latency can be under 1 ms.

Messages are typically read from JMS—for example, a queue in the SOA Suite WebLogic Server – or the EDN (backed by JMS). However, tables can be used as an event source as well, and through custom adapters, we can consume messages from virtually any source, including files, sockets, NoSQL database, and JMX.

The OEP server provides an HTTP Pub/Sub event channel based on the Bayeux protocol; this allows the OEP application to consume messages pushed from a Bayeux-compliant server as well as allows clients to subscribe to messages published by the OEP server. Clients can also publish to an HTTP channel without having to be explicitly connected to the HTTP Pub/Sub server.

Event messages are typically processed by CQL processors—nodes in the event processing network (EPN) that receive messages from stream sources and act on them to produce new event messages. The outcome of a CQL query is typically a stream of events.

OEP provides additional facilities, such as the ability to record events flowing through an event processing network and store them. They can later be played back from the event repository—very useful for testing.

The OEP Visualizer is a web application that is the administration console that enables you to view, develop, configure, and monitor aspects of Oracle Event Processing applications. OEP applications can be deployed, paused and resumed, and uninstalled from the Visualizer. Current operations can be monitored, including all console output. It also has support for visual and run-time CQL Query editing. Events published on an HTTP Pub/Sub channel can be monitored in the Visualizer, asynchronously pushed by the server to the browser.

Car Park Management Using Event Processor

Saibot Airport makes a lot of money from the car parks around the airport. Close monitoring and careful management of the parking process is important for that reason and because it is an important aspect in the evaluation by travelers in airport surveys. Indicating, at the right time, that a car park is full, for example, prevents people from needlessly driving in circles to find a free spot. However, too early warnings mean that people are unnecessarily forced to park their cars on the more remote car parks—not necessarily improving their experience.

In this section, we will see how an OEP application is created to process all events signaling a car entering or leaving a car park and thus deriving the number of cars currently inside the car park. The application will publish a special event when the car park is declared full. And it will publish a similar event when spaces become available again.

Preparation of the Development Environment

OEP 12*c* applications are developed in JDeveloper. These applications are deployed to and run on an instance of the OEP server. This server is not part of the integrated WebLogic Server and is separate from the SOA Suite 12*c* run-time environment based on WebLogic. The OEP run time is an OSGi server that needs to be installed separately.

Install OEP 12*c* according to online instructions on the book's website and create the *SaibotOEP* domain as described. Create a connection to your local OEP server in JDeveloper. Using this connection, from the context menu you can start and stop the server, watch its logging output and deploy, suspend, activate, and undeploy OEP applications.

When the OEP server is running, you can open the log window inside JDeveloper—using the right mouse button menu option Open OEP Server Log Page. Alternatively, you can use the OEP Visualizer tool that runs in the browser at: host:port/wlevs/. This tool includes the console output window—under Domain | defaultServer | Services | Console Output, as shown in Figure 16-2.

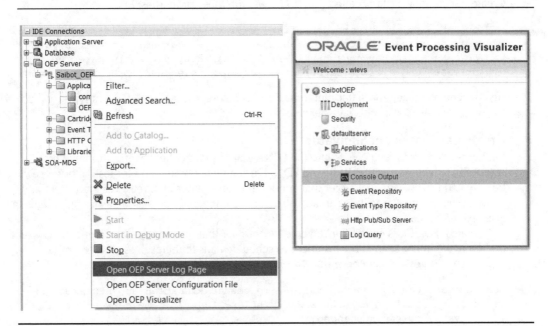

FIGURE 16-2. *Showing the OEP connection in JDeveloper (and the available actions) on the left and the Event Processing Visualizer browser application on the right*

The Saibot Parking OEP Application

In JDeveloper, create a new application based on the template OEP Application. Call the application *SaibotParking*. Create an OEP project *CarParking_step1* inside the application—based on the Empty OEP project template. The application is created with an empty Spring context file called CarParking_step1.context.xml—which will contain definitions of beans, events, channels, and processors and a file called processor.xml that is used to store the CQL queries. The EPN diagram visualizes the Event Processing Network that is defined in the context file. The MANIFEST.MF file finally contains OSGi definitions—for the application itself and all its bundle dependencies.

Define Event CarMovementEvent

Events in OEP can be defined entirely declaratively or based on a Java bean (a POJO). We will adopt the latter approach. Create a Java Class *CarMovementEvent* which is a POJO with these properties:

```
private String carparkIdentifier;
private Integer entryOrExit; // 1 for arrival, -1 for exit
private String licencePlate;
private Long arrivalTime;
```

Generate getter and setter methods for these properties.

Open the EPN diagram. Click on the tab Event Types. Add a new event type to the CarParking_step1.context.xml. The new event is called *CarMovementEvent* and is based on the Java bean with that name.

Create a second Java Class, called *CarParkEvent* with these properties:

```
private String carparkIdentifier;
private Integer carCount; // number of cars currently in the carpark
private Float percentageFull; // % of capacity currently taken up
private Long averageStayDuration; // in nanoseconds, OEPs unit of time
```

Again, generate getter and setter methods. And, as before, create an OEP event type—called *CarParkEvent*—based on this Java bean.

Create Car Movement Simulator

OEP uses adapters to feed events into the EPN. Adapters can collect events from external sources—such as JMS, HTTP, RMI, and EDN. During development and for testing purposes, it can be very handy to create an adapter that generates events rather than retrieves them from an external source. Any Java Class can act as such an event generator, as long as it implements the *StreamSource* interface.

Create a Java Class called *CarMovementController* that implements this interface, as well as the *Runnable* interface to allow instances to schedule calls to themselves. A very simple implementation of a generator of *CarMovementEvents* looks like this:

```
public class CarMovementController implements RunnableBean, StreamSource {
    private static final int SLEEP_MILLIS = 100; // time between events
    private boolean suspended;
    private StreamSender eventSender;
    private static Random rand = new Random();
```

```java
    public static int randInt(int min, int max) {
        int randomNum = rand.nextInt((max - min) + 1) + min;
        return randomNum;
    }
    private String randChar() {
        return new Character((char) randInt(65, 90)).toString();
    }

    public void run() {
      suspended = false;
      while (!isSuspended()) { // Generate messages forever...
        generateCarMovementEvent();
        try { synchronized (this) {
              wait(SLEEP_MILLIS * randInt(1, 5) / 2);
            }
        } catch (InterruptedException e) {
            e.printStackTrace();
        }
      }
    }
    private void generateCarMovementEvent() {
      CarMovementEvent event = new CarMovementEvent();
      event.setEntryOrExit(1);
      event.setCarparkIdentifier("1");
      event.setLicencePlate(randChar() + randChar() + "-" + randInt(1, 999) +
"-" + randChar() + randChar());
      eventSender.sendInsertEvent(event);
    }
    public void setEventSender(StreamSender sender) {
        eventSender = sender;
    }
    public synchronized void suspend() {
        suspended = true;


    }
    private synchronized boolean isSuspended() {
        return suspended;
    }
}
```

This class generates at a somewhat random rate car arrival events with randomly generated license plates. Later, more advanced incarnations of this class will derive car exit events as well and will generate events covering five different car parks.

NOTE
It pays off to spend considerable effort on creating the event generator.
It is a key element in the development and testing of the OEP
application and ideally it should cover all use cases you want to be
able to process.

Create the Event Reporting Bean

The output from the OEP application can be reported through outbound adapters to external receivers, such as a JMS destination, an RMI client, a Socket endpoint, or the Event Delivery Network. During development and for testing purposes, it is frequently convenient to work with an internal event receiver. A simple Java Class that implements the *StreamSink* can be used to receive the outcomes from the event processor and, for example, write them to the console. Create Java Class *CarParkReporter* that implements that interface and that write simple logging lines based on the events it receives:

```java
public class CarParkReporter implements StreamSink {

    public void onInsertEvent(Object event) {
        if (event instanceof CarParkEvent) {
            CarParkEvent cpe = (CarParkEvent)event;
            System.out.println("Current number of cars parked in Car Park "
                    +cpe.getCarparkIdentifier()+" : "+cpe.getCarCount()
                    +" percentage full "+(cpe.getPercentageFull())+"%"
                    +" The average stay of cars is "
                    +(0.1*Math.round(1E-08*cpe.getAverageStayDuration()))
                    +" seconds."
            );
        }
        if (event instanceof CarMovementEvent) {
            CarMovementEvent cpe = (CarMovementEvent)event;
            System.out.println("Car with licence plate "+cpe.getLicencePlate()
                    +" just "+ ( cpe.getEntryOrExit()==1?"arrived at":"left from")
                    +" car park "+cpe.getCarparkIdentifier()
            );
        }
    }
}
```

Create the Event Processing Network

Open the EPN diagram. Drag an Adapter component to the diagram. Call the adapter *carMovementEventGenerator* and select the *CarMovementController* as the Java Class to implement the adapter.

Drag a Channel component to the diagram. Set the name of the channel to *carMovementInputChannel* and select the *CarMovementEvent* as the event type to flow through this channel. Connect the Adapter to the left hand side of the channel—to specify that the output from the adapter is the input for the channel.

Add a Processor component to the diagram. Set its name to *carMovementProcessor* and accept the default processor.xml file for the Configuration Location. Connect the *carMovementInputChannel* to the input (left-hand side) of the processor.

Add a second Channel component, called *carParEventChannel*. Set its event type to *CarParkEvent*. Connect the output from the *carMovementProcessor* to the input side of this channel.

Add a Bean component to the diagram. Call it *carParReporter* and select Java class *CarParkReporter* as its implementation class.

Connect the output from the *carParEventChannel* to this bean. Also connect the output from the *carMovementInputChannel* to the *carParkReporter*.

The diagram should now look like Figure 16-3. This is the visualization of the configuration defined in CarParking_step1.context.xml.

The element still lacking from the application is the actual CQL query that processes and in this cases aggregates the *carMovement* events. Open file processor.xml. It contains the *carMovementProcessor* element with a query with id *ExampleQuery*. Replace the query element with this snippet:

```
<query id="CarparkSummary"><![CDATA[
   IStream(select    sum(car.entryOrExit) as carCount, car.carparkIdentifier
           from      carMovementInputChannel as car
           group by carparkIdentifier) ]]>
</query>
```

Deploy and Test

The application can be deployed. Upon deployment, the *CarMovementController* will immediately start producing events and the processor will also immediately kick into action.

Right click on the project in the application navigator. From the context menu, select Deploy | oep_profile–1. The deployment wizard appears. Accept the default deployment action—*Deploy OSGi bundle to target platform*. Press Next. On the second page, check whether the *Saibot_OEP* server is the target server. If it is and the server is running, press Finish to perform deployment.

Check the log window—either in JDeveloper or in the Visualizer console. You will notice a steady flow of messages—one announcing a car that arrives and a second one that gives an update on the current number of cars in car park number one. CQL will publish a result in this case whenever the previous result is superseded by a new one—that is, with every new car that enters the parking lot.

Such an update of the car count is not really required for every car that enters. We may want to settle for a summary update every 5 seconds. This is easily accomplished by rewriting the from clause as:

```
from      carMovementInputChannel [range 1 DAY slide 5 second] as car
```

Here we have specified that the results from the query are to be calculated over 1 day worth of (input) events and should be produced once every 5 seconds. Make this change and redeploy the application. The summary messages will be less abundant than before.

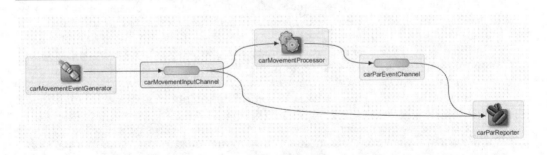

FIGURE 16-3. *The EPN diagram for processing carMovementEvents and sending all output to the carParkReporter bean*

More Event Intelligence

OEP can do much more than just count and aggregate. In this section, we will look at how we can correlate events, detect "missing" events and derive business intelligence from them. Chaining OEP processors—within or across applications—is commonly done to derive varying conclusions from a certain base set of data signals at different levels of granularity; this can be done across applications or within. We will use several processors inside our application.

In this section, we determine for cars that leave how long have they stayed in the car park; we could use that to automatically calculate the parking fees. We next extend our summary with the average stay duration of cars. We look for cars that have out-stayed their welcome: our car parks are short stay only, intended for parking up to 36 hours. Cars that have been in the car park for more than 48 hours become candidate for towing.

Instead of going through every detailed little step and filling this chapter with a lot of long code fragments, the reader is kindly requested to download the book's resources—and in particular the projects CarParking_step2 and _step3 under the Chapter 16 source folder. These projects contain all sources, the salient points of which are discussed below.

An important role is played by the *CarMovementController*—the event generator. This class has been extended to:

- Generate events for cars that leave a car park (when the initial event for the car arrival is generated, the randomly derive time for departure is recorded for the car in a *TreeSet* sorted on departure time; whenever a car arrives at the car park, the *TreeSet* is inspected to see whether the top of the list should depart in which case car exit events are generated).

- Generate events for a set of (currently five) different car parks—each with a specific capacity; the generator respects the capacity, ensuring that not more cars are admitted to the car park than the capacity allows.

It is common to want to enrich events at some point during the processing. For example, because events have to be placed in context, such as which car park did the car arrive at, what is that car park's capacity or its location, and what name should be passed in the business event published to JMS or EDN.

Having to call out to, for example, a relational database each time an event has to be enriched can be quite expensive and is quite unnecessary for (fairly) static data. OEP supports the use of caches to store such data and allows joining to caches in CQL queries. OEP has its own internal (local) cache implementation system. Alternatively it supports use of Coherence (local and distributed) as well as third party caching solutions.

In the current example of the car parks, a cache is defined in the context file, using the internal caching mechanism. A Java class—*CarParkCacheLoader*—is created to provide the static data for the cache. A bean based on this class is configured as the cache-loader for the cache. The CQL query in the *carParkEvent* processor uses the cache to enrich the *CarParkEvent* with the name of the car park. In the next section, the car park's capacity is also retrieved from the cache and used to determine to what extent the car park is filled with cars.

In order to make use of caches, the MANIFEST.MF file has to be edited. The bundle com.bea.cache.jcache has to be added to the list of dependencies.

Car Stay Duration—Derived per Car and Promoted per Car Park

One thing OEP excels at is correlating events. It can find patterns across events that arrive at various points in time. In this example, we will have OEP associate the arrival and exit events for the same car. These events together constitute the "car stay" for which we could calculate the parking fee. By taking all these car stay events into consideration, we can have OEP calculate the average stay duration—per car park. Figure 16-4 shows the EPN for this approach.

CQL to Compose CarStayDone Events

The key CQL operator we leverage to correlate events into meaningful patterns is called MATCH_RECOGNIZE. The query used in the carStayDoneProcessor uses the following clause:

```
... from   carInputChannel
match_recognize (
  partition by carparkIdentifier, licencePlate
  measures A.licencePlate as licencePlate
  ,        A.carparkIdentifier as carparkIdentifier
  ,        A.arrivalTime as arrivalTime
  ,        B.element_time - A.element_time as stayduration
  pattern (A B)
  define
    A as entryOrExit= 1
  , B AS entryOrExit = -1
) as stayed
```

The crucial element in a MATCH_RECOGNIZE expression is the pattern that should be detected in the event stream. In this case, the pattern consists of events A and B that both apply to the same car park and car (through the license plate) as defined by the partition by clause. Additionally, for this one car, A is the arrival event (*entryOrExit* equals 1) and B the subsequent exit event. Whenever these two events have been found—with no other events in between with different values for the *entryOrExit* attribute—the query will produce an event of type *CarStayDone*. The *stayduration* measure is calculated using the pseudo column *element_time*. Every event is time stamped by OEP in such a way that the difference between the *element_time* value for two events is equal to the time lapse (in nanoseconds) between the two events.

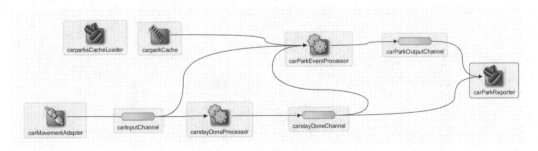

FIGURE 16-4. *The Event Processing Diagram for the CarPark events—deriving Car Stay Complete events and Average Car Stay Duration insight with cache-based enrichment*

CQL to Calculate the Average Car Stay Duration

Using the *CarStayDone* events published to the *carstayDoneChannel*, it becomes quite simple to derive the *CarParkEvents* that report the average stay duration for each car park—with an update published whenever a car leaves a car park. The CQL snippet below takes care of this. Note that the average duration in this case is calculated over the last 100 cars that have left the car park.

```
<query id="CarparkAvgStayQuery"><![CDATA[
    IStream(select -1 as carCount
            ,          carparkIdentifier as carparkIdentifier
            ,          '' as description
            ,          avg(carstayDuration as averageStayDuration
            from carstayDoneChannel [rows 100]
            group by carparkIdentifier
        )
]]></query>
```

When you inspect the contents of the processor.xml file, you will notice that for *carParkEventProcessor*, there are two query elements in the <rules> element. You can define multiple queries in a processor—and each of them is continuously executed. They all need to provide the same event type, obviously, to feed into the output channel. Note how the view *CarparkStatusView* contains the join between the *CarparkStatus* view and the *carparkCache*—which is used to enrich the *CarParkEvent* with the name of the car park that is retrieved from the cache.

Find Towing Candidates

As discussed before, frequently the absence of an expected event is what we should detect and what should result in a new business event to be published. In our case of airport parking, the missing event is the car that does not leave our short stay car park in time.

The event generator has been extended to also come up with cars that will not depart any time soon. Our OEP application should be able to detect such cars—that do not leave within 120 seconds (on the time scale of our sample application). See the sources in project CarParking_step3 for this step.

A new event was defined—*AbandonedCarEvent*—based on a POJO with that name. Java class *AbandonedCarsMonitor* implementing the *StreamSink* interface was created to receive these events and write a log message for them. The *abandonedCarsProcessor* was added to process the events from the *carInputChannel*, detect the abandoned cars and report on them to the *abandonedCarsOutputChannel*, as shown in Figure 16-5.

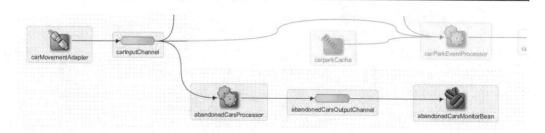

FIGURE 16-5. *The EPN flow for detecting and reporting on abandoned cars—using the missing event detection pattern*

The next CQL snippet is at the heart of the processor.

```
from    carInputChannel
match_recognize (
  partition by carparkIdentifier, licencePlate
  measures A.licencePlate as licencePlate
  ,        A.carparkIdentifier as carparkIdentifier
  ,        A.arrivalTime as arrivalTime
  INCLUDE TIMER EVENTS
  pattern (A NotExit*)
  duration 120 seconds
  define
  A as entryOrExit= 1
  , NotExit AS entryOrExit!= -1
) as abandoned
```

Again, we inspect the *CarMovementEvents* on the *carInputChannel*. We are looking for the pattern A—entry of a certain car, followed by the *NotExit* event—which has been defined as an event for which the *entryOrExit* value is not equal to –1. A car that has entered the car park can do nothing than at some point leave that car park again generating an event with entryOrExit = –1 at that point. And if it does, it is not abandoned.

OEP allows us to mix in system-generated timer events with the regular event stream—using the INCLUDE TIMER EVENTS instruction, combined with the clause DURATION 120 SCONDS. These tell OEP that in every partition of the event stream—for every license plate and car park combination for which we have seen a first *CarMovementEvent*—a system event should be added every 2 minutes if and when there has not been a real event in that two minute timeframe. Subsequently, when such a timer event *is* added for a certain car—because for 120 seconds there has not been a real event, which should have been the "car exit" event—the pattern will match for that car because the system-generated timer event does not have *entryOrExit* equals –1. In fact, timer events do not have attribute values at all.

Publish Car Park Nearly Full events to JMS Destination

As part of car park management, it is important that Saibot staff has good insight into the fullness of each car park. When a car park crosses the 90 percent full marker—and it is not just a fluke peak but it has already been over 85 percent for some time—the car park is declared full. Another car park may be opened and the road signage is updated accordingly.

We will first extend the OEP application to calculate the state of all car parks—using the current car count that we already calculated and the capacity of the car park retrieved from the cache. The percentage filled is added to the summary that already reports the car count. Next, a message is published to a JMS destination to alert any listener about the car park situation.

See the sources in project *CarParking_step4* for this step.

Calculate the Percentage Full for Each Car Park

The *CarParkEvent* processor's CQL statement that joins with the *carparkCache* is extended to calculate the percentage full for the car park. This number is added to the *CarParkEvent* and reported in the *CarParkReporter* bean. The essential CQL snippet is shown here:

```
<view id="CarparkStatusView"><![CDATA[
   RStream(  select carCount, car.carparkIdentifier as carparkIdentifier
          ,         R.name as description
          ,         to_char(100*carCount/R.capacity) as percentageFull
          from    CarparkStatus[now]   as car
          ,         carparkCache as R
          where car.carparkIdentifier = R.identifier
        )
]]></view>
```

Publish the CarParkNearlyFull Event

A new event is defined: *CarParkNearFullEvent* based on a Java class with that name. It is reported on by the extended *CarParkReporter*. A new processor is added (shown in Figure 16-6): the *carParkNearlyFullProcessor* that reads from the *carparkCache* and the *carInputChannel* with *CarMovementEvents* and publishes to the new *carParkNearlyFullChannel*.

This processor has to check the car park's car count (the first view) and compare it to the capacity of the car park that it can pull from the cache (the second view). The third view produces the lowest car count in the last 30 seconds (comparable to perhaps 5 minutes in real life). Finally in the view itself, we produce a car park nearly full event when the current car park fullness percentage is >= 90 and the lowest percentage over the last 30 seconds is 85 or higher—so we do not start publishing a panicky event the first time we cross the 90 percent boundary for only a very brief moment. Note how multiple views can be defined in a processor, referring to each other, similar to inline views in an SQL statement.

```
<processor>
  <name>carParkNearlyFullProcessor</name>
  <rules>
    <view id="CarparkStatus"><![CDATA[
       IStream(select   sum(car.entryOrExit) as carCount
              ,           car.carparkIdentifier
```

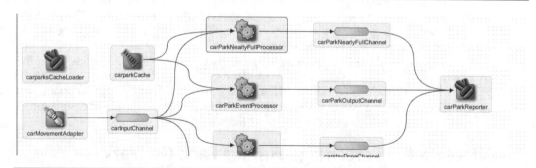

FIGURE 16-6. *The EPN diagram with the flows for spotting nearly full car parks*

```
                      from      carInputChannel as car
                      group by carparkIdentifier) ]]>
   </view>
   <view id="CarparkNearlyFullView"><![CDATA[
      RStream(  select  car.carCount
                   ,         car.carparkIdentifier
                   ,         to_char(100*car.carCount/R.capacity)
                             as percentageFull
                   ,         R.capacity as carParkCapacity
                   from      CarparkStatus [now]  as car
                   ,         carparkCache as R
                   where     car.carparkIdentifier = R.identifier
         )
   ]]></view>
   <view id="CarparkStatusView"><![CDATA[
      RStream(  select  min(carCount) as recentLowCarCount
                   ,         carparkIdentifier
                   from      CarparkStatus [range 30 second]  as car
                   group by carparkIdentifier
            )
   ]]></view>
   <query id="CarparkNearlyFullQuery"><![CDATA[
      IStream(  select  carCount
                   ,         c1.carparkIdentifier as carparkIdentifier
                   ,         percentageFull
                   from      CarparkNearlyFullView[now] as c1
                   ,         CarparkStatusView[now] as c2
                   where     c1.carparkIdentifier = c2.carparkIdentifier
                   and       percentageFull >= 90
                   and       (100*c2.recentLowCarCount/c1.carParkCapacity) >= 85
         )
   ]]></query>
```

Publish from OEP to JMS

The *CarParkNearFull* event has to be pushed outside the OEP application, so the world—or at least carpark management staff at Saibot Airport—learns about it. OEP can publish events to various outbound channels. In this case, we will use JMS. We have to configure the JMS Destination, add an outbound JMS adapter in the OEP application and extend its manifest file, and create a bean that converts the OEP event to the JMS message.

Configure JMS Destination on WebLogic

Add a JMS Queue (or Topic) to your desire, for example, in the *SaibotJMSModule* (see Chapter 6) in the WebLogic Server that runs SOA Suite, and, for example, called jms/facilities/CarParkNearlyFullQueue.

Add an Outbound JMS Adapter

Open the EPN diagram and drag an outbound JMS adapter on to it. The JMS Adapter wizard appears—though not the same one as used in SOA composites and Service Bus services. In OEP

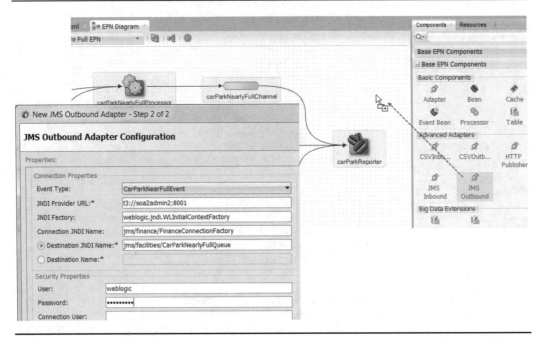

FIGURE 16-7. *Configuring the outbound JMS adapter—connected to the CarParkNearlyFullQueue*

we do not use the same JCA adapters. Set the name to carpark-nearly-full-jms-outbound-adapter. Press Next. Configure the adapter as shown in Figure 16-7.

Connect the *carParkNearFullChannel* to the freshly added JMS adapter.

Add Dependencies to Project and OSGi Manifest

The OEP project properties have to be edited. Add a dependency on the Java EE library (to cover the standard JMS API dependencies). A dependency has to be added on the JAR com.bea.wlevs. adapters.jms_12.1.3.0_0.jar. This file is located in the oep\modules directory under the OEP Home directory.

Similarly, in order to successfully deploy the OEP application, its MANIFEST.MF file needs to be extended with two new bundle dependencies introduced because of use of JMS.

Add these two lines:

```
com.bea.wlevs.adapters.jms.api;version="12.1.3",
javax.jms,
```

Create Message Converter

The JMS adapter can process the events produced by the EPN in an OEP application into JMS MapMessages with entries named after the event properties. For this to happen, an instance-property with name *eventType* and value *CarParkNearFullEvent* has to be configured on the JMS adapter in the Spring context file.

This automatic conversion does not work for complex event properties—such as List—and may not always produce the desired result. It is easy and common to create and configure a message converter on a JMS adapter that will process the event into the desired *MapMessage*.

In this case, create Java class *CarParkNearlyFullEventConverter* that implements interface *OutboundMessageConverter*. Provide code in the *convert* method—that takes a JMS session and your own OEP Event object as input and returns a List<Message>. A simple code snippet is shown here:

```
    public List<Message> convert(Session session, Object inputEvent) throws
MessageConverterException, JMSException {
        CarParkNearFullEvent event = (CarParkNearFullEvent) inputEvent;
        MapMessage message = session.createMapMessage();
        message.setString("carparkIdentifier", event.getCarparkIdentifier());
        message.setFloat("percentageFull", event.getPercentageFull());
        List<Message> messages = new ArrayList<Message>();
        messages.add(message);
        return messages;
}
```

Then define a bean in the Spring context file and configure the bean as the converter for the JMS adapter, using the following configuration:

```
<bean id="carParkNearlyFullEventConverter"
class="saibot.airport.facilities.parking.jms.CarParkNearlyFullEventConverter"/>
<wlevs:adapter id="carpark-nearly-full-jms-outbound-adapter" provider="jms-
outbound">
  <wlevs:instance-property name="converterBean" ref="carParkNearlyFullEventCon
verter"/>
</wlevs:adapter>
```

Deploy and Run—and Listen

With the application completed, you can now deploy it to the OEP server. The output from the reporter bean will immediately be visible in the log window. From this moment on, messages can also be published to the JMS Queue—whenever a car park is seen to be almost full. You can check on the contents of the JMS Queue in several ways—in the WebLogic console, using the QBrowser, through an SOA composite or Service Bus service with inbound JMS adapter or transport, or through a custom JMS client. The latter is included in the online sources—in the project *CarParkNearlyFullQueueListener*. Note that you probably have to change the connection properties in the source.

Figure 16-8 shows a fragment of the logging output produced by the OEP application.

```
Sabot_OEP- Log     Build - Issues
++ Car with licence plate AX-558-AE leaves carpark 18 after a stay of 10 seconds.
Current number of cars parked in Car Park 18 : 93 - Traveller Parking Area II percentage full 37.0% The average stay of cars is 74.3 seconds
****** Here is a car that will be abandoned : RQ-885-FO
******* Carpark Traveller Parking Area I is close to filling up. Number of cars parked : 115 (Capacity = 120, current percentage full: 95.0%
++ Car with licence plate SF-178-TN leaves carpark 16 after a stay of 138 seconds.
Current number of cars parked in Car Park 16 : 114 - Traveller Parking Area I percentage full 95.0% The average stay of cars is 72.600000000
!!!!!!!Abandoned Car identified in in Car Park 16 : licence plate BD-767-QE - parked since Fri Sep 19 09:26:54 CEST 2014
```

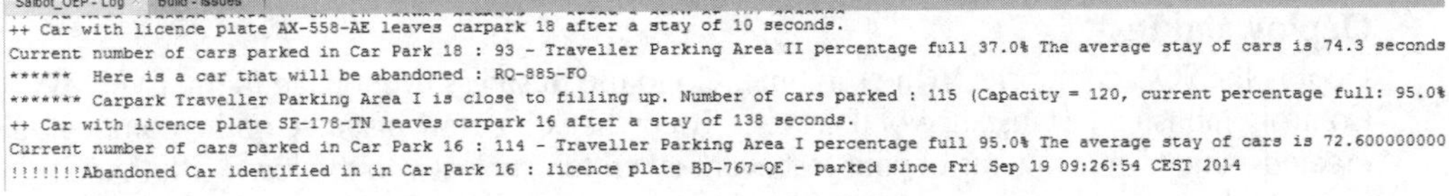

FIGURE 16-8. *Some of the logging produced by the OEP application for various car park– related events*

Publish Car Park Nearly Full Events to Event Delivery Network

The messages published to the JMS destination can of course be read by inbound JMS adapters in SOA composite applications and then turned into business events on the Event Delivery Network (EDN). However, OEP can publish events directly onto the EDN—as we will see next. Note that OEP also has an inbound EDN adapter that allows it to read and process the business events published on the Eevent Delivery Network.

The EDN event is defined—as introduced in Chapter 15—using an EDL file with an associated XSD definition of the payload. These files are imported into the OEP application and referenced from an outbound EDN adapter. A smatter of SQL/XML is added to the CQL query to produce the EDN event's payload in the right format. An SOA composite application subscribed to the EDN event will be triggered whenever OEP produces the *CarParkNearFullEvent*.

The sources for this next step are found in project *CarParking-step5*.

SOA Composite Application for Responding to a Nearly Full Car Park

Create a new SOA application called *SaibotParkingStaff* with a project with that same name based on the *empty* template. In his application, we will first define the EDN event and then create a Mediator that subscribes to the event and writes a line to a log file through a File Adapter.

Define EDN Event

Create an XSD file called FacilitiesEvents.xsd in the Schemas folder, with target namespace *saibot. airport/facilities*. Define an element *CarParkAlmostFullEvent* and associated type *carParkAlmostFullEventType* with children to hold the key attributes of the event. These describe the payload for the EDN event. Check in the online resources for an example.

Right click on the Events folder and select New | Event Definition from the menu. Enter *FacilitiesEvents* as the name for the EDL file and use the same namespace as in the XSD document. Create a new event called *CarParkAlmostFullEvent* based on the XSD element with that same name.

Mediator to Consume Event

Add a Mediator to the composite, called *CarParkAlmostFullHandler*. Select the template *Subscribe to Events*. Select the *CarParkAlmostFull* event as the one to subscribe to.

Create a File Adapter binding—*writeCarParkAlmostFullEntryInAlertLog*—that appends a line to a file called *CarParkAlertLog.txt*. Each line contains details taken from the EDN event, describing a car park that is nearly full. Connect the Mediator to the File Adapter binding. Create the XSL Map to transform from the EDN event to the input to the File Adapter binding and add it to the routing rule.

Deploy and Test

Deploy the SOA composite to the run time. Go to the Business Event page in the EM FMW Control. Publish a test instance of the event. Then check if a new instance of the composite is created—and if the contents of your test event is written correctly to the log file. If that is successful, you can proceed to the next section.

Extend OEP Application with EDN Integration

In order to connect the OEP application with the SOA Suite Event Delivery Network, we have to configure the EDN Outbound Adapter and add a processor to transform the OEP message into the XML format required for the EDN event.

Add and Configure EDN Outbound Adapter

Add an EDN Outbound Adapter to the EPN. Set the name to *CarparkAlmostFull-edn-outbound-adapter*. Click next. Configure the EDN adapter with the JNDI provider URL set to t3://host:port (e.g., localhost:7101 for the Integrated WLS). Browse for the FacilitiesEvents.edl file that you have created in the previous section in the SOA composite application *SaibotParkingStaff*. Select the *CarParkAlmostFullEvent* as the event to publish from OEP to EDN. Check the checkbox *Raw XML Content*. This tells the EDN adapter, that the event passed into it, already has the proper XML payload.

Click Finish to complete the creation of the EDN Outbound Adapter. You will receive a message to the effect that JDeveloper has imported the EDL file and the associated XSD document into the OEP application.

Create Processor to Prepare EDN Events with Proper Payload

Add a new processor to the EPN, called *carParkNearlyFullEventToEDNProcessor*. This processor will prepare the *CarParkAlmostFullEvent* for the EDN adapter, with the proper XML payload. Connect the *carParkNearlyFullChannel* to the input of this processor. Create a new channel *CarParkAlmostFullEventChannel* that reads from this processor and publishes to the outbound EDN adapter.

Now we need to prepare the CQL statement for the processor to create the EDN events' payload. Since we have configured the EDN adapter to process raw XML, we will have to provide the exact payload for the EDN event. The code snippet below shows how we can use SQL/XML instructions to compose the XML in the right namespace.

```
<query id="CarParkAlmostFullEventEDNEventQuery"><![CDATA[
        select XMLELEMENT(
            NAME "CarParkAlmostFullEvent",XMLATTRIBUTES('saibot.airport/
facilities' as "xmlns"),
            XMLELEMENT(NAME "CarParkIdentifier"
            , ''||carparkIdentifier),
            XMLELEMENT(NAME "CarParkName"
            , description),
            XMLELEMENT(NAME "PercentageFull" ,to_char(percentageFull)),
            XMLELEMENT(NAME "Capacity" ,to_char(capacity)),
            XMLELEMENT(NAME "CurrentCarCount" ,to_char(lowestRecentCount)),
            XMLELEMENT(NAME "LowestRecentCarCount" ,to_char(percentageFull))
        ) as xmlContent
        from carParkNearlyFullChannel [now] ]]></query>
```

This query will make our processor create OEP events with an XML content that is exactly according to the EDN event's payload schema. The EDN adapter will take these events and turn them into regular events on the EDN.

Deploy and Test/Run

Before our OEP server can successfully talk to the SOA Suite 12*c* Event Delivery Network, we have to properly set its expectations regarding the EDN set up. In the default case, EDN is based on WebLogic JMS and we have to add JVM startup parameters to let EDN know that.

Open the file startwlevs.sh (or .cmd depending on your OS). Almost at the end of the file is the call to run the wlevs.jar. In this line you need to add the following string, just prior to the "–jar":

```
-Dedn.jms.topic="jms/fabric/EDNTopic" -Dedn.jms.connection-factory="jms/
fabric/EDNConnectionFactory"
```

After making this change (re)start the OEP Server.

You can now deploy the OEP application. The log console should display a message indicating that OEP has created an *EdnJmsConnectionFactory* object—through which it will communicate with EDN.

Sit back and relax—watch for the event report in the log console. Then check the EM FMW Control for a new instance of the SOA composite, triggered by the EDN event—published by the OEP application, as is shown in Figure 16-9. That last part is not visible as such in the flow trace in EM FMW: the origin of the EDN event is unclear.

Credit Card Theft Detection

Another interesting use case for OEP is described in detail in the online resources—along with all code samples. It concerns the shopping area at Saibot Airport, where a series of credit card thefts have taken place. Upon investigation, it became clear that on each occasion, the perpetrator stole the credit card in the crowded main terminal area, made his way toward the exit and in between, within 15 minutes, made three or more purchases with the credit card in the

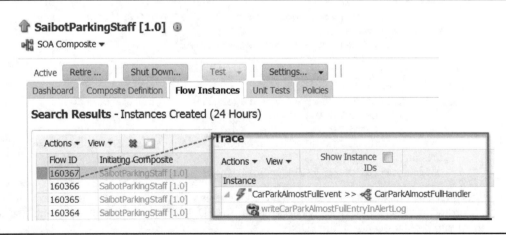

FIGURE 16-9. *Instances of the SaibotParkingStaff SOA composite triggered by the CarParkAlmostFull EDN event published by the OEP application CarParking*

range of $200 to $500. He sometimes back traced a little, entering a shop a little further from the main exit than the previous one.

OEP is set up to process a stream of credit card purchase events, which contain the amount, the credit card number and the shop identifier. With OEP, the pattern described above and shown in Figure 16-10 is to be detected. When it is found, it is to be reported in the form of an EDN event to be taken care of by an SOA composite. Online you will also find sources for an ADF web application that visualizes the suspicious transactions, much in the same way as Figure 16-10 does.

Some salient aspects of this *CreditCard* processing application:

- Use of the listAgg operator to aggregate multiple events into a Java Collection
- Use of custom Java Classes from within CQL queries
- Use of XMLParse to add XML content inside XML Element with child elements, based on a string [prepared in a custom Java class from a List of shop identifiers and purchase amounts] to produce richer, more complex EDN event payloads
- Use of keywords *within* and *subset* in the CQL query to respectively find a pattern only if it occurs within a certain period of time (15 minutes) and to allow aggregation over all or some of the events that constitute the pattern

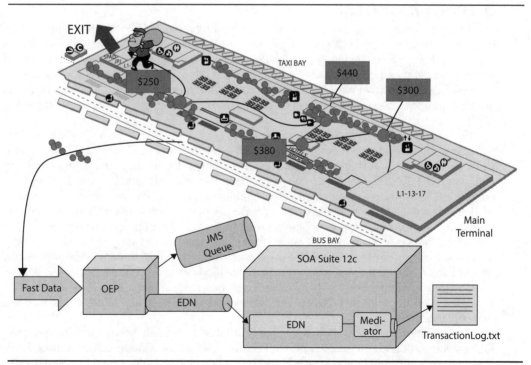

FIGURE 16-10. *The credit card transactions pattern OEP is set up to detect: a series of mid amount range purchases, in a short time window, roughly along the route from main terminal to the exit*

This next snippet shows some crucial aspects of the CQL query that finds fishy transactions:

```
select its.creditCardNumber as creditCardNumber,totalSum as sumAmounts
, delta as shoppingDuration, shops as shops, purchaseAmounts as
purchaseAmounts
  from creditCardMidRangePurchaseChannel
        MATCH_RECOGNIZE (
        PARTITION BY creditCardNumber
          MEASURES C.creditCardNumber as creditCardNumber
          , sum(allPurchases.amount) as totalSum
          , C.element_time - A.element_time as delta
          , listAgg(allPurchases.shopIdentifier) as shops
          , listAgg(allPurchases.amount) as purchaseAmounts
          PATTERN ( A+  B?  A+ C) within 30000 milliseconds
          SUBSET allPurchases = (A,B,C)
          DEFINE
          A as A.shopIdentifier >= A.shopIdentifier
           , B as B.shopIdentifier < A.shopIdentifier and A.shopIdentifier -
B.shopIdentifier < 7
            ,C as A.shopIdentifier - C.shopIdentifier < 7
        ) as its
```

Stream Explorer

Stream Explorer was released by Oracle as an extension on top of OEP 12c. Stream Explorer is a browser based user interface targeted at business users. Through the attractive user interface, see Figure 16-11, with focus on functional details, users can quickly create explorations on top of streams and define ways to visualize these. In doing so, they are creating OEP applications—that if necessary can be further refined by developers in JDeveloper. Stream Explorer can be accessed from the browser when the OEP Server is running, using the URL http://host:port/sx, for example http://127.0.0.1:9002/sx.

The business user defines Streams for the input. Such a Stream can be a (CSV) file, an HTTP Subscriber, EDN event, a JMS destination, a Database Table, or a REST service. These streams carry shape instances. A shape is a record (event) definition that consists of the properties and their types. The Streams can perhaps be preconfigured for the LoB user by the tech savvy IT colleague. The business user can then define Explorations on the Streams, which are based on predefined templates. The business user can make use of many predefined templates that are categorized by industry. These templates represent specific ways of processing events.

The business user has to provide values for template parameters such as the aggregation interval, the aggregation function or the event property to group by. Multiple explorations can be chained; this means that the outcome of one exploration can provide the input for a next.

Downstream destination to which the outcome of an exploration can be sent include a CSV file, an HTTP Publisher, EDN, a JMS destination, a REST service, or BAM—the Business Activity Monitor.

Stream Explorer is a web application that is installed in the Jetty Server that also runs the OEP engine and the OEP Visualizer Admin Console. OEP applications configured using Stream Explorer can be exported to be imported and refined |extended | augmented in JDeveloper by

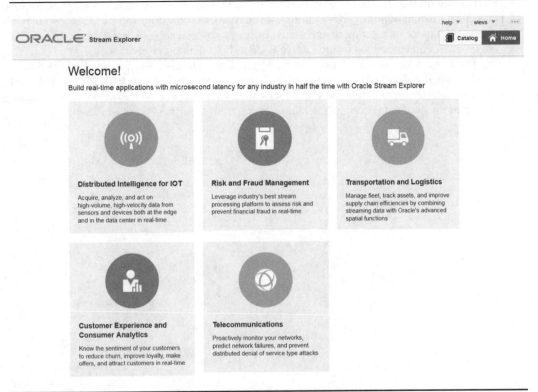

FIGURE 16-11.   *The user friendly home page of the Stream Explorer*

the IT specialists. The Stream Explorer applications contain an Event Processing Network and CQL-based event processors that were constructed using templates.

The near future of Stream Explorer holds interaction with NoSQL sources and destinations, BAM visualizations, support for machine learning algorithms, data redaction on sensitive data, Coherence cache integration, and location-based features.

Summary

Real-time findings—insight, alert, action, based on vast and possibly fast data from a variety of sources—published to various types of channels for onward processing is in a nutshell what Oracle Event Processor can do for us. By constantly scanning streams of events arriving at unpredictable moments, OEP is able to look out for abnormal conditions, meaningful patterns, relevant aggregates, and even important event absences.

Event processing applications use CQL—the Continuous Query Language, that is similar in syntax to SQL and can join event channels, caches, and relational data sources to produce coarser grained, higher value output events. OEP connects on both inbound and outbound edges with SOA Suite and Java applications through JMS, Coherence, and the Event Delivery Network.

By focusing on the core competencies of OEP—light weight, multichannel interaction, cross instances|sessions|transactions|conversations—it is easy to see how, for example, OEP can play an important role for monitoring of and across business processes. Note that the core of the OEP engine has been embedded inside Oracle BAM to help with precisely that.

The support for integration from OEP with the Event Delivery Network in the SOA Suite provides great potential to implement EDA (Event-Driven Architecture) with SOA Suite or at least make the service architecture more event-enabled. Finally, the Stream Explorer product lowers the threshold for starting to leverage event processing from a business point of view.

PART
V

Process Orchestration

CHAPTER
17

The Human Task Service

W hen services are long running—for example, because human involvement is required—we at some point move from composite service orchestration to the realm of process execution. What we still may be lacking in our composite applications—to have them really face the business challenges we know will be thrown at us—is something we could call the "ghost in the machine." After all is said and done by the service components discussed so far—and that is quite a lot, let's make no mistake about that—there is still a category of activities that we do not have the solution for yet. Some things simply cannot be done by fully automated components such Mediators, BPEL processes, adapters, or even Business Rule components. We need something more when it comes to one of the following areas:

- Business logic that involves strategic insight, negotiation skills, creativity, intuition, an understanding of abstract paintings, or capacity to improvise—for example, the final selection from the candidates for a job opening, the slogan for the marketing campaign, or the final bid on an auctioned item

- Recovering from unexpected fault situations

- Processing (and deciding upon) unstructured information such as pictures, PDF attachments, or cryptic content or weighing subtleties lost on (non-AI) computer systems

- Gathering additional information via human channels and from unstructured sources and providing data to the system

- Informing other humans—verbally, in specific terminology or in terminology other than one of the supported languages; in person or via telephone, chat, or sign language; with proper regard for cultural habits and personal sensitivities

- Performing manual operations—wrapping a package, physical verification (signature), measurement

- Conferring with one or more humans to reach consensus and broad support for a decision

- Decisions and choices that we consider too important or far reaching to (already) trust to an automated facility

For these specific areas and situations, we need humans participating in the processing of composite application instances. And just like all other service engines, for the sake of the SCA engine, humans in a composite should come with a WSDL interface and communication specified in XSD too. And that is what the SOA Suite's Human Task Service provides: the interface between the services world of the composite application and the people performing activities in the context of the application (Figure 17-1).

Human tasks typically implement stand-alone tasks around a set of data—potentially with complex escalation, voting, and routing logic. These tasks typically implement activities in a workflow or business process, which may contain other tasks as well as service calls. Chapter 18 discusses how both BPEL and BPM are used to define and implement those workflows. In this chapter, we will focus on defining individual human tasks.

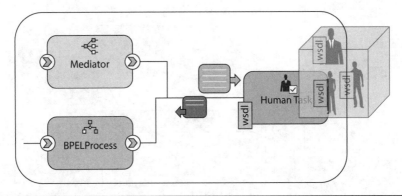

FIGURE 17-1. *The Human Task Service (Engine) integrates people into composite applications*

Introducing the Human Task Service

The Human Task Service acts as the proxy for all human actors. It accepts service request messages, just like other service engines do. Service calls to the Task Service are based on a generic WSDL that defines a number of standard operations to be performed on a task, such as initiate, update, and cancel a task. When the task is completed, the task outcome is forwarded to the initial Task Service invoker—frequently a BPEL (or BPMN, see Chapter 19) process—through a callback from the Task Service. Intermediate developments around the task—such as assignment, escalation, and delegation—can also be reported through callbacks and using events.

The interaction with the Human Task Service is inherently asynchronous because humans react distinctly asynchronously. The overall result of executing the task is only reported back to the task invoker at some later moment—and given the involvement of people and potentially complex task-routing flows, this callback may be hours, days, or even longer after the task initiation.

Architecture of the Human Task Service

When a BPEL or (much less common) a Mediator component requires a task to be performed by a human agent, it calls the generic Task Service and specifies which preconfigured task should be performed. All the various human tasks that the Task Service can make people execute are defined in task definition files. The definition of a task describes many details, including the possible outcomes of the task, the users or roles involved in handling the task, the deadline associated with the task, the data passed into the task, and the parameters that can be updated and returned as part of the task result. More advanced settings in the task definition determine the notification, allocation, collaboration, delegation, and escalation of tasks. The Task Service is the central coordinator that takes responsibility for the execution of the specific task instance. The task instance is created as a result of the initiate task request from a composite application instance and is based on the task definition. It decouples the machine from the man or woman.

The Task Service works with other services provided by the SOA Suite infrastructure to perform allocation and routing, handle notifications to task participants, and deal with the authorization and storage of digitally signed tasks. Note that the Task Service and other Workflow Services are not only available as service component in SOA composite applications, but can be

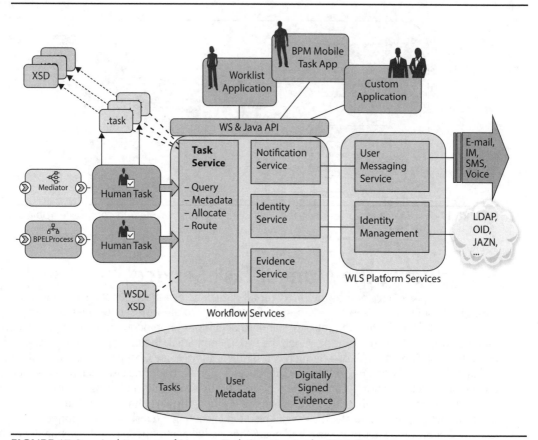

FIGURE 17-2. *Architecture of Human Task Services in the SOA Suite*

interacted with through a SOAP/WS and Java API by other applications that are unrelated to the SOA Suite (Figure 17-2). A frequent use case is the retrieval of task instances for a particular user from a custom-developed user interface.

The task definition files specify parameters—based on elements defined in XSD files. These parameters carry the data specific to the task instance and make it available to the user performing the task. Parameters can be editable. If so, the user can change the data in these parameters, and these changes are returned to the component that invoked the Task Service together with the outcome of the task instance.

The Task Service needs a way to make people aware of the tasks they should execute, and it must offer those people a way to read the task details, update the task's payload, delegate, or escalate a task when necessary, and determine the final task outcome. People, of course, need a user interface to interact with a computer system—you cannot simply send SOAP messages to them. The Task Service can use the User Messaging Service (UMS) to send notifications via various channels such as email, IM (chat), voice, and SMS. The SOA Suite ships with the Worklist application, a prebuilt web application that provides a user interface for all task participants.

It presents the tasks on the user's to-do list, shows the details for a selected task, and allows the user to perform the actions on the task that may be required.

Actionable Email

As a special feature, simple tasks with a limited number of predefined outcomes and no output parameters (or editable payload, which is the better way of putting it for human tasks) can entirely be dealt with from an email. Such an "actionable email" contains hyperlinks for each of the potential task outcomes, and the user can complete the task by simply clicking the desired outcome. A reply email will be sent in which the user can even provide some comments or add attachments. The UMS receives the incoming message and hands it to the Workflow Services that are configured to listen on a specific mailbox for such messages. The email contains an identifier that is used to map the received email to the task. The outcome specified in the email is applied to the task.

Exploring the Task Service in Detail

We will take an in-depth look at how Human Task Service components enable us to engage human agents in our composite applications. In three steps, we will discover some of the intricacies of the Task Service, including integration into BPEL components, notification, payload manipulation, callbacks, and task routing. We will also discuss the integration with identity stores regarding to whom—roles or individuals—a task is assigned or escalated.

First, we will design a simple task that asks a human decision maker to pick one of two possible outcomes (yes or no). Input parameters are passed into the task to provide the user with context for the decision. The only output from this task is the chosen outcome. This task is initially designed to be assigned to a specific user, but it will turn out to be much better to assign the task to a group of users—or more specifically to a role—because, for example, individual users may come and go while the task requirements stay the same. Later in this chapter, we will take on this more robust approach of allocating tasks to roles.

The task is to be integrated into a BPEL process that invokes it when a decision is needed from the human agents and will then wait for its asynchronous response. We will see how the default (out-of-the-box) Worklist application presents the task to the user and allows the user to act on it.

We will then add notification functionality and have the task assignees receive an email that informs them of this new task and invites them to inspect and handle the task using the Worklist application. Because this task only supports two predefined outcomes and has no other output parameters, it could be handled entirely from an actionable email—and that is what we will do next. This introduces an alternative to the Worklist application as an interface for dealing with tasks.

We next step it up a little: the human actor gets to do more than just select one of several predefined outcomes. He or she can manipulate the task's payload as well. This allows the actor to provide some information that cannot be predefined. This data is entered by the user in the generated task form that will be embedded in the default Worklist application. That same form presents the user with the input parameters for the task.

We then look at the advanced task-routing capabilities offered by the Human Workflow Services. We will see how we can define a task that requires multiple participants to make a contribution. We will specify deadlines for the task, create an escalation scheme, and even look at handling leaves of absence for designated task participants. Note that even though multiple actors are involved, they still collaborate on the same task. Real business processes, where multiple, diverse tasks are lined up in logical flows, mixed together with service calls, are discussed in the next two chapters. We will see how such task-and-service-spanning flows can be created using BPEL processes or BPMN service components.

Simple Task Seeking Human Approval for Aircraft Service Proposal

In Chapter 12, we discussed a composite service that orchestrates an RFP around aircraft services such as catering, cleaning, and fueling. Companies providing such services to aircrafts can participate in RFPs by exposing a web service interface called *AircraftServiceProvider*. This interface accepts a request for a proposal (to deliver specified quantities and qualities of cleaning|catering|fueling|... services to a certain aircraft at a certain point in time). In an asynchronous callback, the proposal is to be delivered to the composite service orchestrating the RFP.

Previously, we have not discussed how a provider of aircraft services would arrive at such a proposal. The implementation we used in Chapter 12 returned a hard coded proposal—which is of course not a very realistic scenario. In the current chapter, we will assume that an automated facility, possibly powered by business rules and some calculation engine, will prepare the proposal. However, it is then up to a human actor—an account manager—to confirm (or reject) that machine generated proposal.

In a second iteration in the next section, we will allow that human actor to refine that proposal. And finally we discuss the workflow we have to put in place for approving this customized proposal.

Add Human Task to Composite Application

The SOA composite *AircraftServiceProvider* is shown in Figure 17-3. It exposes an asynchronous service interface that receives a request for a proposal, stews on it for some time and then delivers the proposal in a callback. Internally it uses two BPEL components. The first orchestrates the flow and invokes the second one—*ComposeProposal*—to generate the proposal.

This generated proposal is currently returned unchecked to the RFP issuer. That has to change: an explicit approval has to be given by our human account manager.

Add Human Task Activity in BPEL Process

Open the BPEL component *AircraftServiceRequestProcessor*. Add a Human Task component to the BPEL process, after the scope *RetrieveGeneratedProposal*, as shown in Figure 17-4.

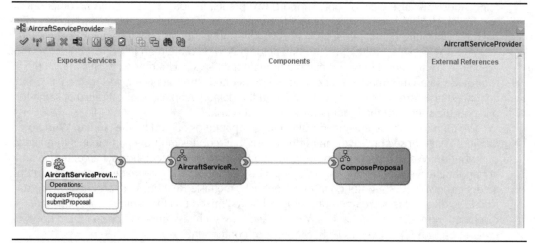

FIGURE 17-3. *Composite AircraftServiceProvider with automated proposal generation*

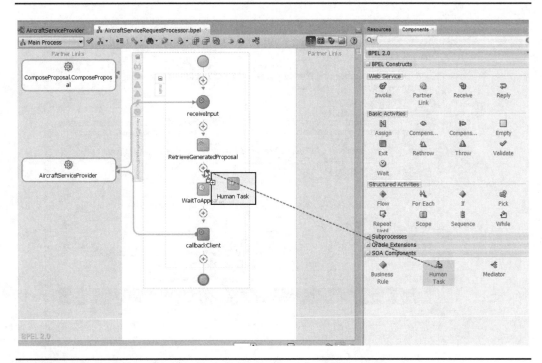

FIGURE 17-4.   *Adding a Human Task component to the BPEL process*

Even though the Human Task is not a BPEL activity, JDeveloper will understand this action. It will create a Human Task scope in the BPEL process—that will contain the appropriate activities for the interaction with the human workflow engine. We next need to edit this scope to actually select an existing or create a new task definition and have it added it to the SOA composite. JDeveloper will then create the necessary BPEL variables and activities to invoke the generic Human Task Service for this specific task definition.

Double click the HumanTask activity that is added to the BPEL process. There is no existing task in this composite that we can select to initiate. Therefore, please click on the plus icon in the first page of the multitabbed editor to create a new task definition.

The dialog to create a new Task Definition appears. Set the name to *AssessProposal*. Accept the default Outcomes—APPROVE and REJECT—since these correspond to the ones we require for this task. Define two parameters for the task—one based on the request for proposal (mapped to the *inputVariable* in the BPEL process) and one mapped to the generated proposal (mapped to the *outputVariable*). This is shown in Figure 17-5.

Press OK to complete the definition of the Human Task definition and again press OK to complete the configuration of the BPEL Task activity that initiates this task. At this point, JDeveloper will do its magic: create the BPEL scope, variables, activities, and if-then-else logic for dealing with the potential outcomes.

The BPEL process flow now looks like Figure 17-6.

It is useful to also check the underlying source code added to the BPEL process, to get a better understanding for what is actually taking place behind the scenes.

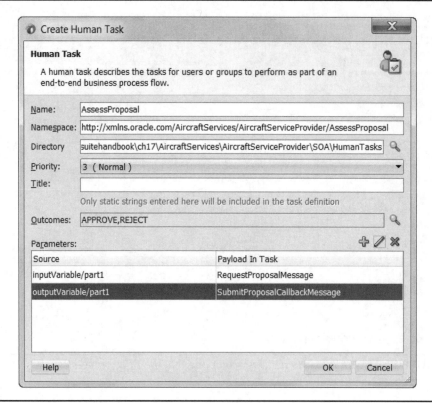

FIGURE 17-5. *Configuring the new task AssessProposal*

Add an Assign activity to the scope for the REJECT outcome. In this case, we have to specify in the response message that we cannot provide the requested service—by setting the *CanDo* element to false and erasing the other elements.

Meanwhile, the composite itself has been extended as well, as shown in Figure 17-7. The task *AssessProposal* is a first class citizen—an SCA component at the same level as the BPEL process components and for example Mediator or Business Rule components. A Human Task definition can be edited outside the scope of the BPEL process and can be reused by other components than the BPEL process from whose context we have just created the task.

Refine Task Definition AssessProposal

Double click on the task definition. The task editor appears—the tool for configuring all details of the task. On the tab labeled General, set the Task Title to a mixed text and XPath expression, as shown in Figure 17-8:

```
Approve or Reject Proposal for RFP <% /task:task/task:payload/ns0:SubmitPr
oposalCallbackMessage/ns0:RFPIdentificationNumber %> for $ <% /task:task/
task:payload/ns0:SubmitProposalCallbackMessage/ns0:Price%>
```

The title is composed from some hard coded texts and some dynamic details from the task payload.

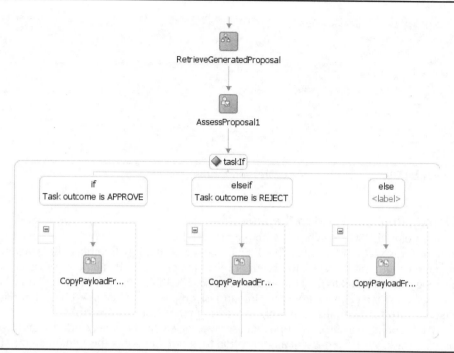

FIGURE 17-6. *The BPEL process after adding the Task AssessProposal*

Open the Assignment tab. Drag a Single Participant from the component palette to Stage 1 in the workflow. Double click this participant to edit the participant type. We will take a shortcut that you should not take in real life: add a participant of type user and set the user's name to the hardcoded string *weblogic,* as shown in Figure 17-9. Every task of the *AssessProposal* task type will now be assigned to this user. We will see later in this chapter how to assign tasks to role(s) which is a more flexible and robust way of assigning tasks.

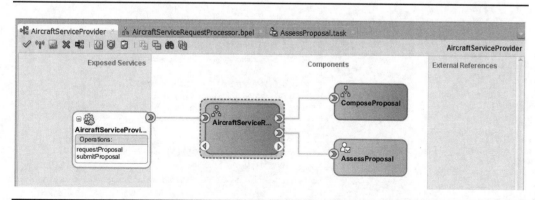

FIGURE 17-7. *The SOA composite with the new Human Task AssessProposal*

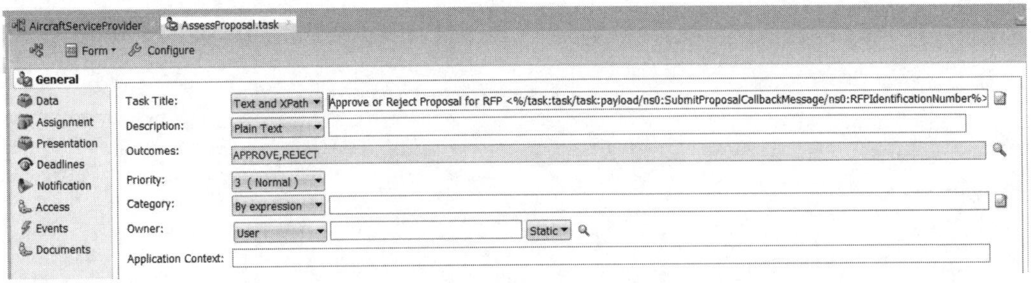

FIGURE 17-8. *Configuring the expression for the task title*

Deploy, Run, and Perform the Task

At this point, the SOA composite with human task inside can be deployed. Invoke the exposed *AircraftServiceProvider* service. The BPEL process will run, it will retrieve the generated proposal and then it will initiate a task to accept or reject the proposal. This task is assigned to user *weblogic* and handed to the Human Task engine. The BPEL engine will cease processing and start waiting for a callback from the Human Task engine (aka Human Workflow Service). See Figure 17-10 for a visualization of this situation in the EM FMW Control.

At this point, we can only hope that user *weblogic* will check her to-do list and work on the assigned task. We have not sent a notification to inform her about this pending request for a decision; we will configure the task a little later on to have this happen.

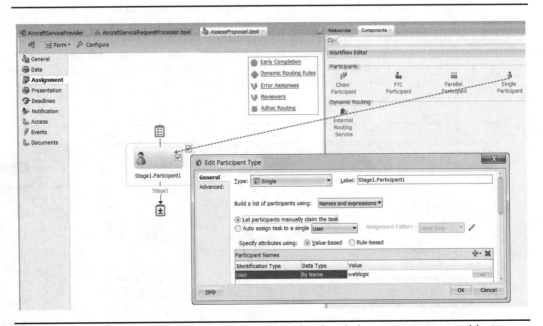

FIGURE 17-9. *Configure the assignment to a single, hard coded participant: user weblogic*

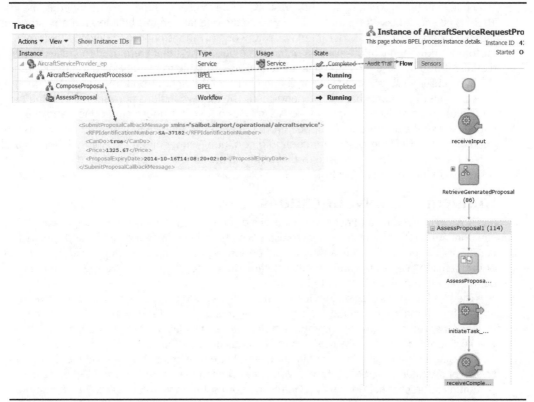

FIGURE 17-10. *The BPEL process has triggered a task and is now waiting for task completion*

The out-of-the-box Worklist application that can be used to inspect, manage and perform tasks can be accessed at this url: http://host:port/integration/worklistapp, with port identifying the *soa* managed server.

Open this BPM Worklist application and login as *weblogic*. The pending task should be listed for *weblogic*, as shown in Figure 17-11.

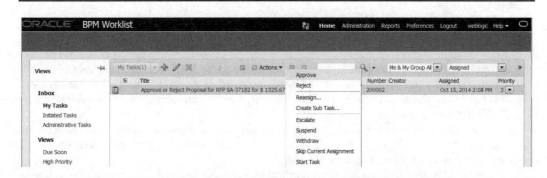

FIGURE 17-11. *The BPM Worklist application with the task(s) assigned to weblogic*

Note that the only details about the task available to user *weblogic* are included in the title. There is no special task form (not yet, we will create one later in this chapter) nor any other insight into the task payload in this user interface. Many organizations choose to develop their own custom Worklist application—on top of the same public APIs that were used to create the shipped worklist. Through these APIs, all payload details are available to be presented to the end user.

When user *weblogic* selects the task and clicks on the Actions button, a dropdown menu appears with the actions that can be performed. The top two actions correspond with the two outcomes we have defined for this task: Approve and Reject. Choose either one—and see what happens next: the task should disappear from the current view—that by default only shows the open tasks. The BPEL process instance should continue—either along the Approve branch or the Reject branch—and the composite instance should produce its response accordingly. You can verify this in the EM FMW Control.

Configure Task Notifications

It is not a very good idea to depend on a user's discipline to regularly check for pending tasks. We can configure notifications to be sent to users who have been assigned tasks—and specify the conditions under which notifications should be sent (assignment, upcoming deadlines, successful or problematic task completion, or other notable task lifecycle events). We specify in the task definition when notifications are to be sent.

The UMS (User Messaging Service) facility in SOA Suite takes care of the actual sending of the notification. It makes use of address details in the identity store used with your SOA Suite instance, as well as the user's communication preferences that can be set through the BPM Worklist application. Here the user can indicate, using rules that can evaluate task payload and metadata at run time, whether a notification should be sent at all and if so whether the default EMAIL or the alternative SMS, Mobile, Voice, or IM channels should be used. A configured communication channel obviously requires the corresponding UMS driver to be configured.

Configure Notification Emails for Task AssessProposal

In order to have emails sent to notify user *weblogic* about newly assigned tasks, we have to take care of a number of aspects:

- UMS Mail Driver configured with an outbound mail server
- Workflow properties at SOA Suite instance level
- Email address for user *weblogic* in identify store (embedded LDAP in WebLogic)
- Notification settings in task definition
- Optionally: user communication preferences in BPM Worklist application

The first and second bullets were taken care of in the set up for Chapter 6 when the outbound UMS adapter was discussed. To set the email address for user *weblogic*, you have to edit the user properties in the default security realm for the embedded LDAP server in WebLogic. The default notification settings in the task should already ensure that an email is sent when the task is assigned. Additional notifications for other events can be configured on the Notification tab in the task definition editor.

On that same tab, we can specify what certain parts of the notification emails should look like—such as the subject. On the advanced tab, we can configure reminders to be sent prior to the due date or expiration time for the task.

When the above steps have been performed using the detailed instructions on the book's site, the SOA composite can be redeployed. When a request is sent, the Human Task engine will send a notification email to the mail address configured for user *weblogic*. The mail contains minimal details about the task. When we have generated a task form in an upcoming section in this chapter, this form will also define the HTML content included in the mail.

Deadlines, Escalation, and Delegation

Tasks can be defined without expiry date or deadline. However, it is common to specify when a task is no longer relevant (expiry) and what the latest moment is at which the assigned user can complete the task. The Deadlines tab in the task editor is used to specify the expiry or renewal period for a task—either as a fixed duration or one that is derived dynamically, for example, from task payload details. Additionally, we can specify when the assignees should be reminded of their task.

To try out the *remind* notifications as well as the *automatic expiry*, open the *Deadlines* tab and configure the task to expire after 1 hour. Also specify that some action is requested within 1 hour. On the *Notification* tab, configure a single reminder 30 minutes prior to expiration (or due date), as is shown in Figure 17-12.

Deploy the component, send a request to its service and wait. You should receive an immediate email to notify about the task assignment. After 30 minutes, a second email arrives, to notify about the pending task expiration—in 30 minutes time. When you do not react, the task will expire after exactly one hour. The BPEL process is notified about the expiration of the task—and resumes processing in the *else* branch. In this branch, we should cater for alternative results than the predefined outcomes that under normal conditions are the result from the task.

The Deadline tab allows us to configure a task not only to be expired but also to be escalated after a fixed or dynamically derived period of time, when no action has been taken by the original assignees. Escalation means that the task is assigned to someone higher up in the hierarchy from the person(s) to whom the task was originally assigned. The hierarchical order of users is read from the identity store. We can indicate the maximum number of levels of escalation to be used for a task as well as the highest level to which the task can be escalated—before it fails altogether. In a subsequent section we will see how we can also create a workflow within a task where the task is escalated up the command chain after a user has completed the task—probably to have the end result checked and confirmed or overruled.

Escalation is one of the task events for which we can have notifications sent, events published, and callbacks made.

Another mechanism for reassigning a task is through delegation. Task assignees can be permitted—and by default they are—to delegate a task assigned to them to another user. This delegation is seen as an assignment in terms of notifications and events. Reassign is an option in the actions menu in the BPM Worklist application.

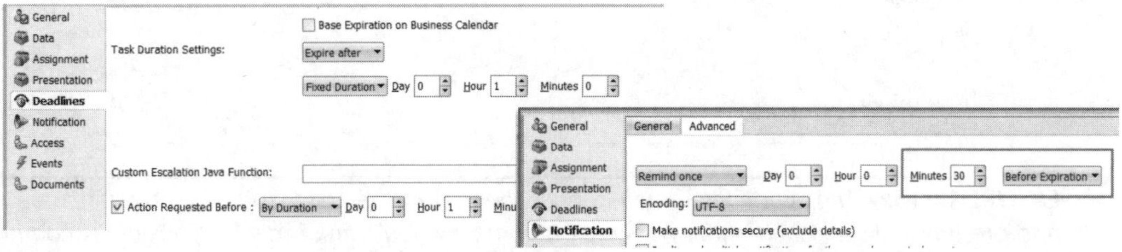

FIGURE 17-12. *Task is configured to be acted upon within 1 hour; notification is configured to be sent 30 minutes before expiration—and therefore 30 minutes after creation*

Actionable Email

Simple tasks can be handled entirely through email. With a so called actionable email, the Human Task Service will send users a notification email that contains hyperlinks for all possible outcomes. Users can complete the task by clicking on one those links. A reply will be sent to the email address that has been configured as the one receiving responses to actionable emails and will lead to the same processing as if the user had selected that outcome from the *Actions* menu in the Worklist application. Users can also provide comments in the response email and add attachments—just like they can in the Worklist application.

To work with actionable emails, the corresponding checkbox should be set on the Advanced section of the Notification tab for the task.

Additionally, the UMS Mail Driver has to be configured for inbound email communications and the Human Workflow facility has to be enabled for the reception of actionable email replies. The Human Workflow component will make sure that the reply address of actionable emails is set correctly. The book's website provides a resource describing the required configuration steps.

Figure 17-13 shows what the actionable email looks like—and what happens when one of the predefined outcomes is selected.

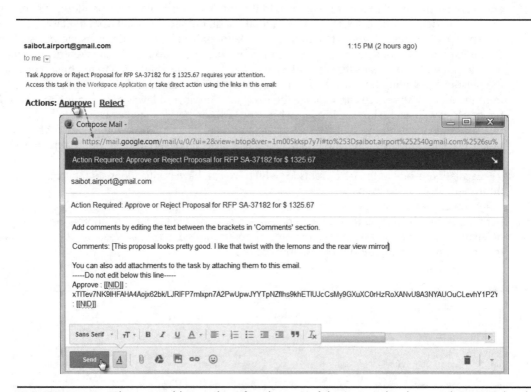

FIGURE 17-13. *The actionable email notifies the user of the assigned task, provides some details and presents links for each of the possible outcomes; when a link is clicked, a reply is composed to be sent to the email address configured on the SOA Suite to process actionable email responses*

When the reply mail is processed, the end result is the same as when the user have would dealt with the task in the BPM Worklist application or through a custom user interface on top of the APIs for the Human Task engine.

Assign to Group

Assigning a task to a single user, by name, is not a very good idea. Users could be unavailable because of sickness or vacation or because they have left the organization altogether, and we would have to change the code and redeploy the application to deal with that. It is a much better idea to assign tasks to logical groups or roles. Who fulfills the role in the organization is not the concern of the task definition or the SOA composite. It is defined through the identity store—outside the SOA Suite and without impact on the deployed composites.

When a group is assigned a task, the notifications are sent to all group members. Each group member can claim and execute the task. In the most common case of the single participant, the one who grabs the task first, is the only one to work on it. As soon as the task has been claimed, other group members no longer have access to the task.

We will now create a group, add members to that group and assign the *AssessProposal* task to the group.

Create Group, Users, and Members

Through the WebLogic Admin Console on our SOA domain, we can add groups and users to the embedded LDAP directory. Subsequently, users can be added as members to the groups. Tasks can be assigned to these groups—and thereby indirectly to the members of the groups.

Open the WebLogic console, click Security Realms in the Domain Structure tree, and then click *myrealm* in the Summary window. The list of current users—which should at least contain the *weblogic* user—is presented. Click the New button in order to add a new user. Enter details for the following users: Sherlock, Scrooge, Dick, Tom, Harry, Matthew, and Mark. Specify at least usernames and passwords and ideally email address as well to receive notifications for assigned tasks. It is okay for multiple users to have the same email address, as far as the human workflow engine is concerned—which makes it easier to set up these demo users. Note that Tom, Dick, and Harry are peers that report to Matthew who reports to Mark.

It is not entirely trivial to create this user hierarchy because the WebLogic Administration Console does not have support for it. The book's website has a reference to resource that explains how to define the hierarchical relationships using an LDAP browser (JXplorer).

Then create the following groups: Auditor, Finance, Account Manager, Sales Manager, and CEO.

Finally create group memberships, linking Sherlock => Auditor, Scrooge => Finance, Tom, Dick, and Harry => Account Manager, Matthew to => Sales Manager, and Mark => CEO.

Assign the Task to the Group

Open the Assignment tab. Click on the Stage1.Participant.

In the popup—shown in Figure 17-14—select the radio button Auto Assign Task to a single User and select the Assignment Pattern Least Busy.

Change the Identification Type for the participant from user to group. Click on the browse icon in the Value column to browse the identity store for the group. Select the group Account Manager.

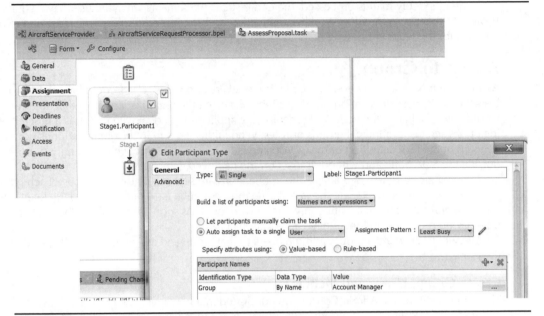

FIGURE 17-14. *Configure the task assignment to the Group Account Manager*

To poise the escalation mechanism—open the Deadlines tab and set the task to escalate after 15 minutes.

Deploy and Run

With this updated task definition, deploy the SOA composite. Send a request to the exposed service of the SOA composite to initiate a new task.

Login to the BPM Worklist application, as Tom. You should see the newly created task—available for Tom to work on. Logout and login as Dick. This user too should see the task, because of his membership of the Account Manager group to which the task was assigned. The same applies to Harry.

If Dick claims the task or even executes it, it is no longer available to Tom and Harry: only one of them has to complete the task. After initially claiming the task, Dick can also release the task if for some reason he cannot complete it after all. The task then reappears in the *to-do* lists for all three account managers.

If no one touches the task for 15 minutes, an automatic escalation takes place. Login to the BPM Worklist application as Matthew before the 15 minutes are up, and there should not be any tasks visible. However, when an *AssessProposal* task is unattended for 15 minutes, the manager of the original assignees—Matthew, who is the manager of Tom, Dick, and Harry—gets the now escalated task assigned. And if he does not react within 15 minutes, the task is moved up the hierarchy once more, to Mark whom Matthew reports to. Figure 17-15 shows the audit trail for the human task with the automatic escalation.

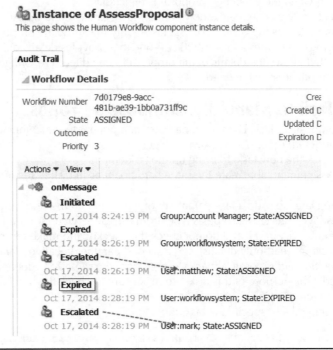

FIGURE 17-15. *Task Assignment to group Account Manager and subsequent escalation*

NOTE
In addition to the out-of-the-box behavior in the Human Task component for task assignment and task escalation, we can also configure our own custom Java classes to implement this logic. Based on our knowledge of the tasks and of our workforce, we can implement customized logic to ensure appropriate allocation— implement Java interface IDynamicAssignmentPattern—and escalation—implement interface IDynamicTaskEscalationFunction. Additionally, we can configure custom Java event listeners— implementing the IRoutingSlipCallback interface—to get notified about task related events and react to them.

Handcraft Proposal When Rejecting the Generated Proposal

Rejecting a generated proposal has serious consequences right now: it means a complete exit from the RFP process. That may not necessarily be our intention. Instead, it would be better to be able to create a new task to handcraft a proposal—a task for the account manager to take on and that is initiated when the generated proposal is rejected.

In this section, we will create a new Human Task—assigned to the Account Manager. It uses the same parameters as the *AssessProposal* task—only this time, the proposal details are editable. This task obviously requires a user interface—one that provides details on the requested aircraft services and that allows the details of the proposal to be edited. We will generate a task form that the Worklist application will embed.

Create Task to Manually Compose a Proposal

Open the composite editor. Drag a Human Task component to the composite diagram. Call the new task *HandcraftProposal*—as shown in Figure 17-16.

Double click the new task, to bring up the task editor.

On the Assignment tab, create the same participant as in task *AssessProposal*: group *Account Manager*.

Open the Data tab. Add a task parameter of type other. In the Add Task Parameter dialog, select requestProposalMessageType as type (from AircraftService.xsd). Call this parameter RequestAircraftServiceInRFP and do not check the checkbox to make this parameter editable because it contains read-only details. Add a second parameter, called *HandcraftedProposal* and based on type SubmitProposalCallbackMessage from the same XSD document. This parameter will be edited—the purpose of this task—so make sure to check the box for *Editable in Worklist*—as shown in Figure 17-17.

On the General tab, specify the task title:

```
Handcraft Proposal for RFP <%/task:task/task:payload/task:RequestAircraftServi
ceInRFP/ns0:RFPIdentificationNumber%>
```

You do not need to edit the outcomes: this task can work with the two default outcomes of *Approve* and *Reject*.

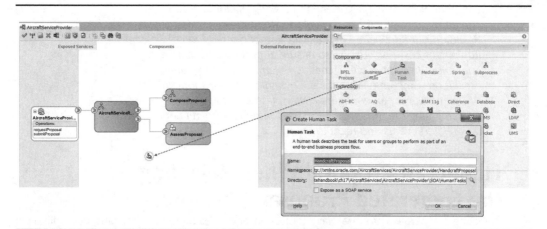

FIGURE 17-16. *Create new Human Task HandcraftProposal in composite*

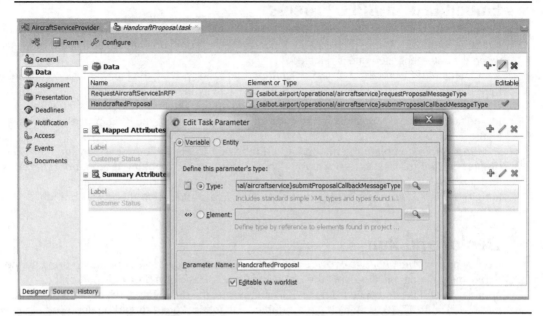

FIGURE 17-17.   *Creating two task parameters based on XSD type definitions*

We do not change any of the default settings for deadlines or notifications. That means among other things that this task is not actionable. That is correct because the task involves not just selecting one out of several possible outcomes. It requires the human actor to edit the properties of the proposal, which is not supported through actionable emails.

Generate the Task Form

The user interface for a task can be generated by JDeveloper. This results in an ADF web application. This application can be further customized by hand. Alternatively, custom user interfaces can be built on top of the same Human Task APIs that the generated form leverages—either using ADF or using other technologies for creating a user interface. The book's website provides resources describing the creation of such custom user interfaces.

From the *Form* dropdown at the top of the task editor, choose the option Auto-Generate Task Form. In the Create Project dialog that appears, enter *HandcraftProposalTaskForm* as the name for the ADF web project that should be created.

At some point during the generation process—that will take multiple dozens of seconds or even minutes—there may be one or more dialogs you have to respond to. Accepting the default settings will suffice for now.

The end result of all the processing is a new JDeveloper project that contains the sources for the task form application. You can inspect the generated sources and you can make changes to them if you like. This application is deployed later on to our SOA Suite run time to be visually embedded in the BPM Worklist application. Note that the task definition contains a reference to the ADF taskflow that contains the task form.

Embed Task in BPEL Process

The task to manually edit the proposal has been defined but is not yet instantiated anywhere in our SOA composite. We require the Account Manager to come up with a handcrafted proposal when the auto-generated one is rejected.

Open the BPEL Process *AircraftServiceRequestProcessor*. Drag the Human Task component from the component palette and drop it as the last activity in the Reject branch.

Select task *HandcraftProposal* from the drop-down list. The two parameters that were defined for the task are listed. Map them to the corresponding variables in the BPEL process, as shown in Figure 17-18.

Press OK to complete the dialog and add the task to the BPEL process. Inside the *Reject* branch created for task *AssessProposal* is now the scope for invoking task *HandcraftProposal* and three if-else branches for the outcomes Approve, Reject and others. Drag the activity *WithdrawProposal* from just prior to *HandcraftProposal* to the *Reject* branch following this task.

Deploy and Run

Deploy project *AircraftServiceProvider* using the *AircraftServiceProvider* profile to bring up the deployment dialog. Because now the *HandcraftProposalTaskForm* project is part of the application and is referenced from the SOA composite, the deployment wizard will present a new page, see Figure 17-19, on which we can indicate that this project should be deployed along with the SOA composite.

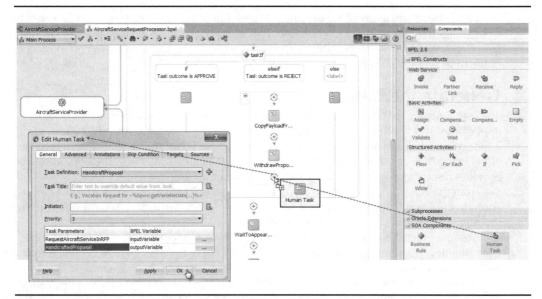

FIGURE 17-18.   *Add task HandcraftProposal to the BPEL Process AircraftServiceRequestProcessor*

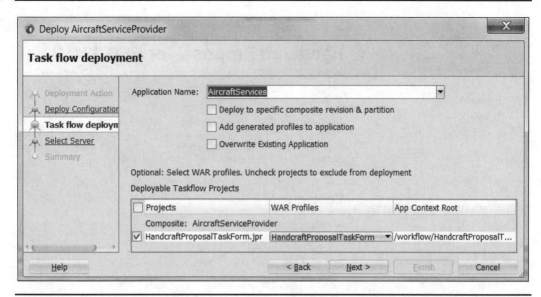

FIGURE 17-19. *Instructing the deployment wizard to deploy the generated task form project along with the SOA composite*

After you press finish, deployment will commence and another dialog may appear—regarding MDS repositories. When that happens, select mds-soa for the repository and set soa-infra for the partition.

When deployment is complete, send a new request message to the exposed service. The ensuing task to *AssessProposal* should be completed with the REJECT outcome. At this point, the new *HandcraftProposal* task is triggered, assigned to the *Account Manager* group.

In case a mail address would have been specified for one of the account managers, a notification email would be sent that—unlike the notification mail for the *AssessProposal* task—contains all task details. The task form is rendered in rich HTML in the notification mail—see Figure 17-20.

The mail contains a link into the Worklist application that presents the task form with this task's details and all controls to manipulate the task and the editable parameter—as shown in Figure 17-21. After editing the properties of the handcrafted proposal, the task can be concluded by either clicking the Approve or the Reject button. The latter means complete withdrawal from the RFP process; the former results in an updated proposal, confirmed by the Account Manager himself.

The properties that were set through the task form for the handcrafted proposal are returned by the Task engine to the BPEL process that instantiated the task. These properties are copied to the *outputVariable* in the BPEL process—as configured in the BPEL Human Task activity for this task.

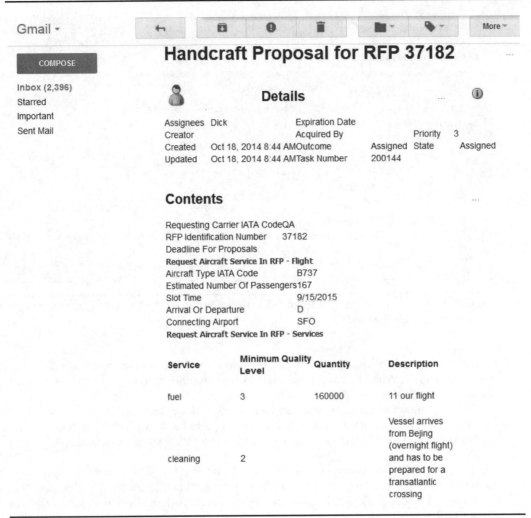

FIGURE 17-20. *The notification mail contains the task details included in the task form*

Update Initial Task AssessProposal to Include Workflow for Approving Manual Proposals

In the previous section, we have given the Account Managers a lot of freedom. From approving or rejecting the generated proposal, they are now in the driving seat themselves: able to fine tune proposals as they see fit when the generated version is rejected.

There needs to be some additional control now: when Account Managers go outside the boundaries that apply to the automated proposal generation system, their proposals have to be checked by peers, superiors, and other stakeholders.

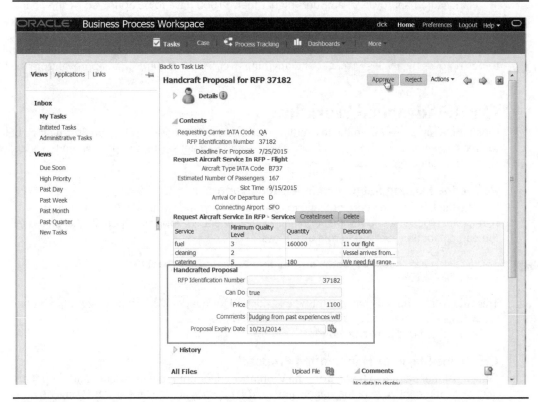

FIGURE 17-21.   *The auto generated task form for an instance of the Handcraft Proposal task*

Human tasks can be created with fairly advanced workflows that go a long way in supporting these requirements. We can have a single task consist of various stages—parallel or sequential—performed conditionally and by different roles. There is an important limitation: the task definition remains the same and all users share the same task payload and task form (unless of course they are given a custom task user interface).

In our example, we will extend the *AssessProposal* task definition. This task is to be used in the BPEL process for the assessment of both the generated proposal as well as the handcrafted one. The task can be included twice in the BPEL process or it can be included once in an inline BPEL subprocess that is invoked twice, when the generated proposal is received as well as when the handcrafted proposal is done.

For the generated proposal, the workflow can stay the same: just a single participant (the Account Manager) with time-based escalation if the proposal assessment is not done on time.

For a handcrafted proposal, the workflow will be considerably more complex.

The group of Auditors has demanded that they should be notified of each handcrafted proposal. They cannot influence the proposal directly, but they need to know about it for registration, compliancy and other reasons. The Human Task Service provides a participant type called FYI that we use for this.

Handcrafted approvals of amounts higher than $1000 have to be approved by the finance department.

Finally, any handcrafted approval has to undergo a peer review by all Account Managers. At least two have to approve—and they should also form a majority. Proposal over $1500 have also to be approves by a Sales Manager and anything over $3000 requires final approval from the CEO as well.

Create Advanced Workflow

Open the Assignment tab in the task editor for task *AssessProposal*. Follow the instructions below to create the workflow shown in Figure 17-22—with parallel stages and participant types to deal with handcrafted proposals.

Refine the Existing Stage for Generated Proposals

Change the label for the current Stage to *Generated Proposals*. Change the label for the participant type to *AccountManagerInitialReviewGeneratedProposal*. Open the Advanced tab for the participant type. Set a skip rule as follows:

```
not(/task:task/task:payload/ns0:SubmitProposalCallbackMessage/
ns0:CanDo='true')
```

This rule will ensure this participant type is skipped for handcrafted proposals. A little bit later on we will set element CanDo to false for handcrafted proposals.

Close the participant type editor.

Create the Stage for Handcrafted Proposals

Drag a parallel participant type from the Workflow Editor component palette, and drop it on the anchor on the right edge of the stage *Generated Proposals*. Set the label for this stage to

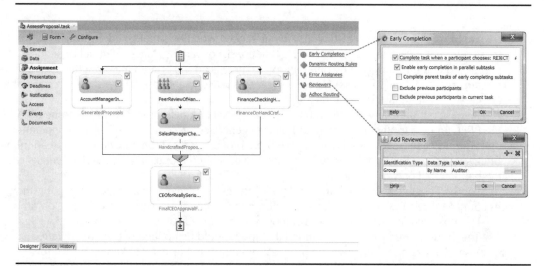

FIGURE 17-22. *The complete workflow for task AssessProposal—with conditional parallel and sequential tasks*

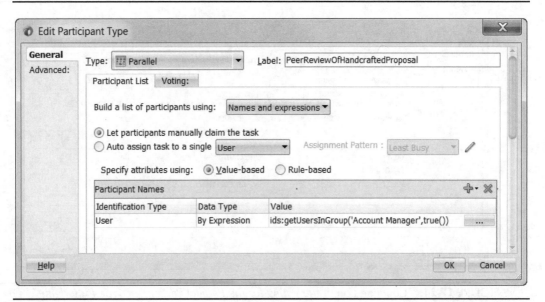

FIGURE 17-23. *Configuring the participants for the Account Managers' vote on the handcrafted proposal*

HandcraftedProposals. Open the editor for the participant type—see figure 17-23. Set the label for the participant type to *PeerReviewOfHandcraftedProposal.*

In this case, we should not simply assign the task to single participant for the group Account Manager. That would be interpreted by the Human Task engine as: we need but a single vote from anyone in group Account Manager. What we really want is to have all account managers review the handcrafted proposal—or at least the majority of them. In order to achieve this, we configure the participant type using an XPath expression that will explicitly select all users in group Account Manager at the time of creating the assignment for this participant type.

Set the Identification Type to *User*, the Data Type to *By Expression* and the Value to:

```
ids:getUsersInGroup('Account Manager',true())
```

Open the *Voting* tab. This is where we can specify that votes from a (substantial) subset of all account managers are enough to settle the matter. Create rows for the outcomes APPROVE and REJECT, both with the *Outcome Type* set to *By Percentage* and the *Values* set at 51 and 35, respectively. This indicates that just over one third (which would currently mean two out of three) of the Account Managers can cause a handcrafted proposal to be rejected. A small majority (also at present two of the three) on the other hand can tip the scale toward approve. The Default Outcome—in case no one votes—is REJECT. Figure 17-24 shows this configuration.

On the Advanced tab, set a skip rule to specify when this participant type does *not* have to act (for generated proposals with CanDo set to true):

```
/task:task/task:payload/ns0:SubmitProposalCallbackMessage/ns0:CanDo='true'
```

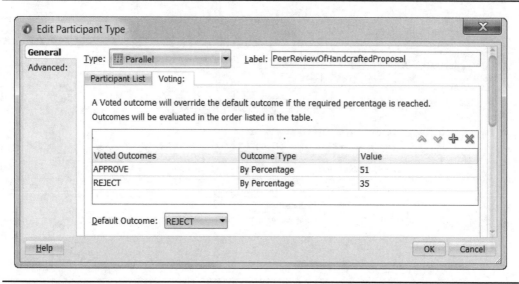

FIGURE 17-24. *Configuration of the Voting for the Parallel Participant Type for judging handcrafted proposals*

NOTE
The Peer Review by the Account Managers of a handcrafted proposal should ideally not include the account manager who created the proposal. The task assignment patterns in SOA Suite unfortunately do not provide such smartness out of the box—nor would it be able to assign a task to the same user who executed an earlier task in the same SOA composite instance. In order to achieve such behavior—we have to implement custom allocation algorithms.

When Human Tasks are created in the context of BPM Suite— see also in Chapter 19—then this four eyes principle and the task stickiness (to a previous actor) can be applied out of the box.

Drag a Single Participant from the palette and attach it to the bottom edge of the parallel participant type *PeerReviewOfHandcraftedProposal*. This single participant is the Sales Manager who only has to act for handcrafted proposals with a price of $1500 or higher.

Assign the task in this participant type to the Group Sales Manager. Define a skip rule with this expression:

```
/task:task/task:payload/ns0:SubmitProposalCallbackMessage/ns0:Price < 1500 or
/task:task/task:payload/ns0:SubmitProposalCallbackMessage/ns0:CanDo='true'
```

Involvement of the Finance Department

To cater for the requirement from the finance department to be involved with any handcrafted proposal with a value of over $1000, we need to add another Single Participant from the component palette. Because the involvement from finance takes place in parallel to the sales department's activities, we can attach the participant to the right edge of the participant type for the Peer Review. Set the stage label to *FinanceOnHandCraftedProposals*. Set the participant type label to *FinanceCheckingHandcraftedProposals*.

Assign the task in this participant type to the role Finance. On the *Advanced* tab, set a skip rule with this expression:

```
/task:task/task:payload/ns0:SubmitProposalCallbackMessage/ns0:Price < 1000 or
/task:task/task:payload/ns0:SubmitProposalCallbackMessage/ns0:CanDo='true'
```

Early Completion

As soon as one of the participant types in our workflow decides to reject the handcrafted proposal, we can immediately consider the task complete: a single rejection suffices for total rejection. This behavior for the workflow can be configured using the *Early Completion* link in the box on the right hand side of the workflow editor.

Click on the link to define the condition under which immediate conclusion should be performed. Specify that the task is to be completed when one of the participants chooses REJECT as the outcome, as shown in Figure 17-22.

Note: For the parallel participant type this means that when the outcome of the vote is REJECT, the immediate completion takes place—not when just one of the voters selects the REJECT outcome.

Read Only Access for Auditors

The auditors require read only access to every handcrafted proposal. We can achieve this very quickly by specifying the Auditor group as a Reviewer for this task—using the Reviewers link in the same box as the *Early Completion* link, as shown in Figure 17-22. This will result in every instance of task *AccessProposal* being visible—but not editable—to members of the Auditor group, including generated proposals.

Alternatively, we can create a parallel participant type, similar to the stage and participant type for the Finance department, including a similar skip rule. However, for the Auditor group, we would use type *FYI Participant*, which results in members of the Auditor group being notified of instances of the *AssessProposal* task for handcrafted proposals and read only access to the details for these task instances.

Generate the Task Form for AssessProposal

In very much the same way as we have done for *HandcraftProposal*, generate the task form for the *AssessProposal* Task. Set name of the project to *AssessProposalTaskForm*. Accept all defaults.

Add a Second Appearance of Task AssessProposal to the BPEL Process

The extended version of *AssessProposal* is to be used for the handcrafted proposal. In the BPEL process *AircraftServiceRequestProcessor* we have to add a Human Activity based on task *AssessProposal* to the Approve branch following Human Activity *HandcraftProposal*. Map its parameters as before to the *inputVariable* and *outputVariable*.

To let the task know it is dealing with a handcrafted proposal, we set the *CanDo* element in *OutputVariable* to false, in an Assign activity just before the newly added Human Activity.

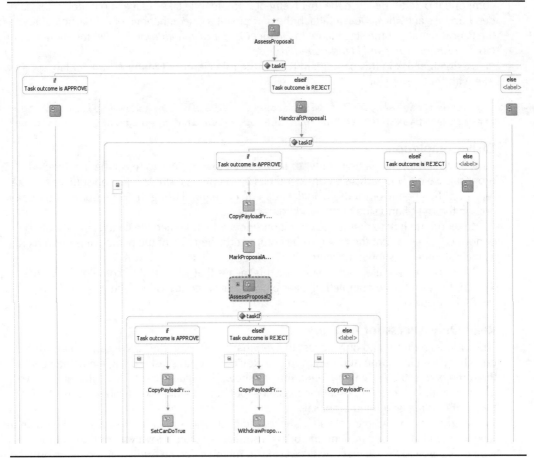

FIGURE 17-25. *BPEL Process AircraftServiceRequestProcessor with the two calls to the AssessProposal task*

Copy activity *WithdrawProposal* from the Reject branch under the first occurrence of *AssessProposal* to the same location in the Reject branch of this second occurrence—to once again reset all proposal properties when also the handcrafted proposal is withdrawn.

Finally, add an activity to the Approve branch under the Human Activity to assess the handcrafted proposal. This activity should set element *CanDo* in the *OutputVariable* to *true*. See Figure 17-25 for the relevant sections from the BPEL process.

Deploy and Run

Deploy the SOA composite *AircraftServiceProvider*. Make sure that the generated project *AssessProposalTaskForm* with the task form for the *AssessProposal* task is included in the deployment. Mark the checkbox *Override existing application*.

Send a request to the service exposed by the SOA composite. The first Assess Proposal task is initiated, for the generated proposal. The task is assigned to the Account Managers. Complete this task by rejecting the proposal as either Tom, Dick, or Harry.

A second task will appear for the Account Managers: to handcraft a proposal. Work on this task in the BPM Worklist application and make sure to set the price to an interesting value, say $5000. Complete the task by selecting the *Approve* outcome.

The *AssessProposal* task is triggered again. This time, the three members of group AccountManager have to do a group vote on the handcrafted proposal. Subsequently, the task is brought to the attention of both the Sales Manager(s) and the finance department—because of the substantial price of the proposal. When both have approved, the task progresses to the next stage where the CEO will be engaged as well, because this proposal is way over the $3000 limit that was set for CEO involvement.

This flow can be tracked in the EM FMW Control and is also visible to users acting on the task in the task form. Figure 17-26, for example, shows the information available to the CEO about the workflow traversed by the task before the moment he has to Approve or Reject the handcrafted proposal. Note that Harry never got to vote: when two votes were in from the Account Manager group, the task engine considered the step complete and progressed to the Sales Manager.

Advanced Features for Human Tasks

Human tasks in SOA Suite do not end with what you have read in this chapter so far. There is a series of advanced features and options that are beyond the scope of this book but should still be mentioned, no matter how briefly.

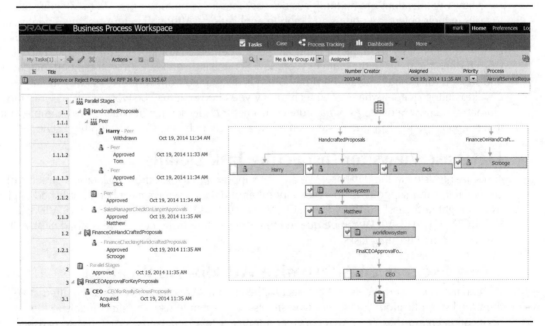

FIGURE 17-26. *Task workflow history as shown in the task form to the users participating in the task*

Business Rules for Task Allocation

When creating the participant list, we can select individual users or groups from the identity management system or use an XPath expression for creating straightforward logic to derive the task actors. There is a third, more advanced option:

You can define state machine routing rules using Oracle Business Rules. This action enables you to create Oracle Business Rules that are evaluated:

- After a routing slip task participant sets the outcome of the task
- Before the task is assigned to the next routing slip participant

This action enables you to build complex routing behavior into tasks.

Upon selection of this rule-based option, a rule dictionary is created that contains predefined functions such as CreateResourceList and a series of fact types for various aspects of the task, including the parameters. This function creates a fact of a type understood by the Task Service and that contains the assignees for the task. A rule set is created in the dictionary that works on the facts that the Task Service passes to the Business Rule component. The rule set can use this function in its actions. The task definition refers to this rule set.

Java and WebService API for Human Workflow Services

The Human Workflow Services can be accessed through a Web Service API as well as a Java API—based on EJBs that can access the SOA Suite both locally for classes running in the JVM as well as remotely. The APIs allow applications to browse, query, and manipulate tasks—and can thus be used to develop custom applications that expose, modify, and/or complete tasks to assignees through tailor-made user interfaces.

Many organizations are building custom user interfaces on top of this API to integrate access to tasks in their enterprise portals and mobile applications. Although in terms of alignment with Oracle's strategic development technology and deployment ease on WebLogic, ADF is an obvious candidate technology for implementing such task oriented UI components, it is perfectly possible to go further afield. Since the Human Workflow Service is a service with well-defined interfaces and support for various interaction protocols, it is decoupled from whatever client you may develop on top of it, in whatever UI technology you choose. It may be worthwhile to wrap the Human Workflow Services API in a more consumer friendly service interface—for example, one that supports the REST protocol—to even allow a purely rich client UI development style.

Database Views for Inspecting Task Details

Tasks are persisted in the database. We are not supposed to access those task tables directly, of course, nor is this supported. However, a number of database views have been published to give us an insight in the tasks directly from SQL. Views such as WFUNATTENDEDTASKS_VIEW and WFPRODUCTIVITY_VIEW can be queried to report on task instances. There is no PL/SQL API for querying or manipulating tasks.

Using Excel as an Alternative Worklist Application

We can use Excel worksheets that connect to the Human Workflow Services as an alternative for the Worklist application. Such Excel worksheets can be sent to users as attachments to the notification email. They can provide a great number of task details in a structured spreadsheet format. These worksheets can contain buttons that act like the actionable links in emails and send task updates to the Task Service. The Excel worksheets are powered by ADF DI (Desktop Integration) and can be created in a similar way to the ADF Faces browser-based task form.

Human Task Callbacks

The Workflow Service can be configured to call back (to the task initiating the BPEL process) or call out (to a Java class or the Event Delivery Network) upon certain events and status changes that take place for the task. The events that can trigger such a call are Assign, Update, Complete, Stage Complete, and Subtask Update. The callback sends a notification about what just happened with the task, including relevant details such as the user who updated the task, the new assignee, and the values of task parameters. Callbacks are configured for a task in the task editor on the Events tab. Three types of callbacks can be discerned:

■ **Java callbacks** A custom class that implements the interface IRoutingSlipCallback can be registered to be called upon task update.

■ **Business events** A task can be configured to produce events on the Event Delivery Network. These events are specified in a pre-seeded EDL file: HumanTaskEvent.edl. Mediators and BPEL components can subscribe to these task events.

■ **BPEL callbacks** When a human task is added to a BPEL process, the process is extended with a Receive activity based on the onTaskCompleted operation in the callback interface. However, the BPEL process can be made to accept other callbacks from the Task Service as well. On the bottom of the Events tab in the task editor is a check box marked "Allow task and routing customization in BPEL callbacks." When you check that box, open the Human Task activity editor in the BPEL process, and click OK, the BPEL process is extended again with a while loop and a Pick activity that has onMessage branches for the various callbacks the task can make. The BPEL process can do various things with the information received in a callback. Among those things is the option to invoke the Task Service to update the task instance—for example, with new parameter values or by ending the task.

Custom Task Allocation and Escalation Mechanisms

The Task Service works with a number of built-in algorithms for assigning tasks to users—such as least busy and round-robin. If you have a need for a specific, custom method for assigning a task to a user or a group (e.g., based on task properties or parameter values), you can register a Java class that is invoked at run time to determine the assignee. In the same way the Task Service can work with a custom task-escalation method implemented in a registered Java class.

Summary

A business process typically consists of a combination of human activities and automated service calls that make computers perform some work. These actions are wired together in a process flow with additional logic, including decision points, loops, and parallel paths. The Human Task Service component introduced in this chapter enables the implementation of the human activity in SOA composite applications. To the SCA engine, it seems almost as if the human actors come with a WSDL interface, just like truly automated services. Human tasks can be handled by the assignees through a generated or custom-created user interface and in some cases through actionable emails. The result of the human activity consists of the task outcome and possibly an updated task payload. Both are returned to the invoker of the Human Task component, which will frequently be a BPEL process component.

We saw in the last step—the process around the acceptance of a handcrafted proposal—that a single task can be defined as a workflow with fairly complex routing that takes the task and its payload to various participants, who can be selected dynamically, work in parallel, and under specific conditions only. However, it is still a single task, a single packet of data, which is routed to human actors only. The routing logic is limited, and service calls are not part of the task route. The definition of the Proposal Approval flow was pushing the human task to the limits.

To implement business processes that consist of various tasks with different payloads and have both services and human agents to execute activities, we need to step outside the scope of a single human task component. Such a process can be implemented using a BPEL process that embeds multiple human tasks, service calls, and the flow logic to wire them all together. We will discuss such workflows in Chapter 18.

In Chapter 19, we will also meet another service engine: the BPMN service engine that runs business processes developed using the Business Process Model Notation. Such BPMN processes also combine human operations and service invocations. Note that this engine is not part of the SOA Suite 12*c* license—it is part of the BPM Suite. Technically however, it is completely integrated in the SOA Suite's SCA environment.

BPMN allows for a more intuitive, business-driven definition of processes and workflows than the combination of BPEL and Human Task. In addition, the run-time BPM Process Composer tool—somewhat similar to the SOA Composer we used for run-time editing of business rules and Domain Value Maps—allows business analysts and other run-time participants to inspect and maintain process definitions through their web browser.

CHAPTER
18

Business Process
Oriented BPEL

B PEL is short for Business Process Execution Language. So far, we have used BPEL for the creation of composite services and asynchronous, sometimes longer running interactions. We have not really been working from the notion of business processes and certainly not yet in terms that business representatives would understand.

In this chapter, we will start from the description of a business process—for the security accreditation of new staff at the airport. This description is turned into the high-level design of a BPEL process—using flows and decision logic, human tasks for various actors, and event handlers. Finally, we will implement the BPEL process.

The objective of this chapter is to get a feel for designing and implementing long-running business processes with BPEL. Compensation is introduced in BPEL—used to undo the business effects of earlier process activities when at a later stage the process is interrupted. Additionally, the LDAP adapter is introduced for interaction with LDAP-based user directories.

In Chapter 20, we will discuss how we can provide operational business insight into these business processes with process analytics and through BAM dashboards. In Chapter 19, we take a brief look at using BPM Suite for designing and implementing a similar business process. When you have BPM Suite at your disposal, it generally is the better option for business processes. BPEL in comparison is a more technical language, better suited to service orchestration than to the implementation of business processes.

Designing the Business Process: Security Accreditation for New Airport Personnel

New employees and temporary staff hired by Saibot Airport itself or by one of the many aircraft service providers, shops and restaurants, cleaning companies, delivery services, customs and immigration services, and other parties active on the airport need various levels of security clearance. This chapter discusses the process that starts with a request for new accreditation for a staff member by a designated requestor, and that ends with either the accreditation awarded or the request denied. Over the course of the process, the original requestor can enquire after the current status of the request and/or cancel the request.

We will first explore the description of the business process as provided by the business analyst. Then we will turn this description into an abstract BPEL process—one that cannot yet be implemented, but that can be used in its visual representations for detailed discussions with the business analyst.

Description of the Business Process

Many organizations are registered as business partners of Saibot Airport. Employees of these organizations can acquire security accreditation at the airport in order to access areas they need to visit in accordance with their roles and responsibilities. Each of these organizations has registered one or more of their staff as requestors—which means they are identified as people who can request security clearance for others employees in their company.

A requestor can send in a request for security accreditation for a colleague. In their request, they have to provide their own and their organization's identifier, the personal details of the employee they make the request for (including employee number, first and last name, birthdate, gender, SSN, picture), the required security level (from the range of 0 to 5), and the motivation for this level. They have to specify the start date and, if known, the end date for the accreditation. Optionally, they can provide references from other staff that can vouch for the new employee.

Provided the request progresses successfully through the initial validation, the almost instantaneous (synchronous) response from the process will be a unique request identification number that can be used for future correspondence. The final asynchronous response carries that same identification as well an indication of the outcome of the request for accreditation with optionally a motivation in case of a denial or the assigned user ID and badge number when the accreditation has been awarded. In the latter case, emails are sent to the requestor and the newly accredited staff member with these same details.

Using the unique request identifier, the requestors can cancel their request at any moment. They can also enquire after the status of running accreditation processes.

The business process consists of three stages: the initial validation, the security check and—upon a successful check—the registration of the new staff member.

Stage One: Initialization and Validation

In this first stage, the request message is screened. The indicated organization and requestor are looked up in the identity store (an LDAP directory) and their security levels are established. Some basic validation is done for the request message. If the lookup operations are unsatisfactory or the validation fails, the process returns an immediate fault message. When the first stage is performed successfully, it will be concluded with the assignment of the accreditation request unique identifier and a synchronous response message that contains that identifier.

Second Stage: The Security Check

For any staff member for which accreditation is requested, a national security background check is performed, provided by a national security agency. This check returns either OK, Not OK, or Unclear. In that latter case, Saibot Airport has to enter discussions with all parties involved. These discussions may result in a new request—possibly with amended or additional information—to perform the national security check, that again may end with OK, Not OK, or Unclear.

In parallel with the national security check, Saibot performs its own check. The thoroughness of this check depends both on the requested security level for the new staff member and on the current security level for the requestor and the requesting company: the more trust already exists, the less demanding the check can be. A business rule—which should be easily adjustable—will decide for the accreditation request what scrutiny level should be applied. This level ranges from 0 to a maximum of 4.

When the level assigned is 1 or more, a human actor—an accreditation evaluator—has to evaluate the request for accreditation. At level 2 a positive evaluation should be reviewed by a peer. At level 3 their team leader is involved afterwards and at level 4 as a final check, a senior security officer has to approve the request.

Saibot Airport also performs a thorough background check, which involves checking out references, reviewing past activities, exploring social media, and other deep dive investigations. This check is performed randomly on a fairly small number of subjects—because of the cost and time it takes. A business rule determines for each accreditation request whether this background check is to be performed. If it is, it happens in parallel to the national security check and the standard Saibot security evaluation. The background check is considered a separate process.

Third Stage: The Registration

The third stage is executed if and when the security checks in stage two result in a positive outcome. In this third stage, the new staff member can be added to relevant systems and have the security badge created.

The staff member has to be registered with the *PersonnelService* that will record personal details for this new member of airport family and also assign a staff identification number.

The staff member is also registered in the LDAP directory with attributes such as name, email address, username and temporary password, manager, organization, and security level. Note that this registration in the LDAP directory should take place just prior to the specified start date for the security accreditation.

A service is invoked to have a security badge prepared with the picture and some personal details. This service will asynchronously return the badge ID that has been awarded.

When all is said and done, the asynchronous callback is made as well as emails are sent to both the requestor and the new staff member with details such as the user ID, the staff ID, and the security badge number that can be collected. A business event is to be published announcing the new staff member. This event includes the Saibot staff ID, company, name, start date, and security level.

Note: If the random background check is performed—can take up to 5 days—and it fails, compensation has to be performed to undo the accreditation of the staff member.

Designing the Still Abstract BPEL Process

The next step to take from the description of the process in the previous section is to start the design of the BPEL process. By creating the flow in a visual way, we get a better handle on the structure in the narrative about the process. The visual process design can be discussed with the business analyst and perhaps other stakeholders and it will likely give rise to more detailed questions and explorations. This abstract design—full of empty BPEL Scope activities—cannot be executed of course, but it will later on serve as the starting point for the implementation when these empty scopes are fleshed out with real activities.

Create a new SOA Application *AirportAccreditationService* with a project of that same name. Add a BPEL process called *AirportAccreditationRequestProcessor* and accept the default WSDL for the Asynchronous BPEL Process template. Uncheck the checkbox to expose this BPEL process as a SOAP service.

Open the BPEL editor.

Add Top Level Scopes for Main Process Stages

Add a scope to the BPEL process called *AirportSecurityAccreditationProcess*. This scope encompasses the entire processing described above by the business analyst. Inside this scope, add three consecutive scopes for the main stages of the process: *InitializationandValidation*, *SecurityChecks,* and *Registration*. To handle the asynchronous requests for a status update or to cancel the accreditation request, add two event handlers to the scope, as shown in Figure 18-1.

Refine Stage InitializationandValidation

Expand the scope for the first stage. For this stage the process description mentions validation and retrieval of information about the requestor and the originating company. Add scopes for these two activities as well as one for composing and returning the synchronous response, as shown in Figure 18-2.

NOTE
The alert icons appear because the BPEL standard does not allow scopes to be empty and JDeveloper warns us about this validation issue. As long as we do not try to deploy the SOA composite, these alerts can be ignored. One way to get rid of all warnings is by adding an Empty activity to all offending scope activities.

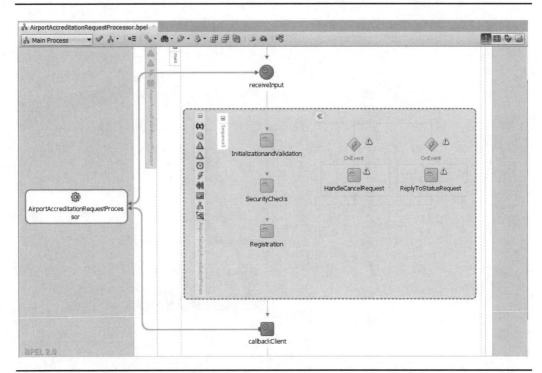

FIGURE 18-1.   *High level BPEL process design for the AirportAccreditationRequest business process*

Detailed Design for Stage Two: Security Checks

Expand the scope for stage security check. We will next create the design shown in Figure 18-3.

Add a flow component with three parallel branches for the *RandomThoroughCheck*, the *NationalSecurityCheck,* and Saibot Airport's *InternalScreening*.

The *RandomThoroughCheck* can be fleshed out with a scope to *DetermineIfDoRandom* followed by an *IfDoRandom* activity with an if-branch containing a scope *DoThoroughBackgroundCheck* and an empty else-branch.

The *NationalSecurityCheck* branch contains a scope *RequestNationalSecurityCheck* followed by an If activity that caters for three outcomes: if OK, elsif N[OT]OK, and else Unclear. In the latter case, a *Discuss* scope is required. After this step, the national security check can be requested again. In other words, the process should be able to loop back at this stage. BPEL does not support anything like *goto*. In order to make the process return to an earlier stage is by enclosing in a loop construct—repeat until, for each, while—the entire section of the process within which such a return step must be supported. In this case, add a *while* activity in the *NationalSecurityCheck* branch and move the scope *RequestNationalSecurityCheck* and the ensuing If activity inside this while loop. Now we can either break out of the loop—for OK and Not OK, or return—for the Unclear case.

The *InternalScreening* branch consists of a scope to *DetermineScreeningIntensity* in which the scrutiny level is set for the current accreditation request. Next follow a Flow activity with two parallel branches. The first one performs automated evaluation of the accreditation request. The

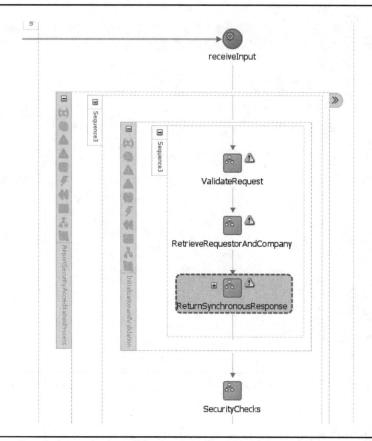

FIGURE 18-2.   *Details for stage one of the business process*

second one has an If activity that checks if automated processing suffices. For when it does not, the else case contains scope *ManualRequestProcessing*.

Detailed Design for Stage Three: Registration

Expand scope *Registration*. Add two Flow activities. The first one has parallel branches *RecordInLDAP*, *RegisterWithPersonnelService,* and *PrepareBadge*. The second Flow activity takes care of communications. It has parallel branches *PublishBusinessEventAboutNewStaffMember*, *NotifyNewStaffMember,* and *NotifyRequestorAndCompany*. The Registration scope should now look like Figure 18-4.

Next Steps

The design of the BPEL process is both a start for the actual implementation and a visual aid to discuss design details with the business analyst. Now that we captured the process in a picture that presents a clear flow, steps—some parallel and some sequential, decision points, and synchronous and asynchronous interactions, we can hopefully confirm the high-level design, uncover additional functional details and start the implementation.

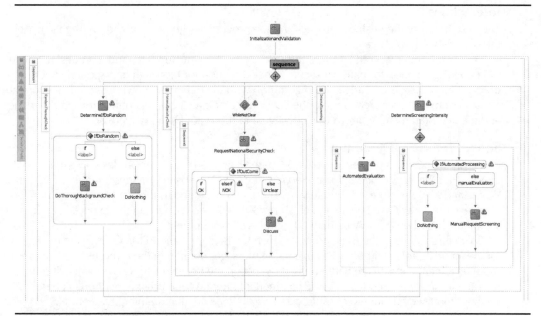

FIGURE 18-3. *Detailed design for stage SecurityChecks*

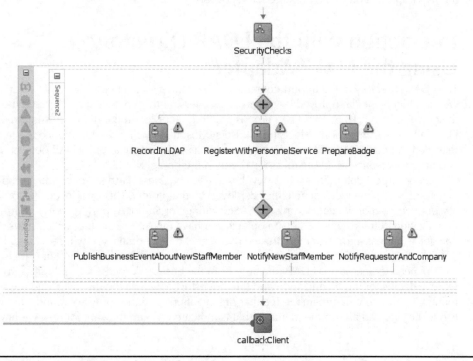

FIGURE 18-4. *Detailed yet abstract design for stage registration*

Interactions

The description of the business process and the process design have provided insights in the interactions we have to cater for.

Incoming: Initial accreditation request, request for a status update, and a request to cancel.

Outgoing: request for national security check, request for thorough background check, and for preparation of a security badge and registration with the personnel service as well as information retrieval from and user creation into the LDAP directory; also emails notifications to the requestor and the new staff member and a business event to the Event Delivery Network.

Service Interface Definition

Based on the business process description, a first stab has been made at designing the service interface for the *AirportAccreditationService*. The book's website provides a reference to the WSDL and XSD resources for this service. These can be added to the SOA composite project.

Next, create a SOAP Service called *AirportAccreditationService* in the Exposed Services swimlane, based on the service defined in the WSDL document.

Wire this service to the BPEL process. Open the BPEL process editor. Change the message type for the *inputVariable* and *outputVariable* to the messages defined in the AirportAccreditationService .wsdl document. Update the partnerLink reference in the Receive and Response activities to refer to the *AirportAccreditationService* partnerLink. Remove the original partnerLink based on the AirportAccreditationRequestProcessor.wsdl. Remove all remaining references to *AirportAccreditationRequestProcessor* in the BPEL process and the composite.xml file.

You can make the BPEL process buildable and deployable by adding Empty activities to all scopes and by specifying the conditions for the If, Elsif, and While conditions. The end result is the *step1* application in the book's code repository.

Interaction with the LDAP Directory Using the LDAP Adapter

The LDAP Directory at the airport contains user accounts for staff employed by Saibot Airport as well as all personnel employed by the many business partners active at and around the airport—as shown in Figure 18-5. These two groups are both recorded in the directory—InternalStaff and ExternalStaff—with person objects for all users. Most users will have a reference to their manager recorded. All business partners are also recorded as organizational unit LDAP objects. The users can have a reference to an organizational unit in their *ou* attribute.

Saibot Airport determines a trust level with each business partner—depending on past experiences and the types of activities deployed by the partner. This trust level is recorded in the attribute *destinationIndicator* using the SASEC rating (for Saibot Airport Security). Both organizationalUnit as well as person objects can have this SASEC setting, which starts at 0 and can get as high as 4 for extremely trusted partners and individuals. We will see how a higher SASEC rating results in a quicker, less intense screening process when new staff is registered.

We need to access this LDAP directory from the business process for multiple purposes: retrieve details for the organization and the requestor as well as the manager, and register the identity for the new staff member. If either organization or requestor is not found—the whole deal is off. The same applies to the manager that is indicated. When they are found—we have the

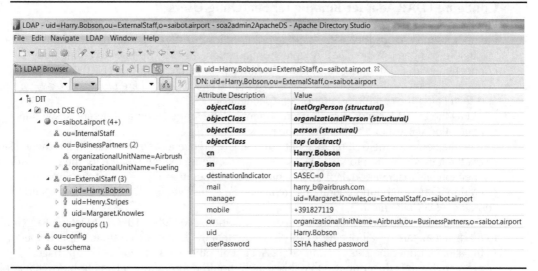

FIGURE 18-5. *Overview of business partners and ExternalStaff members in Saibot Airport's LDAP directory*

SASEC values used by the Business Rule—as well as the email addresses to send notifications to when the new staff member is accepted.

Using a Mediator, the BPEL process will be decoupled from the two LDAP Adapter binding references that take care of the *search* and *add* operations respectively.

Implement Retrieve User from LDAP

The LDAP Adapter is a JCA Adapter, similar to the UMS, JMS, and Database Adapter. It can be used in the inbound direction—triggered by specific changes in an observed LDAP directory—and in the outbound direction to search for LDAP entries, and to create, modify, and delete such entries. The LDAP Adapter supports LDAP v3.0. It can be used against most major LDAP implementations—including OUD (Oracle Universal Directory), OVD (Oracle Virtual Directory), OID (Oracle Internet Directory), Active Directory, and many others. Note that it does not support the Embedded LDAP directory in WebLogic.

Usage of the LDAP Adapter is configured as an adapter binding using an Adapter configuration wizard in JDeveloper. This binding refers to the JNDI name of an adapter connection that is configured in the run time WebLogic domain for the LDAP Adapter deployment—just as is the case with the Database Adapter. This connection describes how to access a particular LDAP directory instance. Details about installing and configuring ApacheDS as LDAP directory—a simple, lightweight, easy to install directory - and of configuring the LDAP Adapter in this run-time environment for accessing that LDAP directory can be found on the book's website. We assume that there will be an LDAP Adapter connection with a JNDI name of eis/ldap/SaibotLdap. We also assume that a top level domain object has been created with its dc and o attributes set to saibot. airport, as shown in Figure 18-5.

Configure LDAP Adapter Binding for Searching Users

Open the SOA composite that contains the BPEL process (you can take the *step1* application in the book's source repository as the starting point, or look at *step2* as final result for this section).

Before you can use the LDAP Adapter configuration wizard, you have to configure a connection to an LDAP directory. On the Resource palette, create a new LDAP Connection, configured as shown in Figure 18-6. Note: Username and password are *uid=admin, ou=system,* and *secret* after the default installation of ApacheDS.

Drag the LDAP Adapter from the component palette to the External References swim lane. The configuration wizard for the adapter appears.

Set the name for the outbound adapter binding reference to *RetrieveUser*. In the second step, select the IDE connection to the LDAP server and configure the JNDI name for the LDAP Adapter connection (eis/ldap/SaibotLdap). In the third page—Operation Type—select the *Search* operation. Other outbound operations are *add*, *delete*, *modify*, *modify DN*, *compare*, and *"execute a DSML Request."*

In step 4, we have to configure the search operation, see Figure 18-7. Set Default Search Base to ou=ExternalStaff, o=saibot.airport. This indicates that the LDAP search should only be performed in the subtree under the *ExternalStaff* node. Accept all other default settings on this page.

In step 5, select the attributes that this search should return. Only select attributes that apply to the object class(es) that the entries implement. Select from object classes *inetOrgPerson, organizationalPerson*. The attributes we require include: *givenName, mail, destinationIndicator*

FIGURE 18-6. *Configuring an LDAP connection to the ApacheDS Directory*

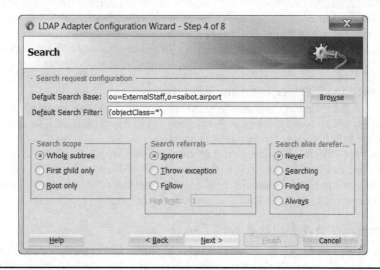

FIGURE 18-7. *Configure the Default Search Base for the LDAP Adapter's search operation*

(that contains the SASEC level), and *ou*. Accept the defaults in steps 6, 7, and 8, press finish to complete the adapter binding configuration.

JDeveloper generates a WSDL and XSD describing the interface that the LDAP adapter presents to the other components in the SOA composite.

Provide Business Process with Proper Search Service

Clearly, a BPEL process that attempts to be as close to a business process as possible should not have to bother itself with LDAP [adapter] specifics, such as *dn* and *cn*. The process wants to just provide a user ID and get the user details returned, including the security level, the email address and the organization unit.

The WSDL file LDAPService.wsdl with its associated schema definition LDAPService.xsd describes a fairly business friendly interface that the BPEL process can interact with. Add a mediator component—*LDAPMediator*—to the SOA composite, to provide the bridge from this interface to the technical service exposed by the LDAP Adapter. Have the mediator implement the LDAPService.wsdl and have it expose as a SOAP service, for easy testing. Wire the mediator to the LDAP adapter binding and select Mediator Operation *getUser* as the one to route.

Double click on the mediator component to bring up the editor. Click on the transformation icon for the request in the routing rule for the *getUser* operation and have a new XSL Map generated to map from *GetUserRequest* to *searchRequest*. Set a text constant to the *baseDN* element and a concatenation for the *searchFilter*, as shown in the next code snippet:

```
    <tns:searchRequest>
      <baseDN>ou=ExternalStaff,o=saibot.airport</baseDN>
      <searchFilter>
        <xsl:value-of select="concat('(&amp;(objectClass=person)(uid=',/
ns0:GetUserRequest/ns0:UserId,'))')"/>
      </searchFilter>
    </tns:searchRequest>
```

Also create an XSL Map to transform the search result to the response message structure described in LDAPService.xsd. Simply map the *value* child element for all *searchResultEntry* children to the corresponding elements in the *GetUserResponse*.

At this moment, you can deploy the SOA composite and verify that you invoke the service exposed by the mediator to retrieve details for one of the users stored in the LDAP directory.

Invoke the LDAPService from the BPEL Process

The first need from the BPEL process for LDAP interaction is to look up details for the requestor. The BPEL process has received the user ID for the requestor. This provides the input to the LDAPService.

Wire the *LDAPMediator* to the BPEL process.

Open the BPEL editor. Open nested scope *RetrieveRequestorAndCompany*. Add an Invoke activity called *RetrieveRequestor*, linked to the *LDAPMediator* partner link. Have local variables created for the input and the output. Add an assign activity to set the input, based on the requestor's user ID in the global *inputVariable*. Let's ignore the response for now.

Implement Add User to LDAP

Adding a user to the LDAP directory is done in a similar fashion, using a second LDAP adapter binding that is subsequently wired to and exposed from the *LDAPMediator* and then linked to from the BPEL process.

Configure the LDAP Adapter Binding for Adding User Entries

Drag the LDAP Adapter once more from the components palette to the External References lane. Set the name to *AddUser*. Configure the connections on the second page in the same way as before. Choose the *Add* operation in step 3.

In step 4, see Figure 18-8, we have to specify the object classes associated with the entry to add. Select *inetOrgPerson*, *organizationalPerson*, and *person*. Also select the following attributes to associated with the new entry: *destinationIndicator*, *employeeNumber*, *givenName*, *mail*, *manager*, *mobile*, *ou*, *title*, *uid*, and *userPassword*.

Accept the default in step five and press Finish in step 6. The adapter binding is generated, as are the WSDL and XSD files that describe the interface of the adapter binding.

Expose AddUser through LDAP Mediator

Wire *LDAPMediator* to the *AddUser* LDAP adapter binding and select the mediator operation *AddUser* as the one to route to, as shown in Figure 18-9.

Open the mediator editor. Generate the XSL Map for transforming the *AddUserRequest* to the input for the *addUser* adapter binding. Most mappings are straightforward; only those LDAP attributes that contain references to other LDAP entries are a little bit more complex—*DN*, *manager*, and *ou*. The salient parts of the XSLT document are in this snippet:

```
    <tns:addRequest>
      <dn>
        <xsl:value-of select="concat ('uid=', /ns0:AddUserRequest/ns0:UserId,
',ou=ExternalStaff,o=saibot.airport ' )"/>
      </dn>
      <requestAttributes>…
        <manager>
          <value>
            <xsl:if test="/ns0:AddUserRequest/ns0:ManagerId != ''">
              <xsl:value-of select="concat ('uid=', /ns0:AddUserRequest/
```

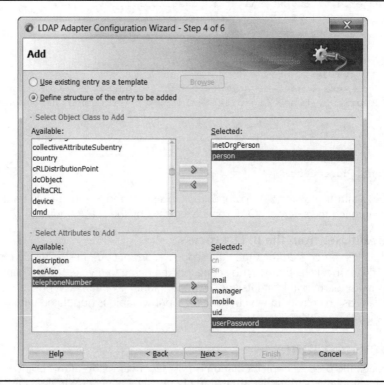

FIGURE 18-8.   *Configuring the attributes to add on the new LDAP entry*

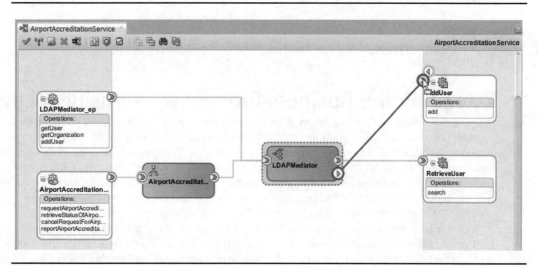

FIGURE 18-9.   *The LDAP Mediator provides operations on the LDAP directory*

```
ns0:ManagerId, ',ou=ExternalStaff,o=saibot.airport ' )"/>
            </xsl:if>
        </value>
      </manager>
      <ou>
        <value>
          <xsl:value-of select="concat('organizationalUnitName=',/
ns0:AddUserRequest/ns0:OrganizationId,',ou=BusinessPartners,o=saibot.
airport')"/>
        </value>
      </ou>
    </requestAttributes>
  </tns:addRequest>
```

You could again deploy the SOA composite at this point and test the newly implemented operation *AddUser* through the external SOAP service exposed by the *LDAPMediator*.

Invoke AddUser from the BPEL Process

Open the BPEL process editor. Open the scope *RecordInLDAP*, nested inside the *Registration* scope. Add an Invoke activity to this scope. Set the name to *InvokeAddUser* and select the *LDAPMediator* partner link and its *addUser* operation. Have a local input variable generated.

Add an Assign activity in which the local input variable is populated with the appropriate data from the global *inputVariable*.

Deploy and Run

Even though the process implementation is nowhere near ready, at this point we do have a deployable implementation that is capable of creating a new entry in the LDAP directory. So deploy it and make a call to the *requestAirportAccreditation* operation. Because we have not yet implemented the synchronous Reply activity, the request will time out. When you inspect the content of the LDAP directory, the new user should have been added. The BPEL process flow trace is shown in Figure 18-10.

NOTE
The implementation at this point can be found in the step2 application in the source code repository.

Extending the Business Process with Business Logic

The scope of this book does not allow us to describe the step by step implementation of the business process. The book's website does provide these details as well as the source code for the implementation. We will start from the *step3* application in the source code repository—which contains global and local variables, the various interactions of the BPEL process (with dummy implementations of external services) as well as the human tasks for discussing unclear outcomes of the national security check and performing the internal manual review by Saibot's security staff.

The SOA composite is shown in Figure 18-11.

We will take a look in this section at the implementation of the process so far.

We will then add a business rule for determining the required scrutiny level for the internal check by Saibot Airport's own security staff. After deployment, we will see how we can dynamically influence this business rule.

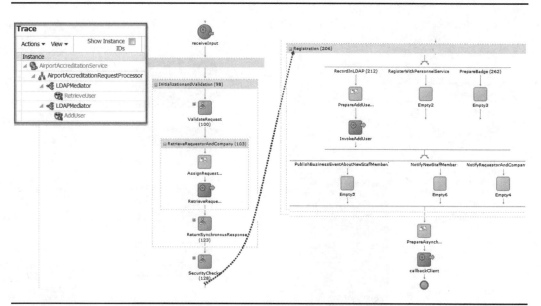

FIGURE 18-10. *The flow in the BPEL process including the two LDAP actions: retrieve and add user*

The Process Implementation So Far

Two global variables have been defined in the BPEL process: one keeps track of the current status—to be used by the event handler for the *retrieveStatus* operation—and one to collect process state produced in various scopes.

No fault handling has been implemented—we assume happy flow all along.

A number of very simplistic service implementations have been added: *ThoroughBackgroundCheck, NationalSecurityCheck, BadgeService,* and *PersonnelService*. Each service is implemented by a BPEL process component that at present does next to nothing. Since our objective is exploring the capabilities of the BPEL process component to implement a substantial business process and our focus is on the *Airport Accreditation* process, it seems justified to have such naïve implementations in the periphery.

Human Tasks

Two Human Tasks have been created—following the steps introduced in Chapter 17. One task is for conducting discussions with the agency that performs the national security check—to handle situations where that check resulted in the outcome *Unclear*. The other task is a little bit more complex—because it contains a four step workflow. The internal security screening at Saibot Airport is performed by a security officer—unless it can be handled automatically. Depending on the scrutiny level, the initial finding of the security officer may have to be reviewed by a peer, a team lead, and a senior security officer. These stages as well as the skip rules have been defined in the *ManualScreening* task.

At present for simplicity's sake, the human tasks do not have generated task forms—so the information available to perform the task consists of almost nothing. The tasks do make use of

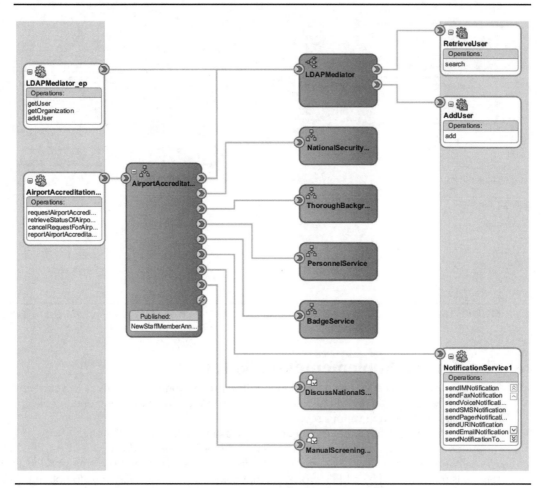

FIGURE 18-11. *The SOA composite AirportAccreditationService after step 3*

actionable emails. Note that these tasks assume the following groups to be present in the identity store—most likely the embedded LDAP directory in the WebLogic domain: *SecurityOfficer, SecurityTeamLead, SeniorSecurityOfficer.*

Publish Event

In the second part of the Registration stage, emails are sent to the requestor and the new staff member. Additionally, an EDN event—*NewStaffMemberAnnouncement*—is published with the salient details about the new staff member. The event is defined in the SecurityEvents.edl file using definitions in the SecurityEvents.xsd schema definition. A BPEL Invoke activity is used to publish the event to the Event Delivery Network (where currently no one is subscribed to it). Figure 18-12 shows how the event is published.

Trace

Instance	Type	Usage
▲ 🛡 AirportAccreditationService	Service	🛡 Service
▲ 🔧 AirportAccreditationRequestProcessor >> ⚡ "NewStaffMemberAnnouncement	BPEL	
▲ ◀ LDAPMediator	Mediator	
🔲 RetrieveUser	Reference	🔲 Reference
◀ LDAPMediator	Mediator	
🔧 NationalSecurityCheckService	BPEL	
🔧 ManualScreeningOfSecurityAccreditationRequest	Workflow	
▲ ◀ LDAPMediator	Mediator	
🔲 AddUser	Reference	🔲 Reference
🔧 PersonnelService	BPEL	
🔧 BadgeService	BPEL	
NotificationService1	Reference	🔲 Reference
NotificationService1	Reference	🔲 Reference

FIGURE 18-12. *Flow trace for running the AirportAccreditationService process as it stands after step 3*

Add Business Rule to Decide on Required Internal Screening Level

A business rule will provide the decision logic for deciding on the scrutiny with which to execute the internal security screening—depending on the SASEC (trust level 0–4) for both the company and the requestor as well as the required security level (0..5) for the new staff member. The rule will produce the scrutiny level to be applied in the internal screening procedure. This level ranges from 0 to a maximum of 4.

Create Business Rule Component InternalSecurityScreeningEvaluation

Open the composite editor and add a business rule component to the composite application. Set the name of the rule to *InternalSecurityScreeningEvaluation*. Specify an input and output fact, based respectively on the elements *decideInternalScreeningLevelInputType* and *decideInternalScreeningLevelOutputType* in the XSD document AirportAccreditationService.xsd.

The business rule editor will open. Facts have already been defined, based on the input and output variables set up for the business rule. Add three value sets: *ScrutinyLevel* (data type *int*, values 0..4), *SASECLevel* (data type *int*, values 0..4), and *SaibotSecurityLevel* (data type *int*, values 0..5). Associate the properties in the input and output fact types with the corresponding value set.

We need to add the decision logic itself—for which a decision table seems well suited. Select the initial Rule Set and set its name to *InternalSecurityEvaluation*. Click on the plus icon for creating a new Decision Table. The decision table editor appears. Set the name to *InternalScrutinyLevelDecisionTable*.

Add three condition rows—for the three properties of the fact *DecideInternalScreeningLevelInputType*. Add as action: modify *DecideInternalScreeningLevelOutputType*, set a parametrized value for property *internalScreeningLevel*.

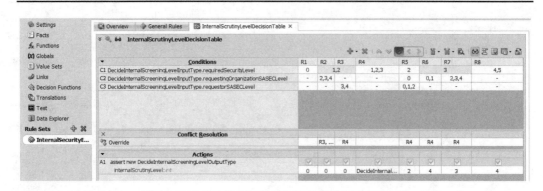

FIGURE 18-13. *Decision Table to decide on the scrutiny level for internal screening based on existing trust levels and the required security level for the new staff member*

At this point, you can define the rules as you see fit: what screening level output is required for which given combination of the existing SASEC trust levels and the requested security level for the new staff member? Use the Gap Analysis to ensure that you have covered all cases.

The result of defining the decision rules could look like Figure 18-13.

Integrate Business Rule into the BPEL Process

Wire the new Business Rule component to the BPEL Process component. Open the BPEL process editor. Add two local variables to scope *DetermineScreeningIntensity*. Their names are *decideInternalScreeningLevelInput* and *decideInternalScreeningLevelOutput* and they are based on the corresponding elements in AirportAccreditationService.xsd. These variables will be the input and output for the business rule. Add Assign activities to set the value for *decideInternalScreeningLevelInput* and to retrieve the value from *decideInternalScreeningLevelOutput* into the existing variable *ScrutinyLevel*.

Drag a business rule component to the scope *DetermineScreeningIntensity* and select Rule Dictionary *InternalSecurityEvaluation*. Define a copy rule for the input fact, taking variable $decideInternalScreeningLevelInput and mapping it to the *DecideInternalScreeningLevelInput* element in the *parameterList* element in variable $dsIn. For the output, map element *DecideInternalScreeningLevelOutput in the resultList of $dsOut* to variable $decideInternalScreeningLevelOutput.

The final result of all steps discussed in this section can be found in the *step4* application in the source code repository. You can deploy the SOA composite in this application and try out a few requests for airport accreditation for new staff members, using varying levels of required security level and/or existing SASEC trust level.

Run Time Adjustment of Decision Logic

As was discussed first in Chapter 11, the SOA Composer (http://host:port/soa/composer) can be used to inspect and modify the logic in business. You may want to try modifying one of the rules in the table, publish these changes and verify the effect of the change by submitting a new accreditation request that will trigger this rule.

Add Correlation and Implement Event Handlers

In order for the requestor to learn about the status of the accreditation request or to cancel the request, we have to configure correlation. The service operations *retrieveStatus* and *cancelRequest* will leverage correlation to make sure that requests end up in the right running instance. These operations are to be implemented in the event handlers.

In this section, we add the correlation definition and the implementation for the *retrieve status* and *cancel request* event handlers

Define Correlation through Properties and Property Aliases

Correlation is based on unique identifiers for the BPEL process. Each request for airport accreditation is assigned a unique identifier, which is returned to the requestor in the *AirportAccreditationRequestIdentifier* element in the synchronous response. Subsequent requests that concern a particular accreditation request and therefore have to be correlated into a specific SOA composite instance have to provide that identifier value.

Configuring Correlation Set and Properties

As we discussed in Chapter 12, correlation is based on a correlation set that consists of one or more properties. The following steps are taken to enable correlation for the current BPEL process, as shown in Figure 18-14. Open the BPEL process editor. From the dropdown menu in the header bar, select option Correlation Sets. Select the child node Correlation Sets under the node *AirportSecurityAccreditationProcess* and click on the plus icon to add a correlation set. Enter *AirportAccreditationRequestSet* as the name for the new set. Add a property called *AirportAccreditationRequestIdentifier* with type String.

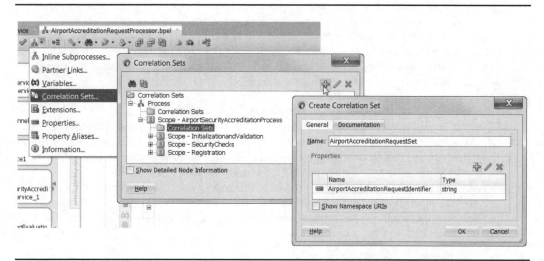

FIGURE 18-14. *Configuring Correlation Set AirportAccreditationRequestSet*

Specify Property Aliases

For each interaction with the BPEL process that triggers or leverages the correlation set, we have to specify how the correlation property's value is mapped to the (in this case response) message. From the dropdown menu in the header bar, select option Property Aliases.

In the Property Aliases editor, create alias for property *AirportAccreditationRequestIdentifier* mapped to the corresponding element in the message elements *RequestForAirportAccreditationResponse*, RetrieveStatusOfAirportAccreditationRequestRequest, CancelRequestForAirportAccreditationRequest.

Define the Initialization of the Correlation Set

The value for the correlation set for a process instance is established once. In the current case, that happens when the initial, synchronous response is returned using the *RequestForAirportAccreditationResponse*. This fact is configured on the Reply activity. Open the editor for this activity. On the Correlations, select correlation set *AirportAccreditationRequestSet* and specify *yes* in the column marked *Initiate*. Close the editor.

Implement the Event Handlers for Asynchronous Request Processing

The scope *AirportSecurityAccreditationProcess* has two event handlers for handling the requests for a status update and a cancellation of the accreditation request. On both event handlers, we have to configure the correlation set to ensure that these requests are routed into the correct process instance—based on the *AirportAccreditationRequestIdentifier*.

Processing a Request for a Status Update

Open the event handler for operation *retrieveStatusOfAirportAccreditationRequest*. Open the Correlations tab. As before, add correlation set *AirportAccreditationRequestSet*. This time, because this request has to be handled in a running process instance, set the value *no* under *Initiate*.

Add a Reply activity to the scope under the event handler. Set its name to *ReplyWithCurrentStatus*. Select the *AirportAccreditationService* partner link and operation *retrieveStatusOfAirportAccreditationRequest* on that partner link. Have a local variable created to provide the input for the status response. Add an Assign activity just before the Reply activity—to set the proper data in this local variable.

Processing a Request to Cancel the Accreditation Request

Open the event handler for operation *cancelAirportAccreditationRequest*. Open the Correlations tab. As before, add correlation set *AirportAccreditationRequestSet*. This time, because this request has to be handled in a running process instance, set the value *no* under *Initiate*.

Add a Reply activity to the scope under the event handler. Set its name to *ReplyWithCurrentStatus*. Select the *AirportAccreditationService* partner link and operation *retrieveStatusOfAirportAccreditationRequest* on that partner link. Have a local variable created to provide the input for the status response. Add an Assign activity just before the Reply activity—to set the proper data in this local variable.

Reorganize the Initialization Stage

The correlation set is initialized in the synchronous Reply activity *ReturnSynchronousResponse*. Currently, that activity is part of the scope (*AirportSecurityAccreditationProcess*) on which the event handlers are defined. That will cause a problem at run time: when a scope commences that has event handlers that rely on a correlation set, that set needs to have been initialized prior to the start of that scope. Therefore we need to move the synchronous reply out of scope *AirportSecurityAccreditationProcess*—to have the correlation set initialized before that scope is entered.

Add a new scope *SynchronousInitialization* to the process, before scope *AirportSecurityAccreditationProcess*. Move scopes *ValidateRequest*, *RetrieveRequestorAndCompany*, and *ReturnSynchronousResponse* from the latter to the former. Also move the definitions of variables *globalProcessStatus* and *globalProcessState* from the *AirportSecurityAccreditationProcess* scope to the main process definition.

Deploy and Try Out

After making the changes described in this section, the implementation of the SOA composite is similar to what can be found in the *step5* application in the source code repository. You can deploy the SOA composite in this application and try to retrieve the status for a few requests for airport accreditation. Subsequently you can try to cancel your requests. When you wait with cancelling the request until the badge is being prepared, you will find that despite your cancellation of the request, the user will already have been added to the LDAP directory.

Compensation, discussed in the next section, is what we typically implement in BPEL processes—especially when they are complex and/or longer running—to have the process itself undo its results when it is cancelled.

Fault Handling and Compensation

Although, of course, we would like to think that everything in our BPEL processes always happens according to our plan for a happy flow, in actual practice that is unlikely to happen. Several types of faults and exceptions are bound to occur and should be catered to. Sometimes we can recover from exceptions—by retrying an operation after a little waiting time or through an alternative execution path. However, some exceptions we have to accept as irrecoverable. And sometimes exceptions are used as a deliberate shortcut to quickly complete processing of the process—so we do not even want to recover from them.

For a process instance that runs into an irrecoverable exception, we may need to roll back some of the work that was already done by the process before it failed with the exception. In BPEL terminology that is called compensation.

This section goes beyond the initial discussion of faults and fault handling in Chapter 8. It discusses some types of faults and exception handling—dealing with the nonhappy flow—and also introduces compensation as a mechanism in BPEL to undo the logical effects of steps in the process that should be rolled back because of the abortion of the logical transaction.

The implementation after implementing the steps described in this section can be found in the *step 6* application in the source code repository.

Exceptions and Fault Handling

We can discern a number of exception categories—from fairly technical to more functional and business process-oriented. At a rather technical level, we have to prepare for the unavailability of infrastructure components or other technical problems with services invoked from the BPEL process.

The external references may also return (predefined) business exceptions in response to the calls from our process, in the form of SOAP faults as specified in the WSDL for the service. Business exceptions are normal situations in business processes, ranging from "the product in the order is sold out" and "credit card payment is not validated by the card issuer" to "no slots are available anymore on Christmas Day."

Between these categories is the type of fault that is returned due to validation errors ("the XML request message does not comply with the XSD definition") and security issues ("the authentication failed" and "you are not authorized to invoke this service"). Our BPEL process can also cause faults because of programming errors (e.g., by performing erroneous XPath operations).

Finally, the last category of exceptions is the type of exception we willingly throw to cause the current scope to be immediately terminated—almost a programmer's trick for want of a break activity in BPEL.

If one of the exceptions described previously occurs in a BPEL process—and we do not catch it—the process instance ends up in a faulted state. If the instance is synchronously invoked by a partner, the partner will receive a SOAP fault as a reply. If the instance is part of an asynchronous conversation, its invoker will continue to wait for the response message because there won't be one.

In Chapter 8, we have already worked with faults and exception handling in a BPEL process. We will reiterate a little of what was discussed there and then advance from there. Let's see how we catch faults in a BPEL process—to prevent faults from causing a process to fault out.

Catching Faults

The main process activity, as well as every scope in a BPEL process, can have a faultHandler associated with it that contains one or more Catch activities that can each handle a specific type of fault (or all faults) when it occurs in the scope they are defined against—or in one of that scope's descendants or nested scopes. Each fault type in a BPEL process is identified through its name. Catch activities specify the fault type they want to catch through that name. Here's an example of a Catch for the standard fault *selectionFailure*, which is thrown, for example, when an XPath expression has returned an empty result:

```
<faultHandlers>
   <catch faultName="bpws:selectionFailure">
     <sequence>
       <empty name="HandleSelectionFailure_gracefully"/>
       <terminate name="Terminate_process_isNOTgraceful"/>
     </sequence>
   </catch>
</faultHandlers>
```

The BPEL 2.0 standard specifies 20 standard faults, all in the same namespace: ambiguousReceive, completionConditionFailure, conflictingReceive, conflictingRequest, orrelationViolation, invalidBranchCondition, invalidExpressionValue, invalidVariables, joinFailure, ismatchedAssignmentFailure, missingReply, missingRequest, scopeInitializationFailure, selectionFailure, ubLanguageExecutionFault, uninitializedPartnerRole, uninitializedVariable, unsupportedReference, xsltInvalidSource, xsltStylesheetNotFound.

All these faults are typeless, meaning they don't have associated messageTypes. Therefore, a Catch activity for one of these faults should not specify a fault variable.

Other faults have data associated with them—for example, the run-time faults thrown by the BPEL run-time engine as the result of problems with the running of the BPEL service component or the web services it invokes. A number of such run-time faults are predefined: bindingFault, remoteFault, and replayFault. These faults are included in the http://schemas.oracle.com/bpel/ extension namespace. They are associated with the messageType RuntimeFaultMessage, which contains three parts—each of type string—called code, summary, and detail, respectively.

A Catch activity for a fault that has associated data can specify a faultVariable that will be initialized with the fault's data when the Catch is activated. In addition to fault-specific Catch elements, we can make use of the catchAll. When no fault-specific Catch is around to take care of the current fault, this all-purpose safety net steps in to handle it. We find out the name of the fault our catchAll is dealing with using the Oracle BPEL-specific XPath function bpelx:getFaultAsString(), which we can use, for example, to assign the name of the fault to a local variable.

NOTE
If a scope does not have an explicit catchAll fault handler, it still has an implicit catchAll that the BPEL engine will execute. In this implicit handler, it performs compensation—if compensation handlers have been defined—for any scopes in the parent of the failed scope that have already been executed at the time of the exception. When this has been done, the fault is rethrown, to be caught at the next embedding scope level, by either an explicit fault handler or a similar implicit one.

So far we have discussed faults that originate in our external partners or in the BPEL run-time engine. There is another category of faults: The faults defined in our own process and thrown in our own logic. These faults are used to control the flow in the BPEL process. By throwing a fault, we interrupt the execution of a scope and hand control to a fault handler for that type of fault. Thus, we can make out-of-line jumps across the process that can be very useful. So in reality, it is more of a control (or flow) type of activity than an exception in the meaning we discussed before.

We use the BPEL Throw activity to instantiate a fault of a specific type. The type of the fault thrown does not need to be predefined in the WSDL or BPEL process—we can just throw any fault (name) we like. We can associate data with the fault by specifying the faultVariable attribute. Here is an example of throwing a fault when the requesting company in an airport accreditation request could not be found:

```
<scope name="RetrieveRequestorAndCompany">
    <variables>
     ...
        <variable name="faultVariable" messageType="ns1:requestForAirportAccredi
tationFaultMessage"/>
     ...
    <sequence name="Sequence4">
     ...
    <if name="IfCompanyNotFound">
      <condition>string-length($RetrieveCompany_getOrganization_OutputVariable.
part1/ns2:OrganizationUnit)
=0</condition>
      <sequence name="Sequence17">
```

```
        <assign name="SetFaultVariable">
          <copy>
            <from>concat("Company could not be found ",$inputVariable.part1/
ns1:RequestingOrganizationId)</from>
            <to>$faultVariable.part1/ns1:FaultDescription</to>
          </copy>
          ... more copy rules omitted
          <throw name="ThrowRequestingOrganizationNotFound"
                 faultName="ns12:requestingOrganizationNotFound"
faultVariable="faultVariable"/>
</sequence>
<else>
    ...
```

The variable used as the fault variable—faultVariable in this case—needs to have been defined earlier in the scope or on some higher level. It needs to be based on a message type—not a simple or complex XML element—in one of the WSDL documents associated with the application.

Faults that are thrown like this can be caught by higher-level faultHandlers. In this example, the *ThrowRequestingOrganizationNotFound* fault is thrown inside the *RetrieveRequestorAndCompany* scope and it is handled by a Catch action at the parent of the parent of this scope (scope *SynchronousInitialization*):

```
<scope name="SynchronousInitialization">
    <variables>
        <variable name="ReplyFault_requestAirportAccreditation_OutputVariable"
              messageType="ns1:requestForAirportAccreditationResponseMessage"/>
    </variables>
    <faultHandlers>
      <catch bpelx:name="handleOrganizationNotFound"
          faultName="ns12:requestingOrganizationNotFound"
          faultVariable="organizationNotFoundVariable"
          faultMessageType="ns1:requestForAirportAccreditationFaultMessage">
        <sequence name="Sequence19">
          <reply name="ReplyFault"
                      faultName="ns1:invalidAccreditationRequest"

                 variable="organizationNotFoundVariable"
                 partnerLink="AirportAccreditationService" portType="ns1:Ai
rportAccreditationService"
                 operation="requestAirportAccreditation"/>
          <exit name="TerminateProcessDueToUnknownRequestingOrganization"/>
        </sequence>
    </catch>
    ... other fault handlers
    </faultHandlers>
```

When we invoke the accreditation service and feed unknown organization data in, the *requestingOrganizationNotFound* fault will be thrown and handled by the handler shown overhead.

Sometimes we can recover from the faults—by retrying an operation after a little waiting time or through an alternative execution path. However, some exceptions we have to accept as irrecoverable. The best we can do for such faults is ensure that we provide relevant information to the stakeholders. That ranges from instructions to administrators on how to deal with the failed process to feedback to the service consumer. The latter can take place through a normal response message that somehow conveys the outcome (or lack thereof) of the service or through SOAP Faults as specified in the WSDL. The latter is done in one of two ways, depending on whether the BPEL process was invoked synchronously or asynchronously. In the synchronous case, the fault is returned via the Reply activity, as is shown in the preceding snippet.

In the case of an asynchronous conversation, the BPEL process sends a response to the consumer by calling an operation on the callback portType. If the process wants to communicate about faults with asynchronous consumers, it should specify the callback portType to include an operation that deals with such messages. Note that others ways to communicate a fault in a service is through a notification—an email or chat message to a human operator or an event on the Event Delivery Network.

SOA Suite Fault Management Framework

Outside BPEL processes and SOA composite applications, at the level of the Fusion Middleware Control, we can use the Fault Management Framework to also catch faults that occurred in BPEL processes or other service components. This framework—introduced in Chapter 5 in conjunction with the Mediator—allows us to define fault policy bindings that prescribe automatic actions to be taken when a certain fault occurs. Such automated actions include retrying the faulted operation, executing Java logic that may provide an alternative workaround, and engaging a human administrator to handle the exception. The EM Fusion Middleware Control provides insight into all exceptions and allows the administrator to recover from recoverable faults.

Compensation for Faults

There are many steps in the business process for airport accreditation at which the conclusion can be reached that the request will be denied—or cancelled. At that point, all activities in the process can and should be aborted as there is no point in continuing them; throwing an exception is typically a quick way to escape from the normal flow and escalate the inability to continue to a higher (scope) level.

It might then be the case that activities have already been performed that should be undone. If, for example, the request to prepare a badge has already resulted in the creation of that badge when a negative outcome from the thorough background check is received, then the earlier creation of the badge should be rolled back or, as is the formal BPEL terminology, be compensated.

We will discuss in this section how we can define *compensation handlers* for BPEL scopes. These handlers contain snippets of BPEL logic that when executed provide the logical compensation for what the execution of the scope has already resulted in.

Introducing Compensation in BPEL

Through a compensation handler that we create for a certain scope, we program the logic that should be executed to undo the side effects produced by that scope. For every scope that makes changes, calls services, and causes transactions to occur, we should consider implementing such a compensation handler that undoes those changes or at least takes the appropriate action. Note that an appropriate action to execute when a scope needs to be compensated could consist of sending an email to an administrator instructing her to make certain manual service calls or even database changes in those cases where the services that were called do not expose a compensate or rollback operation.

It is important to realize that a compensation handler is only ever executed for a scope that has been completed successfully. Compensation handlers are executed automatically for scopes that have been completed successfully and are nested in a parent scope that contains another nested scope that caused the compensation itself (e.g., when an exception is thrown). Scopes that already have completed may have committed transactions themselves or invoked services that completed transactions. Compensating for those local or remote transactions is not a simple technical rollback but usually a functional challenge that requires from external services that they publish compensation operations (unhire car, destroy badge, remove freshly created LDAP entry, and so on).

We can also explicitly invoke compensation handlers through the *compensateScope* activity, which we can execute for a specific scope from a *faultHandler* or *compensationHandler* on the parent scope.

Implementing Compensation for Faults in the Airport Accreditation Process

In the case of the *AirportAccreditationService*, we want to compensate for the registration with the *PersonnelService*, the LDAP registration and the badge creation when the random but thorough background check returns with a rejection of the accreditation request. The negative actions that need to be performed for the compensation are defined in the compensation handlers for the scopes that perform the positive actions.

As an example, let's focus on compensating the creation of the user account in the LDAP directory. The compensating action here is clearly the removal of the user from the directory. Therefore, a new LDAP adapter binding is required to delete an entry.

The WSDL for the *LDAPService* and its associated XSD are extended to cater for the operation remove user. The *LDAPMediator* is wired to the new LDAP Adapter binding. The routing rule is configured and the XSL Map created.

A compensation handler has to be defined on the scope that encloses the activities to compensate. In the BPEL process, locate the Parallel Flow *Registration*. Add a scope *ScopeRecordInLDAP* inside the sequence *RecordInLDAP*. Add the activities in the sequence— assign and invoke (the *LDAPService* that adds a user account)—to the scope, so they can be compensated for.

Add a compensation handler to this scope. In this compensation handler, add an Invoke activity to the *removeUser* operation on the partnerLink for the *LDAPMediator*. Have a local variable created for the input to *removeUser*. Add an Assign activity that sets the user id in this input variable. Figure 18-15 shows the scope and its compensation handler.

In order to demonstrate that a fault in one scope will trigger the compensation of the other, successfully completed sibling scopes under the same parent, locate the scope *PrepareBadge* and add a *throw* activity under the *receive* of the (asynchronous) reply from batch service. Have this activity throw a user defined fault. Deploy the SOA composite and make a request for accreditation. Initially, the new user account will be added to the LDAP Directory. However, once the fault is thrown after the *BadgeService* has done its work, through compensation, this user account is removed again.

Figure 18-15 shows how the fault in scope *PrepareBadge* triggered the implicit *CatchAll* with automatic compensation for all successfully completed sibling scopes. The compensation handler for scope *RecordInLDAP* invokes the *removeUser* operation on the *LDAPMediator* to remove the user account that the scope had previously successfully added.

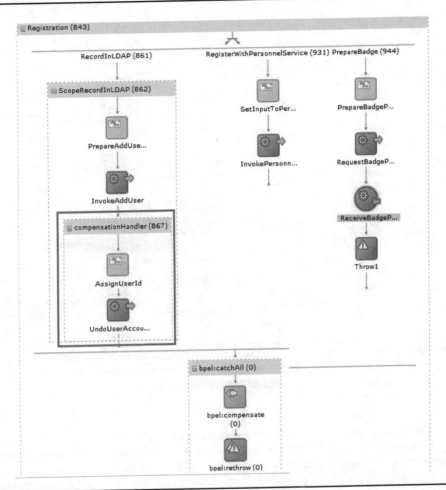

FIGURE 18-15. *BPEL flow trace of a fault thrown after activity ReceiveBadgePreparationResponse causing the implicit catchAll to be executed that does compensation for all sibling scopes that have already were complete—in this case executing the compensationHandler for ScopeRecordInLDAP*

Explicit Compensation

When the *Airport Accreditation* process is cancelled, any steps already performed should be compensated. Compensation for a scope can only be explicitly invoked from a fault handler on the parent scope. So in order to compensate any scopes already completed inside the scope *AirportSecurityAccreditationProcess* on which the cancel request event handler is defined, we need a fault handler on that scope that is triggered by the fault *ExitProcess*, that will be thrown in the event handler for the *cancel request* operation. Add the *compensateScope* activity to the fault handler, targeted at scope *Registration,* see Figure 18-16.

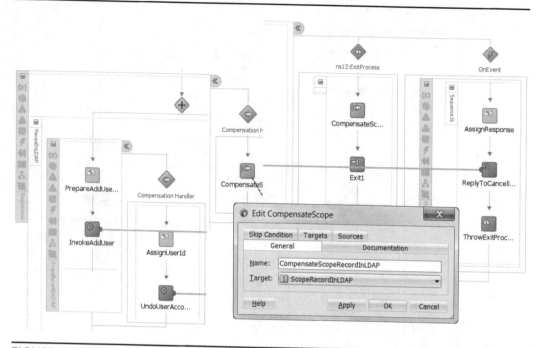

FIGURE 18-16. *Compensation Handler on ScopeRecordInLDAP to remove the user that is added in the scope, Compensation Handler on parent scope Registration and explicit compensateScope in fault handler at next level parent scope*

Add a compensation handler to scope *Registration* that explicitly performs *compensateScope* for the scope *RecordInLDAP*. This is necessary because the explicit *compensateScope* does not automatically traverse to *compensationHandlers* in child scopes.

When now the *cancel* operation is invoked when the process is still somewhere in scope *AirportSecurityAccreditationProcess* and after it has completed scope *Registration*, then the compensation mechanism will take care of compensating the creation of the user in the LDAP: the *eventHandler* for the cancel operation throws the fault; the fault handler catches the fault and executes *compensateScope* on scope Registration. The compensation handler on this scope subsequently performs *compensateScope* on scope *RecordInLDAP* which invokes the *LDAPMediator* to remove the user that was added from the LDAP. Figure 18-17 provides insight in this chain of events.

NOTE

A compensateScope activity will only execute the compensation handler for the scope it explicitly targets. The compensation handlers for the nested scopes are not automatically called as well—these should be called by the compensation handler in the parent scope.

Oracle SOA Suite 12c Handbook

The previous chapter showed the implementation of a very mildly complex business process using a BPEL process component. We have seen how a business process or workflow typically consists of a combination of human activities and automated service calls that make IT systems perform some work to accomplish a business goal. These actions are wired together in a flow with additional logic, including decision points, loops, and parallel paths. BPEL supports these business process implementations—although it sometimes feels like a somewhat rigid, technical tool for implementing the process.

In this chapter, we will meet two new components—BPMN process and case management. The first runs highly structured business processes designed using the Business Process Modeling Notation (BPMN). The second is used for creating more flexible, dynamically adjustable case-based business processes.

BPMN is an industry standard for modeling and visualizing business processes. Its original focus was not so much the execution of business processes but purely the ability to describe these processes in a clear, unequivocal notation. The initial users of BPMN, therefore, were business analysts who wanted to visualize and communicate the business processes as they took place. They then also started to refine and redesign these processes using BPMN.

Many tools became available that supported the visual editing and publication of BPMN process models. Some advanced tools then also introduced process simulation, and at some point the first BPMN run-time engines appeared on the stage. These engines are very similar to BPEL engines, in that they take the process blueprint and create concrete process instances based on the blueprint. Oracle provides one such BPM(N) engine, and SOA composite applications can incorporate BPMN components run by that engine—which turns out to be the same engine on the inside that runs the BPEL process components in the SOA Suite. We will see in this chapter how we can embed BPMN components in composite applications—and how such BPMN components can call out to services, possibly exposed by other composite applications. We do this by reimplementing the *AirportAccreditationService* from the previous chapter as a BPMN-based process rather than a BPEL process.

...ine comes with a special run-time editor called the Process Composer ...used for run-time editing of business ...

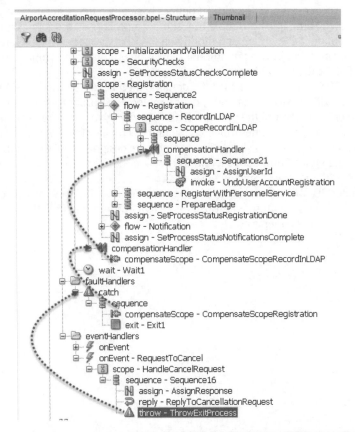

FIGURE 18-17. *The flow triggered by the ExitProcess exception in the event handler, the explicit compensateScope activities to the compensationHandler that undoes the user creation*

Summary

BPEL is used for the implementation of a wide range of service oriented components. Originally positioned as the Business Process executor, it is used for fairly short lived web services coordination at one end and long running process orchestrations at the other. Both extremes consist of activities—human and automated—executed as service invocations, both include flow logic, loops, exception handling, and state manipulation. There is not a clear demarcation between the definitions of composites services and business processes. In this chapter, we have discussed a business process that can be fairly long running, involves many different activities— both automated services and human tasks—and is partly driven by externalized business logic. It should be clear that implementing business processes with BPEL is very well possible.

At the same time, BPEL is a fairly technical tool that has some shortcomings when it comes to designing and implementing business processes. When it comes to communicating with business analysts or even end users, BPEL is not a perfect communication vehicle. The language for designing the process is a little rigid—it defines basically a tree structure that flows in a single direction (downward). It is not simple to just draw a process—abstract design—and test run it or even just simulate it. Designing and modifying the BPEL process is a developer's job—performed in JDeveloper and requiring a fair amount of technical skills, for example around web services and regarding XML manipulation.

Chapter 20 will introduce the BPMN component that can be used in SOA composite applications. With BPMN we can design and implement a process orchestration that aligns closer to the business definition of the process. It also provides some features—such as flexible loop-backs, the notion of swim lanes (roles) in the process design, four-eyes and same-actor task allocation patterns as well as simulation of a process design. The design of the BPMN based process can be created and published in the browser based Process Composer tool. Note that this component requires a BPM Suite license.

In Chapter 20, we will look at collecting analytics from business processes—both BPEL and BPMN—and visualizing those with Business Activity Monitoring (BAM) to provide operational insight to the business operators.

606

CHAPTER

- An organization's interactions with a potential new employee
- A court case—from initial filing of a suit until the final ruling and perhaps the appeal as well
- A repair job on a car
- A security background check on an airport employee

ACM acknowledges the fact that even though all instances of a certain case type are similar, they can also be very different. Not just in the content of the case but also in the way it is executed. Depending on the situation, certain steps that are usually executed are sometimes by-passed or the order in which steps are executed is very different from the normal pattern—if there even is such a thing as the normal pattern. Instead of defining upfront for all instances of the process or case how it is to be executed, ACM takes the agile view of the world and embraces change and variation—without giving up all semblance of organization and coordination.

ACM still provides structure. A number of elements that (potentially) play a role in a (type of) case are defined at design time. These elements are used by the ACM engine to guide stakeholders at run time and to ensure that nonoptional steps are taken and mandatory rules are followed. Even though many aspects of a case can be flexible and determined to a large degree by case workers and the contents of a case, that does not mean that freedom rules supremely and no conditions apply at all.

In this chapter, we will design and implement a simple case that should be started for new staff at the airport in the highest security category. Senior security officers will coordinate the case—instead of a process orchestration engine.

For structured business processes that closely follow protocols or where variations are known at design time and driven by business rules, where straight through processing is the norm and human intervention the exception, BPMN is the way to go. When there is much variation between various situations and expert knowledge and human decision making plays a large role in deciding how to execute each instance, ACM is probably the appropriate approach.

NOTE
This chapter can only scratch the surface when it comes to the rich, complex BPMN process components and Adaptive Case Management components and how to use them for designing and implementing applications.

Business Process Management

Business Process Management (BPM) is concerned with the management (design, improvement, execution, simulation, and so on) of *business* processes in an organization. It is a holistic approach to aligning all aspects of an organization with the ultimate business objectives and the needs of whoever the customers are. It promotes agility, flexibility, and innovation, and attempts to integrate business and (information) technology in order to achieve these goals. It is important to note that not everything within an organization can be modeled as structured processes: Ad hoc questions by users, for example, can be modeled in processes but are usually not part of business process design. Also, out-of-the-ordinary events such as earthquakes are dealt with by an organization even though they are most likely not modeled as business processes.

BPM focuses on business processes—defined as a series of value-added automated or human activities that together achieve a business objective and that may involve participants across the entire organization and outside of it. The adoption of BPM in an organization mandates the use of a modeling technique such as BPMN for analyzing and improving business processes as well as possibly the utilization of a BPM run-time engine to automate and monitor the execution of these processes. Note that BPM and SOA are very complementary because automated processes often use services to have activities performed!

The BPM cycle consists of the following stages:

Business process analysis   In this phase, we identify business processes, capture and analyze existing processes, and/or design new ones. It is an activity that is usually executed by business analysts. Once the business processes have been modeled, they can be analyzed and simulated (e.g., using what-if scenarios) to optimize them for reduced risk, duration and cost, and for increased flexibility.

Business process execution   The processes that are modeled are abstract and need to be translated into concrete processes that can be deployed and run.

Business process monitoring   The processes need to be monitored. When problems occur, we can rectify them by assigning tasks to other people, rerouting actions to other locations, and so on.

Business process optimization   After some time we evaluate the process. We can use historical data about the process to see what bottlenecks exist, what activity is the most time consuming, and so on. This is input for the next step: optimizing the process. Optimizing the process starts the cycle again, beginning with business process analysis.

BPM from an Architectural Point of View

There are different types of processes, with each their preferred way of designing and implementing. Note that many real life business processes are a combination of these types.

One category is formed by human-centric processes, where most of the work is done by humans, the process is very strict and well-defined, and the most important challenge is to assign workload evenly and to monitor and control the progress of tasks. This is what is traditionally known as *workflow*.

Another category is document-centric processes. These are very dynamic processes that evolve around documents, such as contracts or a press release for a website. Typically you will see this embedded in document management and content management systems. There will be processes for scanning, editing, approving, and publishing the documents.

The third category is called rule-centric processes. A rule-centric process is one that has many alternative paths, depending on existing business rules and on decisions made by the human expert. This is what we call adaptive case management. Every case has multiple possible outcomes, depending on the case data. Rules engines and decision services are often appropriate for this type of process.

The final category of processes is system-centric processes. This is what is traditionally called *orchestration*. One of the biggest improvements in system-centric processes in recent years has been the shift from deferred batch processing to straight-through processing of every single item as soon as it materializes.

Note that in reality processes are typically a mix of these categories.

Apart from having different types of processes, we can discern different levels of process design. The highest level (of abstraction), describes the value-added chains that may string several business processes together. The second level contains the end-to-end processes. The third (and lowest) level is the one that is relevant for developers and end users: This is the process that will actually be implemented and executed. It contains implementation details about the types of activities (automated, human step, and so on), and describes in detail the flow logic with loops and parallel flows that can be left out of the model at the second level.

Design Guidelines

As with SOA, certain principles apply when you design and execute processes:

Processes should have the right level of abstraction. When defining the automated steps in business processes, we do not define the applications that execute those steps, but just the service interfaces that provide the required functionality. In short, we orchestrate autonomous services instead of IT systems. This also holds for human interaction: We define the task definition, not the actual implementation. The implementation of those services is outside the scope of BPM. This makes it easier to separate technical changes from changes in the process or the business logic.

Scope of processes (designs) should be aligned with business objectives, business value, responsibilities: the scope of processes or the question where one stand-alone process ends and the next begins—can be a matter of debate.

Decoupling processes should ensure flexibility and reduce change impact. Interactions between processes should be carefully designed; for example, when one process is typically executed in response to a specific step in another process, but this other process does not have a responsibility or interest for making that happen, events are the preferred way of facilitating this chain, instead of a direct process call.

Processes should not be too generic (but also not too specific). Designing business services is different from designing a process. In processes we are looking for efficiency and possibilities for improvement—goals that are at odds with generic, all-purpose designs that have reuse as an important goal.

In addition to many other aspects of process design that deserve mentioning, there is one that I would like to highlight as it is so frequently overlooked: *Parallel execution flows should be used whenever possible.* One of the ways to speed up a process is to have activities not wait for unrelated events. For example, if we need the outcome of the National Security Check, we do that in parallel to the internal screening process.

Tools to Facilitate BPM Efforts

Oracle BPM Suite 12c and Oracle SOA Suite 12c offer several options for BPM. To design processes, you can use either browser-based Process Composer or JDeveloper.

Process Composer is less technical and provides support for some aspects of business architecture and abstract business process design. The Process Composer supports several diagram types to model processes and other Enterprise Architecture (EA) artifacts. The first type is the value-added chain. This diagram specifies the functions in a company that directly influence the real added value of the company. Others include Key Performance Indicators and Key Risk Indicators and of course Business Process Modeling Notation (BPMN).

BPMN is based on flow charting for Business Process Modeling. BPMN became an OMG final adopted standard in February 2006. The 2.0 release of the BPMN standard was published in early 2011. The specification defines the notation and semantics of a so-called business process diagram (BPD)—a standardized, cross-industry way of visualizing business processes in a structured manner. A BPD consists of flow objects, connecting objects, swimlanes, and artifacts. Business processes can be designed in BPMN using many different tools. These tools usually have some capability to publish the models as webpages on an organization's intranet, making the process visualizations available to all employees.

After we design the process, we want to actually execute it. This means that the business analyst is done and a developer comes in to enrich the process definition with data to make it executable. Unlike other modeling approaches, such as Visio or brown paper, the BPMN processes can also run on a server, and in such cases will never be out of sync with the living code (because they are living code). Note: During modeling and before redeployment there is a (temporary) gap between the design time and run-time representation of the process.

A BPMN process is created as a component inside a SOA composite application and is deployed and executed as part of the application, in the same way BPEL processes as well as Human Task and Business Rule components are. Note, however, that the license for SOA Suite does not cover the BPMN Studio, Process Composer, and the run-time engine. You will need the additional BPM Suite license to be able to design, simulate, and run BPMN process components.

Introducing BPMN Service Components

Business processes described through BPMN are workflows that combine human operations, business rules, and service invocations. The focus is often somewhat more on the business process and the human activities in comparison to BPEL, which plays a slightly more technical role and has its primary focus on service orchestration, with the task service and the human actors providing just another service. BPMN can be very system oriented as well—although at a slightly higher, more abstract level than BPEL.

BPMN can be used by both technical staff and business users, and is well suited to bringing these parties together. One of the main reasons for using BPMN in addition to or even instead of BPEL processes is exactly this fact—that business analysts and even end users can typically understand, help maintain, or even own definitions of business processes, as opposed to BPEL, which is not intuitively readable for business users.

Comparing BPMN and BPEL

BPMN is in several areas more intuitive and process oriented than BPEL—which is a rather technical language for service orchestration and composition. Creation of conditional flows and transitions, and even loops and iterations, for example, is quite straightforward in a BPMN process and requires no understanding of technical constructs or XML manipulation. In BPMN, we can easily go back to earlier process activities.

BPMN—quite unlike BPEL—makes use of "swimlanes" that represent organizational units or business roles or IT systems that execute activities. Activities are assigned to a swimlane. This provides clear insight into the responsibilities for and contributions from each part of the organization to a business process. Additionally, the organization's hierarchy can be defined along with calendars that specify per organization unit or role the working hours, normal business days, and special holiday rules. Oracle BPM processes can have inclusive and parallel complex gateways enabling early release and aborting pending flows within the parallel or inclusive gateway structure.

Manipulation of data objects included in the business process (instance) is largely done through data associations that define how data is passed to and from script tasks, business rules, human tasks, external services, and external processes. These associations use data objects and expressions that are similar to but more (business) user friendly than the XSD elements and the XPath expressions used in BPEL processes. For extensive data conversions, BPMN processes can use XSL(T) transformations as well—although leveraging helper components such as BPEL or Mediator may be the better option.

BPMN processes integrate with human tasks to provide the implementation of human activities in the same way BPEL processes do. Integration of business rules is straightforward to perform calculations on behalf of a business process or execute logic that returns the values that determine which conditional flows are to be executed. Calls to other services as well as to other business processes are easily included as well.

A BPMN process can also contain manual tasks. These represent activities that are part of the business process but are not managed by the BPMN service engine. They are included to provide a complete overview of the business process but are otherwise ignored. Note that these manual tasks are not the same as human tasks—although also executed by humans, those are still under the control of the SOA Suite's Human Workflow service engine. BPEL processes would have to use the Empty activity to approximate this concept of a manual task.

BPMN processes can broadcast signals and can be initiated by the reception of signals, similar to BPEL processes. Some of these signals correspond to events on the SOA Suite Event Delivery Network. This provides a second, more decoupled interaction mechanism between BPMN processes and other service components and composite applications—in addition to direct service calls. BPMN has an easy-to-leverage correlation mechanism that acts between BPMN process instances.

A BPMN process can expose a web service interface that can be invoked to initiate a new instance. Reception of a signal (which equals an EDN event) can also initiate a new instance, as can a timer event. The latter can cause an instance to be started at a specific date and time or on a specific interval. BPEL does not have a timer-based initiation mechanism—although using ESS (Chapter 14) it can be emulated.

Both Process Composer and BPM Studio—the JDeveloper extension for BPMN—have support for simulation of business processes. Through the simulations, analysts can examine what-if scenarios for a business process and achieve process optimization based on the results. BPEL does not offer anything like this. Additionally, Process Composer has a feature called Player. With the Player, trial runs can be made for a process—long before its implementation is complete. The Player demonstrates the flow through the process, allows the process designer to determine the outcomes of the service calls in process as well as for human tasks.

BPMN processes can collect metrics during execution that can be collected and monitored using process analytics. These metrics can be tracked in the BPM Business Process Workspace application and Oracle BAM (see Chapter 20 for more details).

Running BPM process instances can be manipulated with the Alter Flow feature. With Alter Flow, the process token—the indicator of the current stage(s) in the process instance—can be moved (so activities can be skipped or executed again). Additionally, the process data objects can be manipulated. Instances can also be temporarily suspended and resumed at a later stage.

When an update to the process definition is deployed—for example, with a bug fix or a small functional change—running instances of the process can be migrated: they continue running and will do so based on the new process definition, including the fixes and changes.

Auxiliary Applications for BPMN Processes

The Business Process Workspace application (commonly at http://host:8001/bpm/workspace) has prebuilt dashboards per business process for monitoring process performance, task performance, and workload, and it also allows creation of custom dashboards. In a similar way to the BPM Worklist application discussed in the previous chapter, it also provides access to human tasks that need to be performed.

The BPM Process Composer (whose default location is http://host:8001/bpm/composer) provides a visual representation of the processes through a browser-based application that can make them accessible to a wide audience. The Process Composer supports some business architecture and high level design modeling. Through this application, business analysts may create, document, simulate, try out (play), and refine the business processes. These refinements can either be deployed to the run-time SCA container or pushed back to JDeveloper, where the developer can evaluate and complete them before deployment. Process Composer is rapidly catching up with BPM Studio in terms of its capabilities—including the ability to implement process activities rather than just model them. The composer is the main mechanism for working on BPM processes in the Oracle Process Cloud Service.

The BPM Suite 12c also contains a native mobile app, geared toward tablets, through which to organize, manage, and work on tasks. The app is designed to work in online as well as offline mode with synchronization capabilities. The REST APIs consumed by this app can just as well be used to build custom web or mobile applications.

Airport Accreditation Request Handling in a BPMN Process

The previous chapter introduced the business process for handling a request for accreditation at the airport for new staff at one of the many business partners of Saibot Airport. In that chapter, the implementation was done entirely using a BPEL process component and while that is certainly an option—there are quite a few reasons to assume BPMN may be a better tool for the job.

We will take the SOA composite *AirportAccreditationService* and use a BPMN component to implement what in the previous chapter was done in the *security checks* stage in the BPEL process. Note that it is not common of course to first implement a business process and BPEL and then do it again in BPMN. It is done here to clearly show how BPMN adds support for true business process modeling and implementation on top of the components available in Oracle SOA Suite 12c, which is the real subject of this book.

Outline SecurityCheck Process in Process Composer

Start JDeveloper and open project *AirportAccreditationService*. As a first step, we need to upgrade the project to support BPM. Open the project properties and click on the node *Features*. Click on the plus icon to add a Project Feature. Select BPM from the list of features to add and click on OK to close the dialog.

NOTE
Upgrading the project with the BPM feature means that you enter the realm of the BPM Suite license. Tread carefully if you do not actually possess that license, as to not inadvertently use features that will force you into footing a much larger bill than you were counting on.

Open the composite editor. Add a BPMN component from the component palette to the composite application. Call it *SecurityCheckProcess* and accept default type Asynchronous Service. This component will expose an external SOAP Service.

Define a single input argument called *OriginalAccreditationRequest*, based on the XSD element *RequestForAirportAccreditationRequest*. Also define two output arguments: AccreditationApproved of type boolean and SecurityCheckComment of type string. Press Finish.

The BPMN Component is added to the composite application—both in the composite.xml file and in the composite diagram—along with the external web service it exposes. The initial implementation of the process is extremely simple: a Start and an End node that represent the reception of a request message and the sending of the asynchronous response, as shown in Figure 19-1.

Open the Business Catalog for the business process using the menu option Window | Catalog. In the Catalog there is an overview of all assets available for modeling and implementing the process—both in JDeveloper and in the Process Composer.

Publish to Process Asset Manager

We will do the design of the *SecurityCheckProcess* in the Process Composer, assuming the role of business analyst. In order to make the project available in Process Composer, we either have to export the BPM process to a file and import that file from the browser environment. A more elegant exchange or better said collaboration mechanism is the Process Asset Manager or PAM. The PAM is a database backed repository—part of the SOA Infra database—that supports multi user access, locking, change history, and version control.

The book's website has a reference to a resource that describes in detail how to create the PAM connection in the IDE and how to bring up the PAM navigator. After following those steps, we can publish the project to the PAM from the context menu on the *AirportAccreditationService* project node using the option Save to PAM.

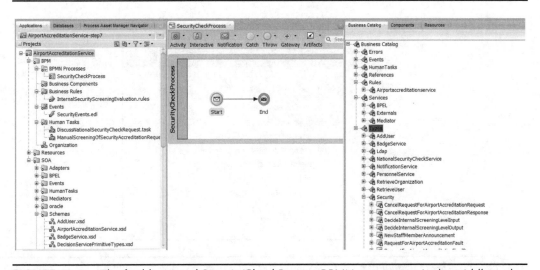

FIGURE 19-1. *The freshly minted SecurityCheckProcess BPMN component in the middle and the Business Catalog with available assets on the right*

A dialog appears where we have to select a Process Space—or create a new one—as the target for publishing the project. Create a new space called *SaibotProcessSpace*. Press OK. A second dialog wants us to provide some (check in) comment. Then press OK. At this moment, the project definition is transferred into the PAM and thereby made available to the Process Composer. Depending on the access privileges defined on the space—other users can also start inspecting or even editing the process definition.

Open the Process Composer

In your favorite browser, access the url http://host:port/bpm/composer. The *AirportAccreditationService* project is listed in the *SaibotProcessSpace*. Click on the entry to bring up the project with the process inside. The project home page is shown next. It lists all BPM process components—just one—and an overview of other assets such as [Business] Rules—also just one, Human Tasks—two of those—and Business Components - 51, based on the XSD definitions in the project. Note that all these assets can be edited from within the Process Composer with functionality that is similar to but also in some cases quite a bit broader and richer than the SOA Composer.

We will assume a somewhat naïve approach in this chapter, for simplicity. This does not represent a best practice for real-life modeling a BPM process. Click on the Data Objects icon in the header bar for the process diagram. In the popup that appears—see Figure 19-2—define the following five process data objects: *requiredScreeningLevel* (Integer), *internalScreeningOutcome* (boolean), *needForRandomThoroughCheck* (boolean), *thoroughCheckOutcome* (boolean), and *nationalSecurityCheckOutcome* (String). These objects are similar to some of the BPEL variables used in the previous chapter. Click on Close when you are done.

TIP
Using the option Business Components in the project level menu, we can define more complex data structures that can be used as the foundation for the process data objects.

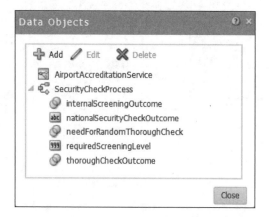

FIGURE 19-2. *Defining Data Objects for the BPM process*

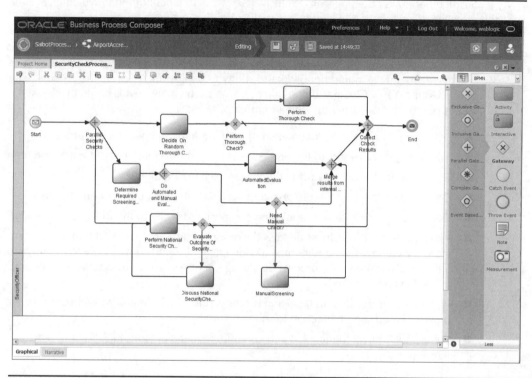

FIGURE 19-3.   *The design of SecurityCheckProcess with all activities still in draft*

Click on the business process *SecurityCheckProcess*—to bring up the process editor. Click on the white area under the single process lane and create a new lane, called Security Officer. At a later stage, we will add this lane—or process role—to a security group in the LDAP directory.

Hover over the gray area to the left of the first lane. Click on the edit icon. Select *Automatic Handler* from the drop-down list to replace value of *Unassigned Role*.

Create the business process as shown in Figure 19-3, by dragging the activities (for this moment, only use the abstract Activity element) and Gateways to the diagram and linking them with flows.

Gateways play an important role in BPMN processes as they determine conditional steps and parallel activities. A Parallel Gateway is a starting point for multiple flows that will all be executed—nonconditionally—in parallel. An Exclusive Gateway will have two or more outgoing flows of which exactly one—depending on the associated boolean conditions—will be executed. An Inclusive Gateway is similar to an Exclusive Gateway; the difference is that it allows multiple paths to be taken instead of exactly one for the Exclusive Gateway.

All flows coming out of an Inclusive or Exclusive Gateway need either be Unconditional or have a condition defined against them.

Define the following conditions on flows:

■ nationalSecurityCheckOutcome=="Unclear" for the flow to *Discuss National SecurityCheck*

■ requiredScreeningLevel>0 for the flow to *ManualScreening*

■ needForRandomThoroughCheck==true for the flow to *Perform Thorough Check*

Set all other flows outgoing from Exclusive Gateways to Unconditional, which means that these are the default flows that kick in when all conditions evaluate to false.

Make all process steps Draft. You do this by: hovering with the mouse cursor over each process activity, click on the edit icon and click on the *Implementation* link. In the property editor that appears, check the box marked Is Draft. This means that the implementation for these steps is not yet available—but that it should not block the ability to deploy and execute the process. Do not forget to press the Apply Changes button after making each change—it is easily overlooked!

At this point, you can continue with a number of steps:

- Provide further details—documentation and implementation—for the process.

- Add business indicators to the process—used for monitoring in dashboards and reports.

- Try to test run the process using the Player—see in line frame.

- Create a simulation of the process, to investigate process optimization options.

- Deploy the process (and its enclosing composite) directly to the BPM Suite run time.

- Run reports on the business process definition—from the main menu under the circular icon in the upper left hand corner, a wide range of reports is available to publish process details (on requirements, process data usage, process service interaction, issues and more) in various formats.

- Provide details for human tasks and business rules, including BPM WebForms for the browser-based user interaction for human tasks.

- Publish the project to the PAM and continue refinement work in BPM Studio aka JDeveloper.

Publish the process definition to the Process Asset Manager using the Publish icon—a little globe with an up arrow. Provide a useful check-in comment.

On the home page of the Process Composer, toggle from Modeler view to Administrator view, as shown in Figure 19-4. Click on the Unlock icon for the project—to allow further development in JDeveloper to be saved to the PAM.

FIGURE 19-4. *Unlocking the project to allow uploading to PAM of changed sources from JDeveloper*

TIP
*The book's source code repository contains folder CH19/
AirportAccreditationService-step7 with the situation at this point.*

Add Process Implementation Details in JDeveloper

The business analyst has done his job in Process Composer—and potentially even more than just analysis—and now the work is continued in JDeveloper. The process activities will be mapped to services, business rules, and human tasks. Two process data objects will be added. The data mapping and manipulation in the process will be defined. Correlation is added—to allow for cancellation of running processes. And the SOA composite including the BPM process component will be deployed.

Check Out the Process from the PAM

The Project Asset Manager holds the latest published version of the project. Open the PAM Navigator. Right click on the *AirportAccreditationService* project and select Check Out from the context menu. Accept the project's root folder as the target for the checkout operation. The latest definitions created and published in composer are now available for refinement in JDeveloper.

Define and Initialize Process Data Objects

An important aspect of business processes is obviously the data associated with the process. This data is received from inbound messages, created during the execution of process activities and used for flow logic and the preparation of the process result. Additionally, KPIs and other business indicators used for monitoring the process are partially based on the process data.

In the composer, we have defined a number of simple typed process data objects. Let us now create some additional, more complex data objects to hold the contents from the request message that triggers the process.

Define Business Objects in Business Catalog   Open the Business Catalog window. Right click on the root node and from the context menu click on New | Module. Create a new module to hold our object definitions; call it, for example, *BusinessObjectsModule*.

Next, click on the new module's node. Select New | Business Object from the context menu. Set the name to *AirportAccreditationProcessState*. Mark the checkbox Based on External Schema and browse to the *AirportAccreditationProcessState* element in the AirportAccreditationService.xsd. Click twice on OK.

The business object editor appears that allows you to inspect—but not to change—the attributes of the object. There are attributes for the SASEC for the requestor and the organization, as well the email ID for the requestor and the *AirportAccreditationRequestIdentifier* to hold the unique identifier assigned to the accreditation request.

Define a Process Data Object Based on a Business Object   Open the Structure Window for the business process. Right click on the node Process Data Object and select New from the context menu. Set the name for the new data object to *accreditationProcessState* and the type to the just created business component *AirportAccreditationProcessState*. Likewise, create a new process data object called *originalAccreditationRequest* based on the XSD element *RequestForAirportAccreditationRequest*.

Define an Input Argument Based on a Business Object   Based on the
AirportAccreditationProcessState element used for the Process Data Object, we can also add an
additional input argument for the business process. Click on the Start [Message] node in the
process diagram. The editor appears. Open the Implementation tab. Add a new argument
ValidatedAccreditationDetails based on business object *AirportAccreditationProcessState*.

TIP
*Use the last option in the Type dropdown which is Browse... This
options gives access to all XSD complex types and elements in the
project to use as the type for an input or output argument.*

Create Data Associations from Input Arguments to Process Data Objects   Data associations
are used to map data from inbound messages to process data objects—and the other way round.
We will now specify how the data in the request message, that triggers the business process, is
copied to the two process data objects.

Click on the Data Associations link. The Data Association editor opens—a tool very similar to
the Assign editor in the BPEL process. Map the two input arguments on the left to the corresponding
Process Data Objects on the right, as shown in Figure 19-5. The result is that when the a new
process instance is triggered with the reception of a request message with the two input arguments,
the two process data objects are initialized with the data from these arguments.

All we need to do is a *top level assignment* because the input arguments and the data are of
the same type.

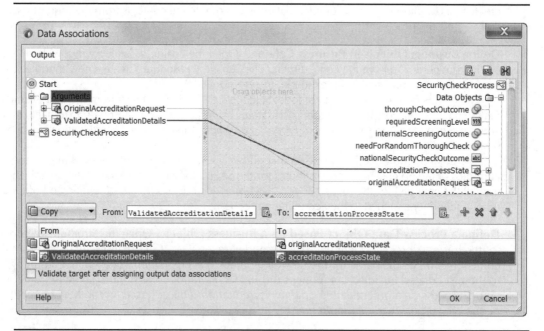

FIGURE 19-5.   *Mapping the input arguments to two of the process data objects*

Map to Business Rule to Determine the Required Internal Screening Level

We already have created a business rule to execute activity *Determine Required Screening Intensity*. This rule is currently called from the BPEL process. Click on this process activity. It should no longer be a draft activity—so uncheck the Is Draft checkbox. Open the Implementation tab. Set the Implementation Type to Business Rule Task. Select the *InternalSecurityScreeningEvaluation* business rule as the implementation for this step. We could also have created (the outline of) a new business rule component by clicking the plus icon.

The business rule has a predefined interface. We need to create the data associations that map from the process data objects to the input arguments of the business rule—and from its outcome to the destination process data object *requiredScreeningLevel*. Click on the link for data associations and create the associations as shown in Figure 19-6. The two *SACLevel input* arguments of type Integer and the corresponding attributes in the *accreditationProcessState* process data object are String values; therefore: you need a number() conversion function in an XPath expression in these two data associations.

At this point, you can deploy the composite and make a test call to the start operation exposed by the *SecurityCheckProcess* operation. Most of the process is still draft only. However, by using various input levels for the SASEC levels and the *requiredSecurityLevel*, we can try out the business rule and see the effect of the conditions on the exclusive gateway.

You can see the graphical process flow by clicking on the entry for the *SecurityCheckProcess* in the composite flow trace, see Figure 19-7. This viewer even allows you to replay the process instance so you can see the order and parallel synchronization of steps as well as the gateways where specific paths were selected.

Implement Human Task Activity Discuss National Security Check

Open Activity *Discuss National SecurityCheck*. The implementation is to be provided by a human task. Uncheck the checkbox Is Draft. Open the Implementation tab. Select User Task as the Implementation Type. We could use the existing Human Task *DiscussNationalSecurityCheckRequest* as the implementing task. Instead, let's create a new task definition using the plus icon.

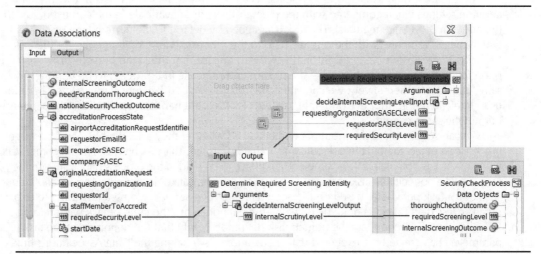

FIGURE 19-6. *Data associations for the input and output to and from the business rule*

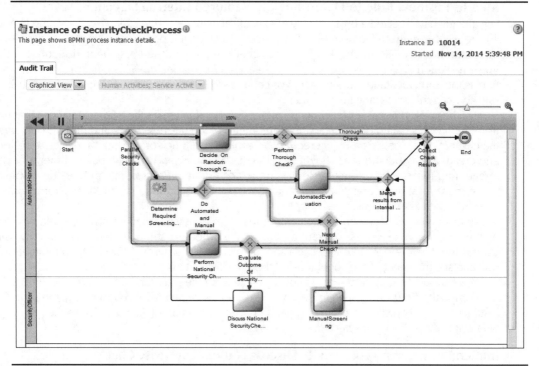

FIGURE 19-7. *Process Flow Trace for an instance of the Security Check Process where the business rule decided that manual screening was required*

The Create Human Task popup appears, as shown in Figure 19-8. It has a few interesting addition settings when compared with the Human Task editor available in the context of just BPEL (without the BPM Suite features). The task is assigned by default to the current lane participant—which means someone with the role we map to the process swim lane that contains the task—*SecurityOfficer* in our case. Additionally, we can ensure that the same person (*previous lane participant*) gets assigned this task—if we want certain tasks in a process to be handled by the same individual. Alternatively, we can check the box for *Exclude Previous Participants*. This allows us to implement the "four eye principle," where two tasks are handled by people in the same role, but not the same people.

We can specify the task's input parameters—and whether they are editable—and the target process data object to hold the task outcome, if that is relevant. This task has just one outcome—OK—when the task is completed. This value does not have to be held in the process data. Click on the plus icon to add a noneditable task parameter—based on process data object *originalAccreditationRequest*. Also add a task parameter based on the *accreditationProcessState*. Adding a task parameter based on a process data object is done by dragging the data object to the table of task parameters.

Click on OK to complete the human task definition. Verify that the definition of the task input parameters has created the expected data associations, by clicking the Data Associations link.

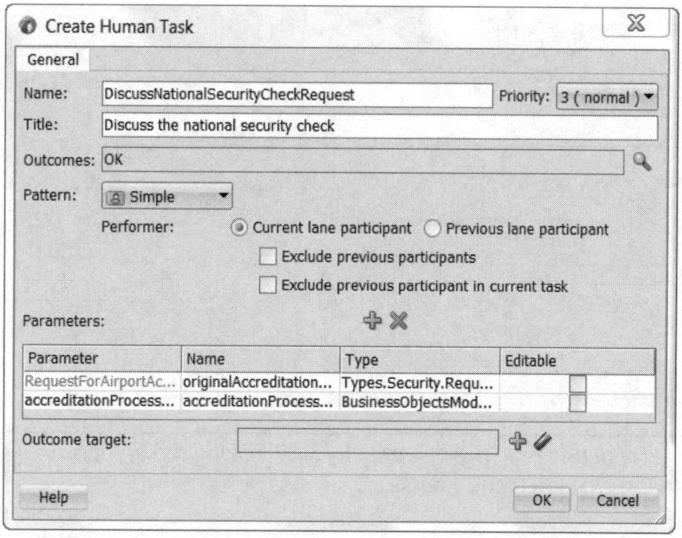

FIGURE 19-8.   *Configuring the Human Task to discuss the "unclear" cases for the National Security Check*

Even though we could do it, deploying the process at this stage to inspect the human task is not useful because the task is triggered only in case of an Unclear result from the activity *Perform National Security Check* that is not yet implemented. You can check though in the composite editor how by now we have created wires from the BPMN component to a human task and a business rule component—just like we did from the BPEL process.

Implement the Service Call to Perform the National Security Check

The National Security Check is provided through a BPEL process component in the composite application. It is an asynchronous service that performs a callback. Invoking services is one of the core competencies of the BPM process engine, and dealing with asynchronous responses comes natural—in a way that is very similar to BPEL.

Double click in the process editor on activity *Perform National Security Check*. Uncheck the *Is Draft* checkbox. Set the *Implementation Type* to Send task, as shown in Figure 19-9. Set the type of Message Exchange to Service Call. Select the *NationalSecurityCheckService* as the service to invoke. The operation gets automatically selected. Create a Data Association for the input to the service; this can be anything you like because the service implementation is a little frivolous right now.

Handling of the asynchronous callback to receive the response message is done using a separate activity, of type Receive Task, also shown in Figure 19-9. Add this activity, based on the NationalSecurityCheckService.Callback. Create a Data Association for the result element in the response message to the process data object *nationalSecurityCheckOutcome* that is used in the exclusive gateway to determine whether or not the human task to discuss the National Security Check should be routed to.

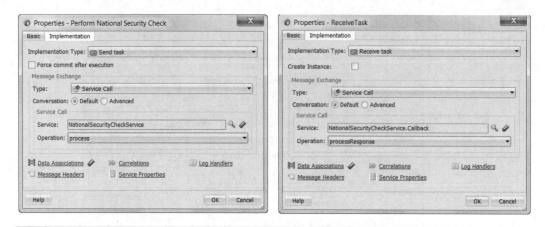

FIGURE 19-9. *Configuring the process activity for invoking the asynchronous NationalSecurityCheckService and handling its callback response*

At this point, you can deploy the process again. The *NationalSecurityCheckService* will be invoked for each process instance. In about 10 percent of the cases it will trigger the human task of discussing the National Security Check.

NOTE
The task is associated with the lane participant—the process role SecurityOfficer. *A mapping is required between this role and an enterprise group or user in order to actually assign the task to a user. This can be done in the BPM Workspace application, as shown in Figure 19-10. Open the menu option Administration. Select option Roles in the navigation bar on the left-hand side. Select the record for AirportAccreditationService.SecurityOfficer. Click on the new icon to bring up a group and user browser. Select user weblogic to add as a role mapping for this role.*

Add Other Implementations for Service Calls You have seen now how to map the business process activities to services. In the same way, add the implementation for activities:

- Perform Thorough Check—implement with a Send Task and a Receive Task to interact with the asynchronous BPEL process ThoroughBackgroundCheck
- ManualScreening—implement with a human task

Groovy Script to Derive the Need for Random Thorough Check
BPM supports activities of type Script Task. These can run snippets of Groovy code that can access the process data objects and read many predefined variables regarding the process instance. Use of Groovy script in BPM processes should be limited and be done with care—just as is the case with embedded Java in BPEL. For complex transformations for example, where Data Associations

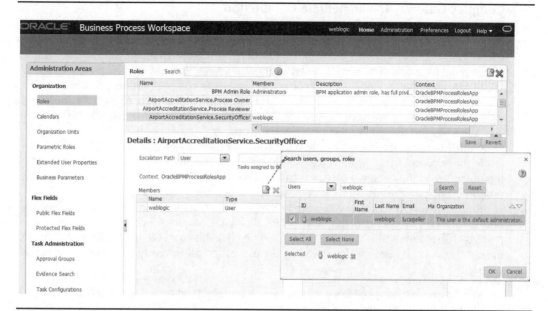

FIGURE 19-10. *Creating a role mapping between the process swim lane and actual LDAP groups and users*

would become extremely complex or impossible to create and maintain, such Script Tasks may just be a nice way out.

In the *SecurityCheckProcess* we need to determine whether or not to perform the thorough but random background check. We do this by calculating a random number in such a way that the random check is performed in only 10 percent of the cases. Using a Groovy-based script task is a good way of implementing this logic.

Open the editor for activity *Decide On Random Thorough Check*. Uncheck checkbox Is Draft and change the implementation type to *Script Task*. Close the activity editor. Right click on the activity and pick option Go To Script from the context menu.

Click on Select Imports. Add an import for java.util.Random. For manipulating complex process data objects, ensure to also import the corresponding class from package oracle .scripting.catalog.

Enter the following code for this script task that will set the process data object *needForRandomThoroughCheck* based on a random number evaluation:

```
try {
        def java.util.Random random = new java.util.Random()
        def int randInt = random.nextInt(100)
        this.needForRandomThoroughCheck = randInt > 90
}
catch(Exception e){
    this.needForRandomThoroughCheck = true
}
```

Complex Gateway for Immediate Completion

There is something inherently inefficient in the current design of the process. As soon as one of the parallel checks produces a negative outcome, we should abort the entire process because the overall result will now always be negative. However, the simple parallel gateway will wait at the merge point for all flows to complete; we do not make efficient use of that knowledge.

BPMN provides us with another type of gateway—the complex gateway that we can use as a smart merge point for multiple flows. The complex gateway is configured with a condition that indicates an early release from the gateway. When this condition holds true, the process token can move beyond the gateway and continue the process. At that point, we have the option to abort the flows that had not yet reached the complex gateway or to leave them running.

In the SecurityChecks process we want to complete the process as soon as we have established the outcome. In the negative case, we can reach our conclusion as soon as one of the check produces a negative result. So we can make meaningful use of the complex gateway.

Right click on the parallel gateway *Parallel Security Checks*. From the context menu, select option Change Gateway configuration to | Parallel and Complex. The icon on the gateway merge point is changed from plus sign to asterisk. Double click this icon. On the implementation tab, mark the checkbox *Abort Pending Flows*. Specify the expression for the early break out of the gateway:

```
activationCount > 0 and (nationalSecurityCheckOutcome == "NOTOK" or
internalScreeningOutcome == false or thoroughCheckOutcome == false and
needForRandomThoroughCheck == true)
```

The activationCount is a predefined variable that indicates at a gateway—how many of the incoming flows have already completed.

NOTE
In order for this expression to not break out too early, it is useful to initialize the process data objects with an appropriate value.

Deploy the process with this new complex gateway configuration. Send in a few security check requests. Handle the manual screening task in the BPM Workspace, approving some and rejecting others. Check in the graphical process flow trace if the process instances for the ones you rejected were indeed cut short—the longer running National Security Check not completed, as shown in Figure 19-11.

TIP
The tree view mode of the process trace page provides a step by step overview of the proceedings through the process instance, including an audit trail of the data exchanged from and to the process instance.

The state of the sources at this point is in the source code repository as *step8*.

Integrate BPMN Component from BPEL Process

It is the intention to replace the security check scope in the BPEL process constructed in the previous chapter with the *SecurityCheckProcess* implemented using a BPMN component in this section. The BPM process exposes a standard asynchronous web service interface—that BPEL can work with quite well.

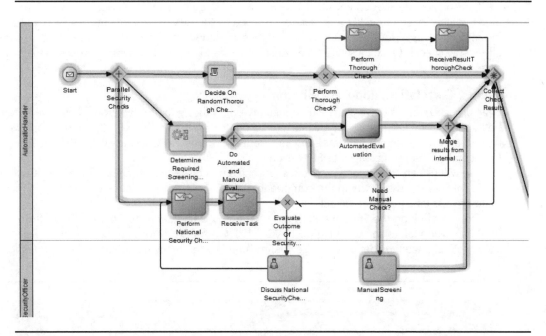

FIGURE 19-11. *An instance of the SecurityChecksProcess cut short at the complex gateway after a rejection in the manual screening task, causing the National Security Check to be aborted*

One step more interesting is the ability to communicate between the BPEL process and the BPM process in mid-flight. After all, when the accreditation request is cancelled—through a call that handled by the event handler on the BPEL process—this should also come to the attention of the *SecurityCheckProcess* because that process can then abort, freeing up valuable resource to get on with other important work. Our challenge is twofold: how to deliver a message to one specific running instance of a BPM process—and how to process such an inbound message in mid-flight to make the parallel running flows in the process abort. As with BPEL, we will use correlation to be able to associate inbound messages with a running instance.

Initiate SecurityCheckProcess from BPEL

Open the BPEL process editor for the *AirportAccreditationRequestProcessor* component. Locate the scope *SecurityChecks*. Remove all of its contents including the scope level variables. Also remove the partner links from the process for the partners that were used only from this scope *SecurityChecks*.

Open the composite editor. Wire the BPEL process to the BPMN component. Add an invoke activity called *InvokeSecurityCheckProcess* to the partner link created for the wire to the *SecurityCheckProcess* component. Have a local variable created. Also add a *receive* activity to handle the asynchronous response from the process. Have a local variable created for that response.

Add an assign activity to prepare the input to the *SecurityCheckProcess* based on the *inputVariable* and the variable *globalProcessState* variable.

Now deploy the SOA composite. Make one or more test calls to the *AirportAccreditationService* (note: not the *SecurityCheckProcess* service exposed by the BPMN component). The BPEL process is instantiated, does some LDAP interaction and then calls the *SecurityCheckProcess* to do take care of all security checks. Once these are done, the result is handed back to the BPEL process—that currently ignores it.

Events, Correlation, and Cancellation

BPM processes can receive events at almost any point during their execution. These events can be handled asynchronously. The events can be dealt with in parallel with the normal process flow or they can suspend or completely interrupt the normal flow. Just as with BPEL, events can be incoming request messages or EDN events.

We will use an activity of type event subprocess to receive the cancellation request. Click on the Event Subprocess activity in the component palette. Subsequently, click somewhere in the main process lane to create the activity.

Double click on the Start event. Set the name to *Cancel Security Checks*. Open the Implementation tab as shown in Figure 19-12. Mark the checkbox for Interrupting Event. Select Message Exchange Type define interface. Define an input argument *accreditationRequestIdentifier*

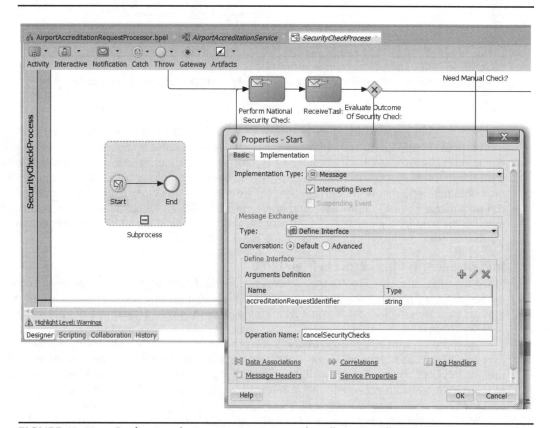

FIGURE 19-12.   *Configuring the interrupting event to handle a cancellation request*

of type String. Set the operation name to *cancelSecurityChecks*. Note that this name will be added to the WSDL describing the interface of the interface of this process.

Click on OK to complete the event handler's definition. When you next save the process definition, the WSDL is updated with the new operation.

The interaction between BPEL and BPM process components leverages WS-Addressing. The BPEL process instance that initiated the BPM process will unfailingly deliver additional messages to the same partner link at the same instance of the BPM process. We can now proceed to invoke the cancel operation on the BPM process from the cancellation event handler in the BPEL process without configuring custom, explicit correlation.

Open the BPEL process editor. Locate the *OnEvent* handler for operation cancelRequestForAirportAccreditation. Under the reply activity, add an Invoke activity associated with the new *cancelSecurityChecks* operation on the *SecurityCheckProcess* partner link. Have a local input variable generated. Add an Assign activity before the Invoke to set the value for this input variable. In order to achieve the intended effect—cancellation of the BPM process—we do not actually need this input.

Deploy the composite application. Send a request message for airport accreditation. The request identifier is returned. After a dozen seconds, when the BPM process has started, send a cancellation request, using this identifier. Correlation with the BPEL process resolves in execution of the event handler. A synchronous reply is returned. Subsequently the BPM process instance is invoked and will execute its event subprocess that interrupts and aborts the instance. Next, the exception handling in the BPEL process takes care of ending this process as well.

Explicit Correlation to Cancel BPM Process from Third Parties   In situations where we cannot rely on this close handshake between BPEL and BPM components, we will have to use explicit correlation. For example, if we want to cancel the *SecurityCheckProcess* directly through its own web service interface instead of through the BPEL process.

As with BPEL, we have to define the correlation in a few steps:

- Define the correlation identifier itself—in our case called *securityCheckRequestIdentifier* and of type String

- At all interaction points we have to specify how the correlation identifier maps to the incoming (or outgoing) messages—and whether the interaction point is the one where the identifier is first populated and fixated for the process instance

Click on the Start event activity to open the editor. Click on the *Correlations* link. The Correlation Definition window appears as shown in Figure 19-13. Click on the *create* icon behind the Property field. Create a new Correlation Property called *securityCheckRequestIdentifier*. Click on OK.

Mark the checkbox Initiates—because the value of the correlation identifier is set when this Start activity receives the incoming message. Click on the expression editor icon to specify how at this interaction point the value of the correlation identifier is taken from the inbound message:

```
ValidatedAccreditationDetails.airportAccreditationRequestIdentifier
```

In a similar way, but of course without initiating the correlation identifier a second time, we configure the correlation on the event subprocess that handles the cancellation. Click on the Message activity *Cancel Security Checks* to bring up the editor. Open the Implementation tab and click on the *Correlations* link. Select property *securityCheckRequestIdentifier* from the dropdown

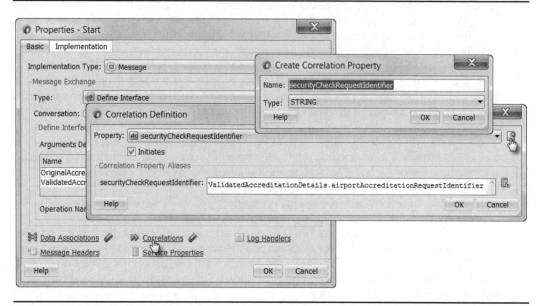

FIGURE 19-13. *Configuration of the correlation property and the initial correlating interaction*

list. Set the expression for the property alias to the *accreditationRequestIdentifier* element in the interface definition for this interaction point.

Figure 19-14 shows the two interaction points where correlation takes place. At #1 when the process instance is initiated the value in the *airportAccreditationRequestIdentifier* element in the inbound message determines the identity of the process instance. When a message arrives at #2, it has to carry the correct value in its *accreditationRequestIdentifier* element, in order to be correctly linked up with the intended running instance.

Deploy the composite application. Invoke the *SecurityCheckProcess* interface for the BPMN component directly—so not through the BPEL component. Set a value for the *airportAccreditationRequestIdentifier* element you can easily remember. After a few seconds, send a cancellation message to the cancel operation on the same web service interface, using the remembered value for the *accreditationRequestIdentifier* element. Through correlation, your second message is hooked up with the running process instance where it triggers the interrupting event subprocess that calls an end to the process instance.

The sources under *step9* in the source repository contain this state of the composite application.

Enabling Business Users to Create the Human Task UI

An important aspect of the execution of business processes is typically the human contribution: the human task activity. Essential for the quality and efficiency for this human involvement is the user interface through which the human actors can make their contribution. In Chapter 17, we have briefly seen how the UI for a human task can be generated in JDeveloper as an ADF web

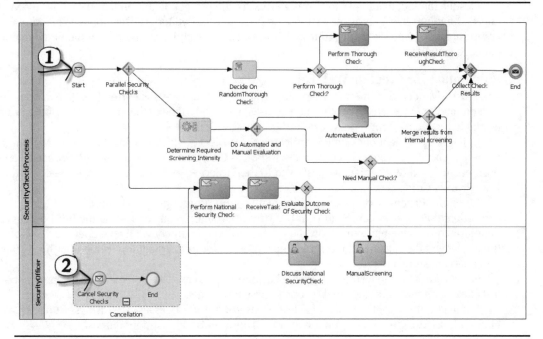

FIGURE 19-14.   *The two interaction points in the SecurityCheckProcess where correlation takes place*

application that developers can fine tune with all the power of the ADF framework at their disposal. Alternative user interfaces can be created on top of the human workflow APIs.

However, these are typically IT tasks to be performed by technical experts. In BPM Suite, an effort has been made to allow business users themselves to create the user interface. Through a browser-based interface, without advanced technical skills, the outline of the human interaction for a specific task can be created through simple drag and drop. These Web Forms are seamlessly integrated into the BPM workspace where users work on their tasks.

The Web Forms can be used as a way for business users to extend their model of the business process with a few prototypes for how they envision the interaction to take place—as an extended design for the developers. Or these Web Forms can be included in the production system—possibly fine-tuned by a developer using advanced mechanisms such as rules (JavaScript for validation and calculation) and styles.

We will very briefly go through the steps of creating and trying out a Web Form for one of the human activities in the *SecurityCheckProcess*, to get a feel for it.

Quick Tour of Web Forms

Web Forms are created in the Process Composer as part of a BPM project. They can be created and designed first and attached to a human task as a second step—that is called the Form First method, where the fields in the form determine the payload that will be available to the human task associated with the form. Alternatively, a Web Form is created in Process Composer from a human task definition. This Data First approach takes the task's payload as the starting point for the Web Form.

Despite the fact that the Web Forms are part of the project definition that is saved to PAM and checked out into JDeveloper, they cannot be inspected nor edited in JDeveloper. When the composite application is deployed from JDeveloper, the Web Forms are part of the deployment package though.

Preparation for Creating Web Forms

The most advanced definition of the project with the BPM process is currently in JDeveloper. In order to add the Web Forms for the human tasks, we need to make the current state of the project available for access from Process Composer.

In JDeveloper, right click on the project in the project navigator. Select Save to PAM from the content menu. Enter some check-in notes and press OK. The project with the BPM process, one business rule and two human tasks is saved to the Project Asset Manager, ready to be opened from Process Composer.

Open the Process Composer and navigate to the project home page for *AirportAccreditationService*. With your business user hat on, you can review the BPM process definition to see where it stands now after these fabled refinements in JDeveloper. Because of all the implementation details, there is definitely more color in the diagram—remember how draft processes are shown in gray.

You could use the Player to explore the business process and its implementation step by step—by just clicking on the player icon in the upper right-hand corner.

On the home page, the project navigator has nodes for Processes (1), Business Rules (1), and Human Tasks (2). There is also a node for Web Forms, currently without entries.

Create Web Form ManualScreeningForm

Navigate to the definition for the Human Task *ManualScreeningOfSecurityAccreditationRequest*. The third tab holds the Data definition: the payload for the task. On the Basic tab, under Presentation, we can start the creation of the Web Form, see Figure 19-15.

Set the Type radio group to Web Form. Click on the plus icon and enter the name for the Web Form, for example *ManualScreeningForm*. Mark the checkbox *Based on payload*. Note: If you do not check this box, Process Composer will assume that the form will drive the payload of the task and the existing data definition is overridden.

Click on the edit icon to bring up the WYSIWYG editor for the Web Form. On the left of the page are three areas with the palette of form elements, the detailed property palette for the current element and the data sources aka the elements of the task payload.

By simply clicking the icon for a data source, a form element is added for that specific element. When you click the item for an element with child elements, form controls are added for all these child elements.

Once the element is on the form, you can click on it and edit the properties such as the display type, the prompt and hint text, the decorator (icon), and if applicable the set of allowable values.

Components can be rearranged by drag and drop. Layout components can be added to bring structure and appeal to the page—including messages, collapsible sections with subheaders, panels (columns), tabs, and tables for organization of components.

Through Form Rules—snippets of server side JavaScript—the developer (perhaps not so much the business user at this stage) can add additional functionality to the Web Form. These rules can add dynamic behavior—such as hiding and showing of items, calculating values for and validating values in components and even retrieving data for lists and dropdown elements

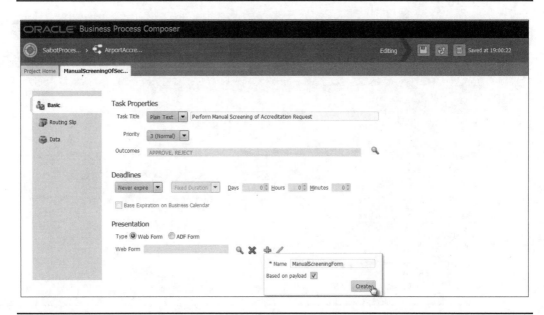

FIGURE 19-15.   *Creating the Data First Web Form for a Human Task in the Process Composer*

from REST services. Rules are created and edited from the left most icon in the icon bar overhead the form.

For our little tentative exploration of Web Forms, it is enough to just add a few components, for example for the payload elements First Name, Last Name, and Social Security Number as shown in Figure 19-16. Using the running man icon, you can get a preview of what the form will look and taste like to the end users—including tabs, sections, and any dynamic behavior you may have added.

Using the Player to Inspect the Process and the Forms

A quick way to inspect the workings of a BPM process and the associated Web Forms inside Process Composer is with the Player. This tool uses a run-time environment that emulates the real-world behavior of business processes. As the application runs, process player displays a visual representation of a BPMN process showing the path the process instance follows through the process flow. When the process hits a human task during its execution, the Player will allow the user to run the associated form for the task as a specific user or simply provide the outcome of the task. The Player will simply skip over activities marked as draft. Activities involving calling out to services will be executed as configured.

When running process player on a business process, Process Composer validates the project definitions and deploys the current draft version of the BPM project to a newly created partition called Player in the runtime environment. When using process player, you do not have to publish or manually deploy the project to view changes while designing a process.

To run the *SecurityCheckProcess* with the Player, click on the icon in the top right-hand corner. You will be invited to provide the SOAP message that is the initial input to the process. You can

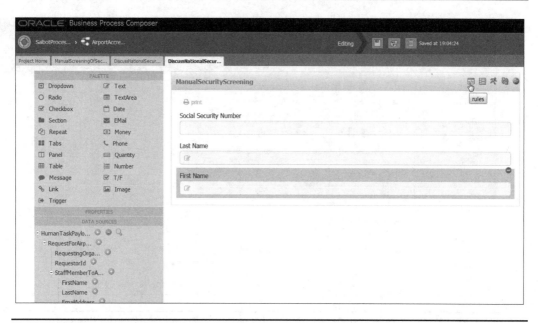

FIGURE 19-16. *The Web Form editor in Process Composer for creating the UI for a Human Task*

use an exact copy, SOAP envelope and all, of the test messages you use in SoapUI for testing the web service exposed by the BPM process. Subsequently, the Player takes over. It shows the visual overview of the project (Figure 19-17) and it will gradually apply color to the flows and activities, as these are traversed and executed. When the *ManualScreening* human task is reached, you can open a popup window from the icon shown on the task. In this window, you can select the user whose identity to assume—for example, for testing assignment and notification rules—and whether to launch the Web Form or immediately provide the outcome of the task activity.

If you choose to launch the form, it would present you with the real data from the payload of the task—based on the original request message that was fed into the process, possibly modified through the earlier activities in the process flow.

Web Forms in the Real Run-Time Environment   Obviously the Player provides a sandbox—no matter how serious and valuable. The Web Forms need to be deployed to and used in the real world at some point. Deployment of the Web Forms happens along with the rest of the project. This can be done in several ways—one of which is deployment straight from Process Composer. On the main menu—click on the circular icon in the top left-hand corner—are the deployment options. Alternatively, deployment can be done through JDeveloper after first publishing the project to the PAM and checking it out into JDeveloper.

When the BPM process is running normally and tasks are instantiated and available for the user to act upon, then the Web Form is embedded in the BPM Workspace page, as shown in Figure 19-18.

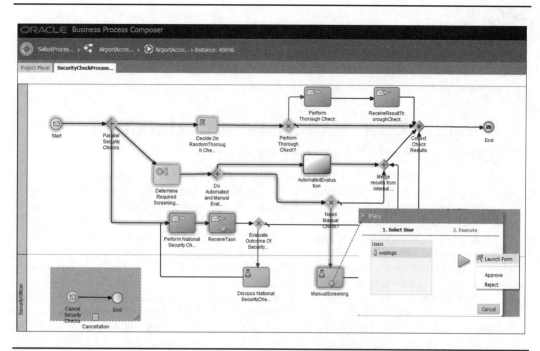

FIGURE 19-17. *The Player in action for the SecurityCheckProcess—providing the option to launch the Web Form for the human activity ManualScreening*

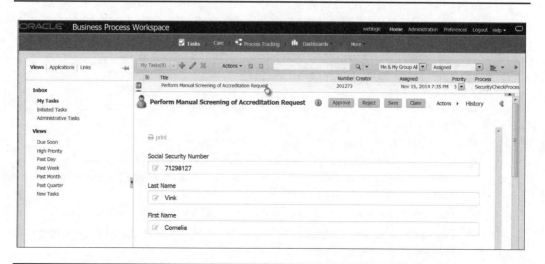

FIGURE 19-18. *BPM Workspace showing the embedded Web Form for the Manual Screening activity*

TIP
Before you can use the Player for the first time, you have to configure it. To do so, go to the home page of Process Composer, enter the Administrator view, and click on Player. In the form that appears, you need to provide the administrator credentials for the SOA Suite runtime, for example weblogic.

Adaptive Case Management to Handle Top Security Level Accreditation

Our highly structured business process is adequate for regular accreditation requests. However, for security clearance at the very highest level, this semi-automated process with its rigid flow is not good enough. Requests for top level security clearance are rare and when they occur, they are always for quite specific people and roles. These requests deserve and require special, tailored attention from one or more senior security officers. That does not mean that all bets are off: in most cases, the steps taken while processing the accreditation request are similar. However, the order and frequency of the steps may vary considerably—at the discretion of the senior security officer handling the request.

This is very much a situation where traditional BPMN falls short because it does not offer the kind of flexibility and tailoring that is apparently required. In these circumstances, adaptive case management comes to the rescue. As soon as we learn that the accreditation request is for the highest security level—and after performing basic validation and data gathering—we can start a case for the request.

Introducing Adaptive Case Management

ACM provides structure in a process that is very fluid. A number of elements that (potentially) play a role in a (type of) case is defined at design time. These elements are used by the ACM engine to guide stakeholders at run time and to ensure that nonoptional steps are taken and mandatory rules are followed. Even though many aspects of a case can be flexible and determined to large degree by case workers and the specific contents of a case, that does not mean that freedom rules supremely and no conditions apply at all.

Elements that define the case include

- The milestones that can be reached in a case and the conditions that need to be satisfied for meeting a milestone

- The activities that can be executed over the course of the case

- Data that is associated with the case; in addition to structured data, it is common to also have documents associated with a case instance (that may be structured for human actors, but are less so to the system)

- Stakeholders that are involved with the case and influence it in some way

- Events that may occur over the lifetime of the case, either triggered by activities within the case or from the outside

- The possible outcomes of the case

The glue tying much of these elements together is formed by the rules that determine when activities can or should be executed, how an activity can be initiated automatically, when a milestone is reached and how the case data can be modified. These rules embody much of the business knowledge around a specific type of case. They bring the order in the chaos—and they limit the flexibility and freedom of the case workers in order to guide. Very careful definition of these rules is crucial in order to provide the required structure (for productivity, quality, consistency) without needlessly (and frustratingly) restricting the professionals working on a case—and the other stakeholders interacting with it.

Activities in ACM are containers of actions—both human and automated. When the rules determine that an activity is available in a particular case (instance), the associated actions can be started—either automatically or instigated by a case worker. Some activities will always be available during (most of) the lifetime of a case instance, such as "add document," "add comment," "send email."

Audit Trail or Case Event Log

Typically during the execution of a case (instance) a detailed log is maintained of all events that happen on the case. Any activity that is triggered, performed or withdrawn, any milestone reached or revoked, any comment or document added, any event occurring—everything is recorded. ACM tooling (such as Oracle BPM Suite) manages this audit trail and can reproduce—even after the case (instance) has been closed—a detailed overview of the history of the case.

You can use subcases to manage activities that contribute to the resolution of a parent case. Subcases are similar to case activities, are instantiated at run time within the context of a parent case and using the data of the parent case. Subcases are deployed as a separate composite from the parent case project. They are linked to the parent using the same case link mechanism that can be used to link case instances to one another that have some meaningful relationship. The case management user interface lists all related cases for the current case and allows direct navigation to them.

Case Contents: Data and Documents

In addition to the case's audit trail, key constituents are structured data and documents. When the case is initiated, at least the bare essential information for the case is populated based on the starting trigger—frequently a web service request. Over the lifetime of the case, case activities can act on the data in the case as can the case workers through the case management user interfaces. The same applies to the documents in the case, which can be manipulated by automated actions as well by the human actors involved with the case.

TIP
By default BPM Suite is configured to use an Oracle Database document store for the case document. A specialized enterprise content management system is recommended for production use. Support is provided for WebCenter Content and Alfresco CMIS.

ACM and BPM

It is quite common to have highly structured activities in a case that itself is extremely flexible and variable. Even though we may not be able to predict exactly how the interaction around a case takes place and what steps will be executed in which order before reaching a certain milestone, we may have a highly structured set of actions taking place inside a specific activity.

For example, the case around a complex order of specialized goods can vary greatly before the exact order has been defined and agreement has been reached over the financial details but when it comes to picking and shipping the order, it is a very well-known process that has to be executed.

Or a court case may require a variable number of actions before the case comes before a judge, but when it comes to the ruling—it is a structured process (even defined in legislation to some extent) that has be to executed. We know of course how to define and execute such structured processes: using BPMN and a BPM(N) engine. That is exactly what we frequently will do in ACM: implement activities through BPMN processes.

Introducing the Top Security Accreditation Case

For the highest security classification, the standard procedure will not do. The vetting of individuals that will have virtually unrestricted access to sensitive information and areas at Saibot Airport is a highly tailored process—adapted at the specific person, his or her organization and the precise role.

We know the structured information that is involved with the case as well as the stakeholders. A substantial set of documents may be gathered and added to the case as well. It is also clear which stages the process will go through and what the main activities in and deliverables from each stage are. Sometimes activities are skipped, sometimes they are repeated once or even multiple times. Occasionally, a top ranked officer steps in to force the case ahead or throw it out completely. For audit reasons, we need to keep—and store for 10 years—a detailed record of all the steps taken, decisions made, and information collected in the process of awarding top level security access.

The possible outcomes of the case are Granted and Denied—along with standard outcomes such as Aborted and Suspended.

The stages identified in the process are, for example,

- Documentation—collecting relevant personal documents (identification, working history, certificates), financial statements from banks and debt registration agencies, records from previous security enquiries, and information about the employing organization and the specific job the person will fulfill.

- Extended National Security Check—performed in conjunction with the national security authorities; this could well prove to be a subcase; for the moment we consider it a combination of a human activity to gather the required documents and one to liaise with the external authorities.

- Desk Research—investigation into known activities and publications using public archives and social media; these are largely unstructured, human activities.

- References Check—one or more following up on personal references, possibly including questionnaires and personal interviews.

- Interviews—a series of conversations with the person under scrutiny; depending on the function as well as the outcomes of initial talks, there may be additional rounds of interviews.

- Biometrics—the subject has to come in to have her iris scanned, her fingerprints taken and perhaps other bodily characteristics investigated and recorded; these data are used for access means for the most sensitive areas. Yet before that they are cross referenced with security authorizes at home and abroad. Note that this is largely conducted according to a very structured even strict protocol that could very well be implemented using a BPMN process.

- Wrap up—conclusion and filing of all relevant records.

Each of these stages can be demarcated by a milestone that signifies the successful conclusion of the stage.

Stakeholders involved with this case include the various levels of security staff at Saibot Airport, the applicant for the high security position who is the subject of the investigation, the applying organization who will employ him or her, external partners who may perform part of the research and the auditor who do not participate but monitor.

Deadlines can be defined on case and on individual milestones—to ensure, for example, regulations regarding waiting periods are satisfied. They are expressed as duration, relative to XPath-based expressions potentially involving the current date and case data. When the deadline expires while the milestone is not yet complete, a milestone deadline event is raised.

In addition to the standard case events that are published when a milestone is complete or a deadline expires, there are custom events relevant to the case such as a criminal investigation is launched involving the subject or one of her close relatives or the applying organization has been acquired by another organization.

Create the Outline of the Top Security Accreditation Case

Adaptive case management is an impressive topic in its own right. In this section, we can only show the bare minimum of what it involves to design and implement a case. It should be enough to get you an idea of how to get started and how to integrate ACM cases with BPM processes and SOA Suite constructs.

Create the First Iteration of the BPM Project with the ACM Case

Create new BPM Project, called *TopSecurityAccreditationCase*. Note that you can define only one case per BPM project. A case can be added to an already existing BPM project that doesn't already include one. Select template *Composite with Case Management*. Accept the default name and namespace.

The case is created as an SCA component, along with a business rule component that contains the rules for the case. When you open the composite editor, you will see these two components and the service exposed by the case components, with operations to start, close, abort, suspend, and reopen.

Double click the case component, to bring up the case editor, see Figure 19-19. Set the title for the case, define two outcomes—*Granted* and *Denied*—and define the following milestones: *Documentation, National Check, Desk Research, References Assessment, Interview Sessions, Biometrics, Wrap Up*.

Open the Data & Documents tab. Add two simple editable String parameter— *AirportAccreditationRequestIdentifier* and *SubjectsMobilePhone*.

At this point, we can already deploy the composite application with the case definition. It will not do a lot, but the idea of how the case is presented and how case actors work with it in the BPM Workspace becomes already quite clear.

After deploying the case, send a SOAP request message with the following payload to the *startCase* operation in the service exposed by the composite:

```
<typ:startCaseInputMessage
    xmlns:typ="http://xmlns.oracle.com/CaseService/types"
    xmlns:case="http://xmlns.oracle.com/bpm/case" >
  <case:case>
    <case:caseHeader>
```

```
        <case:identificationKey>123</case:identificationKey>
      </case:caseHeader>
    </case:case>
  </typ:startCaseInputMessage>
```

Instead of *123* you can use any value that uniquely identifies the instance of the case.

This will start a new instance of the case—as you can see on the Case tab in the BPM Workspace application and Figure 19-20.

In this case management user interface, you can inspect all details for the current case—of which there are not yet many. You can set values for the case data, upload documents, inspect milestones, and mark milestones complete. Cases can be linked to other cases. All case workers can already share this common view of the case and the associated data, even if the case does not yet orchestrate any actions or has rules to automatically act on milestones.

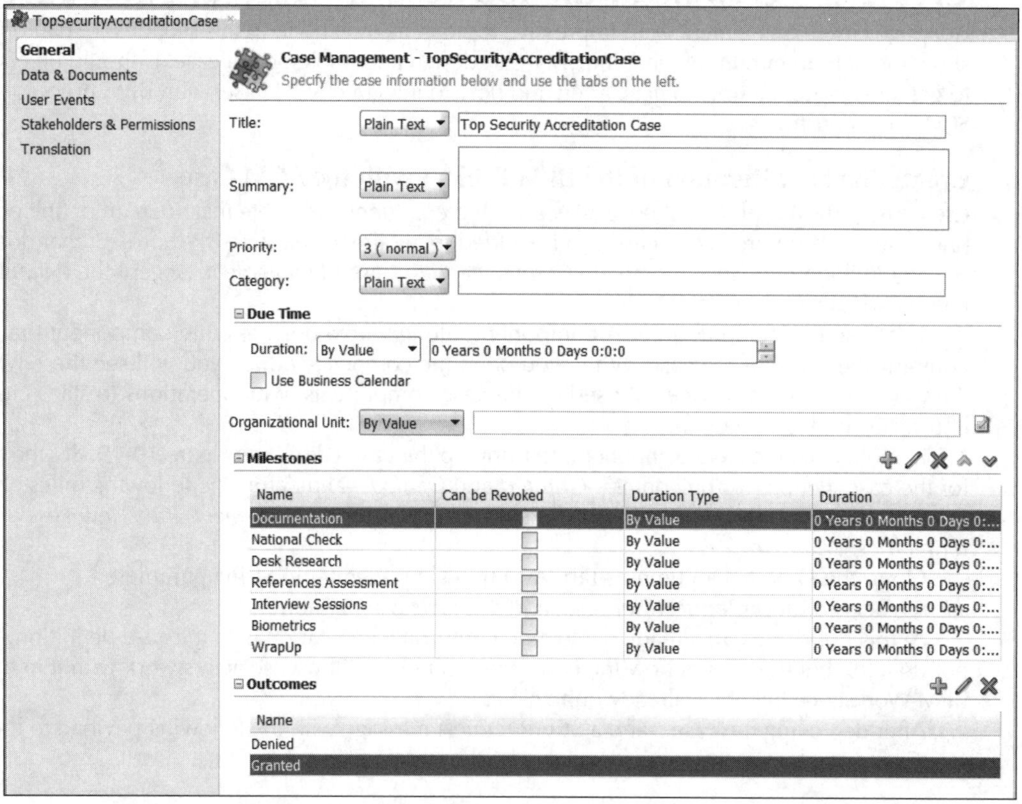

FIGURE 19-19. *The general properties for the TopSecurityAccreditationCase—including the possible outcomes and the milestones. No deadlines have been set for either case or milestones*

FIGURE 19-20. *The case tab in the BPM Workspace application showing an instance of the Top Security Accreditation Case with the case data, a manually completed milestone and more*

Provide Complex Data Input for the Case

A typical case has more interesting data to deal with than just two simple String parameters. Let's add the airport accreditation request as a parameter to the case. Open the Data & Documents tab.

Click on the plus icon to create a new parameter. Set the name of the parameter to *originalRequestForAirportAccreditation*. Mark the checkbox External—to indicate that the value for this parameter is provided by an external partner (when the case is initiated). Click on the plus icon to create the business object on which to build this parameter. The Create Business Object dialog appears. Set the name of the new Business Object to *RequestForAirportAccreditation*. Check the box for *Based on External Schema*. Click on the icon to import a schema file and select XSD document AirportAccreditationService.xsd in the *AirportAccreditationService* project to import. Select type *RequestForAirportAccreditationRequest* in this document.

Click on the browse icon for the Destination Module. In the dialog that appears, create a new module called *CaseDataModule*. All these steps should lead to a new parameter *originalRequestForAirportAccreditation* based on business object *RequestForAirportAccreditation* that takes its structure from XSD element *RequestForAirportAccreditationRequest*.

In order to be able to work with the data in this parameter, we need to create a form to display the parameter. Click on the Case Form icon in the header of the parameter table. Enter *RequestForAirportAccreditationForm* as the name for the new project to create with this parameter form. JDeveloper will now take some time to create a new project and in it the artifacts that constitute the user interface for this complex parameter.

Once the generation is complete, open the application level dropdown menu and create a new EAR style deployment profile for the application, called *TopSecurityAccreditationCaseForms*. Include the newly generated project in this deployment profile, under Application Assembly.

Next, deploy both the SOA composite *TopSecurityAccreditationCase* in the regular way as well as this new application deployment. If during the latter you get questions about MDS deployment, select the *mds-soa* repository and the *obpm* partition.

When this is done, the case can handle complex input data and it knows how to find the ADF Web Application to display and manipulate that data.

Let's try it out by sending a new request message—this time one that contains a request for airport accreditation. The salient aspects of the request message are:

```
<typ:startCaseInputMessage
    xmlns:typ="http://xmlns.oracle.com/CaseService/types"
    xmlns:case="http://xmlns.oracle.com/bpm/case" >
  <case:case>
    <case:caseHeader>
      <case:identificationKey>5434</case:identificationKey>
    </case:caseHeader>
    <case:data>
      <case:name>originalRequestForAirportAccreditation</case:name>
      <case:data>
        <sec:RequestForAirportAccreditationRequest
            xmlns:sec="saibot.airport/security">
          <sec:RequestingOrganizationId>Airbrush</
sec:RequestingOrganizationId>
          <sec:RequestorId>Margaret.Knowles</sec:RequestorId>
          <sec:StaffMemberToAccredit>
            <sec:FirstName>Cornelia</sec:FirstName>
            <sec:LastName>Vink</sec:LastName>
            <sec:EmailAddress>cor.vink@airbrush.com</sec:EmailAddress>
          </sec:StaffMemberToAccredit>
          <sec:RequiredSecurityLevel>4</sec:RequiredSecurityLevel>
        </sec:RequestForAirportAccreditationRequest>
      </case:data>
    </case:data>
  </case:case>
</typ:startCaseInputMessage>
```

After sending this message, the case is instantiated. In the case management user interface, the new form can be opened to allow inspection and editing of the data in the case, as shown in Figure 19-21.

Case Activities and Rules

The case really comes alive when it contains activities that it triggers based on rules driven by actions, data, milestones, and other events.

Add Case Activities

A case activity is one single item that the case worker can perform. Case activities can be mandatory, conditional, or optional. Case activities can be manual or automatic. Manual case activities require a case worker to initiate them while, automatic case activities are initiated by the case runtime. Business rules are used to decide which case activities to activate for automatic or manual initiation, or to withdraw when no longer applicable. Rules are also used to mark a milestone as achieved or revoked.

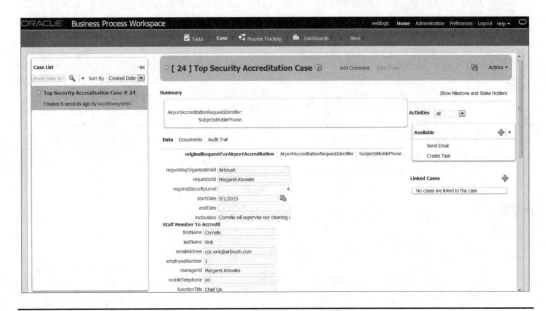

FIGURE 19-21. *The complex parameter form in the BPM Workspace case manager—for inspecting and manipulating the case data*

You can create a case activity based on a BPMN process or on a human task. There is a third option of creating a custom case activity based on a Java class (one that implements the oracle. bpm.casemgmt.caseactivity.ICaseActivityCallback interface).

In the case of a human task that is promoted as case activity, BPM Studio creates the input and output parameters based on the human task payload arguments. The case activity can pass input parameters to the underlying human task. You can also configure the case activity to read the output parameters of the human task and store their value.

When you promote a BPMN process as case activity, BPM Studio generates output arguments for all the arguments in the multiple endpoints of the BPMN process. However, if you want to cover the input arguments of a process that contains multiple start points, then you must create a case activity for each of the start points. You can use synchronous and asynchronous BPMN processes.

NOTE
Because the options to manipulate the case data are fairly limited and mapping the right data from the case to and from a human task can be hard to achieve, in actual practice, most tasks will probably be triggered through a small BPMN process to handle the data manipulation.

If you want a case activity to run after another case activity, then you must define a rule for the second activity that activates it only once the first activity completes.

Add human tasks *GatherIdentificationPapers* and *ExtendedNationalSecurityCheck*. Add a single participant in *stage1* on the assignment tab for each task—for example, associated with user *weblogic*.

In the project navigator, in the folder SOA | Human Tasks, Right-click human task *GatherIdentificationPapers* and select *Promote as Case Activity* on the context menu. The *Crease Case Activity* popup appears for you to confirm the name and display name for the new activity. After pressing OK, a wire is created between the Case component and the Human Task.

The Case Activity editor appears. In this editor, apart from the input and output parameters for the activity, is the configuration for whether the activity is manually or automatically activated, required, repeatable, only conditionally available (which means: enabled by a business rule) or associated with a special permission.

Now also promote human task *ExtendedNationalSecurityCheck* to case activity.

TIP
If you want to reopen the Case Activity editor at a later moment, you can do so from the entries in the folder BPM | Case | Activities under the project node in the project navigator.

If you were to deploy the composite application at this stage, and create a new instance, you can add instances of the two new case activities to the case. Next, you can initiate them—which in this case means they are assigned to user *weblogic* and show up in the BPM Workspace task list. Once completed, the case audit trail is updated with the completion details for these tasks.

Orchestrate the Case through Business Rules

The rule dictionary that was created along with the case is loaded with facts and devoid of rules. The facts are primarily standard case facts—available in any case—and facts derived from Schema definitions in this particular case.

Rules can be created that are triggered by activities being activated or completed, data being updated or by milestones being reached or revoked. These rules can use API calls to manipulate the cases, milestones, and activities.

An example of a typical case rule is completing activity *GatherIdentificationPapers* marks milestone *documentation* complete.

Open business rule dictionary *TopSecurityAccreditationCaseRules*. Check out the Facts and the Value Sets in this dictionary. Open the Rule Set. From the Overview tab, create a new decision table. Call the table *MilestoneRules*.

Add two conditions in the table—for CaseEvent.activityEvent.activityEvent (to filter on the subtype of activity event) and for CaseEvent.activityEvent.activityName. Create a new rule in the table—that means a new column—and cell values of COMPLETED (select the value in the Value Set) and "GatherIdentificationPapers." This rule is triggered when there is an activity event that reports that activity *GatherIdentificationPapers* is COMPLETED.

Next create an action in the table. The action consists of *call reachMileStone* with both arguments parametrized. Enter the values *documentation* (select from Value Set) and some comment on the milestone in the corresponding cells for the first rule. The decision table should look like Figure 19-22.

Much of the intelligence of a case is recorded in these rules. With every event in the case, the rules are evaluated by the case manager, to allow them to apply their logic to the case by, for example, changing the status of activities or updating milestones.

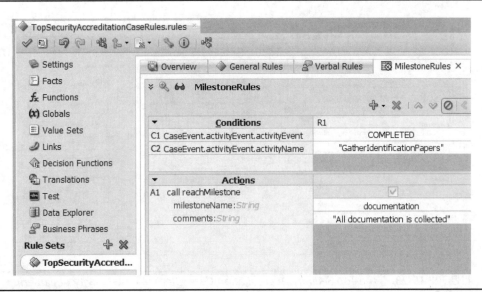

FIGURE 19-22.   *Rule dictionary for the case—evaluated after each case event, deciding on the activation of activities and completion of milestones; here calling milestone documentation after activity completion*

Deploy the composite application once more. Send a request to the startCase operation to create a new instance of the case. Navigate to this instance in the *Case* tab of the BPM Workspace application. Click on the green icon to add activity *Gather Identification Papers*. The activity is now added to the list of available activities. Click on this activity to initiate it.

Open the *Tasks* tab. There should be a task to *Gather Identification Papers* waiting, based on this action in the case. Complete this task and return to the *Case* tab. At this point, see Figure 19-23, the task should be listed as completed. More interestingly, the *Documentation* milestone is now listed as completed. This is the result of the rule that was just created and that was now triggered by the completion of the case activity of gathering documents. Check out the Audit Trail. This page provides a step by step overview of all events in the case and clearly shows how the conclusion of the activity triggered the milestone.

Integration of the Case in the AirportAccreditationProcess

The *TopSecurityAccreditationCase* does not live on its own. It is the somewhat rare extension of the process orchestrated inside the *AirportAccreditationService* (BPEL)—or perhaps of the *SecurityCheckProcess* (BPM). As a final step in this chapter, the case should be integrated into either of these two. As an optional step for the highest security level in the BPEL scope *SecurityChecks* or as an extra parallel flow with its own Exclusive Gateway in the BPM process.

The call to the case is a simple *Invoke* (BPEL) or *Send Message* (BPM). The original airport accreditation request is handed over to the case and the *caseId* and the *caseNumber* are returned

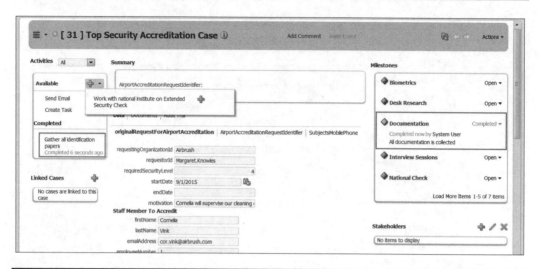

FIGURE 19-23. *The Top Security Accreditation Case after the case activity of gathering identification papers was completed—resulting in reaching milestone documentation*

in a synchronous response. Whenever the *AirportAccreditationService* is invoked with a request for accreditation with required security level equal to 5, the case will be triggered.

Summary

The objectives of an organization can only be achieved through the execution of business processes. This chapter introduced Business Process Management as a means to improve the performance of an organization through a constant focus on its business processes in an iterative cycle of design, execution, and improvement. BPM describes a structured approach to analyzing, designing and modeling, simulating, executing, and monitoring the business processes. BPMN offers a language for formally describing processes. In addition, BPMN run-time engines such as Oracle BPM are capable of executing the processes based on this formalized definition.

In addition to the highly structured business processes that are handled very nicely with the BPMN style process design and implementation, there is a different category of business process that is far less well defined. In this category, the process revolves around a case—documents and data that represent a "conversation." The case is worked on by several actors who can add content, manipulate data, and perform actions with regard to the case. The activities that can be executed on the case are well defined—but the order in which they are performed, the number of times they are repeated, and even whether or not they are performed at all is decided at run time—partially based on business rules and partially determined by case actors with the right privileges. Because of the dynamic adjustment of each case instance, this type of business process is Adaptive Case Management.

ACM processes contain activities that are either human tasks or BPMN processes. The latter are used for automated actions such as service calls as well as sections of structured business process execution.

This chapter introduced the BPMN service component in SOA composite applications. Note that in order to legally use BPM with the SOA Suite, you need an additional license.

BPMN components contain business process definitions that are created from a purely business perspective, without focus on technical aspects and implementation details. A process is defined through flows—conditional, parallel, iterative—in combination with various types of activities allocated to different business roles. The process can be simulated—long before any implementation details have been specified. Note that the initial design, simulation and (high level) implementation can be done through the browser-based Process Composer tool, which is targeted at nondeveloper roles.

In a next iteration—probably where the developer takes over from the analyst—the implementation for the process activities is created, typically in JDeveloper. The implementation of the activities is provided by other service components in the composite application—such as human tasks, business rules, and BPEL processes—or through external references bound to the composite application.

The SOA composite application with BPMN processes inside is deployed in the same way as the composite applications discussed in previous chapters. However, the run-time BPM environment offers various additional browser-based applications through which instances of BPM processes can be created and monitored (BPM Process Workspace) and the BPM process definition can be published, reviewed, and refined (BPM Process Composer).

Another way to implement business processes is through BPEL components. BPEL supports a similar set of flow, logic, and data-mapping facilities and can have more or less the same interaction with other service components and reference bindings. Although the Oracle BPM and BPEL engines share a common process core to handle the things that they both share like Security, Audit Trails, Service Invocation, and data persistence, there is a separate engine for BPM and BPEL. The design experience for BPEL is far more technically oriented and less business (analyst) friendly than BPMN. If you approach applications from a business process perspective and your organization has acquired the BPM license, you will be able to make excellent use of BPMN components in your composite applications. Note that BPMN does not replace BPEL, which has a major role for designing and running complex, orchestrated services.

CHAPTER
20

Monitoring for Insight into Business Process Execution

K nowing at run time what exactly is going on inside the SOA Suite can be useful at various moments for various purposes. At a technical level, the state of the platform and the infrastructure is important to know about in order to be able to guarantee the performance and scalability and even availability of the overall environment and the individual constituents. At a more functional level, insight in the proceedings in the BPEL and BPM engines is equivalent to insight into the execution of the business processes that form the essence of the organization. To some extent, what is orchestrated and recorded in these engines represents an important part of what the company *is*.

Learning by monitoring is relevant at an operational, near real-time level where hiccups in individual process instances have to be identified and dealt with as soon as possible, to prevent a consumer from having a negative experience. At a more tactical level, we will be watching for aggregations across process instances to spot trends and patterns—peaks through the day, the week, and the year—and, for example, learn about bottlenecks and opportunities for process improvement. Typically we will have to satisfy SLA rules that states response time and quality measures that we need to adhere to. Monitoring helps us stay on course regarding the SLA as well as demonstrate our achievements to our customer. Some organizations have a costing and budgeting structure that is based on number of executions of specific types of business processes. In these cases, there is an obvious need for monitoring and reporting on the activities taking place in SOA and BPM Suite.

This chapter discusses monitoring at the functional end of the spectrum. We will look at the mechanisms in BPEL and BPMN for exposing relevant metadata about individual process instances that help track and understand what is happening. This kicks off with sensors and sensor actions in BPEL processes that complement the composite sensors we first met in Chapter 5. Sensors record data in a database schema that is exposed at instance level in the EM FMW Control. Primarily for aggregation across instances, that data can be accessed using plain SQL and any programming language or reporting tool that speaks SQL. The sensors can also publish findings to JMS, for real time, cross instance processing, for example, in OEP or for reporting in BAM.

We then discuss process analytics in both BPEL and BPMN processes—fine-grained aspects of process instances that are gathered at run time into a star data object schema. This data object schema is hosted in the BAM infrastructure. BAM (Business Activity Monitoring) is shipped with not only the data objects for capturing the process analytics published from business process instances, it also provides an extensive set of dashboards and visualizations that provide insight in these process analytics. In short, this means that by flipping a few switches to instruct the tools about the (level of) information to publish for a particular process, the tools publish out of the box real-time dashboards that provide considerable insight in the business process activity at operational and tactical level.

By adding business process specific information to the process analytics mix, we are able to create custom BAM reports that go beyond the generic dashboards' focus and provide context and additional detail. We can, for example, see how aggregates vary with specific business aspects such as product group, security level, customer category, and other attributes that are meaningful to the business at hand. This chapter shows how to configure the BPEL and BPMN processes to publish these custom metadata elements and how to leverage them in custom BAM visualizations and key performance indicators (KPIs).

The BPM Workspace contains the Process Monitor—a tool that provides insight in the execution history of BPMN processes. This monitor visualizes a BPMN process and shows an overlay with aggregations per activity and flow, based on historic execution data—captured in the BAM data objects also used for the Process Analytics dashboard reports. Process Monitor can be used to optimize process execution by identifying bottlenecks and other performance problems.

Service Bus is not typically your first stop to gain insight in the execution of business processes. However, Service Bus can certainly provide information that is relevant for functional monitoring and SLA observation. Through Message Reports and Pipeline Alerts, first discussed in Chapter 3, we can expose metadata from within service execution. With SLA Alerts, we can publish aggregated information regarding the volume of service executions and the response times. Especially when Service Bus is on the edge of our services landscape, its findings are indicative for the end-to-end execution and the external experience. One light weight and optimally decoupled way of reporting findings is through publishing to a JMS Queue. This approach is commonly used with Service Bus [SLA] Alerts.

BAM ships with out of the box data objects for capturing process analytics and prebuilt dashboards that leverage these analytics. We discuss how we can extend the analytics with custom business indicators and how we can create custom dashboards on top of the process analytics data objects. We will also look the creation of our own data objects that can capture any data to be used to create even more custom reports and visualizations. BAM, for example, is frequently used to capture events from JMS channels and use them for near real-time reporting and alerting. As such, BAM is a frequent companion to event processing applications based on OEP. This chapter demonstrates how the car park management discussed in Chapter 16 can be facilitated using a BAM dashboard to show the car park occupancy, car influx, and abandoned cars listing.

BPEL Monitoring Using Sensors

BPEL processes can report data about their execution using two different mechanisms. One produces process analytics into a BAM star schema, to be discussed a little bit later. The other is based on sensors that produce signals for specific activities that are executed, variables that are updated or faults that occur. These signals can be pushed to be reported in the EM FMW control along with other instance details. These values are stored in tables in the SOA Infra database schema where they can be accessed using SQL. Alternatively or additionally, the sensor values can be published to a local JMS Queue or Topic, to a custom Java handler or to the JMS Adapter (for remote destinations).

Three types of sensors can be added to a BPEL process:

- Variable sensors that report any change in a BPEL process variable—including the new value, a timestamp, and the name of the activity that caused the change

- Activity sensors that report selected stages—activation, completion, retry, fault, compensation—in the execution of an activity, including the name and type of the activity and the timestamp for the reported stage

- Fault sensors that report the occurrence of a specific fault—including the activity that triggered the fault, a timestamp and the detail fault message

Associated with each sensor are one or more sensor actions that describe how the sensor registration is published. Sensors and sensor actions are defined with the BPEL editor running in *monitor* mode.

Monitoring AirportAccreditationProcessor with BPEL Sensors

The business process for handling airport accreditation requests was introduced and implemented in the previous chapters. This process is very important at Saibot airport—to ensure a smooth influx of new staff in a way that is in line with security regulations. Both monitoring the execution of individual process instances as well as the longer term state of the entire business process across all accreditation requests is quite relevant.

In this section, we will be using various BPEL sensors to provide easy insight in the current state of a single process instance as well as some aggregated values for execution times.

Variable sensors are used to associate specific metadata with a process instance—in this case the requesting organization and the required security level. This helps us in analyzing possible issues with a process instance. It also provides context for all instances that will help in the analysis of all accreditation requests and the way they were processed: did processing requests from specific organizations or for certain security levels result in different performance characteristics than others?

Activity sensors will detect whether specific activities have been executed and if so—when and for how long? In this case we will specifically track the scope that invokes the *SecurityChecks* process—because that seems to be the bottleneck in the execution of the BPEL process. Additionally, we monitor the Throw activity that is executed when an accreditation request is received for an unknown organization.

TIP
Even without specifically creating sensors—and depending on configured audit level—a lot of run-time information is recorded that describes the execution of composite instances. This information— stored in tables in the SOA Infra database schema—is used to populate the overviews in the EM FMW Control. We can access this data ourselves directly, using either SQL or the Java API.

Decorate the BPEL Process with Sensors and Sensor Actions

Open the *AirportAccreditationRequestProcessor* process in the BPEL editor. In the header bar, switch to monitor mode using the icon in the upper right-hand corner, see Figure 20-1.

Right click on scope *SecurityChecks* and select Create | Sensor from the context menu. A popup window appears to configure an Activity Sensor for this activity. Specify a name, for example, *SecurityChecksActivitySensor*. Set the *Evaluation Time* as *All*—to have this sensor report at the start, end, fault, retry, and compensation of the activity. Add an activity variable sensor—to report the value of a specific variable with each of the activity reports. Such a sensor consists of an XPath expression to retrieve a specific value that the activity probably uses or manipulates.

Click on the green plus icon to create a Sensor Action that applies to this activity sensor. Call the sensor action DB_FOR_FMW and set the Publish Type to Database. Do not specify a Filter condition. Close the popup windows and complete the definition of the sensor.

The Structure Window displays the Sensor and the Sensor Action that was just created, see Figure 20-1. Click on the node *Variable* and subsequently on the green plus icon—in order to create a variable sensor.

Call this sensor *statusSensor*. Set $globalProcessStatus as the Target [expression]. Add sensor action DB_FOR_FMW. This sensor will report every change in the value of the *globalProcessStatus* variable over the course of an instance of the BPEL process.

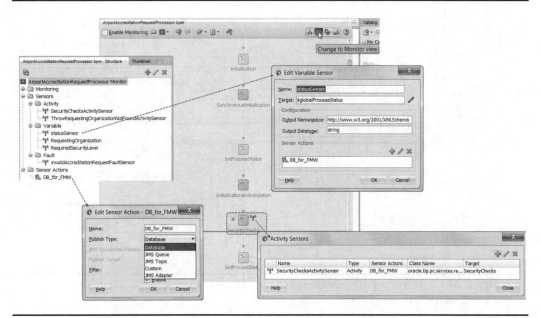

Figure 20-1. *The BPEL process editor in the Monitor View with the SecurityChecksActivitySensor to report on the SecurityChecks Scope activity using the DB_FOR_FMW sensor action*

You can add additional sensors, as shown in Figure 20-1: variable sensors that report the elements *RequestingOrganizationId* and *RequiredSecurityLevel,* respectively, in the original request message and an activity sensor for the Throw activity in *IfCompanyNotFound.*

TIP
When you start creating sensors, it will soon be very obvious that a good way of naming your activities—including scope and sequence— is more than useful: it is imperative to create sensors that produce intelligible monitoring information.

NOTE
The Monitor View of the BPEL Process editor offers more than only sensors. It has a checkbox to Enable Monitoring and it supports creation of Business Indicators (Dimensions, Measures), Intervals and Counters. These are included only for backward compatibility with the 11g release that offered the Monitor Express, a tool that has now been deprecated and succeeded by the Process Analytics in BAM. Oracle recommends you no longer use Monitor Express.

Monitoring Using the Sensor Signals
After deploying the sensor-enabled SOA composite, you can make one or more test requests for airport accreditation. Subsequently, you inspect the in-flight and completed instances in the EM FMW Control. The message flow trace tells us quite a bit about the progress made with

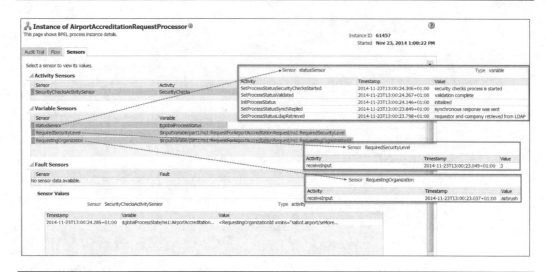

Figure 20-2. *Sensor values reported in the EM FMW Control for an instance of the AirportAccreditationRequestProcessor*

this particular instance. When we drill down to the BPEL process, depending on the audit setting, we can see a detailed audit trail.

The result of the sensors is that on the third tab of the BPEL instance report—Sensors—we see the detailed information we configured the sensors to expose. These details give us insight in the execution of the instance—when, how, how long—and the metadata for this particular instance— requesting organization, required security level. Figure 20-2 shows the sensor overview for a particular instance midway through the process. We can easily tell that the *SecurityChecksProcess* was started at 1PM and that this particular request for accreditation was submitted by Airbrush and required security level 3. The variable sensor *statusSensor* provides compact insight in the steps in the process thus far.

In this case, we used a sensor action to publish the sensor signal to the database for publication through the EM FMW Control. We could also have sent the signals to a JMS destination of a custom Java handler.

SQL Access to Sensor Data   The sensor data published in the EM FMW Control is read from a set of standard tables in the SOA Infra database schema. These tables are wrapped in views that we can use to retrieve information from in a programmatic way. This allows us to get details about individual instances of the BPEL process or to query for aggregate numbers across a bunch of process instances.

The first query we can use to learn about instances of BPEL process components joins together table CUBE_INSTANCE—with entries for every instance of a BPEL process—with view BPEL_ PROCESS_INSTANCES that is a programmer friendly wrapper around that same table. The underlying table can provide the composite instance id and the ECID.

```
select c.flow_id composite_instance_id
,      c.ecid
,      b.instance_key
```

```
,        b.COMPOSITE_NAME
,        b.COMPONENT_NAME
,        b.STATE_TEXT
,        b.STATUS
,        b.eval_time
,        b.creation_date
from     BPEL_PROCESS_INSTANCES b
         join
         CUBE_INSTANCE c
         on (b.instance_key = c.cikey)
```

Figure 20-3 compares the results from this query with the information shown in the EM FMW Control, for an inflight instance of the *AirportAccreditationService*.

The output from activity sensors can be queried from a database view BPEL_ACTIVITY_SENSOR_VALUES. This query returns the results from activity sensors—especially the number of times an activity was executed and the time it took to execute.

```
select   sensor_name
,        ACTIVITY_NAME||' ('||ACTIVITY_TYPE||')' activity
,        count(*) number_of_instances
,        avg(eval_time/1000) avg_execution_time_seconds
from     BPEL_ACTIVITY_SENSOR_VALUES
group
by       sensor_name
,        ACTIVITY_NAME||' ('||ACTIVITY_TYPE||')'
```

Trace

Actions ▾ View ▾ Show Instance ▢ IDs

Instance	Type	Usage	State	Ti
◢ 🔵 AirportAccreditationService	Service	📬 Service	✔ Completed	Nov 23, 2014 1:00:22
◢ 🔧 AirportAccreditationRequestProcessor	BPEL		➜ **Running**	Nov 23, 2014 1:00:22
◢ 🔶 LDAPMediator	Mediator		✔ Completed	Nov 23, 2014 1:00:23
📇 RetrieveUser	Reference	📬 Reference	✔ Completed	Nov 23, 2014 1:00:23
◢ 🔶 LDAPMediator	Mediator		✔ Completed	Nov 23, 2014 1:00:23
📇 RetrieveOrganization	Reference	📬 Reference	✔ Completed	Nov 23, 2014 1:00:23
◢ 🗐 SecurityCheckProcess	BPMN		✔ Completed	Nov 23, 2014 1:00:24
🔧 NationalSecurityCheckService	BPEL		✔ Completed	Nov 23, 2014 1:00:25
🗄 InternalSecurityScreeningEvaluation	Decision		✔ Completed	Nov 23, 2014 1:00:25
🗄 ManualScreeningOfSecurityAccreditationRequest	Workflow		✔ Completed	Nov 23, 2014 1:00:26
🔧 PersonnelService	BPEL		✔ Completed	Nov 23, 2014 1:21:40
🔧 BadgeService	BPEL		➜ **Running**	Nov 23, 2014 1:21:40
◢ 🔶 LDAPMediator	Mediator		✔ Completed	Nov 23, 2014 1:21:40
📇 AddUser	Reference	📬 Reference	✔ Completed	Nov 23, 2014 1:21:40

COMPOSITE_INSTANCE_ID	INSTANCE_KEY	COMPOSITE_NAME	COMPONENT_NAME	STATE_TEXT	STATUS	EVAL_TIME	CREATION_DATE
60196	61467	AirportAccreditationService	BadgeService	open.running	initiated	97	23-NOV-14 01.21.42
60196	61466	AirportAccreditationService	PersonnelService	closed.completed	initiated	191	23-NOV-14 01.21.40
60196	61463	AirportAccreditationService	NationalSecurityCheckService	closed.completed	initiated	60110	23-NOV-14 01.00.26
60196	61462	AirportAccreditationService	SecurityCheckProcess	closed.completed	initiated	1274721	23-NOV-14 01.00.24
60196	61457	AirportAccreditationService	AirportAccreditationRequestProcessor	open.running	ScopeRecordInLDAP	1279345	23-NOV-14 01.00.22

Figure 20-3. *Comparing EM FMW Control and a direct database query with details about a SOA composite instance*

One result row from this query is:

```
SecurityChecksActivitySensor | SecurityChecks (scope) | 43 | 3506.76
```

This indicates 43 requests have been processed by the scope *SecurityChecks* with an average processing time of just under 1 hour.

To drill even further down into the process instances using the results from variable sensors, we can leverage the view BPEL_ACTIVITY_SENSOR_VALUES.

```
select INSTANCE_KEY
,      sensor_name
,      VARIABLE_NAME
,      nvl(VARCHAR2_VALUE , to_char( NUMBER_VALUE) ) variable_value
,      UPDATER_NAME||' ('||updater_type||')' updating_activity
,      creation_date
from   BPEL_VARIABLE_SENSOR_VALUES
```

Figure 20-4 shows an example of the result of this query.

When we combine these results with the outcome from the activity sensors, we can try to analyze the average duration of the security checks process against required security level or requesting organization.

Results from Fault sensors can be inspected through the view BPEL_FAULT_SENSOR_VALUES.

NOTE
SOA composite applications without BPEL process component do not have a means of publishing sensor values. To learn more about instances of these composites beyond their occurrence and perhaps some attributes through composite sensors, we could make use of the custom callout option on a Mediator component to invoke Java code that can publish details about the instance to for example a JMS destination.

TIP
In Chapter 5, we first worked with Composite Sensors to provide metadata for instances of SOA composite applications. Based on the messages sent into or out of a SOA composite application, attributes meaningfully describing each instance are published to the EM FMW Control or to a JMS Queue. From that queue, the sensors values can be consumed into a BAM application to be reported in a custom dashboard.

CE_KEY	SENSOR_NAME	VARIABLE_NAME	VARIABLE_VALUE	UPDATING_ACTIVITY	CREATION_DATE
61457	RequestingOrganization	inputVariable	Airbrush	receiveInput (receive)	23-NOV-14 01.00.23.0
61457	RequiredSecurityLevel	inputVariable	3	receiveInput (receive)	23-NOV-14 01.00.23.0
61457	statusSensor	globalProcessStatus	requestor and company retrieve...	SetProcessStatusLdapRetrieved (assign)	23-NOV-14 01.00.23.7
61457	statusSensor	globalProcessStatus	synchronous response was sent	SetProcessStatusSynchReplied (assign)	23-NOV-14 01.00.23.8
61457	statusSensor	globalProcessStatus	initialized	InitProcessStatus (assign)	23-NOV-14 01.00.24.1
61457	statusSensor	globalProcessStatus	notifications complete	SetProcessStatusNotificationsComple...	23-NOV-14 01.22.43.7

Figure 20-4. *SQL query result from view BPEL_VARIABLE_SENSOR_VALUES*

BPEL Process Analytics Reported Using BAM

Both the BPEL and BPM process engines are prepared to deliver process analytics to a set of BAM data objects. With just a few declarative steps, we can configure any BPEL process to report details about its execution to this BAM environment. As part of the out of the box installation, BAM contains a number of prebuilt business queries, business views, and dashboards on top of these data objects that provide a lot of operational and tactical insight in the business process activities.

In this section we will first configure the AirportAccreditationProcessor for the out of the box process analytics. We will review some of the shipped reports to see the information we have access to without hardly any effort at all. Next, we will create a few process specific business indicators and see how we can leverage those in several custom BAM queries, KPIs, and views that we can combine in a custom dashboard.

Out of the box Process Analytics with BPEL and BAM

Generic process analytics and the reporting on top of those do not provide any business or process specific information, obviously. They focus on generic aspects, such as the number of process instances and executions of individual activities and the processing time aggregates— max, min, avg—for processes as a whole as well as individual activities. The current status for running instances as well as the history overview can be reported on.

Enabling Process Analytics

The production of process analytics is driven by declarative settings at the level of the SOA composite and each BPEL (and BPMN) process for which you want analytics to be produced. Additionally, you need to configure a property in an MBean to enable publication to BAM for your entire WebLogic SOA domain and of course the domain must contain a running BAM [managed] server.

Configure MBean for Domain Wide Process Analytics Publication to BAM   Open the EM Fusion Middleware Control console. Select the WebLogic Domain | SOA domain node in the Target Navigation pane. In the dropdown menu, select option System MBean Browser. In the MBeans tree, locate and expand the node Application Defined MBeans. Expand down to the node oracle.as.soainfra.config and under this node the node for the server running your SOA Suite run-time environment. This node contains a grandchild MBean called AnalyticsConfig | analytics. Select this node, as shown in Figure 20-5, and set its attribute DisableProcessMetrics to false (note the confusing double negative, meaning that we actually want to enable process metrics).

Make sure you apply these changes.

Configure Analytics at Composite Level   At composite level can be specified at what level of detail the process analytics should be produced. This level can subsequently be overridden or inherited at the level of BPEL processes.

Open the composite editor for *AirportAccreditationService*. Click on the Process Analytics icon, as shown in Figure 20-6. In the popup window, select the radio button Generate [Sampling Points] For All Activities. This will result in process analytics for all BPEL process activities being sent to the BAM data objects.

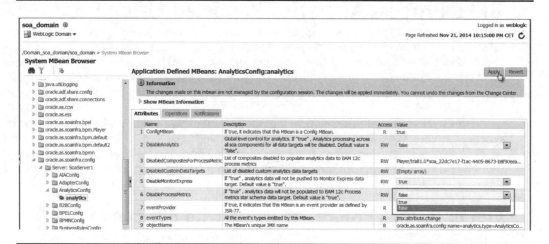

Figure 20-5. *Configuring the Analytics MBean for Process Analytics publication to BAM*

Configure Process Analytics at BPEL Process Level   Open the BPEL Process editor for *AirportAccreditationRequestProcessor*. Change to Analytics view, using the icon in the upper right-hand corner. Note how the components palette now contains the components Counter Mark, Interval Start, Interval Stop, and Single Mark. All these components can be dragged on top of the BPEL process to define spots where to record values, increment counters and produce analytic input. We will use these process specific business indicators a little later on. Let's first focus on the out of the box features.

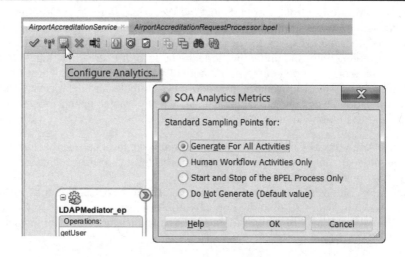

Figure 20-6. *Configuring production of Process Analytics*

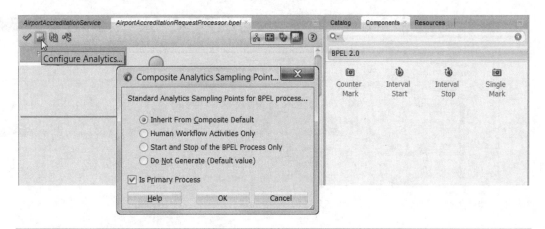

Figure 20-7. *Configure Analytics at the level of the BPEL process*

Click on the icon for configuring analytics. In the popup window, shown in Figure 20-7, select radio button *Inherit From Composite Default* and check the box *Is Primary Process*.

Reviewing Out Of The Box Process Analytics BAM Dashboards

After having made these simple declarative settings regarding analytics for the composite application *AirportAccreditationService* and its key BPEL process, deploy the SOA composite. Subsequently, send a few accreditation requests to the service and handle them through the associated human tasks. This way, some analytics will be collected into the BAM data objects.

Next, open the BAM Composer at the URL http://host:port/bam/composer. Open the Administrator tab. Open the Data Objects folder. The folder *oracle/processanalytics* contains two objects—*AirportAccreditationService Process* and *AirportAccreditationService Activity*—that were generated when the *AirportAccreditationService* composite was deployed with Analytics support enabled. The details for all BPEL processes in new instances of the composite are collected into these two data objects. Select one of them and then open the Data tab for the data object to get a taste of the records that are collected. Figure 20-8 shows some data collected in the BAM data object for BPEL process executions for instances of SOA composite *AirportAccreditationService*. Remember that it takes nothing more than some simple configuration settings to have this data published from the SOA Suite run time to this BAM star schema.

Now select the Home tab. Open—if it is not open already—the BAM project called Process Analytics that is shipped with the SOA Suite. An overview is shown of all the many dashboards available in this project. You can try out a few of these, to get a feel for the information on offer.

Open for example *Analysis of Open Processes,* see Figure 20-9, that gives a straightforward overview of the currently open instances of each of the monitored composites and BPEL processes.

Analysis of Open Processes (Detail) produces a table with a list of all currently open processes. *Bottleneck Analysis of Open Processes* shows a Treemap with an overview of all process activities. The size of the tiles represents the relative occurrence of the activities and they are colored based on average execution time. *Process Summary Dashboard* lists per process the number of new and

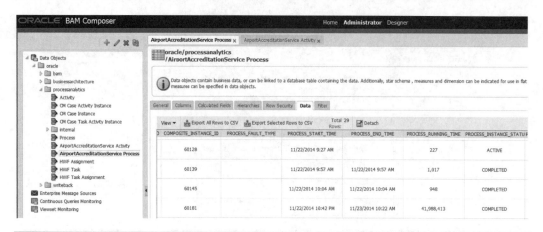

Figure 20-8. *Some of the data in the data object AirportAccreditationService Process generated for capturing process analytics for the SOA composite AirportAccreditationService*

closed instances for the current day, as well as the numbers of open process instances that are due soon, overdue, or not yet due. *Processes opened today* lists some details for the instances that were newly created today and the time for which they have been open. *Trend Analysis for Processes* (Figure 20-10) shows a graphical overview of the average processing time per process instance and the inflow of new and outflow of completed process instances.

Custom Reports and Process Specific Business Indicators

The standard reports provide some relevant insights into the execution of process instances. It is easy to extend this out of the box set-up:

- Add process specific business indicators to the process analytics, to provide some context for the process instances and the data they report; this is done in the BPEL process editor's analytics view

- Create custom business queries, business views, KPIs, and dashboards in the BAM Composer to provide business users and functional administrators with additional information

In this section, we will add a few specific elements to the BPEL process analytics and subsequently leverage these in custom BAM components.

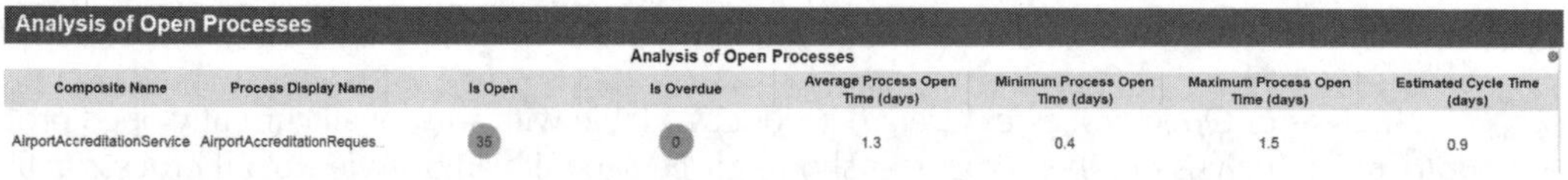

Analysis of Open Processes

			Analysis of Open Processes			
Composite Name	Process Display Name	Is Open	Is Overdue	Average Process Open Time (days)	Minimum Process Open Time (days)	Maximum Process Open Time (days)	Estimated Cycle Time (days)
AirportAccreditationService	AirportAccreditationReques...	35	0	1.3	0.4	1.5	0.9

Figure 20-9. *The Analysis of Open Processes dashboard, listing some data on the open process instances*

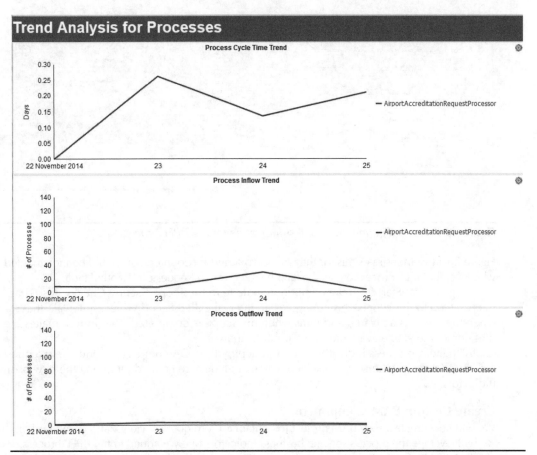

Figure 20-10. *Trend Analysis Dashboard—showing daily number of instances and their average processing time*

Configure Custom Business Indicators for Process Analytics

Open the BPEL editor and ensure it is in analytics view.

In the structure window, select node Business Indicators | Dimensions. Click on the green plus icon to create a new dimension, called RequestionOrganization. Specify the XPath expression to derive the value for this dimension from the RequestionOrganizationId element in the $inputVariable that holds the request message. Subsequently create a second dimension called RequestedSecurityLevel, deriving its value too from the $inputVariable—this time the RequiredSecurityLevel element.

Also create two Counters, called AccreditationRequestCounter and UnknownRequestorCounter. Counters need to be associated with specific points in the BPEL process in order to get assigned their values. These points are called counter marks. You can drag counter marks from the component palette and drop them at the desired location in the BPEL process. Subsequently, you can associate the counters that should be incremented at that particular point with the counter mark.

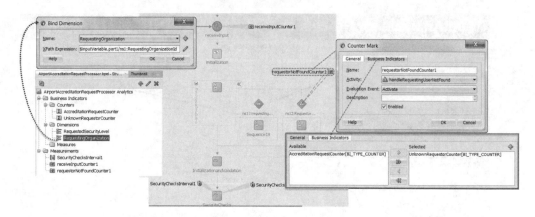

Figure 20-11. *Configuring the business indicators for the BPEL process*

Figure 20-11 demonstrates this for the UnknownRequestorCounter that should be incremented whenever the BPEL process enters the fault handler for the RequestorNotFound fault.

Drag Interval Start from the component palette to the scope SecurityChecks. Also drag Interval Stop to this scope. This configures an interval called SecurityChecksInterval1 that starts when the scope is activated and ends when the scope is completed. That in turn makes the duration of the scope available in the process analytics.

With these business indicators set up, redeploy the SOA composite. Send a few requests for Airport Accreditation—to make sure some analytics are created including the new business indicators.

Create Custom BAM Components

We will now create a new BAM project to contain custom queries, views, and dashboard. In those we will leverage the process specific business indicators that we added to the BPEL process.

Open BAM Composer and navigate to the Designer tab. Click on the down arrow behind the current project name (probably Process Analytics). From the dropdown menu, select Create. In the dialog that appears, provide a name such as *AirportAccreditationsDashboard* and a fitting display name. Press OK to have the project created.

Data Objects   Click on the node Data Objects. A list of existing Data Objects is presented that you can select objects from to use in this new project. Select the Logical Data Objects *AirportAccreditationService Activity* and *AirportAccreditationService Process*. Click Add to close the dialog.

Click on the second data object. An overview appears of the definition of the data object. Click on the Columns tab. Scroll down to find columns B_REQUESTEDSECURITYLEVEL and B_REQUESTINGORGANIZATION—that were generated based on the dimensions that were defined in the BPEL process. If you click on the Data tab, you will find the values from your most recent request messages recorded in these columns.

If you check the columns for data object *AirportAccreditationService Activity*, you will find similar entries for the dimensions and also columns corresponding to the counters: B_UNKNOWNREQUESTOR_COUNTER and B_ACCREDITATIONREQUESTCOUNTER. This data object contains records for each BPEL activity (because of the abundant sample point generation we configured at composite level) as well as entries for each counter mark and for each interval. Column ACTIVITY_DISCRIMINATOR indicates the type of record: STANDARD, MEASUREMENT_ INTERVAL or MEASUREMENT_COUNTER.

Business Queries   Business Queries underpin Business Views and KPIs in BAM. Business Queries describe a data set retrieved from the data objects with specific filters, aggregations, and column selections. BAM supports four types of business queries: Continuous Query (real time, streaming data based), Group SQL Query, Tree Model Query, and Flat SQL Query.

Click on the node Business Queries. In the dialog window that appears, set the name and the display name to AccreditationRequestsPerDayPerSecurityLevel. Select Group SQL Query as the query type. Click the Create button.

In the Business Query editor, select data object *AirportAccreditationService Process*. Mark the checkbox for Count(*) as the Measure. Click on the *preview* icon in the bottom left-hand corner. The query we have composed so far is executed and a single number is printed out.

In the Dimensions column, mark the checkbox for Process Start Time. A dialog appears to configure the Time Grouping. Set the time unit to day or hour—to indicate whether the process instances should be counted per day or per hour. Leave Continuous Time Series unchecked unless you want to see entries in the output for every day or hour that does not have any instances. Press OK to close the dialog.

Press the preview icon again. Now you will probably see multiple records, with the instance count per day or hour.

Next you may add another level of grouping: for example, grouping by the business indicator *required security level*. From the Legend dropdown, select RequestedSecurityLevel BI. Press preview again. Now press the little bar chart icon. The result is shown in Figure 20-12.

Press Save to persist the definition of the business query.

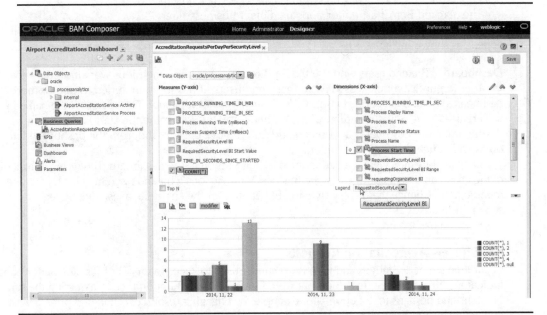

Figure 20-12. *Configuration of the business query AccreditationRequestsPerDayPerSecurityLevel*

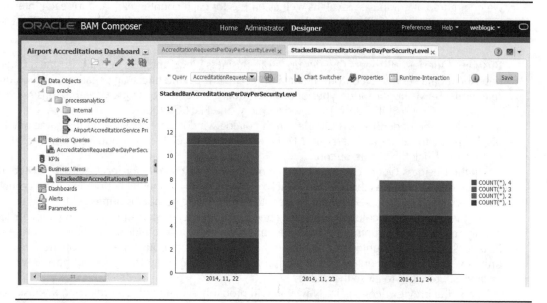

Figure 20-13. *The Business View showing the Accreditation Requests stacked per day and colored per security level*

Business Views   In order for any kind of visualization of this business query to be presented in a dashboard, we have to define a business view based on the query. Click on the node Business Views. In the dialog that appears, set the name to StackedBarAccreditationsPerDayPerSecurityLevel. Select Bar Chart | Stacked Bar Chart as the chart type. Click on Create.

The Stacked Bar Chart editor appears. Select business query *AccreditationRequestsPerDayPerSecurityLevel* as the under this chart. Press Save. The chart will appear, as shown in Figure 20-13.

Dashboard   The end users who use the BAM reports to perform their jobs work from dashboards. In order to publish a business view to these end users, it has to be included in one or more dashboards. Click on the node Dashboards. Enter *AirportAccreditationsDashboard* as the name in the create dialog. Select template *Type 1*. The templates determine the start layout of the dashboard. Note however that you can add and remove cells to and from the dashboard later on as well. Click on the Create button.

Drag the business view created in the previous section to the dashboard. The display properties of the chart can be edited. Click on the Business View Actions icon and open the Display Properties menu option. Change the display style to 3D, set titles for the chart, the axes, and the legend, as shown in Figure 20-14.

Save the dashboard.

KPI on New Accreditation Requests

In addition to charts, gauges and lists, BAM can be used to keep watch over KPIs (key performance indicators). KPIs are specific values that we consider of critical importance to assessing the state of affairs and perhaps to act upon—for example, by engaging resources, changing price levels, contacting business partners.

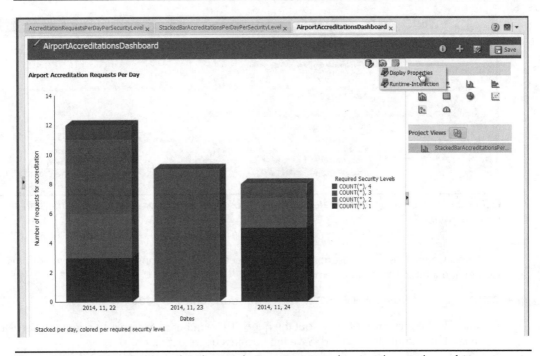

Figure 20-14. *The Dashboard with a single Business View showing the numbers of Airport Accreditation Requests per day—colored per security level*

In this case, we consider the number of accreditation requests we have received in the last hour one of our KPIs. We think we are equipped to handle up to six requests per hour. When there is a sudden influx of requests, we need to respond quickly—to honor the specifications in our SLA. Before, we monitored the average processing time for the requests, but it turned out we could only react when the processing time deteriorated. By looking at the influx, we hope to be able to act in time.

Add Derived Attribute to Data Object To make life easier on ourselves when we create the business query, we start by adding a derived attribute to the data object *AirportAccreditationService* Process. This attribute will tell us for each process instance how long it has been running (in seconds). Click on the data object. Open the tab Calculated Fields. Click on the green plus icon to add a new calculated field. Set the name of the field to TIME_IN_SECONDS_SINCE_STARTED. Set the expression that derives its value to:

```
DATEDIFF(SQL_TSI_SECOND,{Process Start Time},NOW())
```

Figure 20-15 shows the definition of this calculated field.

Create Business Query for the Instances Started in the Last Hour Click on the node Business Queries. The dialog for a new business query appears. Set the name to *AccreditationRequestsInLastHour*. Choose Group SQL Query as the query type.

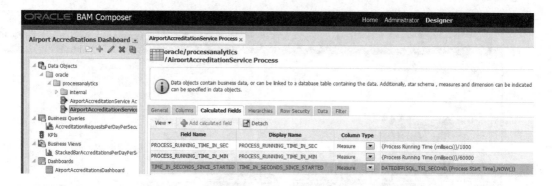

Figure 20-15. *Creating a Calculated Field to expose the number of seconds since the start of the process instance*

Select Count(*) as the Measure and do not select any Dimensions. Click on the green plus icon to add a filter. Set the filter expression to:

```
TIME_IN_SECONDS_SINCE_STARTED is less than 3,600
```

Click on the preview icon to try out the query. The number of accreditation requests received in the last hour should be reported. Save the business query definition.

Create a KPI for the Instances Started in the Last Hour   Click on the KPIs node. Set the name of the new KPI to *RecentAccreditationRequestsKPI*. Select Scheduled KPI as the type of KPI. Click on the Create button.

Select the business query that was created in the previous step. The only available measure is COUNT(*), which is auto selected. Specify a schedule frequency of *Every Minute* (just for demo's sake).

Set the Threshold Constant to 6. Specify a low-to-medium threshold at 5 and the medium-to-high threshold at 7. Define actions for both medium and high range values: send an email to ask for help. Configure the mail message and include the number of emails in the subject.

The KPI definition should look now like Figure 20-16.

Save the KPI definition.

NOTE
In order for BAM to actually send emails, you need to configure the UMS Email Driver Properties on the managed server on which BAM is running. You do this in the same way as you did for the managed server running SOA Suite. Subsequently, you also have to configure the Sender Email ID on the BAM Properties page.

Create KPI Watchlist Including the KPI for Recent Instances   The Business View type used to present a KPI is the KPI Watchlist. Click on the node Business Views. Set the name to AirportAccreditationKPIWatchlist and select KPI Watchlist as the category and the View Type. Click on the Create button.

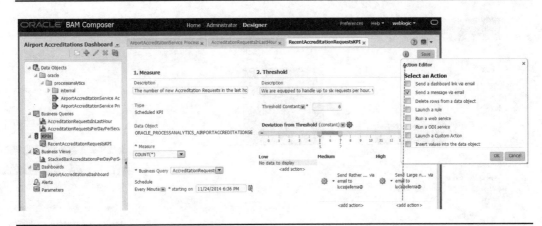

Figure 20-16. *Definition of the KPI to monitor the number of new accreditations requests in the last hour*

Open the dropdown list in the top right-hand corner and mark the KPI that you just created. The KPI is shown, like Figure 20-17. Click on Save.

Add KPI Watchlist to Dashboard   Open the dashboard. Click on the *Dashboard Actions* icon in the upper right-hand corner of the cell that contains the stacked bar chart. From the dropdown menu that appears, select Add New Cell Below. An empty cell is added below the existing cell.

Drag the KPI Watchlist to the new cell. This is all it takes to expose it in the dashboard.

When you open the dashboard, you can set business view filters on dimensions and all characteristics of the process instances available from the underlying data object. Figure 20-18 shows the dashboard with the stacked bar chart filtered on instances with the requested security level less than 3.

Figure 20-17. *The KPI Watchlist containing just a single KPI and its most recently observed values*

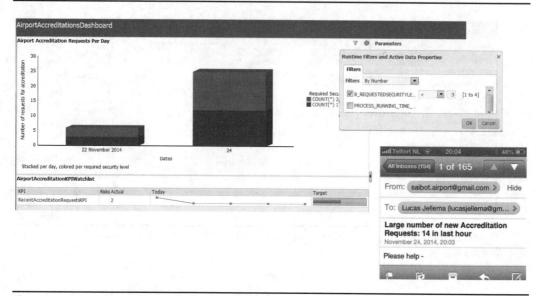

Figure 20-18. *The Airport Accreditations Dashboard with a filter on the stacked bar chart business view; also: the email alert sent out because of the KPI definition*

TIP
All the process analytics data that we accessed from BAM Data Objects are stored in tables in the SOA Infra database schema. You can use SQL to access these Process Star schema data objects by their database views, such as BPM_PV_PROCESS_V and BPM_PV_ACTIVITY_V, that can be joined to dimension views BPM_PV_PROCESS_DEFINITION_V and BPM_PV_ACTIVITY_DEFINITION_V.

Process Analytics in BPM Processes

Oracle BPM Suite is well equipped to provide operational insight in its proceedings to business operators and process owners. Throughout the execution of BPM process instances, data is collected that can be used to monitor in flight instances or to analyze recently completed instances. With simple switches, we can influence the level detail to be recorded for each process instance—as well as the instance specific metadata to be recorded.

Business Process Analytics enables you to monitor the performance of your deployed processes. It measures the key performance indicators in your project and stores them in a database. Process analysts can view the metrics stored in the BAM 12*c* using Process Workspace dashboards or—preferably—Oracle BAM 12*c* Process Analytics dashboards.

The Business Process Analytics support in BPM is very similar to what we have discussed in the previous section for BPEL. The BAM data objects and prebuilt dashboards coincide and the design time part of it is very similar as well. Additionally, BPM offers the Process Monitor, a visualization of a BPM process with an overlay of the metrics collected for each step in the process.

In this section we will briefly discuss the design steps to configure process analytics for BPMN processes as well as an example of the run-time results.

Design Time Configuration of Process Analytics

At design time the project as well as the composite and the individual BPMN process and its activities can be configured for the production of process analytics. The configuration for the composite is of course the same as we have seen before.

Process Analytics Configuration of Project and Process

The configuration of process analytics for a BPM project is also done at project level. Right click the project node in the application navigator and select BPM | Project Preferences from the context menu. A window appears, as shown in Figure 20-19. On the General page, set the Analytics View Identifier to a unique, meaningful identifier, for example, SAIBOTSECU. This value will be reported in the analytics recorded in the data objects and is used to generate project specific database synonyms for easier access to the data for this particular project.

On the Process Analytics Summary page, you can specify the overall settings regarding sampling—in other words: the level of granularity for creating individual log records for executing activities. The Data Targets tab is used to enable publication to BAM 12c for this project and optionally also to BAM 11g. The Business Indicators tab lists the business indicators that have been configured for the project.

Click on OK to close the window.

Open the BPMN process editor. Right click on the diagram. From the context menu, select option Properties. Open the Advanced tab. Here is an opportunity to override the project level settings at process level, as shown in Figure 20-20.

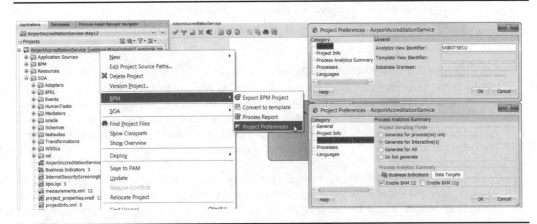

Figure 20-19.   *Configuring the BPM project level settings for process analytics*

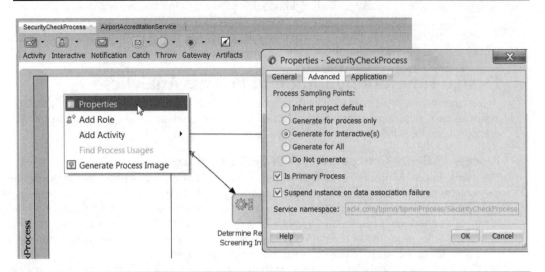

Figure 20-20. *Configuration of Process Analytics Sampling Points at process level*

NOTE
In the original AirportAccreditationService composite, the BPEL process invoked the BPMN SecurityChecks process. With that set up, there were no process analytics recorded for the SecurityChecks process—only for the BPEL process. This seems a general limitation: a BPMN process invoked by a fronting BPEL process does not get its analytics reported. In order to produce process analytics, I have removed the BPEL process from the composite [and moved it to its own composite].

Configuration of Business Indicators

We have met business indicators such as dimensions and measures in our earlier discussion of process analytics for BPEL processes. In BPM processes too we can work with such indicators. They are configured a little bit differently though. A business indicator is implemented as a Project Data Object—rather than being just a snapshot of values from Process Data Objects. We need to explicitly set the values of these objects in order to expose values for the business dimensions.

To expose the dimension *requestingOrganization* from the *SecurityChecks* process, open the structure window. Expand the node Business Indicator Bindings and right click the node Dimension. Choose the option New in the context menu. The Bind Dimension dialog appears. Specify the name for the Project Data Object to be created for the dimension. Click on the green plus icon to create the dimension. A second popup appears. Specify the name of the dimension and its data type. Figure 20-21 shows these steps—as well as the result: a new dimension and an associated, implementing Project Data Object.

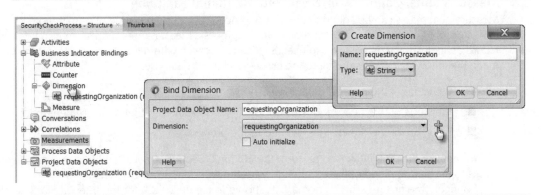

Figure 20-21.   *Configuring a new dimension for the project*

At this point, nothing has been done yet to set a value for this new dimension. Somewhere in the BPMN process do we have to explicitly set the object to the appropriate value.

Open the editor for the Start activity. Open the Data Associations. Add an association from the OriginalAccreditationRequest's *requestingOrganizationId* attribute to the *requestingOrganization* project data object, as shown in Figure 20-22.

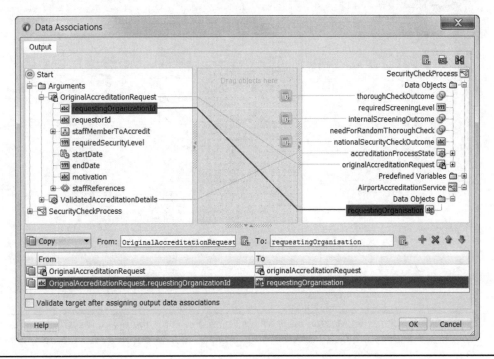

Figure 20-22.   *Setting the value for the project data object that represents the dimension requestingOrganization*

Measurements, Counters, Interval, and Additional Sampling

Measurement marks can be added to the BPMN process to record the value of one or more business indicators of type measure at a certain point in the process. Measurement marks can also be used to record an interval: the time it takes to execute a certain stretch within the process. At a measurement mark, the following data is stored into the Process Analytics database:

- The value of the process default measures
- The value of the measure business indicators associated to that measurement mark
- The value of the dimensions defined in the process

To monitor the time it takes to perform the National Security Check, add two measurement marks to the start and end of the parallel flow for the National Security Check.

Configure the first measurement mark as shown in Figure 20-23, for the Interval Start. Set the name to *StartofNationalSecurityCheckFlow*.

Even if all you want to do is measure the interval, you still need to associate a business indicator of type measure with the measurement mark that tracks the interval. The quickest way to get this over with: click on the green plus icon to create a new business indicator. The Bind Measure dialog appears. Accept the default name. Click on the green plus icon to create the measure. Accept the

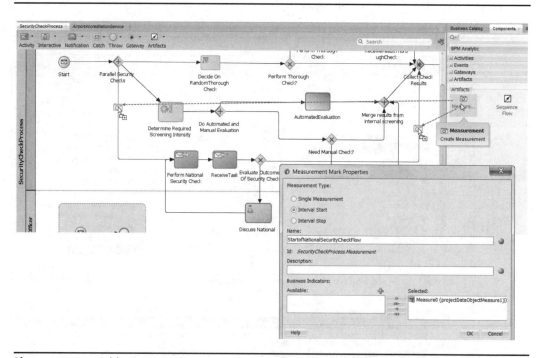

Figure 20-23. *Add two Measurement Marks for recording the interval across the National Security Check. Use a "dummy" measure to satisfy the demand to have one in a Measurement Mark*

default name and type. Click OK. Click OK again to close the Bind Measure dialog. Select the newly create business indicator.

Configure the second measurement mark for the Interval Stop and select *StartofNationalSecurityCheckFlow* as the interval to conclude at this point.

Also create a new counter to count the number of manual security checks being performed. In the structure window, click on the node Business Indicator Bindings | Counter. Right click and select Create. In the dialog that appears, set the name to *ManualCheckCounter*. Click OK.

Right click Human Task *ManualScreening* in the process editor. From the context menu, select option *Add Counter Mark*. A popup appears with a list of all counters, including the *ManualCheckCounter*. Check the box for this counter to indicate that when this activity is executed, the counter should be activated. Click on OK.

Finally, regardless of the project and process level settings, we can explicitly make any activity in the process be a sampling point. Open the editor for the activity. On the Basic tab, expand the Sampling Point panel and select radio button Generate.

Deploy the composite—and send a few requests for a security check.

Leveraging Process Analytics at Run Time

Once the composite with the process configured for process analytics has been deployed and some instances of the process have been created, analytics will have been produced into the underlying database tables in the SOA Infra schema and accessible through BAM Data Objects, the Process Monitor, the standard Workspace Dashboards, and even straight SQL.

SQL Access to Process Analytics

Database synonym BPM_PV_PRCS_SAIBOTSECU_V is created during deployment. Remember that SAIBOTSECU is the Analytics View Identifier that we configured on the project. This synonym refers to an underlying view (BEAM_VIEW_#). Selecting from BPM_PV_PRCS_SAIBOTSECU_V provides insight in instances of the *SecurityChecks* process.

For example, to list the number of times the manual check was executed, based on the counter *ManualCheckCounter* that we configured earlier on, we could use the following SQL query, grouping by the dimension *requestingOrganization*:

```
select  B_REQUESTINGORGANIZATION requesting_organization
,       count(B_MANUALCHECKCOUNTER) number_of_times_executed
from    BPM_PV_PRCS_SAIBOTSECU_V
group
by      B_REQUESTINGORGANIZATION
```

Out of the Box BAM Process Analytics

The same dashboards in the out of the box BAM project Process Analytics that we have seen before in conjunction with our BPEL process are used to monitor the execution of the BPMN process. These reports provide generic overviews of running and completed instances and the activities that take the longest to complete.

Just as before, we can of course create a custom BAM project with our own, tailored business queries, business views, and dashboards, based on the data objects created for exposing the process analytics for the *SecurityChecksProcess*.

Process Monitor

The Process Monitor—accessible from the BPM Workspace—enables you to monitor and optimize process execution by identifying bottlenecks and other performance problems in BPM processes. Use the process monitor dashboard to select the process to monitor, the time interval over which to view statistics, and to view information and see alerts that enable you to identify process issues that are affecting performance. The Process Monitor is driven by the data collected in the BAM process analytics data objects. It shows a visualization of the business process and overlays it with the metrics that were collected.

Activities that have processing issues such as bottlenecks, appear with a yellow or red halo around them. The alert types identified in the monitor are:

- Time Problem
- Queue Problem
- Major Increment From Average
- Bottleneck

A bottleneck appears when there are activities that are taking significantly longer than the average execution time, and there is a queue problem at the same time. In other words, there are many instances of an activity and the execution time for each of the instances is expected to be too long. As a result, process execution time is negatively affected.

The bottleneck detection algorithm considers the average execution time per activity and deviation from the average, and calculates a threshold value. When activities are over the threshold, they can impact the overall processing times. An estimate of currently running activities is calculated. The total execution time and deviation are calculated to give a threshold value. When total activity execution time is over this threshold, a queue problem is indicated.

For each activity in the process, the monitor shows metrics including the number of completed instances, the average | minimum | maximum time to completion.

Standard Dashboards

The BPM Workspace provides a number of predefined dashboards that present the standard metrics gathered during the execution of a process as graphs and drill-downs. The information displayed is based on data previously computed in a process cube schema and does not depend on process analytics. Figure 20-24 shows an example of one of the Performance per process report that indicates an average processing time of about 1.4 minutes for the *SecurityCheckProcess*. When the *ManualScreening* activity is performed, it takes an average of 1.8 minute to complete, considerably longer than the *ManualCheck* activity. When the bars in the chart are clicked on, the list of instances at the bottom gets refreshed to see the instances making up the aggregate information.

Custom Dashboards

The BPM Workspace offers the option to create new pages from within the browser. These pages can contain custom charts and lists, based on the process execution metrics collected in the underlying star schema tables. This feature supports organizations who were already using this mechanism in the 11g release and migrated to 12c. Oracle however recommends going forward to use BAM 12c to create custom dashboards—as discussed earlier in this chapter.

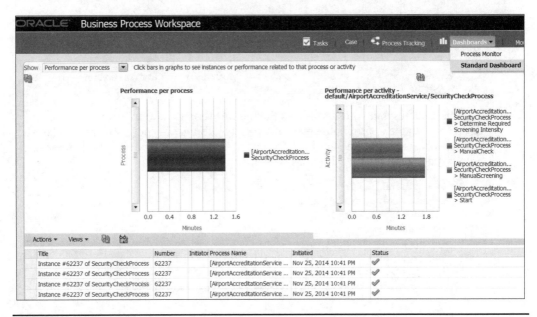

Figure 20-24. *Standard reports in BPM Workspace providing insight in performance and workload per process*

Managing BAM from the Command Line

The BAM product includes a command line facility—BAMCommand—through which a number of power commands can be executed in silent mode as part of an automated process. The most important commands available in this command line:

- Export [Project | one or more Data Objects | Data in on or more Data Objects | ...]
- Import [a selection from a previously exported file]
- Clear [Data Object]
- Delete [on or more Data Objects | Project | ... any combination of objects]

The command line interface is available on the server on which the BAM instance was installed. BAMCommand can be executed from the FMW_HOME\soa\bam\bin directory on the Windows platform and from FMW_HOME/soa/bam/bin on Linux/UNIX platforms—provided the JAVA_HOME environment variable has been set. Note that BAMCommand can be used against a remote machine. That means that you can use it from a machine with JDeveloper running on it against the server running the run-time SOA Suite environment.

A useful command to export a BAM project along with all associated data objects, business queries, business views, KPIs, alerts, and dashboards—but without the current data content—is this one:

```
bamcommand -cmd export -name "AirportAccreditationsDashboard" -type
project -file "C:\AirportAccreditationsDashboardProject.zip"
```

This assumes that you have edited the file BAMCommandConfig.xml in the bin directory with the appropriate details for your environment—including the database connection details for the SOA Infra schema and the host, portname and WebLogic administrator's account for the BAM Server:

```
<BAMCommandConfig>
   <host>soa2admin2</host>
   <port>9001</port>
   <username>weblogic</username>
   <password>weblogic1</password>
   <dbusername>SOAINFRA</dbusername>
   <dbpassword>Wwelcome01</dbpassword>
   <dburl>jdbc:oracle:thin:@10.10.10.5:1521:soarepos</dburl>
</BAMCommandConfig>
```

Business Activity Monitoring beyond Process Analytics

Even though we have been using BAM throughout this chapter, you have not yet properly been introduced to the BAM component. This will be rectified in this section, which also demonstrates how we can leverage BAM outside the context of process monitoring.

BAM Dashboards can be created for many more data sets than just the analytics gathered from BPM and BPEL process execution. BAM can work with various data sources, collecting data from them into its own in-memory data structures, and allowing definition of queries and data visualizations on top of these data objects. One of the characteristics of BAM is its ability to respond in near real-time to data changes—refreshing aggregates, lists and charts without using intervention.

A typical source for data reported in BAM is JMS: events from the Event Delivery Network and Oracle Event Processor, Service Bus Alerts, as well as messages from custom Java applications flow through JMS to be processed by BAM.

Introducing Business Activity Monitoring aka BAM

Real-time insight into what is happening in your organization, through the actual values of relevant KPIs, presented on a visually attractive dashboard, with special alerts being raised and appropriate action being taken upon violations of predefined rules, such as crossing thresholds—that, in short, is the promise of BAM.

BAM maintains an active set of data that is constantly being refreshed, added to, and updated. Reports and charts can be defined against the data objects—and are updated in the browser that displays them whenever the underlying data objects are refreshed by incoming events.

Rules can be specified to identify exceptional situations that may require instant action. These rules are evaluated when the data objects they are defined against are refreshed. When a rule is violated, a visual alert can be displayed in the dashboard and the configured actions can be executed—including sending an email and calling a web service. The rules can be quite advanced, thus allowing BAM to do a fair bit of filtering, aggregation, and pattern matching against its data objects and the events that update them.

BAM works both with data persisted in a relational database as well as streaming data collected for example from JMS destinations. Based on Oracle Coherence, the persistence engine receives data object modifications (insert, update, and delete), caches them, and passes them to the Continuous Query Service. Modifications to archived stream and archived relation data objects are persisted.

The Continuous Query Service (CQS) is a BAM-specific wrapper around the Continuous Query Language (CQL) engine [also used] within OEP. The CQS is a pure push system: query results are delivered automatically. On top of CQS, Oracle BAM provides real-time pattern matching, trend analysis, rolling-window computations, and both static and dynamic thresholds. You can use predefined easy-to-use business query and KPI templates, insulated from the underlying CQL. You can archive the event streams for fuller analysis later.

The report cache receives and caches query results, then pushes the results to dashboards. The report cache holds the query results as viewsets. A viewset includes a data snapshot and the changes since the last snapshot for business views in the same project that use the same query and row security filters. Viewsets minimize time-consuming query re-execution and ensure that views are incrementally updated using a push-based mechanism.

The alert service compares query results to alert events and conditions. If these events and conditions are satisfied, the alert service executes the corresponding alert actions and notifications. The BAM server can also take initiative in the form of two types of outbound actions: sending emails and calling web services, which in turn, of course, can start SOA composite applications, create human tasks, write files, update databases, and produce JMS messages. For email notifications, the alert service uses the Oracle User Messaging Service (UMS).

BAM is accessed through BAM Composer, a browser-based web application, both for development activities such as creating the data objects and designing the reports, as well as for accessing the live dashboards. BAM Composer has three major sections: Administrator, Designer, and Home. Depending on the role of the user, these sections may or may not be accessible.

Use Case Scenarios for BAM

Business Activity Monitoring is the business front-end of the SOA Suite. It is where we come full circle: Having started with (high-level) Business Process Analysis, including the definition of processes, interactions, business objectives, and KPIs, the BAM Dashboard is the live visualization of the execution of those business processes and their effect on the KPIs. Any organization with an interest in how its processes are performing should consider creating BAM reports—usually as a complement to their Business Intelligence initiatives based on more historically oriented, longer-term data warehouses. Once again, BAM is very much for real-time insight.

BAM complements OEP with the visual presentation of findings and the ability to take actions. At the same time, there is some overlap with OEP, because both products analyze events in real time, aggregating and detecting patterns, both using the same CQL-based engine to do so. OEP is geared toward more intense event streams with generally simple, virtually meaningless, almost payload-less signals and events. OEP is not meant as the final destination for events: It emits events that report its findings to downstream consumers to take advantage of. BAM is one of the usual suspects as a consumer.

BAM for Business   Typical users of BAM are business representatives responsible for the execution of specific business processes and their managers. Whether monitoring the status of physical equipment, tracking the vital life signs for the newborn babies in the maternity ward, managing the waiting times and number of calls processed by the hospital's helpdesk, analyzing the load on and efficiency of the emergency room, or studying the efficiency of the invoicing process and the effect of the "get better, pay faster" campaign, BAM can be used to collect the data, events, and statistics needed for deriving the values of performance indicators and visualizing the progress of the operations, as well as to put together the dashboard that updates in real time.

BAM even allows business users to create or enhance reports and dashboards themselves—just like they could do in Excel. When the developer has set up the data objects in BAM—and made sure that those are loaded with the live data feeds—it is an easy, declarative, browser-based task to create the charts, lists, and KPI visualizations.

BAM for System Administration   In addition to its importance for analyzing and visualizing the events on the business and process level, BAM dashboards can be very useful for lower-level, more-detailed technical tasks, such as operational control of computer applications and service infrastructures, including the SOA Suite and the applications it is running.

Events at this level include the number and time of invocations of composites and components, the time it takes to complete each instance, the number and types of faults that occur, the values of variables, changes in environment settings, and so on. The data available from these events can be retrieved from various systems across the enterprise. The data is aggregated in dashboard reports that help to provide insight into bottlenecks in the system—both historic and actual—in terms of performance and functionality (looking at the number of faults originating from specific components). The BAM server can take even some forms of corrective action, or at the very least can alert administrators when the performance of a specific component seems to be degrading very rapidly. Monitoring of Service Level Agreements could also be supported if not implemented using BAM.

The BAM Product Architecture

Oracle Business Activity Monitoring is a product that consists of several components, including a web application (BAM Composer), application server components, and a database. The BAM server runs in its own WebLogic Server (default name, bam_server1). This server is managed from the WebLogic Administration console—for configuring users, groups, application roles, adapter settings—and the Enterprise Manager Fusion Middleware Control for most operational tasks, such as performance and load monitoring and configuring the email driver. The SOA Infra database schema contains all BAM metadata (such as data object definitions and report definitions) and all active data for the data objects.

BAM Web Services   BAM exposes a number of web services for programmatic access—from SOA composite applications or any type of web service consumer. The Oracle BAM web services allow users to build applications that publish data to the Oracle BAM Server. Any client that can talk to standard web services can use these APIs to publish data to—create, update, and delete—as well as retrieve data from Oracle BAM Data Objects. Through these services, rules defined in BAM projects can explicitly be fired.

User Administration   Users of Business Activity Monitoring are all defined in the Identity Store that is configured with WebLogic Server. Initially this will be the default, file-based repository.

Management of the user accounts takes place primarily in WebLogic and to a smaller extent in BAM Composer. In WebLogic, a number of BAM-specific groups have been defined during installation: BAMAdministrator, BAMArchitect, BAMContentCreator, BAMContentViewer, BAMUsers. These groups have been granted the corresponding BAM application roles. When a user is added to one of these groups that user inherits the application role that defines the level of access in the BAM web application.

Privileges on specific reports, data objects, and even rows within data objects can be assigned in BAM Composer.

Real-Time Monitoring of Saibot Airport Carpark Events

In Chapter 16, we discussed event processing and the notion of real-time evaluation of signals, messages, and events. We used the OEP component, for example, to monitor the car parks at Saibot Airport: the influx of cars arriving, the gradually increasing occupation rate and the eventual necessity to open the further removed car parks. OEP was used to process the low-level events and interpret them into business events. We will now use BAM to consume the results produced by OEP and visualize them for human consumption and action.

OEP publishes its findings to JMS and we will create BAM data objects that capture these JMS messages to make them available to real-time business queries. The step of creating business views and dashboards on top of these data objects is the same as previously the creation of views on top of static business queries.

Revisit the OEP Car Park Application

The Car Park application that we created in Chapter 16 with Oracle Event Processor processed a continuous stream of events representing cars entering or leaving one of the car parks around the airport. The OEP application aggregates these events and calculates the current occupancy rate of each car park. Regularly, the current status for each car park is published to a JMS Queue, by the OEP application. The JMS messages are Map Messages with properties for the car park identifier, the current number of cars, and the capacity of the car park.

The source code for Chapter 16 includes a simple Java application that listens to the JMS Queue and prints out the messages.

Create Data Object on Top of JMS

A BAM Data Object can be defined on top of a JMS Queue. The JMS messages are mapped to the data object structure and retained for a specified period of time in the BAM server. An Enterprise Message Source is defined in BAM to represent and connect to the JMS Destination. This EMS also defines the mapping between the JMS messages and the data object records.

The steps we have to go through are:

■   Define the data object that the JMS messages are mapped into.

■   Define an Outbound Connection in the BAM Adapter deployment to connect to the JMS provider.

■   Create the Enterprise Message Source linking the data object to the JMS queue and its message type.

Create Data Object CarParkEvent   Open BAM Composer. Click on the Administrator link. Click on the Data Objects node, to create a new Data Object. Set the name and the display name to CarParkEvent. Set the type to Simple Data Object. Check the box Archived. Set the Continuous Query Type to STREAM, the Replay Unit to Hours and the Replay Amount to 1. Accept the other defaults and press Create.

The Data Object editor opens. Navigate to the Columns tab. Add the following columns: carparkIdentifier (int, Dimension), percentageFull (float, Measure), capacity (int, Attribute), description (varchar, Attribute), currentCarCount (int, Measure), lowestRecentCount (int, Measure). On the General tab, select DATAOBJECT_CREATED as the Timestamp Column.

Press Save.

Create Outbound Connection in BAM Adapter Deployment   In order to have our BAM server reach out to the JMS Queue with the car par messages from OEP, we need to create an outbound connection in the BAM Adapter, similar to the connections we created earlier in the book for the Database and the JMS adapter.

Open WebLogic Console. Open the Deployments overview. Expand the BamServer application. Under this node, there is the entry BeamAdapter.rar for the BAM Adapter. Click on the link for that entry.

The Settings dialog appears. Click on the Configuration tab and on the Outbound Connection Pools sub tab. Click on new to create a new connection. On the first page of the wizard, accept the only available option. On the second page, set the connection's JNDI name to eis/bam/saibot/carparkqueue. Complete the wizard. Save—if so prompted—the configuration plan for the adapter.

Open the properties page for the new connection. Set the property FactoryProperties to the following value (replacing the host and port with your SOA domain host and the port number for the server on which the JMS Queue is accessed) also provide the correct password for weblogic.

```
java.naming.factory.initial=weblogic.jndi.WLInitialContextFactory;java.naming.
provider.url= t3://host:port;java.naming.security.principal=weblogic;java.
naming.security.credentials=weblogic1;
```

Press enter and subsequently click on the save button.

Create Enterprise Message Source   An Enterprise Message Source (EMS) provides direct Java Message Service (JMS) connectivity to the Oracle BAM Server. Map messages are supported as well as Text messages with an XML payload. EMS maps from a message directly to a BAM data object. You can also use an XSL Stylesheet to perform a transformation in between.

Each EMS connects to a specific JMS topic or queue, and the information is delivered into a data object. Use the BAM Composer Administrator page to configure EMS definitions.

The default JMS provider is Messaging for Oracle WebLogic Server. Oracle Advanced Queuing (AQ) JMS is supported as is Tibco JMS.

To create an Enterprise Message Source for the JMS Queue with car park events, click the node Enterprise Message Sources. The Enterprise Message Sources dialog appears. Set CarParkEventQueue as the name and the display name. Click on Create.

The EMS editor is shown. Set the Outbound Connection JNDI to *eis/bam/saibot/carparkqueue*. Set the Topic/Queue Name to *jms/facilities/CarParkNearlyFullQueue*. Set the JMS Message Type to Map Message.

Select *CarParkEvent* as the Data Object for the Source to Data Object mapping. Set Operation to Insert. Create mappings for all data object fields, using the Data Object Field name for the Tag/Attribute name to map from.

Press Save. Then press Start to try out the capture into the Data Object of the JMS messages published by the OEP application.

When you next check the Data tab in the Data Object editor for data object *CarParkEvent*, you will see the first few rows appearing.

Supporting Data Object to Capture Continuous Query Results   A little bit later, we will create a business query of type continuous query. This type of query can produce results that are used for alert rules and actions. Business views cannot be based on the outcome of continuous queries. What can be done though is have the continuous business query publish its findings into an intermediate data object. This data object *can* be used in business views.

To prepare for the continuous query that will continuously report the status for each of our car parks, let's create the supporting data object in advance.

Click on the node *Data Objects*. The *Create Data Object* dialog appears. Enter *ContinuousCarParkResult* as the name. Select Simple Data Object as the type. Set the *Continuous Query Type* to *RELATION*. Click *Create*.

Add two columns: *carParkIdentifier* (int, dimension) and *currentCarCount* (decimal, measure). Save the changes.

Create the CarParkMonitor Project

Click on the link Designer. Click on the dropdown menu behind the project name and select create. Enter the name and display name for the new project as *CarParkMonitor*. Click on Create.

Click on the node *Data Objects* in the new project. Select the data objects *CarParkEvent* and *ContinuousCarParkResult* to add to the new project.

Create Business Queries

Create a business query to continuously capture the results from the Enterprise Message Source. Click on the node Business Queries. Set the name to *CurrentStatusPerCarpark*. Set the type to *Continuous Query* and click on *Create*.

The Business Query editor appears, as shown in Figure 20-25. Select the *Moving Aggregation Template*. Select *CarParkEvent* as the Data Object. Select Measure *currentCarCount* with aggregation function *Average*. Group by *carparkIdentifier*. Select *All* for the output. Click on Save.

After saving the business query, we can add actions associated with the continuous query. One would be to send an email whenever the query is executed and a new result is produced. Another one would be the action to hand over the results from the continuous query to the intermediate data object—*ContinuousCarParkResult*. Click on the *Action* link. Select the action *Insert Values into the Data Object* in the popup that appears. When the action appears in the page, click on the link <select data object>. In the popup that appears now, select data object *ContinuousCarParkResult* as the *insert* (or rather *upsert*) target. Select *upsert* as the operation type. Map the columns *carParkIdentifier* (mark as *Upsert Key*) and *currentCarCount* to the output values from the business query. Press OK to complete the action. Then press Save to complete the definition of the Business Query.

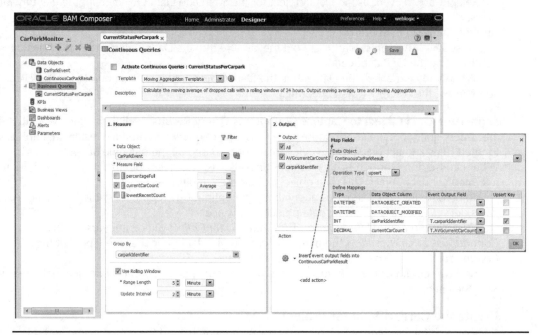

Figure 20-25. *Configuring Business Query CurrentStatusPerCarpark on top of the CarParkEvent data object*

NOTE
The configuration of the action for the continuous business query leads actually to the creation of an alert.

Every 2 minutes, the average is recalculated for every car park that produced new car events. This results in the supporting data object *ContinuousCarParkResult* being an object with the most recent situation—thanks to the action configured on the business query.

Click on the node Business Queries to create the query that makes the current car park car count available. Set the name to *CurrentCarCountPerPark*. Select *Flat SQL Query* as the type.

In the Business Query editor, select Data Object *ContinuousCarParkResult* and select fields *carParkIdentifier* and *currentCarCount*. Press Save. Click on the preview icon to check the current result from the query. Every two minutes, a new result will be available.

Business Views to the Current Car Park Status

Defining a business view that produces the current car count per car park has now become very simple: it is just a matter of leveraging business query *CurrentCarCountPerPark*.

Click on the node Business Views. Set name and display name to *CurrentCarCountPerParkList*. Select Table | List as View Typ. Click on Create.

Select *CurrentCarCountPerPark* as the Query driving the list. Press Save to complete this business view. The data currently in the underlying data object already shows up.

Wrap Up

This only scratches the surface of what you could do with BAM. The data produced by the OEP application regarding car movements and the car park occupancy can be presented and acted on in many ways that would also far better illustrate the capabilities of the product. We have discussed some of the main features though and you can surely build from there.

Summary

Process Monitoring—operational insight at near-real time (down to individual instances) as well as tactical insight across with aggregation across multiple process instances.

BPEL Processes can be configured with sensors that are associated with sensor actions. Through these the process can publish operational data at run time. This data can be collected in database tables and/or be exposed in different ways. The sensor values are available in the EM FMW Control to provide additional insight in process instances and their progress. The values can also be used in user defined reporting to spot trends and evaluate results against SLA value.

Both BPEL and BPMN processes can leverage the process analytics facility to publish run-time data that provide insight into the process execution. As part of configuration of process analytics, we can define business indicators—dimensions, measures, intervals, and counters—that should be exposed for process instances. The values for these business indicators can be used to calculate metrics aggregated per category and to get insight into the frequency of conditional flows and the execution bottlenecks.

The Process Analytics published by BPEL and BPMN processes are gathered in database tables in the SOA Infra database schema. These tables are exposed through predefined data objects in BAM. BAM also ships with a predefined project that contains many out of the box dashboards to provide insight into the operational and tactical state of the processes. Additionally, BAM allows us to create such dashboards ourselves.

Business Activity Monitoring (BAM) is a product in the SOA Suite that we can use to monitor the live proceedings of much more than the BPEL and BPMN processes. BAM is good at gathering data from various sources—including streaming ones—and exposing them in an abstracted way for business designers to create queries on top of that themselves are the source for business views—visualizations and KPIs. BAM has a built in event processing engine that has considerable overlap with OEP. It can do real-time analysis, pattern recognition, aggregation, and other types of processing that help keep the business user informed.

CHAPTER
21

Governance

S OA produces **B**usiness **A**gility through **D**ecoupling, which is not at all a bad thing. Business agility consists of various qualities: The ability to quickly create new functionality by reusing existing, established components. The ability to quickly change functionality by modifying components without impact and ripple through effects. The ability to roll out interconnected networks of components that interact yet are not tightly coupled.

To realize that potential, any implementation of SOA does not only require development tools and a run-time engine such as provided by Oracle SOA Suite—although that is a sine qua non condition. Additionally, a process—supported by tooling—to govern the initial creation and subsequent lifecycle of components and to guarantee their quality and reuse potential is essential in order to reap any benefits from SOA. An organization has to understand the state and scope of their SOA portfolio by communicating and managing the lifecycle of the services, and by identifying and highlighting the dependencies between services and consumers.

This chapter scratches the governance iceberg by discussing some of the key topics. Organizing reuse of shared, common assets using the SOA Suite MDS facility and a counterpart approach for Service Bus projects is one of these. The use and management of templates to provide blueprints and stepping stones to boost and guide development is another of the topics discussed. Versioning of services is introduced—a key aspect of lifecycle management and an important challenge in any SOA environment. Some of the facilities and common practices in SOA Suite are covered. The chapter talks about granularity—common topic in the SOA discourse: how big should components be, in order to strike the right balance in reuse potential and manageability? The notion of partitions as a logical clustering of SOA composites that even provides some management features is briefly touched upon. Finally, some tools are listed that may support governance processes.

The topic of governance is vast. Entire books are written on the subject. This chapter cannot aim for more than providing a brief introduction that offers some inspiration and early guidance as well as a demonstration of the key mechanisms in this area available in SOA Suite.

Reuse, Dependencies, and Coexistence

Reuse requires a paradigm shift—it requires developers to shake off their not-invented-here intuition and look for already existing functionality (services) outside their own scope and span of control. It also requires project leads to not only focus on the immediate functional needs for their current project but at least pay some attention—and some budget—to the more generic requirements that will make a component truly reusable.

Very easy access to the reusable assets is of course essential. These assets need to be easy to find, easy to understand and trust, and easy to adopt. Organizations that really want to achieve reuse need to work on a culture—and before that probably an obligatory but also stimulating process—that makes it hard and/or expensive not to reuse or to create nonreusable services if they could be reusable, and rewarding those who do reuse or develop reusable services. In order to build an inventory of reusable assets, the design and development of new artifacts need to be done in the spirit of reuse and flexibility—and not with only the immediate utilization of the artifact in mind. Developers are not only developing and delivering services for their project but possibly for all projects within their organization (or even outside the organization). This usually requires them to make a service more generic than would be the case if it concerns only a local project's artifact.

Additionally, when assets are being reused, new challenges stare us in the face, such as dependency management, ownership, versioning, and lifecycle management of the reused assets.

Because of the reuse, the number of involved parties and dependent assets has increased. Evolving the reusables or discontinuing them is no longer a matter of a single owner or team—much more is at stake. One cannot just modify a service because one of its users asks for a change. What if other consumers will "break" due to a modification?

Traditionally, stand-alone applications were developed by dedicated teams that remained attached to the application during subsequent stages in its lifecycle. The assets that formed the application were completely owned, controlled, and exclusively used and modified by this relatively small team.

Packaged applications and SaaS offerings have been introduced in most organizations. The evolution of those applications is largely out of the hands of an organization—it can only decide to upgrade to a next release or (temporarily) refrain from doing so. Yet many organizations will have custom extensions and integrations developed around these off-the-shelf applications that are managed in a similar way to the stand-alone custom applications. However, the manufacturer of the packaged application is in a somewhat different situation—one that is close to where, as a result of a service-oriented approach, most development teams will be.

Services are usually initially designed and built for one or more specific consumers at the time being, but they are created with additional future reuse in mind. Reuse and flexibility are things we want to achieve. However, reuse can also lead to new challenges. When a service is deployed, it might be—and hopefully will be—used by others than just the consumer it was originally built for. In a Service-Oriented Architecture, most assets therefore end up very much not (exclusively) owned by any team or even department: They are (in theory, at least) co-owned by the enterprise, targeted at widespread reuse, and not naturally controlled by an individual or group. Note, however, that every service needs to have a designated *owner* who is responsible for the services delivered. Because the service delivers business value, it is a business unit that owns it. And this unit needs to work together with other interested parties in the enterprise when it intends to evolve the service artifacts.

Management of the lifecycle of these assets is important, especially given the extent of reuse we are trying to achieve. To realize reuse, the availability of assets needs to be made public, and the assets need to be found, understood, and trusted. Once reuse has happened, the process of evolving those assets becomes more involved: Multiple parties have a stake in the assets and may have specific requirements with regard to their evolution. The designated owner of an asset—or the body governing the lifecycle of the asset—needs to be aware of all the usages of the asset. Other aspects of governance include: How do we ascertain that assets have the required quality and deliver on their (functional) promise? How do we define and record the required service and security levels and subsequently (at an operational level) monitor the actual performance of assets?

Implementing Governance

Before the management of the assets themselves is in full swing, governance is also required to enforce the architectural principles laid down for the organization. What processes must be implemented to ensure that all teams stick to the rules and are stimulated to do so (not only the service police!)? And how do we ensure that teams do not create the same or overlapping assets? How do we decide which reusable assets should be created? What should the interface be for a new reusable service, and how much functionality should it comprise? Or at a higher level, what should the process look like that determines which assets will be created and how they should look? How do we organize the process to create and control the canonical data model?

We also need strategic governance to link corporate goals to SOA and to have a process in place to check and possibly modify the governance processes for SOA. (And, of course, governance processes themselves are also subject to improvement and change. How do we govern this evolution?)

Governance must be implemented at every stage of the SOA lifecycle to track ongoing changes to the architecture, design, and implementation—and to define, implement, and execute the processes around the creation of new assets and changes to existing ones. An architecture board or (SOA) competence center can be considered with representatives from different departments to align SOA initiatives—and to help overcome each department's not-invented-here tendencies, which stand in the way of true reuse and flexibility. Governance should be aimed at stimulating and enforcing desired behavior. And the one most important behavior we try to achieve is collaboration—opening up applications can only be successful when we open up inward-looking departments and have them collaborate with other units in the organization.

Governance should be aimed at getting all involved parties to do the right things and to do these things right. Not only by laying down rules that are enforced, but mostly by inspiring the people involved, leading the way by setting the right example, and taking care of clear, timely, and open communication. Acting in a truly service-oriented, decoupled, reuse-focused way will take time. Knowledge and skills are required, as well as internalization of the objectives and approach. Ownership must be taken and cannot just be assigned. Coaching of teams that start out in the spirit of SOA by members of the architecture board or representatives from more experienced teams is valuable in order to inspire confidence, to help prevent making common mistakes and reinventing the wheel, and to guide the way through the acronym jungle, the technology challenges, and the adopted practices and mantras of the organization.

All of this requires organizational courage—and real leadership. Governance is not a problem you can simply throw money at, nor can you hire consultants to do it for you. It is an organizational change. Therefore, an important aspect of SOA governance, especially in the early stages of adoption of SOA in an organization, is spreading the word (evangelizing), demonstrating the success, celebrating the measurable results, and thus building the case for SOA. Think big, act small, start successful.

Asset Registration and Publication

Reuse can only happen when assets are first of all identified as reusable and then created and subsequently made available to potential consumers. The latter requires assets to be discoverable, along with metadata that clearly states the status, QoS provided, and meaning of assets and also helps establish the credibility through insight in the current usage of assets, QoS, and the satisfaction of the current consumers. The exact location, security measures, conditions for reuse, and future plans for the asset should be clear as well.

Registration is essential as part of SOA governance—to record a description and status of a service and some of its assets (XSD, WSDL, and so on) as well as to gather and record metadata and metrics. Subsequently, the metadata about the assets must be made available throughout the enterprise. A central repository, here called the "asset manager," provides a single source of truth for what was intended—the to-be architecture design—and what has been and is being implemented (the as-is architecture).

Note that there is typically a grow path here: Start with a run-time registry, which can be very lightweight with only service descriptions and an indication of the status and owner of service. Later on the organization could move to a more elaborate registry. The next stage along the path could be the move to a thin repository (initially only XSD and WSDL artifacts) and finally to a complete repository. The registry is by far the most important when starting with SOA. A full-blown design-time repository loaded with metadata is quite possibly overkill in the early days of SOA adoption in an organization.

At the advanced stage, assets must be managed across every stage of the lifecycle, from conception to implementation, and from deployment to retirement. Ideally, an asset manager includes functionality for automated harvesting of assets and metadata on assets, as well as customizable asset-approval workflows, notifications, and event infrastructure.

The assets themselves as well as this metadata must be easily searchable. The asset manager or SOA artifact registry is the primary means for architects, designers, and developers to learn about the assets available for reuse.

The administration of assets and their metadata can be done in various ways with different levels of sophistication. Most organizations will start out with spreadsheets and text documents, based on predefined templates, collected in a central directory. As the number of assets and the volume of metadata increases, simple content management systems, custom-developed administration tools, or standard governance tools may be adopted.

Lifecycle Stages for SOA Assets

One of the concerns of SOA governance is the evolution of services and other SOA assets or artifacts (these terms are used interchangeably). An organization that starts with SOA must have clear rules about what happens when a service needs to be changed. This applies to change management, configuration management, release management, and for the planning of projects. It also needs to label each asset in such a way that everyone involved understands the status of an asset. The following are examples of the possible states of a service (or other SOA artifact):

- **Identified** The service is identified, either by a project as something they need or in the to-be architecture.

- **Development** A service is being created but not yet in production.

- **Released** The service is released and ready to be used or already used by service consumers.

- **Deprecated** The service is still working, but (new) service consumers are not supposed to use it anymore because the organization plans to discontinue the service. Information that could be stored with this status is a pointer to the alternative and/or a planned retirement date for the service. Services should be deprecated before a replacement has been made available. Some organizations introduce an additional service state called "Sunset." This state is a specialization of Deprecated in that it not only declares the intent to discontinue the service, but also provides an official date for retirement. Note that sometimes the label deprecated is used at the operation level to indicate operations for which new implementations have been provided and that should no longer be consumed by new clients. This happens for example when a new [major] version of service is created in steps, with initially only a subset of all operations implemented in the upcoming new version.

- **Retired** The service is not available anymore.

The states apply to the service as whole. It is not meaningful to have separate states for the service implementation, contract, and interface.

To use services, the organization needs to be aware of the state of the services. Knowing who owns a service and what interface and contract are associated with it is also very important in deciding whether the service can be reused in a certain situation. These and other governance issues can be addressed using tools. But more importantly, the organization has to define and communicate this information to stakeholders in order for services to be (re)used safely. Required information includes the state, owners, and terms and rules for reusing and changing the services (e.g., payment, security, and so on). This information is typically published through the SOA Asset Manager.

Granularity

A crucial aspect in designing services—and indeed other IT assets as well—is their granularity. The size or the functional scope of services matter tremendously. A service on the one hand is just a somewhat arbitrary clustering of operations that provide the functionality. On the other hand, a service is also the unit for many operations—from design and development to administration, the service is the unit for reuse, versioning, testing, planning, governance, deployment, access privileges and authorization policies, monitoring, billing, and SLAs. And as such, it matters a great deal what the granularity of the service is. Note that similar considerations apply to SOA composites and Service Bus projects, to XSD documents, and XQuery, and XSLT transformations.

In many cases, initial decisions regarding the granularity can be reversed or at least amended. Because the implementation of a service is encapsulated, changing the implementation has no or only very little impact. Having a pipeline in a Service Bus project with an operational branch that for some operations calls out to local pipelines and for others to a proxy service in another Service Bus project is perfectly acceptable and allows the implementation of a service to be decoupled from its interface. The same applies to a SOA composite where the exposed service can be wired to a Mediator that for some operations leverages local service components—such as BPEL processes— and for others calls out to external reference bindings.

Changing the interface of a service, however, has a direct impact on all consumers as well as on the implementation and should be avoided as much as possible.

Granularity of SOA Composite Applications

When designing and developing services that are implemented by service composites (aka SOA composite applications), we have to decide on both the granularity of those services and their implementation. How much functionality should be assembled into a single composite application? When should we break up a composite or merge multiple composites together? There are no one-size-fits-all answers. "It depends" is really all you can say, in general.

Well, there is a little bit more that we should realize about service composites— considerations that help decide on how to organize the service composites. Two things are of primary importance:

- **Reusability** If a service component is to be (offered as) reusable, it should be in a separate composite—which you might want to use from a non-SCA context. When it is not, it should be put inside the composite to which it belongs.

- **Flexibility (or the required frequency of changes)** When a piece of functionality will see lots of changes and we don't want to impact other components, that, too, warrants a new composite.

Services and their associated SOA composite applications are the levels that make sense to consumers and business analysts—they don't even care about a more fine-grained level because that is encapsulated away from them.

As we have seen, composites are the level of reuse. Only at the composite level can services be exposed as reusable units, based on encapsulated components, because the composite is also the level of encapsulation. In addition to the services exposed at the composite level—that provide the reusability—a composite will also publicly expose those references from its internal components that cannot be satisfied internally. This could be seen as somewhat breaking the strict encapsulation requirements.

The service composite (application) is the level at which developers work in JDeveloper. There is nothing smaller than the composite—developers can work on service components like BPEL processes and Business Rule components, but always in the context of a composite.

The composite is also the level of deployment—composites are deployed in their entirety. You cannot redeploy part of a composite. Multiple composites can be deployed together, but they are not grouped together in the eyes of the SCA container. The only type of grouping available in the SOA Suite is the partition, a logical clustering of composites, with no functional consequences. Composites can be migrated between environments and shipped to remote teams or external parties—not individual service components.

Governance and Lifecycle Management

In addition to the unit of deployment, the composite is (unavoidably) also the unit of versioning. We can create and discern the version of composites—not versions of something smaller (such as individual components) or something larger (such as a collection of composites). Versioning is a means to enable the modification/evolution of composites that are reused by more than one consumer. Consumers can gradually move to the new version and are not forced to use the new version as soon as it is introduced. Multiple versions of the same composite will be available at run time.

It seems likely that from a governance perspective, we will look at individual artifacts that stretch beyond the boundaries of composites (such as event definitions, XSDs, and WSDLs) on the one hand, and service composites on the other. Talking about lifecycle management, ownership, availability, performance, and the Service Level Agreement only seems to be meaningful with respect to a composite, not to individual service components, given the way these are represented in the tooling, both at run time and at design time. When it is important that governance be done, for example, on individual human tasks or business rules, these should live inside their own composite rather than being embedded in complex composites as internal components.

Security policies—discussed in detail in Chapter 24—are applied mainly at the composite level (some simple policies can be attached to individual components).

Testing

Testing is supported by an out-of-the-box unit testing framework in SOA Suite, next to a plethora of external, standard black-box web service test tools such as SoapUI. All external tests work at the composite level, interacting with the publicly exposed service. The shipped unit-testing framework also supports unit testing of service components, even those that are not publicly exposed.

We can add test suites with test cases to a composite application. The test cases consist of assertions—conditions on the contents of messages—and are associated with wires inside composite applications. Testing applies to interactions at the component level, including components that are not exposed at the composite level. The scope of test cases is at the level of such an interaction.

Test suites that bundle test cases are associated with service composites. Test suites are the unit of running tests; therefore, the service composite is indirectly the unit of testing too. The structure of the composites, however, is not relevant when it comes to determining exactly what you can have unit tested.

Tracing Composite Instances and Messages

Composite sensors—defined at the entrance points of composites (services) as well as the exit points (references)—can be used to monitor the values of important variables. The results from these sensors can be used to locate composite instances. Monitoring and the management of instances, including purging of instances, are done at the composite level.

However, message flow traces go across composites: When we inspect the route of a message from the moment it enters the SCA domain until the time that the response is returned, the flow trace is reported across composite applications. It is not at all intuitive to find out from the message flow trace, which composites participated in it. Usually it is not entirely relevant either, until the time of an error that you want to be able to pin down a specific composite (or version of a composite).

Even more importantly, communication within a service composite is usually equally expensive as communication between composites running in the same SCA container. The container will leverage native bindings for such intra container interactions between different composites with the same minimal overhead that is achieved for communication between components in the same composite.

Exception Handling

Error or exception handling in SOA composite applications can be configured at different levels, each with a different purpose. BPEL components can have exception handling inside to be used for handling business faults.

The fault policy infrastructure in SOA Suite can be instructed to activate certain fault policies when faults occur in a specific component or when faults occur anywhere in the composite. This is useful for technical (or unexpected) fault handling.

Faults can be handled per component or per composite. We cannot define fault policy bindings for multiple composites at the same time. Recovery from faulted instances is at the composite level. Note that transactions may very well involve (instances of) multiple composites and/or components if that is how the message flows.

Splitting and Merging SOA Composites

Does it matter very much how we design the SOA composite applications? Are early decisions irreversible? Is it very hard to break up or combine composite applications later on? Fortunately, although the answer is, of course, "yes" to the first question, it is a resounding "no" to the other two. We have to be aware of what we can and cannot do with composites—and we have to get going in some direction. However, it is fairly easy to change directions and design the composites differently later on.

Splitting Up a SOA Composite   For example, we may have started out with a single composite application that contains all the service components, interacts with many references (adapters and external web services), and exposes a substantial number of services. Then, at some moment, we may come to the conclusion that certain parts of the composite should branch out—for example, because they need to be modified quickly to meet a new business requirement, are subject to a different security scheme than the rest of the composite, or should be shipped offsite to be deployed somewhere else. Whatever the reason, the procedure for creating two composites from one is straightforward.

First, we have to copy the existing composite application in its entirety, so we get a "Part One" and "Part Two" that are exactly the same at this point. Open Part One (one of the two clones of the composite) and then follow these steps:

1. Drag services to the composite level (the exposed services swim lane) that are currently provided to components that will be in Part Two (if they are not already publicly exposed).

2. Drag the references currently satisfied by Part Two components to the composite-level references swimlane.

3. Replace wires to Part Two components with wires to the new composite-level references—primarily in Mediator and BPEL components.

4. Remove the Part Two components from the composite.

5. You may need to change the name of the composite (at least either of the two must be renamed, but for clarity's sake it is probably best if both are given new names).

6. Remove all resources that were only referenced by the Part Two components that have now been removed from the composite.

Now open Part Two. Perform the reverse of the operations just executed for Part One on the components in Part Two. For example, drag services to the composite level that are currently provided to Part One components (if they are not already publicly exposed), and expose as public any reference that is provided by a Part One component.

Note that sometimes instead of copying an entire application and subsequently removing and renaming components and other artifacts, it may be better to create a new application from scratch and only copy individual artifacts such as XSD and XSLT documents, for example using the SOA Template mechanism to be discussed later in this chapter.

Merging Two SOA Composite Applications Together   The reverse procedure from breaking composites into multiple smaller parts is quite straightforward as well. Constructing a composite application by merging together components from multiple composites can be useful when composites have been created on a too-fine-grained level. We may conclude that reuse will only occur for one out of a related collection of composites or that versioning and deployment will always concern a combination of composites.

The steps for the merge procedure are roughly as follows:

1. Pick one of the composites (usually the one with the largest number of components) as the merge target.

2. Iterate through the other composites. Identify the components that must be merged into the target. Right click one of these and select menu item *Create Component Template* from the context menu (see the section on templates later in this chapter for more details). A wizard appears that allows you to select all resources to be copied to the target application. This includes other service components and associated WSDL and XSD documents, XQuery and XSLT files, and other artifacts. These resources are included in the template file that you can have JDeveloper write to the file system.

3. Open the project that is the merge target. Open the composite editor and drag the new component template from the SOA Templates section in the component palette to the diagram. This will create the components in the target project and add all associated resources.

4. The dependencies from the components thus copied to the destination composite need to be satisfied: Wires need to be created from these components to the providers of the required services in their new "composite environment." Some of these dependencies may result in references at the composite level. Note that it may also be the case that the original components in the composite have promoted references that can now be satisfied within the composite itself by the components merged into the composite.

5. For the services that we want to have publicly exposed from the newly added components, create wires from these components to the composite level.

Partitions

Logical groupings or event parallel containers of SCA composites; out of the box, there is a single partition called *default*. New partitions can easily be added. The name of a partition cannot be changed. The name of a partition is part of the endpoint for services exposed by composites deployed in the partition. Partitions cannot be nested. Partitions are not like managed servers or nodes that can be stopped or started as a unit. Partitions only provide a logical grouping of their contents.

Deploying composites to partitions enables you to:

- Make inspecting composites and composites instances easier by logically grouping SOA composites.

- Assign a specific work manager group to a partition in order to isolate [resources used for] request processing and set specific constraints on resource usage by execution of the composites in the partition.

- Perform the following bulk lifecycle management tasks on all SOA composite applications within a specific partition: Start, Shut down, Retire, Activate, Undeploy.

- Secure access to partitions (see Chapter 24).

During deployment of a SOA composite, the target partition is selected. Once deployed, composites cannot be moved to a different partition. However, the exact same composite (revision) can be deployed to multiple partitions.

TIP
Development teams frequently want separate environment to discern between work in progress and components that are ready for the first round of system testing. When there is not a full blown TEST environment available, a partition can be used to create an isolated environment where these somewhat stable incarnations of composites can be deployed without being interfered with by active development activity.

Templates in SOA Suite

Templates are one of the vehicles in SOA Suite 12c that facilitate reuse. Through templates—developers have a head start with the development of new components, because part of the implementation is already available in the template. From a governance point of view, in addition to the reuse advantage there is another important benefit to be had: templates provide a structure for the component based on that template—and of course this structure could and should be the best practice defined by the organization. As such, the template provides the blueprint or the mold for the way implementations should be created. Templates are usually semi-finished products that are to be completed through configuration and further implementation. However, they can also provide complete, ready-made building blocks—for example, to take care of validation, logging, exception handling or other fairly generic functions in Service Bus projects or SOA composites.

As we have discussed in earlier chapters, SOA Suite has templates for Service Bus pipelines and for SOA composite projects, Service Components (such as BPEL processes and Mediators) and custom BPEL activities. The next two sections describe how to create these templates, how to use them, and how to manage them.

Templates for SOA Composite Applications

Templates for SOA composites can be defined at three levels: an entire project, a specific Service Component (BPEL process, Mediator, Human Task, Business Rule, Spring Component or BPMN component), or a scope in a BPEL process. They can be reused across projects and shared across development environments.

Creating and Updating a Template

The context menu for the project node in the application navigator has an entry *Create SOA Template*. The context menu for Service Components has the item *Create Component Template* and a BPEL scope's right click menu has the option *Create Custom Activity Template*. In each case, the item leads to the creation of a template—which is implemented through an archive file with the .tmpl extension—which can be opened with unzip utilities such as 7Zip.

The template file contains a manifest file that has the metadata for the template as well as optionally a template-icon.png file for the icon to be displayed in the component palette (not for project templates). Furthermore, the file contains all the sources that make up the template. Before the template file is created, a wizard is presented that lists all files that will be included in the template (because of the object that was initially selected) and allows the developer to select additional files to include.

The location where the template is to be stored can also be configured in the wizard. This is either a folder on the file system or in the MDS repository (see the next section for more details on what MDS is). The default location is the one set through the preferences editor under Tools | Preferences | SOA | Templates.

The template file itself cannot be opened in JDeveloper for an update of its definition. You can recreate the template from the original sources, effectively replacing the existing definition with the modified version. There is no out of the box support for versioning of templates. By adding a version label to name of templates can you achieve some form of versioning?

TIP
A reusable stand-alone [BPEL] subprocess cannot be turned into a Component Template. However, when for any other component in the composite application the right click Create Component Template option is activated, the subprocess and its dependencies can be added to be part of the template. Any minimalistic component can be used to provide the vehicle to create a template with the subprocess, and thus turn the subprocess into a truly reusable subprocess.

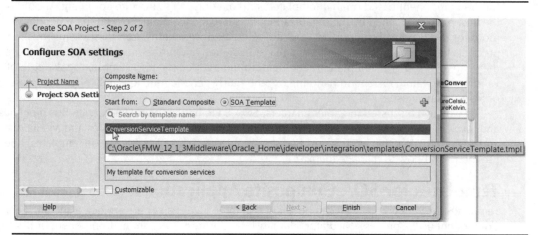

FIGURE 21-1. *Using a custom template in the new project wizard*

Using a Template

The usage of a template depends on the type of template. A project template can be leveraged when you create a new project. In the new project wizard, in the second page, there is a radio button to toggle between Standard Composite [Templates] and [Custom] SOA Templates, see Figure 21-1. When you select a custom project template, the new project will contain all sources that were included in the template.

When the composite editor is open, the component palette contains section SOA Template that presents the custom Service Component Templates (as shown in Figure 21-2). One of these component templates can be dragged to the composite editor. The wizard is shown for creating a component from the template—with all its dependencies. The name of the new component can be defined in the wizard and any conflicts with existing sources can be resolved.

Custom Activity Templates can be used when a BPEL process is edited. The Component Palette contains a section *Custom Activity Templates* from which a template can be dragged to the BPEL process in the same way regular BPEL activities are added to the process.

In all these three cases, there is no inheritance between the template and the usage of it, meaning that future changes to source templates are not visible to applications. If you make changes to the source template, a current user of the template does not (automatically) see the change. However, a Component Template can be applied again. By choosing *Overwrite* as the *Action* to resolve the conflict with the existing sources, you can effectively propagate the changes in the template. Note that any local modifications to the component that was based on the template are lost because of this overwrite.

Management of Templates

Management of templates is fairly straightforward. Most actions are performed in the Preferences editor, which is launched from the main menu using Tools | Preferences. Select the node SOA | Templates to get a list of all configured locations for templates—both on the file system and in MDS. Locations can be added and removed and individual templates can be removed as well. New file system locations can be added. When that is done, all .tmpl files in that location are

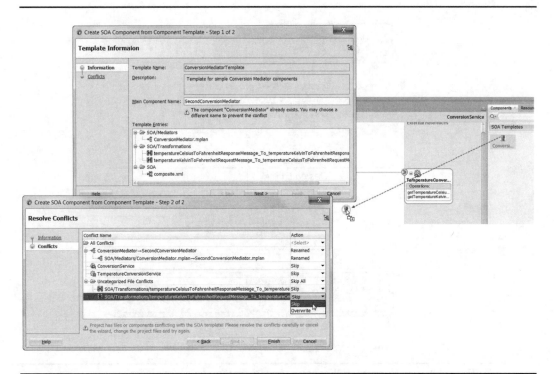

FIGURE 21-2.   *Creating a service component from a custom template*

scanned and the templates are presented—both in the preferences editor and in the relevant component palettes.

Template files can be added and removed at the file system and in the registered MDS folders as well. JDeveloper will pick them up and present them to the developer for consumption. Development of templates is done no differently from development of regular SOA composites. Sharing of the templates can be done by simply sharing the .tmpl files.

Templates for Service Bus Pipelines

In Service Bus projects we can create pipelines based on a pipeline template. Unlike templates for SOA composite applications, pipeline templates are not copied when used, but inherited instead. The link between a pipeline based on a template and that template remains intact and any subsequent change to the template is inherited by all pipelines based on that template. Note however that you can break the link to the template and make the pipeline stand on its own with a local copy of the contents of the template.

A pipeline template is ideally created in a project that is a dedicated container for templates— as illustrated in Figure 21-3. This project has to exist in the same application as the one containing the consuming projects in order for the template to be available. Note that the project with the templates also has to exist in the run-time environment. The link from the pipeline to the template

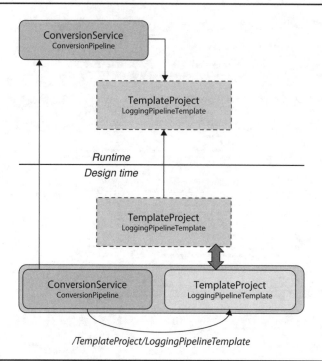

FIGURE 21-3. *The ConversionPipeline is based on the LoggingPipelineTemplate in the TemplateProject; this link exists both at design time and at run time; changes in the template are inherited immediately*

continues to exist after deployment. This also means that when a changed pipeline template is deployed, the functionality of previously deployed services may change as a result.

Unlike the templates used for SOA composite applications, the pipeline template can contain activities and stages that are read only to the consumer of the template. Additionally, placeholders can be included in the template that provides consumers very specific options for completing or complementing the template's functionality in a guided way.

Managing and Reusing Artifacts Using MDS and a Common Project

Many development and deployment strategies that involve reuse sooner or later end up having to rely on copying artifacts. When an XSD definition or XSLT stylesheet is reused, it seems always necessary at some point to create physical duplicates of these artifacts. And in general, duplication of assets in the long run becomes a problem that frustrates the very reuse we try to achieve. Although some level of duplication is acceptable—between environments such as System Test, Acceptance Test, Production, and across multisite production environments—in general it should be prevented. The effort required to keep duplicate artifacts synchronized is huge and typically will fail at some point. On the other hand, if we do not replicate the thing that stores all artifacts, it becomes a single point of failure, also during development.

SOA Suite provides a central store for shared artifacts that can be accessed at design time from JDeveloper and at run time from deployed SOA composite applications. This central store, the MDS repository, along with the Metadata Services on top of it, helps to organize reuse of cross-application artifacts such as canonical data model definitions, SOA composite templates, and business event definitions. Note that the MDS repository is an intrinsic part of the SOA Suite run-time environment, not something that you need to install separately and additionally. However, also note that during development, the JDeveloper IDE can make use of a local, file system–based MDS repository.

Service Bus does not interact with MDS—neither at run time nor at design time, except for the ability to import objects from and export objects to the design time MDS. Working with common, shared artifacts in Service Bus projects is typically done using a single, generic, shared project that holds these artifacts.

Using MDS to Share and Consume Resources

Resources in the MDS can be directly accessed at design time as well as at run time in SOA composite applications using a URL that starts with "oramds:". This URL is valid at design time as well as at run time, resolved against the local or the central MDS service. When a composite application is developed in JDeveloper, it can refer to artifacts in the MDS, and when that application is deployed, those same references into the central MDS are valid.

The MDS repository is organized in partitions, container structures similar to file system directories. Resource names must be unique within a partition. MDS contains three types of resources: (pre)seeded, application specific, and shared.

The pre-seeded resources are the run-time artifacts shipped with the SOA Suite and required out of the box. This includes RuntimeFault.wsdl, HumanTaskEvent.edl, and ws-addressing.xsd. These resources are stored in the partition path /soa/shared.

The second category contains SOA composite applications and their artifacts (business rules, DVMs, and so on) that end up in the MDS repository when they are deployed to the SOA Suite container. Each composite, and in fact each revision, has its own store (or MDS partition) for artifacts such as XSD, WSDL, XSLT, EDL, adapter configurations, and the composite.xml file. These application-specific artifacts are in a path that starts with /apps/.

The last category of shared resources is created by users and deployed in a special type of archive (MAR, or Metadata Archive). It consists of artifacts that are shared by multiple applications. Examples are XSD with common (canonical) definitions, Domain Value Map definitions, and EDL files with business event definitions. Using MDS to store shared artifacts and references to MDS to reuse those artifacts is an important method for reducing duplication (such as local copies) of artifacts.

We will see in the next sections how to add documents to the MDS repository and how to subsequently reference these objects, and how to transfer them to the run-time environment to be used in running services based on SOA composite applications.

Then we will investigate how this all works out for Service Bus projects that cannot leverage MDS. Here we will work from the notion that references in Service Bus projects can be across projects: all projects contribute to a shared folder structure at run time and all artifacts anywhere in this folder structure are potentially accessible. This conclusion has led in many organizations to an approach where corporate-wide standards like schemas, transformation and shared services are in a shared project. This scenario can be handled by having a separate development system for the shared project and providing a read-only copy of the shared project in each departmental development system. When any shared resource changes, all the departmental systems are updated by importing and exporting the required resources.

When deploying resources into a stage system or a production system, the shared project along with all the impacted departmental projects should be deployed together to avoid any semantic errors that might cause the deployment to fail.

SOA Composite Based on Resources in MDS

In this section the interaction with the file based design time MDS facility is explored. Artifacts are transferred into this repository, then used for the creation of a SOA composite application. This application is deployed but only after the required MDS artifacts are transferred to the run-time MDS environment.

Prepare the Design Time MDS Repository

When you install JDeveloper from the quick start installer, a design time MDS connection called SOA_DesignTimeRepository is created. This connection refers to a directory on the local file system. Right click and select Properties in the context menu to find out which folder is currently configured as the home of this design time MDS environment. The designated directory can be changed if you want to.

The source folder for this chapter contains a folder called StartingPoint that contains two subfolders WSDLs and Schemas. Copy these two folders to folder *apps* under the root directory for the design time MDS repository. Create folder *apps* if it does not already exist. Figure 21-4 shows the situation on the file system on the left and in the MDS browser on the Resource palette in JDeveloper (after refreshing) on the right.

TIP
Moving artifacts to the design time MDS repository can also be done from within a JDeveloper project. Just select the artifacts to transfer— of the types supported by MDS—and select menu option Share using SOA Design-Time MDS Repository from the context menu. Select the target folder, configure the way dependencies should be processed and complete the wizard. Note that in this transfer operation, the sources are not just copied to the MDS repository, they are actually removed from the project. Any references to these sources are replaced upon transfer with references (oramds:) to their counterparts in MDS.

The transfer operation cannot be reversed: resources in MDS cannot be transferred directly from MDS to a SOA composite project. Of course a simple copy on the file system can be used to add duplicates of the artifacts in MDS to the project. However, all oramds: references to these artifacts need then to be replaced [with a search and replace in files most likely].

Create a SOA Composite Application Based on MDS Artifacts

Create a new SOA Application called SOAConversionService with a project ConversionService based on the Empty Composite template.

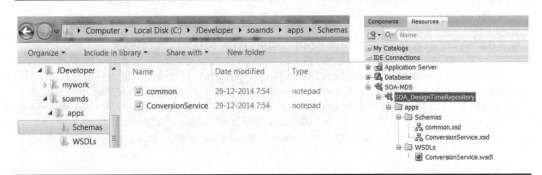

FIGURE 21-4. *The file-based design time MDS repository on the file system (left-hand side) and from within JDeveloper (on the right-hand side)*

Create a SOAP Service binding based on WSDL document ConversionService.wsdl in the apps\WSDLs folder in MDS. In the popup in which you edit the service binding you can browse for an existing WSDL document. The WSDL Chooser offers various sources for the WSDL document: Application Server, File System (under which Application and Project), Project Libraries, SOA-MDS, UDDI, and WSIL. In this case, pick SOA-MDS and locate ConversionService.wsdl. Ensure that the checkbox for importing the WSDL document and its dependencies into the project is *not* checked, because we will want to retain the references to the resources in the MDS repository.

After completing the configuration of the service binding, you will find that no WSDL or XSD documents were added to the project—as shown in Figure 21-5. When you inspect the source of the composite.xml file, you will find that the WSDL document is referenced directly in the MDS repository using the *oramds:* designator that JDeveloper knows how to interpret—as well as the run-time SOA composite engine.

Add a BPEL component called TemperatureConvertor based on the ConversionService.wsdl document. Now JDeveloper will create a WSDL document called ConversionServiceWrapper.wsdl that imports the ConversionService.wsdl document and defines the partnerLinkTypes for the

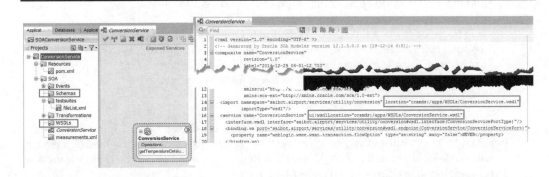

FIGURE 21-5. *The ConversionService project references the WSDL document in the MDS repository*

BPEL process. Implement the BPEL process—using an Assign activity with the formula for calculating the Fahrenheit temperature as (1.8*celsiusTemperature + 32).

Deploying a SOA Composite Application with MDS References

With the SOA composite ConversionService implemented, deploy it to the SOA Suite run time. Although it is a simple application and the implementation is correct, deployment will still fail—most likely with an MDS-00054 error complaining that the file /apps/WSDLs/ConversionService .wsdl does not exist. This file exists really in exactly that directory—however only in the design time MDS repository. We need to make sure that it is available in the run-time MDS before deploying applications that refer to it through an oramds: reference.

There are several ways to get resources into the central, run-time MDS repository. The easiest is probably the Transfer option on the MDS connection in JDeveloper. Before we can use that mechanism however, we need to have a connection in JDeveloper to the run-time MDS environment.

Create the Connection to the Run-Time MDS Repository   Because the run-time MDS repository is stored in a database, we need to have a database connection first to the MDS database schema that was created by the RCU utility when the standalone SOA Suite run-time environment was created. When that database connection is created and tested, open the context menu for node IDE Connections | SOA-MDS (in the Resources palette) and select *New SOA-MDS Connection*. Provide a name for the connection, select DB Based MDS as the connection type, and select the database connection to the MDS schema. From the dropdown labeled Select MDS partition, select the *soa-infra* partition. Test the connection and upon success, click on OK.

The connection is added under the node SOA-MDS. Expand it to check whether the child node soa is present. Under this node are the out of the box shared artifacts that were installed along with the SOA Suite.

TIP
When the run-time environment is the integrated WebLogic Server, then the MDS run-time repository is file based. The creation of the connection to this repository is done using information about its location that you learn in EM FMW Control. Click on the node Metadata Repositores | mds-soa. From the drop-down menu on top of the right-hand side of the page (under mds-soa), select option Target Information. A popup appears that shows the file system location for the mds-soa instance.

In JDeveloper, open the Resources window. Open the context menu for node IDE Connections | SOA-MDS and select New SOA-MDS Connection. Provide a name, select File-Based MDS as the connection type and specify the directory from the Target information popup as MDS Root Folder.

Transfer from Local File-Based MDS to the Central, DB-Based MDS   Transferring artifacts between MDS repositories is a very simple thing to do. Just right click on the source MDS connection—in this case the SOA_DesignTimeRepository—and select the option Transfer in the context menu, as is shown in Figure 21-6.

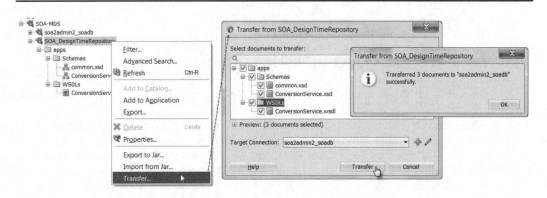

FIGURE 21-6. *Transfer files from the design time MDS repository to the run-time MDS repository*

A popup window appears in which to select the documents to transfer. The folder structure will be honored and copied across when necessary. When the selection is complete, press Transfer. At this point, the documents are copied from the local file system–based MDS environment to the central shared database backed run-time MDS repository. Note that the transfer operation can be made in the reverse direction as well.

Deploy Again and Investigate   Try once more to deploy the SOA composite ConversionService. This time, deployment will succeed because now all referenced objects are indeed available in the run-time MDS to be retrieved from the oramds: references included in the deployed application. You can invoke the ConversionService to verify it is doing its job.

When you inspect the WSDL for the ConversionService, from the EM FMW Control, for example, you will see that imports the ConversionService.xsd document from a special URL that in facts references the MDS directly.

Service Bus, Common Project, and MDS

Service Bus projects cannot directly reference objects in MDS. The oramds: reference that is so convenient in SOA composite applications is meaningless in Service Bus—both at design time and at run time. We use a different mechanism in Service Bus to manage and consume shared resources; frequently we use a *common project* as alternative approach.

Simply put: just like SOA composites can reference WSDL, XSD, XQuery, XSLT, DVM, and EDL definitions and so on in MDS, Service Bus projects can reference files in another project. We can create a generic, shared or common project that contains shared resources, organized in a folder structure just like MDS. When a Service Bus project needs to use one of these resources, it can reference it in the common project. Only a single instance of each shared resource needs to be deployed to the run time. Only a single instance would be needed in the design time as well—if it were not for the fact that the ability to reference objects in other projects is restricted to other projects that live under the same application and common parent folder. What we may end up doing is create a CommonProject that is the editable master copy of all reusable objects. This project is copied to any Service Bus application that requires the shared resources (which is typically every application). These copies are supposed to be read only—synchronized as closely as possible with the master.

In this section, we will work with such a common project and see how it compares to MDS.

Create the Common Project and Transfer Objects from MDS

Create a new Service Bus application called Common with a Service Bus project called CommonProject. This project is to hold the common, shareable resources for all other Service Bus projects.

Open the SOA_DesignTimeRepository SOA-MDS connection. Locate the file ConversionService .wsdl and right click on it. Select Service Bus | Import Resource from the context menu, as is shown in Figure 21-7. The Import Service Bus Resources wizard appears. Specify the import location—a new folder called WSDLs in the Service Bus project. On page for step 2, confirm the selected file and its dependencies (the by now familiar two XSD documents). Click on Finish to execute the import operation.

JDeveloper copies the selected resources from MDS into the CommonProject and creates the same folder structure as in MDS.

Create a Service Project that Consumes the CommonProject

Create a new Service Bus application called SBConversionService with a project called ConversionService.

Next, copy the folder Common/CommonProject—which contains the CommonProject.jpr file and the folders WSDLs and Schemas—into folder SBConversionService. Add the CommonProject to the application SBConversionService by opening the jpr file. Now we can reference the artifacts in the CommonProject from project ConversionService—because the CommonProject is in the same application and its sources are under the same parent folder. We have to regard this local clone of the CommonProject as a read-only copy that we may reference but should not change in any way.

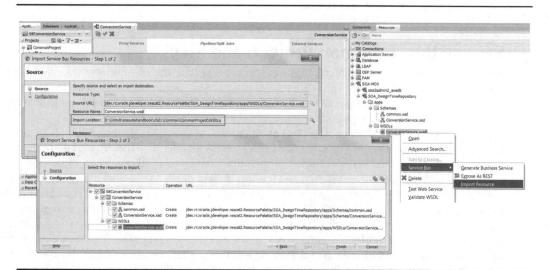

FIGURE 21-7. *Import resources from MDS to a Service Bus project*

TIP
*Instead of copying the CommonProject folder, you could create a local
symbolic link called CommonProject referencing the original folder.
This would of course automatically ensure synchronization since there
would be only a single instance of the CommonProject. Alternatively,
you could implement synchronizing the folder as a step in a build
script—such as Maven or Ant—that is run as part of an automated
build process.*

In the ConversionService project, create a ProxyService called ConversionServicePS that is
based on the ConversionService.wsdl definition in the WSDLs folder in the CommonProject. Also
have a Pipeline generated, called ConversionPipeline—as shown in Figure 21-8. This pipeline
also references the ConversionService.wsdl. Note that this WSDL document is not copied to
the ConversionService project—it is referenced in its original CommonProject context, using the
reference /CommonProject/WSDLs/ConversionService.wsdl. Within an application, all Service
Bus really looks at for addressing objects are the folders—not so much the projects.

Next, implement the pipeline. Add a *pipeline pair* and add a single *replace* activity—either
request or response pipe—to manipulate the contents of $body, once again using the formula 1.8*
celsiusTemperature-from-the-request + 32.

Deploy project ConversionService to the run-time environment. You would perhaps expect a
deployment issue because the project references external artifacts. Deployment is successful though.

Open the Service Bus Console. You will find that the CommonProject is deployed along with
ConversionService—all of it, not just the required artifacts. Note that the master copy of the
CommonProject can also be deployed on its own—from the context of the Common application.
This deployment overrides the one done along with the ConversionService—as the last deployment
always wins over those done before.

Feel free to invoke the ConversionService on the Service Bus to verify its successful conversion
of any Celsius temperature you can throw at it.

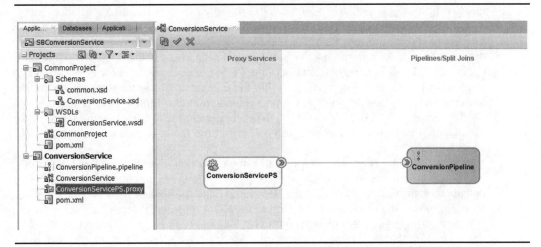

FIGURE 21-8. *The ConversionService with references to the local copy of the CommonProject*

Canonical Data Model and Message Definitions

Enterprises are fueled by information. And every organization has its very own information structures. Data about patients and diagnoses are relevant to hospitals and data about slots and flights make the clock tick for airports. There is of course a lot of overlap too in data objects that are relevant to virtually every organization—such as customers, products and invoices—even though the terms used for these objects can vary across organizations.

The Canonical Data Model or CDM for an organization describes the business objects or entities relevant to that organization with their attributes and their relationships. The CDM expresses these objects and characteristics in the terminology that is actually used by the people working in the organization and executing the business processes. It is not the technical language used in database designs. The CDM also describes constraints that apply to the entities, the relationships, and the properties. What is the data type of properties and what range or set of values is allowed for a property? Is a property value required for an entity—or can it be unknown or not applicable? How many references to another type of entity can or must an entity have?

The CDM provides the universal language throughout the enterprise. It lays the foundation for the structure of the messages exchanged in the Service-Oriented Architecture. Events, request and response messages are inspired by and modeled after the structures defined in the CDM. For this to happen—the CDM cannot just be a set of Wiki pages or an Excel sheet. The CDM needs to be expressed in XSD documents.

Most organizations engaging in SOA will have gone or will go through the preceding paragraphs at some point. Then they need to make a decision on how to proceed when they start to design the request and response messages for the service operations.

Initially, most messages were designed in a service specific XSD document that is imported from the WSDL for the service. And this service specific XSD document imports the XSD documents created for the CDM—closely coupling almost every service interface directly to a set of centrally managed XML Schema Definitions. When the CDM is complete and very stable, this may feel like a workable strategy. One however has the distinct disadvantage of creating message definitions that are not very specific—and potentially quite complex because of the references to probably a web of nested XSD documents with each their own namespace. By referencing entities in the CDM XSD documents, all properties and child elements of these entities become part of the message describing the input to or output from a specific service operation. Most of the time, any particular operation will only operate on a subset of the CDM definition of an entity or return only a small aspect of the entity as it is modeled in the CDM. Looking at the message definitions in the service interface definition is then not telling you the complete story. It suggests you need to provide much more information than an operation will actually require and make use of, and it indicates a much more extensive response message than the operation will actually produce.

When the CDM is not yet complete and stable—which in most organizations is and will be the case for years to come—such a direct dependency in almost every service definition on the CDM XSD documents becomes a major headache when the CDM evolves. Modifications to the CDM means updates to the CDM representation in XSD documents. However, direct dependencies exist on these documents across the service landscape. These changes therefore instantly affect all these services—potentially rendering them invalid. Even applying a versioning strategy to the CDM—as has been tried in many cases—will not really resolve the problem. Such a strategy typically involves defining releases or versions of the CDM including a version label in the namespace of the CDM XSDs. This means that the service interfaces and the message definitions all refer to a specific version of the CDM. That version is stable—from the moment a new version is started. However, upgrading any service to a newer version of the CDM now has a massive impact on the server itself and on all its consumers because all message definitions will change due to the changed namespace.

The following has found to be a better approach that allows for very specific message definitions for service operations and for a flexible evolution of the CDM. Instead of tying the XSD describing the request and response messages for service operations directly to the XSD documents that define the CDM, this XSD does not import any of these XSDs with the CDM definitions. Every service has its very own, stand-alone XSD document that contains the full definition of the messages for the operations in the service, all of them entirely in the same service specific namespace. Each message is inspired by and compliant with the definitions in the CDM XSDs—according to the following rules:

- The elements used in the service specific message definition need to have the same name and type as is used in the CDM XSDs.

- The elements need to be in the same order as they are in the CDM XSDs.

- Elements that are optional in the CDM XSDs can be left out completely from the message definition [if they are irrelevant to that message].

- Constraints on elements in the message specific definition can be tighter than those in the CDM XSDs. That means, for example, mandatory instead of optional, numeric instead of string, a shorter maximum length, a longer minimum length, a smaller set of allowable values, or a more narrow value range.

- Elements required in the message definition and not included in the CDM XSDs— such as metadata or search parameters—can be added—either at the highest level in the message definition or as the last element(s) [with an X prefix] in elements derived from the CDM.

Figure 21-9 visualizes this approach for defining service operation specific messages that are loosely coupled with the Canonical Data Model.

Obviously, this way of working requires some discipline. And some tools would be really useful to support this approach. For example, a tool that verifies whether message definitions are indeed compliant with the CDM according to the rules outlined above. And a tool to help compose a message definition from the CDM XSDs in the prescribed way by picking and choosing the desired CDM elements and their properties and tightening the associated constraints. The tool would create the message definition with all selected elements copied to a single namespace XSD document without imports of the underlying CDM XSD definitions. Ideally, this tool could also compare message definitions with the CDM after it has evolved, point out the discrepancies and allowing a developer to propagate changes in the CDM to previously derived message definitions.

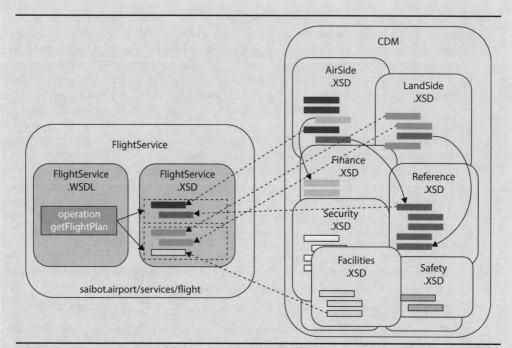

FIGURE 21-9. *Message definitions for service operations are derived from yet not tightly coupled to the XSDs describing the Canonical Data Model*

Updating MDS Resources

The evolution of resources in MDS obviously does not stop after their first introduction into MDS. The artifacts cannot be changed in situ in MDS. However, they can be transferred from MDS to any JDeveloper project to be edited and then be transferred again, back to MDS. Existing artifacts can be overwritten with updated definitions in the transfer operation.

In the next few steps, we will look at updating all three MDS resources in the context of the Service Bus common project. These resources are transferred to MDS – overwriting the existing definitions. This will have an immediate effect on the SOA composite application that now has to implement an extended service interface. The composite is reimplemented—including a call to the Service Bus implementation of the ConversionService created in such a way as to prevent both a duplication of the WSDL and a design time dependency on the run-time availability of this service.

Finally the resources are updated in the MDS run time and the MDS cache is forcibly refreshed.

Update MDS Resources from Common ServiceBus Project

Open the Service Bus application *Common* and expand *CommonProject*, the master copy of this container of shared Service Bus resources. Open common.xsd and add a new element *temperatureKelvinType*—a simple type based on float and restricted to values of zero or higher. Next, extend ConversionService.xsd with elements *temperatureKelvinToFahrenheitRequestMessage* (based

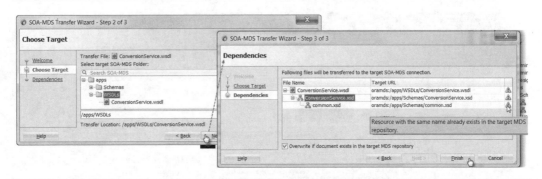

FIGURE 21-10. *Transfer modified artifacts from Service Bus CommonProject to design time MDS*

on the new temperatureKelvinType) and *temperatureKelvinToFahrenheitResponseMessage* (based on the existing temperatureFahrenheitType). Finally extend the service interface in ConversionService .wsdl with operation *getTemperatureKelvinToFahrenheit* and its corresponding messages.

These updated resources provide the foundation for the next iteration of the SOA composite. They should therefore be made available in [the design time] MDS. Right click on ConversionService .wsdl and from the context menu, select Service Bus | Publish to SOA Designtime Repository. The SOA-MDS Transfer Wizard opens. Select folder apps | WSDLs as the target for the transfer operation, as shown in Figure 21-10. Click next to proceed to the Dependencies page. The wizard lists all files selected for transfer as well as the dependencies for these files (the two XSD files). It also marks files that have counterparts in the transfer destination with alert icons. Mark the checkbox *Overwrite if document exists in the target MDS repository* near the bottom of the page. Click on Finish to have the update documents transferred to the design time file based MDS repository.

Extend SOA Composite Based on Updated MDS Resources

Open SOA composite SOAConversionService. Open the composite editor in project ConversionService. The service binding should already display the new operation *getTemperatureKelvinToFahrenheit* that is defined in the ConversionService.wsdl document in MDS. Clearly, JDeveloper inspects this resource in MDS when interpreting the composite.xml file and its dependencies before opening the composite editor.

Add a Reference binding of type SOAP. As the WSDL URL, select WSDLs/ConversionService .wsdl in MDS, as shown in Figure 21-11. Uncheck the checkbox for copying the WSDL and its dependent artifacts into the project. When you close the editor for the reference binding, you will be presented with a warning indicating that this WSDL is just an abstract document—without actual binding and endpoint for making the call to the web service. Acknowledge this warning— we will do something about it later. The reference binding is added to the project and is shown in the composite editor.

Add a Mediator component, based on the same WSDLs/ConversionService.wsdl in MDS. Wire this component to the reference binding, for the operation *getTemperatureKelvinToFahrenheit* in the Mediator to operation *getTemperatureCelsiusToFahrenheit* in the target. Open the mediator for editing. Create transformations for the request and the response. Note that the request transformation should subtract 273 from the request Kelvin temperature to produce the Celsius value to pass on. The transformation of the response message can just pass the value as is.

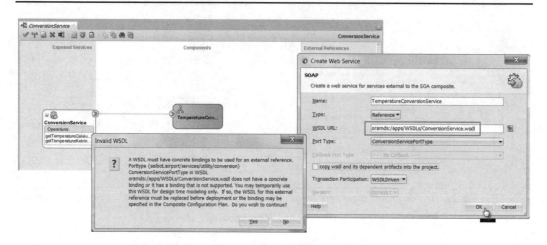

FIGURE 21-11. *Create a reference binding based on a WSDL definition in the local MDS*

Back in the composite editor, remove the BPEL component. Wire the service binding to the Mediator component and create a second routing rule, this one for the operation *getTemperatureCelsiusToFahrenheit*, which is routed to the same operation in the reference binding. Because request and response messages for both operations are based on the same XSD element, we do not need transformations.

Provide the Concrete Endpoint for the Abstract Reference Binding
Before we can deploy the application, we have to do something about the abstract service definition warning we received when creating the reference binding for the WSDL in MDS. We need to specify the concrete endpoint for the external *ConversionService* that we want this composite to invoke.

Open the composite.xml file in source mode. Locate the <reference> element under the <composite> root. The <binding.ws> child element has to be set with proper values.

This reference binding should refer to the ServiceBus project *ConversionService* deployed in the previous section. Locate the run-time wsdl for this service—properly something like http://host:port/ConversionService?wsdl. Open the WSDL document and locate the name of the service and the port. The port attribute of the binding.ws element should be set with targetNamespace#wsdl .endpoint(service/port) and the location attribute holds the location of the run-time WSDL document. The resulting entry in the composite.xml file look very much like this:

```
<binding.ws
  port="saibot.airport/services/utility/conversion#wsdl.endpoint
      (ConversionServicePortTypeSOAP11BindingQSService
      /ConversionServicePortTypeSOAP11BindingQSPort)"
  location="http://10.10.10.21:8011/ConversionService?wsdl"
  soapVersion="1.1"
/>
```

Save the change and deploy the composite application.

Deploy the Extended SOA Composite

The deployment should succeed, however, when you try to invoke the new operation—you will not be able to do so. In fact, when you inspect the WSDL document for the freshly (re)deployed composite, you will not even see the new operation. Deploying the SOA composite based on the modified definitions of the WSDL and XSD documents in the local MDS repository did not affect the corresponding document in the central, run-time database based MDS.

To ensure the run-time MDS has access to the updated WSDL and XSD definitions, use the Transfer operation once more, to transfer the contents of the apps folder in the local, file based MDS repository to the run-time MDS environment.

After a successful transfer—you will probably still not be able to invoke the new operation. And when you check the WSDL document via the url http://host:port/endpoint?wsdl, you will still see the old definition. This is caused by the caching mechanism in the run-time MDS facility. In order to enhance performance, resources are read from MDS once after the SOA Suite is started and then cached in memory to prevent subsequent read operations against the MDS database schema. When the extended WSDL and XSD documents were transferred to the run-time MDS, the database was updated. However, there is no internal mechanism to set the MDS cache dirty and force and update of the cached resources.

When you attempt to access the WSDL and XSD artifacts directly from MDS, using URLs constructed like:

```
http://host:port/soa-infra/services/default/ConversionService/
ConversionService?XSD=../Schemas/common.xsd
```

or

```
http://host:port/soa-infra/services/default/ConversionService/
ConversionService?WSDL=../WSDLs/ConversionService.wsdl
```

You will see the resource definition retrieved from the underlying database rather than the cache—and therefore the updated definition with Kelvin support.

Clear the MDS Cache   There is a way to clear the MDS cache. Open the EM FMW Control. Click on the soa-infra node. Open the dropdown menu and select Administration | System MBean Browser. Browse under Application Defined MBeans for oracle.mds.lcm, as shown in Figure 21-12. Expand the subtree for the managed server running the SOA composite engine. Then find the MBean *Application: soa-infra | MDSAppRuntime | MDSAppRuntime*. Open the *Operations* tab and click on *clearCache*. Press the Invoke button to execute the operation.

Once the cache is cleared, the next attempt to invoke the new operation will probably succeed. SOA Suite will not find the WSDL in the cache and therefore retrieve it from the MDS database, which will of course result in the updated definition which includes the new operation to deal with Kelvin temperatures. A call to either operation in the *ConversionService* composite will go through the Mediator that invokes the Service Bus counterpart, though only operation *getTemperatureCelsiusToFahrenheit* because the new operation is not yet implemented.

TIP
If the refresh of the cache does not work – which occasionally it does not – restarting the managed server is the undesirable, alternative way of resetting the cache.

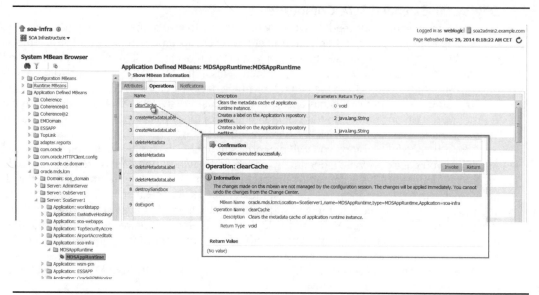

FIGURE 21-12. *Invoke clearCache on the MDSAppRuntime MBean to clear the MDS cache and force refreshing with updated MDS resources*

Updating the Service Bus Project ConversionService

At this point, the master *CommonProject* in application *Common* contains the extended definition of the WSDL for the *ConversionService*. It was the source for the definition that is now in both design time and run-time MDS. The clone of the *CommonProject* in the *SBConversionService* application still contains the original definitions, which is usually not a good thing. We will walk through the steps of upgrading the Service Bus implementation of the *ConversionService*.

Discrepancies in the State of the CommonProject

One of our objectives from a governance perspective is that it should not make any difference whether the master copy of *CommonProject* in the Common application is deployed to the run-time Service Bus environment or one of its clones such as the one under *SBConversionService*.

At this point however, it *does* make a difference. Let's for example deploy the master copy—with the updated definition. Deployment should be quick and easy. Now when you inspect the WSDL for the *ConversionService*, it mentions the new operation for converting Kelvin temperatures. Given the fact that the *ConversionService* does not rely on a local copy of the interface definition ConversionService.wsdl but instead references the document in the *CommonProject* and that project has just been redeployed, this is exactly what could be expected. However, it does mean a discrepancy between the interface definition and the actual implementation. Invoking this new operation will end in an ugly error.

Also note that by redeploying the *ConversionService*—tagging along its local, currently out-of-synch clone of *CommonProject*—will remove the discrepancy but also revert the update to ConversionService.wsdl and the other changes artifacts in the *CommonProject*.

Update the Implementation of the ConversionService

Ideally after every change in the *CommonProject*, all local clones are immediately synchronized. Or at least at the time when Service Bus projects are deployed they should have a fully up to date local clone of the *CommonProject*.

At this point, simply copy the *Common/CommonProject* folder once more to the *SBConversionService* directory. Merge and override at every opportunity.

Open the pipeline editor. Add an operational branch as the first activity with branches for both operations in the WSDL. Move the pipeline pair created earlier to handle the Celsius temperature conversion to the branch for operation *getTemperatureCelsiusToFahrenheit*. Copy the pipeline pair to the branch for operation *getTemperatureKelvinToFahrenheit*. Next, edit the *Replace* activity in the latter branch—ensure that the correct *temperature* element is taken from the $body variable and that 273 is subtracted before the multiplication with 1.8 is performed.

Deploy the *ConversionService*. This will bring the local *CommonProject* along. Fortunately, it is now a perfect copy of the master *CommonProject*, fully in synch, so this is not a problem. Figure 21-13 shows where we can find the WSDL file and how it is referenced at design time and run time and from Service Bus and SOA Composite.

After deployment, invoke the *ConversionService* to convert a Kelvin temperature value to Fahrenheit to verify its correct implementation.

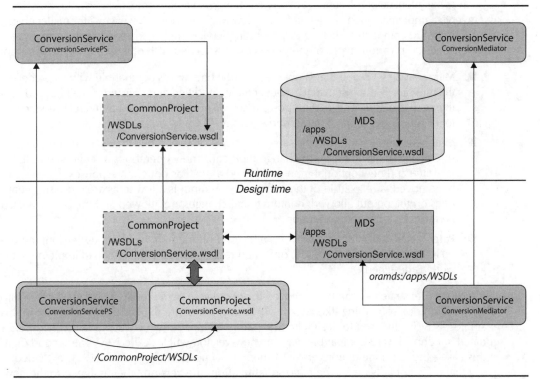

FIGURE 21-13. *An overview of the design time and run-time repositories of shared and reusable artifacts for SOA composite applications (MDS) and Service Bus (a common project)*

Versioning

When we talk about the various states of a service through its lifecycle, a discussion on versioning cannot be far away. A discussion that applies to services—and other components such as data models (including XSDs), business processes and business events.

Versioning is a tool to multiple ends. One is to allow multiple incarnations to be managed in parallel—to minimize impact of change yet allow evolution. To have a fallback option—a previous state of an object with known characteristics to return to when a later change for whatever reason should be undone. To organize parallel development and bugfixing.

Another important aspect of versioning is identification. In order to have control over the development and bugfixing process, over loosely coupled reuse and over the composition of releases and run-time environment, it must be clear at all times which version of a component is and should be around. The version label is as much part of the component identifier as the [local] name and the namespace (or package, folder structure, etc.).

Usually it does not pay off to apply versioning to the components inside the implementation of a service—such as Mediator, Pipeline, or Human Task. A PL/SQL package whose only purpose is to be a part of a service implementation probably does not have a publicly advertised version either—although a reusable PL/SQL package probably does or should.

Versioning of Services

As soon as the interface or the contract of service changes in a noncompatible way, it is best to create a new service implementation altogether for the new major version. However, with smaller changes that are backward compatible, sticking to the existing service implementation may be useful.

We can discern various types of [new] versions associated with different levels of disruption.

- **Major**—a new version that is not (necessarily) backwards compatible with its predecessor; the interface is not just extended but actually modified and consumers will have to adapt their calls; to all intents and purposes a new major version is just a different service (with a lot of similarities to the one it is derived from).

- **Minor**—a new version with the same interface—or at least one that is backward compatible so consumers do not have to change their calls; new operations are allowed in the interface and new optional input is allowed as well as optional response elements can be removed; a relaxation of the constraints on input is allowed as are more stringent rules on the output allowed; nonfunctional changes are allowed as well, such as better performance, cheaper execution.

- **Patch**—a new version that provides a fix for a problem in the previous version; there is no (designed) change intended, only a correction to make the intended implementation work as designed.

Version label strategies can be employed in accordance with these types of versions. Version labels usually look something like x.y.z—where x, y, and z are digits. The first digit—x in this example—is typically used to designate the major version. So when a service at version 1.3 is updated in nonbackward compatible way, the new version will be called 2.0. The second digit—y in this case—indicates the minor version. When the same service at version 1.3 is extended in a way that does not falls under the *major* qualification, the version label assigned to the new incarnation would be 1.4. And when the 1.3 version of the service is fixed, the result would be labeled 1.3.1.

Major New Version

The creation of new major version of a service is a fairly rare event—something that happens at most only a few times in the first years in the life of a service—and not even for all services. It is such an event that when it does happen it has a substantial impact.

There is rather important and consequential distinction between major versions on the one hand and the other version types on the other. Multiple major versions of a service can coexist in a run-time environment, for prolonged periods. Only one minor or patch version under a specific major version label can be active in an environment.

Consumers of a service have to decide which major version of a service they will invoke. When they switch to a different major version, they will have to reconfigure their invocations. Major versions have different names, namespaces, and endpoints. That is required of course in order for them to coexist. The major version digit will therefore make an appearance in both namespace and endpoint and most likely in the name of the version as well. For example, saibot. airport/services/utility/conversion/2 (for the namespace of the 2.0 version of the ConversionService) and http://host:port/utility/conversionservice/2 (for the endpoint of that service).

Creating a major new version of a service will in practice most likely involve creating a duplicate of the JDeveloper project and all its sources for the latest minor version under the previous major version. Although copying and cloning is usually something to avoid, in this case it is the most obvious thing to do because the new major version is so completely different from its predecessor and will even coexist with that predecessor as it will with other versions, that creating a new major version is just the birth of a new service that happens to be able to adopt [copies of] some existing resources as its own.

Service Bus gives us full control over the endpoint of a service. It requires uniqueness on the name of the root folder of projects, hence the name of that folder will have to reflect the major version label. It is up to the Service Bus which service implementation to route requests to that are received by a proxy service that represents a specific version of the business service. This implementation does not have to follow strict versioning rule—as only the Service Bus needs to invoke it and needs to recognize it as the implementation of a specific service version.

For SOA composites we do not have complete control over the endpoint as we will discuss in the next section. However, we can have multiple composite applications with the same [local] name—as long as they have a different revision label or live in different partitions.

Endpoints, States, and Versions of SOA Composite Applications

SOA composite applications can be in one of several states—as determined by the administrator. A composite can be:

- Active—ready for action; can create new instances and complete existing instances
- Shut down—effectively dead, performs no action at all; using Start Up a composite in this state can be revived
- Retired—cannot create new instances; existing instances are allowed to complete normally; can process requests and events through (mid process) correlation.

SOA composite applications are identified at run time by their name in combination with their revision identifier and the partition they live in. Multiple revisions of a composite can coexist. When a SOA composite is deployed, a Revision ID is assigned. This Revision ID is part of the identification as well as of the endpoint of the services exposed by the composite. These services applications are available at an endpoint that looks like this URL:

```
http://host:port/soa-infra/services/default/...
              ...ConversionService!2.0/ConversionService
```

There is some logic built into this URL: It first identifies the partition (*default* in this example) and the composite (ConversionService), then it names a specific revision of the composite (2.0) and finally the service (also ConversionService in this case). Consumers of the service can use this full-blown URL that determines exactly which version of the (services exposed by the) composite they will access. Alternatively and much more commonly, they can use a URL that does not contain the revision information, like this:

```
http://host:port/soa-infra/services/default/...
              ...ConversionService/ConversionService
```

In this case, they leave it to the SOA Suite to decide which version of the composite will be accessed to handle the request. This is where the concept of the default revision makes its appearance: When we deploy a composite application, we can indicate whether that revision will be the default revision; we can also designate the default revision of a composite through the EM FMW Control using the Set A Default button on the composite revision's dashboard. This default revision is the version that will handle all requests to the composite that do not explicitly name the revision in the URL. It is also the version that will be activated by inbound adapters (e.g., Database, JMS, or File). Note that EDN events will be consumed by all revisions of the composite.

Figure 21-14 shows the EM FMW Control with several revisions of the ConversionService composite application. It shows the current state for revision 1.1 as *Active*. Buttons are available to change the state to Retire[d] or Shut Down and also to set this revision as the default revision for the ConversionService composite.

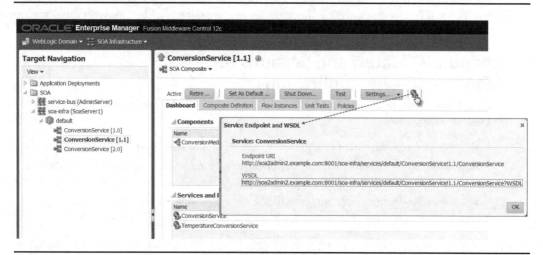

FIGURE 21-14. *Several revisions of the ConversionService composite have been deployed to the default partition; the endpoint and some available operations are shown for the selected revision 1.1*

Versioning of Web Services

Versioning of services is a little more complex than versioning in a traditional architecture. The number of artifacts that each potentially have their own individual lifecycle is much larger than in traditional monolithic applications. And even though through decoupling we try to minimize direct dependencies between these artifacts, they still rely on each other and on their interface definitions (WSDL and XSD). The impact of changing the interface of a single service artifact can be quite huge.

Another aspect of versioning in our service-oriented world is the fact that unlike with the monolithic applications, we can have multiple versions of the same artifacts active at the same time. Provided, of course, that we carefully manage the access of the consumers to the specific version they can work with.

Because a service consists of three parts, all three parts can change independently. Suppose we have a service that can be invoked to retrieve the flight plan for a flight. The interface definition for the operation getPlan has two parameters: flight number and the date for the specific flight. The implementation will return the result code and the flight plan (if it could be found). The contract of this service states that you need to authenticate with an X509 certificate and that HTTPS is used to encrypt the message during transport.

Now the business decides that flight plan information is confidential and that they want the message itself to be encrypted using WS-Security instead of just securing the transport layer. Do we consider this a new service, or a new version of the existing service?

What if we fix a bug in the (encapsulated) implementation of the service? Do we consider this a new version of the service, even if the contract and the interface are unchanged, or just a new version of the component that implements it? Or does this constitute a new service altogether? And what if the interface is changed, but the change is fully backward compatible, such as a new operation or support for a new optional input parameter? Should we then declare a new version of the service or an entirely new service?

Many books and blogs have been written about this topic. In our experience it is a best practice to keep it simple. In general, when the interface, the component, or the contract changes, it is a good idea to consider this to be a new service altogether. In our repository we can deprecate the old service and then retire it as soon as the new service is live, or as soon as all the consumers have switched to the new service. This is clear for the service consumers and keeps the complexity of backward compatibility to a minimum.

Redeployment of SOA Composite Applications

The SOA Suite provides various ways of dealing with changes to composite applications: A deployed application can be replaced through redeployment with a changed implementation, a new version of a deployed application can be deployed in parallel with the existing application, and an application can be renamed and deployed as an entirely new application.

When a composite application is changed and redeployed, all URLs—whether version specific or relying on the default revision—stay the same and continue to work. No consumer may even have to know that the redeployment has taken place, except for two important facts: During redeployment, there will be a period of unavailability that may result in timeout exceptions for service consumers. Even more dramatically, the status of still running instances initiated by the composite revision that is redeployed is changed to "stale." Stale instances have ceased running—they are effectively aborted. And, of course, it is obvious that when the WSDL changes during the redeployment, the consumer may no longer be compatible with the deployed composite and the consumer will very much become aware of the redeployment.

Revision Label Strategy for SOA Composite Applications

A major new version of service could and probably should have a SOA composite whose name reflects that major version label. Alternatively, you could use the revision identifier of the composite to indicate the major version. Because only one revision can be set to be the default revision, consumers of another major version would then have to use the explicit endpoint including the revision identifier rather than rely on the default.

Minor new versions of a service exposed by a SOA composite can just be redeployed using the same revision identifier, replacing the existing one. Before starting redeployment of the composite, you can first retire it. This will prevent new instances from being started. Running instances will continue normally. Short-running instances can be allowed to complete. Then redeployment is performed and the composite can be activated again. Note that the composite is unavailable to consumers as soon as it is retired.

Long-running instances of a composite application (typically using Human Task, BPEL, or BPM—BPMN and Case) do not survive redeployment of that composite, and redeployment is probably not a useful strategy for composite applications that can be long running. Instead, the existing composite can still be retired before or after the changed composite is deployed as a different revision that is set as the default revision. We would then temporarily have multiple minor versions: one for already running instance and a new one for new instances. As soon as the running instances on the retired composite revision have completed, this revision can be removed.

Tools for Governance

Governance of SOA assets is a challenge. One that requires good processes, qualified people fulfilling key roles and an organization wide mindset. Without these, the objectives of governance and of SOA will not be fully achieved. Although by no means a replacement for these requirements, tools can make life easier and may help to do governance in a more efficient and effective way.

Tools can help to organize the workflows that are part of the processes and even to automate some of the tasks involved. Tools can most certainly help to gather and disseminate information. This is pivotal to achieve reuse; after all in order to reuse a component, we have to know it exists, we need to know what it is and how we can use it and we need to know where it is and how to access it (at design time as well as run time). We want to know the owner of a component, someone to contact in case of questions or problems. Essential to governance are the tools that help to publish and advertise and subsequently to find assets, which help to build understanding and trust of these assets, that support dependency and impact analysis across assets and that help to improve assets by promoting interaction between stakeholders.

In the initial stages of applying SOA and implementing services, simple tools are typically quite adequate. Getting all involved parties to use the tools for sharing and consuming information is crucial and simple tooling with low thresholds is required. Usage of Microsoft Excel and Google Sheets to record services and their vital characteristics is common as are company Wiki platforms or intranet portals.

When organizations progress to a more advanced, more extensive and complex stage of doing SOA and SOA governance, they commonly move on to more specialized tools. Examples are a formal Service Registry (usually based on UDDI) or a product like WSO2 Governance Registry. Oracle offers a number of governance products too, from the fairly lightweight API Catalog and the Service Bus extension API Manager to the complete Enterprise Repository with its wide range of functions for asset harvesting, analysis and management.

Note that any tooling approach should ideally integrate well with the source code control system (Subversion, Git), the build management and continuous delivery tooling (Hudson, Jenkins, Bamboo), the issue tracking facility (Jira) and the run-time monitoring tools (Enterprise Manager).

Oracle Enterprise Repository

The OER provides organizations with a central repository of metadata about software assets, facilities for importing and harvesting such metadata from design-time and run-time SOA environments, functionality for providing access to the metadata, and BPM processes for coordinating the lifecycle of the metadata (and the underlying assets). The OER has a number of special integration points with the SOA Suite and JDeveloper that make it an attractive option for supporting SOA governance in organizations that primarily use Oracle's SOA technology.

Fundamentally the Enterprise Repository (OER) is a very generic data store that contains things that have relations to other things. They don't come more universally applicable than this. The things stored in the OER are assets—such as WSDL, XSD, and XSLT artifacts—but also noncode elements such as design documents, test scenarios, payment/cost models, and application screen designs. The OER ships with a number of predefined assets and asset types, as well as definitions of meaningful relationship types between these asset types.

Assets are registered in the OER by their creators, owners, architects, or sponsors. Upon registration and throughout their lifecycle, metadata providing additional information about the assets is recorded. Users may browse the repository in order to learn more about the assets they intend to use in some way, or to first discover assets that they might want to reuse. Browsing can be done through the OER web console and also directly from JDeveloper via a connection on the Resource Palette.

Oracle Enterprise Repository ships with a tool called the Harvester. The Harvester can read artifacts from various sources, including the file system, a running WebLogic Server, and a run-time SOA Suite environment. The Harvester connects to the indicated environment, retrieves the artifacts, and offers these artifacts as assets to the configured OER instance

Note that OER is an enterprise-level infrastructure for governance. It is relevant only in larger organizations with fairly mature SOA environments where processes have evolved sufficiently and departments have embraced service orientation. Implementing OER is not the first step organizations should take when starting to adopt SOA.

Oracle API Catalog

Build on top of the same infrastructure as the full blown OER product, the API Catalog is much more lightweight with a much more focused objective: easily collect and publish APIs from Oracle and non-Oracle environments to build a catalog of APIs that helps to streamline processes and optimizes reuse to foster API adoption. The word API is very close to the notion of a service and can here be assumed to mean the same thing.

The API Catalog offers a browser based visually attractive user interface (Figure 21-15) where existing APIs can be browsed, searched, and explored. The out of the box metadata model for APIs provides the technical and non-technical information you need to discover, understand, and use APIs, without undue complexity.

FIGURE 21-15. *Oracle API Catalog—browser based user interface for exploring APISs*

Creating, editing, and publishing API definitions can be done in the same UI in a simple way. Descriptive information for the API can be entered and linked to other external supporting information to facilitate the discovery, understanding and use of the API. Even easier is the option to use automatic introspection of Oracle SOA Suite and Oracle Service Bus projects, as well as, other deployed APIs. Users can provide ratings and reviews of the APIs on "My APIs" page and view the ratings and reviews from other users of the API.

Developers can benefit from the direct integration in JDeveloper with API Catalog, allowing them to easily locate, understand, and consume APIs. Note that this is the same integration mechanism as used with Oracle Enterprise Repository.

Summary

SOA governance is a term that covers a wide range of activities, agreements, and processes aimed at making SOA a success in an organization by ensuring that the key SOA objectives are realized: agility through decoupling and reuse. At a higher level of abstraction and detachment than design and implementation of concrete SOA components, SOA governance tries to instill a fairly new way of thinking among the many stakeholders involved with the SOA initiatives. It also puts supporting procedures in place, identifies proven best practices, and possibly provides tools to support communication, coordinated execution of agreed-upon workflows, and automated quality assurance. SOA governance first and foremost strives to provide everyone involved with inspiration, timely information, and required facilities to think and act "service oriented." SOA governance is part of and/or related to other types of governance such as corporate governance, Enterprise Architecture governance, and general IT governance.

Granularity is the term used to indicate that size matters. Reuse, versioning, deployment, authorization, SLAs, and billing are all done at the level of services. It is important therefore what the coarseness of these services is. Too small, and the number of objects that must be governed becomes perhaps unwieldy. Too large and the flexibility will suffer. Clear guidelines are wanted on how operations are to be clustered in services and how the implementation of services should be distributed over components—from Service Bus projects and SOA composites, XQuery functions and BPEL components inside the composites and projects to PL/SQL packages, Java classes, and web services.

One of the very tangible aspects of SOA governance is the publication of metadata about potentially reusable SOA assets—such as services, schema definitions, and business events. This metadata should make it possible to discover assets; understand their meaning, history, and planned future; assess their applicability and trustworthiness; and get hold of the physical location or the contents of the assets themselves. From the perspective of the owners of assets, the governance infrastructure supports the asset lifecycle management and provides insight in the dependencies and extent of reuse of the assets. As such, it should enable the organization to measure and demonstrate the results and the success of the implementation of SOA concepts.

Meta Data Services (MDS) are a built-in facility in the SOA Suite that offers capabilities to share artifacts across composite applications and across design-time and run-time environments. MDS is an important weapon against unwanted duplication of documents such as XSD, WSDL, EDL, and XSLT. This chapter demonstrated how artifacts can be deployed to the MDS repository— at design time and run time—and reused from it. It also explained how for Service Bus we can use a common project with shared assets as a counterpart—because Service Bus does not support direct interaction with MDS.

One of the important resources shared through MDS and the Service Bus common project is the set of XSD documents that describes the canonical data model (CDM). It very much depends on the approach adopted by an organization with regard to the construction of service operation specific messages based on the CDM if and how the CDM is to be managed. Clarity on this is, however, imperative in all cases.

Templates provide a powerful mechanism to achieve reuse as well as steer development teams in the desired direction through blueprints and configurable semi-finished building blocks. Managing these templates is crucial. For the pipeline templates in Service Bus, management is very similar to the management of other reusable assets. For SOA composite templates—that are copied rather than inherited from—things are a little different.

Organizations perform lifecycle management on all their IT assets. A versioning strategy for the services—and the underlying implementations—is crucial. How are versions identified and what types of versions are discerned? Different major versions of a service can probably coexist— and therefore need different endpoints, namespaces, and names. Guidelines for use of the source code control system—such as Subversion or Git—for managing multiple versions of the underlying sources are also crucial, as well as procedures for using tags and branches.

Early on in their adoption of SOA, organizations should implement a service inventory. Its purpose is to record and communicate information about all services and other relevant SOA-related artifacts (including canonical data models and policies) that are available to all stakeholders. This SOA governance infrastructure can be as simple and informal as a wiki or a bunch of spreadsheets to communicate the services and other reusable artifacts, or more advanced using tools such as the Oracle API Catalog, API Manager, or even the Enterprise Repository.

CHAPTER
22

Building and Deploying

I n order to start producing real business value, organizations have to move beyond mere development of IT components such as services and process implementations. These components need to be brought into production where they can be used for real. This chapter discusses the steps that follow after initial development that lead to production software.

It briefly (re)visits the ways to verify and improve quality using refactoring, debugging, automated testing, and auditing. When the software has reached a stage where development is done, it goes through the automated build and release pipeline—compilation, packaging, and deployment. SOA Suite 12*c* comes with Maven support that helps implement this automated build also known as continuous integration. We will look at each of the major build and release phases for Service Bus projects, SOA composite applications and associated artifacts such as MDS documents and Java EE resources. The WebLogic Scripting Tool (WLST) is introduced to aid automated creation and manipulation of the run-time target environment next to Maven.

SOA Suite applications are not isolated—they interact with their environment in many ways. Read from file systems, invoke web services publish to JMS queues. Environments differ—server names, directory locations, service endpoint will not be the same all the way from Development through Test to Production environment. Depending on where the applications are deployed, external references need to adapt. SOA Suite has mechanisms—configuration plan, customization file, global token—to tailor components at deployment time to a specific target environment. These mechanisms can be applied for deployment from JDeveloper, from EM FMW Control and in automated procedures using Maven and WLST.

The Finishing Touches

Initially in a development cycle, many developers will focus on producing software that does the job. Hands down coding, quick development/deployment round trips in their local environment. At some point, when the code seems to be working, there will be more room for quality aspects such as naming conventions, project structure, adherence to quality standards, and an inspection of less trivial and nonhappy flows through the software. Of course, attention to these aspects should not be left for a later stage—but to some extent it typically does happen. SOA Suite provides a number of facilities in JDeveloper that are very useful for these activities: the integrated debugger, various refactoring options, SOA composite test suites, and the audit framework.

Integrated Debugger

The integrated debugger in JDeveloper made appearances earlier in the book when we used it to debug both SOA composite applications and Service Bus projects. The debugger can be used with the integrated WebLogic Server as well as with a remote, stand-alone SOA Suite run-time environment—provided it does not run in WebLogic production mode or as a cluster.

Debugging has some requirements and limitations. The SOA composite application name and the JDeveloper project name must be the same. Any SOA composite application encountered during a debugging session must reside in the currently active workspace in JDeveloper. Only one client at a time can connect to the SOA debugger. Breakpoints cannot be set on REST services. Debugging does not extend across languages, for example, into XQuery or XSLT or into Java code executed in a Java Callout or Java Embedded BPEL activity.

Breakpoints can be created in JDeveloper on both ends of wires and for both directions along that wire—request and response. This means that any message received by or returned from a service binding, a component or a reference binding (in SOA composite applications) and a proxy service, pipeline, split-join, or business service (in Service Bus projects) can be intercepted and inspected. Additionally, breakpoints can be created on activities in Pipelines, BPEL, and BPM(N) processes. When these breakpoints are hit, values of variables can be inspected and manipulated.

TIP
You can inspect adapter properties through a breakpoint on an adapter binding. This allows you to check exactly what values are set for all JCA properties such as header fields that determine the run-time behavior, what message is fed to a JCA adapter, what contents is read from or written to a file and even exactly which SQL statement is to be executed by the Database Adapter.

Debugging SOA Composite Application ConversionService
Open the composite editor for the SOA composite that you want to debug. Add breakpoints on one or more wire ends and possibly inside a BPEL process.

Start debugging for the composite using Shift F9, from the context menu on the project node or from the Run menu. A popup appears in which you are asked to confirm the host name for the SOA Suite run time against which debugging will be done as well as the port used for debugging.

JDeveloper connects to the debugger process. Then, the SOA composite application will be built and deployed. JDeveloper is now primed for debugging. Right click the service handle for the service you want to invoke for debugging. The context menu contains the option Initiate WS Debugging. When you select that option, the HTTP Analyzer is opened—ready to send a request message to the service. Enter the details for this message—either by entering the form fields or by copy and pasting (and editing) the XML content and press the button Send Request. The service is invoked and the debugger stops at the first breakpoint in the SOA composite.

When this happens, you can inspect the data associated with the debug session. The tool bar in JDeveloper provides the *step* options available right now. As with most debugging mechanisms, you can choose step over, step into, step out, and resume to continue after the breakpoint was hit.

Prepare Stand-Alone SOA Suite Domain for Debugging To enable debugging on a stand-alone SOA Suite environment, the following properties need to be set in the domain specific setDomainEnv.sh file (on Linux) or setDomainEnv.cmd (on Windows). You can select different port numbers.

```
export SOA_DEBUG_FLAG="true"
export SOA_DEBUG_PORT="5004"
```

NOTE
When you change these settings, you need to restart the server to have them take effect.

Debugging Service Bus Project ConversionService
Open the overview editor for the Service Bus project that you want to debug. Add breakpoints inside pipelines and Split-Join components. In Service Bus projects, you cannot breakpoints on the wires.

Start debugging for the project using Shift F9, from the context menu on the project node, from the Run menu or from the context menu on a proxy service, pipeline or business service. A popup may appear in which you are asked to confirm the host name for the SOA Suite run time against which debugging will be done as well as the port used for debugging.

NOTE
When you are debugging against a remote environment, you have to make sure the current state of the Service Bus project is deployed to that environment before commencing the debug session.
You also have to ensure that the active Run Configuration has its Remote Debugging checkbox checked: open the Project properties editor, click on the Run/Debug node and click on the edit button for the active run configuration. Next, select the node Tool Settings | Debugger | Remote. Set the protocol to Attach to Service Bus. Specify the Host and Post to connect to.

JDeveloper connects to the debugger process of the server run time. The service test console is opened—ready to send a request message to the service exposed by the proxy service, pipeline, or business service. Provide the message details, press the Execute button and the service is invoked. The debugger stops at the first breakpoint in a pipeline or Split-Join component.

When this happens, you can inspect the data associated with the debug session. The tool bar in JDeveloper provides the *step* options available right now. As with most debugging mechanisms, you can choose *step over*, *step into*, *step out,* and *resume* to continue after the breakpoint was hit.

When the service is activated through a different channel than through the test console in JDeveloper, debugging will also take place—there is nothing special about this route, except convenience.

Refactoring

Refactoring is the process of reorganizing source code in a project to improve structure, accessibility and maintainability and to align with coding conventions. Refactoring typically involves moving and renaming artifacts, removing obsolete objects, copy and paste, search and replace, and other actions that should impact the sources only in a nonfunctional way.

Project standards usually involve the folder structure and the way artifacts should be named. Other aspects in SOA applications that can be the target of refactoring are namespace definitions, XSD structures and the organization of BPEL processes, and Service Bus pipelines. To make the project comply with standards and conventions, developers usually will have to do some refactoring at some point in the development cycle. Given all the interdependencies between the artifacts, this can be a cumbersome and delicate job.

JDeveloper provides some valuable support for these activities. The context menu for most SOA sources has a sub menu called Refactor, as shown in Figure 22-1. The options Rename and Move (to a selected folder) are usually available in this menu and perform the operations you would expect them to—with full understanding of the dependencies on and references to the objects undergoing the manipulation. This means that the references to an object are updated according to the renaming or relocation the object is undergoing.

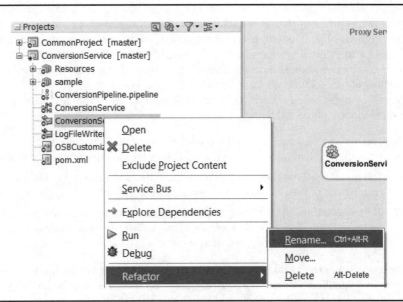

FIGURE 22-1. *Refactor options available in JDeveloper for most source artifacts*

TIP
You can use the menu option Explore Dependencies to investigate dependencies from and to the context object, for example, to gauge the effect your refactor operation may have.

Refactoring support in JDeveloper does currently not extend to the ability to update namespace definitions, change the name of XSD elements or perform other desirable updates that have ripple through effects. The Search and Replace in Files operations—available in the Search menu—are helpful with these types of changes. The replace operation will first present an overview of all intended changes—to give you full control over what will happen. Note that these operations also update files that are not accessible in source mode in JDeveloper, such as the proxy service and pipeline definitions in Service Bus projects.

As we have seen in the previous chapter, templates can be used to help transfer artifacts from one project to another and thus help refactor at the project level. Within a project, copy and paste can be used across sources—for example, to copy a stage from one pipeline to another.

SOA Composite Test Suites

It would seem like a contradiction in terms to test constituents of a SOA composite application on their own because—with the exception of the simplest BPEL process components or the Mediator, which only does an echo of the request message—all components or other subentities in composite applications seem to have dependencies. Messages are passed to other components, external services are engaged to provide information, and interaction is sought with technology adapters. Stand-alone units are hard to find.

Fortunately, the SOA Suite comes with a unit-testing framework that allows us to define testable units inside composite applications by arbitrarily selecting services, components, and references. All calls from within this *unit* to external references—other components, technology adapter references, or to external services—can be handled by the unit-testing framework and responded to with predefined mock response messages. When the unit test is done, no real calls are made to any element outside of the unit, so we can test the unit in isolation.

We define a test suite for such a custom defined unit and create test cases in it. Each test case is the combination of the following:

■   The request message sent into the unit to one of the services it exposes (called *initiation*). Note that we can also emulate events that enter the composite during the test.

■   The mock response messages to be fed into the unit during the test for each of the wires coming out of the unit (known as *emulation* in the unit-testing framework).

■   The expected result that the unit should produce for the test case given the request message (indicated with an *assertion*). This is usually a response but can be any other message traveling out of the unit as well.

The assertion does not take into account any possible side effects the test case may have—for example, in a situation where not all outgoing wires have been plugged through an emulation and the execution of the unit test should result in a change in a file or a database table. The unit-testing framework does not have special setup and tear-down facilities to prepare for and clean up after the test.

Test suites for automated unit tests are created in JDeveloper as part of the composite application that they test. They are deployed along with the application. A test suite can be executed directly from JDeveloper, the EM FMW control as well as from an Ant script, a WLST command or Maven build phase.

Test suites consist of a logical collection of one or more test cases. Each test case contains a set of commands to perform as the test instance is executed. The execution of a test suite is known as a test run. Each test corresponds to a single SOA composite application instance.

An automated test of an individual BPEL process service component can be included in a new or existing SOA composite application test suite to verify the execution of BPEL activities and the manipulation of BPEL variables. There are no facilities to automate the testing of human task, mediator, or Spring service components. We have seen the facility in the Business Rule dictionary editor to test business rules.

Creating a SOA Composite Test Suite

Open the *ConversionService* project with a SOA composite application with that name (shown in Figure 22-7). Right click the node SOA | test suites and select *Create Test Suite* from the context menu. Enter a name for the test suite in the popup window and press OK. Create a test for the new suite: provide a name and a description. Next, as shown in Figure 22-2, select the operation to be tested.

When you press Next, you will be prompted for the request message that you want to send to the selected service operation to initiate the test. Subsequently, the wizard asks you to provide the message that should be the response message in this test. This is the message that the actual response will be compared to in order to determine the successful execution of the test. Click on *Finish* to complete the Test Case.

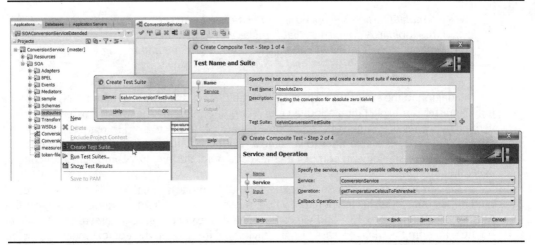

FIGURE 22-2. *Creating a composite test suite*

The Test Case is opened—showing the SOA composite application in read-only mode. By clicking on the wires, you can create the emulated responses that these wires should return instead of actually calling out to whatever component or external service is on the other end of the wire. In Figure 22-3 for example, the wire from the *KelvinToFahrenheitProcessor* BPEL process component to the *TemperatureConversionService* reference binding is right clicked upon. The emulated response from this service can be defined; this response will be used during the execution of the test—and the external service will not be invoked. By defining the emulated responses, we determine which components are part of the test case and which ones are not (because their action is replaced by the emulated response). As part of the emulated response, we can set the delay—how long should the framework pause before producing the emulated response as the mock result.

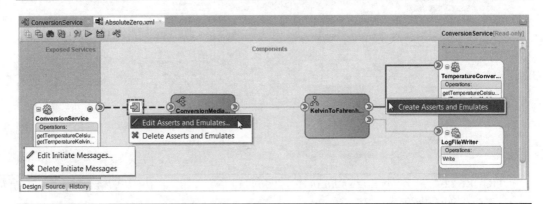

FIGURE 22-3. *Editing the AbsoluteZero test case for the ConversionService composite*

TIP
We can emulate business events using the Emulate Event Messages icon in the toolbar. A composite that is triggered through the consumption of an EDN event can thus be tested using the unit-testing framework.

In addition to the emulated responses, we can define assertions. An assertion is a statement that expresses our expectation about a certain condition. During the test, the assertions are verified by the testing framework. Assertions that are not found to hold true are reported as test failures. You can create assertions to validate an entire XML document, a part section of a message, a non-leaf element, or a leaf element at a point during SOA composite application execution.

In the *Absolute Zero* test case, we expect the BPEL process to call out to the reference binding, sending a Celsius temperature value to convert to a Fahrenheit value. We expect this Celsius value to be –273.15—and we can express this expectation as an assertion. Double click on the wire from the BPEL process or right click the wire to open the context menu and select Create Asserts and Emulates.

Select operation *getTemperatureCelsiusToFahrenheit* and click on the green plus icon to create an assertion about the messages sent along the wire for this operation. In the Create Assert popup, select option Assert Input, as shown in Figure 22-4. Select the temperature element in the request message as the *assert target* or the message content element that the assertion is concerned with.

Select Number for the type to *Compare By*. The Assert Value should be –273.15 in this case, because that is the value the BPEL process should send out. Click OK to complete this assertion. You can of course add more assertions, both on the request messages from the BPEL process or on the response messages to be returned by the external reference. Note: It does not make a lot of sense to both emulate the response messages and express assertions about them.

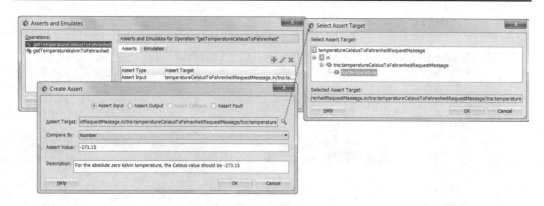

FIGURE 22-4. *Configuring an Input Assertion about the message the BPEL process sends out to the Reference Binding*

Creating a BPEL Component Test

An automated test of an individual BPEL process service component can be created by right clicking the BPEL component in the test case overview. The context menu offers the option Create Component Test that will create the BPEL test. This BPEL test enables you to simulate the interaction between a BPEL process and its web service partners before deployment in a production environment.

After providing a name for the BPEL Component Test, the BPEL process editor opens in read-only mode. The structure window shows folders Asserts, Fast Forward, and Assert Execution Counts. By right clicking one of these folders, you can create new entries. Alternatively, you can right click activities and create or edit assertions from the context menu.

Assertions can be created on the values of variables and the occurrence and contents of faults. Additionally, assertions can be created on the number of executions of an activity—to verify that loops go through the expected number of iterations. Figure 22-5 shows a BPEL component test for the *KelvinToFahrenheitProcessor*. It contains assertions on two variables after their values have been assigned to verify the correctness of these assignments.

TIP
BPEL processes may contain Wait activities to, for example, instruct a process to wait until a deadline expires. When running a test, it usually does not make sense to wait for the full duration that would be required during actual business execution. By defining a FastForward as a special assertion on a Wait activity, you can specify how long the wait should be for the wait when a component test is executed.

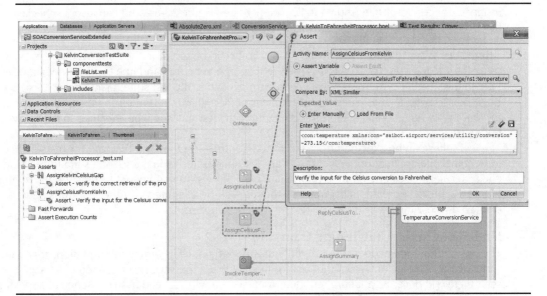

FIGURE 22-5. *A BPEL component test with two variable assertions on Assign activities*

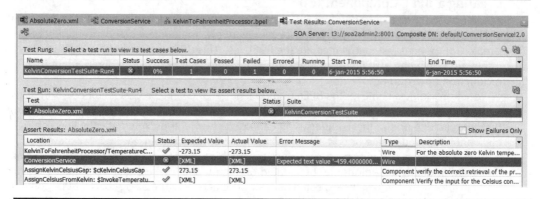

FIGURE 22-6. *Test Results from running the Composite Test Suite showing one failure: the response message from the tested ConversionService is not in accordance with the expected value*

Running a Test Suite

When you have created the initiating messages for the service to be tested, the emulations for the wires that should not actually be executed, and the assertions to test whether the externally exposed service or one of the internal wires produced the expected result, you can run the test suite from JDeveloper. Either click on the run icon or pick Run from the context menu on the test suite folder or even the individual test case in the application navigator.

The composite will be redeployed if recent changes were applied to it. Then, the test(s) are executed—and a special instance of the SOA composite is created in the run time, marked as a test instance. The test results are shown in JDeveloper—see Figure 22-6—and can also be checked in the EM FMW Control on the Unit Tests tab for the composite application.

Alternative Ways to Run a Test Suite   A Test Suite can be run from the command line in WLST, using the sca_test command (WLST is the WebLogic Server command line facility, to be introduced later in this chapter). An Ant task is available for executing the test suite: using the `ant-sca-test.xml` script. In automated build processes orchestrated by Maven using the SOA Suite plugin for Maven—to be introduced later in this chapter—the test suites will be executed in the *verify* build phase.

Test suites can be executed from EM FMW Control—on the Unit Tests tab for the selected SOA composite application. Select the entire test suite or individual tests of a suite to run, and click Execute. You will be prompted for a name for this test run, a timeout setting and the number of test instances to create. Subsequently, the test will be executed and the Test Runs page is displayed where the results from the test run will be reported.

Limitations in the Unit-Testing Framework

The unit-testing framework is undoubtedly useful, but it does have several limitations that you should be well aware of. We cannot test for the fact that a message is sent; when a message is not sent, there will never be a failure reported. An assertion will succeed in the absence of a message, even though the message should have been sent. In our example, we cannot test if a request for a conversion is sent to the external *TemperatureConversionService*. We can only check a message that is actually sent against our expectations. But the test will not tell us that an expected message was in fact not sent at all. Note that by testing a message against some absurd expectation that will never be met, we can trap messages that should not be sent as violations.

We cannot emulate (the response from) one-way services and thereby prevent a real call from being made. This means that in our test, the call out to the outbound file adapter service that logs the conversion request will always be made. Side effects from one-way services invoked from the unit under test scrutiny cannot be prevented, nor can those side effects be tested for by the framework.

Quality Auditing

JDeveloper has an audit framework that checks the project sources against the predefined rules. What rules to apply is determined in customizable audit profiles against which a project can be checked. The rules vary from spotting errors that prevent successful compilation to indicating deviations from suggested conventions. In addition to the rules shipped with JDeveloper, we can add our own audit rules to check adherence to our organization's standards and guidelines.

An audit report can be requested in JDeveloper from the Build menu, against a selected profile. This can be done for a project as a whole or for any individual artifact. The rules and profiles can be managed in the preferences editor: menu option Tools | Preferences | Audit.

The same audit rules and profiles can also be applied from the command line, producing an XML or HTML report with an overview of the audit findings. The command line instruction for performing the audit operation on a project is:

```
<ORACLE_HOME>\jdeveloper\jdev\bin\ojaudit -profile auditrules <path to
project>\ConversionService.jpr
```

Many organizations use various tools to check sources against standards. It is convenient to centrally organize this quality assurance and collect all findings in a grand overview. One tool often used for this is SonarQube, an open source quality management platform. The url https://java.net/projects/sonarqube-ojaudit points to a plugin for SonarQube that runs the JDeveloper audit mechanism and merges the results with the other outcomes.

Automating the Build Pipeline Using Maven

SOA Suite and Fusion Middleware provide support for enterprises that adopt continuous integration techniques to develop applications. This support ranges from integration with source code control systems such as Subversion and Git, the ability to perform operations such as compile, package, and deploy from the command line in a way that can easily be scripted and features to parametrize the deployment packages. Most of the support for continuous integration hinges on use of and integration with Maven.

Maven is an open source project management and build management system that is part of the Apache ecosystem. Maven is based on the central concept of a build lifecycle. The process for building and distributing a particular artifact or project is clearly defined. Build lifecycles are further defined by a set of build phases. A build phase represents a stage in the lifecycle. Build phases are executed sequentially to complete the lifecycle. Build phases consist of goals that perform the actual tasks. The key phases in the default lifecycle are *validate*, *compile*, *test* (run unit tests that do not require deployment to a run time), *package* (take the compiled code and package it in its distributable format, such as jar, ear, war), *integration-test* (which does deployment to the run-time environment and runs tests against that environment), *verify*, *install* (into a local Maven repository), *deploy* (into a remote Maven repository).

An important Maven concept is the repository. A repository in Maven is used to hold build artifacts and dependencies of varying types. There are strictly only two types of repositories: local and remote. The local repository refers to a copy on your own installation that is a cache of the remote downloads, and also contains the temporary build artifacts that you have not yet released. Remote repositories refer to any other type of repositories that are often shared between users, accessed by a variety of protocols such as `file://` and `http://`. These repositories might be a truly remote repository set up by a third party to provide their artifacts for downloading or a central, internal repository set up on a file or HTTP server within an organization, used to share private artifacts between development teams and for releases. Dependencies in software to be compiled and packages on third party libraries are resolved against these repositories.

The Maven Project Object Model (POM), defined in a pom.xml file, ensures that the project is built correctly. It defines the actions to take for each of the build phases using so called plugin elements. It also defines the dependencies of these actions on other plugins and their associated jar file.

A project's POM can reference a predefined parent POM and thus inherit from its parent— and all the parent's ancestors—predefined actions that always apply for a specific type of project. SOA Suite composite application and Service Bus projects inherit from shipped POMs that define among others the actions to perform for compile, package and deploy. The POM can contain references to repositories that provide dependencies beyond the local repository.

In this section, we will use Maven to automate the build process of SOA Suite artifacts— from compilation to deployment. In the next section, we will introduce the mechanisms for environment specific customization. The scope of this book does not allow an introduction of Maven and all it entails. The book's website provides some references to resources that can help you get started.

Preparation for Using Maven

Support for Maven is integrated in Fusion Middleware. When you run the SOA Suite Quickstart Installer or install any Fusion Middleware component, the Maven integration is available. A few additional steps are required to get going with Maven and SOA Suite 12c.

Install Maven

Even though SOA Suite 12c ships with a distribution of Maven, it is recommended to install the latest production version of Maven. This installation requires a Java Development Kit (JDK) and the configuration of several environment variables—M2, M2_HOME, PATH. Follow the standard Maven installation instructions to set up Maven. Verify the success of the installation on the command line using mvn –v to show the version of MVN and some other environment settings.

The Maven settings file is called settings.xml and is usually kept in the .m2 directory inside your home directory. The local repository is by default located in ${user.home}/.m2/repository/. An alternative location can be configured in the settings.xml file using the <localRepository> element.

Prime Maven Repository for SOA Suite Activity

During SOA Suite–related build activities, Maven will require resources that are specific for SOA Suite. This involves both the parent POM files from which our project POMs will inherit and the so called archetypes that describe project structures for SOA Suite project as well as the Maven plugins and the libraries (jar files). These resources have to be loaded into the local Maven repository once. SOA Suite ships with a special plugin that can be executed to perform the population of the repository with these SOA Suite 12c and Fusion Middleware resources. Before this plugin can be used, it needs to be installed itself.

The installation of the plugin is straightforward. It is located in the directory ORACLE_HOME\ oracle_common\plugins\maven\com\oracle\maven\oracle-maven-sync\12.1.3—with ORACLE_HOME set for the installation of JDeveloper (or WebLogic). In this directory, perform the command:

```
mvn install:install-file -DpomFile=oracle-maven-sync.12.1.3.pom -Dfile=oracle-
maven-sync.12.1.3.jar
```

NOTE
You may need to change the names of the pom and jar files in this directory; their names should end with synch.12.1.3 and not with synch-12.1.3 as is the case on some environments.

This action adds the plugin to the local Maven repository (directory com\oracle\maven\ oracle-maven-sync) where it can now be used to upload the SOA Suite resources. On the command line, enter the following command:

```
mvn com.oracle.maven:oracle-maven-sync:push -DoracleHome=ORACLE_HOME
-DoverwriteParent=true
```

This command may run for a fairly long time while it copies a large number of files from the Fusion Middleware installation to the Maven repository.

The next command is used to rebuild the index of archetypes. Some Maven repository managers do this automatically.

```
mvn archetype:crawl -Dcatalog=M2_HOME/archetype-catalog.xml
```

where M2_HOME is the home directory for Maven that also contains the settings.xml file.

The next command can be used to retrieve details about the Oracle SOA Suite 12c Maven Plugin for Composite applications:

```
mvn help:describe -DgroupId=com.oracle.soa.plugin -DartifactId=oracle-soa-
plugin -Dversion=12.1.3-0-0
```

With the values com.oracle.servicebus.plugin for the groupId and oracle-servicebus-plugin for the artifactId you can find out about the plugin for Service Bus projects.

Configuring JDeveloper for Maven

The configuration of JDeveloper for Maven is done in the Preferences editor, opened with Tools | Preferences from the main menu. By default, it is set up for the embedded Maven distribution. You can change this by selecting the External Version option and selecting the directory that contains your Maven distribution.

The local and additional remote repositories can be configured and some repository administration tasks, such as indexing, can be performed. The reference to the settings.xml file can be configured. The Phases and Goals can be configured to specify which context menu options will be available for executing Maven actions on our POM files.

Maven Enabling a Project

When a new project is created for a SOA composite or a Service Bus implementation, JDeveloper automatically creates a POM file for the project—as well as one for the application as a whole. The project level pom.xml file is presented in the Resources folder, the one created for the application is under Build Files in the Application Resources window.

The groupId in the two pom-files is set to the name of the application. This may not be desirable, for example, because the naming standards in your organization for Maven dictate a different layout for groupId, possibly including a namespace like structure. You can change the groupId as you see fit.

The pom.xml at project level configured the plugin *oracle-soa-plugin* that we inspected before. This plugin determines the actions executed in the build phases. This pom.xml also defines many project specific properties that are used by the plugin. Some of these properties are populated using built-in Maven properties such as ${project.basedir} and ${project.artifactId}. Others are passed on the command line when Maven is executed or inherited: this pom.xml inherits from the standard POM *sar-common*. This POM does not actually perform any tasks; it is a customization vehicle in which we can add default values for properties—like oracleServerUrl, oracleUsername, and oraclePassword—so that we do not have to specify them over and over in every project POM. The file is called *sar-common-12.1.3-0-0.pom* and is located in the Maven Repository in folder com\oracle\soa\sar-common\12.1.3-0-0. The sar-common itself inherits in turn from another POM—oracle-common—that is defined in this Maven repository artifact: com\oracle\maven \oracle-common\12.1.3-0-0\oracle-common-12.1.3-0-0.pom.

TIP
Instead of using the New Gallery for creating an application or a project, a JDeveloper application or project can also be created based on a Maven Archetype—with File | New | Maven | Generate from Archetype and using the archetypes oracle-soa-project or oracle-service-bus-project to create a new project. When following this procedure, wizards are presented to set the relevant properties for the new project.

Automated Compilation Using Maven

The *SOAConversionService* application that was created in the previous chapter contains the *ConversionService* project with a SOA composite application with that same name. We will work on the compilation of this composite using Maven—first within JDeveloper and subsequently from the command line.

Use Maven Goals in JDeveloper

The standard make, build and deploy operations in JDeveloper do not use Maven. Instead, under the covers these make use of *ant* tasks. For example, when you run make for the ConversionService project, the file ant-sca-compile.xml is engaged by JDeveloper.

To run a Maven Phase, we use the right mouse click context menu on the pom.xml file. Right click on this file in the ConversionService project and select *Run Maven Phase "Clean."* This will run the clean phase for our project, which removes any previously created build artifacts. When you check the log window, you will see the output from this Maven activity. You can also see the command used to run Maven. The value for the property ${env.ORACLE_HOME} is passed on the command line, referring to the same ORACLE_HOME directory that was used in the previous section.

Compile the Project with MDS References

Run the Maven Phase *Compile*. This will perform compilation—similar to what the *make* operation would do.

In this case, you will probably find this compilation unsuccessful—failing with an MDS-0054 error code and complaining about a problem with loading a WSDL document from an *oramds:* url.

Under Descriptors | ADF META-INF in the Application Resources window, you will find the adf-config.xml file. Open the file in source view. This file contains references to the SOA Design Time MDS Repository. Using the property ${soamds.apps.home}, it refers to whatever location is defined for the local file based MDS repository. Unfortunately, Maven cannot interpret this property.

Change the value for the property metadata-path to the hard coded directory used for the SOA Design Time MDS Repository, for example:

```
<property name="metadata-path" value="C:/JDeveloper/soamds"/>
```

You also need to add the following element inside the <configuration> element of the oracle-soa-plugin <plugin> to enable compilation to resolve the MDS references:

```
<appHome>${project.basedir}/..</appHome>
```

Again, execute the Maven Compile action. This time, the Maven build is probably successful. We know that our sources are correct and all references can be successfully evaluated. No build artifacts are produced at this point though.

NOTE
Even when a SOA composite does not explicitly reference oramds: resources, there can still be references to MDS. If the SOA composite were to contain a Human Task, a Business Rule, or another component that references an out of the box MDS artifact, the adf-config.xml file would contain an entry for the /soa/shared namespace, referring to the seed partition in the integration *folder in ORACLE_HOME.*
In this case you need to make sure the following two elements are inside the <configuration> element of the oracle-soa-plugin <plugin> to enable compilation to resolve these other MDS references:

```
<appHome>${project.basedir}/..</appHome>
<oracleHome>${env.ORACLE_HOME}/soa</oracleHome>
```

Compile the Project from the Command Line

Using Maven to compile the project from within JDeveloper is not especially useful. Using the standard make operation is actually easier—a single shortcut key combination—and does basically the same thing. The real value in using Maven lies in the ability to automate the entire building process (from whatever build tool we feel like using). To get a taste of this, open a command line window.

Navigate to the project directory for the *ConversionService* project (the one that contains the pom.xml file) and type the following command

```
mvn compile -Denv.ORACLE_HOME=ORACLE_HOME
```

(Where you replace the second ORACLE_HOME with the value that is applicable for your environment.)

The output written to the command line should be the same as inside JDeveloper because you are performing the exact same operation as we executed earlier inside the IDE.

TIP
When running Maven from the command line, you can pass values for any of the properties defined in the pom.xml file—and override the values that are set in the file. Just add an entry to the command line with the format –DpropertyName=propertyValue.

Packaging with Maven

A logical next step to take in the build process after compilation is packaging. This phase takes the compiled code and packages it in its distributable format, such as a JAR, WAR, EAR, SAR, or GAR file. The output from this phase is written by default to the *target* directory under the project's base directory.

Default SOA Composite Packaging

From JDeveloper—using the *Run Mave Phase "package"* item in context menu for the pom.xml file—or on the command line using the instruction

```
mvn package -Denv.ORACLE_HOME=ORACLE_HOME
```

Maven can be made to execute the *package* phase. This will result in the SAR file for the Composite application being created in the *target* directory. This SAR file can be deployed (for example, from the Enterprise Manager FMW Control) or be copied to an artifact repository.

Customize the Packaging Phase with the Design MDS Artifacts

When it comes to packaging the project, one could argue though that we are not done yet. There are more resources associated with the project—and required at run time—than are now packaged in this jar. For starters, we have the WSDL and XSD resources in the local SOA Design Time MDS repository that have to be available in the run-time MDS for deployment to be successful. As a first step, we have to ensure that these resources are packaged in a way that allows deployment in the next step in the process.

A Maven POM can be extended. We can add additional pipelines to perform additional tasks and we associate these plugins with build phases. A plugin can make use of a wide array of predefined plugins, or be created from scratch. In this case, we want to create a jar-file that contains the relevant documents from the file-based MDS repository. We can use a predefined Maven plugin for this.

Add the following plugin entry to the <plugins> section of the pom.xml file. This plugin leverages the maven-assembly-plugin that can be used to create zip and jar files and many other file assemblies, in the target directory of the project. Which files and directories to include is configured in the file SOADesignTimeMDSAssembly.xml references in the <descriptor> element.

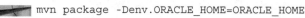

```
<plugin>
  <groupId>org.apache.maven.plugins</groupId>
  <artifactId>maven-assembly-plugin</artifactId>
```

```
        <configuration>
          <descriptor>${project.basedir}/misc/SOADesignTimeMDSAssembly.xml</
descriptor>
          <finalName>Assembly</finalName>
        </configuration>
        <executions>
          <execution>
            <phase>package</phase>
            <goals>
              <goal>single</goal>
            </goals>
          </execution>
        </executions>
      </plugin>
```

Create the file SOADesignTimeMDSAssembly.xml in directory *misc* that describes the file assembly. This file could look like this:

```
<assembly>
  <id>SOADesignTimeMDS</id>
  <formats>
    <format>jar</format>
  </formats>
  <includeBaseDirectory>false</includeBaseDirectory>
  <fileSets>
    <fileSet>
      <directory>${designTimeMDSHome}/apps</directory>
      <outputDirectory>apps</outputDirectory>
      <includes>
        <include>**/*.*</include>
      </includes>
      <excludes>
        <exclude>**/*.tmpl</exclude>
      </excludes>
    </fileSet>
  </fileSets>
</assembly>
```

This specifies that all files and directories under the app folder under the directory indicated by the property ${designTimeMDSHome} are to be added to the archive of type jar. Only files with extension tmpl should be excluded (these are the SOA Composite templates stored in the MDS repository; we only use them at design time).

In order for this plugin to be executed correctly, the referenced property has to be defined. This can be done with an entry like the following in the <properties> element in the pom.xml.

```
<designTimeMDSHome>C:/JDeveloper/soamds</designTimeMDSHome>
```

When you now execute the Maven *package* phase once more, a jar file Assembly-SOADesignTimeMDS.jar will be created in the *target* directory. It contains all documents from the design time MDS repository.

Deployment by Maven

Maven is first of all a framework to automate the build process. Deployment to a run-time environment is not the primary objective. The terms *install* and *deploy* are used in the context of Maven to indicate the transfer of the packaged artifacts to a repository—from where a deployment process or an automated build server such as Hudson or Jenkins can retrieve them.

However, the Maven build phase integration-test takes care of deployment to a run-time environment for the purposes of running integration tests. The SOA Suite Maven plugin has a *deploy* goal that deploys the SAR file to a run-time environment. This goal is mapped to the pre-integration-test phase in the default lifecycle, not the deploy phase, as deployment to a run-time environment is normally done in the pre-integration-test phase in Maven.

Configuration for Out Of The Box Deployment of SOA Composite Applications

You can try out the *integration-test* build phase for the pom.xml file. It will fail, because it attempts to deploy the SAR file without knowing the target server's location or the credentials to connect to that server.

Open the pom.xml file, locate the properties *serverUrl*, *user* and *password*, and provide the relevant values for them, something like:

```
<serverUrl>http://soa2admin2:8001</serverUrl>
<user>weblogic</user>
<password>weblogic1</password>
```

Alternatively set values in the *sar-common-12.1.3-0-0.pom* file from which the pom.xml inherits.

When you retry to execute the *integration-test* build phase, you will most likely run into failure again—probably with an error message about a file not found. The problem is with the naming of the SAR file. The standard deploy goal in the SOA Suite Maven plugin expects *sca_ConversionService_rev1.0.jar* and the file was called *sca_ConversionService_rev1.0-SNAPSHOT.jar* during packaging. This is remedied by changing the value of the <composite.revision> element from 1.0 to ${project.version}.

Run the Maven *integration-test* build phase. SOA Composite applications without references to MDS documents that are not yet available in the run-time MDS repository would at this point be deployed successfully. However, for the ConversionService, chances are that deployment fails once more—this time because the resources referenced from the SOA composite in the MDS are not available in the run-time MDS repository. Which is, of course, correct, because we have done nothing yet in our continuous integration pipeline to actually load them into that repository. See the next section on how to resolve this situation.

TIP
The install *phase will go beyond the integration-test and also install the Maven build results into the local repository—provided all previous phases are successful. For the* ConversionService *project, this results in a folder SOAConversionService\ConversionService\1.0-SNAPSHOT in the local repository, that contains the POM and the JAR files with relevant resources.*

Some of the properties in the POM file that you can set to influence the deployment process are *composite.revision* and *composite.partition* to set the revision identifier and the destination partition.

The *overwrite* property determines whether an existing composite with the same name and revision should be overwritten and *forceDefault* determines if the deployed SOA composite should become the *default* revision. Property *keepInstancesOnRedeploy* indicates if running instances should kept on running—in which case deployment may be aborted—or should be halted.

Customized Deployment to MDS Run-Time Using WLST

In the previous chapter, we have transferred documents manually from the SOA Design Time MDS Repository to the run-time MDS environment using an IDE mechanism in JDeveloper. Although convenient, this is not an acceptable approach in an automated build process. We need to extend the POM for our project to make it also perform the deployment to the run-time MDS.

In a previous section, we have already prepared for this when we created the jar file Assembly-SOADesignTimeMDS.jar with the documents from the design time MDS repository. We will now use a plugin—the weblogic-maven-plugin—that allows us to run WLST script as part of a Maven build phase.

Introducing WLST for Programmatic Management of WebLogic Domains

The WebLogic Scripting Tool is a command-line scripting environment that allows interactive and scripted (file-based, batch-wise) execution of administrative actions for the core WebLogic Server as well as other Fusion Middleware components such as WebCenter, MDS, the Identity Infrastructure, and SOA Suite. It is based on the Java scripting interpreter Jython (aka Python for the Java platform), which supports local variables, conditional variables, and flow control statements. WLST provides an additional set of scripting functions (commands) that are specific to WebLogic Server.

We can create WLST scripts that perform various activities, including configuring WLS domains and servers, creating JDBC and JMS resources and Adapter connections, configuring the User Message Service, and managing SOA composite applications. These scripts cater to different environments and adapt themselves to the specific environment for which they are used because they can inspect the destination environment and set local variables, perform logical evaluations, and conditionally execute specific code branches.

The WLST command-line interface is accessed from the command line under Windows or Unix/Linux in the ORACLE_HOME\wlserver\common\bin directory using the wlst.cmd (or wlst.sh) command script. There are many WLST commands—both for managing WebLogic and Java EE resources in general and for management of SOA composite applications and Service Bus projects in particular. For example, here's how to list all currently deployed composites—for all partitions:

```
sca_listDeployedComposites('localhost', '7101', 'weblogic',
'weblogic1')
```

And here's how to "undeploy" a composite application:

```
sca_undeployComposite('http://localhost:7101','Project1', '1.0')
```

Note: When this latter statement is executed, you will be prompted for the username and password.

This statement will help you retrieve documents from a [remote] run-time MDS environment and export them into a file archive called mds.jar:

```
exportMetadata(application='soa-infra', server='SoaServer1',toLocatio
n='c:/temp/mds.jar', docs='/apps/**', remote='true')
```

The WLST can run scripts using the execfile('someFile.py') command. A simple .sh or .bat script can be created that starts WLST and runs a potentially complex script that prepares a managed server by creating and configuring Java EE resources such as data sources and a database adapter connection pool, a JMS queue, and a connection factory, and then compiles, packages (or exports), and deploys one or more composite applications and executes test cases for those applications. WLST also provides commands for starting and stopping, activating and retiring, and undeploying individual composites.

Create a new document DeployDesignTimeMDStoRunTime.py in the *misc* directory in the *ConversionService* project. Add the following content to this document (note: indentation is essential for Python based programs):

```
def main():
  try:
    archive = sys.argv[1]
    targetServer = sys.argv[2]
    pAdminServerUrl= sys.argv[3]
    pUser= sys.argv[4]
    pPassword = sys.argv[5]
    connect(pUser, pPassword, pAdminServerUrl)
    edit()
    startEdit()
    importMetadata(application='soa-infra', server=targetServer,
fromLocation=archive, docs='/apps/**', remote='true')
    save()
    activate()
  except:
    print('--> something went wrong, bailing out')
    stopEdit('y')
    raise SystemExit
  disconnect()
main()
```

The pivotal element in this script is the *importMetadata* statement that performs the import of documents from a jar-file to the specified target MDS environment.

Next, add the following plugin entry to the pom.xml:

```
<plugin>
    <groupId>com.oracle.weblogic</groupId>
    <artifactId>weblogic-maven-plugin</artifactId>
    <version>12.1.3-0-0</version>
    <executions>
      <execution>
        <id>import-MDS</id>
        <phase>pre-integration-test</phase>
        <goals>
          <goal>wlst</goal>
        </goals>
        <configuration>
          <middlewareHome>C:\Oracle\FMW_12_1_3Middleware\Oracle_Home</
middlewareHome>
          <fileName>${project.basedir}/misc/DeployDesignTimeMDStoRunTime.
py</fileName>
          <args>${project.basedir}/target/Assembly-SOADesignTimeMDS.jar
SoaServer1 t3://soa2admin2:7001 ${user}
                ${password}</args>
        </configuration>
      </execution>
    </executions>
  </plugin>
```

This plugin entry takes care of running the WLST script and passing the relevant argument values.
Execute the Maven *integration-test* build phase. Thanks to the newly added plugin, the import of the relevant resources to the MDS repository is executed in the *pre-integration-test* phase. Now we can perform a complete compilation, packaging, and deployment of our SOA composite application to the specified run-time environment.

TIP
Maven has taken over many of the responsibilities previously assumed by Ant. However, the two are not mutually exclusive. Ant can complement Maven by performing tasks for which no Maven plugins are available. Running an Ant task from Maven can be accomplished by using the maven-antrun-plugin. For example, the following plugin in the pom.xml file executes an Ant task to copy a file from the Maven project directory to the file system location of the SOA Design MDS Time Repository:

```
<plugin>
    <artifactId>maven-antrun-plugin</artifactId>
    <executions>
      <execution>
        <id>copy-SOADesignTimeMDS</id>
        <phase>compile</phase>
        <goals>
          <goal>run</goal>
```

```
      </goals>
      <configuration>
        <tasks>
          <property name="CDMSchemasArchive" value="${project.basedir}/
target/CDMSchemasArchive.zip"/>
          <copy file="${CDMSchemasArchive}" todir="C:/JDeveloper/soamds"/>
        </tasks>
      </configuration>
    </execution>
  </executions>
</plugin>
```

Testing as Part of the Maven Build Process

Testing is of course very much part of the build process. Unit testing has its own phase in Maven (*test*) and integration testing against the freshly deployed artifacts is executed by the SOA Suite Maven plugin when we run the build phase *verify*. More specifically: it will execute the SCA Test Suites that are part of the project. However, before Maven can do so successfully, we need to perform a little preparation.

Preparing the SOA Composite Application for Automated Testing

In order to be able to perform the automated tests with the SCA composite test suites in the project, the SOA Suite Maven plugin needs to have some connection details. They are provided to the plugin in the following way.

Create a file called jndi.properties in the same directory as the pom.xml file. The contents of this file is similar to this:

```
java.naming.factory.initial=weblogic.jndi.WLInitialContextFactory
java.naming.provider.url=t3://soa2admin2:8001/soa-infra
java.naming.security.principal=weblogic
java.naming.security.credentials=weblogic1
dedicated.connection=true
dedicated.rmicontext=true
```

A reference to this file has to be set in the pom.xml, through the property jndi.properties:

```
<jndi.properties.input>${basedir}/jndi.properties</jndi.properties.input>
```

Execute Integration Tests

To have Maven execute the SCA Test Suites—after first performing the compile, package, and deploy steps, run the Maven build phase verify against the pom.xml file in JDeveloper or run the command line instruction:

```
mvn verify -Denv.ORACLE_HOME=ORACLE_HOME
```

The test results are written to the output and to the directory indicated in the scatest.result property.

Using Maven for Service Bus Projects

The previous sections were all on Maven for SOA composite applications. Let's now take a look at how things pan out for using Maven for Service Bus projects.

Preparing Service Bus Project for Maven

Depending on how the Service Bus project was initially created, you may need to edit the pom.xml file. When the project was created from the Maven Archetype for Service Bus, the following is not necessary. However, if the project was created directly as Service Bus project in the New Gallery, you probably have to change the <parent> section in the pom.xml to:

```
<parent>
  <groupId>com.oracle.servicebus</groupId>
  <artifactId>sbar-project-common</artifactId>
  <version>12.1.3-0-0</version>
</parent>
```

Sometimes the pom.xml file is created without this required reference to the sbar-project-common parent POM. This POM is located in the local repository in com\oracle\servicebus \sbar-project-common\12.1.3-0-0\sbar-project-common-12.1.3-0-0.pom. Any settings and customizations you want to apply to all your Service Bus projects can be defined in this file, or possibly in its parent—Oracle—common, defined in this file: com\oracle\maven\oracle-common\12.1.3-0-0\oracle-common-12.1.3-0-0.pom.

Compile and Package Service Bus Project with Maven

After possibly making the change described above, the Service Bus project can be compiled and packaged with Maven, either in JDeveloper and on the command line, using the same command as before for the SOA Composite application:

```
mvn package -Denv.ORACLE_HOME=ORACLE_HOME
```

The result of packaging is written as sbconfig.sbar to the folder .data/maven under the project.

Deploy Service Bus Project with Maven

Before the Service Bus project can be deployed to a run-time environment, the connection details for that environment need to be supplied. Add the following <properties> element to the project's pom.xml file, with of course appropriate values for your environment:

```
<properties>
  <oracleServerUrl>http://soa2admin2:7001</oracleServerUrl>
  <oracleUsername>weblogic</oracleUsername>
  <oraclePassword>weblogic1</oraclePassword>
</properties>
```

Using the build phase pre-integration-test—or anything that comes beyond—either in JDeveloper or on the command line—you can now have the Service Bus project deployed to the run-time environment.

Instead of adding these connection properties to pom.xml file, you can also pass them on the command line:

```
mvn pre-integration-test -Denv.ORACLE_HOME=ORACLE_HOME -DoracleServerUrl=
http://soa2admin2:7001 -DoracleUsername=weblogic -DoraclePassword=weblogic1
```

NOTE
The regular Deploy action in JDeveloper will include project dependencies. The ConversionService project has dependencies on the CommonProject and deploying the former from JDeveloper automatically brings along the latter, as we have seen in the previous chapter. This is not the case with deployment by Maven: here you get exactly what [the project] you ask for. Deployment with Maven of project ConversionService without prior deployment of the CommonProject fails with an OSB-398016 error message because of a failure to find the referenced WSDL file.

Defining the complete and properly ordered build process is evidently quite important. One way of doing that is through the use of application level POMs. Open the pom.xml file for the entire Service Bus Application SBConversionService—in the Application Resources window under Build Files. This POM contains the modules section:

```
<modules>
    <module>System</module>
    <module>CommonProject</module>
    <module>ConversionService</module>
</modules>
```

This is an instruction to Maven that states: upon building this [application level POM], perform the build for the indicated modules in the order in which they are defined—and finally perform the build for the application level POM itself. This takes care of first building the CommonProject and only then taking on the ConversionService.

Environment Friendly

SOA composite applications as well as Service Bus projects will be deployed to environments that will be similar but probably not equal. Development and various testing and production environments will use different servers with possibly different ports, directory structures, polling times, and different values for other properties that govern the behavior of service components or adapter services as well as different security policies. Also, some environments will be configured for high availability, will have additional components such as Web Servers, and will be clustered or have different transactions settings and so on. This might influence the configuration settings for non-concurrent adapters.

The archive that gets deployed consists of the sources as they have been developed. However, during deployment a configuration plan (for SOA composite application) or a customization file (for Service Bus projects) can be applied. These are used to add policies and replace designated properties and references to service endpoints and the physical location of WSDL and XSD documents with environment-specific values as they apply to the deployment target environment. This means that a single archive can be customized for each target environment through the creation and application of configuration plans or customization files that have been especially prepared for those environments. An archive can reference only one configuration plan or customization file during deployment. Configuration plans and customization files can be shared across composites and Service Bus projects though.

As we shall see in the next chapter—most properties that we can automatically customize during deployment using configuration plans and customization files, can also manually be configured through the Enterprise Manager FMW Control, WLST, and the Service Bus Console after deployment.

One clear guideline can be stated thanks to these mechanisms: the code developed by our development teams shall not contain any hardcoded environment specific values (that may turn out to not be applicable to every target environment). So no service endpoints, WSDL locations or directory names are allowed in the checked in sources.

Configuration Plans for SOA Composite Applications

A configuration plan is, by and large, an elaborate set of search-and-replace expressions expressed in XML that prescribe which settings from the base application should be replaced with environment-specific values. When the configuration plan is applied, the composite.xml file (and the import statements in the listed WSDL and XSD files) are scanned for the search expressions that, when encountered, are replaced with the value defined in the configuration plan. Replacement is done for the following values:

- References to (the location of) WSDL files can be replaced in the composite.xml and WSDL files.

- References to (the location of) XSD files can be replaced in the composite.xml and also in WSDL and XSD files.

- Values for port and location attributes in binding elements (specifying the endpoints of references) can be replaced.

- Values for properties at any level in the composite.xml can be replaced. Note that only values for properties that are explicitly defined in the composite.xml can be customized through the configuration plan; for example, the (implicit) default values of technology adapter bindings are not adapted through the configuration plan unless they have been explicitly included in the composite.xml file.

Additionally, the configuration plan can add policy references for service/reference bindings and components. Note that it will not remove or make changes to existing policy attachments.

A configuration plan is created in JDeveloper using the option Generate Config Plan in the context menu on the composite.xml file. The sca_generatePlan() command is available through WLST for the creation of a configuration plan. We need to provide the name of the configuration plan; typically, the name will refer to the environment the plan is intended for—using abbreviations such as dev, tst, acc, and prd. The configuration plan itself is a simple XML file that is, by default, created in the root of the project.

Right after the creation of the plan by JDeveloper, it will not yet cause any replacements to be made when applied during deployment. At this point, the plan only provides the skeleton in which we can specify the replacements that should be made. JDeveloper creates entries for replaceable properties and attributes at the composite and component level as well as for services and reference bindings. Here are two examples:

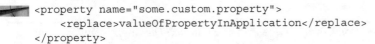

```
<property name="some.custom.property">
    <replace>valueOfPropertyInApplication</replace>
</property>
```

and

```
<reference name="HW_Service">
    <binding type="ws">
        <attribute name="port">
            <replace>com.me/HW#wsdl.endpoint(HW_ep/HW_pt)</replace>
        </attribute>
        <attribute name="location">
            <replace>http://devhost:8001/soa-infra/services/HW_ep?WSDL</replace>
        </attribute>
    </binding>
```

Additionally, it contains suggestions for search-and-replace rules for the import section of the composite.xml file—where WSDL documents are imported. The plan contains an example of a policy that could be attached to service or reference bindings and components. Finally, the wsdlAndSchema element in the generated plan can be used to specify rules to search and replace references to (the location of) imported WSDL and XSD documents; these rules can be applied to all WSDL and XSD documents that are part of the composite application—not just the composite. xml file.

Create Configuration Plan for a SOA Composite Application

We will generate and edit a configuration plan for the extended *ConversionService* composite, shown in Figure 22-7. It still converts temperature values—Kelvin and Celsius to Fahrenheit—and it still leverages an external temperature conversion service whose endpoint is defined in the composite.xml file.

The composite contains a BPEL process that starts with a Pick activity that—similar to the operational branch in a Service Bus pipeline—detects the desired operation and subsequently either converts from Kelvin or from Celsius to Fahrenheit. After returning the conversion result, this BPEL process invokes a File Adapter to write a log entry for the conversion to a log file. The location and name of this log file are governed by properties in the composite.xml file.

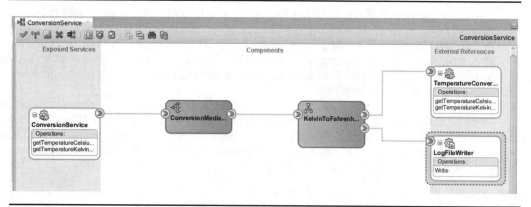

FIGURE 22-7. *The extended ConversionService with an outbound File Adapter and a Reference Binding TemperatureConversionService for an external service*

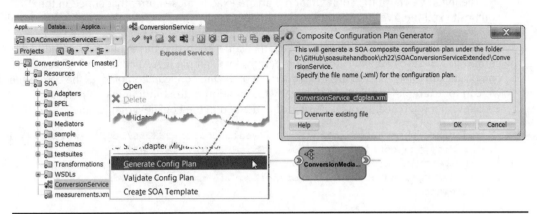

FIGURE 22-8. *Generate the Configuration Plan for SOA composite application ConversionService*

To generate the configuration plan, right click the composite.xml (aka the node *ConversionService*) and select menu item *Generate Config Plan* in the context menu, as shown in Figure 22-8.

The Composite Configuration Plan Generator pops up and asks for a name for the configuration plan. Accept the proposed value and press OK. This is to just keep things simple this time round; in real life you would create a configuration plan for a specific environment and assign a name accordingly.

The configuration plan is generated and opened in the text editor. The plan (shown in Figure 22-9) contains entries that replace some attributes and properties defined in the composite.xml file, such as the *location* for the external service invoked from the *TemperatureConversionService* reference and the LOG_FILE_DIRECTORY property for the *LogFileWriter* File Adapter binding.

```
ConversionService        ConversionService_cfgplan.xml
Q  Find
53      <reference name="KelvinToFahrenheitProcessor.kelvintofahrenheitprocessor_client"/>
54      <reference name="TemperatureConversionService"/>
55      <reference name="LogFileWriter"/>
56      <reference name="TemperatureConversionService">
57          <binding type="ws">
58              <attribute name="port">
59                  <replace>saibot.airport/services/utility/conversion#wsdl.endpoint(ConversionServicePortTypeSOAP11BindingQSService/Convers
60              </attribute>
61              <attribute name="location">
62                  <replace>http://10.10.10.21:8011/ConversionService?wsdl</replace>
63              </attribute>
64          </binding>
65      </reference>
66      <reference name="LogFileWriter">
67          <property name="LOG_FILE_DIRECTORY">
68              <replace>/tmp</replace>
69          </property>
70          <binding type="jca"/>
71      </reference>
72  </composite>
```

FIGURE 22-9. *The configuration plan generated for the ConversionService SOA composite*

The initial values in the configuration plan are exactly those currently defined in the composite.xml file. We can of course change them to have them reflect the specific situation in the target environment for which we want to use this configuration plan.

The configuration plan can only replace the values for properties explicitly defined in the composite.xml. We can explicitly add properties, for example JCA Adapter properties, to composite.xml to be able to have them operated on by the configuration plan. In the composite.xml we can for example add property FileNameConvention to the binding.jca entry for the LogFileWriter reference, to override the value defined in the LogFileWriter.jca file:

```
<reference name="LogFileWriter" ui:wsdlLocation="WSDLs/LogFileWriter.wsdl">
.. <binding.jca config="Adapters/LogFileWriter_file.jca"/>
   <property name="FileNamingConvention" type="xs:string" many="false" overri
de="may">TemperatureConversionServiceLogFile.txt</property>…
  </reference>
```

When you again generate the configuration plan for the ConversionService composite, you will find a new entry to replace the value for this property—allowing us to customize the name of the log file [per environment] through the configuration plan.

Edit the configuration plan to apply customized values for the LOG_FILE_DIRECTORY and FileNamingConvention properties:

```
<reference name="LogFileWriter">
  <property name="LOG_FILE_DIRECTORY">
    <replace>/tmp/conversionLogs</replace>
  </property>
  <property name="FileNamingConvention">
    <replace>TemperatureConversionLogbook.txt</replace>
  </property>
  <binding type="jca"/>
</reference>
```

To find out the effects of these changes in the configuration plan, you can use the option Validate Config Plan on either the node for the configuration plan or the composite.xml. This option will produce a report that lists all components, attributes, and properties that are eligible for changes based on the configuration plan. For each of these it shows whether a value will be changed when the configuration plan is applied for real and if so, what the change would be.

Applying a Configuration Plan during Deployment
Configuration plans can be attached to composite applications during deployment. The applicable plan can be selected as part of the deployment dialog in JDeveloper and in the EM FMW Control as well as in the Ant, WLST, and Maven deploy commands. When a configuration plan is attached during deployment, then prior to moving the composite to the SOA Suite, the composite.xml file is extracted from the service archive, the replace actions are performed, and the result is put back in the archive. The same happens to all artifacts processed by the configuration plan files in the service archive, such as WSDL and XSD.

Attaching a Configuration Plan upon Deployment from JDeveloper   On the Deploy Configuration page in the deployment wizard is the section labeled *SOA Configuration Plan*. In this section is a list of all configuration plans available in the current project. Select one of these

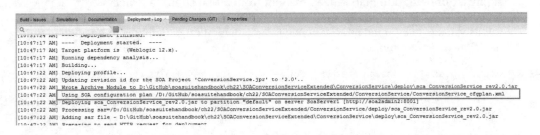

FIGURE 22-10. *Output from the deployment process—reporting on the application of the configuration plan*

configuration plans or the option *Do not attach*. Instead of selecting a configuration plan using a radio button, there is an option to browse for a configuration plan that may be located elsewhere on the file system or in MDS. Check the checkbox *Use the following SOA configuration plan for all composites* to make use of this option. When deploying multiple SOA composite applications at once, the configuration plan selected here is applied to all of them.

The output from the deployment process in the log window—Figure 22-10—indicates the application of the configuration plan.

By checking the properties for the LogFileWriter adapter binding in the EM FMW Control (see Figure 22-11) we can tell that the values defined in the configuration have been used to overwrite the values in the composite.xml file.

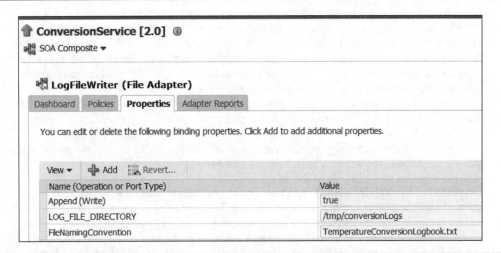

FIGURE 22-11. *Properties for the LogFileWriter adapter binding are set based on the configuration plan*

Apply a Configuration Plan in Deployment from a Maven Build Process   The SOA Maven plugin checks the value for the property *configplan* in the pom.xml file. When this property is set, its value is interpreted as a reference to a configuration plan that is to be applied during deployment. For example,

```
<configplan>${scac.input.dir}/ConversionService_cfgplan.xml</configplan>
```

This entry makes the SOA Maven plugin look for a configuration plan called ConversionService_cfgplan.xml and located in the SOA directory in the project.

Attaching Configuration Plans with Ant and WLST   The ant-sca-deploy.xml script can be invoked with the following optional parameter to apply a plan:

```
-Dconfigplan=<location and name of configuration plan file>
```

The WLST command sca_deployComposite can be invoked with a last optional parameter to specify the configuration plan:

```
sca_deployComposite(...,
configplan="c:/temp/ConversionServiceConfigPlan.xml")
```

Exporting Composite Applications from the Console   The resulting service archive that is created when you export a composite application through the EM FMW Control contains the composite application, including the environment-specific values that were applied from the attached configuration plan at the time of deployment.

When the exported archive is redeployed, you can attach another configuration plan that may overwrite these properties yet again.

Exposing BPEL Process Constants as Customizable Properties

We have seen how the configuration and behavior of composite applications can be manipulated, prior to deployment, by attaching the right configuration plan and at any point after the application has been deployed from the FMW Enterprise Manager. In addition to the standard properties in bindings and the technology adapter we tweaked in the previous section, we can also expose custom properties from our composite application that influence the application behavior and that can be altered at run time to implement changes in the behavior.

Custom SCA properties in the composite.xml can be defined at the component (or composite) level and be used in BPEL processes. These properties can be accessed using special XPath operations, for example, in the BPEL Assign activity. The value of these properties can be set during deployment from a configuration plan and afterward also inspected and modified through the System MBean browser in the run-time environment.

Configuring the kelvinCelsiusGap Property in composite.xml   Defining SCA properties is done in the composite.xml file, at the composite level or at the component/service/reference level—either directly in the source file or through the Property Inspector.

A property definition consists of the name and type of the property—and may also indicate whether the value can be overridden, whether multiple values are allowed, and what the source of the property value is when the component-level property inherits its value from a composite-level property. Note that the name for properties for BPEL components has to start with "preference."

In this case, the property is called preference.kelvinCelsiusGap, is of type float, and has the initial value of 273.15:

```
<component name="KelvinToFahrenheitProcessor" version="2.0">
  <implementation.bpel src="BPEL/KelvinToFahrenheitProcessor.bpel"/>
...
  <property name="preference.kelvinCelsiusGap" type="xs:float">273.15</property>
</component>
```

When we generate a new configuration plan for the *ConversionService* composite, the following entry is created to support environment-specific customization of the property value:

```
<component name="KelvinToFahrenheitProcessor">
        <property name="preference.kelvinCelsiusGap">
            <replace>273.15</replace>
        </property>
</component>
```

Accessing the kelvinCelsiusGap Property in the BPEL Process The BPEL process needs to be altered to have it make use of the *kelvinCelsiusGap* property. Values of BPEL component properties are retrieved in Assign operations using the getPreference() XPath function that is part of the BPEL XPath Extension Functions. We have to pass the name of the property to the getPreference() function—without the prefix "preference." The following copy operation populates the BPEL variable *cKelvinCelsiusGap* with the value set in the property that was defined on the BPEL component in the composite.xml file:

```
<assign name="AssignKelvinCelsiusGap">
  <copy>
    <from>number(ora:getPreference('kelvinCelsiusGap'))</from>
    <to>$cKelvinCelsiusGap</to>
  </copy>
</assign>
```

The hard coded value 273.15 has been removed from the BPEL process and is now set as property in the composite.xml. In fact, we probably should use some ridiculous value for this property in the composite.xml and only provide a sensible value in the configuration plan. That at least should be the approach for properties whose values will depend on the environment—which is hardly the case for this specific example.

Customization of SOA Composite Applications

SOA Suite supports a special type of customization that is primarily used when an application is used across different divisions in a large enterprise or sold as a product and has to be tailored for specific industries, customers or sites. On top of a base implementation, typically small but significant changes may be required to cater for a certain situation—which can be a region in the world or a specific industry in which the application will be used. These changes can be defined as customizations. This has the advantage of keeping the changes separate from the base artifacts. That not only streamlines the development process for the customizations. It also means that upgrades of the base application do not wipe out the customizations.

The Create Project wizard presents the checkbox Customizable that has to be checked to create a SOA composite application that can be customized later on (indicated by the ui:customizable attribute in the <composite> element in composite.xml). Customization of BPEL processes is only allowed on Scopes that have been configured in the base application to be customizable.

Customizations are performed with JDeveloper running in the Customization Developer role. The SAR created by packaging the base application is loaded. The customization layer and value are selected to define for which target situation the customization is to be created: for which industry, which region or which specific site is the customized version of the application destined? Subsequently, customizations are applied and finally the SAR is generated for the customized version. When a SAR arrives for a new version of the base application, all customizations defined for the previous version can be applied again to this new one.

Global Tokens in SOA Composite Applications

Global tokens are variables that can be used in composite.xml files for which the value is provided at run time by the run-time environment into which the SOA composite application has been deployed. These tokens are used in the binding element of references to identify the location of services to be invoked from a SOA composite application. By using tokens such as ${ServiceBusHost}, ${ServiceBusPort}, and ${FinanceServicesHost} in the binding elements and defining the values for these tokens in the SOA Suite run-time environments, we do not have to set these common values in an environment specific configuration plan for every SOA composite. Global tokens cannot only be used for the host, port, and protocol attributes in the binding element but only for values for <property> elements in a <reference>.

Use Global Tokens in the ConversionService SOA Composite

The ConversionService SOA composite has a reference called TemperatureConversionService on an external service that has to convert Celsius temperature values to Fahrenheit values. The location of this external service is defined in the <binding.ws> element in the reference in composite.xml file. We have seen how we can create a configuration plan with a search and replace instruction to provide a specific value for this location, overriding whatever was put in at development time. Now we will use a token and leave it to the run-time engine to provide an appropriate value for its environment.

Create an empty XML-file in the project—in the SOA folder—called token-file.xml.

Open the composite editor. Click on the Binding URL Tokenizer icon in the top bar, as shown in Figure 22-12. This brings up a window with a list of all binding elements in the composite .xml—in this case only the *TemperatureConversionService* binding. Select that binding and click on the edit icon.

A second window appears where tokens can be defined for the attributes protocol, host and port. First select the token file that you just created. This allows JDeveloper to record the current

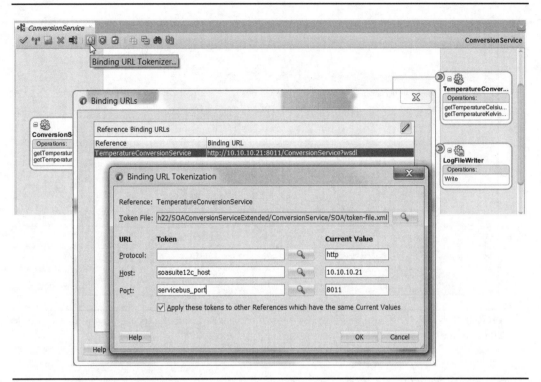

FIGURE 22-12. *Define tokens for the protocol, host and port attributes in reference binding elements*

values in composite.xml for the attributes that will be replaced by tokens. You could later on use this token file to load names and [initial] values for tokens to the run-time SOA Suite environment. The token file has no other purpose.

Set the token names for Host and Port to soasuite12c_host and servicebus_port, respectively. When you press OK, the values for these attributes will be updated in the composite.xml—tokens taking the place of the actual values. The current values are written to the token file.

```
<reference name="TemperatureConversionService" ui:wsdlLocation="oramds:/apps/
WSDLs/ConversionService.wsdl">
...<binding.ws port="saibot/conv#wsdl.endpoint(CVPTSvc/CVPTSOAPPort)"
        location="http://${soasuite12c_host}:${servicebus_port}/
ConversionService?wsdl" supports="" soapVersion="1.1"/>
</reference>
```

The effect of the checkbox *Apply these tokens to other References which have the same Current Values* is what it says it is: if there are other bindings in the composite.xml file with attributes set to these current values that are replaced by tokens, then these values are replaced with the tokens too.

FIGURE 22-13. *The composite.xml shown in EM FMW Control after deployment with the tokens still in place*

Deploy the SOA composite *ConversionService*—without applying a configuration plan. When you inspect the composite's definition in the EM FMW Control, you will find the tokens still in, as shown in Figure 22-13.

When you test the service exposed by this composite, an exception will be thrown to the effect of: java.net.MalformedURLException: Variable "soasuite12c_host" not defined in mdm-url-resolver.xml.: Variable "soasuite12c_host" not defined in mdm-url-resolver.xml. This means that the run-time environment does not yet know about the global tokens used in the composite.xml.

Figure 22-14 shows how to open the editor for the tokens—from the dropdown menu for the SOA infra node, option SOA Administration | Token Configurations.

Edit the tokens manually—as shown in the figure—or load the token file using the Browse and Append buttons. After making the required changes, you unfortunately need to restart the SOA Infrastructure to have the changes take effect.

After the restart, the tokens {servicebus_port} and {soasuite12c_host} will be replaced in the binding.ws element of the composite.xml file of any deployed SOA composite application. Now you can test the service again—successfully.

Tokens are supported for the host, port, and protocol attributes in the ws.binding location and any property under the reference tag. The latter means that you could for example use a global token to the set central logging directory in properties used to define the value for the logical directory used in outbound file adapters:

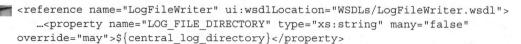

```
<reference name="LogFileWriter" ui:wsdlLocation="WSDLs/LogFileWriter.wsdl">
    ...<property name="LOG_FILE_DIRECTORY" type="xs:string" many="false"
override="may">${central_log_directory}</property>
```

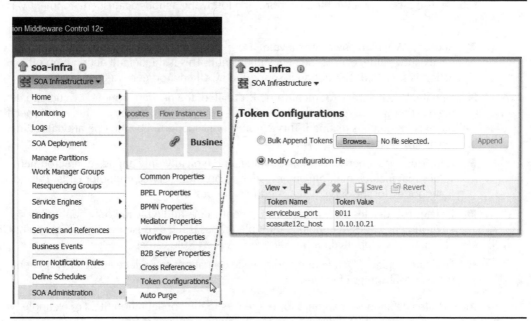

FIGURE 22-14. *Define the Global Tokens through the EM FMW Control*

TIP
There is one token that can be used in composite.xml files without having to be explicitly defined through EM FMW Control: the predefined global token variable named `${serverURL} can be used` *in resource URLs. During run time, this token is replaced by the setting for the Server URL property of the SOA Infrastructure Common Properties page in Oracle Enterprise Manager Fusion Middleware Control. Using this token is a convenient way to refer to services that will be running on the same server as the consuming SOA composite application.*

Configuration Files for Service Bus Projects

For Service Bus projects, we have a mechanism similar to the configuration plans for SOA composite applications for customizing a project for a specific environment. This mechanism uses *configuration files*. Configuration files are XML-based files that define environment values, operational settings, and reference mappings used by Service Bus. By creating and executing a configuration file against a Service Bus instance, you can quickly update the properties that are specific to the environment in which the projects are running without having to manually update the properties one at a time. Configuration files can be applied in the Service Bus Console and during or after deployment from Maven, WLST, or Ant.

You can use a configuration file to perform the following actions against environment variable values:

- Replace. When an environment value is replaced, the new environment value replaces the existing value, even if the new value is null. This is the default action if no other action is specified. This action is supported by all environment values.

- Update. When an environment value is updated, the new environment value updates the existing value except if the new value is not specified. If a new value is not specified, the existing value is retained. This action is only supported by the operational settings environment values.

- Add. This adds a new environment value, and typically only applies to environment values that include multiple entries, such as business service endpoint URIs. This action is supported for the Service SLA Alert Rule values.

- Delete. This deletes an existing environment value, and typically only applies to environment values that include multiple entries, such as business service endpoint URIs. This action is supported for the Service SLA Alert Rule values.

- Find and Replace. Define find and replace operations to replace entire environment values or substrings of values.

You can also define new mappings for references in the configuration file. For example, you can map a proxy service to a different pipeline in the new environment.

NOTE
A huge and unfortunate limitation with configuration files is that they cannot modify the values of JCA properties or other Endpoint properties on a Business Service. To achieve this, organizations have created workarounds using custom Ant tasks and/or WLST scripts to perform search and replace operations in the sources of the Service Bus project.

One very obvious use case for configuration files is to set the endpoint(s) for external services that are accessed from business services by finding and replacing the Service URI variable in the particular project. Another common use case is the replacement of a specific server name and port number in all references in a project.

Create a Service Bus Configuration File

A configuration file can be generated and downloaded from the Service Bus Console, as shown in Figure 22-15. Open the Admin tab in the console and click on the link Create Configuration File. Select the projects that you want the file to be able to customize and click on the Create button. The generated plan is downloaded from the browser. Alternatively, with some tenacity, you can create a WLST script that can generate the configuration file for you; the book's website references a relevant blog article.

You can add the configuration file to the Service Bus project in JDeveloper and open it for editing. The file contains many references and properties that were extracted from the selected project(s) and that can be customized using this file.

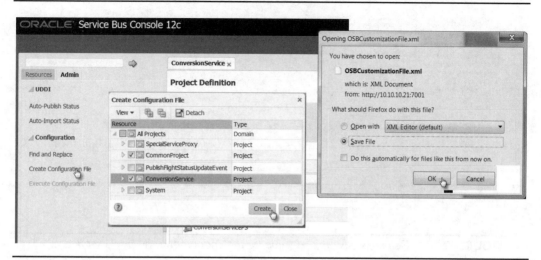

FIGURE 22-15. *Create a Configuration File in the Service Bus Console for the ConversionService project*

As a very simple example, let's customize the endpoint for the proxy service ConversionServicePS to /utilities/ConversionService (rather than the initial value of just / ConversionService). The entry in the configuration file is:

```
<xt:replace>
  <xt:envValueType>Service URI</xt:envValueType>
  <xt:value xsi:type="xs:string" xmlns:xs="http://www.w3.org/2001/XMLSchema">/
utilities/ConversionService</xt:value>
</xt:replace>
```

in the cus:actions element under the cus:customization element for owner ConversionService/ ConversionServicePS, as shown in Figure 22-16.

Apply a Service Bus Configuration File
Configuration files can be applied in the Service Bus Console and during deployment from Maven, WLST, or Ant.

Apply Configuration File in the Service Bus Console   One very direct, manual way of applying a configuration file to a live environment is from the Service Bus console. Create an editing session. On the Admin tab, click on the link Execute Configuration File. A window appears that invites you to select a configuration file on your local file system. Select the OSBCustomizationFile.xml file that was edited for the ConversionService project. The second page of the wizard shows an overview of the changes that will be brought by the application of the configuration file (see Figure 22-17). Click on Finish to have the changes applied.

Before you activate the editing session in the Service Bus console you can inspect the changes. In particular, you can check the Endpoint URI on the Transport tab for the ConversionServicePS proxy service, which should be modified based on the configuration file.

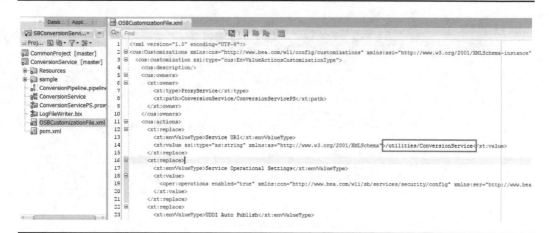

FIGURE 22-16. *Definings customized value for the Endpoint for the proxy service ConversionServicePS in the ConversionService project*

Apply Configuration File during Deployment in Maven Build Process The Maven Service Bus plugin knows how to apply a configuration during the deployment of a Service Bus project. By setting the property *customization* in the project's POM with a reference to the configuration file, the plugin is instructed to apply the customizations in the configuration file as part of the deployment. For the ConversionService project that could be done with this entry in the pom.xml.

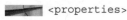

```
<properties>
   ...
   <customization>${project.basedir}\OSBCustomizationFile.xml</customization>
</properties>
```

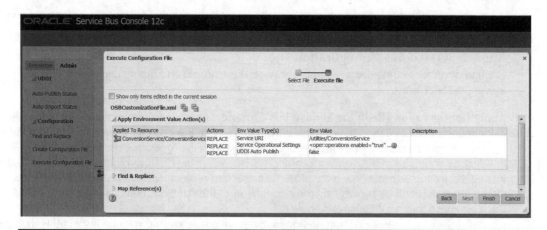

FIGURE 22-17. *Overview of the changes that the application of the selected Configuration File will cause*

Orchestrating Builds with a Build Manager

Using Maven and with the aid of configuration plans and configuration files and WLST, we are capable of automating the build and deployment pipeline—from compilation through packaging all the way to tailored deployment to a selected environment. A logical next step would be to orchestrate the build process across projects from a build manager—such as Hudson, Jenkins, or Bamboo and an artifact repository such as Nexus or Artifactory. Such a build manager can initiate the Maven build pipeline at the appropriate moment, which can be schedule or trigger based with the trigger, for example, being a check in into the source control system.

To get going with a build manager, it typically is integrated with your source code control system—Subversion or Git being the most likely candidates—and configured to leverage the local Maven environment. Subsequently, jobs are defined that execute Maven build phases in selected POMs to do the actual work. Jobs can be chained to handle the dependencies that exist between projects.

Summary

This chapter hovers between development and operations. It talks about the stages of development where testing the functionality and inspecting the quality are the last steps by the developers before their artifacts are to be handed over. Some relevant mechanisms in JDeveloper were discussed: refactor, debug, Composite Test Suites, and audit rules. Note that we will usually be dealing with continuous build, continuous integration or even continuous delivery—a repetitive activity that frequently or even continuously takes the developed deliverables and processes them to deployed artifacts in test or even production environments.

The build process that takes the sources of an application and turns it into a deployable unit was discussed next with a thorough introduction of the Maven support for SOA composite applications and Service Bus projects. We saw how to automate the steps to not only produce the deployable units but also do the actual deployment. Next steps are usually the definition of smoke tests to verify if the deployed applications are up and available. This may include invoking a side effect free *ping* operation on each deployed service—or perhaps a *deepPing* that has the service calling out to all the services it depends on to verify these dependencies are satisfied when the service is invoked for real.

SOA applications will be deployed to different environment—for example, the development, integration test, acceptance test, and production environments. These environments require different settings for properties such as service endpoints, host names and port numbers, directory names and so on. Using configuration plans and global tokens for SOA composite applications and configuration files for Service Bus projects—we can fine-tune environment specific settings during deployment to a specific environment.

In the next chapter, we will see how some settings can not only be inspected after deployment but also be manipulated at run time.

CHAPTER
23

Run-Time Administration

A t run time is where the action is. Only when SOA components have been deployed to and are actually used at run time can they deliver the business value they were created for. To ensure their successful operation, we cannot just sit back and relax. We have to monitor the traffic through the SOA Suite carefully. This allows us to react when things go wrong and to prevent this from happening when we spot telltale signs that indicate pending issues.

Monitoring the run-time execution characteristics help ensure that we comply with the SLAs for performance, security, throughput, and availability that we signed up. It tells us about requests that have ended in failure and need attention and helps us spot bottleneck components. The results from monitoring will prompt us to recover failed conversations and processes. They may also suggest changes in configuration of the deployed components as well as the establishment of (fault) policies to automate some of the recovery.

Part of the flexibility a SOA implementation can deliver is achieved through the run-time reconfiguration we can apply. Redirecting our components to changed endpoints for external services, changing the values of business parameters or the logic of business rules, adjusting the rules for task allocation and assignment, and changing the schedules for execution of batch processes are examples of such run-time administrative tasks.

Purging the remainders of past events is another of the run-time responsibilities we have to take care of. The SOA Suite run-time infrastructure can collect substantial volumes of data during its operation—data used for monitoring, auditing, and reporting. At some point, this data loses its value or should be transferred to a data warehouse. In both cases, the data should be purged from the SOA Suite infrastructure.

This chapter introduces a number of the most common and most important run-time activities and supporting facilities for SOA Suite. These are relevant for developers and administrators alike to monitor and manage their respective environments. First we discuss how to observe and learn what is happening, then we go into (re)acting to what is witnessed and finally we discuss prevention and longer term actions.

Monitor

Through monitoring we want to learn what is (relevant about what is) happening. And we want to know what is happening because we may have to respond with immediate action or longer term correction in order to ensure the run-time behavior that is required, desired, and committed to.

Monitoring takes place in various dimensions. Events are observed live, at real time or operational level and at an aggregated, tactical level. Monitoring is done by automated facilities and by human actors. And monitoring is done at varying degrees of functionality—from business level focused on business processes to technical level with focus on non-functional aspects such as performance and availability.

The main objective of monitoring is to learn about things that are out of the ordinary—that are unexpected and probably in a bad way. When processes are stuck or aborted with faults, when services take much longer to respond than is allowed in the SLA or when components cannot be reached at all—we need to know about it. So we can act to make things better again.

Sometimes our infrastructure and tooling can recover itself when deviations are detected. Sometimes a human administrator can step in and easily correct the problem. And sometimes it will take careful analysis of log files and other run-time data to find the cause of an issue and to determine whether the platform and its configuration were at fault, an external service has broken down or whether perhaps a programming error has slipped through the testing process.

Tactical monitoring is not done to respond instantaneously to findings. Instead, it produces aggregates and summaries that tell us whether we met the SLA targets for our services and processes. These reports also help spot trends that we can use for capacity planning of resources—both human and machine wise.

This section discusses some of the mechanisms at our disposal in SOA Suite and Fusion Middleware to monitor and analyze the proceedings at run-time. We will look at log files: how to find them, search through them to and interpret them. We will discuss how to enrich them with our own logging details. We will look at automated monitoring using SLA Alerts and BAM Alerts. And we once again visit the Enterprise Manager FMW Control that provides a lot of insight in the internal run-time activities.

Log files

Log files are the main mechanism for Fusion Middleware to report on its activities. Log files are persistent, can be searched and inspected in a multitude of tools including EM FMW Control and through WLST, and can be automatically processed by analysis tools including Splunk and other big data utilities.

The Oracle Diagnostic Logging (ODL) framework is the primary facility for most Fusion Middleware applications to log what they are doing. A notable exception to this is WebLogic Server which uses its own log format and file. ODL allows you to limit the amount of diagnostic information saved, including the maximum log file size. It provides several log handlers to manage log messages for individual product components, and also provides a standard log message format. Once a log file reaches a specified size it is renamed, and a new log file is created. Once total log file storage reaches a specified size, the oldest log file is removed.

ODL logs entries in a consistent, structured way using predefined fields and name/value pairs that make them easy to search, to interpret and to process with automated facilities. These fields include:

- Timestamp,
- Organization ID
- Message type (level of severity)
- Component ID
- The Execution Context with the ECID—execution context identifier, see below—and the RID or relationship identifier that lists all IDs for threads that contributed to the conversation
- Operating system process ID and thread ID
- Host address and ID
- User identifier
- Message text

The default format is plain text; alternatively, XML can be configured. The following message types are defined for ODL, in decreasing order of severity: INCIDENT_ERROR, ERROR, WARNING, NOTIFICATION (levels 1 and 16), and TRACE (levels 1, 16, and 32). The level values of 16 and 32 indicate a finer level of granularity and a very detailed trace (of debug information), respectively.

Here is an example of a log entry from managed server SoaServer1 at trace level 16 produced on January 7, 2015 during the execution of an instance of SOA composite *ConversionService* on behalf of an anonymous user:

```
[2015-01-07T08:56:09.889+01:00] [SoaServer1] [TRACE:16] [] [oracle.mds.
oramds.internal] [tid: [ACTIVE].ExecuteThread: '18' for queue: 'weblogic.
kernel.Default (self-tuning)'] [userId: <anonymous>] [ecid: 43219d3f-3215-
4cc4-998b-51de1f26d543-00007a47,0:1] [APP: soa-infra] [composite_name:
ConversionService] [[..DBMetadataStore : MDS Repository connection = (JNDI
Location = jdbc/mds/MDS_LocalTxDataSource)..]]
```

A key element in ODL is the ECID or Execution Context Identifier. An ECID is a globally unique identifier associated with the execution of a particular request. An ECID is generated when the request enters the Fusion Middleware platform and is passed onward from that moment on, to be used in every log entry created in the context of that conversation, across WebLogic managed servers and even domains. This ECID is the red thread that ties all activities and log entries together to paint the complete picture for the complete FMW conversation for a particular request.

Log Configuration

Log configuration is done per managed server. In EM FMW Control, select the node for the server under WebLogic Domain | <name of SOA Domain> [| <name of cluster>] | <name of Managed Server>. From the dropdown menu, select Logs | Log Configuration, as shown in Figure 23-1.

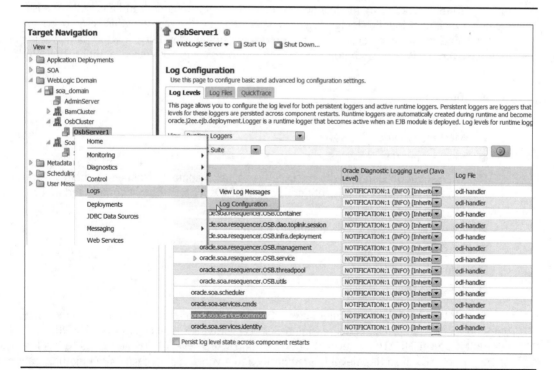

FIGURE 23-1. *Log Configuration for a selected Managed Server—with a list of the SOA Suite loggers, all currently and out of the box associated with the odl-handler*

Most entries from the SOA Suite are written to the server-name-diagnostic.log file which is by default located in directory DOMAIN_HOME/servers/server_name/logs. You can create new log files and change the location of the log files by configuring log handlers.

For ODL logging to work, both loggers and log handlers need to be configured. Loggers send messages to handlers, and handlers accept messages and output them to log files. Loggers are associated with a handler and have a ODL logging level setting that determines the amount of information passed to the handler. SOA Suite includes a variety of loggers to handle messages for various modules and your own (Java) components can add even more loggers. You can view and configure these loggers in Fusion Middleware Control or using WLST commands.

The handler determines which log file to write to, in what format and from which log level upward. They define the rotation policy for the log files. The handler can also be configured to write supplemental attributes to the log file. See Figure 23-2 for an example of the configuration of a log handler.

Logging Policy and Policy Logging
Each message sent to and returned from a (proxy) service and each message sent from and returned to a business service (in Service Bus) or a reference binding (in SOA composites) can be logged to the message log for the domain. The log of messages includes special message headers such as security headers. This message logging does not happen all the time and for all services. It is governed by attaching the OWSM (Oracle Web Services Manager, introduced in detail in Chapter 24) log policy oracle/log to the service binding, proxy service, business service, or reference binding.

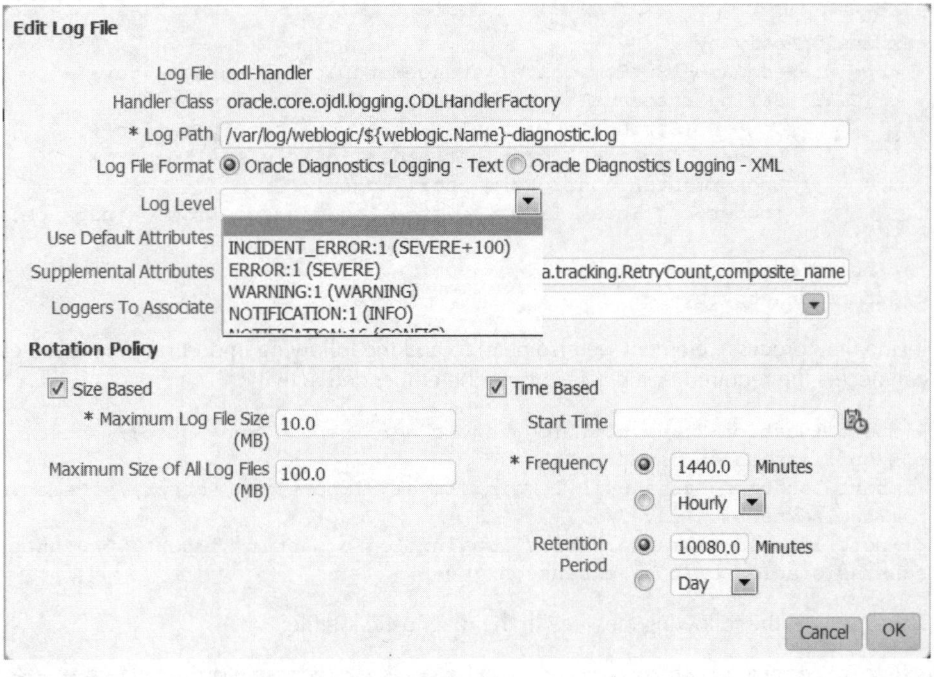

FIGURE 23-2. *Configuration for the log handler odl-handler*

This log policy can be attached at design time in JDeveloper or at run-time in EM FMW Control (for SOA composites) and Service Bus Console. Because there are no unique Java Classes associated with individual services, configuring a log handler to write service messages would affect all services. Through the use of the log policy on individual services, there is a more fine grained mechanism for switching on and off the logging of service messages.

OWSM policies are also used to configure security constraints (see Chapter 24), for example, for authentication, role authorization, encryption, and digital signing. The Oracle Fusion Middleware Audit Framework can be configured through *audit policies* to generate logging about security events associated with actions related to these OWSM security policies.

Logging from SOA Composite Applications

Many components in SOA Suite produce logging output. It depends on the settings for their associated loggers and the subsequent handler what subset of that output is actually persisted to the log files. We can add to this out of the box set of details with our own, SOA composite specific logging to allow tracking of relevant information. The OWSM logging policy discussed in the previous section is one way of configuring a SOA composite for the generation of logging; note that this policy can be associated not only with service and reference bindings but also with the internal components of the composite, such as BPEL Process or Mediator components.

Additionally, wherever we can plug custom Java into the composite application, we can produce custom logging output. Three obvious examples are the Java Embedded activity in BPEL processes (introduced in Chapter 8), the Mediator Java Callouts and the Spring Java component.

To add custom logging to a BPEL process, to provide us with fine grained and process specific logging details, we have to add a Java Embedded activity. This activity is implemented like this in the BPEL component *KelvinToFahrenheitProcessor* in SOA Composite *ConversionService*:

```
<extensionActivity>
  <bpelx:exec name="SetCompositeInstanceMetaData" language="java">
  <![CDATA[String instanceTitle  = "Temperature Conversion " +
              (String)getVariableData("ConversionOperation");
        Logger logger = Logger.getLogger("oracle.soa.Logger");
        LogFormatter.configFormatter(logger);
        logger.log(Level.INFO, "custom log message from "+instanceTitle);
]]>
  </bpelx:exec>
</extensionActivity>
```

Inside the <process> element we also need to add the following import statements, to ensure we can access the required Java classes inside the embedded activity:

```
<import location="java.util.logging.Logger" importType="http://schemas.oracle.
com/bpel/extension/java"/>
<import location="java.util.logging.Level" importType="http://schemas.oracle.
com/bpel/extension/java"/>
<import location="oracle.fabric.logging.LogFormatter" importType="http://
schemas.oracle.com/bpel/extension/java"/>
```

This results in the following message in the diagnostic.log file:

```
[2015-01-07T12:42:40.721+01:00] [SoaServer1] [NOTIFICATION] [] [oracle.soa.
Logger] [tid: [ACTIVE].ExecuteThread: '19' for queue: 'weblogic.kernel.
```

```
Default (self-tuning)'] [userId: weblogic] [ecid: 43219d3f-3215-4cc4-998b-
51de1f26d543-000091a9,0:2] [APP: soa-infra] [J2EE_APP.name: soa-infra] [J2EE_
MODULE.name: fabric] [WEBSERVICE.name: ConversionService] [WEBSERVICE_PORT.
name: ConversionServicePort] [oracle.soa.tracking.FlowId: 140149] [oracle.
soa.tracking.InstanceId: 140377] [oracle.soa.tracking.SCAEntityId: 110023]
[composite_name: ConversionService!1.0] [FlowId: 0000Kf4D2^j5yW^5xVO5yW1KeI
HU000015] custom log message from Temperature Conversion Kelvin2Fahrenheit
```

By using the preconfigured logger oracle.soa.Logger, life was made a little bit easier. Normally you would use your own logger identification, for example, saibot.airport.utilities.Logger. This does not need to be an existing class. However, an entry for this logger should be set up in the ODL framework—and should be associated with a log handler through EM FMW Control as we saw before in Figures 23-1 and 23-2.

Service Bus Logging with Log Action

Service Bus components produce log messages about a wide range of events, including startup and shutdown information, errors, warning messages, access information on HTTP requests, and additional information. In addition to logging standard actions, Service Bus adds entries to the diagnostic log file for any pipelines and split-joins that have log actions and that have logging enabled.

The *ConversionService* Service Bus project contains the *ConversionPipeline* that performs the Celsius to Fahrenheit conversion. It contains a stage that publishes a log entry to a File Adapter to a custom log file. We now add a stage called *ReportToLoggingFramework* after this stage *CalloutToLogWriter*. Add a Log action in this stage. Configure this action as shown in Figure 23-3—with

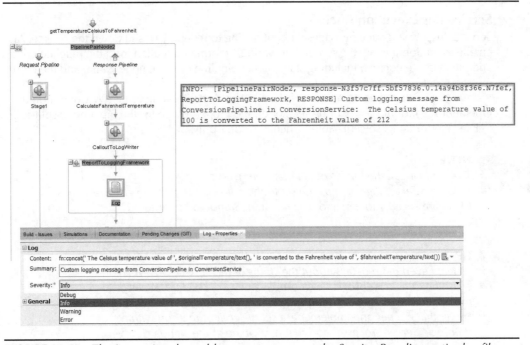

FIGURE 23-3. *The Log action that adds custom output to the Service Bus diagnostics log file (and the log file entry that is produced)*

Severity set to Information, some summary message and the content composed from instance data such as the original and converted temperature values.

Java Callouts invoke custom Java code that of course can also write custom logging in similar way as was described in the previous section for BPEL processes.

TIP
Selective Tracing is a facility that allows you to increase the logging level for specific loggers and for a specific context. This gives a greater capability to collect needed diagnostic log information in a production environment with reduced overhead. For example, when there is an issue in production or another environment that lends itself to filtering by an available context criteria and increasing the log level globally results in too much overhead or irrelevant information, a Selective Tracing session can be executed that only increases the log level for one composite, only one logger, limited to one server in the cluster, and for a preset period of time. In an environment where dozens of composites are deployed this can dramatically reduce the volume and overhead of the logging without sacrificing relevance. The information is written to the server diagnostic log and is exportable from Enterprise Manager.
   Selective Tracing can be administered either from EM FMW Control or through WLST.

Service Bus Execution Trace

Service Bus lets you trace messages without having to redeploy or shutdown the service. After you enable execution tracing, the system logs various information culled from the pipeline context and the message context, including stage name; pipeline or route node name; and the current message context.

You can enable execution tracing for a pipeline or split-join in EM FMW Control on the Operations tab for the server or project, or on the Properties tab for the pipeline or split-join: next to Execution Tracing, select Enabled. Then click on Apply.

NOTE
To see tracing in the log file or standard out (server console), WebLogic Server logging must be set to the following severity levels: Minimum severity to log: Info; Log file: Info; Standard out: Info.

TIP
To learn even more details about the status of the Service Bus, you can enlist the Oracle WebLogic Diagnostic Framework (WLDF). WLDF is a monitoring and diagnostics framework included with Oracle WebLogic Server that defines and implements a set of services that run within WebLogic Server processes and that participate in the standard server lifecycle. Using WLDF, you can capture the diagnostic data generated

by a running server, and set watches and notifications when certain conditions are met. Defining watches and notifications helps you collect the diagnostic data to identify problems, enabling you to isolate and diagnose faults when they occur. The Diagnostic Framework provides several predefined dumps, including diagnostics specific to Service Bus. Diagnostic dumps can be created using the WLST commands listDumps(), describeDump(), and executeDump().

Inspecting Log Entries in EM FMW Control

The contents of log files can of course be inspected by looking through the actual files on the server. For diagnosing specific problems or for access without authorization on the server, it can be much more convenient to review log files through the EM FMW Control. The log messages can be accessed using the managed server drop-down menu option Logs | View Log Messages.

Messages can be searched for by many attributes, including web service name, SOA Instance ID,ECID, timestamp, user, host, message level, and message content. Once a message of interest is located, it can easily be associated with related messages—either by timestamp (all messages in a certain timeframe) or by ECID (all messages connected to the same conversation)—see Figure 23-4.

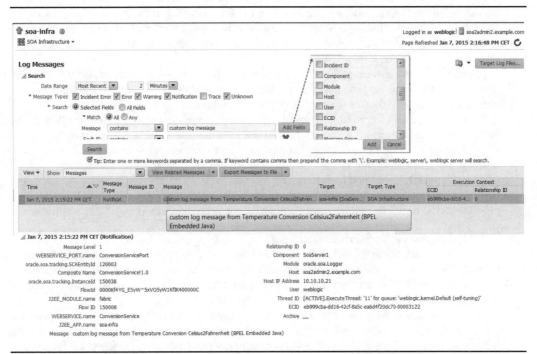

Figure 23-4. *Searching and Reviewing Log Messages through EM FMW Control—showing the custom log message written from a BPEL Process component in the SOA composite application ConversionService*

Alerts

Alerts support the most active form of monitoring. Alerts take the initiative of pushing information about the run-time affairs. Usually alerts are associated with specific conditions and KPIs. When these conditions are met, information is brought to the attention of human operators or automated facilities to assess and possibly act on.

SOA Suite has a number of built in alert facilities. Service Bus has the pipeline alert activity—from within individual executions of a service—and the concept of SLA alerts that monitor conditions on aggregated values across multiple instances. The aggregation and evaluation against predefined conditions and even KPIs can be implemented using OEP and BAM; these products can do powerful processing based on signals published from within the SOA Suite, usually over JMS, for example, from Service Bus message reports or pipeline alert or from SOA composites using composite sensors, BPEL sensors, or a JMS adapter. Fault policies for SOA composites can also publish alerts upon the occurrence of specific business faults or system faults.

Service Bus SLA Alert

The purpose of SLA alerts is to take the initiative to inform the operations team of issues relating to the health of Service Bus services or to the quality of service provided. SLA alert rules trigger alerts for proxy services, business services, pipelines, and split-joins based on the conditions you define for each service. You define alert rules to specify unacceptable service performance according to your business and performance requirements. SLA alerts are automated responses to SLA alert rules violations and are displayed on the Dashboard and the Alert History page. For a service for which monitoring is enabled, an alert rule is evaluated at discrete intervals, for example, once every 5 minutes. An alert can be generated for every violation of the rule or only once for a series of sequential violations.

Alert rules can monitor aggregate values for specific metrics—such as maximum, minimum, and average for response time and elapsed time (for pipelines) and count for the number of messages, errors, and (business service endpoint) failovers.

Alerts can be sent to multiple types of destinations, including email addresses, JMS queues, SNMP traps, custom reporting providers, and the local alert log. An SLA alert or a Pipeline alert is associated with an Alert Destination that can have one or more of the afore mentioned destinations associated with it.

Alerts are only generated if alerting and monitoring are enabled for the Service Bus domain. For SLA alerts, SLA alerting must be enabled for both the individual service and the domain. For pipeline alerts, pipeline alerting must be enabled for both the individual pipeline and the domain.

SLA Alert on Excessive Service Load   SLA Alert Rules are configured in the Service Bus Console, for Proxy Services, Pipelines, Business Service, and Split-Join components. Select the component to which you want to attach the SLA Alert Rule—for example, the proxy service *ConversionServicePS*—and then open the tab labeled SLA Alert Rules. Note: An active edit session is required in the console to make any changes.

On the SLA Alert Rules tab for *ConversionServicePS,* click on the green plus icon. We will create an Alert Rule that raises the alarm when the proxy service is invoked more than 5 times per minute—because that is really way beyond anything we expected and catered for. Figure 23-5 visualizes the definition of an SLA Alert Rule.

Set the name of the alert rule to *NotTooManyConversionsPerMinute*. Set a rule description. Select the desired alert destination to determine how the alert is to be raised. For now a simple

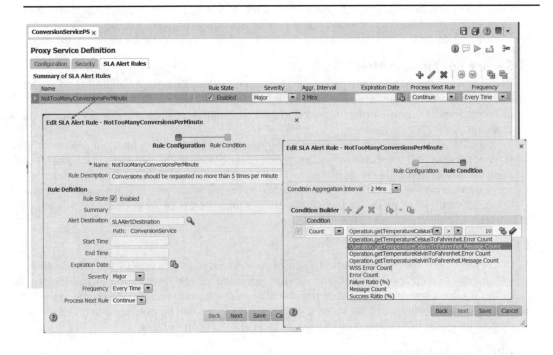

Figure 23-5. *Configuration of an SLA Alert Rule for proxy service ConversionServicePS to publish an alert when the message count grows beyond 5 messages per minute*

destination configured for alert logging will do—to see the alert reported in the console. To have a more activist alert, you should probably use a destination associated with emails or SNMP traps.

Configure a (daily) start time and end time as well as an expiration date for the alert (or leave these fields blank). Specify the severity of the alert, whether subsequent occurrences of the alert should be triggered once or every time and whether other rules should be evaluated after this one has resulted in an alert. Press Next to move to the next page where the rule condition(s) can be specified.

Select *2 Mins* as the aggregation interval. This means that the condition is tested each time (aka the sample interval) the monitoring subsystem aggregates enough samples of data to constitute one aggregation interval. For a 2-minute aggregation interval, the sample interval is 1 minute and for an aggregation interval of 1 hour, the sample interval is 10 minutes.

Define a rule condition that checks if the Message Count for operation *getTemperatureCelsiusToFahrenheit* exceeds 10. This means that the alert is triggered every time the number of requests to this operation in the last 2 minutes is higher than 10.

Click on Save to complete the wizard for the SLA Alert Rule. Then click on the save icon for the Proxy Service editor and finally commit the editing session in the Service Bus Console. The SLA Alert Rule is now active and monitoring the service activity for us.

Make a substantial number of calls to the service exposed by the proxy service and request the Celsius to Fahrenheit Temperature conversion. Open the EM FMW Control and click on the node SOA | service-bus. Open the Alert History tab and press Search. If you have made enough calls—and have waited for at least 2 minutes after activating the SLA Alert Rule—you will see something similar to Figure 23-6: a list with one or more reports of the incidence of the alert.

Service Bus Pipeline Alert

Chapter 3 introduced another type of alert: the pipeline alert. Instead of monitoring aggregates across service executions, the pipeline alert is used to report from within and about a single instance. These alerts are also be reported to alert destinations that can be associated with various channels.

Pipeline alerts are configured as part of the pipeline—either at development time in JDeveloper (Figure 3-28 shows an example) or at a later stage in the Service Bus Console. Pipeline alerts are associated with a severity level—ranging from *information* to *fatal*. At run time, the Service Bus is configured per individual pipeline to keep track of pipeline alerts and if so, starting at what severity level, as shown in Figure 3-30. See Figure 3-29 for an example of inspecting the contents of a pipeline alert in EM FM Control.

Composite Sensors

In Chapter 5, the concept of composite sensors was introduced as a way to add meaningful tags to instances of a composite in order to support searching for and interpreting such instances. The values for these sensors can be written to the SOA infra database and exposed through the EM FMW Control. Additionally, the value of a composite sensor can be published to a JMS destination—and from there used to trigger any action you can think of.

BPEL Sensor Actions

In Chapter 20, we discussed BPEL Sensors and Sensor Actions. Sensors are declaratively configured in BPEL processes to track metrics for the execution of single or multiple activities, the occurrence of faults and the modification of variables. When the sensor is activated, it executes one or more sensor actions. The available sensor actions are similar to the alert destinations available for SLA alerts and pipeline alerts: record sensor value in a database table, publish to JMS queue or topic or execute a custom Java class. The latter can of course perform many actions— from simple logging to using various methods to reach out to administrators.

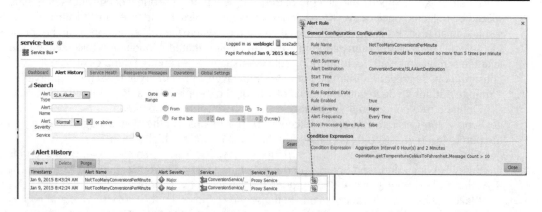

Figure 23-6. *SLA Alert reported in EM FMW Control with unexpected high number of service calls*

Implementing a Custom Sensor Action   A *custom* sensor action to handle a published sensor value can easily be triggered from a BPEL sensor. It gets passed in the current execution context including composite, component, activity, and variable values. To create a custom sensor action, we need to create a Java class that implements a specific interface. First we have to add library *SOA Workflow* to the project—to make the required Java Classes available.

A very simple example of a custom sensor action is created like this:

```
package oracle.soa;
... left out import statements
public class SensorDataPublisher implements DataPublisher {
    private static final Logger logger =
                        Logger.getLogger("oracle.soa.SensorDataPublisher");
    public SensorDataPublisher () {
      LogFormatter.configFormatter(logger);
    }
    public void publish( ITSensorAction sensorAction
                        , ITSensorActionData actionData
                        , Element element) throws Exception {
      ITHeaderInfo header = actionData.getHeader();
      System.out.println( "Custom Sensor Data Publisher "
                        +   header.getSensor().getSensorName()
                        + " published for  "+header.getCompositeName());
        StringBuilder sb = new StringBuilder();
        sb.append("Logging by sensor ").
          append(header.getSensor().getSensorName()).
          append(", evaluated at ").
          append(data.getActivityData().getEvalPoint());
        logger.log(Level.WARNING, sb.toString());
    }
}
```

Using *oracle.soa* as a package name I just a somewhat lazy way to use the oracle.soa logger already defined in WebLogic and associated with odl-handler to write messages to the diagnostics log file. You need to define your own logger in case of a custom package name.

Next, open the BPEL process editor for the process *KelvinToFahrenheitProcessor*. Switch the editor to Monitor mode. Click on the monitor icon and select *Sensor Actions* from the drop-down menu, as shown in Figure 23-7. A popup window appears in which you can manage sensor actions. Create a new sensor action called *SensorDataPublisher* of type Custom. Set the Java Class as the Publish Target and check the box labeled *Enable*.

The sensor action is now ready to be associated with an actual sensor. Right click any activity in the BPEL process. Select Create | Sensor from the context menu. Specify the name for your sensor. Select an Evaluation time—for example, Completion—and add the *SensorDataPublisher* sensor action to this sensor. Note that any sensor action can be associated with many different sensors and any sensor can trigger various sensor actions for execution. Also note that for sensors of type Activity Variable Sensor, the value of the variable is passed to the custom sensor—to be dealt with in the Java code.

You can deploy the SOA composite with the Java class for the custom sensor action and call the service to perform a Kelvin to Fahrenheit conversion. The log file will have an entry produced by the sensor action, as shown in Figure 23-8.

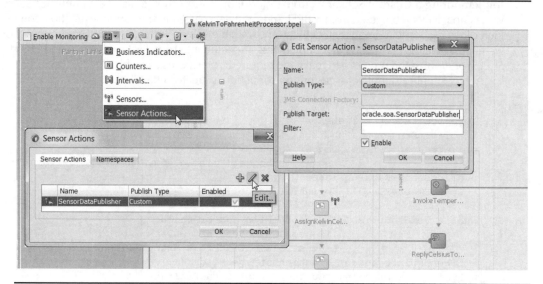

Figure 23-7. *Configure a Custom Sensor Action associated with Java Class SensorDataPublisher*

Fault Policy with Alert

The fault policy framework is used to handle faults thrown by instances of SOA composite. This framework was introduced in Chapter 5, where we saw how fault handling can consist of retrying or aborting an instance or engaging a human actor. An additional option is the association of a policy for a specific fault with alerts—allowing an email or JMS message to be sent when the fault is handled or a message to be written to the log file.

Alerts are configured on the Alerts tab in the editor for the fault-policy.xml file, as shown in Figure 23-9. For JMS alerts, properties jmsDestination and connectionFactory have to be set in a property set with the appropriate JNDI names. For an email style alert, the To and optionally Cc addresses can be specified. For log alerts, a logger has to be set.

Fault handlers link specific faults under certain conditions to actions and alerts. In Figure 23-9, any data validation fault in a Mediator component is associated with two alerts and an action to abort the instance.

This fault policy can be associated with the *ConversionMediator* component. In the source code for this chapter, you will find that the routing rule for the Kelvin temperature conversion references a Schematron validation file that states that Kelvin temperatures cannot be below zero.

```
[2015-01-08T23:20:15.213+01:00] [SoaServer1] [WARNING] [] [oracle.soa.SensorDataPublisher] [tid: [ACTIVE].ExecuteThread:
'19' for queue: 'weblogic.kernel.Default (self-tuning)'] [userId: <anonymous>] [ecid: a9eb7bbd-2881-443c-8d88-43db552f3
35d-0000509b,0.258] [APP: soa-infra] [J2EE_APP.name: soa-infra] [J2EE_MODULE.name: fabric] [WEBSERVICE.name: ConversionS
ervice] [WEBSERVICE_PORT.name: ConversionServicePort] [oracle.soa.tracking.FlowId: 160008] [oracle.soa.tracking.Instance
Id: 160035] [oracle.soa.tracking.SCAEntityId: 120003] [composite_name: ConversionService!1.0] [FlowId: 0000KfBcZpG5yW^5x
VO5yW1KfMpz00000D] Logging by sensor ActivitySensorOnReplyKelvinToFahrenheit, evaluated at completion
```

Figure 23-8. *Log entry in diagnostics log file produced by custom sensor action*

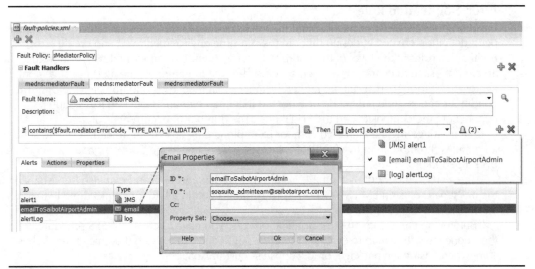

Figure 23-9.   *Configuration of alerts to be triggered by specified fault occurrences*

When we deploy the SOA composite application and call the service to convert a Kelvin temperature of –10, the fault policy is activated and the fault handler executed. This results in an email sent with a report of the fault occurrence and the instance of the SOA composite aborted, and listed in the Error Hospital, see Figure 23-10.

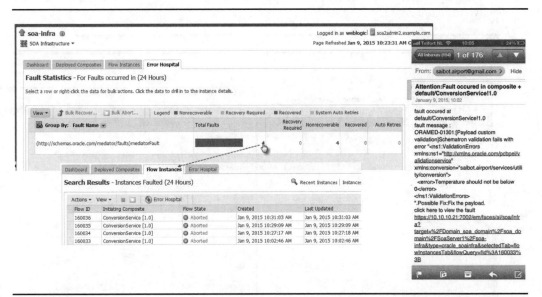

Figure 23-10.   *Fault policy triggered by a validation fault resulting in an email, an aborted instance and (not shown) a JMS message and a log file entry*

Error Notification Rules

The fault policy alert described in the previous section produces alerts for individual instances as per a definition created at design time. In the run-time environment, you can create error notification rules at the level of the entire SOA Infrastructure or an individual partition that cause an alert message to be triggered when specific fault criteria are met. The alert message contains aggregated information about the faulted instances that meet the conditions for the rule. These conditions can include fault code or type, the JNDI name of an associated JCA adapter connection, the composite and the HTTP host. The number of occurrences of a fault can also be a criteria for triggering the alert. You can, for example, create an error notification rule to send out an email when more than five faults of a specific type occur in the *ConversionService* composite over a period of 2 hours.

The alerts can be sent over email, instant messaging, and SMS and can also be visualized in the dashboard page in EM FMW control. The emails contain a URL that links directly to the list of faulted instances.

Before you can create an error notification rule, you have to create an ESS schedule defining the frequency with which to evaluate the error notification rule. Note that this schedule has to live somewhere inside the package /oracle/apps/ess/custom/soa.

The menu option Error Notification Rules is available in the drop-down menu for both the SOA infra node in the EM FMW Control as well as for every partition node. On the page that this option takes you to—shown in Figure 23-11—are all current error notification rules listed. These can be edited and new rules can be created.

The creation of an rule requires you to provide a name, select the ESS schedule according to which to evaluate the rule and the channels to use for sending an alert message. Then you need to specify the conditions that will cause the alert to be triggered, such as the period over which to evaluate and the type of fault to look out for. Complete the rule definition. Then, depending on the schedule, evaluation takes place and if necessary alerts are triggered and notifications sent, as shown in Figure 23-12.

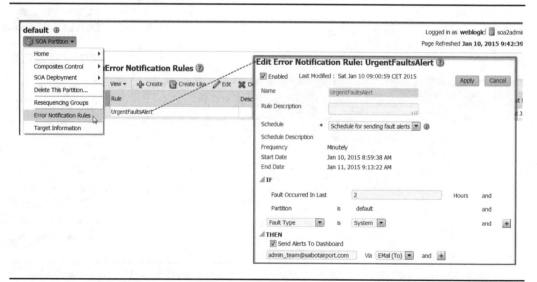

Figure 23-11. *Creating an Error Notification Rule for sending alerts upon selected error conditions*

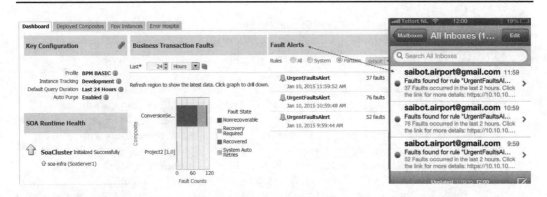

Figure 23-12. *Fault Alerts announce recent faults on the EM FMW Control dashboard and in emails*

Oracle Event Processor

Chapter 16 introduced the Oracle Event Processor (OEP). OEP is created for near-real time processing and interpretation of various types of signals. Clearly, OEP could very easily consume messages from JMS or read entries directly from log files or database tables and perform aggregations and other CQL driven evaluations on these data points.

OEP could well be set up to help detect components with deteriorating response times, too long running activities or processes, rapidly growing and threshold approaching requests volumes, etc. The signals OEP should process can be published to a JMS destination using BPEL Sensors and Pipeline Alerts as well as being read from log files. OEP will in turn have publish its findings. It can do so through the adapters—for example, for JMS, CSV file, Coherence Cache, or EDN—or it can execute custom Java to do additional things such as send email.

BAM Alerts

Business Activity Monitoring from its name seems exclusively oriented on business functionality. However, the BAM platform can very easily be used to monitor non-functional behavior of the SOA Suite as well. Similar to OEP, BAM can be configured to consume JMS messages and poll other channels and it has capabilities to process these signals continuously in near-real time (in fact, it has an embedded OEP engine to perform this feat). Alerts can be configured in BAM—usually associated with business driven KPIs but easily extended to non-functional KPIs such as those laid down in Service Level Agreements (SLA).

It would be a very realistic approach to create a BAM Dashboard that reports on the key nonfunctional metrics regarding SOA Suite behavior and that executes alerts when SLA derived KPIs are threatened or even violated. The alert action can range from notifications presented in the dashboard to emails sent, data object operations performed, web services invoked, external methods invoked, or other alerts triggered. There is a lot of similarity between the SLA Alert Rules in Service Bus and these BAM Alerts. The latter obviously require more setting up in separate BAM project. It is able to monitor across the entire SOA Suite and beyond with signals published by Service Bus projects, SOA composite applications and potentially other sources as well.

More Products for Run Time Operations

In addition to the facilities already built in to the SOA Suite, Oracle offers a number of additional products that can be used for monitoring and other run-time administrative activities.

Oracle Enterprise Manager (OEM) is Oracle's integrated enterprise information technology (IT) management product line. It provides centralized and consolidated management capabilities to help achieve the best service levels for applications. Enterprise Manager Cloud Control uses agents and plugins to discover targets to monitor and to collect data on configuration settings and live action. OEM covers a very wide range of Oracle (Database, Fusion Middleware, Exadata) and non-Oracle products. It offers pluggable capabilities for specific products and management challenges.

The SOA Management Pack Enterprise Edition is an option for OEM. It provides administrators with a consolidated browser-based view of the entire SOA environment, enabling them to monitor and manage all their components from a central location. This streamlines the correlation of availability and performance problems for all components across the SOA environment. The SOA Management Pack leverages RUEI and BTM, explained below, and provides facilities for SOA infrastructure management.

A central repository is provides that stores SOA Suite configuration across nodes. Through this repository, insight is provided in historic configuration changes. A baseline can be created for a working configuration and comparisons can be made between configurations across nodes and across domains. The management pack helps to automate SOA Suite patching, deployment, and server provisioning, as well as to automate deployment of Service Bus projects and SOA composite applications. Administrators can provision new Service Bus and SOA Suite domains based on Middleware Provisioning Profiles in the Enterprise Manager 12c software library. The provisioning process allows for configuration parameters to be set on the domains being provisioned.

Oracle Real User Experience Insight (aka Oracle RUEI) is used to monitor HTTP conversations that constitute a user session with a web application or interactions with web services such as those exposed by components deployed to the SOA Suite. RUEI collects data on individual sessions—for problem diagnosis and replay—as well as statistics across sessions to trap performance bottlenecks, traffic trends, and evaluate real-time characteristics against KPIs such as SLA goals. RUEI could best be used at a perimeter around the entire SOA Suite, covering all of Service Bus, SOA composites, and other components engaging in interactions.

Oracle Business Transaction Management (BTM) monitors the bigger picture across all the technical components that contribute to what constitutes a business transaction. Individual service executions, database manipulations, and adapter actions can execute technical transactions. A faulted technical transaction might mean a failed business transaction. BTM aids with transaction visibility, business KPI monitoring, and proactive exception management, aimed at increased reliability of their business transactions. It does so across various technical components, including SOA Suite, BPM Suite, Database, Java EE applications on WebLogic and non-Oracle components running on .NET, JBoss, and IBM WebSphere.

Enterprise Manager 12c provides a complete Application Performance Management (APM) solution for custom applications and Oracle applications. APM delivers Business Driven Application Management with end-to-end monitoring that includes:

- Live monitoring of actual web service performance with RUEI

- Synthetic transaction monitoring of traffic artificially created by software to mimic the load that would be expected to test the performance and availability of business-critical services in the infrastructure as part of service level management, also with RUEI

- Monitor and trace transactions and transaction instances and monitor business metrics included in transaction content with BPM

Monitor through Enterprise Manager Fusion Middleware Control

The EM FMW Control provides various user interfaces to track activities and monitor status of many aspects of the SOA Suite run-time platform and the requests processed on it. Through Message Reports we can learn similar details about executions in Service Bus. In previous chapters we have seen how the console provides insight in running and (recently) completed instances of SOA composites. We have seen how log files collect potentially vast amounts of data—that can also be reviewed to some extent in the EM FMW Control.

We will now discuss how we can enrich the data presented in the console, to make it easier to find and interpret. Additionally, we will introduce additional pages for monitoring the health of services and references, components and adapter bindings in SOA composite applications and in Service Bus projects.

Monitor SOA Composite Instances

Instances of SOA composite instances can be monitored on the Flow Instances tab at domain wide level, per partition and per SOA composite application. Instances can be searched by many different attributes—including the identifier and name of either the flow instance or the composite instances, the timestamp, initiating user and the current state of the instance and the value of composite sensors. Figure 23-13 shows the Search Options pane where the query can be constructed. Note the ability to save custom search definitions that you can reuse. Also note the option to create a bookmarkable link—one that will take you immediately to the result of the current set of search conditions.

As we have seen many times in the book, we can open the Flow Trace for a selected flow instance. The flow trace shows all composites and components that played a role in the processing of this particular instance. The instance identifier for each of these can be listed—and used to cross reference for example with log files and database tables.

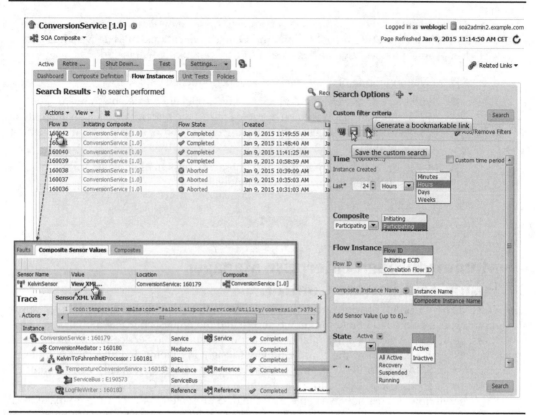

Figure 23-13. *Overview of Flow Instances involving the SOA composite ConversionService retrieved using the Search Options pane*

TIP
The Flow ID uniquely identifies a business flow within an Oracle SOA Suite domain. A business flow that crosses two Oracle SOA Suite domains has a single flow correlation ID (a GUID value that uniquely identifies a business flow that extends across domains) and two flow IDs. Similarly, a business flow that originates outside of Oracle SOA Suite cannot create a flow ID because it does not have access to the Oracle SOA Suite schema. However, it can create a flow correlation ID.

As we saw in Chapter 5, developers can define composite sensors at design time, in JDeveloper. And when appropriately configured, the values of composite sensors are available to search on and inspect in the EM FMW Control. Through the SOA Composer console, additional composite sensors can be configured at run time—to provide more hooks to search for or do analysis on composite instances.

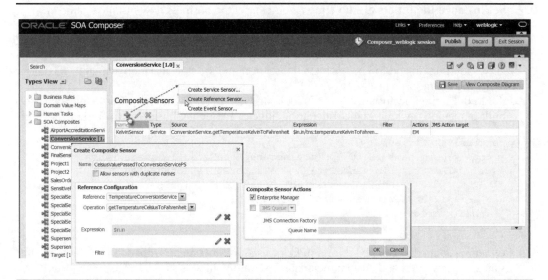

Figure 23-14.   *Define a new Composite Sensor at run time in the SOA Composer*

Open the SOA Composer, select the SOA composite application and create an editing session. Click on the green plus icon—demonstrated in Figure 23-14—and create a new reference sensor.

In the popup window provide a name for the sensor. Select the reference *TemperaturConversionService* (currently configured to call out to the Service Bus) and the *getTemperatureCelsiusToFahrenheit*. Set the expression to $in.in and ensure that the Sensor Action *Enterprise Manager* is enabled.

Click on OK to complete the sensor definition. Then on Save and finally on Publish to commit the current editing session. From this moment on, the new sensor is active.

When a call has been made to convert a value from Kelvin to Fahrenheit, the instance will have two sensor values associated with it, as shown in Figure 23-15.

NOTE
The SOA Suite run time in the Integrated WebLogic Servicer does not support these run-time composite sensor definitions.

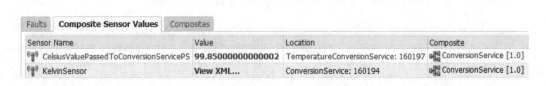

Figure 23-15.   *The result of the two Composite Sensor for the ConversionService SOA composite*

Set Instance Identifiers at Run Time   You can set the business flow instance name or composite instance name of a SOA composite application at run time for Mediator and BPEL Process Manager. The name appears in the Name column on the Flow Instances page of a SOA composite application in EM FMW Control as well as in log file entries. A business flow instance corresponds to an end-to-end business transaction and the flow instance name covers potentially many SOA composite instances.

In BPEL, the flow instance name is set in an Embedded Java activity. This extension uses the built-in method setFlowInstanceTitle(String title) for setting the business flow instance name:

```
<extensionActivity>
  <bpelx:exec name="SetCompositeInstanceMetaData" language="java">
  <![CDATA[String instanceTitle  = "Temperature Conversion " +
             (String)getVariableData("ConversionOperation");
         setFlowInstanceTitle(instanceTitle);]]>
  </bpelx:exec>
</extensionActivity>
```

Other metadata that can be set for a BPEL process instance in an Embedded Java activity: title, status, index values, and custom metadata. This information is stored in the cube_instance and ci_indexes database tables where instances of BPEL processes and their custom index values are recorded. The data can be used to search for and report on specific instances in SQL and through the Java API. A call can be made to addAuditTrailEntry to create custom entries in the audit trail for the BPEL process instance.

The name of the composite instance, rather than the business flow instance, can also be set—although apparently for backward compatibility only. This name shows up in the flow trace window on the composites tab that lists all SOA composites that were involved in a business flow instances.

The composite instance's name can be set in Mediator or BPEL. In a BPEL embedded Java activity, use setCompositeInstanceTitle("the composite instance title") to set the instance name. In Mediator, use the XPath expression function oraext:setFlowInstanceTitle() in an assign activity.

```
<assign>
  <copy expression="med:setFlowInstanceTitle('the title to assign')"
        target="$out.property.tracking.flowInstanceTitle"
        xmlns:med="http://schemas.oracle.com/mediator/xpath"/>
</assign>
```

Using a Mediator component to set the flow instance title seems the better practice, as it is more straightforward and therefore less error prone and easier to maintain.

When both a Mediator component and a BPEL Process component set the name of the instance, whoever does it last will have the upper hand.

Service Component Metrics

The EM FMW Control gives access to a vast collection of reports that provide insight in the what is and has recently been going on in the SOA Suite. Number of instances and faults, trends, average processing times are all readily available. Many details are presented in charts as well as in table layout.

The Dashboard tab for SOA composites lists the components inside the composite as well as all external services and references such as adapter bindings. Each of these entries is a clickable

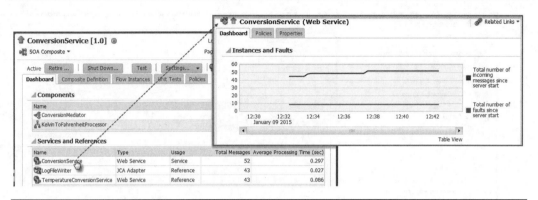

Figure 23-16. *Run-time metrics for SOA composite ConversionService and its service binding*

link—leading to detail pages. Figure 23-16 shows the dashboard for the *ConversionService* composite with some metrics for its services and references. The popup shows more recent performance details for the externally exposed *ConversionService*.

The dashboard for the BPEL process component lists all activities, the number of times they have been executed and the average time required for these executions. The Mediator dashboard lists the number of executions—and faults—per routing operation and per routing rule and also shows the average processing time.

For adapter bindings, there is a lot of relevant data about its activity, including its integration with the JCA service of WebLogic. Figure 23-17 shows an example for the File Adapter binding *LogFileWriter*.

TIP
The information presented in the EM FMW Control is primarily retrieved from tables in the SOA Infra database schema. You could create read only custom user interfaces against these same tables—when all out of the box features and the official Java API fall short of what you need. Note that Oracle does not in any way guarantee that these tables will continue to have the same structure in future releases. The most important tables are:

- *SCA_FLOW_INSTANCE (with an entry for every flow executed by one or more SOA composite applications), SCA_ASYNC_CPNT_STATE an AUDIT_TRAIL (both with entries for each component visited in the flow), AUDIT_DETAILS, SCA_FLOW_TO_CPST, SCA_ENTITY (with all services, references and components in SOA composites), SCA_ SENSOR_VALUE (containing the values of composite sensors); except for SCA_ENTITY, all table records are linked by the value in the FLOW_ID column.*

- *BPEL instances are primarily recorded in tables CUBE_INSTANCE (also with column FLOW_ID) and CI_INDEXES.*

- *Mediator instance details are stored in MEDIATOR_AUDIT_DOCUMENT.*

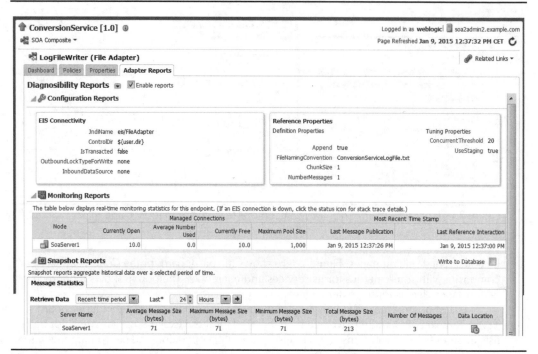

Figure 23-17. *Run-time Reports for the File Adapter binding LogFileWriter*

Service Bus Message Reports

Chapter 3 discussed Message Reports for Service Bus. These are produced from within pipelines with a report activity. This activity publishes a message, associated with key value pairs to define key identifiers and values that can be extracted from any message context variable or message payload. The keys provide a convenient way to find and identify messages—similar to how composite sensors help identify instances of SOA composites.

Messages are published to a JMS Queue with little overhead to the reporting thread—the thread processing the request. The default reporting provider consumes the messages from that queue and writes data to a database table. Alternative reporting providers can be configured for complementary processing of the reports. The messages stored in the database can be searched through and reviewed through the EM FMW Control. Figures 3-31 through 3-34 give an example of configuring the Message Report activity and searching and inspecting the results in EM FMW Control.

Service Bus Service Health metrics

Service Health metrics can be monitored in EM FMW Control. There are no automated actions associated with these metrics such as is the case for the SLA Alerts. These metrics include for each service the average execution time, the number of requests processed, number of errors and specifically the number of validation or security related errors. For pipelines, flow metrics are reported that include message count, error count, and response times down to each pipeline pair.

The Service Bus—Service Health page displays health statistics for all services in the domain that have monitoring enabled. This is a subset of all statistics; you can click a service name to view the complete set of statistics for that service. Note that a similar page is available at project level and at service level. See Figure 3-27 for an example.

You can use the Service Health page to reset monitoring statistics for all services in a domain or project, or just for one specific service. When you reset statistics, the system deletes all monitoring statistics that were collected for the service, project, or domain since you last reset statistics. However, the system does not delete the statistics being collected during the current aggregation interval for the service. After a statistics reset, the system immediately starts collecting monitoring statistics for the service again.

(Re)Act

Knowing what is going on is crucial for effective administration. This knowledge prompts, guides or at the very least enables an administrator to evaluate plan and perform necessary actions. The previous section outlined many ways for learning about the state of affairs in the SOA Suite.

Responding to this knowledge or to information received from other channels, for example, with regard to changes in the environment, is the next essential step to continue providing the business with the agreed or even improved service levels for performance, availability, etc. Many of the nonfunctional aspects of applications running in the SOA Suite can be configured at run time, primarily through the EM FMW Control console, the WebLogic Server Admin console, and the Service Bus console. Through for example WLST scripts, some of the run-time configuration tasks can be automated.

Some functional aspects of the SOA Suite applications can be changed at run time as well, depending to what extent such customization has been designed and implemented into these application. Through the use of, for example, SCA properties, Domain Value Maps, and Business Rules that can all be manipulated at run time, many functions can be created with built in customizability. Applying functional changes at run time is not without risks: if a change is applied that has not been thoroughly tested (and even when it has), it can affect the functionality of services and business processes in unintended, harmful ways.

Dynamically Adjusting Application Behavior

One of the main objectives of SOA in general is to achieve business agility. Agility can be defined in various ways, but a central element of all definitions will be an ability to adapt to changes in a flexible, quick, and controlled manner. A constant willingness and preparedness to embrace change is what we try to instill in people as well as install in the applications we develop both by leveraging the intrinsic facilities of SOA Suite for absorbing changes in the environment and embedding a degree of dynamic customizability in the SOA composite applications.

A portion of the changing requirements we face for our composite applications can be resolved by an administrator, at run time, without the need for changing and redeploying the application. For example, endpoints of external services that are invoked from composite applications can be adjusted. The configuration of technology adapter services is another aspect that can be altered at run time. When it comes to the more functional aspects of the application, there are several options to make those subject to on-the-fly manipulation too. When applications make use of SCA properties and facilities such as Domain Value Maps and business rules that can be edited at run time, parts of their behavior become manageable.

Run-Time Management of Adapter Configuration and Reference Endpoint Settings

SOA Suite has built-in support for run-time adjustment of various types of properties. The administration pages for composites and their service and reference bindings offer access to the same properties that we can replace using configuration plans during deployment. When we inspected the effect of the configuration plan in the previous chapter, we visited those pages that we can now also use to apply run-time modifications to those same properties.

Changing the Endpoints of Services   A possible change that we may need to make to a deployed composite application is a readjustment of the endpoint of one of the services referenced by the composite. The service referenced by the composite may simply be moved to a different server, and we need to use a different address to access it. Or it may be the case that the owner of the service offers a new, improved version of his service that we want to make use of (and because the port and message definitions have not changed, we will be able to). Or a virtualization layer—wrapper service, enterprise service bus, service registry—is to be inserted between the composite and the referenced service and therefore the reference binding needs to switch to a different address.

Whatever the occasion, when the endpoint of a referenced service needs to be changed, the steps are as follows: Select the SOA composite application for which the reference binding needs adjustment. On the tab Dashboard, click on the reference that needs changing. The Reference Binding dashboard opens. Click the Properties tab. The new endpoint address for the referenced service can be entered into the Endpoint Address field, as shown in Figure 23-18. Click the Apply button to save this change.

From then on, whenever the composite invokes the reference, the call is routed to this new address. When you inspect the source on the Composite Definition tab, you will find that new endpoint has been set as the *endpointURI* property for the binding.ws element.

Figure 23-18.   *Changing the endpoint address of a reference binding of an external service*

Modifying Properties for the Composite, Components, and Technology Adapter Services

Both the custom properties that we may define on the composite or one of the components (as we will see in the next section), as well as the standard properties for the technology adapters, can be manipulated in the EM FMW Control. Earlier we checked the effect of the configuration plan on the properties logging directory for the outbound file adapter service. The console pages that we used for this inspection can also be used for manipulation of the values of these properties.

All aspects of the composite application and its adapter bindings that are controlled through properties that can be set at design time are also up for adjustment at run time. The value of these properties can be inspected and modified through the System MBean browser: open the drop-down menu for the soa-infra node. Select Administration | System MBean Browser. Navigate to oracle.soa.config under Application Defined MBeans. Open the sub tree for the managed server. In the folder SCA Composite, expand the node for the relevant application—*ConversionService* is shown in Figure 23-19. Select the component for which a property needs to be adjusted, in this case the BPEL process component. Click on the link for properties. The properties defined for this component are presented in a popup window. Here you can modify the value, for example, for property *preference.kelvinCelsiusGap*. When you press Apply, the new value is effective immediately.

To set the JCA adapter properties that are exposed as SCA properties for an adapter such as the outbound file adapter in the *ConversionService* composite, you can go through the Properties tab in the Adapter Binding page accessed from the composite dashboard in EM FMW Control, as shown in Figure 22-11.

Many properties for the JCA Adapter binding are accessible through an MBean—to be inspected and set at run time. See Figure 23-20 for an example for the same outbound file adapter binding.

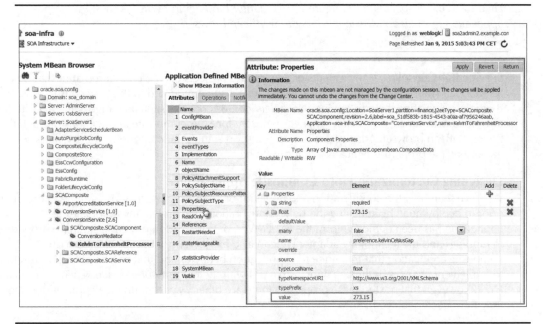

Figure 23-19. *Manipulating the values of SCA properties at run time through the MBean browser*

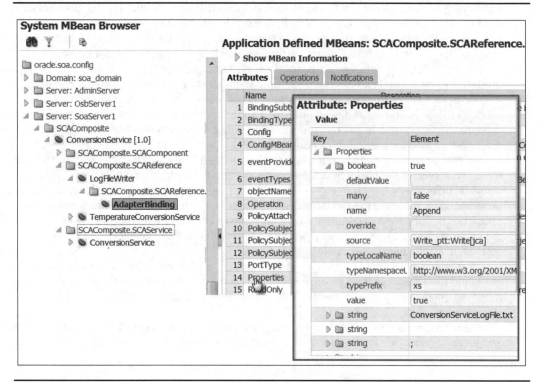

Figure 23-20.   *Inspect and Configured JCA Adapter binding properties for a SOA composite application through an MBean in the System MBean browser*

Service Bus Console   Many aspects of Service Bus projects can be configured at design time in JDeveloper. Then again, many of these aspects can also be modified in the Service Bus console. By merely activating the edit session in the Service Bus console, such a change is in effect in the run-time environment—similar to changes wrought for SOA composite applications through the System MBean browser. Adapter properties, transport settings, and endpoints for business services are among the properties typically set at run time.

Designing Customization into Composite Applications

We have seen how the configuration and behavior of composite applications can be manipulated, prior to deployment, by attaching the right configuration plan and at any point after the application has been deployed from the EM FMW Control. In addition to the standard properties in bindings and the technology adapter we can also expose custom properties from our composite application that influence the application behavior and that can be altered at run time to implement changes in the behavior, as we did with the property *preference.kelvinCelsiusGap*. Note, however, that next to these properties there are other ways to influence applications after they have been deployed.

Several customization strategies are available to turn a hard coded value in an application into one that can be manipulated at run time. Such a value can be:

■ Set using a Business Rule component (that itself can be manipulated in the SOA Composer at run time)

■ Retrieved with XPath functions from a Domain Value Map that is stored in the MDS repository and can be manipulated at run time from the SOA Composer

■ Read from a database table, PL/SQL package, or properties file

■ Retrieved from a Web Service, singleton BPEL process (probably to be considered an antipattern so steer clear of this), EJB, or (static) Java object (which may act as a properties cache)

■ Read from properties defined in the composite.xml file and manipulated through the MBean browser in the EM FMW Control

For simple properties that are used in BPEL processes, using custom SCA properties at the component (or composite) level is the leanest approach that is also supported declaratively, out of the box. These properties are defined in the component element in the composite.xml—for example, for Mediators and BPEL components. These properties can be accessed inside these components using special XPath operations (e.g., in the BPEL Assign activity).

Note that the SOA Suite development team itself designed many run-time customizations into their product and as a result there are a large number of settings we can adjust at run time. Sometimes through nice user friendly user interfaces and almost always (also) through the System MBean browser.

Error Hospital and Fault Recovery

One of the recurring tasks for administrators is the recovery of faulted SOA composite instances. Service Bus interactions are usually synchronous and faults are typically returned to the consumer. However, for asynchronous and one-way service calls as well as for instances initiated through the consumption of an event or for long running SOA composites and business processes, simply returning an error to the consumer is typically not the desired approach or may not even be possible at all. For these cases, we need to design and implement a fault handling strategy.

Fault handling can be implemented inside Service Bus pipelines, in BPEL processes and in BPM processes. However, there comes a time—especially for system faults associated with unavailable partner applications or platform configuration issues—where the fault will be thrown from the instance to the SOA infrastructure, where it becomes the responsibility of the administrators.

To a large extent, these faults can be handled automatically at infrastructure level—using fault policies that retry, turn into a human task or employ a custom resolution. However, the final resort for many cases—including those where the fault was unexpected and not catered for—the SOA composite instance will end up as faulted—transferred to the Error Hospital.

The Error Hospital page is available at the SOA Infrastructure level, where system-wide faults data is aggregated. When accessed at the partition level, the Error Hospital page is limited to faults data associated only with that partition. Use the Error Hospital page to view an aggregate count of errors that have occurred in all SOA Composites deployed in the SOA Infrastructure and drill down to inspect individual instances. Search criteria can be used to list specific selections of faulted instances. Faults can be queried by fault code or type, by JNDI name of an associated JCA adapter connection, by partition and composite and by HTTP host.

Bulk recovery can be initiated on a selected group of similar faults in a single operation. For example when a database has been down and is now running again, and we want to retry all faulted instances that were stuck as a result of the downtime. The *autoretries* feature allows the SOA infrastructure to continuously retry a recoverable fault. When a fault is in *recovery required* state and an autoretry is setup, then an automated system call is generated at a certain interval to try and recover the error.

Recovery of Faulted Instances of SOA Composites

A fairly easy to recover category of faulted instances are those instances that failed to access an external component because it was not available at the address currently configured. When the referenced database, web service or file system is available again or the connection properties are corrected, these instances will probably succeed when restarted.

We will explore this situation for the *ConversionService* SOA composite.

Making the ConversionService Fail   The *ConversionService* composite calls out to the proxy service *ConversionServicePS* exposed by the Service Bus project. Through the Service Bus console, change the endpoint for this proxy service on the transport tab. The next time the composite tries to invoke the proxy service, it will fail because the service is no longer available at the endpoint we have configured in the reference binding. Because the Kelvin to Fahrenheit conversion is a synchronous operation, there is no recovery available for the faulted SOA composite instance.

Adding Asynchronous Processing   Next, we add an asynchronous—potentially long running—implementation of the temperature conversion using an asynchronous BPEL process component, shown in Figure 23-21.

When the asynchronous BPEL process is faced with the fault that originates at the reference binding *TemperatureConversionService*, instead of throwing the towel, it will hang on—available for recovery rather than flat out termination of the instance, shown in Figure 23-22.

Of course, as long as the endpoint for the proxy service is not corrected, retrying will not produce a recovered instance but instead result with another fault. When that happens, the instance

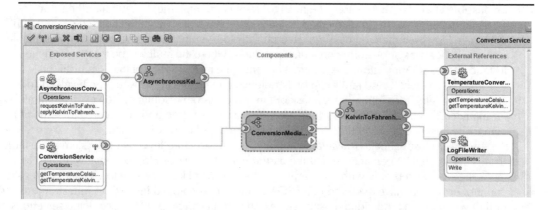

Figure 23-21.   *ConversionService SOA composite with asynchronous and synchronous operations exposed*

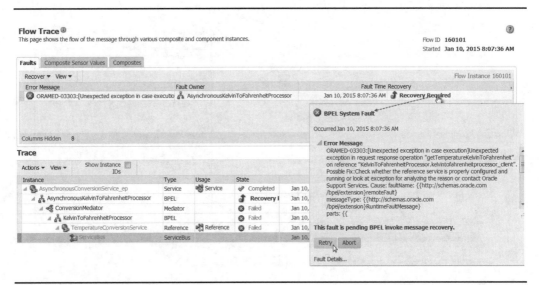

Figure 23-22. *Failed SOA composite instance can be retried and thus perhaps recovered*

will once again be eligible for recovery. Note that automatically retrying failed instances because of this type of run-time fault—under the assumption that an unavailable service will soon become available again—is something we can configure using fault policies, probably with a maximum number of attempts configured as well as an exponentially growing delay between attempts.

Recover the Failed Instances   Make a number of calls, both to the synchronous and the asynchronous temperature conversion operation. Next, check the Error Hospital. Like Figure 23-23, it will show a number of faulted instances—some of which are recoverable starting from the asynchronous calls and others are permanently failed.

Select the entry with recoverable instances. The icon for Bulk Recovery becomes active. Click on the icon. A popup window appears in which you can schedule the bulk recovery of the four instances that require recovery. You can set scheduling properties such as when the recovery should take place and upon failure, how frequently should it be reattempted and how many instances should be operated upon simultaneously (batch size). A job is created with ESS, the enterprise schedule, to perform the recovery. Recovery consists of trying to get the instance going from the point where it failed and is currently stuck. Recovery will of course only succeed if the cause of the fault has been removed.

After creating the job to perform bulk recovery from the Error Hospital, you can track the progress of the job through the ESS pages in EM FMW control. As long as the endpoint of the proxy service is not returned to the original value configured in the *ConversionService* SOA composite, the job for bulk recovery will keep on running. The first job execution after the endpoint is fixed will at last result in recovered and now successfully completed instances.

Note that in addition to bulk recovery, the Error Hospital also offers an option to perform bulk abort on stuck instances—making all these instances terminate.

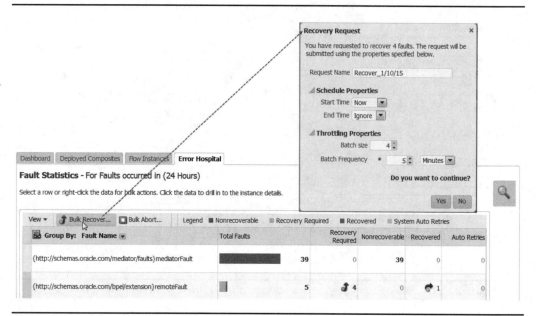

Figure 23-23. *Error Hospital with faulted instances and bulk recovery of some of them*

Prevent or Pro-Act

Even better than rapidly resolving a problematic situation is preventing the situation from occurring at all. There are several recurring tasks to perform as part of the operations around the SOA Suite to preempt problems. These are typically focused on optimal use of system resources. This includes balancing the load over the available resources and preventing unmanageable loads from even reaching the SOA infrastructure. It also entails freeing up resources as quickly as possible, for example, by timely removal of no longer needed remnants of past activity.

Careful capacity planning and clever use of physical resources is the foundation for a healthy run-time environment. If the available infrastructure is simply not dimensioned to handle the load it will be subjected to, then all bets are off. Analysis of the expected (peak) work volume and the required server capacity, nor the design of the network topology and the cluster setup are within the scope of this chapter.

We will merely look at some of the things to do and use given a certain infrastructure layout and capacity: how to protect the infrastructure from total collapse under a peak load, how to influence fair sharing of resources and how to clean up after ourselves to ensure continued smooth operations.

Throttling the Work Volume

Throttling lets you control the volume of requests handled by the SOA Suite run time in order to improve performance and stability by preventing message overload. The SOA Suite clearly cannot process an unlimited number of concurrent service requests, events and process instances. How many requests it can handle depends on the available resources and the work required for each task. Through throttling, we cannot increase the SOA Suite's capacity for processing, but we can prevent a large demand from clogging the infrastructure, bringing it to a standstill that affects all consumers. We do so by deferring the work, distributing the requests over time and by a balanced allocation of resources.

The Service Bus provides a throttling mechanism that enables us to limit the number of concurrent requests processed by a business service and defer the surplus of requests. The inbound Database Adapter gives us another mechanism to process requests at a regulated rate. In mature environments often dedicated load balancers—either software or hardware—are applied to handle traffic load, especially when it comes from outside the organization's boundaries.

Throttling Service Bus Business Services

By configuring throttling for a business services, we restrict the number of threads concurrently used to make outbound calls from the business service.

Throttling can only be configured at run time, in the EM FMW Control. To configure throttling for the business service *ConversionServiceBS* in the project *ThrottlingAndCachingWrapperConversionService*, open the EM FMW Control, click on the service-bus node and then click the name of the project. The Service Bus Project home page appears. On the Operations tab, perform a search and click on the business service. Open the Properties tab—as shown in Figure 23-24.

On this tab, various operational settings are configured—such as detailed message tracing, result caching enablement, offline endpoint URIs settings, monitoring, and throttling.

We specify the *maximum concurrency* to indicate the highest number of threads that can be used at any moment to do work on behalf of the business service. The (in memory) throttling queue is where the requests are held that cannot be processed immediately because no threads are available as a result of the maximum concurrency setting. We configure the maximum size of this queue, which can be zero when we do not want any message to be held for deferred processing. Note the queue is in memory and messages that are placed in this queue are not recoverable when a server fails or when you restart a server. Once a message has been in the throttling queue for an interval greater than the value of message expiration configured for the business service or throttling group, it becomes an expired message and is removed from the queue. When the queue is full, the message in the queue with the lowest priority is removed if a new incoming message has a higher priority.

The settings shown in Figure 23-24 allow two threads to work in parallel on making calls for the business service. A maximum of three messages can be stored on the queue for deferred processing when a thread becomes available. Messages are held on the queue for no longer than 200 milliseconds. When the message is discarded from the queue or cannot even be added to the queue—a throttling error is thrown.

The effect of throttling can be demonstrated using for example a SoapUI test suite with multiple test cases that are executed in parallel, each with several requests to the proxy service in the Service Bus project. When the test suite is executed, there is an almost concurrent load of 10 or more requests put on the business service. Only two can be processed concurrently, three can be deferred for a short while and other requests will be flat out refused. A number of test steps is likely to fail. By fiddling with the throttling settings and reexecuting the test suite, you can get a good feel for the effects of throttling.

Note that throttling does not allow us to control the rate of requests made from the business service. If a call is completed quickly, the thread can quickly process the next request and make

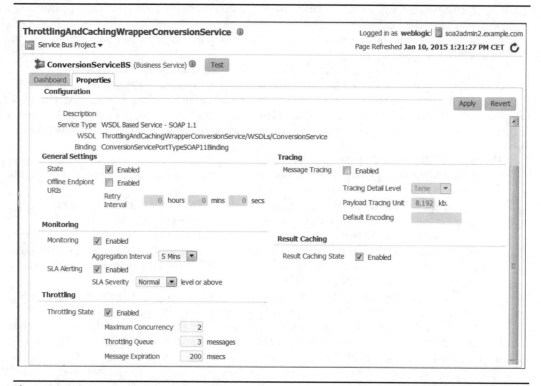

Figure 23-24. *Operational properties for the Service Bus Business Service ConversionServiceBS in EM FMW Control*

another call. When the service invoked from the business service is an asynchronous or one-way service, the load is hardly reduced by throttling the business service. Also note that throttling the business service to a single thread means that the requests (of the same priority) are processed in the exact order in which they arrived at the business service.

TIP
A Business Service is the link from Service Bus to an external service. We can configure multiple endpoints for a business service—with two objectives in mind: to provide an alternative for when the service is not available on one endpoint and to balance the load across the various endpoints. In the Operations tab for a business service, using the General Setting Offline Endpoint URIs we can instruct Service Bus to mark the business service's endpoint URIs offline when they are not responding—either temporarily or permanently, see Figure 23-24. When an unresponsive endpoint is temporarily considered offline, the URI is retried after the specified time interval. If the endpoint responds, the URI becomes online again, or else it remains offline and the process repeats itself.

Messaging Throttling with Database Adapter

A Service Bus project or a SOA composite can be activated through an incoming request message, an EDN event or an activation by an inbound adapter. The database adapter can be used in inbound mode, where it will poll a table for records to process. Each record retrieved from the table for processing will result in an activation as discussed above. By tuning the polling properties, we can control the rate with which services are activated—not the number of concurrent threads but the exact number of instances per time interval.

The relevant properties that govern polling are the polling interval, the number of threads and the (number of) Database Rows per Transaction—and make sure distributed polling is enabled. The number of instances activated also depends on whether the SOA Suite is running on multiple nodes. For example: with a polling interval of 10 seconds, two threads, a value of 4 for Database Rows per Transaction and the SOA Suite running on two nodes, the maximum activation rate is 2 [nodes] * 2 [threads] * 4 [records per polling iteration] * 6 [times a polling interval per minute] or 96 instances per minute.

Using a database table as a queue for requests yet to be processed in conjunction with an inbound database adapter to throttle the rate with which these requests are handled is a fine way of managing the workload on the SOA Suite run-time infrastructure when the requests are handled asynchronously and we want to control the rate of SOA composite execution.

Balanced Resource Allocation

The perceived performance and ultimate stability of infrastructures such as the SOA Suite depends on the smart allocation of the limited system resources. Performing all the work according to first-in-first-out ignores the possible differences in priorities between tasks. Finding the right balance in assigning resources—primarily CPU threads—across workloads in such a way that all work can eventually be completed with regard for the relative priorities is important.

In SOA Suite, we can create clusters of tasks—through partitions containing SOA composites or more fine grained using proxy services or business services. We can also create objects that represent a set or share of system resources; these objects are called *work managers*. By associating a partition, a proxy service or a business service with such a work manager we effectively apply work execution rules, which are used by the WebLogic Server in order to prioritize work and allocate threads.

Work managers are configured through the WebLogic Server Administration console. A work manager has a name, references through the Max Threads Constraint a thread pool of a fixed number of threads shared between all work managers associated with it and can have a maximum capacity (of concurrently handled requests). A work manager can also be associated with the *Fair Share Request Class* that specifies the average thread-use time required to process requests and the *Response Time Request Class* that specifies a response time goal in milliseconds. A request class expresses a scheduling guideline that WebLogic Server uses to allocate threads to requests. Request classes help ensure that high priority work is scheduled before less important work, even if the high priority work is submitted after the lower priority work. Request classes define a best effort.

The WebLogic Admin Console provides insight in the number of pending and completed requests of each work manager. For example, to check on the work managers used for executing SOA composite instances, log in to console and list the Deployments. In the table, browse for and click on soa-infra. Navigate to the tab Monitoring and select sub tab Workload. Details about pending and completed requests in the work managers and deferred requests in the thread pools are displayed.

Resource Management in Service Bus Using Work Managers

When a proxy service receives a request to process, it retrieves a thread from the thread pool associated with the work manager it is configured for. All the work done on the request is done in this thread—from the proxy service, all pipelines including blocking callouts until routing has taken place to the business service. When the request is sent to the target, the thread is released back to the pool.

When the response from the target is received, the muxer—the dispatcher component that handles all responses—hands off the response to a new thread that is used to execute the response pipeline. This thread is retrieved from the thread pool associated with the work manager assigned to the business service.

By assigning appropriate work managers to proxy services and business services, we can influence their chance of easily getting a thread to perform their work. Configuring a work manager for a proxy service or business service is done using the property *dispatch policy* on the Transport Details tab. The value for this property should match the name of a work manager created in the WebLogic Admin Console.

If a work manager is not assigned to the proxy service, it will use the WLS Default work manager.

TIP

By configuring a proxy service or business service with a work manager that is associated with a thread pool of exactly one thread, we effectively apply a throttling policy that restricts the service to sequential processing (one at a time) of all requests.

Partition-Based Load Balancing

Each partition is associated with a *work manager group*. A work manager group consists of work managers dedicated to managing the threads used for processing SOA Suite background work for a given partition. Work manager groups isolate partition configuration and request processing. A work manager group can be shared by multiple partitions. Work managers are included, for example, for different types of mediator activity, various BPMN tasks, and adapter actions. These work managers can be configured through the WebLogic Server Admin console. The configuration of the work managers thus associated with a partition governs the resources used for executing instances of SOA composite application in the partition.

Work manager groups are created in the EM FMW Control. The drop-down menu for the soa-infra node contains menu option Work Manager Groups that gives access to an overview of the existing work manager groups, the partition they are associated with and the work managers they contain. Additionally, the metrics—completed, active pending and stuck requests are presented as well. New work manager groups can be created. When this happens, a new set of work managers in created and added to the new group. These work managers can then be fine-tuned in WebLogic Server Admin console.

To set the work manager group for a partition, open the drop-down menu for the soa-infra node and select *Manage Partitions*. A list of partitions is presented. You can create a new partition and edit or delete existing partitions. Select the partition for which the work manager group is to be set. Click on the edit icon. In the *partition editor* popup, select the required work manager group and click on Apply. The managed server has to be restarted for the work manager group change to take effect.

Purging

The normal operations in the SOA Suite produce potentially enormous amounts of data—primarily in the form of log files and database records and largely depending on the workload and a plethora of configuration settings. The data thus produced can quickly become unwieldy. It consumes storage resources—and it may seriously hamper administrative operations. Querying instance data, analyzing problems, retrieving aggregations and reports, inspecting dashboards, patching, upgrading and performing bulk operations may all be slowed down if we do not periodically get rid of obsolete data. To ensure an optimal performance of your run-time environment, frequent purging of older data associated with flow instances, adapter reports, and fault alerts is essential. Smart use of partitioning in the SOA infra database can help balance query performance as well as speed up purge operations. And by using strict logging settings we can help restrict the volume of data produced by SOA Suite run-time activity to begin with.

The collection of log files can become quite voluminous, depending on the settings we apply both for how much information should be written to the log files—through the log levels defined for the loggers—and how large the files can grow, how long they should be retained and what their rotation policy should be. Most of these settings are configured through the log handler configuration, discussed earlier in this chapter and visualized in Figure 23-2.

The analytics defined for BPEL and BPMN processes—introduced in Chapter 20—can grow to fairly large data collections that we probably should create a scheduled purging strategy for. The same could apply to message reports and pipeline alerts produced by Service Bus projects. And somewhat ironically, any scheduled job will itself leave traces in the form of logging records that should be removed. ESS includes a facility to set up purging policies that define a schedule for removing audit records from scheduled job runs after a certain period.

Most attention in the area of purging should probably be given to the instance data produced by executing SOA composite instances.

SOA Composite Instance Data

Each SOA composite instance is associated with database records. Depending on the complexity of the composite application and, especially, the audit level that is configured for the entire soa-infra system or for individual SOA composites, the number of data records for a single instance can be quite large. It is strongly recommended to set the audit level (soa-infra drop-down menu, SOA Administration | Common Properties) to *Production* (or even to *Off*) in your production environment. You can override this setting for a specific SOA composite when there is a need for it.

In that same drop-down menu, the option SOA Administration | Auto Purge takes you to a page where you can configure a schedule for automatically purging details for past instances, see Figure 23-25. The key properties to define for auto purge are the interval for executing the purge job and the retention time for completed instances to specify which instances can be removed.

In addition to the *Auto Purge*, you can delete selected SOA composite instances in the Flow Instances tab at the level of the entire soa-infra, a complete partition or a specific SOA composite application. Using the search pane, you can retrieve your choice of instances. Using Click, CTRL+Click, SHIFT+Click you can compose a selection that with the icon for *Delete Selected* can all be deleted in one stroke.

Alternatively, you can run purge scripts in SQL to remove the instance data from the SOA infra database. Use one of the overloaded *delete_instances* procedures in the PL/SQL package *soa* in the SOA infra database schema.

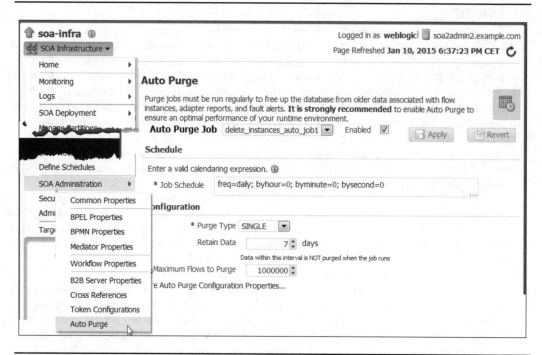

Figure 23-25. *Configuring the Auto Purge schedule(s) to rid the SOA infrastructure of obsolete instance data*

Summary

All the development effort in the world will be meaningless unless the developed products are successful at run time. The run-time value is achieved in a series of stages—that include deployment, configuration, monitoring and fault recovery, and problem resolution. This chapter discussed at length the many ways to learn about what is or was going on inside SOA Suite. Through log files, on screen reports and various types of alerts, data are provided, which describes the run-time activity of the SOA Suite.

This information is used to react to problems such as faulted instances, limited availability of services and unsatisfactory response times. Through the EM FMW Control and the Service Bus Console, many configuration settings determining primarily nonfunctional aspects of the service implementations can be modified. Developers can intentionally build customization into their artifacts, to allow run-time adjustments to satisfy changing requirements.

Ideally, the information gathered though monitoring is leveraged to be proactive and prevent the occurrence of future problems—for example, by extending capacity, freeing up resources by purging historic information and applying throttling mechanisms to prevent overload of the run-time environment.

CHAPTER
24

SOA Suite and Security

I f security is such an important topic, how can it be then that this is the last chapter? A fair
   question, with several possible answers. Security is towering over all other topics and/or it
   touches on all other areas already discussed. Security is to a large degree a cross cutting
concern that could have been discussed at almost any point in the book. Security is such a vast
topic that it really requires a book of its own—you can see this chapter as a stepping stone toward
this other book, and no more than that. Well, regardless of all these true answers to a valid
rhetorical question, it is only too often that security is an afterthought. So in that sense, this final
chapter should leave you with an urge to start at least thinking about security measures from the
beginning of your next project. Last in, first out, as it were.

Security can be compared with fire control. Ideally we prevent fires at all, by putting sensible
safety measures in place. Additionally we monitor for any signs of danger despite our prevention.
And once we detect such a warning sign, we act to stop the fire from spreading. Note that we also
run regular fire drills, to test our measures, detection mechanisms and procedures. Finally, we
keep a log of our findings and activities, for future analysis and accountability.

Some of the primary objectives organizations would have with IT security include:

- Prevent what is not supposed to happen, including disclosure of information to unauthorized
  parties, (D)DoS-attacks undermining availability, tempering of data in illicit ways.
- Allow what *is* supposed to happen.
- Monitor traffic and activities to detect any breach of security and respond appropriately.
- Create an audit trail recording selected activities for example for compliancy reporting.

In this chapter, we will look at various aspects of security in and round the SOA Suite. First we
will discuss access of human actors—administrators—to the SOA Suite run-time tooling and the
contents of service messages handled by service components. Next we look at accessibility of the
services themselves: how to prevent unwarranted use of the services exposed from the SOA Suite?
We briefly introduce many terms and concepts and some of the key standards with regard to
services and security. You may want to start with this second section—titled *Introduction of
Security in the World of Web Services*—if you are new to security (in SOA environments) or if
your main interest is securing of individual services rather than securing the platform.

Service security also stretches to the content of the messages sent to and from the services: we
need to protect the confidentiality of certain messages (prevent unauthorized parties from reading
them) as well as their integrity (make sure these messages cannot be tampered with).

Finally, after discussing various inbound challenges we also discuss how we can invoke
services from Service Bus and SOA composite applications, which are themselves protected by
security measures.

Human Access to Run-Time SOA Suite Tooling

People with access to the run-time tools used to monitor and administrate SOA Suite can see and do
many things. Abort process instances, open up or remove access to services, inspect the contents of
messages and change the logic in business rules. Clearly, access to these means has to be controlled
carefully and in accordance with the security governance rules defined for the organization.

In this section, we will discuss the roles required to access the relevant run-time tools. We
will look at how various sets of permissions acting on clusters of composite applications can be
withheld or granted. Finally we discuss how to hide sensitive pieces of information from
administrator's eyes through encryption.

Note that we are not discussing access to services or human tasks that are part of the custom developed software deployed on top of the SOA Suite platform but instead of access to the administrative tools that are part of the platform's run-time infrastructure.

Role-Based Authorization to Access Run-Time Tools

To be able to access the run-time administrative tooling—WebLogic Console, Enterprise Manager Fusion Middleware Control Console, SOA Composer, Service Bus Console, and BPM Workspace primary among them—one needs a user account defined in the identity store configured for the WebLogic domain. By default this is the embedded LDAP directory, accessed in WebLogic Admin Console under Security | myrealm. To access the SOA Suite run-time tools at all, a user needs a membership in one of the enterprise groups Monitors (preferred as it is the least powerful), Operators, Deployers, or Administrators. All other—fine grained—privileges are taken care of from the EM FMW Control.

In addition to the enterprise group to even rank as a user in the eyes of the soa-infra territory, the user account needs to be granted roles associated with the SOA partitions he gets access to. Access control of information is provided at partition level: users can only view the partitions and composites in those partitions to which they have access. EM FMW Control pages such as Flow Instances and Error Hospital show instance data filtered by partition, as does the audit trail. Application roles and partition roles consist of various combinations of Java permission classes and actions that describe in detail things to see or do.

We will now create a new user and grant some access privileges to a specific partition and its composites.

Create an Enterprise User in Embedded LDAP

Enter the WebLogic Administration Console (http://host:port/console). In the Domain Structure tree on the left of the page, click on Security Realms. Click on *myrealm*. Open the tab *Users and Groups*. Create a new user and specify a password. Open the tab Groups and create a membership for the new user in the group Monitors. Alternatively, create users from EM FMW Control: click on the WebLogic Domain | soa_domain node and select Security | Users and Groups from the dropdown menu. This takes you to the Users and Groups page.

Login to the EM FMW Control using the new account. This should succeed. However, there is not a whole lot you can do right now.

Try to login to the BPM Workspace (possible, yet no tasks are currently assigned to the user) and the SOA Composer (will fail with a message, correctly stating that the user is not authorized to access SOA metadata.

Grant SOA Partition Level Application Roles to the User

In order to allow the user to see and do more, application roles should be granted on the partition(s) that are relevant to the user.

For each partition that is created, SOA Suite will automatically create the following five partition specific application roles:

- Composer. For making changes to SOA composite application artifacts, such as business rules, security policies, fault policies, and so on.

- Deployer. For deploying new SOA composite applications, upgrading existing SOA composite applications, and managing the continuous integration and build process.

- Tester. For performing testing on preproduction systems typically using a combination of command line tools, Oracle Enterprise Manager Fusion Middleware Control, and custom user interfaces.

- Monitor. For the successful operation of deployed SOA composite applications in the partition.

- ApplicationOperator. For handling user complaints and making decisions on requests that result in faults in the automated process. An administrator receives notifications regarding these transactions and can take steps to recover from the fault or terminate the transaction. This role does not include the Deployer and Tester roles.

The name of the application role is specified using the name of the partition followed by _<role name>, such as *default_Composer*, and *finance_Monitor*.

The exact permissions associated with these application roles can be inspected in the EM FMW Control. Click on the node SOA | soa-infra and select Security | Application Policies from the drop-down menu. Click on the find icon to list all application roles. Then click on any application role. The associated permissions will be listed in the detailed Permissions table at the bottom of the page, as shown in Figure 24-1 for application role *finance_Monitor*.

Some of the permission actions that are discerned are change-state, test, delete, manage-fault, manage-alerts, read-alerts, migrate, read, write, lifecycle, provision. Note that in addition to the generated application roles, we can edit these roles or create our own, custom roles with custom clusters of permissions on selected resources.

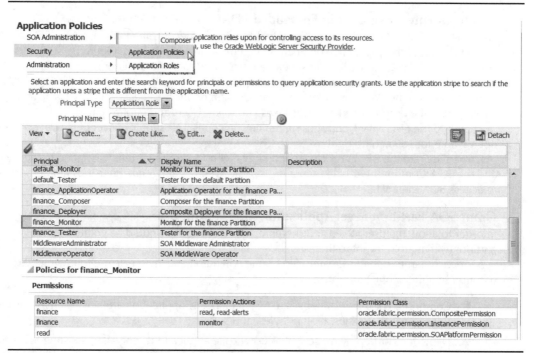

FIGURE 24-1. *Overview of the Application Roles and the associated Permissions for the role finance_Monitor. New roles can be created as well as permissions added or removed*

To grant an application role to a user, click on menu item Security | Application Roles in the SOA Infrastructure drop-down menu. A table with all Application Roles appears. Click on a role. Its current memberships appear in the detail table. Click on the Edit icon to open the application role editor where display name, description, and the role memberships can be modified.

Edit the application role default_monitor and add the newly created user as a member. Press OK to save this change.

Login to the EM FMW Control as the new user. Verify that this user can see the *default* partition. Check the tabs and menu options available to the user when you select the *default* partition—and compare to any other partition. When you also grant the application role *default_deployer*, you will notice more tabs and options becoming accessible to the user.

NOTE
The Application roles MiddlewareOperator and MiddlewareAdministrator *are Oracle SOA Suite-wide—not limited to a specific partition. The latter role provides backup for operational roles and super user access to perform any tasks required for the continued operation of Oracle SOA Suite. The former provides capabilities to ensure the continued operation of Oracle SOA Suite, including permissions to adjust operational settings such as the audit level; to configure error notification rules; to enable, disable, and monitors composites; and manages composite sensors. Needless to say that these roles should be handed out to users with the utmost care.*

Additionally, there are other SOA Suite-wide, more tailored roles: SOA Designer, SOAAuditViewer, SOAAuditAdmin, SOAMonitor, SOAOperator, and SOAAdmin with specific sets of permissions.

Access Privileges for Service Bus Tooling

To grant users access to specific data and functions in the Service Bus components such as the Service Bus Console and the SB sections of EM FMW Control, you define user accounts, groups, application roles, and policies, just as we discussed above. Through the run-time Service Bus Console, development can be done on all types of resources in Service Bus projects; without formal deployment cycle, the run-time service resources can be modified. Needless to say, access to the privilege to make such changes should be zealously governed. To give users access to administrative functions, such as creating proxy services, you assign them to predefined application roles with predefined access privileges. You can also create user groups and assign those groups to the predefined roles in order to give the same access permissions to a group of users. You cannot change the access privileges for the application roles, but you can grant individual access permissions to users and groups along with the default roles.

Service Bus provides eight default application roles, each of which provide a specific set of access permissions that are common to a specific category of user.

- MiddlewareAdministrator—administrative security role with complete access to all resources and services in Service Bus.

- Developer—designed for use in development and testing environments only, and is not intended for production; has full access to Service Bus features in the SB Console and

FMW Control; but unlike MiddlewareAdministrators, Developers cannot add, edit, or delete users or application roles, or see sessions owned by other users.

- Composer—full access to monitoring and management features in FMW Control (except import and export); view-only access to SB Console. The responsibilities of this role will increase in future releases.

- Deployer—full access to the monitoring and management features in FMW Control and SB Console, with the exception of updating security policies and resolving resequencing errors.

- Tester—read-only access to SB Console, and to the monitoring and management features in FMW Control. This role has full access to the Test Console in both.

- MiddlewareOperator—access to certain monitoring tasks and session management, and has read access to all Service Bus resources; also create, view, edit, and delete alert rules and alert destinations, and to view and edit operational settings.

- ApplicationOperator—read-only access to the SB Console and FMW Control. It has full access to the Resequence Groups tab. Application operators receive notifications on faults and can take corrective action by recovering faults, skipping the message, or aborting a transaction.

- Monitor—granted to users who monitor SLA alerts, pipeline alerts, resources, and services in SB Console and FMW Control.

To grant users access privileges allowing them to use features of Service Bus, they should first be made a member of the Monitors group. Next, in EM FMW Control, right click on the node SOA | service-bus. Select menu option Security | Application Roles from the context menu. In the page that appears, select Application Stripe Service_Bus_Console in the drop-down field and press the search icon. The eight roles for Service Bus that were mentioned previously are listed now. To grant one of these application roles to the user, click on the role and then on the Edit icon. In the Application Role editor page that you are taken to, the application role can be granted to Users, Groups and other Application Roles.

Hide Sensitive Data in Logging and Consoles

Even though human actors may require access to the composites and their instances in a certain partition for administrative responsibilities, that does not necessarily mean they should be able to see the entire contents of the messages processed by these composite instances. While visibility of some data may be required for monitoring and fault handling purposes, other data may be so sensitive that administrators should not be able to read it, even in case of errors—neither in the console nor in log files.

SOA Suite provides a mechanism through which sensitive data can be encrypted, as soon as the message containing that data enters the run-time environment until such as time as the message leaves again. All that can be seen in the run-time tooling, the SOA Infra database table or the log files of the sensitive data elements—such as social security numbers, credit card numbers, passwords—is unintelligible encrypted data. Note that this mechanism complements message security policies that enforces message encryption on messages en route to or from SOA Suite. These policies are discussed later in this chapter.

We will go through a simple example of applying this field level encryption to a simple service operation. This turns out to be the first example of applying a security policy to a service binding and a reference binding. This mechanism of applying policies on top of services—without distorting the implementation of the service at all—is typical of the quite powerful way in which SOA Suite approaches security as a decoupled, cross cutting concern.

Configure Encryption/Decryption Key in the Credential Store Framework

The key to be used for encryption and decryption of sensitive data elements in the messages processed by our composites is retrieved from the Credential Store Framework (CSF). CSF is a facility into which to store credentials—security data that certify the authority of entities—that can be used at run time by security policies. CSF stores password credentials—a username and password—and generic credentials that can hold any credential object.

To create a credential to use for the encryption of sensitive data, open EM FMW Control. Click on the WebLogic Domain | domain node and select menu option Security | Credentials. On the Credentials page, check if a map called oracle.wsm.security already exists. If it does not, click on the green plus icon to Create Map and create this map. Click on Create Key. In the dialog that opens, select map oracle.wsm.security, set the Key to *pii-csf-key (pii = personal identifiable information)*, enter username and password of the WebLogic root account (weblogic most likely), and optionally provide a description, as shown in Figure 24-2. Click on OK to create the key. This name of the key is the default that you can replace with another if you want.

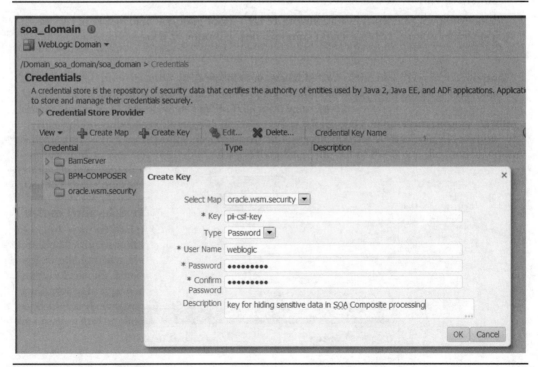

FIGURE 24-2. *Configuring the key pii-csf-key for the encryption of sensitive data in messages processed in SOA composite applications*

Encrypt the Request Message at the Composite Edge

Encryption of sensitive data is configured at the Service Binding of a composite. Before the processing of the request message in the composite starts, the encryption already has taken place. We will assume a simple SOA composite application called *SuperSensitiveComposite*, with a single BPEL process. The composite exposes a service with a single operation that takes a request messages that contain a social security number. This element should be treated as sensitive and has to be encrypted inside the SOA Suite runtime. Note again that what we are about to do will do nothing to protect the message or the social security number outside of the SOA Suite; that is what security policies are used for.

To achieve this, open the composite editor. Right click on service binding. Select menu option Protect Sensitive Data | Encrypt Request Data, as shown in Figure 24-3.

A popup appears that specifies the oracle/pii_security_policy as the one to apply, see Figure 24-4. This policy can be enabled and disabled in this popup using the icon in the upper right hand corner. Click on the edit icon to define one or more XPath expressions for the elements in the request messages that should be encrypted. A two-step wizard appears. In the first step, define the XPath expression(s) for the to-be encrypted message content. In the second step, specify key pii-csf-key—or your own defined key name—as the reference to the credential in the CSF.

If you now deploy the composite application and send a request message with a *socialSecurityNumber*, you will discover in the BPEL audit trail that whatever value you set for this element has been replaced by an encrypted value, see Figure 24-5.

Sensitive Values at the Reference Binding

The configuration of the encryption of the Social Security Element at the service binding in the SOA composite was certainly effective. So effective that the call to the back-end system that does the final processing of the message will contain the encrypted value—unless we take some

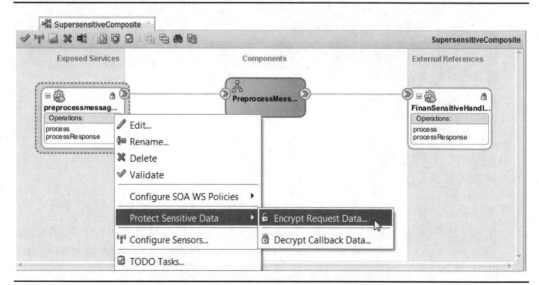

FIGURE 24-3. *Configure encryption for sensitive data elements in inbound messages*

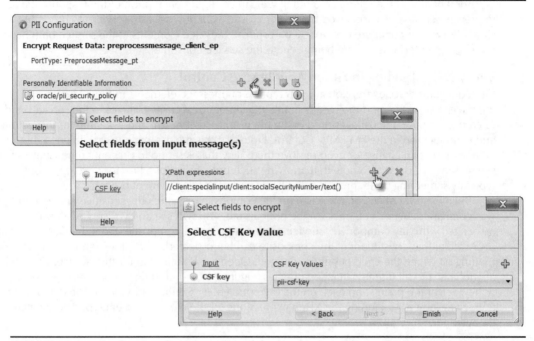

FIGURE 24-4. *Configuring the encryption of the sensitive socialSecurityNumber element*

action. This action consists of configuring Decryption of selected message elements in the Reference Bindings where the outgoing calls take place from the SOA composite.

The little lock icon visible on the reference binding in Figure 24-3 is indicative of the decryption [policy] that has been configured. By right clicking on the reference binding and selecting menu option Protect Sensitive Data | Decrypt Request Data, we can configure decryption on the element that contains the social security number in the message sent to the business service.

FIGURE 24-5. *The payload as shown in the BPEL Audit Trail now contains an encrypted value*

Additionally, at the reference binding we can configure encryption of the response message— to prevent sensitive data received by the composite from downstream services to be visible and similarly, we can configure decryption of response message elements at the service binding to prevent encrypted values from being sent to the service consumer.

Verify Policy Binding in Fusion Middleware Control

Our configuration of encryption and decryption on message elements in the JDeveloper user interface, resulted behind the scenes in the attachment of security policies to the services and references of the composite—stored in the file wsm-assembly.xml and available for inspection and manipulation in the EM FMW Control. Note that this means that a user with enough authorization can change or even remove the policy that is set up to prevent administrators from seeing sensitive data. Also note that applying such policies is not a task for developers but typically something done through scripting as part of the deployment process.

Open the EM FMW Control. Click on the composite on which the sensitive data encryption was configured. When you click on the policies tab, you will see an overview of all policies associated with any component, service or reference in this composite. From the Dashboard tab, every individual constituent of the composite can be inspected. Click, for example, on the service binding on which the encryption was defined. Open the Policies tab for this service. The tab lists all globally and all directly attached policies (Figure 24-6), including the oracle/pii_security_ policy. Select the policy and click on the Override Policy Configuration icon. The details for the policy are shown—including the XPath expressions for the elements to encrypt. These details can be overridden as well.

Encryption and Decryption of Message Elements in Service Bus

Service Bus pipelines are very likely also carriers of sensitive data that should be hidden from view. Consoles and logging contain not a lot, if any, information when the lean SB machine is executing services. However, through message reports, log actions, and pipeline alerts, there is the possibility of sensitive data being exposed. This can be prevented using the same approach as with SOA composites.

Open the overview editor for the Service Bus project. Right click the proxy service for which message elements have to be encrypted. Select the context menu Configure OSB WS Policies. The Policies tab in the proxy service editor opens.

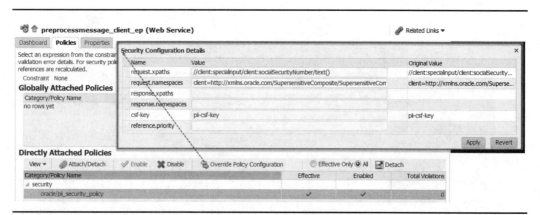

FIGURE 24-6.   *Details of Policy Attachment to the Service Binding*

Scroll down the page to the last category: Personally Identifiable Information. Click on the plus icon to configure the policy. The oracle/pii_security_policy is displayed. Click on the edit icon to configure the message elements to encrypt and the CSF key to use, just as we did earlier in this section for the service binding in a SOA composite application.

For business services, the same procedure is followed to configure the PII policy to decrypt elements leaving the Service Bus.

Introduction of Security in the World of Web Services

Before going into any implementation details regarding web service security, we have to set the stage by introducing a number of terms and technologies. For the purpose of this chapter, we will use some working definitions that you should know and of whose fairly limited scope in this book you should be aware.

Some Security Terminology

A few definitions and introductions to determine the scope of these terms as assumed here is in order. Note that the limited space in this chapter means that we can do no justice to this topic and really provide hardly more than some introduction and a little inspiration.

Identity Management

Identity management is the administration of identities and relevant information (name, job title, password). It provides services for the retrieval and administration of identity information. Identities can represent both human actors, such as employees, patients, suppliers, and applications, as well as virtual entities, such as (internal and external) services, organizations as a whole and applications. Different rules, responsibilities, and administration may apply to each of these categories.

Identity management includes identity propagation: the mechanism to "pass" identity information within a chain of IT components invoking each other. For example, a client might invoke an order service that in turn invokes a payment service. Usually you want a service provider to authenticate the original consumer: the person (or service) that started the chain of service calls, and not some intermediary component such as an ESB. The *initial* service consumer is allowed (or denied) access to your services and information, not intermediary infrastructure components (middleware) that can never act on their own accord. In this example, the payment service needs to authenticate and authorize the client, not the order service or ESB. This implies that intermediary components between service consumer and provider need to be able to transport identity information such as certificates and possibly transform these from one format or protocol into another (e.g., from SSO token into a username/password combination, or from HTTP Basic Authentication to a WS-Security username token).

Every identity in the identity store usually maps to a specific person or IT component. These identities can be members of a larger organization structure such as a department of the company. This results in a hierarchy of identities. In case of external organizations that are allowed access to your services, you should consider the tradeoff between using specific identities (employee "Doe" of organization "Acme") versus more general identities (organization "Acme" as a whole). Specific identities result in better traceability and can provide for more fine-grained access control, whereas more "coarse-grained" identities result in less administrative burden. You might want to avoid generic identities such as "consultant" and "trainee" altogether due to lack of traceability.

Provisioning is the process of synchronizing identity-related information between various identity management systems (in an automated fashion). One of these systems is usually the "source" identity store that provisions (sends) changes to other identity management solutions.

When identity propagation and administration span more than one organization (crossing an organization's boundary), we speak of "identity federation."

A best practice is to use as little centralized identity stores as possible. This avoids duplicate or inconsistent identities and decreases user management efforts. Be careful in allowing externally hosted services and other organizations direct access to your identity management solution. Consider provisioning to an external organization's IAM solution as an alternative in such cases to minimize security risks.

Authentication

Authentication (or identification) is the process of verifying that an identity is who he, she, or it claims to be. Authentication mechanisms are usually based on something an identity knows (username/password combination), something an identity possesses (key, telephone, private key), a unique property of an identity (fingerprint or iris pattern), or a combination of all these.

Best practice is to define a limited set of authentication levels based on the mechanisms described here. For example, "basic" authentication requires knowledge (username/password), "medium" authentication requires knowledge and possession (username/password and token), and "high" authentication requires verification through a biometric property (iris scan).

Authentication also includes Single Sign-On (SSO), a mechanism in which an identity only needs to authenticate once while getting access to several IT components. SSO improves user friendliness and results in a better user experience. For example, a user logs on to a Windows workstation and because of SSO does not need to log in to Outlook and intranet applications. SSO is all about trust: A service needs to verify and trust the SSO component to which it delegates authentication. It also needs to trust the identity-related information received by the SSO component. SSO infrastructure can be used for identity propagation using, for example, Security Assertion Markup Language (SAML) tokens. Identity propagation can be seen as a way to achieve SSO. Single Sign-Off is the opposite of Single Sign-On.

Authorization

Authorization involves the administration, establishment, and enforcement of access rights for *authenticated* identities within a given context. Authorization should be based on the function someone or some organization needs to do and know; no more, no less. A best practice is to avoid "super users"; that is, staff (usually management and IT administrators) who over time have gathered more privileges than they are entitled to.

A very common authorization model is Role-Based Access Control (RBAC). In this model, identities belong to one or more groups. Access rights to IT components are granted to groups instead of being directly coupled to identities (no "lock-in" on specific employees). This greatly reduces the cost and effort to administer authorizations and keeps them up to date. Groups are often based on attributes that do not frequently change over time, such as organizational units (finance, IT, marketing) and functions (senior controller, database administrator, nurse), even when the identities belonging to those roles *do* change. RBAC can furthermore simplify "separation of concerns" so that different roles (and thus different persons if we ensure that combinations or roles cannot be assigned to the same person) need to be involved in decision making within a single process. We used RBAC earlier in this book when discussing the assignment of human tasks.

A frequently used term is "anonymous" to indicate an unauthenticated identity as well as a special authorization role that usually indicates that everyone has the right to access certain information or services, including unauthenticated identities.

"Hard" IT Security

This type of security includes confidentiality and integrity of data and more technical security, including the protection of networks and infrastructure using firewalls, (reverse) proxies, intrusion detection systems (IDS), intrusion prevention systems (IPS), virus scanners, and so on.

Confidentiality (or exclusivity) of information is about restricting access to data and messages to those identities that are allowed to view (and possibly modify) this data. Integrity (or reliability) of information is about ensuring data and messages to be complete, valid, and unaltered by (possibly malicious) unauthorized identities. Encryption using public key infrastructure (PKI) is a common implementation to ensure confidentiality and detection of integrity violations. See the "WS-Security (WSS)" section for more information on the use of encryption for message confidentiality and integrity.

Together with confidentiality and integrity, availability forms the so-called "CIA triad." Availability of information, availability threats (denial-of-service attacks, single points of failure), and measures to ensure availability (clustering, failover) are out of scope for this book.

"Hard" IT security is often divided into various layers such as network security, platform and operating system security, application security, integrity and confidentiality, content security, and mobile security. For each layer, specific measures can be applied to increase overall security. Examples of such measures include dividing networks in segments and specifying fixed network routes (network security), having a central list of allowed and disallowed file extensions for inbound and outbound traffic (content security), and the use of hardening (platform and application security). *Hardening* refers to the process of securing a system (operating system, application, and so on) by means of ridding it of all unnecessary features (e.g., removing unnecessary OS services).

"Soft" security, such as security education and awareness (employees Twittering sensitive information), as well as "physical" security, including fire alarms, metal detectors, and bodyguards, are out of scope for this chapter and this book.

Logging, Monitoring, and Auditing

Logging, monitoring, and auditing encompass:

- Recording of all access to and manipulation of sensitive data—even when the activity was correctly authorized

- Storing and accessing relevant events and related information such as the time and location of (failed) authentication attempts

- Notifying stakeholders (such as administrators) in case of suspicious behavior, for example, when an identity accesses a secured service from different geographical locations within a few minutes

Functionality and processes in an SOA are spread over different loosely coupled components. Some logging and monitoring needs to be executed on a higher level—composite service or process level—than on the level of an elementary service. This gives rise to the need for a central logging and monitoring component that is able to combine and correlate decentralized logs and enable monitoring on the process level.

Transport versus Message Security

In the realm of services, there are two levels typically at stake when implementing authentication—confidentiality and integrity. One focuses on the transport layer and the other on the messages themselves. Because we do not have an explicit login step—as with human users of a web application—we need a fully automated mechanism that covers both authentication and authorization.

Transport security secures a message only during transport between service consumer and service provider by using a secured transport layer—for example, using HTTP over SSL/TLS (HTTPS). That means messages are not protected in intermediary components such as an ESB and are equally unprotected directly after being received by the service endpoint. This implies that even though the message was secure during transport, *after* its delivery to an SOA composite, the message contents are directly visible to the components within the composite and are also readable to administrators who can view the message flow within composites in a console such as Enterprise Manager. This might not be acceptable for very sensitive information such as credit card data or patients' medical records.

Message security secures the message itself, often through encryption of the payload using, for example, PKI and WS-Security (WSS). Because message security can provide security in the scope you want and need—and also in intermediaries and after the message has been received—it is generally preferable over transport security in implementing stricter security requirements, although usually the two are used together. The difference is shown in Figure 24-7. The top part of the figure displays message security, and the lower part displays transport security.

Both transport and message security can be used for authentication purposes and to guarantee message integrity and confidentiality. The following sections dive into the most common implementations in Oracle SOA Suite for transport security using SSL/TLS and message security using WS-Security, as well as how authentication, integrity, and confidentiality can be achieved.

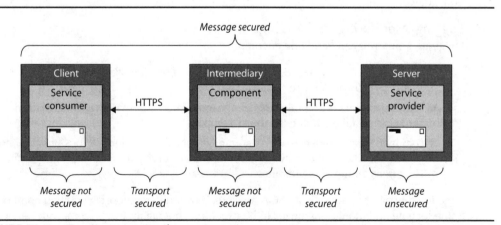

FIGURE 24-7. *Transport security (bottom) versus message security (top)*

Secure Sockets Layer (SSL) or Transport Layer Security (TLS)

A frequent interaction pattern in a service-oriented landscape is invocation of web services using SOAP or REST over HTTP. The HTTP transport layer can be secured using TLS (Transport Layer Security). TLS is an encryption protocol and IETF standard for securing network communications such as over the Internet. Secure Sockets Layer (SSL) is the predecessor of TLS. TLS can be used in combination with other protocols such as HTTP, FTP, SMTP, and LDAP. TLS is a possible implementation to realize a virtual private network (VPN). Current versions are TLS 1.2 and SSL 3. Applying TLS can significantly reduce the overhead involved by removing the need to encode keys and message signatures into XML before sending associated with message level security.

This section won't go into the nitty-gritty details of the protocol but rather outlines its mechanism. TLS can be applied one way (or unilaterally), meaning that the server authenticates to the client using a signature. Server authentication is required, for example, for online banking. A client wants to know that he is really using the bank's online banking application and not some look-a-like website used by a hacker to retrieve his banking data (known as "website spoofing").

Authentication in SSL/TLS is achieved by means of a signature that's generated by the server using its private key. The private key used for authentication should only be known to the server. The client validates the signature using the corresponding public key by means of a trusted digital certificate that is issued by a Certificate Authority (CA). If validation succeeds, the client knows that the server is who it claims to be (server authentication). This ends the "handshake" between server and client. Two-way TLS (mutual authentication) is also possible. This means that the client also sends a signature using its private key to the server so the server can verify the client's identity.

The public and private key pair and a mutually agreed random number are then used to encrypt, hash, and decrypt the information that is sent from client to server, and vice versa, thus ensuring integrity and confidentiality. To use SSL, you must set up keystores and truststores in your environment.

SSL/TLS support—enabling HTTPS communication—is realized through Oracle WebLogic Server on which SOA Suite runs. We will discuss a little later how to enable secure message transport by invoking a service over HTTPS.

WS-Security (WSS)

WS-Security is the most important web service standard to achieve message security. The WS-Security standard is supported by the policy-based security framework of Oracle Web Services Manager that can be used to secure SCA composites and Service Bus services. WSS is an OASIS standard that uses SOAP messaging to secure messages independent of the transport layer that is used. WSS provides end-to-end security, from service consumer to service provider, through all intermediate components as compared to the point-to-point security between servers provided by SSL/TLS. OASIS released WSS version 1.0 in 2004 and version 1.1 in 2006. WS-Security supports authentication, confidentiality, and integrity:

- **Authentication.** WSS adds authentication data—which identifies the service consumer—to a SOAP message using one of the different token types: UserNameToken Profile (username with clear text or digest password combination), X.509 Certificate Token Profile, SAML Token Profile, or Kerberos Token Profile.

- **Confidentiality.** The identity that sends a message uses the public key of the identity that *should* receive the message (e.g., the service provider) to encrypt the message contents using an encryption algorithm such as RSA. Only the owner of the corresponding private key (again, the service provider) is able to decrypt the message contents.

- **Integrity.** The identity that sends a message uses its private key to generate a signature. The signature contains a "digest" of the message contents; this is called "hashing." You cannot re-create a message from its digest. Any change in the message can be detected because the digest in the signature no longer corresponds to the altered contents of the message. The identity that receives the message uses the sender's public key to decrypt the signature. If the signature is decrypted successfully, it knows the sender is authentic because only the holder of the private key could have created a signature that can be decrypted using the public key. The receiver can then use the digest to verify the message contents have not been altered during transport. The XML Digital Signature (XML-DSig) standard is often used as XML syntax for digital signatures.

Figure 24-8 shows what it looks like when all these WS-Security aspects are applied to a SOAP message (header and body).

Consider the following unsecured SOAP message. This is a sample request message for the Acme Web Service that exposes the operation "echoMe":

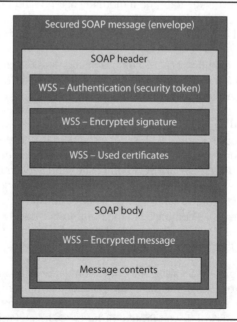

FIGURE 24-8. *Secured SOAP message with WS-Security*

```
<soapenv:Envelope
    xmlns:soapenv="http://schemas.xmlsoap.org/soap/envelope/"
    xmlns:acme="http://acmewebservice/">
  <soapenv:Header/>
  <soapenv:Body>
    <acme:echoMe>Hello World!</acme:echoMe>
  </soapenv:Body>
</soapenv:Envelope>
```

We now use the WS-Security standard to apply security to the Web Service request message enforcing authentication, integrity, and encryption. When trying to invoke the web service without adding the corresponding WS-Security information, we might get the following fault message:

```
<env:Envelope xmlns:env="http://schemas.xmlsoap.org/soap/envelope/">
  <env:Header/>
  <env:Body>
    <!-- Fault message -->
    <env:Fault xmlns:wsse="http://docs.oasis-open.org/wss/2004/01/...
                        ...oasis-200401-wss-wssecurity-secext-1.0.xsd">
      <faultcode>wsse:InvalidSecurity</faultcode>
      <faultstring>Missing <wsse:Security> in SOAP Header</faultstring>
      <faultactor/>
    </env:Fault>
  </env:Body>
</env:Envelope>
```

With the required WS-Security information applied, the header of the resulting secured message may look like this (depending on the selected encryption algorithms, key identifier type, and so on):

```
<soapenv:Header>
  <wsse:Security xmlns:wsse="http://docs.oasis-open.org/wss/2004/01/...
                        ...oasis-200401-wss-wssecurity-secext-1.0.xsd">
<!-- X.509 certificate used for encryption -->
    <wsse:BinarySecurityToken ValueType="wsse:X509v3">
    MIICUTCCAbqgA...awxekHKkTWS2az
    </wsse:BinarySecurityToken>
    <!-- X.509 certificate used for signature -->
    <wsse:BinarySecurityToken ValueType="wsse: X509v3">
    MIICRzCCAbCgA...9ssBsDFmgT2AS0=
    </wsse:BinarySecurityToken>
    <Signature>
      <SignedInfo>
        <!-- message hash (digest) -->
        <DigestValue>odVp0oTtu7BRBJhAxgxSMQssRdI=</DigestValue>
        <!-- signature -->
        <SignatureValue>H7MoXu2JdPx2...HOVdTqrylXDAg=</SignatureValue>
      </SignedInfo>
    </Signature>
```

```
          <!-- clear text authentication -->
          <wsse:UsernameToken>
             <wsse:Username>acme</wsse:Username>
             <wsse:Password>mypassword</wsse:Password>
          </wsse:UsernameToken>
          <!-- timestamp -->
          <Timestamp>
             <Created>2010-04-16T21:10:09Z</Created>
             <Expires>2010-04-17T05:10:09Z</Expires>
          </Timestamp>
       </wsse:Security>
    </Header>
```

The following snippet shows a SOAP message body containing the encrypted request data:

```
<soapenv:Body>
    <!-- header indicating the message body contains encrypted data -->
    <xenc:EncryptedData
        Id="_Dff7ySASsISfb2H31osV8A22"
        Type="http://www.w3.org/2001/04/xmlenc#Content">
       <!-- encryption algorithm -->
       <xenc:EncryptionMethod Algorithm="http://www.w3.org/2001/04/...
                                                ...xmlenc#aes128-cbc"/>
       <!-- encrypted message data -->
       <xenc:CipherData>
          <xenc:CipherValue>LljX08Z3ujA3lsA1+p0E...TaG3WiWm7qA==</xenc:CipherValue>
       </xenc:CipherData>
    </xenc:EncryptedData>
```

Note that applying security such as WS-Security introduces additional challenges. Messages are encrypted and additional information is scarce (because elaborate error messages containing implementation details may pose an additional security risk and therefore *exception shielding* is applied). The very reason to shield unauthorized people also results in the administrator's job becoming more difficult.

Security Products around SOA Suite

The implementation of security for services in SOA Suite leverages platform facilities in WebLogic and SOA Suite and usually external products—software and hardware appliances—as well, to, for example, manage and store identities and provide perimeter security.

The first line of defense with regards to external service consumers is typically composed of a firewall, a load balancer, and an API management facility such as Oracle API Gateway (to handle message screening, do first level throttling to prevent DDOS, do IP filtering and protect against SQL Injection). Oracle Mobile Security Suite and/or Oracle Access Manager (OAM) can also be part of this perimeter guard.

Once requests have made it from the DMZ inside the corporate firewall, they may arrive at the edge of WebLogic domain running the SOA Suite run-time engines. At this point, it is typically the combination of OPSS (Oracle Platform Security Services) and OWSM (Oracle Web Services Manager), possibly with OAM, that enforces the security measures.

Introducing OPSS—Oracle Platform Security Services

OPSS is WebLogic's abstraction layer on top of security functionality and tooling. OPSS provides a set of APIs that can be used by Java and Java EE applications to realize security. These APIs cover authentication, authorization, SSO, auditing, policy management, user and role management, and so on. OPSS supports the SAML, XACML, JACC, and JAAS standards. OPSS is used by Oracle's own components running on WebLogic Server, including Oracle SOA Suite and OWSM. OPSS takes care, for example, of the authentication and authorization of requests, using the security providers that it was configured to use and interacting with possibly a wide variety of LDAP implementations—including OUD, Microsoft Active Directory, OVD, OID, Novell eDirectory, and OpenLDAP.

Introducing Oracle Web Services Manager

Oracle Web Services Manager (OWSM) provides a policy framework to manage and secure web services consistently across your organization. It provides capabilities to build, enforce, run and monitor web service policies, such as security, reliable messaging, MTOM, and addressing policies. OWSM can be used by both developers, at design time, and system administrators in production environments. OWSM provides business agility to respond to security threats and security breaches by allowing policy changes to be enforced in real time without the need to interrupt the running business processes.

OWSM is used to secure Java EE (JAX-WS and JAX-RS) Web Services and Oracle Infrastructure Web Services such as SOA composites, ESS, ADF, and Service Bus services. This section provides an overview of OWSM's architecture and briefly discusses all relevant concepts of OWSM, such as policies, assertions, policy store, and policy administration. OWSM is tightly integrated with Oracle WebLogic Server and collaborates closely with the OPSS.

Architecture of OWSM

OWSM's policy framework is based on the WS-Policy standard. A *policy* is a concrete, bounded, and specific piece of security functionality—for example, an authentication policy that verifies a given username/password using an LDAP server or a management policy that logs request and response messages. One or more policies can be applied to a service to provide both inbound and outbound security, thereby fulfilling its security requirements. A policy is reusable, meaning that the same policy can be applied to more than one service. Policies often need to be *configured* for the specific service they are applied to—for example, when providing a username/password combination for an authentication policy.

Figure 24-9 depicts the various components of the OWSM framework.

The actual enforcement of policies that are applied to services is achieved using *policy interceptors*. These make sure that inbound and outbound messages are intercepted and the policies are also executed.

For some policies, the actual security implementation is delegated to Oracle WebLogic Server using the Oracle Platform Security Services (OPSS) APIs—for example, authentication and authorization policies that leverage WebLogic's LDAP-based authentication and authorization provider.

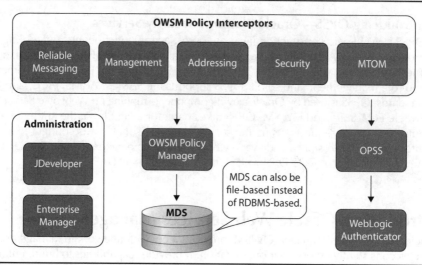

FIGURE 24-9. *Overview of OWSM*

Policy definitions and other metadata—such as policy sets, assertions templates, and policy usage data—are stored in the Meta Data Store (MDS), in the OWSM Repository. Access to the policy definitions in the MDS is achieved through OWSM Policy Manager. This means that policies are centrally managed (MDS, Policy Manager, and Enterprise Manager) and enforced at run time per service.

You can use Enterprise Manager as well as WLST scripting to define, apply, configure, manage, and monitor policies. JDeveloper can only be used to *apply* policies to services.

Policies and Policy Assertions

Policy assertions are the smallest building blocks when it comes to security (Figure 24-10). Assertions provide a basic security capability such as a logging capability, encryption capability, or authentication capability. Policies are created by combining one or more assertions in a sequence (a "pipeline") to provide a larger reusable piece of security functionality—for example, a policy that contains an assertion to log an inbound encrypted message, followed by an assertion to decrypt that message, and finally another logging assertion to log the decrypted message. Another example is a policy containing an authentication and subsequent authorization assertion.

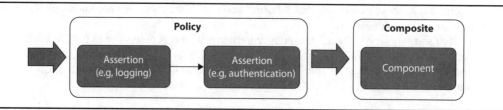

FIGURE 24-10. *Policies are composed of assertions*

OWSM provides a set of out-of-the-box policies and assertion templates on which concrete assertions are based. Next to that, OWSM provides a mechanism to create your own policies and assertions.

OWSM differentiates assertions and policies into the following categories:

- **Security.** Policies for identity propagation, authentication, authorization, confidentiality, and integrity. These policies, among others, implement the WS-Security 1.0 and 1.1 standards. This is the only OWSM policy type that can be applied to JAX-WS Web Services.

- **WS-Addressing.** Policies that support the WS-Addressing standard for including transport information in messages.

- **Message Transmission Optimization Mechanism (MTOM) attachments.** Policies that support the transmission of binary content (attachments) between services. MTOM is applied to reduce message size.

- **Reliable messaging.** Policies that support the WS-Reliable Messaging standard. This standard is used for guaranteed (one-time) delivery of messages and to guarantee the order in which messages are delivered.

- **Management.** Policies that provide logging capabilities for messages (request, response, and fault messages).

Applying Policies

Policies can be applied to service consumers as well as service providers. Suppose message confidentially is required between a service and its clients, and message security is used to realize this. In this case, the service consumer—for example, a reference binding in a composite—can apply a policy to encrypt an outbound message, whereas the service provider uses a policy to decrypt the inbound message.

Looking specifically at SOA composites, policies can be applied to the following:

- **Service bindings.** Securing exposed services for inbound messages

- **Reference bindings.** Applying security to outbound messages

- **Components.** A subset of management (logging) and security (authorization) policies can be applied to components within a composite

Policies can be associated with services using Enterprise Manager, WSLT or JDeveloper. Policy definition, configuration, and management can only be done through Enterprise Manager and partially with WLST.

Policy Enforcement

Policies are enforced using so-called "interceptors." Policies are executed in a specific order based on their type, as shown in Figure 24-11.

Policies are often "two-way," meaning that they are enforced on inbound and outbound communication channels, but in reverse order. For example, if you attach a policy that enforces encryption through WS-Security to an exposed synchronous two-way service (request/reply), you will enforce encryption on the incoming payload (request) as well as the outbound payload (response). This is only the case for applicable policies; for example, applying authorization to a request message will not result in outbound authorization for the response message that is sent back to the client.

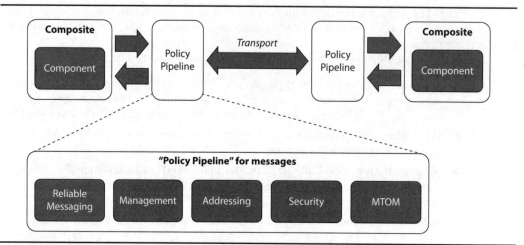

FIGURE 24-11. *Policies are executed in a specific order*

Local Optimization

Oracle SOA Suite uses various protocols and bindings based on its run-time environment and configuration. In case composites run in the same Oracle WebLogic Server or Oracle WebLogic Server cluster, local optimization is applied for invocations from one composite to the other, where possible. This means native Java calls are used instead of the SOAP protocol. In this case, some OWSM policies will not be enforced. If you want to make sure policies are enforced, you can use one or both of the following options:

Disable local optimization between composites. This will result in OWSM policies being enforced but also introduces a slight performance penalty. You can turn off local optimization by adding a property to a reference in the composite.xml file of the client composite. The composite will invoke another composite using SOAP/XML via HTTP rather than the optimized native binary binding.

```
<reference name="MyExternalService" ui:wsdlLocation="MyReference.wsdl">
   <property name = "oracle.webservices.local.optimization">false</property>
</reference>
```

Set the "local optimization control" property of a policy in Enterprise Manager. You can indicate per policy if local optimization is used.

Policy Administration and Monitoring

Oracle provides the following tools for the administration of policies:

■ **Enterprise Manager Fusion Middleware Control Console.** Enterprise Manager is the most comprehensive tool available for policy administration and monitoring. During the remainder of this chapter, you will explore some of its security-related capabilities. These include applying policies to composites, configuring policies and assertions that are applied to composites, viewing the available policies and assertions, run-time monitoring of policies, assertions and possible security violations, and configuring new policies.

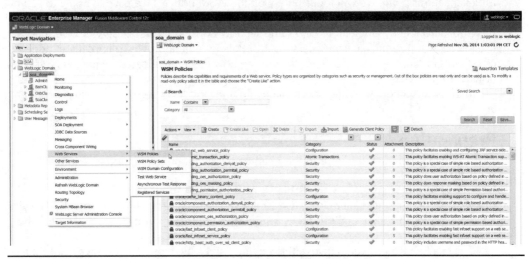

FIGURE 24-12.   *Using Enterprise Manager to view the available policies*

- **JDeveloper.**   JDeveloper can (only) be used to apply policies to composites. This chapter shows an example of how to do this.

- **WLST (WebLogic Scripting Tool).**   WLST provides OWSM-specific scripts for policy administration, such as importing and exporting policies. WLST is outside the scope of this chapter.

Let's inspect the policies and assertions that are available "out of the box." Log in to Enterprise Manager. In the overview panel, open the WebLogic Domain node, right-click the SOA Suite domain, and select Web Services | WSM Policies (Figure 24-12).

This will open the Web Services Policies overview. Here, you can filter on category (MTOM, security, and so on), view policy descriptions, and more. Click the Web Services Assertion Templates link to view the available assertion templates. The out-of-the-box policy and assertion template names have a specific format. It is a best practice to follow these naming conventions when we create our own policies and assertions later on.

Custom Policy Assertions

You can create custom policy assertions if you need security features above and beyond those provided by the default set of out-of-the-box policy assertions. A custom policy assertion is implemented in Java. The custom assertion class must extend oracle.wsm.policyengine.impl. AssertionExecutor. The execute method that needs to be implemented takes an input parameter of type IContext that provides access to many aspects of the request and the message and allow inspection and even manipulation of these. The book's website provides a resource that describes the creation and application of a custom policy assertion in great detail.

Authentication and Authorization of Services

In this section, we will enforce authentication and authorization policies for a very simple service exposed by a SOA composite application. The functionality implemented in the composite is irrelevant at this point, we will focus purely on the WSM policies we have to apply to achieve the non-functional, security requirements. Subsequently we will front the service with a Service Bus public front end—and enforce the same security constraints on this service. We will also use the Service Bus mechanism Access Control Policies that allows us to implement additional constraints for accessing the service. We will see how the authenticated identity can be passed to downstream services.

In the next section, we will add message and transport level security to ensure confidentiality and integrity of the message.

Preparation

To be able to go through the steps in this chapter, a little bit of preparation is required.

Create SpecialService SOA Composite and Service Bus Project

Create a SOA composite called *SpecialService* with a synchronous BPEL process that accepts a simple request message and produces a similarly simple response message. Deploy the SOA composite.

Create a SoapUI project to invoke this service and create a request message. Make a test call and verify that a response is returned. We will be extending this SoapUI project in several iterations, as we step up the security level of the *SpecialService*.

Also create Service Bus project *SpecialServiceProxy* with a proxy service and associated pipeline based on the same WSDL as the composite *SpecialService*. Have the pipeline prepare some sort of response—although it does not really matter what.

At a later stage we will first have the pipeline invoke the SOA composite and later do it the other way round—to give you a taste of invoke a secured service from both SOA composites and Service Bus projects.

Configure Users and Groups

In EM FMW Control, right click on Web Logic Domain | soa_domain (or whatever the name is of your domain). In the context menu, select Security | Users and Groups.

On the Users tab, create new users *airprofs* and *skyfly* with their respective passwords.

Open the Groups tab and create group *GoldPartners*. Add user airproofs to this group.

Authentication Using WS-Security

So where do we check the authentication details that are sent as part of the request message? In other words, where and how is authentication enforced and how is this information delegated to our identity and access management solution?

We will use an OWSM policy to enforce authentication of service clients using WS-Security. When we add this policy to the composite, OWSM will intercept the inbound request message and enforce authentication. This is achieved by extracting the username and password from the request message and delegating authentication to Oracle WebLogic Server's default authenticator, which in turn will validate the username and password.

Apply Authentication Policy to Composite Revision 1.1

Deploy the original SOA composite again, but this time as revision 1.1. The composite is unchanged—and will remain unchanged. The difference with revision 1.0 is that 1.1 will have a security policy applied to it. Note the separation of concerns: Security stays outside the composite and is in this case even applied after deployment.

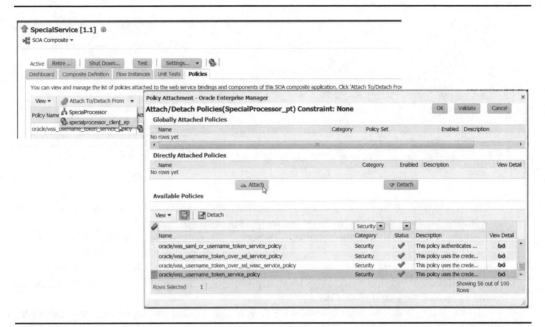

FIGURE 24-13. *Attaching oracle/wss_username_token_service_policy to the service binding in composite SpecialService*

We will use Enterprise Manager to apply the authentication policy to the SOA composite. Log in to Enterprise Manager, expand the SOA node, and click on the node for the 1.1 revision of *SpecialService*. Open the Policies tab. Click *Attach To/Detach From* and select the service binding, as shown in Figure 24-13. This opens the Attach/Detach Policies dialog. In this dialog, filter on policies that are in the Security category and select the policy named oracle/wss_ username_token_service_policy. Click on Attach to associate this policy with the service binding.

This policy will accept a WS-Security UserNameToken as the authentication mechanism—both plain text as well as digest. Click OK to apply the policy to the SOA composite. The policy is enabled by default. You can enable and disable policies per SOA composite using Enterprise Manager.

Put the Authentication Policy to the Test

Open the SoapUI project. Clone the existing request message for the *SpecialService*. Send the cloned request—or the original one: at this moment that does not make a difference. The response message will not contain a confirmation of the successful processing of the request message, but instead a fault message with the following description (Figure 24-14):

```
InvalidSecurity : error in processing the WS-Security security header
```

Return to Enterprise Manager and refresh the Policies tab. You will see that there is one security violation. Note that the violation is not listed in the Authentication column as you might have expected; only the number of incorrect authentication attempts is increased by one because of

FIGURE 24-14. *Fault message after invoking a secured SOA composite*

our failed attempt. In this case, the security headers (and authentication details) were missing altogether—so there was even a failed authentication attempt.

Return to SoapUI to add the required WS-Security authentication headers. Select the cloned Request message in the Navigator view. In the Request Properties view, add the following properties: **USER1** as the username and **weblogic1** as the password. Right-click in the cloned Request message and select Add WSS Username Token. A new dialog opens. Select PasswordText as the password type and click OK.

This will add a WS-Security UserNameToken to the request message. Note that this OWSM policy does not require WS-Security Timestamp information to be included in the message.

The request message now looks like the following:

```
<soapenv:Envelope xmlns:soapenv="http://schemas.xmlsoap.org/soap/envelope/"
xmlns:spec="saibot.airport.finance/SpecialProcessor">
    <soapenv:Header>
        <wsse:Security soapenv:mustUnderstand="1" xmlns:wsse="http://docs.oasis-open.
org/wss/2004/01/oasis-200401-wss-wssecurity-secext-1.0.xsd" xmlns:wsu="http://docs.
oasis-open.org/wss/2004/01/oasis-200401-wss-wssecurity-utility-1.0.xsd">
            <wsse:UsernameToken wsu:Id="UsernameToken-794F8784F30DC1
3B7214173674009531">
                <wsse:Username>USER1</wsse:Username>
                <wsse:Password Type="http://docs.oasis-open.org/wss/2004/01/oasis-
200401-wss-username-token-profile-1.0#PasswordText">weblogic1</wsse:Password>
                <wsse:Nonce EncodingType="http://docs.oasis-open.org/wss/2004/01/
oasis-200401-wss-soap-message-security-1.0#Base64Binary">vzsvquKCZte2STUsiir2ew==</
wsse:Nonce>
                <wsu:Created>2014-11-30T17:10:00.950Z</wsu:Created>
            </wsse:UsernameToken>
        </wsse:Security>
    </soapenv:Header>
    <soapenv:Body>
        <spec:process>
            <spec:name>Lex Jellema</spec:name>
            <spec:ssn>16082002</spec:ssn>
            <spec:amount>123</spec:amount>
        </spec:process>
```

```
    </soapenv:Body>
</soapenv:Envelope>
...
```

Invoke the service again. This time, a valid response is returned.

Edit the request message in SoapUI and enter an invalid password. The response after the service has been invoked now returns the same fault message as before. It does not reveal a whole lot—as it should not do. It only tells us we have failed to invoke the service because of a security issue.

Return to Enterprise Manager and refresh the Policies view for the *SpecialService* composite. The overview will list a new authentication violation.

You can more closely inspect a security violation in the Flow Instances tab for the composite in Enterprise Manager. Note that this does not show any authentication details or other very meaningful information. We cannot see, for example, who sent the request message that failed authentication. For this, we have to resort to the Fusion Middleware Audit Service.

We have now added authentication enforcement to the composite. As you might have guessed, every identity that is in the identity store is considered a valid user—as long as the correct username and password are provided. The notion of different authorizations is not yet configured.

Authorization Using WS-Security

Not every identity in our identity store should be allowed to access the *SpecialService* composite— not even after successful authentication. That is where authorization comes into play. We need to make sure that the authenticated identity actually has the required privileges to access the service. We will apply a second policy to the service for this purpose.

Apply an Authorization Policy to the SpecialService Composite

Now we add a policy to the SOA composite to make sure that only identities belonging to the GoldPartners group may access the service. Deploy the SOA composite again, now as revision 1.2 and first apply the authentication policy from the previous step to ensure authentication is enforced. After all, an identity needs to be authenticated before it can be authorized.

OWSM provides some out-of-the-box authorization policies—for example, oracle/binding_authorization_denyall_policy, which denies all roles access, and oracle/binding_authorization_permitall_policy, which permits all roles access to a service. We will need to create our own policy based on such an out-of-the-box policy so that only members of the group GoldPartners can access the composite.

Log in to EM FMW Control. In the overview panel, open the WebLogic Domain node, right-click the SOA Suite domain, and select Web Services | WSM Policies. Inspect the policies oracle/binding_authorization_denyall_policy and oracle/binding_authorization_permitall_policy by selecting them and clicking View. Next, we create a new policy that is based on these authorization policies. Select either one of the two authorization policies and click Create Like, as shown in Figure 24-15.

In the Create Policy view, enter *saibotairport/binding_authorization_permit_gold_partners_* policy as the policy name, as shown in Figure 24-16. In the Roles region, click the radio button Selected Roles as the Authorization Setting. Add GoldPartners as an authorized role.

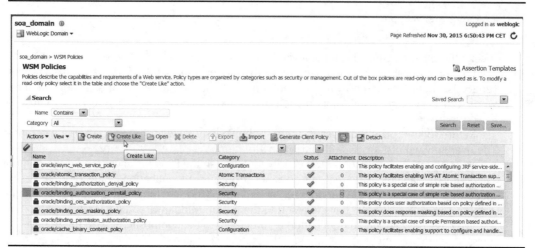

FIGURE 24-15. *Creating a new OWSM policy based on an existing policy*

Use Enterprise Manager to add this newly created policy to revision 1.2 of composite *SpecialService* (Figure 24-17).

TIP
Oracle Entitlement Server (OES) is a product used for managing fine grained authorization. OES is integrated with OWSM to provide such detailed authorization, for example, at operation level. Two OWSM policies used for this are oracle/binding_oes_authorization_policy and oracle/component_oes_authorization_policy.

soa_domain > WSM Policies > Policy Create Like
saibot_binding_authorization_permit_gold_partners_policy

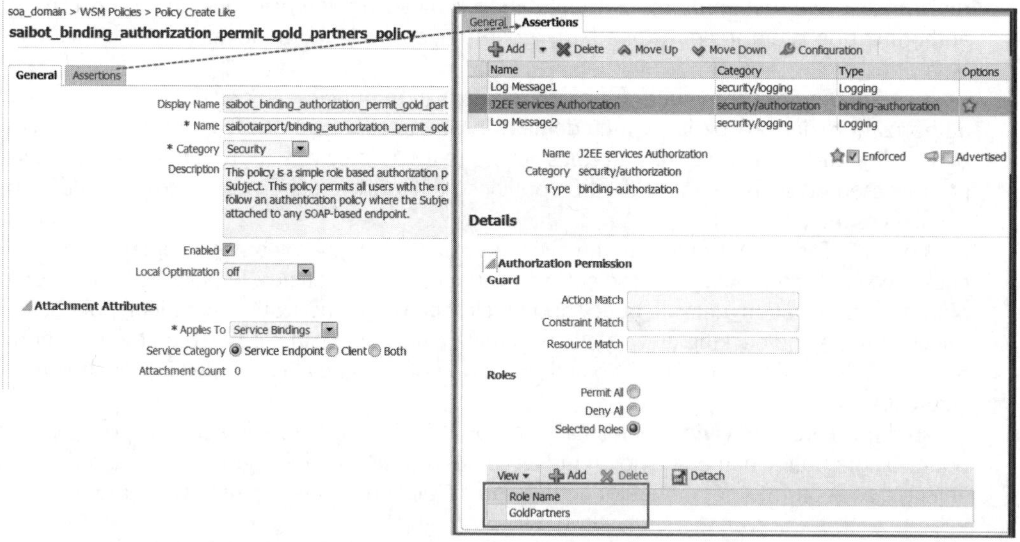

FIGURE 24-16. *Configuring the new custom OWSM policy*

FIGURE 24-17. *The SpecialService composite after the policies have been attached to it*

Trying Out the Authorization Policy

It is time to test the authorization capabilities of the service. Open SoapUI and clone the request with WS Security User Name Token. Use YYY as the username—an identity that is not a member of the GoldPartners group and that should therefore not be able to access the service. Invoke the service.

The response message is the same as on previous occasions where we failed the security requirements.

Return to EM FMW Control and browse to the Policies view for SpecialService (1.2). The overview will list an authorization violation.

In SoapUI, replace the credentials in the request message with those for the YYY and then invoke the service again. This time you should see a valid response message.

> **NOTE**
> *Authorization on the data level is out of scope for this chapter. We will not check that a Gold Partner can only request information regarding its own aircrafts. You could, for example, expand the composite to check for this or apply Oracle Virtual Private Database (VPD) or Oracle Database 12c Real Application Security and identity propagation from the composite to the database to enforce authorization on the data (database row) level.*

Retrieving User Identity in BPEL Process

It may be useful to learn about the current user identity inside a BPEL process. For example, to retrieve additional LDAP properties for that user or to pass the user identity onward, for example in a call to the database adapter to set the database session context.

The following steps are required to access the WSSE header in the BPEL process.

Define XSD for the WS Security Header   We need an XSD describing the WS Security Header in order to create a BPEL variable with the correct structure. Add a file called wsse.xsd to the project with the following content:

```
<schema attributeFormDefault="unqualified" elementFormDefault="qualified"
        targetNamespace=http://docs.oasis-open.org/wss/2004/01/oasis-200401-
wss-wssecurity-secext-1.0.xsd
```

```
      xmlns:tns=http://docs.oasis-open.org/wss/2004/01/oasis-200401-wss-
wssecurity-secext-1.0.xsd
      xmlns="http://www.w3.org/2001/XMLSchema">
  <element name="Security">
    <complexType>
      <sequence>
        <element name="UsernameToken" type="tns:UsernameToken"/>
      </sequence>
    </complexType>
  </element>
  <complexType name="UsernameToken">
    <sequence>
      <element name="Username" type="string"/>
      <element name="Password" type="string"/>
    </sequence>
  </complexType>
</schema>
```

Import the WS Security Schema into the WSDL File   Add the following entry inside the wsdl:types element in the SpecialService.wsdl file:

```
<xsd:schema xmlns:xsd="http://www.w3.org/2001/XMLSchema">
    <xsd:import namespace="http://docs.oasis-open.org/wss/2004/01/oasis-
200401-wss-wssecurity-secext-1.0.xsd" schemaLocation="../Schemas/wsse.xsd"/>
</xsd:schema>
```

Create a BPEL Variable to Hold the WS Security Header   In the BPEL process, create a variable based on the Security element in the wsse.xsd file.

```
<variable name="WSSESecurity" element="wsse:Security"/>
```

Also, add the wsse namespace prefix in the BPEL process element:

```
xmlns:wsse="http://docs.oasis-open.org/wss/2004/01/oasis-200401-wss-
wssecurity-secext-1.0.xsd"
```

Configure the BPEL Receive Activity to Save the WS Security Header   The BPEL Receive activity can be configured to take the content of a SOAP Header element and store it in a BPEL variable. In this case, we want the WSSE Security header to be stored in the WSSESecurity variable. This is one by adding the following attribute to the Receive activity:

```
bpelx:headerVariable="WSSESecurity"
```

Figure 24-18 shows how this is done in the BPEL process editor.

Use the contents of the BPEL Variable including the User Identity   At this point, the WS Security header is captured in the Receive activity into the WSSESecurity variable. From that variable, the information can be used like any BPEL variable. Using XPath functions such as ids:getUserProperty() we can retrieve LDAP attributes for the user identity.

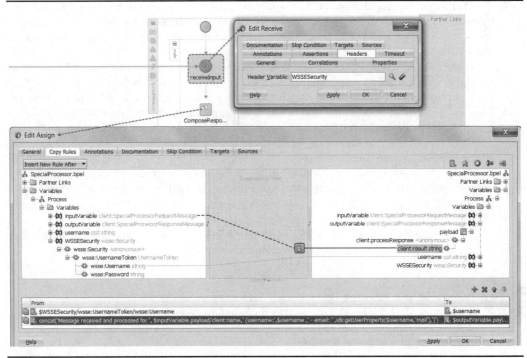

FIGURE 24-18. *Capturing the WS Security header into a BPEL variable and leveraging the username to retrieve the LDAP mail attribute for the current user*

Authentication and Authorization on Service Bus Proxy Services

Frequently, the first—and sometimes the only—port of call for service consumers will be a proxy service on the Service Bus rather than a SOA composite. It is therefore important to also—and perhaps even more so—be able to apply authentication and authorization policies to these proxy services. In this section we will discuss this and see how in Service Bus pipelines we can access the user identity. Additionally, we will briefly look at another type of access policy that we can define for proxy services: access control policies that regulate access according to additional conditions, such as time of day.

Apply Authentication Policy to Service Bus Proxy Service

The Service Bus project *SpecialService* exposes a proxy service with a simple operation *process* very similar to the operation exposed by the SOA composite *SpecialService* that we discussed overhead. Our challenge is first to ensure this proxy service can only be invoked by known users (authentication) and second by authorized users—just like we did for the service exposed by the *SpecialService* SOA composite.

Deploy the Service Bus project to the run-time Service Bus environment. Send a test request, for example from a fresh SoapUI project, based on the WSDL for this service: http://host:port/finance/SpecialService?WSDL. This request will yield a response, even though it does not contain any WS Security details.

Open the Service Bus Console—at http://host:port/servicebus—and click on the proxy service *SpecialService*. Create an edit session. Open the Security tab, as shown in Figure 24-19. Click on the child tab Policies. Click on the Attach [policies] icon. In the popup that appears, filter on Category Security and locate the oracle/wss_username_token_service_policy. Click on Attach to associate this policy with the proxy service.

Click on OK to close the popup, on the Save icon to persist the changes and on Activate to enable these changes.

Make another test call from SoapUI to the proxy service *SpecialService*. Because the request message does not include a WS Security header with authentication details, the request will be denied and a fault is returned that reads: *OSB-386200: General web service security error*.

Just like we did before, add the WSS Username Token to the request in SoapUI and send the message again. This time, the response should be produced without any problem.

NOTE
When a Service Bus proxy service does not have a security policy attached to it, then any security header included in the request to this proxy service is forwarded in the request sent to the next service in the call out or route from the pipeline.

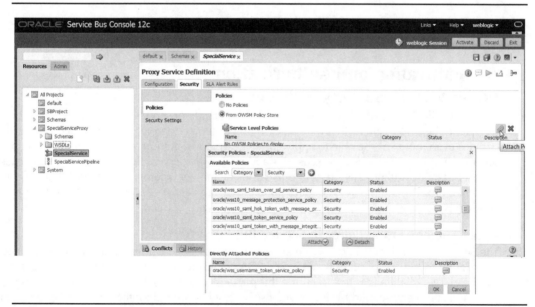

FIGURE 24-19. *Attaching the authentication policy to the Proxy Service in the Service Bus Console*

TIP
*Other authentication policies are available as well, such as wss11_*
x509_token_with_message_protection_service_policy. This policy has
OWSM verifying a signature in the SOAP message using the client's
public key in the server keystore—taken from the client certificate.
The name of the user in the identity store must match with the
common name of the client certificate in order for authentication to
be completed successfully.

Enforce Role-Based Authorization for the Service Bus Proxy Service

Restricting access to the proxy service to only identities that are member of the GoldPartners role is as easy as attaching the same customized policy to the proxy service that before we also applied to the service exposed by the SOA composite.

Once again, open the Proxy Service editor in the Service Bus Console. Create a new edit session, click on the Security tab and the Policies subtab. Click on the attach icon and select the customized policy *saibotairport/binding_authorization_permit_gold_partners_policy* and attach it to the proxy service, as shown in Figure 24-20. Click on OK, save the changes and activate the edit session.

Verify that the authorization policy is now active by invoking the service once with a WS Security Username Token for a user who is in the *GoldPartners* role and once for a user who is not.

Get Hold of Username in Service Bus Pipeline

The following expression can be used to access the username that was processed by the WS Security Username Token policy:

```
{$inbound/ctx:security/ctx:messageLevelClient/ctx:username/text()}
```

With the username, we can for example determine if the user is in a specific role or group or pass the user identity to a database adapter to set the session context.

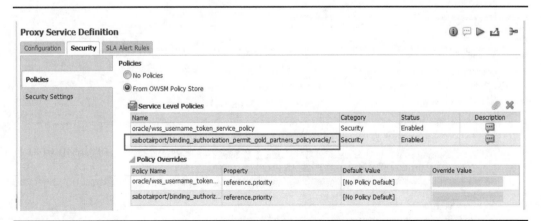

FIGURE 24-20. *Enforcing Role-Based Authorization for the Proxy Service using the customized policy*

Access Control Policies on Service Bus Proxy Services

A Service Bus access control policy specifies conditions under which users, groups, or roles can access a proxy service. For example, you can create a policy that always allows users in the *GoldPartners* role to access a proxy service (at any time) and that allows users in the *SilverPartners* role to access the proxy service only between midnight and 4:00 AM on weekdays. The access control policies are defined in the Service Bus console.

For all proxy services in a project, you can create a transport-level policy, which applies a security check when a client attempts to establish a connection with the proxy service. Only requests that satisfy the specified conditions are allowed through. Similar policies can be defined at individual proxy service, message or operation level.

To enforce the rule that the proxy service *SpecialService* can only be invoked between 4:00 AM and 10:00 AM, you have to go through the following steps.

Open Service Bus console and click on the *SpecialService* proxy service in the *SpecialServiceProxy* project. Activate a change session. Click on the *Security* tab and open the subtab *Security Settings*. Click on the *SpecialService* link under Message Access Control. The editor for access control policies appears.

Click on *Add Conditions*. Now you can choose the predicate to use for this particular condition. Open the drop-down *Predicate List*. The list contains predicates such as Role, Group, User, Access occurs before the specified day of the month, Context element's value equals a string constant, Access occurs on specified days of the week.

In this case, pick the predicate *Access occurs between specified hours* and click Next. The next page shows the arguments for the selected predicate—in this case Starting Time, Ending Time, and GTM offset. Enter values 4:00:00 AM and 10:00:00 AM and your GMT offset, for example GMT+1:00. Press Finish to complete the definition of the predicate.

You return to the policy editor, shown in Figure 24-21. You can add more conditions, and combine them with AND and OR conditions. Press Save then Close to persist the policy definition.

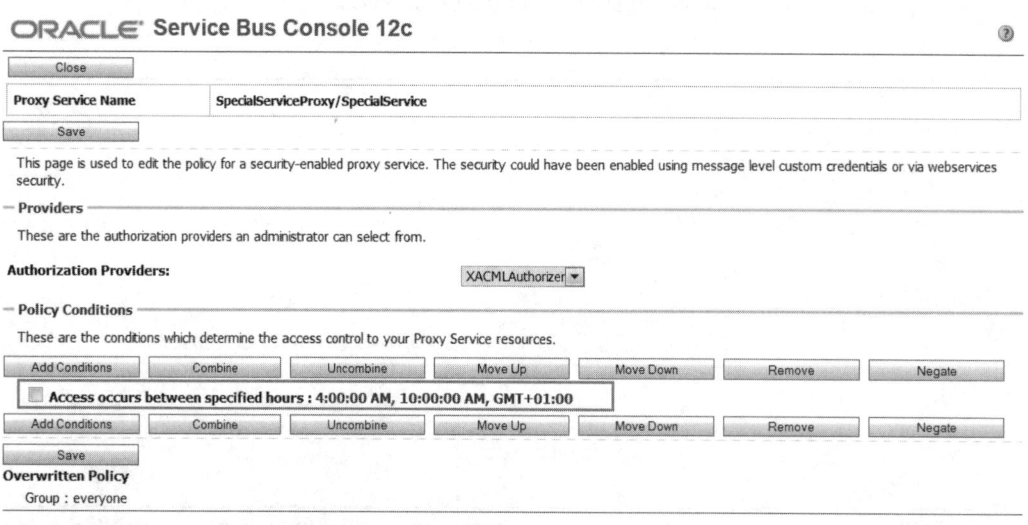

FIGURE 24-21. *Editing the Message Access Control policy for the proxy service SpecialService*

Activate the editing session to make the changes active.

If you invoke the proxy service outside the hours specified, you will be denied access with an error message whose core is: *OSB-386102: Message-level authorization denied.* Invoking the proxy service during the opening hours will work as before.

Confidentiality and Integrity of Message Content

Although we have enforced authentication and authorization for this service, it is far from secure. Third parties that intercept request and response messages to this service are able to see the message contents and the username and password used by partners to invoke the service. Furthermore, Saibot Airport is at this point still unable to guarantee messages have not been altered during transport or even tell whether that has happened. In other words, we need to add message integrity and confidentiality capabilities to the service.

For this we can either use WS-Security or SSL/TLS. Or both. As explained in the section "Transport Versus Message Security," both WS-Security and SSL/TLS apply data encryption so that intercepted messages remain confidential (unreadable) and add a checksum (or hash) so that data integrity can be verified.

Realizing and Enforcing Transport Level Security

Both WS-Security and SSL/TLS (can) use PKI as the underlying encryption mechanism to enable integrity and confidentiality. OWSM provides policies to ensure data integrity and confidentiality. These policies are either based on WS-Security for message security or enforce that SSL/TLS is used in the transport layer (in order to accept a message). The keys used by OWSM for WS-Security policies can be managed through Enterprise Manager. Transport layer security is managed by the underlying Oracle WebLogic Server. The same keys can be used as for message security or different key stores can be leveraged. The key management for SSL/TLS is provided by Oracle WebLogic Console.

The OPSS KSS demo identity and demo trust keystores—kss://system/demoidentity and kss://system/trust—are preconfigured when you create the SOA Suite domain. These keystores can be managed through EM FMW Control: right click on the Domain node and from the context menu select Security | Keystore. New keystores can be created here as well.

Both WebLogic Server and OWSM are by default configured with these key stores. Check for example in the WebLogic Server Administration Console, on the Domain | Security | Advanced page, and see that the "Use KSS For Demo" check box is enabled. In order to get SSL going, no additional set up is required, except switching on the SSL listen port.

The demo keystores and the demo certificates can be used for development and testing purposes. However, for production environments it is recommended to use "real" keystores containing actual certificates that are signed by trusted certificate authorities. For now, we will use the default demo keystores and certificates.

Configure SSL/TLS in WebLogic Console

We are going to enable integrity and confidentiality based on transport security; therefore, we'll make use of SSL/TLS. We will be using one-way SSL/TLS. We need to configure SSL/TLS for Oracle WebLogic Server and apply an authentication policy to the *SpecialService* that enforces use of SSL/TLS. Note that alternatively we can terminate SSL at the Apache or Oracle HTTP Server that is the first port of call for incoming HTTP requests and the finale departure point for HTTP responses.

In the WebLogic Console, select the server that runs the SOA Suite runtime and open the Configuration tab and the SSL subtab to inspect the SSL settings. You can, among other things, configure whether you want to use one-way or two-way SSL. In two-way SSL, the client also needs to send a certificate that needs to be accepted by the server. Two-way SSL can be used for mutual authentication. In our case, however, client authentication is achieved through WS-Security. Therefore, we do not require two-way SSL. For now, we will accept the default values—and thus one-way SSL. The relevant settings are:

- The location of identity (certificate and private key) and trust (trusted CAs) and the SSL attributes for the private key alias and password

and in the Advanced section:

- Hostname Verification, Export Key Lifespan (the number of times WebLogic Server can use an exportable key between a domestic server and an exportable client before generating a new key), Two Way Client Cert Behavior control (set to Client Certs Not Requested for one-way SSL). Inbound and Outbound SSL Certificate Validation.

We can simply accept all default values.

Select the General tab and make sure that the check box SSL Listen Port Enabled is checked so that incoming SSL/TLS connections are supported. Make a note of the listen port, for example 8002 or 7102.

NOTE
The tab Keystores gives an overview of the Identity and Trust Key Stores. The default settings make use of the demo keystores. Those should not be used in production environments, but provide all the functionality we need to try out SSL communication.

Add Transport Security to the SpecialService

We will now add transport security to our SOA composite. Deploy the SOA composite as version 1.3. Instead of adding the authentication policy oracle/wss_username_token_service_policy that we used in the previous versions, we will now use the *oracle/wss_username_token_over_ssl_service_policy,* as visualized in Figure 24-22. This policy enforces that the message is sent over SSL/TLS rather than using a non-secured protocol; it will we rejected when not sent over a secure transport. Also apply our own role authorization policy to it.

NOTE
You may wonder how as a consumer of a web service you are supposed to know that a service should be invoked over SSL and that a WS Security User Token should be included. Open the live WSDL document for the SpecialService. You will find a Policy element for the wss_username_token_over_ssl_service_policy that tells consumers about the policies that should be satisfied by requests. This information should also be recorded in the service contract and exposed through the service catalog.

Test from SoapUI to See Secured Transport in Action

Open the project for *SpecialService* in SoapUI. Clone the request with the Usertoken.

The policy oracle/wss_username_token_over_ssl_service_policy also requires request messages to include a WS-Timestamp header containing the creation and expiration time of the message.

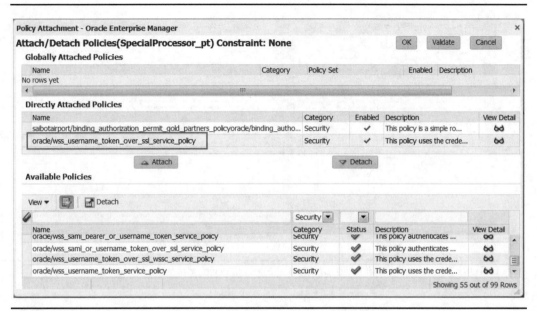

FIGURE 24-22. *Attaching the policy that enforces the messages to be sent over SSL*

The WS-Timestamp header can be placed either before or after the WS-Security UserNameToken header. The order of these elements is not specified by the WS-Security standard. Right-click the cloned request message and select Add WS-Timestamp. Enter **3600** as the Time-To-Live value.

NOTE
When using headers containing timestamps, you may need to regenerate these headers in SoapUI because they can become outdated after a while and will be rejected by OWSM.

Invoke the service. The following fault message is returned:

```
...<env:Fault xmlns:ns0="http://docs.oasis-open.org/wss/2004/01/oasis-200401-
wss-wssecurity-secext-1.0.xsd">
    <faultcode>ns0:InvalidSecurity</faultcode>
    <faultstring>InvalidSecurity : error in processing the WS-Security
security header</faultstring>
    <faultactor/>
</env:Fault>
```

This error is returned because SpecialService (1.3) can only be accessed over HTTPS due to the policy we have applied to it. Our attempt to call it on unsecured HTTP was rejected. We will try again, this time using HTTPS.

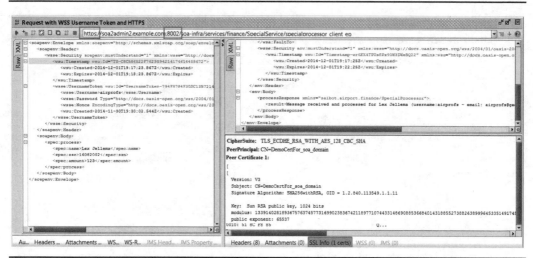

FIGURE 24-23. *The call in SoapUI to the SpecialService protected by an SSL policy*

Add a new endpoint for the request; this time, use the endpoint derived from the WSDL, but replace "http" with "https" and replace the port number (default is 8001) with the SSL port number, as configured in the Oracle WebLogic Server Console (the default SSL port is 8002).

Now invoke the service, calling the new endpoint. This time, the correct response message will be returned by the SOA composite. Click the "SSL Info (1 certs)" tab in the response window to see the certificate returned by Oracle WebLogic Server, as shown in Figure 24-23.

NOTE
A very special type of transport level security can be set up in the WebLogic Administration Console on the Security | Filters tab for the domain configuration. Here we can define network filters to prevent any requests arriving from unknown IP addresses.

Implementing Message Level Confidentiality and Integrity

In the previous section, we have made sure that the communication from consumers to our WebLogic infrastructure takes place in a secure manner. The entire HTTP message is encrypted by the consumer using our public certificate and using our private key; WebLogic takes care of decryption. En route, the communication cannot be overheard—or at least not understood. As soon as the message arrives in WebLogic, it is decrypted and becomes readable. That may be too early: it could be that the message contains sections that are too sensitive to be exposed even within our own infrastructure. For such messages and these sections, or when communication for some reason cannot take place over SSL, we may want to apply message level encryption—for confidentiality—and signing—for integrity. We may also want to implement a mechanism for nonrepudiation or undeniability that allows us to provide a message was indeed sent by a certain party.

Message Level Encryption

The OWSM policies oracle/wss11_message_protection_service_policy and oracle/wss11 _username_token_with_message_protection_service_policy are among those that can be used to enforce message protection (integrity and confidentiality) for inbound SOAP requests in accordance with the WS-Security 1.1 standard. This policy uses the symmetric key technology for signing and encryption, and the WS-Security's Basic 128 suite of asymmetric key technology for endorsing signatures.

To sign and encrypt SOAP messages, you use public and private signature and encryption keys that you store in the OWSM keystore for the WebLogic domain. By default, OWSM uses the KSS (Keystore Service). Alternatively, it can be configured to use Java Key Store (JKS), PKCS11, or a hardware security module.

The keystore configuration is domain wide: all web services and web service clients in the domain use this keystore. The keystore contains an organization's private keys and the certificates associated with those private keys. A truststore contains certificates from a Certificate Authority (CA), or other entities that this entity trusts. The keystore and the truststore can be maintained together in a common store.

The consumer of a service protected by these policies needs a copy of the public key of the server encryption certificate. This public base64-encoded certificate is published in the WSDL for web services that implement a message-protection policy regardless of whether the policy encrypts or decrypts data.

If the public key certificate is not found in the WSDL, the certificate must be in the client's keystore as before.

See the book's website for resources on applying message protection policies.

NOTE
The assertion templates support partial signing and encryption as well as full signing and encryption of the message body. For those assertion templates or predefined policies that provide SOAP message protection, the default behavior is to protect the entire SOAP message body by signing and encrypting the entire SOAP body. You can configure the assertions and policies to protect selected elements, if you wish—for example, for reasons of performance or content based message routing.

Invoke Protected Services from SOA Suite

Part of the security challenge we have to address obviously includes our ability to make our services call out to secured services. SOA composites references and Service Bus business services invoke internal and external services that may require communication over SSL and authentication using a username token to also enforce role based authorization. We will discuss in this section how we can leverage OWSM policies in an outbound direction to handle the security aspects of the interaction with the invoked service. The Service Key provider that we can use with Service Bus provides a means to use a predefined identity for calls to secured services.

Service Bus Calls to Secured Web Services

To see how we can make calls to secured web services from business services in Service Bus projects, add a simple business service to the *SpecialServiceProxy* project and route to this business service in the pipeline. This business services calls out to the web service exposed by the *SpecialService* composite.

Invoke Service with WS Security Username Token Policy

When the composite's service is protected with the *oracle/wss_username_token_service_policy*, the business service has to provide a username token in the request. This can be done using the *oracle/wss_username_token_client_policy* attached to the business service. This policy will create the WS Security header element in the SOAP message sent from the business service to the remote, secured service. We need to tell the policy how to find the username and password used for creating this header element. This can be done with a key entry in the Credentials Store Provider.

Open the EM FMW Control. Click on SOA Domain and from the context menu select Security | Credentials. In the Credentials page that opens, click on Create Key—as shown in Figure 24-24. Select oracle.wsm.security as the map, set Key to *OurSpecialAccount* and the Type to Password. Enter the username and password that you want to use when invoking the secured service—for example, the user AirProfs created earlier on. Press OK to save the new key into the credential store.

After deploying the Service Bus project, open the Service Bus Console. Find the business service and open its Security tab. Set the Policies radio group to From OWSM Policy Store. Select the *oracle/wss_username_token_client_policy* to attach. This policy has several properties associated with it—one of which is csf-key. This property is set with the name of a key in the Credential Store Provider—in this case *OurSpecialAccount*, as shown in Figure 24-25. The policy will retrieve this key and use its username and password when composing the security header.

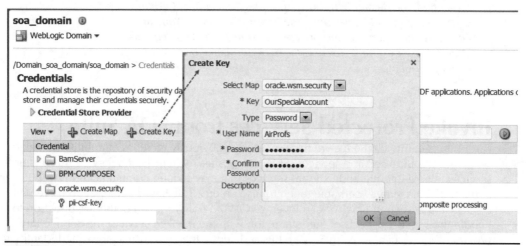

FIGURE 24-24. *Storing a username and password under key OurSpecialAccount in the Credential Store Provider*

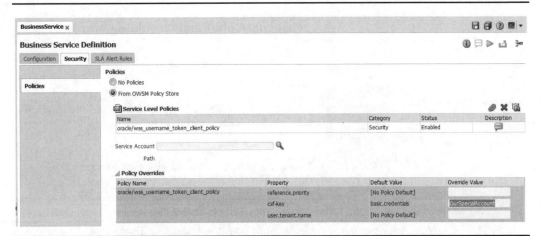

FIGURE 24-25. *Configuring the oracle/wss_username_token_client_policy policy for the Business Service and associating it with the username and password stored under key OurSpecialAccount*

If the secured service also enforces use of SSL, you can use the *oracle/wss_username_token _over_ssl_client_policy* to take care of both the username token as well as the SSL handshake (although for SSL some configuration is still required at infrastructure level in WebLogic or optionally the HTTP server fronting WebLogic).

Using Service Accounts with Business Services

Service Bus supports a concept called Service Accounts. A service account provides a user name and password that proxy services and business services use for outbound authentication or authentication to a local or remote resource, such as an FTP server or a JMS server. For example, if a business service is required to supply a user name and password for transport-level authentication with a web service, you create a service account that specifies the user name and password, then you configure the business service to include the service account credentials in its outbound requests.

The account details are not maintained as part of the proxy or business service definition—but as separate entity that can be referenced from many different service definitions.

We will now create a Service Account and use it in the Business Service. In Service Bus Console, create a new edit session. Click on the *SpecialServiceProxy* project. Click on the new icon and select Service Account from the list of object types. Create the new Service Account *AirprofsServiceAccount* of type Static and associated with user *airprofs* and its password. Note that Service Accounts can also pass the username and password received in the proxy service (Pass Through) or map the identity that was received in the proxy to a predefined username and password combination (Mapping).

Open the Security | Policies tab for the Business Service. Clear the override value for the csf-key property that we previously set to *OurSpecialAccount*. Click on the Service Account browse icon and select the newly created Service Account *AirprofsServiceAccount*, as shown in Figure 24-26. Click on Save and Activate the edit session. Send a request to the *SpecialServiceProxy* service.

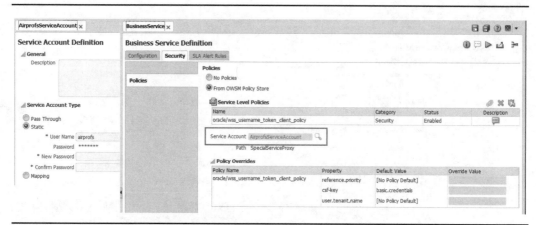

FIGURE 24-26. *Associating a Service Account with the Username Token Policy*

This should result in a valid response—because the user *Airprofs* set up in the Service Account can be authenticated by the OWSM policy attached to the *SpecialService* composite.

Try to change the username of password defined in the Service Account and send another test request. That one should fail.

NOTE
*The XPath function fn-bea:lookupBasicCredentials('AirprofsServiceAcc
ount') can be used to retrieve username and password for the Service
Account for use inside the pipeline.*

Service Key Provider

If a business service requires the use of PKI technology for digital signatures, or SSL authentication, you create a service key provider, which provides private keys paired with certificates.

Use the Oracle WebLogic Server Administration Console to configure a PKI credential mapping provider. In any WebLogic Server domain that hosts Service Bus, you can configure at most one PKI credential mapping provider. Such a PKI credential mapping provider maps Service Bus service key providers to key-pairs that can be used for digital signatures and encryption (for WS Security) and for outbound SSL authentication. You store the key-pairs that the PKI credential mapping provider uses in a keystore. You can store the PKI credential mappings in WebLogic Server's identity keystore or in a separate keystore.

The Service Key Provider itself can be created in JDeveloper and in the Service Bus Console. It refers to an Encryption Key in the keystore that your security realm's PKI credential mapper uses. Keys can be selected in the provider for encryption and digital signing as well as an SSL client authentication key for two-way SSL.

Both a proxy service and a business service can be associated with the service key provider. Proxy services use the Public Key Infrastructure (PKI) credentials for decrypting inbound SOAP messages and verifying Digital Signatures. Business Service use the PKI credentials from Service Key Provider associated with the Proxy Service that initiates the pipeline that invokes them, for SSL communication, encrypting and signing outbound messages.

SOA Composite Calls to Secured Web Services Requiring Authentication

Calls from SOA composites can be made to secured services. OWSM Policies can be attached to reference bindings to impact outbound communication and take care of aspects such as adding WS Security headers, encrypting or signing messages and using SSL for transport. Security policies can be attached in EM FMW Control—as we have seen before—and also in JDeveloper, as we will see now.

Our simple example here will be the *SpecialService* composite invoking the *SpecialServiceProxy* Service Bus proxy service which enforces authentication – and perhaps role based authorization based on this authentication—using the policy oracle/wss_username_token_service_policy.

Send WS Username Token from SOA Composite

Open the composite editor in JDeveloper for *SpecialService*.

Right click the Reference Binding SOAPReference, as shown in Figure 24-27. Select Configure SOA WS Policies in the context menu. The Configure SOA WS Policies editor appears, where we can attach policies to the reference—to impact the calls to the service *SpecialServiceProxy*.

Click on the plus icon in the category Security. Select the oracle/wss_username_token_client _policy. Click on the edit icon. The Config Override Properties dialog opens. Set the value of property csf-key to *OurSpecialAccount*, referring to the key we created earlier in the Credential Store Provider. See Figure 24-27 for details.

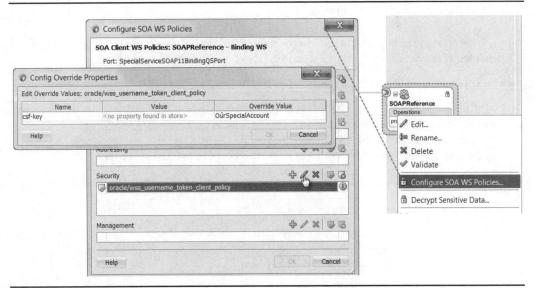

FIGURE 24-27. *Attaching the oracle/wss_username_token_client_policy to the outbound reference binding—and configuring the OurSpecialAccount key to provide username and password*

Press OK several times to save these changes. The file wsm-assembly.xml has been created as a result—or at least has been updated, to include the *policySet* element for this reference with the PolicyReference for this particular policy.

Deploy the composite application. Send a test request to the service exposed by the composite. This should result in a successful invocation of the *SpecialServiceProxy* as you can tell from the message flow trace and the response message.

Manipulate WS Security Header from BPEL Process

Instead of having an outbound OWSM policy to control the outbound messages and add WS Security headers, we can create the headers in the Invoke activity inside the BPEL process. This is done through the *inputHeaderVariable* extension attribute on the Invoke activity that can create the security header from a variable that is based on an XSD element following the exact structure of the WS Security header. In the earlier paragraph *Retrieving User Identity in BPEL Process* we have used such a variable in the Receive activity to capture the security header. Now we will use this same variable to create and send one.

NOTE
Manipulating the security headers from the BPEL process is not recommended. It can be convenient during development, for example to spot problems with the secure interactions. However, ideally all security header inspection and manipulation is externalized from the SOA composite implementation, primarily through security policies. There is the option to create custom security policy implementations that may perform specific logic that otherwise might end up undesirably in the BPEL process.

Remove the policy attachment on the reference binding. Open the BPEL process editor. Verify that the variable WSSESecurity exists and is based on the Security element:

```
<variable name="WSSESecurity" element="wsse:Security"/>
```

Add an Assign activity just prior to the Invoke to the partner link for *SpecialServiceProxy* and set the values for the username and password elements in variable WSSESecurity.

Open the editor for the Invoke activity. Open the Headers tab. Select variable WSSESecurity as the Input Header Variable (see Figure 24-28). Press OK to close the editor.

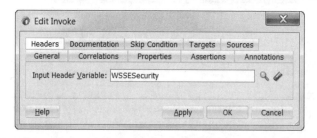

FIGURE 24-28. *Configure the Invoke activity with an input header variable to produce the WS Security Header*

The following attribute is added to the Invoke element in the source file:

```
bpelx:inputHeaderVariable="WSSESecurity"
```

Deploy the SOA composite—without the policy attachment and with this programmatic creation of the WS Security header. Make a test call to the SpecialService and verify if again a successful call is made to the secured *SpecialServiceProxy*.

In the assign activity, instead of hard coding username and password, we could have used other means to retrieve the credentials to use at this particular point in time. It would however always involve plain text passwords.

TIP
OWSM policies can be attached not just at service and reference bindings but also at individual components in a SOA composite application. The set of policies to attach to components is limited—not focusing on transport or authentication for example—but does include authorization and logging policies.

Pass Identity

Passing from a service to another service the identity responsible for the request can be done in several ways. One option is through the WS Security token in the header—which we can potentially use even if the invoked service does not enforce authentication but only has an interest in the identity. We have seen how we can set this header through the outbound OWSM policy or programmatically from BPEL (and also in a Service Bus pipeline). Using a Service Account of type Pass with a business service in Service Bus, we can easily pass on the user identity without any intervention at all—but only when the password is sent in clear text.

When the invoked service has a functional interest in the user's identity—and perhaps does not enforce authentication at all—it may make more sense to include the identity in the message payload instead of "abusing" the security header.

Another more standard option is the use of a SAML token to provide a detailed assertion of the identity and its attributes. The SAML token also specifies what entity is "issuing" the assertion. Various methods are available for handing over SAML tokens and ensuring their trustworthiness. When we are only interested in passing the identity we can use the simplest method, called *bearer confirmation*. Several OWSM policies can be used on the business service or reference binding from which the identity is passed, including oracle/http_saml20_token_bearer_client_policy.

For REST services, use of XML is far less common. A standard way of defining and passing identity for these services is using JSON Web Token (JWT) as a means of representing claims to be transferred between two parties. JWT is a compact token format intended for space-constrained environments such as HTTP Authorization headers. Several OWSM policies know how to process a JWT token and perform authentication and identity extraction from it, for example, oracle/http_jwt_token_service_policy.

Auditing

Auditing the occurrence of relevant events is one of the cornerstones of enterprise security. Auditing serves several purposes, such as compliance, monitoring, and analytics. From auditing we require the ability to trace and prove what has happened, by whom and why, especially regarding sensitive operations and data. Auditing also helps detect and analyze attempts to thwart security policies.

Given the scope of this chapter, our discussion of auditing will only scratch the very surface of this topic. The book's website contains additional resources for delving into this topic.

Fusion Middleware Audit Framework

Fusion Middleware contains the Audit Framework, a centralized audit framework across the middleware family of products, including platform facilities like OPSS and OWSM and custom Java EE applications. This framework is configured using audit policies to prescribe what events should be recorded for which components. Events are written to file and optionally to an Audit Database as well (created by the RCU component). The OPSS Common Audit Framework generates SQL scripts to create Oracle database views. Component reporting applications can use these views to query audit event data from audit database tables.

WebLogic Auditing Provider

The WebLogic Auditing provider is an optional security provider that collects, stores, and distributes information about operating requests and the outcome of those requests for the purposes of nonrepudiation. To use this provider, configure an auditing provider in the WebLogic Server Administration Console, on the Providers | Audit tab for the security realm.

Subsequently, in the domain wide Configuration | General tab set the Configuration Audit Type. Alternatively, include the following Java option in the server's startup command:

```
-Dcom.bea.wli.sb.security.AuditWebServiceSecurityErrors=true
```

All auditing information recorded by the WebLogic Auditing provider is saved in WL_HOME\
yourdomain\yourserver\logs\DefaultAuditRecorder.log by default. You can specify a new directory location for the DefaultAuditRecorder.log file on the command line with the following Java startup option:

```
-Dweblogic.security.audit.auditLogDir=c:\saibotairport\audit
```

Logging Policy

A much more rudimentary form of auditing is provided by the OWSM logging policy: *oracle/log _policy*. This is a policy that instructs OWSM to record the contents of the messages processed—both request and response and including the security headers. The latter can be very handy while debugging security set up and handling faults. This policy can be attached to proxy service and business service in Service Bus projects and, to service and reference bindings as well as any individual component in SOA composite applications.

The logging policy writes its output to the file that is configured for the owsm-message-handler in the SOA server Log Configuration as shown in Figure 24-29.

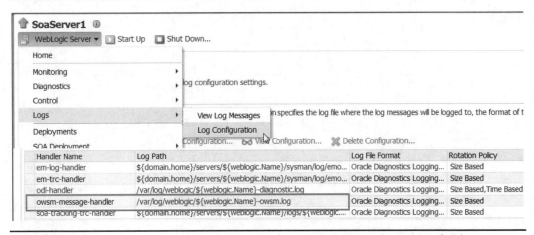

FIGURE 24-29. *Configuration of the OWSM log file where the output is written for the OWSM log policy*

Summary

IT security has become increasingly important over the last decades. This is even more true for businesses and organizations dealing with sensitive information, including airports. This chapter introduced general security concepts such as identity and access management, encryption, transport versus message security and the access of human actors to the SOA Suite run-time environment.

Oracle SOA Suite and WebLogic Server on which it runs provide numerous security capabilities. One of these is Oracle Web Services Manager (OWSM), which can be used to secure Web Services. This chapter described the main features and workings of OWSM and provided a step-by-step case on how to use OWSM to secure your SOA composites and protect valuable and sensitive data.

Security requires a holistic approach. Securing SOA composites alone is not enough. You also need to consider securing Oracle WebLogic Server itself (e.g., access to the various consoles and the file system on which it runs) as well as the surrounding environment and infrastructure including DMZ, web servers and more physical aspects such as the building and the power supply. Also remember to secure access to the human tasks that are created and managed by Oracle SOA Suite.

Security involves prevent, detect and record. While obviously most attention is usually given to the prevention of breaches and incidents, detecting anomalies, and acting rapidly to resolve any problems is very important too—especially given the fact that one hundred percent prevention is not feasible. Monitoring—such as discussed in Chapters 20 and 23—and real-time event analysis, using OEP as discussed in Chapter 16 are very much part of the holistic security approach. Accurate audit trails that capture any irregularities as well as all relevant regular are part of that approach as well.

SOA Suite and the Fusion Middleware infrastructure components offer most pieces of this security puzzle.

Index

C

T

X

Join the Largest Tech Community in the World

 Download the latest software, tools, and developer templates

 Get exclusive access to hands-on trainings and workshops

 Grow your professional network through the Oracle ACE Program

 Publish your technical articles – and get paid to share your expertise

**Join the Oracle Technology Network
Membership is free. Visit oracle.com/technetwork**

@OracleOTN facebook.com/OracleTechnologyNetwork

Reach More than 700,000 Oracle Customers with Oracle Publishing Group

Connect with the Audience that Matters Most to Your Business

Oracle Magazine
The Largest IT Publication in the World
Circulation: 550,000
Audience: IT Managers, DBAs, Programmers, and Developers

Profit
Business Insight for Enterprise-Class Business Leaders to Help Them Build a Better Business Using Oracle Technology
Circulation: 100,000
Audience: Top Executives and Line of Business Managers

Java Magazine
The Essential Source on Java Technology, the Java Programming Language, and Java-Based Applications
Circulation: 125,000 and Growing Steady
Audience: Corporate and Independent Java Developers, Programmers, and Architects

For more information or to sign up for a FREE subscription:
Scan the QR code to visit Oracle Publishing online.

Beta Test Oracle Software

Get a first look at our newest products—and help perfect them. You must meet the following criteria:

- ✓ Licensed Oracle customer or Oracle PartnerNetwork member

- ✓ Oracle software expert

- ✓ Early adopter of Oracle products

Please apply at: pdpm.oracle.com/BPO/userprofile

If your interests match upcoming activities, we'll contact you. Profiles are kept on file for 12 months.